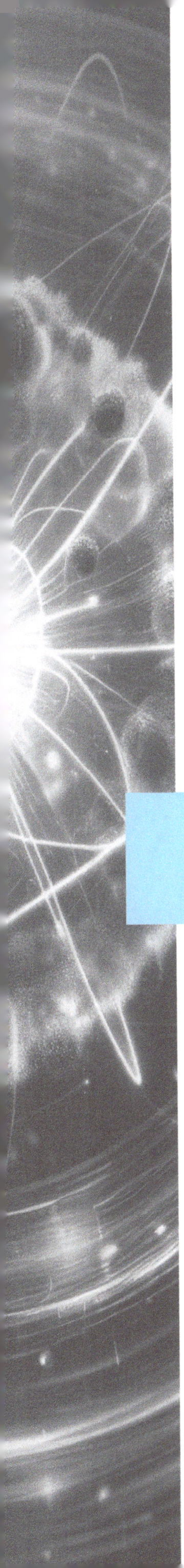

Master the NCERT

Line by Line MCQs from Latest NCERT Books

for NEET/JEE

PHYSICS XII

Master the NCERT

Line by Line MCQs from Latest NCERT Books

for NEET/JEE

PHYSICS XII

KESHAV MOHAN

Co-authored by
Dharmendra Singh
Sunny Kumar

arihant
SUCCESS AND NOTHING LESS

arihant
SUCCESS AND NOTHING LESS

Arihant Prakashan (Series), Meerut

Administrative & Production Offices

Regd. Office

'Ramchhaya' 4577/15, Agarwal Road, Darya Ganj, New Delhi -110002
Tele: 011- 47630600, 43518550

Head Office

Kalindi, TP Nagar, Meerut (UP) - 250002
Tel: 0121-7156203, 7156204

Sales & Support Offices

Agra, Ahmedabad, Bengaluru, Bareilly, Chennai, Delhi, Guwahati, Hyderabad, Jaipur, Jhansi, Kolkata, Lucknow, Nagpur & Pune.

PRICE ₹495.00

PO No : TXT-XX-XXXXXXX-X-XX

Published by Arihant Publications (India) Ltd.

For further information about the books published by Arihant, log on to www.arihantbooks.com or e-mail at info@arihantbooks.com

Follow us on

Preface...

For any aspirant of competitions, a proper grip over NCERT books is the necessity now. After rationalisation of syllabus in competitions like NEET/JEE Main and their syncing with different State Boards, it is very much expected that their test papers will contain most of the questions from NCERT. To cater this situation the need of dual synchronous preparation i.e., study of NCERT for school and competitive exams simultaneously is increasing day by day.

Arihant's **Master the NCERT** Series is framed, developed, and now revised with the same philosophy of such synchronous preparation. These books serve as the complete resource for gripping NCERT with learning, practice and assessment tools. The specialised features of this revised edition are-

- **3 Levels Chapter Analysis** is incorporated in the beggining of each Chapter.
- **Key Notes** are more elaborative and enriched with NEET exclusive features like **NEET PYQ markings, Marks Maximizer, Caution Points & PYQ Notes.**
- **Concept Master** is present at places as concept explanatory videos of key notes.
- Exercise portion is scientifically designed for step-by-step mastering through **Concept Builders,** followed by **Topical MCQs, Numericals Type, Assertion and Reason, Statement based, Matching, NCERT Exemplar's or Past Years Questions** and **Skill Boosters.**
- Questions of Exercises are tagged with NCERT page numbers.
- For Assessment of self-preparation levels **MCQs Based Online Chapter Tests** and **3 Online Mock Tests** are incorporated with this revised edition.

The variety in types of questions framed will also be helpful in analysis of self – performances and exposure to face tough problems of competitive exams.

Huge efforts have been made from our side to keep this book error free, but inspite of that if any error or whatsoever is skipped, then that will be purely incidental. Please write to us your feedbacks for further improvement of the book.

Authors

Key Features

3 Level Chapter Analysis

On the first page of each chapter, NEET Analysis of 5 years is given on following 3 basis -

(i) Topics

(ii) Special format Questions

(iii) Chapter weightage

Topicwise No. of Ques asked in 5 Years (NEET)

Topics	No. of Questions				
	2024	2023	2022	2021	2020
Coulomb's Law	–	–	–	–	1
Electric Field	–	–	–	–	1
Electric Dipole	–	–	1	2	1
Dipole in a Uniform External Field	–	1	–	–	–
Continuous Charge Distribution	–	–	–	–	–
Gauss's Law	–	1	–	–	–
Applications of Gauss's Law	–	–	–	–	–

Special Type of Ques Asked in 5 Years (NEET)

Types	Years				
	2024	2023	2022	2021	2020
A-R	–	–	–	–	–
Statement Based	–	–	–	–	–
Matching	–	–	–	–	–

Last 5 Years Weigtage (NEET)

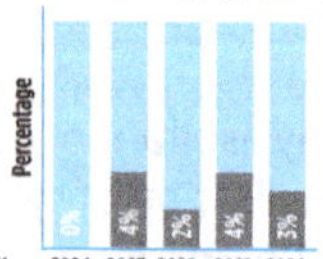

Marks Maximiser

- **Force on a charge placed at the vertex of an equilateral triangle**

  Force on a charge q_3 due to other two charges q_1 and q_2 in an equilateral triangle is given by

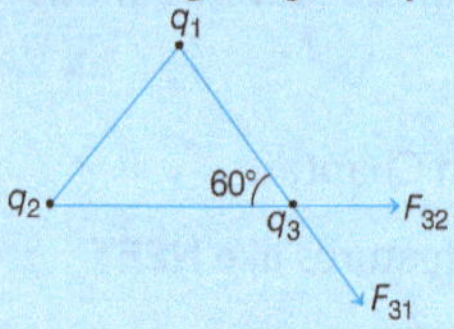

$$F_{net} = \sqrt{F_{31}^2 + F_{32}^2 + 2F_{31}F_{32}\cos 60^\circ} = \sqrt{F_{31}^2 + F_{32}^2 + F_{31}F_{32}}$$

Marks Maximiser

Specialised box matter with NEET/JEE exclusive important information which may or may not be present in NCERT.

Forces Between Multiple Charges

"Total force on a given charge due to number of charges is the vector sum of individual forces acting on that charge due to the presence of other charges". This is termed as the **principle of superposition.**

A system of multiple charges is shown in the figure.

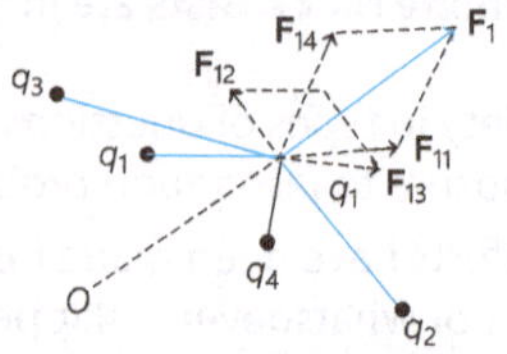

If the charges $q_1, q_2, q_3, \ldots, q_n$ are present in a system, then total force F_1 on charge q_1 due to all other charges is given by

$$\mathbf{F}_1 = \mathbf{F}_{12} + \mathbf{F}_{13} + \mathbf{F}_{14} + \ldots + \mathbf{F}_{1n}$$

i.e. $$\mathbf{F}_1 = \frac{1}{4\pi\varepsilon_0}\left(\frac{q_1q_2}{r_{12}^2}\hat{\mathbf{r}}_{12} + \frac{q_1q_3}{r_{13}^2}\hat{\mathbf{r}}_{13} + \ldots + \frac{q_1q_n}{r_{1n}^2}\hat{\mathbf{r}}_{1n}\right)$$

$$= \frac{q_1}{4\pi\varepsilon_0}\sum_{i=1}^{n}\frac{q_i}{r_{1i}^2}\hat{\mathbf{r}}_{1i}$$

Physics Through Concept Master

Unique video support to explain difficult Topics/Concept of NCERT in simple and easy to understand language.

Key Features

PYQ Notes

1. **Electric field due to an insulating sphere** [NEET 2023]

Field due to a uniformly charged insulating sphere is given by

(i) **Outside the sphere,** i.e. $r < R$

$$E = \frac{q}{4\pi\varepsilon_0 r'^2}\hat{r}$$

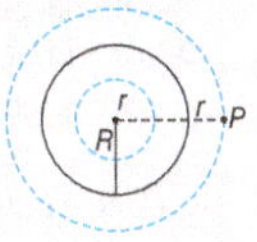

(ii) **At the surface of sphere,**
i.e. $r = R$

$$E = \frac{q}{4\pi\varepsilon_0 R^2}$$

(iii) **Inside the sphere,**
i.e. $r > R$

$$E = \frac{1}{4\pi\varepsilon_0}\frac{Qr}{R^3}$$

$$= \frac{\rho r}{3\varepsilon_0}$$

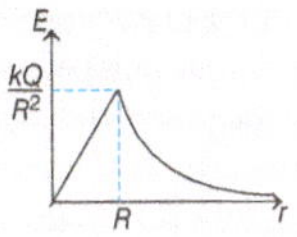

PYQ Notes

NEET / JEE specific important points, which were asked in past years but not incorporated in present Rationalised NCERT .

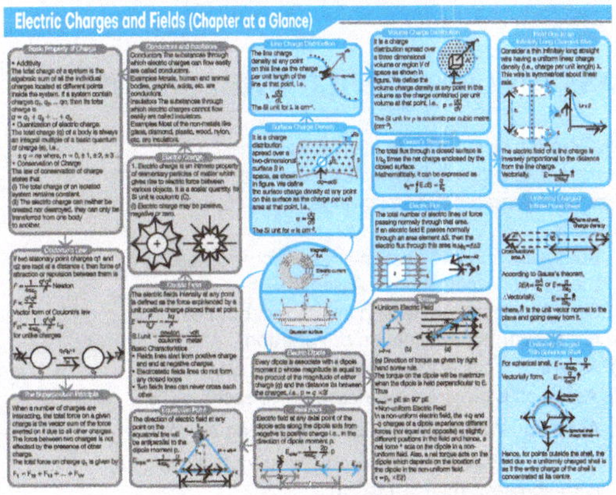

Chapter at a Glance

Completely Coloured Glorified Infographics to map all the key points of a chapter for quick review. These are present at the end of all Chapters.

Step by Step

Mastering NCERT

- Concept Builders
- Topical Questions
- Assertion and Reason Questions
- Statement Based
- Matching Type
- Numerical Type
- NCERT Exemplar
- Past Exams MCQs
- Skill Boosters

Concept Builders

1 On rubbing two bodies, the mass of one body slightly gets......... (increases/decreases)

2 The property which differentiates the two kinds of charges is called the polarity of charge. [T/F]

3 If the sizes of charged bodies are very small compared to the distance between them, then we treat them as ...... (zero/ point) charge.

4 A positively charged glass rod can attract neutral piece of paper. [T/F]

5 If an uncharged bob is placed in an electric field, then its time period of oscillation remains the same. [T/F]

12 Electric field lines cannot cross each other because if they do so, then they will have more than one tangent which is not possible. [T/F]

13 In a non-uniform electric field, a dipole will have translatory as well as rotatory motion. [T/F]

14 The strength of electric field at an axial point of a short dipole is .... (half/twice) the strength at same distance on the equatorial line.

15 If three charges $+q$, $+q$ and $+q$ are placed at the vertices of an equilateral triangle of side a, then what is the force on a charge $+Q$ placed at the centre of the triangle?

Step by Step Mastering NCERT

The scientifically designed practice exercise with all possible type of questions to be asked in competition like NEET/JEE.

Concept Builders

These are present as simple teasers like T/F, Fill ups and one word question. Thus, structured to build foundation stone of NCERT concepts.

Concept Builders

1 On rubbing two bodies, the mass of one body slightly gets......... (increases/decreases)

2 The property which differentiates the two kinds of charges is called the polarity of charge. [T/F]

3 If the sizes of charged bodies are very small compared to the distance between them, then we treat them as ...... (zero/ point) charge.

4 A positively charged glass rod can attract neutral piece of paper. [T/F]

5 If an uncharged bob is placed in an electric field, then its time period of oscillation remains the same. [T/F]

Key Features

Topical Questions

NEET/JEE like MCQs from line by line text of NCERT with complete tagging of pages. All these MCQs are arranged as per the Topic headings of NCERT.

Topical Questions

Electric Charge

1 The discharge of electric charges through our body due to rubbing of insulating surfaces generates NCERT Pg. 1

(a) static electricity
(b) current electricity
(c) electric potential
(d) electrodynamics

2 If a plastic rod rubbed with fur is made to touch two small pith balls suspended nearby, then which figure shows their final configuration? NCERT Pg. 1

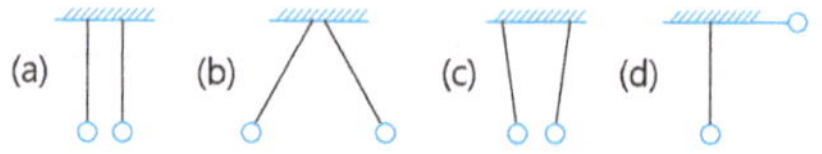

A-R Questions

Most Important special format MCQs category. All of these are also tagged with NCERT page numbers as well .

Assertion and Reason Questions

Direction (Q. Nos. 1-10) *In the following questions, a statement of Assertion is followed by a corresponding statement of Reason. Of the following statements, choose the correct one.*

(a) Both Assertion and Reason are correct and Reason is the correct explanation of Assertion.
(b) Both Assertion and Reason are correct but Reason is not the correct explanation of Assertion.
(c) Assertion is correct but Reason is incorrect.
(d) Assertion is incorrect but Reason is correct.

1 **Assertion** When we produce charge q_1 on a body by rubbing it against another body which gets a charge q_2 in the process, then $q_1 + q_2 = 0$.
Reason Charge on an isolated system remains constant.
NCERT Pg. 4

Statement Type Questions

In NEET Physics paper such types (Statement I & II) of statement based questions are asked.
Such Type of Questions are covered in step by step practice with NCERT page tagging.

Statement Based Questions

Direction (Q. Nos. 1-8) *In the following questions, two statements (I and II) are given. In the light of the given statements, choose the correct answer from the options given below.*

(a) Both Statement I and Statement II are incorrect.
(b) Statement I is correct but Statement II is incorrect.
(c) Statement I is incorrect but Statement II is correct.
(d) Both Statement I and Statement II are correct.

1 **Statement I** When bodies are charged by rubbing, there is a transfer of electrons from one body to other, no new charges are created nor destroyed.

Matching Type Questions

Step by step practice includes the matching type MCQs. These are placed just after statement based MCQs and all are tagged with NCERT page numbers.

Matching Type Questions

1 Match the Column I (charge) with Column II (property) and select the correct answer from the options given below. NCERT Pg. 1

	Column I		Column II
A.	Like charges	1.	of two types
B.	Unlike charges	2.	repel each other
C.	Charge can be	3.	attract each other
D.	Charges are	4.	neutralised, if they are equal and opposite

Key Features

NCERT Exemplar Questions

1 In figure, two positive charges q_2 and q_3 are fixed along the Y-axis, exert a net electric force in the positive x-direction on a charge q_1 fixed along the X-axis. If a positive charge Q is added at $(x, 0)$, the force on q_1

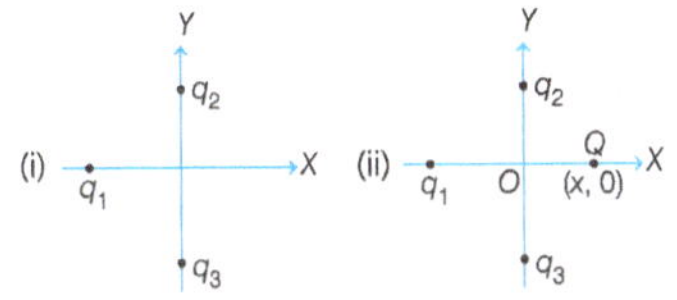

(a) shall increase along the positive X-axis
(b) shall decrease along the positive X-axis
(c) shall point along the negative X-axis
(d) shall increase but the direction changes because of the intersection of Q with q_2 and q_3

NCERT Exemplar's Questions

NCERT Exemplar books are considered as one of the best problem books for competitive exams. Each chapter has selected exemplar problems to provide consolidation for preparations.

Past Exams Questions

NEET

1 An electric dipole is placed at an angle of 30° with an electric field of intensity 2×10^5 NC^{-1}. It experiences a torque equal to 4 N-m. Calculate the magnitude of charge on the dipole, if the dipole length is 2 cm.
NCERT Pg. 27, NEET 2023

(a) 6 mC (b) 4 mC (c) 2 mC (d) 8 mC

11 A point charge of 10 μC is placed at the origin. At what location on the X-axis should a point charge of 40 μC be placed, so that the net electric field is zero at $x = 2$ cm on the X-axis? NCERT Pg. 14, JEE Main 2023

(a) $x = 8$ cm (b) $x = -4$ cm
(c) $x = 4$ cm (d) $x = 6$ cm

Past Exams' Questions

Selected PYQs with NCERT page tagging are present as the final check of preparation.

Skill Boosters

1 A glass rod rubbed with fur is used to charge a gold leaf electroscope and the leaves are observed to diverge. The electroscope disc is then exposed to X-rays for a short period. Then,

(a) the divergence of leaves is not affected
(b) the leaves diverge further
(c) the leaves will collapse
(d) the leaves will melt

2 A foreigner student who grow up in a tropical country but is studying in United States may not have experience with static electricity sparks or shocks. The student most probably gets his/her first shock in

(a) during a thunderstorm (b) while having a stroll in rain
(c) in summer (d) in winter

Skill Boosters

Brain Teasers present at the end of step by step practice to provide extra edge for preparation.

Decoding the Questions

Answers and explanatory solutions of selected questions for better gripping of NCERT concepts.

Step by Step

Decoding the Questions

Concept Builders

1 decreases
2 True (T)
3 point
4 True (T)
5 True (T)
6 Quantisation of charges
7 9×10^9 N
8 different
9 directly
10 intensity, potential
11 $\mathbf{E}(r) = \frac{1}{4\pi\varepsilon_0} \sum_{i=1}^{n} \frac{q_i}{r_{ip}^2} \hat{r}_{ip}$

atmosphere. Due to this excess charge, the possibility of generation of spark increases and the inflammable material may catch fire.

In order to prevent this, metallic ropes are suspended from the carrier to keep its body in the contact with earth.

11 (b) If a sphere having charge q is put in contact with an identical uncharged sphere, then the charge q would get redistributed such that overall charge on the system remains conserved.

Also, by symmetry we can say that, charge on each sphere would be

If F is maximum, then $\frac{dF}{dq} = 0$

i.e. $\frac{d}{dq}\left(\frac{1}{4\pi\varepsilon_0} \frac{qQ - q^2}{r^2}\right) = 0$

$\Rightarrow \quad Q = +2q$

16 (b) If the two charges are placed in contact with each other and then separated, charges on them will be redistributed and net charge on them will be the difference of two,

i.e. $q_{net} = |q_1 - q_2|/2$

This net charge have same polarity, so after placing them at a distance d, they experience a force of repulsion.

Contents

01

Scan for **Physics Through Concept Master** Videos

Electric Charges and Fields

Topicwise No. of Ques asked in 5 Years (NEET)

Topics	2024	2023	2022	2021	2020
Coulomb's Law	–	–	–	–	1
Electric Field	–	–	–	–	1
Electric Dipole	–	–	1	2	1
Dipole in a Uniform External Field	–	1	–	–	–
Continuous Charge Distribution	–	–	–	–	–
Gauss's Law	–	1	–	–	–
Applications of Gauss's Law	–	–	–	–	–

(No. of Questions)

Special Type of Ques Asked In 5 Years (NEET)

Types	2024	2023	2022	2021	2020
A-R	–	–	–	–	–
Statement Based	–	–	–	–	–
Matching	–	–	–	–	–

(Years)

Last 5 Years Weigtage (NEET)

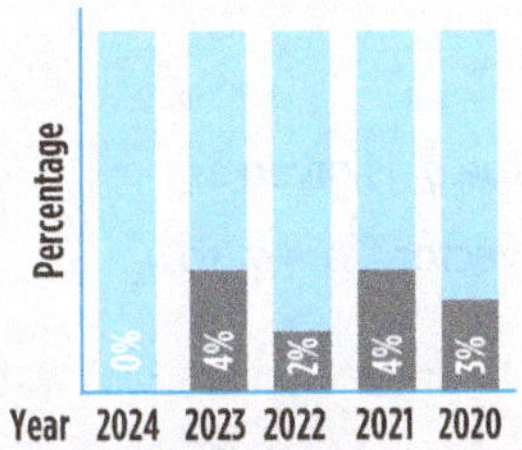

- Electrostatics deals with the study of forces, fields and potentials arising from static charges.

Electric Charge

- The physical property of a matter that causes it to experience a force when placed in an electromagnetic field is called **electric charge**. There are two types of charges, i.e. **positive charge** and **negative charge**.
- **Like charges** repel each other while **unlike charges** attract each other as shown in figure below.

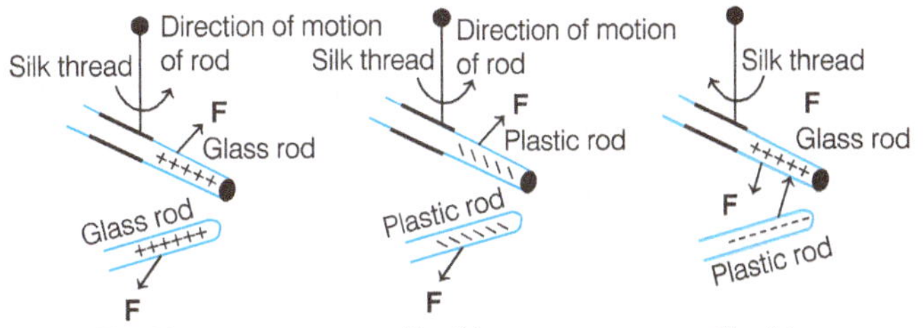

Fig. (a) Fig. (b) Fig. (c)

Two like charges on two glass rods [Fig. (a)] and two plastic rods [Fig. (b)] repel each other, whereas two unlike charges on glass rod and plastic rod [Fig. (c)] respectively, attract each other.

- The property which differentiates the two kinds of charges is called the **polarity of charge**.
- If an object possesses an electric charge, it is said to be **electrified** or **charged**. When it has no charge, it is said to be **electrically neutral**.

Gold-leaf electroscope is a simple apparatus to detect the charge on a body.

- A body can be **charged positively by losing some of its electrons** and similarly, **can be charged negatively by gaining electrons**.

Conductors and Insulators

- Those substances which allow electricity to pass through them easily are called **conductors**.
- They have electric charges (electrons) that are comparatively free to move inside the material.
- Metals, human & animal bodies and earth are conductors.
- Most of the non-metals like glass, porcelain, plastic, nylon, wood offer high resistance to the passage of electricity through them, they are called **insulator**.
- When some charge is transferred to a conductor, it readily gets distributed over the entire surface of the conductor. In contrast, if some charge is put on an insulator, it stays at the same place.
- When we bring a charged body in contact with the earth, all the excess charge on the body disappears by causing a momentary current to pass to the ground through the connecting conductor (such as our body).
- The process of sharing the charges with the earth is called **grounding** or **earthing**. It provides a safety measure for electrical circuits and appliances.

Basic Properties of Electric Charge

- If the sizes of charged bodies are very small as compared to the distances between them, we treat them as point charges.

  All the charge content of the body is assumed to be concentrated at one point in space.
- **Additivity of Charges** The net electric charge on a body is equal to the algebraic sum of all the electric charges distributed on the different parts of the body.

  If a system contains n-charges $q_1, q_2, q_3, \ldots, q_n$, then

$$q_{total} = q_1 + q_2 + q_3 + \ldots + q_n$$

- **Charge is conserved** In an isolated system consisting of many charged bodies, charges may get redistributed due to interactions among the bodies but total charge is always conserved.
- It is not possible to create or destroy net charge carried by any isolated system although the charge carrying particles may be created or destroyed in a process.
- **Quantisation of Charge** The charge on a body is always an integral multiple of e (basic unit of charge, i.e. charge on an electron). This is called quantisation of charge.

  i.e. $q = ne$

  where, $n = 1, 2, 3, \ldots$

  The charge on an electron is taken to be negative.
- The **SI unit** of charge is **coulomb** and it is denoted by **symbol C**.

  The value of basic unit of charge is given as

$$e = 1.602192 \times 10^{-19}\ \text{C}$$

  The charge of magnitude – 1C contains 6.24×10^{18} electrons.

Coulomb's Law

- If two point charges q_1, q_2 are separated by a distance r in vacuum, then the magnitude of the force F between them is given by **NEET 2020, 19**

$$F = k\frac{|q_1 q_2|}{r^2}$$

where, $k = \dfrac{1}{4\pi\varepsilon_0} = 9 \times 10^9\ \text{N-m}^2/\text{C}^2$

and ε_0 = permittivity of free space

$= 8.854 \times 10^{-12}\ \text{C}^2\text{N}^{-1}\text{m}^{-2}$.

- The **force between two charges q_1 and q_2 located at a distance r** in a medium is expressed as

$$F_{medium} = \frac{1}{4\pi\varepsilon}\cdot\frac{q_1 q_2}{r^2}$$

where, ε = absolute permittivity of the medium.

- In **dielectric medium of dielectric constant K, force decreases by a factor K**.

$$\frac{F_{vacuum}}{F_{medium}} = \frac{1}{4\pi\varepsilon_0}\cdot\frac{q_1 q_2}{r^2} \Big/ \frac{1}{4\pi\varepsilon}\cdot\frac{q_1 q_2}{r^2} = \frac{\varepsilon}{\varepsilon_0} = \varepsilon_r = K$$

i.e. $F_{medium} = \dfrac{F_{vacuum}}{K}$

where, ε_r = relative permittivity of the medium,

the ratio of permittivity of the medium to the permittivity of free space is called **relative permittivity**.

- **Coulomb's Law in Vector Form** Let the position vectors of charges q_1 and q_2 be $\mathbf{r}_1$ and $\mathbf{r}_2$ respectively as shown in figure below

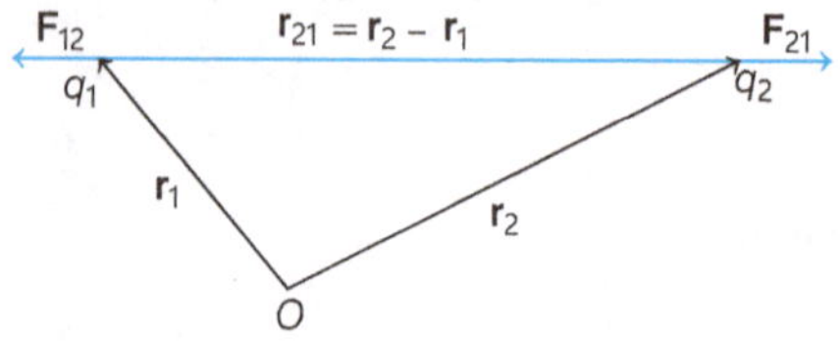

- The force $\mathbf{F}_{21}$ on charge q_2 due to charge q_1 is given as

$\mathbf{F}_{21} = \dfrac{1}{4\pi\varepsilon_0}\cdot\dfrac{q_1 q_2}{r_{21}^2}\hat{\mathbf{r}}_{21}$, where $\hat{\mathbf{r}}_{21}$ is unit vector from q_1 to q_2.

$$\therefore \quad \hat{\mathbf{r}}_{21} = \frac{\mathbf{r}_{21}}{r_{21}}$$

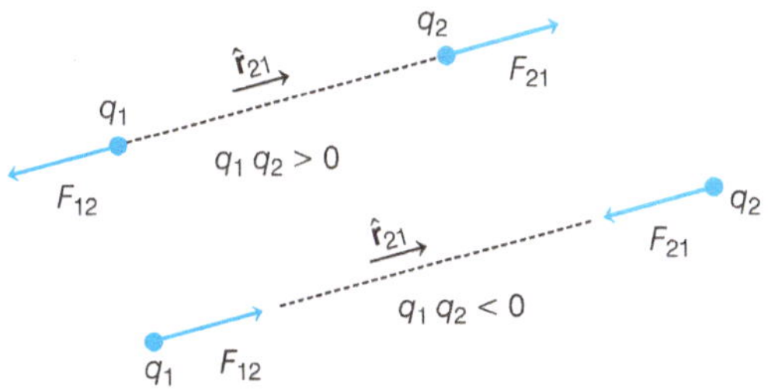

- The force $\mathbf{F}_{12}$ on charge q_1 due to charge q_2 is given as

$$\mathbf{F}_{12} = \frac{1}{4\pi\varepsilon_0} \cdot \frac{q_1 q_2}{r_{12}^2} \hat{\mathbf{r}}_{12} = -\frac{1}{4\pi\varepsilon_0} \cdot \frac{q_1 q_2}{r_{21}^2} \hat{\mathbf{r}}_{21}$$

- Coulomb's law agrees with the Newton's third law, i.e. $\mathbf{F}_{12} = -\mathbf{F}_{21}$

Forces between Multiple Charges

"Total force on a given charge due to number of charges is the vector sum of individual forces acting on that charge due to the presence of other charges". This is termed as the **principle of superposition**.

A system of multiple charges is shown in the figure.

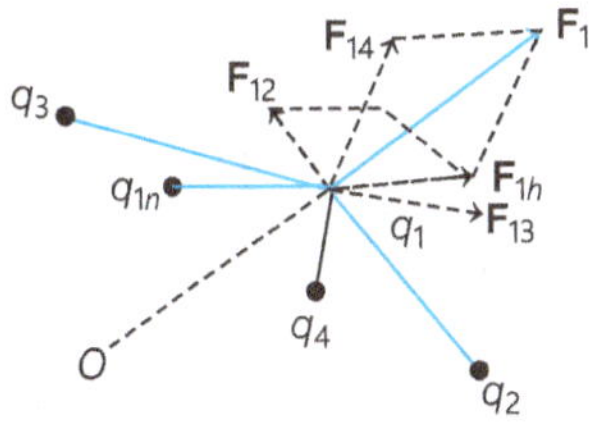

If the charges $q_1, q_2, q_3, \ldots, q_n$ are present in a system, then total force F_1 on charge q_1 due to all other charges is given by

$$\mathbf{F}_1 = \mathbf{F}_{12} + \mathbf{F}_{13} + \mathbf{F}_{14} + \ldots + \mathbf{F}_{1n}$$

i.e.
$$\mathbf{F}_1 = \frac{1}{4\pi\varepsilon_0}\left(\frac{q_1 q_2}{r_{12}^2}\hat{\mathbf{r}}_{12} + \frac{q_1 q_3}{r_{13}^2}\hat{\mathbf{r}}_{13} + \ldots + \frac{q_1 q_n}{r_{1n}^2}\hat{\mathbf{r}}_{1n}\right)$$

$$= \frac{q_1}{4\pi\varepsilon_0}\sum_{i=1}^{n}\frac{q_i}{r_{1i}^2}\hat{\mathbf{r}}_{1i}$$

For Concept Master Video

Marks Maximiser

- **Force on a charge placed at the vertex of an equilateral triangle**

Force on a charge q_3 due to other two charges q_1 and q_2 in an equilateral triangle is given by

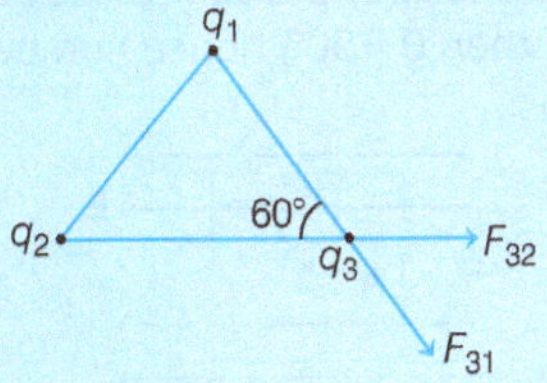

$$F_{\text{net}} = \sqrt{F_{31}^2 + F_{32}^2 + 2F_{31}F_{32}\cos 60°} = \sqrt{F_{31}^2 + F_{32}^2 + F_{31}F_{32}}$$

Electric Field

- It is the region surrounding an electric charge or a group of charges, in which another charge experiences a force. Its **unit** is N/C and it is a **vector quantity**.
- The electric field produced by the charge Q at a point r is given as $\mathbf{E}(\mathbf{r}) = \frac{1}{4\pi\varepsilon_0} \cdot \frac{Q}{r^2}\hat{\mathbf{r}}$ **NEET 2020**

where, $\hat{\mathbf{r}} = \frac{\mathbf{r}}{r}$ is a unit vector from the origin to the point $\mathbf{r}$.

- If the position of charge q is denoted by vector $\mathbf{r}$, then it experiences a force $\mathbf{F}$ equal to the charge q multiplied by the electric field $\mathbf{E}$ at the location of q.

Thus, $\mathbf{F}(\mathbf{r}) = q\mathbf{E}(\mathbf{r})$.

- The charge Q which is producing the electric field is called a **source charge** and the charge q, which tests the effect of a source charge is called a **test charge**.
- **Electric field vector E** (also known as electric field intensity) at any point is given by

$$\mathbf{E} = \lim_{q_0 \to 0} \frac{\mathbf{F}}{q_0}$$

where, q_0 is a small positive test charge which experiences a force $\mathbf{F}$ at given point.

- **Direction of electric field intensity** is taken from positive charge to negative charge.
- **Electric Field due to a System of Charges** If a system of charges $q_1, q_2, q_3, \ldots, q_n$ with position vector $\mathbf{r}_1, \mathbf{r}_2, \mathbf{r}_3, \ldots, \mathbf{r}_n$ relative to origin O, then Coulomb's law and the superposition principle can be used to determine the net field at a point P denoted by the position vector $\mathbf{r}$.

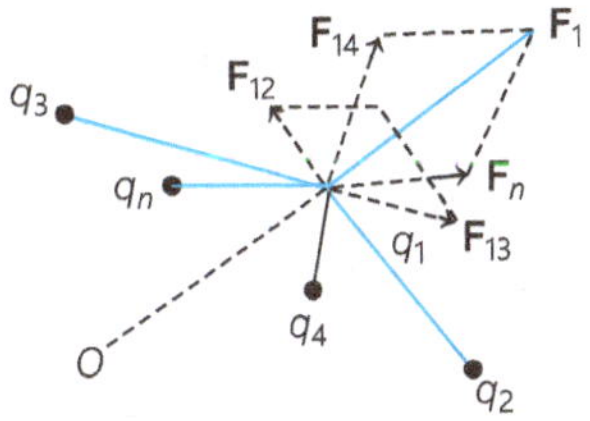

By the superposition principle, the electric field $\mathbf{E}$ at $\mathbf{r}$ due to system of charges is (as shown in above figure)

$$\mathbf{E}(\mathbf{r}) = \mathbf{E}_1(\mathbf{r}) + \mathbf{E}_2(\mathbf{r}) + \ldots + \mathbf{E}_n(\mathbf{r})$$

$$= \frac{1}{4\pi\varepsilon_0}\frac{q_1}{r_{1p}^2}\hat{\mathbf{r}}_{1p} + \frac{1}{4\pi\varepsilon_0}\frac{q_2}{r_{2p}^2}\hat{\mathbf{r}}_{2p} + \ldots + \frac{1}{4\pi\varepsilon_0}\frac{q_n}{r_{np}^2}\hat{\mathbf{r}}_{np}$$

$$\Rightarrow \mathbf{E}(\mathbf{r}) = \frac{1}{4\pi\varepsilon_0}\sum_{i=1}^{n}\frac{q_i}{r_{ip}^2}\hat{\mathbf{r}}_{ip}$$

where, $\hat{\mathbf{r}}_{ip}$ is directed from ith charge to point P.

Physical Significance of Electric Field

- Electric field is a characteristic of the system of charges and is independent of test charge that you place at a point to determine the field.
- Since, force is a vector quantity. So, electric field is a vector field.
- The effect of any motion of charge q_1 on charge q_2 cannot arise instantaneously. There will be some time delay between the effect (force on q_2) and the cause (motion of q_1).
- The accelerated motion of charge q_1 produces electromagnetic waves, which then propagate with the speed c, reaches q_2 and cause a force on q_2.

  Although, electric field can be detected only by its effect (force) on charge, but it evolves according to laws of its own. It can also transport energy.

Electric Field Lines

- Electric field line is an imaginary line drawn around a charge. **The tangent on these lines at any point gives direction of field at that point.**
- The density of the field lines represents the magnitude of electric field. The dependence of electric field strength on the distance and its relation to the number of field lines is shown in the figure.

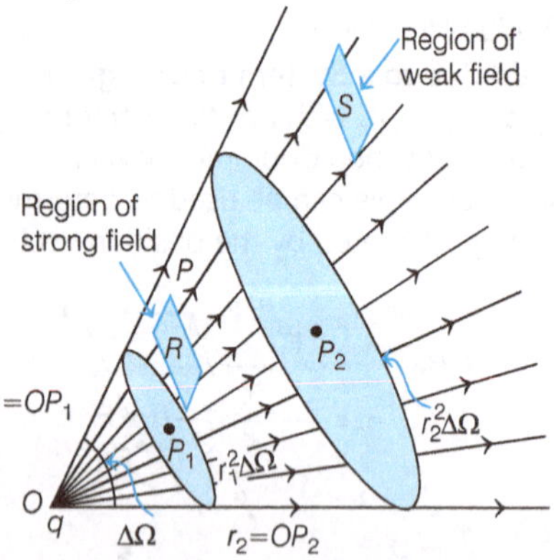

- **The field lines follow some important general properties**
  - (i) Field lines start from positive charges and ends at negative charges. If there is a single charge, they may start or end at infinity.
  - (ii) In a charge free region, electric field lines can be taken to be continuous curves without any breaks.
  - (iii) Two field lines can never cross each other (if they did, the field at the point of intersection will not have a unique direction, which is absurd).
  - (iv) Electrostatic field lines do not form any closed loops. This follows from the conservative nature of electric field.
  - (v) Electric field lines are always perpendicular to the surface of the conductor, both while entering and leaving.
  - (vi) **Electric field lines due to some simple charge configuration** are shown in the figure.

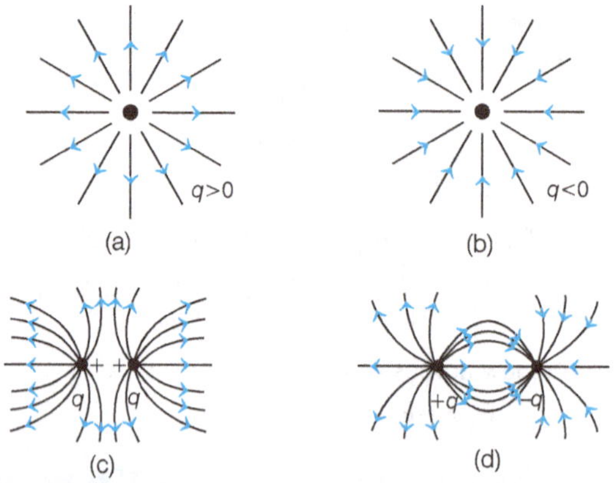

Electric Flux

- Electric flux is a measure of flow of electric field through a surface. Mathematically, electric flux is the product of an area element $\Delta \mathbf{S}$ and normal component of $\mathbf{E}$ integrated over a surface as shown in figure alongside.

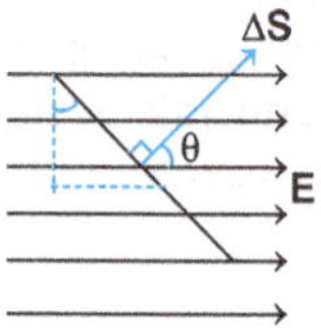

i.e. $\phi_E = \int \mathbf{E}\cdot\Delta\mathbf{S} = \int \mathbf{E}\cdot\hat{\mathbf{n}}\,\Delta S = \int E\,\Delta S\cos\theta$

where, θ is the angle between the directions of electric field $\mathbf{E}$ and area vector $\Delta\mathbf{S}$ of the surface

and $\hat{\mathbf{n}}$ is the unit vector normal to area element ΔS as shown in figure below

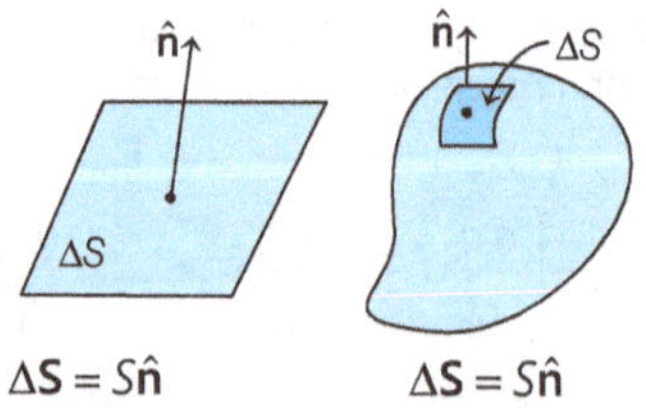

$\Delta\mathbf{S} = S\hat{\mathbf{n}}$ $\Delta\mathbf{S} = S\hat{\mathbf{n}}$

The **SI unit of electric flux** is N-m^{2}C^{-1} or V-m.

- **If the area element ΔS is normal to E at a point** as shown in figure alongside, then $\theta = 0°$, hence number of field lines crossing it is proportional to $\mathbf{E}\Delta S$.

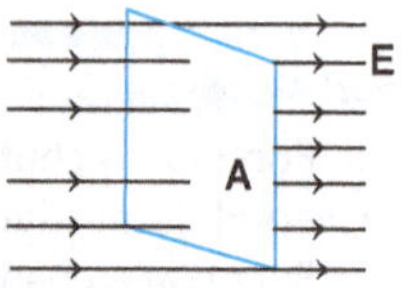

- **If the area element ΔS is parallel to E at a point** as shown in figure below, then $\theta = 90°$, hence number of field lines crossing it is zero.

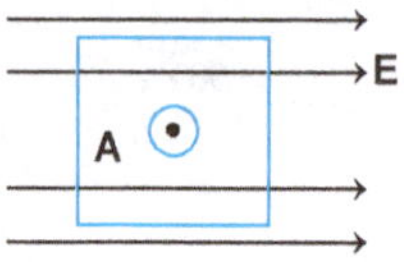

- Electric field in a region can be non-zero even though electric flux may be zero but its *vice-versa* is not possible.

Electric Dipole

- An electric dipole is a system formed by two equal and opposite point charges placed at a small distance apart.

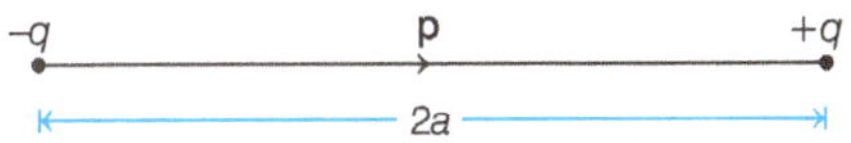

- The product of the magnitude of either charge q and the distance between the charges $2a$ is called **electric dipole moment** (**p**).

  i.e. $\mathbf{p} = q \times 2\mathbf{a}$

  It is a **vector quantity** and its SI unit is C-m.

- The direction of electric dipole moment is from $-q$ to q.
- The total charge of the electric dipole is zero, this does not mean that the field due to the electric dipole is zero.
- **Electric field at an axial point of a dipole**

  Electric field due to a dipole at an axial point P as shown in the figure is given by

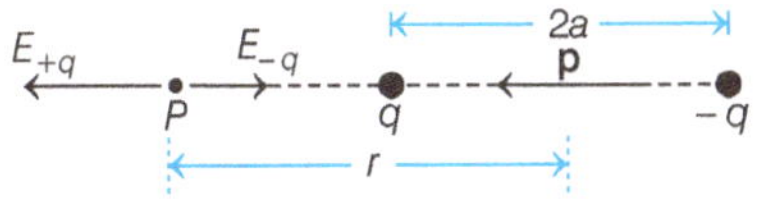

$$\mathbf{E} = \frac{1}{4\pi\varepsilon_0} \cdot \frac{2pr}{(r^2 - a^2)^2} \quad \text{[direction of } \mathbf{E} \text{ is same as of } \mathbf{p}]$$

$$\mathbf{E} = \frac{1}{4\pi\varepsilon_0} \cdot \frac{2\mathbf{p}}{r^3} \quad [\text{when } r >> a]$$

- **Electric field at an equitorial point of a dipole**

  Electric field due to a dipole at an equitorial point P as shown in the figure is given by

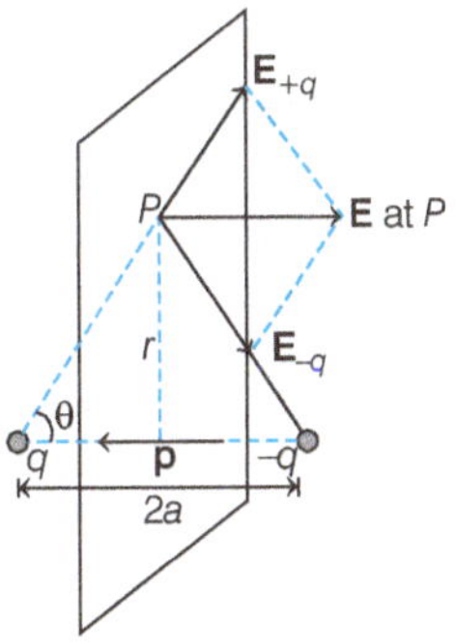

$$\mathbf{E} = -\frac{1}{4\pi\varepsilon_0} \cdot \frac{p}{(r^2 + a^2)^{3/2}}$$

[direction of **E** is opposite to that of **p**]

$$\mathbf{E} = -\frac{\mathbf{p}}{4\pi\varepsilon_0 r^3} \quad [\text{when } r >> a]$$

Physical Significance of Dipoles

- In most molecules, the centres of positive charges and of negative charges lie at the same place. Therefore, their dipole moment is zero, e.g. CO_2 and CH_4.
- But in some molecules, the centres of negative charges and of positive charges do not coincide. Therefore, they have a permanent electric dipole moment, even in the absence of an electric field. Such molecules are called **polar molecules**, e.g. H_2O.

Dipole in a Uniform External Field

- When a dipole of dipole moment **p** is placed at an angle θ from the direction of a uniform electric field **E** as shown in figure below, then it experiences a torque and its magnitude is given by

$$\tau = pE \sin\theta$$

In vector form, $\tau = \mathbf{p} \times \mathbf{E}$

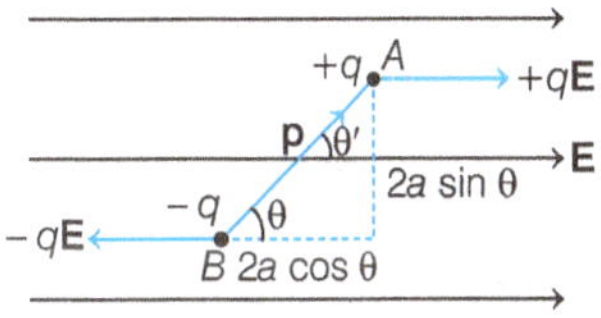

- Direction of torque is perpendicular to the plane of paper and inwards.
- The two charges of electric dipole experience equal and opposite forces, which cancel each other and hence net force on electric dipole in uniform electric field is zero.
- When dipole is parallel or anti-parallel to E, then torque is zero at $\theta = 0°$ or $180°$ and maximum, $\tau_{max} = \mathbf{pE}$ at $\theta = 90°$.
- The dipole tends to align in a direction, where it experiences minimum torque. So, it aligns parallel or anti-parallel to the direction of uniform electric field.
- **When an electric dipole of dipole moment p is placed parallel or anti-parallel to the direction of a non-uniform electric field**, **E** as shown in figure below, then in either case, the net torque is zero, but there is net force on the dipole in the direction of increasing electric field.

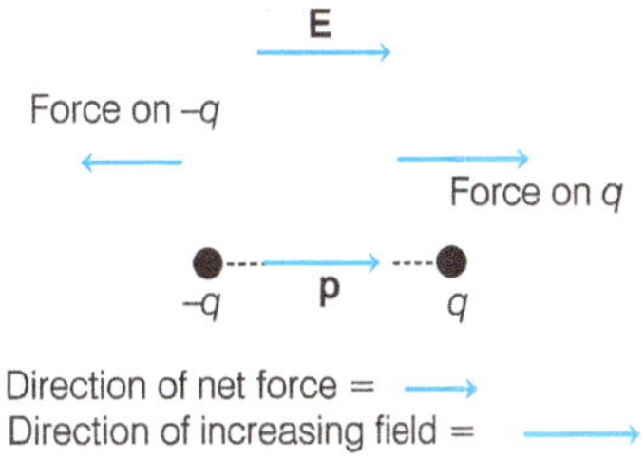

(a)

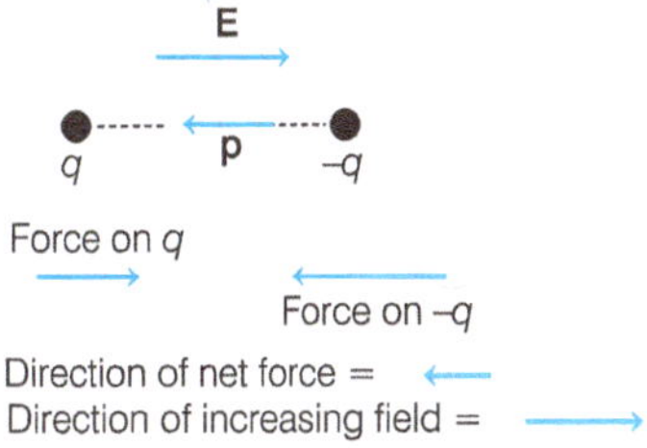

(b)

Continuous Charge Distribution

There are three types of continuous charge distribution and according to charge distribution, there are three types of charge density as given below

(i) **Linear Charge Density** It is charge per unit length of a long wire. If ΔQ charge is distributed uniformly on line element Δl of the wire, then linear charge density (λ) is given as $\lambda = \frac{\Delta Q}{\Delta l}$ C/m.

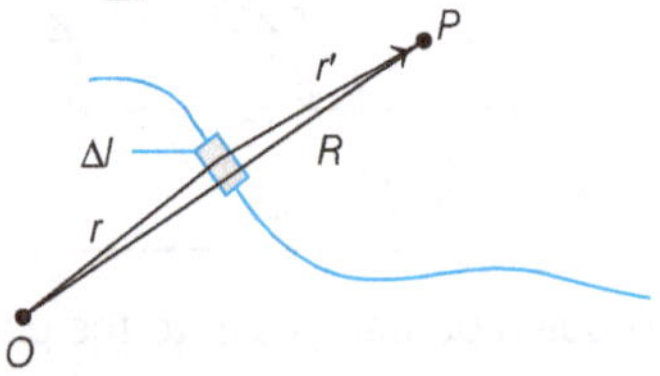

(ii) **Surface Charge Density** It is charge per unit area of a surface. If ΔQ charge is distributed uniformly on area element ΔS, then surface charge density (σ) is given as $\sigma = \frac{\Delta Q}{\Delta S}$ C/m^2.

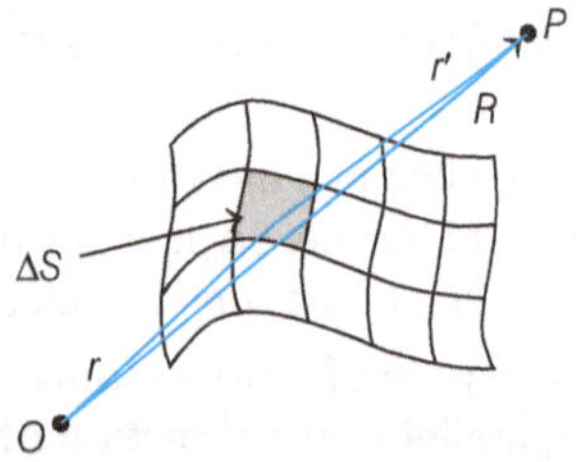

(iii) **Volume Charge Density** It is charge per unit volume of a bulk material. If ΔQ charge is distributed uniformly on volume element ΔV, then volume charge density (ρ) is given as $\rho = \frac{\Delta Q}{\Delta V}$ C/m^3.

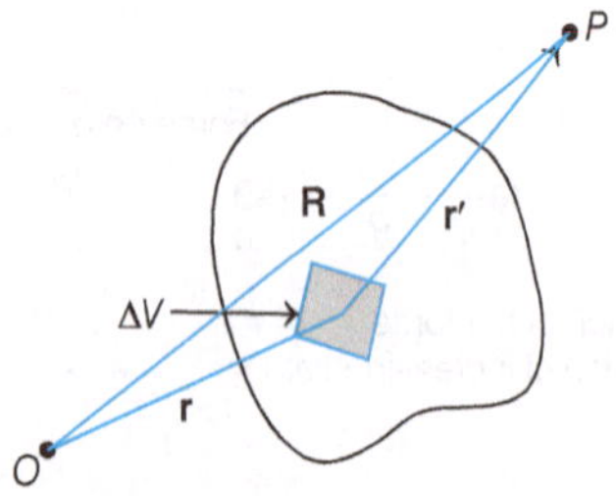

- **Electric field due to charge $\rho \Delta V$ is** given by

$$\Delta \mathbf{E} = \frac{1}{4\pi\varepsilon_0} \cdot \frac{\rho \Delta V}{r'^2} \hat{\mathbf{r}}'$$

where, r' is the distance between the charge element and P, and $\hat{\mathbf{r}}'$ is a unit vector in the direction from charge element to P.

- The **total electric fields due to different volume elements** is given as

$$\mathbf{E} \cong \frac{1}{4\pi\varepsilon_0} \sum_{\text{all } \Delta V} \frac{\rho \Delta V}{r'^2} \hat{\mathbf{r}}'$$

Gauss's Law

- It states that the surface integral of the electric field intensity (i.e. total electric flux) over any closed surface (called Gaussian surface) **S** as shown in figure below in free space is equal to $\frac{1}{\varepsilon_0}$ times the net charge q enclosed within the surface.

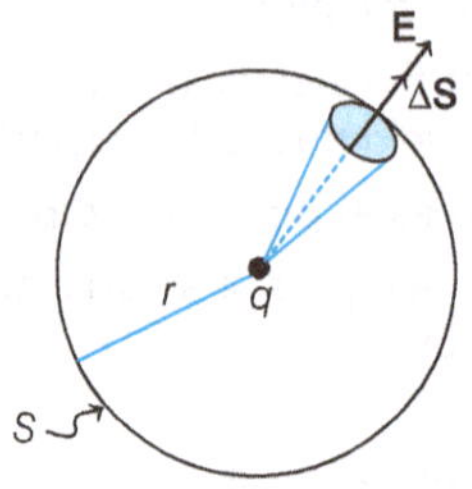

Hence, $\phi_E = \oint \mathbf{E} \cdot d\mathbf{S} = \frac{1}{\varepsilon_0} \sum_{i=1}^{n} q_i = \frac{q_{\text{enclosed}}}{\varepsilon_0}$

where, $q = \sum_{i=1}^{n} q_i$ is the algebraic sum of all the charges inside the closed surface.

- **Some important points regarding Gauss's law**

(i) It is true for any closed surface, no matter what its shape or size.

(ii) The term q on the right side of Gauss's law, includes the sum of all charges enclosed by the surface.

(iii) In the situation when the surface is so chosen that there are some charges inside and some are outside it, then the electric field is due to all the charges, i.e. due to both inside and outside S. The term q on the right side of Gauss's law, however represents only the total charge inside S.

(iv) The surface which is chosen for the application of Gauss's law is called **Gaussian surface**. The Gaussian surface can pass through a continuous charge distribution.

(v) Gauss's law is often useful towards a much easier calculation of the electrostatic field when the system has some symmetry.

(vi) It is based on the inverse square dependence on distance contained in the Coulomb's law. Any violation of Gauss's law will indicate departure from the inverse square law.

Applications of Gauss's Law

Gauss' law can be used to determine the electric field due to symmetric charge configurations.

S.No.	Field due to	Formula	Terminology	Variation of *E* with *r*
(i)	Infinitely long line charge 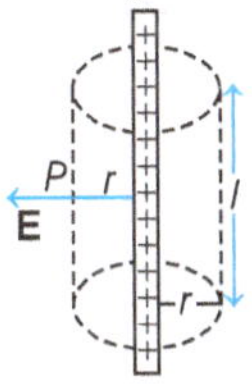	$\mathbf{E} = \frac{\lambda}{2\pi\varepsilon_0 r}\hat{\mathbf{n}}$ $= \frac{2k\lambda}{r}\hat{\mathbf{n}}$	• λ is linear charged density. • $\hat{\mathbf{n}}$ is the radial unit vector. • **r** is perpendicular distance of point charge.	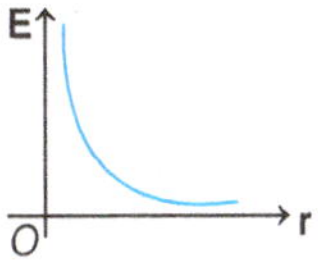
(ii)	Uniformly charged infinite plane sheet 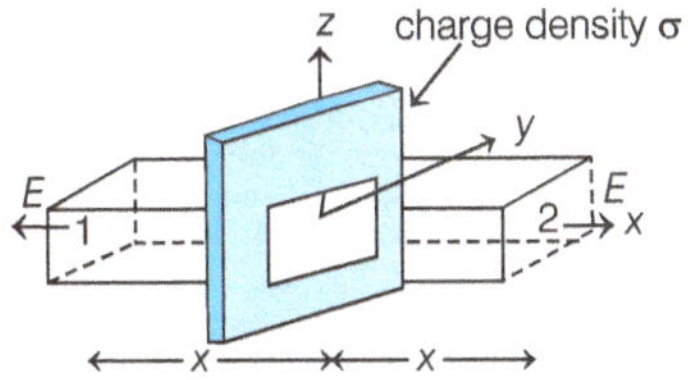	$\mathbf{E} = \frac{\sigma}{2\varepsilon_0}\hat{\mathbf{n}}$	• σ is surface charged density. • $\hat{\mathbf{n}}$ is the unit vector normal to the planes and going away from it. • **E** is directed away from the plate if σ is positive and towards the plate, if σ is negative.	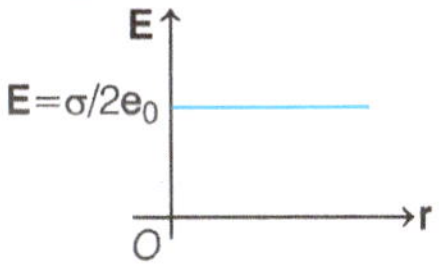
(iii)	Uniformly charged thin spherical shell. 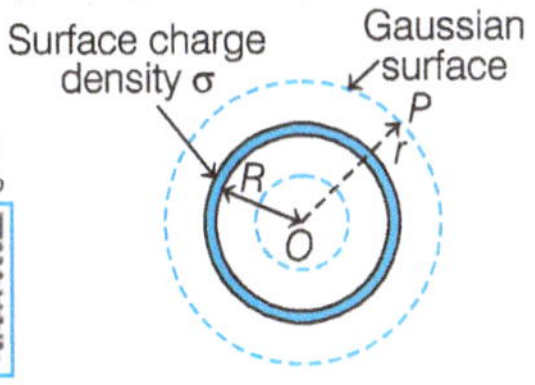 For Concept Master Video	• $r \geq R$ $\mathbf{E} = \frac{q}{4\pi\varepsilon_0 r^2}\hat{\mathbf{r}}$ • $r < R$ $\mathbf{E} = 0$	• r is the radius of Gaussian surface charged density. • R is radius of shell.	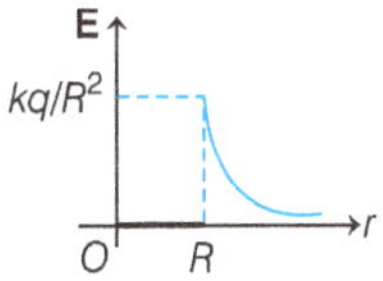

Caution Points

- There is a force known as strong force which holds all the positive charge present in a nucleus. It acts in a very small range of 10^{-14}m. This force gives structure to the atoms.
- The reason for the relatively large value of k and the unit of charge 1C arises because charge is defined based on magnetic effects, which are weaker than electric effects.
- Under rotation, charge is not only scalar but also invariant for reference frame in relative motion.
- Conservation of total charge in an isolated system is independent of the scalar nature of charge and refers to the invariance of charge over time in a specific frame of reference.
- The quantisation of electric charge is fundamental, unexplained law of nature, whereas there is no analogous law for quantisation of mass.
- Electric field from discrete charge configurations is not defined at the discrete charge locations. For continuous volume charge distributions, fields are defined anywhere in the distribution, but for surface charge distributions, the electric field is discontinuous across the surface.
- Charge configuration with zero total charge creates some electric field which is not zero, but as we move farther compared to the size of configuration, its field weakens faster than $\frac{1}{r^2}$. An electric dipole can be a good example of this fact.

PYQ Notes

1. Electric field due to an insulating sphere [NEET 2023]

Field due to a uniformly charged insulating sphere is given by

(i) **Outside the sphere,** i.e. $r < R$

$$E = \frac{q}{4\pi\varepsilon_0 r'^2}\hat{\mathbf{r}}$$

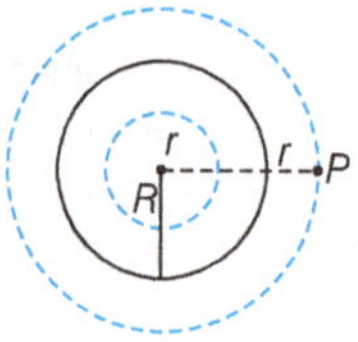

(ii) **At the surface of sphere,**

i.e. $r = R$

$$\mathbf{E} = \frac{q}{4\pi\varepsilon_0 R^2}$$

(iii) **Inside the sphere,**

i.e. $r > R$

$$\mathbf{E} = \frac{1}{4\pi\varepsilon_0}\frac{Q\mathbf{r}}{R^3}$$

$$= \frac{\rho r}{3\varepsilon_0}$$

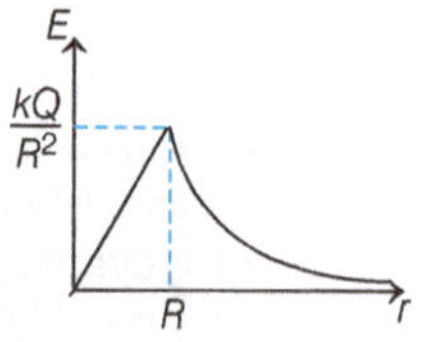

2. Field due to a finite wire [JEE Main 2023]

Electric field due to a finite wire with uniform charged density λ is given by

$$\mathbf{E} = \frac{2k\lambda}{r}\sin\frac{\theta}{2}$$

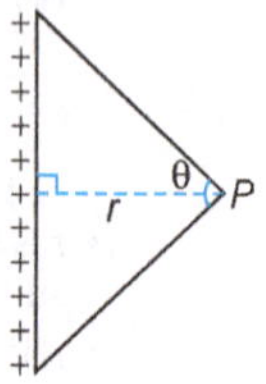

3. Field due to a cylinder [JEE Main 2022]

Electric field due to a cylinder of charge density ρ at a distance r from axis of cylinder is given by

$$E = \frac{\rho R^2}{2\varepsilon_0 r}$$

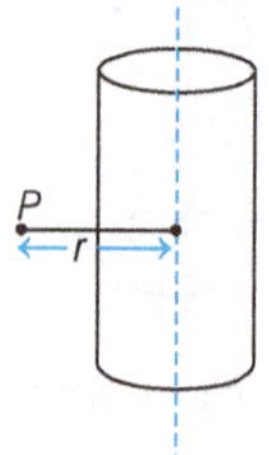

4. Variation of electric field with distance for conducting sphere [NEET 2019]

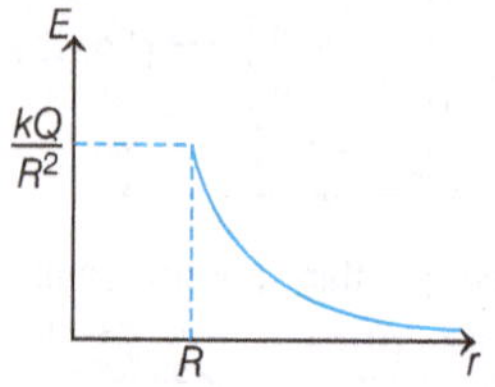

Step by Step

Mastering NCERT

- Concept Builders
- Topical Questions
- Assertion and Reason Questions
- Statement Based
- Matching Type
- Numerical Type
- NCERT Exemplar
- Past Exams MCQs
- Skill Boosters

Concept Builders

1 On rubbing two bodies, the mass of one body slightly gets ....

2 The property which differentiates the two kinds of charges is called the polarity of charge. [T/F]

3 If the sizes of charged bodies are very small compared to the distance between them, then we treat them as ...... (zero/ point) charge.

4 A positively charged glass rod can attract neutral piece of paper. [T/F]

5 If an uncharged bob is placed in an electric field, then its time period of oscillation remains the same. [T/F]

6 What does the equation $q = ne$ represents?

7 What is the force of repulsion between two positive charges of 1 C each, kept 1 m apart in vacuum?

8 Electric field is .... (same/different) at different points on the surface of an irregularly shaped charged conductor.

9 Electric field at any point on the surface of a conductor is .... (directly / inversely) proportional to the surface charged density.

10 Force characteristic of field is .... (intensity / potential) and work characteristic of field is .... (intensity / potential).

11 What is the formula for the electric field due to system of charges in vector form?

12 Electric field lines cannot cross each other because if they do so, then they will have more than one tangent which is not possible. [T/F]

13 In a non-uniform electric field, a dipole will have translatory as well as rotatory motion. [T/F]

14 The strength of electric field at an axial point of a short dipole is .... (half/twice) the strength at same distance on the equatorial line.

15 If three charges $+q$, $+q$ and $+q$ are placed at the vertices of an equilateral triangle of side a, then what is the force on a charge $+Q$ placed at the centre of the triangle?

16 Torque on a dipole becomes zero when it aligns itself .... (perpendicular / parallel) to the electric field.

17 If the electric flux entering and leaving a closed surface in air are ϕ_1 and ϕ_2 respectively, then the electric charge enclosed within surface will be $\varepsilon_0(\phi_2 + \phi_1)$. [T/F]

18 The electric field of a uniformly charged infinity plane sheet decreases with increase in distance r from it. [T/F]

19 If charge q is placed at one of the vertices of a closed cube of side l, then what will be the electric flux through face of the cube which does not pass through that vertex?

20 Electric field due to a uniformly charged thin spherical shell is maximum at the .... (centre/surface) of the shell.

Topical Questions

Electric Charge

1 The discharge of electric charges through our body due to rubbing of insulating surfaces generates **NCERT Pg. 1**

(a) static electricity

(b) electric current

(c) gravitational field

(d) magnetic field

2 If a plastic rod rubbed with fur is made to touch two small pith balls suspended nearby, then which figure shows their final configuration? **NCERT Pg. 1**

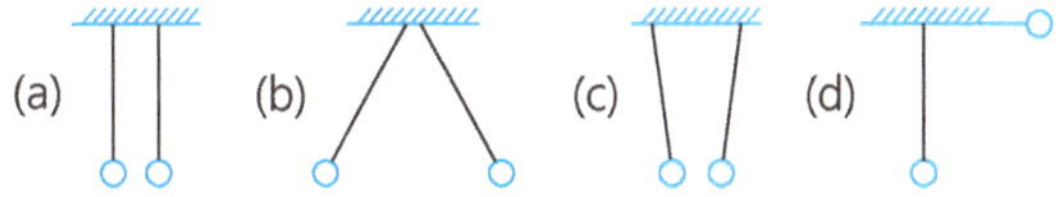

3 A soap bubble is given a negative charge, then its radius NCERT Pg. 2
(a) decreases
(b) increases
(c) remains unchanged
(d) nothing can be predicted as information is insufficient

4 One metallic sphere A is given positive charge, whereas another identical metallic sphere B of exactly same mass as that of A is given equal amount of negative charge. Then, NCERT Pg. 2
(a) mass of A and mass of B still remain equal
(b) mass of A increases
(c) mass of B decreases
(d) mass of B increases

5 In general, metallic ropes are suspended from the carriers to the ground which take inflammable material. The reason is NCERT Pg. 2
(a) their speed is controlled
(b) to keep the gravity of the carrier nearer to the earth
(c) to keep the body of the carrier in contact with the earth
(d) nothing should be placed under the carrier

6 When a glass rod is rubbed with a silk cloth, charge appears on both. This observation is consistent with law of conservation of charge as NCERT Pg. 2
(a) charge on both causes attraction
(b) charge on both causes repulsion
(c) charges appearing on both bodies are equal and opposite
(d) charge on first body is more than that of second body

7 When a glass rod is rubbed with a silk cloth, then the glass rod NCERT Pg. 2
(a) loses electron
(b) gains electron
(c) neither loses nor gains electron
(d) behaves as a plastic rod

8 The apparatus used to detect charge on a body is known as NCERT Pg. 3
(a) electric charge accumulator
(b) gold-leaf electroscope
(c) silver-leaf electroscope
(d) electric charge separator

Conductors and Insulators

9 Which of the following material has electric charges that are free to move inside it? NCERT Pg. 3
(a) Human body (b) Dry air
(c) Ebonite (d) Plastic

10 Most of the non-metals are NCERT Pg. 3
(a) conductor (b) insulator
(c) semiconductor (d) superconductor

Basic Properties of Electric Charge

11 Suppose charge on a metallic sphere is q. If the sphere is put in contact with an identical uncharged sphere, the charge will spread over the two spheres. By symmetry, charge on each sphere will be NCERT Pg. 4
(a) q (b) $\frac{q}{2}$ (c) $2q$ (d) zero

12 If a body gives out 10^9 electrons per second, how much time is required to get a total charge of 1 C from it? NCERT Pg. 4
(a) Around 198 min (b) Around 198 h
(c) Around 198 days (d) Around 198 yr

13 The number of electrons that must be removed from an electrically neutral silver dollar to give it a charge of + 2.4 C is NCERT Pg. 5
(a) 2.5×10^{19} (b) 1.5×10^{19}
(c) 1.5×10^{-19} (d) 2.5×10^{-19}

14 An object of mass 1 kg contains 4×10^{20} atoms. If one electron is removed from every atom of the solid, the charge gained by the solid of 1 g is NCERT Pg. 5
(a) 2.8 C (b) 6.4×10^{-2} C
(c) 3.6×10^{-3} C (d) 9.2×10^{-4} C

Coulomb's Law

15 A certain charge Q is divided into two parts q and $(Q-q)$. How the charge Q and q must be related, so that when q and $(Q-q)$ is placed at a certain distance apart experience maximum electrostatic repulsion? NCERT Pg. 6
(a) $Q = 4q$ (b) $Q = 3q$ (c) $Q = 2q$ (d) $Q = 4q + C$

16 Two electrical charged particles of different magnitudes when placed at a distance d from each other, experience a force of attraction F.
These two particles are then put in contact and again placed at the same distance from each other.
What is the nature of new force between them?
NCERT Pg. 6
(a) Attractive
(b) Repulsive
(c) Attractive or repulsive depending upon magnitude of charges present on them
(d) Cannot predicted

17 Force between two charges varies with distance between them as **NCERT Pg. 6**

(a) 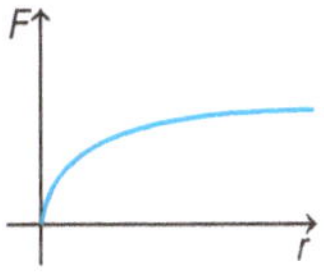

(b) 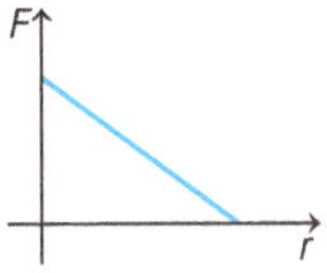

(c) 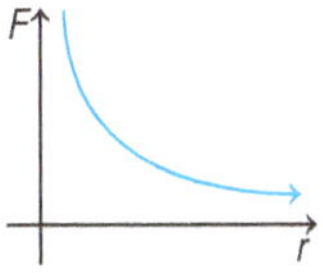

(d) 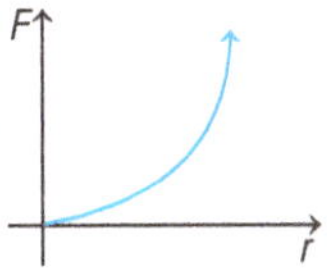

18 If point charges $Q_1 = 2\times10^{-7}$ C and $Q_2 = 3\times10^{-7}$ C are at 30 cm separation, then find electrostatic force between them. **NCERT Pg. 6**

(a) 2×10^{-3} N
(b) 6×10^{-3} N
(c) 5×10^{-3} N
(d) 1×10^{-3} N

19 For two charges q_1 and q_2, if force between them for some separation in air is F, then force between them in a medium of permittivity ε will be **NCERT Pg. 6**

(a) $\frac{\varepsilon_0}{\varepsilon}F$
(b) $\frac{\varepsilon}{\varepsilon_0}F$
(c) $\varepsilon\varepsilon_0 F$
(d) $\frac{F}{\varepsilon_0\varepsilon}$

20 The ratio of the forces between two small spheres with constant charge (i) in air (ii) in a medium of dielectric constant K is **NCERT Pg. 6**

(a) $1:K$
(b) $K:1$
(c) $1:K^2$
(d) $K^2:1$

21 Two point charges placed at a certain distance r in air exert a force F on each other. Then, the distance r' at which these charges will exert the same force in a medium of dielectric constant K is given by **NCERT Pg. 6**

(a) r
(b) r/K
(c) $r/\sqrt{K}$
(d) $r\sqrt{K}$

22 F_G and F_e represents gravitational and electrostatic force respectively, between electron and proton at a distance of 10 cm. The ratio of F_G/F_e is of the order of **NCERT Pg. 6**

(a) 10^{42}
(b) 10^{-39}
(c) 1
(d) 10^{-43}

23 The electrostatic force acting on a sphere of charge 8μC due to another sphere of charge –20μC in air is 9 N. The distance between two sphere is **NCERT Pg. 6**

(a) 0.2 m
(b) 0.4 m
(c) 4 m
(d) 2 m

24 Two small spheres each having the charge $+Q$ are suspended by insulating threads of length L from a hook. This arrangement is taken in space, where there is no gravitational effect, then the angle between the two suspensions and the tension in each thread will be **NCERT Pg. 6**

(a) $180°, \frac{1}{4\pi\varepsilon_0}\frac{Q^2}{(2L)^2}$
(b) $90°, \frac{1}{4\pi\varepsilon_0}\frac{Q^2}{L^2}$
(c) $180°, \frac{1}{4\pi\varepsilon_0}\frac{Q^2}{2L^2}$
(d) $180°, \frac{1}{4\pi\varepsilon_0}\frac{Q^2}{L^2}$

25 Suppose the spheres A and B with charge 6.5×10^{-7} C have identical sizes and distance between their centres is 50 cm. A third sphere of the same size but uncharged is brought in contact with the first, then brought in contact with the second and finally removed from both. What is the new force of repulsion between A and B? **NCERT Pg. 6**

(a) 5.7×10^{-3} N
(b) 1.5×10^{-2} N
(c) 0.24 N
(d) 0.24×10^{-2} N

26 Charge q_2 of mass m revolves around a stationary charge q_1 in a circular orbit of radius r. The orbital periodic time of q_2 would be **NCERT Pg. 6**

(a) $\left(\frac{4\pi^3 mr^2}{kq_1q_2}\right)^{1/2}$
(b) $\left(\frac{kq_1q_2}{4\pi^2 mr^2}\right)^{1/2}$
(c) $\left(\frac{4\pi^2 mr^4}{kq_1q_2}\right)^{1/2}$
(d) $\left(\frac{4\pi^2 mr^3}{kq_1q_2}\right)^{1/2}$

Forces between Multiple Charges

27 Four charges equal to $-Q$ are placed at the four corners of a square and a charge q is at its centre. If the system is in equilibrium, the value of q is **NCERT Pg. 11**

(a) $-\frac{Q}{4}(1+2\sqrt{2})$
(b) $\frac{Q}{4}(1+2\sqrt{2})$
(c) $-\frac{Q}{2}(1+2\sqrt{2})$
(d) $\frac{Q}{2}(1+2\sqrt{2})$

28 ABC is an equilateral triangle. Three charged particle each having charge $+q$ are placed at each corner as shown in figure. The net electric force on charge which is at point A, is **NCERT Pg. 11**

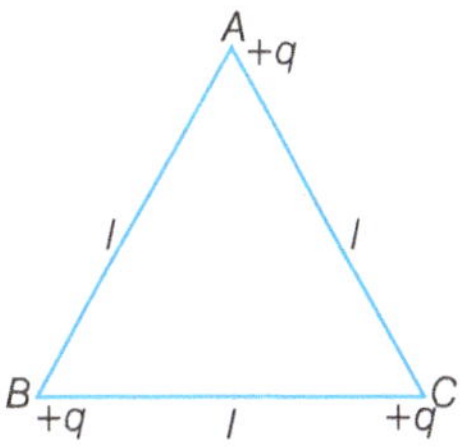

(a) $\frac{q^2}{4\pi\varepsilon_0 l^2}$
(b) $\frac{\sqrt{3}q^2}{4\pi\varepsilon_0 l^2}$
(c) $\frac{\sqrt{2}q^2}{4\pi\varepsilon_0 l^2}$
(d) zero

29 Equal charges q are placed at the four corners A, B, C, D of a square of length a. The magnitude of the force on the charge at B will be **NCERT Pg. 11**

(a) $\frac{3q^2}{4\pi\varepsilon_0 a^2}$

(b) $\frac{4q^2}{4\pi\varepsilon_0 a^2}$

(c) $\frac{q^2}{4\pi\varepsilon_0 a^2}\left(\frac{1+2\sqrt{2}}{2}\right)$

(d) $\frac{q^2}{4\pi\varepsilon_0 a^2}\left(2+\frac{1}{\sqrt{2}}\right)$

30 Three charges $-q_1, +q_2$ and $-q_3$ are placed as shown in the figure. The x-component of the force on q_1 is proportional to **NCERT Pg. 11**

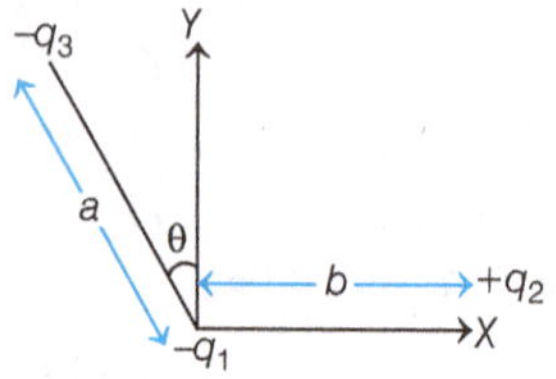

(a) $\frac{q_2}{b^2}-\frac{q_3}{a^2}\cos\theta$ (b) $\frac{q_2}{b^2}+\frac{q_3}{a^2}\sin\theta$

(c) $\frac{q_2}{b^2}+\frac{q_3}{a^2}\cos\theta$ (d) $\frac{q_2}{b^2}-\frac{q_3}{a^2}\sin\theta$

31 Net force on charge placed at A is **NCERT Pg. 11**

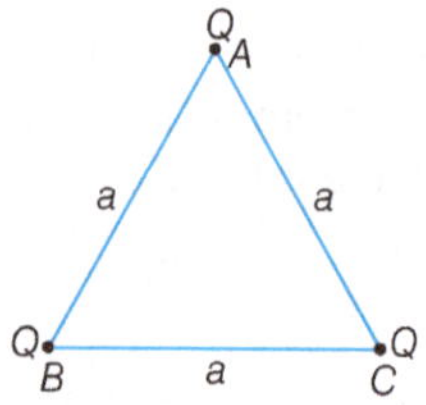

(a) $\sqrt{2}\frac{kQ^2}{a^2}$ (b) $\frac{\sqrt{3}kQ^2}{a^2}$

(c) $\frac{kQ^2}{\sqrt{2}a^2}$ (d) zero

Electric Field

32 The electric field in a certain region is acting radially outward and is given by $E = Aa$. A charge contained in a sphere of radius a centred at the origin of the field will be **NCERT Pg. 14**

(a) $4\pi\varepsilon_0 Aa^2$

(b) $A\varepsilon_0 a^2$

(c) $4\pi\varepsilon_0 Aa^3$

(d) $\varepsilon_0 Aa^3$

33 The bob of a simple pendulum has mass 2g and a charge of 5.0 μC. It is at rest in a uniform horizontal electric field of intensity 2000 V/m. At equilibrium, the angle that the pendulum makes with the vertical is (Take, $g = 10\text{ m/s}^2$) **NCERT Pg. 14**

(a) $\tan^{-1}(2.0)$

(b) $\tan^{-1}(0.2)$

(c) $\tan^{-1}(5.0)$

(d) $\tan^{-1}(0.5)$

34 An electron of mass m_e initially at rest moves through a certain distance in a uniform electric field in time t_1. A proton of mass m_p also initially at rest takes time t_2 to move through an equal distance in this uniform electric field. Neglecting the effect of gravity, the ratio of t_2/t_1 is nearly equal to **NCERT Pg. 14**

(a) 1836

(b) $(m_e/m_p)^{1/2}$

(c) $(m_p/m_e)^{1/2}$

(d) 1

35 Two point charges q_1 and q_2 of $+10^{-8}$ C and -10^{-8} C respectively are placed 0.1 m apart. **NCERT Pg. 14**

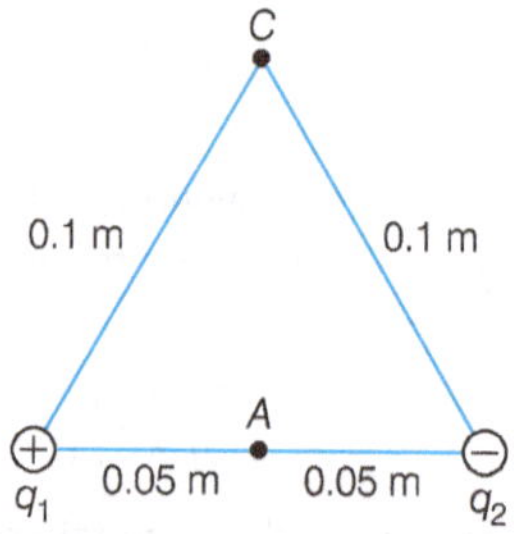

Then, ratio of magnitudes of electric fields at A and C is

(a) 4 : 1 (b) 1 : 4 (c) 8 : 1 (d) 1 : 8

36 Three identical positive point charges below are placed at the vertices of an isosceles right angled triangle as shown. Which of the vectors numbered coincides in direction with the electric field at the mid-point M of the hypotenuse due to the given system of charges? **NCERT Pg. 14**

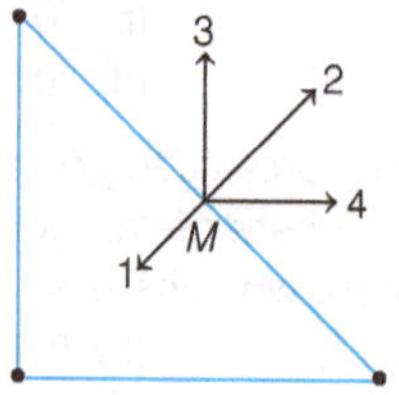

(a) 1 (b) 2 (c) 3 (d) 4

37 Charges q, $2q$, $3q$ and $4q$ are placed at the corners A, B, C and D of a square as shown in the figure. The direction of electric field at the centre of the square is along NCERT Pg. 14

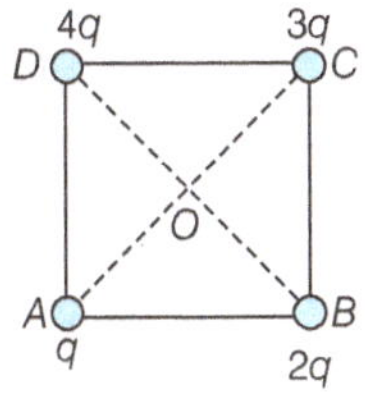

(a) AB (b) CB (c) BD (d) AC

38 If an infinite number of charges each equal to 5×10^{-9} C are placed along the X-axis at $x = 1$m, $x = 2$m, $x = 4$m, $x = 8$m and so on. If charges are alternatively positive and negative, the intensity of the electric field at the point $x = 0$ is (in volt/m) NCERT Pg. 14

(a) 30 (b) 36 (c) 18 (d) zero

39 A charge of 2C is placed on the X-axis at 1m from the origin along −ve X-axis. Infinite number of charges each of magnitude 2C are placed on X-axis at 1m, 2m, 4m, ... from origin along +ve X-axis. The first charge is positive and alternate charges are of opposite in nature. The electric field intensity at the origin NCERT Pg. 14

(a) $\frac{1}{10\pi\varepsilon_0}$ along −ve X-axis.

(b) $\frac{1}{10\pi\varepsilon_0}$ along + ve X-axis.

(c) $\frac{1}{\pi\varepsilon_0}$ along +ve X-axis.

(d) $\frac{1}{\pi\varepsilon_0}$ along −ve X-axis.

40 A charge Q is placed at the centre of a square. If electric field intensity due to the charge at the corners of square is E_1 and the intensity at the mid-point of the side of square is E_2, then the ratio of $\frac{E_1}{E_2}$ will be NCERT Pg. 14

(a) $\frac{1}{\sqrt{2}}$ (b) $\sqrt{2}$ (c) $\frac{1}{2}$ (d) 2

41 A charged cork ball of mass 2 kg is suspended by light insulated string in electric field (**E**) as shown, find the charge on ball, if it is in equilibrium. NCERT Pg. 14

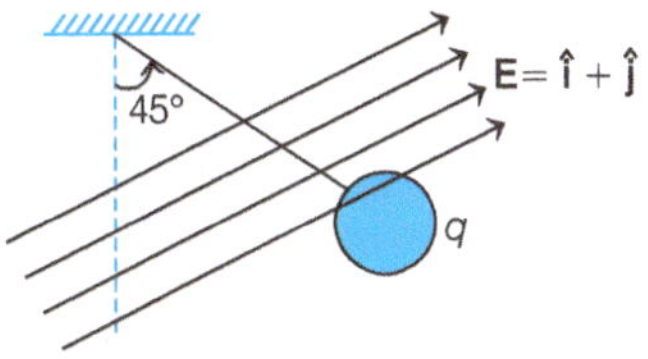

(a) 2C (b) 5C (c) 10 C (d) 20 C

42 A wire is bent into a semi-circular ring of radius r with charge q distributed uniformly over it. The net field **E** at the centre is NCERT Pg. 14

(a) $\frac{q}{4\pi^2\varepsilon_0 r^2}\hat{j}$ (b) $\frac{q}{2\pi^2\varepsilon_0 r^2}\hat{j}$

(c) $-\frac{q}{4\pi^2\varepsilon_0 r^2}\hat{j}$ (d) $-\frac{q}{2\pi^2\varepsilon_0 r^2}\hat{j}$

43 How many electrons should be removed from a coin of mass 1.6 g, so that it may float in an electric field of intensity 10^9 N/C directed upward? NCERT Pg. 14

(a) 9.8×10^7 (b) 9.8×10^5

(c) 9.8×10^3 (d) 9.8×10^1

44 The charge on a body is 4C. If the charge on it is doubled, then new electric field becomes NCERT Pg. 14

(a) half (b) double

(c) unchanged (d) thrice

45 A force of 2.5 N acts on a charge of 5×10^{-4} C. The intensity of electric field at that point is NCERT Pg. 14

(a) 1500 N/C (b) 2000 N/C

(c) 5000 N/C (d) 3000 N/C

Electric Field Lines

46 In the diagram shown below, NCERT Pg. 19

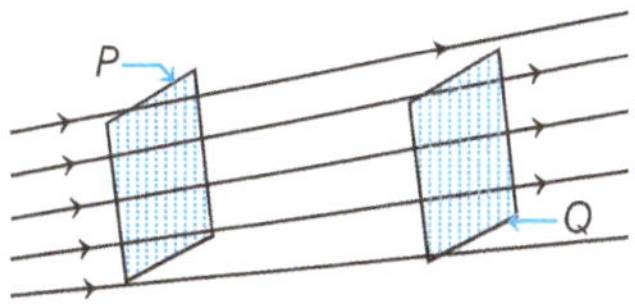

(a) field strength at P is less than field strength at Q

(b) field strength at P and Q are equal

(c) field is more strong at P and less strong at Q

(d) Cannot be determined from the figure

47 A metallic solid sphere is placed in a uniform electric field. Which of the following path of electric line of force is correct? NCERT Pg. 19

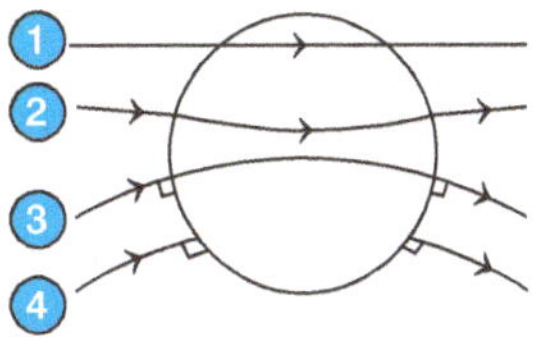

(a) 1 (b) 2 (c) 3 (d) 4

48 A point charge q is kept at corner of a cube, then total electric field lines passing through the surface containing the corner having charge, is NCERT Pg. 19

(a) zero (b) $\frac{q}{96\varepsilon_0}$ (c) $\frac{q}{12\varepsilon_0}$ (d) $\frac{q}{24\varepsilon_0}$

49. Figure shows the electric field lines around three point charges *A*, *B* and *C*. Which of the following charges are positive? **NCERT Pg. 19**

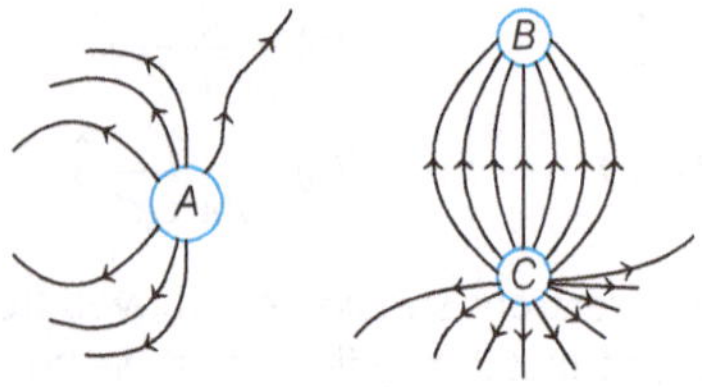

(a) Only *A*
(b) Only *C*
(c) Both *A* and *C*
(d) Both *B* and *C*

50. Which of the following represents the electric field lines due to a combinations of two negative charges? **NCERT Pg. 19**

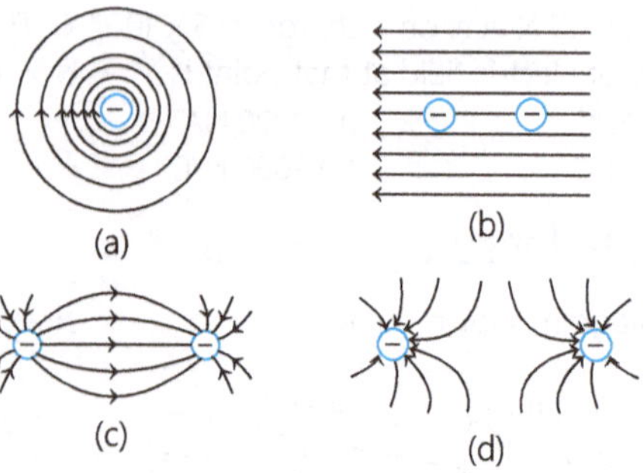

51. A non-uniform electric field is represented by the diagram. At which of the following points, the electric field is greatest in magnitude? **NCERT Pg. 19**

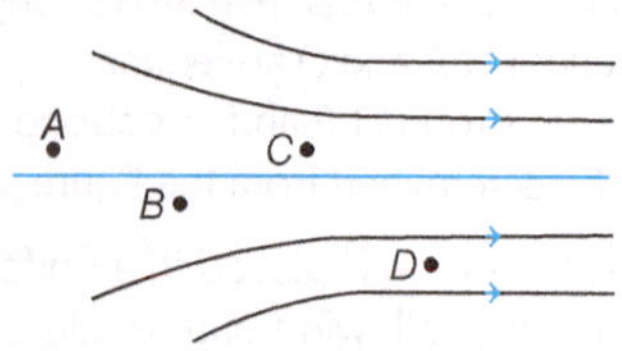

(a) *A* (b) *B*
(c) *C* (d) *D*

52. Which of the following statements is not true about electric field lines? **NCERT Pg. 19**

(a) Electric field lines start from positive charge and end at negative charge.
(b) Two electric field lines can never cross each other.
(c) Electrostatic field lines do not form any closed loops.
(d) Electric field lines cannot be taken as continuous curve.

53. Which of the following curves represent electric field lines correctly? **NCERT Pg. 19**

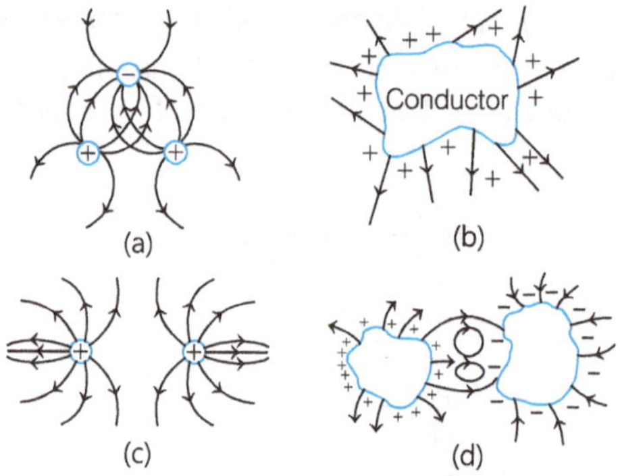

54. Which of the following figures represents the electric field lines due to a single positive charge? **NCERT Pg. 19**

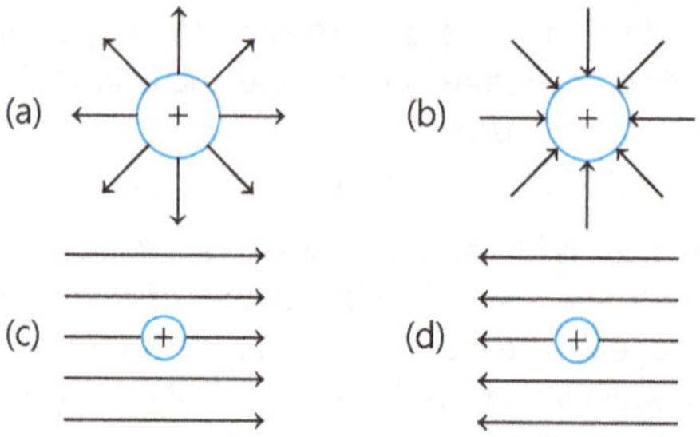

55. Which of the following figures represent the electric field lines due to a single negative charge? **NCERT Pg. 19**

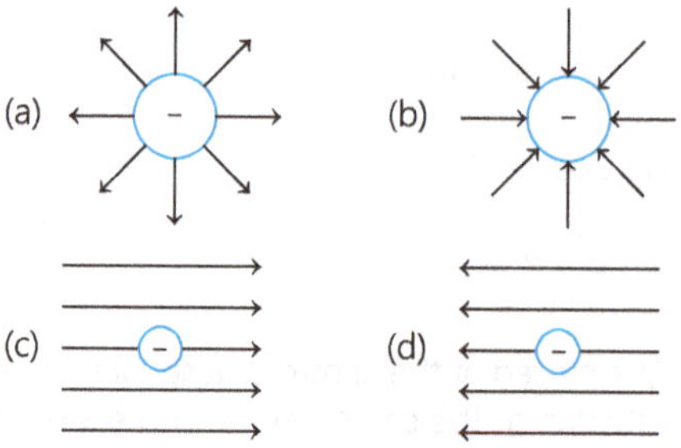

56. Which of the following figure represents the electric field lines due to a combination of one positive and one negative charge? **NCERT Pg. 19**

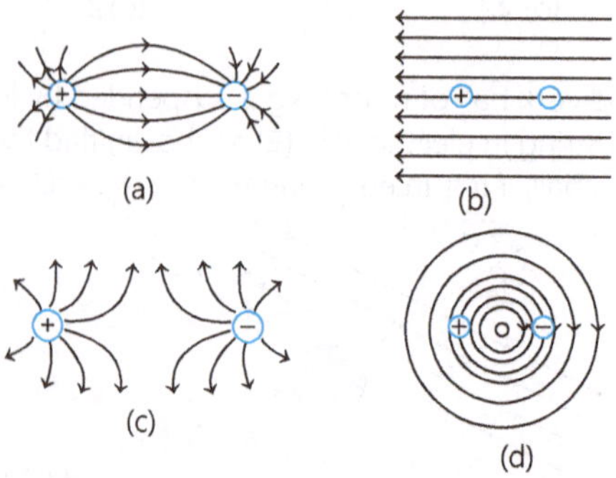

Electric Flux

57 If an area is tilted in the direction of field such that normal to plane of area makes θ angle with the direction of field, then number of field lines passing through the area is NCERT Pg. 21

(a) equal to $E\Delta S$
(b) proportional to $E\Delta S \cos\theta$
(c) equal to $E\Delta S \cos\theta$
(d) proportional to $E\Delta S \cos\theta / r^2$

58 Consider a region inside which there are various types of charges but the total charge is zero. At points outside the region, NCERT Pg. 21

(a) the electric field is necessarily zero
(b) the electric field is due to the dipole moment of the charge distribution only
(c) the dominant electric field is $\propto \frac{1}{r^3}$, for large r, where r is the distance from a origin in this region
(d) None of the above

59 Electric flux emanating through a surface element $d\mathbf{S} = -5\hat{\mathbf{i}}$ placed in an electric field $\mathbf{E} = 4\hat{\mathbf{i}} + 4\hat{\mathbf{j}} + 4\hat{\mathbf{k}}$ is NCERT Pg. 21

(a) 10 unit
(b) 60 unit
(c) 30 unit
(d) 20 unit

60 If an electric field is given by $10\hat{\mathbf{i}} + 3\hat{\mathbf{j}} + 4\hat{\mathbf{k}}$, calculate the electric flux through a surface of area 10 unit lying in YZ-plane. NCERT Pg. 21

(a) 100 unit (b) 10 unit
(c) 30 unit (d) 40 unit

Electric Dipole

61 Determine the electric dipole moment of the system of three charges, placed on the vertices of an equilateral triangle as shown in the figure. NCERT Pg. 23

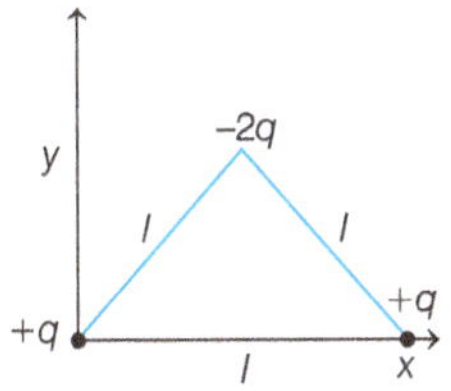

(a) $\sqrt{3}\, ql \frac{\hat{\mathbf{j}} - \hat{\mathbf{i}}}{\sqrt{2}}$ (b) $2ql\,\hat{\mathbf{j}}$
(c) $-\sqrt{3}\, ql\,\hat{\mathbf{j}}$ (d) $(ql)\frac{\hat{\mathbf{i}} + \hat{\mathbf{j}}}{\sqrt{2}}$

62 The ratio of electric fields on the axis and at equator of an electric dipole will be NCERT Pg. 23

(a) 1 : 1 (b) 2 : 1
(c) 4 : 1 (d) None of these

63 In given figures, $OP = OQ = 15$ cm, $OA = OB = 2.5$ mm NCERT Pg. 23

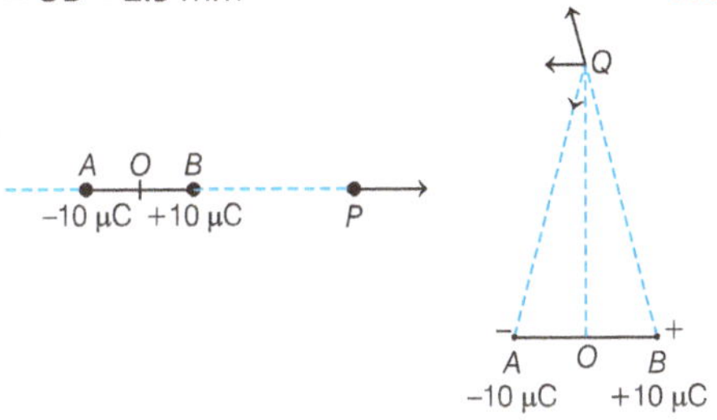

Magnitudes of electric field at P and Q are respectively

(a) 2.6×10^5 NC^{-1}, 2.6×10^5 NC^{-1}
(b) 1.3×10^5 NC^{-1}, 1.3×10^5 NC^{-1}
(c) 2.6×10^5 NC^{-1}, 1.3×10^5 NC^{-1}
(d) 1.3×10^5 NC^{-1}, 2.6 NC^{-1}

64 The electric force on a point charge situated on the axis of a short dipole is F. If the charge is shifted along the axis to double the distance, the electric force acting will be NCERT Pg. 23

(a) $4F$ (b) $\frac{F}{2}$
(c) $\frac{F}{4}$ (d) $\frac{F}{8}$

Dipole in a Uniform External Field

65 When a dipole is placed in an uniform external field, then NCERT Pg. 27

(a) net force on dipole is zero but torque is non-zero
(b) torque is zero but net force is non-zero
(c) torque and net force both are non-zero
(d) both torque and net force are zero

66 Two small identical electrical dipoles AB and CD, each of dipole moment p are kept at an angle of 120° as shown in the figure. If this system is subjected to electric field ($\mathbf{E}$) directed along X-axis, then the magnitude and direction of the torque acting on this is NCERT Pg. 27

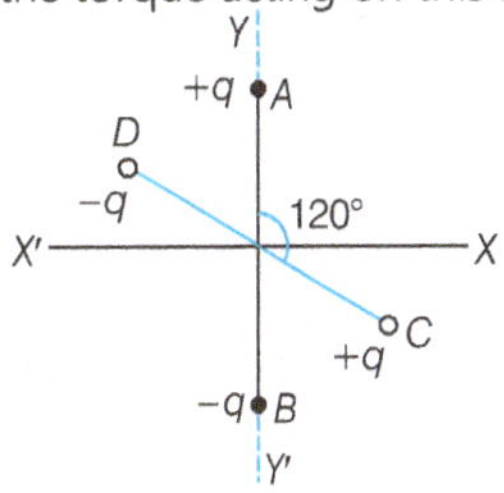

(a) $pE \sin\theta$, along Z-axis
(b) $2pE \sin\theta$, along Z-axis
(c) $\frac{\sqrt{3}}{2} pE \sin\theta$, along Z-axis
(d) $\frac{1}{2} pE \sin\theta$, along Z-axis

67 An electric dipole consists of two opposite charges each of magnitude 1×10^{-6} C separated by a distance 2 cm. The dipole is placed in an external field of $10 \times 10^5 \frac{N}{C}$.
The maximum torque on the dipole is **NCERT Pg. 27**
(a) 0.2×10^{-3} N-m
(b) 1.0×10^{-3} N-m
(c) 20×10^{-3} N-m
(d) 4×10^{-3} N-m

68 An electric dipole is placed at an angle 60° with an electric field of strength $4 \times 10^5 \frac{N}{C}$. It experiences a torque equal to $8\sqrt{3}$ N-m. Calculate the charge on the dipole, if dipole is of length 4 cm. **NCERT Pg. 27**
(a) 10^{-1} C (b) 10^{-2} C
(c) 10^{-3} C (d) 10^{-4} C

Continuous Charge Distribution

69. A uniformly charged conducting sphere of 4.4 m diameter has a surface charge density of 80 μC m^{-2}. The charge (in 10^{-3} C) on the sphere is **NCERT Pg. 28**
(a) 8.6 (b) 4.9
(c) 5.7 (d) 3.7

70. A positive charge Q is uniformly distributed along a circular ring of radius R. A small test charge q is placed at the centre of the ring as shown in figure. Then, **NCERT Pg. 28**

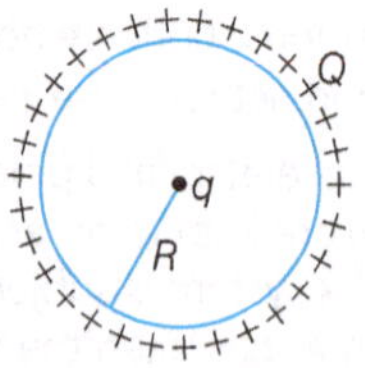

(a) if $q > 0$, and is displaced away from the centre in the plane of the ring, it will be pushed back towards the centre
(b) if $q < 0$ and is displaced away from the centre in the plane of the ring, it will never return to the centre and will continue moving till it hits the ring
(c) if $q < 0$ it will perform SHM for small displacement along the axis
(d) All of the above

71. A metallic spherical shell has an inner radius R_1 and outer radius R_2. A charge is placed at the centre of the spherical cavity. The surface charge density on the inner surface is **NCERT Pg. 28**

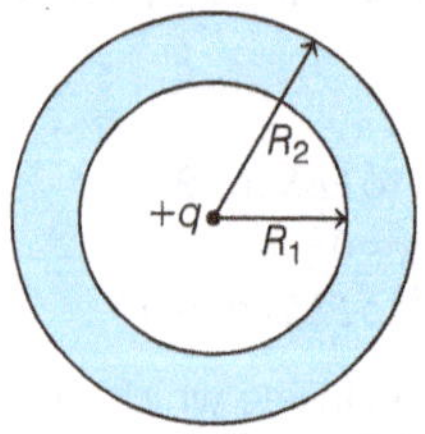

(a) $\frac{q}{4\pi R_1^2}$ (b) $\frac{-q}{4\pi R_1^2}$ (c) $\frac{q^2}{4\pi R_2^2}$ (d) $\frac{q}{4\pi R_2^2}$

72. The linear charge density of a rod of length 3m is $\lambda = (3x^2 + 5x + 2)$C/m, where x is the distance from one end of the rod. The total charge present on the rod is **NCERT Pg. 28**
(a) 39.5 C (b) 42.5 C
(c) 55.5 C (d) 60 C

73 Two non-conducting solid spheres of radii R_1 and R_2 and carrying uniform volume charge densities $+\rho$ and $-\rho$ respectively are placed such that they partially overlap as shown in the figure. At all points in the overlapping region, **NCERT Pg. 28**

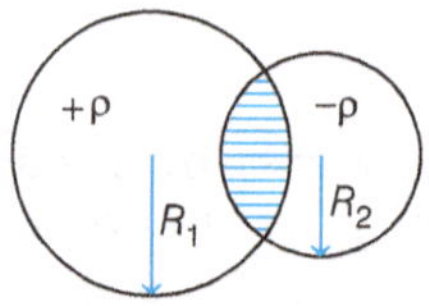

(a) the electrostatic field is zero
(b) the electrostatic potential is constant
(c) the electrostatic field is constant in magnitude
(d) None of the above

Gauss's Law

74 Consider the charge configuration and spherical Gaussian surface as shown in the figure. When calculating the flux of the electric field over the spherical surface, the electric field will be due to **NCERT Pg. 29**

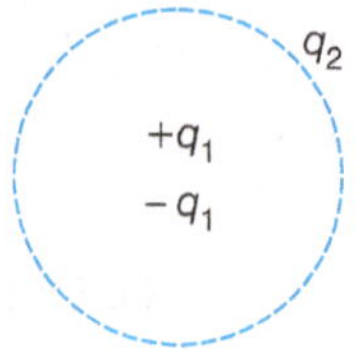

(a) q_2 (b) only the positive charges
(c) all the charges (d) $+q_1$ and $-q_1$

75 If $\int_S \mathbf{E} \cdot d\mathbf{S} = 0$ over a surface, then NCERT Pg. 29

(a) the electric field inside the surface and on it is zero
(b) the electric field inside the surface is necessarily uniform
(c) the number of flux lines entering the surface must be equal to the number of flux lines leaving it
(d) None of the above

76 Total electric flux coming out of a unit positive charge put in air is NCERT Pg. 29

(a) ε_0 (b) ε_0^{-1}
(c) $(4p\varepsilon_0)^{-1}$ (d) $4\pi\varepsilon_0$

77 If same charge q is placed inside a sphere and cube having radius 1m and side 2m, respectively. What will be the ratio of flux passing through them? NCERT Pg. 29

(a) 1 : 1 (b) 1 : 8 (c) 8 : 1 (d) 1 : 2

78 Eight dipoles of charges of magnitude e each are placed inside a cube. The total electric flux coming out of the cube will be NCERT Pg. 29

(a) $\frac{8e}{\varepsilon_0}$ (b) $\frac{16e}{\varepsilon_0}$ (c) $\frac{e}{\varepsilon_0}$ (d) zero

79 Refer to the arrangement of charges in figure and a Gaussian surface of radius R with Q at the centre, then NCERT Pg. 29

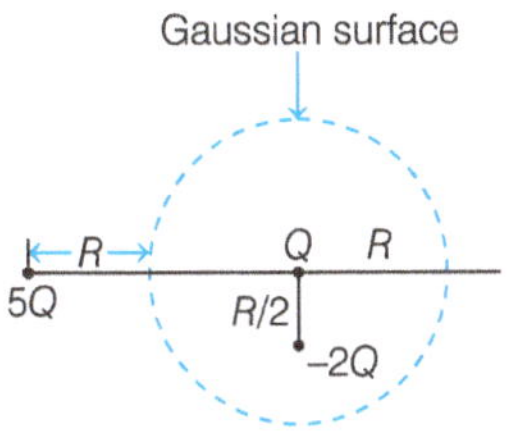

(a) total flux through the surface of the sphere is $\frac{-Q}{\varepsilon_0}$
(b) field on the surface of the sphere is zero
(c) flux through the surface of sphere due to 5 Q is $-\frac{5Q}{\varepsilon_0}$
(d) field on the surface of sphere due to $-2Q$ is same everywhere

80 Shown in the figure is a shell made of a conductor. It has inner radius a and outer radius b and carries charge Q. At its centre is a dipole **p** as shown. In this case, NCERT Pg. 29

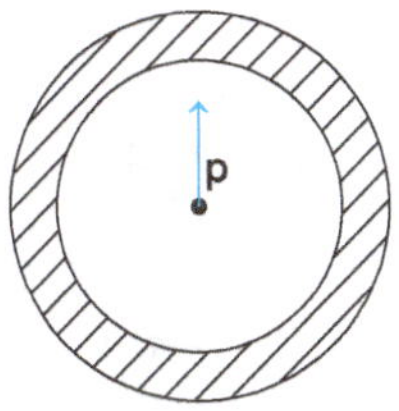

(a) surface charge density on the inner surface is uniform and equal to $\frac{\left(\frac{Q}{2}\right)}{4\pi a^2}$
(b) electric field outside the shell is the same as that of a point charge at the centre of the shell
(c) surface charge density on the outer surface depends on $|\mathbf{p}|$
(d) surface charge density on the inner surface of the shell is zero everywhere

81 The electric flux through a Gaussian surface A that encloses the charged particles in free space is [Given $q_1 = -14$ nC, $q_2 = 78.85$ nC, $q_3 = -56$ nC] NCERT Pg. 29

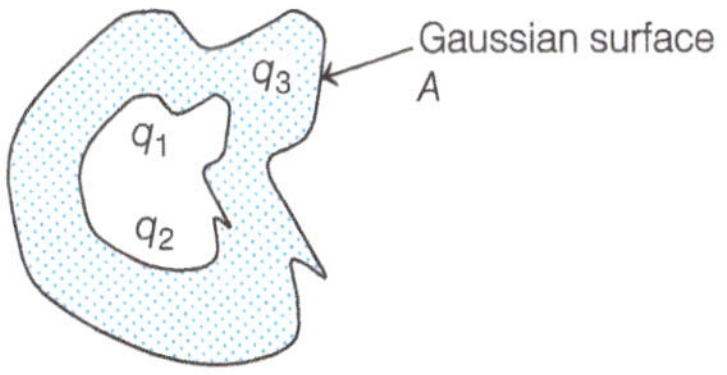

(a) 10^3 N-m^{2}C^{-1} (b) 10^3 CN^{-1}m^2
(c) 6.32×10^3 N-m^{2}C^{-1} (d) 6.32×10^3 CN^{-1}m^2

82 A hollow cylinder has a charge q coulomb within it. If ϕ is the electric flux in units of volt-metre associated with the curved surface B, the flux linked with the plane surface A in units of volt-metre will be NCERT Pg. 29

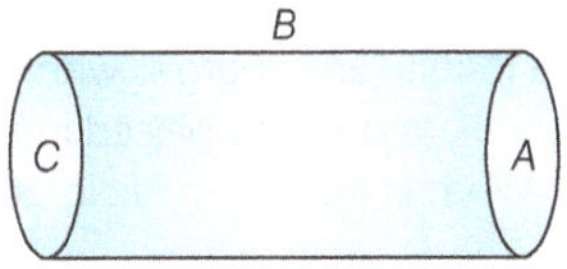

(a) $\frac{1}{2}\left(\frac{q}{\varepsilon_0} - \phi\right)$ (b) $\frac{q}{2\varepsilon_0}$ (c) $\frac{\phi}{3}$ (d) $\frac{q}{\varepsilon_0} - \phi$

Applications of Gauss's Law

83 Two infinite plane parallel sheets separated by a distance d have equal and opposite uniform charge densities σ. Electric field at a point between the sheets, is NCERT Pg. 33

(a) zero (b) $\frac{\sigma}{\varepsilon_0}$ (c) $\frac{\sigma}{2\varepsilon_0}$
(d) depends upon the location of the point

84 Two large, thin metal plates are parallel and close to each other. On their inner faces, the plates have surface charge densities of opposite signs and of magnitude 17.0×10^{-22} Cm^{-2}. What is E in the outer region of the first plate? NCERT Pg. 33

(a) 17×10^{-22} N/C (b) 1.5×10^{-15} N/C
(c) 1.9×10^{-10} N/C (d) Zero

85 A hollow charged sphere of radius R has a constant surface charge density σ. Of the following graphs the one which shows the variation of the electric field strength E with distance X from the centre of the sphere is **NCERT Pg. 33**

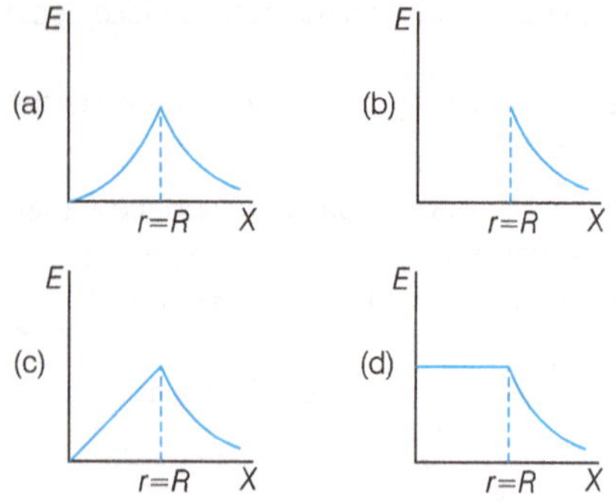

86 The electric field intensity at a point located at distance $r\ (r < R)$ from the centre of a hollow spherical conductor (radius R) having charged Q will be **NCERT Pg. 33**

(a) $\frac{kQR}{r^3}$ (b) $\frac{kQr}{R^3}$ (c) $\frac{kQ}{r^2}$ (d) zero

87 A non-conducting sphere of radius R is uniformly charged. The electric field due to sphere at a distance $r(r < R)$ from the centre is related to r as **NCERT Pg. 33**

(a) $E = 0$ (b) $E \propto \frac{1}{r^2}$ (c) $E \propto \frac{1}{r}$ (d) $E \propto r$

88 Three parallel infinite line charges with linear charge densities $+\lambda$, $+2\lambda$ and $-\lambda$ are placed in a plane as shown in the figure. What is the electric field at point P? **NCERT Pg. 33**

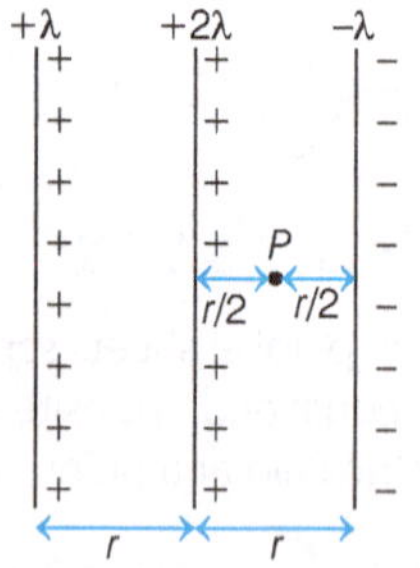

(a) $\frac{2k\lambda}{r}$ (b) $\frac{4k\lambda}{r}$ (c) $\frac{8k\lambda}{3r}$ (d) $\frac{40k\lambda}{3r}$

89 A sphere of radius R has a uniform distribution of electric charge (q) in its volume. At a distance x from its centre, the electric field $\left(\text{at } x = \frac{R}{2}\right)$ will be **NCERT Pg. 33**

(a) $\frac{q}{4\pi\varepsilon_0 R^2}$ (b) $\frac{q}{8\pi\varepsilon_0 R^2}$ (c) $\frac{3q}{4\pi\varepsilon_0 R^3}$ (d) zero.

90 Two parallel infinite line charges $+\lambda$ and $-\lambda$ are placed with a separation distance R in free space. The net electric field exactly mid-way between the two line charges is **NCERT Pg. 33**

(a) zero (b) $\frac{2\lambda}{\pi\varepsilon_0 R}$ (c) $\frac{\lambda}{\pi\varepsilon_0 R}$ (d) $\frac{\lambda}{2\pi\varepsilon_0 R}$

91 A rod of length 2.4 m and radius 4.6 mm carries a negative charge of 4.2×10^{-7} C spread uniformly over its surface. The electric field (in 10^5 NC^{-1}) near the mid-point of the rod, at a point on its surface is **NCERT Pg. 33**

(a) – 8.6 (b) 8.6 (c) – 6.7 (d) 4.7

92 A charged ball B hangs from a silk thread S, which makes an angle θ with a large charged conducting sheet P as shown in the figure. The surface charge density of the sheet is proportional to **NCERT Pg. 33**

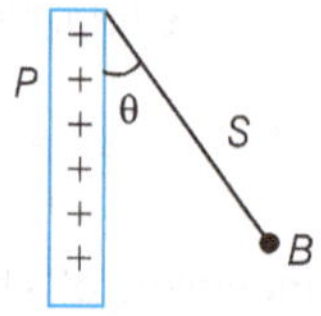

(a) $\cos\theta$ (b) $\cot\theta$ (c) $\sin\theta$ (d) $\tan\theta$

93 Two large thin metal plates are parallel and close to each other. On their inner faces, the plates have surface charge densities of opposite signs and magnitude 27×10^{-22} C m^{-2}. The electric field **E** (in 10^{-10} N C^{-1}) in region II in between the plates is **NCERT Pg. 34**

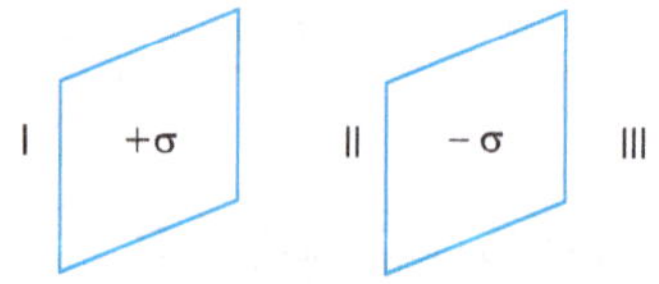

(a) 4.25 (b) 6.28 (c) 3.05 (d) 5.03

94 A non-conducting sphere of radius a has a net charge $+q$ uniformly distributed throughout its volume. A spherical conducting shell having inner and outer radii b and c and net charge $-q$ is concentric with the sphere (see the figure).

Read the following statements. **NCERT Pg. 35**

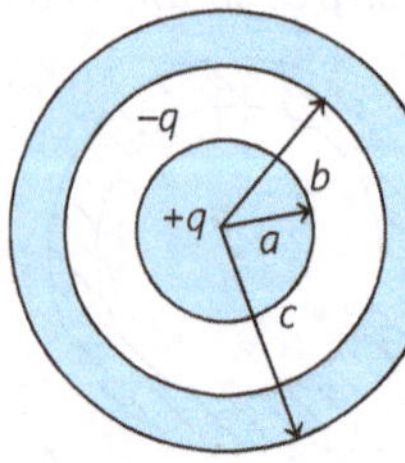

(i) The electric field at a distance r from the centre of the sphere for $r < a$ is $\frac{1}{4\pi\varepsilon_0}\frac{qr}{a^3}$.

(ii) The electric field at distance r for $a < r < b$ is 0.

(iii) The electric field at distance r for $b < r < c$ is 0.

(iv) The charge on the inner surface of the spherical shell is $-q$.

(v) The charge on the outer surface of the spherical shell is $+q$.

Which of the above statements are true?

(a) (i), (ii) and (v)
(b) (i), (iii) and (iv)
(c) (ii), (iii) and (iv)
(d) (ii), (iii) and (v)

95 Consider a thin spherical shell of radius R consisting of uniform surface charge density σ. The electric field at a point outside the shell at a distance x from its centre is **NCERT Pg. 35**

(a) inversely proportional to σ
(b) directly proportional to x^2
(c) directly proportional to R
(d) inversely proportional to x^2

Assertion and Reason Questions

Direction (Q. Nos. 1-10) *In the following questions, a statement of Assertion is followed by a corresponding statement of Reason. Of the following statements, choose the correct one.*

(a) Both Assertion and Reason are correct and Reason is the correct explanation of Assertion.
(b) Both Assertion and Reason are correct but Reason is not the correct explanation of Assertion.
(c) Assertion is correct but Reason is incorrect.
(d) Assertion is incorrect but Reason is correct.

1 **Assertion** When we produce charge q_1 on a body by rubbing it against another body which gets a charge q_2 in the process, then $q_1 + q_2 = 0$.
Reason Charge on an isolated system remains constant. **NCERT Pg. 4**

2 **Assertion** At macroscopic level, quantisation of charge has no practical consequence and can be ignored.
Reason $1\,\mu C$ charge contains 10^{13} times electronic charge e approximately. **NCERT Pg. 4**

3 **Assertion** The charge on a body can be increased or decreased in terms of electronic charge e.
Reason Charge on a body is integral multiple of electronic charge e, this is called quantisation of charge. **NCERT Pg. 4**

4 **Assertion** When bodies are charged through friction, there is a transfer of electric charge from one body to another, but no creation or destruction of charge take place.
Reason This follows from conservation of electric charges. **NCERT Pg. 4**

5 **Assertion** Coulomb force and gravitational force follow the same inverse-square law.
Reason Both laws are same in all aspect. **NCERT Pg. 6**

6 **Assertion** A positive point charge initially at rest in a uniform electric field starts moving along electric lines of force. (Neglect all other forces except electric forces.)
Reason A point charge released from rest in an electric field always moves along the line of force. **NCERT Pg. 14**

7 **Assertion** In a uniform electric field electron move in the opposite direction of electric field.
Reason This is because of the negative charge of an electron. **NCERT Pg. 14**

8 **Assertion** If an electric dipole of dipole moment 30×10^{-5} C-m is enclosed by a closed surface, the net flux coming out of the surface will be zero.
Reason Electric dipole consists of two equal and opposite charges. **NCERT Pg. 29**

9 **Assertion** Upon displacement of charges within a closed surface, **E** at any point on the surface does not change.
Reason The flux crossing through a closed surface is independent of the location of charge within the surface. **NCERT Pg. 29**

10 **Assertion** **E** in outside vicinity of a conductor depends only on the local charge density σ and it is independent of the other charges present anywhere on the conductor.
Reason **E** in outside vicinity of a conductor is given by $\frac{\sigma}{\varepsilon_0}$. **NCERT Pg. 33**

Statement Based Questions

Direction (Q. Nos. 1-8) *In the following questions, two statements (I and II) are given. In the light of the given statements, choose the correct answer from the options given below.*

(a) Both Statement I and Statement II are incorrect.
(b) Statement I is correct but Statement II is incorrect.
(c) Statement I is incorrect but Statement II is correct.
(d) Both Statement I and Statement II are correct.

1 **Statement I** When bodies are charged by rubbing, there is a transfer of electrons from one body to other, no new charges are created nor destroyed.

Statement II When a neutron turns into a proton and an electron. The proton and electron thus created have equal and opposite charges and the total charge is zero, before and after the creation. NCERT Pg. 1

2 **Statement I** If a system contains two point charges q_1 and q_2, the total charge of the system is obtained simply by adding algebraically q_1 and q_2, e.g. (−2 units charge) + (6 units charge) = 4 units charge.

Statement II Total charge of a system having charges of value −2 units and +6 units is 8 units charge. NCERT Pg. 4

3 **Statement I** The charge q on a body is always given by $q = ne$, where n is any integer, positive or negative.

Statement II By convention, the charge on an electron is taken to be negative. NCERT Pg. 4

4 **Statement I** Magnitude of electric field at a point decreases inversely as square of distance of that point from the charge.

Statement II Away from the charge field gets weaker and density of field lines is less, resulting in well separated lines. NCERT Pg. 14

5 **Statement I** A point charge is brought in an electric field, the field at a nearby point will increase or decrease, depending on the nature of charge.

Statement II The electric field is independent of the nature of charge. NCERT Pg. 19

6 **Statement I** No two electric lines of force can intersect each other.

Statement II Tangent at any point of electric line of force gives the direction of electric field. NCERT Pg. 21

7 **Statement I** On bringing a positively charged rod near the uncharged conductor, the conductor gets attracted towards the rod.

Statement II The electric field lines of the charged rod are perpendicular to the surface of conductor. NCERT Pg. 21

8 **Statement I** A metallic shield in form of a hollow shell may be built to block electric field.

Statement II In a hollow spherical shell, the electric field inside it is zero at every point. NCERT Pg. 29

Matching Type Questions

1 Match the Column I (charge) with Column II (property) and select the correct answer from the options given below. NCERT Pg. 1

Column I	Column II
A. Like charges	1. of two types
B. Unlike charges	2. repel each other
C. Charge can be	3. attract each other
D. Charges are	4. neutralised, if they are equal and opposite

Codes

	A	B	C	D		A	B	C	D
(a)	1	2	3	4	(b)	2	1	3	4
(c)	4	1	3	2	(d)	2	3	4	1

2 Match the Column I (type of body) with Column II (electric field) and select the correct answer from the options given below. NCERT Pg. 33

Column I	Column II
A. Infinite plane sheet of uniform charge density	1. 0
B. Infinite plane sheet of uniform thickness	2. $\sigma / 2\varepsilon_0$
C. Non-conducting charged solid sphere at its surface	3. $R\rho / 3\varepsilon_0$
D. Conducting charged solid sphere at its centre	4. σ / ε_0

Codes

	A	B	C	D		A	B	C	D
(a)	2	4	3	1	(b)	3	2	1	4
(c)	1	4	2	3	(d)	2	1	4	3

3 Match the Column I (electric lines of force) with Column II (types of charge) and select the correct answer from the options given below. **NCERT Pg. 19**

Column I		Column II
A.	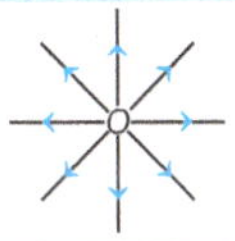	1. A pair of equal and opposite charges
B.	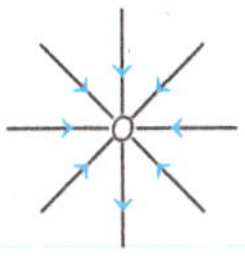	2. A pair of positive charges
C.	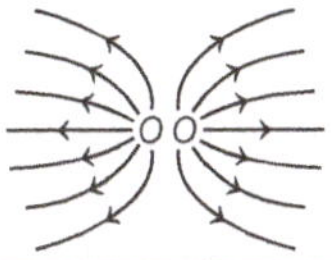	3. A single positive charge
D.	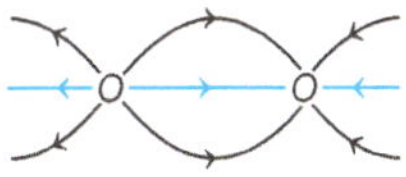	4. A single negative charge

Codes

	A	B	C	D		A	B	C	D
(a)	1	2	3	4	(b)	3	2	1	4
(c)	3	4	1	2	(d)	3	4	2	1

Numerical Type Questions

1 Two particles of same mass of 10 g and charge 2×10^{-7} C are placed on a horizontal table with a separation of L between them such that they stay in limited equilibrium. If the coefficient of friction between each particle and table is 0.25, then the value of L is .... cm. (Take, $g = 10\ \text{m/s}^2$) **NCERT Pg. 6**

2 A cubical volume is bounded by the surfaces $x = 0$, $x = a, y = 0, y = a, z = 0, z = a$.

The electric field in the region is given by $\mathbf{E} = E_0 x\hat{\mathbf{i}}$. where, $E_0 = 6 \times 10^4 \text{NC}^{-1}\text{m}^{-1}$. If $a = 2$ cm, the charge contained in the cubical volume is $Q \times 10^{-14}$C. The value of Q is ....

(Take, $\varepsilon_0 = 9 \times 10^{-12} \text{C}^2 / \text{N-m}^2$) **NCERT Pg. 29**

3 The electric field strength in air at NTP is 3×10^6 V/m. The maximum charge that can be given to a spherical conductor of radius 3 m is $x \times 10^{-3}$C, the value of x is ... . **NCERT Pg. 14**

4 A square of side 10 cm is placed parallel to YZ-plane in a uniform electric field of field intensity $5 \times 10^3 \hat{\text{i}}$ N/C.

If the square is turned to an angle of 30° with X-axis, then the flux is given by .... N-m^2/C. **NCERT Pg. 21**

5 Three charges of 10 μC, – 10 μC and 5 μC are placed in the form of equilateral triangle ABC, having each side equal to 5 cm. The resultant force on the charge at A is .... N. (5μC charge is placed at point A.) **NCERT Pg. 6**

6 The forced experienced by a unit charge when placed at a distance of 10 m from the middle of an electric dipole on its axial line is 2.5 N/C. When it is placed at a distance of 20 m, then the force is reduced to 0.2 N/C. The length of dipole is .... m. **NCERT Pg. 23**

7 A uniform electric field $E = (4m/e)$V / m is created between two parallel plates of length 2 m as shown in figure, (where, m = mass of electron and e = charge of electron). An electron enters the field symmetrically between the plates with a speed of 2m/s. The angle of the deviation θ of the path of the electron as it comes out of the field will be $\tan^{-1}(x)$.

The value of x is ....

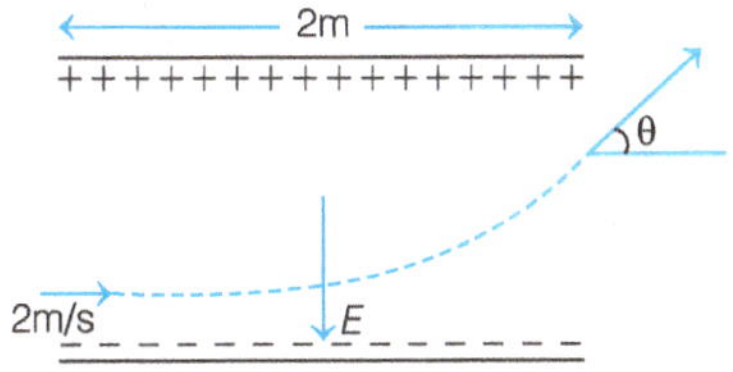

NCERT Pg. 14

8 An infinite number of charges each equal to q are placed only on X-axis at $x = 1, x = 2, x = 4, x = 8$ and so on. The electric field at point $x = 0$ due to this set up is given by $\frac{q}{x\pi\varepsilon_0}$, the value of x is .... **NCERT Pg. 14**

9 Four charges equal to $-Q$ are placed at the four corners of a square and a charge q is at its centre. If the system is in equilibrium, then the value of q is $\frac{Q}{x}(1 + \sqrt{2x})$. The value of x is .... **NCERT Pg. 6**

10 Two identical conducting spheres with negligible volume have 2nC and –1 nC charges, respectively. They are brought into contact and then separated by a distance of 0.6 m. The electrostatic force acting between the spheres is .... $\times 10^{-9}$ N.

[Given, $4\pi\varepsilon_0 = \frac{1}{9 \times 10^9}$ SI unit] **NCERT Pg. 6**

NCERT Exemplar Questions

1 In figure, two positive charges q_2 and q_3 are fixed along the Y-axis, exert a net electric force in the positive x-direction on a charge q_1 fixed along the X-axis. If a positive charge Q is added at $(x, 0)$, the force on q_1

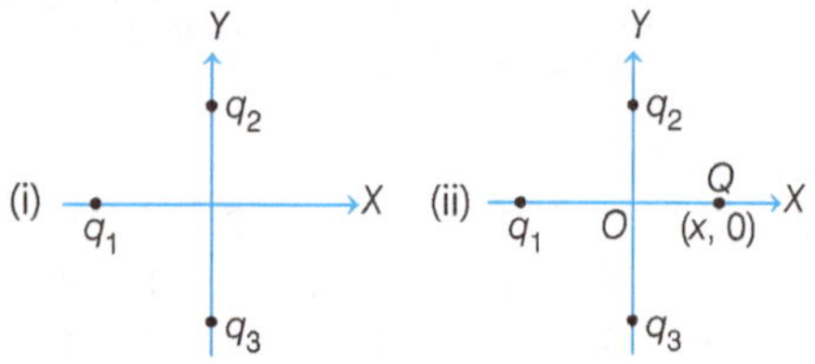

(a) shall increase along the positive X-axis
(b) shall decrease along the positive X-axis
(c) shall point along the negative X-axis
(d) shall increase but the direction changes because of the intersection of Q with q_2 and q_3

2 A positive point charge is brought near an isolated conducting sphere (figure). The best representation of electric field is given by

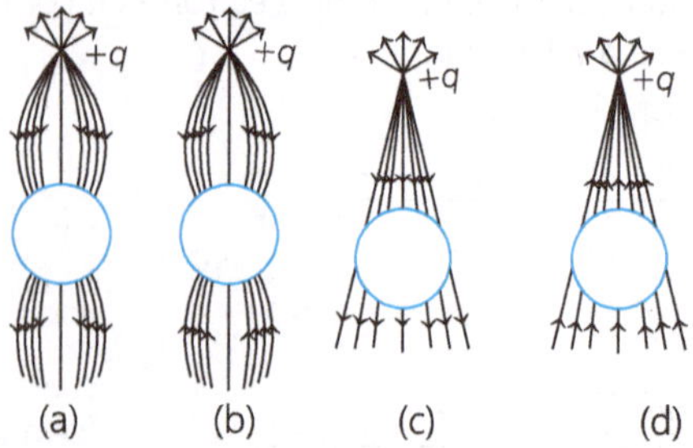

3 The electric flux through the surface

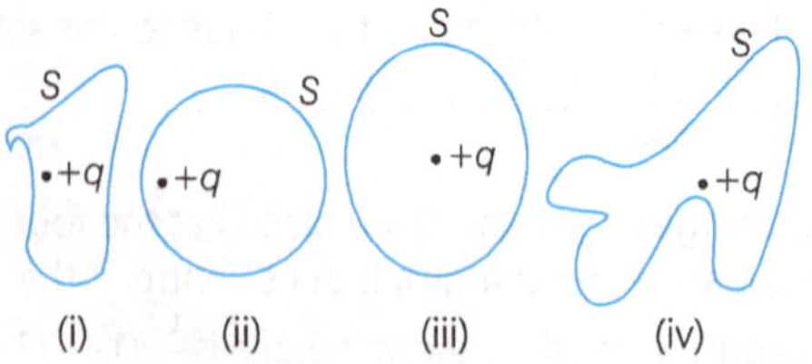

(a) in Fig. (iv) is the largest
(b) in Fig. (iii) is the least
(c) in Fig. (ii) is same as Fig. (iii) but is smaller than Fig. (iv)
(d) is the same for all the figures

4 A metallic spherical shell has an inner radius R_1 and outer radius R_2. A charge Q is placed at the centre of the spherical cavity. What will be surface charge density on the outer surface?

(a) $\frac{-Q}{4\pi R_1^2}$ (b) $\frac{Q}{4\pi R_1^2}$ (c) $\frac{Q}{4\pi R_2^2}$ (d) $\frac{-Q}{4\pi R_2^2}$

5 What will be the total flux through the faces of the cube as given in the figure with side of length a, if a charge q is placed at B, mid-point of an edge of the cube?

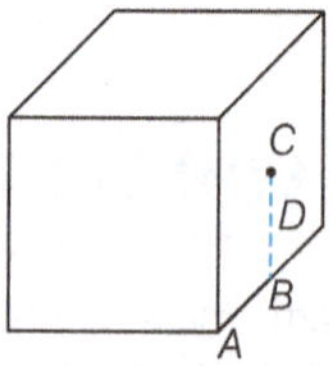

(a) $\frac{q}{8\varepsilon_0}$ (b) $\frac{q}{3\varepsilon_0}$

(c) $\frac{q}{4\varepsilon_0}$ (d) $\frac{q}{2\varepsilon_0}$

6 Two charges q and $-3q$ are placed fixed on X-axis separated by distance d. Where should a third charge $2q$ be placed such that it will not experience any force?

(a) $\frac{d}{3}(1+\sqrt{3})$ to the right of q

(b) $\frac{d}{3}(1+\sqrt{3})$ to the left of q

(c) $\frac{d}{2}(1+\sqrt{3})$ to the left of q

(d) $\frac{d}{2}(1+\sqrt{3})$ to the right of q

7 A point charge $+q$ is placed at a distance d from an isolated conducting plane. The field at a point P on the other side of the plane is

(a) directed perpendicular to the plane and away from the plane
(b) directed perpendicular to the plane but towards the plane
(c) directed radially away from the point charge
(d) directed radially towards the point charge

Past Exams Questions

NEET

1 An electric dipole is placed at an angle of 30° with an electric field of intensity 2×10^5 NC^{-1}. It experiences a torque equal to 4 N-m. Calculate the magnitude of charge on the dipole, if the dipole length is 2 cm. NCERT Pg. 27, NEET 2023

(a) 6 mC (b) 4 mC (c) 2 mC (d) 8 mC

2 Polar molecules are the molecules NCERT Pg. 23, NEET 2021

(a) having zero dipole moment
(b) acquire a dipole moment only in the presence of electric field due to displacement of charges
(c) acquire a dipole moment only when magnetic field is absent
(d) having a permanent electric dipole moment

3 A spherical conductor of radius 10 cm has a charge of 3.2×10^{-7} C distributed uniformly. What is the magnitude of electric field at a point 15 cm from the centre of the sphere? NCERT Pg. 33, NEET (Sep.) 2020

$\left(\frac{1}{4\pi\varepsilon_0} = 9 \times 10^9 \text{ N-m}^2/\text{C}^2\right)$

(a) 1.28×10^5 N/C (b) 1.28×10^6 N/C
(c) 1.28×10^7 N/C (d) 1.28×10^4 N/C

4 The electric field at a point on the equatorial plane at a distance r from the centre of a dipole having dipole moment $\mathbf{p}$ is given by
($r >>$ separation of two charges forming the dipole, ε_0 = permittivity of free space) NCERT Pg. 23, NEET (Oct.) 2020

(a) $\mathbf{E} = \frac{\mathbf{p}}{4\pi\varepsilon_0 r^3}$ (b) $\mathbf{E} = \frac{2\mathbf{p}}{4\pi\varepsilon_0 r^3}$
(c) $\mathbf{E} = -\frac{\mathbf{p}}{4\pi\varepsilon_0 r^2}$ (d) $\mathbf{E} = -\frac{\mathbf{p}}{4\pi\varepsilon_0 r^3}$

5 A sphere encloses an electric dipole with charge $\pm 3 \times 10^{-6}$ C. What is the total electric flux across the sphere? NCERT Pg. 29, NEET (Odisha) 2019

(a) -3×10^{-6} N-m^2/C (b) Zero
(c) 3×10^6 N-m^2/C (d) 6×10^{-6} N-m^2/C

6 A hollow metal sphere of radius R is uniformly charged. The electric field due to the sphere at a distance r from the centre NCERT Pg. 33, NEET (National) 2019

(a) zero as r increases for $r < R$, decreases as r increases for $r > R$
(b) zero as r increases for $r < R$, increases as r increases for $r > R$
(c) decreases as r increases for $r < R$ and for $r > R$
(d) increases as r increases for $r < R$ and for $r > R$

7 Suppose the charge of a proton and an electron differ slightly. One of them is $-e$ and the other is $(e + \Delta e)$. If the net of electrostatic force and gravitational force between two hydrogen atoms placed at a distance d (much greater than atomic size) apart is zero, then Δe is of the order (Given, mass of hydrogen, $m_h = 1.67 \times 10^{-27}$ kg) NCERT Pg. 6, NEET 2017

(a) 10^{-20} C (b) 10^{-23} C (c) 10^{-37} C (d) 10^{-47} C

8 Two identical charged spheres suspended from a common point by two massless strings of lengths l, are initially at a distance d ($d << l$) apart because of their mutual repulsion. The charges begin to leak from both the spheres at a constant rate. As a result, the spheres approach each other with a velocity v. Then, v varies as a function of the distance x between the sphere, as NCERT Pg. 6, NEET 2016

(a) $v \propto x$ (b) $v \propto x^{-1/2}$
(c) $v \propto x^{-1}$ (d) $v \propto x^{1/2}$

JEE Main

9 Five charges $+q$, $+5q$, $-2q$, $+3q$ and $-4q$ are situated as shown in the figure. The electric flux due to this configuration through the surface S is NCERT Pg. 24, JEE Main 2024

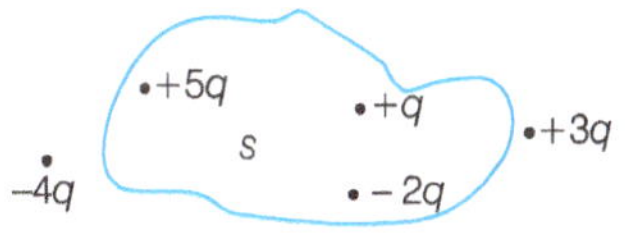

(a) $\frac{3q}{\varepsilon_0}$ (b) $\frac{5q}{\varepsilon_0}$ (c) $\frac{4q}{\varepsilon_0}$ (d) $\frac{q}{\varepsilon_0}$

10 An electric field $\mathbf{E} = (2x\hat{\mathbf{i}})$ NC^{-1} exists in space. A cube of side 2m is placed in the space as per figure given below. The electric flux through the cube is .... Nm^2/C. NCERT Pg. 24, JEE Main 2024

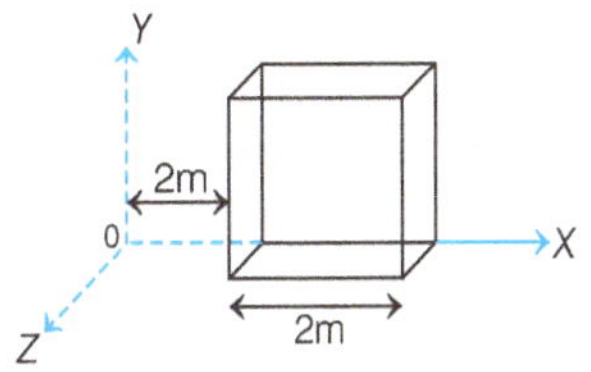

11 A point charge of 10 μC is placed at the origin. At what location on the X-axis should a point charge of 40 μC be placed, so that the net electric field is zero at $x = 2$ cm on the X-axis? NCERT Pg. 14, JEE Main 2023

(a) $x = 8$ cm (b) $x = -4$ cm
(c) $x = 4$ cm (d) $x = 6$ cm

12 Let σ be the uniform surface charge density of two infinite thin plane sheets shown in figure. Then, the electric fields in three different region E_I, E_{II} and E_{III} are

NCERT Pg. 33, JEE Main 2023

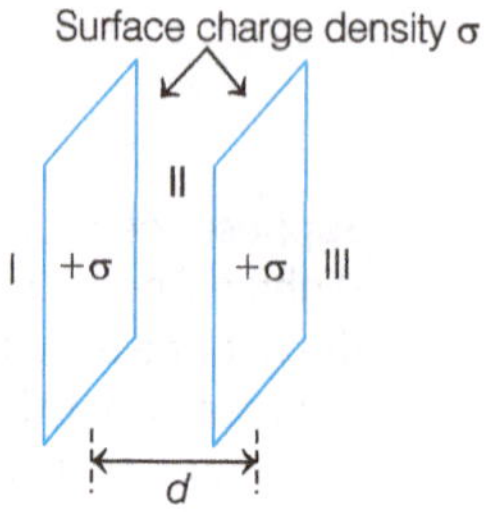

(a) $\mathbf{E}_I = -\frac{\sigma}{\varepsilon_0}\hat{n}$, $\mathbf{E}_{II} = 0$, $\mathbf{E}_{III} = \frac{\sigma}{\varepsilon_0}\hat{n}$

(b) $\mathbf{E}_I = \frac{\sigma}{2\varepsilon_0}\hat{n}$, $\mathbf{E}_{II} = 0$, $\mathbf{E}_{III} = \frac{\sigma}{2\varepsilon_0}\hat{n}$

(c) $\mathbf{E}_I = 0$, $\mathbf{E}_{II} = \frac{\sigma}{\varepsilon_0}\hat{n}$, $\mathbf{E}_{III} = 0$

(d) $\mathbf{E}_I = \frac{2\sigma}{\varepsilon_0}\hat{n}$, $\mathbf{E}_{II} = 0$, $\mathbf{E}_{III} = \frac{2\sigma}{\varepsilon_0}\hat{n}$

13 Find the electric field at point P (as shown in figure) on the perpendicular bisector of a uniformly charged thin wire of length L carrying a charge Q. The distance of the point P from the centre of the rod is $a = \frac{\sqrt{3}}{2}L$.

NCERT Pg. 14, JEE Main 2021

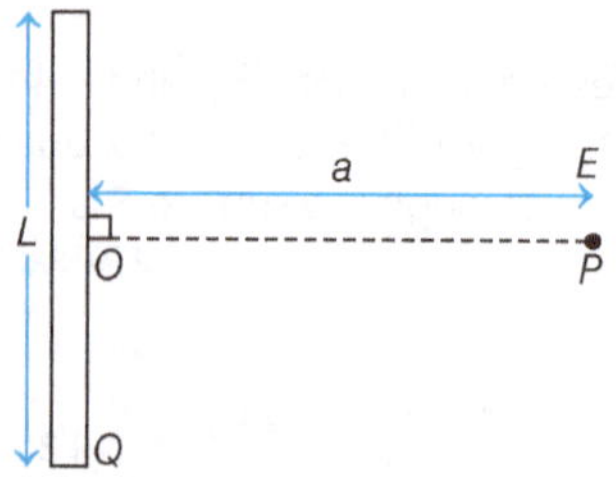

(a) $\frac{\sqrt{3}\,Q}{4\pi\varepsilon_0 L^2}$ (b) $\frac{Q}{3\pi\varepsilon_0 L^2}$

(c) $\frac{Q}{2\sqrt{3}\pi\,\varepsilon_0 L^2}$ (d) $\frac{Q}{4\pi\varepsilon_0 L^2}$

14 An electric dipole is placed on X-axis in proximity to a line charge of linear charge density 3.0×10^{-6} C/m. Line charge is placed on Z-axis, positive and negative charge of dipole is at a distance of 10 mm and 12 mm from the origin, respectively. If total force of 4 N is exerted on the dipole, find out the amount of positive or negative charge of the dipole. NCERT Pg. 33, JEE Main 2021

(a) 815.1 nC (b) 8.8 μC
(c) 0.485 nC (d) 4.44 μC

15 What will be the magnitude of electric field at point O as shown in figure? Each side of the figure is l and perpendicular to each other. NCERT Pg. 14, JEE Main 2020

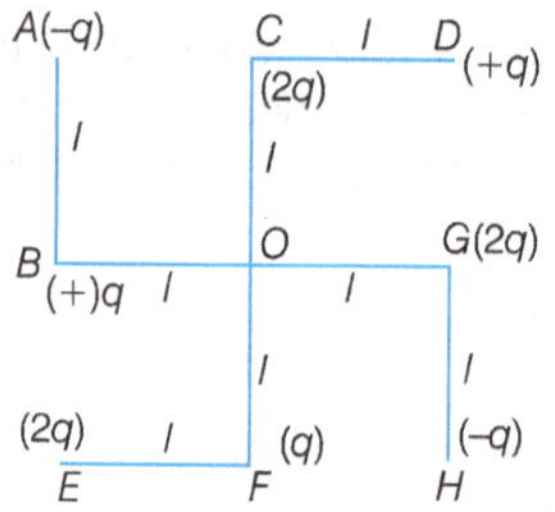

(a) $\frac{1}{4\pi\varepsilon_0}\frac{q}{l^2}$ (b) $\frac{1}{4\pi\varepsilon_0}\frac{q}{(2l^2)}(2\sqrt{2}-1)$

(c) $\frac{q}{4\pi\,\varepsilon_0\,(2l)^2}$ (d) $\frac{1}{4\pi\varepsilon_0}\frac{2q}{2l^2}(\sqrt{2})$

Skill Boosters

1 A glass rod rubbed with fur is used to charge a gold leaf electroscope and the leaves are observed to diverge. The electroscope disc is then exposed to X-rays for a short period. Then,

(a) the divergence of leaves is not affected
(b) the leaves diverge further
(c) the leaves will collapse
(d) the leaves will melt

2 A foreigner student who grow up in a tropical country but is studying in United States may not have experience with static electricity sparks or shocks. The student most probably gets his/her first shock in

(a) during a thunderstorm (b) while having a stroll in rain
(c) in summer (d) in winter

3 A ring of radius 0.1 m is made of thin metallic wire of area of cross-section 10^{-6}m^2. The ring has a uniform charge of π coulomb. Young's modulus of metal of wire is 2×10^{11} N/m^2 and $E_0^{-1} = 36\pi\times 10^9$ Vm / As. When a charge of 10^{-8} C is placed at the centre of the ring, then

(a) tension in the wire is 4.5×10^4 N
(b) tension in the wire is 4.5×10^5 N
(c) change in radius is 2.25×10^{-3} m
(d) change in radius is 2.25×10^{-5} m

4 Two small metal sphere having equal charge and mass are suspended from some point on the ceiling of a damp room with silk threads of equal length. Let centre to centre distance between sphere be x, $x << l$, l is length of silk thread. Due to ionisation of medium, charge leaks off from each sphere and they keep on coming closer to each other at a constant rate.

Let their approach velocity v varies as $v \propto x^{-1/2}$.

If mass of each sphere is m, then the rate at which charge varies with respect to time is

$$\frac{dq}{dt} \propto \frac{N}{2}\sqrt{\frac{2\pi\varepsilon_0 mg}{l}}$$

Value of N is

(a) 7 (b) 9
(c) 3 (d) 11

5 A charged dust particle of radius 5×10^{-7} m is moving in a horizontal electric field of intensity 6.28×10^5 V/m. The surrounding medium is air with coefficient of viscosity $\eta = 1.6 \times 10^{-5}$ N-s/m^2. If this particle is moving with a uniform horizontal speed of 0.02 m/s, then number of excess electrons on the drop are

(a) 30 (b) 18
(c) 60 (d) 15

6 A uniform field of 10^3 V/m is maintained between two very long plates with a separation of 2cm. A particle of mass 1.6×10^{-30} kg with a charge of -1.6×10^{-19} C is projected as shown.

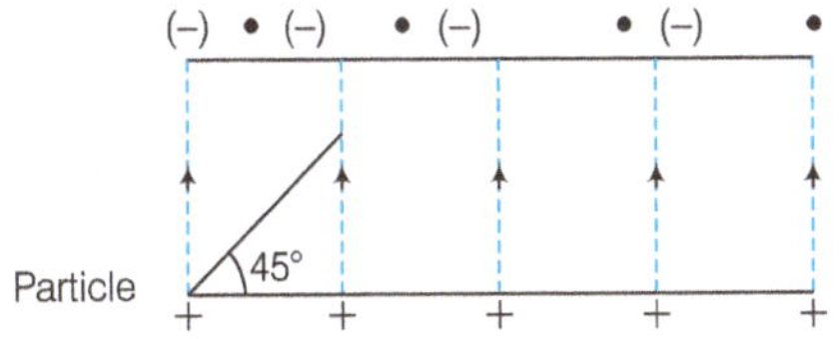

Maximum velocity of projection for which electron does not hit the upper plate is

(a) 2×10^6 m/s (b) 1.5×10^6 m/s
(c) 1.3×10^5 m/s (d) 2.7×10^5 m/s

7 A linear charge having linear charge density λ, penetrates a cube diagonally and then it penetrates a sphere diametrically as

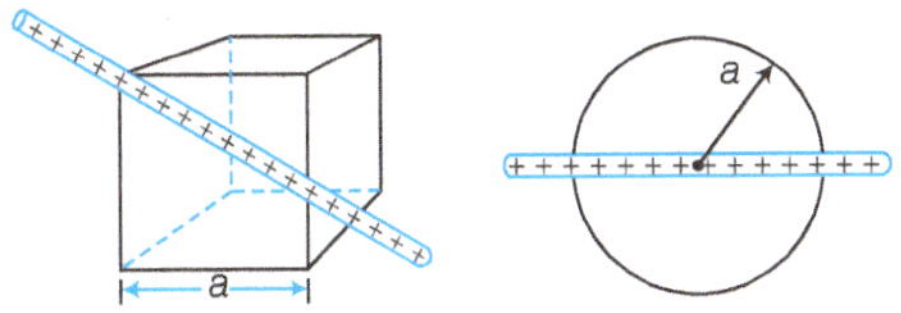

The ratio of flux through cube and through sphere is

(a) $\frac{1}{\sqrt{2}}$ (b) $\sqrt{2}$ (c) $\frac{\sqrt{3}}{2}$ (d) 1

8 S_1 and S_2 are two hollow concentric spheres with charges q and $2q$. Space between S_1 and S_2 is filled with a dielectric of dielectric constants.

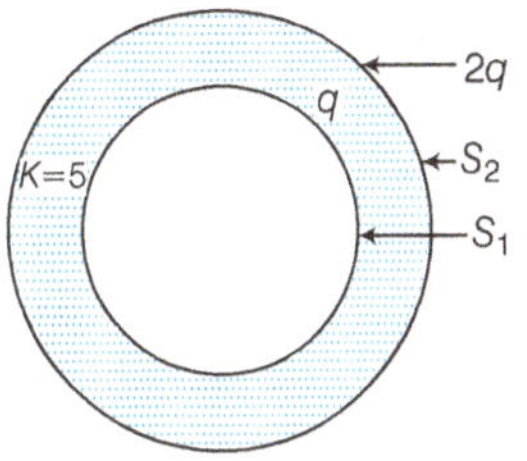

The ratio of flux through S_2 and flux through S_1 is

(a) 10 : 3 (b) 9 : 11 (c) 8 : 7 (d) 11 : 1

9 Two large circular discs separated by a distance of 0.01m are connected to a battery *via* a switch as shown in the figure. Charged oil drops of density 900 kgm^{-3} are released through a tiny hole at the centre of the top disc. Once some oil drops achieve terminal velocity, the switch is closed to apply a voltage of 200 V across the discs. As a result, an oil drop of radius 8×10^{-7} m stops moving vertically and floats between the discs. The number of electrons present in this oil drop is (Neglect the buoyancy force, take acceleration due to gravity = 10 ms^{-2} and charge on an electron (e) = 1.6×10^{-19} C)

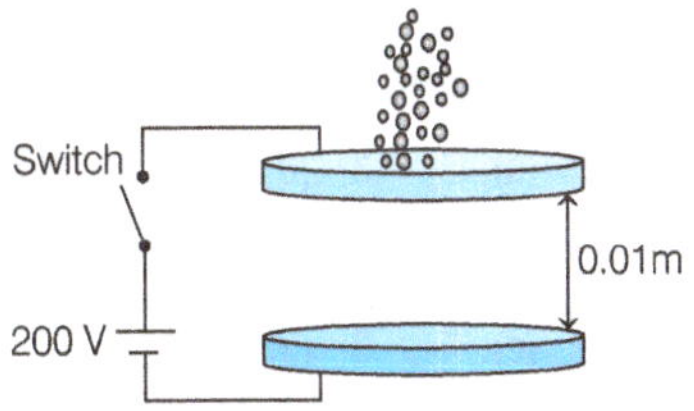

(a) 6 (b) 12 (c) 10 (d) 8

10 A charge Q is distributed uniformly on a ring of radius r. Consider the sphere of equal radius r with its centre at the periphery of the ring. Find the flux of the electric field through the surface of the sphere.

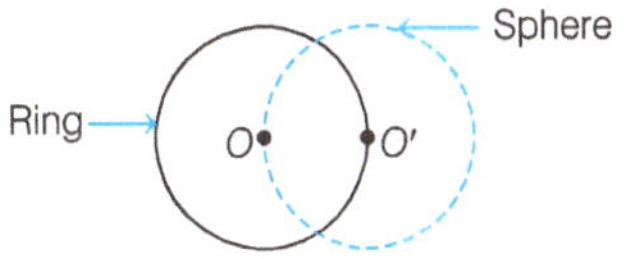

(a) $\frac{Q}{4\varepsilon_0}$ (b) $\frac{Q}{6\varepsilon_0}$ (c) $\frac{Q}{3\varepsilon_0}$ (d) $\frac{Q}{2\varepsilon_0}$

Correct Codes

Topical Questions

1 (a)	2 (b)	3 (b)	4 (d)	5 (c)	6 (c)	7 (a)	8 (b)	9 (a)	10 (b)
11 (b)	12 (d)	13 (b)	14 (b)	15 (c)	16 (b)	17 (c)	18 (b)	19 (a)	20 (b)
21 (c)	22 (b)	23 (b)	24 (a)	25 (a)	26 (d)	27 (b)	28 (b)	29 (c)	30 (b)
31 (b)	32 (c)	33 (d)	34 (c)	35 (c)	36 (b)	37 (b)	38 (b)	39 (b)	40 (c)
41 (c)	42 (d)	43 (a)	44 (b)	45 (c)	46 (c)	47 (d)	48 (a)	49 (c)	50 (d)
51 (d)	52 (d)	53 (c)	54 (a)	55 (b)	56 (a)	57 (c)	58 (c)	59 (d)	60 (a)
61 (c)	62 (b)	63 (c)	64 (d)	65 (a)	66 (a)	67 (c)	68 (c)	69 (b)	70 (d)
71 (b)	72 (c)	73 (c)	74 (c)	75 (c)	76 (b)	77 (a)	78 (d)	79 (a)	80 (b)
81 (a)	82 (a)	83 (b)	84 (d)	85 (b)	86 (d)	87 (d)	88 (d)	89 (b)	90 (b)
91 (c)	92 (d)	93 (c)	94 (b)	95 (d)					

Assertion and Reason Questions

1 (a)	2 (a)	3 (a)	4 (a)	5 (c)	6 (a)	7 (a)	8 (a)	9 (d)	10 (d)

Statement Based Questions

1 (d)	2 (b)	3 (d)	4 (d)	5 (b)	6 (d)	7 (d)	8 (d)

Matching Type Questions

1 (d)	2 (a)	3 (d)

Numerical Type Quesitons

1 (12)	2 (425)	3 (3)	4 (25)	5 (180)	6 (5)	7 (2)	8 (3)	9 (4)	10 (6.25)

NCERT Exemplar Questions

1 (a)	2 (a)	3 (d)	4 (c)	5 (c)	6 (c)	7 (a)

Past Exams Questions

1 (c)	2 (d)	3 (a)	4 (a)	5 (b)	6 (a)	7 (c)	8 (b)	9 (c)	10 (16)
11 (d)	12 (a)	13 (c)	14 (d)	15 (b)					

Skill Boosters

1 (b)	2 (d)	3 (c)	4 (c)	5 (a)	6 (a)	7 (c)	8 (d)	9 (a)	10 (c)

Step by Step

Decoding the Questions

Concept Builders

1 increased or decreased

2 True (T)

3 point

4 True (T)

5 True (T)

6 Quantisation of charges

7 9×10^9 N

8 different

9 directly

10 intensity, potential

11 $\mathbf{E}(r) = \frac{1}{4\pi\varepsilon_0} \sum_{i=1}^{n} \frac{q_i}{r_{ip}^2} \hat{\mathbf{r}}_{ip}$

12 True (T)

13 True (T)

14 twice

15 Zero

16 parallel

17 False (F)

18 False (F)

19 $\frac{q}{24\varepsilon_0}$

20 surface

Topical Questions

3 (*b*) When a soap bubble is given a negative charge, then the charges will repel each other. Hence, its radius increases.

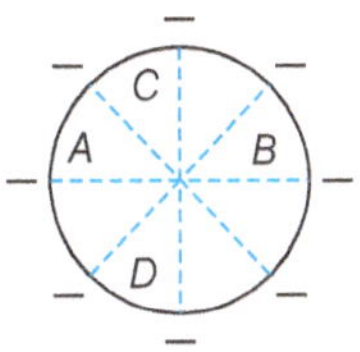

5 (*c*) During the motion of the carriers, its body gets charged because of rubbing with dry air and dust particle of the atmosphere. Due to this excess charge, the possibility of generation of spark increases and the inflammable material may catch fire.

In order to prevent this, metallic ropes are suspended from the carrier to keep its body in the contact with earth.

11 (*b*) If a sphere having charge q is put in contact with an identical uncharged sphere, then the charge q would get redistributed such that overall charge on the system remains conserved.

Also, by symmetry we can say that, charge on each sphere would be $q/2$.

12 (*d*) 1 coulomb of charge is made of $n = \frac{q}{e} = \frac{1}{1.6 \times 10^{-19}}$

$= 6.25 \times 10^{18}$ electrons

$\therefore$ Time required $= \frac{6.25 \times 10^{18}}{10^9}$ s

$= 6.25 \times 10^9 \text{ s} \approx 198$ yr

13 (*b*) Number of electrons, to be removed from silver dollar,

$$n = \frac{q}{e} = \frac{2.4 \text{ C}}{1.6 \times 10^{-19} \text{ C}} = 1.5 \times 10^{19}$$

14 (*b*) Here, number of electrons removed

= number of atoms in 1 g

or $n = \frac{4 \times 10^{20}}{10^3} = 4 \times 10^{17}$

$\therefore$ Charge, $q = ne$

$= 4 \times 10^{17} \times 1.6 \times 10^{-19}$

$= 6.4 \times 10^{-2}$ C

15 (*c*) The electrostatic force of repulsion between the change q and $(Q-q)$ at separation r is given by

$$F = \frac{1}{4\pi\varepsilon_0} \frac{q(Q-q)}{r^2}$$

If F is maximum, then $\frac{dF}{dq} = 0$

i.e. $\frac{d}{dq}\left(\frac{1}{4\pi\varepsilon_0} \frac{qQ - q^2}{r^2}\right) = 0$

$\Rightarrow \quad Q = +2q$

16 (*b*) If the two charges are placed in contact with each other and then separated, charges on them will be redistributed.

i.e. $q_{\text{net}} = |q_1 + q_2|/2$

This net charge have same polarity, so after placing them at a distance d, they experience a force of repulsion.

18 (*b*) Electrostatic force, $F = k\frac{Q_1 Q_2}{r^2}$

$\Rightarrow F = 9 \times 10^9 \times \frac{2 \times 10^{-7} \times 3 \times 10^{-7}}{(30 \times 10^{-2})^2}$

$= 6 \times 10^{-3}$ N

19 (*a*) Force in air, $F = \frac{1}{4\pi\varepsilon_0} \cdot \frac{q_1 q_2}{r^2}$

$F_m = \frac{1}{4\pi\varepsilon_0 \varepsilon_r} \cdot \frac{q_1 q_2}{r^2}$

$F_{\text{medium}} = \frac{\varepsilon_0}{\varepsilon} \cdot \frac{1}{4\pi\varepsilon_0} \frac{q_1 q_2}{r^2}$

$\Rightarrow F_{\text{medium}} = \frac{\varepsilon_0}{\varepsilon} F$

20 (*b*) The force between charges in air is

$F_{\text{air}} = \frac{1}{4\pi\varepsilon_0} \cdot \frac{q_1 q_2}{r^2}$

$F_{\text{medium}} = \frac{1}{4\pi\varepsilon_0 K} \cdot \frac{q_1 q_2}{r^2}$

$\Rightarrow \frac{F_{\text{air}}}{F_{\text{medium}}} = \frac{K}{1}$

21 (*c*) Force exerted between two point charges in air,

$$F = \frac{q_1 q_2}{4\pi\varepsilon_0 r^2}$$

So, force exerted between two point charges in a medium of dielectric constant K is

$$F' = \frac{q_1q_2}{4\pi\varepsilon_0 K(r')^2}$$

Given, $F = F'$

$$\Rightarrow \frac{q_1q_2}{4\pi\varepsilon_0 r^2} = \frac{q_1q_2}{4\pi\varepsilon_0 K(r')^2}$$

$$\therefore \quad r' = \frac{r}{\sqrt{K}}$$

22 (*b*) The electric force between an electron and proton at a distance r is

$$F_e = \frac{-ke^2}{r^2}$$

The corresponding gravitational force between electron and proton is

$$F_G = -G\frac{m_p m_e}{r^2}$$

$$\left|\frac{F_e}{F_G}\right| = \frac{k e^2}{G m_p m_e}$$

$$= \frac{(9\times10^9)(1.6\times10^{-19})^2}{(6.67\times10^{-11})(9.1\times10^{-31})(1.67\times10^{-27})}$$

$$= 2.3\times10^{39}$$

$$\Rightarrow F_G/F_e \approx 10^{-39}$$

23 (*b*) From Coulomb's law,

$$F = \frac{q_1q_2}{4\pi\varepsilon_0 r^2}$$

$$\therefore r^2 = \frac{q_1q_2}{4\pi\varepsilon_0 F}$$

$$= \frac{(9\times10^9)(8\times10^{-6})(-20\times10^{-6})}{9}$$

$$\Rightarrow r = 0.4\text{ m}$$

24 (*a*)

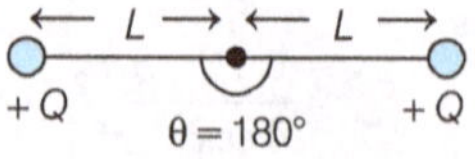

∴Tension in each thread,

i.e. $F = \dfrac{kQQ}{(2L)^2} = \dfrac{1}{4\pi\varepsilon_0}\dfrac{Q^2}{(2L)^2}$

25 (*a*)

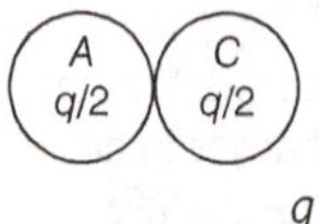

i.e. $\quad q_A = q_C = \dfrac{q}{2}$

When C is touched with B, total charge of B and C

$$= q + q/2 = \frac{3q}{2}$$

When B and C are separated, then charge is equally shared between them, i.e. $q_B = q_C = \dfrac{3q}{4}$

So, finally we have following situation

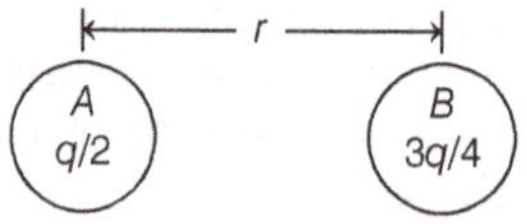

Given, $q_A = q_B = 6.5\times10^{-7}$ C

and $\quad r = 50\times10^{-2}$ m

∴ New force of repulsion between A and B is

$$F = \frac{9\times10^9\times q_Aq_B}{r^2}$$

$$= \frac{9\times10^9\times\frac{1}{2}\times\frac{3}{4}\times(6.5\times10^{-7})^2}{(0.5)^2}$$

$$= 5.7\times10^{-3}\text{ N}$$

26 (*d*) As, Coulomb's attraction = centripetal force

$$\therefore \frac{1}{4\pi\varepsilon_0}\cdot\frac{q_1q_2}{r^2} = mr\omega^2 = \frac{4\pi^2 mr}{T^2}$$

$$\Rightarrow \quad T = \left(\frac{4\pi^2 mr^3}{kq_1q_2}\right)^{1/2}$$

27 (*b*) The given condition can be seen in the figure below

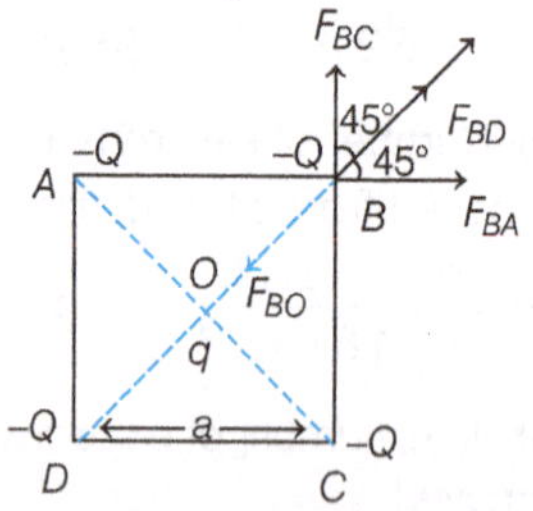

$$F_{BA} = F_{BC} = \frac{Q^2}{4\pi\varepsilon_0 a^2}$$

$$F_{BD} = \frac{Q^2}{4\pi\varepsilon_0(\sqrt{2}a)^2} = \frac{Q^2}{4\pi\varepsilon_0(2a^2)}$$

$$F_{BO} = \frac{-qQ}{4\pi\varepsilon_0\left(\frac{a}{\sqrt{2}}\right)^2} = \frac{-2qQ}{4\pi\varepsilon_0 a^2}$$

Therefore, the net force acting on $-Q$ at point B will be zero,

i.e. $F_{BA}\cos45° + F_{BC}\cos45° + F_{BD} - F_{BO} = 0$

On solving, we get

$$q = \frac{Q}{4}(1+2\sqrt{2})$$

28 (*b*) From Coulomb's law, we have

$$F = \frac{1}{4\pi\varepsilon_0}\frac{q_1q_2}{l^2}$$

$$F_{AB} = F_{AC} = \frac{1}{4\pi\varepsilon_0}\frac{q^2}{l^2} = F$$

$$\Rightarrow F_R = \sqrt{F_{AC}^2 + F_{AB}^2 + 2F_{AB}F_{AC}\cos60°}$$

$$= \sqrt{3}F$$

$$F = \sqrt{3}\frac{1}{4\pi\varepsilon_0}\frac{q^2}{l^2}$$

29 (*c*)

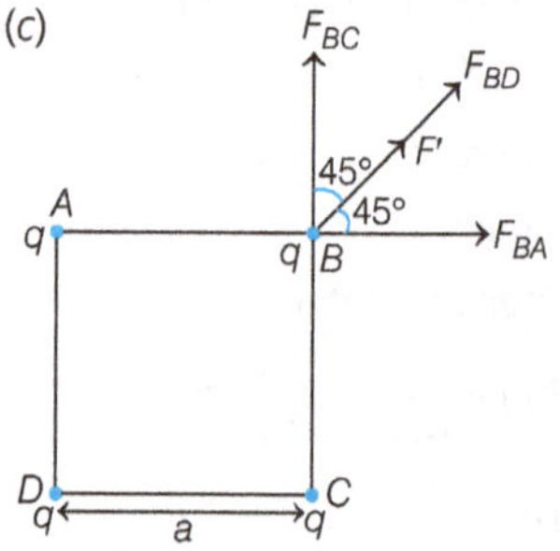

$$F_{net} = \left(\sqrt{2} + \frac{1}{2}\right)F$$

$[\because F_{net} = F' + F_{BD};\ F' = \sqrt{F_{BA}^2 + F_{BC}^2}]$

Here, $F = \dfrac{kq^2}{a^2}$

$$= \left(\frac{2\sqrt{2}+1}{2}\right)\frac{q^2}{4\pi\varepsilon_0 a^2}$$

30 (*b*) According to given figure,

$$F\sin\theta + F' = \frac{kq_1q_3}{a^2}\sin\theta + \frac{kq_1q_2}{b^2}$$

$$\propto \frac{q_2}{b^2} + \frac{q_3}{a^2}\sin\theta$$

31 (*b*) $\therefore F = \dfrac{kQ^2}{a^2}$

$$F_{net} = \sqrt{F^2 + F^2 + 2F^2\cos60°}$$

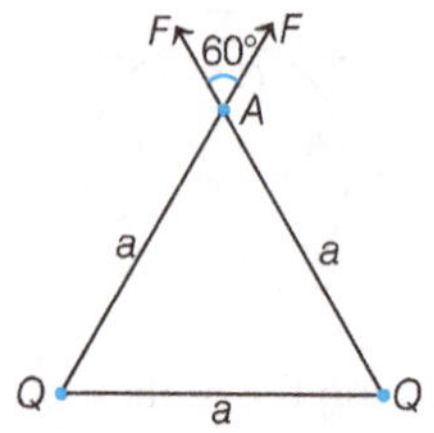

$$= \sqrt{3}F = \frac{\sqrt{3}kQ^2}{a^2}$$

32 (c) Given, electric field,

$$E = Aa \quad \text{...(i)}$$

A charge q contained in a sphere of radius a centred at the origin as shown below

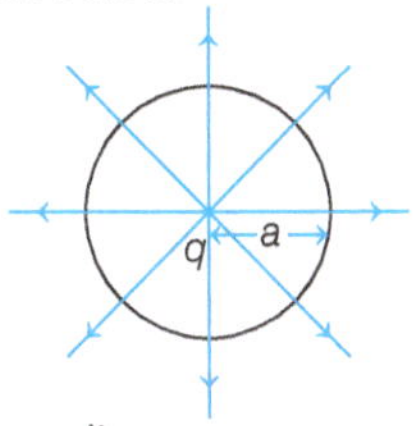

Here, radius, $r = a$

$\therefore$ Electric field,

$$E = \frac{1}{4\pi\varepsilon_0} \cdot \frac{q}{a^2} \quad \text{...(ii)}$$

From Eqs. (i) and (ii),

$$\Rightarrow \quad q = 4\pi\varepsilon_0 A a^3$$

33 (d) Forces on the bob are as shown below

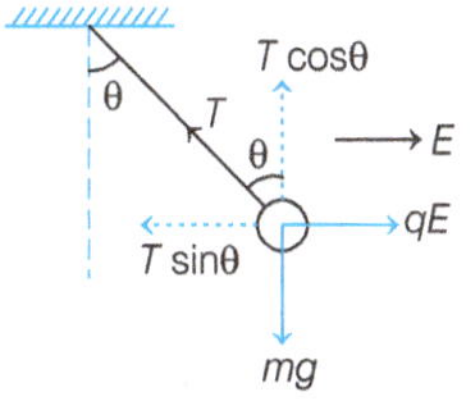

For equilibrium,

$$T\cos\theta = mg \quad \text{...(i)}$$

and $\quad T\sin\theta = qE \quad$ ...(ii)

Dividing Eq. (ii) by Eq. (i), we get

$$\tan\theta = \frac{qE}{mg}$$

$$\Rightarrow \tan\theta = \frac{5\times10^{-6}\times2000}{2\times10^{-3}\times10} = \frac{1}{2} = 0.5$$

$$\Rightarrow \quad \theta = \tan^{-1}(0.5)$$

34 (c) For electron, acceleration $= \frac{eE}{m_e}$

$$s = \frac{eE}{2m_e}\times t_1^2 \quad \text{...(i)}$$

Similarly for proton,

$$s = \frac{eE}{2m_p}\times t_2^2 \quad \text{...(ii)}$$

Dividing Eq. (ii) by Eq. (i), we get

$$\frac{t_2}{t_1} = \left(\frac{m_p}{m_e}\right)^{1/2}$$

35 (c) $E_1 = \frac{kq_1}{r^2} = \frac{(9\times10^9)\times(10^{-8})}{(0.05)^2}$

$= 3.6\times10^4\,\text{NC}^{-1}$

$$E_2 = \frac{kq_2}{r^2} = \frac{(9\times10^9)\times(10^{-8})}{(0.05)^2}$$

$= 3.6\times10^4\,\text{NC}^{-1}$

The magnitude of the total electric field at A is

$$E_A = E_1 + E_2 = 7.2\times10^4\ \text{NC}^{-1} \quad \text{...(i)}$$

This $\mathbf{E}_A$ is directed towards the right.

Now, consider the following given figure

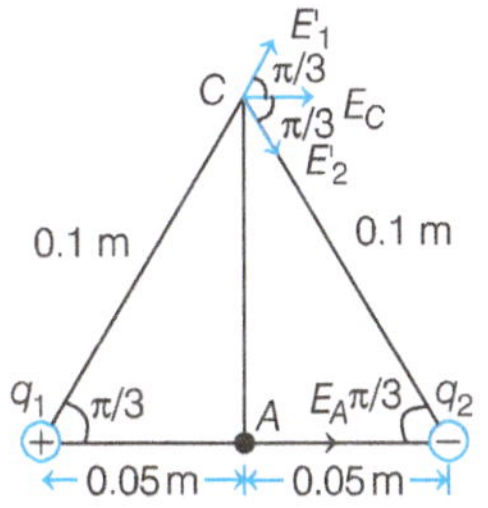

The magnitude of each electric field vector at point C, due to charges q_1 and q_2 is

$$E_1' = E_2'$$

$$= \frac{(9\times10^9)\times(10^{-8})}{(0.1)^2}$$

$$= 9\times10^3\ \text{NC}^{-1}$$

The resultant of these two vectors is

$$E_C = E_1'\cos\frac{\pi}{3} + E_2'\cos\frac{\pi}{3}$$

$$= 9\times10^3\ \text{NC}^{-1} \quad \text{...(ii)}$$

This $\mathbf{E}_C$ points towards the right.

Dividing Eq (i) by Eq. (ii), we get

$$\frac{E_A}{E_C} = \frac{7.2\times10^4}{9\times10^3} = \frac{8}{1}$$

36 (b)

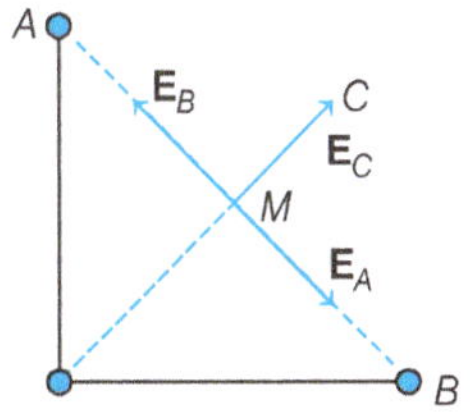

where,

E_A = electric field at M due to charge placed at A,

E_B = electric field at M due to charge placed at B

and E_C = electric field at M due to charge placed at C.

As seen from figure $|\mathbf{E}_B| = |\mathbf{E}_A|$, so net electric field at M,

$\mathbf{E}_{net} = |\mathbf{E}_C|$, in the direction of vector 2.

37 (b)

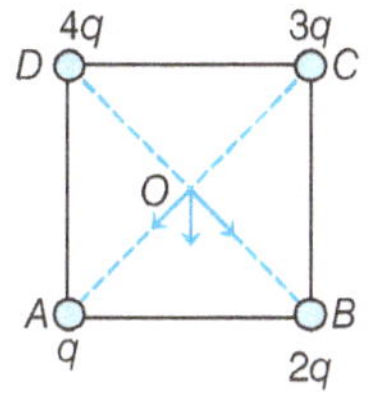

So, the net electric field will be along bisector of angle AOB which parallel to CB.

38 (b)

$$E = \frac{1}{4\pi\varepsilon_0}\cdot q\left[1 - \frac{1}{2^2} + \frac{1}{4^2} - \frac{1}{8^2} + \ldots\right]$$

$$= \frac{q}{4\pi\varepsilon_0}\frac{1}{\left[1-\left(-\frac{1}{4}\right)\right]} = 36\ \text{V/m}$$

39 (b) $E_R = E_1 - E_2$

$$= \frac{1}{4\pi\varepsilon_0}\frac{q}{1} - \frac{1}{4\pi\varepsilon_0}q\left(\frac{1}{1+\frac{1}{4}}\right)$$

$$= \frac{1}{10\pi\varepsilon_0}, \text{ along + ve } X\text{-axis}$$

40 (c)

$$\frac{E_1}{E_2} = \frac{\dfrac{q}{\dfrac{1}{4\pi\varepsilon_0}\left(\dfrac{a}{\sqrt{2}}\right)^2}}{\dfrac{1}{4\pi\varepsilon_0}\dfrac{q}{\left(\dfrac{a}{2}\right)^2}} = \frac{1}{2}$$

41 (c)

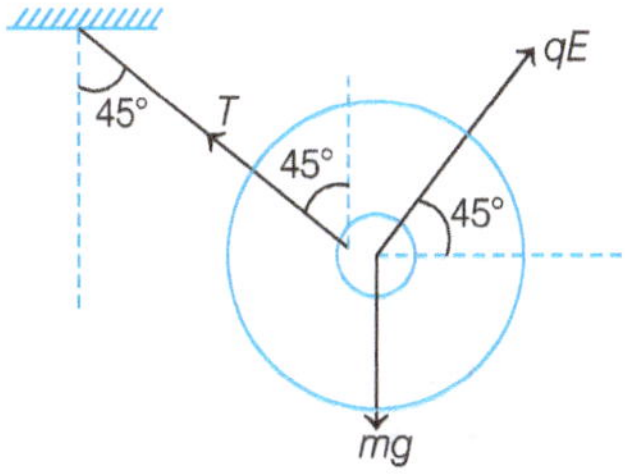

$$\mathbf{E} = \hat{\mathbf{i}} + \hat{\mathbf{j}}$$

$$E = |\mathbf{E}| = \sqrt{2}\ \text{N/C}$$

For equilibrium,

$$T\cos45° + qE\sin45° = mg$$

$$T\sin45° = qE\cos45°$$

$$\Rightarrow \quad T = qE$$

$$qE\cos 45° + qE\sin 45° = mg$$
$$\frac{qE}{\sqrt{2}} + \frac{qE}{\sqrt{2}} = mg$$
$$\sqrt{2}qE = mg$$
$$\Rightarrow \quad q = \frac{20}{2} = 10\,C$$

42 (*d*) Linear charge density, $\lambda = \left(\frac{q}{\pi r}\right)$

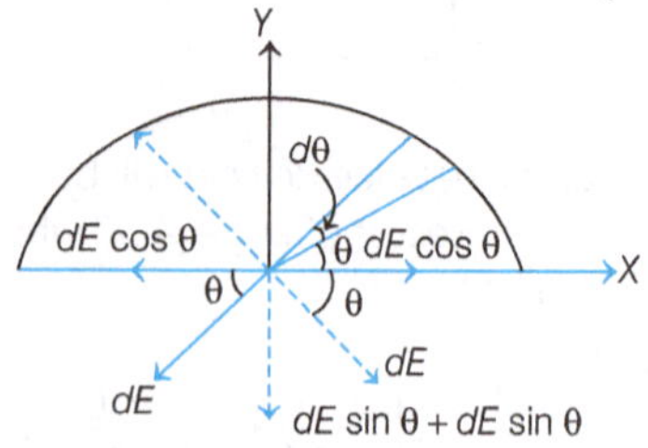

$$E = \int dE \sin\theta(-\mathbf{j})$$
$$= \int_0^{\pi} \frac{k\cdot dq}{r^2}\sin\theta(-\mathbf{j})$$
$$= \frac{q}{2\pi^2\varepsilon_0 r^2}(-\mathbf{j})$$

43 (*a*) $mg = neE$

$$\Rightarrow \quad n = \frac{9.8\times10^{-3}}{10^{-10}} = 9.8\times10^{7}$$

44 (*b*) Given, $Q_1 = 4C$, $Q_2 = 8C$

The electric field at a distance r due to a point charge is

$$E = \frac{1}{4\pi\varepsilon_0}\cdot\frac{Q}{r^2} \Rightarrow E \propto Q$$
$$\therefore \quad \frac{E_2}{E_1} = \frac{Q_2}{Q_1} = 2 \quad \Rightarrow E_2 = 2E_1$$

45 (*c*) Given, $F = 2.5$ N, $q = 5\times10^{-4}$C

$$\therefore \text{Electric field, } E = \frac{F}{q} = \frac{2.5}{5\times10^{-4}}$$
$$= 0.5\times10^{4}$$
$$= 5000 \text{ N/C}$$

59 (*d*) Given, $d\mathbf{S} = 5\hat{\mathbf{i}}$,

$$\mathbf{E} = 4\hat{\mathbf{i}} + 4\hat{\mathbf{j}} + 4\hat{\mathbf{k}}$$

Electric flux is given by

$$\phi = \mathbf{E}\cdot d\mathbf{S} = (5\mathbf{i})\cdot(4\hat{\mathbf{i}} + 4\hat{\mathbf{j}} + 4\hat{\mathbf{k}})$$
$$\Rightarrow \quad \phi = 20 \text{ unit}$$

60 (*a*) Given, $\mathbf{E} = 10\hat{\mathbf{i}} + 3\hat{\mathbf{j}} + 4\hat{\mathbf{k}}$

$$\mathbf{A} = 10\hat{\mathbf{i}}$$

Flux through a surface is given by

$$\phi = \mathbf{E}\cdot\mathbf{A} = (10\hat{\mathbf{i}} + 3\hat{\mathbf{j}} + 4\hat{\mathbf{k}})\cdot(10\hat{\mathbf{i}})$$
$$= 100 \text{ unit}$$

61 (*c*)

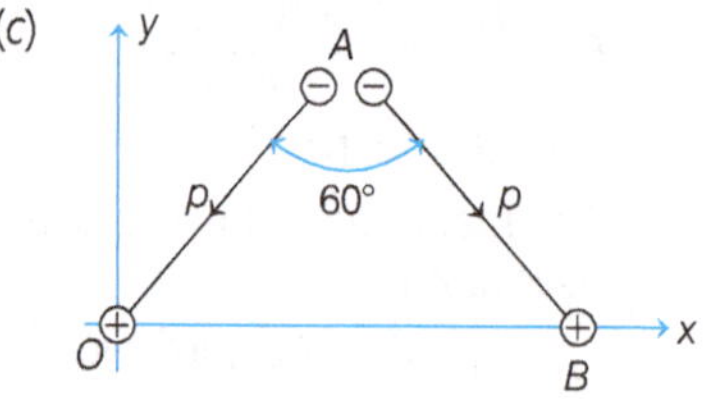

$$p_{\text{net}} = \sqrt{p^2 + p^2 + 2p\cdot p\cos 60°}$$
$$= \sqrt{3}p = \sqrt{3}ql$$

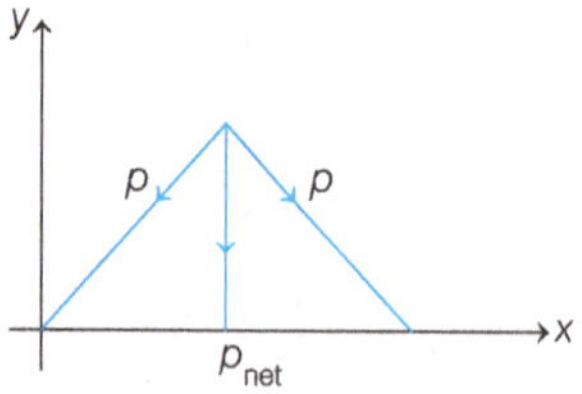

As, resultant is directed along negative y-direction,

$$p_{\text{net}} = -\sqrt{3}p\hat{\mathbf{j}} = -\sqrt{3}ql\,\hat{\mathbf{j}}$$

63 (*c*) $\therefore$ Electric field at a point P on dipole axis is

$$E_P = \frac{2p}{4\pi\varepsilon_0 r^3} = \frac{2(2a\times q)}{4\pi\varepsilon_0 r^3}$$
$$= \frac{2\,(5\times10^{-3}\times10\times10^{-6})\times(9\times10^{9})}{(15\times10^{-2})^3}$$
$$= 2.6\times10^{5}\ \text{NC}^{-1}$$

Now, electric field at a point Q on equatorial plane is

$$E_Q = \frac{p}{4\pi\varepsilon_0 r^3} = \frac{1}{2}E_P$$
$$= \frac{1}{2}\times2.6\times10^{5} = 1.3\times10^{5}\ \text{NC}^{-1}$$

64 (*d*) $E = \frac{1}{4\pi\varepsilon_0}\cdot\frac{2p}{r^3}$ (short dipole)

$$F = q_0E$$
$$F_1 = q_0\left[\frac{1}{4\pi\varepsilon_0}\cdot\frac{2p}{(2r)^3}\right] = \frac{F}{8}$$

66 (*a*) Net dipole moment,

$$p_{\text{net}} = \sqrt{p^2 + p^2 + 2p^2\cos 120°}$$
$$p_{\text{net}} = \sqrt{p^2 + p^2 - p^2} = p$$
$$\tau = p_{\text{net}}E\sin\theta$$

$\Rightarrow \tau = pE\sin\theta = \mathbf{p}\times\mathbf{E}$ and it is along positive Z-axis.

67 (*c*) $\tau = p\cdot E$(As, $\theta = 90°$)

For maximum, $\tau = p\cdot E$

$$\tau = q\times 2aE$$
$$= 1\times10^{-6}\times2\times10^{-2}\times10^{6}$$
$$= 20\times10^{-3}\ \text{N-m}$$

68 (*c*) $\tau = p\cdot E\sin\theta$

$$\tau = q\times 2aE\sin\theta$$
$$= q\times(4\times10^{-2})\times4\times10^{5}\times\sin 60°$$
$$\Rightarrow 8\sqrt{3} = q\times4\times10^{-2}\times4\times10^{5}\times\sqrt{3}/2$$
$$\Rightarrow \quad q = 10^{-3}\ \text{C}$$

69 (*b*) Given, $d = 4.4$ m, $\sigma = 80\,\mu\text{Cm}^{-2}$

$$\therefore \quad r = 2.2 \text{ m}$$

The charge on the sphere is given by $Q = \sigma A = 80\times10^{-6}\times4\pi\times(2.2)^2$

$$= 4.9\times10^{-3}\ \text{C}$$

71 (*b*) As, the net electric field inside a spherical shell is zero. So, net charge inside the shell is also zero.

i.e. $\quad q + q' = 0$

$$\therefore \quad q' = -q$$

$\therefore$ The surface charge density on the inner surface of the shell is

$$\sigma_1 = \frac{q'}{4\pi R_1^2} = \frac{-q}{4\pi R_1^2}$$

72 (*c*) Given, $\lambda = (3x^2 + 5x + 2)$ C/m,

$$l = 3 \text{ m}$$

The net charge present on the rod is $\quad q = \int_0^l \lambda dx = \int_0^3 (3x^2 + 5x + 2)dx$

$$= \left[3\cdot\frac{x^3}{3} + 5\cdot\frac{x^2}{2} + 2x\right]_0^3$$
$$= 55.5\ \text{C}$$

73 (*c*) According to the question,

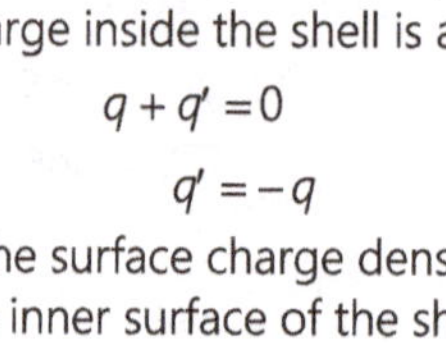

The electric field at P due to charge $\rho\Delta V$ is

$$\mathbf{E}_1 = \frac{1}{4\pi\varepsilon_0}\frac{\rho\Delta V}{(C_1P)^2}$$

$$= \frac{1}{4\pi\varepsilon_0} \frac{\rho \frac{4}{3}\pi(C_1P)^3}{(C_1P)^2}$$

$$= \frac{\rho}{3\varepsilon_0} C_1P, \text{ along } C_1P$$

Similarly,

$$\mathbf{E}_2 = \frac{(-\rho)}{3\varepsilon_0} C_2P, \text{ along } PC_2$$

So, net electric field, $|\mathbf{E}_P| = |\mathbf{E}_1| + |\mathbf{E}_2|$

$$= \frac{\rho}{3\varepsilon_0}(C_1P + C_2P)$$

Since, these two spheres partially overlap.

So, the distance, $C_1P + C_2P \approx C_1C_2$

$$\therefore \quad \mathbf{E}_P = \frac{\rho}{3\varepsilon_0} C_1C_2, \text{ along } C_1C_2$$

Hence, electrostatic field is constant in magnitude.

74 (c) As flux $= \frac{q_{\text{enclosed}}}{\varepsilon_0}$, so flux is due to only charges $+q_1$ and $-q_1$ that makes a sum zero. But q_2 produces its own flux and net flux linked with sphere is zero.

Hence, electric field will be due to all the charges.

75 (c) $\oint_S \mathbf{E} \cdot d\mathbf{S} = \phi_E$ represents electric flux over the closed surface.

When $\oint_S \mathbf{E} \cdot d\mathbf{S} = 0$, it means that the number of flux lines entering the surface must be equal to the number of flux lines leaving it.

76 (b) By Gauss's law,

electric flux through closed surface area, $\phi = \frac{q_{\text{enclosed}}}{\varepsilon_0}$.

If $q_{\text{enclosed}} = 1$ unit, then

$$\phi = \frac{1}{\varepsilon_0} = \varepsilon_0^{-1}$$

77 (a) According to Gauss' law

$$\phi = \frac{q}{\varepsilon_0}$$

As, $\phi_{\text{sphere}} = \phi_{\text{cube}}$

$\therefore \phi_{\text{sphere}} : \phi_{\text{cube}} = 1:1$

78 (d) Net charges of one dipole

$= -e + e = 0$

Net charge of 8 dipoles $= 8 \times 0 = 0$

$\therefore$ Net charge inside cube, $q = 0$

By Gauss's law,

total flux emerging from surface,

$$\phi = \frac{q}{\varepsilon_0} = \frac{0}{\varepsilon_0} = 0$$

79 (a) Total charge inside the given surface is

$$= Q - 2Q = -Q$$

$\therefore$ Total flux through the surface of the sphere, $\phi = \frac{-Q}{\varepsilon_0}$

The field on the surface of sphere is

$$E = \frac{Q}{4\pi\varepsilon_0 R^2}$$

As $\quad E \propto \frac{1}{R^2}$,

so the field due to $-2Q$ is not same everywhere on the sphere.

80 (b) Using Gauss's law at outer surface, let charge on dipole is q,

$$\phi = \frac{\Sigma q}{\varepsilon_0} = E \cdot A$$

or $\quad E = \frac{1}{A\varepsilon_0}\Sigma q$

$$= \frac{(+Q + q - q)}{A\varepsilon_0}$$

$$= \frac{Q}{A\varepsilon_0}$$

$$= \frac{\sigma}{\varepsilon_0} = \text{constant}$$

81 (a) $q_{\text{net}} = q_1 + q_2 + q_3 = 8.85\text{nC}$

$$\phi = \frac{q}{\varepsilon_0} = \frac{8.85 \times 10^{-9}}{8.85 \times 10^{-12}}$$

$$= 10^3 \text{ N-m}^2\text{C}^{-1}$$

82 (a) $\phi_{\text{total}} = \phi_A + \phi_B + \phi_C = \frac{q}{\varepsilon_0}$

$\because \quad \phi_B = \phi$

and $\quad \phi_A = \phi_C = \phi'$

$$\therefore 2\phi' + \phi = \frac{q}{\varepsilon_0}$$

$$\Rightarrow \quad \phi' = \frac{1}{2}\left(\frac{q}{\varepsilon_0} - \phi\right)$$

83 (b) The electric field between two parallel plates is as shown below

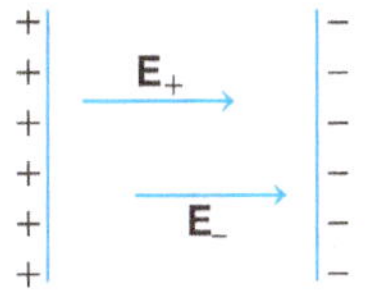

Here, $\quad E_+ = E_- = \frac{\sigma}{2\varepsilon_0}$

$$\Rightarrow \quad E_{\text{net}} = 2\left(\frac{\sigma}{2\varepsilon_0}\right) = \left(\frac{\sigma}{\varepsilon_0}\right)$$

84 (d)

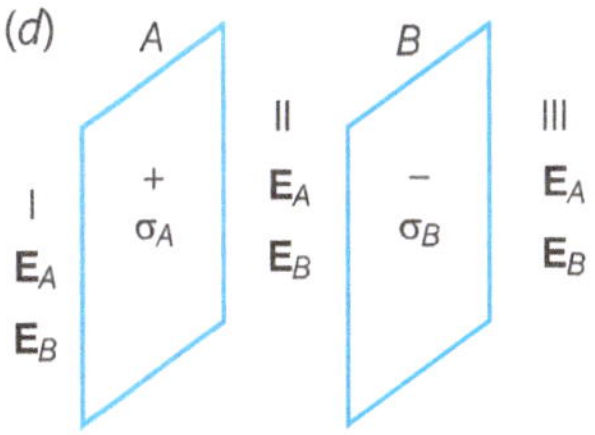

$$\mathbf{E}_\text{I} = \mathbf{E}_A + \mathbf{E}_B$$

$$= \frac{\sigma}{2\varepsilon_0} + \left(-\frac{\sigma}{2\varepsilon_0}\right) = 0$$

87 (d) Electric field due to uniformly charged solid non-conducting sphere is given by

$$E = \frac{1}{4\pi\varepsilon_0}\frac{Q}{R^3} r \text{ (for } r < R)$$

$\therefore \quad E \propto r$

So, electric field increases as r increases.

88 (d) Electric field at point P is given by

$$E = E_1 + E_2 + E_3$$

$$= \frac{2k\lambda}{\frac{3r}{2}} + \frac{2k(2\lambda)}{\frac{r}{2}} + \frac{2k(\lambda)}{\frac{r}{2}}$$

$$\Rightarrow \quad E = \frac{40k\lambda}{3r}$$

89 (b) We know that the electric field due to uniformly charged sphere is given by

$$E = \frac{kqx}{R^3}$$

$$= \frac{1}{4\pi\varepsilon_0}\frac{qx}{R^3}$$

$\therefore$ Electric field at distance $x = \dfrac{R}{2}$ is given by $E = \dfrac{1}{4\pi\varepsilon_0}\dfrac{q}{R^3}\dfrac{R}{2}$

$$E = \frac{1}{8\pi\varepsilon_0}\frac{q}{R^2}$$

90 (b)

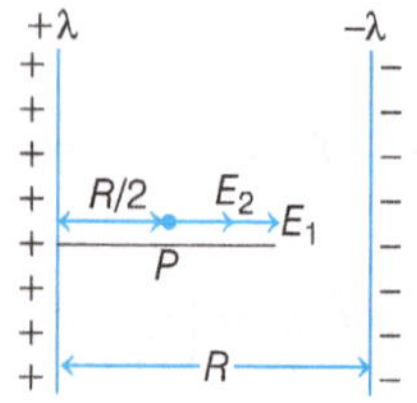

Electric field at point P due to $+\lambda$ is

$$E_1 = \frac{\lambda}{2\pi\varepsilon_0\left(\frac{R}{2}\right)} = \frac{\lambda}{\pi\varepsilon_0 R}$$

Electric field at point P due to $-\lambda$ is

$$E_2 = \frac{\lambda}{2\pi\varepsilon_0\left(\frac{R}{2}\right)}$$

$$= \frac{\lambda}{\pi\varepsilon_0 R}$$

$\therefore$ Net electric field at point P is

$$E_{net} = E_1 + E_2 = \frac{2\lambda}{\pi\varepsilon_0 R}$$

91 (c) Given, $l = 2.4$ m, $r = 4.6$ mm $= 4.6 \times 10^{-3}$ m,

$q = -4.2 \times 10^{-7}$ C

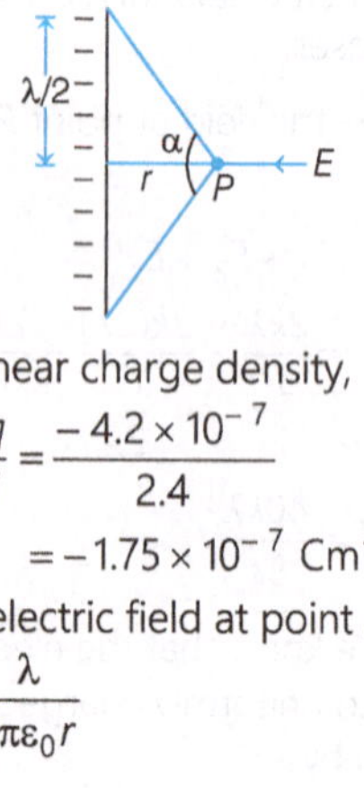

$\therefore$ Linear charge density,

$$\lambda = \frac{q}{l} = \frac{-4.2 \times 10^{-7}}{2.4}$$

$$= -1.75 \times 10^{-7}\ \text{Cm}^{-1}$$

The electric field at point P is

$$E = \frac{\lambda}{2\pi\varepsilon_0 r}$$

$$= \frac{-1.75 \times 10^{-7}}{2 \times 3.14 \times 8.854 \times 10^{-12} \times 4.6 \times 10^{-3}}$$

$$= -6.7 \times 10^5\ \text{NC}^{-1}$$

92 (d) The FBD of the ball B is given as

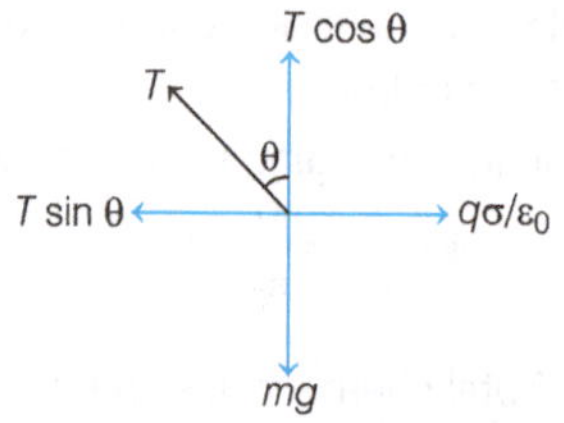

$$\therefore \quad \Sigma F_x = 0 \Rightarrow T\sin\theta = \frac{q\sigma}{\varepsilon_0} \quad \text{...(i)}$$

$$\Sigma F_y = 0 \Rightarrow T\cos\theta = mg. \quad \text{..(ii)}$$

Dividing Eq. (i) by Eq. (ii), we get

$$\tan\theta = \frac{q\sigma}{mg\varepsilon_0} \Rightarrow \sigma \propto \tan\theta$$

93 (c) The electric fields in region II between the plates are shown below.

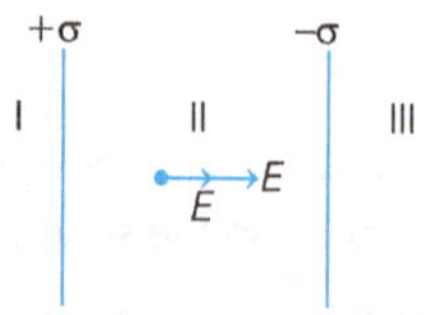

Given, $\sigma = 27 \times 10^{-22}\ \text{Cm}^{-2}$

$\therefore$ The net electric field in region II is

$$E_{net} = 2E = 2\left(\frac{\sigma}{2\varepsilon_0}\right) = \frac{\sigma}{\varepsilon_0}$$

$$= \frac{27 \times 10^{-22}}{8.85 \times 10^{-12}} = 3.05 \times 10^{-10}\ \text{NC}^{-1}$$

95 (d)

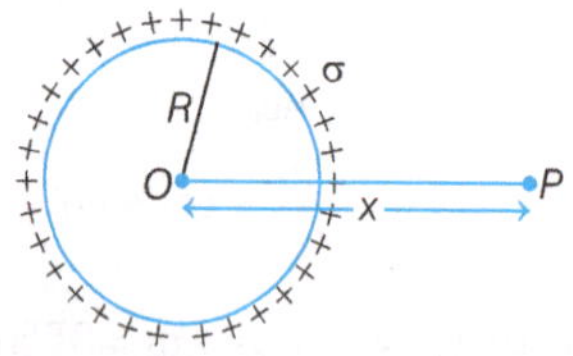

The electric field at point P due to spherical shell is

$$E = \frac{1}{4\pi\varepsilon_0}\cdot\frac{Q}{x^2} = \frac{1}{4\pi\varepsilon_0}\cdot\frac{\sigma(4\pi R^2)}{x^2}$$

$$\therefore \quad E \propto \frac{1}{x^2}$$

Assertion and Reason Questions

1 (a) When we produce charge q_1 on a body by rubbing it against another body which gets a charge q_2 in the process, then q_1 and q_2 both are equal in magnitude but opposite in polarities.

Hence, $q_1 + q_2 = 0$.

2 (a) At macroscopic level, we deal with charges of order $1\mu\text{C} = 10^{-6}$ C, which has $\dfrac{10^{-6}}{1.6 \times 10^{-19}} = 0.625 \times 10^{13}$

$= 10^{13}$ charges.

Addition of a few hundred of e charges do not make any physically observable effect on attraction or repulsion, so quantisation can be ignored.

3 (a) The total amount of charge on the body is

$$n_2 e + n_1(-e) = (n_2 - n_1)e.$$

Thus, the charge on any body is integral multiple of e and can be increased in terms of e.

4 (a) Conservation of electric charges state that the total charge of an isolate system remains the same.

5 (c) Coulomb force and gravitational force follow the same inverse square law. But gravitational force has only one sign which is always attractive, while Coulomb force can be of both signs which are attractive and repulsive.

6 (a) When a positive charge initially at rest is placed in a uniform electric field, then it moves along the electric lines of force.

But if a point charge is released from rest in a direction making an angle with the field, then it follows a parabolic path.

8 (a) Given, dipole moment,

$$p = 30 \times 10^{-5}\ \text{C-m}$$

Using Gauss's law,

$$\phi = \frac{Q_{in}}{\varepsilon_0} = 0 \quad (\because Q_{in} = 0 \text{ for dipole})$$

9 (d) Due to displacement of charge within a closed surface, **E** at any point may change. But net flux crossing the surface will not change. The flux crossing through a closed surface is independent of the location of charge within the surface, as it is same everywhere on its surface.

10 (*d*) **E** in outside vicinity of conductor surface depends on all the charges present in the space and its expression is $\mathbf{E} = \frac{\sigma}{\varepsilon_0}$.

Statement Based Questions

2 (*b*) The Statement II is incorrect and it can be corrected as,

-2 units charge $+ 6$ units charge $= 4$ units charge.

5 (*b*) The electric field will increase, if positive charge is brought in an electric field. Therefore, Statement I is correct but Statement II is incorrect.

7 (*d*) Though the net charge on the conductor is still zero but due to induction, negatively charged region is nearer to the rod as compared to the positively charged region. That's why the conductor gets attracted towards the rod.

Therefore, Both Statement I and Statement II are correct.

8 (*d*) The electrostatic shielding is possible by metallic conductor. Therefore, both Statement I and Statement II are correct.

Matching Type Questions

3 (*d*)

A. Electric lines of forces emerge from a single positive charge and goes to infinity.

B. Electric lines of forces enter into a single negative charge coming from infinity.

C. Electric lines of forces are repelled away when they are produced by the pair of positive charges.

D. The electric line of forces produced by a pair of equal and opposite charges.

Hence, A $\rightarrow$ 3, B $\rightarrow$ 4, C $\rightarrow$ 2 and D $\rightarrow$ 1.

Numerical Type Questions

1 (12) Given, $m_1 = m_2 = 10\,g$

Charge, $q_1 = q_2 = 2 \times 10^{-7}\,C$

$\mu = 0.25$, $g = 10\,m/s^2$

In the condition of limited equilibrium on either charge,

electrostatic force = static friction

$$\frac{kq_1q_2}{L^2} = \mu mg$$

$$\frac{9 \times 10^9 \times 2 \times 10^{-7} \times 2 \times 10^{-7}}{L^2} = 0.25 \times 0.01 \times 10$$

$\Rightarrow \quad L = 0.12 = 12$ cm

2 (425) Drawing the cube given in the question.

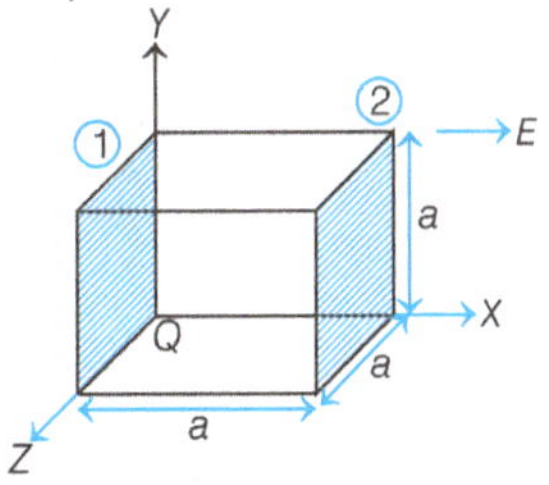

Electric flux, $\phi = \mathbf{E} \cdot \mathbf{A} = EA\cos\theta$

At face 1, $\phi_1 = E_0 x a^2 = (0) a^2 = 0$ $\quad (\because x = 0)$

At face 2, $\phi_2 = \mathbf{E} \cdot \mathbf{A}$

$$= (E_0 a \hat{\mathbf{i}}) \cdot (a^2 \hat{\mathbf{i}}) = E_0 a^3$$

$$= 6 \times 10^4 \times (2 \times 10^{-2})^3$$

$$\phi_2 = 48 \times 10^{-2}\,N/m^2\text{-}C$$

Net flux, $\phi = \phi_2 - \phi_1$

$$= 48 \times 10^{-2}\,N/m^2\text{-}C$$

From Gauss's, law,

$$\phi = \frac{q_{enc}}{\varepsilon_0}$$

$\Rightarrow q_{enc} = \phi\varepsilon_0$

$$= 48 \times 10^{-2} \times 8.85 \times 10^{-12}$$

$\Rightarrow q_{enc} \approx 425 \times 10^{-14}\,C$

3 (3) Given, $E_{max} = 3 \times 10^6\,V/m$,

$r = 3\,m$

We know that,

$$E = \frac{1}{4\pi\varepsilon_0}\frac{q}{r^2}$$

$\Rightarrow \quad q_{max} = 4\pi\varepsilon_0 r^2 E_{max}$

$$= \frac{(3)^2 \times (3 \times 10^6)}{9 \times 10^9}$$

$$q_{max} = 3 \times 10^{-3}\,C$$

4 (25) Given, electric field intensity,

$$\mathbf{E} = 5 \times 10^3 \hat{\mathbf{i}}\,N/C$$

$\Rightarrow |\mathbf{E}| = 5 \times 10^3\,N/C$

Side of square, $S = 10$ cm $= 0.1$ m

Area of square, $A = (0.1)^2 = 0.01\,m^2$

$\therefore$ Flux through the plane,

$$\phi = |\mathbf{E}| \times A\cos\theta$$

$$= 5 \times 10^3 \times 0.01 \cos 0^\circ$$

$$= 50\,N\text{-}m^2/C$$

If the plane makes an angle of 30° with the X-axis, then $\theta = 60^\circ$.

$\therefore$ Flux through the plane,

$$\phi = |\mathbf{E}| \times A \times \cos 60^\circ$$

$$= 5 \times 10^3 \times 0.01 \times \cos 60^\circ$$

$$= 25\,N\text{-}m^2/C$$

5 (180) The charge at point B repels the charge at point A with force F_{AB}

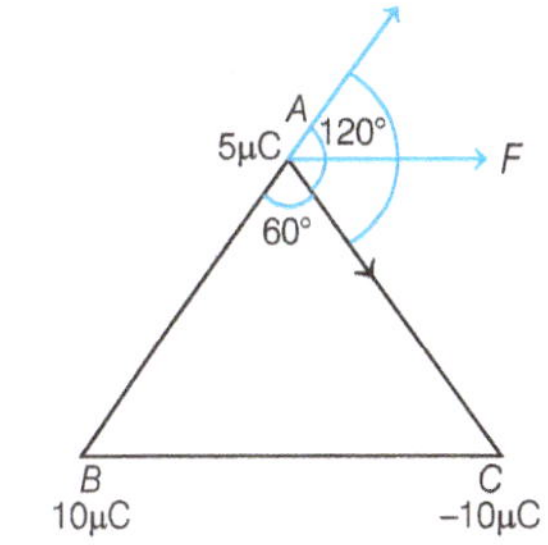

$$F_{AB} = \frac{kq_1q_2}{r^2}$$

$$= \frac{9 \times 10^9 \times 5 \times 10^{-6} \times 10 \times 10^{-6}}{(0.05)^2}$$

$$= 180\,N$$

The charge at C attracts the charge at A with a force F_{AC},

$$F_{AC} = \frac{9 \times 10^9 \times (5 \times 10^{-6}) \times (10 \times 10^{-6})}{(0.05)^2}$$

$$= 180\,N$$

Now, the resultant force on A is given by

$$F = \sqrt{F_{AB}^2 + F_{AC}^2 + 2F_{AB}F_{AC}\cos\theta}$$

$$= \sqrt{180^2 + 180^2 + 2(180)(180)\cos 120^\circ}$$

$$= 180\,N$$

6 (5) $E_{axial} = \frac{1}{4\pi\varepsilon_0}\frac{2pr}{(r^2 - a^2)^2}$

For first case

$r = 10$ m, $E = 2.5$ N/C

$\therefore \quad 2.5 = \dfrac{9 \times 10^9 \times 2p \times 10}{(10^2 - a^2)^2}$ ...(i)

For second case

$r = 20\text{ m}, \; E = 0.2\text{ N/C}$

$\therefore \quad 0.2 = \dfrac{9 \times 10^9 \times 2p \times 20}{(20^2 - a^2)^2}$ ...(ii)

Dividing Eq. (i) by Eq. (ii), we get

$$\frac{2.5}{0.2} = \frac{10}{20} \frac{(20^2 - a^2)^2}{(10^2 - a^2)^2}$$

$\Rightarrow \quad a = 5\text{ m}$

7 (2) Given, electric field,

$E = 4\,m/e\text{ Vm}^{-1}$

Length of plates, $l = 2\text{m}$

Speed of electron, $v_x = 2\text{ ms}^{-1}$

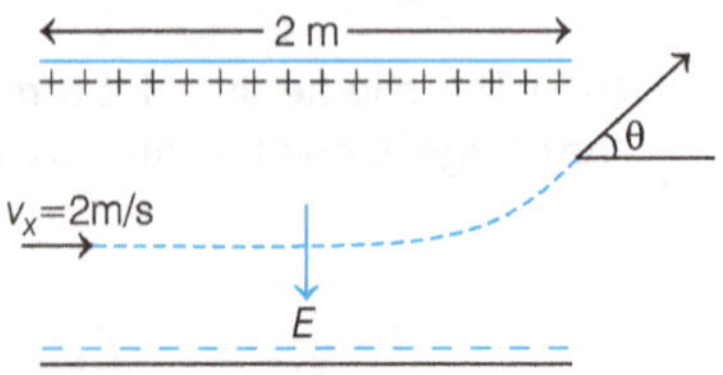

The time taken by the electron to come out of field undeflected is

$$t = \frac{l}{v_x} = \frac{2}{2} = 1\text{s}$$

As we know, $F = qE$

Since, electron is accelerating opposite to the direction of **E**.

$\Rightarrow -m \times a_y = e \times \dfrac{4m}{e}$

$\Rightarrow \quad a_y = -4\text{ ms}^{-2}$

Using first equation of motion,

$v_y = u_y + a_y t$

$\Rightarrow \quad v_y = 0 + (-4)(1)$

or $\quad |v_y| = 4\text{ms}^{-1}$

As the electron is deflected by angle θ, so

$$\tan\theta = \frac{v_y}{v_x}$$

$\Rightarrow \quad \theta = \tan^{-1}\left(\dfrac{4}{2}\right) = \tan^{-1}(2)$

So, the value of x is 2.

8 (3) At the point $x = 0$, the electric field due to all the charges is given by

$$E = \frac{1}{4\pi\varepsilon_0}\left[\frac{q}{1^2} + \frac{q}{2^2} + \frac{q}{4^2} + \frac{q}{8^2} + \ldots\right]$$

$$= \frac{q}{4\pi\varepsilon_0}\left[\frac{1}{1 - \frac{1}{4}}\right] = \frac{q}{3\pi\varepsilon_0}$$

So, the value of x is 3.

9 (4) So, we are considering the equilibrium of charge, placed at the corners of a square.

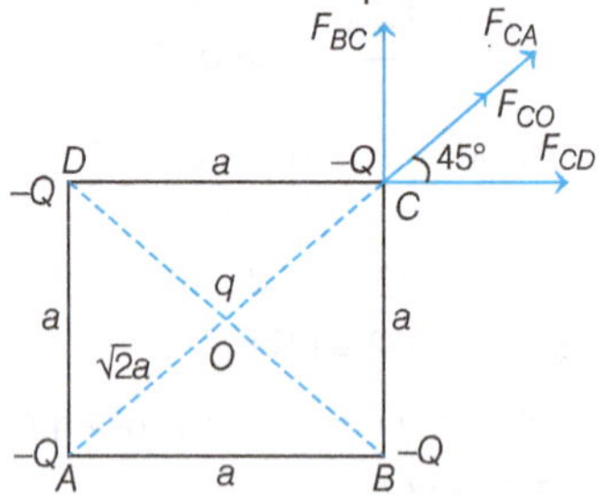

$F_{CD} + F_{CA}\cos 45° + F_{CO}\cos 45° = 0$

$$\frac{1}{4\pi\varepsilon_0}\left[\frac{(-Q)(-Q)}{a^2} + \frac{(-Q)(-Q)}{(\sqrt{2}a)^2} \times \frac{1}{\sqrt{2}} + \frac{(-Q)q}{\left(\sqrt{2}\frac{a}{2}\right)^2} \times \frac{1}{\sqrt{2}}\right] = 0$$

$$q = (\sqrt{4 \times 2} + 1)\frac{Q}{4}$$

$\therefore$ The value of x is 4.

10 (6.25) Force, $F = \dfrac{kq_1q_2}{d^2}$

charge on each sphere after bringing the two spheres in contact,

$$= \frac{2\text{nC} - 1\text{nC}}{2} = 0.5\text{ nC}$$

$$\therefore F = \frac{9 \times 10^9 \times 0.5 \times 10^{-9} \times (0.5 \times 10^{-9})}{(0.6)^2}$$

$= 6.25 \times 10^{-9}\text{N}$

NCERT Exemplar Questions

4 (c) The given condition is as shown below.

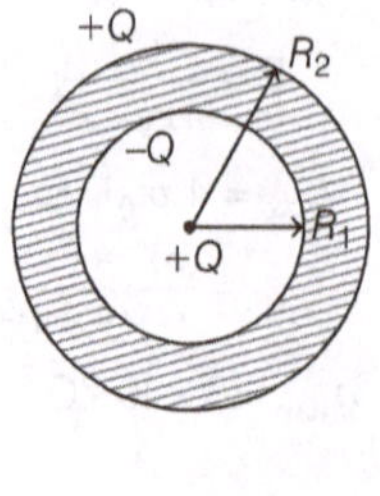

Now, surface charge density on the inner surface of spherical shell is $\sigma = \dfrac{q}{S} = \dfrac{-Q}{4\pi R_1^2}$

$\therefore$ Surface charge density on the outer surface $= \dfrac{+Q}{4\pi R_2^2}$

6 (c)

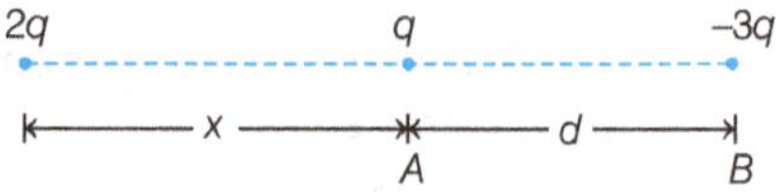

Thus, force of attraction by $-3q$ = force of repulsion by q

$$\Rightarrow \quad \frac{2q \times 3q}{4\pi\varepsilon_0\,(x + d)^2} = \frac{2q \times q}{4\pi\varepsilon_0\,x^2}$$

$$\therefore \quad x = \frac{d}{2} + \frac{\sqrt{3}d}{2} = \frac{d}{2}(1 + \sqrt{3})$$

to the left of q.

Past Exams Questions

1 (c) We know that, $\tau = pE\sin\theta$

$\Rightarrow \quad p = \dfrac{\tau}{E\sin\theta} = \dfrac{4}{2 \times 10^5 \times \sin 30°}$

$\Rightarrow \quad p = 4 \times 10^{-5}$ C-m

$\Rightarrow \quad 2l \cdot q = 4 \times 10^{-5}$

$\Rightarrow \quad q = \dfrac{4 \times 10^{-5}}{2l} = \dfrac{4 \times 10^{-5}}{2 \times 10^{-2}}$

$= 2 \times 10^{-3}\text{ C} = 2\text{mC}$

3 (a) Electric field at a point ($x = 15$ cm) from the centre of the sphere is

$$E = \frac{1}{4\pi\varepsilon_0} \cdot \frac{q}{x^2}$$

$$= 9 \times 10^9 \times \frac{3.2 \times 10^{-7}}{(15 \times 10^{-2})^2}$$

$= 1.28 \times 10^5$ N/C

5 (b) When a sphere encloses a charged dipole,

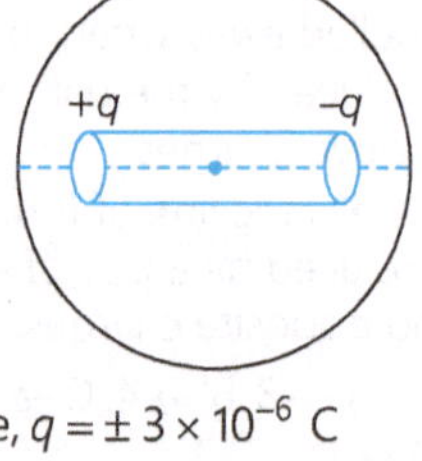

Here, $q = \pm 3 \times 10^{-6}$ C

Thus, according to Gauss's law,

$$\phi_E = \frac{q_{in}}{\varepsilon_0} = \frac{+3\times10^{-6} - 3\times10^{-6}}{\varepsilon_0} = 0$$

6 (*a*)

(i) The electric field at a point outside the hollow sphere is

$$\phi = \oint_S \mathbf{E}\cdot d\mathbf{S} = \frac{Q_{\text{enclosed}}}{\varepsilon_0}$$

[from Gauss' law]

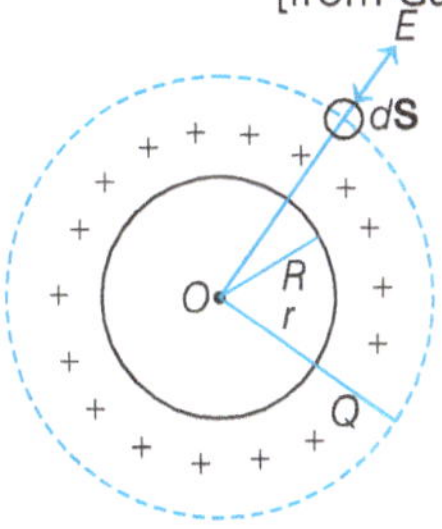

$$\Rightarrow \quad E(4\pi r^2) = \frac{Q}{\varepsilon_0}$$

$$\Rightarrow \quad E = \frac{Q}{4\pi\varepsilon_0 r^2}$$

$$\Rightarrow \quad E \propto \frac{1}{r^2}$$

(ii) The electric field at the surface $(r = R)$,

$$E = \frac{Q}{4\pi\varepsilon_0 R^2}$$

(iii) The electric field inside hollow sphere is

$$E = 0$$

This can be shown graphically as

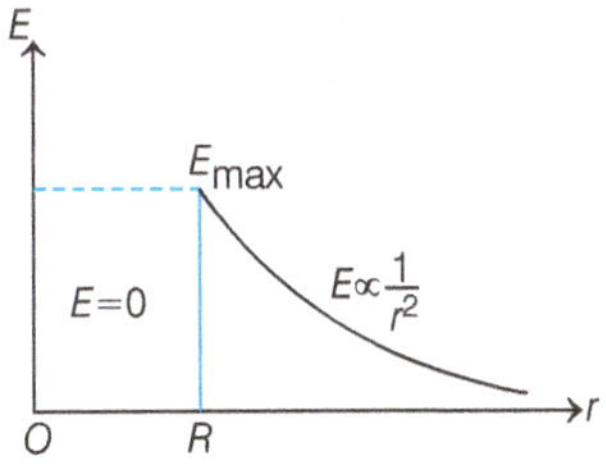

7 (*c*) Net charge on one H-atom,

$$q = -e + e + \Delta e = \Delta e$$

$$F_r = \frac{kq^2}{d^2} = \frac{k(\Delta e)^2}{d^2}$$

$$F_G = \frac{Gm_h^2}{d^2}$$

It is given that, $F_r - F_G = 0$

$$\Rightarrow \quad (\Delta e)^2 = \frac{Gm_h^2}{K}$$

$$(\Delta e)^2 = \frac{(6.67\times10^{-11})(1.67\times10^{-27})^2}{9\times10^9}$$

$$\Rightarrow \Delta e = 1.437\times10^{-37}\ \text{C}$$

8 (*b*)

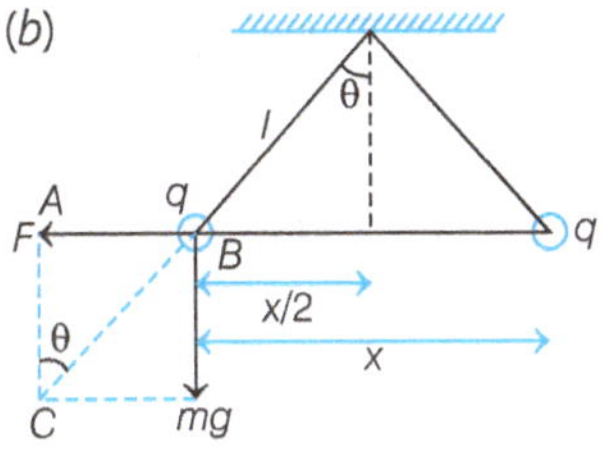

$\because$ In ΔABC, $\dfrac{F}{mg} = \tan\theta$ ...(i)

Therefore, Eq. (i) can be rewritten as

$$\frac{kq^2}{x^2 mg} = \frac{x/2}{\sqrt{l^2 - \frac{x^2}{4}}}$$

$$\Rightarrow \quad \frac{kq^2}{x^2 mg} = \frac{x}{2l} \qquad (\because d << l \text{ given})$$

or $\quad q^2 \propto x^3$

$$\Rightarrow \quad q \propto x^{3/2}$$

$$\Rightarrow \quad \frac{dq}{dt} \propto \frac{d(x^{3/2})}{dx}\cdot\frac{dx}{dt}$$

$$\Rightarrow \quad \frac{dq}{dt} \propto x^{1/2}\cdot v$$

$$\Rightarrow \quad v \propto x^{-1/2}$$

9 (*c*) Total flux $(\phi) = \dfrac{Q_{\text{enclosed}}}{\varepsilon_0}$

$$= \frac{+5q + q - 2q}{\varepsilon_0}$$

$$= \frac{4q}{\varepsilon_0}$$

10 (16) Given, $\mathbf{E} = 2x\hat{\mathbf{i}}\ \text{NC}^{-1}$

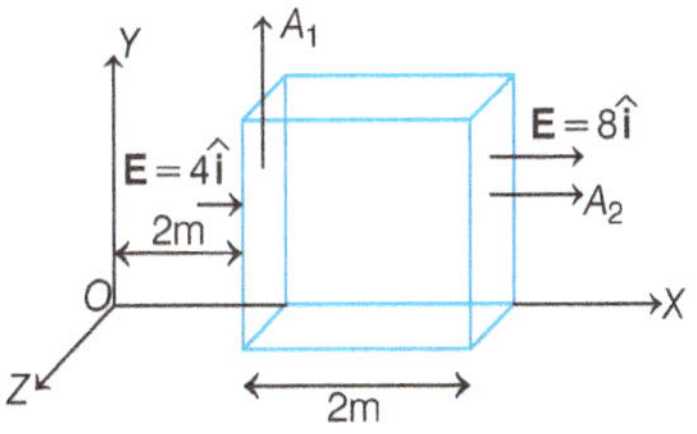

Total flux = Flux at A_2 − Flux at A_1

$$= E\cdot A_2 - E\cdot A_1$$

$$= 2\times4\times4 - 2\times2\times4$$

$$= 32 - 16\ \text{Nm}^2/\text{C}$$

$$= 16\ \text{Nm}^2/\text{C}$$

11 (*d*)

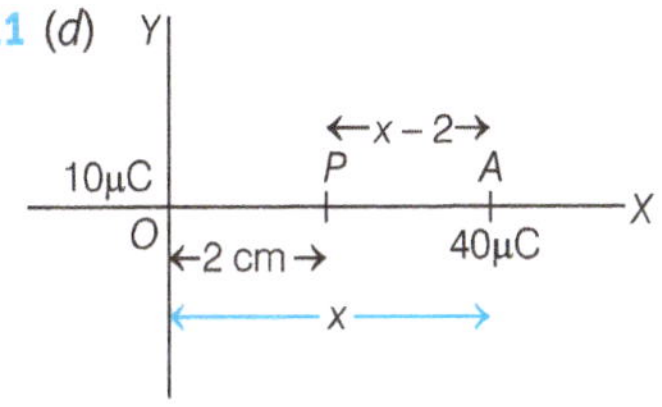

$$E_{OP} = E_{AP}$$

$$\Rightarrow \quad \frac{1}{4\pi\varepsilon_0}\cdot\frac{10^{-5}}{(2\times10^{-2})^2} = \frac{1}{4\pi\varepsilon_0}\cdot\frac{4\times10^{-5}}{(x-2)^2\times(10^{-2})^2}$$

$$\Rightarrow \quad x = 6\ \text{cm}$$

12 (*a*) As $\mathbf{E} = \dfrac{\sigma}{2\varepsilon_0}\hat{\mathbf{n}}$

Situation given is shown below.

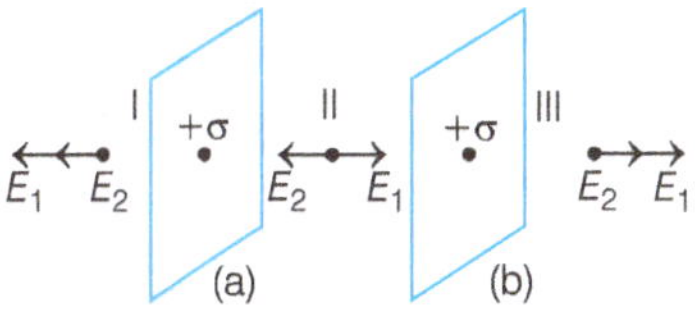

In region I, net field,

$$\mathbf{E}_1 = \mathbf{E}_1 + \mathbf{E}_2$$

$$\mathbf{E}_1 = \left(-\frac{\sigma}{2\varepsilon_0}\hat{\mathbf{n}}\right) + \left(-\frac{\sigma}{2\varepsilon_0}\hat{\mathbf{n}}\right)$$

$$= -\frac{\sigma}{\varepsilon_0}\hat{\mathbf{n}}$$

Similarly, in region II and III,

$$\mathbf{E}_{II} = \left(-\frac{\sigma}{2\varepsilon_0}\hat{\mathbf{n}}\right) + \left(\frac{\sigma}{2\varepsilon_0}\hat{\mathbf{n}}\right) = 0$$

$$\mathbf{E}_{III} = \left(\frac{\sigma}{2\varepsilon_0}\hat{\mathbf{n}}\right) + \left(\frac{\sigma}{2\varepsilon_0}\hat{\mathbf{n}}\right) = \frac{\sigma}{\varepsilon_0}\hat{\mathbf{n}}$$

13 (*c*) Given, length of conductor = L

Charge on conductor = Q

According to figure,

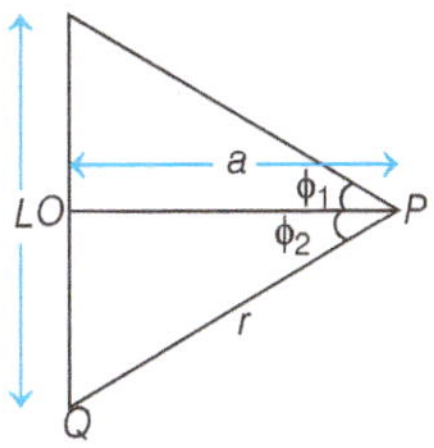

Let $\quad PQ = r = \sqrt{OP^2 + OQ^2}$

$$\Rightarrow \quad PQ = \sqrt{\left(\frac{\sqrt{3}}{2}L\right)^2 + \left(\frac{L}{2}\right)^2}$$

and E be the electric field at point P.

Since, E (due to finite wire)

$$= \frac{k\lambda}{a}(\sin\phi_1 + \sin\phi_2) \quad \text{...(i)}$$

λ = linear charge density $= \frac{Q}{L}$

and $\sin\phi_1 = \sin\phi_2 = \frac{L/2}{L} = \frac{1}{2}$

$$E = \frac{k\lambda}{a} = \frac{1}{4\pi\varepsilon_0}\frac{Q}{L \cdot \frac{\sqrt{3}L}{2}}$$

$$= \frac{1}{2\sqrt{3}\pi\varepsilon_0}\frac{Q}{L^2}$$

14 (*d*) Given, linear charge density,

$$\lambda = 3 \times 10^{-6}\ \text{C/m}$$

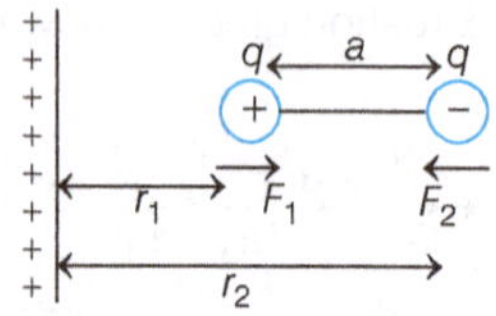

$$r_1 = 10\ \text{mm} = 10 \times 10^{-3}\ \text{m}$$
$$r_2 = 12\ \text{mm} = 12 \times 10^{-3}\text{m}$$

and the separation between charges

$$= r_2 - r_1 = 12 - 10$$
$$= 2\ \text{mm} = 2 \times 10^{-3}\ \text{m}$$

Electric field due to line charge,

$$E = \frac{2k\lambda}{x}$$

$$\mathbf{F}_{\text{net}} = \mathbf{F}_1 - \mathbf{F}_2 = q\mathbf{E}_1 - q\mathbf{E}_2$$

$$\Rightarrow \quad 4 = q\left(\frac{2k\lambda}{r_1} - \frac{2k\lambda}{r_2}\right)$$

$$\Rightarrow \quad 4 = 2k\lambda q\left(\frac{1}{r_1} - \frac{1}{r_2}\right)$$

$$\Rightarrow \quad q = 4.44\ \mu\text{C}$$

15 (*b*) Here, $E_A = \frac{kq}{(\sqrt{2}l)^2} = \frac{kq}{2l^2}$;

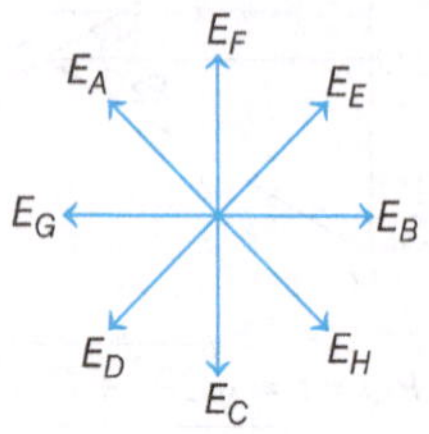

$$E_B = \frac{kq}{(l)^2}$$

E_A and E_H cancel out.

$$E_C = \frac{2kq}{l^2};\ E_D = \frac{kq}{(\sqrt{2}l)^2}$$

$$E_E = \frac{2kq}{(\sqrt{2}l)^2};\ E_F = \frac{kq}{l^2};$$

$$E_G = \frac{2kq}{l^2};\ E_H = \frac{kq}{(l)^2}$$

$$\therefore E_{\text{net}} = \sqrt{(E_C - E_F)^2 + (E_G - E_B)^2} - (E_E - E_D)$$

$$= \frac{kq}{l^2}\sqrt{2} - \frac{kq}{2l^2}$$

$$= \frac{1}{4\pi\varepsilon_0}\cdot\frac{q}{(2l)^2}(2\sqrt{2} - 1)$$

Skill Boosters

1 (*b*) Glass rod is positive charged.

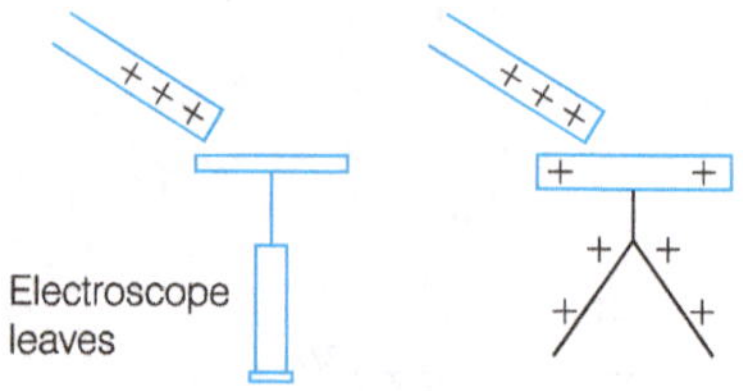

Due to touching, some of positive charge is acquired by leaves of electroscope and so they show divergence.

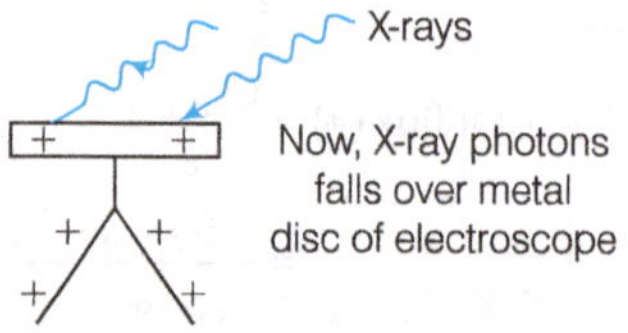

Few of electrons absorbs X-ray photons and rest are ejected from the metal surface.

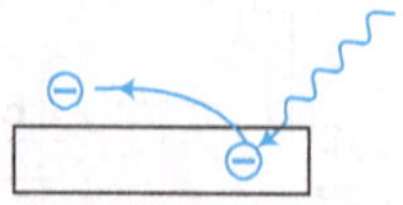

This causes more positive charge on metal disc and on leaves of electroscope.

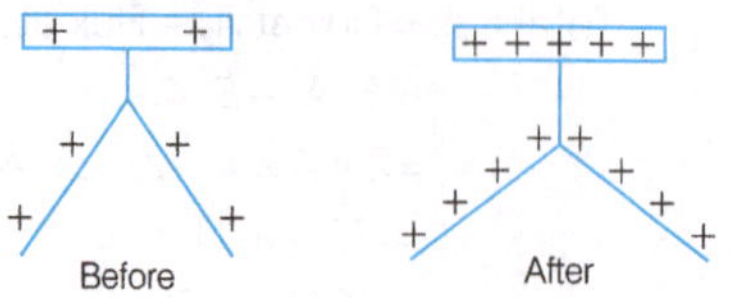

Thus, leaves show divergence.

2 (*d*) During an American winter, cold dry air allows accumulation of significant excess charge giving the potential for a shock.

3 (*c*)

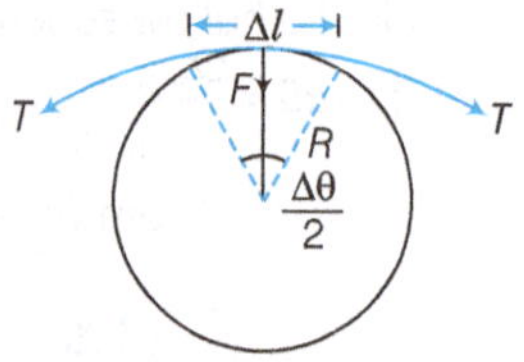

Consider a small segment of length Δl making an angle of $\Delta\theta$ at centre.

Horizontal components of tension cancels out each other and vertical components add upto from these forces **F**.

$$\Rightarrow \quad 2T\sin\frac{\theta}{2} = T\Delta\theta = T\cdot\frac{\Delta l}{R}$$

$$\Rightarrow \quad T = \frac{FR}{\Delta l}$$

where,

$$F = \frac{1}{4\pi\varepsilon_0}\cdot\frac{5\Delta l \times 10^{-8}}{R^2}$$
$$= 4.5 \times 10^4 \times \Delta l$$

So, $T = \frac{F}{\Delta l} \times R$

$$= 4.5 \times 10^4 \times 0.1$$
$$= 4.5 \times 10^3\ \text{N}$$

Also, change in radius

$$\Delta R = R \times \frac{T}{AY}$$
$$= 2.25 \times 10^{-3}\ \text{m}$$

4 (*c*)

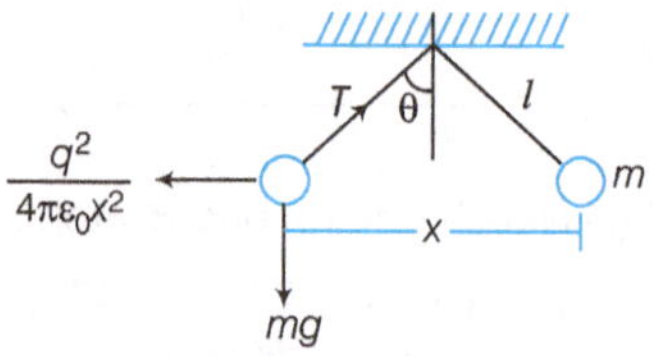

At equilibrium,

$$\frac{q^2}{4\pi\varepsilon_0 x^2}\cos\theta = mg\sin\theta$$

For small θ, $\cos\theta \to 1$ and

$$\sin\theta \approx \theta = \frac{x/2}{l}$$

$$\Rightarrow \quad \frac{q^2}{4\pi\varepsilon_0 x^2} = \frac{mgx}{2l}$$

$$\Rightarrow \quad q = x^{3/2}\cdot\sqrt{\frac{2\pi\varepsilon_0 mg}{l}}$$

$$\Rightarrow \quad \frac{dq}{dt} = \frac{3}{2}\left(x^{1/2}\cdot\sqrt{\frac{2\pi\varepsilon_0 mg}{l}}\right)\left(\frac{dx}{dt}\right)$$

Put $\quad v = \frac{dx}{dt} \propto x^{-1/2}$

$$\Rightarrow \quad \frac{dq}{dt} \propto \frac{3}{2}\sqrt{\frac{2\pi\varepsilon_0 mg}{l}}$$

Hence, $N = 3$

5 (*a*) As particle is moving horizontally only forces acting on it are Stokes' force and electric force.

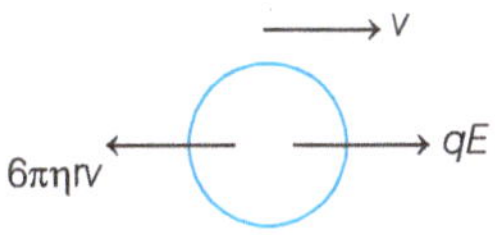

If $v =$ constant, then

$6\pi\eta rv = qE$

$\Rightarrow 6\pi\eta rv = neE$

$\Rightarrow n = \frac{6\pi\eta rv}{Ee}$

$$= \frac{6\times 3.14\times 1.6\times 10^{-5}\times 5\times 10^{-7}\times 0.02}{6.28\times 10^{5}\times 1.6\times \times 10^{-16}}$$

$= 30$

6 (*a*) Particle will not hit the upper plate, if the velocity component normal to plate is zero before reaching the plate.

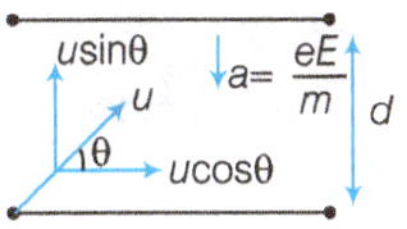

Acceleration due to field (downwards),

$$a_y = \frac{eE}{m}$$

$$v_y^2 = 0 = u^2 - 2(a_y)y$$

where, $y \le d, d =$ distance between plates.

So, $u_{max} = \sqrt{2a_y y}$

$$= \sqrt{\frac{2\times 1.6\times 10^{-19}\times 10^{3}\times 2\times 10^{-2}}{1.6\times 10^{-30}}}$$

$$\Rightarrow \quad u_{max} = 2\times 10^{6}\ \text{m/s}$$

7 (*c*) $\phi_{cube} = \frac{q_{enclosed}}{\varepsilon_0} = \frac{\sqrt{3}\,a\lambda}{\varepsilon_0}$,

$\phi_{sphere} = q_{enclosed} = \frac{2a\lambda}{\varepsilon_0}$

Ratio, $r = \frac{\sqrt{3}\,a\lambda}{\varepsilon_0} \times \frac{\varepsilon_0}{2a\lambda} = \frac{\sqrt{3}}{2}$

8 (*d*) With air in the space between S_1 and S_2,

$\phi_{S_1} = \frac{q}{\varepsilon_0}$ and $\phi_{S_2} = \frac{2q}{\varepsilon_0}$

When a medium of $K = 5$ is filled in space,

$$\phi'_{S_1} = \frac{Q}{K\varepsilon_0} = \frac{\phi_{S_1}}{5} = \frac{q}{5\varepsilon_0}$$

and in this case, flux through S_2,

$\phi'_{S_2} =$ flux of S_1 + flux of charge $2q$

$$= \frac{q}{5\varepsilon_0} + \frac{2q}{\varepsilon_0} = \frac{q+10q}{5\varepsilon_0} = \frac{11q}{5\varepsilon_0}$$

So, $\quad$ ratio $\frac{\phi'_{S_2}}{\phi'_{S_1}} = 11:1$

9 (*a*) $E = \frac{V}{d} = \frac{200}{0.01} = 2\times 10^{4}\ \text{Vm}^{-1}$

When the oil drop floats,

$mg = qE$

$\Rightarrow \frac{4}{3}\pi r^3 \rho g = NeE$

$\therefore N = \frac{4}{3}\pi\frac{(8\times 10^{-7})^3\times 900\times 10}{1.6\times 10^{-19}\times 2\times 10^{4}}$

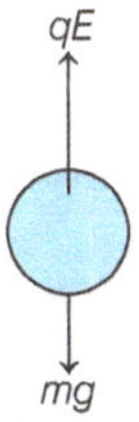

$= \pi\times 64\times 3\times 10^{-2} \simeq 6$

10 (*c*)

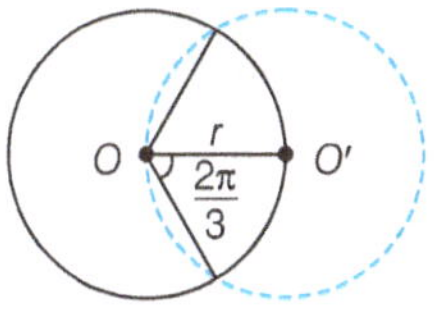

$L_{inside} = \frac{2\pi}{3}r$

$Q_{inside} = \frac{Q}{2\pi r}\times\frac{2\pi}{3}r = \frac{Q}{3}$

By Gauss's law, $\phi = \frac{Q_{inside}}{\varepsilon_0}$

$$\Rightarrow \quad \phi = \frac{Q}{3\varepsilon_0}$$

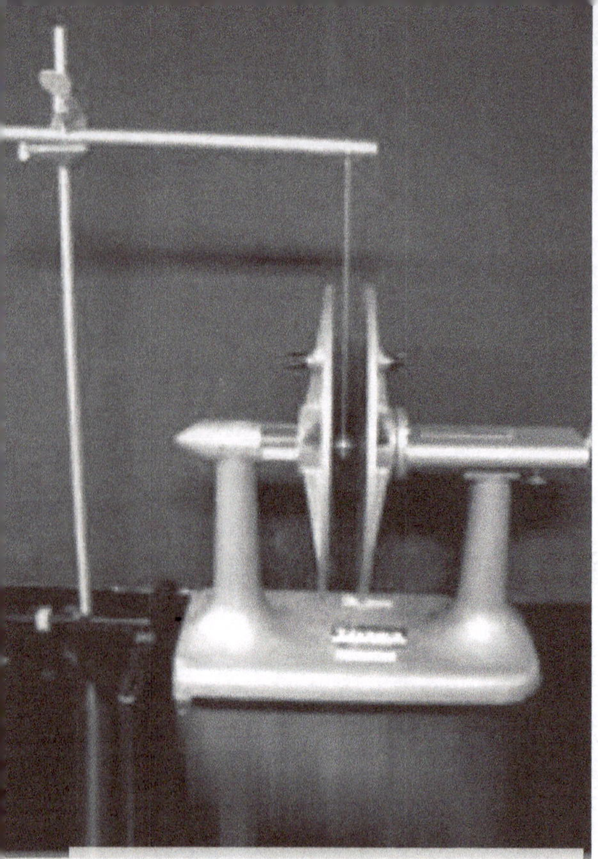

02

Scan for **Physics Through Concept Master** Videos

Electrostatic Potential and Capacitance

Topicwise No. of Ques asked in 5 Years

Topics	No. of Questions				
	2024	2023	2022	2021	2020
Potential due to an Electric Dipole	1	1	–	–	1
Potential due to System of Charges	1	–	1	1	1
Equipotential Surfaces	–	–	1	–	1
Effect of Dielectric on Capacitance	–	–	–	–	1
Combination of Capacitors	2	1	–	1	1
Energy Stored in a Capacitor	–	–	–	1	–

Special Type of Ques asked in 5 Years

Types	Years				
	2024	2023	2022	2021	2020
A-R	–	–	–	–	–
Statement Based	–	–	–	–	–
Matching	–	–	–	–	–

Last 5 Years Weigtage

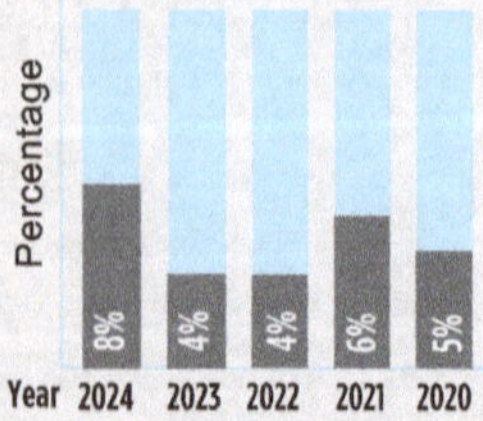

Introduction

- The work done by external force in moving a charged particle q from R to P against electrostatic repulsive force (as shown in figure) is given as

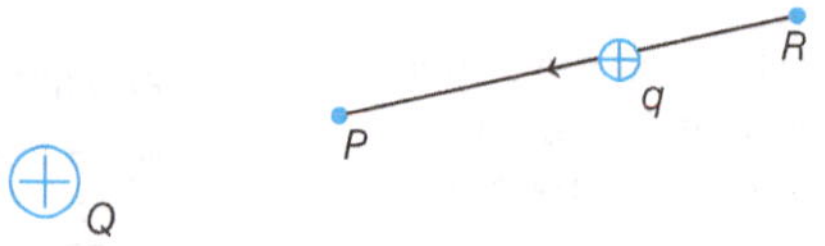

$$W_{RP} = \int_R^P \mathbf{F}_{\text{ext}} \cdot d\mathbf{r} = -\int_R^P \mathbf{F}_E \cdot d\mathbf{r}$$

This work done gets stored as potential energy.

- The electric potential energy difference between two points is defined as the work required to move (without accelerating) charge q from one point to another in electric field of any arbitrary charge configuration.

i.e. $\Delta U = U_P - U_R = W_{RP}$ **NEET 2022**

- The work done by an electrostatic field in moving a charge from one point to another, depends only on the initial and the final positions and is independent of the path taken to go from one point to the other. This is the fundamental characteristics of a conservative force.
- The actual value of potential energy is not physically significant, it is only the difference of potential energy that is significant.

- Potential energy of charge q at a point (in the presence of field due to any charge configuration) is the work done by the external force (equal and opposite to the electric force) in bringing the charge q from infinity to that point,

  i.e. $$W_{\infty P} = U_P - U_\infty = U_P$$

Electrostatic Potential

- Electrostatic potential (V) at a point is equal to work done by an external force in bringing a unit positive charge from infinity to that point.

  i.e. $$V = \frac{W}{q_0}$$

- The work done by external force in bringing a unit positive charge from one point R to another point P is called **potential difference** between those points (P and R).

  i.e. $$V_{RP} = V_P - V_R = \frac{U_P - U_R}{q} = \frac{W_{RP}}{q}$$

  or $$V_{RP} = -\int \mathbf{E} \cdot d\mathbf{l}$$

- **Potential due to a point charge** at a distance r is

  $$V = \frac{1}{4\pi\varepsilon_0} \cdot \frac{Q}{r}$$ NEET 2022, 21

- The variation of electric potential (V) and electric field (E) with distance (r) for a point charge is given below.

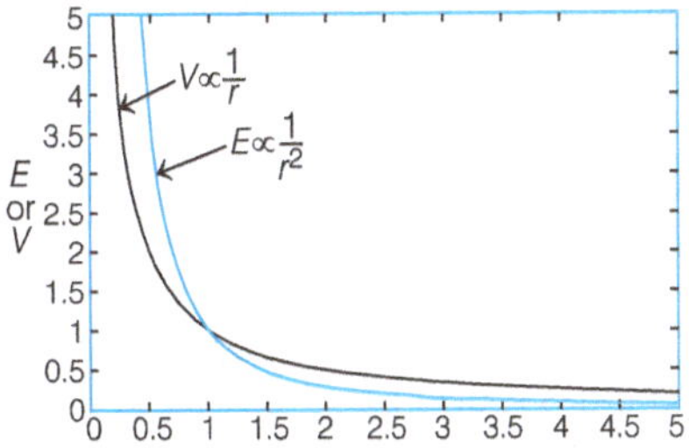

- **Potential due to an electric dipole** at any point P whose position vector is $\mathbf{r}$ with respect to mid-point of dipole is given by

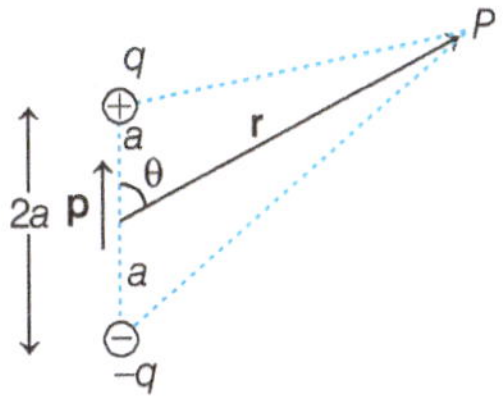

$$V = \frac{1}{4\pi\varepsilon_0} \cdot \frac{p\cos\theta}{r^2} \; (r >> a) \quad \text{or} \quad V = \frac{1}{4\pi\varepsilon_0} \cdot \frac{\mathbf{p} \cdot \hat{\mathbf{r}}}{|\mathbf{r}|^2}$$ NEET 2020

where, θ is the angle between $\mathbf{r}$ and $\mathbf{p}$.

(i) **Potential at axial position** ($\theta = 0°$) is given by

$$V_{\text{axial}} = \frac{1}{4\pi\varepsilon_0} \frac{p}{r^2}$$ NEET 2023

(ii) **Potential at equitorial position** ($\theta = 90°$) is given by

$$V_{\text{equitorial}} = 0$$

- Some important points related to the potential due to an electric dipole are as follows

  (i) The electric potential on the dipole axis is positive for $\theta = 0°$ and negative for $\theta = \pi$. The potential in the equatorial plane ($\theta = \pi/2$) is zero.

  (ii) The electric potential due to dipole falls off at large distance, as $1/r^2$ while potential due to point charge falls as $1/r$.

- **Electric potential at any point P due to system of charges** It is equal to the algebraic sum of potentials due to individual charges.

  i.e. $$V = \frac{1}{4\pi\varepsilon_0} \cdot \left(\frac{q_1}{r_{1P}} + \frac{q_2}{r_{2P}} + \dots \frac{q_n}{r_{nP}} \right) = \frac{1}{4\pi\varepsilon_0} \sum_{i=1}^{n} \frac{q_i}{r_{iP}}$$

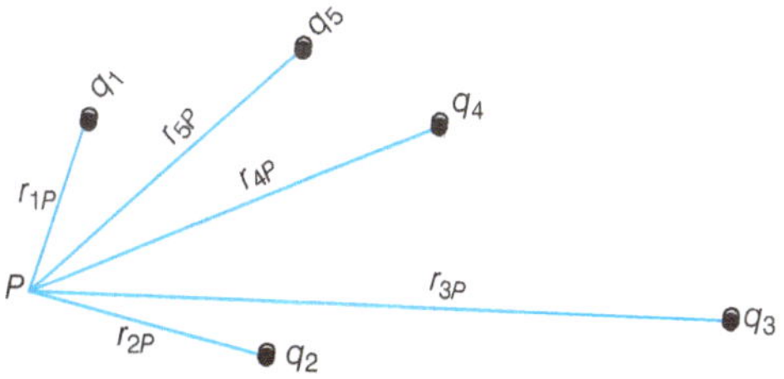

Marks Maximiser

- **Electrostatic potential due to a thin charged spherical shell** carrying charge q and radius R at any point P lying

  (i) inside the shell, $V = \frac{1}{4\pi\varepsilon_0} \cdot \frac{q}{R}$, for $r < R$

  (ii) on the surface of shell, $V = \frac{1}{4\pi\varepsilon_0} \cdot \frac{q}{R}$, for $r = R$

  (iii) outside the shell, $V = \frac{1}{4\pi\varepsilon_0} \cdot \frac{q}{r}$, for $r > R$

  where, r is the distance of point P from the centre of the shell.

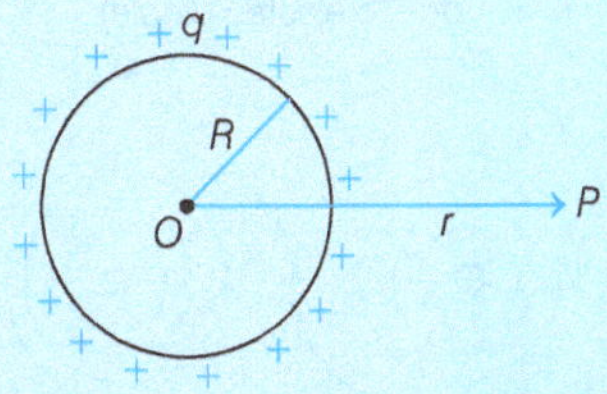

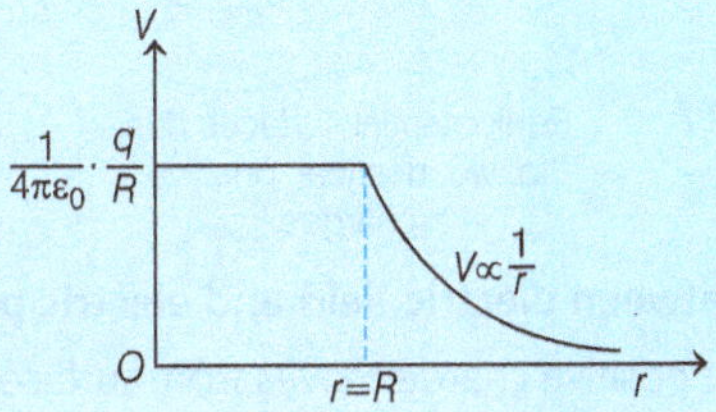

Equipotential Surface

- The surface at which electric potential is same at each point, is called equipotential surface.
- Equipotential surfaces of a single point charge are concentric spherical surface centred at the charge.
- The electric field at every point is normal to the equipotential surface passing through that point.
- For any charge configuration, equipotential surface through a point is normal to the electric field at that point.
- There is no potential difference between any two points on the equipotential surface and no work is required to move a test charge on the equipotential surface.

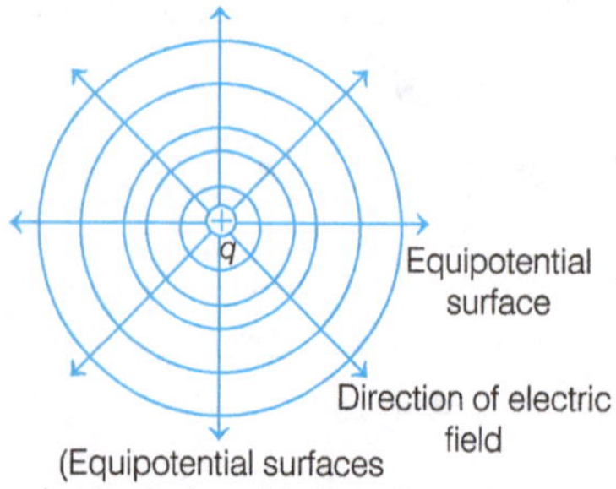

(Equipotential surfaces due to single point charge)

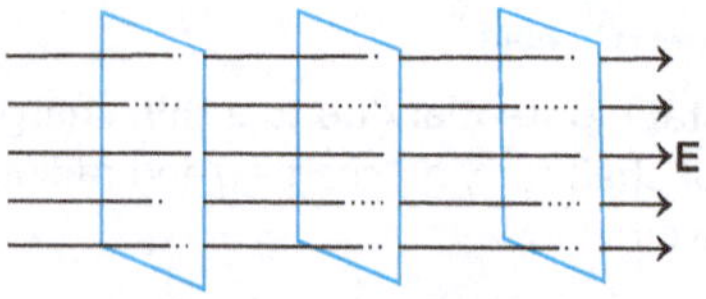

(Equipotential surfaces for uniform electric field)

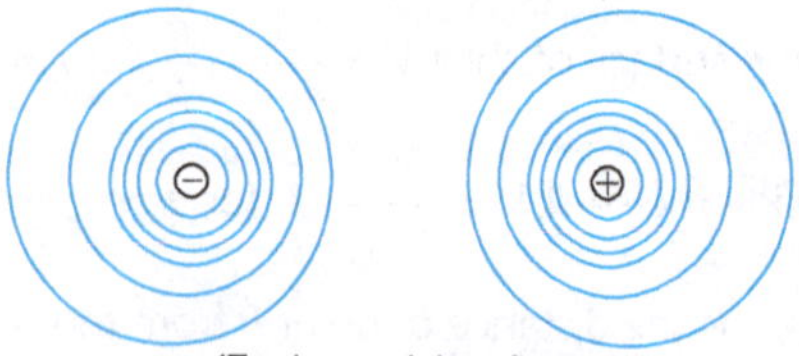

(Equipotential surfaces due to electric dipole)

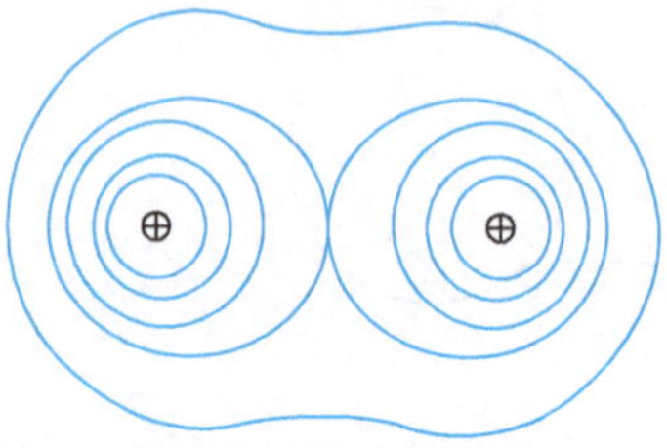

Equipotential surfaces due to two identical positive charges

- **Relation between electric field and electric potential**

  When a unit positive charge moves from surface B to surface A perpendicularly as shown in the next diagram, then

Work done = Potential difference

$$\Rightarrow \quad |\mathbf{E}|\,\delta l = V-(V+\delta V) = -\,\delta V$$

$$|\mathbf{E}| = \frac{-\,\delta V}{\delta l} = \frac{+|\delta V|}{\delta l}$$

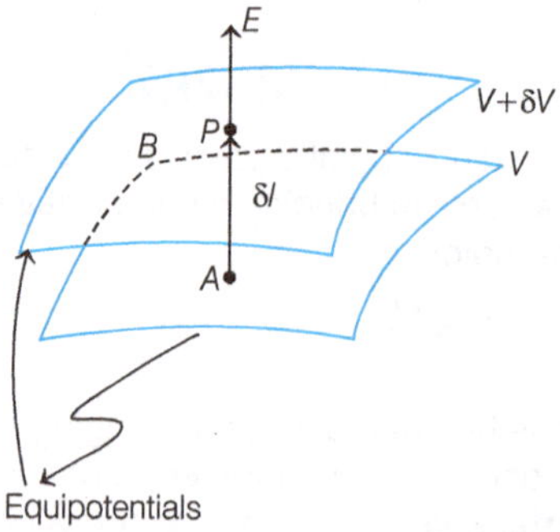

For Concept Master Video

where, δl is the perpendicular distance between two equipotential surfaces and δV is the change in V in the direction of electric field E.

There are two important conclusions concerning the relation between electric field and electric potential.

(i) Electric field is in the direction in which the potential decreases steepest.

(ii) Its magnitude is given by the change in the magnitude of potential per unit displacement normal to the equipotential surface at the point.

Potential Energy of a System of Charges

- Electrostatic potential energy of a system of two point charges is given by

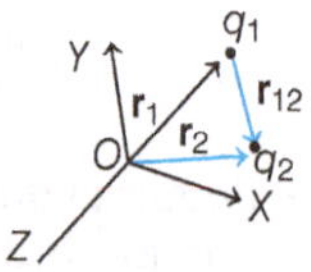

$$U = \frac{1}{4\pi\varepsilon_0}\cdot\frac{q_1 q_2}{r_{12}}$$

  where, q_1 and q_2 are charges and r_{12} is the separation between the point charges.

- The potential energy of the system of three charges is given by

$$U = \frac{1}{4\pi\varepsilon_0}\left(\frac{q_1 q_2}{r_{12}} + \frac{q_1 q_3}{r_{13}} + \frac{q_2 q_3}{r_{23}}\right)$$

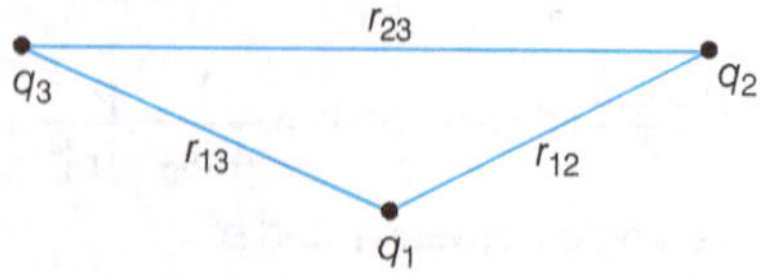

- Potential energy for a system of n charges is given by

$$U = \frac{1}{4\pi\varepsilon_0}\sum_{i=1}^{n}\left[\sum_{j=1}^{n}\frac{q_j q_i}{r_{ij}}\right], \qquad \text{for } (j > i)$$

- The potential energy is a characteristics of the present state of configuration and not the way, the state is achieved.

Marks Maximiser

(i) Electric potential due to uniformly charge ring,

$$V = \frac{1}{4\pi\varepsilon_0} \frac{q}{\sqrt{R^2 + x^2}}$$

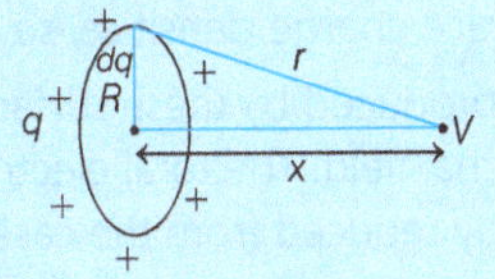

Potential at the centre, $x = 0 \Rightarrow V = \frac{1}{4\pi\varepsilon_0}\frac{q}{R}$

(ii) Electric potential due to uniformly charged disc of change density σ

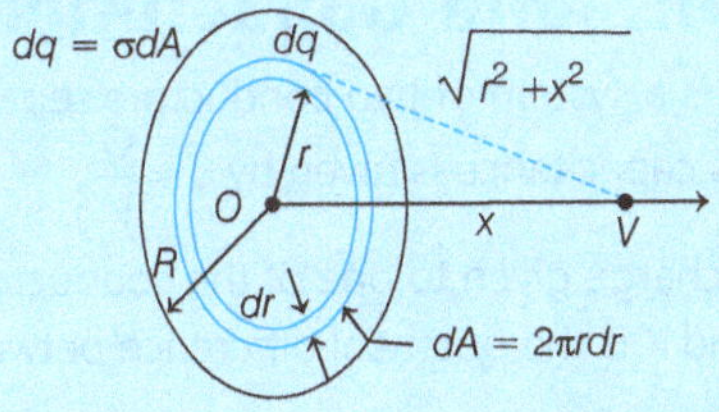

$$V = 2\pi k\sigma\,[\sqrt{R^2 + x^2} - x]$$

Potential at the centre, $x = 0 \Rightarrow V = 2\pi k\sigma R = \frac{\sigma R}{2\varepsilon_0}$

(iii) Potential difference due to uniformly charged long thin wire, $V_2 - V_1 = \frac{\lambda}{2\pi\varepsilon_0}\ln\left(\frac{x_1}{x_2}\right)$

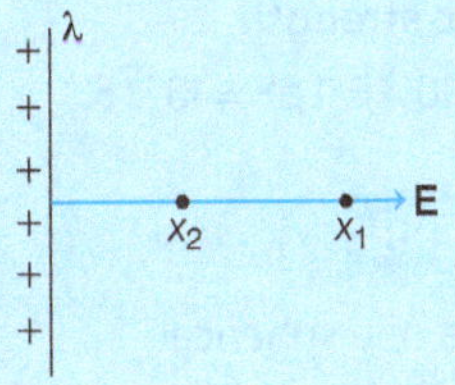

Potential Energy in an External Field

- **Potential energy of a single charge q at** a point with position vector **r**, in an external field is $qV(\mathbf{r})$, where $V(\mathbf{r})$ is the potential at the point due to external electric field **E**.
- **Potential energy of a system of two charges in an external field can** be given as

$$U = q_1V(\mathbf{r}_1) + q_2V(\mathbf{r}_2) + \frac{q_1q_2}{4\pi\varepsilon_0 r_{12}}$$

where, q_1 and q_2 are two point charges at position vectors $\mathbf{r}_1$ and $\mathbf{r}_2$, respectively.

$V(\mathbf{r}_1)$ = potential at $\mathbf{r}_1$ due to the external field

and $V(\mathbf{r}_2)$ = potential at $\mathbf{r}_2$ due to the external field.

- **Potential Energy of a Dipole in an External Field**

If an external torque τ_{ext} is applied in such a manner that it just neutralises the torque and rotates it in the plane of paper from angle θ_0 to angle θ_1 at an infinitesimal angular speed and without angular acceleration, the amount of work done by the external torque will be given by

$$W = pE\,(\cos\theta_0 - \cos\theta_1)$$

- Potential energy of a dipole in a uniform electric field,

$$U(\theta) = -\mathbf{p}\cdot\mathbf{E} = -pE\cos\theta$$

At $\theta = 0°$, $U = -pE$, i.e. minimum. So, dipole will be in **stable equilibrium position**.

At $\theta = 180°$, $U = pE$, i.e. maximum. So, dipole will be in **unstable equilibrium position**.

Electrostatics of Conductors

- **Conductors** are the materials through which electric charge can flow easily.
- In electrostatics, the conductors have following properties
  (i) Inside a conductor, electrostatic field is zero.
  (ii) At the surface of a charged conductor, electrostatic field must be normal to the surface at every point.
  (iii) The interior of a conductor can have no excess charge in the static situation.
  (iv) Electrostatic potential is constant throughout the volume of the conductor and has the same value (as inside) on its surface.
  (v) Electric field at the surface of a charged conductor is given as

$$E = \frac{\sigma}{\varepsilon_0}\hat{\mathbf{n}}$$

where, σ is the surface charge density and $\hat{\mathbf{n}}$ is a unit vector normal to the surface in the outward direction.

For $\sigma > 0$, electric field is normal to the surface outward and for $\sigma < 0$, the electric field is normal to the surface inward.

  (vi) **Electrostatic Shielding** The phenomenon of protecting a certain region of space from external electric field is called electrostatic shielding.

Also, the electric field inside the cavity of a conductor is always zero. It is used to protect sensitive instruments from outside electric influence.The properties of conductors are shown in figures given below.

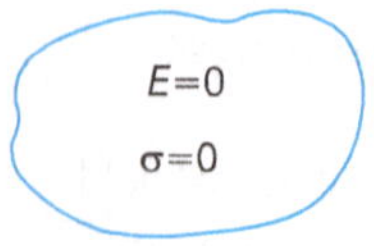

(Electric field is zero inside conductor)

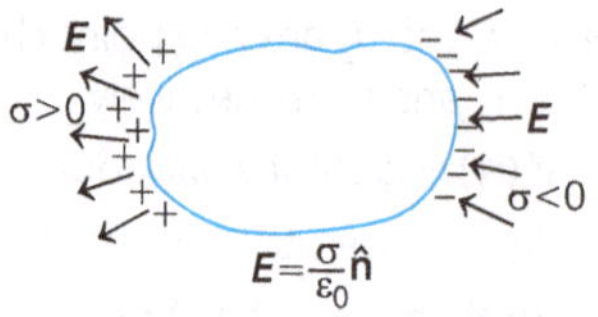

(Electric field is normal to the surface of a conductor)

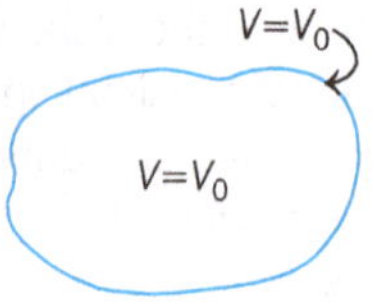

(Electric potential is constant at the surface and inside the conductor)

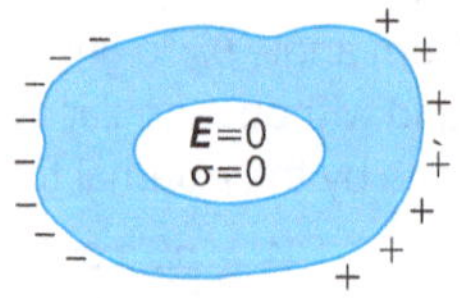

(The cavity inside a conductor is shielded from outside electric influence)

Dielectrics and Polarisation

- **Dielectrics** are non-conducting substances. In contrast to conductors, they have no (or negligible number of) charge carriers.
- In a dielectric, the free movement of charges is not possible. If external field is applied, then it induces dipole moment by stretching or re-orienting molecules of the dielectric.
- The induced dipole moments induces net charges on the surface of the dielectric which produces a field that opposes the external field.

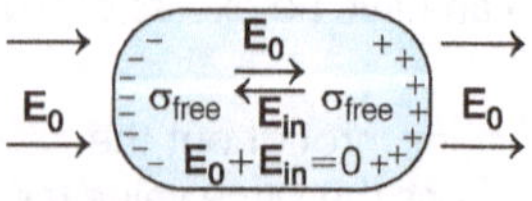

(Behaviour of conductor in external electric field $\mathbf{E}_0$)

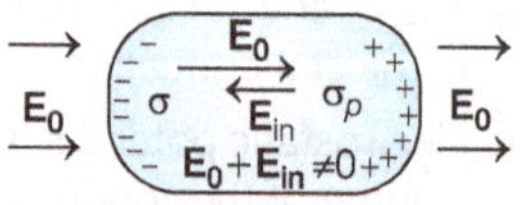

(Behaviour of dielectric in external electric field $\mathbf{E}_0$)

- On the basis of their behaviour in external field, dielectric are of two types.
  - (i) In a **non-polar molecule**, the centres of positive and negative charges coincide. The molecule has no permanent dipole moment, e.g. O_2, H_2, etc.
  - (ii) The **polar molecule** is one in which the centres of positive and negative charges are separated even when there is no external field. Such molecules have a permanent dipole moment. e.g. HCl, H_2O, etc.
- The dielectric in which the induced dipole moment is in the direction of the field and is proportional to the field strength is called **linear isotropic dielectrics**.
- When a polar or non-polar dielectric develops a net dipole moment in the presence of an external electric field, the dipole moment per unit volume is called polarisation and is denoted by **P**.
- For linear isotropic dielectrics, $\mathbf{P} = \varepsilon_0 \chi_e \mathbf{E}$

  where, χ_e is the constant characteristic of a dielectric and is known as the **electric susceptibility** of the dielectric medium.
- When dielectric slab is placed inside the electric field, then due to polarisation, every volume element ΔV of slab has a dipole moment $\mathbf{P}\Delta V$ in the direction of the field.
- The polarised dielectric is equivalent to two charged surfaces with induced surface charge densities, says σ_p and $-\sigma_p$.

  The electric field produced by these surface charges opposes the external field. The total electric field in the dielectric is thereby reduced from the case when no dielectric is present.
- Surface charge density $\pm\sigma_p$ arises from bound (not free) charges in the dielectric.

Capacitors and Capacitance

- A capacitor is a system of two conductors separated by an insulator. Its capacitance is given by $C = \frac{Q}{V}$

  where, Q is charge given to one of the conductor of capacitor and V is the potential difference between the conductors.
- The SI unit of capacitance is Farad.
- The capacitance C depend not only on the geometrical configuration (shape, size and separation) of the system of two conductors. It also depends on the nature of the insulator (dielectric) separating the two conductors.
- The maximum electric field that a dielectric medium can withstand without breakdown (of its insulating property) is called its **dielectric strength**.
- $1\mu F = 10^{-6} F$, $1 nF = 10^{-9} F$, $1 pF = 10^{-12} F$.

Marks Maximiser

- The capacitance of a spherical capacitor, when its outer sphere is earthed,

$$C = 4\pi\varepsilon_0 \left(\frac{R_1 R_2}{R_2 - R_1}\right)$$

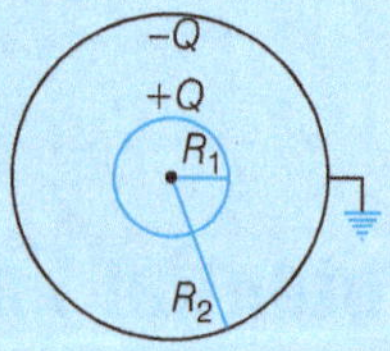

The Parallel Plate Capacitor

- It consists of two large plane parallel conducting plates separated by a small distance as shown in the figure below.

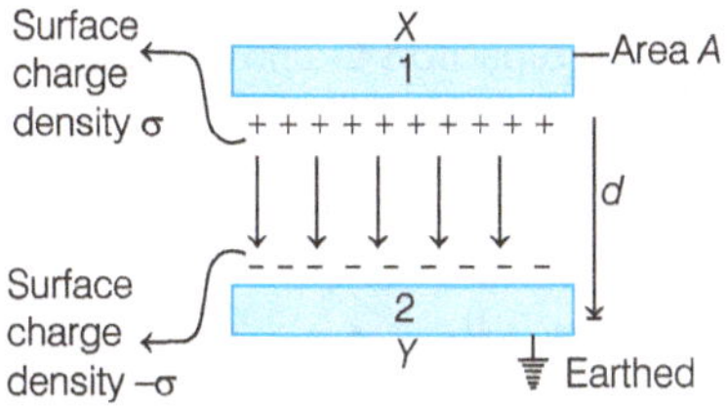

- Intensity of the electric field between the plates of a capacitor, $E = \frac{\sigma}{\varepsilon_0} = \frac{q}{A\varepsilon_0}$
- Potential difference between the plates, $V = Ed = \frac{qd}{A\varepsilon_0}$

  where, d is the distance between the conductor plates.
- The capacitance C of the parallel plate capacitor is given by

$$C = \frac{q}{V} = \frac{\varepsilon_0 A}{d}$$ **NEET 2020**

Effect of Dielectric on Capacitance

- Electric potential between the plates of capacitor, when dielectric material of dielectric constant K is introduced, is given by

$$V = \frac{\sigma d}{\varepsilon_0 K} = \frac{Qd}{A\varepsilon_0 K}$$

- The capacitance C with dielectric between the plates, is given as $C = \frac{Q}{V} = \frac{\varepsilon_0 KA}{d}$ and $K = \frac{\varepsilon}{\varepsilon_0} = \frac{C}{C_0}$

  where, ε is permittivity of dielectric medium.
- When a dielectric fully occupies the intervening region between the plates of a capacitor, the dielectric is polarised by the field, the effect is equivalent to two charged sheets having surface charge densities $+\sigma_p$ and $-\sigma_p$.

  The electric field in the dielectric is $E = \frac{\sigma - \sigma_p}{\varepsilon_0}$.

  For linear dielectric $\sigma - \sigma_p = \frac{\sigma}{K}$

For Concept Master Video

Combination of Capacitors

- In the **series combination of capacitors**, equivalent capacitance C_s of n capacitors is given by

$$\frac{1}{C_s} = \frac{1}{C_1} + \frac{1}{C_2} + \frac{1}{C_3} + \ldots + \frac{1}{C_n}$$ **NEET 2023**

- In the **parallel combination of capacitors**, the equivalent capacitance C_p of n capacitors is given by

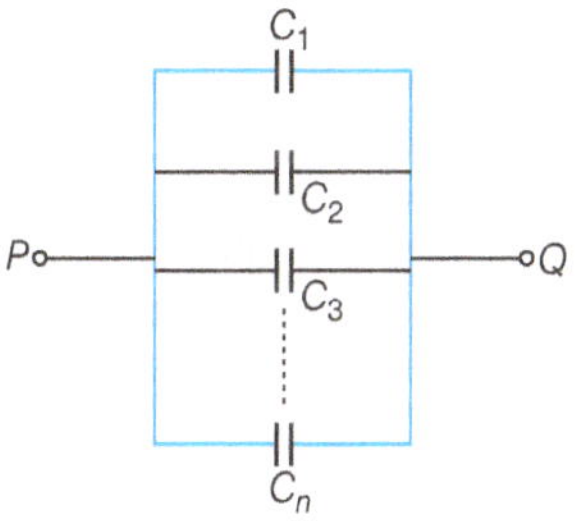

$$C_p = C_1 + C_2 + C_3 + \ldots C_n$$ **NEET 2023**

Energy Stored in a Capacitor

- The work done in the transfer of charge q between two plates of capacitor is

$$W = \frac{1}{2} qV = \frac{1}{2} CV^2 = \frac{q^2}{2C}$$ **NEET 2021**

  This work done is stored in the form of potential energy of the system.
- Total energy stored in the capacitor is given by

$$U = \frac{1}{2}\varepsilon_0 E^2 \times Ad = \frac{1}{2}\varepsilon_0 E^2 V$$ **NEET 2021**

  where, V is volume of capacitor.
- The electrostatic energy density (energy per unit volume) in a region with electric field **E** is $U = \frac{1}{2}\varepsilon_0 E^2$.

Caution Points

- The configuration of capacitor is made such that there is considerable electric field strength in the region of space of capacitor and small potential difference between two plates of the capacitor.
- The torque on an electric dipole in a uniform electric field **E** is

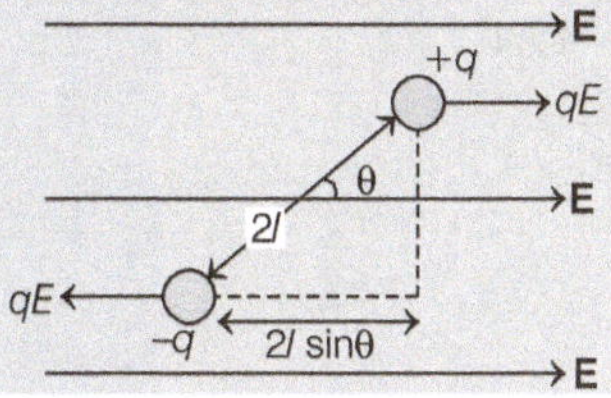

$$\tau_R = -(qE)\cdot(2l\sin\theta)$$

$\Rightarrow \quad I\alpha = -pE\sin\theta \qquad [\because p = q(2l)]$

where, I is the moment of inertia of the system of two charges.

For small value of θ, $\sin\theta \approx \theta$

$$\alpha = -\left(\frac{pE}{I}\right)\cdot\theta \qquad \ldots(i)$$

From equation of SHM, $\alpha = -\omega^2\theta \qquad \ldots(ii)$

Comparing Eqs. (i) and (ii), we get

$$\omega = \sqrt{\frac{pE}{I}}$$

Hence, the electric dipole oscillates about **E** and finally, damped and aligns with **E** in case of dissipative mechanism.

PYQ Notes

1. The electric potential at the centre of a uniformly charged circular arc of linear charge density λ is given by

   $\therefore$ Electric potential at O, $V_o = \left(\dfrac{\lambda}{4\pi\varepsilon_0}\right)\theta$

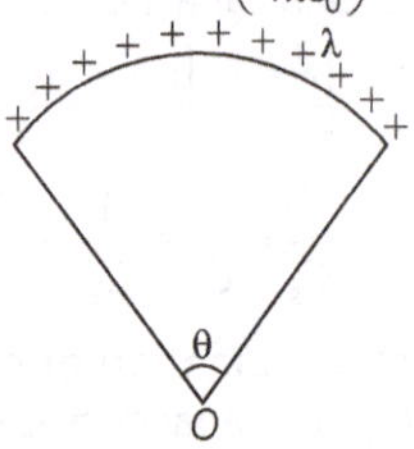

   where, θ is in radian

   [JEE MAIN 2023]

2. When two uniformly charged spherical conductors are connected by a conducting wire, then the charge flows from a conductor at higher potential to that at lower potential. This flow of charge stops, when the potential of both the conductors becomes equal.

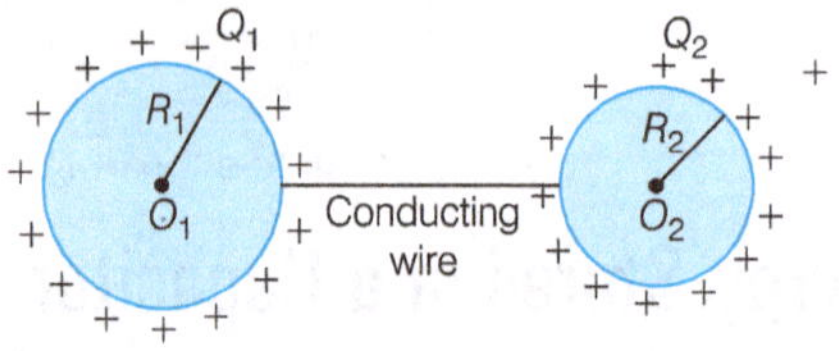

   At equilibrium, $V_1 = V_2$

   $$\therefore Q_1 = \left(\frac{R_1}{R_1 + R_2}\right)(Q_1 + Q_2)$$

   $$Q_2 = \left(\frac{R_2}{R_1 + R_2}\right)(Q_1 + Q_2)$$

   [NEET 2019]

3. Capacitance of a parallel plate capacitor, when it is partially filled with dielectric materials of dielectric constants K_1 and K_2 is given by

   $$C = \frac{\varepsilon_0 A}{(d - t_1 - t_2) + \dfrac{t_1}{K_1} + \dfrac{t_2}{K_2}}$$

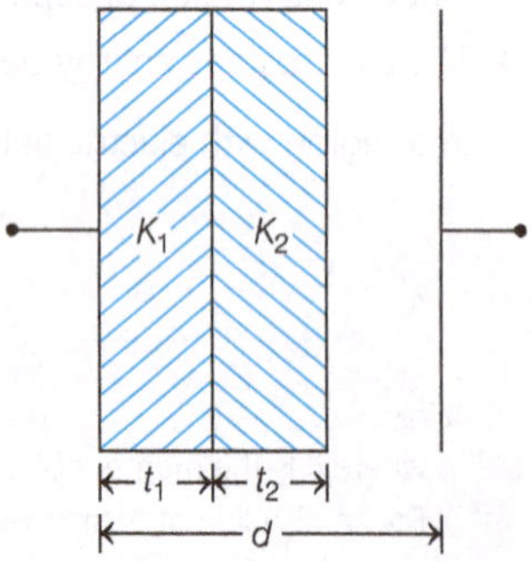

   [JEE MAIN 2021, NEET 2020]

4. When two capacitors C_1 and C_2 with potential V_1 and V_2 are connected to each other, then sharing of charges between them takes place according to law of conservation of charge.

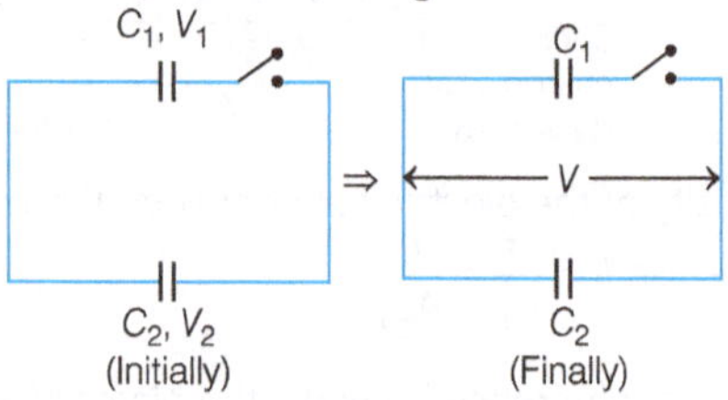

   The common potential (V) after sharing of charges is given by

   $$V = \frac{C_1V_1 + C_2V_2}{C_1 + C_2} = \frac{Q_1 + Q_2}{C_1 + C_2}$$

   The heat loss or energy loss after sharing of charges is given by

   $$H = \frac{1}{2}\left(\frac{C_1C_2}{C_1 + C_2}\right)(V_1 - V_2)^2$$

   [NEET 2016, NEET 2019]

5. The electrostatic force between the plates of a parallel plate capacitor C having a charge Q and area A is given by

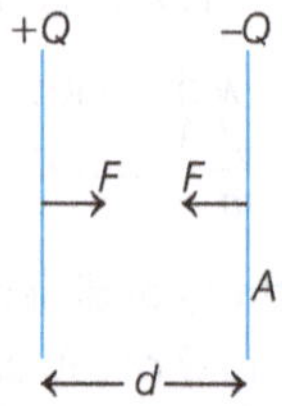

   $$F = QE = Q\left(\frac{Q}{2A\varepsilon_0}\right) = \frac{Q^2}{2A\varepsilon_0}$$

   [NEET 2018]

6. The quantity $\varepsilon_0 E + P$ is called the **electric displacement** and is denoted by D.

   Thus, $D = \varepsilon_0 E + P$

7. The ratio of the magnitudes of D and E is given as

   $$\frac{D}{E} = \varepsilon_0 K$$

   $\Rightarrow$ $D = \varepsilon_0 KE$

   and $P = D - \varepsilon_0 E = \varepsilon_0 (K - 1)E$

   Also, for electric susceptibility, $\chi_e = \varepsilon_0 (K - 1)$.

Step by Step

Mastering NCERT

- Concept Builders
- Topical Questions
- Assertion and Reason Questions
- Statement Based
- Matching Type
- Numerical Type
- NCERT Exemplar
- Past Exams MCQs
- Skill Boosters

Concept Builders

1 Is there any kind of material which when placed between the plates of a capacitor reduces its capacitance?

2 A solid conducting sphere can hold more charge than a hollow sphere of same radius. [T/F]

3 At the centre of the line joining two equal and similar charges $V \neq 0, E = 0$. [T/F]

4 The potential difference on the capacitor plates remains constant when battery remains connected across it, even after the introduction of a dielectric slab. [T/F]

5 The electric potential of a point charge is......... . (spherically/cylindrically) symmetric while that of an electric dipole is ...... (spherically/cylindrically) symmetric.

6 In series combination, the equivalent capacitance is .... (smaller/larger) than the smallest individual capacitance.

7 The electrostatic potential at a point can be zero where electric field is not zero. [T/F]

8 With rise in temperature dielectric constant of liquid increases. [T/F]

9 Due to polarisation of a dielectric slab, the value of electric field .... (reduce/increase).

10 Electric potential at any equatorial point of an electric dipole is .... (one/zero)

11 The dielectric constant of a perfect insulator is infinite. [T/F]

12 Charge always resides on the surface of the .... (conductor/ non-conductor)

13 Two plates of unequal area .... (can / cannot) form a capacitor.

14 Total energy stored in any setup of capacitors is sum of the energies stored in individual capacitors whatever be the mode of combination. [T/F]

15 If plates of a parallel plate capacitor (initial separation d) is moved away with some velocity, then the rate of change of capacitance with time is proportional to $\frac{1}{d^2}$. [T/F]

16 Force of attraction between the plates of a parallel plate capacitor is .... (independent/dependent) of separation between the plates.

17 The potential energy of a dipole when its dipole moment p is parallel to the external field E is .... $(+pE/-pE)$

18 We can give as much charge to a capacitor as we wish. [T/F]

19 When a dielectric is placed between the plates of a parallel plate capacitor, then it's capacitance .... (increases/decreases) but potential difference .... (increases / decreases).

20 In the cavity of a hollow charged conductor, electric field is .... (zero/non-zero) while electric potential is (zero/non-zero).

Topical Questions

Electrostatic Potential

1 Work done by external forces in moving a charge q from R to P as shown in figure is NCERT Pg. 46

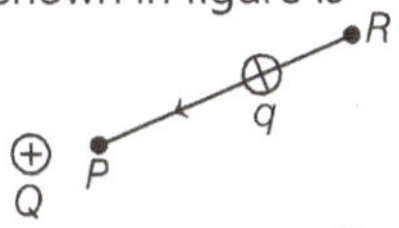

(a) $-\int_R^P \mathbf{F}_E \cdot d\mathbf{r}$
(b) $\int_R^P \mathbf{F}_E \cdot d\mathbf{r}$
(c) $\int_R^P 2\,\mathbf{F}_E \cdot d\mathbf{r}$
(d) $\int_R^P \frac{\mathbf{F}_E}{2} \cdot d\mathbf{r}$

2 A point charge $(+q)$ is taken along two different paths say AMB (path 1) and ACB (path 2) such that A, M and B lie on the circle and $+q$ (another charge) is placed at the centre (as shown in the figure), so the work done along path ACB and path AMB are related as NCERT Pg. 46

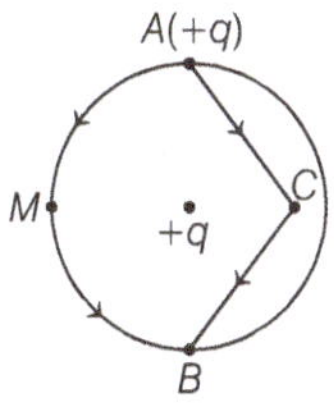

(a) $W_{AMB} > W_{ACB}$
(b) $W_{ACB} > W_{AMB}$
(c) $W_{ACB} = W_{AMB}$
(d) None of these

3 A uniform electric field E exists between two charged plates. What would be the work done in moving a charge q along the closed path $ABCDA$? **NCERT Pg. 46**

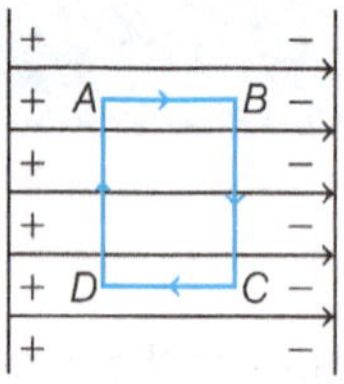

(a) $\oint \mathbf{E} \cdot d\mathbf{l}$ (b) $-\oint \mathbf{E} \cdot d\mathbf{l}$
(c) Zero (d) None of these

4 If 100 J of work has to be done in moving an electric charge of 4 C from a place, where potential is -10 V to another place where potential is V volt, find the value of V. **NCERT Pg. 47**

(a) 5 V (b) 10 V (c) 25 V (d) 15 V

5 If dW is the work done in bringing an infinitesimal small test charge dq from infinity to a point P, then potential at point P is **NCERT Pg. 47**

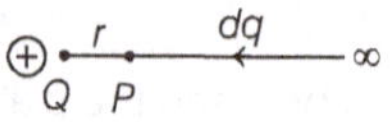

(a) $\dfrac{dW}{dq}$ (b) $-\dfrac{dW}{dq}$ (c) $dW \cdot dq$ (d) $\dfrac{dq}{dW}$

6 In a region, electrostatic potential varies along X-axis according to the equation $V = (4x^{3/2})$V, where x is in metre. The magnitude of electric field at $x = 4$ m is **NCERT Pg. 47**

(a) 24 V/m (b) 6 V/m (c) 12 V/m (d) 22 V/m

7 What is the work done in moving a $2\,\mu$C point charge from corner A to corner B of a square $ABCD$ in figure, when a $10\,\mu$C charge exists at the centre of the square? **NCERT Pg. 47**

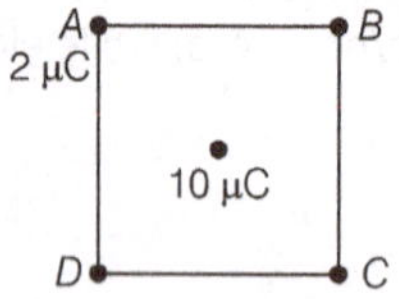

(a) Zero (b) 5 J (c) 2 J (d) 20 J

Potential due to a Point Charge

8 In the given figure, total work done W by the external force from $r' = \infty$ to $r' = r$ is **NCERT Pg. 48**

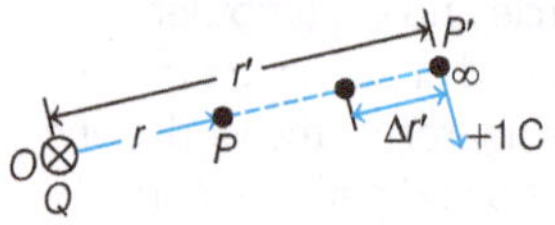

(a) $-\dfrac{Q}{4\pi\varepsilon_0 r}$ (b) $\dfrac{Q}{4\pi\varepsilon_0 r}$ (c) $\dfrac{2Q}{4\pi\varepsilon_0 r}$ (d) $-\dfrac{2Q}{4\pi\varepsilon_0 r}$

9 As per this diagram, a point charge $+q$ is placed at the origin O. Work done in taking another point charge $-Q$ from the point A [coordinate $(0, a)$] to another point B [coordinate $(a,0)$] along the straight path AB is **NCERT Pg. 48**

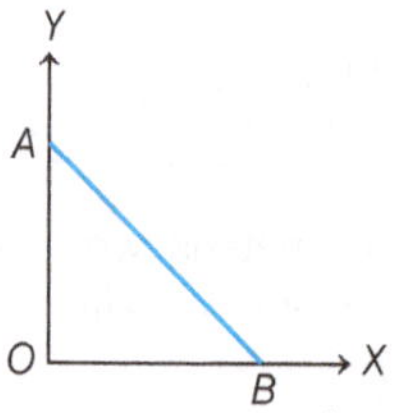

(a) zero (b) $\left(\dfrac{-qQ}{4\pi\varepsilon_0 a^2}\right)\sqrt{2}a$

(c) $\left(\dfrac{qQ}{4\pi\varepsilon_0 a^2}\right) \cdot \dfrac{a}{\sqrt{2}}$ (d) $\left(\dfrac{qQ}{4\pi\varepsilon_0} \dfrac{1}{a^2}\right)\sqrt{2}a$

10 The figure given below shows the variation of potential V or electric field E with r for a point charge Q. **NCERT Pg. 49**

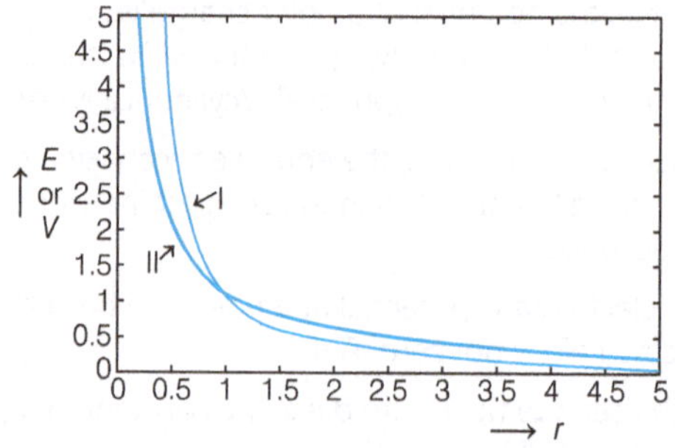

Which of the given curves represent E *versus* r or V *versus* r?

(a) I → E *versus* r, II → V *versus* r
(b) I → V *versus* r, II → E *versus* r
(c) Both represent E *versus* r
(d) Both represent V *versus* r

Potential due to an Electric Dipole

11 The variation of electric potential of an electric dipole with distance r is **NCERT Pg. 50**

(a) $V \propto \dfrac{1}{r^3}$ (b) $V \propto \dfrac{1}{r^2}$

(c) $V \propto \dfrac{1}{r}$ (d) $V \propto r$

12 The potential in the equatorial plane of a dipole of a dipole moment p is **NCERT Pg. 50**

(a) infinite (b) zero
(c) maximum (d) equal to p

13 In the figure given below, O is the centre of line joining AB. Two charges of opposite nature and same magnitude are placed at points A and B, respectively. NCERT Pg. 51

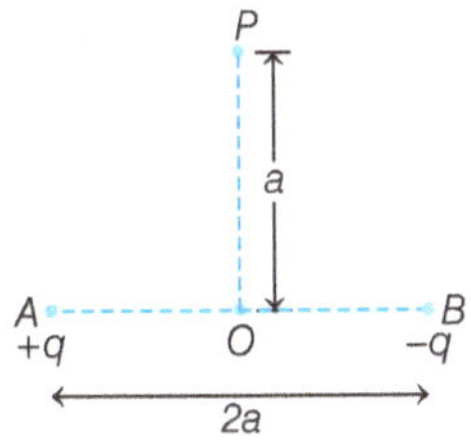

The potential at point P is

(a) $\frac{2kq}{a\sqrt{2}}$ (b) zero (c) $\frac{kq}{a\sqrt{2}}$ (d) $\frac{kq}{2a}$

Potential due to System of Charges

14 Two charges 3×10^{-8} C and -2×10^{-8} C located 15 cm apart. At what point on the line joining the two charges, the electric potential is zero? NCERT Pg. 51

(a) 9 cm (b) 42 cm (c) 18 cm (d) 20 cm

15 A charge $2Q$ is placed at each corner of a cube of side a. The potential at the centre of the cube is NCERT Pg. 51

(a) $\frac{8Q}{\pi\varepsilon_0 a}$ (b) $\frac{4Q}{4\pi\varepsilon_0 a}$

(c) $\frac{8Q}{\sqrt{3}\,\pi\varepsilon_0 a}$ (d) $\frac{2Q}{\pi\varepsilon_0 a}$

16 An infinite number of charges each equal to Q are placed along the X-axis at $x = 1, 2, 4, 8......$ The potential at the point $x = 0$ due to this set of charges is NCERT Pg. 51

(a) $\frac{Q}{4\pi\varepsilon_0}$ (b) $\frac{2Q}{4\pi\varepsilon_0}$ (c) $\frac{3Q}{4\pi\varepsilon_0}$ (d) $\frac{Q}{\pi\varepsilon_0}$

17 Four charges $+3\mu$C, -1μC, $+5\mu$C and -7μC are arranged on the circumference of a circle of radius 0.5 m. The potential at the centre is NCERT Pg. 51

(a) zero (b) 18×10^4 V

(c) -18×10^4 V (d) 288×10^3 V

18 Four point charges $+q, +q, -q$ and $-q$ are placed, respectively at corners A, B, C and D of a square of side a. The electric potential at centre O of square is NCERT Pg. 51

(a) $\frac{1}{4\pi\varepsilon_0}\frac{q}{a}$ (b) $\frac{1}{4\pi\varepsilon_0}\frac{2q}{a}$

(c) $\frac{1}{4\pi\varepsilon_0}\frac{4q}{a}$ (d) zero

19 A metallic sphere of radius R is charged to a potential V. The magnitude of electric field at a distance r $(r>R)$ from the centre of the sphere is NCERT Pg. 51

(a) $\frac{V}{r}$ (b) $\frac{Vr}{R^2}$ (c) $\frac{VR}{r^2}$ (d) zero

20 The electrostatic potential of a uniformly charged thin spherical shell of charge Q and radius R at a distance r from the centre is NCERT Pg. 52

(a) $\frac{Q}{4\pi\varepsilon_0 r}$ for outside points and $\frac{Q}{4\pi\varepsilon_0 R}$ for inside points of the shell

(b) $\frac{Q}{4\pi\varepsilon_0 r}$ for both points inside and outside the shell

(c) zero for points outside and $\frac{Q}{4\pi\varepsilon_0 r}$ for points inside the shell

(d) zero for both points inside and outside the shell

21 A hollow metal sphere of radius 10 cm is charged such that the potential on its surface becomes 80 V. The potential at the centre of the sphere is NCERT Pg. 52

(a) 80 V (b) 800 V

(c) 8 V (d) zero

22 Three concentric metal shells A, B and C of respective radii a, b and c $(a<b<c)$ have surface charge densities $+\sigma, -\sigma$ and $+\sigma$ respectively. The potential of shell B is NCERT Pg. 52

(a) $\frac{\sigma}{\varepsilon_0}\left[\frac{a^2-b^2}{a}+c\right]$ (b) $\frac{\sigma}{\varepsilon_0}\left[\frac{a^2-b^2}{b}+c\right]$

(c) $\frac{\sigma}{\varepsilon_0}\left[\frac{b^2-c^2}{b}+a\right]$ (d) $\frac{\sigma}{\varepsilon_0}\left[\frac{b^2-c^2}{c}+a\right]$

23 There are 8 drops of a conducting fluid. Each has radius r and they are charged. They are then combined to form a bigger drop of 1V. Find potential of smaller drop. NCERT Pg. 52

(a) 0.25 V (b) 4 V

(c) 2 V (d) 8 V

24 A hollow metal sphere of radius 5 cm is charged such that the potential on its surface is 10 V. The potential at the centre of the sphere is NCERT Pg. 52

(a) 0 V

(b) 10 V

(c) Same as at point 5 cm away from the surface

(d) Same as at point 25 cm away from the surface.

25 A charge Q is distributed over two concentric hollow spheres of radii r and $R(R>r)$ such that the surface charge densities are equal. Find the potential at the common centre. NCERT Pg. 52

(a) $\frac{Q}{4\pi\varepsilon_0}\times\frac{(r+R)}{(R+r)^2}$

(b) $\frac{Q(R^2+r)^2}{4\pi\varepsilon_0(r+R)}$

(c) $\frac{Q(r+R)}{4\pi\varepsilon_0(R^2+r^2)}$

(d) None of the above

26 A solid conducting sphere having a charge Q is surrounded by an uncharged concentric conducting hollow spherical shell. Let the potential difference between the surface of the solid sphere and that of the outer surface of the hollow shell be V. If the shell is now given a charge of $-3Q$ the new potential difference between the two same surfaces is **NCERT Pg. 52**

(a) V (b) $2V$
(c) $4V$ (d) $-2V$

Equipotential Surfaces

27 Choose the incorrect statement. Equipotential surfaces **NCERT Pg. 54**

(a) are closer in regions of larger electric fields compared to regions of lower electric fields.
(b) will be more crowded near sharp edges of a conductor.
(c) will be more crowded near regions of larger charge densities.
(d) will always be equally spaced.

28 For a uniform electric field **E**, along the X-axis, the equipotential surfaces are plane **NCERT Pg. 54**

(a) perpendicular to Z-axis
(b) parallel to the YZ-plane
(c) perpendicular to YZ-plane
(d) perpendicular to Y-axis

29 Three equipotential surfaces are shown in the figure **NCERT Pg. 55**

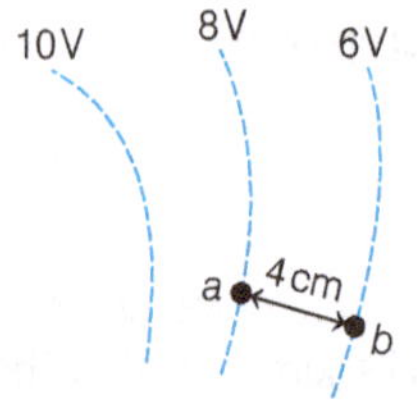

Which of the following option correctly represents the corresponding field lines?

(a)

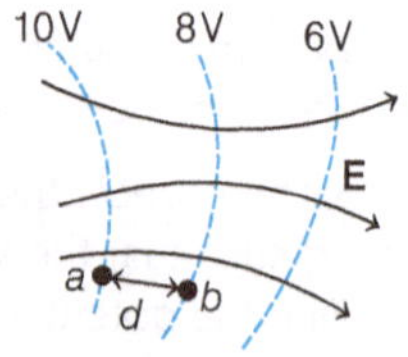

(b)

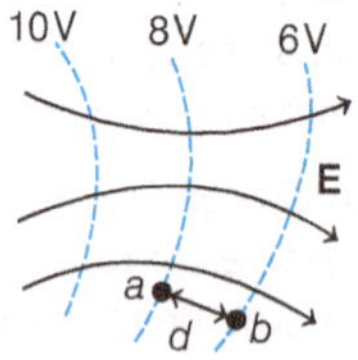

(c)

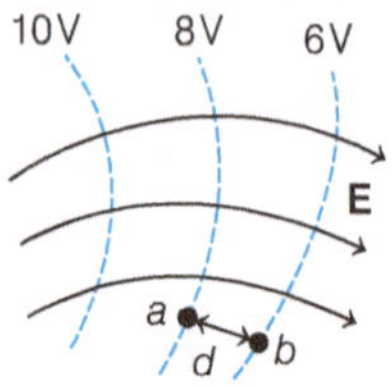

(d) None of these

30 The figure given below shows various equipotential surfaces. **NCERT Pg. 55**

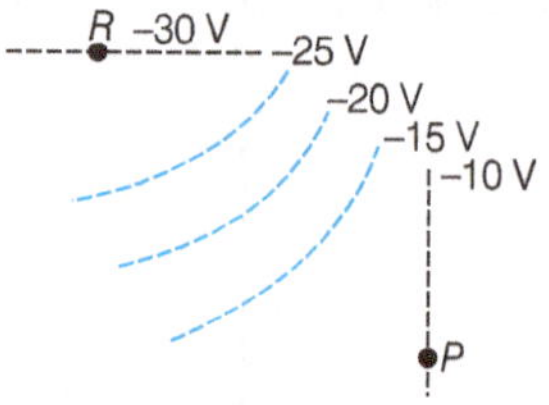

What is the direction of electric field **E** at P and R?

(a) At P, **E** is to the left and at R, **E** is upward
(b) At P, **E** is to the right and at R, **E** is downward
(c) At P, **E** is to downward and at R, **E** is to the left
(d) At P, **E** is to upward and at R, **E** is to the right

31 The electric potential at a certain distance from a point charge is 600 V and the electric field is 200 NC^{-1}. The distance of the point charge (in m) is **NCERT Pg. 55**

(a) 2 (b) 3
(c) 1 (d) 0

32 Uniform electric field of magnitude 100 V/m in space is directed parallel to the line $y = 3 + x$. Find the potential difference between points A (3, 1) and B (1, 3). **NCERT Pg. 55**

(a) 100 V (b) $200\sqrt{2}$ V
(c) 200 V (d) Zero

33 The electric potential V is given as a function of distance x (metre) by $V = (5x^2 - 10x - 9)$ V.
The value of electric field at $x = 1$ m is **NCERT Pg. 55**

(a) 20 V/m (b) 6 V/m
(c) 11 V/m (d) zero

34 Figure shows a set of equipotential surfaces. The magnitude and direction of electric field that exists in the region is **NCERT Pg. 55**

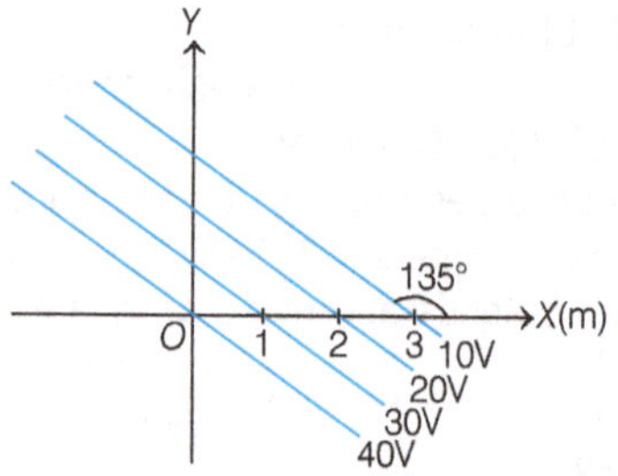

(a) $10\sqrt{2}$ V/m at 45° with-X-axis.
(b) $10\sqrt{2}$ V/m at $-45°$ with X-axis.
(c) $5\sqrt{2}$ V/m at 45° with X-axis.
(d) $5\sqrt{2}$ V/m at $-45°$ with X-axis.

35 The electric potential figure shows the variation of electric field intensity E *versus* distance x. What is the potential difference between the points at $x = 2$m and at $x = 6$m from O? NCERT Pg. 55

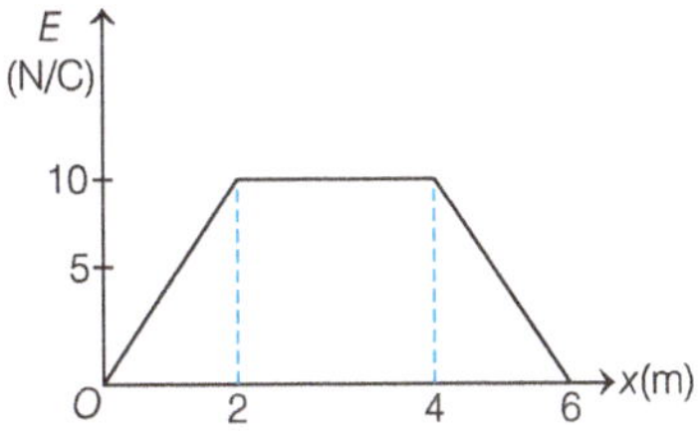

(a) 30V (b) 60V (c) 40 V (d) 80 V

Potential Energy of a System of Charges

36 The total potential energy of a system of three charges q_1, q_2 and q_3 located at r_1, r_2 and r_3, respectively is NCERT Pg. 56

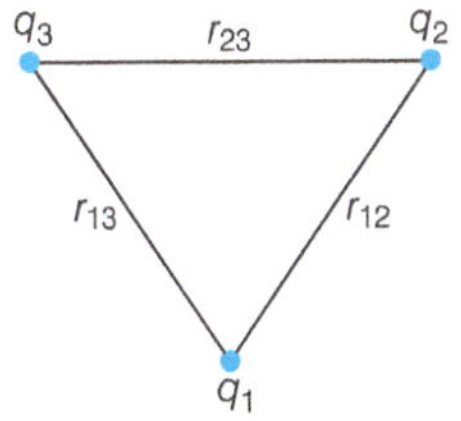

(a) $\frac{1}{4\pi\varepsilon_0}\left(\frac{q_1q_2}{r_{12}} + \frac{q_1q_3}{r_{13}} + \frac{q_2q_3}{r_{23}}\right)$

(b) $\frac{1}{4\pi\varepsilon_0}\left(\frac{q_1q_2}{r_{12}} - \frac{q_1q_3}{r_{13}} + \frac{q_2q_3}{r_{23}}\right)$

(c) $\frac{1}{4\pi\varepsilon_0}\left(\frac{q_1q_2}{r_{12}} + \frac{q_1q_3}{r_{13}} - \frac{q_2q_3}{r_{23}}\right)$

(d) $\frac{1}{4\pi\varepsilon_0}\left(\frac{q_1q_2}{r_{12}} - \frac{q_1q_3}{r_{13}} - \frac{q_2q_3}{r_{23}}\right)$

37 Three charges Q, $+q$ and $+q$ are placed at the vertices of a right angle isosceles triangle as shown below. The net electrostatic energy of the configuration is zero, if the value of Q is NCERT Pg. 56

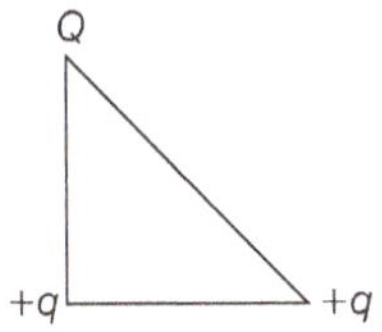

(a) $-2q$ (b) $\frac{-q}{1+\sqrt{2}}$ (c) $+q$ (d) $\frac{-\sqrt{2}q}{\sqrt{2}+1}$

38 Two charges of equal magnitude q are placed in air at a distance $2a$ apart and third charge $-2q$ is placed at mid-point. The potential energy of the system is NCERT Pg. 56

(a) $-\frac{q^2}{8\pi\varepsilon_0 a}$ (b) $-\frac{3q^2}{8\pi\varepsilon_0 a}$

(c) $-\frac{5q^2}{8\pi\varepsilon_0 a}$ (d) $-\frac{7q^2}{8\pi\varepsilon_0 a}$

39 Three point charges $+q$ $-2q$ and $-2q$ are placed at the vertices of an equilateral triangle of side a. The work done by some external force to increase their separation to $2a$ will be NCERT Pg. 56

(a) $\frac{1}{4\pi\varepsilon_0}\frac{2q^2}{a}$ (b) $\frac{1}{4\pi\varepsilon_0}\frac{q^2}{2a}$

(c) $\frac{1}{4\pi\varepsilon_0}\frac{\delta q}{a^2}$ (d) zero

40 Two charges q_1 and q_2 are placed 30 cm apart, as shown in the figure. A third charge q_3 is moved along the arc of a circle of radius 40 cm from C to D. The change in the potential energy of the system is $\frac{q_3}{4\pi\varepsilon_0}K$, where K is NCERT Pg. 56

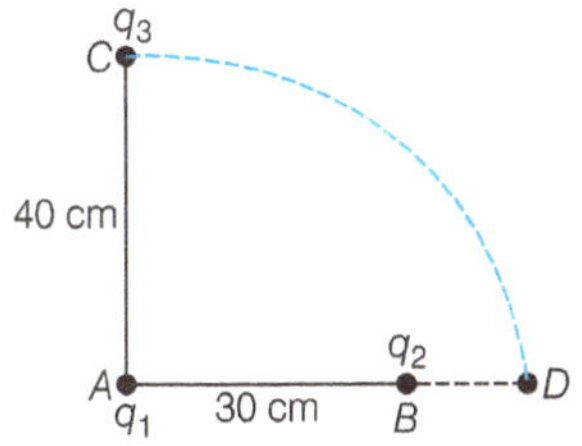

(a) $8q_2$ (b) $8q_1$ (c) $6q_2$ (d) $6q_1$

41 The potential difference between a cloud and the earth is 10^7 V. Calculate the amount of energy dissipated when the charge of 100 C is transferred from the cloud to the ground due to lightning bolt. NCERT Pg. 56

(a) zero (b) 10^9 J

(c) 60 J (d) 10^7 J

42 Four charges are arranged at the corners of a square $ABCD$ of side d, as shown in the figure. The work required to put together this arrangement is NCERT Pg. 57

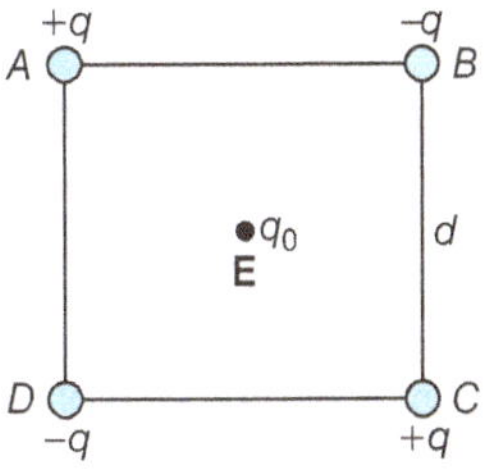

(a) $\frac{-q^2}{4\pi\varepsilon_0 d}(4-\sqrt{2})$ (b) $\frac{-q^3}{4\pi\varepsilon_0 d}(4-\sqrt{2})$

(c) $\frac{-q^4}{4\pi\varepsilon_0 d}(4-\sqrt{2})$ (d) $\frac{q^2}{4\pi\varepsilon_0 d}(4-\sqrt{2})$

Potential Energy in an External Field

43 In the figure, proton moves a distance d in a uniform electric field E as shown in the figure. Does the electric field do a positive or negative work on the proton? Does the electric potential energy of the proton increase or decrease? NCERT Pg. 58

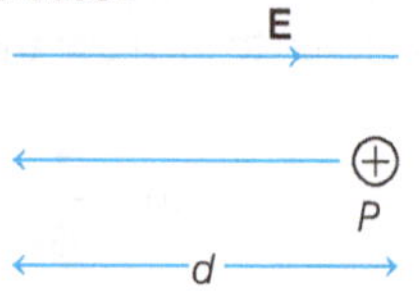

(a) Negative, increase (b) Positive, decrease
(c) Negative, decrease (d) Positive, increase

44 Suppose a system of two charges as shown below placed in an external electric field

$E = A(1/r^2)$, where $A = 9 \times 10^5$ C / m^2.

What would be the electrostatic energy of the configuration? NCERT Pg. 59

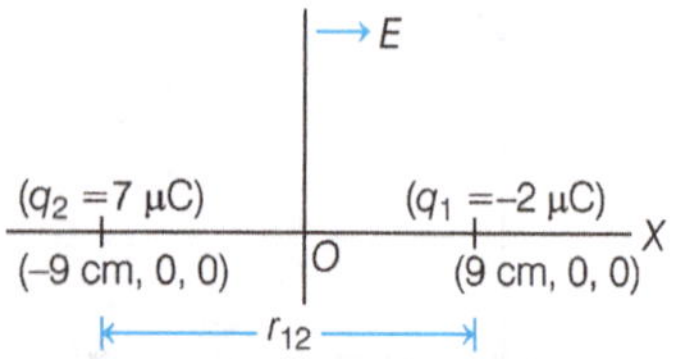

(a) 49 J (b) 49.3 J (c) −49.3 J (d) 45 J

45 A positive charge is moved from low potential point A to a high potential point B. Then, the electric potential energy. NCERT Pg. 59

(a) increases
(b) decreases
(c) will remain same
(d) Nothing definite can be predicted

46 An electric field of 1000 V/m is applied to an electric dipole at angle of 45°. The value of electric dipole moment is 10^{-29} Cm. What is the potential energy of the electric dipole? NCERT Pg. 60

(a) -9×10^{-20} J (b) -10×10^{-29} J
(c) -20×10^{-18} J (d) -7×10^{-27} J

47 An electric dipole made up of positive and negative charges each of 3.5 μC and placed at a distance 4.2 cm apart is placed in an electric field of 5.87×10^5 NC^{-1}. What will be the maximum torque which the field can exert on the dipole? Also, obtain the work that must be done to turn the dipole from 0° to 180°. NCERT Pg. 60

(a) 86.289×10^{-3} Nm^{-1}, 1.72×10^{-1} J
(b) 75.26×10^{-3} Nm^{-1}, 1.72×10^{-1} J
(c) 86.289×10^{-3} Nm^{-1}, 3.72×10^{-3} J
(d) 55.26×10^{-3} Nm^{-1}, 1.72×10^{-3} J

48 A molecule of a substance has a permanent electric dipole moment of magnitude 10^{-29} Cm. A mole of this substance is polarised (at low temperature) by applying a strong electrostatic field of magnitude 10^6 Vm^{-1}.

The direction of the field is suddenly changed from an angle of 60° to 0°. Estimate the heat released from the substance in aligning its dipoles along the new direction of the field. NCERT Pg. 60

(a) −3 J (b) 3 J (c) −6 J (d) 6 J

Electrostatics of Conductors

49 If a conductor is given an excess of charge, then it NCERT Pg. 62

(a) resides on its surface
(b) move to its centre
(c) escape from its surface
(d) distributes equally inside it

50 Consider a cavity in a conductor as shown in the figure below, the electric field and charge density in the cavity are NCERT Pg. 62

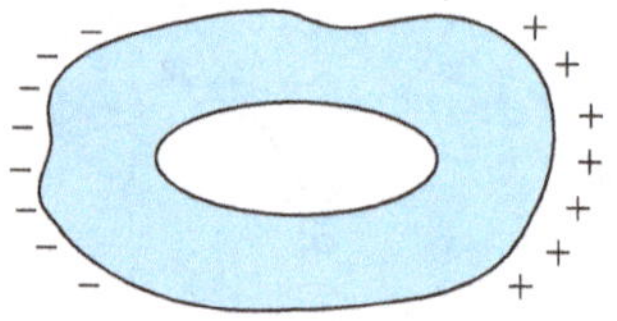

(a) $E > 0, \sigma > 0$ (b) $E < 0, \sigma < 0$
(c) $E = 0, \sigma = 0$ (d) $E > 0, \sigma < 0$

51 Read the following statements regarding to electrostatics of conductors. Which of the following is correct? NCERT Pg. 62

(a) Inside the conductor, electrostatic field is zero.
(b) At the surface of a charged conductor, electrostatic field must be parallel to the surface at every point.
(c) Electrostatic potential continuously varies throughout the volume of the conductor.
(d) Electrostatic field at the surface of a charged conductor is zero.

Dielectrics and Polarisation

52 If dielectric constant and dielectric strength be denoted by K and X, respectively, then a material suitable for using it as a dielectric in a capacitor must have NCERT Pg. 65

(a) high K and high X (b) high K and low X
(c) low K and high X (d) low K and low X

53 When a dielectric is placed in an electric field, the electric field inside the dielectric NCERT Pg. 65

(a) increases (b) decreases
(c) constant (d) zero

54 The dielectric constant of helium at 0°C and 1 atmospheric pressure is 1.00074. Find the dipole moment induced in each helium atom, when the gas is in electric field of intensity 10 Vm^{-1}. NCERT Pg. 66

(a) 2.4×10^{40}Cm (b) 2.4×10^{-39}Cm
(c) 2.6×10^{-39}Cm (d) 1.5×10^{40}Cm

Capacitors and Capacitance

55 Two capacitors C_1 and C_2 are charged to 120 V and 200 V, respectively. It is found that by connecting them together, the potential on each one can be made zero. Then, NCERT Pg. 67

(a) $5C_1 = 3C_2$ (b) $3C_1 = 5C_2$
(c) $3C_1 + 5C_2 = 0$ (d) $9C_1 = 4C_2$

56 A capacitor of capacitance C is charged with a battery of potential V and then disconnected. Now, a charge $+Q$ is given to negative plate, then potential difference between the plates is NCERT Pg. 67

(a) V (b) $V - \frac{Q}{C}$ (c) $V - \frac{Q}{2C}$ (d) $V - \frac{2Q}{C}$

The Parallel Plate Capacitor

57 Consider two parallel plates of area A each having surface charge densities σ and $-\sigma$ separated by distance d as shown in figure below. The electric field in outer region I (region above the plate 1) is NCERT Pg. 68

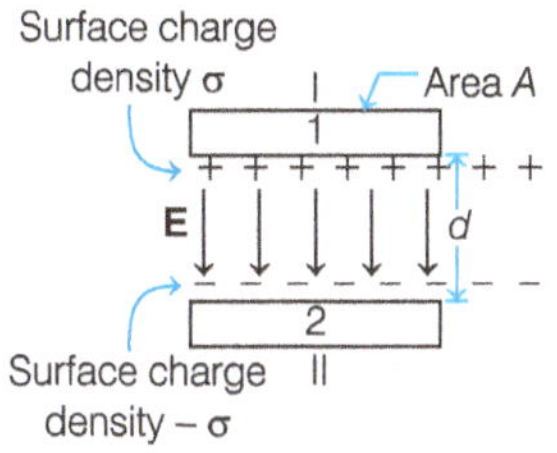

(a) $\frac{\sigma}{2\varepsilon_0}$ (b) $-\frac{\sigma}{2\varepsilon_0}$ (c) zero (d) $\frac{2\sigma}{4\varepsilon_0}$

58 A parallel plate capacitor with plates of area 1 m^2 each, are at a separation of 0.1 m. If the electric field between the plates is 100 N/C, the magnitude of charge on each plate is $\left(\text{Take, } \varepsilon_0 = 8.85 \times 10^{-12} \frac{C^2}{N\text{-}m^2}\right)$ NCERT Pg. 69

(a) 9.85×10^{-10} C (b) 8.85×10^{-10} C
(c) 7.85×10^{-10} C (d) 6.85×10^{-10} C

59 A parallel plate capacitor is charged and then charging is disconnected. If the plates are now pulled apart with insulated handles. NCERT Pg. 69

(a) The capacitance increases
(b) Potential energy decreases
(c) Potential difference increases
(d) Charge and potential difference both remains same

60 A parallel plate capacitor has 1μF capacitance. One of its two plates is given + 2 μC charge and the other plate + 4 μC charge. The potential difference developed across the capacitor is NCERT Pg. 69

(a) 1 V (b) 5 V (c) 2 V (d) 3 V

Effect of Dielectric on Capacitance

61 A parallel plate capacitor is made of two circular plates separated by a distance of 5 mm and with a dielectric of dielectric constant 2.2 between them. When the electric field in the dielectric is 3×10^4 V/m, then charge density of the positive plate will be closed to NCERT Pg. 69

(a) 6×10^{-7} Cm^{-2} (b) 3×10^{-7} Cm^{-2}
(c) 3×10^4 Cm^{-2} (d) 6×10^4 Cm^{-2}

62 A parallel plate air capacitor has a capacitance 18 μF. If the distance between the plates is tripled and a dielectric medium is introduced, the capacitance becomes 72 μF. The dielectric constant of the medium is NCERT Pg. 69

(a) 4 (b) 9 (c) 12 (d) 2

63 In a parallel plate capacitor, the separation between the plates is 3 mm with air between them. Now, a dielectric of dielectric constant 2 is introduced between the plates due to which the capacitance increases. In order to bring its capacitance of the original value, the separation between the plates must be made NCERT Pg. 69

(a) 1.5 mm (b) 2.5 mm
(c) 4 mm (d) 6 mm

64 The capacitance of a parallel plate capacitor with air in between the plates is 3 μF. With the introduction of a dielectric medium between the plates, the capacitance becomes 15 μF. The permittivity of the medium is NCERT Pg. 69

(a) 5 $C^2 N^{-1}m^{-2}$ (b) 15 $C^2N^{-1}m^{-2}$
(c) 0.44×10^{-10} $C^2N^{-1}m^{-2}$ (d) 8.845×10^{-11} $C^2N^{-1}m^{-2}$

65 A capacitor of capacitance 15 nF having dielectric slab of $\varepsilon_r = 2.5$, dielectric strength = 30 MV/m and potential difference = 30 V. Calculate the area of the plate. NCERT Pg. 70

(a) 6.7×10^{-4} m^2 (b) 4.2×10^{-4} m^2
(c) 8.0×10^{-4} m^2 (d) 9.85×10^{-4} m^2

66 A slab of material of dielectric constant K has the same area as the plates of a parallel plate capacitor but has a thickness $(3/4)d$, where d is the separation of the plates. How is the capacitance changed, when the slab is inserted between the plates? NCERT Pg. 70

(Given, C_0 is the capacitance of the capacitor with air as medium between plates)

(a) $\frac{4KC_0}{K+3}$ (b) $\frac{K+3C_0}{4K}$ (c) $\frac{K-3C_0}{4K}$ (d) $\frac{4KC_0}{K-3}$

67 A parallel plate capacitor with air between the plates is charged to a potential of 500 V and then insulated. A plastic plate is inserted between the plates filling the whole gap. The potential difference between the plates become 75 V. The dielectric constant of the plastic plate is **NCERT Pg. 70**

(a) $\frac{10}{3}$ (b) 5 (c) $\frac{20}{3}$ (d) 12

Combination of Capacitors

68 The parallel combination of two air filled parallel plate capacitors of capacitance C and nC is connected to a battery of voltage, V. When the capacitors are fully charged, the battery is removed and after that a dielectric material of dielectric constant K is placed between the two plates of the first capacitor. The new potential difference of the combined system is **NCERT Pg. 71**

(a) $\frac{(n+1)V}{(K+n)}$ (b) $\frac{nV}{K+n}$

(c) V (d) $\frac{V}{K+n}$

69 A parallel plate capacitor has the space between its plates filled by the two slabs of thickness $\frac{d}{2}$ each, having dielectric constants K_1 and K_2 and d is the plate separation of the capacitor. The capacity of the capacitor is **NCERT Pg. 71**

(a) $\frac{2\varepsilon_0 d}{A}\left(\frac{K_1+K_2}{K_1K_2}\right)$ (b) $\frac{2\varepsilon_0 A}{d}\left(\frac{K_1K_2}{K_1+K_2}\right)$

(c) $\frac{2\varepsilon_0 A}{A}(K_1+K_2)$ (d) $\frac{2\varepsilon_0 A}{d}\left(\frac{K_1+K_2}{K_1K_2}\right)$

70 A parallel plate capacitor having cross-sectional area A and separation d has air in between the plates. Now a thin conducting slab of same area but thickness t is inserted between the plates as shown. The new capacitance of the capacitor will be **NCERT Pg. 71**

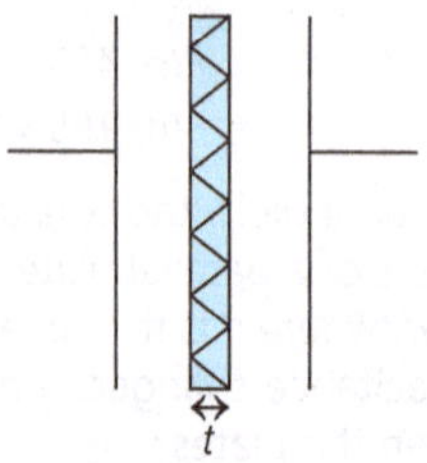

(a) $\frac{A\varepsilon_0}{d}$ (b) $\frac{A\varepsilon_0}{d-t}$

(c) $\frac{A\varepsilon_0}{t}$ (d) zero

71 Find the capacitance of the parallel plate capacitor as shown in the figure below. **NCERT Pg. 71**

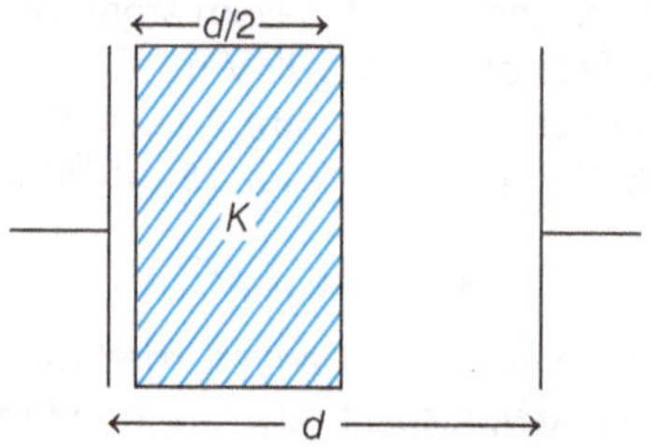

(a) $\frac{2KA\varepsilon_0}{(K+1)\,d}$ (b) $\frac{2KA\varepsilon_0}{d}$ (c) $\frac{(K+1)A\varepsilon_0}{2d}$ (d) $\frac{2\,KA\,\varepsilon_0}{(K^2+1)\,d}$

72 The two plates of a parallel plate capacitor having charges Q_1 and Q_2 are given. The capacitance of the capacitor is C. When the switch is closed, mark the incorrect statement. Assuming both Q_1, Q_2 to be positive. **NCERT Pg. 72**

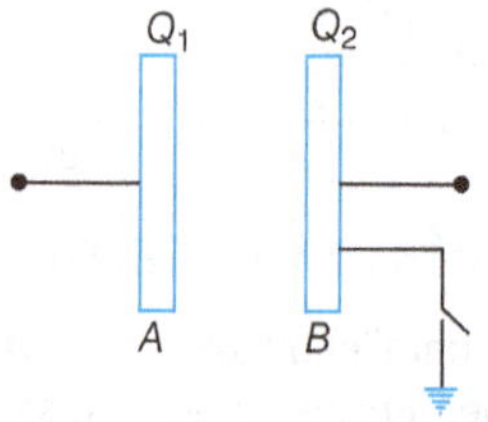

(a) The charge flown through switch is zero.
(b) The charge flown through switch is Q_1+Q_2.
(c) Potential difference across the capacitor plates is $\frac{Q_1}{C}$.
(d) The charge of the capacitor is Q_1.

73 A parallel plate capacitor is charged and the charging battery is then disconnected. If the plates of the capacitor are moved further apart by means of insulating handles, then which of the following statement is correct? **NCERT Pg. 72**

(a) The charge on the capacitor increases.
(b) The voltage across the plates increases.
(c) The capacitance increases.
(d) The electrostatic energy stored in the capacitor decreases.

74 A parallel plate air capacitor of capacitance C_0 is connected to a cell of emf V and then disconnected from it. A dielectric slab of dielectric constant K, which can just fill the air gap of the capacitor, is now inserted in it. Which of the following statement is incorrect? **NCERT Pg. 72**

(a) The potential difference between the plates decreases K times.
(b) The energy stored in the capacitor decreases K times.
(c) The change in energy is $\frac{1}{2}C_0V^2(K-1)$.
(d) The change in energy is $\frac{1}{2}C_0V^2\left(\frac{1}{K}-1\right)$.

75 A gang capacitor is formed by interlocking nine plates with each other. The distance between the consecutive plates is 0.885 cm and the overlapping area of the plate is 5 cm^2. The capacity of the unit is NCERT Pg. 72

(a) 1.06 pF (b) 4 pF
(c) 6.36 pF (d) 12.72 pF

76 A capacitance of 2 μF is required in an electrical circuit across a potential difference of 1 kV. A large number of 1 μF capacitors are available which can withstand a potential difference of not more than 300 V. The minimum number of capacitors required to achieve this is NCERT Pg. 72

(a) 16 (b) 24 (c) 32 (d) 2

77 An infinite number of identical capacitors each of capacitance 1 μF are connected as shown in the figure. Then, the equivalent capacitance between *A* and *B* is NCERT Pg. 72

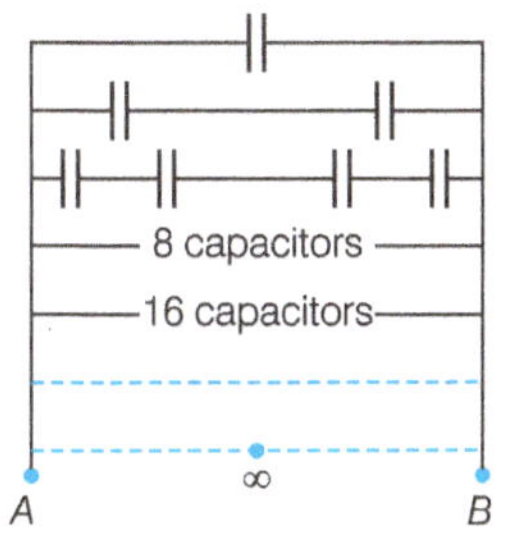

(a) 1 μF (b) 2 μF (c) $\frac{1}{2}$ μF (d) ∞

78 In the circuit shown, find *C* if the effective capacitance of the whole circuit is to be 0.5 μF. All values in the circuit are in μF. NCERT Pg. 72

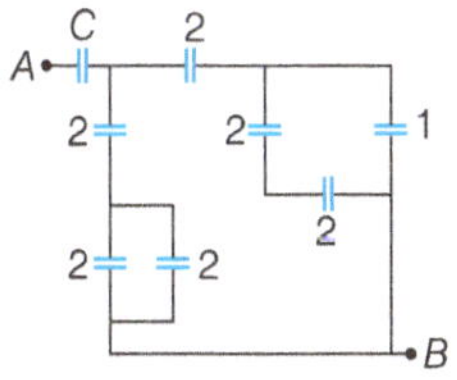

(a) $\frac{6}{5}$ μF (b) 4 μF (c) $\frac{7}{10}$ μF (d) $\frac{7}{11}$ μF

79 A number of condensers, each of the capacitance 1 μF and each one of which gets punctured, if a potential difference just exceeding 500 V is provided. An arrangement suitable for giving capacitance of 2 μF across which 3000 V may be applied requires atleast NCERT Pg. 72

(a) 6 component capacitors
(b) 12 component capacitors
(c) 72 component capacitors
(d) 2 component capacitors

80 In the circuit shown in the figure, the potential difference across the 4.5 μF capacitor is NCERT Pg. 72

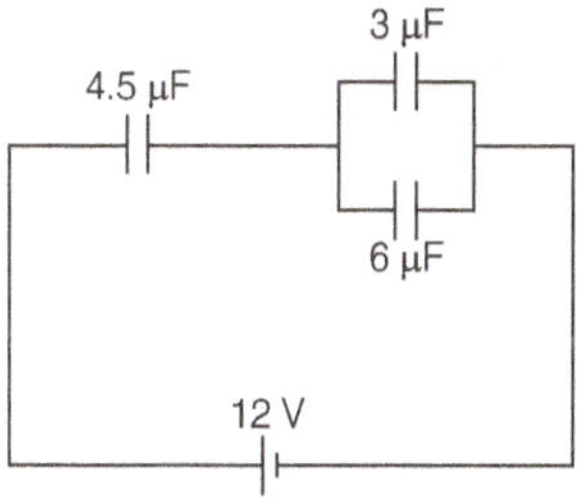

(a) $\frac{8}{3}$ V (b) 4 V
(c) 6 V (d) 8 V

81 The equivalent capacitance of the following circuit between terminals *A* and *B* is (all capacitors are identical and have capacitance 4 μF) NCERT Pg. 72

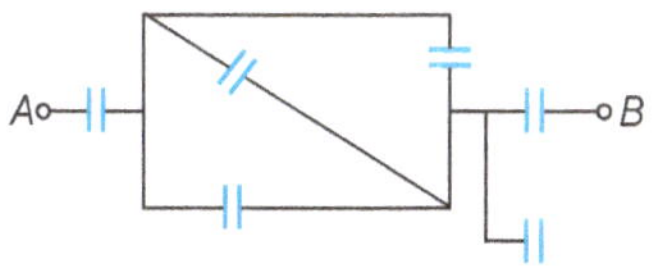

(a) 12 μF (b) $\frac{12}{7}$ μF
(c) $\frac{28}{3}$ μF (d) 27 μF

82 Two identical capacitors are joined in parallel and charged to a potential *V*. Now these are separated and connected in series. i.e., the positive plate of one is connected to negative of the other, while open plates are kept open ended NCERT Pg. 72

(a) The charges on the plates connected together finally become zero
(b) The charges on the free plates are enhanced
(c) The energy stored in the system increases
(d) The potential difference between the free plates becomes 2*V*

83 The capacitor, whose capacitance is 6μF, 3μF and 2μF, respectively are connected with 12 V battery as shown in figure. The charge on 3μF capacitor will be NCERT Pg. 72

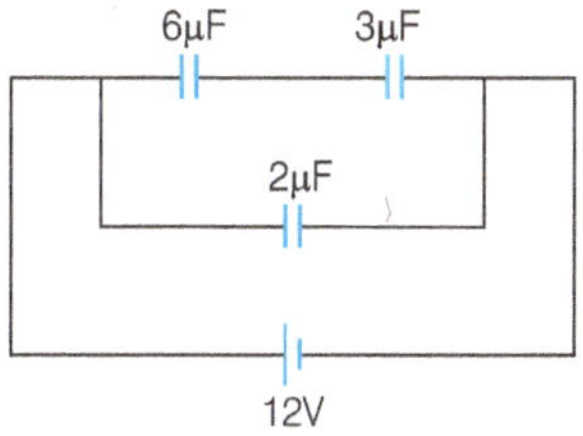

(a) 12 μC (b) 24 μC
(c) 8 μC (d) 16 μC

84 The equivalent capacitance of four identical capacitors, as shown in the figure is 15 μF. The value of each capacitor is NCERT Pg. 72

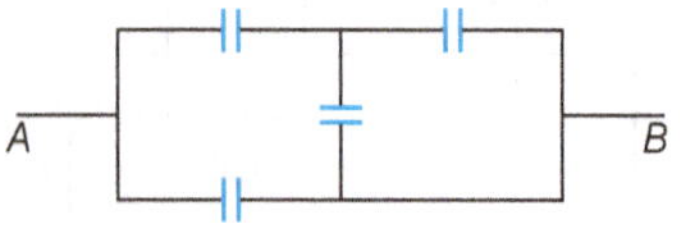

(a) 6 μF (b) 5 μF (c) 8 μF (d) 9 μF

85 Five capacitors, each of capacitance value C are connected as shown in the figure. The ratio of capacitance between P and R, and the capacitance between P and Q, is NCERT Pg. 72

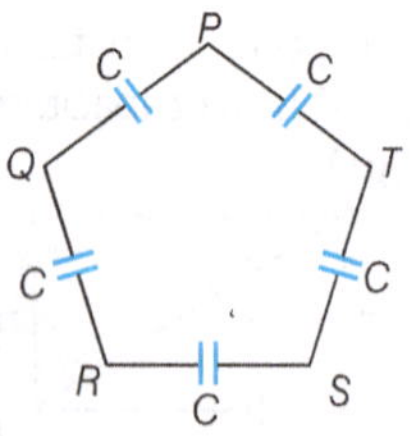

(a) 3 : 1 (b) 5 : 2 (c) 2 : 3 (d) 1 : 1

86 In the arrangement shown in the figure, find the equivalent capacitance between A and B (symbols have their usual meaning) (each capacitor has identical dimensions) NCERT Pg. 72

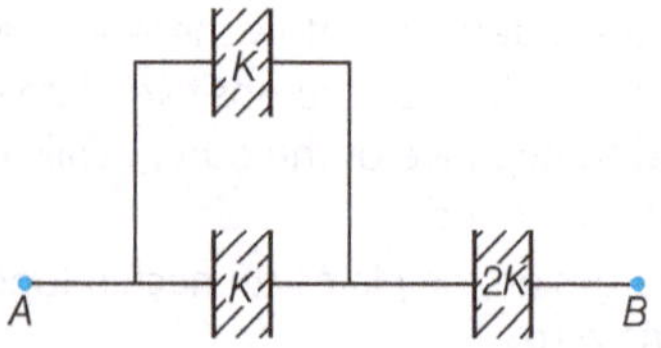

(a) $\frac{3A\varepsilon_0 K}{d}$ (b) $\frac{4A\varepsilon_0 K}{d}$ (c) $\frac{A\varepsilon_0 K}{d}$ (d) $\frac{2A\varepsilon_0 K}{d}$

87 The expression for the equivalent capacitance of the system shown is (A is the cross-sectional area of one of the upper plates) NCERT Pg. 72

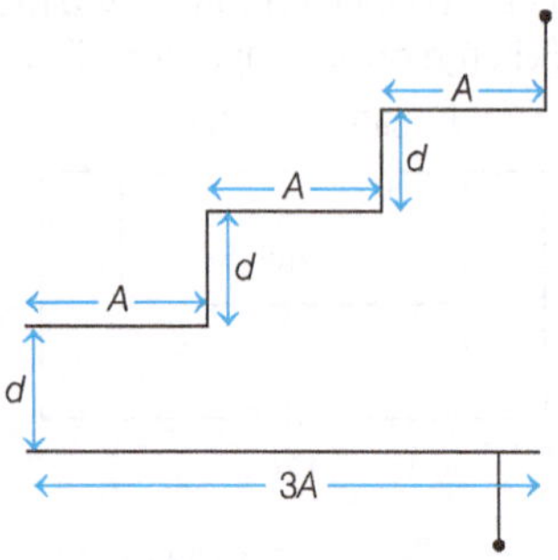

(a) $\frac{\varepsilon_0 A}{3d}$ (b) $\frac{3A\varepsilon_0}{d}$ (c) $\frac{11A\varepsilon_0}{6d}$ (d) $\frac{6A\varepsilon_0}{d}$

88 A 10 μF capacitor is charged to a potential of 50 V and is connected to another uncharged capacitor in parallel. Now, their common potential becomes 20 V. The capacitance of second capacitor is NCERT Pg. 72

(a) 15 μF (b) 20 μF (c) 25 μF (d) 40 μF

Energy Stored in a Capacitor

89 The charge q on a capacitor varies with voltage V as shown in figure. The area of the triangle AOB represents NCERT Pg. 73

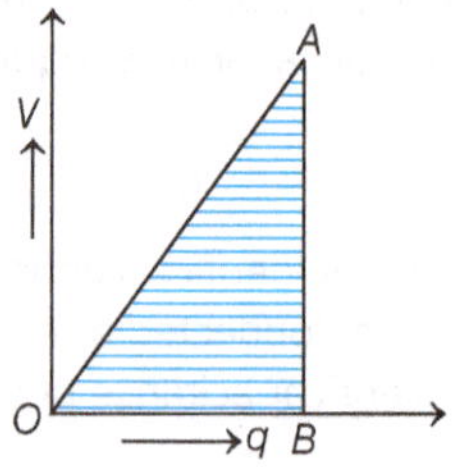

(a) Electric field between the plates
(b) Electric flux between the plates
(c) Energy density
(d) Energy stored by the capacitor

90 A 900 pF capacitor is charged by 100 V battery in the figure. How much electrostatic energy is stored by the capacitor? NCERT Pg. 74

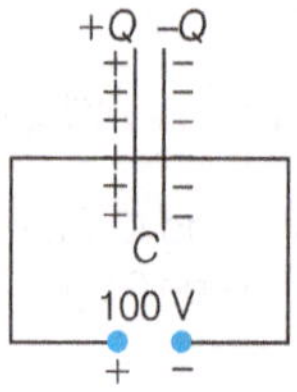

(a) 45×10^{-6} J (b) 4.5×10^{6} J
(c) 4.5×10^{-6} J (d) 0.45×10^{5} J

91 A parallel plate capacitor having capacitance 12 pF is charged by a battery to a potential difference of 100 V between its plates. The charging battery is now disconnected and a porcelain slab of dielectric constant 6.5 is slipped between the plates. The work done by the capacitor on the slab is NCERT Pg. 74

(a) 560 pJ (b) 508 pJ
(c) 692 pJ (d) 600 pJ

92 A capacitor with capacitance 5 μF is charged to 5 μC. If the plates are pulled apart to reduce the capacitance to 2 μF, how much work is done? NCERT Pg. 74

(a) 6.25×10^{-6} J
(b) 2.16×10^{-6} J
(c) 2.55×10^{-6} J
(d) 3.75×10^{-6} J

93 In the given circuit, find the heat produced between A and B (given $C = 1\,\mu F$) NCERT Pg. 74

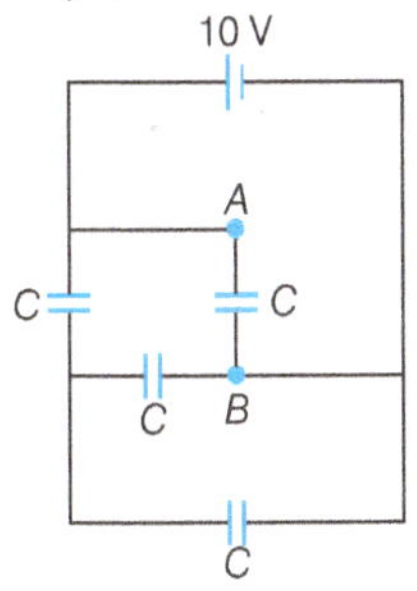

(a) 50 μJ (b) 60 μJ (c) 70 μJ (d) 100 μJ

94 A series combination of n_1 capacitors, each of value C_1, is charged by a source of potential difference 4V. When another parallel combination of n_2 capacitors, each of value C_2, is charged by a source of potential difference V, it has the same (total) energy stored in it as the first combination has. The value of C_2 in terms of C_1 is NCERT Pg. 74

(a) $\frac{2C_1}{n_1 n_2}$ (b) $16\frac{n_1}{n_2}$ (c) $2\frac{n_2}{n_1}C_1$ (d) $\frac{16C_1}{n_1 n_2}$

95 A parallel plate capacitor has a uniform electric field E (Vm^{-1}) in the space between the plates. If the distance between the plates is d(m) and area of each plate is $A(m^2)$, the energy (J) stored in the capacitor is NCERT Pg. 74

(a) $\frac{1}{2}\varepsilon_0 E^2$ (b) $\varepsilon_0 EAd$ (c) $\frac{1}{2}\varepsilon_0 E^2 Ad$ (d) $E^2 Ad/\varepsilon_0$

96 A parallel plate capacitor is connected to a 5V battery and charged. The battery is then disconnected and a glass slab is introduced between the plates, then the quantities that decrease are NCERT Pg. 74

(a) charge and potential difference
(b) charge and capacitance
(c) capacitance and potential difference
(d) energy stored and potential difference

97 A parallel plate capacitor have plate area A and plate separation d is charged by a battery of voltage V. The battery is then disconnected. The work needed to pull the plates to separation $2d$ is NCERT Pg. 74

(a) $\frac{AV^2\varepsilon_0}{d}$ (b) $\frac{2AV^2\varepsilon_0}{d}$ (c) $\frac{AV^2\varepsilon_0}{2d}$ (d) $\frac{3AV^2\varepsilon_0}{2d}$

98 A 40 μF capacitor in a defibrillator is charged to 3000 V. The energy stored in the capacitor is sent through the patient during a pulse of duration 2 ms. The power delivered to the patient is NCERT Pg. 74

(a) 45 kW (b) 90 kW (c) 180 k (d) 360 kW

99 A 900 pF capacitor is charged by 100 V battery, then which of the following statement is correct? NCERT Pg. 74

(a) The charge on the capacitor is 4.5×10^{-8}C.
(b) The energy stored by the capacitor is 9×10^{-6} J.
(c) If capacitor is disconnected from the battery and connected to another 900 pF capacitor, then energy stored by the system is 2.25×10^{-6} J.
(d) None of the above

Assertion and Reason Questions

Direction (Q. Nos. 1-10) *In the following questions, a statement of Assertion is followed by a corresponding statement of Reason. Of the following statements, choose the correct one.*

(a) Both Assertion and Reason are correct and Reason is the correct explanation of Assertion.
(b) Both Assertion and Reason are correct but Reason is not the correct explanation of Assertion.
(c) Assertion is correct but Reason is incorrect.
(d) Assertion is incorrect but Reason is correct.

1 **Assertion** Work done by the electrostatic force in bringing the unit positive charge from infinity to the point P, is positive.

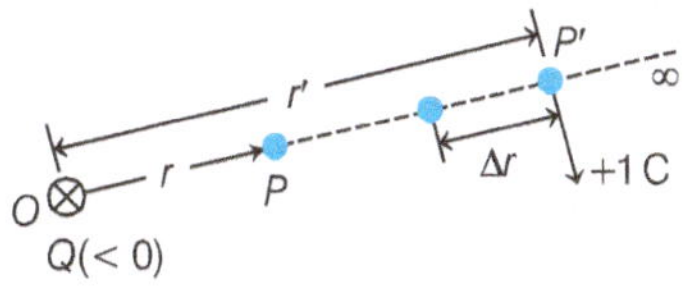

Reason For $Q < 0$, the force on unit positive charge is attractive, so that the electrostatic force and the displacement (from infinity to P) are in the same direction. NCERT Pg. 46

2 **Assertion** If a positive charge comes close to a negative charge, then the potential energy of the system increases.

Reason The potential energy of system of two charges is inversely proportional to the separation between two charges. NCERT Pg. 55

3 **Assertion** The expression of potential energy $U = \frac{1}{4\pi\varepsilon_0}\frac{q_1 q_2}{r_{12}}$, is unaltered whatever way the charges are brought to the specified locations.

Reason The potential energy is negative of work done by conservative force. NCERT Pg. 56

4 **Assertion** A capacitor can be given only a limited quantity of charge.

Reason Charge stored by a capacitor depends on the shape and size of the plates of capacitor and the surrounding medium. NCERT Pg. 61

5 **Assertion** In the absence of an external electric field, the dipole moment per unit volume of a polar dielectric is zero.

Reason The dipoles of a polar dielectric are randomly oriented. NCERT Pg. 65

6 **Assertion** Polar molecules have permanent dipole moment.

Reason In polar molecules, the centre of positive and negative charges coincides even when there is no external field. NCERT Pg. 65

7 **Assertion** Capacity of a parallel plate capacitor increases when distance between the plates is decreased.

Reason Capacitance of a capacitor is directly proportional to distance between them. NCERT Pg. 68

8 **Assertion** A parallel plate capacitor is connected across a battery through a key. A dielectric slab of dielectric constant K is introduced between the plates. The electric field inside the capacitor becomes K times.

Reason The surface density of charge on the plate remains constant or unchanged. NCERT Pg. 68

9 **Assertion** If three capacitors of capacitances $C_1 < C_2 < C_3$ are connected in parallel and in series, then their equivalent capacitances.

$$C_p > C_s$$

where, C_p and C_s are the equivalent capacitances in parallel and series, respectively.

Reason $\frac{1}{C_p} = \frac{1}{C_1} + \frac{1}{C_2} + \frac{1}{C_3}$ and $C_s = C_1 + C_2 + C_3$

where, C_p and C_s is the equivalent capacitance in parallel and series, respectively. NCERT Pg. 68

10 **Assertion** When a capacitor is charged to a certain potential and a dielectric material is placed between its plates without disconnecting the battery, then the charge on the capacitor remains constant.

Reason By inserting dielectric material between the plates of a capacitor, its capacitance increases. NCERT Pg. 69

Statement Based Questions

Direction (Q.Nos.1-8) *In the following questions, Statement I and Statement II are given. Read the statements and choose most appropriate answer from the options given below.*

(a) Both Statement I and Statement II are false.
(b) Statement I is true but Statement II is false.
(c) Statement I is false but Statement II is true.
(d) Both Statement I and Statement II are true.

1 **Statement I** For a non-uniformly charged thin circular ring with net charge is zero, the electric field at any point on axis of the ring is zero.
Statement II For a non-uniformly charged thin circular ring with net charge is zero, the electric potential at each point on axis of the ring is zero. NCERT Pg. 47

2 **Statement I** At any point inside the sphere, electric intensity is zero.
Statement II At any point inside the conducting sphere, the electrostatic potential is equal to potential on the surface.

3 **Statement I** Two equipotential surfaces cannot cut each other.
Statement II Two equipotential surfaces are parallel to each other. NCERT Pg. 54

4 **Statement I** In metals, the positive ions are made up of the nuclei and the bound electrons remain held in their fixed positions.
Statement II In electrolytic conductors, the charge carriers are both positive and negative ions. NCERT Pg. 61

5 **Statement I** Conductors having equal positive charge and volume, must also have same potential.
Statement II Electric potential depends only on charge and volume of conductor. NCERT Pg. 61

6 **Statement I** In an external electric field, the positive and negative charges of a non-polar molecule are displaced in opposite directions.
Statement II In non-polar molecules, displacement stops when the external force on the constituent charges of the molecule is balanced by the restoring force. NCERT Pg. 65

7 **Statement I** Electric field vector **(E)**, electric displacement vector **(D)** and electric polarisation vector **(P)** are mutually perpendicular to each other.

Statement II Electric field vector **(E)**, electric displacement vector **(D)** and electric polarisation vector **(P)** are mutually parallel to each other. NCERT Pg. 66

8 **Statement I** Increasing the charge on the plates of a capacitor means increasing the capacitance.
Statement II Capacitance is directly proportional to charge. NCERT Pg. 68

Matching Type Questions

1 Match the Column I (potential) with Column II (value) for electric potential at different points P_1, P_2, P_3 and P_4 as shown in the figure with respect to an electric dipole. NCERT Pg. 51

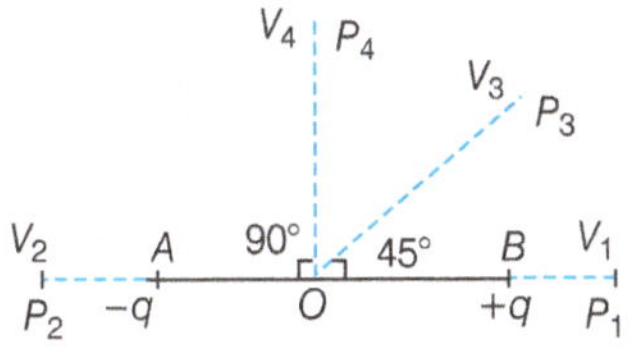

Each points P_1, P_2, P_3 and P_4 are at equal distance r from mid-point O of the dipole.

Column I		Column II
A. V_1	1.	0
B. V_2	2.	$\frac{p}{4\sqrt{2}\pi\varepsilon_0 r^2}$
C. V_3	3.	$\frac{-p}{4\pi\varepsilon_0 r^2}$
D. V_4	4.	$\frac{p}{4\pi\varepsilon_0 r^2}$

Choose the correct answer from the options given below.

Codes

	A	B	C	D		A	B	C	D
(a)	3	4	2	1	(b)	1	2	3	4
(c)	4	3	2	1	(d)	4	3	1	2

2 Consider a dielectric inserted between the plates fully occupying the intervening region. The surface charge densities on the charged plates are $\pm\sigma$. Match the Column I (parameter of capacitor) with Column II (value). NCERT Pg. 69

Column I		Column II
A. Electric field E	1.	$Qd / A\varepsilon_0 K$
B. Potential difference V across the plates	2.	$(\sigma - \sigma_p) / \varepsilon_0$
C. The capacitance C, with dielectric between the plates	3.	C / C_0
D. Dielectric constant of the substance (K)	4.	$\varepsilon_0 KA/d$

Choose the correct answer from the options given below.

Codes

	A	B	C	D		A	B	C	D
(a)	1	2	3	4	(b)	2	1	4	3
(c)	3	4	1	2	(d)	4	2	3	1

3 Match the Column I (charge on capacitor) with Column II (value). NCERT Pg. 72

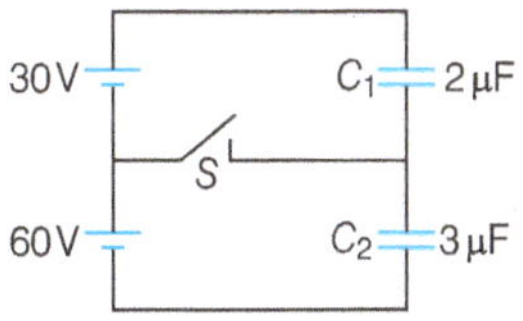

Column I		Column II
A. Charge on both the capacitors (S open)	1.	108 μC
B. Charge on C_2 (S closed)	2.	240 μC
C. Charge on C_1 (S closed)	3.	60 μC
D. Charge on C_1 and C_2 (S closed)	4.	180 μC

Choose the correct answer from the options given below.

Codes

	A	B	C	D
(a)	1	2	3	4
(b)	4	3	2	1
(c)	1	4	3	2
(d)	1	3	2	4

4 A capacitor C_1 of capacitance C is charged to a potential difference V_0. The terminals of the charged capacitor are then connected to an uncharged capacitor C_2 of capacitance $C/2$. Match the Column I (energy of capacitor) with Column II (value). NCERT Pg. 74

Column I		Column II
A. Final energy of capacitor C_1	1.	$-(1/6)\, CV_0^2$
B. Final energy of capacitor C_2	2.	$(1/3)\, CV_0^2$
C. Final energy of the system	3.	$(2/9)\, CV_0^2$
D. Change in energy on joining the capacitors	4.	$(1/9)\, CV_0^2$

Choose the correct answer from the options given below.

Codes

	A	B	C	D
(a)	1	2	2	4
(b)	3	4	2	1
(c)	4	3	2	1
(d)	1	2	2	3

Numerical Type Questions

1 For a charged spherical ball, electrostatic potential inside the ball varies with r as $V = 2ar^2 + b$. Here, a and b are constants and r is the distance from the centre. The volume charge density inside the ball is $-\beta a\varepsilon$. The value of β is ....
ε = permittivity of the medium. NCERT Pg. 48

2 216 identical drops of mercury are charged to a potential of 2 V each. The drops are joined to form a single drop. The potential of this drop is .... V. NCERT Pg. 48

3 A capacitor C_1 of capacitance 10 μF is charged to a potential of 30 V using a battery. The battery is then removed and the charged capacitor is connected to an uncharged capacitor C_2 of capacitance 10 μF as shown in figure.

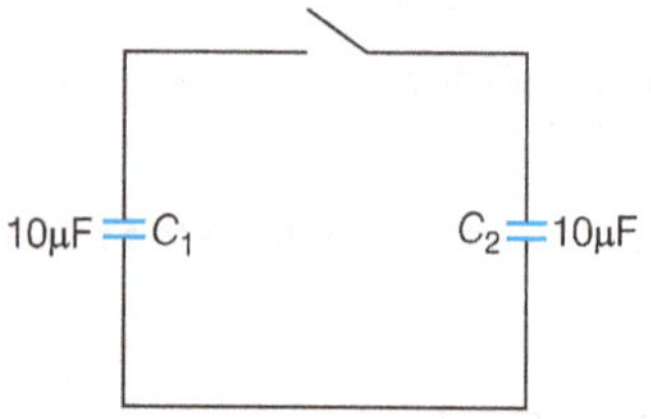

When the switch is closed, charge flows between the capacitors. At equilibrium, the charge on the capacitor C_2 is .... μC. NCERT Pg. 69

4 A parallel plate capacitor has plate area 105 m^2 and plate separation of 15 m. The space between the plates is filled upto a thickness of 5 m with a material of dielectric constant of 10. The resultant capacitance of the system is $x \times 10^{-13}$F. NCERT Pg. 70

The value of $\varepsilon_0 = 8.85 \times 10^{-12} C^2 / N\text{-}m^2$.

The value of x to the nearest integer is ....

5 A parallel plate capacitor with air between the plates has a capacitance of 18 pF. The separation between the plate becomes half and the space between them is filled with a medium of dielectric constant 3.5. Then, the capacitance becomes $\frac{x}{4}$ pF. The value of x is NCERT Pg. 70

6 A capacitor has capacitance 15 μF when it's parallel plates are separated by air medium of thickness d. A slab of material of dielectric constant 1.5 having area equal to that of plates but thickness $\frac{d}{2}$ is inserted between the plates. Capacitance of the capacitor in the presence of slab will be ...... μF. NCERT Pg. 70

7 A 2 μF capacitor C_1 is first charged to a potential difference of 100 V using a battery. Then, the battery is removed and the capacitor is connected to an uncharged capacitor C_2 of 8 μF. The potential on C_2 in equilibrium condition is ...... V.
(Round off to the nearest integer) NCERT Pg. 70

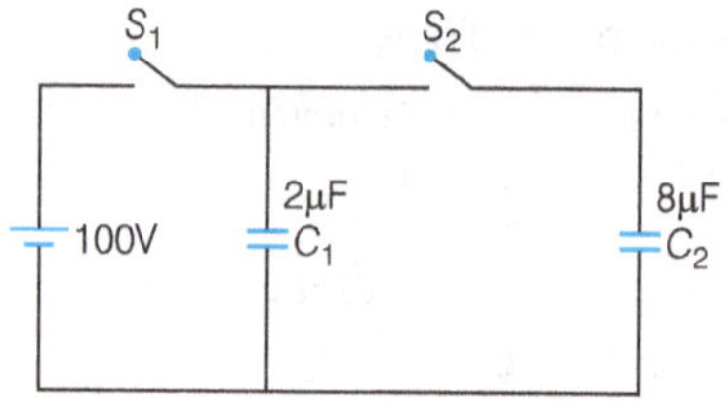

8 Four identical rectangular plates with length, $l = 5$ cm and breadth, $b = \frac{6}{5}$ cm are arranged as shown in figure.

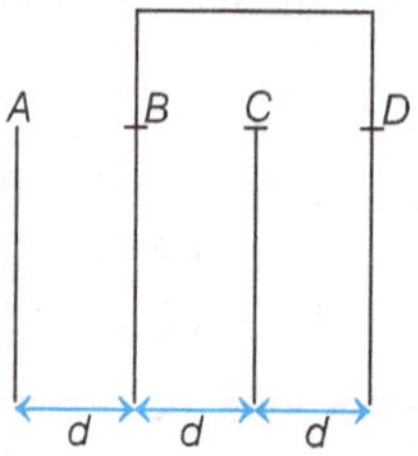

The equivalent capacitance between A and C is $\frac{x\varepsilon_0}{d}$. The value of x is .... NCERT Pg. 72

9 A 80 pF capacitor is fully charged by a 20 V supply. It is then disconnected from the supply and is connected to another uncharged 80pF capacitor is parallel. The electrostatic energy that is lost in this process by the time, the charge is redistributed between them is (in nJ). NCERT Pg. 74

10 A 400 pF capacitor is charged by 200 V supply. It is then disconnected from the supply and is connected to another uncharged 400 pF capacitor. Energy stored in each capacitor is $x \times 10^{-6}$ J. The value of x is .... NCERT Pg. 70

NCERT Exemplar Questions

1 A positively charged particle is released from rest in an uniform electric field. The electric potential energy of the charge

(a) remains constant because the electric field is uniform

(b) increases because the charge moves along the electric field

(c) decreases because the charge moves along the electric field

(d) decreases because the charge moves opposite to the electric field

2 Figure shows some equipotential lines distributed in space. A charged object is moved from point A to point B.

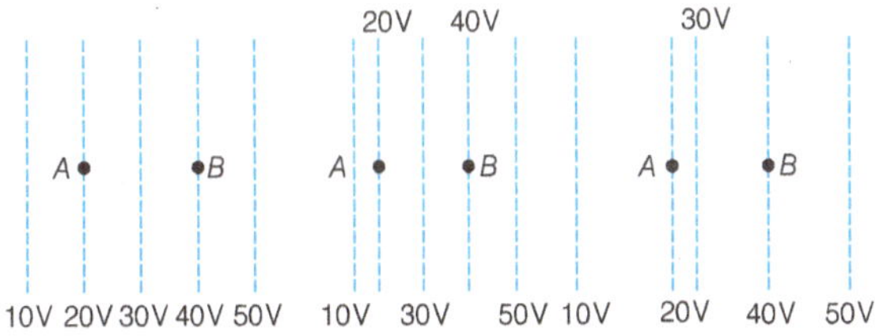

Fig. (i) Fig. (ii) Fig. (iii)

(a) The work done in Fig. (i) is the greatest

(b) The work done in Fig. (ii) is least

(c) The work done is the same in Figs. (i), (ii) and (iii)

(d) The work done in Fig. (iii) is greater than Fig. (ii) but equal to that in Fig. (i)

3 Equipotentials at a great distance from a collection of charges whose total sum is not zero, are approximately

(a) spheres (b) planes

(c) paraboloids (d) ellipsoids

4 A parallel plate capacitor is made of two dielectric blocks in series. One of the blocks has thickness d_1 and dielectric constant K_1 and the other has thickness d_2 and dielectric constant K_2 as shown in figure. This arrangement can be thought as a dielectric slab of thickness $d\ (=d_1 + d_2)$ and effective dielectric constant K, then K is`

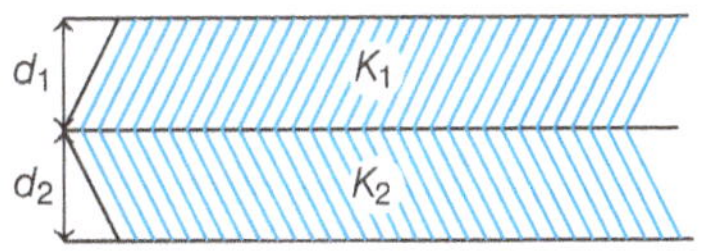

(a) $\dfrac{K_1 d_1 + K_2 d_2}{d_1 + d_2}$ (b) $\dfrac{K_1 d_1 + K_2 d_2}{K_1 + K_2}$

(c) $\dfrac{K_1 K_2 (d_1 + d_2)}{(K_1 d_2 + K_2 d_1)}$ (d) $\dfrac{2K_1 K_2}{K_1 + K_2}$

Past Exams Questions

NEET

1 Given below are two statements. One is labelled as Assertion (A) and the other is labelled as Reason (R).

Assertion (A) The potential V at any axial point, at 2 m distance r from the centre of the dipole of dipole moment vector **p** of magnitude, 4×10^{-6} C m, is $\pm 9 \times 10^3$ V.

(Take, $\dfrac{1}{4\pi\varepsilon_0} = 9 \times 10^9$ SI units)

Reason (R) $V = \pm \dfrac{2p}{4\pi\varepsilon_0 r^2}$, where r is the distance of any axial point, situated at 2 m from the centre of the dipole. NCERT Pg. 48, NEET 2024

In the light of the above statements, choose the correct answer from the options given below.

(a) Both A and R are true and R is the correct explanation of A.

(b) Both A and R are true but R is not the correct explanation of A.

(c) A is true but R is false.

(d) A is false but R is true.

2 A thin spherical shell is charged by some source. The potential difference between the two points C and P (in V) shown in the figure is

(Take, $\dfrac{1}{4\pi\varepsilon_0} = 9 \times 10^9$ SI units)

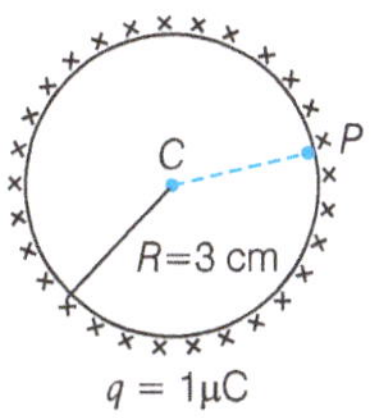

NCERT Pg. 47, NEET 2024

(a) 3×10^5 (b) 1×10^5

(c) 0.5×10^5 (d) zero

3 If the plates of a parallel plate capacitor connected to a battery are moved close to each other, then

A. the charge stored in it, increases.

B. the energy stored in it, decreases.

C. its capacitance increases.

D. the ratio of charge to its potential remains the same.
E. the product of charge and voltage increases.

NCERT Pg. 74, NEET 2024

Choose the most appropriate answer from the options given below

(a) A, B and E only (b) A, C and E only
(c) B, D and E only (d) A, B and C only

4 In the following circuit, the equivalent capacitance between terminal A and terminal B is

NCERT Pg. 70, NEET 2024

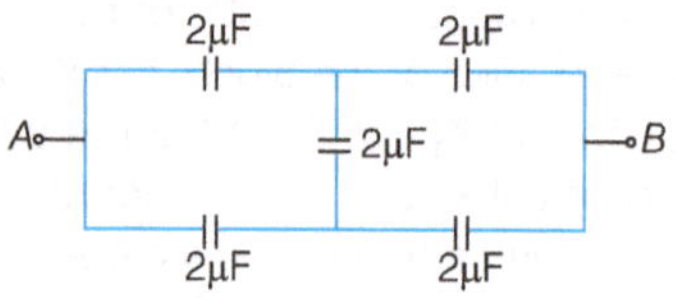

(a) 2 μF (b) 1 μF (c) 0.5 μF (d) 4 μF

5 The equivalent capacitance of the system shown in the following circuit is

NCERT Pg. 72, NEET 2023

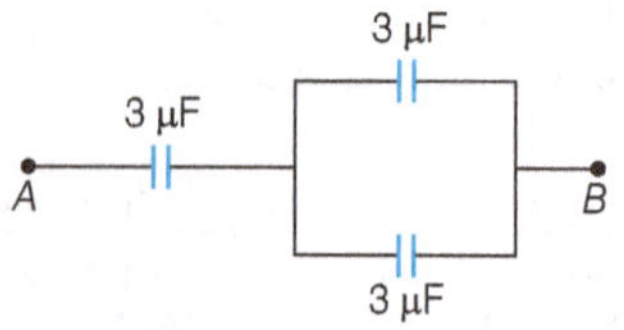

(a) 3 μF (b) 6 μF (c) 9 μF (d) 2 μF

6 Two hollow conducting spheres of radii R_1 and $R_2 (R_1 > R_2)$ have equal charges. The potential would be

NCERT Pg. 52, NEET 2022

(a) more on smaller sphere
(b) equal on both the spheres
(c) dependent on the material property of the sphere
(d) more on bigger sphere

7 Twenty seven drops of same size are charged at V_1 potential each. They combine to form a bigger drop. The potential of the bigger drop is V_2. Find the ratio V_2 / V_2. Ignore the change in density of the fluid on combining the drops.

NCERT Pg. 52, NEET 2021

(a) –2 (b) 3 (c) 14 (d) 9

8 Two charged spherical conductors of radii R_1 and R_2 are connected by a wire. Then, the ratio of surface charge densities of the spheres (σ_1 / σ_2) is

NCERT Pg. 52, NEET 2021

(a) $\frac{R_1}{R_2}$ (b) $\frac{R_2}{R_1}$ (c) $\sqrt{\left(\frac{R_1}{R_2}\right)}$ (d) $\frac{R_1^2}{R_2^2}$

9 A capacitor of capacitance $C = 900$ pF is charged fully by 100 V battery B as shown in fig. (a). Then, it is disconnected from the battery and connected to another uncharged capacitor of capacitance $C = 900$ pF as shown in fig. (b). The electrostatic energy stored by the system (b) is

NCERT Pg. 74, NEET 2021

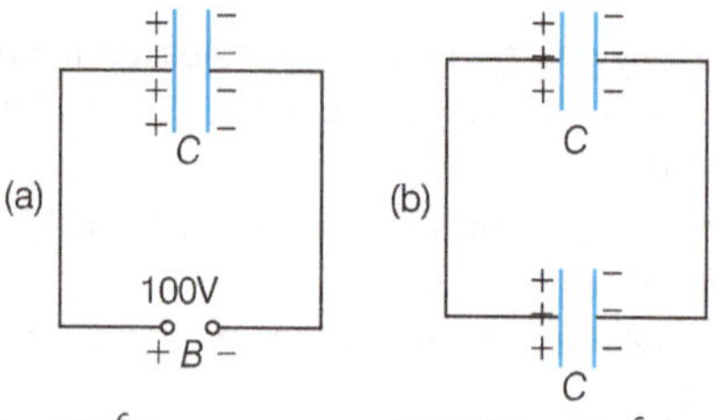

(a) 3.25×10^{-6} J (b) 2.25×10^{-6} J
(c) 1.5×10^{-6} J (d) 4.5×10^{-6} J

10 The equivalent capacitance of the combination shown in the figure is

NCERT Pg. 71, NEET 2021

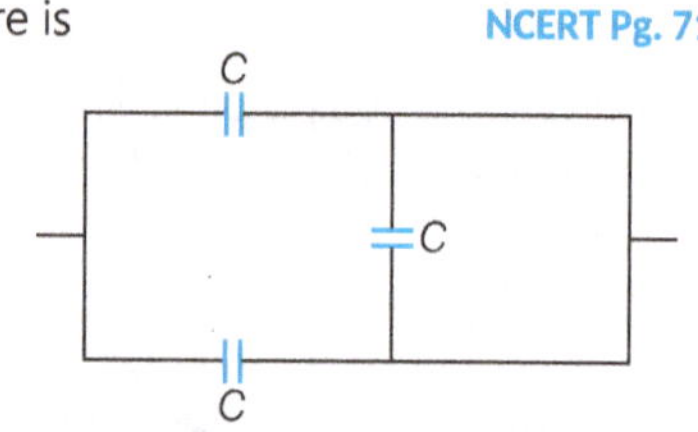

(a) $3C$ (b) $2C$ (c) $C/2$ (d) $3C/2$

11 A short electric dipole has a dipole moment of 16×10^{-9} C-m. The electric potential due to the dipole at a point at a distance of 0.6 m from the centre of the dipole, situated on a line making an angle of 60° with the dipole axis is $\left(\frac{1}{4\pi\varepsilon_0} = 9 \times 10^9 \text{ Nm}^2 / \text{C}^2\right)$

NCERT Pg. 52, NEET 2020

(a) 200 V (b) 400 V (c) zero
(d) 50 V

12 A parallel plate capacitor having cross-sectional area A and separation d has air in between the plates. Now, an insulating slab of same area but thickness $d/2$ is inserted between the plates as shown in figure having dielectric constant $(K = 4)$. The ratio of new capacitance to its original capacitance will be

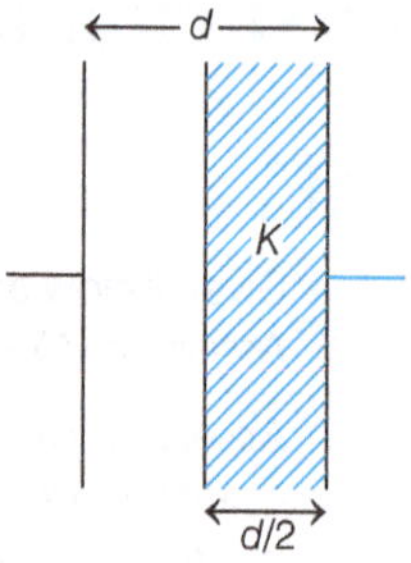

NCERT Pg. 71, NEET 2020

(a) 2 : 1 (b) 8 : 5
(c) 6 : 5 (d) 4 : 1

13. The electrostatic force between the metal plates of an isolated parallel plate capacitor C having a charge Q and area A, is

NCERT Pg. 74, NEET 2018

(a) proportional to the square root of the distance between the plates
(b) linearly proportional to the distance between the plates
(c) independent of the distance between the plates
(d) inversely proportional to the distance between the plates

14. The diagrams below show regions of equipotentials.

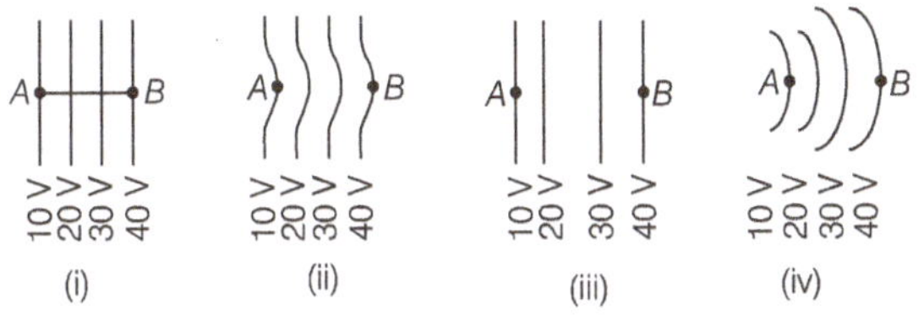

A positive charge is moved from A to B in each diagram. **NCERT Pg. 55, NEET 2017**

(a) Maximum work is required to move q in figure (iii)
(b) In all the four cases, the work done is the same
(c) Minimum work is required to move q in figure (i)
(d) Maximum work is required to move q in figure (ii)

15. A capacitor of $2\,\mu$F is charged as shown in the figure. When the switch S is turned to position 2, the percentage of its stored energy dissipated is **NCERT Pg. 80, NEET 2016**

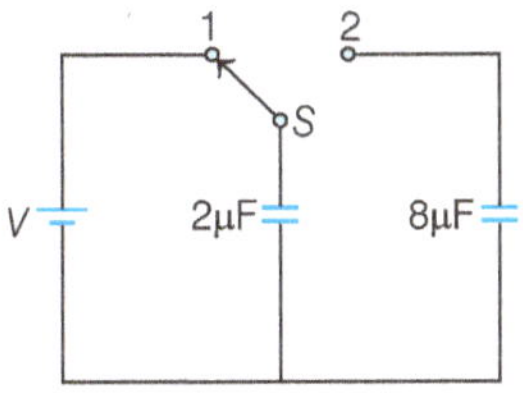

(a) 20% (b) 75%
(c) 80% (d) 0%

JEE Main

16. The distance between two plates of a capacitor is d and its capacitance is C_1, when air is the medium between the plates. If a metal sheet of thickness $\frac{2d}{3}$ and of the same area as plate is introduced between the plates, the capacitance of the capacitor becomes C_2. The ratio $\frac{C_2}{C_1}$ is **NCERT Pg. 70, JEE Main 2023**

(a) 3 : 1 (b) 1 : 1
(c) 4 : 1 (d) 2 : 1

17. A parallel plate capacitor of capacitance 2F is charged to a potential V. The energy stored in the capacitor is E_1. The capacitor is now connected to another uncharged identical capacitor in parallel combination. The energy stored in the combination is E_2. The ratio E_2 / E_1 is **NCERT Pg. 70, JEE Main 2023**

(a) 1 : 2 (b) 1 : 4 (c) 2 : 3 (d) 2 : 1

18. Two identical thin metal plates has charges q_1 and q_2, respectively, such that $q_1 > q_2$. The plates were brought close to each other to form a parallel plate capacitor of capacitance C. The potential difference between them is **NCERT Pg. 69, JEE Main 2022**

(a) $\frac{(q_1 + q_2)}{C}$ (b) $\frac{(q_1 - q_2)}{C}$ (c) $\frac{(q_1 - q_2)}{2C}$ (d) $\frac{2(q_1 - q_2)}{C}$

19. A charge Q is distributed over two concentric conducting thin spherical shells radii r and R $(R > r)$. If the surface charge densities on the two shells are equal, the electric potential at the common centre is **NCERT Pg. 52, JEE Main 2020**

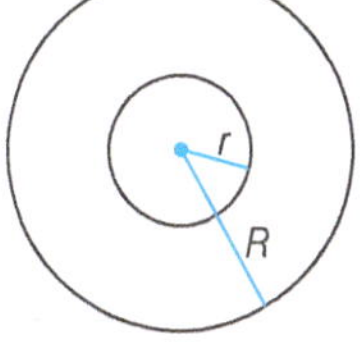

(a) $\frac{1}{4\pi\varepsilon_0}\frac{(R + r)}{2(R^2 + r^2)}Q$ (b) $\frac{1}{4\pi\varepsilon_0}\frac{(2R + r)}{(R^2 + r^2)}Q$

(c) $\frac{1}{4\pi\varepsilon_0}\frac{(R + 2r)Q}{2(R^2 + r^2)}$ (d) $\frac{1}{4\pi\varepsilon_0}\frac{(R + r)}{(R^2 + r^2)}Q$

Skill Boosters

1 Consider a uniform electric field in a region as shown below.

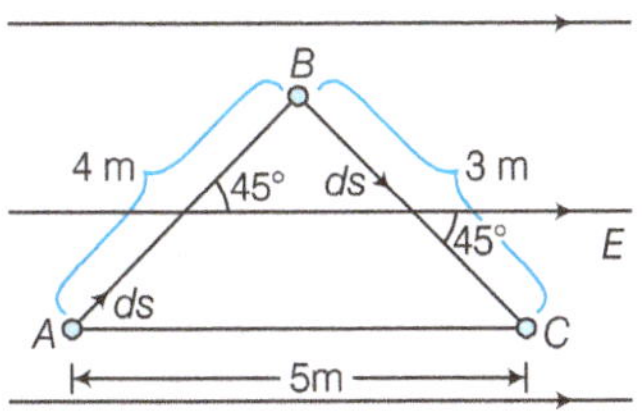

Then, potential difference between points A and C is given by

(a) $V_A - V_C = -\int_{AB} Eds\cos 45° - \int_{BC} Eds\cos 45°$
(b) $V_A - V_C - V_C = -\int_{AB} Eds\cos 45° - \int_{BC} Eds\cos 45°$
(c) $V_A - V_C = 5\,E$
(d) $V_C - V_A = 5\,E$

2 Two identical thin rings, each of radius R, coaxially placed a distance R apart. If Q_1 and Q_2 are respectively the charges, uniformly spread on the two rings, the work done in moving a charge q from the centre of one ring to that of the other is

(a) zero
(b) $q(Q_1 - Q_2)(\sqrt{2} - 1)/\sqrt{2}\,(4\pi\varepsilon_0 R)$
(c) $q\sqrt{2}\,(Q_1 + Q_2)/(4\pi\varepsilon_0 R)$
(d) $q(Q_1/Q_2)(\sqrt{2} + 1)\sqrt{2}\,(4\pi\varepsilon_0 R)$

3 Electric potential at the point P on axis of the charged disc with a hole is

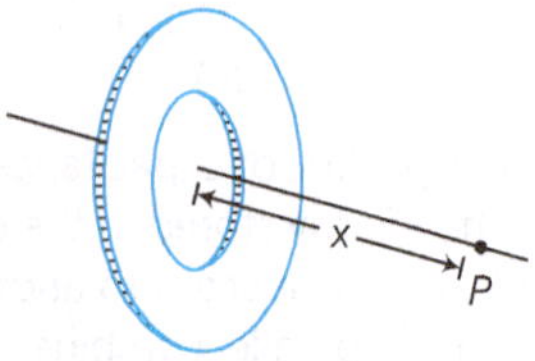

(Given, hole radius $= a$, outer radius $= b$ and charge density on surface $= \sigma$)

(a) $k\sigma(\sqrt{x^2+b^2} - \sqrt{x^2+a^2})$

(b) $\frac{k\pi\sigma}{4}(\sqrt{x^2+b^2} - \sqrt{x^2+a^2})$

(c) $4\pi k\sigma(\sqrt{x^2+b^2} - \sqrt{x^2+a^2})$

(d) $2\pi k\sigma(\sqrt{x^2+b^2} - \sqrt{x^2+a^2})$

4 A non-conducting disc of radius a and uniform positive surface charge density σ is placed on ground with its axis vertical. A particle of negligible mass 'm' and positive charge q is dropped along the axis of disc from height H with zero initial velocity. For particle, $\frac{q}{m} = \frac{4\varepsilon_0 g}{\sigma}$.

Potential energy (U) *versus* height (H) curve for the particle is

(a)
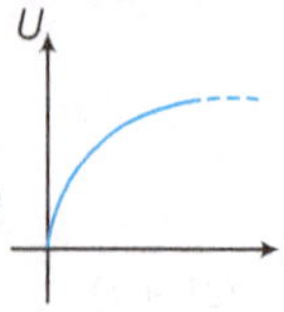

(b)
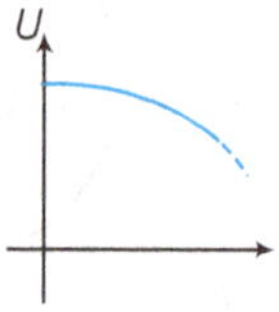

(c)
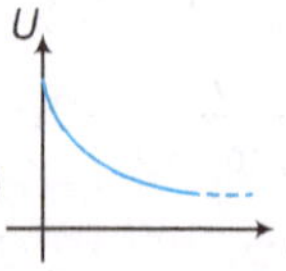

(d)
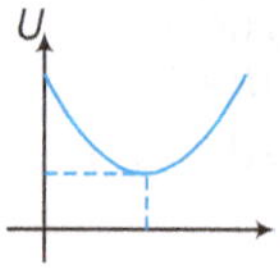

5 Two large metal plates are maintained at potentials $+V_0$ and $-V_0$ at a distance d from each other. A small conducting ball of mass m and radius R $(R << d)$ is suspended between the plates. The thread supporting the ball is a thin copper wire connected to the ground so that potential of ball is fixed at $V = 0$.

The ball hangs vertically in equilibrium when V_0 is sufficiently small.

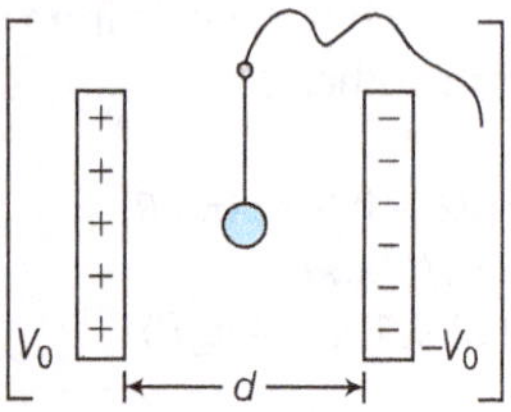

The equilibrium of ball is unstable when V_0 exceeds the critical value of $V_0 = \left(\frac{d^2mg}{N(4\pi\varepsilon_0 RL)}\right)^{1/2}$

The value of N in the above expression is

(a) 2 (b) 3 (c) 4 (d) 6

6 A massless rigid rod of length L carries two small spheres each of mass m and charge q at each of its ends. This rod is held in a region of uniform electric field **E** such that the rod makes a small angle θ (around 3 to 5°) with the direction of field.

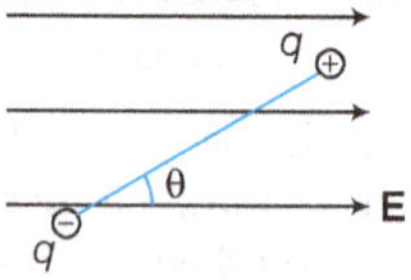

Least time required by rod to become parallel to field is

(a) $\frac{\pi}{2}\sqrt{\frac{mL}{2qE}}$ (b) $\frac{\pi}{4}\sqrt{\frac{mL}{qE}}$

(c) $2\pi\sqrt{\frac{mL}{2qE}}$ (d) None of these

7 The variation of electric field between two charges q_1 and q_2 along the line joining charges is as shown below.

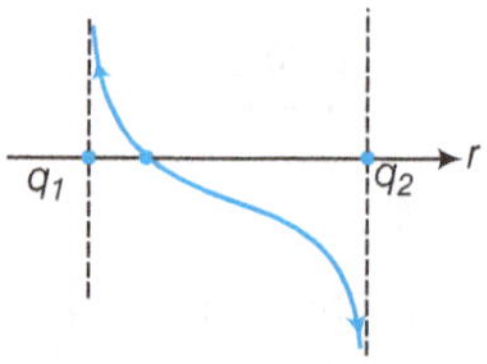

Then,

I. q_1 and q_2 are positive and $q_1 < q_2$.

II. q_1 and q_2 are positive and $q_1 > q_2$.

III. q_1 is positive, q_2 is negative and $q_1 < q_2$.

IV. q_1 and q_2 are negative and $q_1 < q_2$.

Correct option is

(a) I and II (b) I and IV (c) II and III (d) II and IV

8 A rectangular surface in XOY-plane extends from $x = 0$ to $x = w$ and $y = 0$ to $y = h$. If an electric field $\mathbf{E} = ay\hat{\mathbf{i}} + bz\hat{\mathbf{j}} + cx\hat{\mathbf{k}}$ exists in the region, then flux through the surface is

(a) $\frac{cw^2b}{2}$ (b) $\frac{chw^2}{2}$ (c) $\frac{c^2hw}{2}$ (d) $\frac{cw^2a}{2}$

9 Two spherical shells are as shown in figure.

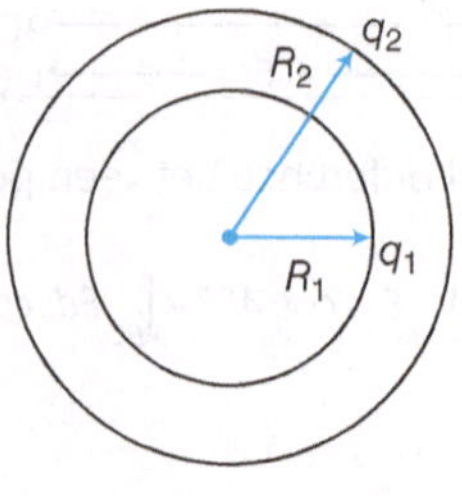

Let r be the distance of a point from their common centre. Then, electric field for $R_1 < r < R_2$.

(a) is constant for q_2 and vary for q_1
(b) is zero for q_2 and vary for q_1
(c) is constant
(d) is zero.

10 A point charge Q is placed at a distance $\frac{r}{2}$ above an imaginary Gaussian sphere of radius r as shown.

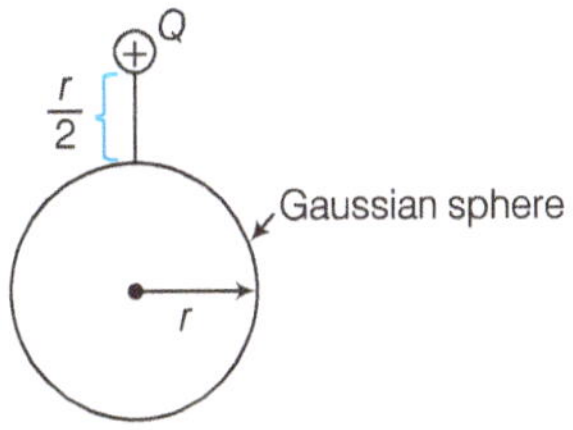

Let E, denotes magnitude of electric field over the Gaussian surface. Value of $E_{max} - E_{min}$ is

(a) $\frac{24\,Q}{25\pi\varepsilon_0 r^2}$ (b) $\frac{20\,Q}{17\pi\varepsilon_0 r^2}$ (c) $\frac{12\,Q}{13\pi\varepsilon_0 r^2}$ (d) $\frac{7\,Q}{5\,\pi\varepsilon_0 r^2}$

Correct Codes

Topical Questions

1 (a)	2 (c)	3 (c)	4 (d)	5 (a)	6 (c)	7 (a)	8 (b)	9 (a)	10 (a)
11 (b)	12 (b)	13 (b)	14 (a)	15 (c)	16 (b)	17 (a)	18 (d)	19 (c)	20 (a)
21 (a)	22 (b)	23 (a)	24 (b)	25 (c)	26 (a)	27 (d)	28 (b)	29 (c)	30 (a)
31 (b)	32 (d)	33 (d)	34 (a)	35 (a)	36 (a)	37 (d)	38 (d)	39 (d)	40 (a)
41 (b)	42 (a)	43 (a)	44 (b)	45 (a)	46 (d)	47 (a)	48 (b)	49 (a)	50 (c)
51 (a)	52 (a)	53 (b)	54 (b)	55 (b)	56 (c)	57 (c)	58 (b)	59 (c)	60 (a)
61 (a)	62 (c)	63 (d)	64 (c)	65 (a)	66 (a)	67 (c)	68 (a)	69 (b)	70 (b)
71 (a)	72 (a)	73 (b)	74 (d)	75 (b)	76 (c)	77 (b)	78 (d)	79 (c)	80 (d)
81 (b)	82 (d)	83 (b)	84 (d)	85 (c)	86 (c)	87 (c)	88 (a)	89 (d)	90 (c)
91 (b)	92 (d)	93 (a)	94 (d)	95 (c)	96 (d)	97 (c)	98 (b)	99 (c)	

Assertion and Reason Questions

1 (a)	2 (d)	3 (b)	4 (a)	5 (a)	6 (c)	7 (c)	8 (c)	9 (c)	10 (d)

Statement Based Questions

1 (c)	2 (d)	3 (b)	4 (d)	5 (a)	6 (d)	7 (c)	8 (a)

Matching Type Questions

1 (c)	2 (b)	3 (c)	4 (b)

Numerical Type Questions

1 (12)	2 (72)	3 (150)	4 (885)	5 (504)	6 (45)	7 (20)	8 (4)	9 (8)	10 (2)

NCERT Exemplar Questions

1 (c)	2 (c)	3 (a)	4 (c)

Past Exams Questions

1 (c)	2 (d)	3 (b)	4 (a)	5 (d)	6 (a)	7 (d)	8 (b)	9 (b)	10 (b)
11 (a)	12 (b)	13 (c)	14 (b)	15 (c)	16 (a)	17 (b)	18 (c)	19 (d)	

Skill Boosters

1 (c)	2 (b)	3 (d)	4 (d)	5 (c)	6 (a)	7 (b)	8 (b)	9 (b)	10 (a)

Step by Step

Decoding the Questions

Concept Builders

1 No
2 False (F)
3 True (T)
4 True (T)
5 spherically, cylindrically
6 smaller
7 True (T)
8 False (F)
9 reduce
10 zero
11 False (F)
12 conductor
13 can
14 True (T)
15 True (T)
16 independent
17 $-pE$
18 False (F)
19 increases, decreases
20 zero, non-zero

Topical Questions

4 (*d*) Since, $V_B - V_A = \dfrac{W_{AB}}{q_0}$,

$$V - (-10\text{V}) = \frac{100\text{ J}}{4\text{C}} = 25\text{ V}$$

or $\quad V = 25\text{ V} - 10\text{ V} = 15\text{ V}$

6 (*c*) $|E| = \left.\dfrac{dV}{dx}\right|_{x=4} = \left.-\dfrac{d}{dx}(4x^{\frac{3}{2}})\right|_{x=4}$

$$= \left.4 \times \frac{3}{2} x^{\frac{1}{2}}\right|_{x=4}$$

$$= 6 \times (4)^{\frac{1}{2}} = 12\text{ V/m}$$

8 (*b*) Electrostatic force between any two positive charges q_1 and q_2 separated by a distance r is given by

$$\mathbf{F}_{21} = \frac{q_1 q_2}{4\pi\varepsilon_0 r^2}\hat{\mathbf{r}}$$

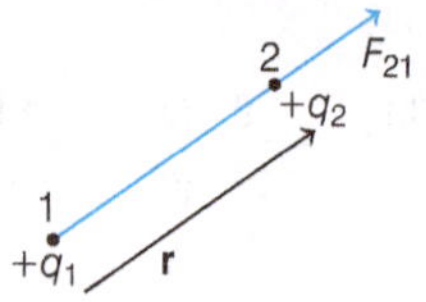

In this case $q_1 = +Q$, $q_2 = +1\text{C}$ and $r = r'$

$$\Rightarrow \quad \mathbf{F} = \frac{Q \times 1}{4\pi\varepsilon_0 (r')^2}\hat{\mathbf{r}}' \quad \text{...(i)}$$

Total work done W by the external force is obtained by integrating Eq. (i) from $r' = \infty$ to $r' = r$

$$\therefore \quad W = -\int_\infty^r \frac{Q}{4\pi\varepsilon_0 (r')^2} dr'$$

$$= \left|\frac{Q}{4\pi\varepsilon_0 r'}\right|_\infty^r = \frac{Q}{4\pi\varepsilon_0 r}$$

9 (*a*) Potential at point A due to a point charge q at origin O,

$$V_A = \frac{1}{4\pi\varepsilon_0} \cdot \frac{q}{a}$$

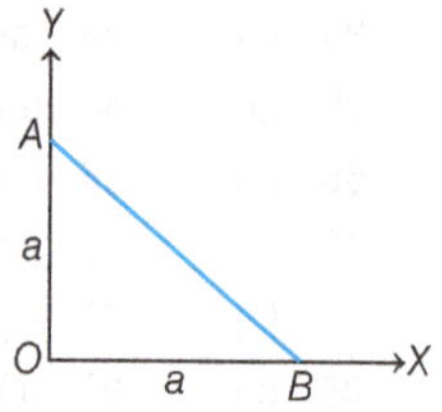

Similarly,

Potential at point B, $V_B = \dfrac{1}{4\pi\varepsilon_0} \cdot \dfrac{q}{a}$

So, work done in taking a test charge $-Q$ from A to B,

$$W = (V_A - V_B) \times Q = 0$$

10 (*a*) $E = \dfrac{KQ}{r^2} \Rightarrow E \propto \dfrac{1}{r^2}$

and potential,

$$V = \frac{KQ}{r} \Rightarrow V \propto \frac{1}{r}$$

So, for the values of r such that $0 < r < 1$, the value of E would be more than that of V.

And for $r > 1$, the value of E would be less as compared to that of V.

$\therefore$ From the given graph, it can be concluded that curve I represents E *versus* r and curve II represents V *versus* r.

14 (*a*)

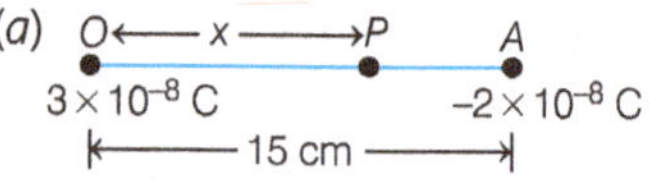

According to question,

$$\frac{1}{4\pi\varepsilon_0}\left[\frac{3 \times 10^{-8}}{x \times 10^{-2}} - \frac{2 \times 10^{-8}}{(15 - x) \times 10^{-2}}\right] = 0$$

$$\Rightarrow \quad \frac{3}{x} - \frac{2}{15 - x} = 0$$

which gives $x = 9$ cm

If x lies on the extended line OA, the required condition is

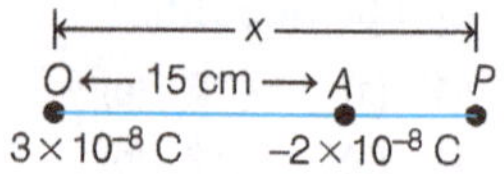

$$\frac{3}{x} - \frac{2}{x - 15} = 0$$

which gives $x = 45$ cm

Thus, electric potential is zero at 9cm and 45cm away from the positive charge on the side of the negative charge.

15 (*c*) Let V_1 be the potential at the centre of the cube due to one charge

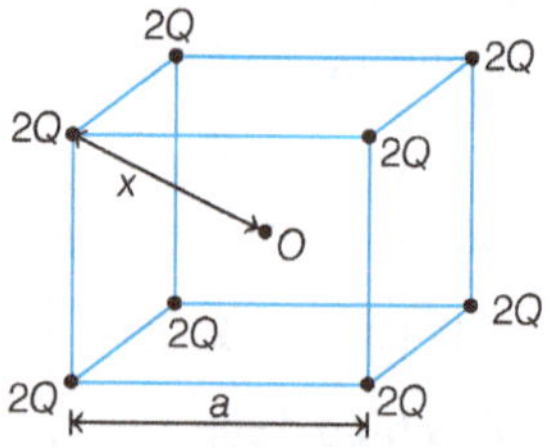

$$\Rightarrow \quad V_1 = \frac{1}{4\pi\varepsilon_0} \cdot \frac{2Q}{x}$$

Distance of centre of cube from its corner, $x = \dfrac{a\sqrt{3}}{2}$.

Potential at centre of cube due to all eight corners of the cube,

$$V = 8V_1$$

$$= 8\left[\frac{1}{4\pi\varepsilon_0} \frac{2Q \times 2}{\sqrt{3}a}\right]$$

$$= \frac{32Q}{4\pi\varepsilon_0 \sqrt{3} \times a} = \frac{8Q}{\sqrt{3}\pi\varepsilon_0 a}$$

16 (b) $V = \dfrac{Q}{4\pi\varepsilon_0}\left[\dfrac{1}{r_1}+\dfrac{1}{r_2}+\dfrac{1}{r_3}\ldots\right]$

$= \dfrac{Q}{4\pi\varepsilon_0}\left[\dfrac{1}{1}+\dfrac{1}{2}+\dfrac{1}{4}+\dfrac{1}{8}+\ldots\right]$

$= \dfrac{Q}{4\pi\varepsilon_0}\cdot\dfrac{1}{\left(1-\dfrac{1}{2}\right)}$

$= \dfrac{Q}{4\pi\varepsilon_0\left(\dfrac{1}{2}\right)} = \dfrac{2Q}{4\pi\varepsilon_0}$

18 (d)

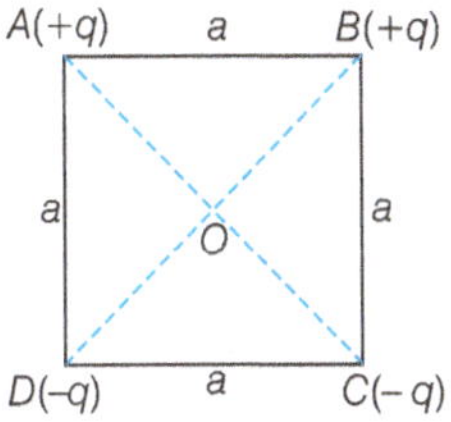

The electric potential at O,

$V = \dfrac{1}{4\pi\varepsilon_0}\left(\dfrac{Q_A}{r_A}+\dfrac{Q_B}{r_B}+\dfrac{Q_C}{r_C}+\dfrac{Q_D}{r_D}\right)$

$r_A = r_B = r_C = r_D = \dfrac{\sqrt{2}a}{2} = \dfrac{a}{\sqrt{2}}$

$\therefore V = \dfrac{1}{4\pi\varepsilon_0}\left[\dfrac{2\times q}{\left(\dfrac{a}{\sqrt{2}}\right)}+\dfrac{2\times(-q)}{\left(\dfrac{a}{\sqrt{2}}\right)}\right]$

$= 0$

19 (c) The potential of metallic sphere

$V = \dfrac{kQ}{R}$

$\therefore \quad Q = \dfrac{VR}{k}$

The magnitude of electric field at a distance r is

$E = \dfrac{kQ}{r^2} = \dfrac{k}{r^2}\left(\dfrac{VR}{k}\right) = \dfrac{VR}{r^2}$

22 (b)

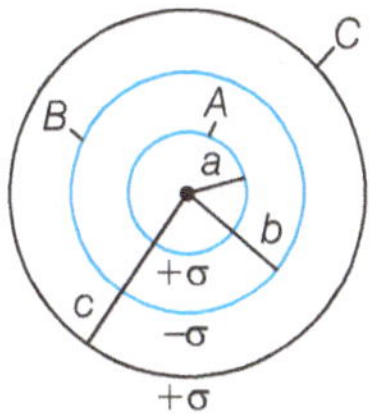

$\therefore \quad V_B = \dfrac{k(Q_A+Q_B)}{b} + \dfrac{kQ_C}{c}$

$= \dfrac{1}{4\pi\varepsilon_0}\left[\dfrac{\sigma 4\pi a^2}{b} - \dfrac{\sigma 4\pi b^2}{b} + \dfrac{\sigma 4\pi c^2}{c}\right]$

$V_B = \dfrac{\sigma}{\varepsilon_0}\left(\dfrac{a^2-b^2}{b}+c\right)$

23 (a) For bigger drop, $V = \dfrac{kQ}{R} = 1\text{V}$

Now, $\dfrac{4}{3}\pi R^3 = 8\times\dfrac{4}{3}\pi r^3$

$\therefore \quad r = \dfrac{R}{2}$

Also, $\rho_{\text{smaller}} = \rho_{\text{bigger}}$

$\Rightarrow \quad \dfrac{q}{\dfrac{4}{3}\pi r^3} = \dfrac{Q}{\dfrac{4}{3}\pi R^3}$

$\Rightarrow \quad q = \dfrac{Q}{8}$

$\therefore$ Potential of smaller drop,

$V = \dfrac{kq}{r} = \dfrac{k\left(\dfrac{Q}{8}\right)}{\left(\dfrac{R}{2}\right)}$

$= \dfrac{1}{4}\left(\dfrac{kQ}{R}\right) = \dfrac{1}{4}\times 1 = \dfrac{1}{4}\text{ V}$

$= 0.25\text{ V}$

25 (c) Given, $\sigma_1 = \sigma_2$

$\Rightarrow \quad \dfrac{q}{4\pi r^2} = \dfrac{Q-q}{4\pi R^2}$

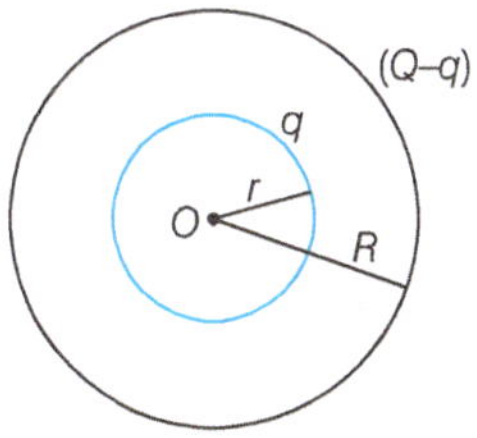

$\Rightarrow \quad \dfrac{q}{r^2} = \dfrac{Q}{R^2} - \dfrac{q}{R^2}$

$\therefore \quad q = \left(\dfrac{r^2}{R^2+r^2}\right)\cdot Q$

$Q - q = \left(\dfrac{R^2}{R^2+r^2}\right)\cdot Q$

$\therefore$ The electric potential at the common centre of the shell,

$V_0 = \dfrac{1}{4\pi\varepsilon_0}\cdot\dfrac{q}{r} + \dfrac{1}{4\pi\varepsilon_0}\cdot\dfrac{(Q-q)}{R}$

$= \dfrac{Q(r+R)}{4\pi\varepsilon_0(R^2+r^2)}$

26 (a) $\Delta V = V_1 - V_2$

$= \left[\dfrac{1}{4\pi\varepsilon_0}\cdot\dfrac{Q}{R_1}\right] - \left[\dfrac{1}{4\pi\varepsilon_0}\cdot\dfrac{Q}{R_2}\right] = V$

$\Rightarrow \Delta V' = V_1' - V_2'$

$= \left[\dfrac{1}{4\pi\varepsilon_0}\cdot\dfrac{Q}{R_1} + \dfrac{1}{4\pi\varepsilon_0}\cdot\dfrac{3Q}{R_2}\right]$

$- \left[\dfrac{1}{4\pi\varepsilon_0}\cdot\dfrac{Q}{R_2} + \dfrac{1}{4\pi\varepsilon_0}\cdot\dfrac{3Q}{R_2}\right]$

$\Rightarrow \Delta V' = V_1' - V_2'$

$= \left[\dfrac{1}{4\pi\varepsilon_0}\cdot\dfrac{Q}{R_1} - \dfrac{1}{4\pi\varepsilon_0}\cdot\dfrac{Q}{R_2}\right] = V$

27 (d) The electric field intensity is larger near sharp edges of charged conductor and also near regions of larger charge densities. Therefore, equipotential surfaces are not always equally spaced.

30 (a) Electric field lines are perpendicular to the equipotential surfaces and point in the direction of decreasing potential. So, at P, electric field **E** is to the left and at R, **E** is upward.

31 (b) As electric field, $E = |V/r|$

$\therefore$ The distance of point charge,

$r = \dfrac{V}{E} = \dfrac{600\text{ V}}{200\text{ NC}^{-1}} = 3\text{ m}$

32 (d) The potential difference between points A and B is

$V_B - V_A = -\int_{a_1}^{a_2} E\,dx - \int_{b_1}^{b_2} E\,dy$

$= -100\int_3^1 dx - 100\int_1^3 dy = 0$

33 (d) $E = -\left.\dfrac{dV}{dx}\right|_{x=1} = 10x - 10|_{x=1}$

$= 10\times 1 - 10 = 0$

34 (a) $E = \left|\dfrac{-dV}{dr}\right| = \left|\dfrac{V_2 - V_1}{x\sin 45^\circ}\right|$

$= \dfrac{10}{(1)\sin 45^\circ} = 10\sqrt{2}$ at 45° with x-axis

$(\because x = 1)$

35 (*a*) $V_{x=2} = -\frac{1}{2} \times 2 \times 10 = 10\text{ V}$

$$V_{x=6} = -\left[\left(\frac{1}{2} \times 2 \times 10\right) + [(4-2) \times 10] + \left(\frac{1}{2} \times 2 \times 10\right)\right]$$

$$= -[10 + 20 + 10] = -40\text{ V}$$

$$\Delta V = V_{x=2} - V_{x=6} = 30\text{ V}$$

36 (*a*) To bring charge q_1 first from infinity to $\mathbf{r}_1$, no work is required. So, while bringing charge q_2 from infinity to $\mathbf{r}_2$, q_1 produces a potential V_1, so work is done in this step can be given as

$$W_1 = q_2 V_1(\mathbf{r}_2) = \frac{1}{4\pi\varepsilon_0} \frac{q_1 q_2}{r_{12}} \quad \text{...(i)}$$

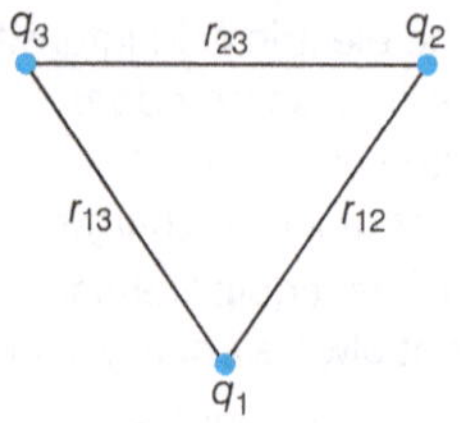

Now, work done in bringing q_3 from infinity to the point $\mathbf{r}_3$ is

$$W_2 = \frac{1}{4\pi\varepsilon_0}\left(\frac{q_1 q_3}{r_{13}} + \frac{q_2 q_3}{r_{23}}\right) \quad \text{...(ii)}$$

The total work done in assembling the charges at the given locations is obtained by combining Eqs. (i) and (ii).

This work done is stored as potential energy and given by

$$U = W_1 + W_2$$

$$= \frac{1}{4\pi\varepsilon_0}\left(\frac{q_1 q_2}{r_{12}} + \frac{q_1 q_3}{r_{13}} + \frac{q_2 q_3}{r_{23}}\right)$$

37 (*d*) In accordance to the principle of superposition, total energy of the charge system as shown in the figure below is

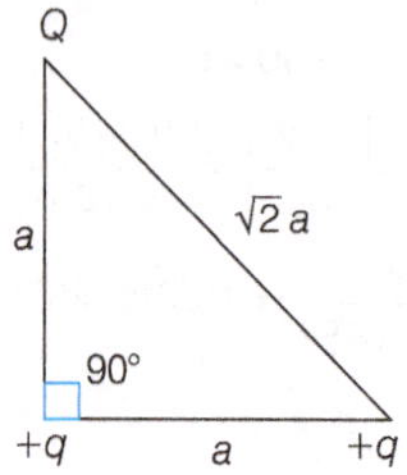

$$U = \frac{Kq^2}{a} + \frac{KQq}{a} + \frac{KQq}{\sqrt{2}a}$$

It is given that, $U = 0$

$$\therefore \quad \frac{Kq}{a}\left[q + Q + \frac{Q}{\sqrt{2}}\right] = 0$$

$$\Rightarrow \quad Q = \frac{-\sqrt{2} \times q}{(\sqrt{2}+1)}$$

38 (*d*) Here, potential energy of the system,

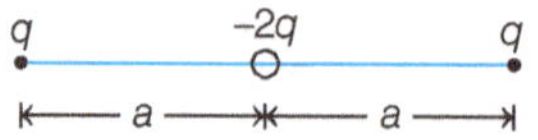

$$U = \frac{1}{4\pi\varepsilon_0}\left[\frac{q_1 q_2}{r_{12}} + \frac{q_1 q_3}{r_{13}} + \frac{q_2 q_3}{r_{23}}\right]$$

$$= \frac{1}{4\pi\varepsilon_0}\left[\frac{qq}{2a} + \frac{q(-2q)}{a} + \frac{q(-2q)}{a}\right]$$

$$= \frac{-7q^2}{8\pi\varepsilon_0 a}$$

39 (*d*) Work done in increasing the separation from a to $2a$ is

$$W = U_f - U_i \quad \text{...(i)}$$

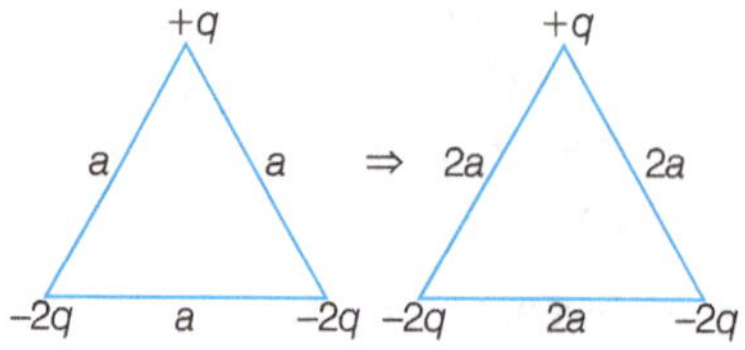

Here, $U_i = \frac{1}{4\pi\varepsilon_0}$

$$\left[\frac{q(-2q)}{a} + \frac{q(-2q)}{a} + \frac{(-2q)(-2q)}{a}\right]$$

$$= \frac{1}{4\pi\varepsilon_0 a}[-2q^2 - 2q^2 + 4q^2] = 0$$

Similarly,

$$U_f = \frac{1}{4\pi\varepsilon_0(2a)}(-2q^2 - 2q^2 + 4q^2)$$

$$= 0$$

Hence, from Eq. (i)

$$W = U_f - U_i = 0$$

40 (*a*) When charge q_3 is at C, then potential energy of the system is

$$U_C = \frac{1}{4\pi\varepsilon_0}\left[\left(\frac{q_1 q_3}{AC} + \frac{q_2 q_3}{BC}\right) + \frac{q_1 q_2}{AB}\right]$$

$$= \frac{1}{4\pi\varepsilon_0}\left\{\left(\frac{q_1 q_3}{0.4} + \frac{q_2 q_3}{0.5}\right) + \frac{q_1 q_2}{0.3}\right\}$$

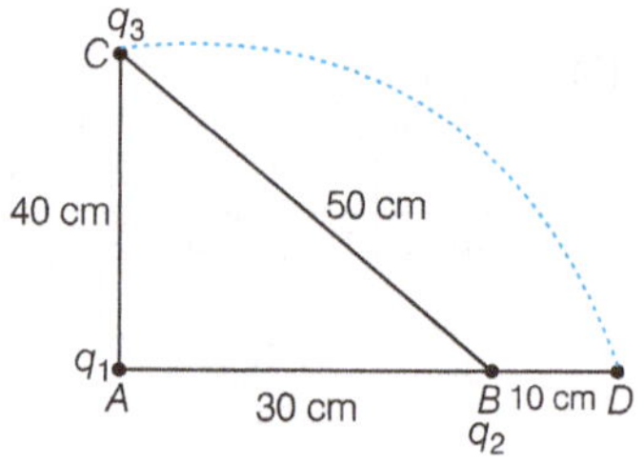

Similarly, when charge q_3 is at D, then potential energy is

$$U_D = \frac{1}{4\pi\varepsilon_0}\left[\left(\frac{q_1 q_3}{AD} + \frac{q_2 q_3}{BD}\right) + \frac{q_1 q_2}{AB}\right]$$

$$= \frac{1}{4\pi\varepsilon_0}\left\{\left(\frac{q_1 q_3}{0.4} + \frac{q_2 q_3}{0.1}\right) + \frac{q_1 q_2}{0.3}\right\}$$

Here, change in potential energy,

$$\Delta U = U_D - U_C$$

$$\frac{q_3}{4\pi\varepsilon_0} K = \frac{1}{4\pi\varepsilon_0}\left(\frac{q_2 q_3}{0.1} - \frac{q_2 q_3}{0.5}\right)$$

$$\left[\because \Delta U = \frac{q_3 K}{4\pi\varepsilon_0}\right]$$

$$\Rightarrow \quad K = \left(\frac{q_2}{0.1} - \frac{q_2}{0.5}\right)$$

$$\Rightarrow \quad K = 8q_2$$

42 (*a*) Suppose, first the charge $+q$ is brought to A and then, the charges $-q$, $+q$ and $-q$ are brought to B, C and D, respectively. The total work needed can be calculated in steps

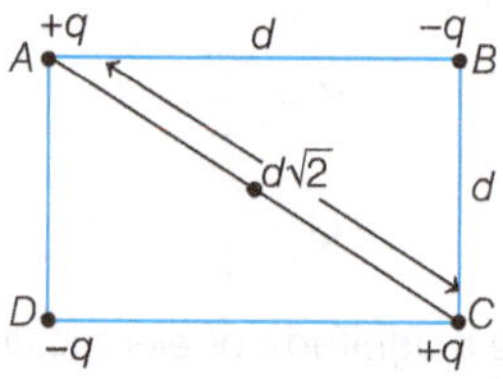

(i) Work needed to bring charge $+q$ to A, when no charge is present elsewhere.

(ii) Work needed to bring $-q$ to B when $+q$ is at A. This is given by (charge at B) × (electrostatic potential at B due to charge $+q$ at A)

$$= -q \times \left(\frac{q}{4\pi\varepsilon_0 d}\right)$$

$$= -\frac{q^2}{4\pi\varepsilon_0 d}$$

(iii) Work needed to bring charge $+q$ to C when $+q$ is at A and $-q$ is at B. This is given by (charge at C) × (potential at C due to charges at A and B)

$$= +q\left(\frac{+q}{4\pi\varepsilon_0 d\sqrt{2}} + \frac{-q}{4\pi\varepsilon_0 d}\right)$$

$$= \frac{-q^2}{4\pi\varepsilon_0 d}\left(1 - \frac{1}{\sqrt{2}}\right)$$

(iv) Work needed to bring $-q$ to D when $+q$ at A, $-q$ at B and $+q$ at C. This is given by (charge at D) × (potential at D due to charges at A, B and C)

$$= -q\left(\frac{+q}{4\pi\varepsilon_0 d} + \frac{-q}{4\pi\varepsilon_0 d\sqrt{2}} + \frac{q}{4\pi\varepsilon_0 d}\right)$$

$$= \frac{-q^2}{4\pi\varepsilon_0 d}\left(2 - \frac{1}{\sqrt{2}}\right)$$

Adding the work done in steps (i), (ii), (iii) and (iv), the total work required is

$$= \frac{-q^2}{4\pi\varepsilon_0 d}\left\{(0) + (1) + \left(1 - \frac{1}{\sqrt{2}}\right) + \left(2 - \frac{1}{\sqrt{2}}\right)\right\}$$

$$= \frac{-q^2}{4\pi\varepsilon_0 d}(4 - \sqrt{2})$$

44 (b)

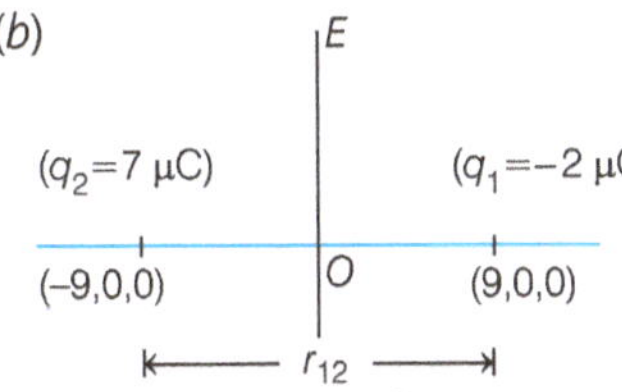

$$E = -\frac{dV}{dr}$$

$$\Rightarrow \int_{\infty}^{r_1} \frac{A}{r^2} dr = -\int_0^{V_1} dV$$

$$\Rightarrow \frac{A}{r_1} = V_1$$

or $V_1 = A / r_1$

and $V_2 = A / r_2$

Total electrostatic energy of the system

$$= q_1 V_1 + q_2 V_2 + \frac{k q_1 q_2}{r_{12}}$$

$$= A\left(\frac{-2 \times 10^{-6}}{0.09}\right) + A\left(\frac{7 \times 10^{-6}}{0.09}\right) + \left(\frac{-9 \times 10^9 \times 7 \times 2 \times 10^{-12}}{0.18}\right)$$

$$= \frac{9 \times 10^5 (5 \times 10^{-6})}{0.09} - 0.7\ \text{J}$$

$= 50\ \text{J} - 0.7\ \text{J} = 49.3\ \text{J}$

45 (a) Given, $V_B > V_A$

The potential energy between two points A and B,

$$U_B - U_A = q(V_B - V_A)$$

As, $V_B > V_A$

$\Rightarrow$ $U_B > U_A$

∴ On moving from point A to B, the potential energy increases.

47 (a) For maximum torque, $\theta = 90°$

$\tau_{max} = pE \sin 90°$

i.e. $\tau_{max} = pE$

$\Rightarrow \tau_{max} = q \times 2l \times E$

$= (3.5 \times 10^{-6}) \times 4.2 \times 10^{-2} \times 5.87 \times 10^5$

$= 86.289 \times 10^{-3}\ \text{Nm}^{-1}$

Work done in rotating the dipole from an angle θ_0 to θ,

$$W = \int_{\theta_0}^{\theta} pE \sin\theta\, d\theta$$

$$= pE [\cos\theta_0 - \cos\theta]$$

Here, $\theta_0 = 0°$ and $\theta = 180°$

$W = pE(\cos 0° - \cos 180°)$

$\Rightarrow W = 2pE$

$= 2 \times q \times 2l \times E$

$= 2 \times (3.5 \times 10^{-6}) \times (4.2 \times 10^{-2}) \times 5.87 \times 10^5$

$= 1.725 \times 10^{-1}\ \text{J}$

$\simeq 1.72 \times 10^{-1}\ \text{J}$

48 (b) Total dipole moment of all molecules,

$p = 6.02 \times 10^{23} \times 10^{-29}\ \text{Cm}$

$= 6.02 \times 10^{-6}\ \text{Cm}$

Initial potential energy,

$U_i = -pE \cos\theta$

$= -6.02 \times 10^{-6} \times 10^6 \times \cos 60°$

$= -6.02 \times \frac{1}{2} = -3.01\ \text{J}$

Final potential energy (when $\theta = 0°$),

$U_f = -6.02 \times 10^{-6} \times 10^6 \times \cos 0°$

$= -6.02\ \text{J}$

Change in potential energy

$= -6.02\ \text{J} - (-3.01\ \text{J}) = -3.01\ \text{J}$

So, there is a loss in potential energy. This must be the energy released by the substances in the form of heat in aligning its dipole.

∴ Heat energy $= -\Delta U$

$= -(-3.01\ \text{J}) = 3.01\ \text{J}$

54 (b) As, polarisation $P = \varepsilon_0 \chi_e E$

and $\varepsilon_r = 1 + \chi_e$

$\Rightarrow$ $P = \varepsilon_0 (\varepsilon_r - 1) E$

If n is the number of helium atoms/m^3 and p is the dipole moment per atom, then

$P = np$

or $p = \frac{P}{n} = \frac{\varepsilon_0 (\varepsilon_r - 1) E}{n}$ ...(i)

Since, at NTP, 1 mole (6.02×10^{23} atoms) of a gas occupies a volume of 22.4 L (i.e., $22.4 \times 10^{-3}\ \text{m}^3$).

$$n = \frac{6.02 \times 10^{23}}{22.4 \times 10^{-3}}$$

$= 2.69 \times 10^{25} / \text{m}^3$ ...(ii)

From Eqs. (i) and (ii), we get

$$p = \frac{(8.85 \times 10^{-12}(1.00074 - 1)(10)}{2.69 \times 10^{25}}$$

$= 2.4 \times 10^{-39}\ \text{Cm}$

55 (b) Two capacitors are given as below

For potential to be made zero after connection, the charge on both capacitors should be equal.

∴ $q_1 = q_2$

$C_1 V_1 = C_2 V_2$

or $120\, C_1 = 200\, C_2$

$\Rightarrow$ $3C_1 = 5C_2$

56 (c) For the capacitor, $C = \frac{\varepsilon_0 A}{d}$

Initial charge, $q = CV$ ...(i)

When $+Q$ charge is given to the negative plate of the capacitor, then

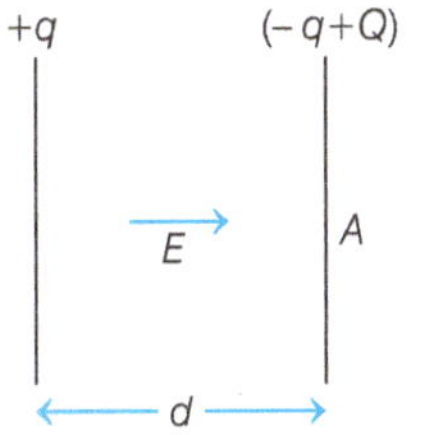

Potential difference across the capacitor

$$V' = Ed = \frac{qd}{2A\varepsilon_0} + \frac{qd}{2A\varepsilon_0} - \frac{Qd}{2A\varepsilon_0}$$

$$= \frac{qd}{A\varepsilon_0} - \frac{Qd}{2A\varepsilon_0} = \frac{q}{C} - \frac{Q}{2C}$$

$$= V - \frac{Q}{2C} \quad \text{[From Eq. (i)]}$$

57 (c)

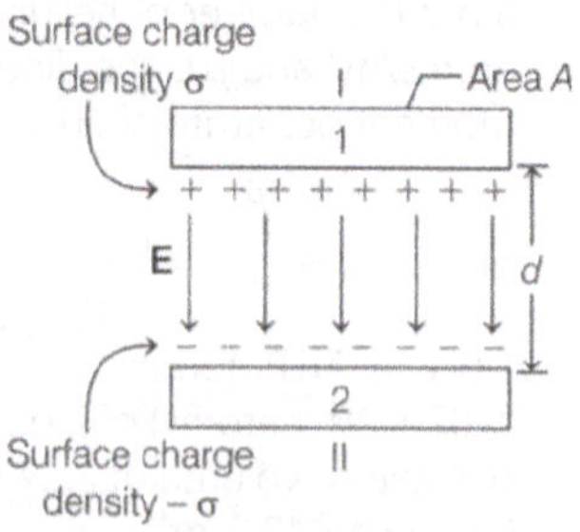

The electric field in outer region I (region above the plate 1) is

$$E = E_\sigma + E_{-\sigma} = \frac{\sigma}{2\varepsilon_0} - \frac{\sigma}{2\varepsilon_0} = 0$$

58 (b) If Q = charge on each plate, then

$$Q = CV = \frac{\varepsilon_0 A}{d} \cdot Ed = \varepsilon_0 AE$$

Here, $A = 1\,\text{m}^2$, $E = 100$ N/C

and $\varepsilon_0 = 8.85 \times 10^{-12} \frac{\text{C}^2}{\text{N-m}^2}$

So, by substituting given values, we get

$$Q = 8.85 \times 10^{-12} \times 1 \times 100$$
$$= 8.85 \times 10^{-10}\ \text{C}$$

59 (c) When the capacitor is disconnected from the battery, then charge, Q = constant

$$\therefore\ Q = CV = \left(\frac{\varepsilon_0 A}{d}\right) V = \text{constant}$$

$$\Rightarrow \quad V \propto d$$

∴ When the separation increases, then the potential difference increases.

60 (a) Charge of capacitor is

$$q = \Delta q_{net} = \frac{4-2}{2} = 1\,\mu\text{C}$$

Potential difference between capacitor plates is

$$V = \frac{Q}{C} = \frac{1\,\mu\text{C}}{1\,\mu\text{F}} = 1\,\text{V}$$

61 (a) Electric field inside dielectric

$$= \frac{\sigma}{K\varepsilon_0} = 3 \times 10^4$$

Thus, charge density,

$$\sigma = K\varepsilon_0 \times 3 \times 10^4$$
$$= 2.2 \times 8.85 \times 10^{-12} \times 3 \times 10^4$$
$$= 5.841 \times 10^{-7} \approx 6 \times 10^{-7}\ \text{Cm}^{-2}$$

62 (c) Initially,

$$C_0 = \frac{\varepsilon_0 A}{d} = 18\,\mu\text{F} \quad \text{...(i)}$$

When $d' = 3d$ and a dielectric medium is introduced,

$$C = \frac{K\varepsilon_0 A}{3d} = 72\,\mu\text{F} \quad \text{...(ii)}$$

On dividing Eq. (ii) by Eq. (i), we get

$$\frac{K}{3} = \frac{72}{18} = 4$$

∴ Dielectric constant, $K = 12$

63 (d) $\frac{C'd'}{K} = Cd$ $(\because \varepsilon_0 A = \text{constant})$

Given, $C' = C \Rightarrow d' = Kd$

$\Rightarrow \quad d' = 2 \times 3 = 6$ mm

64 (c) Capacitance of a parallel plate capacitor with air is $C = \frac{\varepsilon_0 A}{d}$ and capacitance of a same parallel plate capacitor with the introduction of a dielectric medium is

$$C' = \frac{K\varepsilon_0 A}{d}$$

$$\therefore \quad K = \frac{C'}{C} = \frac{15}{3} = 5$$

Also, $K = \frac{\varepsilon}{\varepsilon_0}$

or $\varepsilon = K\varepsilon_0 = 5 \times 8.854 \times 10^{-12}$

$= 0.4427 \times 10^{-10}\ \text{C}^2\ \text{N}^{-1}\text{m}^{-2}$

65 (a) If d be the distance between the plates, then

$$d = \frac{V}{E} = \frac{30}{30 \times 10^6} = 10^{-6}\ \text{m}$$

Capacitance of capacitor,

$$C = \frac{\varepsilon_0\ \varepsilon_r A}{d}$$

$$15 \times 10^{-9} = \frac{8.85 \times 10^{-12} \times 2.5 \times A}{10^{-6}}$$

$$\Rightarrow \quad A = 6.7 \times 10^{-4}\ \text{m}^2$$

66 (a) Let, $E_0 = V_0/d$ be the electric field between the plates, when there is no dielectric and the potential difference is V_0. If the dielectric is inserted, the electric field in the dielectric will be $E = E_0/K$ and the potential difference will be

$$V = E_0\left(\frac{1}{4}d\right) + \frac{E_0}{K}\left(\frac{3}{4}d\right)$$

$$= E_0 d\left(\frac{1}{4} + \frac{3}{4K}\right)$$

$$= V_0 \cdot \left(\frac{K+3}{4K}\right) \quad (\because V = E \cdot d)$$

The potential difference decreases by the factor $\frac{K+3}{4K}$ while the free charge Q_0 on the plates remains unchanged.

∴ The capacitance becomes

$$C = \frac{Q_0}{V} = \left(\frac{4K}{K+3}\right)\frac{Q_0}{V_0}$$

$$= \frac{4KC_0}{K+3} \quad \left[\because C_0 = \frac{Q_0}{V_0}\right]$$

67 (c) For isolated capacitor,

$$Q = \text{constant}$$

$$\therefore \quad C_2 = kC_1$$

$$\Rightarrow \quad \frac{Q}{V_2} = k \cdot \frac{Q}{V_1}$$

$$\therefore \quad k = \frac{V_1}{V_2}$$

$$= \frac{500}{75} = \frac{20}{3}$$

68 (a) When parallel combination is fully charged, charge on the combination is

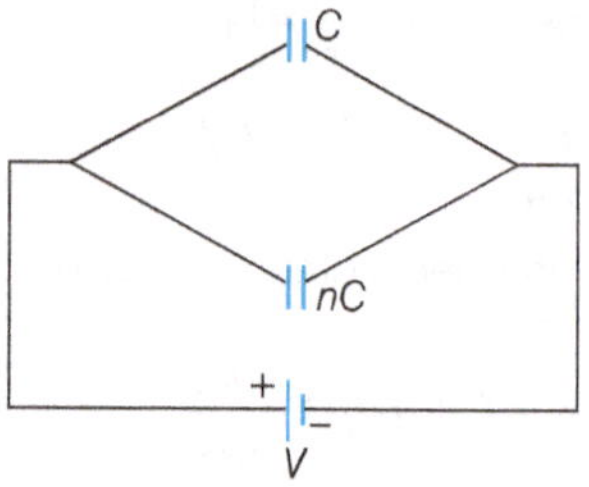

$$Q = C_{eq}V = C(1+n)V$$

When battery is removed and a dielectric slab is placed between two plates of first capacitor, then charge on the system remains same.

Now, equivalent capacitance after insertion of dielectric is

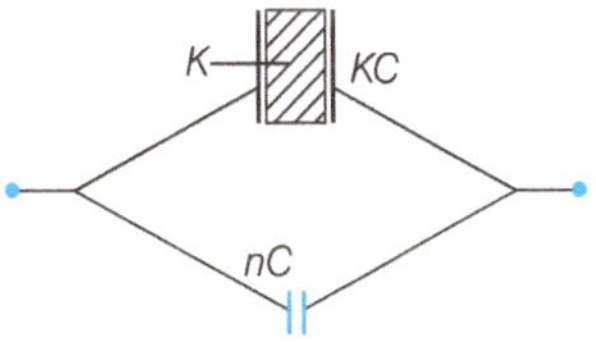

$$C_{eq} = KC + nC = (n+K)C$$

If potential value after insertion of dielectric is V', then charge on system is

$$Q' = C_{eq}V' = (n+K)CV'$$

As $Q = Q'$, we have

$$C(1+n)V = (n+K)CV'$$

$$\therefore \quad V' = \frac{(1+n)V}{(n+K)}$$

69 (*b*) Here, due the insertion of two slabs between the capacitor plates, two new capacitors are formed whose new capacitances are

Capacitance, $C_1 = \dfrac{K_1\varepsilon_0 A}{d/2} = \dfrac{2K_1\varepsilon_0 A}{d}$

and $C_2 = \dfrac{2K_2\varepsilon_0 A}{d}$

$$\therefore \frac{1}{C_s} = \frac{1}{C_1} + \frac{1}{C_2} = \frac{d}{2K_1\varepsilon_0 A} + \frac{d}{2K_2\varepsilon_0 A} = \frac{d}{2\varepsilon_0 A}\left(\frac{K_1+K_2}{K_1K_2}\right)$$

$\therefore$ Capacitance,

$$C_s = \frac{2\varepsilon_0 A}{d}\left(\frac{K_1K_2}{K_1+K_2}\right)$$

70 (*b*)

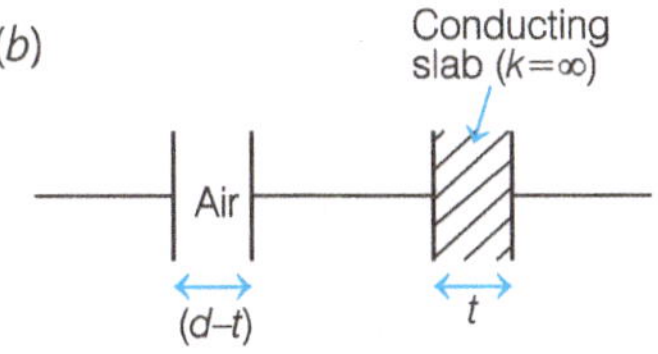

$\therefore$ The equivalent capacitance,

$$\frac{1}{C} = \frac{1}{\left(\frac{\varepsilon_0 A}{d-t}\right)} + \frac{1}{\frac{k\varepsilon_0 A}{t}} \quad (\because k=\infty)$$

$$= \frac{d-t}{\varepsilon_0 A} + 0$$

$$\therefore C = \frac{\varepsilon_0 A}{d-t}$$

71 (*a*) This combination is same as the two capacitors are connected in series and distance between plates of each capacitor is $d/2$.

So, $\quad C_1 = \dfrac{K\varepsilon_0 A}{d/2}$

and $\quad C_2 = \dfrac{\varepsilon_0 A}{d/2}$

Hence,

$$C_{net} = \frac{C_1C_2}{C_1+C_2} = \frac{\left(\frac{2K\varepsilon_0 A}{d}\right)\left(\frac{2\varepsilon_0 A}{d}\right)}{\left(\frac{2K\varepsilon_0 A}{d} + \frac{2\varepsilon_0 A}{d}\right)} = \frac{2KA\varepsilon_0}{(K+1)d}$$

72 (*a*) When we earthed plate *B*, whole of its charge will go to earth. Hence, the charge flown through switch is not zero.

73 (*b*) The statement given in option (b) is correct but rest are incorrect and these can be corrected as, When battery is disconnected, charge remains conserved.

The plates are pulled apart, so capacity will decrease, so there is an increase of voltage.

Now, capacity decreases, hence energy will increase as charge is constant $\left(E = \dfrac{Q^2}{2C}\right)$.

74 (*d*) Initial energy, $U_i = \dfrac{1}{2}C_0V^2$

When dielectric slab is introduced the capacitance becomes *K* times and potential difference decreases *K* times.

$\therefore$ Final energy,

$$U_f = \frac{1}{2}(KC_0)\left(\frac{V}{K}\right)^2$$

or $\quad U_f = \dfrac{1}{K}\left(\dfrac{1}{2}C_0V^2\right)$

So, energy stored in the capacitor decreases *K* times.

$\therefore$ Change in energy $= U_f - U_i$

$$= \frac{1}{2}C_0V^2\left(\frac{1}{K} - 1\right)$$

75 (*b*) According to the question, the given arrangement of nine plates is equivalent to the parallel combination of 8 capacitors.

The capacity of each capacitor,

$$C = \frac{\varepsilon_0 A}{d} = \frac{8.854\times 10^{-12}\times 5\times 10^{-4}}{0.885\times 10^{-2}}$$

$= 0.5$ pF

Hence, the capacity of the unit of 8 capacitors

$= 8C = 8\times 0.5 = 4$ pF

76 (*c*) As each capacitors cannot withstand more than 300 V, so there should be four capacitors in each row became in this condition 1 kV i.e., 1000 V will be divided by 4 (i.e., 250 V not more than 300 V).

Now, equivalent capacitance of one row

$$= \frac{1}{4}\times 1\,\mu F = 0.25\,\mu F$$

[$\because$ in series combination, $C_{eq} = C/n$]

Now, we need equivalent of $2\,\mu F$, so, let we need *n* such rows

$\therefore \quad n \times 0.25 = 2\,\mu F$

[$\because$ in parallel combination $C_{eq} = nC$]

$$n = \frac{2}{0.25} = 8$$

$\therefore$ Total number of capacitors

= number of rows × number of capacitors in each row

$= 8\times 4 = 32$

77 (*b*)

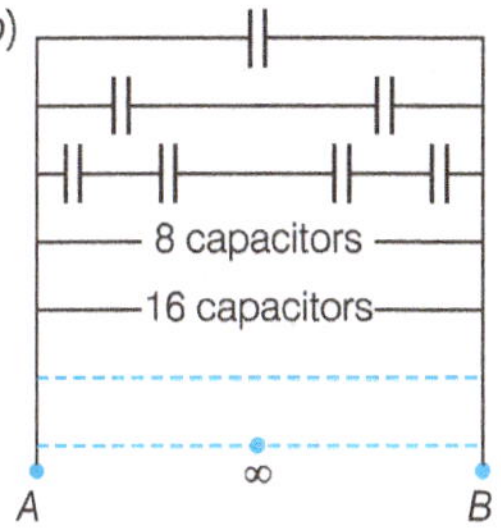

This combination forms a GP,

$$s = 1 + \frac{1}{2} + \frac{1}{4} + \frac{1}{8} + \ldots$$

Sum of infinite GP,

$$s = \frac{a}{1-r} \Rightarrow s = \frac{1}{1-\frac{1}{2}}$$

$$\Rightarrow \quad s = \frac{1}{1/2} \qquad \therefore \; s = 2$$

Hence, capacitance of the combination,

$$C_\infty = 2 \times 1\,\mu F = 2\,\mu F$$

78 (*d*) We simplify given circuit as

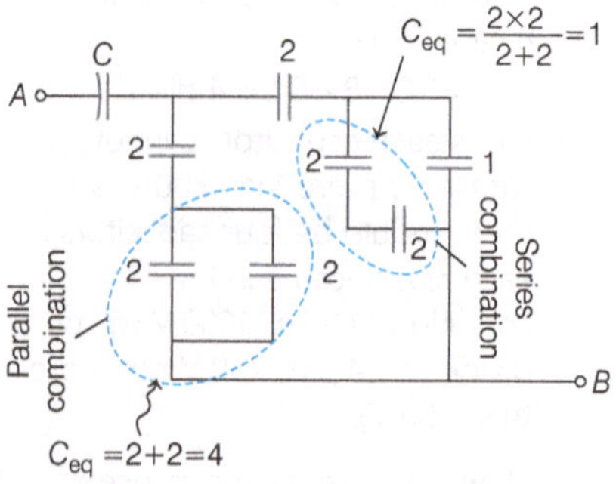

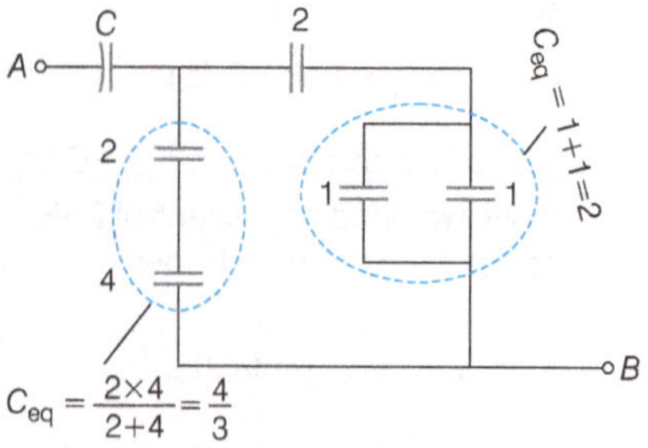

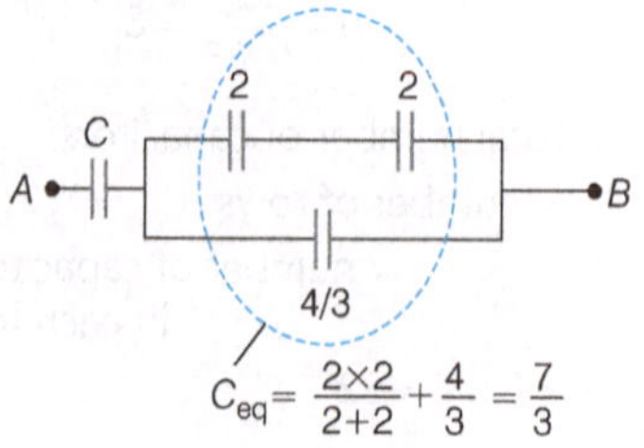

So, $C_{AB} = \frac{C \times 7/3}{C + 7/3} = \frac{1}{2}$ (given)

$$\Rightarrow \quad \frac{7C}{3} = \frac{C}{2} + \frac{7}{6}$$

$$\Rightarrow \quad \left(\frac{14-3}{6}\right) C = \frac{7}{6}$$

$$\Rightarrow \quad C = \frac{7}{11}\,\mu F$$

79 (*c*) Minimum number of conductors in each row

$$= \frac{V_{max}}{V} = \frac{3000}{500} = 6$$

If C_s is capacity of 6 conductors in a row, then

$$\frac{1}{C_s} = \frac{1}{1} + \frac{1}{1} + \frac{1}{1} + \frac{1}{1} + \frac{1}{1} + \frac{1}{1} = 6$$

$$\Rightarrow \quad C_s = \frac{1}{6}\,\mu F$$

Let there be m such rows in parallel.

Total capacity, $C_{net} = m \times C_s$

$$2 = m \times \frac{1}{6}$$

$$\therefore \quad m = 12$$

Total number of capacitors

$$= 6 \times 12 = 72$$

80 (*d*) In the given circuit, net capacitance of 3 μF and 6 μF capacitors being connected in parallel is

$$C' = 3\,\mu F + 6\,\mu F = 9\,\mu F$$

Now, 4.5 μF capacitor and capacitance 9 μF are in series. So, the total capacity of capacitor,

$$C = \frac{9 \times 4.5}{9 + 4.5} = \frac{9 \times 4.5}{13.5} = 3\,\mu F$$

Charge, $q = CV = 3 \times 12 = 36\,\mu C$ [given, $V = 12$ V]

∴Potential difference across 4.5 μF,

$$V' = \frac{q}{4.5} = \frac{36}{4.5} = 8\text{ V}$$

81 (*b*)

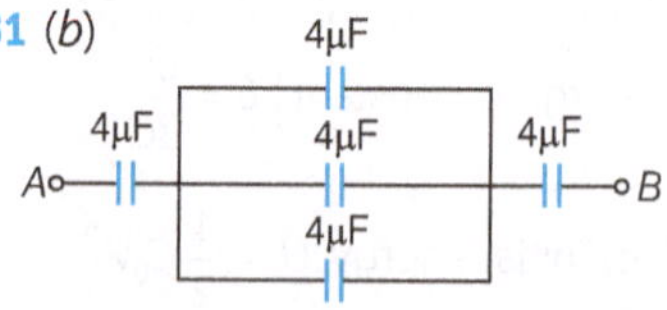

∴The equivalence capacitance between points A and B,

$$\frac{1}{C} = \frac{1}{4} + \frac{1}{(4+4+4)} + \frac{1}{4}$$

$$\therefore \; C = \frac{12}{7}\,\mu F$$

82 (*d*)

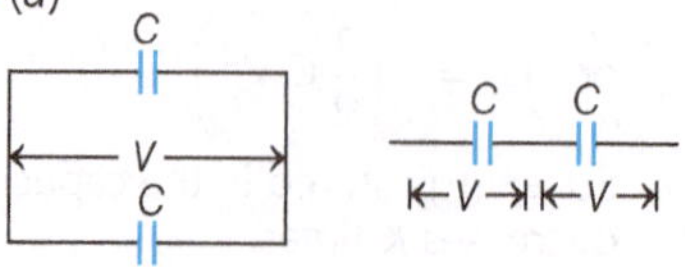

The charge will flow through the capacitor when the circuit is completed.

As the circuit is incomplete. So, the charge remains same on both capacitors.

∵ Initial energy stored = Final energy stored

$$= \left(\frac{1}{2} CV^2\right) \times 2 = CV^2$$

The potential difference between free plates of the system is

$$V' = V + V = 2V$$

83 (*b*) The charge flowing through different capacitor is shown in figure below

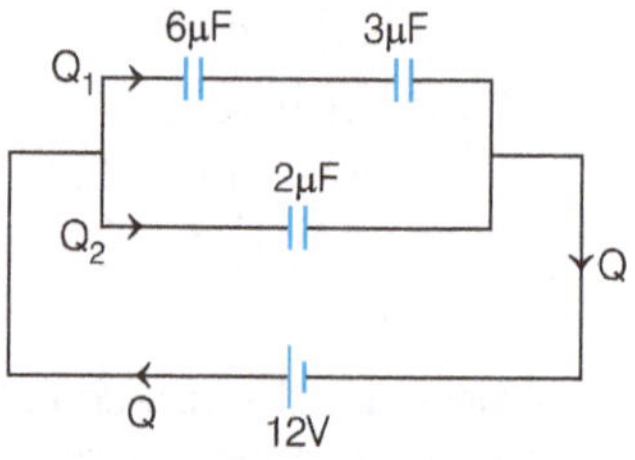

The equivalent capacitance,

$$C = \frac{6 \times 3}{6+3} + 2 = 4\,\mu F$$

$$\therefore \quad Q = CV = 4 \times 12 = 48\,\mu C$$

∴Charge on 3 μF capacitor,

$$Q_1 = \frac{2}{4} \times 48 = 24\,\mu C$$

84 (*d*)

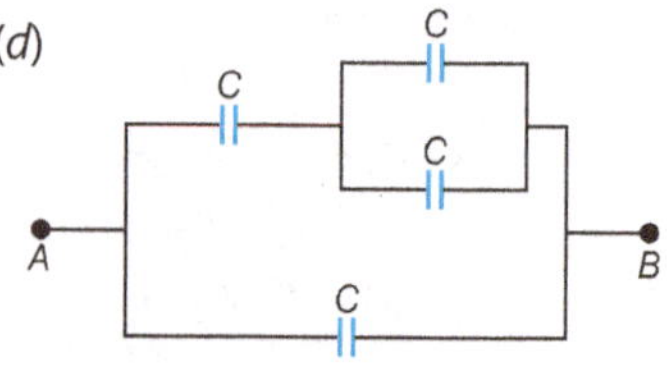

The equivalent capacitance between points A and B is

$$C_{eq} = \frac{C \times 2C}{C + 2C} + C$$

$$15 = \frac{5C}{3}$$

$$\Rightarrow \quad C = 9\,\mu F$$

85 (*c*) C_{eq} between P and R

$$= \frac{C}{3} + \frac{C}{2} = \frac{5C}{6}$$

C_{eq} between P and Q

$$= C + \frac{C}{4} = \frac{5C}{4}$$

$$\text{ratio} = \frac{4}{6} = \frac{2}{3}$$

86 (c) The equivalent capacitance between A and B is given by

$$C_{eq} = \frac{2C_1 \times C_2}{2C_1 + C_2}$$

Given, $C_1 = KC$, $C_2 = 2KC$

$$\therefore \quad C_{eq} = \frac{2 \times KC \times 2KC}{2(KC) + 2KC} = KC$$

$$= \frac{K\varepsilon_0 A}{d}$$

87 (c) The equivalent capacitance is given by

$$C = \frac{\varepsilon_0 A}{d} + \frac{\varepsilon_0 A}{2d} + \frac{\varepsilon_0 A}{3d} = \frac{11}{6}\frac{\varepsilon_0 A}{d}$$

88 (a) $$V_C = \frac{C_1 V_1 + C_2 V_2}{C_1 + C_2}$$

$$\Rightarrow \quad 20 = \frac{10 \times 50 + 0}{10 + C_2}$$

$$\therefore \quad C_2 = 15\,\mu\text{F}$$

90 (c) Given, $C = 900$ pF $= 900 \times 10^{-12}$ F and $V = 100$ V

The charge on the capacitor is

$$Q = CV = 900 \times 10^{-12}\ \text{F} \times 100\ \text{V}$$
$$= 9 \times 10^{-8}\text{C}$$

$\therefore$ The energy stored by the capacitor

$$= (1/2)\,CV^2 = (1/2)\,QV$$
$$= (1/2) \times 9 \times 10^{-8} \times 100$$
$$= 4.5 \times 10^{-6}\ \text{J}$$

91 (b) Energy stored in a charged capacitor is given by

$$U = \frac{1}{2}CV^2 = \frac{1}{2} \cdot QV$$

$$\Rightarrow \quad U = \frac{1}{2} \times 12 \times 10^{-12} \times 100$$

$$U = 6 \times 10^{-10}\ \text{J}$$

After insertion of slab, capacitance will be

$C' = KC$ and final energy,

$$U' = \frac{1}{2} \cdot \frac{Q^2}{C'} = \frac{1}{2}\frac{Q^2}{KC}$$

$$\Rightarrow U' = \frac{1}{K}U = \frac{1}{6.5} \times 6 \times 10^{-10}\ \text{J}$$

($\because$ given, $K = 6.5$)

So, energy dissipated in the process will be equal to work done on the slab, i.e.

$$W = U - U' = \left(1 - \frac{1}{6.5}\right) \times 6 \times 10^{-10}\ \text{J}$$

$$\Rightarrow \quad W = \frac{5.5}{6.5} \times 6 \times 10^{-10}\ \text{J}$$

$$\cong 5.08 \times 10^{-10}\ \text{J or 508 pJ}$$

92 (d) Potential energy stored in a capacitor is

$$U = \frac{1}{2}QV = \frac{1}{2}\frac{Q^2}{C}$$

So, initial energy of the capacitor,

$$U_i = \frac{1}{2}\frac{Q^2}{C_1}$$

Final energy of the capacitor,

$$U_f = \frac{1}{2}\frac{Q^2}{C_2}$$

As we know, work done,

$$W = \Delta U = U_f - U_i$$
$$= \frac{1}{2}Q^2\left[\frac{1}{C_2} - \frac{1}{C_1}\right]$$

$$\Rightarrow \quad \Delta U = \frac{1}{2} \times (5 \times 10^{-6})^2 \left[\frac{1}{2 \times 10^{-6}} - \frac{1}{5 \times 10^{-6}}\right]$$

$$\Rightarrow \quad \Delta U = 3.75 \times 10^{-6}\ \text{J}$$

93 (a) As, potential drop is zero along an ideal conductor, because it has zero resistance.
So, potential at point, $A = 10$ V
and potential at point, $B = 0$ V
$\therefore$ Potential difference across
$AB = (10 - 0)$ V $= 10$ V

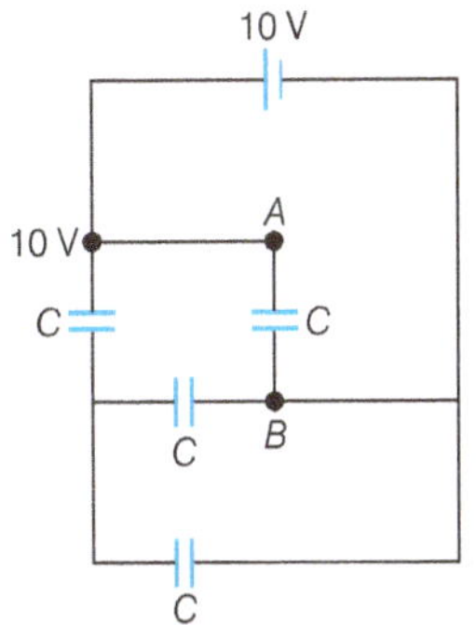

Maximum heat produced

$$= \text{Energy stored} = \frac{1}{2}CV^2$$

$$= \frac{1}{2} \times 10^{-6} \times (10)^2 = 50\,\mu\ \text{J}$$

94 (d) Given, potential difference across capacitor system,

$$\Delta V = 4V$$

Energy stored in a capacitor system,

$$U = \frac{1}{2}C_{eq}\Delta V^2$$

Case I When the capacitors are joined in series,

$$U_{series} = \frac{1}{2}\frac{C_1}{n_1}(4V)^2$$

Case II When the capacitors are joined in parallel,

$$U_{parallel} = \frac{1}{2}(n_2 C_2)V^2$$

Given, $U_{series} = U_{parallel}$

$$\text{or} \quad \frac{1}{2}\frac{C_1}{n_1}(4V)^2 = \frac{1}{2}(n_2 C_2)V^2$$

$$\Rightarrow \quad C_2 = \frac{16\,C_1}{n_1 n_2}$$

95 (c) The energy stored in the capacitor,

$$U = \frac{1}{2}CV^2 = \frac{1}{2}\left(\frac{A\varepsilon_0}{d}\right)(Ed)^2$$

$$\left(\because C = \frac{A\varepsilon_0}{d} \text{ and } V = Ed\right)$$

$$= \frac{1}{2}\varepsilon_0 E^2 Ad$$

96 (d) The quantities, energy stored and potential difference decreases, because $U = \frac{1}{2}\frac{q^2}{KC_0}$ and $V = \frac{q}{KC_0}$ decreases. Because on inserting a dielectric, the capacitance will increase (KC_0), where C_0 is the capacitance when no glass slab is present and K is dielectric constant, q is constant here.

97 (c) As, the battery is disconnected.
$\therefore$ Charge, Q = constant

$$= C_i V = \left(\frac{\varepsilon_0 A}{d}\right)V$$

$$\therefore \quad C_i = \frac{\varepsilon_0 A}{d}$$

$$C_f = \frac{\varepsilon_0 A}{2d}$$

Initial energy, $U_i = \dfrac{Q^2}{2C_i}$

Final energy, $U_f = \dfrac{Q^2}{2C_f}$

$\therefore$ Work done to increase plate separation,

$$W = U_f - U_i$$
$$= \frac{Q^2}{2}\left(\frac{1}{C_f} - \frac{1}{C_i}\right)$$
$$= \frac{Q^2}{2}\left(\frac{2d}{\varepsilon_0 A} - \frac{d}{\varepsilon_0 A}\right)$$
$$= \left(\frac{\varepsilon_0{}^2 A^2 V^2}{2d^2}\right)\left(\frac{d}{\varepsilon_0 A}\right) = \frac{\varepsilon_0 A V^2}{2d}$$

98 (*b*) The energy stored in capacitor is

$$U = \frac{1}{2}CV^2$$
$$= \frac{1}{2} \times 40 \times 10^{-6} \times (3000)^2$$
$$= 180\ \text{J}$$

The power delivered by the capacitor,

$$P = \frac{U}{t} = \frac{180}{2 \times 10^{-3}} = 90\ \text{kW}$$

99 (*c*) The charge on the capacitor is

$$Q = CV$$
$$= 900 \times 10^{-12}\ \text{F} \times 100\ \text{V}$$
$$= 9 \times 10^{-8}\text{C}$$

The energy stored by the capacitor is

$$= \frac{1}{2}CV^2 = \frac{1}{2}QV$$
$$= (1/2) \times 9 \times 10^{-8}\ \text{C} \times 100\ \text{V}$$
$$= 4.5 \times 10^{-6}\ \text{J}$$

In the steady situation, the two capacitors have their positive plates at the same potential and their negative plates at the same potential. Let the common potential difference be V'. The charge on each capacitor is $Q' = CV'$.

By charge conservation law, $Q' = Q$, this implies $V' = V/2$. The total energy of the system is

$$= \frac{1}{2}Q'V' = \frac{1}{4}QV$$
$$= 2.25 \times 10^{-6}\ \text{J}$$

Assertion and Reason Questions

1 (*a*) For $Q < 0$, the force on unit positive charge is attractive, so that the electrostatic force and displacement are in same direction. So, due to this reason, work done by the electrostatic force in bringing the unit positive charge from infinity to point P is positive.

2 (*d*) The potential energy of system of two charges is

$$U = \frac{1}{4\pi\varepsilon_0} \cdot \frac{q_1 q_2}{r}$$
$$\Rightarrow \quad U \propto \frac{1}{r}$$

When a positive charge comes close to a negative charge, then its potential energy decreases.

4 (*a*) The maximum amount of charge a capacitor can have depends on the shape and size of capacitor and also on the surrounding medium.
Thus, a capacitor can be given only a limited quantity of charge.

5 (*a*) Polar dielectric molecules are the one in which centres of positive and negative charges are separated even when there is no external field. It means, they have permanent dipoles.

So, in the absence of any external electric field, the different permanent dipoles are oriented randomly due to thermal agition. So, the total dipole moment is zero.

6 (*c*) A polar molecule is one in which the centres of positive and negative charges are separated, when there is no external field. Such molecules have a permanent dipole moment.

7 (*c*) Capacitance of a capacitor is inversely proportional to distance between the plates. So, capacity of a parallel plate capacitor increases when distance between the plates is decreased.

8 (*c*) Surface density of parallel plate capacitor without a dielectric slab is given as

$$\sigma = \frac{q}{A} = \frac{CV}{A} \qquad \text{...(i)}$$

Surface density of a parallel plate capacitor in the presence of dielectric slab is,

$$\sigma' = \frac{q'}{A} = \frac{C'V'}{A} = \frac{(KC)V}{A}$$
$$(\text{as } C' = KC, V' = V)$$

So from Eq. (i), the above equation can be written as

$$\sigma' = \frac{Kq}{A} = K\sigma$$

The electric field on introduction of dielectric between plates of a capacitor becomes,

$$E' = \frac{K\sigma}{\varepsilon_0} = KE \qquad \left[\because E = \frac{\sigma}{\varepsilon_0}\right]$$

Thus, the electric field and surface density both become K times on introducing the dielectric between the plates.

9 (*c*) Net capacitance of the capacitors when connected in series is given as

$$\frac{1}{C_s} = \frac{1}{C_1} + \frac{1}{C_2} + \frac{1}{C_3} \qquad \text{... (i)}$$

and when they are connected in parallel, net capacitance is given as

$$C_p = C_1 + C_2 + C_3 \qquad \text{... (ii)}$$

Since, $C_1 < C_2 < C_3$, then comparing Eqs. (i) and (ii), we can say that, $C_p > C_s$.

10 (*d*) When dielectric material is placed between the plates of a capacitor connected to a battery, then the potential difference between the plates remains constant, but its capacitance increases.

As, $\quad Q = CV \Rightarrow Q \propto C$

$\therefore$ Charge on the capacitor also increases.

Statement Based Questions

1 (c) For a non-uniformly charged thin circular ring with net zero charge, electric potential at each point on its axis is zero. Hence, electric field at each point on its axis must be perpendicular to the axis. Therefore, statement I is false but statement II is true.

2 (d) Electric field intensity inside a conducting sphere is always zero, and electrostatic potential inside the sphere is same as on the surface.

3 (b) Statement I is true but Statement II is false. Equipotential surface can or cannot be parallel. It depends on the distribution of charges.

5 (a) Electric potential of a charged conductor depends not only on the amount of charge and volume but also on the shape of the conductor. Hence, if their shapes are different, they may have a different electric potential. Therefore, both Statement I and Statement II are false.

7 (c) Electric field vector (**E**), electric displacement vector (**D**) and electric polarisation vector (**P**) are related as

$$\mathbf{D} = \varepsilon_0 \mathbf{E} + \mathbf{P} \quad \text{...(i)}$$

where, ε_0 is permittivity of free space.

From Eq. (i), it is clear that **D**, **E** and **P** are in same direction, i.e. they are mutually parallel to each other.

8 (a) Both Statement I and Statement II are false. On increasing the charge, potential increases.

But capacity of a capacitor is fixed by geometry of capacitor $\left(C = \frac{\varepsilon_0 A}{d}\right)$.

Capacitance is independent of charge.

Matching Type Questions

1 (c) Electric potential at any point due to electric dipole is given as

$$V = \frac{p\cos\theta}{4\pi\varepsilon_0 r^2}$$

A. At point P_1, $\theta = 0°$

$$\Rightarrow \quad V_1 = \frac{1}{4\pi\varepsilon_0} \cdot \frac{p\cos 0°}{r^2} = \frac{p}{4\pi\varepsilon_0 r^2}$$

B. At point P_2, $\theta = 180°$

$$\Rightarrow \quad V_2 = \frac{1}{4\pi\varepsilon_0} \cdot \frac{p\cos 180°}{r^2} = \frac{-p}{4\pi\varepsilon_0 r^2}$$

C. At point P_3, $\theta = 45°$

$$\Rightarrow \quad V_3 = \frac{1}{4\pi\varepsilon_0} \cdot \frac{p\cos 45°}{r^2} = \frac{p}{4\sqrt{2}\pi\varepsilon_0 r^2}$$

D. At point P_4, $\theta = 90°$

$$\Rightarrow \quad V_4 = \frac{1}{4\pi\varepsilon_0} \cdot \frac{p\cos 90°}{r^2} = 0$$

Hence, A $\rightarrow$ 4, B $\rightarrow$ 3, C $\rightarrow$ 2 and D $\rightarrow$ 1.

2 (b) Electric field in a dielectric is given by

A. $$E = \frac{\sigma - \sigma_p}{\varepsilon_0}$$

B. The potential difference across the plates is

$$V = Ed = \frac{\sigma - \sigma_p}{\varepsilon_0} d$$

For linear dielectric, we except σ_p to be proportional to E_0, i.e., to σ. Thus, $(\sigma - \sigma_p)$ is proportional to σ and we can write

$\sigma - \sigma_p = \frac{\sigma}{K}$, then

$$V = \frac{\sigma d}{\varepsilon_0 K} = \frac{Qd}{A\varepsilon_0 K}$$

C. The capacitance C with dielectric between the plates is

$$C = \frac{Q}{V} = \frac{\varepsilon_0 KA}{d}$$

As, $C_0 = \frac{\varepsilon_0 A}{d}$

and $C = \frac{\varepsilon_0 KA}{d}$,

$$\therefore \quad K = \frac{C}{C_0}$$

Hence, A $\rightarrow$ 2, B $\rightarrow$ 1, C $\rightarrow$ 4 and D $\rightarrow$ 3.

3 (c)

A. When S is open, then

$$C_{eq} = \frac{C_1 C_2}{C_1 + C_2} = \frac{(2\mu F)(3\mu F)}{(2\mu F + 3\mu F)} = \frac{6}{5}\mu F$$

Charge q on both the capacitors will be the same (as these are in series), i.e.

$$q = C_{eq} V = \left(\frac{6}{5}\mu F\right)(30 + 60)\text{ V} = 108\ \mu C$$

B. Charge on C_2, i.e.

$$q_2 = C_2 V_2 = (3\ \mu F)(60\text{ V}) = 180\ \mu C$$

C. When S is closed, charge on C_1, i.e.

$$q_1 = C_1 V_1 = (2\ \mu F)(30\text{ V}) = 60\ \mu C$$

D. Charge on C_1 and C_2

$= 60\ \mu C + 180\ \mu C = 240\ \mu C$

Hence, A $\rightarrow$ 1, B $\rightarrow$ 4, C $\rightarrow$ 3 and D $\rightarrow$ 2.

4 (b)

A. As, $\frac{Q_1}{C_1} = \frac{Q_2}{C_2}$

$$\Rightarrow \quad Q_2 = \left(\frac{C_2}{C_1}\right) Q_1 = \frac{(C/2)}{C} Q_1 = \frac{Q_1}{2}$$

Further as,

$$Q = Q_1 + Q_2 = Q_1 + \frac{Q_1}{2} = \frac{3}{2} Q_1$$

$$Q_1 = \frac{2}{3} Q \text{ and } Q_2 = \frac{1}{3} Q$$

Final energy of capacitor C_1,

$$U_1 = \frac{Q_1^2}{2C_1} = \frac{\left(\frac{2}{3}Q\right)^2}{2C}$$

$$=\frac{2}{9}\left(\frac{Q^2}{C}\right)=\frac{2}{9}\left(\frac{C^2V_0^2}{C}\right)$$

$$=\frac{2}{9}CV_0^2 \qquad (\text{as } Q=CV_0)$$

B. Final energy of capacitor C_2,

$$U_2=\frac{Q_2^2}{2C_2}=\frac{\left(\frac{1}{3}Q\right)^2}{2(C/2)}$$

$$=\frac{1}{9}\left(\frac{Q^2}{C}\right)=\frac{1}{9}CV_0^2$$

C. Final energy of system,

$$U_{\text{final}}=U_1+U_2=\frac{1}{3}CV_0^2$$

D. Inital energy of system,

$$U_{\text{initial}}=\frac{Q^2}{2C}=\frac{(CV_0)^2}{2C}=\frac{1}{2}CV_0^2$$

∴Change in energy,

$$\Delta U=U_{\text{final}}-U_{\text{initial}}=-\frac{1}{6}CV_0^2$$

Hence, A → 3, B → 4, C → 2 and D → 1.

Numerical Type Questions

1 (12)

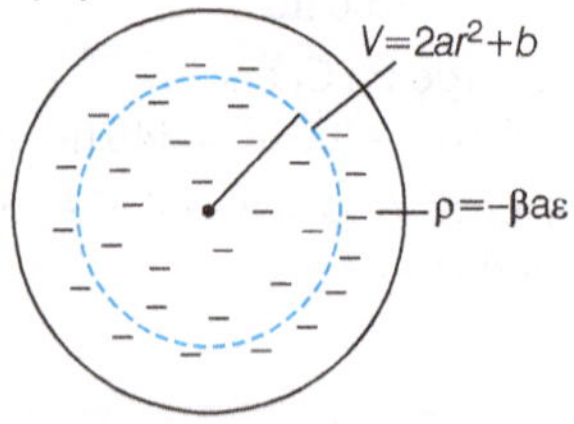

Given, volume charge density inside a charged spherical ball, $\rho=-\beta a\varepsilon$

As, charge density is constant, charge enclosed in a Gaussian sphere of radius r is

$$q=\rho\cdot V=-\beta a\varepsilon\left(\frac{4}{3}\pi r^3\right)$$

By Gauss's law, electric field on surface of Gaussian sphere is

$$E=\frac{1}{4\pi\varepsilon}\frac{q_{\text{enclosed}}}{r^2}$$

$$=\frac{1}{4\pi\varepsilon}\frac{-\beta a\varepsilon\frac{4}{3}\pi r^3}{r^2}=-\frac{\beta}{3}ar$$

Now, using $E=\frac{-dV}{dr}$, we get

$$V=\int_0^V dV=-\int_0^r (Edr)$$

$$\text{or } V=\int_0^r\frac{\beta}{3}ar\,dr=\frac{\beta a}{3}\cdot\left(\frac{r^2}{2}\right)$$

$$\text{or} \qquad V=\frac{\beta}{6}ar^2 \qquad \text{...(i)}$$

But potential is given,

$$V=2ar^2+b \qquad \text{...(ii)}$$

On comparing Eq. (i) and Eq. (ii), we get

$$\frac{\beta}{6}=2 \text{ or } \beta=12$$

2 (72) Now, when all drops are joined into single drop, volume remains constant,

$$\text{i.e., } 216\times\frac{4}{3}\pi r^3=\frac{4}{3}\pi R^3$$

$$\Rightarrow \qquad R=6r$$

$$\because \qquad V=\frac{kq}{r}=2 \qquad \text{...(i)}$$

$$\therefore \qquad V_{\text{net}}=\frac{kQ}{R}$$

where, Q be the charge of bigger sphere.

$$\Rightarrow \qquad V_{\text{net}}=\frac{k\times 216q}{6r} \qquad \text{...(ii)}$$

On dividing Eq. (ii) by Eq. (i) we get

$$\frac{V_{\text{net}}}{V}=\frac{k\times 216q\times r}{6r\times kq}$$

$$=\frac{216}{6}$$

$$\Rightarrow \qquad V_{\text{net}}=2\times 36=72\text{ V}$$

3 (150) Given arrangement is

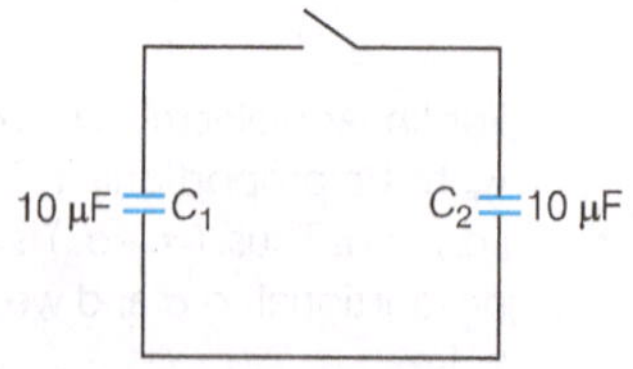

When switch is closed, charge flows from capacitor C_1 to capacitor C_2 till both reaches some common potential.

Now, common potential.

$$V=\frac{Q_1+Q_2}{C_1+C_2}=\frac{10\times 30+0}{20}=15\text{V}$$

Charge on capacitor C_2 after redistribution of charge is

$$Q_2=C_2\cdot V_2'$$

$$=(10\times 10^{-6})\times 15$$

$$=150\times 10^{-6}\text{ C}=150\,\mu\text{C}$$

4 (885) As we know, the expression of the capacitor with dielectric constant.

$$C=\frac{A\varepsilon_0}{\left(d-t+\frac{t}{K}\right)}$$

$$\Rightarrow C=\frac{105\times 8.85\times 10^{-12}}{\left(15-5+\frac{5}{10}\right)}$$

$$\Rightarrow C=8.85\times 10^{-11}\text{ F}=885\times 10^{-13}\text{ F}$$

5 (504) Initial, capacitance of capacitor,

$$C=\frac{\varepsilon_0 A}{d}=18\text{pF} \qquad \text{[Given]}$$

When separation is half and space is filled with dielectric $K=3.5$, capacitance of capacitor becomes

$$C'=\frac{\varepsilon_0 KA}{\frac{d}{2}}=2K\left(\frac{\varepsilon_0 A}{d}\right)$$

$$=2\times 3.5\times 18=\frac{504}{4}\text{pF}$$

6 (45) According to first condition,

$$C_0=\frac{\varepsilon_0 A}{d} \qquad \text{...(i)}$$

According to second condition, Capacitance of the capacitor in the presence of slab,

$$C'=\frac{\varepsilon_0 KA}{\frac{d}{2}}=\frac{\varepsilon_0 A}{d}\times 2K=C_0\times 2K$$

$$=15\times 10^{-6}\times 2\times 1.5=45\,\mu\text{F}$$

7 (20) Initial condition,

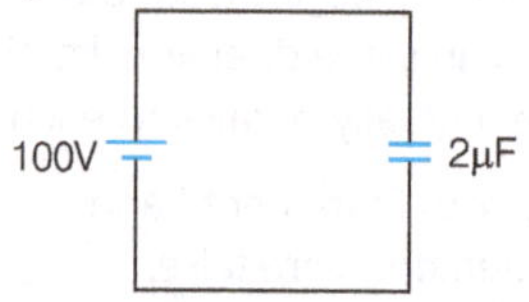

Now, after removing the battery the capacitor is connected.

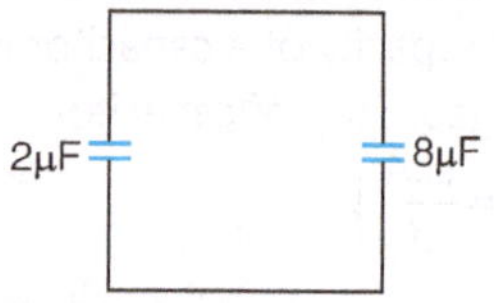

Let, V be the voltage across each capacitor.

So, using the law of conservation of charge,

$$2 + 8 = 2 \times 100 = 200$$

$$\Rightarrow \quad 10V = 200 \Rightarrow V = 20V$$

As we know,

$Q = CV = 8 \times 20 = 160\,\mu C$

8 (4) The given figure can be shown with capacitors as

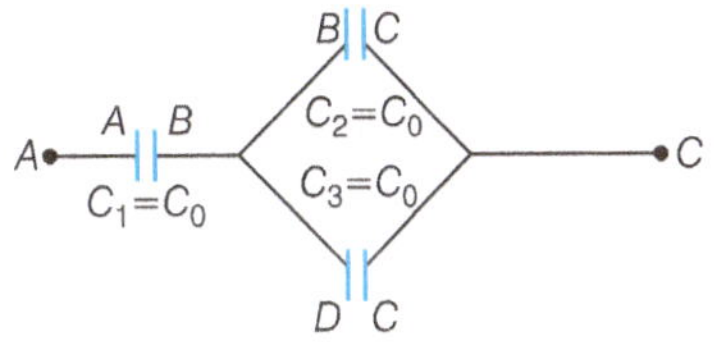

$$C'_{eq} = C_2 + C_3$$

$$\Rightarrow C'_{eq} = C_0 + C_0 = 2C_0$$

$$\Rightarrow \frac{1}{C_{eq}} = \frac{1}{C_1} + \frac{1}{C'_{eq}}$$

$$= \frac{1}{C_0} + \frac{1}{2C_0} = \frac{3}{2C_0}$$

$$\Rightarrow C_{eq} = \frac{2C_0}{3} \quad \text{...(i)}$$

$$\text{As, } C_0 = \frac{\varepsilon_0 A}{d} \quad \text{...(ii)}$$

From Eqs. (i) and (ii), we get

$$C_{eq} = \frac{2}{3}\left(\frac{\varepsilon_0 A}{d}\right)$$

$$\Rightarrow C_{eq} = \frac{2\varepsilon_0}{3d}(l \times b) = \frac{2\varepsilon_0}{3d}\left(5 \times \frac{6}{5}\right)$$

$$\Rightarrow C_{eq} = \frac{4\varepsilon_0}{d} \quad \text{...(iii)}$$

According to question, the equivalent capacitance between A and C is $\frac{x\varepsilon_0}{d}$.

So, comparing it with Eq. (iii), we get

$$x = 4$$

9 (8) Initially, a 80 pF capacitor is fully charged by a 20 V supply as shown in the figure.

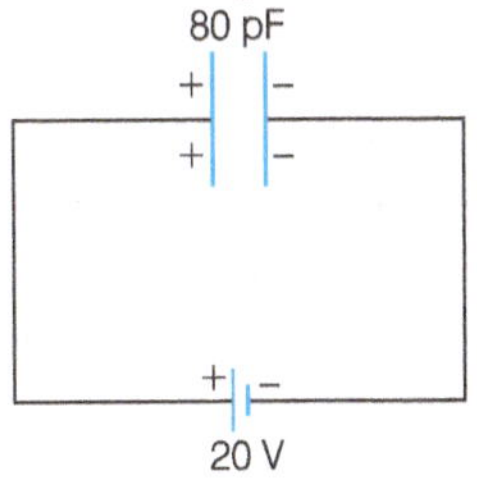

Its energy, $U_1 = \frac{1}{2}CV^2$

$$\Rightarrow U_1 = \frac{1}{2} \times 80 \times 10^{-12} \times (20)^2$$

$$= 16 \times 10^{-9} \text{J}$$

Then, it is connected to another uncharged 80pF capacitor as shown in the figure.

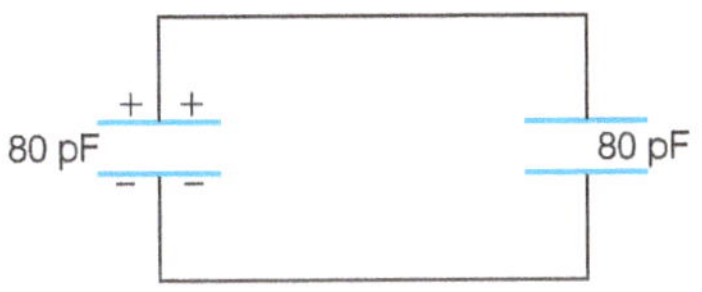

Transfer of charge from charged to uncharged capacitor occurs till both reaches a common potential.

If V = common potential, then

$$V = \frac{\text{total charge}}{\text{total capacitance}}$$

$$\Rightarrow V = \frac{Q_1}{C_1 + C_2} = \frac{C_1 V_1}{C_1 + C_2}$$

$$= \frac{80 \times 10^{-12} \times 20}{80 \times 10^{-12} + 80 \times 10^{-12}}$$

$$= 10 \text{ V}$$

Final energy of system,

$$U_2 = \frac{1}{2}(C_1 + C_2) \cdot V^2$$

$$= \frac{1}{2} \times 2 \times 80 \times 10^{-12} \times (10)^2$$

$$= 80 \times 10^{-10} = 8 \times 10^{-9} \text{J}$$

Loss of energy,

$$\Delta U = U_1 - U_2$$

$$= 16 \times 10^{-9} - 8 \times 10^{-9}$$

$$= 8 \times 10^{-9} \text{ J} = 8 \text{ nJ}$$

10 (2)

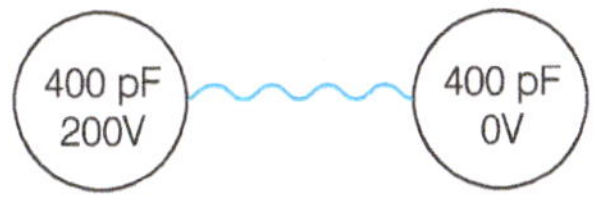

As both capacitors are identical, common potential after equilibrium is obtained is

$$V' = \frac{Q_1 + Q_2}{C_1 + C_2} = \frac{C_1 V_1 + C_2 V_2}{C_1 + C_2}$$

$$= \frac{400 \times 200 + 400 \times 0}{400 + 400}$$

$$= 100 \text{ V}$$

Energy stored in each capacitor will

$$U' = \frac{1}{2}C_1 V'^2 = \frac{1}{2} \times 4000 \times 10^{-12} \times 100 \times 100$$

$$= 2 \times 10^{-6} \text{ J}$$

NCERT Exemplar Questions

1 (c) Electric field always acts along decreasing potential. Thus, when a positively charged particle is released from rest in a uniform electric field, the work done or electric potential energy of the charge decreases because it moves along the electric field, i.e. from high potential to low potential.

4 (c) Since, the two capacitors are in series combination, the equivalent capacitance is given by,

$$\frac{1}{C} = \frac{1}{C_1} + \frac{1}{C_2}$$

$$C = \frac{C_1 C_2}{C_1 + C_2} = \frac{\frac{K_1\varepsilon_0 A}{d_1} \cdot \frac{K_2\varepsilon_0 A}{d_2}}{\frac{K_1\varepsilon_0 A}{d_1} + \frac{K_2\varepsilon_0 A}{d_2}}$$

$$= \frac{K_1 K_2 \varepsilon_0 A}{K_1 d_2 + K_2 d_1} \quad \text{...(i)}$$

But the equivalent capacitances is given by

$$C = \frac{K\varepsilon_0 A}{d_1 + d_2} \quad \text{... (ii)}$$

On comparing Eqs. (i) and (ii), we have

$$K = \frac{K_1 K_2 (d_1 + d_2)}{K_1 d_2 + K_2 d_1}$$

Past Exams Questions

1 (c) We know that, potential at point due to an ideal point at any point on axial line is given

$$V = \pm \frac{1}{4\pi\varepsilon_0} \frac{p}{r^2}$$

Putting the values of p and r, we get

$$V = \pm 9 \times 10^9 \times \frac{4 \times 10^{-6}}{(2)^2}$$

$$= \pm 9 \times 10^3 \text{ V}$$

Hence, A is true but R is false.

2 (*d*) Since, there is no electric field inside the shell the potential at any point inside the shell is equal to the potential on the surface of the shell is

$$V = \frac{1}{4\pi\varepsilon_0}\frac{q}{r}$$

$$V_C - V_P = 0$$

3 (*b*) We know that,

$$C = \frac{\varepsilon_0 A}{d}$$

$$E = \frac{1}{2}CV^2 \text{ and } Q = C\cdot V$$

As the distance between the plates decreases capacitance increases, therefore energy increases and also charge stored is increased. Hence, A, C, and E are correct.

4 (*a*) Given combination of capacitors represent Wheatstone bridge, thus central capacitor can be removed.

Capacitance of each branch,

$$C = \frac{2}{2} = 1\,\mu\text{F}$$

Capacitance between *A* and *B*,

$$C_{net} = 1 + 1 = 2\,\mu\text{F}$$

5 (*d*) Equivalent capacitance of the system,

$$C_{AB} = \frac{3\times(3+3)}{3+(3+3)} = \frac{18}{9} = 2\,\mu\text{F}$$

6 (*a*) Potential on the hollow conducting sphere of radius *R* due to charge *Q* is

$$V = \frac{1}{4\pi\varepsilon_0}\cdot\frac{Q}{R}$$

$$\Rightarrow \quad V \propto \frac{1}{R} \quad \text{[For same charge Q]}$$

$$\Rightarrow \quad \frac{V_1}{V_2} = \frac{R_2}{R_1}$$

Since, $R_1 > R_2$

$$\Rightarrow \quad \frac{R_2}{R_1} < 1$$

$$\therefore \quad \frac{V_1}{V_2} < 1$$

$$\Rightarrow \quad V_1 < V_2$$

Hence, potential will be more on smaller sphere.

7 (*d*) According to the question,

$$V_{bigger} = 27 \times V_{smaller}$$

$$\Rightarrow \quad \frac{4}{3}\pi R^3 = 27 \times \frac{4}{3}\pi r^3$$

$$\Rightarrow \quad R^3 = 27 \times r^3$$

$$\Rightarrow \quad R = 3r$$

Now, the potential of the small drop,

$$V_1 = \frac{Kq}{r} \quad \text{...(i)}$$

The potential of the bigger drop,

$$V_2 = \frac{KQ}{R}$$

$$Q = 27q$$

So, the potential of the bigger drop,

$$V_2 = \frac{K \times 27q}{3r}$$

$$\Rightarrow \quad V_2 = 9\frac{Kq}{r}$$

$$V_2 = 9V \quad \text{[From Eq. (i)]}$$

$$\text{So, } \frac{V_2}{V_1} = 9$$

8 (*b*) When two charged spherical conductors are connected by a conducting wire, then the potential becomes same in both the spherical conductor, i.e.,

$$V_1 = V_2$$

$$\Rightarrow \quad \frac{Kq_1}{R_1} = \frac{Kq_2}{R_2}$$

$$\Rightarrow \quad \frac{q_1}{q_2} = \frac{R_1}{R_2} \quad \text{...(i)}$$

$$\sigma = \frac{q}{4\pi R^2}$$

$$\frac{\sigma_1}{\sigma_2} = \frac{\dfrac{q_1}{4\pi R_1^2}}{\dfrac{q_2}{4\pi R_2^2}}$$

$$\Rightarrow \quad \frac{\sigma_1}{\sigma_2} = \frac{R_1}{R_2}\frac{R_2^2}{R_1^2} \quad \text{[From Eq. (i)]}$$

$$\Rightarrow \quad \frac{\sigma_1}{\sigma_2} = \frac{R_2}{R_1}$$

9 (*b*) The given situation is shown below.

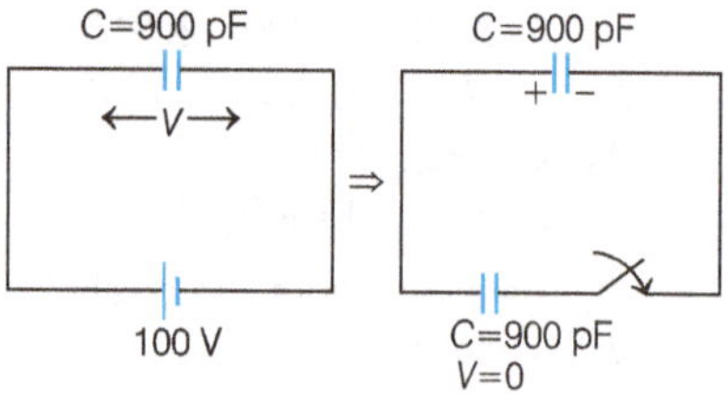

After combination,

Common potential,

$$V = \frac{C_1V_1 + C_2V_2}{C_1 + C_2}$$

$$= \frac{C\times 100 + C \times 0}{C + C} = 50\text{ V}$$

∴ Electrostatic stored potential energy,

$$U = 2 \times \frac{1}{2}CV^2 = CV^2$$

$$= 9 \times 10^{-10} \times 50^2$$

$$= 2.25 \times 10^{-6}\text{ J}$$

10 (*b*) Consider the nodes be *A*, *B*, *E* and *F* as shown in the figure

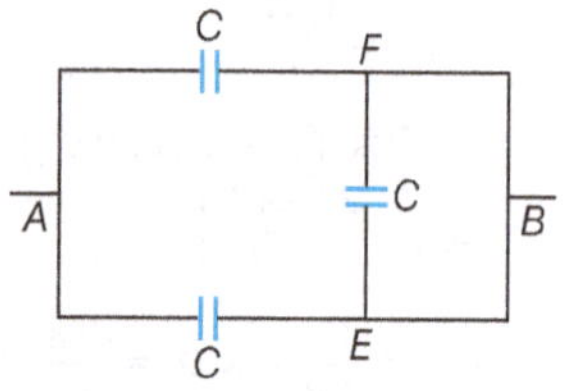

The potential at *F* is equal to the potential at node *E*.

So, *EF* behaves as open circuit.

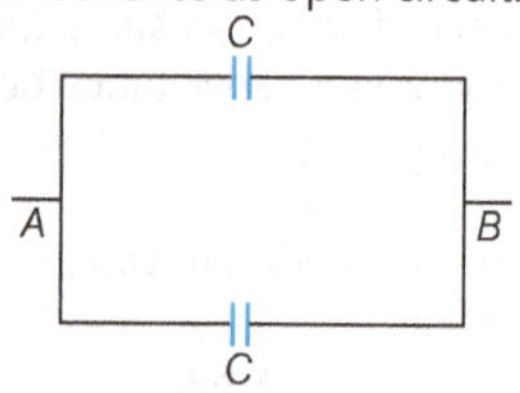

Now, the two capacitors are arranged in parallel. The net equivalent capacitors,

$$C_{eq} = C_1 + C_2$$

$$\Rightarrow \quad C_{eq} = C + C$$

$$\Rightarrow \quad C_{eq} = 2C$$

11 (*a*) Electric potential at a point which is at a distance *r* at some angle θ from electric dipole is

$$V = \frac{p\cos\theta}{4\pi\varepsilon_0 r^2}$$

$$= \frac{9 \times 10^9 \times 16 \times 10^{-9} \times \frac{1}{2}}{(0.6)^2}$$

$$= 2 \times 10^2 = 200 \text{ V}$$

12 (*b*) Capacitance of parallel plate capacitor when medium is air

$$C_0 = \frac{\varepsilon_0 A}{d}$$

According to second condition,

$$A' = A, t = d/2, K = 4$$

$$\therefore \text{ Capacitance, } C = \frac{\varepsilon_0 A}{(d - t) + \frac{t}{k}}$$

$$= \frac{\varepsilon_0 A}{\left(d - \frac{d}{2}\right) + \frac{d/2}{4}} = \frac{8}{5} \cdot \frac{\varepsilon_0 A}{d}$$

$$\therefore \frac{C}{C_0} = \frac{\frac{8}{5} \cdot \frac{\varepsilon_0 A}{d}}{\frac{\varepsilon_0 A}{d}} \Rightarrow C : C_0 = 8 : 5$$

13 (*c*) As we know that, the total work done in transferring a charge to a parallel plate capacitor is

given as $\quad W = \dfrac{Q^2}{2C}$ ...(i)

Since, $\quad W = F \cdot d$ ...(ii)

From Eqs. (i) and (ii), we get

$$W = \frac{Q^2}{2C} = Fd$$

$\Rightarrow \quad F = \dfrac{Q^2}{2Cd}$ ...(iii)

The capacitance of a parallel plate is given as, $C = \dfrac{\varepsilon_0 A}{d}$

$$\therefore \quad F = \frac{Q^2 d}{2\,\varepsilon_0 A d} = \frac{Q^2}{2\,\varepsilon_0 A}$$

This means, electrostatic force is independent of the distance between the plates.

15 (*c*) Consider the given figure,

When the switch S is connected to point 1, then initial energy stored in the capacitor can be given as

$$U = \frac{1}{2}(2\mu\text{F}) \times V^2$$

When the switch S is connected to point 2, energy dissipated on connection across 8 μF will be

$$\Delta U = \frac{1}{2}\left(\frac{C_1 C_2}{C_1 + C_2}\right) . V^2$$

$$= \frac{1}{2} \times \frac{2\,\mu\text{F} \times 8\,\mu\text{F}}{10\,\mu\text{F}} \times V^2$$

$$= \frac{1}{2} \times (1.6\,\mu\text{F}) \times V^2$$

Therefore, % loss of energy,

$$\frac{\Delta U}{U} \times 100 = \frac{1.6}{2} \times 100 = 80\%$$

16 (*a*) Given, dielectric constant for metallic sheet, $K = \infty$

Thickness of metallic plate, $t = \dfrac{2d}{3}$

Distance between two plates of capacitor $= d$

According to question, $C_1 = \dfrac{\varepsilon_0 A}{d}$

$$C_2 = \frac{\varepsilon_0 A}{d - t + \frac{t}{K}} = \frac{\varepsilon_0 A}{d - \frac{2d}{3} + 0} = 3C_1$$

$$\Rightarrow \quad \frac{C_2}{C_1} = 3 : 1$$

17 (*b*) Given, $C = 2\text{F}$

Energy stored, $E_1 = \dfrac{1}{2} CV^2$ ...(i)

Now, common potential,

$$V_C = \frac{C_1 V_1 + C_2 V_2}{C_1 + C_2} = \frac{CV + 0}{2C} = \frac{V}{2}$$

$E_2 = \dfrac{1}{2} CV_C^2 = \dfrac{CV^2}{8}$ ...(ii)

$$\frac{\text{Eq. (ii)}}{\text{Eq. (i)}} = \frac{E_2}{E_1} = \frac{CV^2/8}{CV^2/2} = \frac{1}{4}$$

18 (*c*) The given situation is shown below.

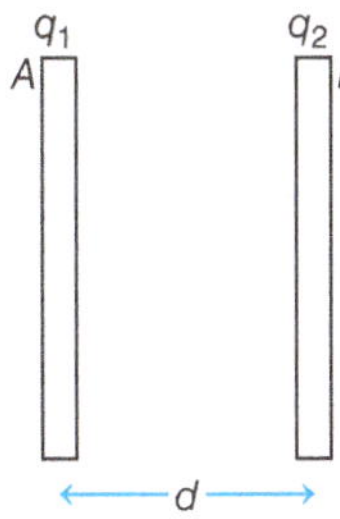

Net electric field inside the parallel plate capacitor,

$$E = \frac{\sigma_1}{2\varepsilon_0} - \frac{\sigma_2}{2\varepsilon_0} = \frac{1}{2\varepsilon_0}(\sigma_1 - \sigma_2)$$

$$= \frac{1}{2\varepsilon_0}\left[\frac{q_1}{A_1} - \frac{q_2}{A_2}\right]$$

$$\therefore \quad A_1 = A_2 = A$$

$$\Rightarrow \quad E = \frac{1}{2\varepsilon_0}\left[\frac{q_1}{A} - \frac{q_2}{A}\right]$$

$$= \frac{q_1 - q_2}{2\varepsilon_0 A}$$

∴ Potential difference between the plates,

$$V = E \cdot d = \frac{(q_1 - q_2)d}{2\varepsilon_0 A}$$

$$= \frac{q_1 - q_2}{2\left(\frac{\varepsilon_0 A}{d}\right)} = \frac{q_1 - q_2}{2C}$$

$$\left(\text{where, } \frac{\varepsilon_0 A}{d} = C\right)$$

19 (*d*)

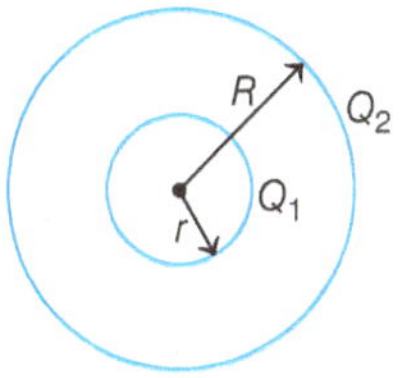

Charge density of inner shell,

$$\sigma_1 = \frac{Q_1}{4\pi r^2}$$

Charge density of outer shell,

$$\sigma_2 = \frac{Q_2}{4\pi R^2}$$

but $\quad \sigma_1 = \sigma_2$

$$\Rightarrow \quad \frac{Q_1}{4\pi r^2} = \frac{Q_2}{4\pi R^2}$$

$$\Rightarrow \quad Q_2 = \frac{Q_1 R^2}{r^2}$$

Also, $\quad Q_1 + Q_2 = Q$

$$\Rightarrow \quad Q_1 + \frac{Q_1 R^2}{r^2} = Q$$

or $\quad Q_1 = \dfrac{Qr^2}{(r^2 + R^2)}$

and $\quad Q_2 = \dfrac{QR^2}{(r^2 + R^2)}$

Potential due to Q_1 and Q_2 at common centre of shells is

$$V = V_{Q_1} + V_{Q_2}$$

$$= \frac{kQ_1}{r} + \frac{kQ_2}{R}$$
$$= \frac{kQr}{r^2 + R^2} + \frac{kQR}{r^2 + R^2}$$
$$= \frac{1}{4\pi\varepsilon_0} \cdot \frac{Q(r + R)}{r^2 + R^2}$$

Skill Boosters

1 (c) Using, $V_f - V_i = -\int_i^f \mathbf{E} \cdot d\mathbf{s}$

$\Rightarrow \quad V_f - V_i = -Ed$

$\Rightarrow \quad V_C - V_A = -5E$

$\Rightarrow \quad V_A - V_C = 5E$

2 (b) $V_{C_1} = V_{Q_1} + V_{Q_2}$

$$= \frac{Q_1}{4\pi\varepsilon_0 R} + \frac{1}{4\pi\varepsilon_0} \frac{Q_2}{R\sqrt{2}}$$
$$= \frac{1}{4\pi\varepsilon_0 R}\left(Q_1 + \frac{Q_2}{\sqrt{2}}\right)$$

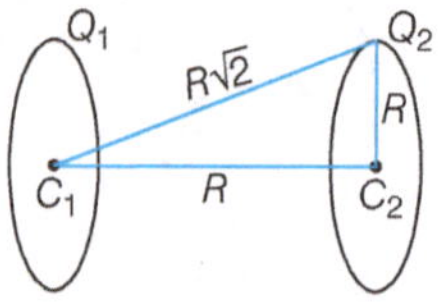

Similarly, $V_{C_2} = \frac{1}{4\pi\varepsilon_0 R}\left(Q_2 + \frac{Q_1}{\sqrt{2}}\right)$

$\therefore \Delta V = V_{C_1} - V_{C_2}$

$$= \frac{1}{4\pi\varepsilon_0 R}\left[(Q_1 - Q_2) - \frac{1}{\sqrt{2}}(Q_1 - Q_2)\right]$$
$$= \frac{Q_1 - Q_2}{\sqrt{2}\,(4\pi\varepsilon_0 R)}(\sqrt{2} - 1)$$

$W = q\Delta V$

$= q(Q_1 - Q_2)(\sqrt{2} - 1)/\sqrt{2}(4\pi\varepsilon_0 R)$

3 (d) Using result of a charged ring, potential at P due to a ring of area dA is

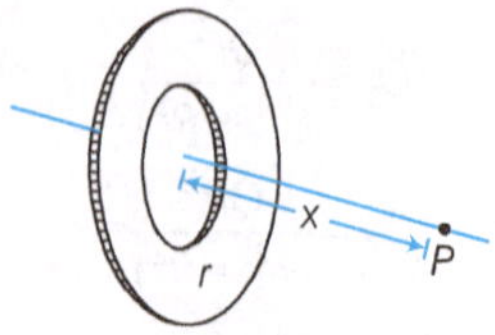

$$dV = \frac{k\,dq}{\sqrt{r^2 + x^2}}$$

$dq = \sigma\, dA = \sigma 2\pi r\, dr$

$$\therefore V = \int_a^b 2\pi\sigma k\left(\frac{r\,dr}{\sqrt{r^2 + x^2}}\right)$$
$$= 2\pi\sigma k\left(\sqrt{x^2 + b^2} - \sqrt{x^2 + a^2}\right)$$

4 (d) Potential due to an elemental ring of thickness dr on its axis is

$$dV = \frac{1}{4\pi\varepsilon_0} \cdot \frac{dq}{x}$$
$$x = \sqrt{H^2 + r^2}$$

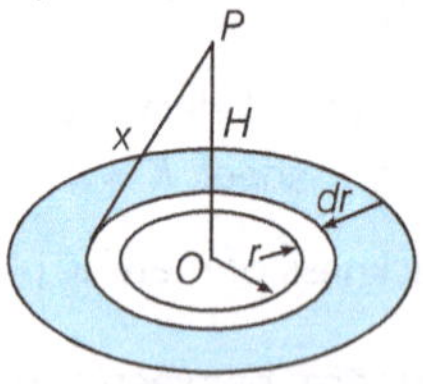

and $\quad dq = 2\pi r dr \sigma$

$$\therefore \quad dV = \frac{\sigma}{2\varepsilon_0} \cdot \frac{r\,dr}{\sqrt{H^2 + r^2}}$$

Potential due to complete disc,

$$V = \int_{r=0}^{a} dV = \frac{\sigma}{2\varepsilon_0}\int_{r=0}^{a} \frac{r\,dr}{\sqrt{H^2 + r^2}}$$

$$\Rightarrow \quad V_{\text{at } P} = \frac{\sigma}{2\varepsilon_0}\{\sqrt{a^2 + H^2} - H\}$$

U-H equation is

$$U = 2mg(\sqrt{a^2 + H^2} - H)$$

which is parabolic and $U = 2mga$

at $H = 0$.

Also, at $H = \frac{a}{\sqrt{3}}$, $U = U_{\min}$.

$\therefore$ Graph will be

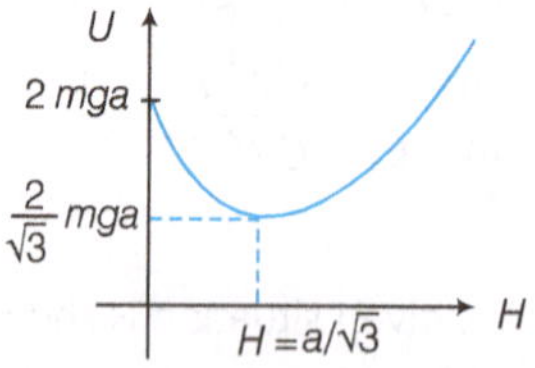

5 (c) Field between plates $= \frac{2V_0}{d}$

If ball swings a small distance x to right. Voltage is lower by

$$-Ex = \frac{-2V_0}{d}x.$$

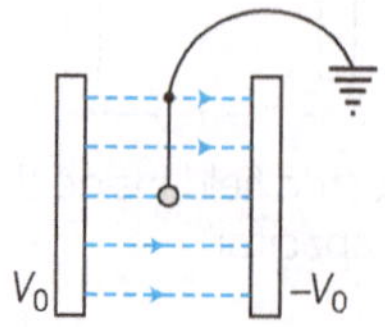

As ground connection keeps ball at zero potential by allowing charge q to flow to ball from the ground.

So, $\left.-\frac{2V_0}{d}x + \frac{kq}{R} = 0\right\}\ k = \frac{1}{4\pi\varepsilon_0}$

$$\Rightarrow \quad q = \frac{2V_0 xR}{kd}$$

$\therefore$ The ball feels the force

$$F = qE = \frac{4V_0^2 xR}{kd^2}$$

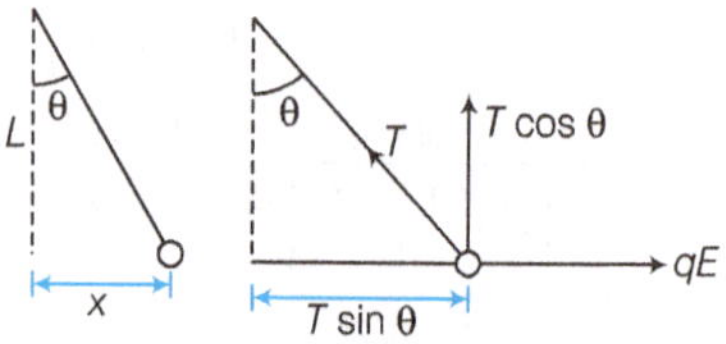

For equilibrium, this force must be balanced by the horizontal component of the string tension T.

From FBD, $\quad T\cos\theta = mg$

and $\quad T\sin\theta = qE$

$$\Rightarrow \tan\theta = \frac{qE}{mg} = \frac{4V_0^2 xR}{kd^2 mg} = \frac{x}{L}$$

For small displacements x.

$$\text{So,} \quad V_0 = \left(\frac{kd^2 mg}{4\,RL}\right)^{1/2}$$

If V_0 is less than this, the only equilibrium position of ball is hanging down between the plates. If V_0 exceeds this value the ball will swing over to one plate or the other.

$\therefore \quad N = 4$

6 (a) Torque on the arrangement is

$$\tau = -\mathbf{p} \times \mathbf{E}$$
$$= qL\,E\sin\theta$$

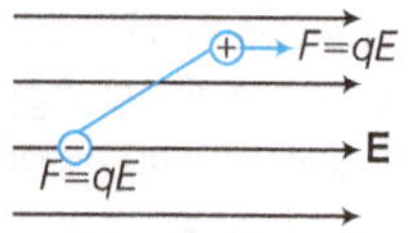

If I = moment of intertia of the arrangement, then

$$I = 2 \times m \times \left(\frac{L}{2}\right)^2 = \frac{mL^2}{2}$$

Also, torque $= I\alpha$

$$qLE\sin\theta = \frac{mL^2}{2}\alpha$$

$$\Rightarrow \quad \alpha = -\frac{2qE}{mL}\sin\theta$$

For small angles,

$$\sin\theta \approx \theta$$

$$\Rightarrow \quad \alpha = \frac{-2qE}{mL}\theta$$

Equation of simple harmonic motion is

$$\Rightarrow \quad \frac{d^2\theta}{dt^2} + \frac{2qE}{mL}\cdot\theta = 0$$

So, time period is

$$T = 2\pi\sqrt{\frac{mL}{2qE}}$$

Time required by rod to get aligned with the field is to complete 1/4th oscillation.

$$\therefore \quad t = \frac{T}{4} = \frac{\pi}{2}\sqrt{\frac{mL}{2qE}}$$

7 (*b*) As field is zero at a point nearer to q_1 and $q_1 < q_2$. Also, both q_1 and q_2 must be positive (or both may be negative).

8 (*b*) Given, $\mathbf{E} = ay\hat{\mathbf{i}} + bz\hat{\mathbf{j}} + cx\hat{\mathbf{k}}$

In XY-plane $z = 0$,

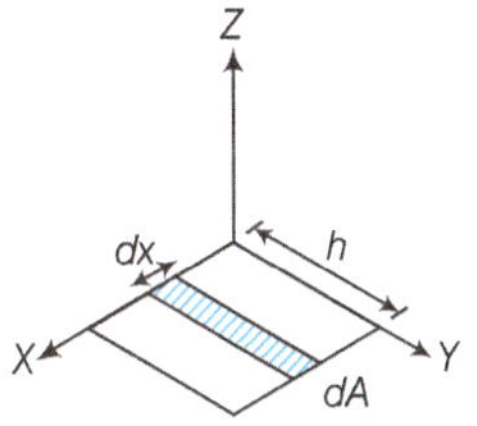

$$\therefore \quad E = ay\hat{\mathbf{i}} + cx\hat{\mathbf{k}}$$

$$d\mathbf{A} = hdx\hat{\mathbf{k}}$$

and flux, $\phi_E = \int \mathbf{E}\cdot d\mathbf{A}$

$$= \int (ay\hat{\mathbf{i}} + cx\hat{\mathbf{k}})\cdot(hdx)\hat{\mathbf{k}}$$

$$\therefore \quad \phi_E = \int_{x=0}^{x=w} ch\,xdx = \frac{chw^2}{2}$$

9 (*b*) For $r < R_1$, $E = 0$ as no charge is inside region $r < R_1$

$\therefore \quad E = 0$ at all points

For $\quad r < R_1, \; \frac{dV}{dr} = -E = 0$

$\Rightarrow \quad V =$ constant for $r < R_1$

For $R_1 < r < R_2$, is constant for q_2 as point lies inside the sphere of radius R_2.

Also, for $R_1 < r < R_2$, charge q_2 does not contribute to the field as it lies outside the surface.

10 (*a*) Minimum distance of charge Q from Gaussian surface is $r/2$ and maximum distance

$$\left(2r + \frac{r}{2}\right) \text{ is } \frac{5r}{2}.$$

So, $E_{max} = \frac{kQ}{d^2}$

$$= \frac{kQ}{(r/2)^2} = \frac{4kQ}{r^2}$$

and $E_{min} = \frac{kQ}{d^2} = \frac{kQ}{\left(\frac{5}{2}r\right)^2}$

$$= \frac{4kQ}{25r^2}$$

$$\therefore E_{max} - E_{min} = \frac{4kQ}{r^2} - \frac{4kQ}{25r^2}$$

$$= \frac{24 \times 4kQ}{25r^2}$$

$$= \frac{24Q}{25\pi\varepsilon_0 r^2}$$

03

Scan for Physics Through Concept Master Videos

Current Electricity

Topicwise No. of Ques asked in 5 Years (NEET)

Topics	2024	2023	2022	2021	2020
Electric Currents in Conductors	–	–	–	–	–
Ohm's Law	–	1	–	–	1
Drift of Electrons and the Origin of Resistivity	–	–	1	–	1
Resistivity of Various Materials	1	–	–	–	1
Temperature Dependence of Resistivity	1	1	1	–	1
Electrical Energy, Power	1	–	2	–	–
Cells, Electromotive Force and Internal resistance	1	–	–	–	–
Kirchhoff's Rules	–	2	–	–	1
Wheatstone Bridge	–	–	1	–	–

Special Type of Ques Asked In 5 Years (NEET)

Types	2024	2023	2022	2021	2020
A-R	–	–	–	–	–
Statement Based	–	–	–	–	–
Matching	–	–	1	–	–

Last 5 Years Weigtage (NEET)

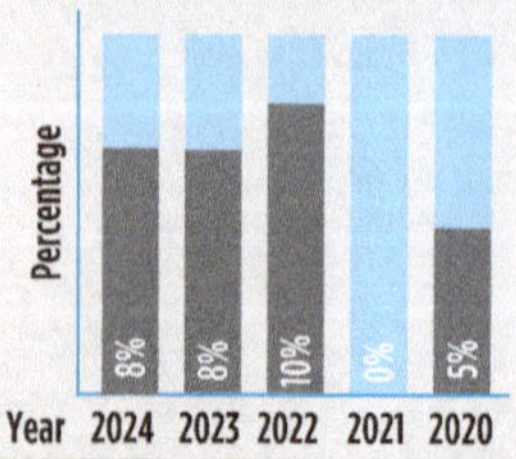

Electric Current

- The rate of flow of electric charge through any cross-sectional area of a conductor is known as electric current.
- If electric current through a conductor is steady, then current,

$$I = \frac{q}{t} = \frac{ne}{t} \qquad (\because q = ne)$$

where, $n =$ number of charged particles constituting the current and $e =$ electronic charge.

- Currents are not always steady and hence more generally, we define the current as $I(t) = \lim_{\Delta t \to 0}\left(\frac{\Delta Q}{\Delta t}\right)$

where, $\Delta Q =$ net charge flowing across a cross-section of conductor.

- Its SI unit is ampere and denoted by A, where $1\text{A} = 1\text{Cs}^{-1}$.

Electric Currents in Conductors

- In conductors, the electric current flows due to movement of negatively charged electrons.
- Electrolytic solutions are the type of conductors in which electric current flows due to the movement of both positive and negative charges.
- When no electric field is present in conductors, the average number of electrons travelling in any direction will be equal to the number of electrons travelling in the opposite direction. So, there will be no net electric current.

- If a conductor in shape of cylinder and charges $+Q$ and $-Q$ are put at the ends of it as shown in figure, then an electric field is created in conductor which is directed from positive charge to negative charge. NEET 2019

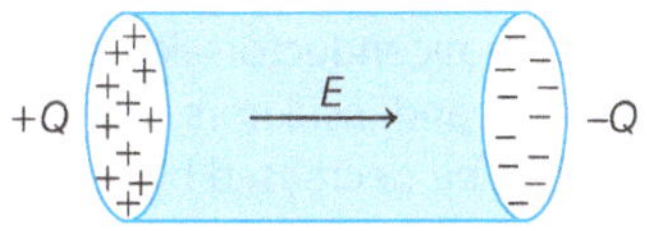

The electrons will be accelerated towards $+Q$ due to electric field and develop current for a very short time.

If we provide continuous supply of charges to ends of conductor by using cells or batteries, then we get continuous current.

Ohm's Law

- It states that, the current flowing through a conductor is directly proportional to the potential difference across its ends.

i.e. $I \propto V$ or $V \propto I$

$\Rightarrow$ $V = IR$ NEET 2019

where, R = resistance of conductor, which is measured in **ohm** (Ω).

- The resistance R, not only depends on the material of the conductor but also on the dimensions of the conductor.
- In general, resistance of a conductor is directly proportional to its length, i.e.

$$R \propto l$$

and inversely proportional to its cross-sectional area,

$$R \propto \frac{1}{A}$$

So, $R \propto \frac{l}{A} \Rightarrow R = \frac{\rho l}{A}$ NEET 2023

where, ρ is constant of proportionality, which is known as **resistivity of the material**. It depends upon the nature of the material and temperature of the conductor but not on the dimensions of conductor.

- Ohm's law can also be written as

$$V = IR = \frac{I\rho l}{A} \qquad \left[\because R = \frac{\rho l}{A}\right]$$

$\therefore$ $V = \left(\frac{I}{A}\right)\rho l$ NEET 2020

where, $\frac{I}{A}$ is current per unit area, which is known as **current density** and denoted as J.

The SI unit of current density is $\frac{\text{A}}{\text{m}^2}$.

- If E is the magnitude of uniform electric field in conductor, then $V = El$

So, from Ohm's law,

$$El = J\rho l$$

$\Rightarrow$ $E = J\rho$

In vector form, $\mathbf{E} = \mathbf{J}\rho$

or $\mathbf{J} = \frac{1}{\rho}\mathbf{E}$

$\Rightarrow$ $\mathbf{J} = \sigma\mathbf{E}$

where, σ is called conductivity.

$$\sigma = \frac{1}{\rho}$$

Drift of Electrons and the Origin of Resistivity NEET 2021

- The average velocity with which the free electrons in a conductor get drifted towards the positive end of a conductor under the influence of an external electric field is known as **drift velocity**.
- The time interval between two successive collisions of electrons is called **relaxation time**. It is denoted by τ.
- When an external electric field is applied to conductor, then force on the electrons will be $F = eE$ and acceleration of the electrons will be $a = \frac{eE}{m}$. Thus, drift velocity in terms of relaxation time, $v_d = \frac{eE}{m}\tau$
- **Electric current in terms of drift velocity,** $I = neA\,v_d$.

where, n = number density of free electrons
and A = cross-sectional area. NEET 2020

- **Current density at any point of conductor,** $J = \frac{I}{A} = ne\,v_d$
- The vector **J** is parallel to **E** and hence $\mathbf{J} = \frac{ne^2}{m}\tau\mathbf{E}$. NEET 2022
- The **relation between conductivity and relaxation time** is given as, $\sigma = \frac{ne^2}{m}\tau$.

Mobility

- The magnitude of the drift velocity per unit electric field is called **mobility** of charge carriers.

i.e. $\mu = \frac{|\mathbf{v}_d|}{E} = \frac{e\tau}{m}$

Its SI unit is $\text{m}^2\text{s}^{-1}\text{V}^{-1}$.

Limitations of Ohm's law

- Ohm's law is not a fundamental law of nature, this is a commonly found property of many substances under a given suitable conditions.
- There are some materials and devices used in electric circuits, where the proportionality of V and I does not hold. The deviations broadly are one or more of the following types
  (i) V ceases to be proportional to I. The dotted line represent the Ohm's law and solid line is V *versus* I for a good conductor as shown in figure.

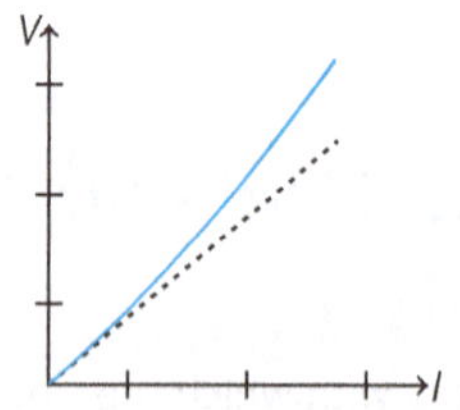

  (ii) If I is the current for a certain V, then reversing the direction of V keeping its magnitude fixed, does not produce a current of the same magnitude as I in the opposite direction. This happens in diodes as shown in figure.

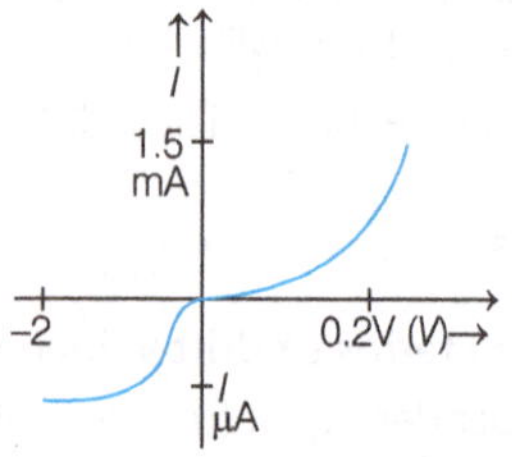

  (iii) The relation between V and I is not unique, i.e. there is more than one value of V for the same current I as shown in figure.
  A material exhibiting such behaviour is GaAs.

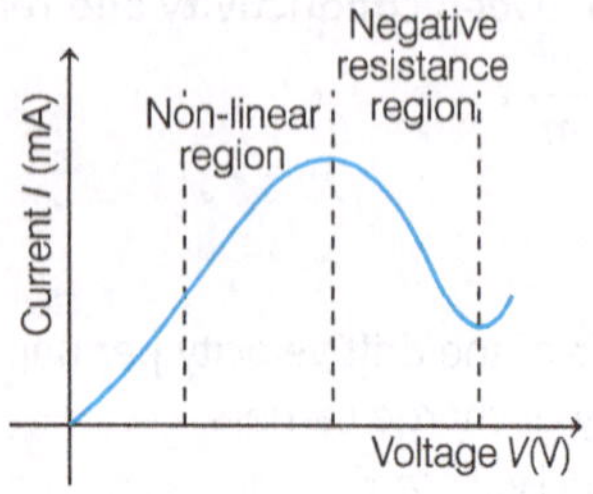

For Concept Master Video

Resistivity of Various Materials

- Materials are classified as conductors, semiconductors and insulators depending on their resistivities.
- Metals have low resistivities in the range of 10^{-8} Ω-m to 10^{-6} Ω-m.
- Insulators like ceramic, rubber and plastic have resistivities 10^{18} times greater than metals or more.
- The resistivities of semiconductors lie between the resistivities of metals and insulators. The resistivities of semiconductors can be decreased by adding suitable impurities.

Temperature Dependence of Resistivity

- Resistivity of a metallic conductor depends on the temperature of conductor and it increases on increasing the temperature. NEET 2022
- The variation of resistivity with temperature is given by
$$\rho_T = \rho_0 [1 + \alpha(T - T_0)]$$
where, ρ_T is the resistivity at a temperature T,
ρ_0 is resistivity at a reference temperature T_0
and α is called the **temperature coefficient of resistivity**. The dimension of α is $[T^{-1}]$.
- The value of α is positive for metallic conductor and in terms of resistance, it is given as $\alpha = \dfrac{R_2 - R_1}{R_1(t_2 - t_1)}$. NEET 2023
- A graph of ρ_T plotted against T can be approximated as a straight line over a limited range of T. For example, variation of resistivity of copper is shown below. It is linear between 70 K to 150 K.

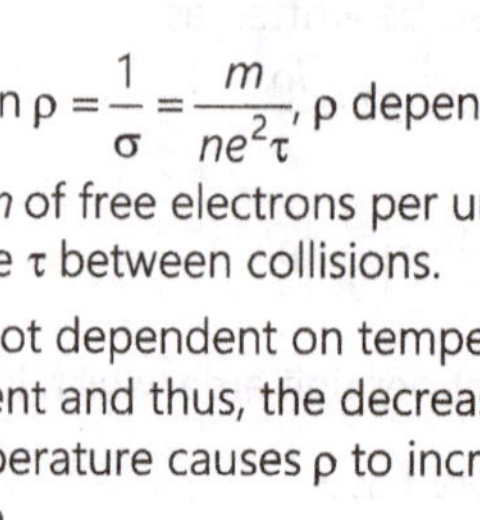

NEET 2020

- From the relation $\rho = \dfrac{1}{\sigma} = \dfrac{m}{ne^2\tau}$, ρ depends inversely both on the number n of free electrons per unit volume and on the average time τ between collisions. NEET 2020
- In a metal, n is not dependent on temperature to any appreciable extent and thus, the decrease in the value of τ with rise in temperature causes ρ to increase as shown in the above figure.
- Some materials like nichrome, manganin and constantan exhibit a very weak dependence of resistivity with temperature.

- Variation in resistivity of nichrome with T is as shown below.

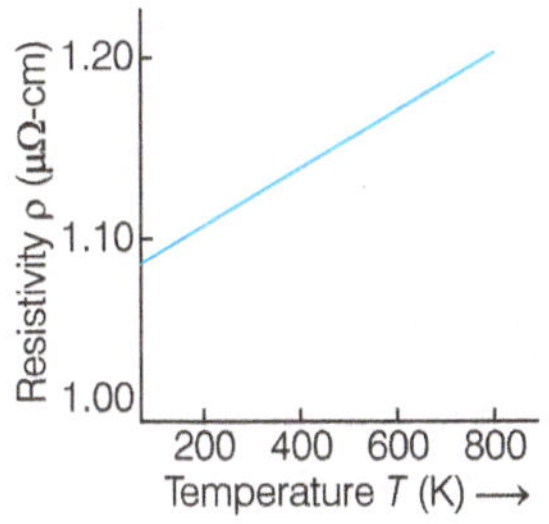

- For insulators and semiconductors, n increases with temperature. This increase in n compensates any decrease in τ, so that for such materials, ρ decreases with temperature.
- The resistivities of semiconductors decreases rapidly with increasing temperature as shown in figure below.

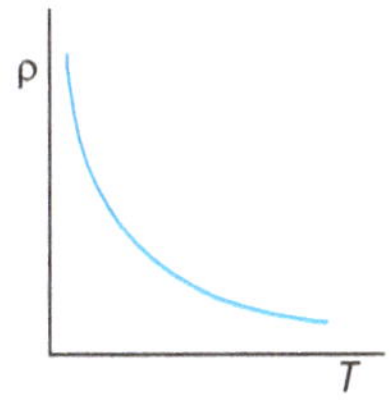

Electrical Energy, Power

- If electric potential at end points A and B of a conductor are denoted by V_A and V_B respectively and I current is flowing from A to B, then potential across AB is,

$$V = V_A - V_B > 0$$

Thus, change in potential energy,

$$\Delta U = \Delta Q(V_B - V_A) = -\Delta QV$$
$$= -I\Delta tV \qquad [\because \Delta Q = I\Delta t]$$

So, **electrical energy is the total work done by the source of emf in maintaining the electric current in the given circuit for Δt time.** It is given as

$$E = W = VI\Delta t = \frac{V^2\Delta t}{R}.$$

- **Electric Power** It is the rate at which electrical energy is supplied per unit time to maintain the flow of current in a conductor and given by $P = VI = I^2R = V^2/R$. NEET 2022, 19

Its SI unit is **watt (W)** and its commercial unit is **horse power (HP)**, where 1 HP = 746 W.

- The power dissipated in the connecting wires is

$$P_c = I^2R_c = \frac{P^2R_c}{V^2}$$

where, P is power delivered by wires of resistance R_c.

*Combination of Resistors

- **In Series**
  - (i) Equivalent resistance, $R = R_1 + R_2 + R_3$.

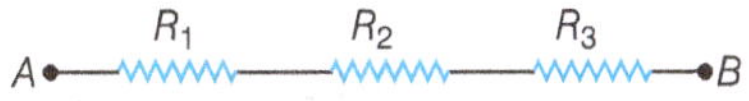

  - (ii) Current through each resistor is same. NEET 2023, 22
  - (iii) Sum of potential differences across individual resistors is equal to the potential difference applied by the source.
- **In Parallel**
  - (i) Equivalent resistance, $\frac{1}{R} = \frac{1}{R_1} + \frac{1}{R_2} + \frac{1}{R_3}$.

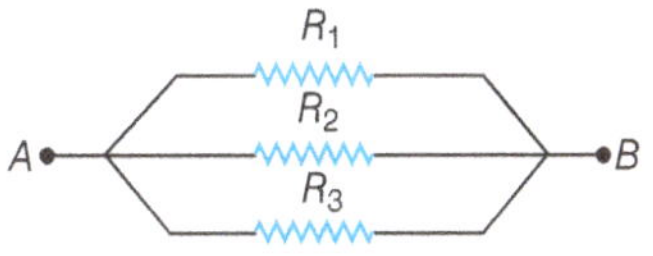

NEET 2023, 21, 20

  - (ii) Potential difference across each resistor is same.
  - (iii) Sum of electric currents flowing through individual resistors is equal to the electric current drawn from the source.

Marks Maximiser

Calculation of resistance in different cases

(i) A wire of resistance R is cut into n equal parts and all parts are connected in parallel, then

$$R_{eq} = \frac{R}{n^2}$$

(ii) A wire of resistance R is bent in the form of a circle as shown in the figure, then resistance between A and B,

$$R_{AB} = \frac{R\alpha\,(2\pi - \alpha)}{4\pi^2}$$

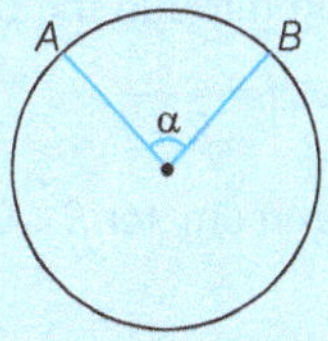

Equivalent resistivity in different cases

(i) If two wires of resistivities ρ_1 and ρ_2, lengths l_1 and l_2 are connected in series, the equivalent resistivity,

$$\rho = \frac{\rho_1 l_1 + \rho_2 l_2}{l_1 + l_2}$$

(ii) If two wires of resistivites ρ_1 and ρ_2, areas of cross-section A_1 and A_2 are connected in parallel, the equivalent resistivity, $\rho = \frac{\rho_1\rho_2(A_1 + A_2)}{\rho_1 A_2 + \rho_2 A_1}$

*This topic is not included in latest rationalised NCERT, but it is given in latest NEET syllabus.

Cells, Emf, Internal Resistance

- **Electrolytic Cell** It is a device which converts chemical energy into electrical energy. The combination of cell produces a battery.
- **Electromotive force or emf of a cell** It is the potential difference across its terminals when no electric current is flowing through it.
- **Internal Resistance of a Cell** It is the resistance offered by the electrolyte of the cell to the flow of current through it.

  In terms of ε and V as shown in the circuit below, it is represented as $r = \left(\frac{\varepsilon}{V} - 1\right)R$.

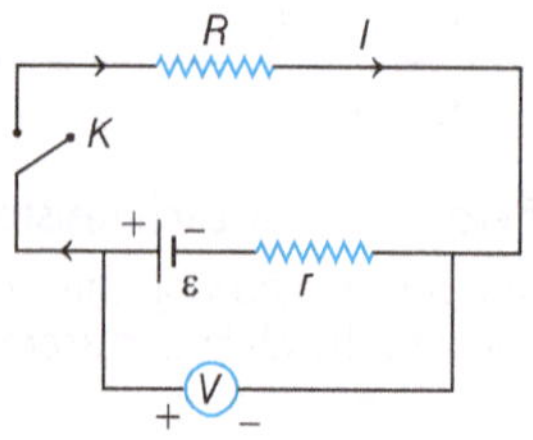

- Internal resistance of a cell depends upon
  (i) surface area of each electrode
  (ii) distance between the two electrodes
  (iii) nature, temperature and concentration of electrolyte.
- The terminal potential difference V during the charging of cell as shown in figure below is given by $V = \varepsilon + Ir$

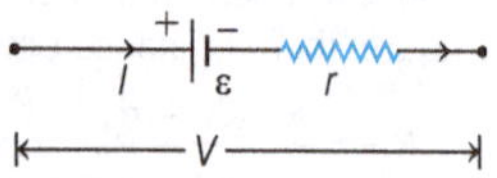

- Electric current flowing through the cell across finite resistance R is given as $I = \frac{\varepsilon}{R + r}$.

  In a cell, current is maximum, for $R = 0$, i.e. $I_{max} = \frac{\varepsilon}{r}$.

Cells in Series and in Parallel

Series Combination

- The series combination of two cells is shown below.

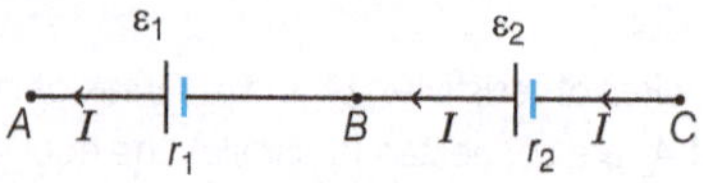

- The equivalent emf of a series combination of the above shown cells is just the sum of their individual emf's, i.e. $\varepsilon_{eq} = \varepsilon_1 + \varepsilon_2$ and the equivalent internal resistance of this combination is just the sum of their internal resistances, i.e. $r_{eq} = r_1 + r_2$. These rules can be extended to any number of cells.
- If polarity of one of the batteries is reversed, then equivalent emf is $|\varepsilon_1 - \varepsilon_2|$ and net internal resistance continue to be same.

Parallel Combination

- The equivalent emf of parallel combination of two cells as shown below and is given by

$$\varepsilon_{eq} = \frac{\varepsilon_1 r_2 + \varepsilon_2 r_1}{r_1 + r_2}$$

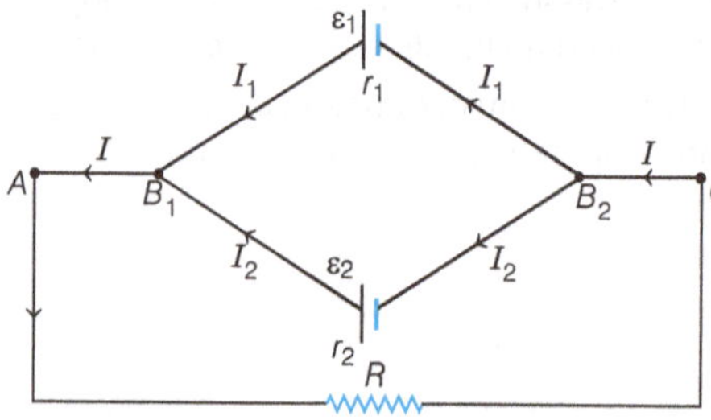

and internal resistance of combination, $r_{eq} = \frac{r_1 r_2}{r_1 + r_2}$.

For m cells, each of emf ε and internal resistance r, then

(i) net emf $= \varepsilon_{net}$

(ii) net internal resistance $= \frac{r}{m}$

(iii) total resistance of the circuit,

$$R_T = R + \frac{r}{m}$$

(iv) current in the circuit,

$$I = \frac{\varepsilon}{R + \frac{r}{m}} = \frac{m\varepsilon}{mR + r}$$

Special Case

(i) If $R << \frac{r}{m}$, then

$I = \frac{m\varepsilon}{r} = m$ times the current due to a single cell.

(ii) If $R >> \frac{r}{m}$, then

$I = \frac{E}{R} =$ the current given by a single cell.

Hence, if R is much smaller than total internal resistance, then connect cells in parallel to get maximum current.

Marks Maximiser

Mixed Grouping

In the following figure, n identical cells are connected in m rows.

(i) Net emf $= m\varepsilon$

(ii) Total resistance $= R + \dfrac{mr}{n}$

(iii) Total current $I = \dfrac{m\varepsilon}{R + \dfrac{mr}{n}}$

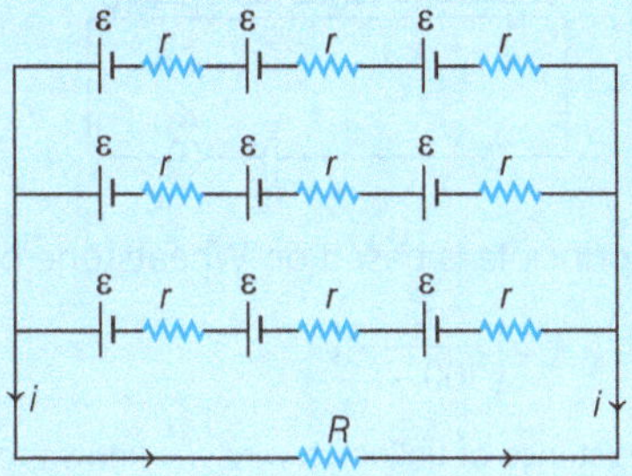

Kirchhoff's Rules

- There are two rules given by Kirchhoff as given below.
    (i) **Junction Rule** At any junction, the sum of the currents entering the junction is equal to the sum of currents leaving the junction, i.e. $\Sigma I = 0$.

    This rule is based on the law of **conservation of charges**. NEET 2019, 20, 23

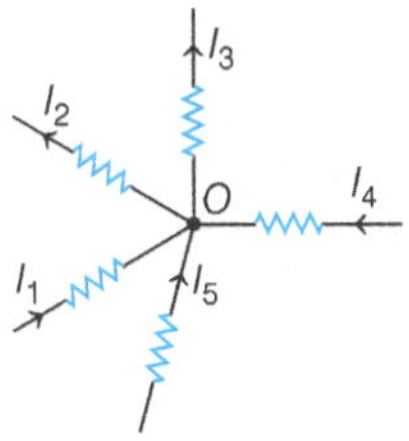

From the given figure, $I_1 - I_2 - I_3 + I_4 + I_5 = 0$

(ii) **Loop Rule** The algebraic sum of changes in potential around any closed loop involving resistors and cells in the loop is zero, i.e. $\Sigma IR + \Sigma \varepsilon = 0$.

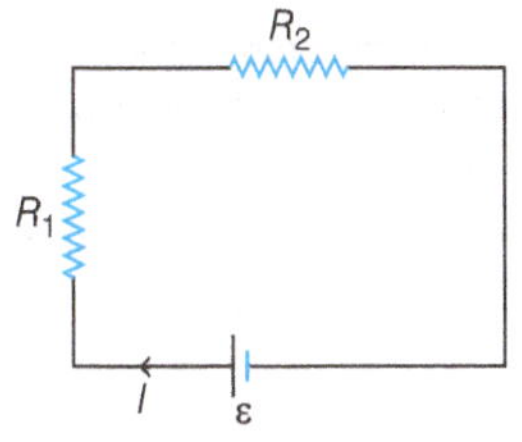

For Concept Master Video

From the figure, $\varepsilon - IR_1 - IR_2 = 0$

- This rule is based on the law of conservation of energy.

Marks Maximiser

Junction Removal

In the following figure the terminal of battery is connected across AB and the circuit is symmetric about DF. Hence, point D can be separated without affecting the circuit as shown in the figure.

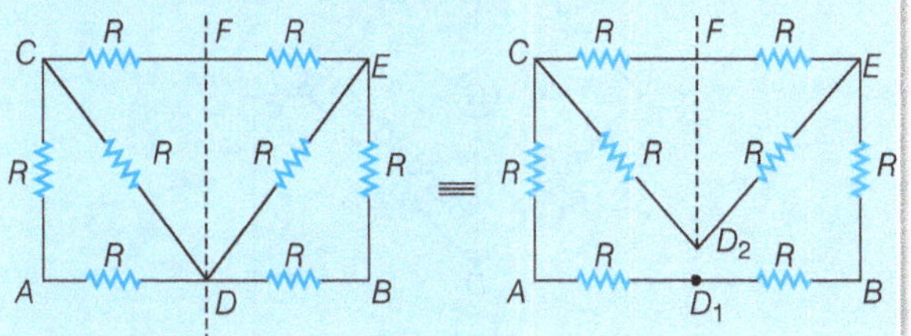

Hence, potential at points D_1 and D_2 are same.

Equipotential points

Two points of a circuit are said to equipotential if they are at same potential.

Using this fact the following circuit can be simplified as shown in the figure. (Points A and 2 are equipotential and points B and 1 are equipotential.) NEET 2020, 19

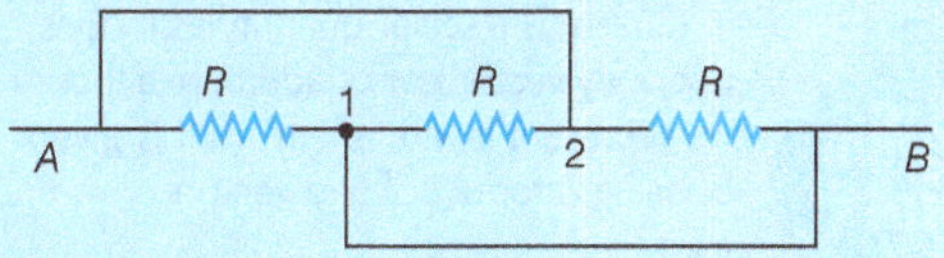

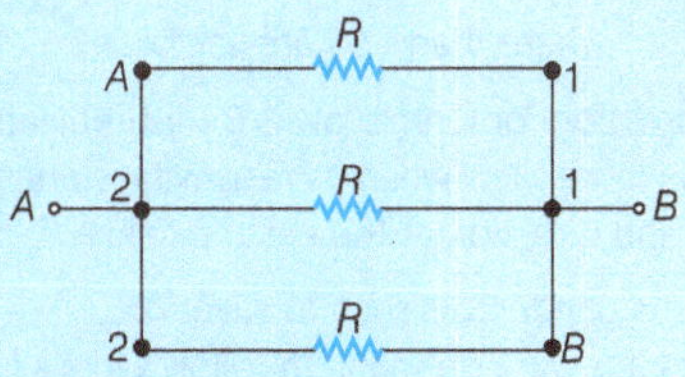

Delta-star transformation

$$R_{12} = \frac{R_1 R_2}{R_1 + R_2 + R_3};$$

$$R_{13} = \frac{R_1 R_3}{R_1 + R_2 + R_3};$$

$$R_{23} = \frac{R_2 R_3}{R_1 + R_2 + R_3}$$

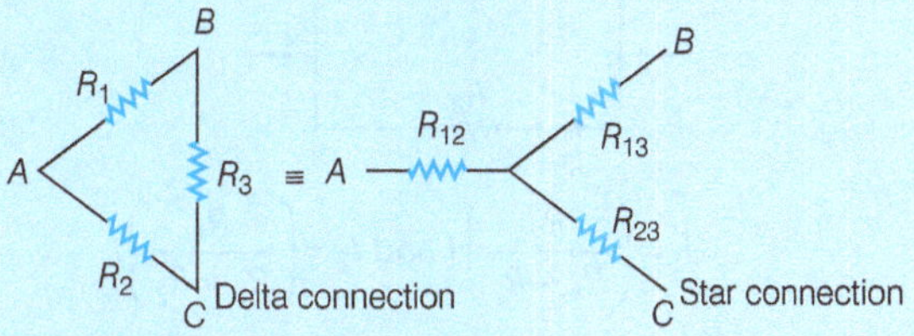

Wheatstone Bridge

- It is an arrangement of four resistors used to measure the resistance of one of them in terms of other three.
- The Wheatstone bridge circuit is shown in figure below.

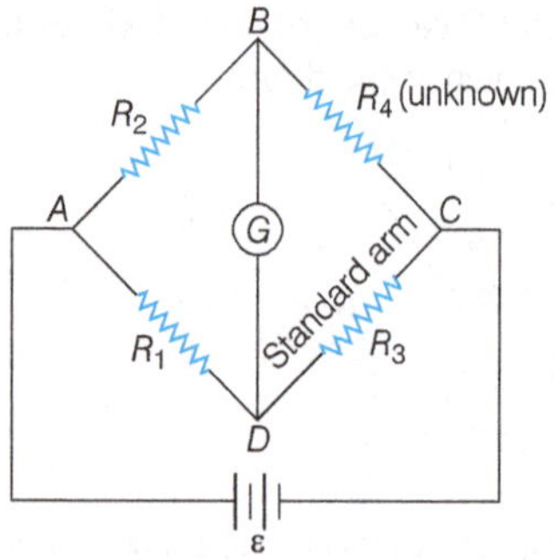

- Across one pair of diagonally opposite points (A and C) a source is connected, as shown in figure, AC is called the **battery arm.**
- Between the other two vertices B and D, a galvanometer G is connected. This line shown as BD in the figure, is called the **galvanometer arm.**
- In case of balanced bridge, the resistors are such that galvanometer current, $I_g = 0$. In this case, $\frac{R_2}{R_1} = \frac{R_4}{R_3}$

  This equation is called the **balance condition** for the galvanometer to give zero or null deflection. NEET 2022, 21

*Meter Bridge

- It is a device which is used to measure resistance of an unknown wire.
- It is shown in given figure.

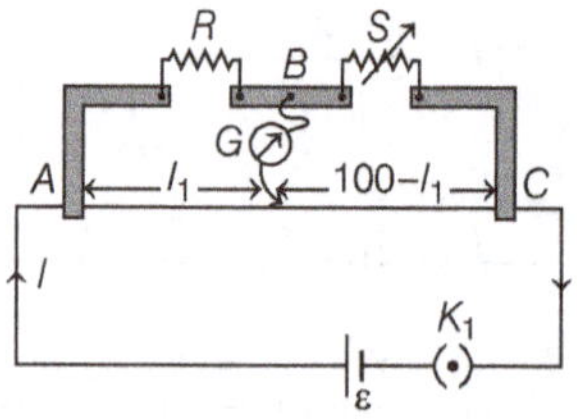

- Its working principle is based on Wheatstone bridge principle, i.e. $R = S\left(\frac{l_1}{100 - l_1}\right)$

  where, R = resistance of unknown wire, S = known resistance and l_1 = distance of null point from first end. **[NEET 2020, 19]**

Caution Points

- Current is a scalar quantity as it does not obey vector law of addition, although we represent it with an arrow. It is given by scalar product of two vectors.
  $I = \mathbf{J} \cdot \Delta\mathbf{S}$
  where, **J** and **ΔS** are vectors.
- Another expression for Ohm's law is $\mathbf{E} = \rho\mathbf{J}$, indicating a material follows Ohm's law when its resistivity is unaffected by magnitude and direction of the electric field.
- Homogeneous conductors such as silver or semiconductors like pure germanium follow Ohm's law within a certain range of electric field values. However, deviations from Ohm's law occur when the electric field becomes too strong in all cases.
- The motion of conduction electrons in an electric field (**E**) consists of two components, i.e., motion from random collision and motion due to **E**.
- The relation $\mathbf{J} = \rho\mathbf{v}$ should be applied to each type of charge carriers separately.
- Total current and charge density in a conducting wire comes from both positive and negative charges.
  $$\mathbf{J} = \rho_+\mathbf{v}_+ + \rho_-\mathbf{v}_-$$
  $$\rho = \rho_+ + \rho_-$$
  For a neutral wire carrying current,
  $$\rho_+ = -\rho_- \Rightarrow \quad \rho = 0$$
  Further, $\mathbf{v}_+ \sim 0$ which gives
  $$\mathbf{J} = \rho_-\mathbf{v}$$
  Thus, $\mathbf{J} = \rho\mathbf{v}$ does not apply to the total current charge density.

PYQ Notes

1. If two resistors R_1 and R_2 are connected in parallel as shown in figure, then you can find the value of I_1 and I_2 using current division rule as

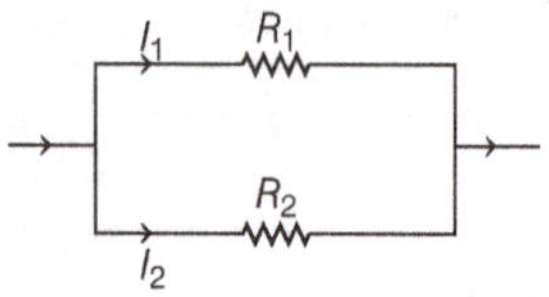

$$I_1 = \left(\frac{R_2}{R_1 + R_2}\right)I \text{ and } I_2 = \left(\frac{R_1}{R_1 + R_2}\right)I$$

[JEE Main 2023]

2. When current I flow through a resistor of resistance R. According to Joule's law of heating, heat produced is $H = I^2Rt = \frac{V^2}{R}t$ **[JEE Main 2021, NEET 2022]**
3. Fuse is used in electric circuit as a protective device. When excess amount of current flows in the circuit, it melts and breaks the circuit. **[NEET 2019]**
4. In steady state, no current will pass through capacitor. Hence, capacitor will act open switch. **[JEE Main 2023, 2017]**

**This topic is not included in latest rationalised NCERT, but it is given in latest NEET syllabus.*

Step by Step

Mastering NCERT

- Concept Builders
- Topical Questions
- Assertion and Reason Questions
- Statement Based
- Matching Type
- Numerical Type
- NCERT Exemplar
- Past Exams MCQs
- Skill Boosters

Concept Builders

1 By maintaining the potential difference between two ends of a conductor, electric current can be kept continuous. [T/F]

2 The direction of electronic current is .... (same/opposite) as that of conventional current.

3 The conventional current is due to the flow of .... (positive/negative) charges and electronic current is due to (positive/negative) charge.

4 If a wire is stretched to double its original length without loss of mass, how will the resistivity of wire be changed?

5 n equal resistors are first connected in series and then connected in parallel. What is the ratio of the maximum resistance to the minimum resistance?

6 It is easier to start a car engine on a warm day than on a cold day. [T/F]

7 Internal resistance of a battery decreases with .... (increase/ decrease) in temperature.

8 What is the range of resistivity of metals ?

9 Relaxation time .... (increases/decreases) with rise in temperature.

10 Thermal energy ...... (decreases/increases) the velocity of electrons in continuous motion.

11 Coefficient of thermal resistance (α) of carbon is negative. [T/F]

12 The heat energy produced in a current carrying wire is inversely proportional to the square of the current. [T/F]

13 Write down the formula for the power transferred per unit volume in a resistor in terms of current density.

14 The power consumed by n equal resistors in parallel combination is .... $\left(n^2 / \frac{1}{n^2}\right)$ times that of power consumed in series combination, if V remains same.

15 A domestic electrical appliance working on a three pin will continue to working even if the top pin is removed. [T/F]

16 According to Kirchhoff's loop rule, the algebraic sum of the emf's in any loop of a circuit is equal to the sum of the products of .... (voltage/current) and (current/resistors) in it.

17 Bending or orienting the wire will also changes the validity of Kirchhoff's junction rule. [T/F]

18 When the Wheatstone bridge is balanced, the potential difference between the two points is .... (maximum/ zero)

19 Wheatstone bridge is most sensitive when the resistance in the four arms are of the same order. [T/F]

20 The Wheatstone bridge method is not applicable for measurement of very high and very low resistances. [T/F]

Topical Questions

Electric Current

1 An electron revolves around the nucleus of an atom. It is making 9.4×10^{18} revolution per second along a path of radius 0.72 Å. The equivalent current is NCERT Pg. 82

(a) 1.0 A (b) 2.5 A (c) 1.5 A (d) 2.0 A

2 In a hydrogen atom, an electron moves in an orbit of radius 5.0×10^{-11} m with a speed of 2.2×10^6 ms^{-1}. The equivalent current is NCERT Pg. 82

(a) 11.2×10^{-3} A (b) 1.9×10^{-3} A
(c) 1.12×10^{-3} A (d) 11.2×10^{4} A

3 Two boys A and B are sitting at two points in a field near an assemblage of charged balls each carrying charge $+3e$. A throws 100 balls per second towards B while B throws 50 balls per second towards A simultaneously. Find the current at the mid-point of A and B. NCERT Pg. 82

(a) $i = 3.4\times 10^{-17}$ A from A to B
(b) $i = 2.4\times 10^{-17}$ A from A to B
(c) $i = 2.8\times 10^{-17}$ A from B to A
(d) $i = 4.8\times 10^{-17}$ A from B to A

4 The current in a wire varies with time according to the equation $i = 4 + 2t$, where i is in ampere and t is in second. The quantity of charge which passes through a cross-section of the wire during the time $t = 2$s to $t = 6$s is **NCERT Pg. 82**

(a) 40 C (b) 48 C (c) 38 C (d) 43 C

Electric Current in Conductors

5 Twenty million electrons reaches from point X to point Y in two microsecond as shown in the figure. Direction and magnitude of the current is **NCERT Pg. 82**

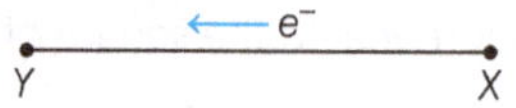

(a) 1.5×10^{-10} A from X to Y
(b) 1.6×10^{-6} A from Y to X
(c) 1.5×10^{-13} A from Y to X
(d) 1.6×10^{-4} A from X to Y

6 In a region 10^{19} α-particles and 10^{19} protons move to the left, while 10^{19} electrons moves to the right per second. The current is **NCERT Pg. 82**

(a) 3.2 A towards left (b) 3.2 A towards right
(c) 6.4 A towards left (d) 6.4 A towards right

Ohm's Law

7 For a wire, $\frac{R}{l} = \frac{1}{2}$ and length of wire, $l = 5$ cm. If potential difference of 1 V is applied across it, then current through wire will be (R = resistance) **NCERT Pg. 83**

(a) 40 A (b) 4 A (c) 25 A (d) 2.5 A

8 The V- I graph for a good conductor makes angle 40° with V-axis. Here, V denotes voltage and I denotes current. The resistance of the conductor will be **NCERT Pg. 83**

(a) sin 40° (b) cos 40° (c) tan 40° (d) cot 40°

9 All the edges of a block with parallel faces are unequal. Its longest edge is twice its shortest edge and third edge is 1.5 times of shortest edge, then ratio of the maximum and minimum resistance between parallel faces is **NCERT Pg. 84**

(a) 8 (b) 4 (c) 2 (d) 14

10 A copper wire of cross-sectional area 2.0 mm^2, resistivity = 1.7×10^{-8} Ω-m, carries a current of 1 A. The electric field in the copper wire is **NCERT Pg. 84**

(a) 8.5×10^{-5} Vm^{-1} (b) 8.5×10^{-4}Vm^{-1}
(c) 8.5×10^{-3} Vm^{-1} (d) 8.5×10^{-2} Vm^{-1}

11 If resistivity of copper conductor is 1.7×10^{-8} Ω-m and electric field is 100 Vm^{-1}, then current density will be **NCERT Pg. 85**

(a) 6×10^{9} Am^{-2} (b) 1.7×10^{-6} Am^{-2}
(c) 1.7×10^{-10} Am^{-2} (d) 6×10^{7} Am^{-2}

12 A charge of 4C is flowing through a copper wire of cross-section 2 mm^2 in 2s. If the conductivity of copper wire be 6.25×10^{7} Sm^{-1}, then electric field in copper wire is **NCERT Pg. 85**

(a) 0.8×10^{-2} N/C (b) 1.6×10^{-3} N/C
(c) 1.6×10^{-2} N/C (d) 3.2×10^{-3} N/C

Drift of Electrons and the Origin of Resistivity

13 A current i is flowing through the wire of diameter d having drift velocity of electrons v_d in it. What will be new drift velocity when diameter of wire is made $d/4$? **NCERT Pg. 86**

(a) $4v_d$ (b) $\frac{v_d}{4}$
(c) $16\,v_d$ (d) $\frac{v_d}{16}$

14 When a current I flows through a wire, the drift velocity of the electrons is v. When current $2I$ flows through another wire of the same material having double the length and double the area of cross-section, the drift velocity of the electrons will be **NCERT Pg. 86**

(a) $v/8$ (b) $v/4$
(c) $v/2$ (d) v

15 A potential difference of 100 V is applied to the ends of a copper wire of 1 m length. What is the average drift velocity of electrons?

(Take, $\sigma = 5.81 \times 10^7 \Omega^{-1}$ or $n_{Cu} = 8.5 \times 10^{28}$ m^{-3}) **NCERT Pg. 86**

(a) 0.43 ms^{-1} (b) 0.83 ms^{-1}
(c) 0.52 ms^{-1} (d) 0.95 ms^{-1}

16 A current of 10 A is passing through a metallic wire of cross-sectional area 4×10^{-6} m^2. If the density of the aluminium conductor is 2.7 g/cc. Considering aluminium gives 1 electron per atom for conduction, then find the drift velocity of the electrons, if molecular weight of aluminium is 27 g. **NCERT Pg. 86**

(a) 1.6×10^{-4} m/s (b) 3.6×10^{-4} m/s
(c) 2.6×10^{-4} m/s (d) 1.5×10^{-4} m/s

17 A conducting wire of cross-sectional area 1 cm^2 has 3×10^{23} charge carrier per m^3. If wire carries a current of 24 mA, the drift velocity of carriers is **NCERT Pg. 86**

(a) 5×10^{-2} ms^{-1} (b) 0.5 ms^{-1}
(c) 5×10^{-3} ms^{-1} (d) 4×10^{-2} ms^{-1}

18 If resistivity of copper is $1.72 \times 10^{-8}\Omega$-m and number of free electrons in copper is 8.5×10^{28} /m^3. Find the mobility. **NCERT Pg. 88**

(a) 4.27×10^{-3}m^2 / C-Ω
(b) 6.8×10^{-3}m^2 / C-Ω
(c) 8.5×10^{-3}m^2 / C-Ω
(d) 3.4×10^{-3}m^2 / C-Ω

Limitations of Ohm's Law

19 Which of the following I-V graph represents ohmic conductors? NCERT Pg. 89

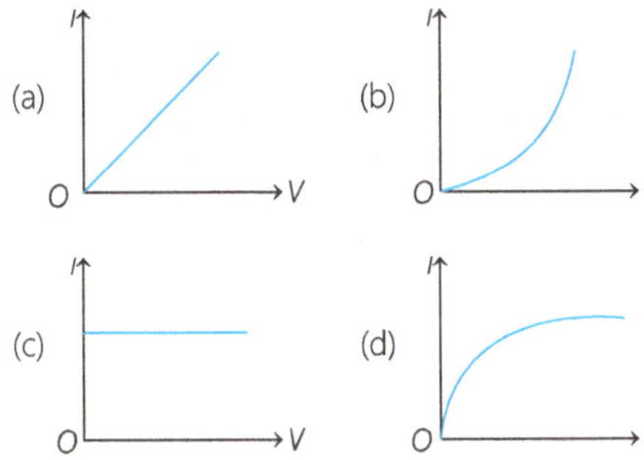

20 The I-V graph given in the figure represents NCERT Pg. 89

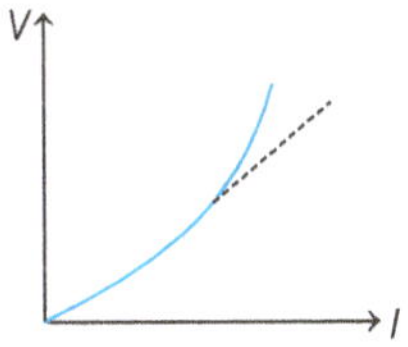

(a) ohmic conductors (b) super conductors
(c) good conductors (d) insulators

21 The I-V characteristic shown in figure represents NCERT Pg. 89

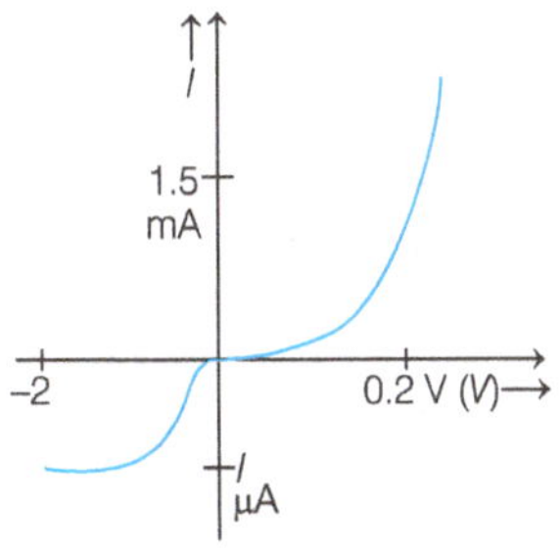

(a) a good conductor
(b) a diode
(c) an insulators
(d) an ohmic conductor

Resistivity of Various Materials

22 Arrangement of the following materials is given in increasing order of their resistivity. Which of the following is correct? NCERT Pg. 89

(a) Copper < Germanium < Ceramic
(b) Germanium < Ceramic < Copper
(c) Ceramic < Copper < Germanium
(d) Ceramic < Germanium < Copper

Temperature Dependence of Resistivity

23 Resistance of a wire at 20°C is 20Ω and at 500°C is 60 Ω. At what temperature, its resistance is 25Ω? NCERT Pg. 90

(a) 160°C (b) 250°C (c) 100°C (d) 80°C

24 Two conductors have the same resistance at 0°C but their temperature coefficients of resistance are α_1 and α_2. The effective temperature coefficient of their series combination is NCERT Pg. 90

(a) $\frac{\alpha_1 + \alpha_2}{4}$ (b) $\alpha_1 \times \alpha_2$
(c) $\alpha_1 + \alpha_2$ (d) $\frac{\alpha_1 + \alpha_2}{2}$

25 The current i and voltage V graph for a given metallic wire at two different temperatures T_1 and T_2 are shown in the figure. It is concluded that NCERT Pg. 90

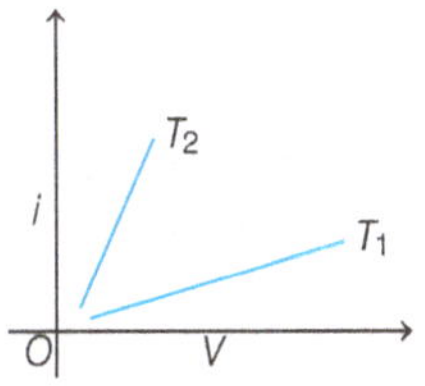

(a) $T_1 > T_2$ (b) $T_1 < T_2$
(c) $T_1 = T_2$ (d) $T_1 = 2T_2$

26 The temperature dependence of resistances of Cu and undoped Si in the temperature range 300-400 K, is best described by NCERT Pg. 90

(a) linear increase for Cu, linear increase for Si
(b) linear increase for Cu, exponential increase for Si
(c) linear increase for Cu, exponential decrease for Si
(d) linear decrease for Cu, linear decrease for Si

27 The resistance of wire in a heater at room temperature is 65 Ω. When the heater is connected to a 220 V supply, the current settles after a few seconds to 2.8 A. What is the steady temperature of the wire? (Temperature coefficient of resistance, $\alpha = 1.70 \times 10^{-4}\ °C^{-1}$) NCERT Pg. 90

(a) 955 °C (b) 1055 °C
(c) 1155 °C (d) 1258 °C

28 The resistance of the wire in the platinum resistance thermometer at ice point is 5Ω and at steam point is 5.25 Ω. When the thermometer is inserted in an unknown hot bath, its resistance is found to be 5.5 Ω. The temperature of the hot bath is NCERT Pg. 90

(a) 100 °C (b) 200 °C
(c) 300 °C (d) 350 °C

29 Figure (a) and figure (b) both are showing the variation of resistivity (ρ) with temperature (T) for some materials. Identify the type of these materials. **NCERT Pg. 90**

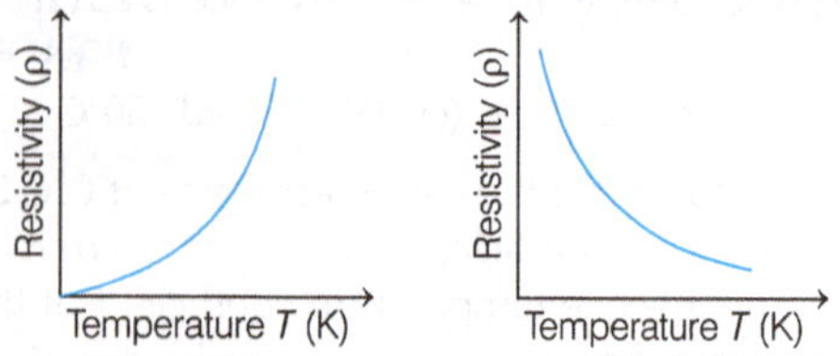

Figure (a) Figure (b)

(a) Insulator and semiconductor
(b) Conductor and insulator
(c) Conductor and semiconductor
(d) Semiconductor and conductor

Combination of Resistors : Series and Parallel

30 Two wires of same metal have the same length but areas of their cross-sections are in the ratio 3 : 1 are joined in series. The resistance of the thicker wire is 10Ω. The total resistance of the combination is **Old NCERT Pg. 107**

(a) (5/2) Ω (b) (40/2)Ω
(c) 40 Ω (d) 100 Ω

31 The equivalent resistance between the points P and Q in the network given here is equal to (given, $r = \frac{3}{2}\Omega$) **Old NCERT Pg. 107**

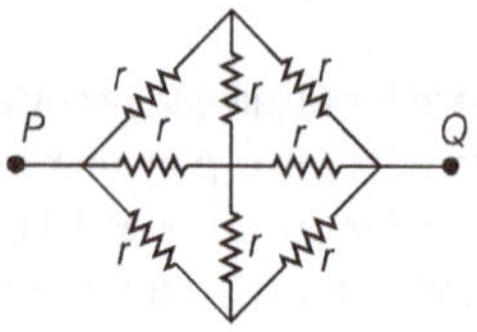

(a) $\frac{1}{2}\Omega$ (b) 1Ω
(c) $\frac{3}{2}\Omega$ (d) 2Ω

32 The potential difference across 8 Ω resistance is 48 V as shown in the figure. The value of potential difference across X and Y points will be **Old NCERT Pg. 107**

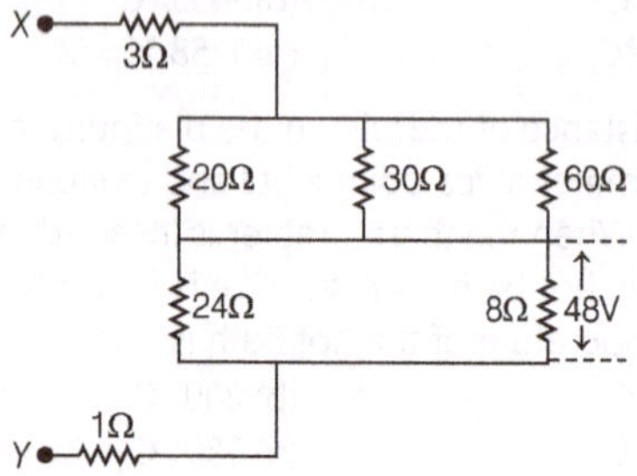

(a) 160 V (b) 128 V
(c) 80 V (d) 62 V

33 Two resistances 400Ω and 800Ω are connected in series with 6 V battery. The potential difference measured by voltmeter of 10 kΩ across 400Ω resistor is **Old NCERT Pg. 107**

(a) 2 V (b) 1.95 V (c) 3.8 V (d) 4 V

34 A uniform metallic wire has a resistance of 18 Ω and is bent into an equilateral triangle. Then, the resistance between any two vertices of the triangle is **Old NCERT Pg. 109**

(a) 12 Ω (b) 8 Ω (c) 2 Ω (d) 4 Ω

35 Two resistances are joined in parallel whose equivalent resistance is (3/5) Ω. One of the resistance wire is broken and the effective resistance becomes 3Ω. The resistance (in ohm) of the wire that got broken was **Old NCERT Pg. 109**

(a) 4/3 (b) 2 (c) 6/5 (d) 3/4

36 A wire of uniform cross-section and length l has a resistance of 16Ω. It is cut into four equal parts. Each part is stretched uniformly to length l and all the stretched parts are connected in parallel. Calculate the total resistance of the combination so formed. (Assume that the stretching of the wire does not cause any change in the density of the material.) **Old NCERT Pg. 109**

(a) 10 Ω (b) 12 Ω (c) 16 Ω (d) 18 Ω

37 Find i in shown figure. **Old NCERT Pg. 108**

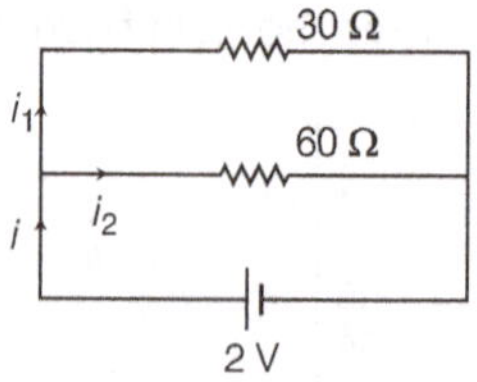

(a) 0.2 A (b) 0.1 A (c) 0.3 A (d) 0.4 A

38 Two resistances R and 2 R are connected in parallel in an electric circuit. The thermal energy developed in R and $2R$ in the ratio **Old NCERT Pg. 107**

(a) 1:2 (b) 1:4 (c) 4:1 (d) 2:1

39 The equivalent resistance of n resistors each of same resistance when connected in series is R. If the same resistances are connected in parallel, the equivalent resistances will be **Old NCERT Pg. 107**

(a) R/n^2 (b) R/n (c) n^2R (d) nR

40 Five resistors are connected as shown in figure. Find the equivalent resistance between the points B and C. **Old NCERT Pg. 108**

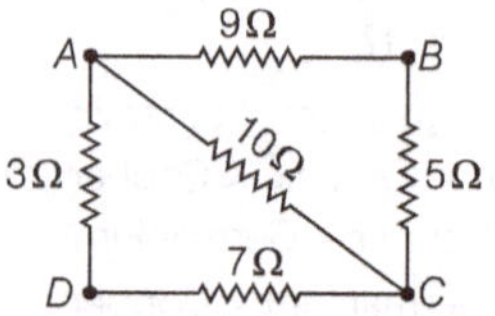

(a) $\frac{70}{19}\Omega$ (b) $\frac{19}{70}\Omega$ (c) $\frac{16}{5}\Omega$ (d) $\frac{15}{8}\Omega$

41 Six equal resistances are connected between points P, Q and R as shown in the figure. Then, the net resistance will be maximum between **Old NCERT Pg. 108**

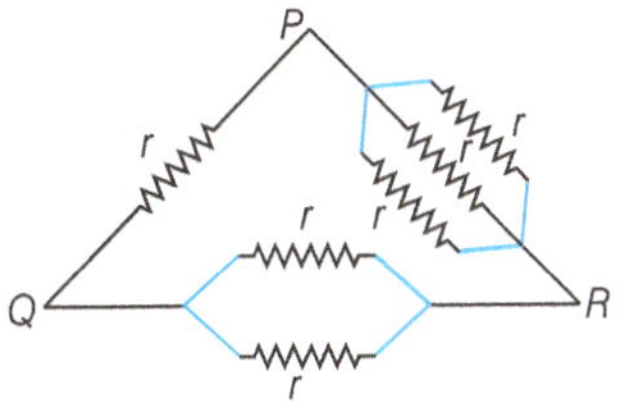

(a) P and Q
(b) Q and R
(c) P and R
(d) equal for any two points

42 A ring is made of a wire having a resistance $R_0 = 12\,\Omega$. Find the points A and B as shown in the figure, at which a current carrying conductor should be connected, so that the resistance R of the sub-circuit between these points is equal to $(8/3)\,\Omega$. **Old NCERT Pg. 108**

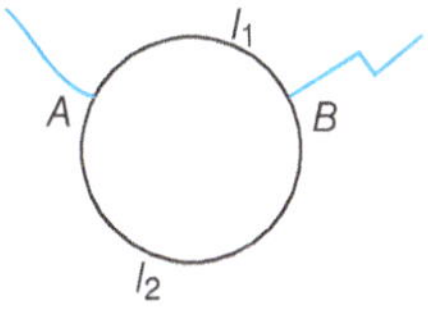

(a) $\frac{l_1}{l_2} = \frac{5}{8}$
(b) $\frac{l_1}{l_2} = \frac{1}{3}$
(c) $\frac{l_1}{l_2} = \frac{3}{8}$
(d) $\frac{l_1}{l_2} = \frac{1}{2}$

43 What is the equivalent resistance across the points A and B in the circuit given below? **Old NCERT Pg. 109**

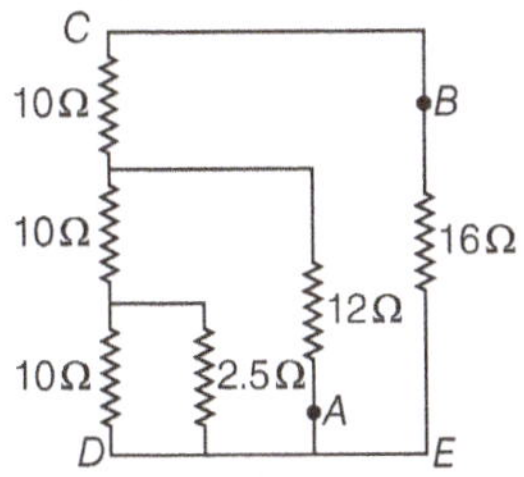

(a) $8\,\Omega$
(b) $12\,\Omega$
(c) $16\,\Omega$
(d) $32\,\Omega$

44 The actual value of resistance R as shown in the figure is $30\,\Omega$. This is measured in an experiment as shown using the standard formula $R = \frac{V}{I}$, where V and I are the readings of the voltmeter and ammeter, respectively. If the measured value of R is 5% less, then the internal resistance of the voltmeter is **Old NCERT Pg. 109**

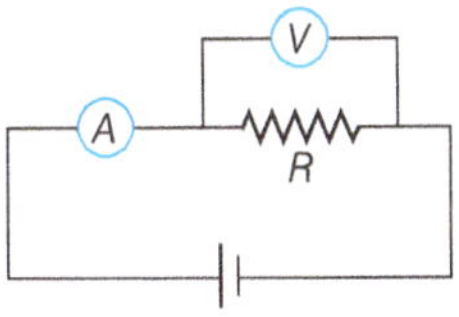

(a) $600\,\Omega$
(b) $570\,\Omega$
(c) $350\,\Omega$
(d) $35\,\Omega$

45 The reading of an ideal voltmeter in the circuit shown is **Old NCERT Pg. 109**

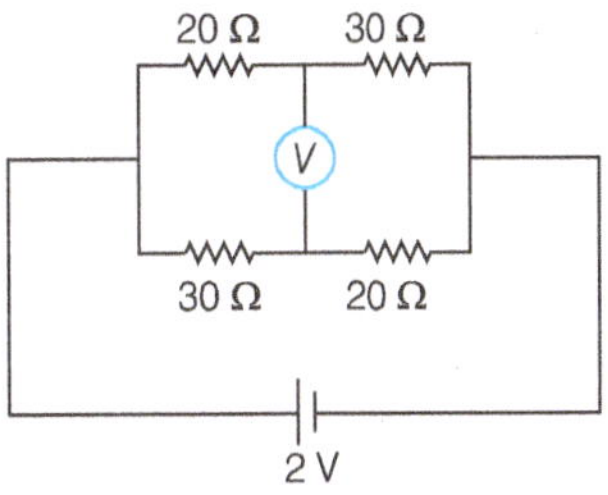

(a) 0.6 V
(b) 0 V
(c) 0.5 V
(d) 0.4 V

46 Find the current in the $8\,\Omega$ resistance in the given circuit. **Old NCERT Pg. 109**

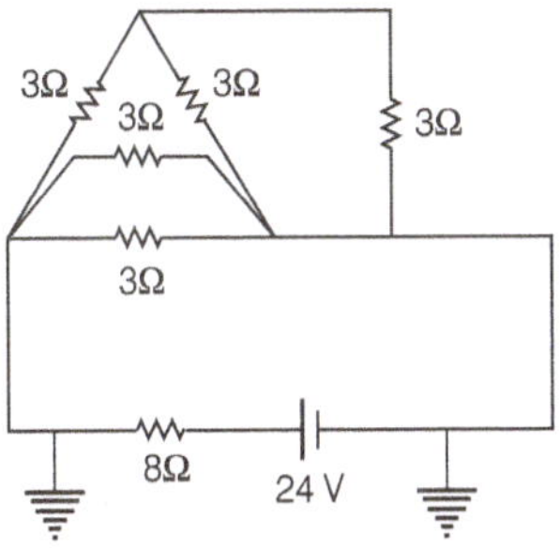

(a) 2 A
(b) 3A
(c) 4 A
(d) 5 A

47 Find $V_P - V_Q$ in the circuit shown in figure. **Old NCERT Pg. 109**

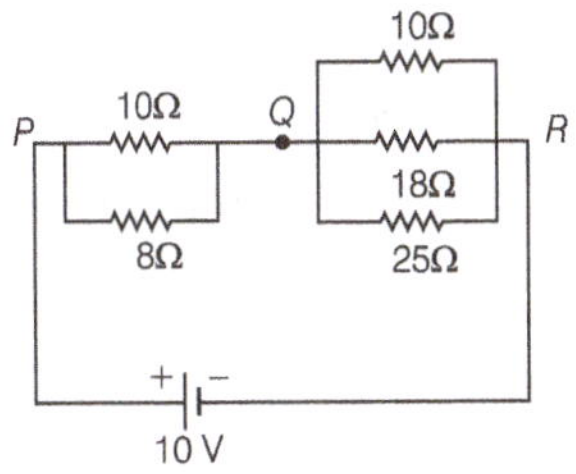

(a) 6.68 V
(b) 8 V
(c) 4.65 V
(d) 7 V

48 The resistive network shown below is connected to a DC source of 16 V. The power consumed by the network is 4 W. The value of R is **Old NCERT Pg. 109**

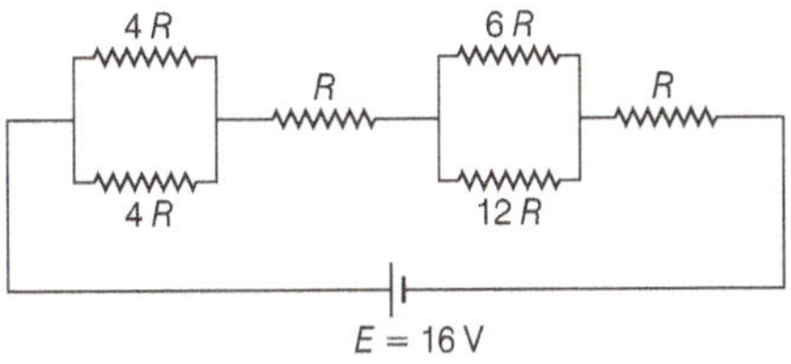

(a) $6\,\Omega$
(b) $8\,\Omega$
(c) $1\,\Omega$
(d) $16\,\Omega$

49 In the circuits shown below, the readings of voltmeters and the ammeters will be Old NCERT Pg. 109

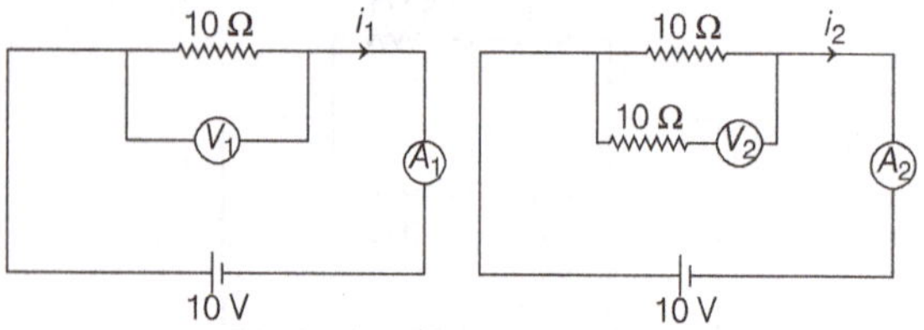

(a) $V_1 = V_2$ and $i_1 > i_2$
(b) $V_1 = V_2$ and $i_i = i_2$
(c) $V_2 > V_1$ and $i_1 > i_2$
(d) $V_2 > V_1$ and $i_1 = i_2$

Electrical Energy, Power

50 A current of 2 mA was passed through an unknown resistor which dissipated a power of 4.4 W. Dissipated power when an ideal power supply of 11 V is connected across it is NCERT Pg. 92

(a) 11×10^{-4} W
(b) 11×10^{-5} W
(c) 11×10^{5} W
(d) 11×10^{-3} W

51 Two cities are 150 km apart. Electric power is sent from one city to another city through copper wires. The fall of potential per km is 8 V and the average resistance per km is 0.5 Ω. The power loss in the wire is NCERT Pg. 92

(a) 19.2 W
(b) 19.2 kW
(c) 19.2×10^4 W
(d) 12.2 kW

52 An electric bulb is marked 100 W, 230 V. If the supply voltage drops to 115 V, what is the heat and light energy produced by the bulb in 20 min? NCERT Pg. 92

(a) 20000 J (b) 25000 J (c) 30000 J (d) 35000 J

53 The number of electrons moving per second through the filament of a lamp of 100 W, operating at 200 V is NCERT Pg. 92

(a) 3.1×10^{18}
(b) 3.1×10^{19}
(c) 4.8×10^{18}
(d) 4.8×10^{19}

54 An electric motor operating on a 50 V DC supply draws a current of 12 A. If the efficiency of the motor is 30%, then estimate the resistance of the windings of the motor. NCERT Pg. 92

(a) 1.5 Ω (b) 2 Ω (c) 2.9 Ω (d) 1 Ω

Cells, EMF, Internal Resistance

55 The internal resistance of a 2.1 V cell which gives a current of 0.2 A through a resistance of 10 Ω is NCERT Pg. 93

(a) 0.2 Ω
(b) 0.5 Ω
(c) 0.8 Ω
(d) 1.0 Ω

56 The cell has an emf of 2V and the internal resistance of this cell is 0.1 Ω, it is connected to resistance of 3.9 Ω, the voltage across the cell will be NCERT Pg. 93

(a) 1.95 V (b) 1.5 V (c) 2 V (d) 1.8 V

57 In the circuit shown, the current through 8 Ω is same before and after connecting E. The value E is NCERT Pg. 93

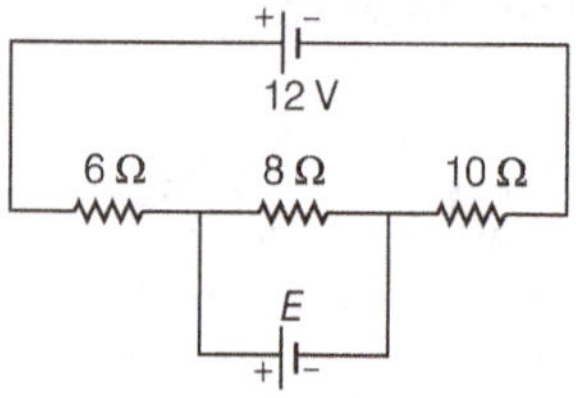

(a) 12 V (b) 6 V (c) 4 V (d) 2 V

58 The terminals of battery of emf 12 V and internal resistance 1 Ω are connected to a circular coil of resistance 16 Ω at two points distance a quarter of circumference of coil. The current flowing in smaller arc of circle is NCERT Pg. 93

(a) 2.4 A
(b) 2.25 A
(c) 0.75 A
(d) 1.66 A

Cells in Series and in Parallel

59 The maximum power dissipated in an external resistance R when connected to a cell of emf E and internal resistance r will be NCERT Pg. 93

(a) $\frac{E^2}{r}$ (b) $\frac{E^2}{2r}$ (c) $\frac{E^2}{3r}$ (d) $\frac{E^2}{4r}$

60 Consider first two cells in series as shown in figure. The potential difference between the terminals A and C of the combination is ($\varepsilon_{eq} = \varepsilon_1 + \varepsilon_2; r_{eq} = r_1 + r_2$) NCERT Pg. 95

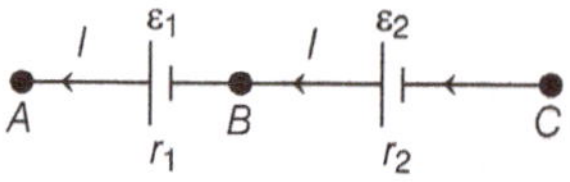

(a) $V_{AC} = \varepsilon_1 - Ir_1$
(b) $V_{AC} = \varepsilon_2 - Ir_2$
(c) $V_{AC} = \varepsilon_{eq} - Ir_{eq}$
(d) $V_{AC} = 2\varepsilon_{eq} - Ir_{eq}$

61 A battery consists of a variable number n of identical cells (having internal resistance r each) which are connected in series. The terminals of the battery are short-circuited and the current I is measured. Which of the graphs shows the correct relationship between I and n? NCERT Pg. 95

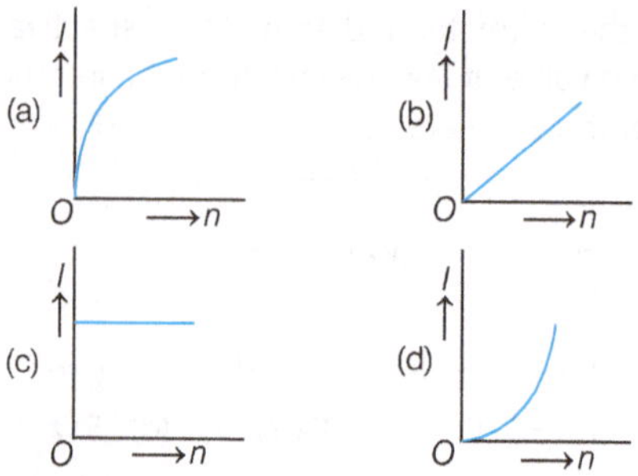

62 Consider a parallel combination of the cells in the figure. New NCERT Pg. 95

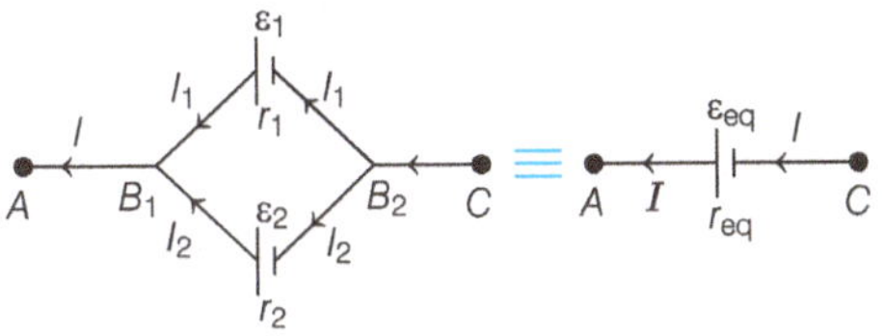

The potential difference across its terminals B_1 and B_2 is NCERT Pg. 95

(a) $V = \varepsilon_{eq} - Ir_{eq}$
(b) $V = \varepsilon_2 - Ir_2$
(c) $V = 2\varepsilon_{eq} - Ir_{eq}$
(d) $V = \varepsilon_1 - 2Ir_1$

63 n identical cells are joined in series with two cells A and B with reversed polarities. EMF of each cell is ε and internal resistance is r. Potential difference across cell A or B is $(n > 4)$ NCERT Pg. 95

(a) $\frac{2\varepsilon}{n}$ (b) $2\varepsilon\left(1-\frac{1}{n}\right)$
(c) $\frac{4\varepsilon}{n}$ (d) $2\varepsilon\left(1-\frac{2}{n}\right)$

64 Two cells having the internal resistance $0.2\,\Omega$ and $0.4\,\Omega$ are connected in parallel. The voltage across the battery terminal is 1.5 V. The emf of first cell is 1.2 V. The emf of second cell is NCERT Pg. 95

(a) 2.7 V (b) 2.1 V
(c) 3 V (d) 4.2 V

65 In the given circuit diagram, the emf and internal resistance of a single battery which is equivalent to a combination of three batteries respectively, are NCERT Pg. 95

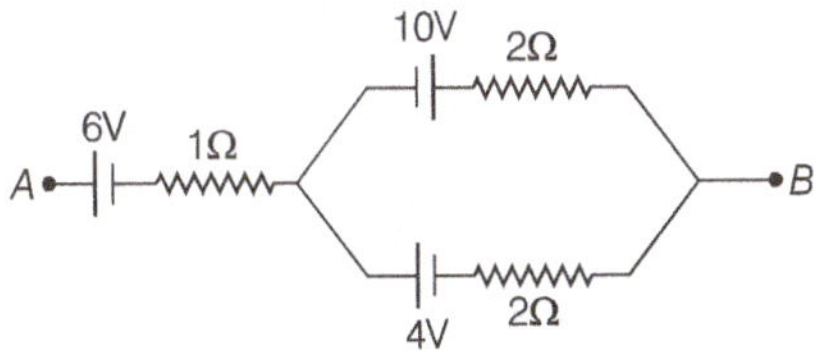

(a) 10V, 4Ω (b) 12 V, 2Ω
(c) 3V, 6Ω (d) 3V, 2Ω

66 To get a maximum current through a resistance of $2.5\,\Omega$, one can use m rows of cells each row having n cells. The internal resistance of each cell is $0.5\,\Omega$. What are the values of m and n, if the total number of cells are 20? NCERT Pg. 95

(a) $m = 2, n = 10$
(b) $m = 4, n = 5$
(c) $m = 5, n = 4$
(d) $n = 2, m = 10$

Kirchhoff's Rules

67 In the given circuit diagram, the currents $I_1 = -0.3$ A, $I_4 = 0.8$ A and $I_5 = 0.4$ A, are flowing as shown. The currents I_2, I_3 and I_6 respectively, are NCERT Pg. 97

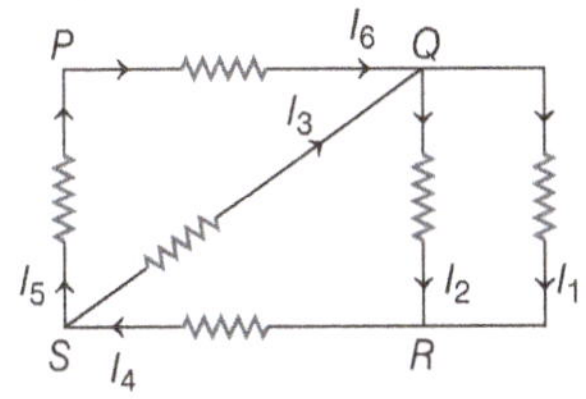

(a) 1.1 A, 0.4 A, 0.4 A (b) 1.1 A, −0.4 A, 0.4 A
(c) 0.4 A, 1.1 A, 0.4 A (d) −0.4 A, 0.4 A, 1.1 A

68 In the circuit given here, the points A, B and C are at potentials 70 V, zero, 10 V, respectively. Then, NCERT Pg. 97

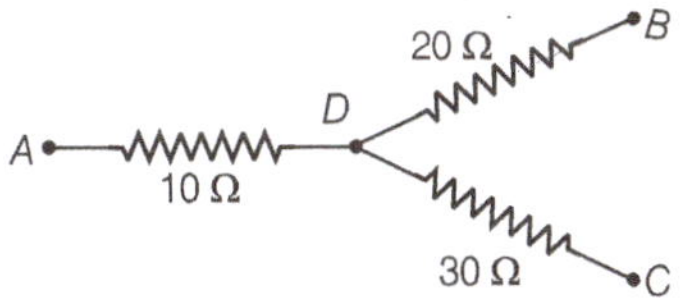

(a) the point D will be at a potential of 60 V
(b) the point D will be at a potential of 20 V
(c) currents in the paths AD, DB and DC are in the ratio of 1 : 2 : 3
(d) currents in the paths AD, DB and DC are in the ratio of 3 : 2 : 1

69 In the circuit, the galvanometer G shows zero deflection. If the batteries A and B have negligible internal resistance, the value of the resistor R will be NCERT Pg. 97

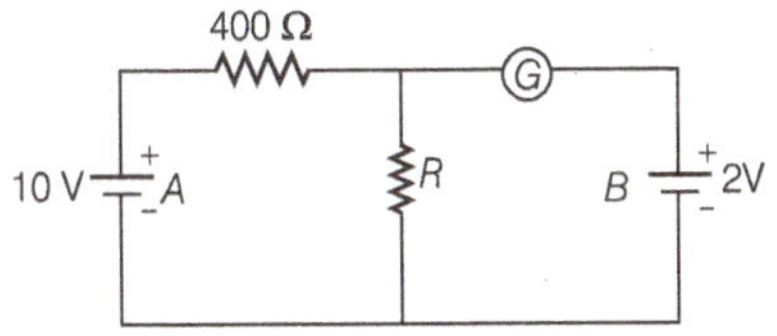

(a) 200 Ω (b) 100 Ω (c) 400 Ω (d) 1000 Ω

70 Four resistors having resistances r_1, r_2, r_3 and r_4 are connected as shown in the given circuit. The ratio $\frac{i_1}{i_4}$ of currents in terms of resistances used in the circuit is NCERT Pg. 97

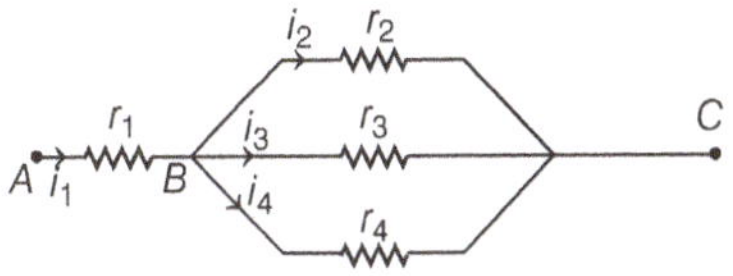

(a) $\frac{r_3r_4 + r_2r_4 + r_2r_3}{r_2r_3}$ (b) $\frac{r_1r_4 + r_1r_2 + r_2r_3}{r_1r_4}$
(c) $\frac{r_2}{r_4} + \frac{r_4}{r_3} + 1$ (d) $\frac{r_2}{r_4} + \frac{r_3}{r_2} + 1$

71 The emf of the battery shown in figure is NCERT Pg. 97

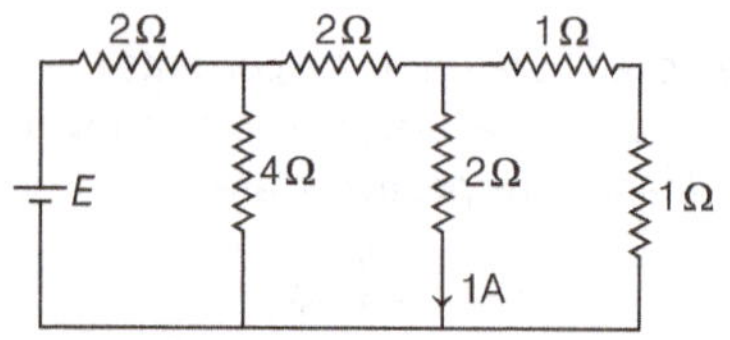

(a) 12 V (b) 13 V (c) 16 V (d) 18 V

72 A battery of emf ε and negligible internal resistance is connected across the diagonally opposite corners of a cubical network consisting of 12 resistors each of resistance R. The equivalence resistance of the network is NCERT Pg. 97

(a) $\frac{5}{6}R$ (b) $\frac{6}{5}R$ (c) $3R$ (d) $12R$

Wheatstone Bridge

73 Find current i in circuit shown in the figure. NCERT Pg. 100

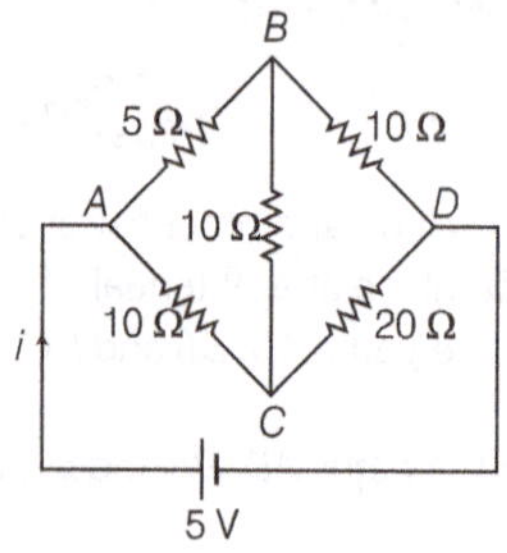

(a) 0.5 A (b) 0.2 A (c) 1 A (d) 2 A

74 The resistances of the four arms P, Q, R and S in a Wheatstone's bridge are 10 Ω, 30 Ω, 30 Ω and 90 Ω, respectively. The emf and internal resistance of the cell are 7 V and 5 Ω, respectively. If the galvanometer resistance is 50 Ω, the current drawn from the cell will be NCERT Pg. 100

(a) 1.0 A (b) 0.2 A (c) 0.1 A (d) 2.0 A

75 In a Wheatstone bridge (see figure), resistances P and Q are approximately equal. When $R = 400\,\Omega$, the bridge is balanced. On interchanging P and Q, the value of R for balance is 405 Ω. The value of X is close to NCERT Pg. 100

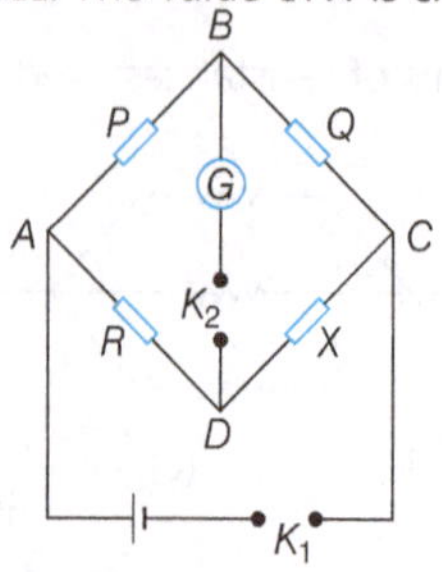

(a) 404.5 Ω (b) 401.5 Ω (c) 402.5 Ω (d) 403.5 Ω

76 The measurement of an unknown resistance R_4 is to be carried out using Wheatstone bridge as given in the figure. Two students perform an experiment in two ways. The first students takes $R_2 = 10\,\Omega$ and $R_1 = 5\,\Omega$ and the second student takes $R_2 = 1000\,\Omega$ and $R_1 = 500\,\Omega$. In the standard arm, both take $R_3 = 5\,\Omega$.

Both find $R_4 = \frac{R_2}{R_1} \times R_3 = 10\,\Omega$ within errors. NCERT Pg. 100

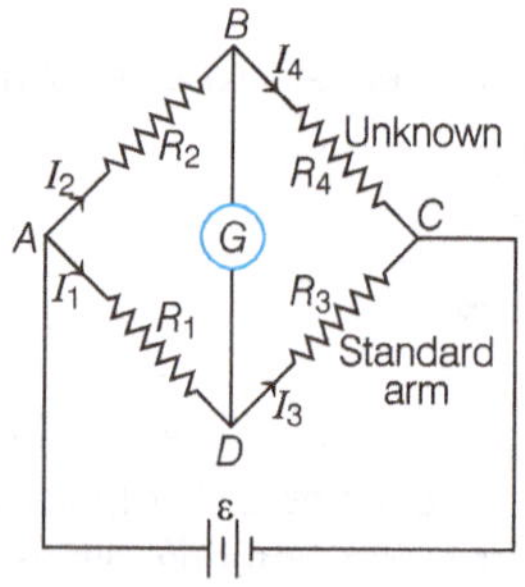

(a) The errors of measurement of the two students are the same

(b) Errors of measurement do not depend on the accuracy with which R_2 and R_1 can be measured

(c) If the student uses large values of R_2 and R_1, the currents through the arms will be very weak. This will make determination of null point accurately more difficult

(d) Wheatstone bridge is a very accurate instrument and has no errors of measurement

77 The four arms of a Wheatstone bridge in figure have following resistances $AB = 100\,\Omega$, $BC = 10\,\Omega$, $CD = 5\,\Omega$ and $DA = 60\,\Omega$. NCERT Pg. 100

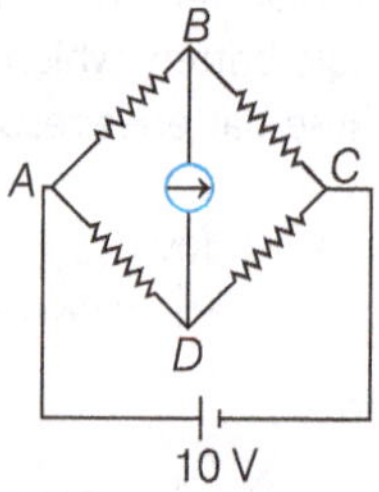

A galvanometer of 15 Ω resistance is connected across BD. Calculate the current through the galvanometer when a potential difference of 10 V is maintained across AC.

(a) 4.87 A (b) 4.87 mA
(c) 4.0 A (d) 4.0 mA

Meter Bridge

78 The meter bridge shown in the balance position with $\frac{P}{Q} = \frac{l_1}{l_2}$. If we now interchange the positions of galvanometer and cell, will the bridge work?

If yes, that will be the balanced condition? Old NCERT Pg. 121

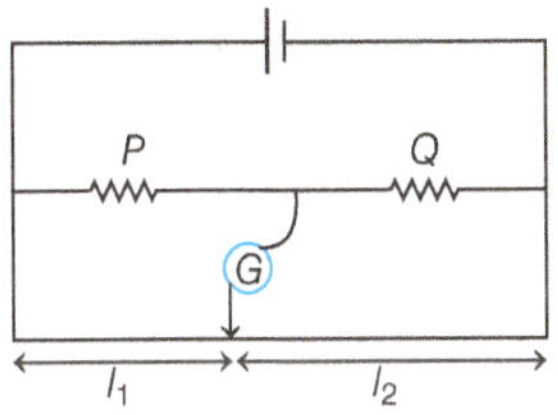

(a) yes, $\frac{P}{Q} = \frac{l_2 - l_1}{l_2 + l_1}$ (b) no, no null point

(c) yes, $\frac{P}{Q} = \frac{l_2}{l_1}$ (d) yes, $\frac{P}{Q} = \frac{l_1}{l_2}$

79 The resistances in the two arms of the meter bridge are 5Ω and $R\Omega$, respectively. When the resistance R is shunted with an equal resistance, the new balance point is at $1.6\,l_1$. The resistance R is Old NCERT Pg. 121

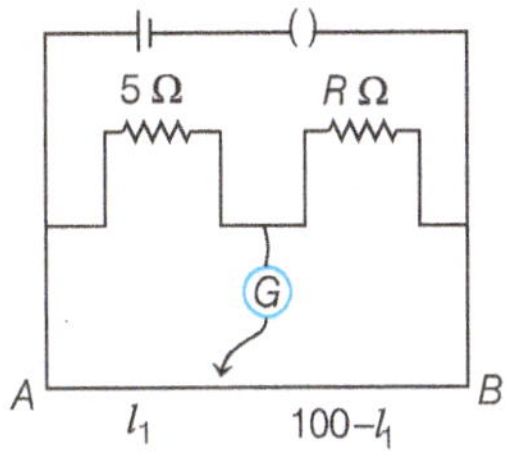

(a) $10\,\Omega$ (b) $15\,\Omega$

(c) $20\,\Omega$ (d) $25\,\Omega$

80 A wire connected in the left gap of a meter bridge balance a $10\,\Omega$ resistance in the right gap to a point, which divides the bridge wire in the ratio 3 : 2. If the length of the wire is 1 m. The length of one ohm wire is

(a) 0.057 m (b) 0.067 m Old NCERT Pg. 121

(c) 0.37 m (d) 0.134 m

Assertion and Reason Questions

Direction (Q. Nos. 1-10) *In the following questions, a statement of Assertion is followed by a corresponding statement of Reason. Of the following statements, choose the correct one.*

(a) Both Assertion and Reason are correct and Reason is the correct explanation of Assertion.

(b) Both Assertion and Reason are correct but Reason is not the correct explanation of Assertion.

(c) Assertion is correct but Reason is incorrect.

(d) Assertion is incorrect but Reason is correct.

1 Assertion In electrostatics, all charges whether free or bound are considered to be at rest.

Reason The charges in motion constitute an electric current. NCERT Pg. 81

2 Assertion The current flowing through a conductor is directly proportional to the drift velocity.

Reason As the drift velocity increases the current flowing through the conductor decreases. NCERT Pg. 82

3 Assertion Charge carriers do not move with acceleration but with a steady drift velocity.

Reason Charge carriers undergo collisions with ions and atoms during transit. NCERT Pg. 85

4 Assertion Increasing the temperature of a metallic conductor leads to an decrease in its electrical conductivity.

Reason Raising the temperature decrease the mobility of charge carriers within the conductor. NCERT Pg. 88

5 Assertion For insulators and semiconductors, number of free electrons increases with increasing temperature.

Reason This increase of number of free electrons is more effective than any decrease in τ, so that for such materials ρ decreases with temperature. NCERT Pg. 89

6 Assertion The average time of collisions τ decreases with increasing temperature.

Reason At increased temperature, average speed of the electrons, which act as the carriers of current increases, resulting in more frequent collisions. NCERT Pg. 90

7 Assertion The drift velocity of electrons in a metallic wire decreases when temperature of the wire increases.

Reason On increasing temperature, conductivity of metallic wire decreases. NCERT Pg. 90

8 Assertion A bulb is connected to a battery of emf E and internal resistance r. The brightness of the bulb is proportional to the square of the voltage across the bulb.

Reason The power dissipated by a bulb is inversely proportional to the square of the voltage across the bulb. NCERT Pg. 93

9 Assertion A 65W-210V bulb glows more than a 100W-210V bulb when they are connected in series across a potential difference.

Reason The resistance of 100W-210V bulb will be more. NCERT Pg. 93

10 **Assertion** Two identical resistors R are connected in parallel across a battery of emf E and internal resistance r. The current flowing through each resistor is $\frac{E}{2r + R}$.

Reason The current flowing through each resistor is equal to the total current flowing through the circuit divided by the number of resistance in parallel. Old NCERT Pg. 107

Statement Based Questions

Direction (Q. Nos. 1-8) *In the following questions Statement I and Statement II are given. Read the statements and choose the most appropriate answer from the options given below.*

(a) Both Statement I and Statement II are incorrect.
(b) Statement I is correct but Statement II is incorrect.
(c) Statement I is incorrect but Statement II is correct.
(d) Both Statement I and Statement II are correct.

1 **Statement I** When the wire of resistance 4Ω is stretched to twice its original length, then resistance of the stretched wire will be 16Ω.

Statement II Resistance of stretched wire is equal to n (ratio of final length and initial length) square times the original resistance. NCERT Pg. 84

2 **Statement I** The drift velocity of electrons in a metallic wire will decrease, if the temperature of the wire is increased.

Statement II Electric field outside the conducting wire which carries a constant current is zero. NCERT Pg. 85

3 **Statement I** A current flows is a conductor only when there is an electric field with in the conductor.

Statement II The drift velocity of electrons increases with decreases of electric field. NCERT Pg. 85

4 **Statement I** Mobility of a current carrier is inversely proportional to the mass of the current carrier.

Statement II The small interval of time between one successive collisions between electron and ion in the conductor is called relaxation time or mean free time (τ). NCERT Pg. 88

5 **Statement I** The graph between resistivity and temperature for a limited range of temperature is straight line for a material like nichrome.

Statement II The resistivity of semiconductor increases with increasing temperature. NCERT Pg. 90

6 **Statement I** A 200W bulb consumes 2 units of electrical energy when it is used for 10 h.

Statement II 1 unit of electrical energy = 1000 kWh NCERT Pg. 92

7 **Statement I** The internal resistance of a cell increases with increase in temperature.

Statement II For a cell in open circuit, the internal resistance is zero. NCERT Pg. 94

8 **Statement I** A bulb does not become dim when another bulb of same power in parallel circuit is switched ON.

Statement II Each component in a parallel circuit has the same voltage across it. NCERT Pg. 95

Matching Type Questions

1 **Column I** gives certain physical terms associated with flow of current through a metallic conductor.
Column II gives some mathematical relations involving electrical quantities. Match Column I and Column II with appropriate relations. NCERT Pg. 89

Column I	Column II
A. Drift velocity	1. $\frac{m}{ne^2\rho}$
B. Electrical resistivity	2. nev_d
C. Relaxation period	3. $\frac{eE}{m}\tau$
D. Current density	4. E/J

Choose the correct answer from the codes given below

	A	B	C	D
(a)	3	4	1	2
(b)	3	4	2	1
(c)	3	1	4	2
(d)	3	2	4	1

2 The thickness of a conductor continuously decreases from its one end A to another end B. It is connected across the terminals of a battery. Match the items of Column I with the respective items of Column II. NCERT Pg. 89

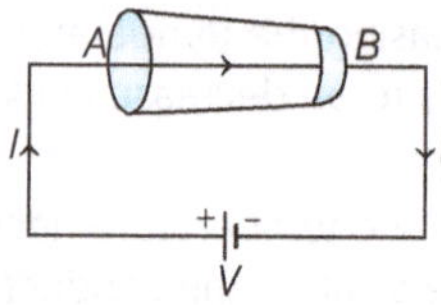

Column I		Column II	
A.	Electric field	1.	Increases linearly
B.	Current density	2.	Increases from A to B
C.	Mobility of the electron	3.	Decreases from B to A
D.	Temperature	4.	No change

Choose the correct answer from the codes given below.

Codes

	A	B	C	D		A	B	C	D
(a)	2	3	4	1	(b)	2	4	1	3
(c)	3	1	4	2	(d)	4	1	3	2

3 A battery A (15V, 1Ω) and a battery B(10 V, 1Ω) are joined to a resistance of 3Ω as shown in figure. NCERT Pg. 93

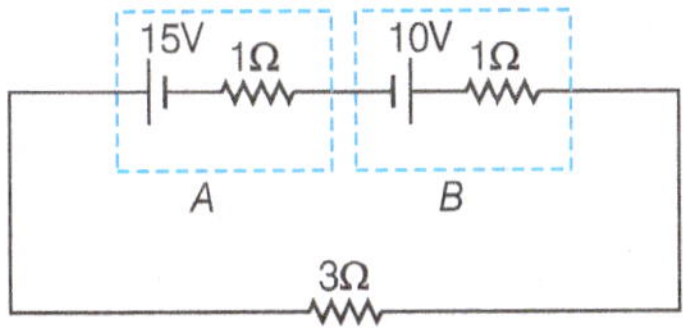

Match the statements given in Column I with Column II.

Column I		Column II	
A.	Potential drop across A	1.	A
B.	Potential drop across B	2.	B
C.	Power is supplied by battery	3.	14 V
D.	Power is consumed by battery	4.	11 V

Choose the correct answer from the codes given below.

Codes

	A	B	C	D		A	B	C	D
(a)	2	3	4	1	(b)	4	2	1	3
(c)	3	4	1	2	(d)	3	1	4	2

4 In given circuit, current in branch AD is I_2. Match the items of Column I with the respective items of Column II. NCERT Pg. 101

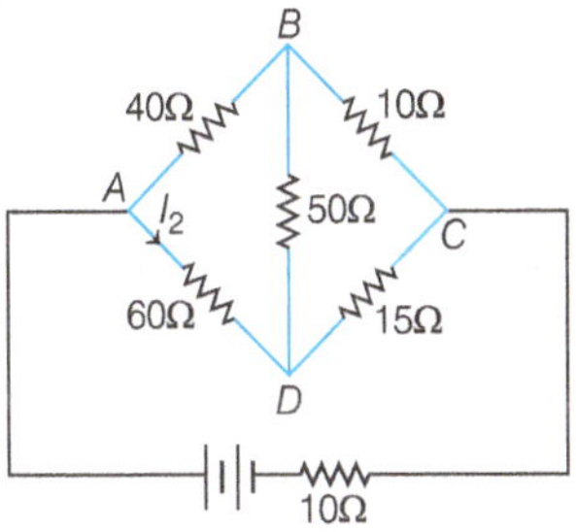

Column I		Column II	
A.	P_{AB}	1.	$22.5I_2^2$
B.	P_{BC}	2.	$15I_2^2$
C.	P_{DC}	3.	$90I_2^2$
D.	P_{AD}	4.	$60I_2^2$

Choose the correct answer from the codes given below.

Codes

	A	B	C	D		A	B	C	D
(a)	3	1	2	4	(b)	2	1	3	4
(c)	3	4	1	2	(d)	2	4	3	1

Numerical Type Questions

1 The current density in a cylindrical wire of radius 2 mm is 8×10^6 Am^{-1}. The current through the outer portion of the wire between radius $R/2$ and R is $n\pi$ A. The value of n is .... NCERT Pg. 85

2 Consider a wire of length 0.1 m with an area of cross-section 1 mm^2 connected to 5V. Then, the current flowing through the metallic wire is .... A. (where, $\mu = 5 \times 10^{-6}$ m^2 V^{-1}s^{-1}, $e = 1.6 \times 10^{-19}$ C and $n = 8 \times 10^{28}$ m^{-3}) NCERT Pg. 85

3 An electron to move a distance $l = 1$ km in a copper wire of cross-section $A = 1$ mm^2. If it carries a current $I = 4.5$ A, then time taken by an electron to move in one kilometre distance is .... $\times 10^6$ s. (Take number density of electrons $n = 10^{28}$) NCERT Pg. 86

4 At 20°C, the temperature coefficient of resistivity of a long cylindrical conductor is close to zero. If this is made by assembling alternate disks of iron and carbon, then the ratio of the thickness of a carbon disk to that an iron disk is $x/1000$. The value of x is ....
[For carbon, $\rho = 3500 \times 10^{-8}\,\Omega$m, $\alpha = -0.5 \times 10^{-3}\,°C^{-1}$ and for iron, $\rho = 9.68 \times 10^{-8}\,\Omega$m, $\alpha = 6.5 \times 10^{-3}\,°C^{-1}$] NCERT Pg. 90

5 A uniform heating wire of resistance 60 Ω is connected across a potential difference of 220 V. The wire is then cut into half and potential difference of 220 V is applied across each half separately. The ratio of power dissipation in first case to the total power dissipation in the second case would be $\frac{x}{4}$, where x is .... NCERT Pg. 93

6 A heater is designed to operate with a power of 1 kW in a 100 V line. It is connected in combination with a resistance of 10 Ω and a resistance R as shown in the

figure. If the heater operates with power of 62.5 W, then the value of R is $x \times 10^{-2}\ \Omega$. The value of x is .... **NCERT Pg. 93**

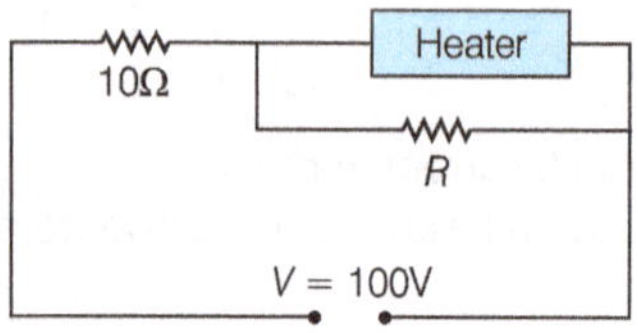

7 A potential V_0 is applied across a uniform wire of resistance R. The power dissipation is P_1. The wire is then cut into two equal halves and a potential of V_0 is applied across the length of each half. The total power dissipation ratio across two wires is P_2. The ratio $P_2 : P_1$ is $\sqrt{x} : 1$. The value of x is .... **NCERT Pg. 93**

8 In the following figure, the value of V_0 will be ...... V. **NCERT Pg. 95**

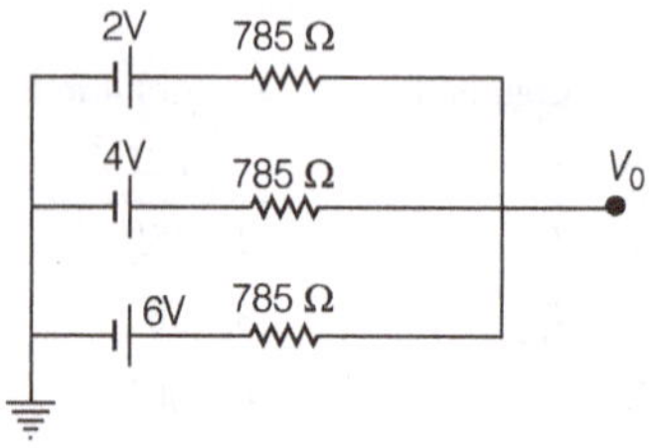

9 The four arms of a Wheatstone bridge have resistances as shown in the figure. A galvanometer of 15Ω resistance is connected across BD. Calculate the current (in mA) through the galvanometer when potential. difference of 10V is maintained across AC. **NCERT Pg. 93**

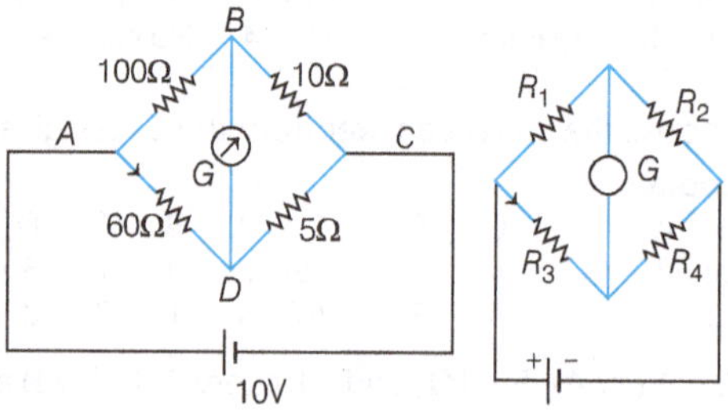

10 The total current supplied to the circuit as shown in figure by the 15V battery is .... A. **Old NCERT Pg. 107**

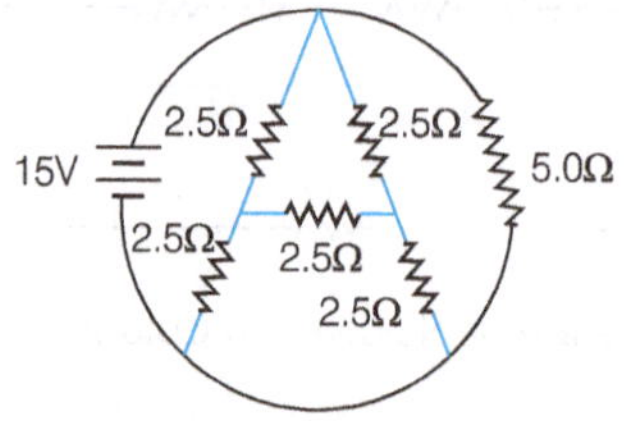

NCERT Exemplar Questions

1 Consider a current carrying wire (current I) is in the shape of a circle. Note that as the current progresses along the wire, the direction of J (current density) changes in an exact manner, while the current I remains unaffected. The agent that is essentially responsible for

(a) source of emf

(b) electric field produced by charges accumulated on the surface of wire

(c) the charges just behind a given segment of wire which push them just the right way by repulsion

(d) the charges ahead

2 Two batteries of emfs ε_1 and $\varepsilon_2 (\varepsilon_2 > \varepsilon_1)$ and internal resistances r_1 and r_2, respectively are connected in parallel as shown in figure.

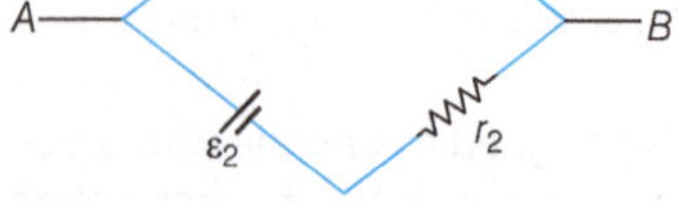

(a) The equivalent emf ε_{eq} of the two cells is between ε_1 and ε_2, i.e., $\varepsilon_1 < \varepsilon_{eq} < \varepsilon_2$

(b) The equivalent emf ε_{eq} is smaller than ε_1

(c) The ε_{eq} is given by $\varepsilon_{eq} = \varepsilon_1 + \varepsilon_2$ always

(d) ε_{eq} is independent of internal resistances r_1 and r_2

3 A resistance R is to be measured using a meter bridge. A student chooses the standard resistance S to be 100 Ω. He finds the null point at $l_1 = 2.9$ cm. He is told to attempt to improve the accuracy. Which of the following is a useful way?

(a) He should measure l_1 more accurately

(b) He should change S to 1000 Ω and repeat the experiment

(c) He should change S to 3 Ω and repeat the experiment

(d) He should give up hope of a more accurate measurement with a meter bridge

Past Exams Questions

NEET

1 The terminal voltage of the battery, whose emf is 10 V and internal resistance 1Ω when connected through an external resistance of 4 Ω as shown in the figure is NCERT Pg. 96, NEET 2024

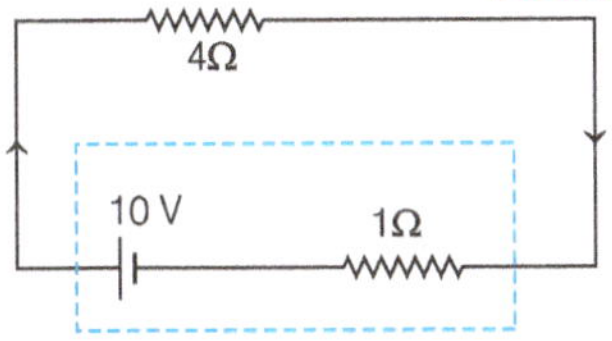

(a) 4 V (b) 6 V (c) 8 V (d) 10 V

2 A wire of length l and resistance 100 Ω is divided into 10 equal parts. The first 5 parts are connected in series while the next 5 parts are connected in parallel. The two combinations are again connected in series. The resistance of this final combination is NCERT Pg. 95, NEET 2024

(a) 26 Ω (b) 52 Ω (c) 55 Ω (d) 60 Ω

3 10 resistors, each of resistance R are connected in series to a battery of emf E and negligible internal resistance. Now, these resistances are connected in parallel to the same battery, so the current is increased n times. The value of n is NCERT Pg. 94, NEET 2023

(a) 100 (b) 1
(c) 1000 (d) 10

4 In circuit diagram, if the galvanometer G does not show any deflection, then the value of R is given by NCERT Pg. 101, NEET 2023

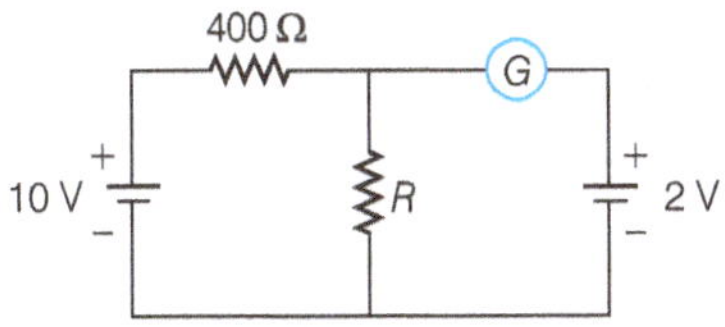

(a) 50 Ω (b) 100 Ω
(c) 400 Ω (d) 200 Ω

5 A copper wire of length 10 m and radius $(10^{-2}/\sqrt{\pi})$ m has electrical resistance of 10Ω. The current density in the wire for an electric field strength of 10(V/m) is NCERT Pg. 86, NEET 2022

(a) 10^4 A/m^2 (b) 10^6 A/m^2
(c) 10^{-5} A/m^2 (d) 10^5 A/m^2

6 A Wheatstone bridge is used to determine the value of unknown resistance X by adjusting the variable resistance Y as shown in the figure. For the most precise measurement of X, the resistances P and Q NCERT Pg. 101, NEET 2022

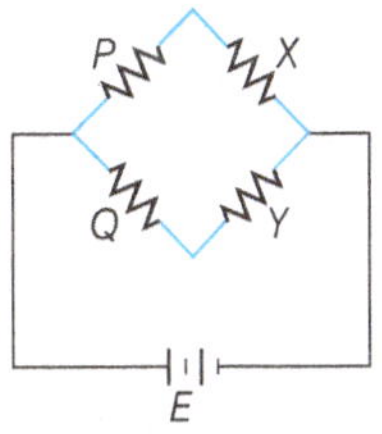

(a) should be approximately equal and are small
(b) should be very large and unequal
(c) do not play any significant role
(d) should be approximately equal to $2X$

7 Three resistors having resistances r_1, r_2 and r_3 are connected as shown in the given circuit. The ratio i_3/i_1 of currents in terms of resistances used in the circuit is NCERT Pg. 96, NEET 2021

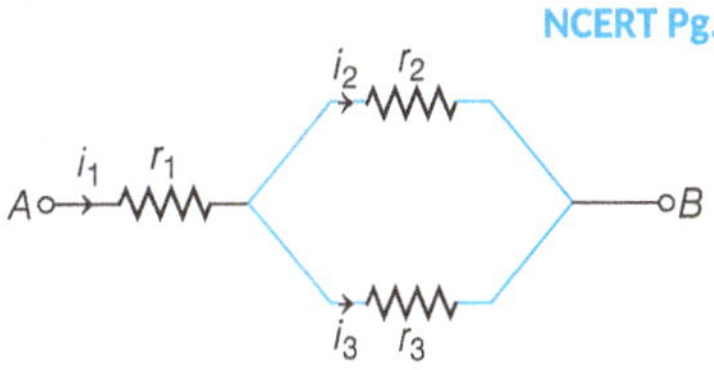

(a) $\frac{r_1}{r_2 + r_3}$ (b) $\frac{r_2}{r_2 + r_3}$ (c) $\frac{r_1}{r_1 + r_2}$ (d) $\frac{r_2}{r_1 + r_3}$

8 A charged particle having drift velocity of 7.5×10^{-4} ms^{-1} in an electric field of 3×10^{-10} Vm^{-1}. Then, the mobility of charge particle is (in m^{2}V^{-1}s^{-1}) NCERT Pg. 86, NEET 2020

(a) 2.5×10^6 (b) 2.5×10^{-6}
(c) 2.25×10^{-15} (d) 2.25×10^{15}

9 A set of n equal resistors, of value R each are connected in series to a battery of emf E and internal resistance R. The current drawn is I. Now, the n resistors are connected in parallel to the same battery. Then, the current drawn from battery becomes $10I$. The value of n is NCERT Pg. 95, NEET 2018

(a) 20 (b) 11
(c) 10 (d) 9

10 The resistance of a wire is R ohm. If it is melted and stretched to n times its original length, its new resistance will be NCERT Pg. 84, NEET 2017

(a) nR (b) $\frac{R}{n}$ (c) n^2R (d) $\frac{R}{n^2}$

11 A filament bulb (500W, 100V) is to be used in a 230V main supply. When a resistance R is connected in series, it works perfectly and the bulb consumes 500W. The value of R is **NCERT Pg. 93, NEET 2016**

(a) 230 Ω (b) 46 Ω
(c) 26 Ω (d) 13 Ω

12 The charge following through a resistance R varies with time t as $Q = at - bt^2$, where a and b are positive constants. The total heat produced in R is **NCERT Pg. 93, NEET 2016**

(a) $\frac{a^3R}{3b}$ (b) $\frac{a^3R}{2b}$ (c) $\frac{a^3R}{b}$ (d) $\frac{a^3R}{6b}$

13 Two metal wires of identical dimensions are connected in series. If σ_1 and σ_2 are the conductivities of the metal wires respectively, the effective conductivity of the combination is **NCERT Pg. 89, AIPMT 2015**

(a) $\frac{2\sigma_1\sigma_2}{\sigma_1 + \sigma_2}$ (b) $\frac{\sigma_1 + \sigma_2}{2\sigma_1\sigma_2}$
(c) $\frac{\sigma_1 + \sigma_2}{\sigma_1\sigma_2}$ (d) $\frac{\sigma_1\sigma_2}{\sigma_1 + \sigma_2}$

14 The resistances in the two arms of the meter bridge are 5 Ω and R Ω, respectively. When the resistance R is shunted with an equal resistance, the new balance point is at $1.6\,l_1$. The resistance R, is **NCERT Pg. 101, AIPMT 2014**

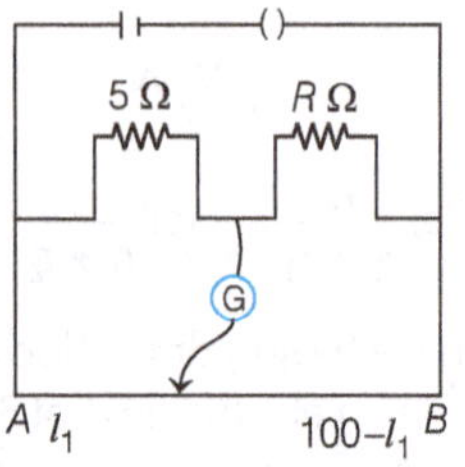

(a) 10 Ω (b) 15 Ω
(c) 20 Ω (d) 25 Ω

JEE Main

15 A wire of resistance R and length L is cut into 5 equal parts. If these parts are joined parallely, then resultant resistance will be **NCERT Pg. 96, JEE Main 2024**

(a) $25R$ (b) $\frac{1}{25}R$ (c) $5R$ (d) $\frac{1}{5}R$

16 A wire of length 10 cm and radius $\sqrt{7} \times 10^{-4}$ m is connected across the right gap of a meter bridge. When a resistance of 4.5 Ω is connected on the left gap by using a resistance box, the balance length is found to be at 60 cm from the left end. If the resistivity of the wire is $R \times 10^{-7}$ Ωm, then value of R is **NCERT Pg. 101, JEE Main 2024**

(a) 63 (b) 70 (c) 66 (d) 35

17 As shown in the figure, a network of resistor is connected to a battery of 24V with an internal resistance of 3 Ω. The currents through the resistors R_4 and R_5 are I_4 and I_5, respectively. The values of I_4 and I_5 are **NCERT Pg. 94, JEE Main 2023**

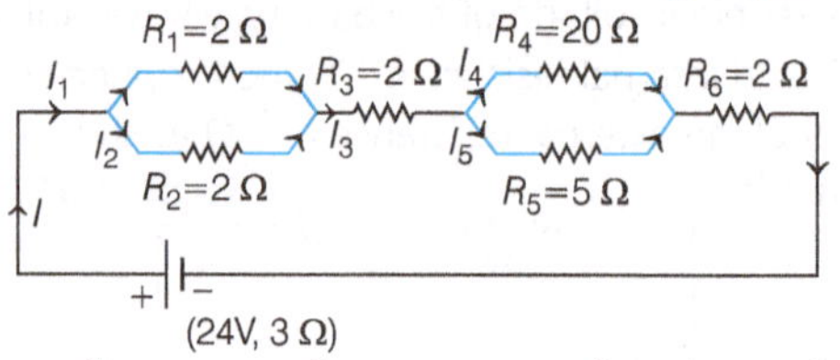

(a) $I_4 = \frac{8}{4}$ A and $I_5 = \frac{2}{5}$ A (b) $I_4 = \frac{2}{5}$ A and $I_5 = \frac{8}{5}$ A
(c) $I_4 = \frac{24}{5}$ A and $I_5 = \frac{6}{5}$ A (d) $I_4 = \frac{6}{5}$ A and $I_5 = \frac{24}{5}$ A

18 The equivalent resistance between the adjacent corners of a regular n-sided polygon of uniform wire of resistance R would be **NCERT Pg. 96, JEE Main 2022**

(a) $\frac{(n-1)R}{n}$ (b) $\frac{(n-1)R}{(2n-1)}$ (c) $\frac{(n-1)R}{n^2}$ (d) $\frac{n^2R}{n-1}$

19 A 1 m long wire is broken into two unequal parts X and Y. The X part of the wire is stretched into another wire W. Length of W is twice the length of X and the resistance of W is twice that of Y. Find the ratio of length of X and Y. **NCERT Pg. 96, JEE Main 2022**

(a) 1 : 4 (b) 1 : 2 (c) 4 : 1 (d) 2 : 1

20 The equivalent resistance between points A and B in the given network is **NCERT Pg. 96, JEE Main 2022**

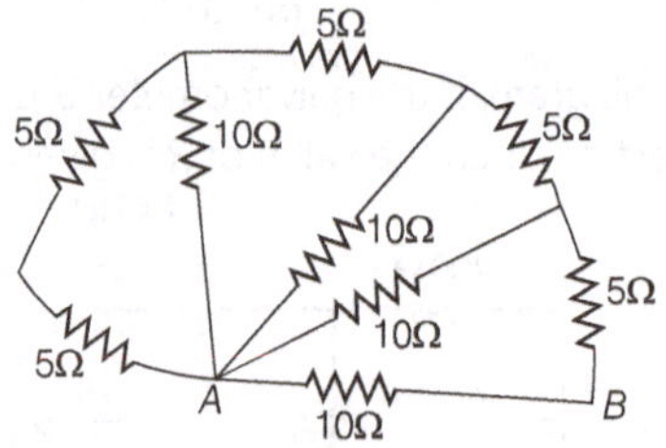

(a) 65 Ω (b) 20 Ω
(c) 5 Ω (d) 2 Ω

21 In the given figure, a battery of emf E is connected across a conductor PQ of length l and different area of cross-sections having radii r_1 and $r_2 (r_2 < r_1)$. **NCERT Pg. 86, JEE Main 2021**

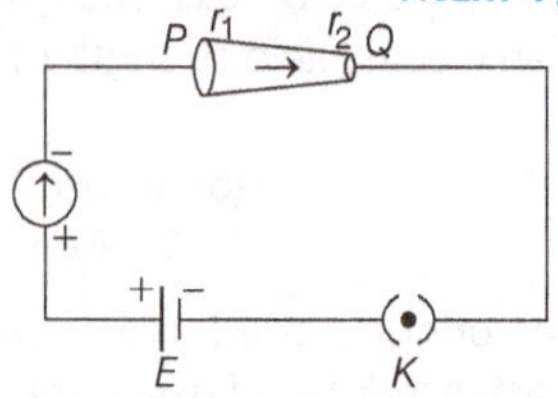

Choose the correct option as one moves from P to Q.
(a) Drift velocity of electron increases
(b) Electric field decreases
(c) Electron current decreases
(d) All of the above

22 A current through a wire depends on time as $i = \alpha_0 t + \beta t^2$, where $\alpha_0 = 20$ A/s and $\beta = 8$ As^{-2}. Find the charge crossed through a section of the wire in 15 s. **NCERT Pg. 86, JEE Main 2021**

(a) 260 C (b) 2100 C
(c) 11250 C (d) 2250 C

23 In the given figure, the emf of the cell is 2.2 V and if internal resistance is 0.6 Ω. Calculate the power dissipated in the whole circuit. **NCERT Pg. 93, JEE Main 2021**

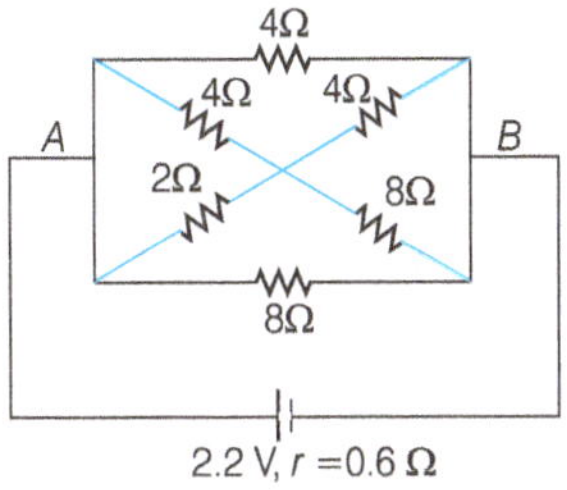

(a) 1.32 W (b) 0.65 W (c) 2.2 W (d) 4.4 W

24 Five identical cells each of internal resistance 1 Ω and emf 5V are connected in series and in parallel with an external resistance R. For what value of R, current in series and parallel combination will remain the same? **NCERT Pg. 94, JEE Main 2021**

(a) 1 Ω (b) 25 Ω (c) 5 Ω (d) 10 Ω

Skill Boosters

1 Mohit run an electric heater for 10 min on a 120 V line. Heater has resistance of 6 Ω. The energy liberated in this period of time is
(a) 7.2×10^3 J (b) 14.4×10^5 J
(c) 43.2×10^4 J (d) 28.8×10^4 J

2 A city power station delivers 750 kW of power at 12000 V, to a factory through a cable of resistance 3Ω. If electricity is delivered at 50000 V instead of 12000 V, then power wasted will be
(a) 1.1×10^5 W (b) 1.1×10^4 W
(c) 1.1×10^6 W (d) 1.1×10^3 W

3 A student tried to make a jumbo battery by using twelve cells each having the same emf. He connected all the cell in series and kept it in a closed box. But some of the cell are wrongly connected. This battery of cells is connected in series with an ammeter and two cells identical with the others. The current is 3A when the cell and the battery aid each other and is 2A when the cells and the battery oppose each other. How many cell in the battery are wrongly connected?
(a) 1 (b) 6 (c) 4 (d) 8

4 In a household wiring, four bulb of power 25W, 40 W, 60W and 100W are connected in series . Which bulb have the highest potential difference across its end ?
(a) 25W (b) 40W (c) 60W (d) 100W

5 Himanshu buy an electric kettle which has two heating coils. When only first coil is switched ON, the boiling begins in 6 min. When only second coil is switched ON, the boiling begins in 8 min. In what time, the boiling begins, if both the coils are switched ON simultaneously in parallel ?
(a) 2.8 min (b) 2 min (c) 3.4 min (d) 5 min

6 In an experiment, two bulbs are connected in series. It is found that second light bulb is less bright than first. By noticing it, four student claim four cause of it. Choose the correct cause.
(a) Student I - The first bulb uses up some of the current.
(b) Student II - Wattage of first bulb is less than the wattage of second bulb.
(c) Student III - Resistance of first bulb is less than the resistance of second bulb.
(d) Student IV - Distance of first bulb from current source is less than the distance of second bulb from current source.

7 In a battery manufacturing plant, different type of batteries are manufacture. Four batteries (battery I, battery II, battery III and battery IV) having 12 V emf and 0.04 Ω internal resistance each being charged with current of 50A, 25A, 60A and 40A. Which of the following options is incorrect about the potential difference across their terminals?
(a) Battery I has 14 V potential difference
(b) Battery II has 13 V potential difference
(c) Battery III has 16 V potential difference
(d) Battery IV has 13.6 V potential difference

8 For a household wiring, copper alloy is used which has $\rho = 1.7 \times 10^{-8}$ Ω-m and $n = 8.49 \times 10^{28}$ m^{-3}. If atomic spacing of copper is about 0.2 nm and an electron on

(Given, average speed of free electrons of copper is about 1.6×10^6 m/s)

(a) 300 (b) 200 (c) 250 (d) 400

9 An electric motor runs for 5 h a day at 220 V. The supply wiring consists of copper wire of 1 mm radius and length 10m. Power consumption per day is 10 commercial units. What fraction of it goes in the joule heating in wires?

[For copper, $\rho = 1.7 \times 10^{-8} \Omega$-m]

(a) $\frac{1}{450}$ (b) $\frac{1}{600}$

(c) $\frac{1}{400}$ (d) $\frac{1}{550}$

10 For the given circuits, galvanometer shows no deflection when switches S_1 and S_2 are closed.

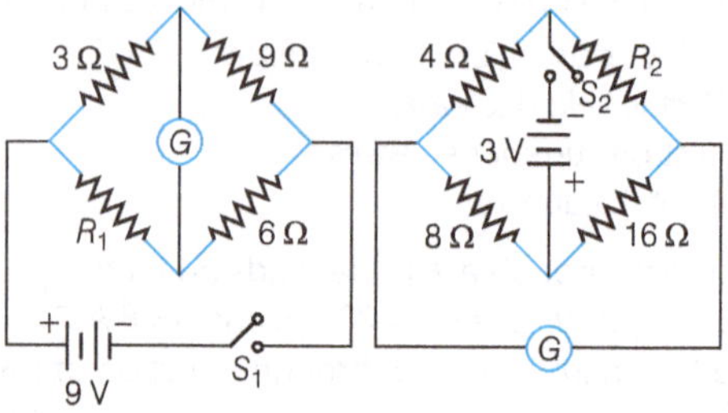

If $R_2 = kR_1$ then the value of k is

(a) 4 (b) 6

(c) 8 (d) 12

Correct Codes

Topical Questions

1 (c)	2 (c)	3 (b)	4 (b)	5 (b)	6 (c)	7 (a)	8 (d)	9 (b)	10 (c)
11 (a)	12 (c)	13 (c)	14 (d)	15 (a)	16 (c)	17 (c)	18 (a)	19 (a)	20 (c)
21 (b)	22 (a)	23 (d)	24 (d)	25 (a)	26 (c)	27 (d)	28 (b)	29 (c)	30 (c)
31 (b)	32 (a)	33 (b)	34 (d)	35 (d)	36 (c)	37 (b)	38 (d)	39 (a)	40 (a)
41 (a)	42 (d)	43 (a)	44 (b)	45 (d)	46 (b)	47 (c)	48 (b)	49 (b)	50 (b)
51 (b)	52 (c)	53 (a)	54 (c)	55 (b)	56 (a)	57 (c)	58 (b)	59 (d)	60 (c)
61 (c)	62 (a)	63 (d)	64 (b)	65 (d)	66 (a)	67 (a)	68 (d)	69 (b)	70 (a)
71 (b)	72 (a)	73 (a)	74 (b)	75 (c)	76 (c)	77 (b)	78 (d)	79 (b)	80 (b)

Assertion and Reason Questions

1 (b)	2 (c)	3 (a)	4 (a)	5 (a)	6 (a)	7 (b)	8 (c)	9 (c)	10 (a)

Statement Based Questions

1 (d)	2 (d)	3 (b)	4 (d)	5 (b)	6 (b)	7 (a)	8 (d)

Matching Type Questions

1 (a)	2 (a)	3 (c)	4 (a)

Numerical Type Questions

1 (24)	2 (3.2)	3 (3)	4 (36)	5 (1)	6 (500)	7 (16)	8 (4)	9 (4.87)	10 (9)

NCERT Exemplar Questions

1 (b)	2 (a)	3 (c)

Past Exams Questions

1 (c)	2 (b)	3 (a)	4 (b)	5 (d)	6 (a)	7 (b)	8 (a)	9 (c)	10 (c)
11 (c)	12 (d)	13 (a)	14 (b)	15 (b)	16 (c)	17 (b)	18 (c)	19 (b)	20 (c)
21 (a)	22 (c)	23 (c)	24 (a)						

Skill oosters

1 (b)	2 (b)	3 (a)	4 (d)	5 (c)	6 (b)	7 (b)	8 (b)	9 (a)	10 (a)

Step by Step

Decoding the Questions

Concept Builders

1 True (T) 2 opposite

3 positive, negative

4 Remains same 5 n^2

6 True (T) 7 increase

8 $10^{-8}\,\Omega$-m to $10^{-6}\,\Omega$-m

9 decreases 10 decreases

11 True (T) 12 False (F)

13 $\frac{P}{V} = J^2\sigma$ 14 n^2

15 True (T)

16 current , resistors

17 False (F) 18 zero

19 True (T) 20 True (T)

Topical Questions

1 (*c*) Given, number of revolution per second

$= 9.4 \times 10^{18}$ rev

$\therefore$ Frequency, $\nu = 9.4 \times 10^{18}$ rev/s

Now, equivalent current,

$$I = \frac{e}{T} = e\nu \qquad \left[\because \nu = \frac{1}{T}\right]$$

$= 1.6 \times 10^{-19} \times 9.4 \times 10^{18}$ $[\because e = 1.6 \times 10^{-19}\ \text{C}]$

$= 1.5$ A

3 (*b*) Let mid-point be C as shown in the figure.

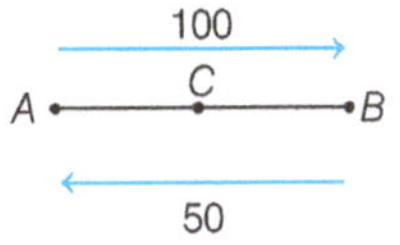

Current from A to B,

$$i_1 = 100 \times 3e = 300e \quad \left(\because i = \frac{ne}{t}\right)$$

Current from B to A,

$$i_2 = 50 \times 3e = 150\,e$$

Net current,

$$i = 300\,e - 150\,e = 150\,e,$$

towards right

$$i = 150 \times 1.6 \times 10^{-19}$$
$= 2.4 \times 10^{-17}$ A from A to B

4 (*b*) The instantaneous charge,

$$dq = i\,dt = (4 + 2t)\,dt$$
$$\Rightarrow q = \int_2^6 (4 + 2t)\,dt = [4t + t^2]_2^6$$
$$= 48\ \text{C}$$

6 (*c*) The total current will be

$$i = n_\alpha q_\alpha + n_p q_p + n_e q_e \quad \text{...(i)}$$

Here, $n_\alpha = n_p = n_e = 10^{19}$,

$q_p = q_e = 1.6 \times 10^{-19}$ C

and $q_\alpha = 2q_p = 2 \times 1.6 \times 10^{-19}$ C

Substituting these values in Eq. (i), we get

$$i = 10^{19} \times (2 \times 1.6 \times 10^{-19}) + 10^{19} \times (1.6 \times 10^{-19}) + 10^{19} \times (1.6 \times 10^{-19})$$

$= 6.4$ A towards left

8 (*d*) The V-I graph for a conductor is as shown in the figure

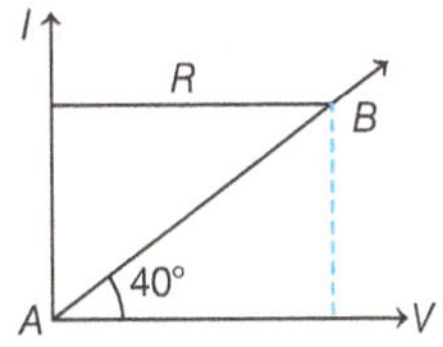

According to Ohm's law, we get

Current, $I = \frac{V}{R}$

Also, slope $AB = \frac{1}{\text{Resistance}} = \frac{I}{V}$

$$\Rightarrow \quad \frac{1}{R} = \tan 40°$$
$$R = \cot 40°$$

or $\quad R = \cot 40°$

9 (*b*) The resistance is given by

$$R = \rho l / A$$

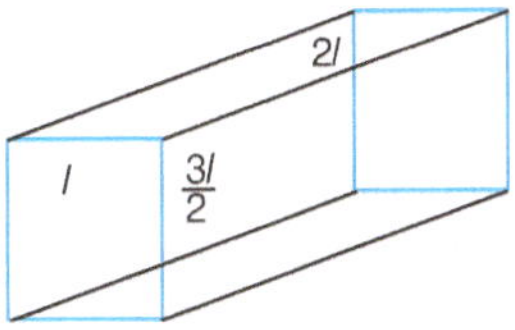

So, from figure, the resistance between parallel faces having area of $(l \times \frac{3l}{2})$,

$$R_1 = \frac{\rho \times 2l}{l \times 3l/2} = \frac{2\rho}{3l/2} = \frac{4\rho}{3l} \quad \text{...(i)}$$

Resistance between parallel faces having area of $l \times 2l$,

$$R_2 = \frac{\rho \times 3l/2}{l \times 2l} = \frac{3\rho}{4l} \quad \text{...(ii)}$$

and resistance between $3l/2$ parallel faces having area of $2l \times \frac{3l}{2}$,

$$R_3 = \frac{\rho \times l}{2l \times 3l/2} = \frac{\rho}{3l} \quad \text{...(iii)}$$

From Eqs. (i), (ii) and (iii), we get

$$R_{max} = R_1 = \frac{4\rho}{3l} \text{ and } R_{min} = R_3 = \frac{\rho}{3l}$$
$$\therefore \quad \frac{R_{max}}{R_{min}} = 4$$

10 (*c*) Electric field, $E = \frac{V}{l} = \frac{IR}{l}$ $[\because V = IR]$

$$= \frac{I\rho l}{Al} = \frac{I\rho}{A} \quad [\because R = \rho l / A]$$
$$\Rightarrow \quad E = \frac{1 \times 1.7 \times 10^{-8}}{2 \times 10^{-6}}$$
$$= 8.5 \times 10^{-3}\ \text{Vm}^{-1}$$

15 (*a*) Electric field

$$= \frac{\Delta V}{l} = \frac{100}{1} = 100\ \text{Vm}^{-1}$$

Drift velocity, $v_d = \frac{i}{n_{Cu} eA}$

and current density,

$$J = \sigma E = \frac{i}{A} \Rightarrow v_d = \frac{\sigma E}{e n_{Cu}}$$
$$= \frac{5.81 \times 10^7 \times 100}{1.6 \times 10^{-19} \times 8.5 \times 10^{28}}$$
$$= 0.43\ \text{ms}^{-1}$$

16 (*c*) Given, $i = 10$ A,

$A = 4 \times 10^{-6}\ \text{m}^2$,

$\rho = 2.7$ g/cc $= 2.7 \times 10^3$ kg/m^3,

$M_w = 27\,g = 27 \times 10^{-3}$ kg

If n be the total number of electrons in the conductor per unit volume, then

$$n = \frac{\text{Avogadro's number}}{V} \times \left(\frac{M}{M_w}\right)$$

$$= 6 \times 10^{23} \times \frac{\rho}{M_w} \qquad \left[\because \rho = \frac{M}{V}\right]$$

$$= 6 \times 10^{23} \times \frac{2.7 \times 10^3}{27 \times 10^{-3}}$$

$\therefore n = 6 \times 10^{28}$

We know that, drift velocity,

$$v_d = \frac{i}{neA}$$

$$= \frac{10}{6 \times 10^{28} \times 1.6 \times 10^{-19} \times 4 \times 10^{-6}}$$

$$= 2.6 \times 10^{-4} \text{ m/s}$$

17 (c) Given, cross-sectional area,

$A = 1\,\text{cm}^2 = 10^{-4}\,\text{m}^2$

Number of electrons per m^3,

$$n = 3 \times 10^{23}$$

Current, $I = 24$ mA $= 24 \times 10^{-3}$ A

Now, drift velocity, $v_d = \dfrac{I}{neA}$

$$= \frac{24 \times 10^{-3}}{3 \times 10^{23} \times 1.6 \times 10^{-19} \times 10^{-4}}$$

$$= 5 \times 10^{-3} \text{ m/s}$$

23 (d) Given, $R_{20} = 20\,\Omega$, $R_{500} = 60\,\Omega$, $R = 25\,\Omega$

$\therefore \quad R_t = R_0\,(1 + \alpha t)$

$\Rightarrow \quad 20 = R_0\,(1 + \alpha \times 20) \quad$ ...(i)

and $\quad 60 = R_0\,(1 + \alpha \times 500) \quad$ ...(ii)

On dividing Eq. (ii) by Eq. (i), we get

$$\frac{1 + 500\alpha}{1 + 20\alpha} = 3$$

$$\Rightarrow \quad \alpha = \frac{2}{440} = \frac{1}{220}\,°\text{C}^{-1}$$

From Eq (i), we get

$$20 = R_0\left(1 + \frac{1}{220} \times 20\right) \quad \text{...(iii)}$$

At $\;R = 25\Omega$,

$$25 = R_0\left(1 + \frac{1}{220} \times t\right) \quad \text{...(iv)}$$

On dividing Eq. (iv) by Eq. (iii), we get

$$\frac{25}{20} = \frac{\left(1 + \frac{1}{220} \times t\right)}{\left(1 + \frac{1}{220} \times 20\right)}$$

$$\Rightarrow \quad \frac{5}{4} = \frac{220 + t}{240}$$

$\therefore \quad t = 80°\,\text{C}$

27 (d) Given, $T_1 = 27\,°\text{C}$,

$R_1 = 65\,\Omega$

$$R_2 = \frac{\text{Supply voltage}}{\text{Steady current}} = \frac{220}{2.8} = 78.6\,\Omega$$

Now, using the relation,

$$R_2 = R_1\,[1 + \alpha(T_2 - T_1)]$$

$$\Rightarrow \quad T_2 - T_1 = \frac{R_2 - R_1}{R_1} \times \frac{1}{\alpha}$$

$$= \frac{78.6 - 65}{65} \times \frac{1}{1.70 \times 10^{-4}}$$

$$= 1231\,°\text{C}$$

$\therefore T_2 = 1231 + T_1$

$= 1231 + 27 = 1258\,°\text{C}$

30 (c) For the same length and same material, $\dfrac{R_2}{R_1} = \dfrac{A_1}{A_2} = \dfrac{3}{1} \Rightarrow R_2 = 3\,R_1$

The resistance of thick wire,

$R_1 = 10\ \Omega$

The resistance of thin wire,

$R_2 = 3\,R_1 = 3 \times 10 = 30\ \Omega$

Total resistance for series

$= R_1 + R_2 = 10 + 30 = 40\,\Omega$

32 (a) The given circuit can be redrawn as follows.

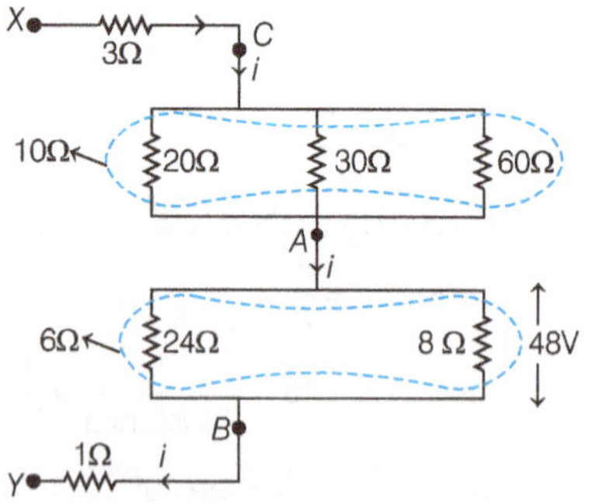

Resistance between A and B

$$= \frac{24 \times 8}{32} = 6\,\Omega$$

Similarly, resistance between C and A

$$\frac{1}{R} = \frac{1}{20} + \frac{1}{30} + \frac{1}{60}$$

$$R = 10\Omega$$

Current between (A) and (B) and current between (X) and (Y) is same as

$$= i = \frac{48}{6} = 8\text{ A}$$

Resistance between X and Y

$= (3 + 10 + 6 + 1) = 20\,\Omega$

$\Rightarrow$ Potential difference between X and $Y = 8 \times 20 = 160$ V

33 (b) Given, resistance of 400 Ω and (10 kΩ) 10000 Ω are in parallel, their effective resistance R_p will be

$$R_p = \frac{400 \times 10000}{400 + 10000} = \frac{5000}{13}\,\Omega$$

Total resistance of circuit,

$$R = \frac{5000}{13} + 800 = \frac{15400}{13}\,\Omega$$

Current in the circuit,

$$i = \frac{V}{R} = \frac{6}{15400/13}$$

$$= \frac{39}{7700}\text{ A} \qquad [\because V = 6\text{V}]$$

Potential difference across voltmeter,

$$V = iR_p = \frac{39}{7700} \times \frac{5000}{13} = 1.95\text{ V}$$

35 (d) The equivalent resistance of parallel combination,

$$R_p = \frac{R_1 R_2}{R_1 + R_2} = \frac{3}{5}$$

and $R_1 = 3\ \Omega$, then $\dfrac{3 \times R_2}{3 + R_2} = \dfrac{3}{5}$

$\Rightarrow \quad 15\,R_2 = 9 + 3\,R_2 \Rightarrow 12\,R_2 = 9$

$$\therefore \quad R_2 = \frac{3}{4}\,\Omega$$

36 (c) Resistance of each part,

$$R' = \frac{R}{4} = \frac{16}{4} = 4\,\Omega$$

and length of each part, $l' = l\,/\,4$.

In stretching l' to l, it is stretched 4 times, so resistance become

$$R'' = \frac{\rho(4l)}{(A/4)} = 4^2\frac{\rho l}{A} = 4^2 R'$$

$$\Rightarrow \quad R'' = 4^2 \times 4 = 64\,\Omega$$

For parallel combination,

$$\frac{1}{R_{\text{eq}}} = \frac{1}{64} + \frac{1}{64} + \frac{1}{64} + \frac{1}{64} = \frac{4}{64}$$

$$\Rightarrow \quad R_{\text{eq}} = \frac{64}{4} = 16\,\Omega$$

40 (a) Resistance in the branch ADC,

$R_1 = 3\,\Omega + 7\,\Omega = 10\,\Omega$

Since, arms ADC ($10\ \Omega$) and AC ($10\ \Omega$) are in parallel, their equivalent resistance,

$$R_2 = \frac{10 \times 10}{10 + 10}\ \Omega = 5\ \Omega$$

Since, R_2 is in series with 9Ω in arm AB, equivalent resistance,
$R_3 = 5\ \Omega + 9\ \Omega = 14\ \Omega$

As R_3 is in parallel with $5\ \Omega$ in arm BC, equivalent resistance between B and C,

i.e. $$R_{BC} = \frac{14 \times 5}{14 + 5} = \frac{70}{19}\ \Omega$$

42 (*d*) Given, resistance of wire,

$$R_0 = R_1 + R_2 = 12\ \Omega$$

Resistance between A and B,

$$R = \frac{R_1 \times R_2}{R_1 + R_2} = \frac{8}{3}\ \Omega$$

$$\Rightarrow R_1R_2 = \frac{8}{3}(R_1 + R_2) = \frac{8}{3} \times 12 = 32\ \Omega$$

We get, $R_1 = 4\Omega$ and $R_2 = 8\Omega$

As $R \propto l$, then $\frac{l_1}{l_2} = \frac{R_1}{R_2} = \frac{4}{8} = \frac{1}{2}$

44 (*b*) Actual value of $R = 30\ \Omega$

So, measured value of R is

$$R' = 30 - (5\% \text{ of } 30)$$

$$= 30 - \frac{5}{100} \times 30 = 28.5\ \Omega \quad \text{... (i)}$$

Now, let us assume that internal resistance of voltmeter R_V. Replacing voltmeter with its internal resistance, we get following circuit.

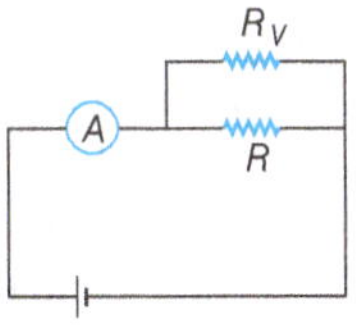

It is clear that the measured value, R' should be equal to parallel combination of R and R_V. Mathematically,

$$R' = \frac{RR_V}{R + R_V} = 28.5\ \Omega$$

Given, $R = 30\ \Omega$

$$\Rightarrow \frac{30R_V}{30 + R_V} = 28.5\ \Omega$$

$$\Rightarrow R_V = \frac{28.5 \times 30}{1.5} = 19 \times 30$$

or $$R_V = 570\ \Omega$$

45 (*d*) The given circuit diagram can be drawn as shown below.

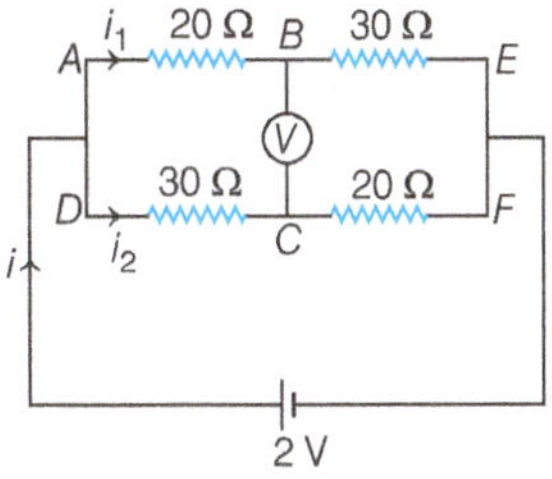

The equivalent resistance of circuit is given by

$$\frac{1}{R_{eq}} = \frac{1}{R_{AE}} + \frac{1}{R_{DF}}$$

$$= \frac{1}{(20 + 30)} + \frac{1}{(30 + 20)}$$

$$= \frac{2}{50} \Rightarrow R_{eq} = 25\ \Omega$$

The current in circuit, $i = \frac{V}{R} = \frac{2}{25}$ A

As the resistance of two branches is same, i.e. $50\ \Omega$.

So, the current, $i_1 = i_2$

$$\Rightarrow \qquad i = i_1 + i_2$$

$$\frac{2}{25} = 2i_1 \Rightarrow i_2 = i_1 = \frac{1}{25}\text{ A}$$

$\therefore$ The voltage across AB,

$$V_1 = V_A - V_B = i_1R_1 = \frac{20}{25}$$

and voltage across CD,

$$V_2 = V_A - V_C = i_2R_2 = \frac{30}{25}$$

$\therefore$ Voltmeter reading $= V_B - V_C$

$$= \frac{30}{25} - \frac{20}{25} = 0.4\text{ V}$$

46 (*b*) The circuit can be redrawn by breaking into two parts,

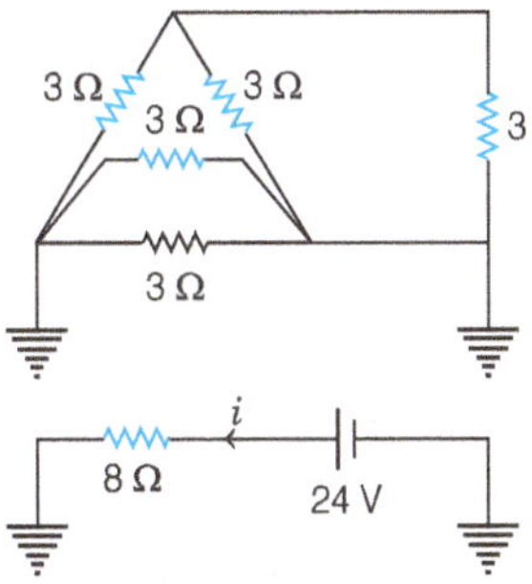

As the other end of 8Ω resistor is grounded, so it is at zero potential.

The potential difference across $8\ \Omega$ resistor $= 24 - 0 = 24$V

$\therefore$ Current in $8\ \Omega$ resistor,

$$i = \frac{V}{R} = \frac{24 - 0}{8} = 3\text{ A}$$

47 (*c*) The circuit is as shown below

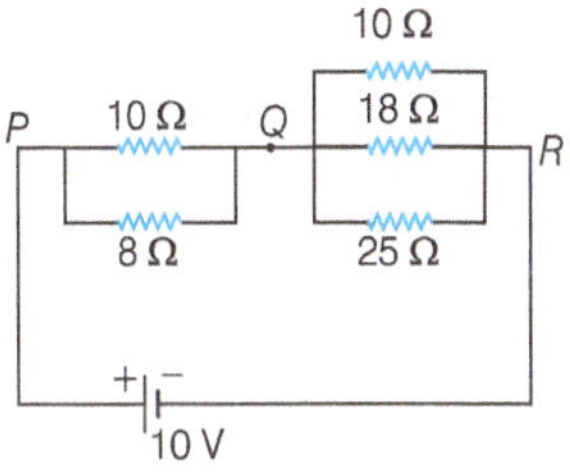

In the given circuit, net resistance between P and Q is R_{PQ} and net resistance between Q and R is R_{QR}, then $R_{PQ} = \frac{10 \times 8}{10 + 8} = \frac{80}{18} = \frac{40}{9}\ \Omega$

and

$$R_{QR} = \frac{10 \times 18 \times 25}{10 \times 18 + 18 \times 25 + 25 \times 10}$$

$$= \frac{4500}{880} = \frac{225}{44}\ \Omega$$

So, circuit will be

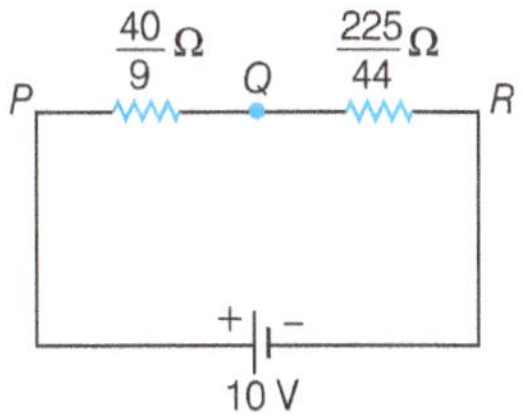

In the series circuit, voltages will be divide in the ratio of their resistances.

$$\therefore \qquad \frac{R_{PQ}}{R_{QR}} = \frac{V_{PQ}}{V_{QR}}$$

$$\therefore \qquad \frac{\left(\frac{40}{9}\right)}{\left(\frac{225}{44}\right)} = \frac{V_{PQ}}{V_{QR}} \quad \text{or} \quad \frac{1760}{2025} = \frac{V_{PQ}}{V_{QR}}$$

Now, $$\frac{V_{PQ}}{V_{PR}} = \frac{V_{PQ}}{V_{PQ} + V_{QR}}$$

$$= \frac{1760}{1760 + 2025}$$

$$\Rightarrow \qquad \frac{V_{PQ}}{10} = \frac{1760}{3785}$$

$$\Rightarrow \qquad V_{PQ} = 4.65\text{ V}$$

or $$V_P - V_Q = 4.65\text{ V}$$

48 (*b*) Given circuit is

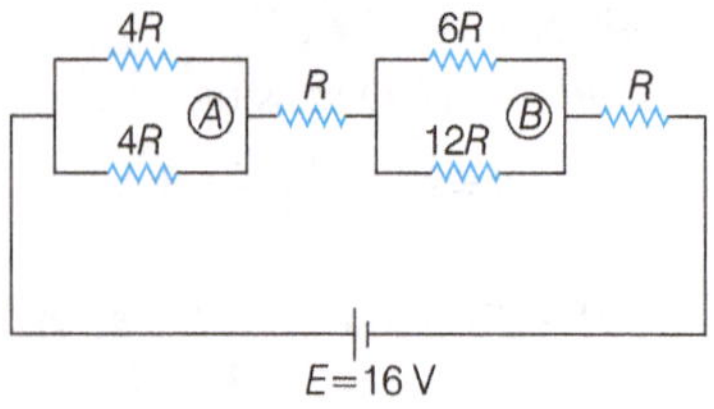

Equivalent resistance of part *A*,

$$R_A = \frac{4R \times 4R}{4R + 4R} = 2R$$

Equivalent resistance of part *B*,

$$R_B = \frac{6R \times 12R}{6R + 12R} = \frac{72}{18} R = 4R$$

$\therefore$ Total resistance of the given network is

$$R_s = 2R + R + 4R + R = 8R$$

As we know, power of the circuit,

$$P = \frac{E^2}{R_s} = \frac{(16)^2}{8R} = \frac{16 \times 16}{8R} \quad \text{...(i)}$$

According to question, power consumed by the network,

$$P = 4 \text{ W}$$

From Eq. (i), we get

$$\therefore \frac{16 \times 16}{8R} = 4 \Rightarrow R = \frac{16 \times 16}{8 \times 4} = 8\Omega$$

49 (*b*) For circuit 1,

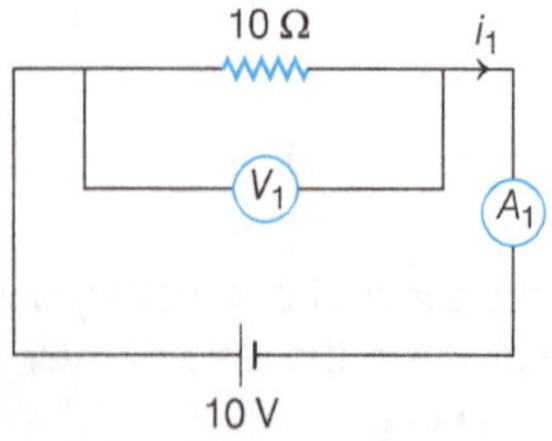

$$R \times i_1 = V \text{ or } 10 i_1 = 10$$

$$\Rightarrow \quad i_1 = \frac{10}{10} = 1 \text{ A}$$

$$\therefore \quad V_1 = i_1 \times R = 1 \times 10 = 10 \text{ V}$$

Similarly, for circuit 2, the addition of 10 Ω to voltmeter does not affect the current and hence

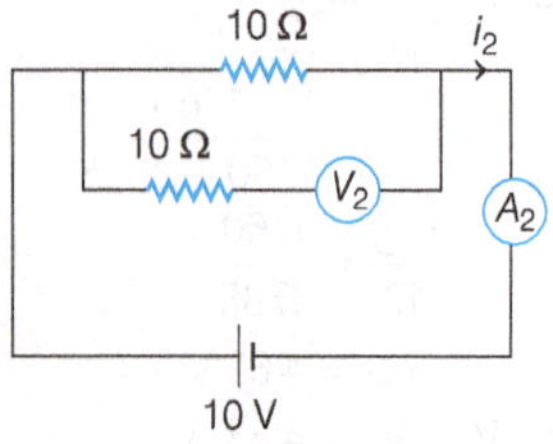

$$R \times i_2 = V \text{ or } 10 i_2 = 10$$

$$\Rightarrow \quad i_2 = \frac{10}{10} = 1 \text{ A}$$

$$\Rightarrow \quad V_2 = i_2 R = 1 \times 10 = 10 \text{ V}$$

$$\therefore \quad V_1 = V_2 \text{ and } i_1 = i_2$$

50 (*b*) Power dissipated by any resistor *R*,

$$P = I^2 R \quad \text{... (i)}$$

$$4.4 = (2 \times 10^{-3})^2 \times R$$

$$\text{or} \quad R = \frac{4.4}{4 \times 10^{-6}} \Omega \quad \text{...(ii)}$$

When this resistance *R* is connected with 11 V supply, then power dissipated is

$$P = \frac{V^2}{R}$$

$$\text{or} \quad P = \frac{(11)^2}{4.4} \times 4 \times 10^{-6}$$

[$\because$ Using Eq. (ii)]

$$\Rightarrow P = \frac{11 \times 11 \times 4 \times 10^{-6}}{44 \times 10^{-1}} \text{ W}$$

$$\text{or} \quad P = 11 \times 10^{-5} \text{ W}$$

51 (*b*) Distance between two cities, $d = 150$ km

Fall of potential per km, $V = 8$ V

Average resistance per km,

$$R = 0.5\,\Omega$$

Power loss per km,

$$P_1 = \frac{V^2}{R} = \frac{8^2}{0.5} = 128 \text{ W}$$

$\therefore$ Total power loss in wire $= P_1 \times d$

$$= 128 \times 150 = 19.2 \text{ kW}$$

54 (*c*) Since, the efficiency of the motor is 30%.

Power dissipated as heat in the motor windings

$$= (100\% - 30\%) = 70\%$$

Total power dissipated as heat in the windings

$$= \left(\frac{70}{100}\right) \times 600 = 420 \text{ W}$$

If *R* is the resistance of the windings of the motor, total power dissipated as heat $= i^2 R$

$$\Rightarrow \quad i^2 R = 420 \text{ W}$$

$$\Rightarrow \quad R = \frac{420 \text{ W}}{(12 \text{ A})^2} = 2.9\,\Omega$$

55 (*b*) As, $i = \dfrac{E}{R + r}$ or $E = i(R + r)$

Given, $i = 0.2$ A, $E = 2.1$ V

and $R = 10\,\Omega$

$$\Rightarrow \quad 2.1 = 0.2\,(10 + r)$$

$$\Rightarrow \quad 10 + r = \frac{2.1}{0.2}$$

$$\therefore \quad r = 10.5 - 10 = 0.5\,\Omega$$

56 (*a*) The situation can be drawn as

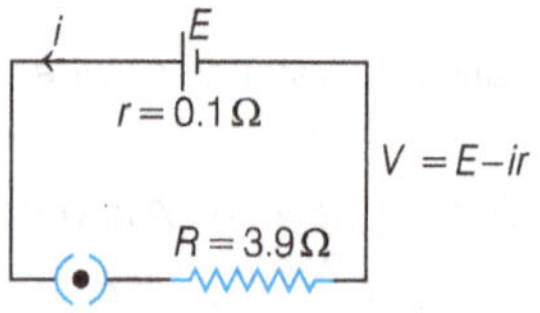

$$\therefore \quad V = E - ir$$

Also, current, $i = \dfrac{E}{R + r}$

$$\Rightarrow \quad V = E - \left(\frac{E}{R + r}\right) r$$

Putting numerical values, we have $E = 2$ V, $r = 0.1\,\Omega$ and $R = 3.9\,\Omega$

$$\Rightarrow \quad V = 2 - \left(\frac{2}{3.9 + 0.1}\right) \times 0.1$$

$$\Rightarrow \quad V = 1.95 \text{ V}$$

57 (*c*) Given that, the current through 8Ω is same before and after connecting *E*.

Now, current in the circuit before connecting *E*,

$$I_1 = \frac{V}{R_{eq}} = \frac{12}{6 + 8 + 10} = \frac{1}{2} \text{ A}$$

Current in the circuit after connecting *E*,

$$I_2 = \frac{1}{2} \text{ A} \quad [\because I_1 = I_2]$$

$\because$ Voltage through the 8Ω resistor is equal to voltage through *E*.

$$\therefore \quad E = IR$$

$$\Rightarrow \quad E = \frac{1}{2} \times 8 = 4 \text{ V}$$

58 (*b*) Total resistance across cells

$$R = 1 + \frac{12 \times 4}{12 + 4} = 4\Omega$$

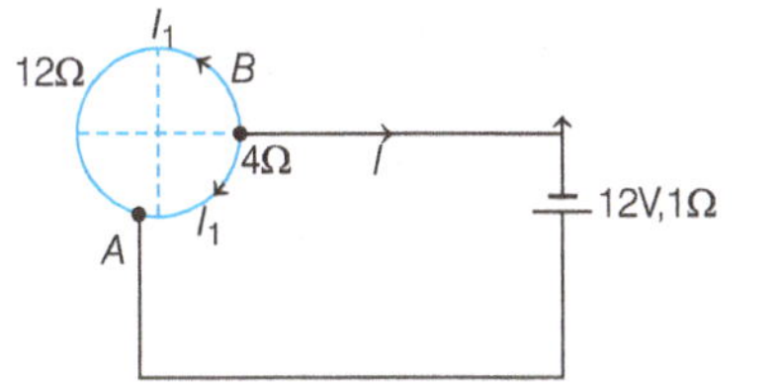

Current through cell $I = \frac{E}{R} = \frac{12}{4} = 3A$

Potential drop across AB

$$v = E - IR = 12 - 3 \times 1 = 9\,V$$

Now, $I_1R_1 = I_2R_2 = V$

$\Rightarrow I_2 \times 4 = 9 \Rightarrow I_2 = \frac{9}{4} = 2.25\,A$

60 (c) The given circuits are as shown below

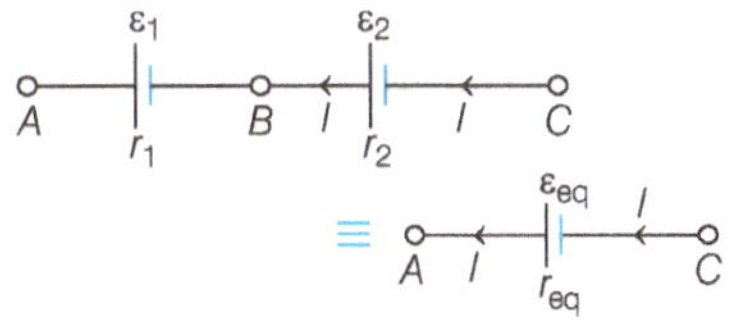

So, potential difference between the terminals A and C is,

$$V_{AC} = V_A - V_C$$
$$= (V_A - V_B) + (V_B - V_C)$$
$$= \varepsilon_1 - Ir_1 + \varepsilon_2 - Ir_2$$
$$= (\varepsilon_1 + \varepsilon_2) - I(r_1 + r_2)$$
$$= \varepsilon_{eq} - Ir_{eq}$$

62 (a) According to given circuit,

$$I = I_1 + I_2$$

If V be the potential difference across B_1 and B_2, then

$$I_1 = \frac{\varepsilon_1 - V}{r_1} \Rightarrow I_2 = \frac{\varepsilon_2 - V}{r_2}$$

Combining these three equations, we get

$$I = I_1 + I_2$$
$$= \frac{\varepsilon_1 - V}{r_1} + \frac{\varepsilon_2 - V}{r_2}$$
$$= \left(\frac{\varepsilon_1}{r_1} + \frac{\varepsilon_2}{r_2}\right) - V\left(\frac{1}{r_1} + \frac{1}{r_2}\right)$$

Hence, $V = \frac{\varepsilon_1 r_2 + \varepsilon_2 r_1}{r_1 + r_2} - I\frac{r_1 r_2}{r_1 + r_2}$

If we want to replace the combination by a single cell, between B_1 and B_2 of emf ε_{eq} and internal resistance r_{eq}, we would have, $V = \varepsilon_{eq} - Ir_{eq}$

63 (d) If two cells are wrongly connected, then $i = \frac{(n-4)\,\varepsilon}{nr}$

Potential difference across A or B,

$$V = \varepsilon + ir = \varepsilon + \frac{(n-4)}{nr}\varepsilon \times r$$
$$= \left(\frac{n + n - 4}{n}\right)\varepsilon = \left(2 - \frac{4}{n}\right)\varepsilon$$
$$\Rightarrow V = 2\varepsilon\left(1 - \frac{2}{n}\right)$$

64 (b) Given that, the resultant voltage across the battery terminal = 1.5 V

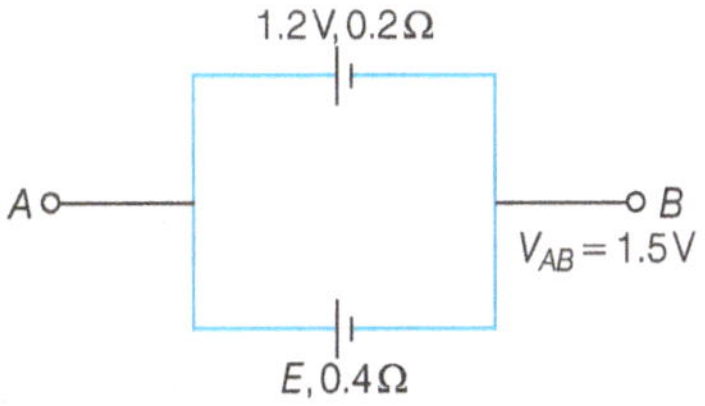

For circuit having two cells of emf E_1 and E_2 with internal resistances of r_1 and r_2 in parallel, the equivalent emf of battery is given by

$$E_{eq} = \frac{E_1/r_1 + E_2/r_2}{1/r_1 + 1/r_2}$$
$$= \frac{\frac{1.2}{0.2} + \frac{E}{0.4}}{\frac{1}{0.2} + \frac{1}{0.4}} = 1.5$$

$\Rightarrow 2.4 + E = 1.5 \times 3$

Solving this, we get $E = 2.1$ V.

65 (d) The given combination consists of two batteries in parallel and resultant of these two in series with third one.

For parallel combination, we can apply

$$E_{eq} = \frac{\frac{E_1}{r_1} - \frac{E_2}{r_2}}{\frac{1}{r_1} + \frac{1}{r_2}} = \frac{\frac{10}{2} - \frac{4}{2}}{\frac{1}{2} + \frac{1}{2}} = \frac{6}{2} = 3\,V$$

Further, $\frac{1}{r'_{eq}} = \frac{1}{r_1} + \frac{1}{r_2} = \frac{1}{2} + \frac{1}{2} = 1$

$\Rightarrow \quad r'_{eq} = 1\,\Omega$

Now, this is in series with third one, i.e.

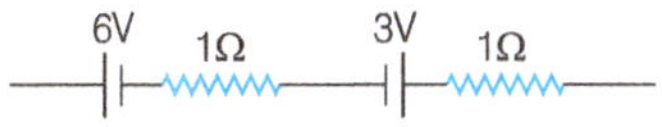

$\Rightarrow \quad r_{eq} = 1 + 1 = 2\Omega$

and $\quad E_{eq} = 6 - 3 = 3\,V$

67 (a) Given circuit with currents as shown in the figure below, [In the question $I_1 = -0.3$ A is given, due to it we change the direction of I_1, in this figure].

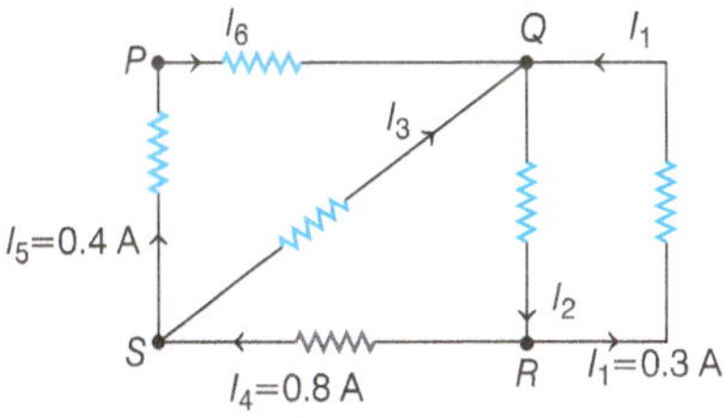

From Kirchhoff's junction rule,

$$\Sigma I = 0$$

At junction S, $I_4 = I_5 + I_3$

$\Rightarrow \quad 0.8 = 0.4 + I_3 \Rightarrow I_3 = 0.4$ A

At junction P, $I_5 = I_6$

$\Rightarrow \quad I_6 = 0.4$ A

At junction Q,

$$I_2 = I_1 + I_3 + I_6 = 0.3 + 0.4 + 0.4$$
$$= 1.1\,A$$

68 (d) Applying Kirchhoff's law at point D as shown, we get

$$i_1 = i_2 + i_3$$
$$\frac{V_A - V_D}{10} = \frac{V_D - V_B}{20} + \frac{V_D - V_C}{30}$$
$$\Rightarrow \quad 70 - V_D = \frac{V_D}{2} + \frac{V_D - 10}{3}$$
$$\Rightarrow \quad V_D = 40\,V$$

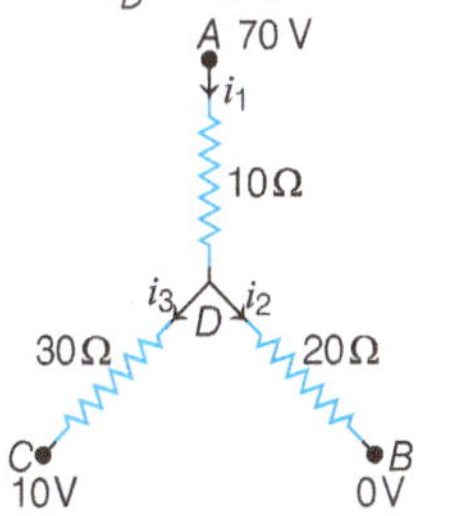

$$i_1 = \frac{V_A - V_D}{10} = \frac{70 - 40}{10} = 3\,A,$$
$$i_2 = \frac{V_D - V_B}{20} = \frac{40 - 0}{20} = 2A$$

and $i_3 = \frac{V_D - V_C}{30} = \frac{40 - 10}{30} = 1\text{A}$

Hence, $i_1 : i_2 : i_3 = 3 : 2 : 1$

69 (*b*) The given circuit can be redrawn as

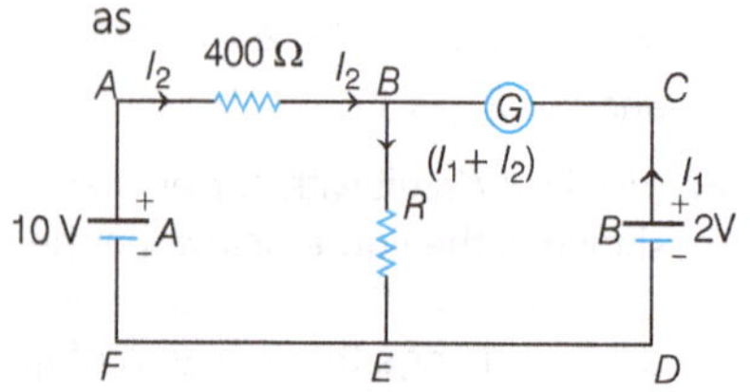

For loop *DCBED*,

$$2 = (I_1 + I_2) R$$

But $I_1 = 0$, then $2 = I_2 R$ ...(i)

For loop *ABEFA*,

$$10 - 400 I_2 - R I_2 = 0 \quad \text{...(ii)}$$

From Eqs. (i) and (ii), $R = 100\,\Omega$

70 (*a*) $V_{BC} = i_2 r_2 = i_3 r_3 = i_4 r_4$ ...(i)

$$i_1 = i_2 + i_3 + i_4 \quad \text{...(ii)}$$

Put values of i_2 and i_3 by Eq. (i) in Eq. (ii).

$$i_1 = \frac{i_4 r_4}{r_2} + \frac{i_4 r_4}{r_3} + i_4$$

$$\Rightarrow \frac{i_1}{i_4} = \frac{r_4}{r_2} + \frac{r_4}{r_3} + 1$$

$$= \frac{r_3 r_4 + r_2 r_4 + r_2 r_3}{r_2 r_3}$$

71 (*b*) The distribution of current is shown in figure.

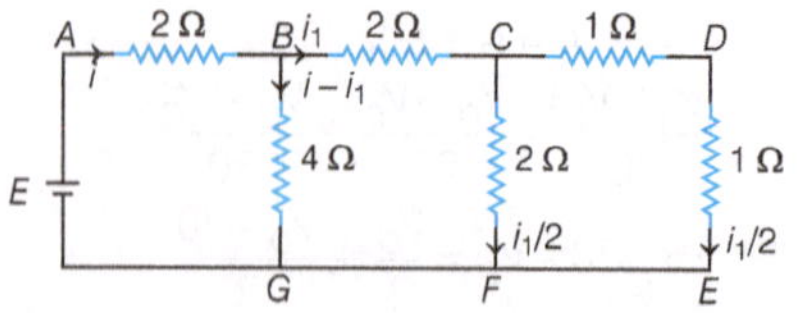

As per question, $\frac{i_1}{2} = 1\text{A}$ (given)

or $i_1 = 2\text{A}$

In a closed circuit *BCFGB*,

$$2i_1 + 2 \times \frac{i_1}{2} - 4(i - i_1) = 0$$

$$\Rightarrow 4 + 2 = 4(i - 2)$$

$$\Rightarrow i = \frac{7}{2}\text{A}$$

Again, in the closed circuit *ABGA*,

$$2i + 4(i - i_1) = E$$

$$\Rightarrow E = 2 \times \frac{7}{2} + 4\left(\frac{7}{2} - 2\right) = 13\text{ V}$$

72 (*a*) In a closed loop, say *ABCC′EA*, apply Kirchhoff's second rule,

$$-IR - \left(\frac{I}{2}\right)R - IR + \varepsilon = 0 \quad \text{...(i)}$$

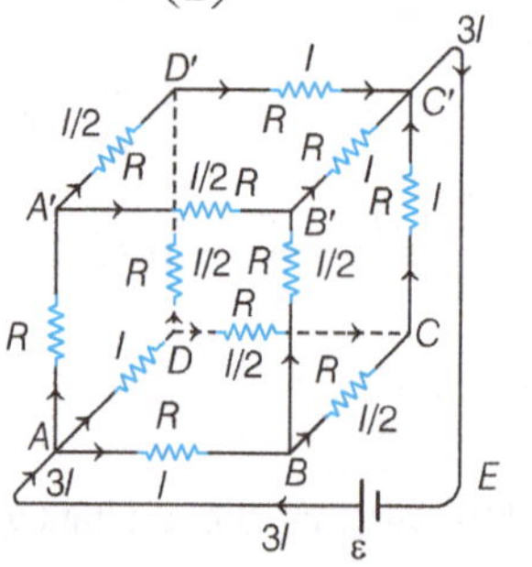

where, *R* is the resistance of each edge and ε the emf of battery.

Thus, $\varepsilon = \frac{5}{2} IR$ [from Eq. (i)]

The equivalent resistance R_{eq} of the network is

$$R_{eq} = \frac{\varepsilon}{3I} = \frac{(5/2)IR}{3I} = \frac{5}{6}R$$

74 (*b*)

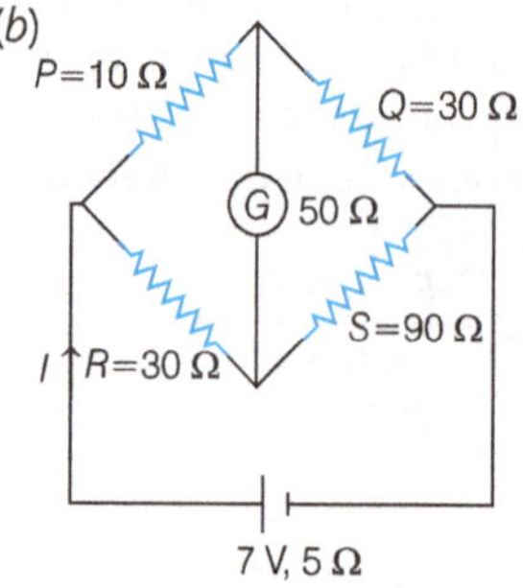

$$\therefore R_{eff} = \frac{(P+Q)(R+S)}{(P+Q)+(R+S)}$$

$$= \frac{40 \times 120}{120 + 40} = \frac{4800}{160} = 30\,\Omega$$

$$\therefore \text{Current, } I = \frac{7}{30+5} \left(\because I = \frac{E}{R+r}\right)$$

$$= \frac{7}{35} = 0.2\text{ A}$$

75 (*c*) In first case when $R = 400\,\Omega$, the balancing equation will be

$$\frac{P}{R} = \frac{Q}{X} \Rightarrow \frac{P}{400\,\Omega} = \frac{Q}{X}$$

$$\Rightarrow P = \frac{400 \times Q}{X} \quad \text{...(i)}$$

In second case, *P* and *Q* are interchanged and $R = 405\,\Omega$

$$\therefore \frac{Q}{R} = \frac{P}{X} \Rightarrow \frac{Q}{405} = \frac{P}{X} \quad \text{...(ii)}$$

Substituting the value of *P* from Eq. (i) in Eq. (ii), we get

$$\frac{Q}{405} = \frac{Q \times 400}{X^2}$$

$$\Rightarrow X^2 = 400 \times 405$$

$$\Rightarrow X = \sqrt{400 \times 405}$$

$$= 402.5$$

The value of *X* is close to $402.5\,\Omega$.

76 (*c*) Given, for first student,

$R_2 = 10\,\Omega$, $R_1 = 5\,\Omega$ and $R_3 = 5\,\Omega$

For second student,

$$R_1 = 500\,\Omega,\ R_3 = 5\,\Omega$$

and $R_2 = 1000\,\Omega$

Now, according to Wheatstone bridge rule, $\frac{R_2}{R_4} = \frac{R_1}{R_3}$

$$\Rightarrow R_4 = R_3 \times \frac{R_2}{R_1} \quad \text{...(i)}$$

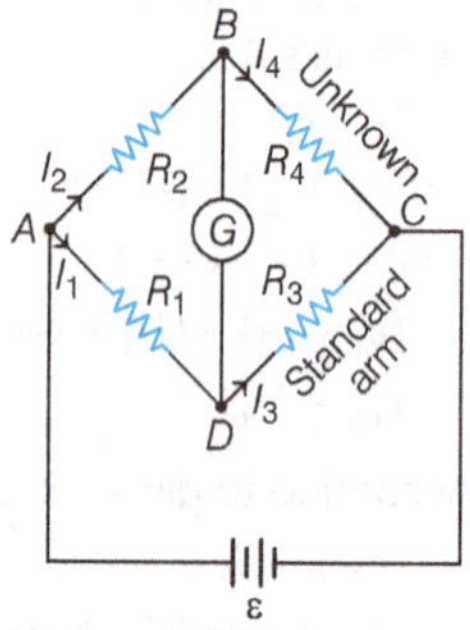

Now, putting all the values in Eq. (i), we get

$R_4 = 10\,\Omega$, for both students. Thus, we can analyse that the Wheatstone bridge is most sensitive and accurate, if resistances are of same value. Thus, the errors of measurement of the two students depend on the accuracy and sensitivity of the bridge, which in turn depends on the accuracy with which R_2 and R_1 can be measured.

When R_2 and R_1 are larger, the currents through the arms of bridge is very weak. This can make the determination of null point accurately more difficult.

77 (*b*) Considering the mesh *BADB*, we have

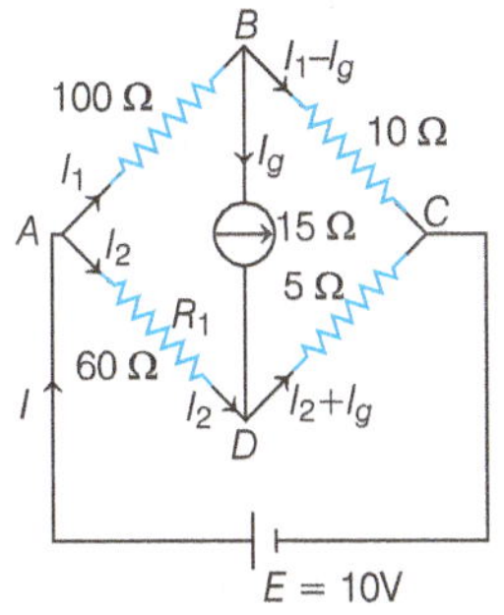

$$100\, I_1 + 15\, I_g - 60\, I_2 = 0$$

$$\Rightarrow \quad 20\, I_1 + 3\, I_g - 12\, I_2 = 0 \quad \text{...(i)}$$

Considering the mesh *BCDB*, we have

$$10\,(I_1 - I_g) - 15\, I_g - 5\,(I_2 + I_g) = 0$$

$$\Rightarrow \quad 10\, I_1 - 30\, I_g - 5 I_2 = 0$$

$$\Rightarrow \quad 2 I_1 - 6\, I_g - I_2 = 0 \quad \text{...(ii)}$$

Considering the mesh *ADCEA*, we have

$$60 I_2 + 5\,(I_2 + I_g) = 10$$

$$\Rightarrow \quad 65\, I_2 + 5 I_g = 10$$

$$\Rightarrow \quad 13 I_2 + I_g = 2 \quad \text{...(iii)}$$

On multiplying Eq. (ii) by 10, we get

$$20\, I_1 - 60\, I_g - 10 I_2 = 0 \quad \text{...(iv)}$$

Subtracting Eq. (iv) from Eq. (i), we get

$$63\, I_g - 2 I_2 = 0$$

$$\Rightarrow \quad I_2 = 31.5\, I_g$$

On substituting the value of I_2 into Eq. (iii), we get

$$13\,(31.5\, I_g) + I_g = 2$$

$$\Rightarrow \quad 410.5\, I_g = 2$$

$$\Rightarrow \quad I_g = 4.87 \text{ mA}$$

79 (*b*) For first case,

$$\frac{5}{l_1} = \frac{R}{(100 - l_1)} \quad \text{...(i)}$$

Now, by shunting resistance *R* with an equal resistance *R*, new resistance in that arm become *R*/2,

$$\text{so} \quad \frac{5}{1.6 l_1} = \frac{R/2}{(100 - 1.6 l_1)} \quad \text{...(ii)}$$

From Eqs. (i) and (ii), we get

$$\frac{1.6}{1} = \frac{(100 - 1.6 l_1)}{100 - l_1} \times 2$$

$$\Rightarrow \quad 160 - 1.6 l_1 = 200 - 3.2 l_1$$

$$\Rightarrow \quad 1.6\, l_1 = 40$$

$$l_1 = \frac{400}{16} = 25 \text{ cm}$$

From Eq. (i), $\frac{5}{25} = \frac{R}{75} \Rightarrow R = 15\,\Omega$

80 (*b*) The circuit diagram is given below.

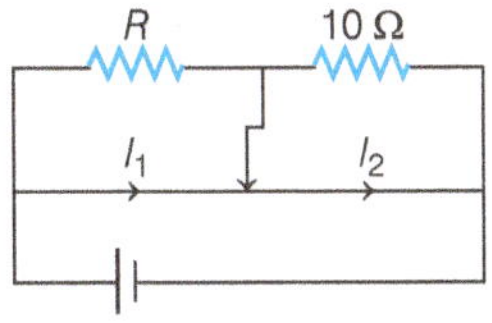

$$\frac{R}{10} = \frac{l_1}{l_2} \Rightarrow \frac{R}{10} = \frac{3}{2} \quad \text{(given)}$$

$$\Rightarrow \quad R = 15\,\Omega$$

Length of 15Ω resistance wire is $= 1$ m

$\therefore$ Length of 1Ω resistance wire $= \frac{1}{15}$

$= 0.0666$ m $= 0.067$ m (Approx.)

Assertion and Reason Questions

2 (*c*) Consider a conductor of length *l* and area of cross-section *A*. Time taken by the free electrons to cross the conductor, $t = \frac{l}{v_d}$

Hence, current, $I = \frac{q}{t} = \frac{Al \times ne}{l / v_d}$

$$\Rightarrow \quad I = Ane\, v_d \Rightarrow I \propto v_d$$

Thus, current is directly proportional to drift velocity. Therefore, Assertion is correct but Reason is incorrect.

4 (*a*) Increasing the temperature of a metallic conductor increases the resistance of the conductor. Since electrical conductivity is inversely related to resistance, an increase in temperature leads to a decrease in conductivity.

Raising the temperature reduces the mean free path of the charge carriers, effectively decreasing their mobility.

9 (*c*) Assertion is correct but Reason is incorrect. Resistance of bulb,

$$R = \frac{V_{\text{rated}}^2}{P_{\text{rated}}}$$

$$\therefore \quad R_1 = \frac{(210)^2}{65} = 678.46\Omega$$

$$\therefore \quad R_2 = \frac{(210)^2}{100} = 441\Omega$$

Statement Based Questions

3 (*b*) Statement I is correct but Statement II is incorrect.

The expression for drift velocity

$$v_d = \frac{\sigma E}{ne}$$

As, $v_d \propto E$, drift velocity increases with increase in electric field.

5 (*b*) Statement I is correct but Statement II is incorrect and it can be corrected as,

Unlike metals, the resistivity of semiconductors decreases with increasing temperature.

6 (*b*) We know that, $P = Q/t$

$$\Rightarrow \quad Q = P \times t$$

$$\therefore \quad Q = 200 \times 10 = 2000 \text{ Wh}$$

$$= 2 \text{ kWh} \quad (\because 1 \text{ unit} = 1 \text{ kWh})$$

$$= 2 \text{ electrical units}$$

Hence, Statement I is correct but Statement II is incorrect.

7 (*a*) Both Statement I and Statement II are incorrect.

The internal resistance opposes the flow of ions. As the temperature increases, ions move faster and more current is produced. This lead to decrease in the internal resistance. The internal resistance represents the opposition to flow of current within cell itself and it is always present to some extent.

Matching Type Questions

1 (*a*) As we know that, the expression of the drift velocity,

$$v_d = \frac{eE}{m}\tau$$

Here, *e* is the electric charge,

E is the electric field,
m is the mass of an electron and
τ is the relaxation time.

Consider the conductor having length l, area of the cross-section A and the charge density n.

Electrical resistivity, $\rho = \frac{m}{ne^2\tau}$

Relaxation period, $\tau = \frac{m}{ne^2\rho}$

Current density,
$$J = \frac{I}{A} = \frac{neAv_d}{A} = nev_d$$

Again, $\frac{E}{J} = \frac{E}{\sigma E} = \frac{1}{\sigma} = \rho$

$\therefore$ Electrical resistivity, $\rho = \frac{E}{J}$

The correct match is
A → 3, B → 4, C → 1 and D → 2.

2 (a) A conductor of non-uniform cross-section is a series combination of many conductors of non-uniform cross-section. So, current I through them remains constant.

A. $E = \frac{V}{l} = \frac{IR}{l} = \frac{I\rho l}{lA} = \frac{I\rho}{A} \Rightarrow E \propto \frac{1}{A}$

$\therefore$ E increases from end A to B.

B. $J = \frac{I}{A} \Rightarrow J \propto \frac{1}{A}$

$\therefore$ Current density J decreases from B to A.

C. $\mu = \frac{v_d}{E} = \frac{eE\tau}{mE} = \frac{e\tau}{m}$ = constant

D. Temperature increases linearly.

The correct match is
A → 2, B → 3, C → 4 and D → 1

3 (c) Current flowing in a circuit is given by
$$I = \frac{15\text{V} - 10\text{V}}{3\Omega + 1\Omega + 1\Omega} = 1\text{A}$$

A. Potential drop across A,
$V_A = \varepsilon - Ir = 15\text{V} - (1\Omega \times 1\text{A}) = 14\text{V}$

B. Potential drop across B,
$V_B = \varepsilon - Ir = 10\text{V} + (1\Omega \times 1\text{A}) = 11\text{V}$

C. Power is supplied by battery A because it is charging battery B and hence it is discharging itself.

D. Power is consumed by battery B because it is being charged by battery A.

The correct match is
A → 3, B → 4, C → 1 and D → 2

4 (a) In the given circuit, Wheatstone bridge is balanced.

As, $P/Q = R/S$
$$\Rightarrow \frac{40}{10} = \frac{60}{15} = 4$$

Hence, $V_{AB} = V_{AD}$

$\Rightarrow 40I_1 = 60I_2$ [Let I_1 flows in AB]
$I_1 = 1.5I_2$

Power across branch $AB = I^2R$
$= (1.5I_2)^2 \times 40 = 90I_2^2$

Power across branch $BC = I^2R$
$= (1.5I_2)^2 \times 10 = 22.5I_2^2$

Power across branch DC
$= I_2^2R = 15I_2^2$

Power across branch AD
$= I_2^2R = 60I_2^2$

The correct match is
A → 3, B → 1, C → 2 and D → 4

Numerical Type Questions

1 (24) Current for a small portion of wire, $dI = J\left(\frac{dV}{l}\right)$

$$\int_0^I dI = \int_{R/2}^{R} \frac{JdV}{l}$$
$$\int_0^I dI = J\int_{R/2}^{R} 2\pi r dr$$
$$I = 8 \times 10^6 \times 2 \times \pi \int_{R/2}^{R} r\,dr$$
$$= 16 \times 10^6 \times \pi\left[\frac{3R^2}{8}\right]$$
$$= 8 \times 10^6 \times \pi \times 3 \times 10^{-6}$$
$$= 24\pi = n\pi$$
$\therefore$ $n = 24$

2 (3.2) Given, $A = 1\text{ mm}^2 = 10^{-6}\text{ m}^2$, $l = 0.1\text{ m}, V = 5\text{ V}$

Due to the applied potential difference across the wire, an electric field is set up in the conductor. So,
$$E = \frac{V}{l} = \frac{5}{0.1} = 50\text{ Vm}^{-1}$$

The current flowing through the wire is given by
$$I = nAev_d = nAe\mu E \quad \left(\text{where, } \mu = \frac{v_d}{E}\right)$$
$$= 8 \times 10^{28} \times 10^{-6} \times 1.6 \times 10^{-19} \times 5 \times 10^{-6} \times 50$$
$$= 3.2\text{ A}$$

3 (3) Time taken by electron to travel in copper wire is $t = \frac{l}{v_d}$

where, $v_d = \frac{J}{ne}$ or $t = \frac{neAl}{I}$
$$t = \frac{10^{28} \times 1.6 \times 10^{-19} \times 10^3 \times 10^{-6}}{4.5}$$
$\Rightarrow t \approx 3 \times 10^6\text{ s}$

4 (36) When temperature changes from T_0 to T_1, then change in the resistance,
$$R - R_0 = R_0\alpha_{av}(T - T_0)$$

Here, disks will be in series, so
$$R_C + R_i = R_{0_C}[\alpha_C(T - T_0) + 1] + R_{0_i}[\alpha_i(T - T_0) + 1]$$
$$= R_{0_C} + R_{0_i} + [R_{0_C}\alpha_C + R_{0_i}\alpha_i][T - T_0]$$

This equation will be constant, when $R_{0_C}\alpha_c + R_{0_i}\alpha_i = 0$

$\because$ $R = \frac{\rho L}{A}$ and $A_C = A_i + A$

$\therefore$ $L_c\rho_c\alpha_c + L_i\rho_i\alpha_i = 0$

or $\frac{L_c}{L_i} = -\frac{\rho_i\alpha_i}{\rho_c\alpha_c}$
$$= -\frac{9.68 \times 10^{-18} \times 6.5 \times 10^{-3}}{3500 \times 10^{-8} \times (-0.50 \times 10^{-3})}$$
$$= 0.036 = \frac{36}{1000} = \frac{x}{1000}$$
$\therefore$ $x = 36$

5 (1) **For case I**

The potential difference of the uniform wire, $V = 220$ V

The resistance of the uniform wire,
$$R_1 = 60\Omega$$

The power dissipation in the first case,

$$P_1 = \frac{V^2}{R_1} = \frac{(220)^2}{60}$$

For case II

The resistance of each half,

$$R_2 = \frac{R_1}{2} = \frac{60}{2} = 30\,\Omega$$

$$\therefore \quad P_2 = \frac{V^2}{R_2} + \frac{V^2}{R_2} = \frac{(220)^2}{30} + \frac{(220)^2}{30}$$

$$= \frac{(220)^2}{15}$$

Thus, the ratio of the total power dissipation in the first case to the second case, $\frac{P_1}{P_2} = \frac{(220)^2/60}{(220)^2/15} = \frac{1}{4}$

On comparing with $\frac{P_1}{P_2} = \frac{x}{4}$

The value of x is 1.

6 (500) The resistance of the heater

$$R' = \frac{V^2}{P} = \frac{(100)^2}{1000} = \frac{10000}{1000} = 10\Omega$$

If the heater has to operate with power $P' = 62.5$ W, then

$$V' = \sqrt{P'R'} = \sqrt{62.5 \times 10} = 25\text{ V}$$

Since voltage drop across heater is 25 V, hence voltage drop across $10\,\Omega$ resistor $= 100 - 25 = 75$ V

Therefore, current in the circuit is

$$I = \frac{75}{10} = 7.5\text{ A}$$

Now, current through heater

$$= \frac{V'}{R'} = \frac{25}{10} = 2.5\text{ A}$$

So, current through resistor,

$R = 7.5 - 2.5 = 5.0$ A

$$\text{Hence, } R = \frac{V'}{5} = \frac{25}{5} = 5\Omega$$

$$= 500 \times 10^{-2}\Omega$$

$$= x \times 10^{-2}\Omega$$

Therefore, $x = 500$

7 (16) According to first condition,

$$P_1 = \frac{V_0^2}{R}$$

According to second condition, when wire is cut into two halves,

$$\text{then } P_2 = \frac{V_0^2}{\frac{R}{2}} + \frac{V_0^2}{\frac{R}{2}}$$

$$\Rightarrow \quad P_2 = \frac{4V_0^2}{R} = 4P_1$$

$$\Rightarrow \quad \frac{P_2}{P_1} = \frac{4}{1} = \frac{\sqrt{x}}{1} \quad \text{(given)}$$

$$\therefore \quad \sqrt{x} = 4 \Rightarrow x = 16$$

8 (4) The given circuit diagram is shown below.

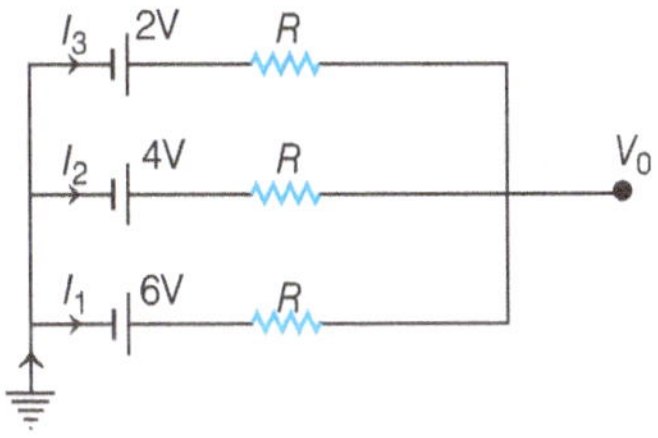

Using Kirchhoff junction rule,

$$I_1 + I_2 + I_3 = 0$$

$$\frac{V_1}{R_1} + \frac{V_2}{R_2} + \frac{V_3}{R_3} = 0$$

$$\because \quad R_1 = R_2 = R_3 = R = 785\,\Omega$$

$$\therefore \quad V_1 + V_2 + V_3 = 0$$

$$6 - V_0 + 4 - V_0 + 2 - V_0 = 0$$

$$\Rightarrow 12 - 3V_0 = 0 \Rightarrow V_0 = 4\text{ V}$$

9 (4.87) As, A is directly connected to the positive terminal of the battery, $V_A = 10$V and $V_C = 0$

By nodal analysis at B,

$$\frac{V_B - 10}{100} + \frac{V_B - V_D}{15} + \frac{V_B - 0}{10} = 0$$

$$53V_B - 20V_D = 30 \quad \text{... (i)}$$

By nodal analysis at D,

$$\frac{V_D - 10}{60} + \frac{V_D - V_B}{15} + \frac{V_D - 0}{5} = 0$$

$$-4V_B + 17V_D = 10 \quad \text{...(ii)}$$

On solving Eqs. (i) and (ii) by substitution method, we get

$$V_D = 0.792\text{ V}$$

$$\Rightarrow \quad V_B = 0.865\text{ V}$$

The current through the galvanometer, $I = \frac{V_B - V_D}{R}$

On substituting the values in the above equation, we get

$$I = \frac{0.865 - 0.792}{15}$$

$$\Rightarrow \quad I = 4.87\text{ mA}$$

10 (9) Circuit diagram is shown below.

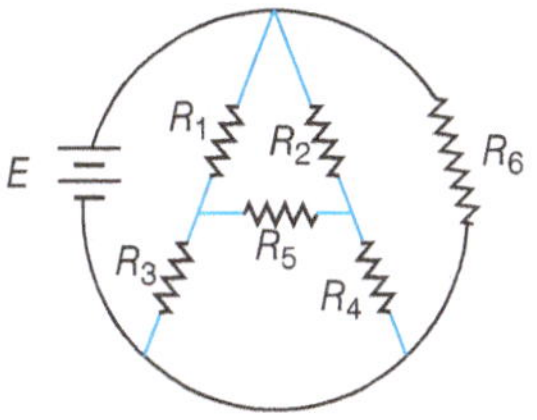

According to the question,

$\frac{R_1}{R_2} = \frac{R_3}{R_4}$, so R_5 is neglected.

$$\therefore \quad \frac{1}{R_{eq}} = \frac{1}{2.5 + 2.5} + \frac{1}{2.5 + 2.5} + \frac{1}{5.0}$$

$$\Rightarrow \quad \frac{1}{R_{eq}} = \frac{1}{5.0} + \frac{1}{5.0} + \frac{1}{5.0}$$

$$\Rightarrow \quad \frac{1}{R_{eq}} = \frac{1+1+1}{5.0}$$

$$\Rightarrow \quad R_{eq} = \frac{5.0}{3}\Omega$$

Now, total current in the circuit is

$$I = \frac{V}{R_{eq}} = \frac{15}{5/3} = 9\text{ A}$$

NCERT Exemplar Questions

1 (*b*) The current density is directed along E and the relationship is given by

$$\mathbf{J} = \sigma\mathbf{E}$$

As direction of E changes, direction of J also changes but current I remains unaffected.

Thus, the agent that is responsible for the given situation in the question, is the electric field produced by charges accumulated on the surface of wire.

2 (*a*) The equivalent emf of this combination is given by

$$\varepsilon_{eq} = \frac{\varepsilon_2 r_1 + \varepsilon_1 r_2}{r_1 + r_2}$$

Also, $\quad \varepsilon_2 > \varepsilon_1$

This suggest that the equivalent emf ε_{eq} of the two cells is

$$\varepsilon_1 < \varepsilon_{eq} < \varepsilon_2$$

$\because$ ε_{eq} is weighted mean of ε_1 and ε_2, so it will lie between ε_1 and ε_2.

3 (c) The percentage error in R can be minimised by adjusting the balance point near the middle of the bridge, i.e., when l_1 is close to 50 cm. This requires a suitable choice of S.

Since, $\frac{R}{S}=\frac{l_1}{(100-l_1)}$

Since, here $R:S::2.9:97.1$, implies that the S is nearly 33 times to that of R. In order to make this ratio 1:1, it is necessary to reduce the value of S nearly (1/33) times, i.e. change the value of S to 3 Ω.

Past Exams Questions

1 (c) Given,

EMF, $\varepsilon=10$ V

Internal resistance, $r=1\Omega$

External resistance, $R=4\Omega$

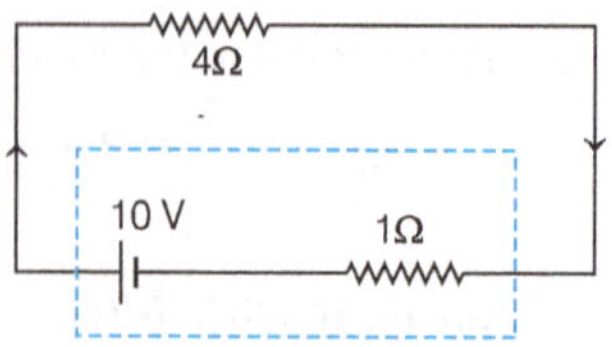

Terminal voltage,

$$V=\varepsilon-Ir$$

and $I=\frac{\varepsilon}{R+r}=\frac{10}{4+1}=2$ A

Thus, $V=10-2\times1=8$ V

2 (b) Given, wire of length l is divided into 10 parts each having $\frac{100}{10}\Omega=10\ \Omega$ resistance.

According to question, 5 parts are connected in series

i.e., $R_1=5\times10=50\,\Omega$

5 parts are connected in parallel

i.e., $R_2=\frac{R}{5}=\frac{10}{5}=2\,\Omega$

Then, both R_1 and R_2 are connected in series

Thus, $R_{net}=R_1+R_2$

$=50+2=52\,\Omega$

3 (a) When 10 resistors, each of resistance R is connected in series, then equivalent resistance,

$R_s=R+R+R+\ldots$ 10 times

$\Rightarrow R_s=10R$

$\therefore$ Current drawn from the battery,

$$I_s=\frac{E}{R_S}=\frac{E}{10R} \quad \ldots(i)$$

In second case, when resistors are connected in parallel, then equivalent resistance,

$$\frac{1}{R_p}=\frac{1}{R}+\frac{1}{R}+\frac{1}{R}+\ldots\text{10 times}$$

$$=\frac{10}{R}\Rightarrow R_p=\frac{R}{10}$$

$\therefore$ Current drawn from the battery,

$$I_p=\frac{E}{R_p}=\frac{E}{R/10}$$

$$=10\times\frac{E}{R}=100\times\frac{E}{10R}$$

$\Rightarrow$ $I_p=100I$

$\therefore$ $n=100$

4 (b) The given situation is shown below.

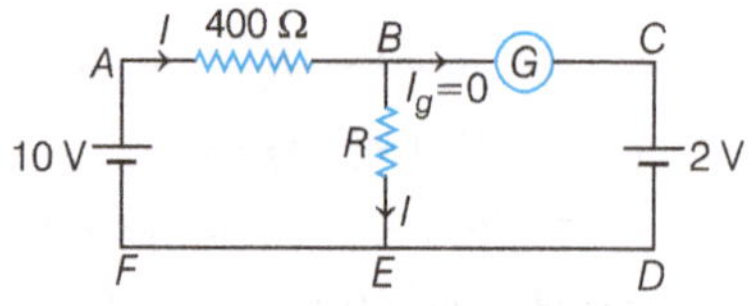

Applying Kirchhoff's voltage law in the loop $ABCDEFA$, we get

$400I+2-10=0$

$\Rightarrow$ $I=\frac{8}{400}=\frac{1}{50}$ A

Applying Kirchhoff's voltage law in loop $ABEFA$, we get

$400I+RI-10=0$

$\Rightarrow$ $(400+R)I=10$

$\Rightarrow$ $(400+R)\times\frac{1}{50}=10$

$\Rightarrow$ $400+R=500$

$\Rightarrow$ $R=100\,\Omega$

5 (d) Given, length, $l=10$ m

Radius, $r=\frac{10^{-2}}{\sqrt{\pi}}$ m

The current density,

$$J=\sigma E=\frac{E}{\rho} \quad \ldots(i)$$

So, $\rho=\frac{RA}{l}=\frac{10\times\pi\times\frac{10^{-4}}{\pi}}{10}$

$=10^{-4}\,\Omega$-m

From Eq. (i), we get

$$J=\frac{10}{10^{-4}}=10^5\,\text{A/m}^2$$

6 (a) For the most precise measurement of unknown resistance X, the resistances P and Q should be approximately equal and should be small, so that it could decrease error in experiment.

7 (b) According to the given circuit diagram in question,

$$i_1=i_2+i_3 \quad \ldots(i)$$

In parallel arrangement of the electrical circuit, the voltage remains same.

$\therefore$ $V=ir$ (Using Ohm's law)

$\Rightarrow$ $i_2r_2=i_3r_3\Rightarrow i_2=\frac{i_3r_3}{r_2}$

Substituting the values in the Eq. (i), we get

$$i_1=\frac{i_3r_3}{r_2}+i_3\Rightarrow\frac{i_1}{i_3}=\frac{r_3}{r_2}+1$$

$\Rightarrow$ $\frac{i_3}{i_1}=\frac{r_2}{r_3+r_2}$

8 (a) Given, drift velocity,

$v_d=7.5\times10^{-4}$ m/s

Electric field, $E=3\times10^{-10}$ V/m

As, mobility, $\mu=\frac{v_d}{E}=\frac{7.5\times10^{-4}}{3\times10^{-10}}$

$=2.5\times10^6\,\text{m}^2\text{V}^{-1}\text{s}^{-1}$

9 (c) When n equal resistors of resistance R are connected in series, then the current drawn is given as

$$I=\frac{E}{nR+r}$$

where, nR = equivalent resistance of n resistors in series and r = internal resistance of battery.

Given, $r=R$

$\Rightarrow$ $I=\frac{E}{nR+R}=\frac{E}{R(n+1)} \quad \ldots(i)$

Similarly, when n equal resistors are connected in parallel, then the current drawn is given as

$$I'=\frac{E}{\frac{R}{n}+R}$$

where, $\frac{R}{n}$ = equivalent resistance of n resistors in parallel.

Given, $I' = 10\,I$

$$\Rightarrow \quad 10I = \frac{E}{\frac{R}{n} + R} = \frac{nE}{(n+1)R} \quad \text{...(ii)}$$

Substituting the value of I from Eq. (i) in Eq. (ii), we get

$$10\left(\frac{E}{R(n+1)}\right) = \frac{nE}{R(n+1)}$$

$$\Rightarrow \quad n = 10$$

10 (c) As volume remains same,

$$A_1 l_1 = A_2 l_2$$

Now, given $l_2 = n l_1$

$$\therefore \text{New area, } A_2 = \frac{A_1 l_1}{l_2} = \frac{A_1}{n} \quad \text{...(i)}$$

Resistance of wire after stretching,

$$R_2 = \rho\frac{l_2}{A_2} = \rho \cdot \frac{n l_1}{A_1 / n}$$

[Using Eq. (i)]

$$= \left(\rho\frac{l_1}{A_1}\right) \cdot n^2 = n^2 \cdot R$$

$$\left[\because R = \left(\rho\frac{l_1}{A_1}\right)\right]$$

11 (c) $P_{rated} = \frac{V_{rated}^2}{R}$

$\therefore$ Current in the bulb, $i = \frac{P}{V}$ $(\because P = Vi)$

$$\Rightarrow \quad i = \frac{500}{100} = 5\text{ A}$$

$\therefore$ Resistance of bulb,

$$R_b = \frac{100 \times 100}{500} = 20\,\Omega$$

$\because$ Resistance R is connected in series.

$$\therefore \text{Current, } i = \frac{E}{R_{net}} = \frac{230}{R + R_b}$$

$$\Rightarrow R + 20 = \frac{230}{5} = 46$$

$$\therefore \quad R = 26\,\Omega$$

12 (d) Given, charge, $Q = at - bt^2$ ...(i)

We know that, current, $I = \frac{dQ}{dt}$

So, Eq. (i) can be written as

$$I = \frac{d}{dt}(at - bt^2)$$

$$\Rightarrow \quad I = a - 2bt \quad \text{...(ii)}$$

For maximum value of t, till the current exist is given by

$$a - 2bt = 0$$

$$\therefore \quad t = \frac{a}{2b} \quad \text{...(iii)}$$

$\because$ The total heat produced (H) can be given as

$$H = \int_0^t I^2 R\,dt$$

$$= \int_0^{a/2b} (a - 2bt)^2 R\,dt \quad \left\{\because t = \frac{a}{2b}\right\}$$

$$= \int_0^{a/2b} (a^2 + 4b^2t^2 - 4abt) R\,dt$$

$$H = \left[a^2t + 4b^2\frac{t^3}{3} - \frac{4abt^2}{2}\right]_0^{a/2b} R$$

Solving above equation, we get

$$H = \frac{a^3R}{6b}$$

13 (a) Net resistance of a metal wire having resistivity ρ, we have

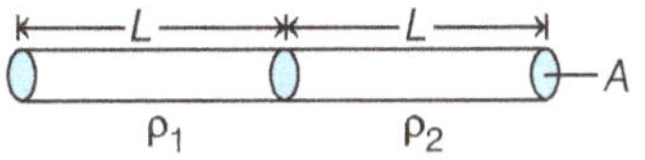

$$R_1 = \rho_1\frac{L}{A}$$

Similarly, $R_2 = \rho_2\frac{L}{A}$

Then, net effective resistance of two metal wires,

$$R_{eq} = R_1 + R_2$$

$$\Rightarrow \quad \rho\frac{2L}{A} = \rho_1\frac{L}{A} + \rho_2\frac{L}{A}$$

$$\Rightarrow \quad 2\rho = \rho_1 + \rho_2$$

As conductivity, $\sigma = \frac{1}{\rho}$, we have

$$\frac{2}{\sigma} = \frac{1}{\sigma_1} + \frac{1}{\sigma_2} \Rightarrow \frac{2}{\sigma} = \frac{\sigma_1 + \sigma_2}{\sigma_1\sigma_2}$$

$\Rightarrow$ Net effective conductivity of combined wires, $\sigma = \frac{2\sigma_1\sigma_2}{\sigma_1 + \sigma_2}$

14 (b) For first case, balanced condition of meter bridge will be

$$\frac{5}{l_1} = \frac{R}{(100 - l_1)} \quad \text{...(i)}$$

Now, by shunting resistance R by an equal resistance R, new resistance in that arm becomes $\frac{R}{2}$.

So, new balanced condition will be

$$\frac{5}{1.6\,l_1} = \frac{R/2}{(100 - 1.6\,l_1)} \quad \text{...(ii)}$$

From Eqs. (i) and (ii),

$$\frac{1.6}{1} = \frac{(100 - 1.6\,l_1)}{100 - l_1} \times 2$$

$$\Rightarrow 160 - 1.6l_1 = 200 - 3.2\,l_1$$

$$1.6\,l_1 = 40$$

$$\Rightarrow \quad l_1 = \frac{40}{1.6} = 25\text{ m}$$

From Eq. (i), $\frac{5}{25} = \frac{R}{75}$

$$\Rightarrow \quad R = 15\,\Omega$$

15 (b) As $R \propto l$

$\therefore$ Resistance of each part will be $\frac{R}{5}$.

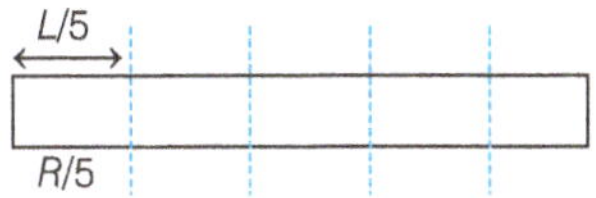

Parallel arrangement is,

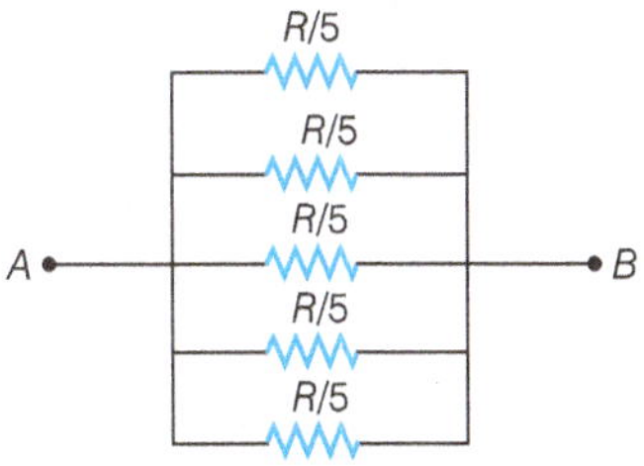

$$R_{eq} = \frac{R/5}{5} = \frac{R}{25}$$

16 (c)

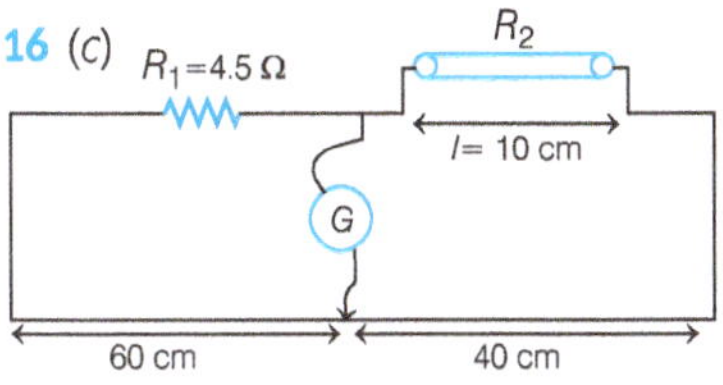

$$r = \sqrt{7} \times 10^{-4}\text{ m}$$

$$l = 10\text{ cm} = 10 \times 10^{-2}\text{m} = \frac{1}{10}\text{m}$$

Under balance condition $\frac{R_1}{l_1} = \frac{R}{l_2}$

Here, $R_1 = 4.5\,\Omega$, $l_1 = 60$ cm

$$l_2 = 100 - l_1 = 40\text{ cm}$$

$$R_2 = R$$

$$\frac{l_1}{l_2} = \frac{R_1}{R_2} \Rightarrow \frac{60}{40} = \frac{4.5\,\Omega}{R}$$

$$R = 3\,\Omega$$

$$R = \rho\frac{l}{A} \Rightarrow 3 = \rho \times \frac{1}{\pi r^2}$$

$$3 = \rho \times \frac{1}{10 \times \pi \times 7 \times 10^{-8}}$$

$$\Rightarrow \quad \rho = 21\pi \times 10^{-7}$$

$$\rho = 21 \times \frac{22}{7} \times 10^{-7} = 66 \times 10^{-7}$$

$$\rho = 66 \times 10^{-7}$$

$$\Rightarrow \quad R = 66$$

17 (*b*) Given circuit is

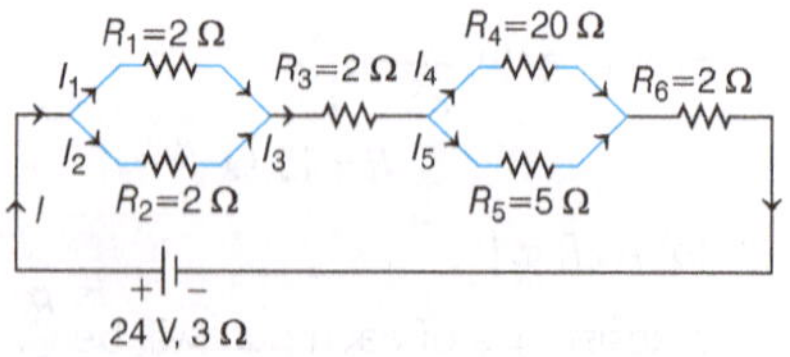

Total resistance of circuit

$$= (2||2) + 2 + (20||5) + 2 + 3$$

$$= \left(\frac{2 \times 2}{2+2}\right) + 2 + \left(\frac{20 \times 5}{20+5}\right) + 2 + 3$$

$$= 3 + 4 + 5 = 12\,\Omega$$

$$I = \frac{24}{12} = 2\text{A}$$

So, current through resistor R_4,

$$I_4 = \left(\frac{5}{25}\right) \times 2 = \frac{2}{5}\text{ A}$$

and current through resistor R_5,

$$I_5 = \frac{20}{25} \times 2 = \frac{8}{5}\text{ A}$$

18 (*c*) When a uniform wire of resistance R is shaped into a regular n-sided polygon, the resistance of each side will be

$$R_1 = \frac{R}{n}$$

Let R_1 and R_2 be the resistances between adjacent corners of a regular polygon.

$\therefore$ The resistance of $(n-1)$ side,

$$R_2 = \left(\frac{n-1}{n}\right)R$$

Since, two parts are in parallel.

Therefore, $R_{eq} = \dfrac{R_1 R_2}{R_1 + R_2}$

$$= \frac{\left(\frac{R}{n}\right)\left(\frac{n-1}{n}\right)R}{\frac{R}{n} + \left(\frac{n-1}{n}\right)R}$$

$$\Rightarrow \quad R_{eq} = \frac{(n-1)}{n^2}R$$

19 (*b*) According to the question,

$$l_w = 2l_x \quad \text{... (i)}$$

$$R_w = 2R_y$$

$$\Rightarrow \quad \rho\frac{l_w}{A_w} = 2\rho\frac{l_y}{A_y} \quad \text{... (ii)}$$

$$\Rightarrow \quad \frac{l_w}{A_w} = \frac{2l_y}{A_y}, \frac{2l_x}{A_w} = \frac{2l_y}{A_y}$$

$$\Rightarrow \quad A_x l_x = A_w l_w \quad \text{...(iii)}$$

From Eqs. (i) and (iii), we get

$$A_x l_x = A_w(2l_x);\ A_x = 2A_w$$

From Eq. (ii), $\dfrac{2l_x}{A_x/2} = \dfrac{2l_y}{A_y}$

$$\Rightarrow \quad \frac{2l_x}{l_y} = \frac{A_x}{A_y} \quad \text{...(iv)}$$

Since, $A_x = A_y$

$$\Rightarrow \quad 2l_x = l_y,\ \frac{l_x}{l_y} = \frac{1}{2}$$

20 (*c*) The given network is shown as

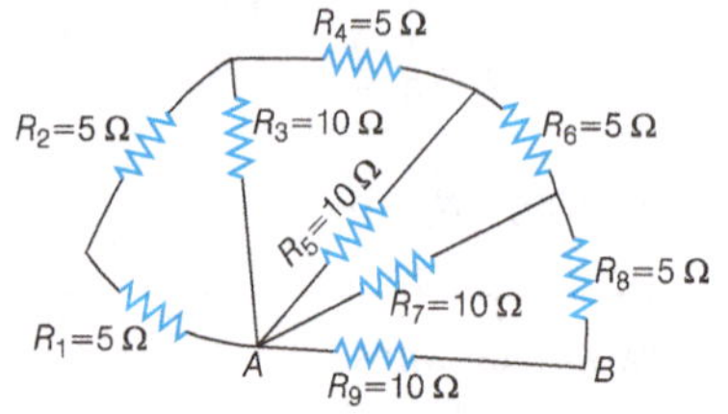

R_1 and R_2 are in series.

$$\therefore \quad R_{12} = R_1 + R_2$$

$$= 5 + 5 = 10\,\Omega$$

Now, R_{12} and R_3 are in parallel,

$$R_{123} = \frac{R_{12} \times R_3}{R_{12} + R_3}$$

$$= \frac{10 \times 10}{10 + 10} = 5\,\Omega$$

Now, R_{123} and R_4 are in series,

$$R_{1234} = 5 + 5 = 10\,\Omega$$

Again, $R_{1234} || R_5$

$$\therefore \quad R_{12345} = \frac{R_{1234} \times R_5}{R_{1234} + R_5}$$

$$= \frac{10 \times 10}{10 + 10} = 5\,\Omega$$

Similarly, on solving we get

$R_{AB} = 5\Omega$

21 (*a*) If we consider only conductor PQ as follows

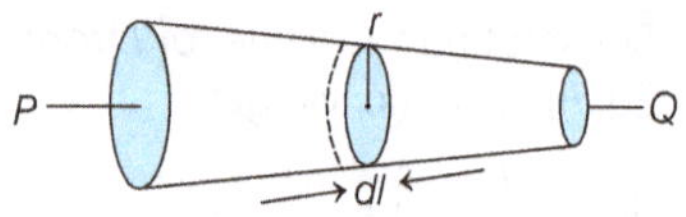

Let dl be the small element of conductor PQ.

$\because$ Current passing through PQ is constant.

So, resistance of this small element dl will be given as

$$dR = \frac{\rho dl}{A} \quad \text{...(i)}$$

$$\because \quad \text{Current, } I = \frac{dV}{dR}$$

$$\Rightarrow \quad dV = IdR \quad \text{...(ii)}$$

From Eqs. (i) and (ii), we get

$$dV = \frac{I\rho dl}{A}$$

$$\Rightarrow \quad dV = \frac{I\rho dl}{\pi r^2} \quad \text{...(iii)}$$

$$(\because A = \pi r^2)$$

We know that,

$$\text{Electric field, } E = \frac{dV}{dl} \quad \text{...(iv)}$$

From Eqs. (iii) and (iv), we get

$$\Rightarrow \quad E = \frac{I\rho dl}{\pi r^2 dl}$$

$$\Rightarrow \quad E \propto \frac{1}{r^2} \quad \text{...(v)}$$

Also, we know that, drift velocity,

$$v_d = \frac{eE\tau}{m} \Rightarrow v_d \propto E \quad \text{...(vi)}$$

$\therefore$ From Eqs. (v) and (vi), we can say, if r decreases, E will increase and due to this, v_d will increase.

22 (*c*) Given, $i = \alpha_0 t + \beta t^2$

where, $\alpha_0 = 20\text{ A/s}$, $\beta = 8\text{ A/s}^2$

We know that, $i = \dfrac{dq}{dt}$

$$\Rightarrow \frac{dq}{dt} = i = \alpha_0 t + \beta t^2 = 20t + 8t^2$$

$$\Rightarrow \quad dq = (20t + 8t^2)dt$$

On integrating both sides, we get

$$\int_0^q dq = \int_0^{15} (20\,t + 8\,t^2)dt$$

$$q = \left[\frac{20t^2}{2} + \frac{8t^3}{3}\right]_0^{15}$$

$$= 10 \times (15)^2 + \frac{8}{3} \times (15)^3$$

$$\therefore \quad q = 11250 \text{ C}$$

23 (c) The given circuit diagram can be drawn as

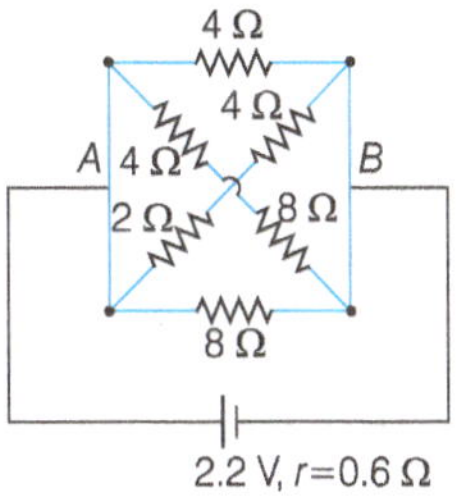

Redrawing the above circuit diagram as

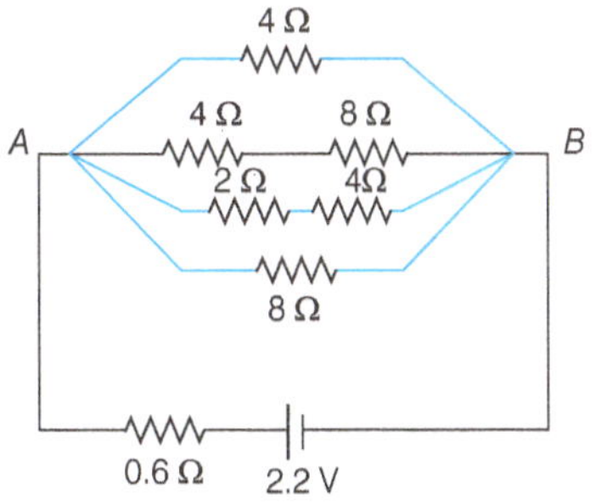

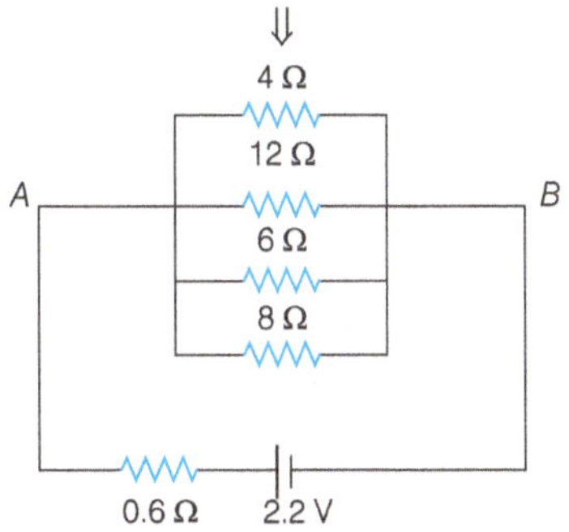

Equivalent resistance of the circuit between points A and B is given as

$$\frac{1}{R_{eq}} = \frac{1}{R_1} + \frac{1}{R_2} + \frac{1}{R_3} + \frac{1}{R_4}$$

$$= \frac{1}{4} + \frac{1}{12} + \frac{1}{6} + \frac{1}{8}$$

$$\Rightarrow \quad R_{eq} = 1.6\,\Omega$$

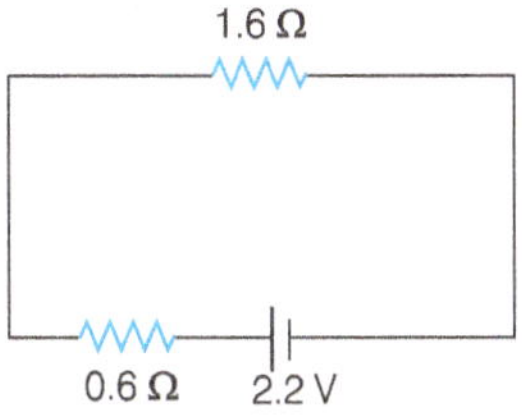

$$R_{total} = 1.6 + 0.6 = 2.2\,\Omega$$

$$P = \frac{V^2}{R_{total}} = \frac{2.2 \times 2.2}{2.2} = 2.2 \text{ W}$$

24 (a) When all cells are connected in parallel as shown below.

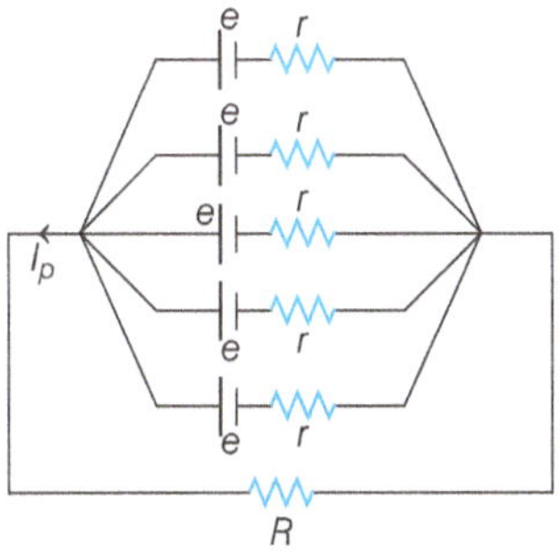

Potential will remain same as,
$V_P = 5$ V

Net resistance in parallel combination will be given as

$$R_p = R + \left[\frac{1}{\frac{1}{r} + \frac{1}{r} + \frac{1}{r} + \frac{1}{r} + \frac{1}{r}}\right]$$

$$= R + \frac{r}{5}$$

$$\Rightarrow \quad R_p = R + \frac{1}{5} \qquad (\because r = 1\,\Omega) \quad \text{...(i)}$$

When all cells are connected in series as shown below

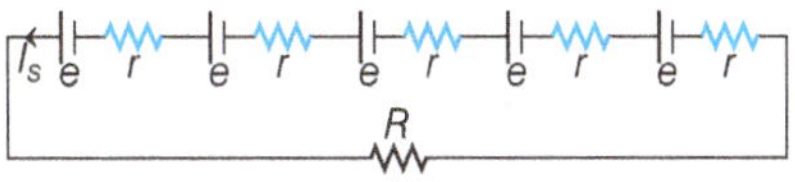

The net potential will increase as cells are connected in series,
$V_s = 5 + 5 + 5 + 5 + 5 = 25$ V

Net resistance,

$$R_s = r + r + r + r + r + R = 5r + R$$

$$R_s = 5 + R \qquad (\because r = 1\,\Omega) \text{...(ii)}$$

Since, $\quad I = V / R$

As current in both series and parallel combination is same,

$$\frac{V_p}{R_p} = \frac{V_s}{R_s} \Rightarrow \frac{5}{R + \frac{1}{5}} = \frac{25}{5 + R}$$

[From Eqs. (i) and (ii)]

$$\Rightarrow \quad 25 + 5R = 25R + 5$$

$$\Rightarrow \quad R = 1\,\Omega$$

Skill Boosters

1 (b) Heat produced, $H = \dfrac{V^2 t}{R}$

$$= (120)^2 \times \frac{10 \times 60}{6}$$

$$= 14.4 \times 10^5 \text{ J}$$

2 (b) $P = VI \quad \Rightarrow \quad I = \dfrac{P}{V}$

Power dissipated $= I^2 R = \dfrac{P^2}{V^2} \cdot R$

$\therefore$ Power dissipated at 12000 V

$$= \frac{(7.5 \times 10^5)^2}{(1.2 \times 10^4)^2} \times 3 = 11719 \text{ W}$$

Power dissipated at 50000 V

$$= \left(\frac{7.5 \times 10^5}{5 \times 10^4}\right)^2 \times 3 = 675 \text{ W}$$

So, difference is $11719 - 675$

$$= 1.1 \times 10^4 \text{ W}$$

3 (a) Let E be the emf of each cell and let n be the number of cells connected wrongly. Then, the net emf of the battery is equal to the emf of correctly connected cells – emf of wrongly connected cells.

$$= (12 - n)E - nE = (12 - 2n)E$$

When the two cells aid the battery, the net emf is

$$E_1 = (12 - 2n)E + 2E = (14 - 2n)E$$

If R is the resistance in the circuit, the current is

$$I_1 = \frac{E_1}{R} = \frac{(14 - 2n)E}{R} \qquad \text{...(i)}$$

When the two cells oppose the battery, the net emf is

$$E_2 = (12 - 2n)E - 2E$$

$$= (10 - 2n)E \qquad \text{...(ii)}$$

Now, the current in the circuit is

$$I_2 = \frac{(10 - 2n)E}{R}$$

Dividing Eq. (i) by Eq. (ii), we get

$$\frac{I_1}{I_2}=\frac{(14-2n)}{(10-2n)}=\frac{(7-n)}{(5-n)}$$

Given, $I_1=3A$ and $I_2=2A$

Thus, $\frac{3}{2}=\frac{(7-n)}{(5-n)}$

which gives, $n=1$.

Hence, one cell in the battery is wrongly connected.

4 (*d*) In series, current is same and power of bulb $=I^2R=P$

and potential drop across any bulb is $\quad V=IR$

$$\Rightarrow \quad V=I\cdot\frac{P}{I^2}=PI$$

Clearly, when bulbs are in series, $V\propto P$. So, bulb of lowest power has lowest potential drop and bulb of highest power has highest potential drop.

5 (c) Amount of heat absorbed by water

= Amount of heat generated by coil

$$=I^2Rt=\frac{V^2}{R}t$$

For Ist coil, $H=I^2R_1\,(6\times 60)$

$$=\frac{V^2}{R_1}(6\times 60)$$

For IInd coil, $H=I^2R_2\,(8\times 60)$

$$=\frac{V^2}{R_2}(8\times 60)$$

As, amount of heat required to heat water is same in both cases.

$$\therefore \frac{V^2}{R_1}(6\times 60)=\frac{V^2}{R_2}(8\times 60)$$

$$\Rightarrow \quad 6R_1=8R_2 \Rightarrow R_1=\frac{3}{4}R_2$$

When resistors are connected in parallel,

$$R_{eq}=\frac{R_1R_2}{R_1+R_2}=\frac{\frac{4}{3}R_1\times R_1}{R_1+\frac{4}{3}R_1}$$

$$=\frac{\frac{4}{3}}{\frac{7}{3}}R_1=\frac{4}{7}R_1$$

$\therefore$ Heat produced in time Δt,

$$\frac{V^2}{R_{eq}}\cdot\Delta t=\frac{V^2}{R_1}(6\times 60)$$

$$\Rightarrow \quad \frac{V^2}{\frac{4}{7}R_1}\Delta t=\frac{V^2}{R_1}\times 6\times 60$$

$$\Rightarrow \quad \Delta t=\frac{4}{7}\times 6\text{ min}$$

$$\approx 3.4\text{ min}$$

6 (*b*) As, maximum power of bulb,

i.e. wattage, $W=\frac{V_s^2}{R}$

where, V_s is specified voltage on the bulb.

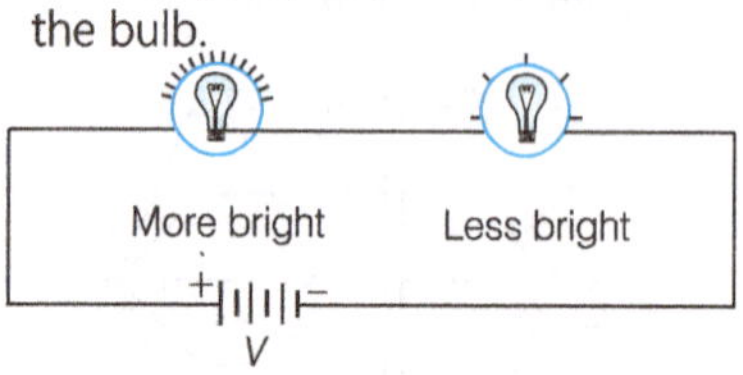

So, resistance of filament of bulb is

$$R=\frac{V_s^2}{W}$$

So, $\quad R\propto\frac{1}{W}$

When bulbs are connected in series, I is a constant.

Power consumed, $P=I^2R$

$$P\propto R\propto\frac{1}{W}$$

So, less wattage bulb will consume more power, so give more brightness.

As, first bulb gives more brightness, then wattage of first bulb is less than the wattage of second bulb. Hence, claim of student II is correct.

7 (*b*) During charging for a battery,

$$V=E+Ir$$

So, V = potential across terminals of cell.

For battery I,

$$V=12+50\times 0.04=14V$$

For battery II,

$$V=12+25\times 0.04=13V$$

For battery III,

$$V=12+60\times 0.04=14.4V$$

For battery IV,

$$V=12+40\times 0.04=13.6V$$

8 (*b*) Mean relaxation time, $\tau=\frac{m}{ne^2\rho}$

$$=\frac{9.11\times 10^{-31}}{(8.49\times 10^{28})\times(1.6\times 10^{-19})^2\times(1.7\times 10^{-8})}$$

$$=2.5\times 10^{-14}\text{ s}$$

Given, $v=1.6\times 10^6$ m/s

Mean free path (on an average) travelled by an electron

$$=l=v\tau=2.5\times 10^{-14}\times 1.6\times 10^6$$

$$=4\times 10^{-8}\text{ m}=40\text{ nm}$$

Average atomic spacing $=0.2$ nm

Number of atomic spacings covered by electron between collisions $=\frac{40}{0.2}=200$

$\therefore \quad X=200$

9 (*a*) Power consumption = 10 units

In 5 h = 10 units

$\Rightarrow$ Energy consumed in 1 h = 2 units = 2 kWh

Hence, power consumed

= 2000 J/s

Current in circuit,

$$I=\frac{P}{V}=\frac{2000}{220}\approx 9\text{ A}$$

Power loss in wires $=I^2R\text{ Js}^{-1}$

$$=\rho\frac{l}{A}\cdot I^2$$

$$=1.7\times 10^{-8}\times\frac{10}{\pi\times 10^{-6}}\times 81$$

$$\approx 4.4\text{ Js}^{-1}$$

Hence, power loss in wires

$$=\frac{4.4}{2000}=\frac{1}{450}$$

10 (*a*) Both the Wheatstone bridges are given balanced.

$$\therefore \quad \frac{3}{R_1}=\frac{9}{6} \text{ and } \frac{4}{8}=\frac{R_2}{16}$$

$$\Rightarrow R_1=\frac{6\times 3}{9}=2$$

$$R_2=\frac{4\times 16}{8}=8$$

Hence, $\frac{R_1}{R_2}=\frac{2}{8}=\frac{1}{4}$

So, $k=4$

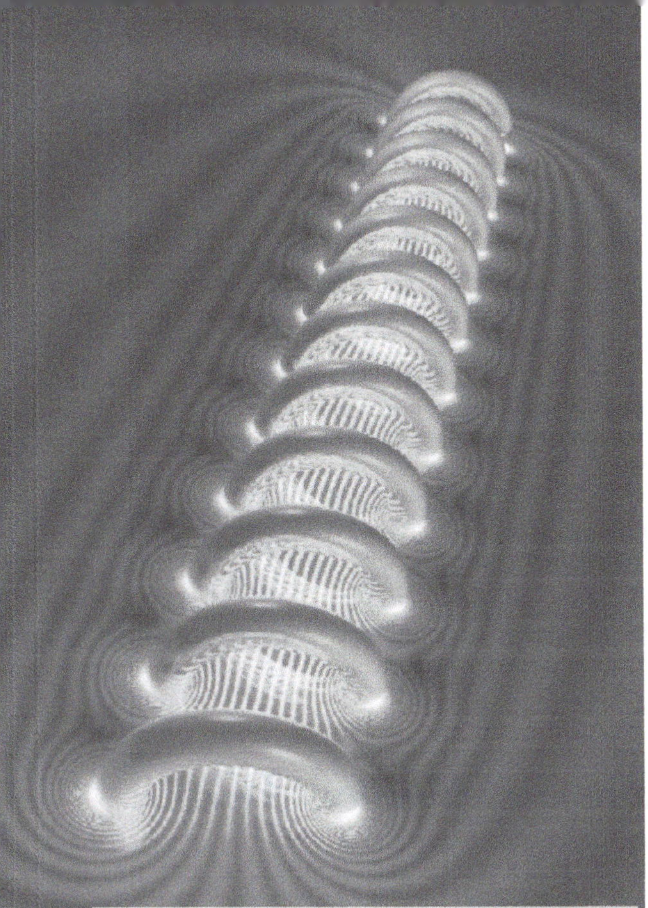

04

Scan for **Physics Through Concept Master** *Videos*

Moving Charges and Magnetism

Topicwise No. of Ques asked in 5 Years

Topics	No. of Questions				
	2024	2023	2022	2021	2020
Magnetic Force	–	1	–	1	–
Motion in Magnetic Field	–	–	–	–	–
Magnetic Field due to a Current Element : Biot-Savart Law	1	–	2	–	–
Ampere's Circuital Law	–	1	2	2	–
The Solenoid	–	–	–	–	1
The Moving Coil Galvanometer	–	–	–	–	–

Special Type of Ques asked in 5 Years

Types	Years				
	2024	2023	2022	2021	2020
A-R	–	–	–	–	–
Statement Based	–	1	–	–	–
Matching	–	–	–	–	–

Last 5 Years Weigtage (NEET)

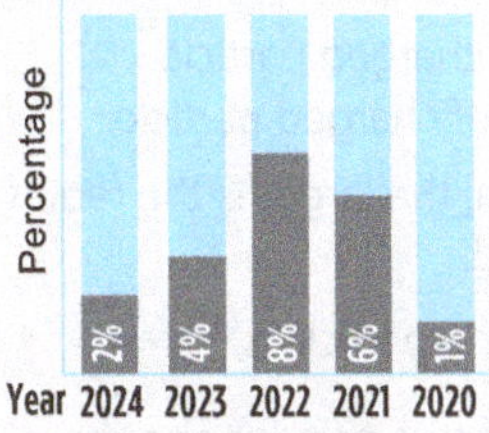

Introduction

- Danish Physicist Hans Oersted concluded that moving charges or an electric current flowing in a conductor produces a magnetic field in the surrounding space.
- Oersted noticed that a current in a straight wire causes a deflection in a nearby magnetic compass needle.
- The orientation of the needles is shown in the figure
  (a) when the current emerges out of the plane of the paper and
  (b) the current moves into the plane of the paper,
  (c) the arrangement of iron filings around the wire.
- The darkened ends of the needles represent **north poles** and brighter ends represent **south poles**. The effect of earth's magnetic field is neglected.

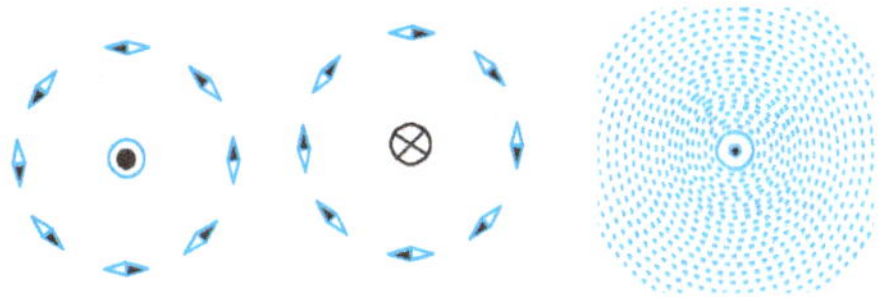

(a) (b) (c)

- A current or a field (electric or magnetic) emerging out of the plane of the paper is depicted by a dot ⊙ and a current or a field going into the paper is depicted by a cross ⊗.

Magnetic Force

- **Source and Fields** Charges at rest produce electric field, while moving charges produce current and magnetic field. Magnetic field is a vector quantity and is denoted by **B**. It has several basic properties which are similar to electric field.
- **SI unit of magnetic field B is newton per ampere per metre. This unit is called tesla (T).**
- A smaller unit (non-SI) called **gauss** (1 G $= 10^{-4}$ T) is also often used.
- **Principle of Superposition** The resultant magnetic field of several sources is the vector addition of magnetic field of each individual source.

Lorentz Force

- It is the force on an electric charge q (moving with a velocity **v** and located at distance **r** at a given time t) due to both, electric and magnetic fields and can be written as

$$\mathbf{F} = q[\mathbf{E}(\mathbf{r}) + \mathbf{v} \times \mathbf{B}(\mathbf{r})]$$
$$= \mathbf{F}_{\text{electric}} + \mathbf{F}_{\text{magnetic}}$$

- The magnetic force on a moving charge q in a uniform magnetic field **B** is $\mathbf{F} = q[\mathbf{v} \times \mathbf{B}] = qvB \sin\theta\hat{\mathbf{n}}$, **NEET 2021**

  where, θ is the angle between **v** and **B**.
- **Magnetic force has following features :**
  (i) It depends on q, **v** and **B**. Force on a negative charge is opposite to that on a positive charge.
  (ii) If particle's velocity is perpendicular to magnetic field, then magnetic force will be maximum.
  (iii) If particle's velocity is parallel to the magnetic field, then magnetic force will be zero.
  (iv) If particle velocity is zero, then $|\mathbf{F}_m| = 0$, it means only a moving charge experience magnetic force.
- The direction of the magnetic force acting on a charged particle is shown below.
  (a) force on positively charged particle with velocity **v** and making angle θ with **B** is given by right hand rule.
  (b) shows a moving charged particle q is deflected in an opposite sense to $-q$ in the presence of magnetic field.

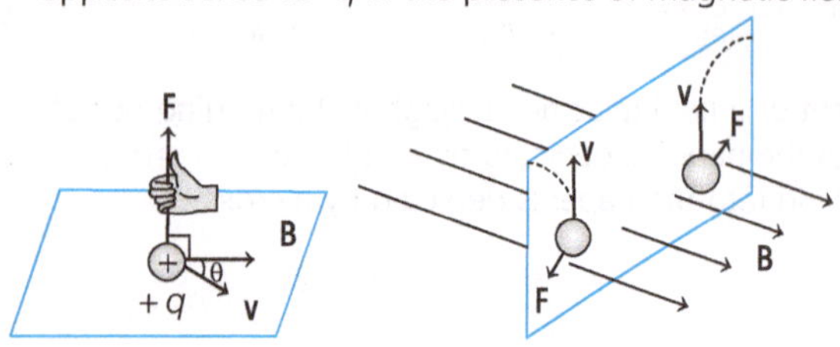

(a) (b)

Magnetic Force on a Current Carrying Conductor

- When a current carrying conductor having current I is placed in uniform magnetic field **B**, then force experienced by the conductor

$$F = I(\mathbf{l} \times \mathbf{B}) \Rightarrow F = IBl \sin\theta$$

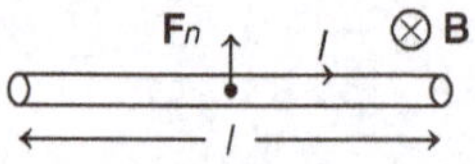

Case I When conductor is placed in the magnetic field and $\theta = 0°$, then

$$F = 0$$

Case II When conductor is placed perpendicular to the direction of magnetic field, then $\theta = 90°$

$$\therefore \quad F_{\text{max}} = IBl$$

- If the wire has an arbitrary shape, we can calculate the Lorentz force on it by considering it as a collection of linear strips

$$\mathbf{F} = \sum_j I d\mathbf{l}_j \times \mathbf{B}$$ **NEET 2023**

Motion in a Magnetic Field

- A moving charge particle q in the presence of external magnetic field **B** experiences a perpendicular force $q[\mathbf{v} \times \mathbf{B}]$, which acts as a centripetal force and produces a circular motion perpendicular to the magnetic field as shown in the figure.

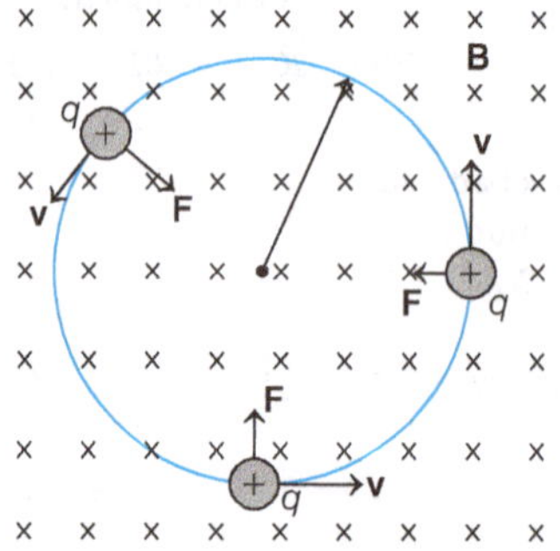

- The force acting on the moving charge is given by

$$F = qvB$$

- The particle will describe a circle, if **v** and **B** are perpendicular to each other. This motion has following features:
  (i) The radius of the circle described by the charged particle is

$$r = \frac{mv}{qB} = \frac{p}{qB} = \frac{\sqrt{2mK}}{qB}$$ **NEET 2019**

  where, p = momentum of charged particle
  and K = kinetic energy of charged particle.

  The larger the momentum, the larger is the radius and bigger the circle described.

  (ii) **Angular frequency** ω of the particle is, $\omega = \frac{qB}{m}$

  which is independent of the velocity or energy.

(iii) **The time taken by the particle to complete one revolution** is $T = \frac{2\pi m}{qB}$.

Note *Time period of circular path does not depend on the velocity of charge particle.*

- If velocity of the charged particle has a component along **B**, then it will make the particle to move along the field, thereby producing a helical motion as shown in the figure.

  However, this component of velocity remains unchanged as the motion along the magnetic field will not be affected by the magnetic field.

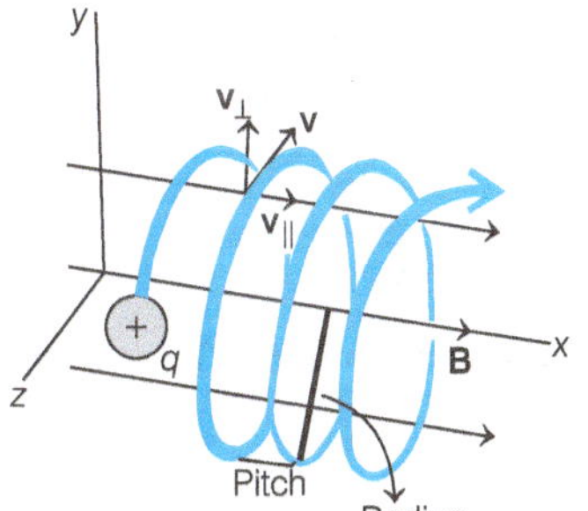

- The distance moved along the magnetic field in one rotation is called **pitch** *P*.

$$P = v_{\|}T = \frac{2\pi m v_{\|}}{qB} = \frac{2\pi m v \cos\theta}{qB}$$

where, $v_{\|}$ = component of the velocity parallel to the magnetic field and θ is the angle between velocity and magnetic field.

For Concept Master Video

- The radius of the circular component of motion is also called the **radius of the helix**, given by $R = \frac{mv_{\perp}}{qB}$.

Magnetic Field Due to a Current Element : Biot-Savart's Law

- According to this law, the magnitude of the magnetic field $d\mathbf{B}$ is proportional to the current I, the element length $|d\mathbf{l}|$ and inversely proportional to the square of the distance r.
- Its direction is perpendicular to the plane containing $d\mathbf{l}$ and $\mathbf{r}$.

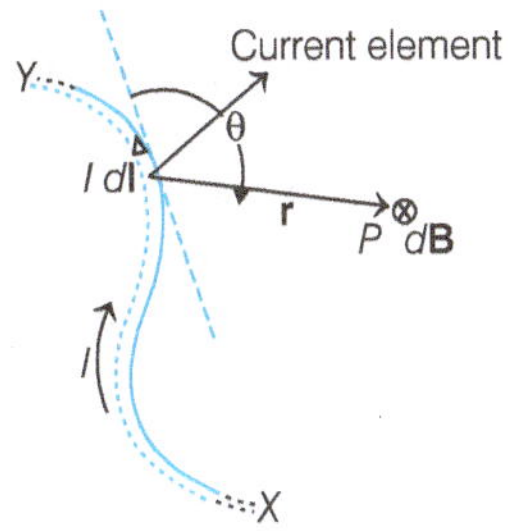

- As shown in the figure, for a finite conductor *XY* carrying current *I*, the magnetic field $d\mathbf{B}$ due to the element $d\mathbf{l}$ of the conductor at point *P* is given by

$$d\mathbf{B} = \frac{\mu_0}{4\pi} \frac{I d\mathbf{l} \times \mathbf{r}}{r^3}$$ NEET 2022

Thus, $$|d\mathbf{B}| = \frac{\mu_0}{4\pi} \frac{I dl \sin\theta}{r^2} \quad \text{...(i)}$$

where, $\frac{\mu_0}{4\pi} = 10^{-7}$ Tm/A and μ_0 is the permeability of free space or vacuum.

Marks Maximiser

Variation of magnetic field with different parameter of Eq. (i).

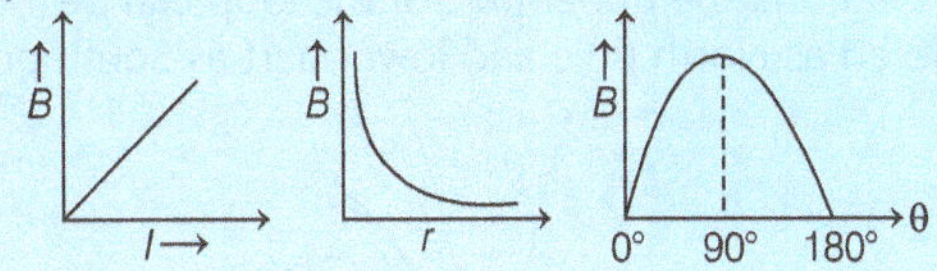

Comparison of Biot-Savart Law with Coulomb's Law

(i) Both are long range, depends inversely on the square of distance from the source to the point of intersect.

(ii) The electrostatic field is produced by a scalar source, namely, the electric charge. The magnetic field is produced by a vector source $I\,d\mathbf{l}$ i.e., current element. NEET 2022

(iii) The electrostatic field is along the displacement vector joining the source and the field point. The magnetic field is perpendicular to the plane containing the displacement vector **r** and the current element $I\,d\mathbf{l}$.

(iv) There is an angle dependence in the Biot-Savart law which is not present in the electrostatic case. The magnetic field at any point in the direction of $d\mathbf{l}$ is zero.

(v) Relation between permittivity of free space ε_0, the permeability of free space μ_0 and speed of light *c* in vacuum is given by $\varepsilon_0\mu_0 = \frac{1}{c^2}$.

Magnetic Field on the Axis of a Circular Current Loop

- Magnetic field at any point *P* along the **axis of circular current carrying loop** as shown in the figure below is

$$\mathbf{B} = \frac{\mu_0 I R^2}{2(x^2 + R^2)^{3/2}} \hat{\mathbf{i}}$$

When $x >> R$, then $B \propto \frac{1}{x^3}$

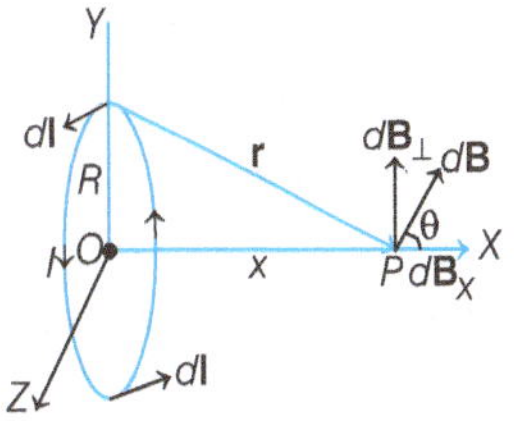

- Magnetic field at the centre ($x = 0$) of a circular current carrying conductor/coil

$$\mathbf{B} = \frac{\mu_0 I}{2R}\hat{\mathbf{i}}$$

where, R is the radius of a circular loop.

- The magnetic field lines due to a circular wire, form closed loops and the direction of the magnetic field is given by right hand thumb rule.
In this diagram, the upper part of the loop can be considered as North pole and lower part as South pole.

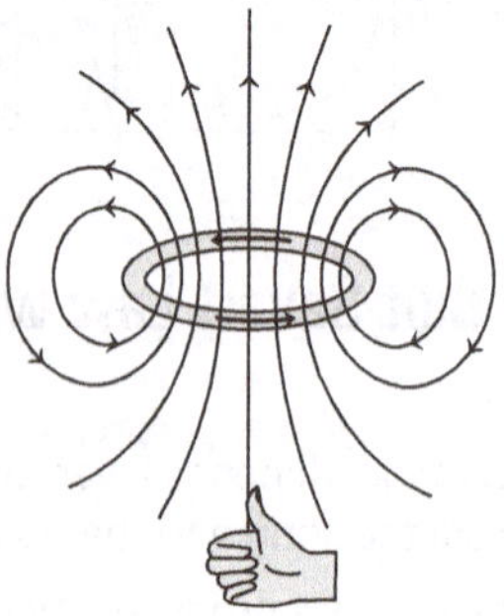

- Magnetic field due to semi-circular arc at centre is given by

$$B = \frac{\mu_0 I}{4R}$$ NEET 2023

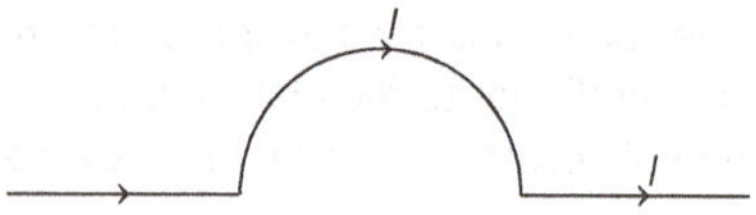

Ampere's Circuital Law

- The line integral of the magnetic field **B** around any closed loop is equal to μ_0 times the total current enclosed by the loop.
i.e., $\oint \mathbf{B} \cdot d\mathbf{l} = \mu_0 I$

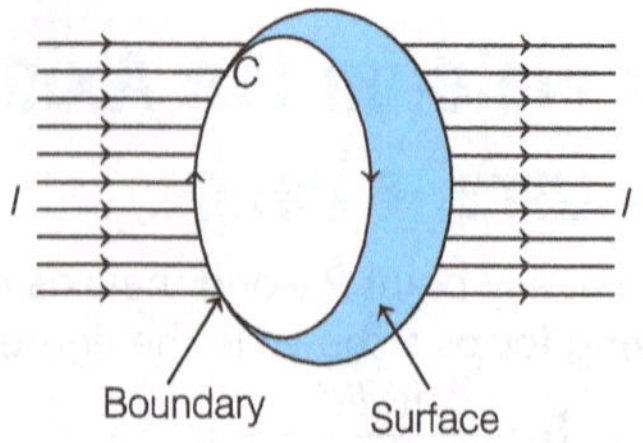

- An amperian loop is possible such that at each point of the loop, either
  (i) **B** is tangential to the loop and is a non-zero constant or
  (ii) **B** is normal to the loop, or
  (iii) **B** vanishes.
- The magnetic field at a distance r outside the wire is tangential and given by

$$B = \frac{\mu_0 I}{2\pi r}$$ NEET 2022

- From the result, some important points can be derived,
  (i) The magnetic field at every point on a circle of radius r is same in magnitude. The magnetic field around a wire possesses **cylindrical symmetry**.
  (ii) The field direction at any point on this circle is tangential to it. The lines of constant magnitude of magnetic field forms concentric circles. The circular lines are called **magnetic field lines**.
  (iii) Even though the wire is of infinite length, the field due to it at a non-zero distance is not infinite.
- The Ampere's circuital law holds for steady currents, which does not fluctuate with time.

Marks Maximiser

Magnetic Field due to Infinitely Long Solid Cylinder or Wire

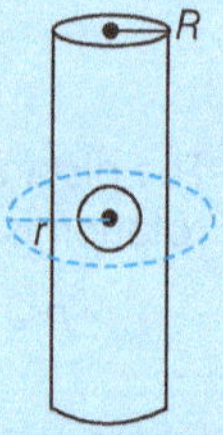

(i) Inside the conductor at a distance r from the centre,

$$B_{in} = \frac{\mu_0 I r}{2\pi R^2}$$

(ii) At the surface, $B_s = \frac{\mu_0 I}{2\pi R}$ (maximum)

(iii) Outside the conductor, $B_{out} = \frac{\mu_0 I}{2\pi r}$

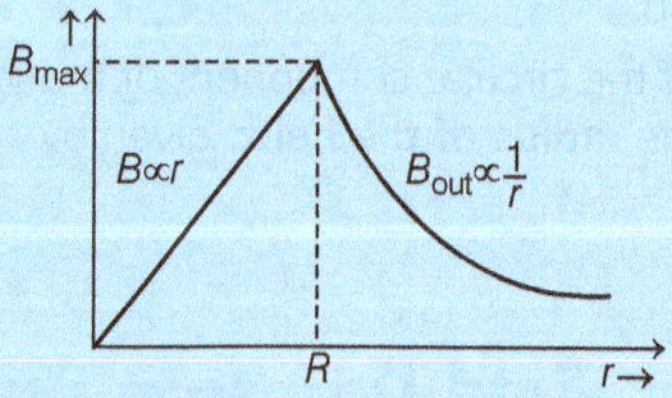

The Solenoid

- A solenoid is a coil which has large length compared to its radius.
- It consists of a long wire wound in the form of a helix, where the neighbouring turns are closely spaced. The net magnetic field is the vector sum of the fields due to all the turns.

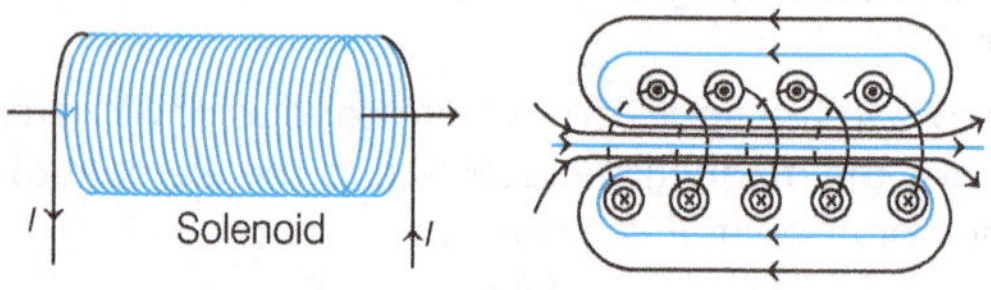

- Considering a rectangular amperian loop as shown below. The magnetic field due to a solenoid

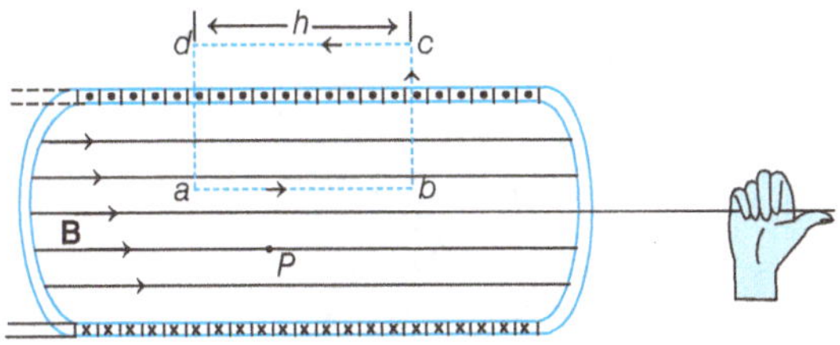

(i) At any point P inside the solenoid, NEET 2022, 20

$$B = \mu_0 nI$$

where, n = number of turns per unit length.

(ii) At the ends of the solenoid, $B = \frac{1}{2}\mu_0 nI$

(iii) The direction of the field is given by the right-hand thumb rule.

The field inside the solenoid is uniform and parallel to the axis and zero outside of it. The solenoid is commonly used to obtain a uniform magnetic field.

Marks Maximiser

Magnetic field on any axial point P inside the solenoid of finite length is given by

$$B = \frac{\mu_0 nI}{2}(\cos\theta_1 - \cos\theta_2)$$

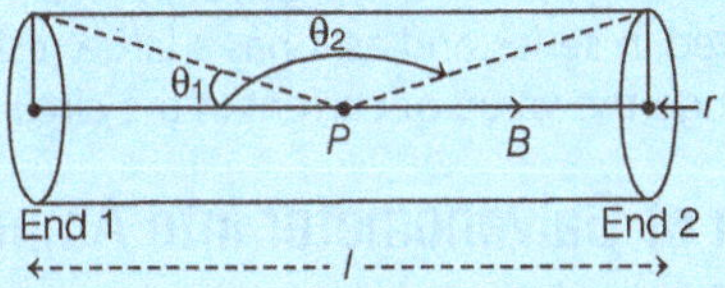

Force between Two Parallel Currents : The Ampere

- If two infinitely long parallel conductors carrying currents I_a and I_b, respectively and are separated by a distance d, then magnetic force experienced by length L of any one conductor due to the other current carrying conductor is $\mathbf{F}_{ba} = \frac{\mu_0}{2\pi}\cdot\frac{I_a I_b}{d}\cdot L$

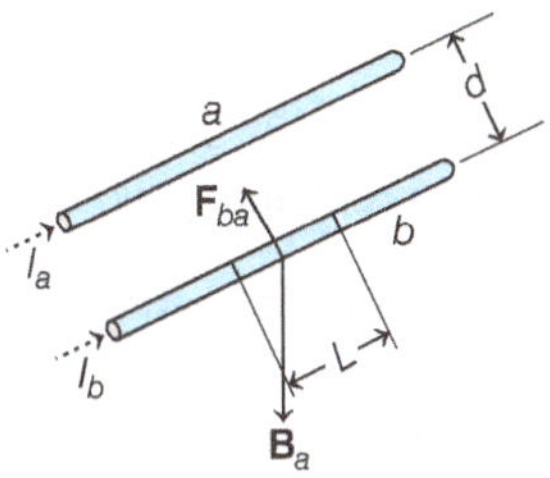

- The force $\mathbf{F}_{ba}$ per unit length, $f_{ba} = \frac{\mu_0 I_a I_b}{2\pi d}$
- The direction of force depends on the direction of current in them as
  (i) **attractive**, if current flow is in same direction.
  (ii) **repulsive**, if current flow is in opposite direction.

Ampere

- **One ampere** is the current which flows through each of the two parallel uniform long linear conductors, which are placed in free space at a distance of 1 m from each other and attract or repel each other with a force of 2×10^{-7} N/m.
- The SI unit of charge, the Coulomb can be defined in terms of ampere. If a steady current of 1 A is setup in conductor, the quantity of charge that flows through its cross-section in 1 s is **one coulomb** (1 C).

Application

Equilibrium of free wire

(i) When upper wire is free to move, $\frac{\mu_0 I_1 I_2}{2\pi h} = \lambda g = \left(\frac{M}{l}\right)g$

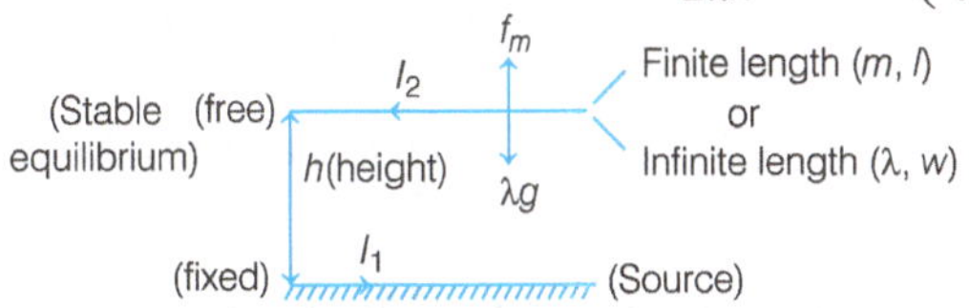

- The system will be in stable equilibrium condition
- If wire is slightly moved and released, then it will execute SHM is vertical plane, and its time period is given by $T = 2\pi\sqrt{\frac{h}{g}}$

(ii) When lower wire is free to move, $\frac{\mu_0 I_1 I_2}{2\pi h} = \lambda g = \left(\frac{m}{l}\right)g$

- The system will be in unstable equilibrium.

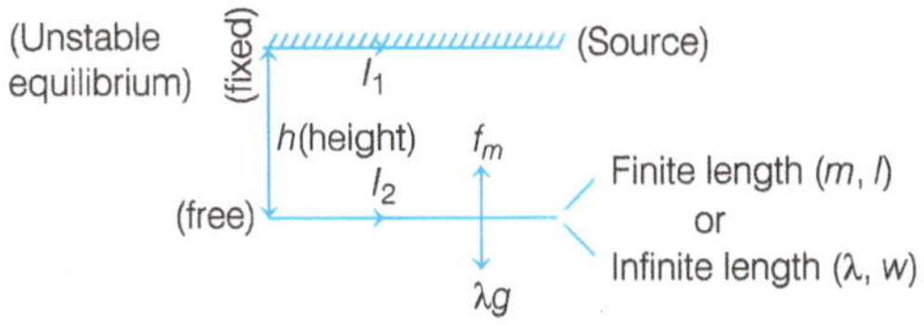

Torque on a Current Loop, Magnetic Dipole

- **The torque on a rectangular loop placed in a uniform magnetic field**

When area vector of the loop makes an arbitrary angle θ with the magnetic field as shown in the figure, then torque is given by

$$\tau = IAB\sin\theta$$

where, θ = angle between plane of coil & magnetic field lines and $A = ab$ is the area of the rectangular coil.

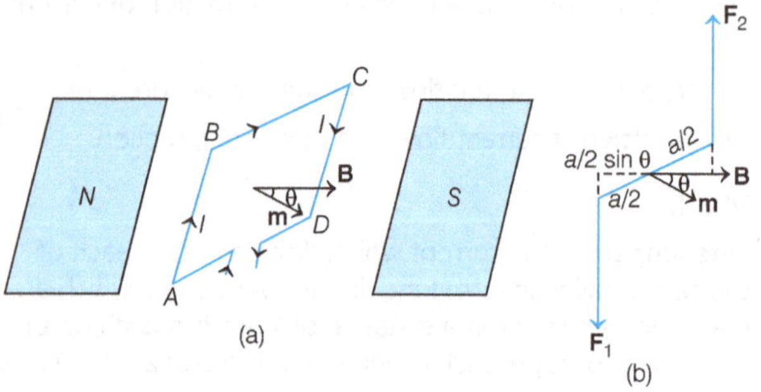

- The magnetic moment of the current loop is $\mathbf{m} = I\mathbf{A}$, where the direction of area vector $\mathbf{A}$ is given by the right-hand thumb rule. Its unit is Am^2.
- The torque can be expressed as vector product of the magnetic moment of the coil and magnetic field.

$$\tau = \mathbf{m} \times \mathbf{B}$$

- Torque τ vanishes when $\mathbf{m}$ is either parallel or anti-parallel to the magnetic field $\mathbf{B}$. This indicates a state of equilibrium as there is no torque on the coil.
- If the loop has N-closely wound turns, then $\mathbf{m} = NI\mathbf{A}$.

  So, $\tau = IAB \sin\theta$ **NEET 2021**

Circular Current Loop as a Magnetic Dipole

- The magnetic field due to a current carrying circular coil on the axial line is given by

$$\mathbf{B} = \frac{\mu_0}{4\pi} \cdot \frac{2\mathbf{m}}{x^3}$$

  and in the plane of the loop of at a distance x is $\mathbf{B} = \frac{\mu_0}{4\pi} \cdot \frac{\mathbf{m}}{x^3}$.

  [when $x >> R$, where R is radius of circular loop].
- A planar current loop is equivalent to a magnetic dipole of dipole moment $\mathbf{m} = I\mathbf{A}$.

The Moving Coil Galvanometer

- This device is used to measure current upto nanoampere.
- When a current flows through the coil of a galvanometer, a torque acts on it. This torque is given by

$$\tau = NIAB$$

- Due to this torque, a deflection ϕ is indicated on the scale by a pointer attached to the spring as

$$\phi = \left(\frac{NAB}{k}\right) I$$

  where, k = torsional constant of the spring or the restoring torque per unit twist.

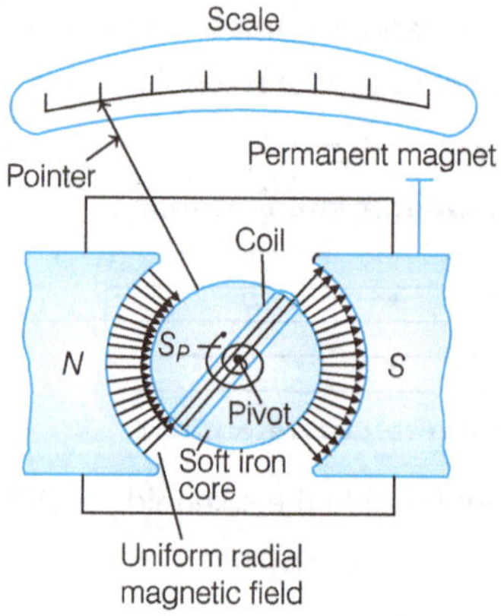

Uses of Galvanometer

(i) It is used to detect electric current in a circuit e.g. Wheatstone bridge.

(ii) It can be converted to an ammeter by putting a low resistance across it.

(iii) It can be converted to a voltmeter by putting a high resistance in series.

- The galvanometer cannot as such be used as an ammeter to measure the value of the currents in a given circuit. There are two reasons for it.

  (i) Galvanometer is a very sensitive device, it gives a full-scale deflection for a current of the order of μA.

  (ii) For measuring currents, the galvanometer has to be connected in series and as it has a large resistance, this will change the value of current in the circuit.

Conversion of Galvanometer into Ammeter

- To use a galvanometer as an ammeter, a small resistance r_s is attached (called **shunt resistance**) in parallel with galvanometer coil. The resistance of this arrangement is

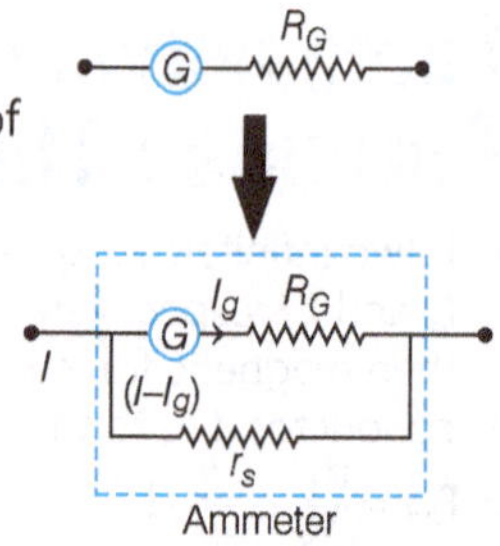

$$\frac{r_s}{R_G} = \frac{I_g}{I - I_g}$$

  where, r_s is very small resistance

  Thus, $r_s = \frac{I_g}{I - I_g} R_G$

- The **current sensitivity** of the galvanometer is the deflection per unit current and given by $\frac{\phi}{I} = \frac{NAB}{k}$

  The sensitivity increases by increasing the number of turns N.
- The **voltage sensitivity** is the deflection per unit volt of applied potential difference, i.e.,

Voltage sensitivity $= \dfrac{\phi}{V} = \dfrac{\phi}{IR}$

$$= \left(\frac{NAB}{K}\right)\frac{I}{V} = \left(\frac{NAB}{K}\right)\frac{1}{R}$$

- The galvanometer can be used as a voltmeter to measure the voltage across a given section of the circuit. For this, it must be connected in parallel with that section of the circuit.

Conversion of Galvanometer into Voltmeter

- A large resistance is connected in series.

$V = I_g (R_G + R) \therefore R = \dfrac{V}{I_g} - R_G$

Here, R is large resistance ($R >> R_G$)

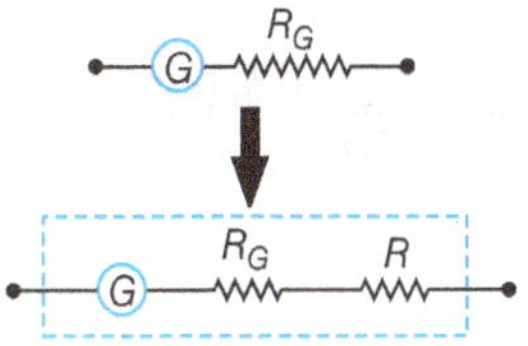

Voltmeter

- An interesting point to note is that increasing the current sensitivity may not necessarily increase the voltage sensitivity. If $N \to 2N$ i.e., we double the number of turns, then $\dfrac{\phi}{I} \to 2\dfrac{\phi}{I}$.

For Concept Master Video

- Thus, the current sensitivity doubles. However the resistance of the galvanometer is also likely double, since it is proportional to the length of the wire. If $N \to 2N$ and $R \to 2R$, thus the voltage sensitivity does not change.

Caution Points

- In the expression, $\mathbf{F} = q(\mathbf{v} \times \mathbf{B} + \mathbf{E})$, if we change the frame with instantaneous velocity **v**, the magnetic force becomes zero. Then, the motion of charged particle is explained by consider an appropriate electric field. However, the resolution of this pradox shows that electricity and magnetism are linked and Lorentz force does not imply a universal preferred frame.
- Ampere's circuital law is dependent on Biot-Savart law. This relation is similar to the relations of Gauss' law and Coulomb's law.

PYQ Notes

- **Magnetic field due to a parallel wires connected to semi-circular wire**

(i) Magnetic field due to the given configuration at point P is given by

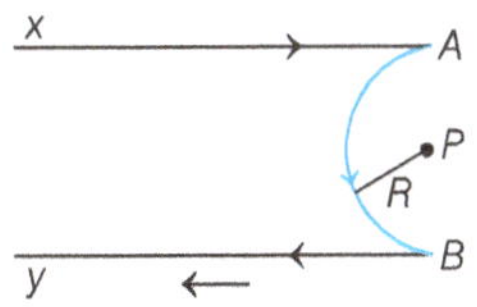

$$B = \frac{\mu_0 I}{4R}\left[1 - \frac{2}{\pi}\right]$$

Its direction is out of the page. [NEET 2023]

(ii) Magnetic field at point O due to the given configuration is

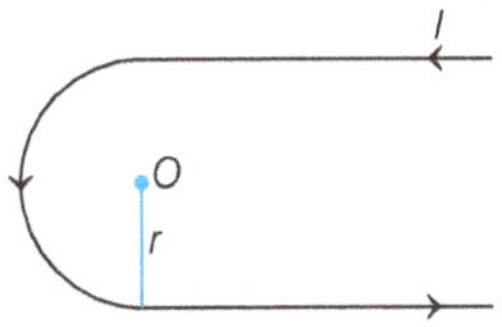

$$B = \frac{\mu_0 I}{4\pi r}[2 + \pi]$$

The direction of field is given by right hand thumb rule, i.e. out of the page. [JEE Main 2023]

- **Magnetic field due to an arc of circle**

The magnetic field at the centre of an arc subtended at an angle θ is given by

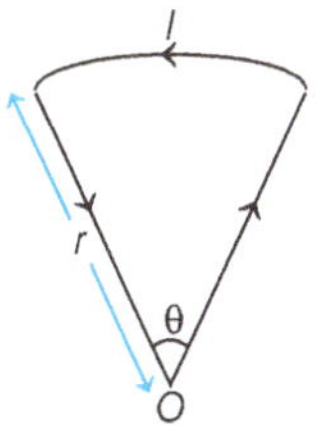

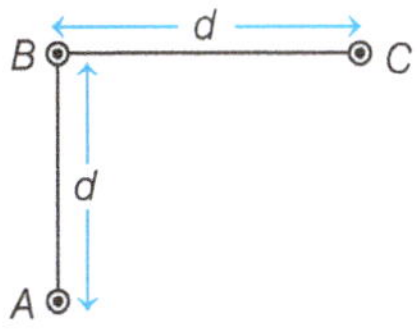

$$B = \frac{\mu_0 I}{2r} \times \frac{\theta}{2\pi}$$

[JEE Main 2019]

- **Magnetic force due to three finite straight wires placed at right angle to each other**

Force on wire B due to A and C is attractive and given by

$$F = \frac{\mu_0 I^2}{\sqrt{2}\,\pi d}$$

[NEET 2017]

- **Magnetic Field due to a long straight wire**

Magnetic field at point P due to long straight wire having current I is given by

$$B = \frac{\mu_0}{4\pi} \cdot \frac{I}{r} [\sin \phi_1 + \sin \phi_2]$$

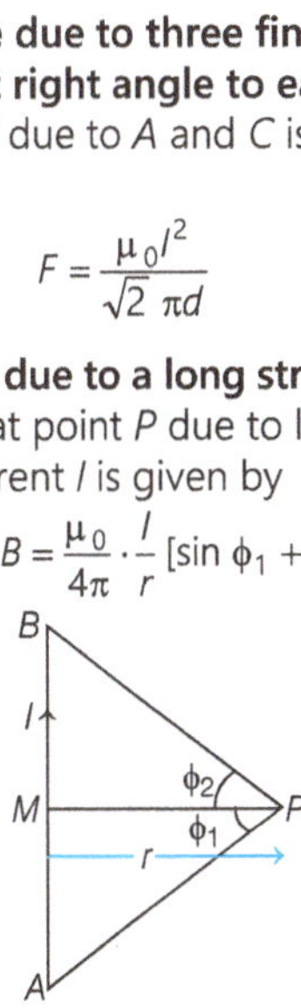

[JEE Main 2021]

Step by Step

Mastering NCERT

- Concept Builders
- Topical Questions
- Assertion and Reason Questions
- Statement Based
- Matching Type
- Numerical Type
- NCERT Exemplar
- Past Exams MCQs
- Skill Boosters

Concept Builders

1 When a charged particle moves perpendicular to the direction of magnetic field, then rate of change of momentum remains constant. [T/F]

2 Magnetic force on a moving charge in a magnetic field depends on .... (velocity / mass) of the charged particle.

3 A .... (radial / linear) magnetic field is used in moving coil galvanometer to make the scale of galvanometer.

4 The graph between magnetic field outside the conductor and distance from the centre is hyperbolic. [T/F]

5 If a current carrying loop of one turn is transformed into a coil of *n* identical circular loops, then how much times the magnetic field at the centre will increase?

6 What will be the magnetic field produced by an electron moving in a circular path of radius *r* and velocity *v*?

7 A solenoid tends to .... (contract/expand) when current flows through it .

8 Graduation on scale in AC ammeter and voltmeter are .... (not equally/ equally) distant.

9 A moving coil galvanometer can measure the alternating current. [T/F]

10 A .... (moving charge / rest charge) is a source of both electric and magnetic fields.

11 The magnetic field is .... (zero / maximum) at points on the axis of a current element and .... (zero/maximum) in a plane passing through the element and perpendicular to its axis.

12 Ampere's circuital law is not independent of the Biot-Savart law. [T/F]

13 An electron does not suffer any deflection while passing a region, it implies that there is no magnetic field in that region. [T/F]

14 In a non-uniform magnetic field, the net magnetic .... (force/ torque) on the current loop is non-zero but the .... force / torque) acting on it may be zero or non-zero.

15 What is the angle between electric and magnetic field if an electron passes undeflected through crossed electric and magnetic fields?

16 The current sensitivity of a moving coil galvanometer cannot be increased by decreasing torsion constant of the spring and the suspension wire. [T/F]

17 What is the resistance of an ideal ammeter and voltmeter ?

18 Higher the range of an ammeter to be prepared from a given galvanometer, ... (higher/ lower) is the value of the shunt resistance required for the purpose.

19 The range of ammeter can be decreased. [T/F]

20 The torque acting on a planar current loop in a magnetic field changes when its shape is changed without changing its area. [T/F]

Topical Questions

Magnetic Force

1 Which of the following statement (s) is/are correct ? NCERT Pg. 109

(a) Moving charges or currents produced a magnetic field in the surrounding space.

(b) The electric field can convey energy and momentum and is established instantaneously.

(c) The magnetic field of several sources is the arithmetic addition of magnetic field of each individual source.

(d) The Lorentz force depends on q, $\mathbf{v}$ and $\mathbf{B}$. Force on a negative charge is same as that on a positive charge.

2 The Lorentz force on a charged particle of charge q moving with velocity $\mathbf{v}$ in presence of both the electric field $\mathbf{E(r)}$ and the magnetic field $\mathbf{B(r)}$ is given by NCERT Pg. 109

(a) $q\left[\mathbf{E}(\mathbf{r})+\frac{1}{2}\mathbf{v}\times\mathbf{B}(\mathbf{r})\right]$ (b) $q[\mathbf{E}(\mathbf{r})+\mathbf{v}\times\mathbf{B}(\mathbf{r})]$
(c) $q[\mathbf{E}(\mathbf{r})-\mathbf{v}\times\mathbf{B}(\mathbf{r})]$ (d) $q[\mathbf{v}\times\mathbf{B}(\mathbf{r})-\mathbf{E}(\mathbf{r})]$

3 A proton is projected with velocity $\mathbf{v}=2\hat{\mathbf{i}}$ m/s in a region, where magnetic field $\mathbf{B}=(\hat{\mathbf{i}}+3\hat{\mathbf{j}}+4\hat{\mathbf{k}})\ \mu$T and electric field $\mathbf{E}=10\hat{\mathbf{i}}\ \mu$V/m, then find out the net force on proton. **NCERT Pg. 109**
(a) 22.6×10^{-25} N (b) 14.14×10^{-25} N
(c) 1.6×10^{-25} N (d) 10.5×10^{-25} N

4 A 2 MeV proton is moving perpendicular to uniform magnetic field of 2.5 T. The magnetic force on the proton is **NCERT Pg. 110**
(a) 8×10^{-12} N (b) 4×10^{-12} N
(c) 16×10^{-12} N (d) 2×10^{-12} N

5 When an electron is kept in a strong magnetic field, then **NCERT Pg. 110**
(a) electron moves in opposite direction of applied magnetic field
(b) electron moves in the direction of applied magnetic field
(c) electron moves in the perpendicular direction of magnetic field
(d) electron remains stationary at same position

6 A horizontal metal wire is carrying an electric current from the north to the south. Using a uniform magnetic field, it is to be prevented from falling under gravity. The direction of this magnetic field should be towards the **NCERT Pg. 110**
(a) north (b) south (c) east (d) west

7 A proton enters a magnetic field of flux density 1.5 Wbm^{-2} with a velocity of $2\times10^{7}\ \text{ms}^{-1}$ at an angle of 30° with the field. The force on the proton will be **NCERT Pg. 110**
(a) 2.4×10^{-12} N (b) 0.24×10^{-12} N
(c) 24×10^{-12} N (d) 0.024×10^{-12} N

8 Which of the following diagram is correct for the direction of magnetic force on a charge moving in a uniform magnetic field? **NCERT Pg. 110**

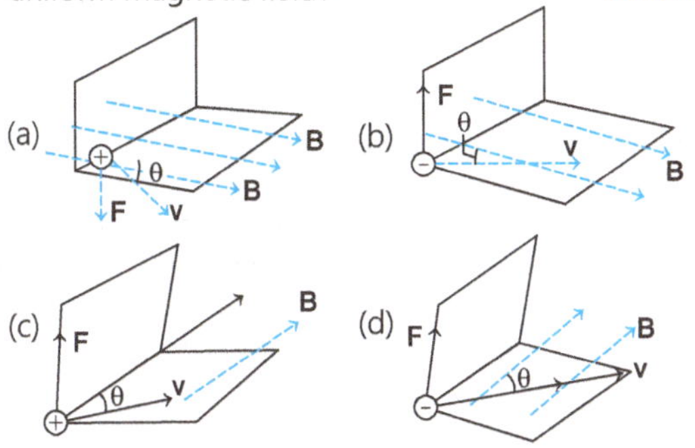

9 If a particle of charge 10^{-12} C moving along the x-direction with a velocity $10^{5}\ \text{ms}^{-1}$ experiences a force of 10^{-10} N in y-direction due to magnetic field, then the minimum magnetic field is **NCERT Pg. 110**
(a) 6.25×10^{3} T in z-direction
(b) 10^{-15} T in z-direction
(c) 6.25×10^{-3} T in z-direction
(d) 10^{-3} T in z-direction

10 An electron beam is moving with velocity of $10^{6}\ \text{ms}^{-1}$ through a uniform magnetic field 0.2 T, which is perpendicular to direction of beam. What is the force acting on an electron? **NCERT Pg. 110**
(a) 3.2×10^{-14} N (b) 1.5×10^{-14} N
(c) 8×10^{-15} N (d) 6.4×10^{-14} N

11 A charge particle having charge 2C is thrown with velocity of $(2\hat{\mathbf{i}}+3\hat{\mathbf{j}})$ m/s inside a region having $\mathbf{E}=2\hat{\mathbf{j}}$ N/C and magnetic field $5\hat{\mathbf{k}}$ T. The Lorentz force acting on particle is **NCERT Pg. 110**
(a) $(30\hat{\mathbf{i}}-16\hat{\mathbf{j}})$ N (b) $(15\hat{\mathbf{i}}+20\hat{\mathbf{j}})$ N
(c) $(15\hat{\mathbf{i}}-30\hat{\mathbf{j}})$ N (d) $(30\hat{\mathbf{i}}+15\hat{\mathbf{j}})$ N

12 An electron is moving with velocity of $10^{6}\ \text{ms}^{-1}$ through uniform magnetic field of 0.1 T which is perpendicular to direction of the motion. What is the force on the electron? **NCERT Pg. 110**
(a) 1.6×10^{-12} N (b) 1.6×10^{-14} N
(c) 5×10^{-9} N (d) 3.2×10^{-14} N

13 An electron is travelling horizontally towards east. A magnetic field in vertically downward direction exerts a force on the electron along **NCERT Pg. 110**
(a) east (b) west
(c) north (d) south

14 A straight wire of mass 200 g and length 1.5 m carries a current of 2 A. It is held in mid-air by a uniform horizontal magnetic field. What is the magnitude of magnetic field? **NCERT Pg. 111**
(a) 1 T (b) 0.65 T
(c) 0.35 T (d) 0.85 T

Motion in Magnetic Field

15 In an experiment, electrons are accelerated from rest by applying a voltage of 500 V. Calculate the radius of the path, if a magnetic field 100 mT is then applied. (Take, charge of the electron $=1.6\times10^{-19}$ C and mass of the electron $=9.1\times10^{-31}$ kg) **NCERT Pg. 112**
(a) 7.5×10^{-2} m (b) 7.5×10^{-4} m
(c) 7.5×10^{-3} m (d) 7.5×10^{-5} m

16 Two particles of masses m_a and m_b with same charge are projected in a perpendicular magnetic field. They travel along circular path of radii r_a and r_b such that $r_a > r_b$. Then, which of the following option is correct? **NCERT Pg. 112**

(a) $m_a v_a > m_b v_b$ (b) $m_a > m_b$ and $v_a < v_b$
(c) $m_a = m_b$ and $v_a = v_b$ (d) $m_b v_b > m_a v_a$

17 A deuteron of kinetic energy 50 keV is describing a circular orbit of radius 0.5 m in a plane perpendicular to magnetic field B. The kinetic energy of the proton that describes a circular orbit of radius 0.5 m in the same plane with the same magnetic field B is **NCERT Pg. 112**

(a) 25 keV (b) 50 keV
(c) 200 keV (d) 100 keV

18 A proton, a deuteron and an α-particle enter a region of perpendicular magnetic field (to their velocities) with same kinetic energy. If r_p, r_d and r_α are the radii of circular paths of these particles, then **NCERT Pg. 112**

(a) $r_\alpha = r_p < r_d$ (b) $r_\alpha = r_d = r_p$
(c) $r_\alpha < r_d < r_p$ (d) $r_\alpha > r_d > r_p$

19 An electron enters a region of magnetic field perpendicularly with a speed of 3×10^7 ms^{-1}. Strength of magnetic field is 6×10^{-4} T. Frequency is **NCERT Pg. 112**

(a) 2 MHz (b) 17 MHz
(c) 20 MHz (d) 2 MHz

20 A particle of mass m and charge q moves with a constant velocity v along the positive x-direction. It enters a region containing a uniform magnetic field B directed along the negative z-direction, extending from $x = a$ to $x = b$.

The minimum value of v required, so that the particle can just enter the region $x > b$ is **NCERT Pg. 112**

(a) $qb\,B/m$ (b) $[q(b-a)B]/m$
(c) $q\,aB/m$ (d) $q(b+a)B/2m$

21 A proton of mass 1.67×10^{-27} kg and charge 1.6×10^{-19} C is projected with a speed of 2×10^6 ms^{-1} at an angle of 60° to the X-axis. If a magnetic field of 0.104 T is applied along Y-axis, then path of proton is **NCERT Pg. 112**

(a) a circle of radius 0.2 m and time period of $\pi \times 10^{-7}$ s
(b) a circle of radius 0.1 m and time period $2\pi \times 10^{-7}$ s
(c) a helix of radius 0.2 m and time period of $2\pi \times 10^{-7}$ s
(d) a helix of radius 0.2 m and time period of $4\pi \times 10^{-7}$s

22 A proton of energy 1 MeV describes a circular path in plane at right angles to a uniform magnetic field of 6.28×10^{-4} T. The mass of proton is 1.67×10^{-27} kg. The frequency of proton is nearly equal to **NCERT Pg. 112**

(a) 10^7 Hz (b) 10^5 Hz
(c) 10^6 Hz (d) 10^4 Hz

23 Which one is a correct figure to represent path of a charge moving at an angle (other than 0° or 90°) in a magnetic field? **NCERT Pg. 112**

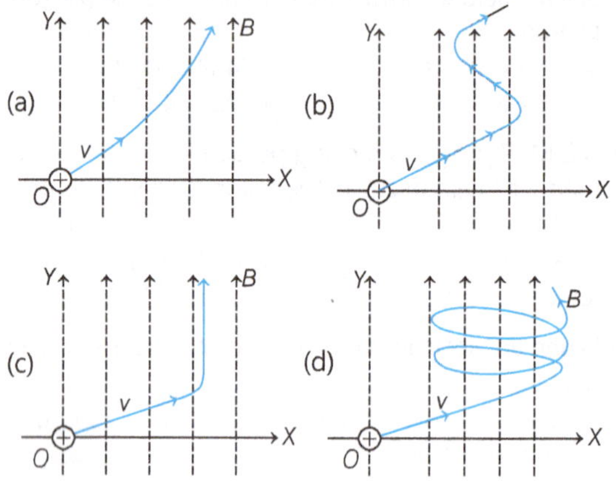

24 An ionised gas contains both positive and negative ions. If it is subjected simultaneously to an electric field along the + x-direction and a magnetic field along the + z-direction, then **NCERT Pg. 112**

(a) positive ions deflect towards $+y$-direction and negative ions towards $-y$-direction
(b) all ions deflect towards $+y$-direction
(c) all ions deflect towards $-y$-direction
(d) positive ions deflect towards $-y$-direction and negative ions towards $+y$-direction

25 An electron moves straight inside a charged parallel plate capacitor. Plates of capacitor have charge density σ. The space between plates is filled with constant magnetic field of induction **B**. **NCERT Pg. 112**

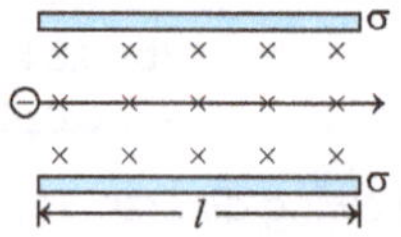

Time taken by electron to pass through the region is

(a) $\dfrac{e\sigma}{\varepsilon_0 lB}$ (b) $\dfrac{\varepsilon_0 lB}{\sigma}$ (c) $\dfrac{\sigma e}{\varepsilon_0 B}$ (d) $\dfrac{\varepsilon_0 B}{e\sigma}$

26 A proton and an α-particle both enter a region of uniform magnetic field B, moving at right angles to the field B. If the radius of circular orbits for both the particles is equal and the kinetic energy acquired by proton is 1 MeV, the energy acquired by the α-particle will be **NCERT Pg. 112**

(a) 4 MeV (b) 0.5 MeV (c) 1.5 MeV (d) 1 MeV

27 A uniform magnetic field acts at right angles to the direction of motion of electrons. As result, the electron moves in a circular path of radius 2 cm. If the speed of the electrons is doubled, the radius of the circular path will be NCERT Pg. 112

(a) 2.0 cm (b) 0.5 cm (c) 4.0 cm (d)1.0 cm

28 Which of the following statement(s) is/are incorrect? NCERT Pg. 112

(a) If a moving charged particle enters into a region of magnetic field from outside, it does not complete a circular path.
(b) If a moving charged particle traces a helical path in a uniform magnetic field, the axis of the helix is parallel to the magnetic field.
(c) The power associated with the force exerted by a magnetic field on a moving charged particle is always equal to unity.
(d) If in a region a uniform magnetic field and a uniform electric field both exist, a charged particle moving in this region cannot trace a circular path.

Magnetic Field due to a Current Element : Biot-Savart Law

29 An element $\Delta l = \Delta x\, \hat{\mathbf{i}}$ is placed at the origin and carries a current $I = 10$ A.

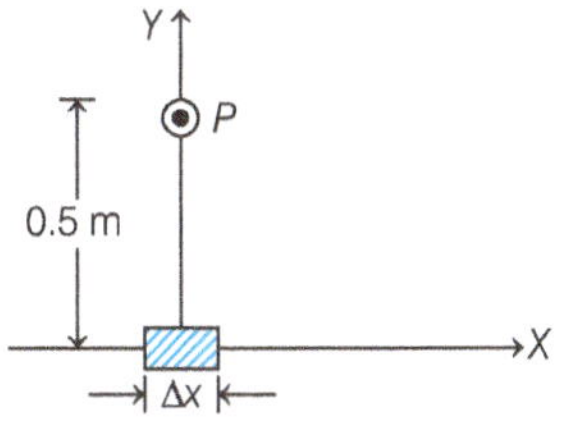

If $\Delta x = 1$ cm, magnetic field at point P is NCERT Pg. 114

(a) $4 \times 10^{-8}\, \hat{\mathbf{k}}$ T (b) $4 \times 10^{-8}\, \hat{\mathbf{i}}$ T
(c) $4 \times 10^{-8}\, \hat{\mathbf{j}}$ T (d) $-4 \times 10^{-8}\, \hat{\mathbf{j}}$ T

30 Two circular coils of radii 5 cm and 10 cm carry equal currents of 2 A. The coils have 50 and 100 turns, respectively and are placed in such a way that their planes as well as their centres coincide. Magnitude of magnetic field at the common centre of coils is NCERT Pg. 116

(a) $8\pi \times 10^{-4}$T, if currents in the coils are in same sense
(b) $4\pi \times 10^{-4}$T, if currents in the coils are in opposite sense
(c) zero, if currents in the coils are in same sense
(d) $8\pi \times 10^{-4}$T, if currents in the coils are in opposite sense

31 Which of the following statement(s) is/are incorrect ? NCERT Pg. 116

(a) Magnetic field possesses cylindrical symmetry.
(b) The lines of constant magnitude of magnetic field are parallel straight lines.
(c) Even though the wire is infinite, the field due to it at a non-zero distance is not infinite.
(d) The direction of magnetic field is given by right-hand rule in which fingers will curl around in the direction of the magnetic field.

32 A straight wire carrying a current of 12A is bent into a semi-circular loop of radius 2.0 cm. What will be magnetic field at the centre of the semi-circular loop? NCERT Pg. 117

(a) $\mathbf{B} = 1.9 \times 10^{-4}$ T, ⊙ (b) $\mathbf{B} = 1.9 \times 10^{4}$ T, ⊙
(c) $\mathbf{B} = 1.9 \times 10^{-4}$ T, ⊗ (d) $\mathbf{B} = 1.9 \times 10^{4}$ T, ⊗

33 Two circular loops having same radius ($R = 10$ cm) and same current ($I = 7/2$ A) are placed along same axis as shown. If distance between their centres is 10 cm, then the net magnetic field at point P is NCERT Pg. 116

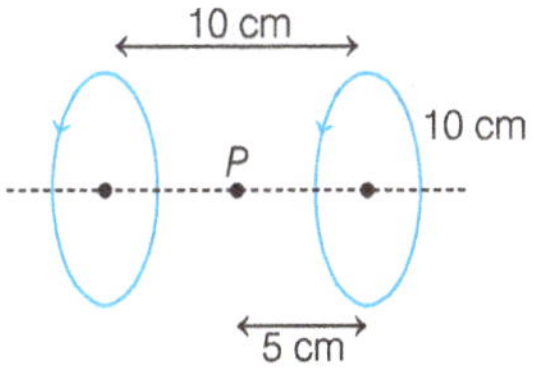

(a) $\frac{50\mu_0}{\sqrt{5}}$ T (b) $\frac{28\mu_0}{\sqrt{5}}$ T
(c) $\frac{56\mu_0}{\sqrt{5}}$ T (d) $\frac{56\mu_0}{\sqrt{3}}$ T

34 The magnetic field at the centre of a circular current carrying-conductor of radius r is B_c. The magnetic field on its axis at a distance r from the centre is B_a. The value of $B_c : B_a$ will be NCERT Pg. 117

(a) $1 : \sqrt{2}$ (b) $1 : 2\sqrt{2}$
(c) $2\sqrt{2} : 1$ (d) $\sqrt{2} : 1$

35 Magnetic field intensity at the centre of a circular current loop, radius 0.4 m, and carrying a current of 3 A is NCERT Pg. 117

(a) 4.7×10^{-6} T (b) 4.8×10^{-5} T
(c) 5.2×10^{-8} T (d) 4.8×10^{-2} T

Ampere's Circuital Law

36 A long straight wire of radius a carries a current distributed uniformly over its cross- section. The ratio of the magnetic fields due to the wire at distances $\frac{a}{3}$ and $2a$, respectively from the axis of the wire is NCERT Pg. 118

(a) $\frac{3}{2}$ (b) 2
(c) $\frac{2}{3}$ (d) $\frac{1}{2}$

37 A tightly wound coil of 100 turns with radius 10 cm, magnitude of carrying-current in coil is 1 A, what will be the magnitude of magnetic field at centre of coil? NCERT Pg. 118

(a) 6.28×10^{-6} T (b) 6.28×10^{-7} T
(c) 6.28×10^{-5} T (d) 6.28×10^{-4} T

38 Which of the following statement(s) is/are incorrect? NCERT Pg. 118

(a) For Ampere's law relation, a sign convention is given by the right-hand rule, in which direction of the thumb gives the sense in which the current I is regarded as positive.
(b) An amperian loop is that at each point of which either **B** is tangential to the loop and is a non-zero constant B or **B** is normal to the loop or **B** vanishes.
(c) When there is a system with a symmetry such as for a straight infinite current carrying wire, the Ampere's law enables an easy evaluation of the magnetic fields.
(d) Ampere's circuital law holds for currents that are accelerated with time.

39 A cylindrical conductor of radius R is carrying a constant current I, having uniform distribution across its cross-section. What will be the magnetic field strength at $r = \frac{R}{2}$ from the axis of cylinder? NCERT Pg. 118

(a) $\frac{\mu_0 I}{2\pi R}$ (b) $\frac{\mu_0 I}{4\pi R}$ (c) $\frac{\mu_0 I}{2R}$ (d) Zero

The Solenoid

40 A long solenoid has 20 turns cm^{-1}. The current necessary to produce a magnetic field of 20 mT inside the solenoid is approximately NCERT Pg. 112

(a) 1A (b) 2 A (c) 4 A (d) 8 A

41 A solenoid of length 0.5 m has a radius of 1 cm and is made up of 500 turns. It carries a current of 5A. What is the magnetic field inside the solenoid? NCERT Pg. 122

(a) 6.28×10^{-3} T (b) 6.28×10^{3} T
(c) 6.28×10^{-5} T (d) 6.28×10^{5} T

42 A very long solenoid is to be constructed by tightly wrapped wire with a magnetic field of 0.168 T at its centre. The radius of solenoid is to be 0.01 m and the wire carries a current of 2 A. If the solenoid is 1.4 m long. What is the length of wire needed in nearest integer (in m)? NCERT Pg. 122

(a) 4220 (b) 5842
(c) 2550 (d) 58800

43 Which of the following statement(s) is/are incorrect ? NCERT Pg. 122

(a) In a solenoid, the net magnetic field is the vector sum of the fields due to all the turns.
(b) Enamelled wires are used for winding, so that turns are insulated from each other.
(c) The field inside the solenoid approaches zero and everywhere outside becomes parallel to the axis.
(d) The solenoid is commonly used to obtain a uniform magnetic field.

44 A long solenoid having 200 turns/cm and carries current I. Magnetic field at its axis is 6.28×10^{-2} Wb/m^2. An another solenoid having 100 turns/cm and carries $I/3$ current, then magnetic field at its axis will be NCERT Pg. 122

(a) 1.05×10^{-4} Wb/m^2
(b) 1.05×10^{-2} Wb/m^2
(c) 1.05×10^{-5} Wb/m^2
(d) 1.05×10^{-3} Wb/m^2

Force Between Two Parallel Currents: The Ampere

45 What is magnetic flux density at a point 9 cm from the long straight wire carrying a current of 6 A? NCERT Pg. 123

(a) 1.33×10^{-5} T (b) 1.7×10^{-4} T
(c) 2.3×10^{-2} T (d) 1.36×10^{-4} T

46 Three long wires carrying current 10 A, 20 A and 30 A are placed parallel to each other as shown in the figure. Points P and Q are in midway of wires. What is ratio of magnetic fields at point P to the Q? NCERT Pg. 123

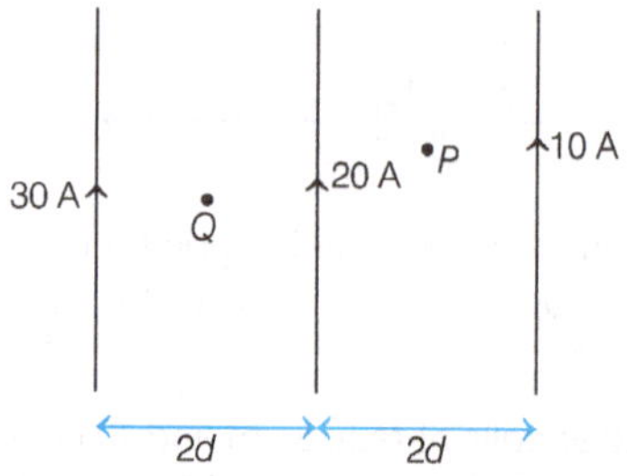

(a) 2 : 1 (b) 3 : 2 (c) 2 : 3 (d) 3 : 1

47 If two parallel current carrying conductors placed 1 m apart in vacuum are placed such that each carries 1 A current, then there is a force of NCERT Pg. 123

(a) 2×10^{-7} Nm^{-1} (b) 2×10^{7} Nm^{-1}
(c) 9×10^{9} Nm^{-1} (d) 9×10^{-9} Nm^{-1}

48 Two long parallel straight wires A and B carrying currents of 4.0 A and 5.0 A in same direction separated by a distance of 4×10^{-2} m.
The force on a 0.20 m section of wire A is NCERT Pg. 123

(a) 2×10^{-5} N (towards B)
(b) 2×10^{-5} N (away from B)
(c) 2×10^{-5} N (towards A)
(d) 2×10^{-5} N (parallel to B)

49 Two very long, straight and parallel wires carry same steady current I flowing in same direction. The distance between the wires is d. At a certain instant of time, a point charge q is at a point equidistant from the two wires in the plane of the wires. Its instantaneous velocity v is perpendicular to this plane.

The magnitude of the force due to the magnetic field acting on the charge at this instant is **NCERT Pg. 123**

(a) $\frac{\mu_0 Iqv}{2\pi d}$ (b) $\frac{\mu_0 Iqv}{\pi d}$ (c) $\frac{2\mu_0 Iqv}{\pi d}$ (d) 0

50 In figure, two parallel infinitely long current carrying wires are shown. If resultant magnetic field at point A is zero, then determine the value of current I. **NCERT Pg. 123**

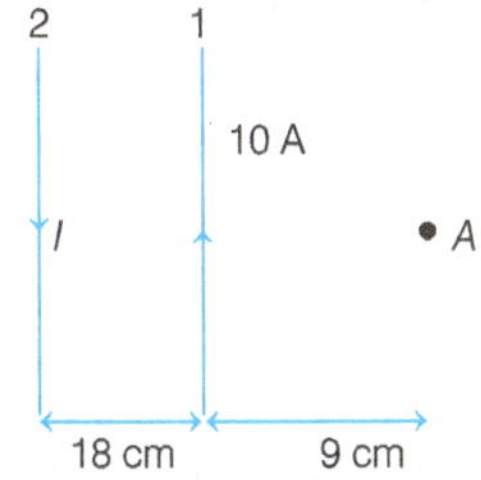

(a) 50 A (b) 15 A (c) 30 A (d) 25 A

51 A rigid square loop of side a and carrying current I_2 is lying on a horizontal surface near a long current I_1 carrying wire in the same plane as shown in figure. The net force on the loop due to the wire will be **NCERT Pg. 123**

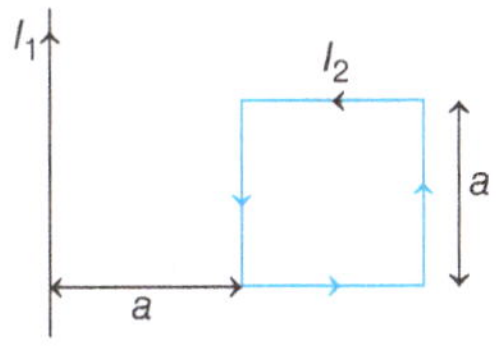

(a) repulsive and equal to $\frac{\mu_0 I_1 I_2}{2\pi}$

(b) attractive and equal to $\frac{\mu_0 I_1 I_2}{3\pi}$

(c) zero

(d) repulsive and equal to $\frac{\mu_0 I_1 I_2}{4\pi}$

52 A current carrying closed loop in the form of a right angled isosceles ΔABC is placed in a uniform magnetic field acting along AB. If the magnetic force on the arm BC is F, then force on the arm AC is **NCERT Pg. 123**

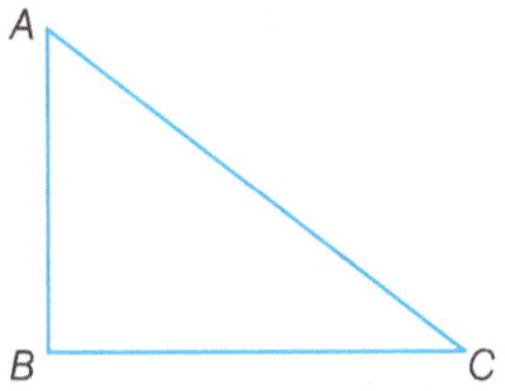

(a) $-F$ (b) F
(c) $\sqrt{2}\,F$ (d) $-\sqrt{2}\,F$

53 Three long, straight and parallel wires carrying currents are arranged as shown in the figure.

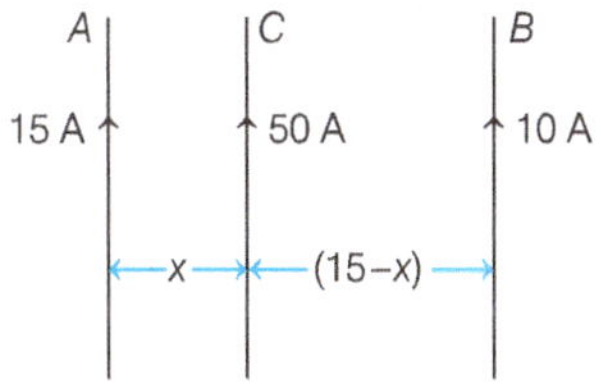

The wire C which carries a current of 50 A is so replaced that it experiences no force. The distance of wire C from wire A is **NCERT Pg. 123**

(a) 9 cm (b) 7 cm (c) 5 cm (d) 3 cm

54 Figure shows, two long parallel wires separated by a distance of 18 cm. There is current of 8 A in wire 1 and 12 A in wire 2. At what point on line joining of the wires, the magnetic field is zero? **NCERT Pg. 123**

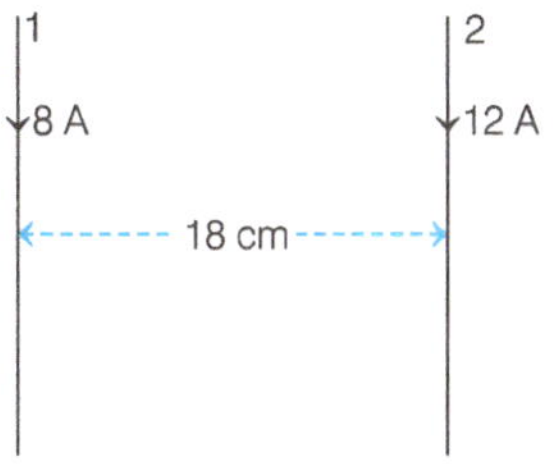

(a) 5.2 cm from wire 1 (b) 9.4 cm from wire 2
(c) 7.2 cm from wire 1 (d) 10.3 cm from wire 2

Torque on Current Loop, Magnetic Dipole

55 Area enclosed by a planar loop is $2 \times 10^{-3} m^2$. If loop carries a current of 2 A, then magnitude of magnetic dipole moment of the loop is **NCERT Pg. 126**

(a) $4 \times 10^3 JT^{-1}$ (b) $8 \times 10^{-3} JT^{-1}$
(c) $4 \times 10^{-3} JT^{-1}$ (d) $2 \times 10^{-3} JT^{-1}$

56 A circular coil of 25 turns and radius 12 cm is placed in a uniform magnetic field of 0.5 T normal to the plane of the coil. If the current in the coil is 6 A, then total torque acting on the coil is **NCERT Pg. 126**

(a) zero (b) 3.4 N-m
(c) 3.8 N-m (d) 4.4 N-m

57 A current loop in a magnetic field **NCERT Pg. 126**

(a) experiences a torque whether the field is uniform or non-uniform in all orientations
(b) can be in equilibrium in one orientations
(c) can be equilibrium in two orientations, both the equilibrium states are unstable
(d) can be in equilibrium in two orientations, one stable while the other is unstable

58 A rectangular loop of sides 10 cm and 5 cm carrying a current I of 12 A is placed in different orientations as shown in the figures.

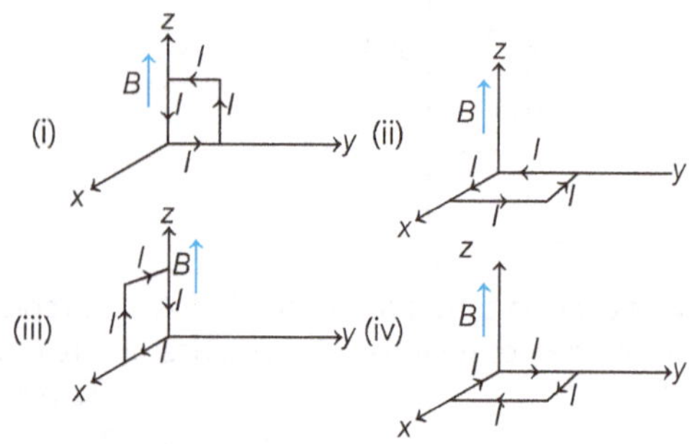

If there is a uniform magnetic field of 0.3 T in the positive z-direction, in which orientations the loop would be in (i) stable equilibrium and (ii) unstable equilibrium? **NCERT Pg. 126**

(a) (i) and (ii) respectively (b) (i) and (iii) respectively
(c) (ii) and (iv) respectively (d) (ii) and (iii) respectively

59 A steady current i flows in a small square loop of wire of side L in a horizontal plane. The loop is now folded about its middle such that half of it lies in a vertical plane. Let μ_1 and μ_2 denotes the magnetic moments due to the current loop before and after folding, respectively. Then, **NCERT Pg. 126**

(a) $\mu_2 = 0$ (b) μ_1 and μ_2 are in the same direction
(c) $\frac{|\mu_1|}{|\mu_2|} = \sqrt{2}$
(d) $\frac{|\mu_1|}{|\mu_2|} = \left(\frac{1}{\sqrt{2}}\right)$

60 An electron is revolving around the nucleus of hydrogen atom of radius 1 Å with a speed of 10^6 m/s. Magnetic dipole moment associated with the electron is **NCERT Pg. 126**

(a) 8×10^{-24} A-m^2 (b) 2×10^{-24} A-m^2
(c) 4×10^{-24} A-m^2 (d) 3.25×10^{-24} A-m^2

61 Magnetic field at the centre of a circular loop of area A is B. The magnetic moment of the loop will be **NCERT Pg. 126**

(a) $\frac{BA^2}{\mu_0\pi}$ (b) $\frac{BA^{3/2}}{\mu_0\pi}$ (c) $\frac{BA^{3/2}}{\mu_0\pi^{1/2}}$ (d) $\frac{2BA^{3/2}}{\mu_0\pi^{1/2}}$

62 A square loop is carrying a steady current I and the magnitude of its magnetic dipole moment is m. If this square loop is changed to a circular loop and it carries the same current, the magnitude of the magnetic dipole moment of circular loop (in A-m^2) will be **NCERT Pg. 126**

(a) $\frac{4m}{\pi}$ (b) $\frac{3m}{\pi}$ (c) $\frac{2m}{\pi}$ (d) $\frac{m}{\pi}$

63 The magnetic moment of an electron orbiting in a circular orbit of radius r with a speed v is equal to **NCERT Pg. 126**

(a) $evr/2$ (b) evr
(c) $er/2v$ (d) None of these

64 A wire of length l metre carrying a current of i A is bent in the form of an equilateral triangle. Its magnetic dipole moment is **NCERT Pg. 126**

(a) $\frac{il^2}{12}$ A-m^2 (b) $\frac{il^2}{4}$ A-m^2 (c) $\frac{il^2}{12\sqrt{3}}$ A-m^2 (d) $\frac{il^2}{6}$ A-m^2

65 A square coil of side 10 cm consists of 20 turns and carries a current of 12 A. The coil is suspended vertically and the normal to the plane of the coil makes an angle of 30° with the direction of a uniform horizontal magnetic field of magnitude 0.80 T. What is the magnitude of torque experienced by the coil? **NCERT Pg. 126**

(a) 0.96 N-m (b) 96 N-m
(c) $0.96 \times \sqrt{3}$ N-m (d) $96 \times \sqrt{3}$ N-m

66 A rectangular coil of wire carrying a current is suspended in a uniform magnetic field. The plane of the coil is making an angle of 30° with the direction of the field and the torque experienced by it is τ_1 and when the plane of the coil is making an angle of 60° with the direction of the field the torque experienced by it is τ_2. Then the ratio $\tau_1 : \tau_2$ is **NCERT Pg. 126**

(a) $1 : \sqrt{3}$ (b) $\sqrt{3} : 1$ (c) 1 : 3 (d) 3 : 1

The Moving Coil Galvanometer

67 A galvanometer of resistance 70 Ω is converted into an ammeter by a shunt resistance $r_s = 0.03\ \Omega$. The value of its resistance will become **NCERT Pg. 130**

(a) 0.025 Ω (b) 0.022 Ω (c) 0.035 Ω (d) 0.030 Ω

68 The resistance of a galvanometer is 50 ohm and the maximum current which can be passed through it is 0.002 A. What resistance must be connected to it in order to convert it into an ammeter of range 0-0.5 A? **NCERT Pg. 130**

(a) 0.2 Ω (b) 0.5 Ω (c) 0.002 Ω (d) 0.02 Ω

69 In the circuit shown, the galvanometer G of resistance 60 Ω is shunted by a resistance $r = 0.02\ \Omega$. The current through R is nearly 1 A. The value of resistance R is nearly **NCERT Pg. 130**

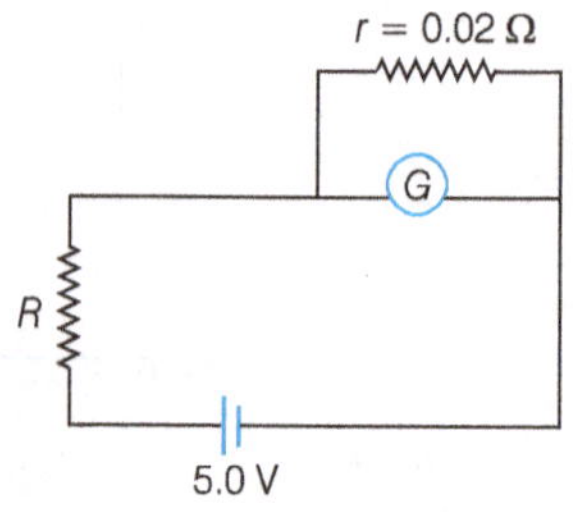

(a) 1.00 Ω (b) 5.00 Ω
(c) 11.0 Ω (d) 6.0 Ω

70 A galvanometer of 50 Ω resistance has 25 divisions. A current of 4×10^{-4} A gives a deflection of one division. To convert this galvanometer into a voltmeter having a range of 25V, it should be connected with a resistance of NCERT Pg. 130

(a) 2500 Ω as a shunt (b) 245 Ω as a shunt
(c) 2550 Ω in series (d) 2450 Ω in series

71 Which of the following statement(s) is/are incorrect ? NCERT Pg. 130

(a) The deflection ϕ indicated on the scale of a moving coil galvanometer by a pointer attached to the spring is given by $\phi = (NAB/k)I$.
(b) The galvanometer can be used as a detector to check, if a current is flowing in the circuit.
(c) Current sensitivity of the galvanometer is the deflection per unit current while voltage sensitivity is the deflection per unit voltage.
(d) In voltage measurement, to keep the disturbance due to the measuring device below one percent a small resistance *R* is connected in parallel with the galvanometer.

72 In two galvanometers *A* and *B*, to produce a deflection of 10 divisions, currents of 3 mA and 5 mA are required, respectively, then NCERT Pg. 130

(a) *A* is more sensitive than *B*
(b) *B* is more sensitive than *A*
(c) Both are equally sensitive
(d) sensitivity of *B* is 5 / 3 that *A*

73 The coil of a galvanometer consists of 100 turns and effective area of 1 cm^2. The restoring couple is 10^{-8} N-m rad^{-1}. The magnetic field between poles is of 5 T. Current sensitivity of this galvanometer is NCERT Pg. 130

(a) 5×10^4 rad/μ A (b) 5×10^6 A^{-1}
(c) 2×10^{-7} A^{-1} (d) 5 rad/μ A

74 When 2A current is passed through a tangent galvanometer, it gives a deflection of 30°. For 60° deflection, the current must be NCERT Pg. 130

(a) 1 A (b) $2\sqrt{3}$ A (c) 4 A (d) 6 A

75 In an ammeter 10% of main current passes through the galvanometer. If resistance of galvanometer is *G*, then resistance of ammeter is NCERT Pg. 130

(a) $\frac{G}{5}$ (b) $\frac{G}{10}$ (c) $\frac{G}{20}$ (d) $\frac{G}{25}$

76 A galvanometer has a coil of resistance 20 Ω and its full scale deflection current is 9 A. Value of shunt resistance that should be connected with it so that it can read a maximum of 99 A current, is NCERT Pg. 130

(a) 10 Ω (b) 2 Ω (c) 1 Ω (d) 9 Ω

77 An ammeter reads upto 1 A. Its internal resistance is 0.81 Ω. To increase the range to 10 A, the value of the required shunt is NCERT Pg. 130

(a) 0.03 Ω (b) 0.3 Ω (c) 0.9 Ω (d) 0.09 Ω

78 If only 2% of main current is to be passed through a galvanometer of resistance *G*, then the resistance of shunt will be NCERT Pg. 130

(a) $\frac{G}{49}$ (b) *G* (c) $\frac{G}{100}$ (d) $\frac{G}{98}$

79 Relation between voltage sensitivity S_V and current sensitivity S_i for a galvanometer of resistance *G* ohms is NCERT Pg. 131

(a) $\frac{S_i}{G} = S_V$ (b) $\frac{S_V}{G} = S_i$ (c) $S_i S_V = G$ (d) $\sqrt{S_i S_V} = G$

80 To increase current sensitivity of a moving coil galvanometer by 50%, its resistance is increased, so that its new resistance is twice of its initial resistance. Its voltage sensitivity changes by a factor of NCERT Pg. 131

(a) increases by a factor of 2
(b) decreases by a factor of (1 / 2)
(c) increases by a factor of 4
(d) decreases by a factor of (1 /4)

81 Current sensitivity of a moving coil galvanometer is 10 div/mA and its voltage sensitivity is 20 div/V. The resistance of galvanometer is NCERT Pg. 131

(a) 100 Ω (b) 200 Ω
(c) 250 Ω (d) 500 Ω

Assertion and Reason Questions

Direction (Q. Nos. 1-10) *In the following questions, a statement of Assertion is followed by a corresponding statement of Reason. Of the following statements, choose the correct one.*

(a) Both Assertion and Reason are correct and Reason is the correct explanation of Assertion.
(b) Both Assertion and Reason are correct but Reason is not the correct explanation of Assertion.
(c) Assertion is correct but Reason is incorrect.
(d) Assertion is incorrect but Reason is correct.

1 **Assertion** A magnetic field interacts with a moving charge and not with a stationary charge.

Reason A moving charge produce a magnetic field.
NCERT Pg. 112

2 **Assertion** Electron moving perpendicular to magnetic field **B** will perform circular motion.

Reason Force exerted by magnetic field on the electron is perpendicular to its velocity. NCERT Pg. 112

3 **Assertion** A charge particle is released from rest in magnetic field, then it will move in a circular path.

Reason Work done by magnetic field is zero. NCERT Pg. 112

4 **Assertion** When a charged particle moves in a region of magnetic field such that its velocity is at some acute angle with the direction of field, its trajectory is a helix.

Reason Perpendicular component of velocity causes a rotating centripetal force and parallel component of velocity does not produces any force. NCERT Pg. 112

5 **Assertion** If we increase the current sensitivity of a galvanometer by increasing number of turns, its voltage sensitivity also increases.

Reason Resistance of a wire also increases with N. NCERT Pg. 112

6 **Assertion** The magnetic field produced by a current-carrying solenoid (n & is kept constant) is independent of its length and cross-sectional area.

Reason The magnetic field inside the solenoid is uniform. NCERT Pg. 122

7 **Assertion** Torque on the coil is minimum, when coil is suspended in a radial magnetic field.

Reason In a radial magnetic field, the magnetic lines of force act perpendicular to the coil. NCERT Pg. 124

8 **Assertion** When the radius of a current carrying loop is halved, its magnetic moment becomes one-fourth.

Reason The magnetic moment of a current carrying loop is directly proportional to the radius of the loop. NCERT Pg. 124

9 **Assertion** A galvanometer can be converted into an ammeter by connecting a low resistance shunt in parallel with it.

Reason The shunt in parallel, decreases the sensitivity of the galvanometer. NCERT Pg. 128

10 **Assertion** The resistance of an ideal voltmeter should be infinite.

Reason The voltmeter is connected in parallel across any element of a circuit. NCERT Pg. 129

Statement Based Questions

Direction (Q. Nos. 1-8) *In the following questions, a statement I is followed by a corresponding statement II. Of the following statements, choose the correct one.*

(a) Both Statement I and Statement II are incorrect.
(b) Statement I is correct but Statement II is incorrect.
(c) Statement I is incorrect but Statement II is correct.
(d) Both Statement I and Statement II are correct.

1 **Statement I** If a current is flowing through a conductor from east to west, then the direction of magnetic field at a point above the conductor is towards north.

Statement II The magnetic field due to a long straight wire carrying current (i) is proportional to i^3. NCERT Pg. 109

2 **Statement I** When a charged particle moves in the region of a perpendicular magnetic field, its speed remains constant.

Statement II Force acting on the charged particle is given by $\mathbf{F} = q(\mathbf{v} \times \mathbf{B})$. NCERT Pg. 112

3 **Statement I** When a charged particle moves in a region of magnetic field such that its velocity is at some acute angle with direction of field, its trajectory is a circle.

Statement II Parallel component of velocity causes a rotating centripetal force and perpendicular component of velocity does not produces any force. NCERT Pg. 112

4 **Statement I** Biot Savart's law gives us the expression for the magnetic field strength of an infinitesimal current element ($Id\mathbf{l}$) of a current carrying conductor only.

Statement II Biot-Savart's law is analogous to Coulomb's inverse square law of charge q, with the former being related to the field produced by a scalar source q while the latter being produced by a vector source $Id\mathbf{l}$. NCERT Pg. 114

5 **Statement I** Graph of force per unit length between two long parallel current carrying conductors and the distance between them is a straight line.

Statement II Two parallel conductors carrying same current i in the same direction attract each other with a force $\frac{\mu_0}{2\pi}\frac{i^2}{R}$ N/m. NCERT Pg. 123

6 **Statement I** A planar circular loop of area A and carrying current I is equivalent to magnetic dipole $M = IA$.

Statement II At large distances, the magnetic field of circular loop and magnetic dipole is same. NCERT Pg. 129

7 **Statement I** Galvanometer cannot as such be used as an ammeter to measure the value of the current in a given circuit.

Statement II Galvanometer gives full scale deflection for a current of the order of microampere. NCERT Pg. 131

8 **Statement I** If we increase the current sensitivity of a galvanometer by increasing number of turns, its voltage sensitivity also increases.

Statement II Magnetic field cannot change kinetic energy of moving charge. NCERT Pg. 131

Matching Type Questions

1 A charged particle with some initial velocity is projected in a region where non-zero electric and magnetic fields are present. Match the entries of Column I with the entries of Column II and select the correct answer from the codes given below. NCERT Pg. 109

Column I	Column II
A. $\mathbf{E}=0, \mathbf{B}\neq 0$ and initial velocity is at any angle with $\mathbf{B}\,(\theta\neq 90°)$	1. Straight line
B. $\mathbf{E}=0, \mathbf{B}\neq 0$ and initial velocity is perpendicular to $\mathbf{B}$	2. Helical path with uniform pitch
C. $\mathbf{E}\neq 0, \mathbf{B}\neq 0, \mathbf{E}\parallel\mathbf{B}$ and initial velocity is $\perp$ to both	3. Circular
D. $\mathbf{E}\neq 0, \mathbf{B}\neq 0, \mathbf{E}$ perpendicular to $\mathbf{B}$ and $\mathbf{v}$ perpendicular to both $\mathbf{E}$ & $\mathbf{B}$	4. Helical path with non-uniform pitch

Codes

	A	B	C	D		A	B	C	D
(a)	2	3	4	1	(b)	1	3	4	2
(c)	2	3	1	4	(d)	4	1	2	3

2 A current carrying wire loop of N-turns, placed in a region of a uniform magnetic field $\mathbf{B}$. Match the Column I (torque and magnetic moment of loop) with Column II (values) and select the correct answer from the options given below. NCERT Pg. 125

Column I	Column II
A. Torque on loop	1. mB
B. Torque on loop when $\mathbf{m}$ is either parallel or anti-parallel to $\mathbf{B}$	2. NIA
C. Magnetic moment of loop	3. zero
D. Torque on loop when $\mathbf{m}$ is perpendicular to $\mathbf{B}$	4. $\mathbf{m}\times\mathbf{B}$

Codes

	A	B	C	D		A	B	C	D
(a)	1	2	3	4	(b)	2	1	4	3
(c)	4	3	2	1	(d)	1	3	4	2

3 Figure shows the construction details of a moving coil galvanometer.

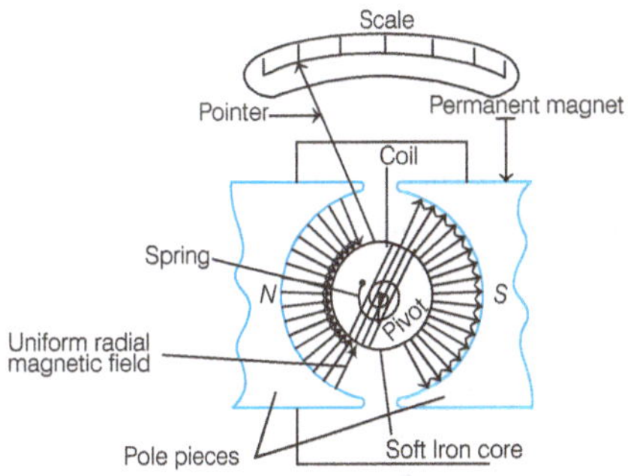

Match the Column I (parts) with Column II (effect) and select the correct answer from the codes given below. NCERT Pg. 130

Column I	Column II
A. Soft iron core	1. produces deflecting torque
B. Pole pieces	2. produces restoring torque
C. Spring	3. produces radial field
D. Coil	4. increases field strength

Codes

	A	B	C	D		A	B	C	D
(a)	1	2	3	4	(b)	1	2	4	3
(c)	2	1	3	4	(d)	4	3	2	1

Numerical Type Questions

1 An electron moving at a speed of 10 km/s in a straight line enters a uniform electric field where it experiences a constant acceleration of 2 km/s^2 in a direction opposite to its motion. It will come back to its initial point after a time .... s. NCERT Pg. 113

2 A proton carrying 1 MeV kinetic energy is moving in a circular path of radius R in uniform magnetic field. The energy of an α-particle to describe a circle of same radius in the same field is x MeV. The value of x is .... NCERT Pg. 113

3 A particle of charge -20×10^{-18} C moving with velocity 10 ms^{-1} along the X-axis enters a region where a magnetic field of induction **B** is along the Y-axis and an electric field of magnitude 10^4 Vm^{-1} is along the negative Z-axis. If the charged particle continues moving along the X-axis, the magnitude of **B** is $x \times 10^3 \text{ Wb m}^{-2}$. The value of x is .... NCERT Pg. 113

4 The magnetic field due to a current carrying circular loop of radius 3 cm at a point on the axis at a distance of 4 cm from the centre is 54 mT. Its value at the centre of the loop is x mT. The value of x is .... NCERT Pg. 116

5 A straight wire carrying a current of 16 A is bent into a semicircular arc of radius 2.5 cm as shown in the figure.

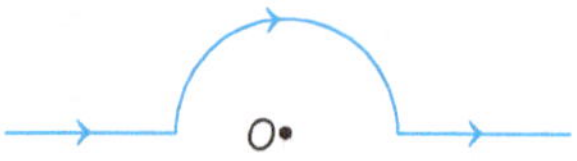

The magnetic field produced by the current at the centre (O) of the arc, is .... $\times 10^{-4}$ T. NCERT Pg. 117

6 Two short magnetic dipoles m_1 and m_2, each having magnetic moment of 2 Am^2 are placed at point O and P, respectively. The distance between OP is 1 m. The torque experienced by the magnetic dipole m_2 due to the presence of m_1 is .... $\times 10^{-7}$ Nm. NCERT Pg. 125

7 A galvanometer of resistance 50 Ω is connected to battery of 3 V along with a resistance of 2950 Ω in series. A full scale deflection of 30 divisions is obtained in the galvanometer. In order to reduce this deflection to 20 divisions, the resistance in series should be .... Ω. NCERT Pg. 130

NCERT Exemplar Questions

1 Two charged particles traverse identical helical paths in a completely opposite sense, in a uniform magnetic field $B = B_0\hat{\mathbf{k}}$. Then,

(a) they have equal z-components of momenta.
(b) they must have equal charges.
(c) they necessarily represent a particle, anti-particle pair.
(d) the charge to mass ratio satisfy $(e/m)_1 + (e/m)_2 = 0$.

2 Biot-Savart's law indicates that the moving electrons (velocity **v**) produce a magnetic field **B** such that

(a) **B** is perpendicular to **v**
(b) **B** is parallel to **v**
(c) it obeys inverse cube law
(d) it is along the line joining the electron and point of observation

3 A circular current loop of magnetic moment **M** is in an arbitrary orientation in an external magnetic field **B**. The work done to rotate the loop by 30° about an axis perpendicular to its plane is

(a) MB (b) $\sqrt{3}\,\dfrac{MB}{2}$ (c) $\dfrac{MB}{2}$ (d) zero

Past Exams Questions

NEET

1 A tightly wound 100 turns coil of radius 10 cm carries a current of 7 A. The magnitude of the magnetic field at the centre of the coil is (Take, permeability of free space as $4\pi \times 10^{-7}$ SI units) NCERT Pg. 121, NEET 2024

(a) 44 mT (b) 4.4 T
(c) 4.4 mT (d) 44 T

2 A wire carrying a current I along the positive X-axis has length L. It is kept in a magnetic field $\mathbf{B} = (2\hat{\mathbf{i}} + 3\hat{\mathbf{j}} - 4\hat{\mathbf{k}})$ T. The magnitude of the magnetic force acting on the wire is NCERT Pg. 110, NEET 2023

(a) $\sqrt{5}\, IL$ (b) $5IL$
(c) $\sqrt{3}\, IL$ (d) $3IL$

3 A thick current carrying cable of radius R carries current I uniformly distributed across its cross-section. The variation of magnetic field B due to the cable with the distance r from the axis of the cable is represented by NCERT Pg. 118, NEET 2021

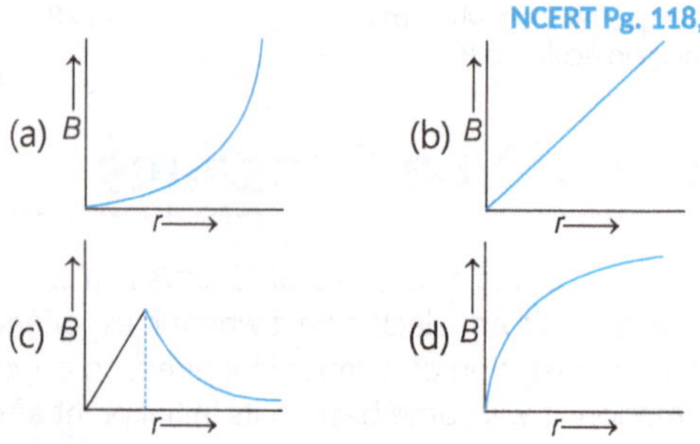

4 A long solenoid of radius 1 mm has 100 turns per mm. If 1 A current flows in the solenoid, the magnetic field strength at the centre of the solenoid is

NCERT Pg. 124, JEE Main 2024

(a) 12.56×10^{-2} T (b) 12.56×10^{-4} T
(c) 6.28×10^{-4} T (d) 6.28×10^{-2} T

5 An infinitely long straight conductor carries a current of 5 A as shown. An electron is moving with a speed of 10^5 m/s parallel to the conductor. The perpendicular distance between the electron and the conductor is 20 cm at an instant. Calculate the magnitude of the force experienced by the electron at that instant

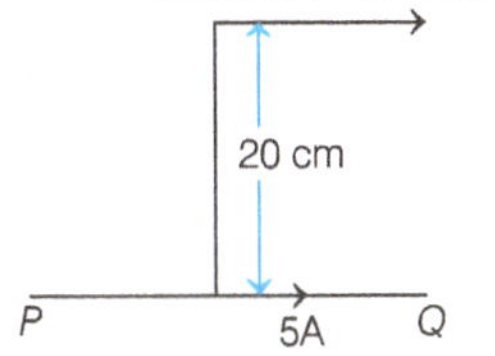

NCERT Pg. 123, NEET 2021

(a) 8×10^{-20} N (b) 4×10^{-20} N
(c) $8\pi \times 10^{-20}$ N (d) $4\pi \times 10^{-20}$ N

6 A long solenoid of 50 cm length having 100 turns carries a current of 2.5 A. The magnetic field at the centre of solenoid is
(Take, $\mu_0 = 4\pi \times 10^{-7}$ TmA^{-1}) NCERT Pg. 122, NEET 2020

(a) 3.14×10^{-4} T (b) 6.28×10^{-5} T
(c) 3.14×10^{-5} T (d) 6.28×10^{-4} T

7 A long straight wire of radius a carries a steady current I. The current is uniformly distributed over its cross-section. The ratio of the magnetic field B and B' at radial distances $a/2$ and $2a$ respectively, from the axis of the wire is NCERT Pg. 118, NEET 2016

(a) $\frac{1}{2}$ (b) 1 (c) 4 (d) $\frac{1}{4}$

8 A long wire carrying a steady current is bent into a circular loop of one turn. The magnetic field at the centre of the loop is B. It is then bent into a circular coil of n turns. The magnetic field at the centre of this coil of n turns will be NCERT Pg. 116, NEET 2016

(a) nB (b) n^2B (c) $2nB$ (d) $2n^2B$

9 A square loop $ABCD$ carrying a current i, is placed near and coplanar with a long straight conductor XY carrying a current I, the net force on the loop will be

NCERT Pg. 122, NEET 2016

(a) $\frac{\mu_0 Ii}{2\pi}$ (b) $\frac{2\mu_0 IiL}{3\pi}$ (c) $\frac{\mu_0 IiL}{2\pi}$ (d) $\frac{2\mu_0 Ii}{3\pi}$

10 A wire carrying current I has the shape as shown in adjoining figure. Linear parts of the wire are very long and parallel to X-axis while semicircular portion of radius R is lying in YZ-plane. Magnetic field at point O is

NCERT Pg. 117, AIPMT 2015

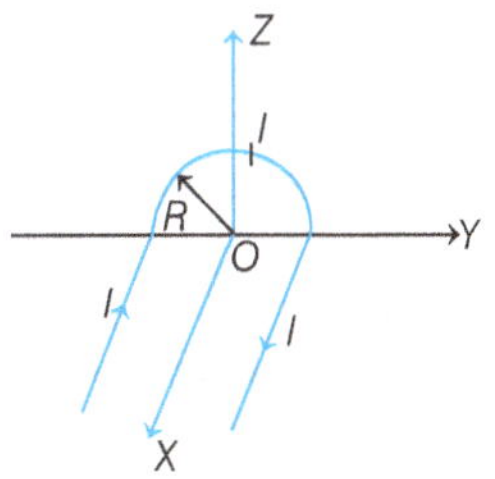

(a) $\mathbf{B} = \frac{\mu_0}{4\pi}\frac{I}{R}(\pi\hat{\mathbf{i}} + 2\hat{\mathbf{k}})$ (b) $\mathbf{B} = -\frac{\mu_0}{4\pi}\frac{I}{R}(\pi\hat{\mathbf{i}} - 2\hat{\mathbf{k}})$
(c) $\mathbf{B} = -\frac{\mu_0}{4\pi}\frac{I}{R}(\pi\hat{\mathbf{i}} + 2\hat{\mathbf{k}})$ (d) $\mathbf{B} = \frac{\mu_0}{4\pi}\frac{I}{R}(\pi\hat{\mathbf{i}} - 2\hat{\mathbf{k}})$

11 A rectangular coil of length 0.12 m and width 0.1 m having 50 turns of wire is suspended vertically in a uniform magnetic field of strength 0.2 Wb/m^2. The coil carries a current of 2 A. If the plane of the coil is inclined at an angle of 30° with the direction of the field, the torque required to keep the coil in stable equilibrium will be NCERT Pg. 125, AIPMT 2015

(a) 0.15 Nm (b) 0.20 Nm (c) 0.24 Nm (d) 0.12 Nm

JEE Main

12 A uniform magnetic field of 2×10^{-3}T acts along positive Y-direction. A rectangular loop of sides 20 cm and 10 cm with current of 5A is in Y-Z plane. The current is in anti-clockwise sense with reference to negative X-axis. Magnitude and direction of the torque is NCERT Pg. 124, JEE Main 2024

(a) 2×10^{-4} N-m along positive z-direction
(b) 2×10^{-4} N-m along negative z-direction
(c) 2×10^{-4} N-m along positive x-direction
(d) 2×10^{-4} N-m along positive y-direction

13 A long straight wire of radius a carries a steady current I. The current is uniformly distributed across its cross section. The ratio of the magnetic field at $\frac{a}{2}$ and $2a$ from axis of the wire is NCERT Pg. 117, JEE Main 2024

(a) 4 : 1 (b) 3 : 4
(c) 1 : 4 (d) 1 : 1

14 An electron is projected with uniform velocity along the axis inside a current carrying long solenoid.

NCERT Pg. 121, JEE Main 2024

Then,
(a) the electron path will be circular about the axis.
(b) the electron will experience a force at 45° to the axis and execute a helical path.
(c) the electron will be accelerated along the axis.
(d) the electron will continue to move with uniform velocity along the axis of the solenoid.

15 In a co-axial straight cable, the central conductor and the outer conductor carry equal currents in opposite directions. The magnetic field is zero.

NCERT Pg. 121, JEE Main 2024

(a) outside the cable
(b) in between the two conductors
(c) inside the inner conductor
(d) inside the outer conductor

16 A long conducting wire having a current I flowing through it, is bent into a circular coil of N turns. Then it is bent into a circular coil of n turns. The magnetic field is calculated at the centre of coils in both the cases. The ratio of the magnetic field in first case to that of second case is **NCERT Pg. 116, JEE Main 2023**

(a) $N^2 : n^2$ (b) $N : n$ (c) $n^2 : N^2$ (d) $n : N$

17 A coil of n number of turns would tightly in the form of a spiral with inner and outer radii r_1 and r_2 respectively. When a current of strength I is passed through the coil, the magnetic field at its centre will be

NCERT Pg. 122, JEE Main 2022

(a) $\dfrac{\mu_0 nI}{2(r_2 - r_1)}$ (b) $\dfrac{\mu_0 nI}{r_2}$

(c) $\dfrac{\mu_0 nI}{r_2 - r_1} \log_e \dfrac{r_1}{r_2}$ (d) $\dfrac{\mu_0 nI}{2(r_2 - r_1)} \log_e \dfrac{r_2}{r_1}$

18 There are two infinitely long straight current carrying conductors and they are held at right angles to each other, so that their common ends meet at the origin as shown in the figure given below. The ratio of current in both conductors is 1 : 1. The magnetic field at point P is

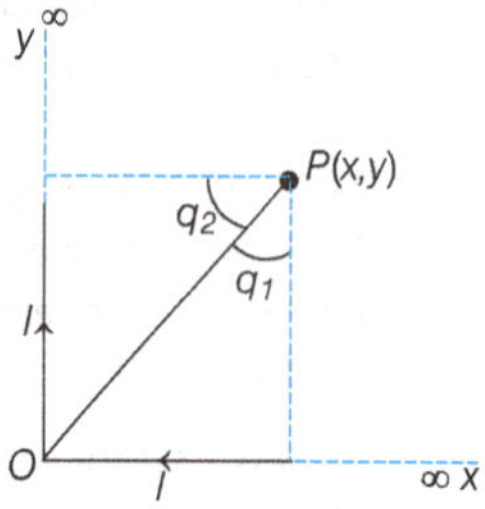

NCERT Pg. 123, JEE Main 2021

(a) $\dfrac{\mu_0 I}{4\pi xy}[\sqrt{x^2 + y^2} + (x + y)]$

(b) $\dfrac{\mu_0 I}{4\pi xy}[\sqrt{x^2 + y^2} - (x + y)]$

(c) $\dfrac{\mu_0 Ixy}{4\pi}[\sqrt{x^2 + y^2} - (x + y)]$

(d) $\dfrac{\mu_0 Ixy}{4\pi}[\sqrt{x^2 + y^2} + (x + y)]$

19 A wire carrying current I is bent in the shape $ABCDEFA$ as shown, where rectangle $ABCDA$ and $ADEFA$ are perpendicular to each other. If the sides of the rectangles are of lengths a and b, then the magnitude and direction of magnetic moment of the loop $ABCDEFA$ is **NCERT Pg. 126, JEE Main 2020**

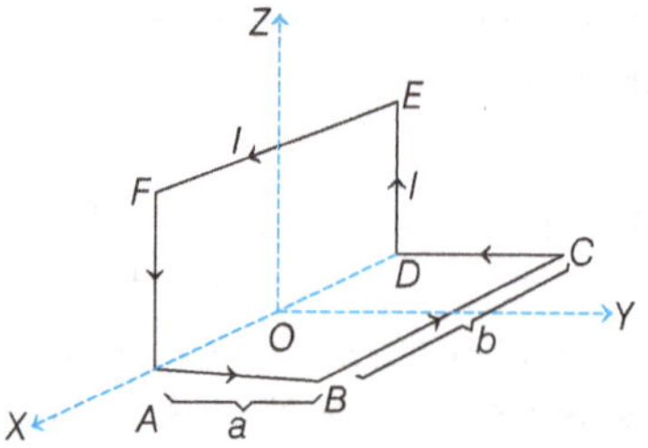

(a) abI, along $\left(\dfrac{\hat{\mathbf{j}}}{\sqrt{2}} + \dfrac{\hat{\mathbf{k}}}{\sqrt{2}}\right)$ (b) $\sqrt{2}\, abI$, along $\left(\dfrac{\hat{\mathbf{j}}}{\sqrt{2}} + \dfrac{\hat{\mathbf{k}}}{\sqrt{2}}\right)$

(c) $\sqrt{2}\, abI$, along $\left(\dfrac{\hat{\mathbf{j}}}{\sqrt{5}} + \dfrac{2\hat{\mathbf{k}}}{\sqrt{5}}\right)$ (d) abI, along $\left(\dfrac{\hat{\mathbf{j}}}{\sqrt{5}} + \dfrac{2\hat{\mathbf{k}}}{\sqrt{5}}\right)$

20 A particle having the same charge as of electron moves in a circular path of radius 0.5 cm under the influence of a magnetic field of 0.5 T. If an electric field of 100 V/m makes it to move in a straight path, then the mass of the particle is (Take, charge of electron $= 1.6 \times 10^{-19}$ C)

NCERT Pg. 110, JEE Main 2019

(a) 1.6×10^{-19} kg (b) 1.6×10^{-27} kg
(c) 9.1×10^{-31} kg (d) 2.0×10^{-24} kg

Skill Boosters

1 For the given figure, a charged sphere of mass m and charge q starts sliding from rest on a vertical fixed circular track of radius R from the position shown below. There exists a uniform and constant horizontal magnetic field of induction B.

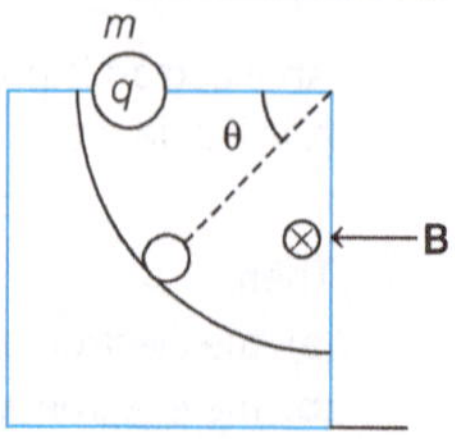

The maximum force exerted by the track on the sphere is

(a) mg (b) $3mg - qB\sqrt{2gR}$
(c) $3mg + qB\sqrt{2gR}$ (d) $mg - qB\sqrt{2gR}$

2 Magnetic force on a charged particle is given by $\mathbf{F}_m = q(\mathbf{v} \times \mathbf{B})$ and electrostatic force $\mathbf{F}_e = q\mathbf{E}$

A particle having charge $q = 1$ C and mass $m = 1$ kg is released from the rest at origin. There are electric and magnetic fields given by

$\mathbf{E} = (10\hat{\mathbf{i}})$ N/C for $x \le 1.8$ m and

$\mathbf{B} = (-5\hat{\mathbf{k}})$ T for $1.8\text{ m} \le x \le 2.4$ m

A screen is placed parallel to YZ-plane at $x = 3.0$ m. Neglect gravity forces.

Time after which the particle will collide the screen is

(a) $\frac{1}{5}\left(3+\frac{\pi}{6}+\frac{1}{\sqrt{3}}\right)$ s (b) $\frac{1}{5}\left(6+\frac{\pi}{3}+\sqrt{3}\right)$ s

(c) $\frac{1}{3}\left(5+\frac{\pi}{6}+\frac{1}{\sqrt{3}}\right)$ s (d) $\frac{1}{3}\left(6+\frac{\pi}{18}+\sqrt{3}\right)$ s

3 From a cylinder of radius R, a cylinder of radius $R/2$ is removed as shown in the figure. Current flowing in the remaining cylinder is I. Magnetic field strength is

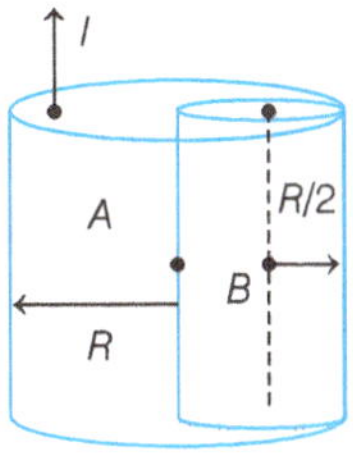

(a) zero at point A

(b) zero at point B

(c) $\frac{\mu_0 I}{3\pi R}$ at point A

(d) $\frac{\mu_0 I}{\pi R}$ at point B

4 A steady current I goes through a wire loop PQR having shape of a right angled triangle with $PQ = 3x$, $PR = 4x$ and $QR = 5x$. The magnitude of the magnetic field at P due to this loop is

(a) $\frac{\mu_0 I}{48\pi x}$ (b) $7\left(\frac{\mu_0 I}{48\pi x}\right)$ (c) $7\left(\frac{\mu_0 I}{\pi x}\right)$ (d) $7\left(\frac{\mu_0 I}{48x}\right)$

5 A current I flows around a closed path in the horizontal plane of the circle as shown in the figure. The path consists of eight arcs with alternating radii r and $2r$. Each segment of arc subtends equal angle at the common centre P. The magnetic field produced by current path at point P is

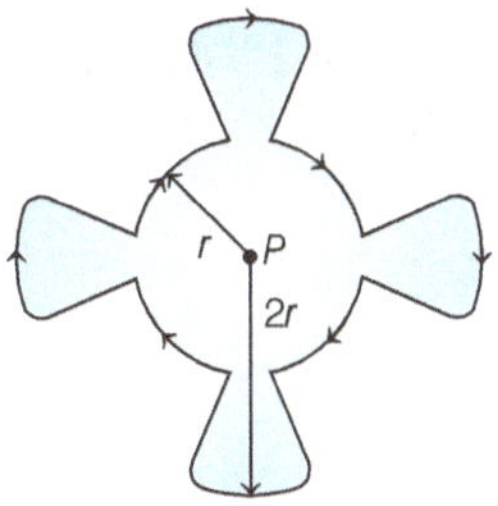

(a) $\frac{3}{8}\cdot\frac{\mu_0 I}{r}$; perpendicular to the plane of the paper and directed inwards

(b) $\frac{3}{8}\cdot\frac{\mu_0 I}{r}$; perpendicular to the plane of the paper and outwards

(c) $\frac{1}{8}\cdot\frac{\mu_0 I}{r}$; perpendicular to the plane of the paper and inwards

(d) $\frac{1}{8}\cdot\frac{\mu_0 I}{r}$; perpendicular to the plane of the paper and outwards

6 Find the magnetic field at point P due to arrangement as shown in the figure.

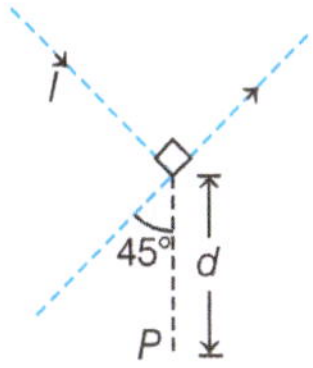

(a) $\frac{\mu_0 I}{\sqrt{2}\,\pi d}\left(1-\frac{1}{\sqrt{2}}\right)$ (b) $\frac{2\mu_0 I}{\sqrt{2}\,\pi d}$

(c) $\frac{\mu_0 I}{\sqrt{2}\,\pi d}$ (d) $\frac{\mu_0 I}{\sqrt{2}\,\pi d}\left(1+\frac{1}{\sqrt{2}}\right)$

7 A charged particle of charge q and mass m enters a uniform magnetic field B at an angle of θ shown in the figure.

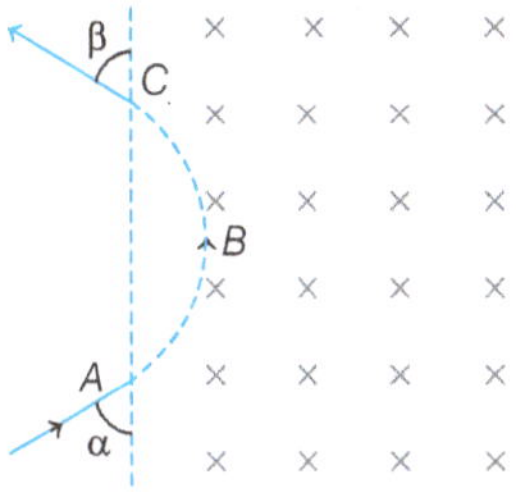

Time spent by the particle in magnetic field is

(a) $\frac{2\,m\alpha}{Bq}$ (b) $\frac{m\alpha}{Bq}$ (c) $\frac{4\,m\alpha}{Bq}$ (d) $\frac{1}{2}\frac{m\alpha}{Bq}$

8 A rectangular coil of N turns pivoted about a vertical axis carrying a current I is placed in the region of a uniform horizontal magnetic field B. When plane of coil makes an angle θ with magnetic field, torque required to percent it rotating is τ_1. When coil rotates through 90°, then torque required will be τ_2. Magnitude of magnetic field B will be

(a) $\frac{\sqrt{\tau_1^2+\tau_2^2}}{NIA}$ (b) $\frac{2\sqrt{\tau_1^2+\tau_2^2}}{NIA}$

(c) $\frac{\tau_1+\tau_2}{2(NIA)}$ (d) $\frac{\tau_1+\tau_2}{NIA}$

9 For the figure, a coil of single turn is wound on a sphere of radius r and mass m. The plane of the coil is parallel to the inclined plane and lies in the equatorial plane of the sphere. If the sphere is in rotational equilibrium, then the value of B is (current in the coil is I)

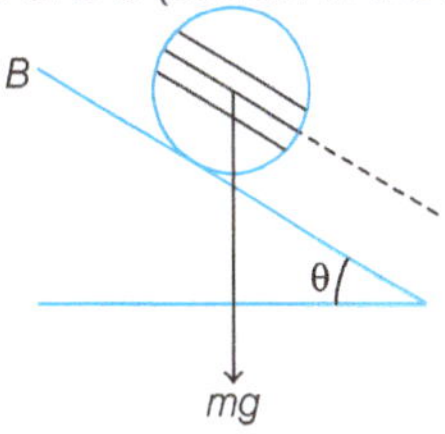

(a) $\frac{mg}{\pi I r}$ (b) $\frac{mg\sin\theta}{\pi I}$

(c) $\frac{mg\sin\theta}{\pi I r}$ (d) None of these

10 A magnetic field $\mathbf{B} = B_0\hat{\mathbf{j}}$ exists in the region $a < x < 2a$ and $\mathbf{B} = -B_0\hat{\mathbf{j}}$ in the region $2a < x < 3a$, where B_0 is a positive constant. A positive point charge moving with a velocity $\mathbf{v} = v_0\hat{\mathbf{i}}$, where v_0 is a positive constant enters the magnetic field at $x = a$. The trajectory of the charge in this region can be like

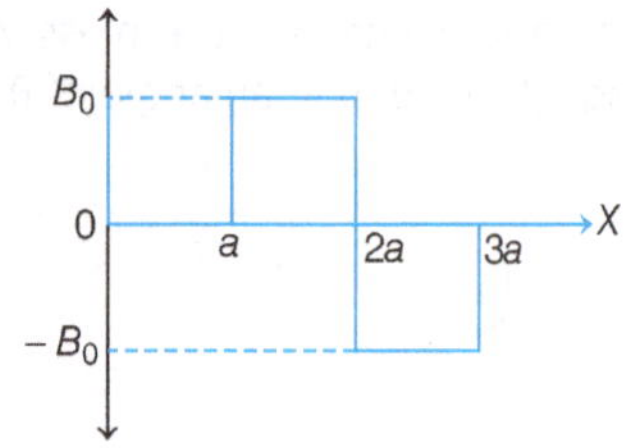

(a)
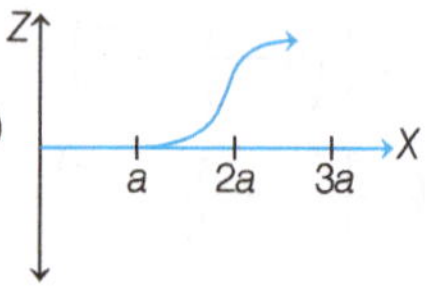

(b)
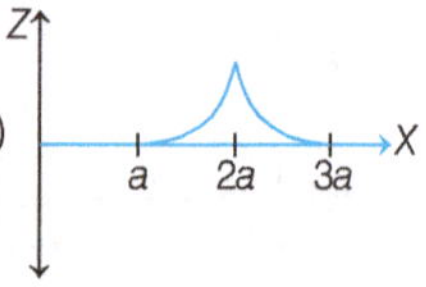

(c)
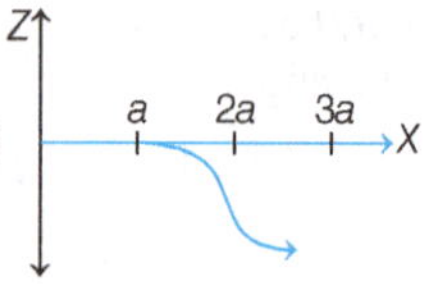

(d)
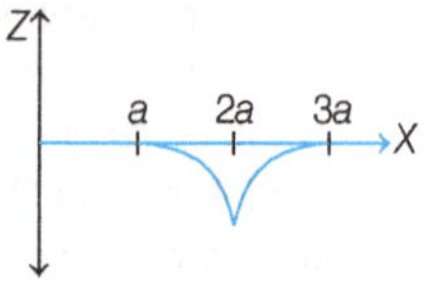

Correct Codes

Topical Questions

1 (a)	2 (b)	3 (a)	4 (a)	5 (d)	6 (c)	7 (a)	8 (c)	9 (d)	10 (a)
11 (a)	12 (b)	13 (d)	14 (b)	15 (b)	16 (a)	17 (d)	18 (a)	19 (b)	20 (b)
21 (b)	22 (d)	23 (d)	24 (c)	25 (b)	26 (d)	27 (c)	28 (c)	29 (a)	30 (a)
31 (b)	32 (c)	33 (c)	34 (c)	35 (a)	36 (c)	37 (d)	38 (d)	39 (b)	40 (d)
41 (a)	42 (d)	43 (c)	44 (b)	45 (a)	46 (d)	47 (a)	48 (a)	49 (d)	50 (c)
51 (d)	52 (b)	53 (a)	54 (c)	55 (c)	56 (a)	57 (d)	58 (c)	59 (c)	60 (a)
61 (d)	62 (a)	63 (a)	64 (c)	65 (a)	66 (b)	67 (d)	68 (a)	69 (b)	70 (d)
71 (d)	72 (a)	73 (b)	74 (d)	75 (b)	76 (b)	77 (d)	78 (a)	79 (a)	80 (d)
81 (d)									

Assertion and Reason Questions

1 (a)	2 (a)	3 (d)	4 (a)	5 (d)	6 (b)	7 (d)	8 (c)	9 (c)	10 (b)

Statement Based Questions

1 (b)	2 (d)	3 (a)	4 (d)	5 (c)	6 (d)	7 (d)	8 (c)

Matching Type Questions

1 (a)	2 (c)	3 (d)

Numerical Type Questions

1 (10)	2 (1)	3 (1)	4 (250)	5 (2)	6 (4)	7 (4450)

NCERT Exemplar Questions

1 (d)	2 (a)	3 (d)

Past Exams Questions

1 (c)	2 (b)	3 (c)	4 (a)	5 (a)	6 (d)	7 (b)	8 (b)	9 (d)	10 (c)
11 (b)	12 (a)	13 (d)	14 (d)	15 (a)	16 (a)	17 (d)	18 (a)	19 (b)	20 (d)

Skill Boosters

1 (b)	2 (a)	3 (c)	4 (b)	5 (a)	6 (a)	7 (a)	8 (a)	9 (a)	10 (a)

Step by Step

Decoding the Questions

Concept Builders

1 True (T) 2 velocity

3 Radial 4 True (T)

5 n^2 times 6 $B = \frac{\mu_0}{4\pi} \frac{ev}{r^2}$

7 contract 8 not equally

9 False (F) 10 moving charge

11 zero, maximum

12 True (T) 13 False (F)

14 force, torque

15 90° 16 False (F)

17 zero, infinite 18 lower

19 False (F) 20 False (F)

Topical Questions

1 (*a*) The electric field can convey energy and momentum and is not established instantaneously but takes finite time to propagate.

The magnetic field of several sources is the vector addition of magnetic field of each individual source.

The Lorentz force depends on q, **v** and **B**. Force on a negative charge is opposite to that on a positive charge.

2 (*b*) When a point charge q is moving with velocity **v** and located at **r** at a given time t in presence of both the electric field **E**(**r**) and the magnetic field **B**(**r**), then it experiences a force called Lorentz force and given by

$$\mathbf{F} = \mathbf{F}_{\text{electric}} + \mathbf{F}_{\text{magnetic}}$$
$$\mathbf{F} = q[\mathbf{E}(\mathbf{r}) + \mathbf{v} \times \mathbf{B}(\mathbf{r})]$$

3 (*a*) Given, velocity of proton,
$\mathbf{v} = 2\hat{\mathbf{i}}$ m/s

Magnetic field, $\mathbf{B} = (\hat{\mathbf{i}} + 3\hat{\mathbf{j}} + 4\hat{\mathbf{k}})\,\mu\text{T}$
Electric field, $\mathbf{E} = 10\hat{\mathbf{i}}\,\mu$ V/m

Charge on proton, $q = 1.6 \times 10^{-19}$ C

Lorentz force,

$$\mathbf{F} = q\mathbf{E} + q(\mathbf{v} \times \mathbf{B}) = q[\mathbf{E} + (\mathbf{v} \times \mathbf{B})]$$
$$= 1.6 \times 10^{-19} [10 \times 10^{-6}\,\hat{\mathbf{i}} + 2\hat{\mathbf{i}} \times (\hat{\mathbf{i}} + 3\hat{\mathbf{j}} + 4\hat{\mathbf{k}}) \times 10^{-6}]$$
$$\mathbf{F} = 1.6 \times 10^{-25} \times [10\hat{\mathbf{i}} - 8\hat{\mathbf{j}} + 6\hat{\mathbf{k}}] \text{ N}$$
$$|F| = 1.6 \times 10^{-25} \times \sqrt{(10)^2 + (-8)^2 + (6)^2}$$
$$= 22.6 \times 10^{-25} \text{ N}$$

4 (*a*) $F = qvB,\ E = \frac{1}{2} mv^2$

$$F = qB\sqrt{\frac{2E}{m}} = 1.6 \times 10^{-19} \times 2.5 \times \sqrt{\frac{2 \times 2 \times 10^6 \times 1.6 \times 10^{-19}}{1.6 \times 10^{-27}}}$$
$$F = 8 \times 10^{-12} \text{ N}$$

5 (*d*) When a charged particle is kept stationary ($v = 0$) in the strong magnetic field, then no force acts on the charged particle.

i.e., $F = Bqv = Bq \times 0$

$F = 0$

Hence, when an electron is kept in a strong magnetic field, then electron remains stationary at same position.

6 (*c*) The magnetic force must be vertically upward to prevent the wire from falling under gravity. As the current in the horizontal wire is from north to south, so according to right hand screw rule, the magnetic field should be from west to east, i.e., towards east.

7 (*a*) Net force on the proton,

$$F = Bqv\sin\theta$$
$$= 1.5 \times 1.6 \times 10^{-19} \times 2 \times 10^7 \times \sin 30°$$
$$= 2.4 \times 10^{-12} \text{ N}$$

8 (*c*) Direction of force on a moving charge in magnetic field can be determine by right hand-rule.

As we know, the direction of **F** is the direction of cross product of velocity **v** and magnetic field **B**, which is perpendicular to the plane containing **v** and **B**.

So for positive charge it acts upward and for negative charge it acts downward, hence diagram (c) is correct.

9 (*d*) As we know, force, $F = qvB$

$\therefore$ Magnetic field, $B = \frac{F}{qv}$

$$= \frac{10^{-10}}{10^{-12} \times 10^5}$$
$$= 10^{-3} \text{ Wb m}^{-2} \text{ or T}$$

So, according to right hand rule, as particle is moving in x-direction and experiences a force in y-direction, then magnetic field is acting along z-direction.

10 (*a*) $F = q(\mathbf{v} \times \mathbf{B}) = qvB\sin\theta$

$$= 1.6 \times 10^{-19} \times 10^6 \times 0.2 \times \sin 90°$$
$$\therefore F = 3.2 \times 10^{-14} \text{ N}$$

11 (*a*) $\mathbf{F} = q(\mathbf{E} + \mathbf{v} \times \mathbf{B})$

$$= 2\,[2\hat{\mathbf{j}} + \{(2\hat{\mathbf{i}} + 3\hat{\mathbf{j}}) \times 5\hat{\mathbf{k}}\}]$$
$$\Rightarrow \mathbf{F} = (30\hat{\mathbf{i}} - 16\hat{\mathbf{j}}) \text{ N}$$

12 (*b*) $F = qvB\sin\theta$

$$= (1.6 \times 10^{-19}) \times (10^6) \times (0 \cdot 1) \sin 90°$$
$$F = 1.6 \times 10^{-14} \text{ N}$$

13 (*d*) Using the Fleming's left hand rule, the direction of force can be determined. According to it, the force experienced will be in south direction.

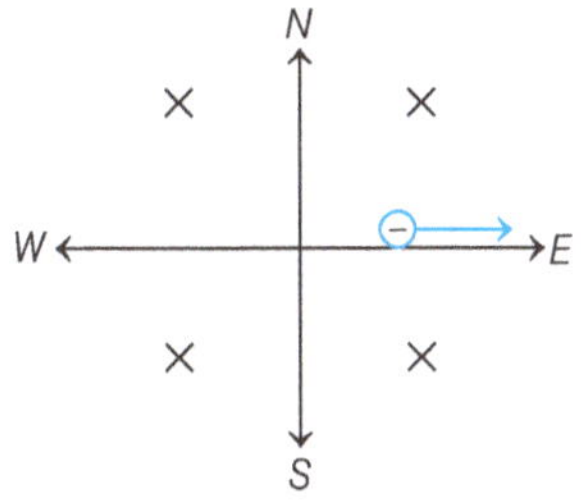

14 (*b*) A straight wire of mass 200 g and length 1.5 m carries a current of 2A. It is held in a mid-air by a uniform horizontal magnetic field. There is an upward force **F** of magnitude IlB. For mid-air suspension, this must be balanced by the force due to gravity as shown in figure.

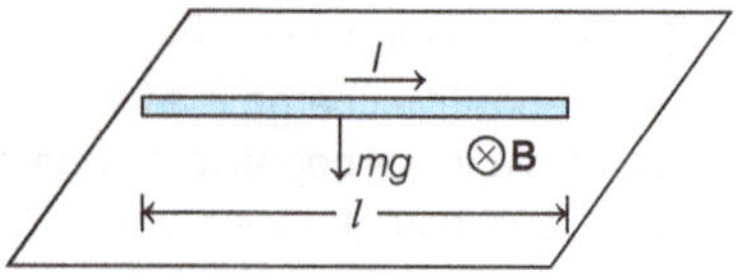

$$mg = IlB \quad [\because m = 200\text{ g} = 0.2\text{ kg}]$$

$$\Rightarrow \quad B = \frac{mg}{Il} = \frac{0.2 \times 9.8}{2 \times 1.5} = 0.65\text{ T}$$

15 (*b*) During the circular motion of accelerated electron in the presence of magnetic field, its radius is given by

$$r = \frac{mv}{Be} = \frac{\sqrt{2meV}}{eB}$$

where, v is velocity and V is voltage.

$$r = \frac{\sqrt{2 \times 9.1 \times 10^{-31} \times 1.6 \times 10^{-19} \times 500}}{1.6 \times 10^{-19} \times 100 \times 10^{-3}}$$

$$r = 7.5 \times 10^{-4}\text{ m}$$

16 (*a*) Radius of path, $r = \frac{mv}{qB}$

Given, $r_a > r_b$

$$\Rightarrow \quad \frac{m_a v_a}{qB} > \frac{m_b v_b}{qB} \quad [\because q_a = q_b \text{ (given)}]$$

$$\Rightarrow \quad m_a v_a > m_b v_b$$

17 (*d*) Radius of the circular orbit that a charged particle traverses is given as

$$\because \quad r = \frac{mv}{Bq} = \frac{\sqrt{2mK}}{Bq}$$

where, K is kinetic energy.

When B is same,we can write

$$r \propto \frac{\sqrt{2mK}}{q}$$

$$\Rightarrow \quad \frac{r_{\text{proton}}}{r_{\text{deuteron}}} = \sqrt{\frac{m_p K_p}{m_d K_d}}$$

$$\Rightarrow \quad \frac{0.5}{0.5} = \sqrt{\frac{m_p K_p}{2m_p K_d}} \quad [\because r_p = r_d = 0.5\text{ m}]$$

[$\because$ mass of deuteron $= 2 \times$ mass of proton]

$$1 = \frac{m_p K_p}{2m_p K_d}$$

$$K_p = 2K_d \quad [\because \text{Given, } K_d = 50\text{ keV}]$$

$$\Rightarrow K_p = 2 \times 50 = 100\text{ keV}$$

18 (*a*) As we know that, radius of circle,

$$r = \frac{mv}{qB}$$

$$K = \frac{1}{2}mv^2$$

$$r = \frac{\sqrt{2mK}}{qB} \quad \Rightarrow r \propto \frac{\sqrt{m}}{q}$$

$$q_\alpha = 2q_p \quad \Rightarrow \quad m_\alpha = 4\,m_p$$

$$q_d = q_p \quad \Rightarrow \quad m_d = 2\,m_p$$

$$r_\alpha = \frac{\sqrt{4m_p}}{2q_p} \propto \frac{\sqrt{m_p}}{q_p} = r_p$$

$$r_d = \frac{\sqrt{2m_p}}{q_p} \propto \sqrt{2}\,\frac{\sqrt{m_p}}{q_p} = \sqrt{2}r_p$$

$$r_\alpha = r_p < r_d$$

19 (*b*) Given, speed, $v = 3 \times 10^7\text{ ms}^{-1}$ and magnetic field,

$$B = 6 \times 10^{-4}\text{ T}$$

Radius,

$$r = \frac{mv}{qB} = \frac{9 \times 10^{-31} \times 3 \times 10^7}{1.6 \times 10^{-19} \times 6 \times 10^{-4}}$$

$$= 28 \times 10^{-2}\text{m}$$

Frequency of an electron,

$$\nu = \frac{v}{2\pi r} = \frac{3 \times 10^7}{2 \times \frac{22}{7} \times 28 \times 10^{-2}}$$

$$= 17\text{ MHz}$$

20 (*b*) The particle moves in a circular path of radius r in the magnetic field. It can just enter the region $x > b$ for $r \geq (b - a)$.

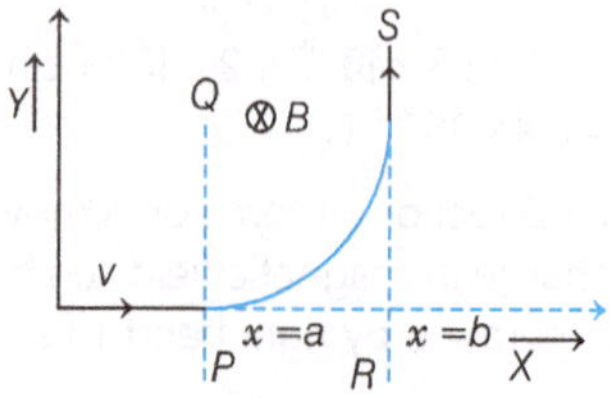

Now, $r = \frac{mv}{qB} \geq (b - a)$

or $v \geq \frac{q(b - a)B}{m}$

$$\Rightarrow \quad v_{\min} = \frac{q(b - a)B}{m}$$

21 (*b*) As, component of velocity **v** is along magnetic field **B**. So, path is helical.

Radius of a helix,

$$r = \frac{mv_\perp}{Bq}$$

$$= \frac{1.67 \times 10^{-27} \times 2 \times 10^6 \sin 30^\circ}{0.104 \times 1.6 \times 10^{-19}}$$

$$\Rightarrow r = \frac{0.2}{2}\text{ m} = 0.1\text{ m}$$

Time period,

$$T = \frac{2\pi m}{Bq} = \frac{2\pi \times 1.67 \times 10^{-27}}{0.104 \times 1.6 \times 10^{-19}}$$

$$= 2\pi \times 10^{-7}\text{ s}$$

22 (*d*) Given, magnetic field,

$B = 6.28 \times 10^{-4}$ T

and mass of proton,

$$m_p = 1.67 \times 10^{-27}\text{ kg}$$

As we know that, frequency of proton,

$$f = \frac{1}{T} = \frac{qB}{2\pi m}$$

$$= \frac{1.6 \times 10^{-19} \times 6.28 \times 10^{-4}}{2 \times \frac{22}{7} \times 1.67 \times 10^{-27}} \approx 10^4\text{ Hz}$$

23 (*d*) When a charge moving at an angle (other than 0° or 90°) in a magnetic field, then it will move in a helical path as shown in option (d).

24 (c) For an ionised gas, as the electric field is switched ON, positive ions will start to move along positive x-direction and negative ions along negative x-direction. Current associated with motion of both types of ions is along positive x-direction.

According to Fleming's left hand rule, force on both types of ions will be along negative y-direction ($-y$ direction).

25 (b) If electric and magnetic fields are E and B respectively, then

Velocity of a particle,

$$v = \frac{E}{B} = \frac{\sigma}{\varepsilon_0 B}$$

[$\because$ for parallel plate capacitor, $E = \frac{\sigma}{\varepsilon_0}$]

$\therefore$ Time taken by electron to pass through the region,

$$t = \frac{l}{v} = \frac{\varepsilon_0 lB}{\sigma}$$

26 (d) Radius in magnetic fields of circular orbit, $R = \frac{mv}{qB} = \frac{\sqrt{2mE}}{qB}$

$$\left[\begin{aligned} &\because \text{Kinetic energy}, E = \frac{1}{2}mv^2 \\ &\therefore mv = \sqrt{2mE} \end{aligned}\right]$$

and total energy of a moving particle in a circular orbit,

$$E = \frac{q^2B^2R^2}{2m}$$

For a proton entering in a region of magnetic field,

$$E_1 = \frac{e^2 \times B^2 \times R^2}{2 \times m_p} \quad \text{...(i)}$$

where, m_p is the mass of proton. Similarly, for an α-particle moving in a uniform magnetic field,

$$E_2 = \frac{(2e)^2 \times B^2 \times R^2}{2 \times (4m_p)}$$

$$(\because m_\alpha = 4m_p) \text{...(ii)}$$

Dividing Eq. (ii) by Eq. (i), we get

$$\frac{E_2}{E_1} = \frac{(2e)^2 \times B^2 \times R^2}{2 \times (4m_p)} \times \frac{2 \times m_p}{e^2 \times B^2 \times R^2}$$

$$\frac{E_2}{E_1} = 1$$

$$\Rightarrow \quad E_2 = E_1 = 1 \text{ MeV}$$

27 (c) The radius of electron moving in a magnetic field is given by

$$r = \frac{mv}{qB} \Rightarrow r \propto v$$

So, as the speed of the electron is doubled, the radius will also be doubled for the electron.

$$\therefore \quad r_2 = 2r_1 = 2 \times 2$$

$$r_2 = 4 \text{ cm}$$

28 (c) As in case of moving charged particle in magnetic field $\mathbf{F}_{mag} \perp \mathbf{v}$, hence power associated will be zero.

29 (a) The magnitude of magnetic field,

$$|d\mathbf{B}| = \frac{\mu_0}{4\pi} \cdot \frac{I\,dl \sin\theta}{r^2}$$

Given, $\Delta dl = \Delta x = 10^{-2}$ m, $I = 10$ A,

$r = 0.5$ m,

$\theta = 90°$

$\Rightarrow \sin 90° = 1$

$$\Rightarrow \quad |d\mathbf{B}| = \frac{10^{-7} \times 10 \times 10^{-2}}{25 \times 10^{-2}}$$

or $\quad \mathbf{B} = 4 \times 10^{-8}\hat{\mathbf{k}}$ T

Since, $dl \times \mathbf{r} = \Delta x\hat{\mathbf{i}} \times y\hat{\mathbf{j}}$

$= y\,\Delta x\,(\hat{\mathbf{i}} \times \hat{\mathbf{j}}) = y\,\Delta x\hat{\mathbf{k}}$

So, the direction of the field is in the + z-direction.

Therefore, $d\mathbf{B} = 4 \times 10^{-8}\hat{\mathbf{k}}$T

30 (a) Magnetic field due to the current carrying coil at the centre is given as $B = \frac{\mu_0 NI}{2R}$

For coil with $R = 5$ cm, $N = 50$, $I = 2$ A,

$$|\mathbf{B}_1| = \frac{4\pi \times 10^{-7} \times 50 \times 2}{2 \times 5 \times 10^{-2}}$$

$$= 4\pi \times 10^{-4} \text{ T}$$

Similarly, for coil with $R = 10$ cm, $I = 2$A, $N = 100$,

$$|\mathbf{B}_2| = \frac{4\pi \times 10^{-7} \times 100 \times 2}{2 \times 10 \times 10^{-2}}$$

$$= 4\pi \times 10^{-4} \text{ T}$$

$\Rightarrow |\mathbf{B}_1| = |\mathbf{B}_2| = 4\pi \times 10^{-4}$ T

If currents are in same sense, then

$B_{net} = |\mathbf{B}_1| + |\mathbf{B}_2| = 8\pi \times 10^{-4}$ T.

If currents are in opposite sense,

$B_{net} = |\mathbf{B}_1| - |\mathbf{B}_2| = 0$.

31 (b) Statement given in option (b) is incorrect and it can be corrected as,

The lines of constant magnitude of magnetic field form concentric circles called magnetic field lines.

32 (c) Given, current, $I = 12$ A,

radius, $R = 2$ cm $= 2 \times 10^{-2}$ m

Magnetic field at the centre of current carrying circular loop,

$$B_c = \frac{\mu_0 I}{2R} = \frac{\mu_0}{2\pi} \cdot \frac{\pi I}{R}$$

Magnetic field at the centre of semi-circular loop,

$$B = \frac{B_c}{2} = \frac{\mu_0}{4\pi}\frac{\pi I}{R}$$

$$= 10^{-7} \times \frac{3.14 \times 12}{2 \times 10^{-2}}$$

$$= 1.9 \times 10^{-4} \text{ T}$$

Thus, $\mathbf{B}$ is 1.9×10^{-4} T normal to the plane of the paper going into it, i.e., ⊗.

33 (c) Given, radius of identical circular loops,

$$R = 10 \text{ cm} = 10^{-1} \text{ m}$$

Current, $I = \frac{7}{2}$ A

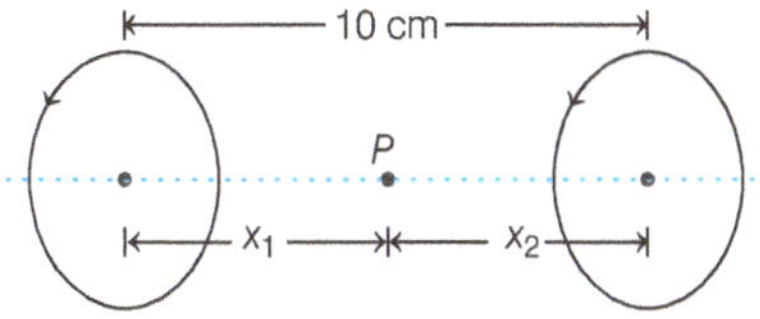

Distance from both circular loops at point P,

$$x_1 = x_2 = x = 5 \text{ cm} = 5 \times 10^{-2} \text{ m}$$

The net magnitude of magnetic field is

i.e., $B = B_1 + B_2$

$$= \frac{\mu_0 IR^2}{2(R^2 + x^2)^{3/2}} + \frac{\mu_0 IR^2}{2(R^2 + x^2)^{3/2}}$$

$$= \frac{\mu_0 IR^2}{(R^2 + x^2)^{3/2}}$$

$$= \frac{\mu_0 \times (7/2) \times (10^{-1})^2}{[(0.1)^2 + (0.05)^2]^{3/2}} = \frac{56\mu_0}{\sqrt{5}} \text{ T}$$

34 (c) Magnetic field at the centre of a current-carrying conductor,

$$B_c = \frac{\mu_0 I}{2r} \quad \text{...(i)}$$

Magnetic field at axial point due to a current-carrying conductor at distance of r,

$$B_a = \frac{\mu_0 I r^2}{2(r^2+d^2)^{3/2}}$$

$$\Rightarrow \quad B_a = \frac{\mu_0 I r^2}{2(2r^2)^{3/2}} \quad (\because d = r)\ldots\text{(ii)}$$

Now, $\dfrac{B_c}{B_a} = \dfrac{\mu_0 I}{2r} \times \dfrac{2(2r^2)^{3/2}}{\mu_0 I r^2} = 2\sqrt{2}$

$$B_c : B_a = 2\sqrt{2} : 1$$

35 (*a*) Magnetic field at the centre of the coil is given by

$$B = \frac{\mu_0 I}{2a}$$

$$B = \frac{(4\pi \times 10^{-7} \times 3)}{(2 \times 0.4)}$$

$$B = 4.7 \times 10^{-6}\ \text{T}$$

36 (*c*) By Ampere's circuital rule, Magnetic field due to wire at a distance $\frac{a}{3}$ from centre,

$$B_1 = \frac{\mu_0}{2\pi}\frac{i\left(\frac{a}{3}\right)}{a^2} = \frac{\mu_0 i}{6\pi a}$$

and magnetic field at a distance $2a$ from centre,

$$B_2 = \frac{\mu_0 i}{2\pi(2a)} = \frac{\mu_0 i}{4\pi a}$$

Ratio of magnetic fields will be

$$\frac{B_1}{B_2} = \frac{\left(\frac{\mu_0 i}{6\pi a}\right)}{\left(\frac{\mu_0 i}{4\pi a}\right)} = \frac{2}{3}$$

37 (*d*) The magnitude of the magnetic field at centre of coil is

$$B = \frac{\mu_0 N I}{2R}$$

$$= \frac{4\pi \times 10^{-7} \times 10^2 \times 1}{2 \times 10^{-1}}$$

$$= 2\pi \times 10^{-4}$$

$$= 6.28 \times 10^{-4}\ \text{T}$$

38 (*d*) Ampere's circuital law holds for steady currents which are not accelerated with time.

39 (*b*) As we know that

$$J = \frac{I}{A} = \frac{I}{\pi R^2}$$

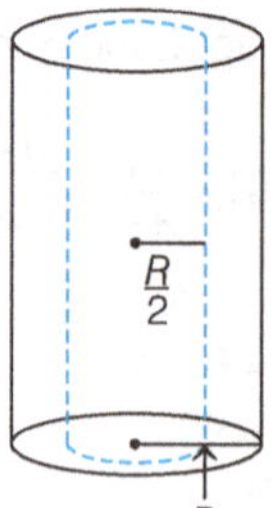

Current at a distance r is given by

$$I_r = \frac{I}{\pi R^2} \times \pi r^2 = I\left(\frac{r}{R}\right)^2$$

From Ampere's circuital law

$$\oint B \cdot dl = \mu_0 I_r$$

$$\Rightarrow \quad B \cdot 2\pi r = \mu_0 I\left(\frac{r}{R}\right)^2$$

$$B = \frac{\mu_0 I}{2\pi r}\frac{r^2}{R^2} = \frac{\mu_0 I}{2\pi R^2} \times r$$

$$B = \frac{\mu_0 I}{2\pi R^2} \times \frac{R}{2} \qquad \left[\because r = \frac{R}{2}\right]$$

$$\therefore \quad B = \frac{\mu_0 I}{4\pi R}$$

40 (*d*) Given, $n = 20$ turns cm^{-1}

$= 20 \times 100$ turns m^{-1}

$= 2000$ turns m^{-1}

and magnetic field, $B = 20$ m T

$= 20 \times 10^{-3}$ T

By the formula, magnetic field,

$$B = \mu_0 n I$$

or $20 \times 10^{-3} = 4\pi \times 10^{-7} \times 2000 \times I$

or $$I = \frac{20 \times 10^{-3}}{4\pi \times 10^{-7} \times 2000}$$

$$\Rightarrow \quad I \simeq 8\ \text{A}$$

41 (*a*) Given, length, $l = 0.5$ m, radius, $r = 1$ cm $= 0.01$ m and current, $I = 5$ A.

Number of turns per unit length is

$$n = \frac{500}{0.5} = 1000\ \text{turns m}^{-1}$$

$\because \quad l/r = 50$, i.e. $l >> r$.

Hence, we can use the long solenoid formula,

Magnetic field, $B = \mu_0 n I$

$= 4\pi \times 10^{-7} \times 10^3 \times 5$

$= 6.28 \times 10^{-3}$ T

42 (*d*) Given, $B = 0.168$ T

$r = 0.01$ m

$I = 2$A

By using, $B = \mu_0 n I$

$$\Rightarrow \quad B = \frac{\mu_0 N}{l} I$$

$$\Rightarrow \quad N = \frac{Bl}{\mu_0 I}$$

Now, the total length of the wire

$$L = N \times 2\pi r = \frac{B \cdot l \times 2\pi r}{\mu_0 I}$$

$$= \frac{0.168 \times 1.4 \times 2\pi \times 0.01 \times 10}{4\pi \times 10^{-7} \times 2}$$

$$\Rightarrow L = 58800\ \text{m}$$

43 (*c*) Statement given in option (c) is incorrect and it can be corrected as, the field outside the solenoid approaches zero and everywhere inside becomes parallel to the axis. Rest statements are correct.

44 (*b*) Here, $B = \mu_0 n I$

$$\frac{B_1}{B_2} = \frac{n_1}{n_2} \cdot \frac{I_1}{I_2}$$

$$\Rightarrow \frac{6.28 \times 10^{-2}}{B_2} = \frac{200}{100} \times \frac{I}{I} \times 3$$

$$B_2 = 1.05 \times 10^{-2}\ \text{Wb/m}^2$$

45 (*a*) Given, $d = 9$ cm $= 9 \times 10^{-2}$ m

$I = 6$ A

Magnetic field due to a straight wire is given by

$$B = \frac{\mu_0 I}{2\pi d} = \frac{4\pi \times 10^{-7} \times 6}{2\pi \times 9 \times 10^{-2}}$$

$$\therefore \quad B = 1.33 \times 10^{-5}\ \text{T}$$

46 (*d*) Magnetic field at point *P* is given by

$$B_P = \left(\frac{\mu_0 I_1}{2\pi r_1}\right) + \left(\frac{\mu_0 I_2}{2\pi r_2}\right) + \left(\frac{\mu_0 I_3}{2\pi r_3}\right)$$

$$= \frac{\mu_0}{2\pi}\left(\frac{30}{3d} + \frac{20}{d} - \frac{10}{d}\right)$$

$$= \frac{\mu_0}{2\pi}\left(\frac{30 + 60 - 30}{3d}\right)$$

$$B_P = \frac{\mu_0}{2\pi}\frac{20}{d}$$

Now, $B_Q = \frac{\mu_0}{2\pi}\left(\frac{30}{d} - \frac{20}{d} - \frac{10}{3d}\right)$

$$= \frac{\mu_0}{2\pi}\left(\frac{90 - 60 - 10}{3d}\right) = \frac{\mu_0}{2\pi}\frac{20}{3d}$$

So, the ratio of magnetic field is

$$\frac{B_P}{B_Q} = \frac{\mu_0}{2\pi}\frac{20}{d} \times \frac{2\pi}{\mu_0}\frac{3d}{20}$$

$$\frac{B_P}{B_Q} = \frac{3}{1}$$

47 (*a*) The force acting per unit length of a current carrying conductor,

$$\frac{F}{l} = \frac{\mu_0}{4\pi}\frac{2I_1I_2}{d}$$

When $d = 1\text{m}, l = 1\text{m}$

and $I_1 = I_2 = 1\text{ A}$

$$F = 10^{-7} \times \frac{2 \times 1 \times 1}{1^2}$$

$$F = 2 \times 10^{-7}\text{ Nm}^{-1}$$

48 (*a*) Given,

$I_1 = 4.0\text{ A}, I_2 = 5.0\text{ A}, d = 4 \times 10^{-2}\text{m}$

and $l = 0.20\text{ m}$

Force on a current carrying wire,

$$F = \frac{\mu_0 I_1 I_2 l}{2\pi d}$$

$$= \frac{4\pi \times 10^{-7} \times 4.0 \times 5.0 \times 0.20}{2 \times \pi \times 4 \times 10^{-2}}$$

$= 2 \times 10^{-5}$ N (towards *B*)

49 (*d*) The given situation can be drawn as below

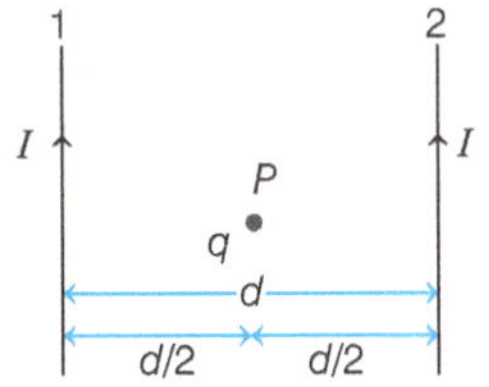

The magnetic field $\mathbf{B}_1$ at mid-point *P* due to first wire is in downward direction, according to right-hand rule. Similarly, magnetic field $\mathbf{B}_2$ due to second wire is in upward direction.

Let the charge *q* is moving with instantaneous velocity **v** in upward direction, then magnitude of force on *q*, due to first wire is

$$F_1 = q(\mathbf{v} \times \mathbf{B}_1) = qvB_1 \sin\theta$$

$$= qvB_1 \sin 180°$$

Similarly, magnitude of force on *q*, due to second wire is

$$F_2 = q(\mathbf{v} \times \mathbf{B}_2) = qvB_2 \sin\theta$$

$$= qvB_2 \sin 0° = 0$$

Thus, net magnitude of force on *q*,

$$F_{net} = F_1 + F_2 = 0$$

50 (*c*) Resultant magnetic field due to current carrying parallel wire 1 (10 A) and wire 2 (*I*A) at point *A* is zero.

i.e., $B_1 = B_2$

$$\frac{\mu_0 I_1}{2r_1} = \frac{\mu_0 I_2}{2r_2}$$

$$\Rightarrow \quad \frac{I_1}{r_1} = \frac{I_2}{r_2} \quad \text{...(i)}$$

As, given, $r_1 = 9\text{ cm} = 9 \times 10^{-2}\text{ m}$

$r_2 = 18 + 9 = 27\text{ cm} = 27 \times 10^{-2}\text{ m}$

∴From Eq. (i),

$$\frac{10}{9 \times 10^{-2}} = \frac{I}{27 \times 10^{-2}}$$

$$\Rightarrow \quad I = 30\text{ A}$$

51 (*d*) Net force experienced by two wires separated by same distance is attractive, if current flow in them in same direction. However, this force is repulsive in nature, if current in them flows in opposite direction.

Force on a wire 1 in which current I_1 is flowing due to another wire 2 which are separated by a distance *r* is given as

$$\mathbf{F} = I_1(\mathbf{l} \times \mathbf{B}_2)$$

or $F = \frac{\mu_0 I_1 I_2}{2\pi r} \cdot l \sin\theta \quad \left[\because \mathbf{B}_2 = \frac{\mu_0 I_2}{2\pi r}\right]$

This given square loop,

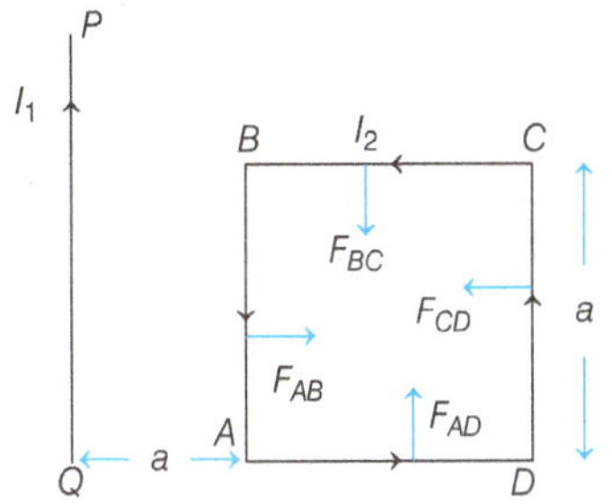

$$F_{AB} = \frac{\mu_0 I_1}{2\pi a} \cdot I_2 a$$

(away from wire *PQ*)

$$F_{BC} = F_{AD} = 0 \quad [\because \theta = 0°]$$

$$F_{CD} = \frac{\mu_0 I_1}{2\pi(2a)} \cdot I_2 a$$

$$= \frac{\mu_0 I_1}{4\pi a} \cdot I_2 a$$

(towards the wire *PQ*)

$$\therefore \quad F_{net} = F_{AB} - F_{CD}$$

$$= \frac{\mu_0 I_1 I_2}{2\pi} - \frac{\mu_0 I_1 I_2}{4\pi}$$

(away from wire)

$= \frac{\mu_0 I_1 I_2}{4\pi}$ (repulsive in nature)

52 (*b*) Consider the given figure

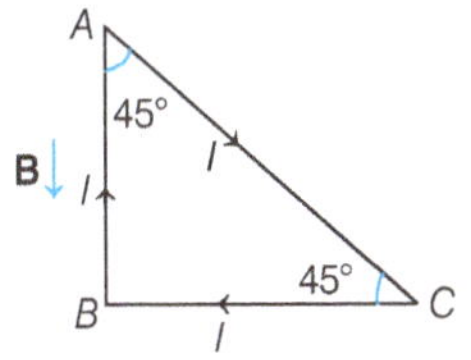

Take, $BC = l$

From figure, $\frac{BC}{AC} = \sin 45°$

$$\Rightarrow \quad \frac{l}{AC} = \frac{1}{\sqrt{2}}$$

$$\Rightarrow \quad AC = \sqrt{2}l \quad \text{...(i)}$$

Since, magnetic field is along *AB*, therefore arm *BC* is perpendicular to the direction of magnetic field *B*, i.e., $\theta = 90°$.

$$\therefore \quad F_{BC} = IB \times BC \times \sin 90°$$

$$= IBl \sin 90°$$

$$F_{BC} = IBl \quad \text{...(ii)}$$

Force on arm *AC*,

$$F_{AC} = IB \times AC \times \sin 45°$$

$$= IB \times \sqrt{2}l \times \frac{1}{\sqrt{2}} \quad \text{[From Eq. (i)]}$$

$$= IBl = F_{BC}$$

$\therefore F_{AC} = F_{BC} = F$ [given, $F_{BC} = F$]

53 (*a*) Consider the given figure

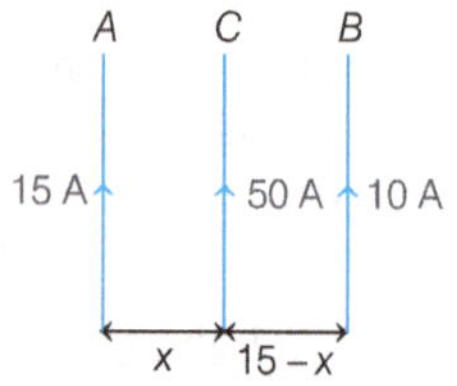

Since, wire C is so replaced that, it experiences no net force, so

$$\frac{F_{AC}}{l} = \frac{F_{BC}}{l}$$

$$\frac{\mu_0 2I_A I_C}{4\pi d} = \frac{\mu_0 2I_B I_C}{4\pi d'}$$

$$\frac{\mu_0}{4\pi} \cdot \frac{2 \times 15 \times 50}{x} = \frac{\mu_0}{4\pi} \times \frac{2 \times 50 \times 10}{15 - x}$$

$$\frac{15}{x} = \frac{10}{(15 - x)}$$

$$225 - 15x = 10x$$

$$\Rightarrow \quad 25x = 225$$

$$\Rightarrow \quad x = 9 \text{ cm}$$

54 (c) From Biot-Savart law,

$$B = \frac{\mu_0 I}{2\pi r}$$

For wire 1

$$B_1 = \frac{4\pi \times 10^{-7} \times 8}{2\pi r} \quad \text{...(i)}$$

for wire 2

$$B_2 = \frac{4\pi \times 10^{-7} \times 12}{2\pi (0.18 - r)} \quad \text{...(ii)}$$

From Eqs. (i) and (ii),

$$\frac{4\pi \times 10^{-7} \times 8}{2\pi r} = \frac{4\pi \times 10^{-7} \times 12}{2\pi (0.18 - r)}$$

$$\Rightarrow \quad \frac{2}{r} = \frac{3}{0.18 - r}$$

$$\Rightarrow \quad r = 0.072 \text{ m}$$

$$= 7.2 \text{ cm}$$

So, magnetic field will be zero at point 7.2 cm from wire 1.

55 (c) Given, area of the loop, $A = 2 \times 10^{-3} \text{m}^2$

Current, $I = 2\text{A}$

$\therefore$ Magnitude of magnetic dipole moment associated with the loop,

$$m = IA = 2 \times 2 \times 10^{-3}$$

$$= 4 \times 10^{-3} \text{JT}^{-1}$$

56 (*a*) The torque acting on the coil

$$|\tau| = |\mathbf{m} \times \mathbf{B}| = mB \sin \theta$$

$$= mB \sin 0°$$

$$\Rightarrow \quad \tau = 0$$

57 (*d*) A current loop in a magnetic field can be in equilibrium in two orientations. For parallel m and B, current loop is stable and for anti-parallel it is unstable.

58 (c) Torque, $\tau = \mathbf{m} \times \mathbf{B}$

$$\Rightarrow \quad |\tau| = |\mathbf{m}||\mathbf{B}| \sin \theta$$

where, m = magnetic moment of coil.

For given orientation (anti-clockwise) shown in Fig. (ii), $\theta = 0° \Rightarrow \tau = 0$

So, for this orientation the loop would be in stable equilibrium.

and for Fig. (iv), $\theta = \pi \Rightarrow \tau = 0$

Therefore, for this orientation (clockwise) the loop would be in unstable equilibrium.

59 (c) Consider the following given figure

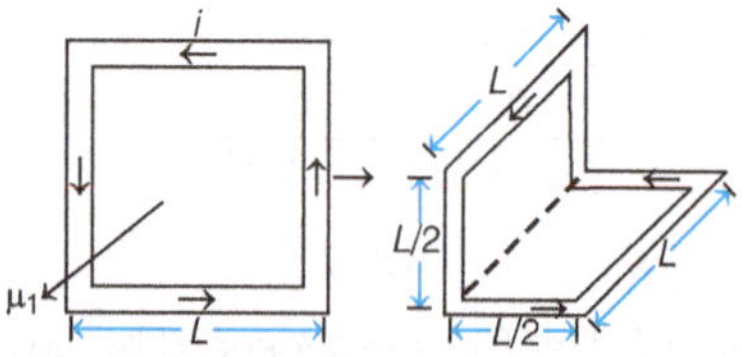

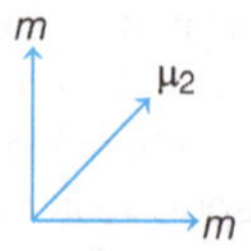

As, we know that initial magnetic moment, $\mu_1 = iL^2$

After folding the loop,

m = magnetic moment due to each part

$$= i\left(\frac{L}{2}\right) \times L = \frac{iL^2}{2} = \frac{\mu_1}{2}$$

Net magnetic moment after folding is

$$\mu_2 = \sqrt{m^2 + m^2} = m\sqrt{2}$$

$$= \frac{\mu_1}{2} \times \sqrt{2} = \frac{\mu_1}{\sqrt{2}}$$

$$\therefore \quad \frac{|\mu_1|}{|\mu_2|} = \sqrt{2}$$

60 (*a*) Given, radius, $r = 1\text{Å} = 10^{-10}$ m and speed, $v = 10^6$ m/s

Current associated with moving electron

$$I = \frac{e}{T} = \frac{e}{\left(\frac{2\pi r}{v}\right)} = \frac{ev}{2\pi r} \quad \text{...(i)}$$

$\therefore$ Magnetic dipole moment associated with revolving electron,

$$m = IA$$

$$= \frac{ev}{2\pi r} \times \pi r^2 \quad \text{[from Eq. (i)]}$$

$$= \frac{evr}{2} = \frac{1.6 \times 10^{-19} \times 10^6 \times 10^{-10}}{2}$$

$$= 0.8 \times 10^{-23} \text{ A-m}^2$$

$$= 8 \times 10^{-24} \text{ A-m}^2$$

61 (*d*) Magnetic field at the centre of circular loop,

$$B = \frac{\mu_0}{4\pi} \frac{2\pi I}{r} = \frac{\mu_0 I}{2r}$$

$$\Rightarrow \quad I = \frac{2Br}{\mu_0}$$

Also, $A = \pi r^2$

or $r = (A/\pi)^{1/2}$

Magnetic moment, $m = IA = \frac{2Br}{\mu_0} A$

On putting the value of r, we get

$$m = \frac{2BA}{\mu_0} \times \left(\frac{A}{\pi}\right)^{1/2} = \frac{2BA^{3/2}}{\mu_0 \pi^{1/2}}$$

62 (*a*) Magnetic dipole moment of a current carrying loop is

$$m = IA \text{ (Am}^2\text{)}$$

where, I = current in loop and

A = area of loop.

Let the given square loop has side a, then its magnetic dipole moment will be

$$m = Ia^2$$

When square is converted into a circular loop of radius r,

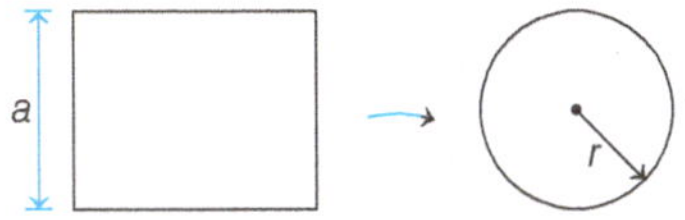

Then, wire length will be same in both area,

$\Rightarrow \quad 4a = 2\pi r$

$\Rightarrow \quad r = \frac{4a}{2\pi} = \frac{2a}{\pi}$

Hence, area of circular loop formed is, $A' = \pi r^2$

$$= \pi\left(\frac{2a}{\pi}\right)^2 = \frac{4a^2}{\pi}$$

Magnitude of magnetic dipole moment of circular loop will be

$$m' = IA' = I\frac{4a^2}{\pi}$$

Ratio of magnetic dipole moments of both shapes is,

$$\frac{m'}{m} = \frac{I \cdot \frac{4a^2}{\pi}}{Ia^2} = \frac{4}{\pi}$$

$\Rightarrow \quad m' = \frac{4m}{\pi}$ (A-m^2)

63 (*a*) An electron orbiting in a circular orbit of radius r with speed v as shown below.

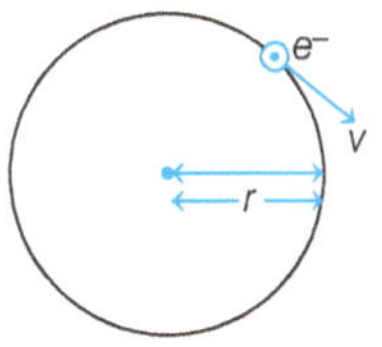

Magnetic moment, $M = NiA$

where, N = number of turns of the current loop

and i = current.

Since, the orbiting electron behaves as a current loop of current i, we can write

$$i = \frac{e}{T} = \frac{e}{\frac{2\pi r}{v}} = \frac{ev}{2\pi r}$$

$$\Rightarrow M = NiA = (1)\left(\frac{ev}{2\pi r}\right)(\pi r^2) = \frac{evr}{2}$$

64 (*c*) Area of equilateral triangle

$$= \frac{\sqrt{3}(\text{side})^2}{4}$$

Here, side $= \frac{l}{3}$

So, $A = \frac{\sqrt{3}}{4}\frac{l^2}{9} = \frac{l^2}{12\sqrt{3}}$

Magnetic moment,

$$m = iA = \frac{il^2}{12\sqrt{3}}$$

$$m = \frac{il^2}{12\sqrt{3}}\ \text{Am}^2$$

65 (*a*) Given, side of square coil = 10 cm = 0.1 m

Number of turns $(n) = 20$

Current in square coil, $I = 12$ A

Angle made by coil, $\theta = 30°$ and magnetic field, $B = 0.80$ T

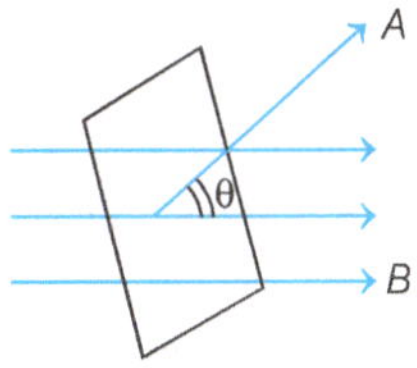

Torque,

$$\tau = NIAB\sin\theta$$

$$= 20 \times 12 \times (10 \times 10^{-2})^2 \times 0.80 \times \sin 30°$$

$$\tau = \frac{2.4 \times 0.80}{2} = 0.96 \text{ N-m}$$

66 (*b*) Torque due to rectangular coil is given by

$$\tau = BA\,I_n \cos\theta$$

$$\theta = 30°,$$

$$\tau_1 = BAI_n \cos 30°$$

Similarly, torque, when coil is making an angle of 60° is

$$\tau_2 = BAI_n \cos 60°$$

So, $\frac{\tau_1}{\tau_2} = \frac{\cos 30°}{\cos 60°} = \frac{\sqrt{3}/2}{1/2}$

$\frac{\tau_1}{\tau_2} = \frac{\sqrt{3}}{1}$; $\tau_1 : \tau_2 = \sqrt{3} : 1$

67 (*d*) To convert a galvanometer into an ammeter resistance is connected in parallel,

Resistance, $R = \frac{R_G r_s}{R_G + r_s}$

Given, $R_G = 70\,\Omega$ and $r_s = 0.03\,\Omega$

$\therefore \quad R = \frac{70 \times 0.03}{70 + 0.03} = 0.02998$

$= 0.030\,\Omega$

68 (*a*) Ammeter circuit is shown in the figure below

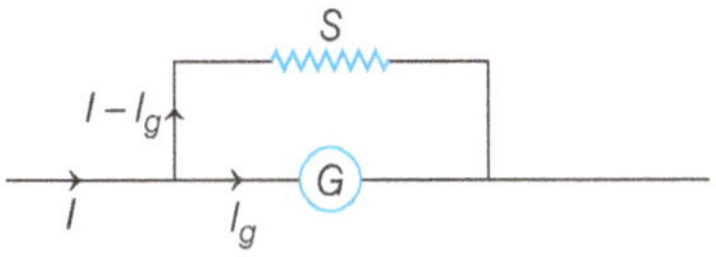

So, $\quad I_g G = (I - I_g)S$

Here, $\quad I_g = 0.002$ A,

$I = 0.5$ A,

$G = 50\,\Omega$

So, shunt resistance required is

$$S = \frac{I_g G}{I - I_g} = \frac{0.002 \times 50}{(0.5 - 0.002)} \approx 0.2\,\Omega$$

69 (*b*) Here, resistance of the galvanometer,

$$R_g = 60\,\Omega$$

When the galvanometer is shunted by a resistance r, its effective resistance,

$$R_P = \frac{R_g r}{R_g + r} = \frac{60 \times 0.02}{60 + 0.02}$$

$\approx 0.02\,\Omega \quad [\because r = 0.02\,\Omega]$

Total resistance of the circuit,

$$R_{net} = R + R_P = R + 0.02$$

Current, $I = \frac{V}{R_{net}} = \frac{5}{R + 0.02}$

$\Rightarrow \quad 1 = \frac{5}{R + 0.02} \quad [\because I = 1\text{ A}]$

$R + 0.02 = 5$

$\Rightarrow \quad R = 5 - 0.02$

$= 4.98 \approx 5\,\Omega$

70 (*d*) Given, resistance of galvanometer, $R_g = 50\Omega$ and $I = 4 \times 10^{-4}$ A

Number of divisions = 25,

$I_g = 25 \times I$

$= 25 \times 4 \times 10^{-4}$

$= 10^{-2}$ A

Consider the given figure

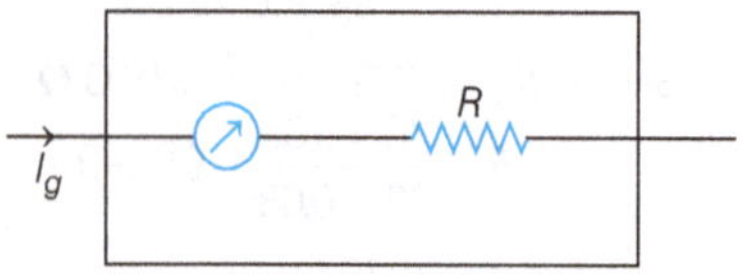

R is the resistance connected in series of galvanometer to convert into voltmeter.

$\therefore \quad V = I_g (R_g + R)$

$25 = 10^{-2} (50 + R)$

$\Rightarrow \quad R = \frac{25}{10^{-2}} - 50$

$= 2500 - 50$

$= 2450\,\Omega$ in series

71 (*d*) Statement given in option (d) is incorrect and it can be corrected as,

When a galvanometer is used as a voltmeter, it must draw a very small current, otherwise the voltage measurement will disturb the original set up by an amount which is very large. So, to keep the disturbance due to the measurement device below one percent, large resistance R is connected in series with the galvanometer.

Rest statements are correct.

72 (*a*) Two galvanometers A and B produce a deflection of 10 divisions, then minimum current is measured by $A \rightarrow 0.3$ mA/div and by $B \rightarrow 0.5$ mA/div, so A is more sensitive than B.

73 (*b*) Given, spring constant,

$k = 10^{-8}$ N-m rad^{-1},

Number of turns, $N = 100$,

Area, $A = 1\text{ cm}^2 = (1 \times 10^{-2})^2\text{ m}^2$

$= 1 \times 10^{-4}\text{m}^2$

and magnetic field, $B = 5$ T

$\therefore \quad S_i = \frac{NBA}{k}$

$= \frac{100 \times 5 \times 1 \times 10^{-4}}{10^{-8}}$

$= 5 \times 10^6\text{ A}^{-1}$

74 (*d*) For tangent galvanometer

$I \propto \tan\theta$

$\Rightarrow \quad \frac{I_1}{I_2} = \frac{\tan\theta_1}{\tan\theta_2}$

$\frac{2}{I_2} = \frac{\tan 30°}{\tan 60°} = \frac{1/\sqrt{3}}{\sqrt{3}}$

$\frac{2}{I_2} = \frac{1}{3}, I_2 = 2 \times 3, I_2 = 6$ A

75 (*b*)

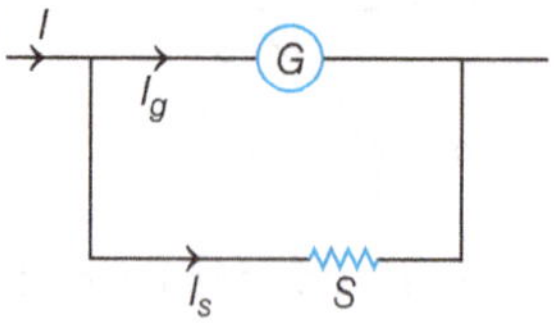

As $I_g = \frac{10}{100} I = 0.1I$

For shunt, $I_s = I - I_g = 0.9I$

$S = \frac{I_g G}{I - I_g} = \frac{0.1IG}{0.9I} = \frac{G}{9}$

Resistance of ammeter is parallel combination of G and S.

$R_A = \frac{G(G/9)}{G + G/9} = \frac{G}{10}$

or alternate solution

$IR_A = 0.1IG \Rightarrow R_A = \frac{G}{10}$

76 (*b*) Given, $I_g = 9$ A, $I = 99$ A,

$R_g = 20\,\Omega$

Out of main current of 99 A, only 9 A current should go through the coil to show full scale deflection. The current through the coil is

$\frac{I_g}{I} = \frac{R_s}{R_s + R_g}$

$R_s = \frac{I_g}{I}(R_s + R_g)$

$= \frac{9}{99}(R_s + 20)$

$R_s = \frac{1}{11}(R_s + 20)$

$11R_s - R_s = 20 \Rightarrow R_s = 2\,\Omega$

$\therefore$ The value of shunt resistance should be $2\,\Omega$.

77 (*d*) Here, $S = \frac{G}{\frac{I}{I_g} - 1} = \frac{0.81}{\frac{10}{1} - 1}$

$= \frac{81}{100} \times \frac{1}{9} = 0.09\,\Omega$

78 (*a*) Given, current passing through the galvanometer is 2% and current remaining is 98%.

$\therefore \quad \frac{I_s}{I} = \frac{G}{S}$

$\frac{G}{S} = \frac{0.98}{0.2}$

$\frac{G}{S} = \frac{98}{2}$

$\therefore \quad S = \frac{G}{49}$

79 (*a*) As we know, current sensitivity,

$S_i = \frac{NBA}{k}$ ...(i)

and voltage sensitivity,

$S_V = \frac{NBA}{kR}$ ...(ii)

From Eqs. (i) and (ii), we get

$\frac{S_i}{S_V} = R$

$\Rightarrow \quad \frac{S_i}{G} = S_V \quad (\because R = G)$

80 (*d*) Voltage sensitivity,

$S_V = \frac{\text{Current sensitivity } S_i}{\text{Galvanometer resistance } R}$

Given, $R_{\text{initial}} = R$,

$R_{\text{final}} = 2R_{\text{initial}} = 2R$

Since, S_i has been increased to 50% of initial value, so

$(S_i)_{\text{final}} = S_i + 50\%$ of S_i

$= 1.5\,S_i$

$\Rightarrow$ New voltage sensitivity,

$S_V' = \frac{1.5S_i}{2R} = \frac{3}{4}S_V \quad \left[\because S_V = \frac{S_i}{R}\right]$

Decrease in voltage sensitivity

$= \left[1 - \left(\frac{3}{4}\right)\right]S_V = \left(\frac{1}{4}\right)S_V$

81 (*d*) Current sensitivity,

$I_g = \frac{NBA}{k} = 10$ div/mA

$= \frac{10}{10^{-3}} = 10000\,\frac{\text{div}}{\text{A}}$

Voltage sensitivity,

$$V_s = \frac{NBA}{kR} = 20 \text{ div/V}$$

Now, $\frac{I_s}{V_s} = R \Rightarrow R = \frac{10000}{20}$

$$R = 500\,\Omega$$

Assertion and Reason Questions

1 (*a*) A stationary charge produces electric field only. However, a moving charge which is equivalent to a current produces a magnetic field in the surrounding space and can interacts with external magnetic field.

2 (*a*) When an electron enters perpendicular to a uniform magnetic field, then a magnetic force acts on the electron in a direction perpendicular to both, the directions of magnetic field and the direction of velocity of electron. Particle moves in uniform circular motion.

Therefore, electron moving perpendicular to magnetic field **B** will perform circular motion.

3 (*d*) When a charge particle of charge q is released from rest ($u = 0$) in the uniform magnetic field B, then magnetic force on the charged particle $F = Bqu \sin\theta = 0$, because $u = 0$. Therefore, the charge particle will not move in circular path.

In the magnetic field, force on charge particle always acts in perpendicular direction to the direction of velocity of charge particle, therefore work done by magnetic field on charge particle is zero.

4 (*a*) Perpendicular component causes rotation, while parallel component displaces particle along the direction of field, thus path will be helical.

5 (*d*) Current sensitivity, $S_i = \frac{NBA}{k}$

$$S_i \propto N$$

and voltage sensitivity, $S_V = \frac{NBA}{kR}$

$$S_V \propto \frac{N}{R}$$

So, when S_i is increased by increasing number of turns N, length of wire used also increases and so resistance R increases.

Hence, S_V may remain same or decrease whereas S_i increases.

Therefore, Assertion is incorrect but Reason is correct.

6 (*b*) The magnetic field due to solenoid having n-number of turns/metre and carrying current I is $B = \mu_0 nI$.

It is obvious that magnetic field is independent of length and cross-sectional area.

Also, magnetic field is uniform inside the solenoid.

Therefore, Assertion and Reason are correct but Reason is not the correct explanation of Assertion.

7 (*d*) A is false but R is true.

The torque on the coil in a magnetic field is given by

$$\tau = IBA \sin\theta$$

When coil is suspended in a radial magnetic field, the angle between the area vector and magnetic field is 90°.

$\therefore \quad \tau = IBA \sin 90° \Rightarrow \tau = IBA$

Which is the maximum value of the torque

8 (*c*) A is true but R is false.

The magnetic moment is given by

$$\mathbf{M} = I\mathbf{A}$$

where, I = Current through loop and A = Area of loop}

Also, $\quad M = I(\pi R^2) \quad$ ...(i)

So, $M \propto R^2$ {Radius of loop}

When $\quad R' = R/2$

$$M = I\left[\pi\left(\frac{R}{2}\right)^2\right]$$

$$M' = \frac{I\pi R^2}{4} \Rightarrow \frac{M}{4} \text{ [using (i)]}$$

$$M' = \frac{M}{4}$$

9 (*c*) A is true but R is false.

A parallel shunt resistance allows the majority of the current to flow through it and provides an alternative path for current to bypass the galvanometer. This is done to increase the range of the galvanometer, so that it can measure large currents. But, the reason is false because the shunt in parallel increases the sensitivity of the galvanometer.

10 (*b*) Both A and R are true but R is not the correct explanation of A.

A voltmeter is connected in parallel with the components across which the potential difference is required to be measured. It must have very high resistance, so that very small current passes through it and the potential difference across that component is not affected.

Statement Based Questions

1 (*b*) Statement I is correct and Statement II is incorrect.

Using the right hand thumb rule, the direction of magnetic field at a point above a current carrying conductor is towards North.

The magnetic field due to a long straight wire, carrying current I is given by

$$B = \frac{\mu_0 I}{2\pi R}$$

$\therefore \quad B \propto I$

2 (*d*) When a charged particle moves in region of a perpendicular magnetic field, the magnetic force is perpendicular to the velocity of the particle. So, no work is done and no change in the magnitude of the velocity.

3 (*a*) If velocity has component along **B**, this component remains unchanged as the motion along the magnetic field will not be affected by the magnetic field.

The motion in a plane perpendicular to **B** is as before a circular one, thereby producing a helical motion.

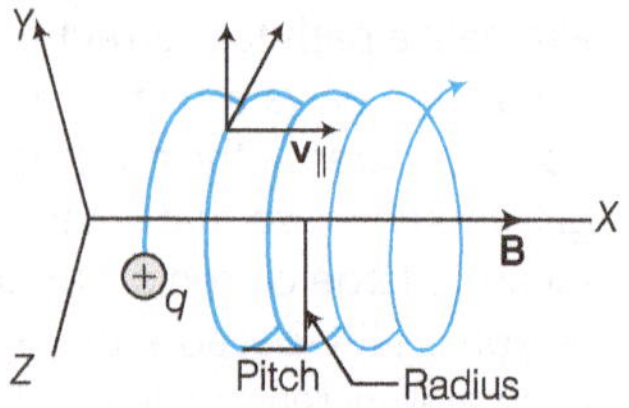

4 (*d*) According to Biot-Savart's law, magnetic field due to small current element $I d\mathbf{l}$, at a distance r from it, is given as

$$d\mathbf{B} = \frac{\mu_0}{4\pi}\frac{(I d\mathbf{l} \times \mathbf{r})}{r^3}$$

Thus, current element $I d\mathbf{l}$ is a vector quantity. Hence, both Statement I and Statement II are correct.

5 (*c*) Force per unit length, $F = \frac{\mu_0}{2\pi}\frac{i^2}{R}$

$$\Rightarrow F \propto \frac{1}{R}$$

Hence, graph of F and R is not a straight line.

8 (*c*) Current sensitivity, $S_i = \frac{NBA}{k}$

and voltage sensitivity, $S_V = \frac{NBA}{kR}$

So, when S_i is increased by increasing number of turns N, length of wire used also increases and so, R increases. Hence, S_V may remain same or decrease whereas S_i increases.

Matching Type Questions

1 (*a*)

A. Since, $\mathbf{E} = 0$ and $\mathbf{B} \neq 0$ the magnetic force will act on it and the path will be helical (with uniform pitch) if $\mathbf{v}$ is at any angle to $\mathbf{B}$ $(\theta \neq 90°)$.

B. Since, $\mathbf{E} = 0$, $\mathbf{B} \neq 0$ and $\mathbf{v} \perp \mathbf{B}$, then a force called Lorentz force, $F = q(\mathbf{v} \times \mathbf{B})$, acts on charged particle, which provides centripetal force to it and hence, the path will be circular.

C. Since, $\mathbf{E} \neq 0, \mathbf{B} \neq 0, \mathbf{E} \,||\, \mathbf{B}$, so path will be helical with non-uniform pitch as both electric and magnetic forces act on it.

D. Since, $\mathbf{E} \neq 0, \mathbf{B} \neq 0, \mathbf{E} \perp \mathbf{B}$ and $\mathbf{v}$ is perpendicular to both $\mathbf{E}$ and $\mathbf{B}$, then the particle will move in a straight line due to the resultant force of magnetic and electric fields.

Hence, A $\to$ 2, B $\to$ 3, C $\to$ 4 and D $\to$ 1.

Numerical Type Questions

1 (10) Time taken by electron when its velocity becomes 0 m/s.

$$t = \frac{v-u}{-a} = \frac{0-u}{-a} = \frac{u}{a}$$

$$= \frac{10 \text{ km/s}}{2 \text{ km/s}^2} = 5 \text{ s}$$

Total time taken to comeback to its initial position,

$$T = t + t = 10 \text{s}$$

2 (1) According to given situation,

$$F_c = F_m$$

$$\Rightarrow \frac{mv^2}{r} = qvB$$

$$\Rightarrow \quad r = \frac{mv}{qB} = \frac{p}{qB} = \frac{\sqrt{2mK}}{qB}$$

$$r_\alpha = \frac{\sqrt{2(4m)K'}}{2qB}$$

$$\frac{r}{r_\alpha} = \sqrt{\frac{K}{K'}}; \text{ but } r = r_\alpha \text{ (given)}$$

Thus, $K = K' = 1$ MeV

So, the value of energy required, 1 MeV and the value of x is 1.

3 (1) Force on a charged particle is

$$\mathbf{F} = q(\mathbf{E} + \mathbf{v} \times \mathbf{B})$$

or $$\mathbf{F} = \mathbf{F}_e + \mathbf{F}_m$$

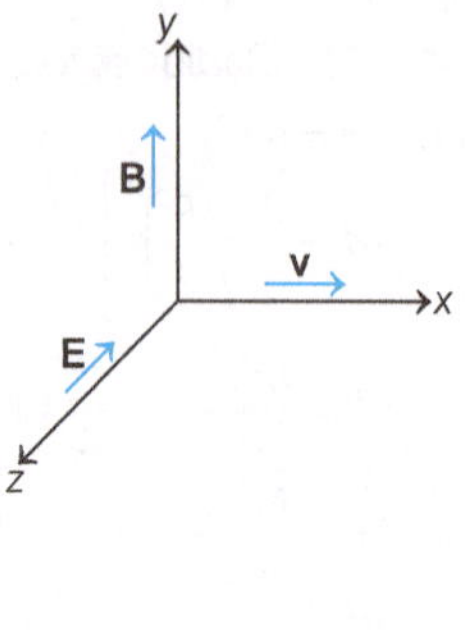

$$\therefore \mathbf{F}_e = q\mathbf{E} = -20 \times 10^{-18} \times 10^4(-\hat{\mathbf{j}})$$
$$= 20 \times 10^{-14}\,\hat{\mathbf{k}}$$

and $$\mathbf{F}_m = -20 \times 10^{-18}(10\hat{\mathbf{i}} \times B\hat{\mathbf{j}})$$
$$= -20 \times 10^{-17} \times B(+\hat{\mathbf{k}})$$
$$= -20 \times 10^{-17}\,B\hat{\mathbf{k}}$$

Since, particle will continue to move along $+X$-axis, so resultant force is equal to zero.

$$\mathbf{F}_e + \mathbf{F}_m = 0$$

$$\Rightarrow 20 \times 10^{-14} = 20 \times 10^{-17} B$$

$$\Rightarrow \quad B = \frac{20 \times 10^{-14}}{20 \times 10^{-17}} = 10^3$$

or $$B = 10^3 \text{ Wb/m}^2$$

Hence, the value of x is 1.

4 (250) Given, $R = 3 \text{ cm} = 3 \times 10^{-2}$ m

$x = 4 \text{ cm} = 4 \times 10^{-2}$ m

$B = 54 \text{ mT} = 54 \times 10^{-3}$ T

Field along axis of coil is given by

$$B = \frac{\mu_0 I R^2}{2(R^2 + x^2)^{3/2}}$$

at centre of the coil, $B' = \frac{\mu_0 I}{2R}$

$$\therefore \quad \frac{B'}{B} = \frac{\mu_0 I / 2R}{\left(\frac{\mu_0 I R^2}{2(R^2 + x^2)^{3/2}}\right)}$$

$$= \frac{(R^2 + x^2)^{3/2}}{R^3}$$

$$\therefore B' = \frac{B \times (R^2 + x^2)^{3/2}}{R^3}$$

$$= \frac{54 \times 10^{-3} \times [3^2 + 4^2]^{3/2}}{3^3}$$

$$= \frac{54 \times 10^{-3} \times 125}{27} = 250 \times 10^{-3}$$

$$B' = 250 \text{ mT}$$

So, the value of x is 250.

5 (2) Magnetic field due to circle at the centre is given by $B = \frac{\mu_0 I}{2R}$

So, magnetic field due to semi-circle is

$$B = \frac{1}{2} \times \frac{\mu_0 I}{2R} = \frac{\mu_0 I}{4R}$$

$$B = \frac{4\pi \times 10^{-7} \times 16}{4 \times 2.5 \times 10^{-2}}$$

$$= 2.0 \times 10^{-4} \text{ T}$$

6 (4) In the given figure,

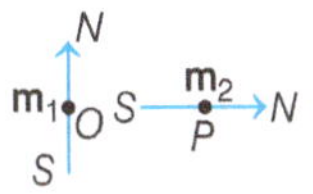

The direction of magnetic moment is from south to north.

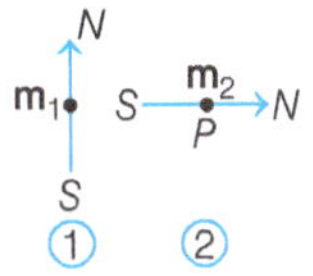

When second magnet is kept in the magnetic field produced by first magnet, the torque acting on second magnet is given by

$$\tau = \mathbf{m}_2 \times \mathbf{B}_1$$

$$|\tau| = m_2 B_1 \sin\theta \qquad (\because \theta = 90°)$$

$$|\tau| = m_2 B_1$$

Point P lie on equitorial position,

so $B_1 = \frac{\mu_0}{4\pi} \frac{m_1}{r^3}$

$$|\tau| = \left(\frac{\mu_0}{4\pi} \frac{m_1}{r^3}\right) m_2$$

$m_1 = m_2 = 2$ A-m^2, $r = 1$ m (given)

$$|\tau| = \frac{10^{-7} \times 2 \times 2}{(1)^3} = 4 \times 10^{-7} \text{ Nm}$$

$$\Rightarrow \qquad |\tau| = 4 \times 10^{-7} \text{ Nm}$$

7 (4450) According to given situation, total internal resistance

$$= (50 + 2950)\,\Omega$$

$$= 3000\,\Omega, \varepsilon = 3 \text{ V}$$

$$I = \frac{\varepsilon}{R} = \frac{3}{3000} = 1 \times 10^{-3} \text{ A}$$

$$= 1.0 \text{ mA}$$

$\therefore$ Current for full scale deflection of 30 divisions is 1.0 mA

$\therefore$ Current for a deflection of 20 divisions

$$I = \left(\frac{20}{30} \times 1\right) \text{mA}$$

or $I = \frac{2}{3}$ mA

Let the resistance be $p\,\Omega$. Then

$$p = \frac{\varepsilon}{I} = \frac{3 \text{ V}}{\left(\frac{2}{3} \times 10^3 \text{ A}\right)}$$

$$= \frac{3 \times 3 \times 10^3}{2}\,\Omega$$

$$= 4500\,\Omega$$

But the resistance of the galvanometer is $50\,\Omega$.

$\therefore$ Resistance to be added

$$= (4500 - 50)$$

$$= 4450\,\Omega$$

NCERT Exemplar Questions

1 (*d*) For given pitch d of a helical path corresponding to motion of a charged particle in a uniform magnetic field, we have,

$$\frac{q}{m} = \frac{2\pi v \cos\theta}{qB} = \text{constant}$$

$$\Rightarrow \qquad \left(\frac{e}{m}\right)_1 + \left(\frac{e}{m}\right)_2 = 0$$

2 (*a*) Magnetic field associated with moving charge,

$$\mathbf{B} = \frac{\mu}{4\pi} q \frac{\mathbf{v} \times \mathbf{r}}{r^2}$$

According to thumb's rule, **B** is perpendicular to **v**.

3 (*d*) The rotation of the loop by 30° about an axis perpendicular to its plane make no change in the angle made by magnetic moment with the direction of magnetic field, therefore the work done to rotate the loop is zero.

Past Exams Questions

1 (*c*) Given, number of turns, $N = 100$

radius, $r = 10$ cm $= 10 \times 10^{-2}$ m

current, $I = 7$A

Magnetic field at the centre of a solenoid,

$$B = \frac{\mu_0 NI}{2r}$$

$$= \frac{4\pi \times 10^{-7} \times 100 \times 7}{2 \times 10 \times 10^{-2}}$$

$$= 44 \times 10^{-4}$$

$$= 4.4 \times 10^{-3} \text{ T}$$

$$= 4.4 \text{ mT}$$

2 (*b*) Given, $\mathbf{L} = L\hat{\mathbf{i}}$

$$\mathbf{B} = (2\hat{\mathbf{i}} + 3\hat{\mathbf{j}} - 4\hat{\mathbf{k}})\text{ T}$$

$$\therefore \quad \mathbf{F} = I(\mathbf{L} \times \mathbf{B})$$

$$= I[L\hat{\mathbf{i}} \times (2\hat{\mathbf{i}} + 3\hat{\mathbf{j}} - 4\hat{\mathbf{k}})]$$

$$= I[2L(\hat{\mathbf{i}} \times \hat{\mathbf{i}}) + 3L(\hat{\mathbf{i}} \times \hat{\mathbf{j}}) - 4L(\hat{\mathbf{i}} \times \hat{\mathbf{k}})]$$

$$= I[0 + 3L\hat{\mathbf{k}} + 4L\hat{\mathbf{j}}]$$

$$= I[4L\hat{\mathbf{i}} + 3L\hat{\mathbf{k}}]$$

$$\therefore \quad F = |\mathbf{F}| = \sqrt{(4LI)^2 + (3LI)^2} = 5LI$$

3 (*c*) Magnetic field inside the conducting cylindrical cable,

$$B = \frac{\mu_0 I}{2\pi R^2} r \Rightarrow B \propto r$$

$\therefore$ The graph of magnetic field B with r is a straight line passing through origin.

For a point outside the cylinder,

$$B = \frac{\mu_0 I}{2\pi R} \Rightarrow B \propto \frac{1}{R}$$

The graph of magnetic field with r is a rectangular hyperbola passing through the outer surface of the cylinder.

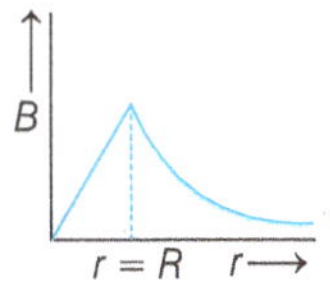

4 (*a*) Given, Radius of solenoid,

$r = 1$ mm

Number of turns per mm $= \frac{100}{1 \text{ mm}}$

$\therefore$ Number of turns per metre

$$= \frac{100}{1 \times 10^{-3} \text{m}}$$

i.e., $n = 10^5$ turns/m

Current flowing through the solenoid, $I = 1$ A

$\therefore$ Magnetic field strength at the centre of the solenoid $B = \mu_0 nI$

$$= 4\pi \times 10^{-7} \times 10^5 \times 1$$

$$= 4\pi \times 10^{-2} \text{ T}$$

$$= 12.56 \times 10^{-2} \text{ T}$$

5 (*a*) Magnetic field due to a current carrying wire at a distance r from the wire.

or $B = \frac{\mu_0 2i}{4\pi r} = \frac{10^{-7} \times 2 \times 5}{20 \times 10^{-2}}$

$$= \frac{1}{2} \times 10^{-5} \text{ T}$$

So,

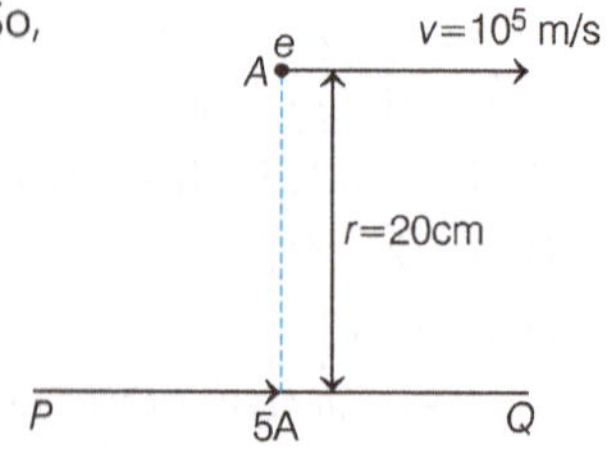

Therefore, force acting on electron

$$\mathbf{F} = q(\mathbf{v} \times \mathbf{B})$$

$$|\mathbf{F}| = 1.6 \times 10^{-19} \times \left(10^5 \times \frac{1}{2} \times 10^{-5}\right)$$

$$= 8 \times 10^{-20} \text{ N}$$

6 (*d*) Given,

$$l = 50 \text{ cm} = 0.5 \text{ m},$$

$$N = 100 \text{ turns and } I = 2.5 \text{ A}$$

∴ Magnetic field at the centre of solenoid is

$$= \mu_0 nI = \mu_0 \left(\frac{N}{l}\right) \cdot I$$

$$= 4\pi \times 10^{-7} \times \frac{100}{0.5} \times 2.5$$

$$= 6.28 \times 10^{-4} \text{ T}$$

Hence, correct option is (d)

7 (*b*) Consider two Amperian loops of radius $\frac{a}{2}$ and $2a$ as shown in the diagram.

Applying Ampere's circuital law for these loops we get,

$$\oint \mathbf{B} \cdot d\mathbf{l} = \mu_0 I_{\text{enclosed}}$$

For the smaller loop,

$$B \times 2\pi\left(\frac{a}{2}\right) = \mu_0 \times \frac{I}{\pi a^2} \times \pi\left(\frac{a}{2}\right)^2$$

$$= \frac{\mu_0 I}{4}$$

$\Rightarrow B = \frac{\mu_0 I}{4\pi a}$, at distance $\frac{a}{2}$ from the axis of the wire.

Similarly, for bigger Amperian loop.

$$B' \times 2\pi(2a) = \mu_0 I$$

[total current enclosed by Amperian loop is 2]

$$\Rightarrow \quad B' = \frac{\mu_0 I}{4\pi a},$$

At distance $2a$ from the axis of the wire.

So, ratio of $\frac{B}{B'} = \frac{\mu_0 I}{4\pi a} \times \frac{4\pi a}{\mu_0 I} = 1$

8 (*b*) $B_{\text{centre}} = \frac{n \cdot \mu_0 i}{2R}$ (For a circular coil)

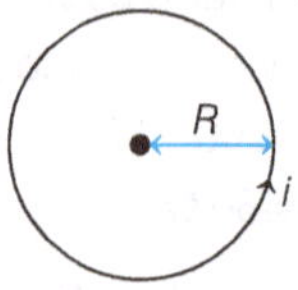

$$B = \frac{\mu_0 i}{2R} = \frac{\mu_0 i(2\pi)}{2(l)} = \frac{\mu_0 \pi i}{l}$$

$$= \frac{\mu_0 ni}{2\left(\frac{l}{2n\pi}\right)} = \frac{n^2 \mu_0 \pi i}{l} = n^2 B$$

9 (*d*) Consider the given figure,

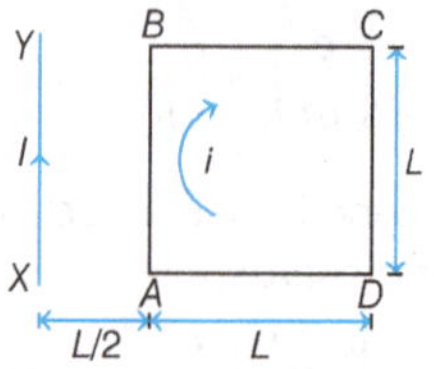

From the above figure, it can be seen that the direction of currents in a long straight conductor *XY* and arm *AB* of a square loop *ABCD* are in the same direction. So, there exist a force of attraction between the two, which will be experienced by F_{BA} as

$$F_{BA} = \frac{\mu_0 IiL}{2\pi\left(\frac{L}{2}\right)}$$

In the case of *XY* and arm *CD*, the direction of currents are in the opposite direction. So, there exist a force of repulsion which will be experienced by *CD* as

$$F_{CD} = \frac{\mu_0 IiL}{2\pi\left(\frac{3L}{2}\right)}$$

Therefore, net force on the loop *ABCD* will be

$$F_{\text{loop}} = F_{BA} - F_{CD}$$

$$= \frac{\mu_0 IiL}{2\pi}\left[\frac{1}{(L/2)} - \frac{1}{(3L/2)}\right]$$

$$F_{\text{loop}} = \frac{2\mu_0 iI}{3\pi}$$

10 (*c*) The magnetic field in the different regions is given by

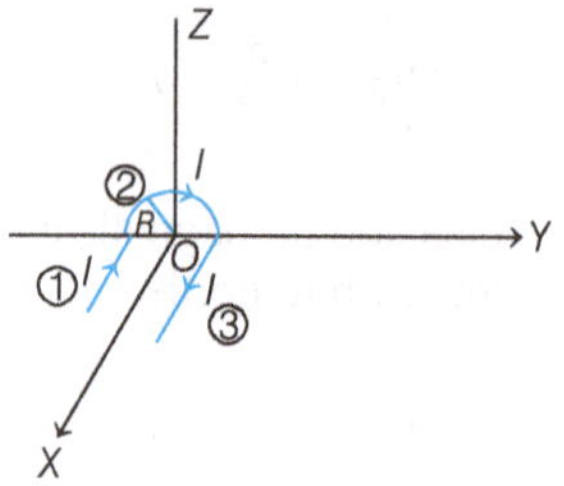

$$\mathbf{B}_1 = \frac{\mu_0}{4\pi} \times \frac{I}{R}(-\hat{\mathbf{k}})$$

$$\mathbf{B}_3 = \frac{\mu_0 I}{4\pi R}(-\hat{\mathbf{k}})$$

$$\mathbf{B}_2 = \frac{\mu_0 I}{4R}(-\hat{\mathbf{i}})$$

Net magnetic field at the centre *O* is $\mathbf{B} = \mathbf{B}_1 + \mathbf{B}_2 + \mathbf{B}_3$

$$= \frac{\mu_0 I}{4\pi R}(-2\hat{\mathbf{k}}) + \frac{\mu_0 I}{4R}(-\hat{\mathbf{i}})$$

$$= -\frac{\mu_0 I}{4\pi R}(2\hat{\mathbf{k}} + \pi\hat{\mathbf{i}})$$

11 (*b*) Given, $N = 50$

$$B = 0.2 \text{ Wb/m}^2, I = 2 \text{ A}$$

$$\theta = 60°$$

$$A = 0.12 \times 0.1 = 0.012 \text{ m}^2$$

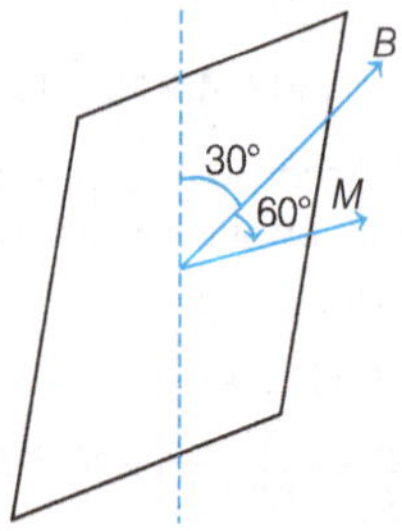

Thus, torque required,

$$\tau = NIAB \sin\theta$$

$$= 50 \times 2 \times 0.012 \times 0.2 \times \sin 60°$$

$$= 50 \times 2 \times 0.12 \times 0.2 \times \frac{\sqrt{3}}{2}$$

$$= 0.20 \text{ Nm}$$

12 (*a*)

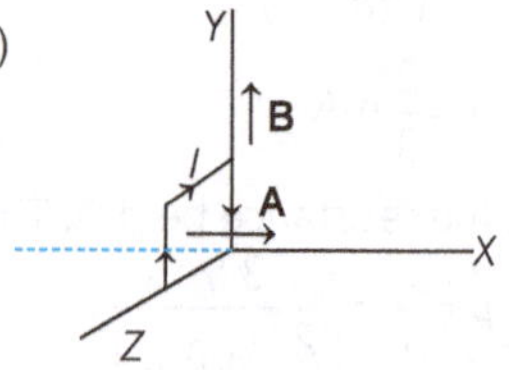

Torque on loop,

$$= \mathbf{m} \times \mathbf{B}$$
$$= I\mathbf{A} \times \mathbf{B}$$
$$= (5 \times 0.02\,\hat{\mathbf{i}}) \times (2 \times 10^{-3}\,\hat{\mathbf{j}})$$
$$= 2 \times 10^{-4}\,\hat{\mathbf{k}} \text{ N-m}$$

13 (*d*) Magnetic field outside of a wire is,

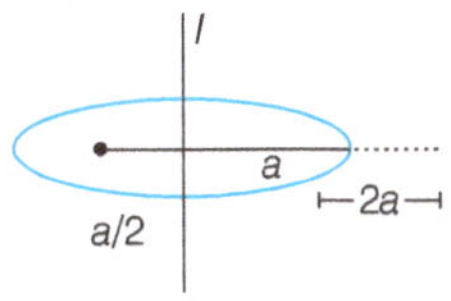

$$B_1 = \frac{\mu_0 i}{2\pi r_1} \quad \text{...(i)}$$

Magnetic field inside of a wire is,

$$B_2 = \frac{\mu_0}{2\pi} \cdot \frac{ir_2}{R^2}$$

Here, $r_1 = 2a$, $r_2 = \frac{a}{2}$ and $R = a$

$$\therefore \quad B_1 = \frac{\mu_0 i}{2\pi(2a)} = \frac{\mu_0 i}{4\pi a} \quad \text{...(ii)}$$

$$\text{and } B_2 = \frac{\mu_0 i\left(\frac{a}{2}\right)}{2\pi a^2} = \frac{\mu_0 i}{4\pi a} \quad \text{...(iii)}$$

From Eq. (ii) and Eq. (iii)

So, $\frac{B_1}{B_2} = 1:1$

14 (*d*) Since, electron is moving uniformly along magnetic field inside a current-carrying solenoid

i.e. $\theta = 0°$

Then using Lorentz force formula,

$$F_{net} = qvB \sin\theta = 0$$

Hence, electron will move in direction of its initial velocity without changing its motion and speed.

15 (*a*)

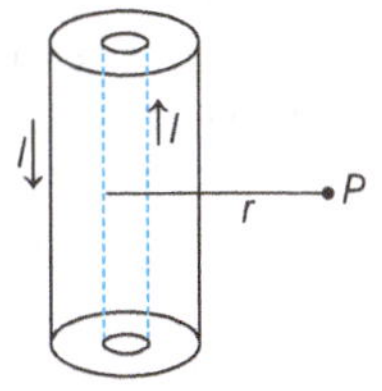

According to Ampere's circuit law,

$$\int \mathbf{B} \cdot d\mathbf{l} = \mu_0 (I_{enclosed})$$

As $I_{enclosed} = 0$ (net current)

$$\Rightarrow \quad B = 0$$

Hence, magnetic field outside is zero.

16 (*a*) Magnetic field at the centre of current carrying coil of R having N number of turns is given as,

$$B = \frac{\mu_0 NI}{2R}$$

For two given situations

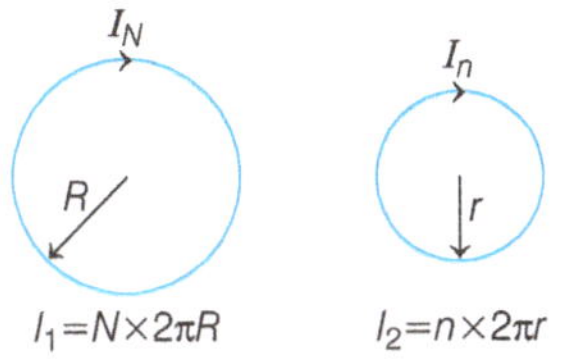

Length remains same, $l_1 = l_2$

$$N \times 2\pi R = n \times 2\pi r \text{ or } \frac{r}{R} = \frac{N}{n}$$

Since, $B_1 = \frac{\mu_0 NI}{2R}$ and $B_2 = \frac{\mu_0 nI}{2r}$

$$\therefore \frac{B_1}{B_2} = \frac{\frac{\mu_0 NI}{2R}}{\frac{\mu_0 nI}{2r}} = \frac{N}{n}\left(\frac{r}{R}\right) = \left(\frac{N}{n}\right)\left(\frac{N}{n}\right)$$

$$\Rightarrow \quad \frac{B_1}{B_2} = \left(\frac{N}{n}\right)^2$$

17 (*d*) Magnetic field at centre due to this strip dr is given as

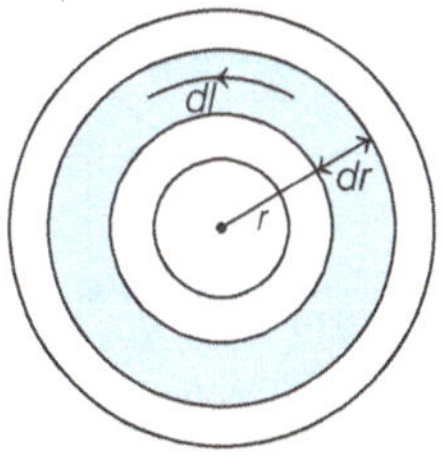

$$dB = \frac{\mu_0}{2r}\,dl = \frac{\mu_0}{2r} \cdot \left(\frac{n}{r_2 - r_1}\right) . dr$$

$$\text{So, } B_{net} = \int dB = \frac{\mu_0 nI}{2(r_2 - r_1)} \int_{r_1}^{r_2} \frac{dr}{r}$$

$$= \frac{\mu_0 nI}{2(r_2 - r_1)} \log_e\left(\frac{r_2}{r_1}\right)$$

18 (*a*) The diagram is given below

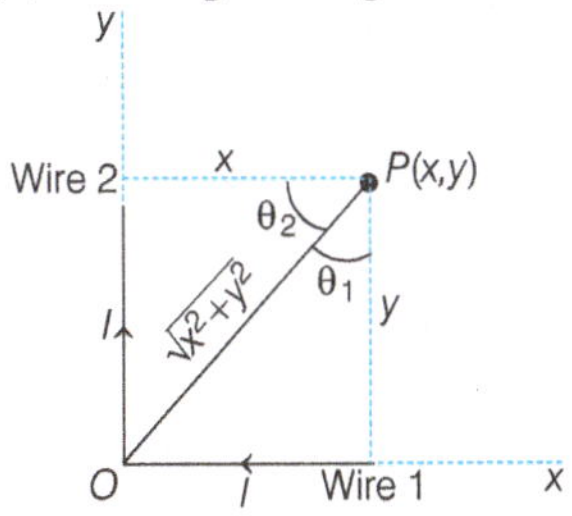

The magnetic field due to the wire 1,

$$B_{wire\,1} = \frac{\mu_0 I}{4\pi y}(\sin 90° + \sin\theta_1)$$

$$= \frac{\mu_0 I}{4\pi y}\left(1 + \frac{x}{\sqrt{x^2 + y^2}}\right)$$

The magnetic field due to the wire 2,

$$= \frac{\mu_0 I}{4\pi x}(\sin 90° + \sin\theta_2)$$

$$B_{wire\,2} = \frac{\mu_0 I}{4\pi x}\left(1 + \frac{y}{\sqrt{x^2 + y^2}}\right)$$

Thus, the total magnetic field,

$$B = B_1 + B_2$$

$$= \frac{\mu_0 I}{4\pi}\left(\frac{1}{y} + \frac{x}{y\sqrt{x^2 + y^2}} + \frac{1}{x} + \frac{y}{x\sqrt{x^2 + y^2}}\right)$$

$$= \frac{\mu_0 I}{4\pi xy}\left[\sqrt{x^2 + y^2} + (x + y)\right]$$

19 (*b*) Given rectangular loop can be viewed as a combination of two loops *ABCDA* and *ADEFA*.

So, magnetic moment is given by

$$\mathbf{m} = \frac{N}{A}$$

$\mathbf{m}$ (loop) $= \mathbf{m}(ABCDA) + \mathbf{m}(ADEFA)$

The area vector of *ABCDA* is along *Z*-axis and that of *ADEFA* is along *Y*-axis as shown in figure,

Now, $\mathbf{m}(ABCDA) = IA\hat{\mathbf{k}} = I(ab)\hat{\mathbf{k}}$

and $\mathbf{m}(ADEFA) = IA\hat{\mathbf{j}} = I(ab)\hat{\mathbf{j}}$

$$\therefore \quad \mathbf{m}\text{ (loop)} = Iab\hat{\mathbf{k}} + Iab\hat{\mathbf{j}}$$
$$= Iab(\hat{\mathbf{k}} + \hat{\mathbf{j}})$$

$$= (Iab\sqrt{2})\left(\frac{\hat{\mathbf{k}}}{\sqrt{2}} + \frac{\hat{\mathbf{j}}}{\sqrt{2}}\right)$$

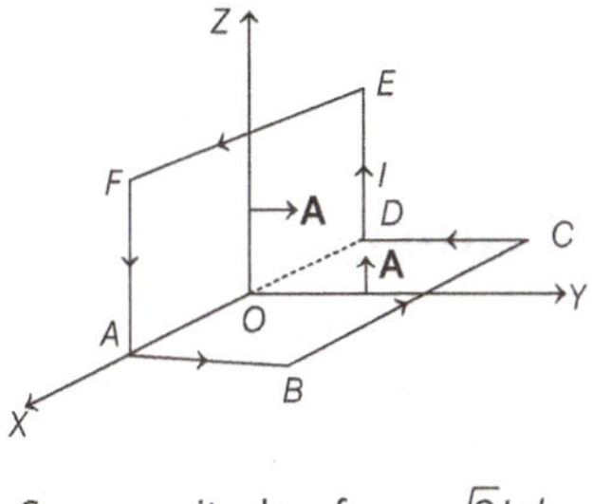

So, magnitude of $\mathbf{m} = \sqrt{2}Iab$

and direction of **m** is along

$$\frac{1}{\sqrt{2}}(\hat{\mathbf{j}}+\hat{\mathbf{k}})$$

20 (*d*) According to given condition, when a particle having charge same as electron move in a magnetic field on circular path, then the force always acts towards the centre and perpendicular to the velocity.

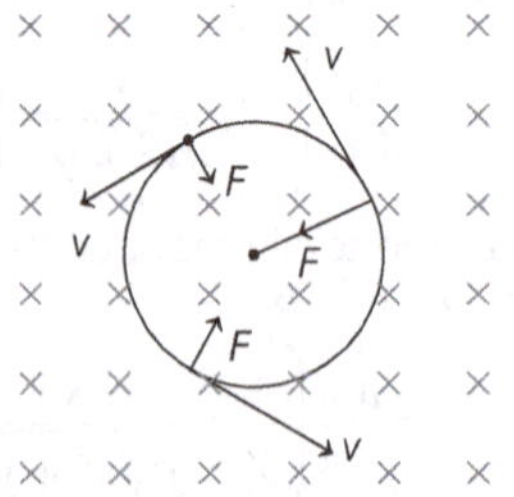

Here, $B = 0.5$ T

$R = 5$ cm

Magnetic force is

$$F_m = q(v \times B)$$

$$= q\,vB\sin 90°$$

$$F_m = qvB \quad \text{...(i)}$$

When the electric field is applied and the particle moves in a straight path, then this is the case of velocity selector.

$\therefore \quad F_e = qE \quad$ ...(ii)

Here, $F_m = F_e$

$\Rightarrow \quad qvB = qE \quad$ ...(iii)

Initially particle moves under the magnetic field, so the radius of circular path taken by the particle is

$$R = \frac{mv}{qB} \quad \text{...(iv)}$$

From Eqs. (iii) and (iv), we get

$$m = \frac{qB^2R}{E}$$

$$m = \frac{1.6\times10^{-19}\times0.25\times0.5\times10^{-2}}{10^2}$$

$$m = 2\times10^{-24}\text{ kg}$$

Skill Boosters

1 (*b*) Magnetic force, $F_m = qvB$ and directed along $\mathbf{v}\times\mathbf{B}$, i.e. radially inwards.

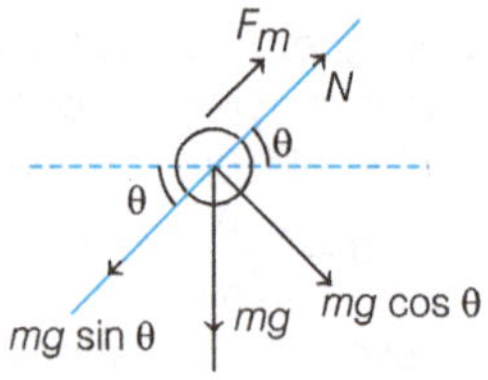

$$N - mg\sin\theta + F_m = \frac{mv^2}{R}$$

$$\Rightarrow N = \frac{mv^2}{R} + mg\sin\theta - qvB \quad \text{...(i)}$$

From conservation of energy,

Loss in gravitational potential energy = Gain in kinetic energy

$$\Rightarrow \quad mgR\sin\theta = \frac{1}{2}mv^2 \quad \text{...(ii)}$$

From Eqs. (i) and (ii), we get

$$N = 3mg\sin\theta - qB\sqrt{2gR\sin\theta}$$

At $\theta = \frac{\pi}{2}$, $N_{max} = 3mg - qB\sqrt{2gR}$

2 (*a*)

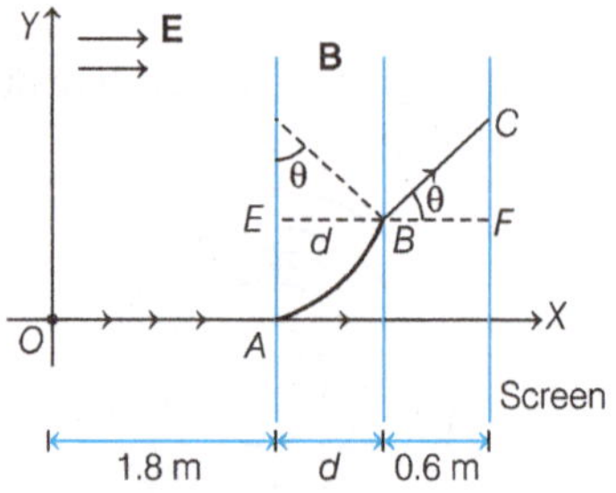

$$v_A = \sqrt{2as} = v \text{ (say)}$$

or $v = \sqrt{2\left(\frac{qE}{m}\right)s}$

$$= \sqrt{\frac{2\times1.0\times10\times1.8}{1}}$$

$$= 6\text{ ms}^{-1}$$

In magnetic field, speed does not change. Hence, particle will collide with 6 ms^{-1}.

In magnetic field, path of the particle is a circle. Radius of circular particle is

$$r = \frac{mv}{Bq} = \frac{(1)(6)}{(5)(1)} = 1.2\text{m}$$

$$d = (2.4 - 1.8)\text{ m} = 0.6\text{ m}$$

Since, $d < r$

$$\theta = \sin^{-1}\left(\frac{d}{r}\right) = \sin^{-1}\left(\frac{0.6}{1.2}\right) = 30°$$

$$AE = r(1-\cos\theta) = 1.2\left(1-\frac{\sqrt{3}}{2}\right)$$

$$= 0.6\,(2-\sqrt{3})$$

$$FC = BF\tan\theta = \frac{0.6}{\sqrt{3}}$$

$\therefore$ y-coordinate $= AE + FC$

$$= 0.6\left(2-\sqrt{3}+\frac{1}{\sqrt{3}}\right)$$

$$= \frac{1.2\,(\sqrt{3}-1)}{\sqrt{3}}\text{ m}$$

Total time, $t = t_{OA} + t_{AB} + t_{BC}$

$$t_{OA} = \sqrt{\frac{2s}{A}} = \sqrt{\frac{2s}{\frac{qE}{m}}} = \frac{\sqrt{2ms}}{qE}$$

$$= \sqrt{\frac{2\times1\times1.8}{(1)(10)}}$$

$$= 0.6\text{ s} = \frac{3}{5}\text{ s}$$

$$t_{AB} = \left(\frac{30°}{360°}\right)T = \left(\frac{1}{12}\right)\left(\frac{2\pi m}{Bq}\right)$$

$$= \frac{(2\pi)(1)}{(12)(5)(1)} = \frac{\pi}{30}\text{ s}$$

$$t_{BC} = \frac{BC}{v} = \frac{0.6\sec\theta}{v}$$

$$= \frac{(0.6)\left(\frac{2}{\sqrt{3}}\right)}{6} = \frac{1}{5\sqrt{3}}\text{ s}$$

$$\therefore \quad t = \frac{1}{5}\left(3+\frac{\pi}{6}+\frac{1}{\sqrt{3}}\right)\text{s}$$

3 (*c*) Cylinder magnetic field B is

$$B = \frac{\mu_0 ir}{2\pi R^2}, \text{ for } r < a$$

$$B = \frac{\mu_0 i}{2\pi r}, \text{ for } r \geq a$$

We can consider the given cylinder as a combination of two cylinders. One of cylinder of radius R carrying current I in one direction and other of radius $\frac{R}{2}$ carrying $\frac{I}{3}$ in other direction.

At point A,

$$B = \frac{\mu_0(I/3)}{2\pi(R/2)} + 0 = \frac{\mu_0 I}{3\pi R}$$

At point B,

$$B = \frac{\mu_0(4I/3)}{2(\pi R^2)}\,\frac{R}{2} + 0 = \frac{\mu_0 I}{3\pi R}$$

4 (*b*) Here, $B_{PR} = 0$ and $B_{PQ} = 0$

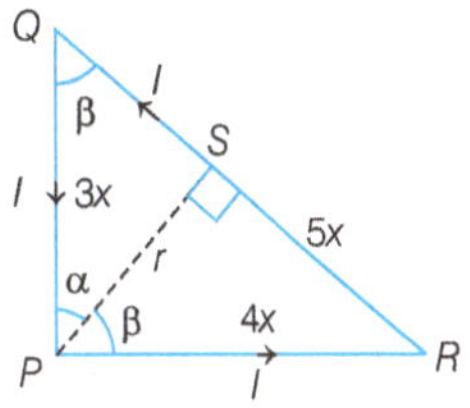

$$\sin\alpha = \frac{3}{5}, \quad \sin\beta = \frac{4}{5}$$

Also, $\sin\alpha = \frac{r}{4x} = \frac{3}{5}$

$$r = \frac{12x}{5}$$

Magnetic field along QR,

$$B = B_{QR} = \frac{\mu_0 I}{4\pi r}(\sin\alpha + \sin\beta)$$

$$= \frac{\mu_0}{4\pi} \cdot \frac{I}{12x/5}\left(\frac{3}{5} + \frac{4}{5}\right) = 7\left(\frac{\mu_0 I}{48\pi x}\right)$$

5 (*a*) Magnetic field along a current carrying wire of radius r, i.e.

$$\mathbf{B}_1 = \frac{\mu_0}{4\pi} \times \frac{I}{r} \times \pi = \frac{\mu_0 I}{4r}$$

Similarly, magnetic field along a current carrying wire of radius $2r$, i.e.

$$\mathbf{B}_2 = \frac{\mu_0}{4\pi} \times \frac{I}{2r} \times \pi = \frac{\mu_0 I}{8r}$$

So, net magnetic field at point P,

$$\mathbf{B} = \mathbf{B}_1 + \mathbf{B}_2 = \frac{\mu_0 I}{4r} + \frac{\mu_0 I}{8r}$$

$$= \frac{3}{8} \cdot \frac{\mu_0 I}{r}$$

i.e. perpendicular to the plane of the paper and directed inwards.

6 (*a*) As, we know

$$\frac{x}{d} = \sin 45° \Rightarrow x = \frac{d}{\sqrt{2}}$$

We can extend the wire and then subtract the field of extended part.

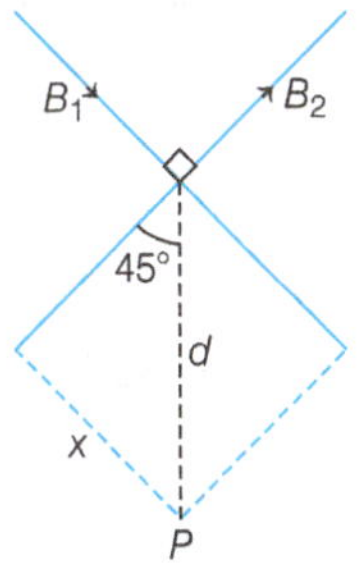

Magnetic field, i.e.

$$B_1 = \frac{\mu_0 I}{4\pi d/\sqrt{2}}(\sin 0° + \sin 90°)$$

$$- \frac{\mu_0 I}{4\pi d/\sqrt{2}}(\sin 0° + \sin 45°)$$

$$= \frac{\mu_0 I}{2\sqrt{2}\pi d}\left(1 - \frac{1}{\sqrt{2}}\right)$$

and similarly, $B_2 = \frac{\mu_0 I}{2\sqrt{2}\pi d}\left[1 - \frac{1}{\sqrt{2}}\right]$

Then, net magnetic field at point P

$$B = (B_1 + B_2) = 2B$$

$$= \frac{\mu_0 I}{\sqrt{2}\pi d}\left(1 - \frac{1}{\sqrt{2}}\right)$$

7 (*a*) Radius of circular path is

$$r = \frac{mv_0}{Bq}$$

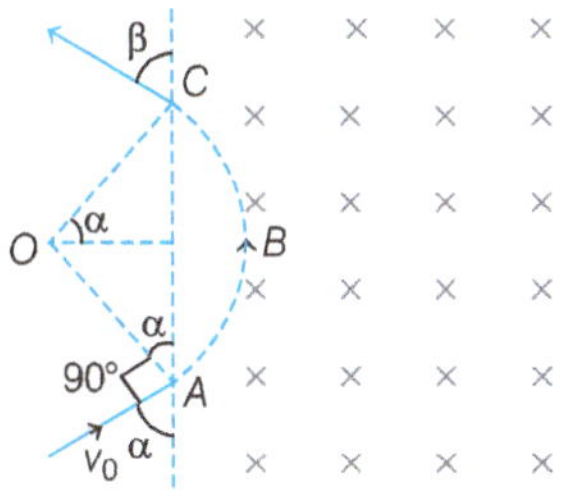

Let O be the centre of circular path, then

$$\angle OCD = \angle OAD$$

$$\Rightarrow \quad 90° - \beta = 90° - \alpha$$

$$\Rightarrow \quad \beta = \alpha$$

$$\Rightarrow \quad \angle AOC = 2\alpha$$

So length of arc

$$ABC = r(2\alpha) = \frac{2mv_0}{Bq}\alpha$$

$$\text{Time }(ABC) = \frac{\text{Arc length } ABC}{\text{Speed}}$$

$$= \frac{2m\alpha}{Bq}$$

8 (*a*) $\tau_1 = NBIA\cos\theta$

$\tau_2 = NBIA\cos(90° + \theta) = NBIA\sin\theta$

$\Rightarrow \tau_1^2 + \tau_2^2 = (NBIA)^2(\cos^2\theta + \sin^2\theta)$

$$\Rightarrow \quad B = \frac{\sqrt{\tau_1^2 + \tau_2^2}}{NIA}$$

9 (*a*) The gravitational torque must be counter balanced by the magnetic torque about O for the equilibrium of the sphere.

$$\tau_m = \pi I r^2 B \sin\theta$$

$$\tau_{gravity} = mgr\sin\theta$$

For equilibrium, $\tau_m = \tau_{gravity}$

or $\quad \pi I r^2 B\sin\theta = mgr\sin\theta$

or $\quad B = \frac{mg}{\pi I r}$

10 (*a*) $\because \mathbf{F}_m = q(\mathbf{v} \times \mathbf{B})$

For region, $a < x < 2a$

$$|\mathbf{F}| = qvB_0$$

The force $\mathbf{F}$ will be in the direction of $(\mathbf{v} \times \mathbf{B})$, i.e. along $(\hat{\mathbf{i}} \times \hat{\mathbf{j}}) = \hat{\mathbf{k}}$

For region, $2a < x < 3a$

$$|\mathbf{F}| = qvB_0$$

$\mathbf{F}$ will be in the direction of $-\hat{\mathbf{k}}$.

Hence, the direction of circular motion will be as shown in graph (a).

05

Scan for **Physics Through Concept Master** *Videos*

Magnetism and Matter

Topicwise No. of Ques asked in 5 Years (NEET)

Topics	No. of Questions				
	2024	2023	2022	2021	2020
The Bar Magnet	2	–	–	1	1
Magnetism and Gauss's Law	–	1	–	–	–
Magnetisation and Magnetic Intensity	–	–	–	–	–
Magnetic Properties of Materials	1	–	1	–	1

Special Type of Ques Asked In 5 Years (NEET)

Types	Years				
	2024	2023	2022	2021	2020
A-R	–	–	–	–	–
Statement Based	–	–	–	–	–
Matching	1	–	–	–	–

Last 5 Years Weigtage (NEET)

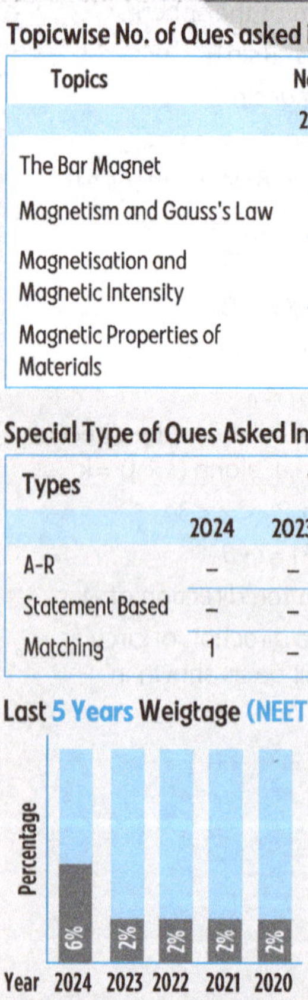

- Magnetic phenomena are universal in nature.
- The word magnet is derived from the name of an island in Greece called **magnesia**, where magnetic ore deposits were found in early 600 BC.
- A magnet is a material that has both attractive and directive properties.
- The phenomenon of attraction of small bits of iron, steel, cobalt, nickel, etc. towards the magnet, is called **magnetism.**

Some of the commonly known ideas regarding magnetism are

- The earth behaves as a magnet with the magnetic field pointing approximately from the geographic south to the north.
- When a magnet (bar magnet) is freely suspended, it points in the north-south direction.
- The tip which points to the geographic north is called the **north pole** and the tip which points to the geographic south is called the **south pole** of the magnet.
- There is a **repulsive force** when north pole (or south pole) of two magnets are brought close together. Conversely, there is an **attractive force** between the north pole of one magnet and the south pole of the other.
- We cannot isolate the north or south pole of a magnet. If a bar magnet is broken into two halves we get two similar bar magnets with somewhat weaker properties. Unlike electric charges, isolated magnetic north and south pole known as magnetic monopoles do not exist.
- A bar magnet is a magnet in shape of bar which produces magnetic field around it. It consists of two equal and non-separable magnetic poles.
- It is possible to make magnets out of iron and its alloys.

Bar Magnet

- A bar magnet is a natural magnetic dipole which produces magnetic field around it.
- **Properties of a bar magnet are**
  - They attract small pieces of iron, nickel and cobalt.
  - The ends of bar magnet where the magnetic force due to bar magnet is maximum are called the **poles** of magnet.
- A freely suspended bar magnet aligns itself in the north-south direction of earth. Pole of a freely suspended magnet which points towards the north of earth is called **north pole** (*N*) and pole that points towards the south of earth is called **south pole** (*S*) of bar magnet.
- Like poles repel each other and unlike poles attract each other.
- Magnetic poles always exist in pairs. Every bar magnet is a magnetic dipole. Mono poles do not exist in magnetism.
- Repulsion is the surest test for distinguishing between a piece of iron and magnet.

Magnetic Field Lines

- The magnetic field lines of a magnet are the imaginary lines which continuously represent the direction of the magnetic field.
- **Important properties of magnetic field lines are**
  (i) The magnetic field lines of a magnet (or a solenoid) form continuous closed loops.
  (ii) The tangent to the field line at a given point represents the direction of the net magnetic field **B** at that point.
  (iii) The larger the number of field lines crossing per unit area, the stronger is the magnitude of the magnetic field **B**. In Fig. (a), **B** is large around region (ii) than region (i).
  (iv) The magnetic field lines do not intersect, for if they did, the direction of the magnetic field would not be unique at the point of intersection.
  (v) The figures (a) , (b), (c) show the **magnetic field lines** of a bar magnet, a current carrying solenoid and an electric dipole, respectively.

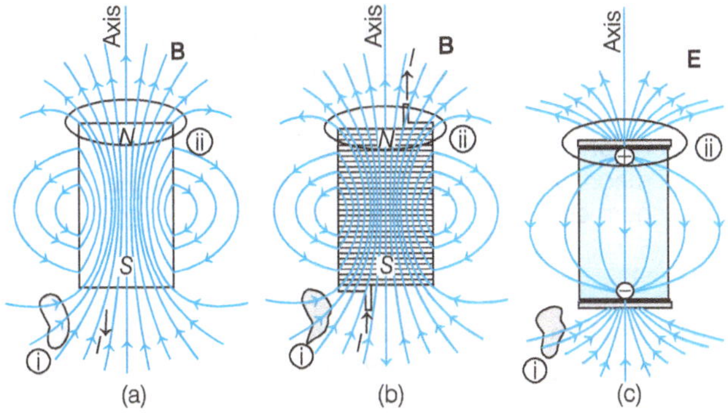

Bar Magnet as an Equivalent Solenoid

- Similarities of magnetic field lines of a bar magnet and a solenoid suggest that a bar magnet may be thought of as a large number of circulating currents in analogy with a solenoid.

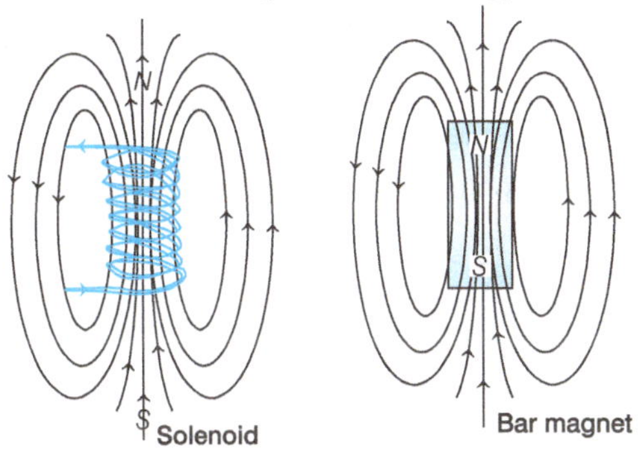

- Cutting a bar magnet in half is like cutting a solenoid, we get two smaller solenoids with weaker magnetic properties.
- The field lines remain continuous, emerging from one face of the solenoid and entering into the other face.
- The magnitude of the magnetic moment of the solenoid is M = (total number of turns × current × cross sectional area) $= n(2l)\, I(\pi a^2)$.
- **A bar magnet and a solenoid produce similar magnetic fields**. The magnetic moment of a bar magnet is thus equal to the magnetic moment of an equivalent solenoid that produces the same magnetic field.
- For axial position magnetic field at a point due to a bar magnet,

$$\mathbf{B}_a = \frac{\mu_0}{4\pi}\frac{2\mathbf{M}}{r^3}$$

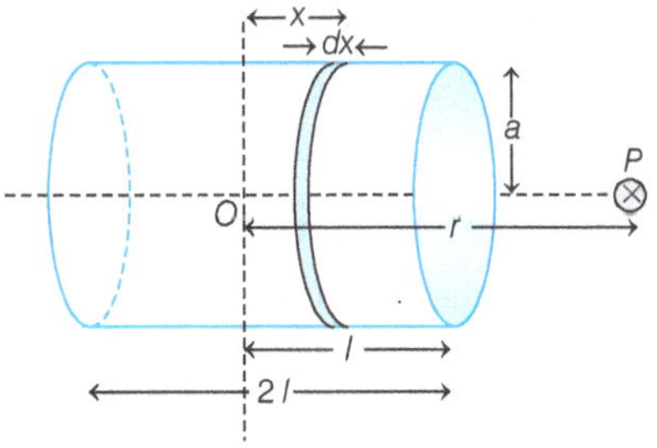

Marks Maximiser

Magnetic field at a general position

$$|\mathbf{B}_{res}| = \left(\frac{\mu_0}{4\pi}\right)\frac{M\sqrt{1+3\cos^2\theta}}{r^3}$$

for axial point, $\theta = 0°$

for equatorial point, $\theta = 90°$

$$\tan\phi = \frac{|\mathbf{B}_n|}{|\mathbf{B}_r|} = \frac{\tan\theta}{2}$$

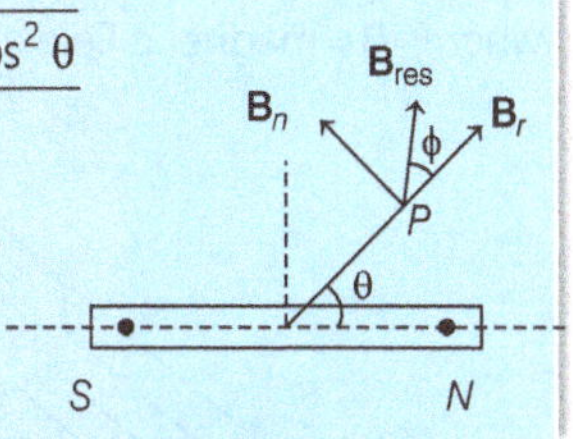

B_n = magnetic field in the normal direction

and B_r = magnetic field in radial direction.

Dipole in a Uniform Magnetic Field

- A magnetic dipole when placed in a uniform magnetic field does not experience any net force. However, it experiences a torque given by

Torque, $\tau = \mathbf{M} \times \mathbf{B}$

$$|\tau| = MB \sin\theta\, \hat{\mathbf{n}}$$

where, θ is the angle from magnetic field along which the dipole has been placed.

- The magnetic potential energy U_m is given by

$$U_m = \int_{90°}^{\theta} \tau\, d\theta = \int_{90°}^{\theta} MB \sin\theta\, d\theta$$ NEET 2021, 20

$$= -MB\cos\theta$$

or $U_m = -\mathbf{M}\cdot\mathbf{B}$

(i) $U_m = 0$, at $\theta = 90°$

(ii) $U_{min} = -MB$ (minimum), at $\theta = 0°$ (most stable position)

(iii) $U_{max} = +MB$ (maximum), at $\theta = 180°$ (most unstable position)

The Dipole Analogy

The analogy between electric and magnetic dipoles is shown below

Physical quantity	Electrostatics	Magnetism
Proportionality	$1/\varepsilon_0$	μ_0
Dipole moment	$\mathbf{p}$	$\mathbf{M}$
Equatorial field for a short dipole	$-\mathbf{p}/4\pi\varepsilon_0 r^3$	$-\mu_0\mathbf{M}/4\pi r^3$
Axial field for a short dipole	$2\mathbf{p}/4\pi\varepsilon_0 r^3$	$\mu_0 2\,\mathbf{M}/4\pi r^3$
External field : Torque	$\mathbf{p}\times\mathbf{E}$	$\mathbf{M}\times\mathbf{B}$
External field : Energy	$-\mathbf{p}\cdot\mathbf{E}$	$-\mathbf{M}\cdot\mathbf{B}$

For Concept Master Video

Magnetism and Gauss's Law

- The number of magnetic field lines leaving the surface is balanced by the number of lines entering it, i.e. **net magnetic flux ϕ_B through any closed surface is always zero.**

$$\phi_B = \sum_{all} \Delta\phi_B = \sum_{all} \mathbf{B}\cdot d\mathbf{S} = 0$$ NEET 2023

where, $\mathbf{B}$ = magnetic field and ΔS = area element.

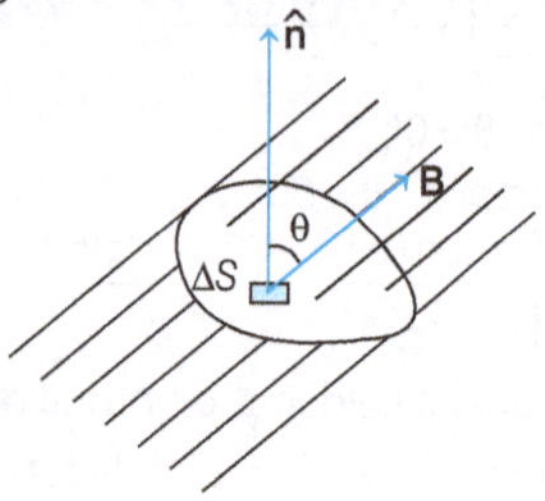

- The Gauss's law of magnetism shows that monopoles does not exist. There is no start point or end point of magnetic field lines.
- As we can say, magnetic flux incoming is equal to magnetic flux outgoing.

Magnetisation and Magnetic Intensity

(i) **Magnetic induction** (B) is the number of magnetic field lines passing normally through a cross-sectional area of material.

Its SI unit is **tesla (T)** or **weber/ metre^2 (Wm^{-2})** and CGS unit is **gauss (G)**.

Also, $1\text{T} = 10^4$ G.

(ii) **Intensity of magnetisation** (I) The net magnetic moment per unit volume.

i.e. $$I = \frac{\text{Magnetic moment}}{\text{Volume of the magnetic substance}}$$

$$I = \frac{M}{V}$$

It is a vector quantity and its SI unit is Am^{-1}. Its dimensional formula is $[M^0L^{-1}T^0A]$

(iii) **Magnetising field Intensity** (H) is a measure of the capability of external magnetic field to magnetise the given substance and given by $H = \frac{B}{\mu_0} - I$.

Its SI unit is Am^{-1} and CGS unit is oersted.

(iv) **Magnetic susceptibility** (χ_m) is the ratio of intensity of magnetisation in a substance to the magnetic field.

i.e. $$\chi_m = \frac{I}{H}$$

It is a scalar quantity with no units and dimensions. It is a measure of how a magnetic material responds to an external field.

(v) **Magnetic permeability** (μ) is the ratio of the magnetic induction to the magnetic intensity.

i.e. $$\mu = \frac{B}{H}$$ NEET 2022, 20

It is a scalar quantity. Its SI unit is Wb/A-m or TmA^{-1} and its dimensional formula is $[MLT^{-2}A^{-2}]$

It measures the degree to which a magnetic material is permeable to field.

(vi) **Relative magnetic permeability** (μ_r) is the ratio of magnetic permeability of the substance to the permeability of free space and given as

$$\mu_r = \frac{\mu}{\mu_0} = \frac{B}{B_0}$$

(vii) **Relation between relative magnetic permeability and magnetic susceptibility** is

$$\mu_r = 1 + \chi_m$$

Magnetic Properties of Materials

In terms of magnetic behaviour, all substances are categorised in three types, diamagnetic, paramagnetic and ferromagnetic

Properties	Diamagnetic	Paramagnetic	Ferromagnetic
Substance placed in uniform magnetic field	Poor magnetisation in opposite direction. Here, $B_m < B_o$ 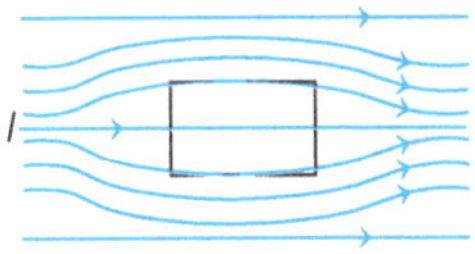	Poor magnetisation in same direction. Here, $B_m > B_o$ 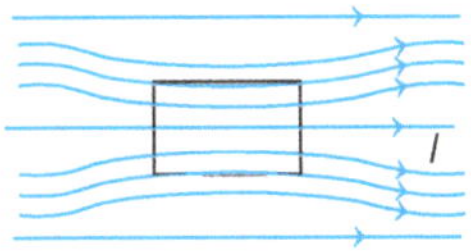	Strong magnetisation in same direction. Here, $B_m >> B_o$ 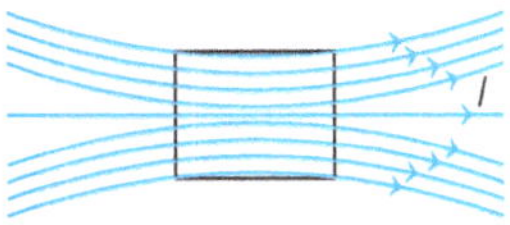
Nature	Weakly repelled by a magnet	Weakly attracted by magnet	Strongly attracted by magnet
Magnetic flux density	Inside a diamagnetic material is less than in air	Inside a paramagnetic material is larger than in air	Inside a ferromagnetic material is much larger, than in air
Cause of magnetism	Orbital motion of electrons	Spin motion of electron	Formation of domain
Behaviour of magnetic field lines	Not pass through them 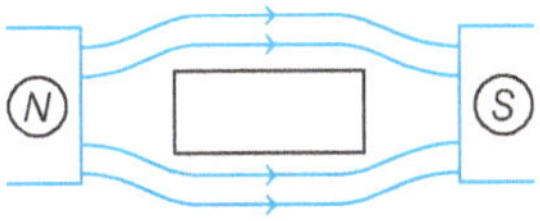	Most of line pass through them 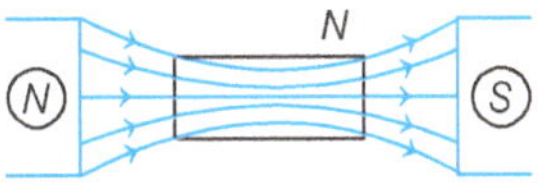	Pass through them 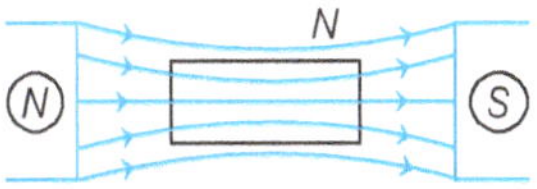
I-*H* curve	*I* is small, negative, varies linearly with field 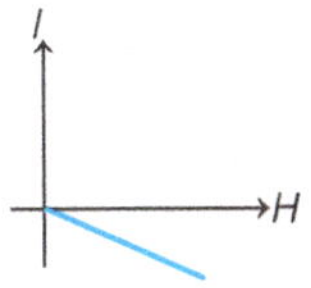	*I* is small, positive, varies linearly with field 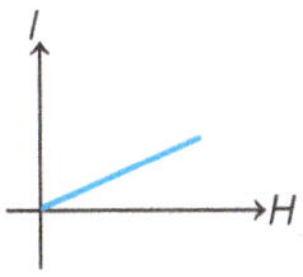	*I* is very large, positive and varies non-linearly with field. 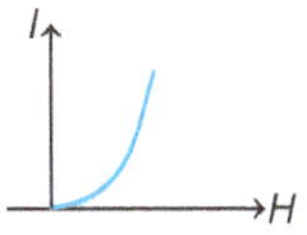
μ_r	$1 > \mu_r > 0$, $(\mu < \mu_0)$	$(1+\varepsilon) \geq \mu_r > 1$, $(\mu > \mu_0)$	$\mu_r >>> 1$, $(\mu >>> \mu_0)$
χ_m -*T* curve For Concept Master Video	χ_m small, negative and temperature independent $\chi_m \propto T^0$ 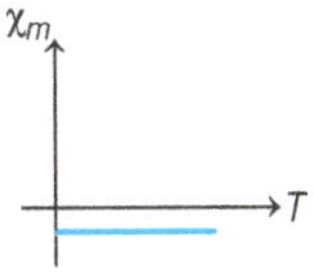	χ_m small, positive and varies inversely with temperature, $\chi_m \propto \frac{1}{T}$ (curie law) 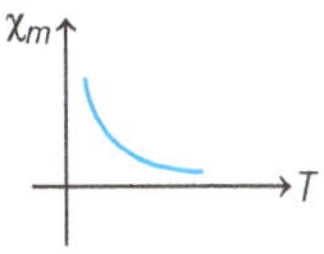	χ_m very large, positive and temperature dependent $\chi_m \propto \frac{1}{T - T_C}$ (Curie-Weiss law) 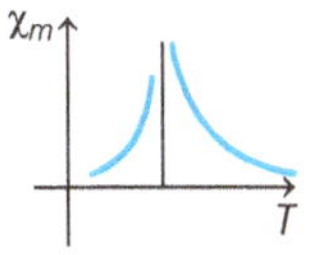 $T_{C(\text{iron})} = 770°C$
Magnetic moment of single atom	Atom do not posses permanent magnetic moment	Atom have permanent magnetic moment which are randomly oriented	Atom have permanent magnetic moment which are organised in domain
Physical state of the material	Solid, liquid or gas	Solid, liquid or gas	Normally solid only
Example	Bismuth, copper, lead, water sodium chloride	Aluminium, sodium, calcium; oxygen, copper chloride	Iron, cobalt, nickel, gadolinium

Hysteresis

- The lagging of intensity of magnetisation (I) or magnetic induction (B) behind the magnetising field (H) during the process of magnetisation and demagnetisation of a ferromagnetic material is called hysteresis.
- The area of hysteresis loop is equal to the energy loss per cycle per unit volume and its different for different material.

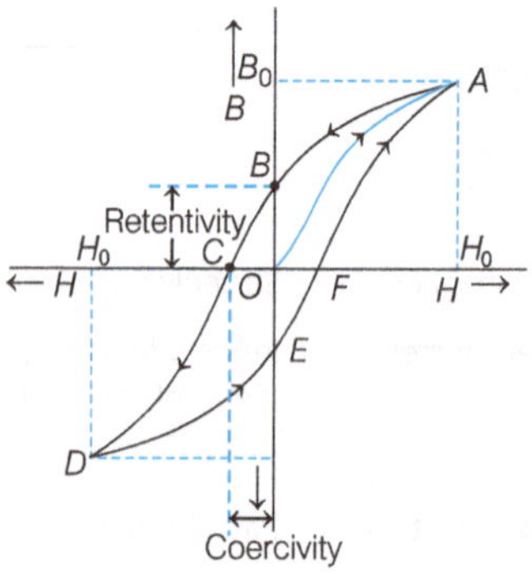

Ferromagnetic Materials

Parameter	Soft Iron	Steel
1. Retentivity	High	Low
2. Coercivity	Low	High
3. Permeability	High	Low
4. Susceptibility	High	Low
5. Intensity of magnetisation	High	Low
6. Hystersis loss	Low	High
7. Uses	electromagnet, cores of transformer	Permanent magnets
8. Hysteresis loop	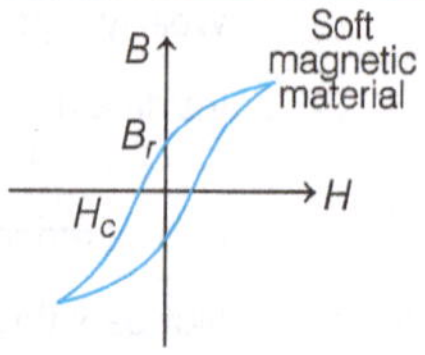	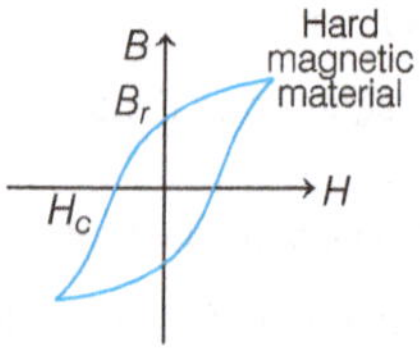

Caution Points

- For diamagnetic materials, the magnetic susceptibility, $\chi = -10^{-5}$ whereas for paramagnetic materials, the magnetic susceptibility $\chi = +10^{-5}$.
- The difference in magnetic susceptibility between diamagnetic and paramagnetic materials is very small but it can lead to radically different behaviour.
- A super conductor is a special kind of material. These materials have two remarkable properties.
  (i) They are perfect diamagnets.
  (ii) They are also perfect conductors.
- Diamagnetism is universal. It is present in all materials but it is weak and hard to detect.
- There exist some other type of magnetic material like as ferromagnetic, anti - ferromagnetic and spin glass. These materials have unique and mysterious properties.

PYQ Notes

- Horizontal and vertical components of Earth's magnetic field.
  If B_E is the net magnetic field on any point on the surface of the earth and δ is the angle of dip, then
  Horizontal component, $H = B_E \cos \delta$
  Vertical component, $V = B_E \sin \delta$
- The value of δ varies from $-90°$ in south pole to $+90°$ in the north pole and its value is zero at equator. **[NEET 2022]**

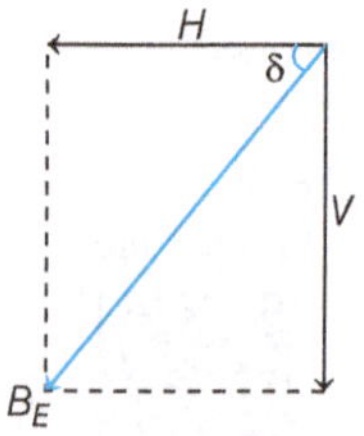

Step by Step

Mastering NCERT

- Concept Builders
- Topical Questions
- Assertion and Reason Questions
- Statement Based
- Matching Type
- Numerical Type
- NCERT Exemplar
- Past Exams MCQs
- Skill Boosters

Concept Builders

1 The earth behaves as a magnet with the magnetic field pointing approximately from the geographic south to the north. [T/F]

2 What is the most elementary form of magnetism?

3 When a magnet of pole strength q_m is cut into two equal parts perpendicular to its axis, the pole strength of each part will be ....(q_m / q_m / 2)

4 The magnetic poles also exist as unlike pairs of equal strength. [T/F]

5 The discrepancy between the orientation of a compass and true north-south direction is known as magnetic .... (inclination/declination)

6 A magnetic demagnetises on .... (heating/cooling)

7 At which angle, the magnetic potential energy is maximum?

8 If a magnetised needle is placed in a uniform magnetic field experiencing some torque, then what will be the force on the needle ?

9 According to Ampere's hypothesis, what is the cause of magnetic effects?

10 Write down the formula for the magnetic field at an equitorial point of a bar magnet.

11 The material having small negative susceptibility are called .... (paramagnetic / diamagnetic) substances.

12 The intensity of magnetisation of a paramagnetic material decreases with the increase in magnetising field. [T/F]

13 The relative magnetic permeability of a diamagnetic material is 1. [T/ F]

14 What does the phenomena of the lagging of magnetic induction behind the magnetising field in ferromagnetic material is called?

15 Soft iron is more suitable than steel for making a permanent magnet. [T/F]

16 What is the cause of magnetism in the paramagnetic substances?

17 Susceptibility of a diamagnetic material does not depend upon temperature. [T/F]

18 Water is a .... (paramagnetic / diamagnetic) substance.

19 The product of magnetic susceptibility and absolute temperature for a paramagnetic substance is a constant. [T/F]

20 For a diamagnetic material χ_m is .... $(+10^{-5} / -10^{-5})$ and for a paramagnetic material χ_m is .... $(+10^{-5} / -10^{-5})$

Topical Questions

The Bar Magnet

1 Which of the following point lies in the region of highest magnetic field strength ? NCERT Pg. 137

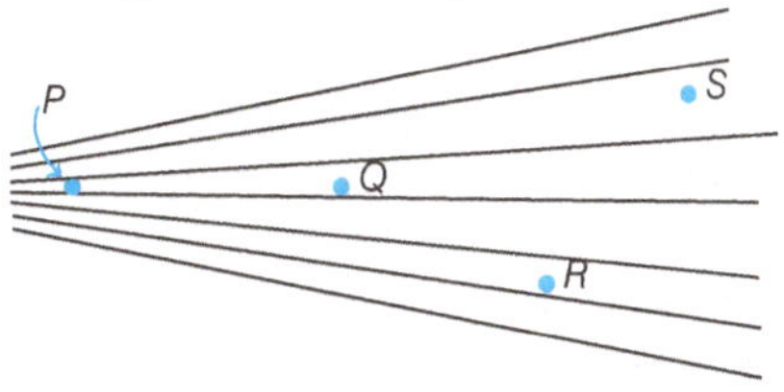

(a) P (b) Q (c) R (d) S

2 Many of the diagrams given in figure below, show magnetic field lines (thick lines in the figure). Which of them correctly show this? NCERT Pg. 137

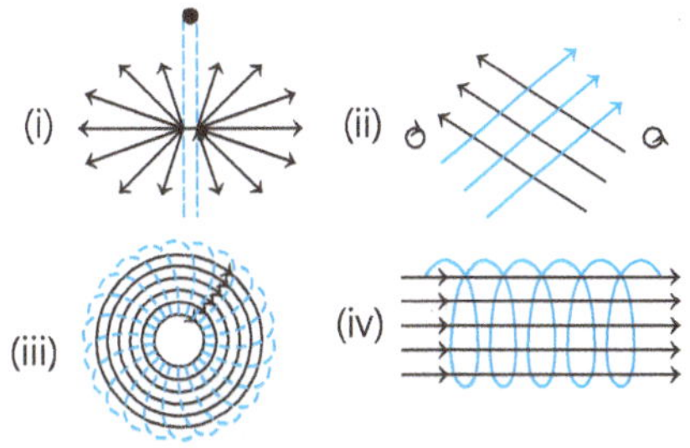

(a) Both (i) and (iv) (b) Both (ii) and (iv)
(c) Both (iii) and (iv) (d) Only (iii)

3 A large magnet is broken into two pieces, so that their lengths are in the ratio 2 : 1. The pole strengths of the two pieces will have ratio **NCERT Pg. 137**
(a) 2 : 1 (b) 1 : 2
(c) 4 : 1 (d) 1 : 1

4 If the bar magnet of magnetic moment 0.40 A-m^2 is replaced by a solenoid of cross- sectional area $2 \times 10^{-4} m^2$ and 1000 turns having same magnetic moment, the current flowing through the solenoid is **NCERT Pg. 138**
(a) -2 A (b) 2 A
(c) 20 A (d) 1 A

5 A horizontal circular loop carries a current that looks anti-clockwise when viewed from above. It is replaced by an equivalent magnetic dipole *N-S*. Which of the following statement is correct? **NCERT Pg. 138**
(a) The line *N-S* should be along a diameter of the loop.
(b) The line *N-S* should be parallel to the plane of the loop.
(c) South pole should be below the loop.
(d) North pole should be below the loop.

6 A current carrying loop is placed in a uniform magnetic field in four different orientations as shown in figure. The potential energy increases in order of **NCERT Pg. 139**

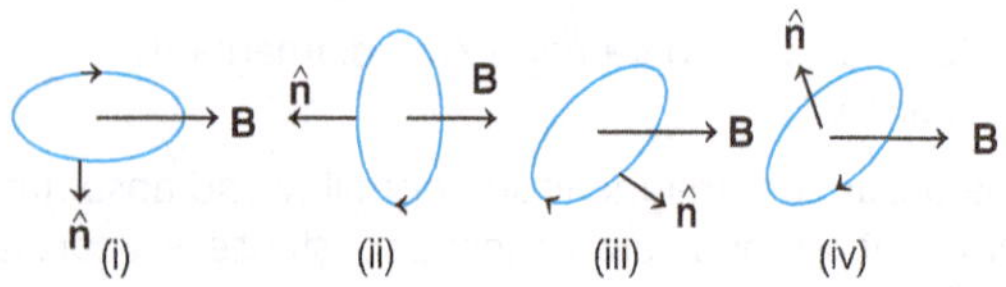

(a) (iii), (i), (iv) and (ii)
(b) (i), (ii), (iii) and (iv)
(c) (ii), (iii), (i) and (iv)
(d) (iv), (iii), (i) and (ii)

7 Following figures show the arrangement of bar magnets in different configurations. Each magnet has magnetic dipole moment *M*. Which configuration has net magnetic dipole moment $\sqrt{2}M$? **NCERT Pg. 139**

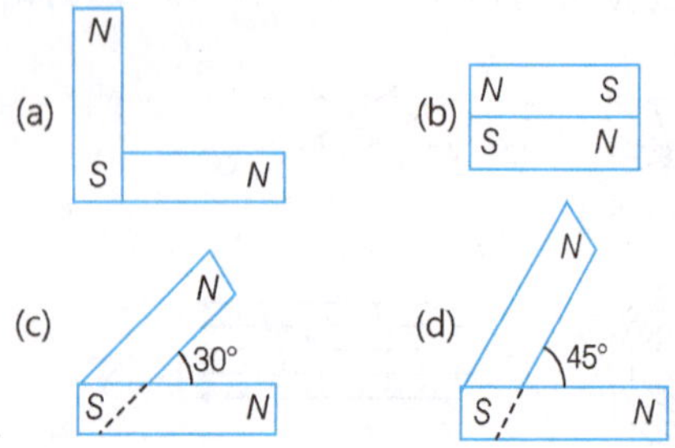

8 A short bar magnet of magnetic moment $0.32\ JT^{-1}$ is placed in a uniform magnetic field of 0.15 T. If the bar is free to rotate in the plane of the field, then the potential energy which would corresponds to its unstable equilibrium is **NCERT Pg. 139**
(a) 4.8×10^{-2} J (b) -4.8×10^{-2} J
(c) 7.5×10^{-2} J (d) 3.6×10^{5} J

9 The rate of change of torque τ with deflection θ is maximum for a magnet suspended freely in a uniform magnetic field of induction *B*, when **NCERT Pg. 139**
(a) $\theta = 0°$ (b) $\theta = 45°$ (c) $\theta = 60°$ (d) $\theta = 90°$

10 A bar magnet of magnetic moment 2.0 Am^2 is placed in uniform magnetic field of 0.2 T. The torque on bar magnet is 0.3464 J, then the angle between bar magnet and magnetic field is **NCERT Pg. 139**
(a) 30° (b) 45° (c) 60° (d) 90°

11 A dipole of magnetic moment $25\hat{\mathbf{j}}$ A - m^2 is placed along the *Y*-axis in a uniform magnetic field $(3\hat{\mathbf{i}} + 18\hat{\mathbf{j}})$ T. The torque acting on it is **NCERT Pg. 139**
(a) $-40\hat{\mathbf{k}}$ N-m (b) $-50\hat{\mathbf{k}}$ N-m
(c) $-60\hat{\mathbf{k}}$ N-m (d) $-75\hat{\mathbf{k}}$ N-m

12 The magnetic moment of a short bar magnet placed with its magnetic axis at 30° to an external field of 600 G and experience a torque of 0.03 N-m is **NCERT Pg. 139**
(a) 1.0 A-m^2 (b) 0.3 A-m^2
(c) 2.2 A-m^2 (d) 0.5 A-m^2

13 A bar magnet of magnetic moment 2.0 Am^2 is placed in parallel position with respect to a magnetic field 0.5 T. The amount of work done required in changing the position of magnet from parallel to anti-parallel is **NCERT Pg. 139**
(a) 3.0 J (b) 4.5 J (c) 2.0 J (d) 2.5 J

14 A magnetic dipole with a magnetic moment of 1.0 Am^2 is placed in a uniform magnetic field of 0.5 T. The angle between the magnetic field is 45°, then the torque on the magnetic dipole is **NCERT Pg. 139**
(a) 0.48 J (b) 0.35 J (c) 8.5 J (d) 0.85 J

15 A bar magnet is held at a right angle to a uniform magnetic field. The couple acting on the magnet is to be halved by rotating it from this position. The angle of rotation is **NCERT Pg. 139**
(a) 60° (b) 45° (c) 30° (d) 75°

16 A magnet of magnetic dipole moment $10\hat{\mathbf{j}}\ Am^2$ is placed along the *Y*-axis in uniform magnetic field $\mathbf{B} = (2\hat{\mathbf{i}} + 3\hat{\mathbf{j}})$T. The torque experienced by the dipole is . **NCERT Pg. 139**
(a) 80 N-m along positive *Y*-axis
(b) 60 N-m along negative *Y*-axis
(c) 30 N-m along positive *Z*-axis
(d) 20 N-m along negative *Z*-axis

17 A magnet of dipole moment M is aligned in equilibrium position in a magnetic field of intensity B. The work done to rotate it through an angle θ in the magnetic field is NCERT Pg. 139

(a) $MB \sin \theta$ (b) $MB \cos \theta$
(c) $MB(1-\cos \theta)$ (d) $MB(1-\sin \theta)$

18 A thin bar magnet is placed in a uniform magnetic field and aligned with the field. The needle is now rotated by an angle of 45° and the work done is W. The torque on the magnetic needle at this position is NCERT Pg. 139

(a) zero (b) $\frac{W}{\sqrt{2}-1}$ (c) $\frac{W}{\sqrt{2}}$ (d) $\sqrt{2}\,W$

19 A bar magnet having a magnetic moment of $2 \times 10^4\ JT^{-1}$ is free to rotate in a horizontal plane. A horizontal magnetic field $B = 6 \times 10^{-4}$ T exists in the space. The work done in taking the magnet slowly from a direction parallel to the field to a direction 60° from the field is NCERT Pg. 139

(a) 0.6 J (b) 12 J (c) 6 J (d) 2 J

20 The work done in turning a magnet of magnetic moment M by an angle of 90° from the meridian, is n times the corresponding work done to turn it through an angle of 60°. The value of n is given by NCERT Pg. 139

(a) 2 (b) 1 (c) 0.5 (d) 0.25

21 The torque and magnetic potential energy of a magnetic dipole is most stable position in a uniform magnetic field (**B**) having magnetic moment (**M**) will be NCERT Pg. 139

(a) zero, $-MB$ (b) zero, MB
(c) $-MB$, zero (d) MB, zero

22 What is the magnitude of axial field due to a bar magnet of length 3 cm at a distance of 75 cm from its, mid-point, if its magnetic moment is 0.6 Am^2? NCERT Pg. 139

(a) 0.284 μT (b) 0.313 μT (c) 0.013 μT (d) 0.113 μT

23 A bar magnet of length 6 cm magnetic moment of $4\ JT^{-1}$. Find the strength of magnetic field at a distance of 200 cm from the centre of the magnet along its equatorial line. NCERT Pg. 139

(a) 3×10^{-8} T (b) 5×10^{-8} T
(c) 3.5×10^{-8} T (d) 4×10^{-8} T

24 A bar magnet of length 3 cm has points A and B along axis at a distance of 24 cm and 48 cm on the opposite ends. Ratio of magnetic fields at these points will be NCERT Pg. 139

(a) 8 (b) 3 (c) 4 (d) $1/2\sqrt{2}$

25 What is the magnitude of the equatorial and axial fields due to a bar magnet of length 5.0 cm at a distance of 50 cm from its mid-point ? The magnetic moment of the bar magnet is 0.40 $A\text{-}m^2$. NCERT Pg. 139

(a) 3.2×10^{-6} T, 6.4×10^{-7} T
(b) 4.2×10^{5} T, 6×10^{-7} T
(c) 5×10^{-6} T, 3.2×10^{-7} T
(d) 3.2×10^{-7} T, 6.4×10^{-7} T

26 Two identical magnets each of magnetic moment M_o tied together, inclined at 120° with each other. The magnetic induction at point P is NCERT Pg. 139

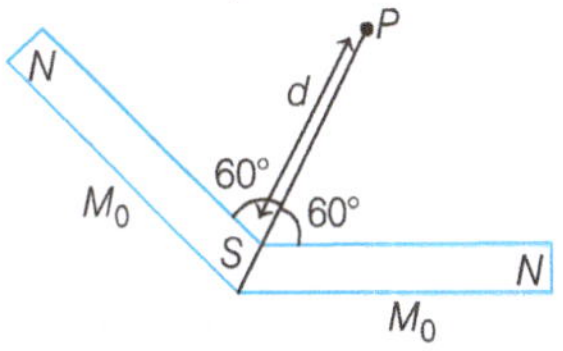

(a) $\frac{\mu_0 M_0}{2\pi d^3}$ (b) $\frac{\mu_0 2M_0}{6\pi d^3}$ (c) $\frac{\mu_0}{2\pi}\frac{2M_0}{d^2}$ (d) $\frac{\mu_0}{8\pi}\frac{2M_0}{d^2}$

27 A magnetic dipole has a magnetic moment of 0.48 JT^{-1}. The magnitude and direction of the magnetic field produced by the magnetic dipole at a distance of 20 cm from the centre of the magnetic dipole equatorial line of it is NCERT Pg. 139

(a) 0.06 G, N-S direction (b) 4.95 G, S-N direction
(c) 0.0195 G, S-N direction (d) 19.5 G, N-S direction

28 Two short bar magnets of magnetic moment 8.0 Am^2 each are arranged at the opposite corners of a square as given in figure. The magnetic induction at corner D is NCERT Pg. 140

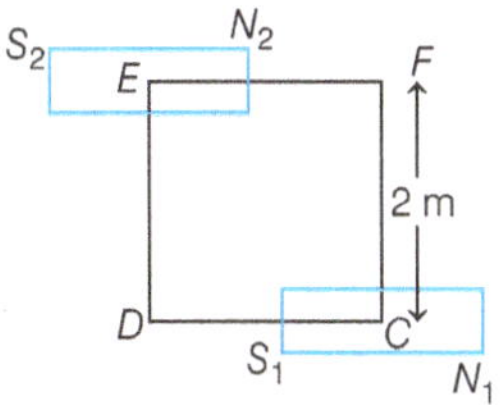

(a) 2 μT (b) 1 μT (c) 0.1 μT (d) 0.2 μT

29 A uniform magnetic field B of 0.5 T is along the positive z-direction. A rectangular loop ($abcd$) of sides 25 cm × 20 cm carries a current I of 5 A. Out of the following different orientations, which one dissipate minimum energy to get in stable equilibrium? NCERT Pg. 139

(a)
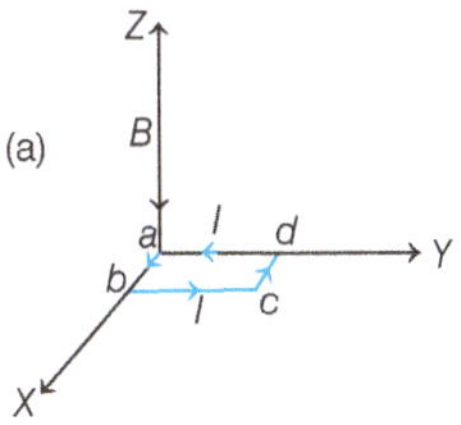

(b)
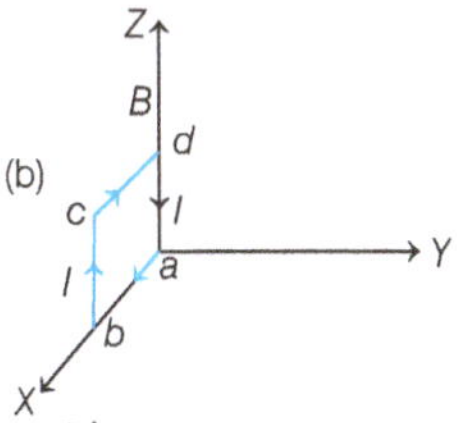

(c)
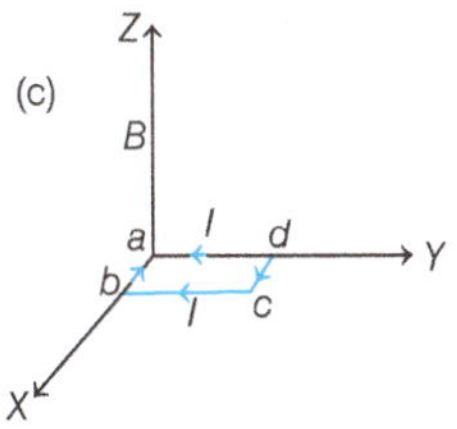

(d)
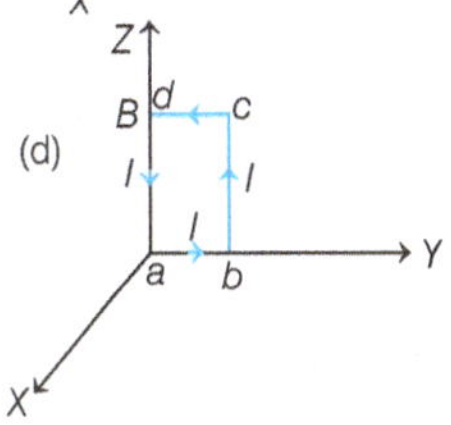

30 A small circular coil of 10 turns, area 1 mm^2 and carrying a current of $\left(\frac{21}{44}\right)$ A is in the middle of a long solenoid of 10^3 turns/m with its axis perpendicular to the axis of the solenoid.

If torque 1.5×10^{-8} N-m can hold the coil in the solenoid, then current flowing in the solenoid is NCERT Pg. 139

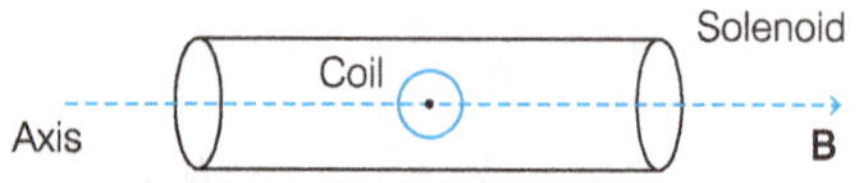

(a) 2.5 A (b) 3.5 A
(c) 1.5 A (d) 2 A

31 Two identical bar magnets of magnetic moment 5.0 A m^2 are placed in air at a separation of 10 m. The axis of these bar magnets are perpendicular to each other. The resultant magnetic field at a mid-point between the magnets is NCERT Pg. 140

(a) $5\sqrt{5} \times 10^{-10}$ T
(b) $2\sqrt{5} \times 10^{-5}$ T
(c) $4\sqrt{5} \times 10^{-5}$ T
(d) $4\sqrt{5} \times 10^{-10}$ T

32 The magnetic induction at a point 1Å away from a charge particle along its axis of spin is
[Here, magnetic moment of charge particle is 1.4×10^{-26} A-m^2] NCERT Pg. 140

(a) 2.8 mT (b) 2.8 μT (c) 0.28 mT (d) 0.28 μ T

33 A circular coil of 16 turns and radius 10 cm carrying a current of 0.75 Å rests with its plane normal to an external field of magnitude 5.0×10^{-2} T. Which of the following statement(s) is/are correct? NCERT Pg. 145

(a) Magnetic moment of the coil is 3.77 JT^{-1}.
(b) If coil oscillates about its stable equilibrium with a frequency of 2/s, then moment of inertia of the coil will be 1.2×10^{-4} kg-m^2.
(c) If coil oscillates about its stable equilibrium with a frequency of 3/s, then moment of inertia of the coil will be 3.2×10^{-4} kg-m^2.
(d) If the moment of inertia is 4×10^{-2}, then coil oscillates with frequency of 3/s.

Magnetism and Gauss' Law

34 The net magnetic flux passing through a hypothetical closed surface enclosing a bar magnet is (in magnitude only) NCERT Pg. 142

(a) 1 (b) less than 1
(c) greater than 1 (d) zero

35 The difference between Gauss' law of magnetism and that for electrostatics is a reflection of the fact that NCERT Pg. 142

(a) isolated magnetic poles are not known to exist.
(b) isolated magnetic poles are exist.
(c) domain of magnetic substance is not align properly.
(d) domain of magnetic substance align properly.

Magnetisation and Magnetic Intensity

36 *S* is the surface of a lump of magnetic material. Which of the following statement is correct? NCERT Pg. 145

(a) Lines of **B** are necessarily continuous across *S*.
(b) Some lines of **B** must be discontinuous across *S*.
(c) Lines of **H** are necessarily continuous across *S*.
(d) Magnetic intensity **H** remains same for inside and outside jump.

37 Obtain the earth's magnetisation assuming that the earth's field can be approximated by a giant bar magnet of magnetic moment 8.0×10^{22} A-m^2. The earth's radius is 6400 km. NCERT Pg. 145

(a) 7.9×10^5 Am^{-1} (b) 73 Am^{-1}
(c) 1.8×10^{-5} Am^{-1} (d) 1.0 Am^{-1}

38 A bar magnet of length 25 cm and cross- section area 1×10^{-4} m^2 has magnetic moment of 1.0 Am^2, then the magnetisation of bar magnet is NCERT Pg. 145

(a) 4.0×10^4 Am^{-1} (b) 6.0×10^{-4} Am^{-1}
(c) 5.0×10^{-4} Am^{-1} (d) 2.5×10^4 Am^1

39 A domain in ferromagnetic iron in the form of cube have 8×10^{10} atoms. If the side length of this domain is 2.0 μm and each atom has a dipole moment of 5×10^{-24} Am^2, then magnetisation of domain is NCERT Pg. 145

(a) 11.8×10^5 Am^{-1} (b) 5×10^4 Am^{-1}
(c) 23.5×10^4 Am^{-1} (d) 5×10^5 Am^{-1}

40 A solenoid has a core of a material with relative permeability of 400. The windings of the solenoid are insulated from the core and carry a current of 3 A. If the number of turns is 1500 per metre, then magnetisation is NCERT Pg. 145

(a) 7.78×10^5 Am^{-1} (b) 8.88×10^6 Am^{-1}
(c) 1.8×10^6 Am^{-1} (d) 10.2×10^5 Am^{-1}

41 An iron rod of 0.2 cm^2 cross-sectional area is subjected to a magnetising field of 1200 Am^{-1}. The susceptibility of iron is 599. The permeability will be NCERT Pg. 146

(a) 7.9×10^5 TmA^{-1}
(b) 8.0×10^{22} TmA^{-1}
(c) 7.5×10^{-4} TmA^{-1}
(d) 1.8×10^{-5} TmA^{-1}

42 A paramagnetic material has a magnetic susceptibility of 10^{-5}. When it is placed in a magnetic field of 0.5 T, then the magnetisation of material is NCERT Pg. 146

(a) 5×10^{-5} Am^{-1}
(b) 25×10^{-5} Am^{-1}
(c) 5×10^{-6} Am^{-1}
(d) 25×10^{-6} Am^{-1}

43 A solenoid has core of material with relative permeability 600 and its windings carry a current of 1.5 A. The number of turns of the solenoid is 600 per metre. The magnetisation of the material is nearly NCERT Pg. 146

(a) 2.5×10^5 Am^{-1} (b) 2.5×10^5 Am^{-1}
(c) 5.3×10^5 Am^{-1} (d) 2.0×10^5 Am^{-1}

44 A long solenoid has 1000 turns per metre and carries a current of 1 A. It has a soft iron core of $\mu_r = 1000$. The core is heated beyond the Curie temperature, T_C. NCERT Pg. 146

Which of the following statement(s) is/are correct?

(a) The **H** field in the solenoid is (nearly) unchanged but the **B** field increases drastically.
(b) The **H** and **B** fields in the solenoid are nearly unchanged.
(c) The magnetisation in the core reverses direction.
(d) The susceptibility in the core diminishes by a factor of about 10^8

Magnetic Properties of Materials

45 Which of the following statement(s) is/are correct?

A. Electric dipole and monopoles exists whereas magnetic monopoles exist but dipole do not exist.
B. Magnetic field lines due to a solenoid at its ends and outside are completely straight and confined.
C. Magnetic field lines inside a bar magnet are parallel.
D. $\chi = +1$ is the condition for a perfect diamagnetic material, where χ is its magnetic susceptibility.

Choose the correct answer from the options given below. NCERT Pg. 147

(a) A and B only
(b) C and D only
(c) B and C only
(d) C only

46 Which of the following statement is incorrect? NCERT Pg. 147

(a) Diamagnetic substances are those which have tendency to move from stronger to the weaker part of the external magnetic field.
(b) Superconductors are metals, cooled to very low temperature which exhibits both perfect conductivity and perfect diamagnetism.
(c) Superconducting magnets can be used for running magnetically levitated superfast trains.
(d) For a paramagnetic material, both χ and μ_0 depend only on the material.

47 If a diamagnetic substance is brought near the north or the south pole of a bar magnet, then it is NCERT Pg. 147

(a) attracted by the both poles
(b) repelled by both the poles
(c) repelled by the north pole and attracted by the south pole
(d) attracted by the north pole and repelled by the south pole

48 The variation of magnetic susceptibility χ with temperature for a diamagnetic substance is best represented by figure NCERT Pg. 147

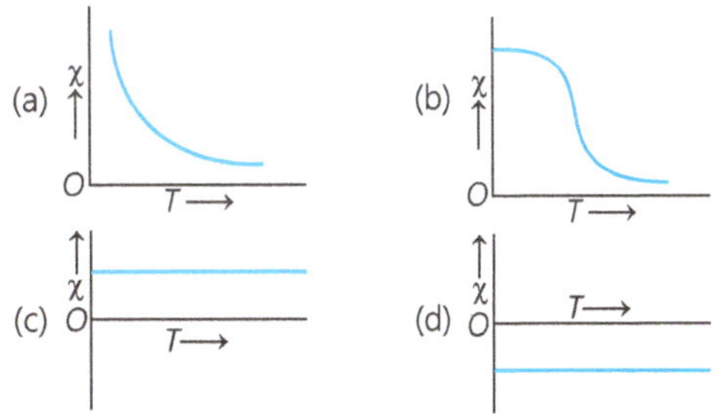

49 If a diamagnetic solution is poured into a U-tube and one arm of this U-tube is placed between poles of a strong magnet, with the meniscus in line with the field, then the level of solution will NCERT Pg. 147

(a) rise
(b) fall
(c) oscillate slowly
(d) remain as such

50 A thin diamagnetic rod is placed vertically between the poles of an electromagnet. When the current in the electromagnet is switched ON, then the diamagnetic rod is pushed up, out of the horizontal magnetic field. The rod gains gravitational potential energy. The work required to do this comes from NCERT Pg. 147

(a) the lattice structure of the material of the rod
(b) the magnetic field
(c) the current source
(d) the induced electric field due to the changing magnetic field

51 The relative permeability of a substance X is slightly less than unity and that of substance Y is slightly more than unity, then NCERT Pg. 147

(a) X is paramagnetic and Y is ferromagnetic
(b) X is diamagnetic and Y is ferromagnetic
(c) X and Y both are paramagnetic
(d) X is diamagnetic and Y is paramagnetic

52 The variation of the intensity of magnetisation (I) with respect to the magnetising field (H) in a diamagnetic substance is described by the graph **NCERT Pg. 147**

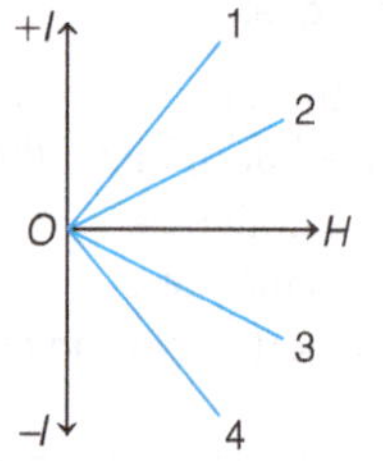

(a) 2 (b) 3 (c) 4 (d) 1

53 Diamagnetic materials are superconductors. These are metals, cooled to very low temperature which exhibits both perfect conducting and perfect diamagnetism when **NCERT Pg. 147**

(a) $\chi = -1, \ \mu_r = 0$
(b) $\chi = -\frac{1}{2}, \ \mu_r = 0$
(c) $\chi = 0, \ \mu_r = 1$
(d) $\chi = 1, \ \mu_r = -\frac{1}{2}$

54 Diamagnetic substances are those which have tendency to move from stronger to the weaker part of external magnetic field. When placed in a non-uniform magnetic field, the diamagnetic substance will **NCERT Pg. 147**

(a) tend to rotate and translate
(b) tend to rotate but without translation
(c) tend to translate but without rotation
(d) shows no movement

55 If a magnetic material is having magnetic susceptibility $(\chi) = -1$, then the relative magnetic permeability (μ_r) and type of magnetic material is **NCERT Pg. 147**

(a) – 1, diamagnetic (b) 1, paramagnetic
(c) 2, ferromagnetic (d) 0, diamagnetic

56 A perfectly diamagnetic sphere has a small spherical cavity at its centre, which is filled with a paramagnetic substance. The whole system is placed in a uniform magnetic field B. Then, the field inside the paramagnetic substance is **NCERT Pg. 147**

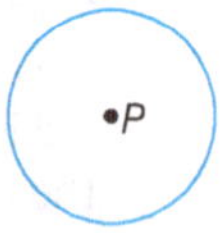

(a) much larger than $|B|$ and parallel to B.
(b) B
(c) zero
(d) much larger than $|B|$ but opposite to B.

57 A paramagnetic substance in the form of a cube with sides 1 cm has a magnetic dipole moment of 20×10^{-6} J/T when a magnetic intensity of 60×10^3 A/m is applied. Its magnetic susceptibility is **NCERT Pg. 148**

(a) 3.3×10^{-4} (b) 3.3×10^{-2}
(c) 4.3×10^{-2} (d) 2.3×10^{-2}

58 A paramagnetic material has 10^{28} atoms/m^3. Its magnetic susceptibility at temperature 350 K is 2.8×10^{-4}. Its susceptibility at 300 K is **NCERT Pg. 148**

(a) 3.726×10^{-4}
(b) 3.672×10^{-4}
(c) 2.672×10^{-4}
(d) 3.267×10^{-4}

59 The magnetic susceptibility of a paramagnetic material at – 73 °C is 0.0075, its value at – 173 °C will be **NCERT Pg. 148**

(a) 0.0075 (b) 0.015
(c) 0.0030 (d) 0.0045

60 Which of the following statement(s) is/are incorrect associated with a ferromagnetic material? **NCERT Pg. 149**

(a) In a ferromagnetic material, the field lines are highly concentrated.
(b) Hard ferromagnets are those which persists magnetisation.
(c) Soft ferromagnetic materials are those in which the magnetisation disappears on removal of the external field.
(d) The relative magnetic permeability of ferromagnets is less than 1.

61 A ferromagnetic material is heated above its curie temperature. Which one is a correct statement? **NCERT Pg. 149**

(a) Ferromagnetic domains are perfectly arranged
(b) Ferromagnetic domains becomes random
(c) Ferromagnetic domains are not influenced
(d) Ferromagnetic material changes itself into diamagnetic material.

62 Ferromagnetic substances are temperature dependent. At very high temperature, ferromagnetic substances become a paramagnet. The domain structure will **NCERT Pg. 149**

(a) disintegrates with temperature
(b) disintegrates with pressure
(c) Never depend on temperature
(d) always depends on pressure

63 Needles N_1, N_2 and N_3 are made of a ferromagnetic, a paramagnetic and a diamagnetic substances, respectively. A magnet when brought close to them will **NCERT Pg. 149**

(a) attract N_1 and N_2 strongly but repel N_3
(b) attract N_1 strongly, N_2 weakly and repel N_3 weakly
(c) attract N_1 strongly, but repel N_2 and N_3 weakly
(d) attract all three of them

64 A domain in ferromagnetic iron is in the form of a cube of side length 1 μm. Estimate the number of iron atoms in the domain. The molecular mass of iron is 55 g/mol and its density is 7.9 g cm^{-3}. NCERT Pg. 149

(a) 8.65×10^{-10} atoms (b) 8.0×10^{-13} atoms
(c) 8.0×10^{5} atoms (d) 8.65×10^{10} atoms

65 The *I-H* curve for a paramagnetic material is represented by figure NCERT Pg. 148

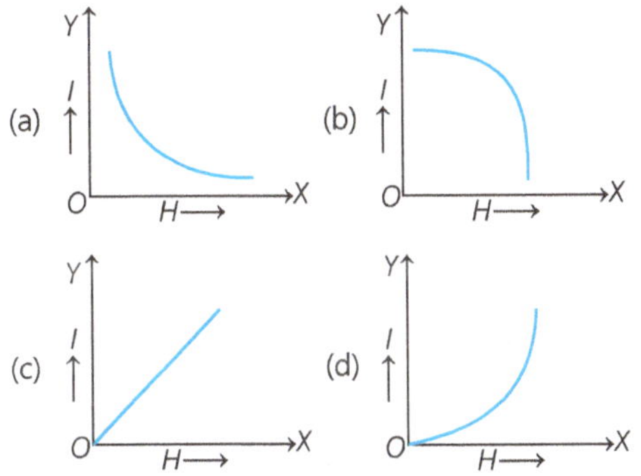

66 The susceptibility of magnesium at 300 K is 1.2×10^{-5}. At what temperature will the susceptibility increase to 1.8×10^{-5}? NCERT Pg. 149

(a) 100 K (b) 200 K
(c) 300 K (d) 400 K

67 The variation of magnetic susceptibility χ with absolute temperature *T* for a ferromagnetic material is given in figure by NCERT Pg. 149

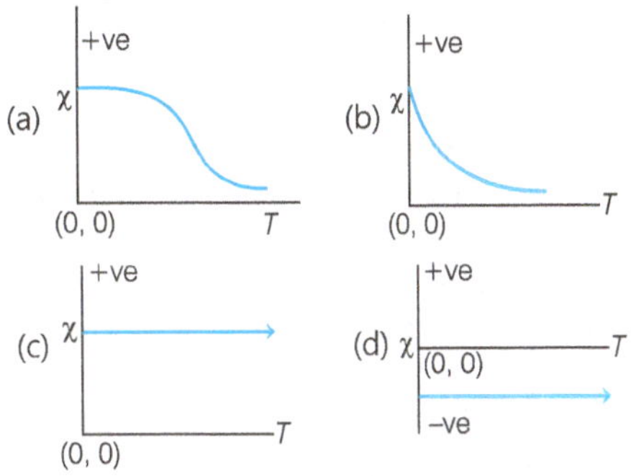

Assertion and Reason Questions

Direction (Q. Nos. 1-10) *In the following questions, a statement of Assertion is followed by a corresponding statement of Reason. Of the following statements, choose the correct one.*

(a) Both Assertion and Reason are correct and Reason is the correct explanation of Assertion.
(b) Both Assertion and Reason are correct but Reason is not the correct explanation of Assertion.
(c) Assertion is correct but Reason is incorrect.
(d) Assertion is incorrect but Reason is correct.

1 **Assertion** The poles of magnet cannot be separated by breaking into two pieces.

Reason The magnetic moment will be reduced to half when a magnet is broken into two equal pieces. NCERT Pg. 137

2 **Assertion** According to Gauss's law for magnetism, the net magnetic flux through any closed surface is zero.

Reason The number of magnetic field lines leaving the surface is balanced by the number of lines entering it. NCERT Pg. 143

3 **Assertion** Susceptibility is defined as the ratio of intensity of magnetisation *M* to magnetic intensity *H*.

Reason Greater the value of susceptibility, smaller is the value of intensity of magnetisation *M*. NCERT Pg. 146

4 **Assertion** When a piece of iron is brought near a strong magnet , it gets magnetised.

Reason Iron is a diamagnetic material. When a diamagnetic material brought in a magnetic field, it aligns its magnetic domain with the external magnetic field. NCERT Pg. 147

5 **Assertion** Paramagnetic substances are those which get weakly magnetised when placed in an external magnetic field.

Reason Paramagnetic substances have tendency to move from a region of weak magnetic field to strong magnetic field. NCERT Pg. 148

6 **Assertion** The ferromagnetic substances do not obey Curie law.

Reason At Curie point, a ferromagnetic substance start behaving as a paramagnetic substance. NCERT Pg. 148

7 **Assertion** A ferromagnetic material can be magnetised to saturation.

Reason Ferromagnetic materials have a high relative permeability. NCERT Pg. 149

8 **Assertion** Ferromagnetic substances have strong tendency to move from weak magnetic field to strong magnetic field.

Reason The individual atoms (or ions or molecules) in a ferromagnetic material possess a dipole moment as in a paramagnetic material. NCERT Pg. 149

9 Assertion Substances which are at room temperature retain their ferromagnetic property for a long period of time are called permanent magnets.

Reason Permanent magnet can be made by placing a ferromagnetic rod inside a solenoid and passing current through it. NCERT Pg. 149

10 Assertion Ferromagnetic substances are those which gets strongly magnetised when placed in an external magnetic field.

Reason Ferromagnetic substances have strong tendency to move from a region of weak magnetic field to strong magnetic field, i.e. they get strongly attracted to a magnet. NCERT Pg. 149

Statement Based Questions

Direction (Q Nos 1 - 8) *In the following questions Statement - I and Statement II are given. Read these statements and choose the most appropriate answer from the options given below.*

(a) Both Statement I and Statement II are incorrect.
(b) Statement I is correct but Statement II is incorrect.
(c) Statement I is incorrect but Statement II is correct.
(d) Both Statement I and Statement II are correct.

1 Statement I The name lodestone (or load stone) given to a naturally occurring ore of iron magnetite means leading stone in magnetism.

Statement II The bar magnet is not analogous to a solenoid. NCERT Pg. 139

2 Statement I The magnetic dipole moment of a wire of length (L m) carrying current (I A), bent in the form of circle is $IL^2/4\pi$ Am^2.

Statement II Magnetic dipole moment of a circular loop is directly proportional to its radius. NCERT Pg. 139

3 Statement I When radius of a circular loop carrying current is doubled, its magnetic moment becomes four times.

Statement II Magnetic moment depends on area of the loop. NCERT Pg. 140

4 Statement I Diamagnetic substances have a small positive susceptibility.

Statement II Diamagnetic substances have tendency to move from stronger to weaker part of the external magnetic field. NCERT Pg. 142

5 Statement I The difference between the Gauss' law of magnetism and that for electrostatics is a reflection of the fact that isolated magnetic poles are not known to exist.

Statement II There are no sources or sinks of magnetic field B, the simplest magnetic element is a dipole or a current loop. NCERT Pg. 142

6 Statement I Susceptibility is defined as the ratio of Intensity of magnetisation (I) to magnetic intensity (H).

Statement II Greater the value of susceptibility, smaller will be the value of intensity of magnetisation (I) NCERT Pg. 145

7 A bar of diamagnetic material placed in an external magnetic field.

Statement I The field lines are attracted and result in the field inside the material will get increased.

Statement II When placed in a non-uniform magnetic field, the bar will tend to move from high to low field. NCERT Pg 147

8 Statement I On heating a ferromagnetic material above curie temperature, it changes into diamagnetic material.

Statement II In a ferromagnetic substance domains are perfectly arranged. When it is placed in a magnetic field NCERT Pg 149

Matching Type Questions

1 Match the Column I (potential energy of magnetic dipole at different orientation) with Column II (value of potential energy in magnetic field) NCERT Pg. 139

Column I		Column II	
A.	Potential energy at $\theta = 90°$	1.	Minimum
B.	Potential energy at $\theta = 0°$	2.	$-\frac{1}{2}MB$
C.	Potential energy at $\theta = 180°$	3.	Zero
D.	Potential energy at $\theta = 60°$	4.	Maximum

Choose the correct answer from the codes given below.

Codes

	A	B	C	D
(a)	3	1	4	2
(b)	1	2	4	3
(c)	2	1	3	4
(d)	1	4	2	3

2 Match the Column I (magnetic quantities) with Column II (their formula). NCERT Pg. 141

Column I		Column II	
A.	Equatorial field for a short dipole	1.	$-\mathbf{M}\cdot\mathbf{B}$
B.	Axial field for a short dipole	2.	$\mathbf{M}\times\mathbf{B}$
C.	External field : torque	3.	$-\mu_0\mathbf{M}/4\pi r^3$
D.	External field : energy	4.	$\mu_0 2\mathbf{M}/4\pi r^3$

Choose the correct answer from the codes given below.

Codes

	A	B	C	D
(a)	3	4	2	1
(b)	3	4	1	2
(c)	3	1	2	4
(d)	4	2	3	1

3 Match Column I (properties or action) with Column II (material or effect) and choose the correct answer from the codes given below. NCERT Pg. 149

ColumnI		Column II	
A.	Reversing poles of a magnet	1.	Compass
B.	Heating a magnet	2.	Alnico
C.	Permanent electromagnet	3.	Alternating current
D.	Directive property of a magnet used in	4.	Demagnetisation

Codes

	A	B	C	D
(a)	3	4	2	1
(b)	3	4	1	2
(c)	4	2	1	3
(d)	1	2	3	4

Numerical Type Questions

1 Two identical bar magnets of magnetic moment 4.0 Am^2 are placed at a separation of 2 m with their axes perpendicular to each other in air. The resultant magnetic field at a mid-point between the magnets is $n\sqrt{5}\times 10^{-7}$ T, then the value of n is .... NCERT Pg. 139

2 A short bar magnet has a magnetic moment of 0.5 Am^2. The magnitude of magnetic field produced by the magnet at a distance of 20 cm from the centre of the magnet on its axis is $x\times 10^{-7}$ T along S-N direction, then the value of x is .... NCERT Pg. 139

3 The magnetic field due to a bar magnet of magnetic moment 4.0 Am^2 at a point 1 m away from it in a direction making an angle of 30° with the magnetic axis is $2\sqrt{p}\times 10^{-7}$ T. The value of p is .... NCERT Pg. 139

4 The pole strength of 12 cm long bar magnet is 25 A m. The magnetic induction at a point 10 cm away from the centre of the magnet on its axial line is $x\times 10^{-6}$ T, then the value of x is .... NCERT Pg. 139

5 A bar magnet is acted upon by two magnetic fields which are inclined to each other at an angle of 75°. One of the fields has a magnitude of 17 mT. The dipole attains stable equilibrium at an angle of 45° with this field . The magnitude of the other field (in mT) is .... NCERT Pg. 139

6 A magnet is 10 cm long and its pole strength is 150 CGS units (1 CGS unit of pole strength = 0.1 Am) . The magnitude of the magnetic field B is $n\times 10^{-6}$ T at a point on its axis at a distance 20 cm from it. Then, the value of n is .... NCERT Pg. 139

7 Two short magnetic dipoles M_1 and M_2 each having magnetic moment of 1.2 Am^2 are placed at point O and P , respectively. The distance between OP is 1.2 m. The torque experienced by the magnetic dipole M_2 due to the presence of M_1 is ....$\times 10^{-9}$ N-m. NCERT Pg. 139

8 A bar magnet has a magnetic moment of 200 Am^2. The magnet is suspended in a magnetic field of $0.30 N A^{-1}m^{-1}$. The torque required to rotate the magnet from its equilibrium position through angle θ is 30 N-m, then θ (in degree) is .... NCERT Pg. 149

9 A rod of ferromagnetic material with dimensions $10 \text{ cm} \times 0.5 \text{ cm} \times 0.4 \text{ cm}$ is placed in a magnetic field of strength $0.5 \times 10^4 \text{ Am}^{-1}$ as a result of which a magnetic moment of 10 Am^2 is produced in the rod. The value of magnetic induction is $x \times 10^{-2}$ T, then x is .... NCERT Pg. 149

NCERT Exemplar Questions

1 A paramagnetic sample shows a net magnetisation of 8 Am^{-1}, when placed in an external magnetic field of 0.6 T at a temperature of 4K. When the same sample is placed in an external magnetic field of 0.2 T at a temperature of 16 K, the magnetisation will be

(a) $(32/3) \text{ Am}^{-1}$
(b) $(2/3) \text{ Am}^{-1}$
(c) 6 Am^{-1}
(d) 2.4 Am^{-1}

2 A toroid of n turns, mean radius R and cross-sectional radius a carries current I. It is placed on a horizontal table taken as xy-plane. Its magnetic moment **m**

(a) is non-zero and points in the z-direction by symmetry
(b) points along the axis of the toroid ($\mathbf{m} = m\,\phi$)
(c) is zero, otherwise there would be a field falling as $\frac{1}{r^3}$ at large distances outside the toroid
(d) is pointing radially outwards

3 In a permanent magnet at room temperature,

(a) magnetic moment of each molecule is zero
(b) the individual molecules have non-zero magnetic moment which are all perfectly aligned
(c) domains are partially aligned
(d) domains are all perfectly aligned

4 Consider the two idealised systems (i) a parallel plate capacitor with large plates and small separation and (ii) a long solenoid of length $L >> R$, radius of cross-section. In (i) **E** is ideally treated as a constant between plates and zero outside. In (ii) magnetic field is constant inside the solenoid and zero outside. These idealised assumptions, however, contradict fundamental laws as below.

(a) case (i) contradicts Gauss' law for electrostatic fields
(b) case (ii) contradicts Gauss' law for magnetic fields
(c) case (i) agrees with $\oint \mathbf{E}.d\mathbf{l} = 0$.
(d) case (ii) contradicts $\oint \mathbf{H}.d\mathbf{l} = I_{en}$

Past Exams Questions

NEET

1 Match List-I with List-II.

List-I (Material)		List-II (Susceptibility (χ))	
A	Diamagnetic	I.	$\chi = 0$
B	Ferromagnetic	II.	$0 > \chi \geq -1$
C	Paramagnetic	III.	$\chi >> 1$
D	Non-magnetic	IV.	$0 < \chi < \varepsilon$ (a small positive number)

Choose the correct answer from the options given below. NCERT Pg. 146, NEET 2024

(a) A-II, B-III, C-IV, D-I
(b) A-II, B-I, C-III, D-IV
(c) A-III, B-II, C-I, D-IV
(d) A-IV, B-III, C-II, D-I

2 An iron bar of length L has magnetic moment M. It is bent at the middle of its length such that the two arms make an angle 60° with each other. The magnetic moment of this new magnet is NCERT Pg. 137, NEET 2024

(a) M
(b) $\frac{M}{2}$
(c) $2M$
(d) $\frac{M}{\sqrt{3}}$

3 In a uniform magnetic field of 0.049 T, a magnetic needle performs 20 complete oscillations in 5 s as shown. The moment of inertia of the needle is 9.8×10^{-6} kg m^2. If the magnitude of magnetic moment of the needle is $x \times 10^{-5}$ Am^2, then the value of x is

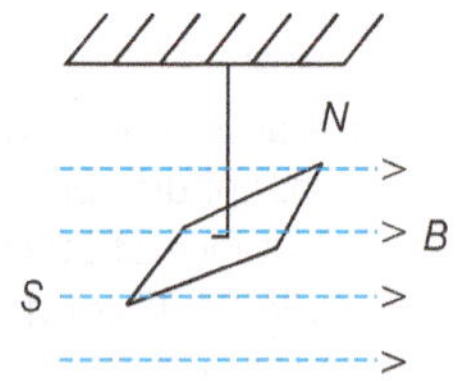

(a) $5\pi^2$
(b) $128\pi^2$
(c) $50\pi^2$
(d) $1280\pi^2$

4 The dimensions $[MLT^{-2}A^{-2}]$ belong to the NCERT Pg. 146, NEET 2022

(a) self-inductance
(b) magnetic permeability
(c) electric permittivity
(d) magnetic flux

5 An iron rod of susceptibility 599 is subjected to a magnetising field of 1200 Am^{-1}. The permeability of the material of the rod is

(Take, $\mu_0 = 4\pi \times 10^{-7}$ T m A^{-1}) NCERT Pg. 146, NEET 2020

(a) 8.0×10^{-5} T m A^{-1} (b) $2.4\pi \times 10^{-5}$ T m A^{-1}
(c) $2.4\pi \times 10^{-7}$ T m A^{-1} (d) $2.4\pi \times 10^{-4}$ T m A^{-1}

6 The net magnetic flux through any closed surface is NCERT Pg. 142, NEET 2016

(a) positive (b) infinity
(c) negative (d) zero

7 A bar magnet is hung by a thin cotton thread in a uniform horizontal magnetic field and is in equilibrium state. The energy required to rotate it by 60° is W. Now the torque required to keep the magnet in this position is NCERT Pg .139, NEET 2016

(a) $\frac{W}{\sqrt{3}}$ (b) $\sqrt{3}\,W$ (c) $\frac{\sqrt{3}W}{2}$ (d) $\frac{2W}{\sqrt{3}}$

8 The magnetic susceptibility is negative for NCERT Pg. 147, NEET 2016

(a) paramagnetic material only
(b) ferromagnetic material only
(c) paramagnetic and ferromagnetic materials
(d) diamagnetic material only

9 Following figure show the arrangement of bar magnets in different configurations. Each magnet has magnetic dipole moment M. Which configuration has highest net magnetic dipole moment? NCERT Pg. 139, AIPMT 2014

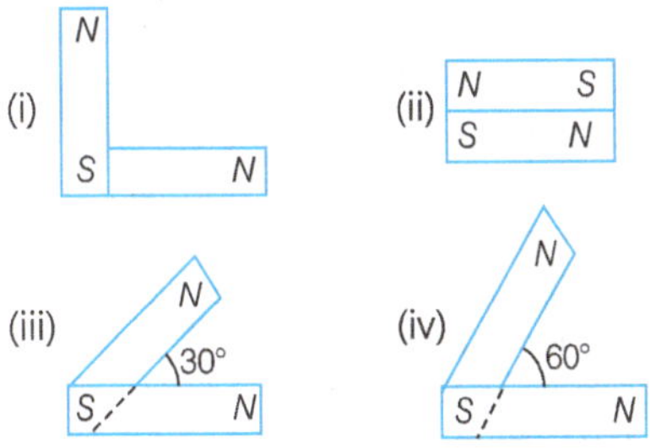

(a) (i) (b) (ii) (c) (iii) (d) (iv)

JEE Main

10 Match List-I with List-II.

	List-I (Y vs X)	List II (Shape of Graph)
A.	Y = magnetic susceptibility X = magnetising field	I. 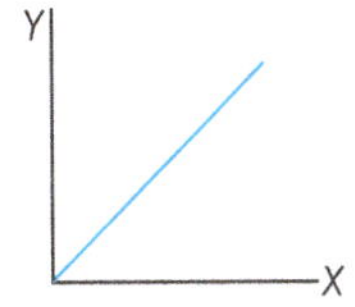
B.	Y = magnetic field X = distance from centre of a current carrying wire for $x < a$ (where a = radius of wire)	II. 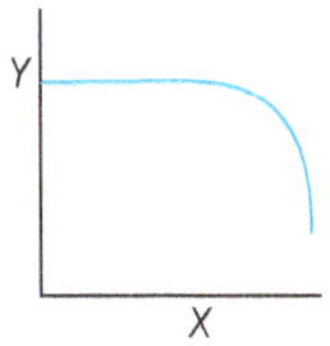
C.	Y = magnetic field X = distance from centre of a current-carrying wire for $x > a$ (where a = radius of wire)	III. 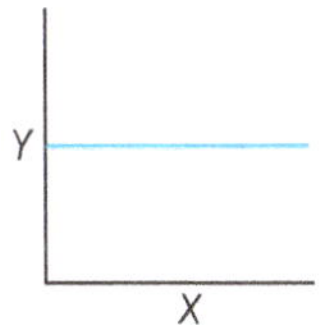
D	Y = magnetic field inside solenoid X = distance from centre	IV. 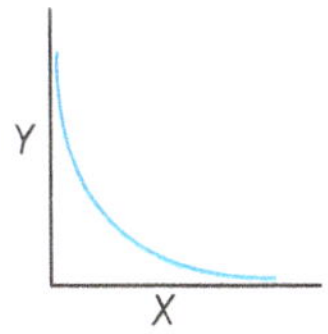

NCERT Pg. 147, JEE Main 2024

Choose the correct answer from the options given below.

	A	B	C	D
(a)	IV	I	III	II
(b)	III	I	IV	II
(c)	III	IV	I	II
(d)	I	III	II	IV

11 Paramagnetic substances

A. align themselves along the directions of external magnetic field.
B. attract strongly towards external magnetic field.
C. has susceptibility little more than zero.
D. move from a region of strong magnetic field to weak magnetic field. NCERT Pg. 147, JEE Main 2024

Choose the most appropriate answer from the options given below :

(a) B, D Only (b) A, C Only
(c) A, B, C, D (d) A, B, C Only

12 A straight magnetic strip has a magnetic moment of 44 Am^2. If the strip is bent in a semicircular shape, its magnetic moment will be .... Am^2.

(Given $\pi = \frac{22}{7}$) NCERT Pg. 145, JEE Main 2024

13 A bar magnet with a magnetic moment 5.0 A-m^{-2} is placed in parallel position relative to a magnetic field of 0.4 T. The amount of required work done in turning the magnet from parallel to anti-parallel position relative to the field direction is NCERT Pg. 139, JEE Main 2023

(a) 2 J (b) zero (c) 4 J (d) 1 J

14 The susceptibility of a paramagnetic material is 99. The permeability of the material in Wb/A- m is [Permeability of free space, $\mu_0 = 4\pi \times 10^{-7}$ Wb/A-m]

NCERT Pg. 148, JEE Main 2022

(a) $4\pi \times 10^{-7}$ (b) $4\pi \times 10^{-4}$
(c) $4\pi \times 10^{-5}$ (d) $4\pi \times 10^{-6}$

15 The magnetic susceptibility of a material of a rod is 499. Permeability in vacuum is $4\pi \times 10^{-7}$ H/m. Absolute permeability of the material of the rod is

NCERT Pg. 146, JEE Main 2021, 20

(a) $4\pi \times 10^{-4}$ H/m (b) $2\pi \times 10^{-4}$ H/m
(c) $3\pi \times 10^{-4}$ H/m (d) $\pi \times 10^{-4}$ H/m

16 An iron rod of volume 10^{-3} m^3 and relative permeability 1000 is placed as core in a solenoid with 10 turns/ cm. If a current of 0.5 A is passed through the solenoid, then the magnetic moment of the rod will be

NCERT Pg. 145, JEE Main 2020

(a) 50×10^2 A-m^2 (b) 5×10^2 A-m^2
(c) 500×10^2 A-m^2 (d) 0.5×10^2 A-m^2

17 A bar magnet is demagnetised by inserting it inside a solenoid of length 0.2 m, 100 turns and carrying a current of 5.2 A. The coercivity of the bar magnet is

NCERT Pg. 145, JEE Main 2019

(a) 1200 A/m (b) 285 A/m
(c) 2600 A/m (d) 520 A/m

Skill Boosters

1 A bar magnet is under the influence of two magnetic fields, which are perpendicular to each other. One of the field has magnitude of 3.0×10^{-2} T, If bar magnet comes to stable equilibrium at angle of 30° with this field, then the magnitude of another magnetic field is

(a) 3×10^{-2} T (b) $\sqrt{3} \times 10^{-2}$ T
(c) 2.4×10^{-2} T (d) $\sqrt{2} \times 10^{-2}$ T

2 If a bar magnet with magnetic moment M and moment of inertia I (about its centre perpendicular to length) is divided into two equal pieces perpendicular to its length and the original magnet oscillates with a period T in a magnetic field B , what would be the period T' for each of the cut pieces when oscillating similarly?

(a) $\frac{5T}{2}$ (b) $\frac{T}{2}$
(c) $\frac{3T}{4}$ (d) T

3 A solenoid of length 94 cm has a ferromagnetic core of relative permeability 800. The winding of the solenoid are insulated from the core and carry a current of 2 A. If total number of turns are 3500, then the magnetic field in the core is

(a) 5.4 T (b) 7.4 T
(c) 2.5 T (d) 4.5 T

4 A sample of paramagnetic salt contains 2.0×10^{24} atomic dipoles, each of dipole moment 1.5×10^{-23} JT^{-1}. The sample is placed under *a* homogeneous magnetic field of 0.84 T and cooled to a temperature of 4.2 K. The degree of magnetic saturation achieved is equal to 15% The total dipole moment of the sample for a magnetic field of 0.98 T and a temperature of 2.8 K is

(a) 3×10^3 JT^{-1} (b) $4\pi \times 10^{-6}$ JT^{-1}
(c) 7.9 JT^{-1} (d) 7×10^4 JT^{-1}

5 A domain of iron in the form of a cube of side length 2 µm.If dipole moment of an atom is 9.27×10^{-27} Am^2, then the intensity of magnetisation is (molecular mass = 55 g/mol and density = 7.92 g/cm^3)

(a) 3×10^8 Am^{-1} (b) 8×10^8 Am^{-1}
(c) 8×10^2 Am^{-1} (d) 3×10^5 Am^{-1}

6 A bar magnet of length 14 cm is placed in the magnetic meridian with its north pole pointing towards the geographic north pole. A neutral point is obtained at a distance of 18 cm from the centre of the magnet. If B_H = 0.4 G, the magnetic moment of the magnet is

(a) 2.880×10^3 JT^{-1} (b) 2.880×10^2 JT^{-1}
(c) 2.880 JT^{-1} (d) 28.80 JT^{-1}

7 A circular coil of 16 turns and radius 10 cm carrying a current of 0.75 A rests with its plane normal to an external field of magnitude 5.0×10^{-2} T. The coil is free to turn about an axis in its plane perpendicular to the field direction. When the coil is turned slightly and released, it oscillates about its stable equilibrium with a frequency of 2.0/s. What is the moment of inertia of the coil about its axis of rotation?

(a) 1.2×10^{-4} g-cm^2 (b) 3×10^{-4} kg-m^2
(c) 0.3×10^{-4} kg-m^2 (d) 1.2×10^{-4} kg-m^2

8 The given diagram shows the arrangement of three bar magnets. If magnetic moment of each magnet is M and angle between two pair magnets is same, then magnetic moment of the combination is

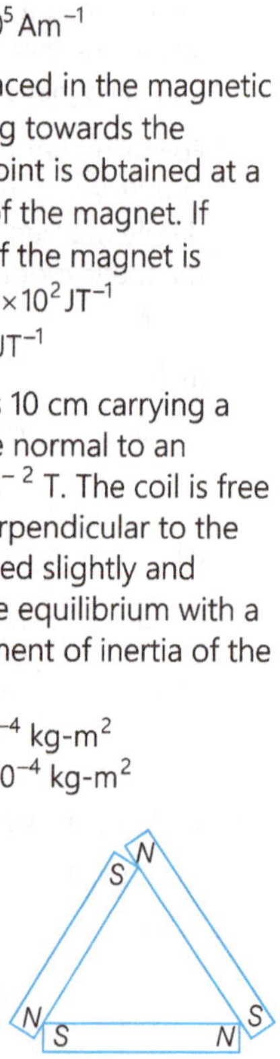

(a) $3m$ (b) m (c) $\frac{m\sqrt{3}}{2}$ (d) zero

9 Two short bar magnets are placed perpendicular as shown in the following diagram. The magnetic field at point P is

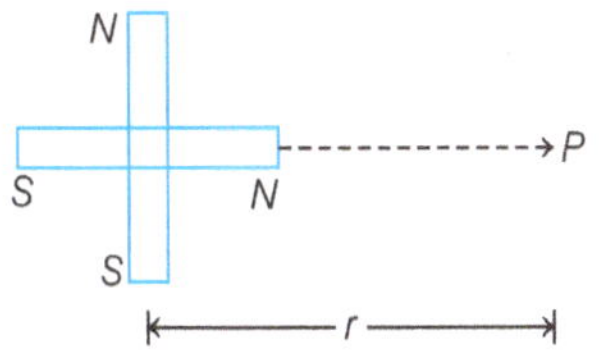

(a) $\frac{\mu_0}{4\pi}\frac{m}{r^3}$ (b) $\frac{\mu_0}{4\pi}\frac{2m}{r^3}$

(c) $\frac{\mu_0}{4\pi}\cdot\frac{m\sqrt{3}}{r^3}$ (d) $\frac{\mu_0}{4\pi}\cdot\frac{m\sqrt{5}}{r^3}$

10 Two bar magnets of identical physical dimensions have magnetic moments M and $2M$, respectively. If these are placed in such a way that their magnetic moment points in same direction, then time period of oscillation is 3s. The new time period, if they are placed in such a way that their magnetic moment points in opposite direction is

(a) $\sqrt{3}$ s (b) $3\sqrt{3}$ s (c) 3 s (d) 65 s

Correct Codes

Topical Questions

1 (a)	2 (d)	3 (d)	4 (b)	5 (c)	6 (a)	7 (a)	8 (a)	9 (a)	10 (c)
11 (d)	12 (a)	13 (c)	14 (b)	15 (a)	16 (d)	17 (c)	18 (b)	19 (c)	20 (a)
21 (a)	22 (a)	23 (b)	24 (a)	25 (d)	26 (a)	27 (a)	28 (c)	29 (a)	30 (a)
31 (a)	32 (a)	33 (b)	34 (d)	35 (a)	36 (a)	37 (b)	38 (a)	39 (b)	40 (c)
41 (c)	42 (c)	43 (c)	44 (d)	45 (d)	46 (d)	47 (b)	48 (d)	49 (b)	50 (c)
51 (d)	52 (b)	53 (a)	54 (a)	55 (d)	56 (c)	57 (a)	58 (d)	59 (b)	60 (d)
61 (b)	62 (a)	63 (b)	64 (d)	65 (c)	66 (b)	67 (a)			

Assertion and Reason Questions

1 (b)	2 (a)	3 (c)	4 (c)	5 (a)	6 (d)	7 (b)	8 (a)	9 (a)	10 (b)

Statement Based Questions

1 (b)	2 (b)	3 (d)	4 (c)	5 (d)	6 (b)	7 (c)	8 (c)

Matching Type Questions

1 (a)	2 (a)	3 (a)

Numerical Type Questions

1 (4)	2 (125)	3 (13)	4 (146)	5 (24)	6 (43)	7 (84)	8 (30)	9 (628)

NCERT Exemplar Questions

1 (b)	2 (c)	3 (d)	4 (b)

Past Exams Questions

1 (a)	2 (b)	3 (d)	4 (b)	5 (d)	6 (d)	7 (b)	8 (d)	9 (c)	10 (b)
11 (b)	12 (28)	13 (c)	14 (c)	15 (b)	16 (b)	17 (c)			

Skill Boosters

1 (b)	2 (b)	3 (b)	4 (c)	5 (c)	6 (c)	7 (d)	8 (d)	9 (d)	10 (b)

Step by Step

Decoding the Questions

Concept Builders

1 True (T)
2 Magnetic dipole
3 q_m
4 True(T)
5 declination
6 heating
7 180°
8 Zero
9 Current loops
10 $\mathbf{B}_{equatorial} = \frac{-\mu_0 \mathbf{M}}{4\pi r^3}$
11 diamagnetic
12 False (F)
13 False (F)
14 Hysteresis
15 False (F)
16 Spin motion of electrons
17 True (T)
18 diamagnetic
19 True (T)
20 $+10^{-5}, -10^{-5}$

Topical Questions

3 (*d*) Pole strength does not depend on length it depends upon cross-section area of magnet.
So, strength of the two pieces will remain same.

4 (*b*) Magnetic moment of solenoid, $M = NIA$

$\Rightarrow 0.40 = 1000 \times I \times 2 \times 10^{-4}$

$\Rightarrow I = 0.40 \times 10^4 / (1000 \times 2) = 2$ A

5 (*c*) When dipole is replaced by equivalent bar magnet, then the line joining *N-S* will be perpendicular to the plane of loop. As current is anti-clockwise, so north pole lies above the loop and south pole lies below the loop.

6 (*a*) In given cases,

(i) $U = -MB\cos 90° = 0$ $[\because \cos 90° = 0]$

(ii) $U = -MB\cos 180° = mB$ $[\because \cos 180° = -1]$

(iii) $U = -MB\cos(360° - \theta)$
$= -MB\cos\theta$ $[\because \cos(360° - \theta) = +\cos\theta]$

(iv) $U = -MB\cos(90° + \theta)$
$= MB\sin\theta$ $[\because \cos(90° + \theta) = -\sin\theta]$

So, correct order of potential energy in increasing order is
(iii) > (i) > (iv) > (ii).

7 (*a*) Magnetic moment is from *S* to *N*,

$M_{net} = \sqrt{M^2 + M^2 + 2M^2\cos\theta}$

Therefore, M_{net} will be $\sqrt{2}M$, if $\cos\theta$ is 0 and $\cos\theta$ will be 0 when θ will be $\theta = 90°$.

8 (*a*) For unstable equilibrium, **M** is to be anti-parallel to **B**. In this case, $\theta = 180°$, thus

$$U = -MB\cos 180°$$
$$= -MB(-1) = MB$$

Hence, $U = (0.32)(0.15) = 4.8 \times 10^{-2}$ J

9 (*a*) As we know, torque,

$$\tau = MB\sin\theta$$

Hence, rate of change of torque with deflection,

$\frac{d\tau}{d\theta} = MB\cos\theta$. It will be maximum when $\cos\theta = 1$, i.e. $\theta = 0°$.

10 (*c*) Torque, $\tau = mB\sin\theta$

$$\sin\theta = \frac{\tau}{MB} = \frac{0.3464}{2.0 \times 0.2}$$
$$\sin\theta = 0.866$$
$$\Rightarrow \quad \theta = 60°$$

11 (*d*) The torque acting on dipole,

$\tau = \mathbf{M} \times \mathbf{B}$
$= (25\hat{\mathbf{j}}) \times (3\hat{\mathbf{i}} + 18\hat{\mathbf{j}})$
$= (25 \times 3)(-\hat{\mathbf{k}}) + (25 \times 18)(0)$ $[\because \hat{\mathbf{j}} \times \hat{\mathbf{j}} = 0]$
$= -75\hat{\mathbf{k}}$ N-m

12 (*a*) Given, $B = 600$ G

$= 600 \times 10^{-4}$
$= 6 \times 10^{-2}$ T

Now torque,

$$\tau = MB\sin\theta$$
$$M = \frac{\tau}{B\sin\theta}$$
$$= \frac{0.03}{6 \times 10^{-2} \times \sin 30°}$$
$$= \frac{0.03 \times 2}{6 \times 10^{-2}}$$
$$= 1.0 \text{ A - m}^2$$

13 (*c*) Work done,

$W = MB[\cos 0° - \cos 180°]$
$= MB[1 + 1]$
$= 2MB$
$= 2 \times 2.0 \times 0.5$
$= 2.0$ J

14 (*b*) The torque on the magnetic dipole,

$\tau = MB\sin\theta$
$= 1.0 \times 0.5 \times \sin 45°$
$= 0.5 \times \frac{1}{\sqrt{2}} = 0.35$ J

15 (*a*) Torque, $\tau = MB\sin\theta$

where, $\theta = 90°$
$\tau = MB$

Given, $\tau_2 = \frac{1}{2}\tau_1$

$\therefore \quad MB\sin\theta = \frac{1}{2}MB$

$\therefore \quad \sin\theta = \frac{1}{2}$

$\Rightarrow \quad \theta = 30°$

Angle of rotation $= 90° - 30° = 60°$

16 (*d*) Torque acting on the dipole,

$\tau = \mathbf{M} \times \mathbf{B}$
$= 10\hat{\mathbf{j}} \times (2\hat{\mathbf{i}} + 3\hat{\mathbf{j}})$
$= 20(\hat{\mathbf{j}} \times \hat{\mathbf{i}}) + 30(\hat{\mathbf{j}} \times \hat{\mathbf{j}})$
$= 20(-\hat{\mathbf{k}}) = -20\hat{\mathbf{k}}$ N-m

17 (c) Work done to rotate a magnet of magnetic dipole moment M in uniform magnetic field B from equilibrium position to angle θ,

$$W=\int dW=\int_0^{\theta}\tau d\theta=\int_0^{\theta}MB\sin\theta$$

$$W=MB(1-\cos\theta)$$

18 (b) We know that,

$$W=MB(\cos 0°-\cos\theta)$$
$$=MB(1-\cos 45°)$$
$$=MB\left(1-\frac{1}{\sqrt{2}}\right)=\left(\frac{\sqrt{2}-1}{\sqrt{2}}\right)MB$$
$$\Rightarrow \quad MB=\frac{\sqrt{2}W}{\sqrt{2}-1} \quad \text{...(i)}$$

Hence, torque, $\tau=MB\sin\theta$

$$\tau=MB\sin 45°=\frac{W\times\sqrt{2}}{\sqrt{2}-1}\times\frac{1}{\sqrt{2}}$$
[from Eq. (i)]
$$=\frac{W}{\sqrt{2}-1}$$

19 (c) When magnetic dipole is rotated from initial position θ_1 to final position θ_2, then work done

$$W=MB(\cos\theta_1-\cos\theta_2)$$

Given, $\theta_1=0°$, $\theta_2=60°$

$$\therefore \quad W=MB(\cos 0°-\cos 60°)$$
$$\Rightarrow \quad W=MB\left(1-\frac{1}{2}\right)$$
$$=\frac{2\times10^4\times6\times10^{-4}}{2}=6\text{ J}$$

20 (a) Work done in rotating the dipole from θ_1 to θ_2 is

$$W=-MB(\cos\theta_2-\cos\theta_1)$$

Case I

$$W_1=-MB(\cos 90°-\cos 0°)=MB \quad \text{...(i)}$$

Case II

$$W_2=-MB(\cos 60°-\cos 0°)$$
$$=-MB\left(\frac{1}{2}-1\right)=\frac{1}{2}MB \quad \text{...(ii)}$$

From Eqs. (i) and (ii), we get

$$W_2=\frac{1}{2}W_1 \quad \text{... (iii)}$$

Given, $W_1=nW_2$ ... (iv)

By comparing Eqs. (iii) and (iv), we get

$$\therefore \quad n=2$$

21 (a) Torque, $\tau=|\mathbf{M}\times\mathbf{B}|=MB\sin\theta$

and magnetic potential energy,

$$U_m=-\mathbf{M}\cdot\mathbf{B}=MB\cos\theta$$

At $\theta=0°$, the dipole will be in most stable situation.

$$\tau=MB\sin\theta=MB\sin 0°=0$$

and $U_m=-MB\cos\theta$
$$=-MB\cos 0°=-MB$$

22 (a) $B_{\text{axial}}=\frac{\mu_0}{4\pi}\left(\frac{2m}{r^3}\right)$

$$=10^{-7}\times\frac{2\times0.6}{(0.75)^3}$$
$$B_{\text{axial}}=2.84\times10^{-7}\text{ T}=0.284\ \mu\text{T}$$

23 (b) Strength of magnetic field on equatorial line,

$$B_{eq}=\frac{\mu_0}{4\pi}\frac{M}{d^3}=10^{-7}\times\frac{4}{8}$$
$$=5\times10^{-8}\text{ T}$$

24 (a) The axial magnetic field,

$$B=\frac{\mu_0}{4\pi}\cdot\frac{2M}{r^3} \quad \Rightarrow B\propto\frac{1}{r^3}$$

Hence, $\frac{B_1}{B_2}=\frac{r_2^3}{r_1^3}=\left(\frac{48}{24}\right)^3=8$

Thus, the ratio of magnetic fields is 8.

25 (d) Magnetic field at equatorial line,

$$B_e=\frac{\mu_0 M}{4\pi r^3}$$
$$=\frac{10^{-7}\times0.40}{(0.5)^3}=\frac{10^{-7}\times0.40}{0.125}$$
$$=3.2\times10^{-7}\text{ T}$$

Magnetic field at axial line,

$$B_a=\frac{\mu_0 2M}{4\pi r^3}=6.4\times10^{-7}\text{ T}$$

26 (a) Here, net magnetic moment is

$$M_{\text{net}}=\sqrt{(M_0)^2+(M_0)^2+2M_0M_0\cos(120°)}$$
$$=M_0$$

Now, magnetic induction at point P,

$$B_P=\frac{\mu_0}{4\pi}\cdot\frac{2M_{\text{net}}}{d^3}$$
$$\because \quad M_{\text{net}}=M_0$$
$$\therefore \quad B_P=\frac{\mu_0}{4\pi}\cdot\frac{2M_0}{d^3}=\frac{\mu_0}{2\pi}\frac{M_0}{d^3}$$

27 (a) The magnetic field produced by magnetic dipole on equatorial line,

$$B=\frac{\mu_0}{4\pi}\cdot\frac{M}{d^3}$$
$$=\frac{10^{-7}\times0.48}{(0.20)^3}=\frac{0.48\times10^{-7}}{8\times10^{-3}}$$
$$=0.06\times10^{-4}\text{ T}$$
$$=0.06\text{ G, } N\text{-}S\text{ direction.}$$

28 (c) The magnetic induction at point D due to magnet at C [axial point],

$$B_1=\frac{\mu_0}{4\pi}\cdot\frac{2M_1}{d^3}$$
$$=\frac{10^{-7}\times2\times8.0}{(2.0)^3}$$
$$=2\times10^{-7}\text{ T along } D \text{ to } C \quad \text{...(i)}$$

Magnetic induction at point D due to magnet at E [equatorial point],

$$B_2=\frac{\mu_0}{4\pi}\cdot\frac{M_2}{d^3}=\frac{10^{-7}\times8.0}{(2.0)^3}$$
$$=1\times10^{-7}\text{ T along } C \text{ to } D \quad \text{...(ii)}$$

Now, total magnetic induction at point D,

$$B=B_1-B_2$$

From Eqs. (i) and (ii), we get

$$B=2\times10^{-7}-1\times10^{-7}$$
$$=1\times10^{-7}\text{ T}$$
$$=0.1\ \mu\text{T}$$

29 (a) Magnetic potential energy of the dipole in a magnetic field,

$U=-\mathbf{M}\cdot\mathbf{B}$

As M and B are same in each case for stable equilibrium, potential energy should be minimum. Minimum potential energy is possible if **M** and **B** are in same direction.

i.e. option (a). Since configuration of option (a) is already in stable equilibrium, hence it will not dissipate any energy.

30 (a) Magnetic field due to a long solenoid on its axis,

$$B=\mu_0 nI_2 \quad \text{...(i)}$$

Magnetic moment of a circular coil, $M = NAI_1$ ...(ii)

Torque, $\tau = \mathbf{M} \times \mathbf{B}$

$$\tau = MB \sin\theta = MB \quad [\because \theta = 90° \text{ (Given)}]$$

$$\tau = (NAI_1)(\mu_0 n I_2) \quad \text{[using Eqs. (i) and (ii)]}$$

$$\Rightarrow I_2 = \frac{\tau}{NAI_1 \mu_0 n} = \frac{1.5 \times 10^{-8}}{(10)(1 \times 10^{-6})\left(\frac{21}{44}\right)(4\pi \times 10^{-7})(10^3)} = 2.5 \text{ A}$$

31 (a) Let point P be a mid-point between the magnets.

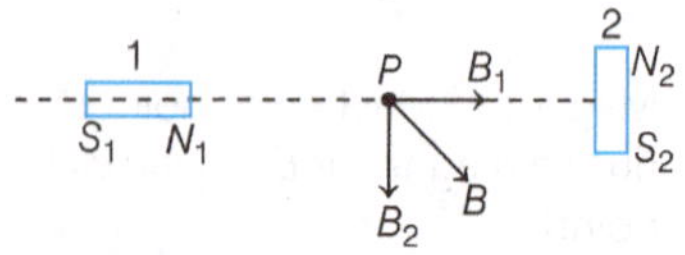

Magnetic field due to magnet 1 (at axial),

$$B_1 = \frac{\mu_0}{4\pi} \cdot \frac{2M_1}{d_1^3}$$

$$\therefore B_1 = 10^{-7} \times \frac{2 \times 5}{(10)^3} = 1 \times 10^{-9} \text{ T}$$

Magnetic field due to magnet 2 (at equatorial),

$$B_2 = \frac{\mu_0}{4\pi} \cdot \frac{M_2}{d_2^3} = \frac{10^{-7} \times 5}{(10)^3} = 5 \times 10^{-10} \text{T}$$

Net magnetic field,

$$B = \sqrt{B_1^2 + B_2^2} = \sqrt{(1 \times 10^{-9})^2 + (5 \times 10^{-10})^2} = \sqrt{(100 \times 10^{-20}) + 25 \times 10^{-20}} = \sqrt{125 \times 10^{-20}} = 5\sqrt{5} \times 10^{-10} \text{ T}$$

32 (a) Magnitude of magnetic field,

$$B = \frac{\mu_0}{4\pi} \cdot \frac{2M}{d^3} = 10^{-7} \times 2 \times \frac{1.4 \times 10^{-26}}{(1 \times 10^{-10})^3} = \frac{10^{-7} \times 2 \times 1.4 \times 10^{-26}}{1 \times 10^{-30}} = 2.8 \times 10^{-3} \text{ T} = 2.8 \text{ mT}$$

33 (b) Frequency of oscillation of the coil,

$$f = \frac{1}{2\pi}\sqrt{\frac{M \times B}{I}}$$

Squaring on both the sides, we get

$$f^2 = \frac{1}{4\pi^2} \cdot \frac{MB}{I}$$

$$\Rightarrow I = \frac{MB}{4\pi^2 f^2} = \frac{0.377 \times 5 \times 10^{-2}}{4 \times 3.14 \times 3.14 \times 2 \times 2}$$

$$\Rightarrow I = 1.2 \times 10^{-4} \text{ kg-m}^2$$

34 (d) The net magnetic flux passing through a hypothetical closed surface enclosing a bar magnet (dipole) is zero because bar magnet has two poles (north and south poles), hence number of magnetic field lines leaving the surface is balanced by the number of magnetic field lines entering it.

35 (a) Here, both laws of magnetism and electrostatic are different but in isolated magnetic poles are not known to exist by Gauss' law of magnetism.

36 (a) Magnetic field lines for magnetic material form continuous lines, so lines of **B** are necessarily continuous across S.

37 (b) Magnetisation,

$$I = \frac{M_{net}}{V} = \frac{8.0 \times 10^{22}}{(4/3)\pi R^3} \quad \left[\because V = \frac{4}{3}\pi R^3\right]$$

$$= \frac{8.0 \times 10^{22}}{(4/3)(3.14)(6.4 \times 10^6)^3} = 73 \text{ Am}^{-1}$$

38 (a) Volume,

$$V = l \times A = 0.25 \times 1 \times 10^{-4} = 2.5 \times 10^{-5} \text{ m}^3$$

Magnetisation,

$$I = \frac{M}{V} = \frac{1.0}{2.5 \times 10^{-5}} = 4.0 \times 10^4 \text{ Am}^{-1}$$

39 (b) Now, volume of cubic domain,

$$V = l^3 = (2.0 \times 10^{-6})^3 = 8.0 \times 10^{-18} \text{m}^3$$

Total dipole moment of all atoms

$$M_{max} = N \times M = 8 \times 10^{10} \times 5 \times 10^{-24} = 40 \times 10^{-14} = 4 \times 10^{-13} \text{Am}^2$$

The magnetisation of domain,

$$I = \frac{M_{max}}{V} = \frac{4 \times 10^{-13}}{8 \times 10^{-18}} = 5 \times 10^4 \text{ Am}^{-1}$$

40 (c) Magnetic intensity of solenoid,

$$H = nI = 1500 \times 3 = 4500 \text{ Am}^{-1}$$

$$\text{Magnetisation} = (\mu_r - 1)H = (400 - 1)4500 = 399 \times 4500 = 1.8 \times 10^6 \text{ Am}^{-1}$$

41 (c) Permeability of core,

$$\mu = \mu_0 \mu_r = \mu_0 (1 + \chi_m) \quad (\because \mu_r = 1 + \chi_m)$$

$$= (4\pi \times 10^{-7})(1 + 599) = 7.5 \times 10^{-4} \text{Tm A}^{-1}$$

42 (c) Magnetisation,

$$I = \chi H = 10^{-5} \times 0.5 = 5 \times 10^{-6} \text{ Am}^{-1}$$

43 (c) Magnetic intensity, $H = nI$

$$= 600 \times 1.5 = 900 \text{ Am}^{-1}$$

Now, magnetisation, $I = \chi H$

$$\because \chi = \mu_r - 1$$

$$\therefore I = (\mu_r - 1)H = (600 - 1)900 = 5.3 \times 10^5 \text{ Am}^{-1}$$

44 (d) Here, for solenoid,

$$\mathbf{H} = ni$$

As we know, $B = \mu_0 \mu_r ni = \mu_0 ni \mu_r = k\mu_r$

where, $k = \mu_0 ni$ = constant.

Thus, from above equation, we find that **B** varies with the variation in μ_r.

Now, for magnetisation in the core, when temperature of the iron core of solenoid is raised beyond Curie temperature, then it will behave as paramagnetic material, i.e. magnetisation does not reverses.

As we know, $(\chi)_{ferro} \approx 10^3$

and $(\chi)_{para} \approx 10^{-5}$

$$\Rightarrow \frac{(\chi)_{ferro}}{(\chi)_{para}} = \frac{10^3}{10^{-5}} = 10^8$$

$$\Rightarrow (\chi)_{para} = \frac{\chi_{ferro}}{10^8}$$

45 (*d*) A. Magnetic dipole exists but magnetic monopole do not exist.

B. Magnetic field lines at the ends of the solenoid are not straight and confined.

D. For a perfectly diamagnetic material, $\chi = -1$.

46 (*d*) The susceptibility of paramagnetic material

$$\chi = C\frac{\mu_0}{T}$$

This is known as Curie's law.

Thus, for a paramagnetic material both χ and μ_0 depend not only on the type of material but also on the sample's temperature.

Thus, the statement given in option (d) is incorrect.

48 (*d*) For diamagnetic substances, the magnetic susceptibility is negative and it is independent of temperature.

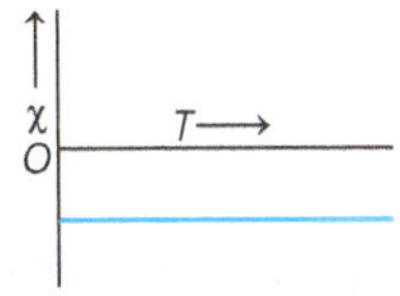

49 (*b*) A diamagnetic liquid moves from stronger part of magnetic field to weaker part. Therefore, the meniscus of the level of solution will fall.

52 (*b*) Intensity of magnetisation of diamagnetic substance is very small and negative.
Here, graph 3 represent negative value of intensity of magnetisation and it is less than that given in graph 4. Therefore, graph 3 represent a diamagnetic substance.

55 (*d*) Here, $\chi = -1$

Then, $\mu_r = 1 + \chi$

$\Rightarrow \mu_r = 1 + (-1) = 1 - 1 = 0$

Since, magnetic susceptibility of given material is less than one. Hence, the given magnetic material is a diamagnetic material.

56 (*c*) As, the sphere is perfectly diamagnetic, it completely expels field as shown below

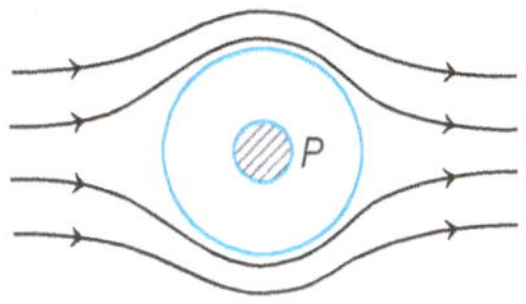

Therefore, there will be no magnetic field inside the cavity of sphere. So, the paramagnetic sample at the spherical cavity at the centre of sphere remains unaffected by external field and field inside paramagnetic sample is zero.

57 (*a*) Intensity of magnetisation,

$$I = \frac{M}{V} = \frac{20 \times 10^{-6}}{10^{-6}} = 20 \text{ A/m}$$

Now, magnetic susceptibility χ is

$$\chi = \frac{\text{Intensity of magnetisation}}{\text{Magnetic intensity}}$$

$$= \frac{I}{H} = \frac{20}{60 \times 10^3}$$

$$\Rightarrow \chi = \frac{1}{3} \times 10^{-3} = 3.33 \times 10^{-4}$$

58 (*d*) From Curie's law for paramagnetic substance, we have

Magnetic susceptibility,

$$\chi \propto \frac{1}{T}$$

$$\frac{\chi_2}{\chi_1} = \frac{T_1}{T_2}$$

$$\chi_2 = \frac{\chi_1 T_1}{T_2}$$

$$\chi_2 = \frac{2.8 \times 10^{-4} \times 350}{300}$$

$$= 3.267 \times 10^{-4}$$

59 (*b*) Here, $\chi_{m_1} = 0.0075$

$T_1 = -73\text{ °C} = (-73 + 273)$ K

$= 200$ K

$T_2 = -173\text{ °C} = (-173 + 273)]$

$= 100$ K

As for paramagnetic material magnetic susceptibility.

$$\chi_m \propto \frac{1}{T} \Rightarrow \frac{\chi_{m_2}}{\chi_{m_1}} = \frac{T_1}{T_2} = \frac{200}{100} = 2$$

$$\chi_{m_2} = 2\chi_{m_1} = 2 \times 0.0075$$

$$= 0.015$$

61 (*b*) On heating, different domains have net magnetisation in them which are randomly distributed. Thus, the net magnetisation of the substance due to various domains decreases to minimum.

62 (*a*) At high enough temperature, a ferromagnet becomes a paramagnet. The domain structure disintegrates with temperature.

64 (*d*) The volume of cubic domain is

$V = (10^{-6})^3 \text{ m}^3 = 10^{-18} \text{ m}^3 = 10^{-12} \text{cm}^3$

[$\because$ side $= 1\ \mu$m]

Mass = Density × Volume

($\because$ Density $= 7.9 \text{ gcm}^{-3}$)

$= 7.9 \text{ gcm}^{-3} \times 10^{-12} \text{ cm}^3$

$= 7.9 \times 10^{-12}$ g

It is given that Avogadro's number i.e. $N_A = (6.023 \times 10^{23})$ of iron atoms have a mass of 55 g. Hence, the number of atoms in the domain is

$$N = \frac{\text{Mass} \times N_A}{\text{Molecular mass}}$$

$$= \frac{7.9 \times 10^{-12} \times 6.023 \times 10^{23}}{55}$$

$$= 8.65 \times 10^{10} \text{ atoms}$$

65 (*c*) In a paramagnetic material,

$$I = C\frac{B}{T} = C\frac{\mu H}{T} \quad [\because B = \mu H]$$

Hence, $I \propto H$. Therefore, the graph between H and I is a straight line represented by in figure below

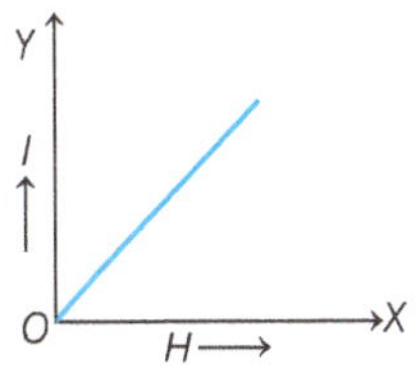

66 (*b*) As magnetic susceptibility,

$$\chi = \frac{C}{T}$$

$$\Rightarrow \quad \frac{\chi}{\chi'} = \frac{T'}{T}$$

$$\Rightarrow T' = \left(\frac{\chi}{\chi'}\right) T = \left(\frac{1.2 \times 10^{-5}}{1.8 \times 10^{-5}}\right) 300$$

$$= 200 \text{ K}$$

67 (*a*) As temperature of ferromagnetic material is raised, its susceptibility χ remains constant upto curie temperature and then decreases as shown in figure.

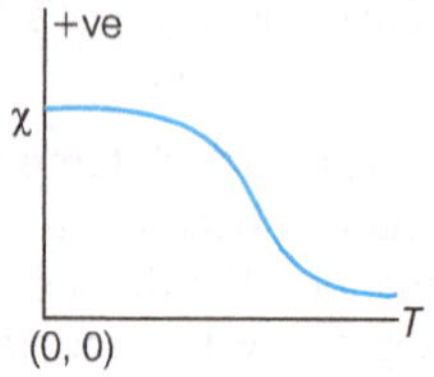

Assertion and Reason Questions

1 (*b*) The poles of magnet cannot be separated by breaking into two pieces.

If a bar magnet is broken into two halves, we get two similar bar magnets with somewhat weaker properties. As magnetic moment will be reduced to half, because magnetic dipole moment is directly proportional to the length between the poles.

2 (*a*) The net magnetic flux passes through a closed surface enclosing a bar magnet is zero because a bar magnet has two poles (one north and other south) and the magnetic flux leaving the north pole is equal to the magnetic flux entering the south pole of bar magnet.

3 (*c*) Susceptibility of the material,

$$\chi = \frac{M}{H} \Rightarrow M = \chi H$$

Thus, it is obvious that greater the value of susceptibility of a material greater will be the value of intensity of magnetisation, i.e. more easily it can be magnetised.

4 (*c*) When a piece of iron is brought near strong magnet, the external magnetic field of the magnet causes the magnetic domains in the iron to align with the field. This is because iron is a ferromagnetic material.

5 (*a*) Paramagnetic substances are those which get weakly magnetised when placed in an external magnetic field, because these substances have tendency to move from a region of weak magnetic field to strong magnetic field, i.e. they get weakly attracted to a magnet.

6 (*d*) At Curie point, a ferromagnetic substance start behaving as a paramagnetic substance. Thus, ferromagnetic substances obey Curie's law.

7 (*b*) Ferromagnetic materials have a high relative permeability, which means that they are strongly attracted to magnetic field.
A ferromagnetic material can be magnetised to saturation when all of the magnetic domains are aligned with external magnetic field.

10 (*b*) Ferromagnetic substances have property that they gets strongly magnetised when placed in an external magnetic field.

They have strong tendency to move from a region of weak magnetic field to strong magnetic field, i.e. they get strongly attracted to a magnet.

Statement Based Questions

1 (*b*) Naturally occurring ore of iron is leading stone (lodestone) in magnetism and magnetic phenomena are universal in nature.

2 (*b*) Statement I is correct and Statement II is incorrect.

Magnetic dipole moment,
$M = IA$ (I = Current, A = Area)
When wire is bent in the form of circle, then
$L = 2\pi R$ (R = Radius of circle)

$$\Rightarrow \quad R = \frac{L}{2\pi}$$

So, $$M = I(\pi R^2) = I\pi\left(\frac{L}{2\pi}\right)^2$$

$$M = \frac{IL^2}{4\pi} \text{ Am}^2$$

3 (*d*) $M = IA = I \times \pi r^2$

$$r' = 2r$$

$$\therefore \quad M' = I \times \pi(2r)^2 = 4M$$

4 (*c*) Statement I is incorrect and it can be corrected as

Susceptibility of a diamagnetic substances is negative and it does not change with temperature.

6 (*b*) Statement I is correct and Statement II is incorrect.

$$\chi_m \propto I$$

Greater value of susceptibility, greater will be the value of magnetisation.

7 (*c*) The magnetic field lines will not increase inside the material. Also, when magnet material placed in non-uniform magnetic field it moves from high field to low field.

Matching Type Questions

1 (*a*) Since, the magnetic potential energy U_m is given by

$$U_m = -\mathbf{M} \cdot \mathbf{B}$$
$$= -MB\cos\theta$$

A. For $\theta = 90°$,
$$U_m = -MB\cos 90° = 0$$

B. For $\theta = 0°$,
$$U_m = -MB\cos 0° = -mB$$

The potential energy is minimum and hence the needle is in most stable position.

C. For $\theta = 180°$,
$$U_m = -MB\cos 180° = +mB$$

The potential energy is maximum and hence the needle is in unstable position.

D. For $\theta = 60°$

$U_m = -MB\cos 60°$

$= -\frac{1}{2}mB$

Hence, A $\rightarrow$ 3, B $\rightarrow$ 1, C $\rightarrow$ 4 andD$\rightarrow$ 2.

2 (*a*)

A. Here, equatorial field for a short dipole is given as $-\frac{\mu_0 \mathbf{M}}{4\pi r^3}$.

B. Axial field for a short dipole is $\frac{\mu_0 2\mathbf{m}}{4\pi r^3}$.

C. External field for torque is $\mathbf{m} \times \mathbf{B}$.

D. External field for energy is $-\mathbf{m} \times \mathbf{B}$.

Hence, A $\rightarrow$3, B$\rightarrow$ 4, C$\rightarrow$ 2, D$\rightarrow$1

3 (*a*)

A. On applying alternating current, the position of north and south poles of a magnet can be changed.

B. On heating, the kinetic energy of molecules of magnet increases. Due to increased kinetic energy, the magnetic domains point in different directions due to which the magnet gets demagnetise.

C. Alnico is made up of aluminum, nickel and cobalt is known as permanent magnet.

D. Directive property of a magnet is used in compass to find the north and south directions.

Hence, A $\rightarrow$ 3, B $\rightarrow$ 4, C $\rightarrow$ 2 and D $\rightarrow$ 1.

Numerical Type Questions

1 (4) Let point *P* be the mid-point between the magnets.

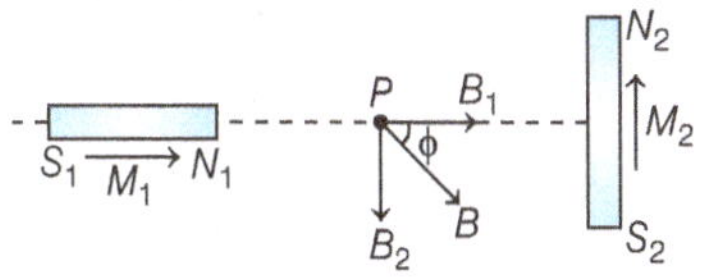

Now, the magnetic field due to magnet 1 at point *P* is

$B_1 = \frac{\mu_0}{4\pi}\frac{2m_1}{r_1^3} = \frac{10^{-7} \times 2 \times 4.0}{(1)^3}$

$= 8 \times 10^{-7}$ T

and magnetic field due to magnet 2 at point *P* is

$B_2 = \frac{\mu_0}{4\pi}\cdot\frac{M_2}{(r_2)^3} = \frac{10^{-7} \times 4.0}{(1)^3}$

$= 4 \times 10^{-7}$ T

The resultant magnetic field at point *P* is

$B = \sqrt{B_1^2 + B_2^2}$

$= \sqrt{(8 \times 10^{-7})^2 + (4 \times 10^{-7})^2}$

$= 4\sqrt{5} \times 10^{-7}$

$= n\sqrt{5} \times 10^{-7}$ T (given)

where, $n = 4$

2 (125) The magnetic field at axis of magnet,

$B = \frac{\mu_0}{4\pi}\cdot\frac{2m}{d^3}$

$= \frac{10^{-7} \times 2 \times 0.5}{(0.2)^3}$

$= \frac{1000 \times 10^{-7}}{8} = 125 \times 10^{-7}$

$= x \times 10^{-7}$ (given)

$\therefore$ The value of *x* is 125.

3 (13) The magnetic field due to bar magnet, $B = \frac{\mu_0}{4\pi}\cdot\frac{m}{r^3}\sqrt{1 + 3\cos^2\theta}$

$= 10^{-7} \times \frac{4.0}{(1)^3}\sqrt{1 + 3(\cos 30°)^2}$

$= 4 \times 10^{-7}\sqrt{1 + 3 \times \frac{3}{4}}$

$= 2 \times 10^{-7} \times \sqrt{13}$

$= 2\sqrt{13} \times 10^{-7}$

$= 2\sqrt{p} \times 10^{-7}$ (given)

$\therefore p = 13$

4 (146) The magnetic moment

$M = m \times 2l = 25 \times 0.12$ A - m^2

The magnetic induction at a point 10 cm away f rom the centre of the magnet on its axial line,

$B = \frac{\mu_0}{4\pi} \times \frac{2Md}{(d^2 - l^2)^2}$

$= 10^{-7} \times \frac{2 \times 25 \times 0.12 \times 0.1}{[(0.1)^2 - (0.06)^2]^2}$

$= 146 \times 10^{-5} = x \times 10^{-5}$ (given)

$\therefore \quad x = 146$

5 (24) The bar magnet reaches in stable equilibrium under the influence of these two fields making an angle

$\theta_1 = 45°$ with B_1 and

$\theta_2 = 75° - 45° = 30°$ with B_2

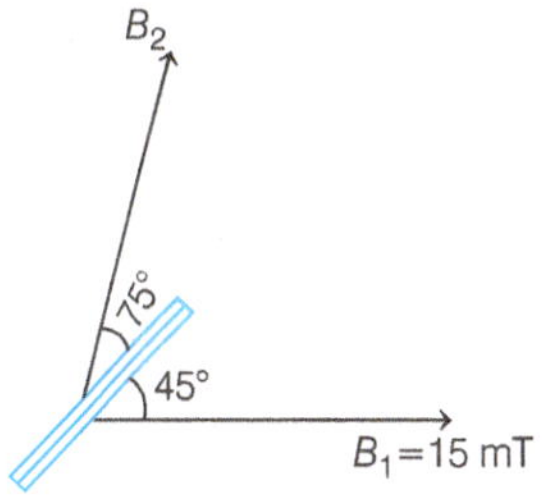

For stable equilibrium, net torque acting on dipole must be zero, i.e,

$\tau_1 + \tau_2 = 0$ or $\tau_1 = \tau_2$

or $mB_1\sin\theta_1 = mB_2\sin\theta_2$

$\Rightarrow B_2 = B_1 \times \frac{\sin\theta_1}{\sin\theta_2} = 17 \times \frac{\sin 45°}{\sin 30°}$

$= 17 \times \frac{1}{\sqrt{2}} \times 2$

$= 24.03$ mT $\approx$ 24 mT

6 (43) Given, pole strength,

$m = 150$ CGS unit

$= 15$ A-m

Now, magnetic field

$B = \frac{\mu_0}{4\pi} \times \frac{2Md}{(d^2 - l^2)^2}$ ...(i)

s we know that,

$M = m \times 2l = 15 \times 0.1 = 1.5$ A m^2

From Eq. (i),

$B = \frac{10^{-7} \times 2 \times 1.5 \times 0.2}{[(0.2)^2 - (0.05)^2]^2}$

$= 43 \times 10^{-6} = n \times 10^{-6}$T (given)

$\therefore \quad n = 43$

7 (84) Torque, $\tau = \mathbf{M_2} \times \mathbf{B_1}$

B_1 is magnetic field at *P* due to short magnet M_1.

$\tau = M_2B_1\sin 90° = 1.2 \times \frac{\mu_0}{4\pi}\cdot\frac{M_1}{(1.2)^3} \times 1,$

$\Rightarrow \quad \tau = 84 \times 10^{-9}$ N-m

8 (30) Given, $M = 200 \text{A m}^2$

$$B = 0.30 \text{ N A}^{-1}\text{m}^{-1}$$
$$\tau = 30 \text{ N m}$$

The torque experienced,

$$\tau = MB\sin\theta$$
$$\therefore \sin\theta = \frac{\tau}{MB} = \frac{30}{200 \times 0.3} = \frac{30}{60}$$
$$\sin\theta = \frac{1}{2} \Rightarrow \sin\theta = \sin 30°$$
$$\therefore \theta = 30°$$

9 (628) Given, volume of the rod,
$V = (10 \times 0.5 \times 0.4) \times 10^{-6}$
$= 2 \times 10^{-6} \text{m}^3$

Magnetic strength,
$H = 0.5 \times 10^4 \text{ A m}^{-1}$

Magnetic moment, $M = 10 \text{ A m}^2$

Now, magnetisation,

$$I = \frac{M}{V} = \frac{10}{2 \times 10^{-6}} = 5 \times 10^6 \text{ A m}^{-1}$$

The magnetic induction,

$$B = \mu_0(H + I)$$
$$= 4\pi \times 10^{-7}[0.5 \times 10^4 + 5 \times 10^6]$$
$$= 6.28 \text{ T} = 628 \times 10^{-2}\text{T}$$
$$= x \times 10^{-2} \text{ (given)}$$
$$\therefore x = 628$$

NCERT Exemplar Questions

1 (b) As we know,

$$M \propto \frac{B \text{ (magnetic field induction)}}{T \text{ (temperature in kelvin)}}$$
$$\Rightarrow \frac{M_2}{M_1} = \frac{B_2}{B_1} \times \frac{T_1}{T_2}$$

Given, $M_1 = 8 \text{ Am}^{-1}$, $B_1 = 0.6$ T and $T_1 = 4$ K, $B_2 = 0.2$ T and $T_2 = 16$ K

$$\Rightarrow \frac{0.2}{0.6} \times \frac{4}{16} = \frac{M_2}{8}$$
$$\Rightarrow M_2 = 8 \times \frac{1}{12} = \frac{2}{3} \text{Am}^{-1}$$

2 (c) In case of toroid, the magnetic field is only confined inside the body of toroid in the form of concentric magnetic lines of force and there is no magnetic field outside the body of toroid. This is because the loop encloses no current. Thus, the magnetic moment of toroid is zero.

In general, if we take r as a large distance outside the toroid, then $m \propto \frac{1}{r^3}$. But this case is not possible here.

3 (d) As we know a permanent magnet is a substance which at room temperature retain ferromagnetic property for a long period of time.

The individual atoms in a ferromagnetic material possess a dipole moment as in a paramagnetic material.

However, they interact with one another in such a way that they spontaneously align themselves in a common direction over a macroscopic volume called domain. Thus, we can say that in a permanent magnet at room temperature, domains are all perfectly aligned.

4 (b) As Gauss' law states,

$$\oint_S \mathbf{E} \cdot d\mathbf{s} = \frac{q}{\varepsilon_0} \text{ for electrostatic field.}$$

It does not contradict for electrostatic fields as the electric field lines do not form continuous closed path.

According to Gauss' law in magnetic field, $\oint_S \mathbf{E} \cdot \mathbf{ds} = 0$

It contradicts for magnetic field, because there is a magnetic field inside the solenoid and no field outside the solenoid carrying current but the magnetic field lines form the closed path.

Past Exams Questions

1 (a) For a diamagnetic material magnetic susceptibility χ is small and negative, is, $0 > \chi \geq -1$.

For a ferromagnetic material, $\chi >> 1$.

For a paramagnetic material, $0 < \chi < \varepsilon$

(ε is a small positive number) and for non-magnetic material, $\chi = 0$.

Hence, correct option is (a).

2 (b)

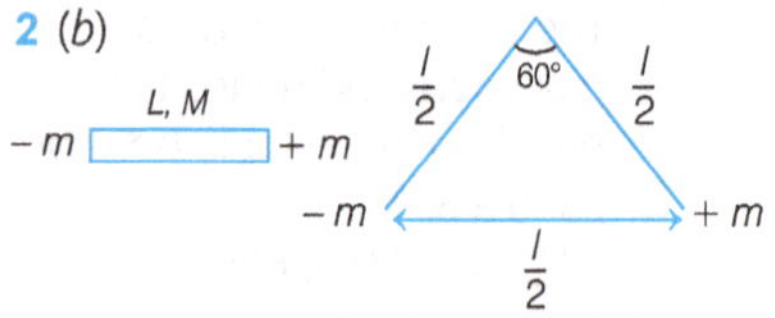

The magnetic moment is given by

$$M = m \cdot L$$

New magnetic moment, $M' = m \cdot L'$

$$= m \cdot \frac{l}{2} = \frac{ml}{2}$$

Thus, $M' = \frac{M}{2}$

3 (d) Given, magnetic field
$B = 0.049$ T

Time period, $T = \frac{5}{20} = \frac{1}{4}$ s

Moment of inertia,

$$I = 9.8 \times 10^{-6} \text{ kg m}^2$$

The time period of oscillation of a magnetic needle in a magnetic field is given by $T = 2\pi\sqrt{\frac{I}{MB}}$

where, M is the magnetic moment of the needle.

Thus, $T = 2\pi\sqrt{\frac{9.8 \times 10^{-6}}{M \times 0.049}}$

$$\Rightarrow \left(\frac{1}{4}\right)^2 = (2\pi)^2\left(\frac{9.8 \times 10^{-6}}{M \times 4.9 \times 10^{-2}}\right)$$
$$\Rightarrow \frac{1}{16} = \frac{4\pi^2 \times 2 \times 10^{-4}}{M}$$
$$\Rightarrow M = 16 \times 8 \times \pi^2 \times 10^{-4}$$
$$= 128\pi^2 \times 10^{-4} \text{ Am}^2$$
$$= 1280\pi^2 \times 10^{-5} \text{ Am}^2$$

4 (b) We know that, magnetic field due to current carrying solenoid,

$$B = \mu_0 nI \Rightarrow \mu_0 = \frac{B}{nI}$$
$$\Rightarrow [\mu_0] = \frac{[B]}{[n][I]} = \frac{\left[\frac{F}{IL}\right]}{[n][I]} \quad [\because F = IBL]$$
$$= \frac{[F]}{[n][L][I^2]} = \frac{[\text{MLT}^{-2}]}{[\text{L}^{-1}][\text{L}][\text{A}^2]}$$
$$= [\text{MLT}^{-2}\text{A}^{-2}]$$

5 (d) As, $\mu_m = \mu_0(1 + \chi)$

$$= 4\pi \times 10^{-7}(1 + 599)$$
$$= 2.4\pi \times 10^{-4} \text{ T mA}^{-1}$$

6 (*d*) Net magnetic flux through a closed surface is zero because the number of field lines leaving the surface are equal to the number of field lines entering the surface.

7 (*b*) Work done in rotating the magnet, $W = MB(\cos\theta_0 - \cos\theta)$

where, M = magnetic moment of the magnet

and B = magnetic field.

$$W = MB(\cos 0° - \cos 60°)$$
$$= MB\left(1 - \frac{1}{2}\right) = \frac{MB}{2}$$

$\therefore \quad MB = 2W \qquad$ ...(i)

Torque on a magnet in this position is given by

$$\tau = \mathbf{M} \times \mathbf{B}$$
$$= MB\sin\theta = 2W\sin 60°$$
[from Eq. (i)]
$$= 2W\frac{\sqrt{3}}{2} = \sqrt{3}\,W$$

8 (*d*) As we know, the relation between the magnetic permeability and susceptibility of material , i.e.

$$\mu_r = 1 + \chi_m \qquad \text{...(i)}$$

$\because$ For diamagnetic substances, $\mu_r < 1$. So, according to Eq. (i) , the magnetic susceptibility (χ_m) of diamagnetic substance will be negative.

9 (*c*) Magnetic moment is from *S* to *N*,

$$M_{net} = \sqrt{M^2 + M^2 + 2M^2\cos\theta}$$

M_{net} will be maximum if $\cos\theta$ is maximum. $\cos\theta$ will be maximum when θ will be minimum.

So, at $\theta = 30°$, M_{net} will be maximum.

10 (*b*) Magnetic susceptibility (χ) of a magnetic material does not depend on magnetising field (H)

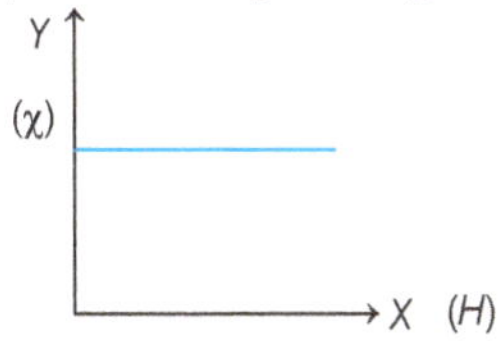

$\therefore \quad$ A → III

Magnetic field due to current carrying wire for $x < a$

$$B = \frac{\mu_0 Ix}{2\pi a^2} \Rightarrow B \propto x$$

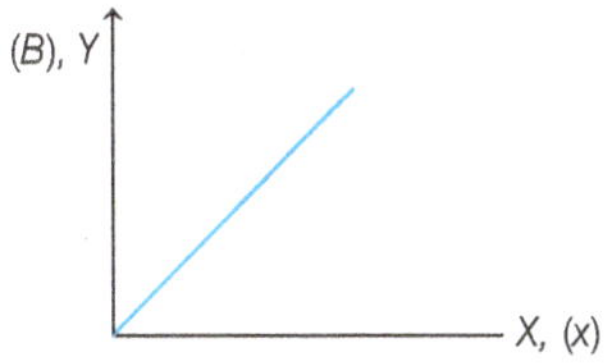

$\therefore \quad$ B → I

Magnetic field due to a current carrying wire for $x > a$

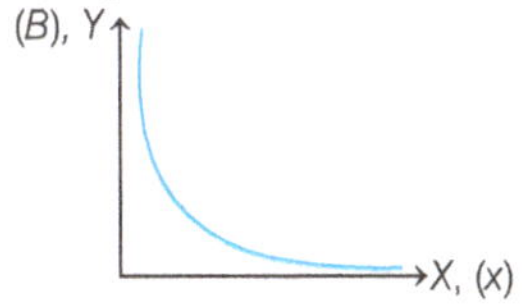

$$\therefore \quad B = \frac{\mu_0 I}{2\pi x} \Rightarrow B \propto \frac{1}{x}$$

$\therefore \quad$ C → IV

Magnetic field inside a solenoid is constant and becomes zero outside the solenoid.

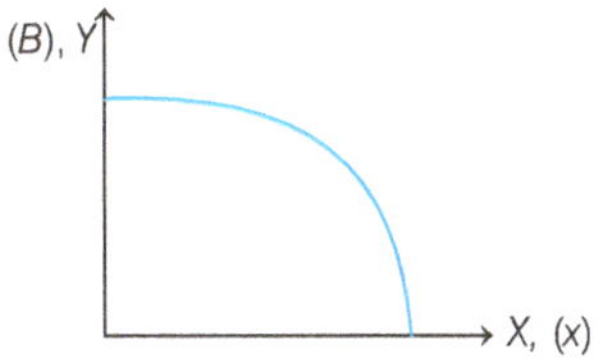

$\therefore$ D → II

11 (*b*) Paramagnetic substances have a weak net dipole moment of their own.

So, they tend to align with external magnetic field and their susceptibility is a small positive member.

12 (*28*) Magnetic moment of straight strip, $M = 44\ \text{Am}^2$

When it is bent in semicircular shape.

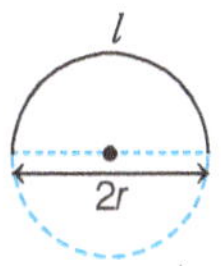

$$l = \pi r \text{ or } r = \frac{l}{\pi}$$

Now, the distance between two poles, $2r = \frac{2l}{\pi}$

Its new magnetic moment is,

$$M' = m \times 2r = m \times \frac{2l}{\pi}$$
$$= \frac{2}{\pi}(m \times l) \qquad (\because m \times l = M)$$
$$= \frac{2}{\pi} \times 44 = \frac{2}{22} \times 44 \times 7$$
$$= 7 \times 4 = 28\ \text{Am}^2$$

13 (*c*) Initial orientation, $\theta_i = 0°$ (parallel to B)

Final orientation, $\theta_f = 180°$
(anti-parallel to B)

Work done in rotating a dipole from θ_i position to θ_f position,

$$W = MB(\cos\theta_i - \cos\theta_f)$$
$$= 5 \times 0.4(\cos 0° - \cos 180°)$$
$$= 2(1 - (-1)) = 4\ \text{J}$$

14 (*c*) We know that, $\mu_R = 1 + \chi$

$$\Rightarrow \frac{\mu_m}{\mu_0} = 1 + 99$$
$$\Rightarrow \mu_m = \mu_0 \times 100$$
$$= 4\pi \times 10^{-7} \times 100$$
$$= 4\pi \times 10^{-5}\ \text{Wb/ A-m}$$

15 (*b*) Absolute permeability of the material,

$$\mu = \mu_0(1 + \chi_m)$$
$$\Rightarrow \quad \mu = 4\pi \times 10^{-7}(1 + 499)$$
$$= 4\pi \times 10^{-7} \times 500$$
$$= 2\pi \times 10^{-4}\ \text{H / m}$$

Skill Boosters

1 (*b*) In stable equilibrium, torque of two magnetic fields, i.e. $\tau_1 = \tau_2$

$$\Rightarrow MB_1\sin\theta_1 = MB_2\sin\theta_2$$
$$\Rightarrow \quad B_2 = \frac{B_1\sin\theta_1}{\sin\theta_2}$$

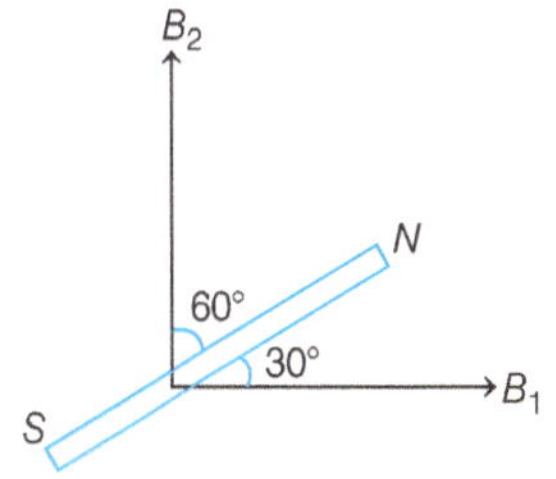

$$= \frac{3 \times 10^{-2} \times \sin 30^\circ}{\sin 60^\circ}$$

$$= \frac{3 \times 10^{-2} \times \frac{1}{2}}{\frac{\sqrt{3}}{2}}$$

$$= \sqrt{3} \times 10^{-2} \text{T}$$

2 (*b*) The moment of inertia of the bar magnet,

$$I = \frac{ml^2}{12}$$

Moment of inertia of each piece of magnet about an axis perpendicular to length passing through its centre,

$$I' = \frac{m}{2}\frac{\left(\frac{l}{2}\right)^2}{12} = \frac{ml^2}{12} \times \frac{1}{8} = \frac{I}{8}$$

and magnetic dipole moment,

$$M' = \frac{M}{2}$$

and time period of oscillation,

$$T = 2\pi\sqrt{\frac{I}{MB}}$$

$$\therefore \quad T' = 2\pi\sqrt{\frac{I'}{M'B}}$$

$$= 2\pi\sqrt{\frac{\frac{I}{8}}{\frac{M}{2}B}}$$

$$\Rightarrow T' = \frac{2\pi}{2}\sqrt{\frac{I}{MB}} = \frac{T}{2}$$

3 (*b*) Number of turns per metre,

$$n = \frac{N}{l} = \frac{3500}{94 \times 10^{-2}}$$

$$= 3723.4 \text{ per metre}$$

Now, the magnetic field in the core,

$$B = \mu_0 \mu_r n I$$

$$= 4\pi \times 10^{-7} \times 800 \times 3723.4 \times 2.0$$

$$= 7.4 \text{ T}$$

4 (*c*) For a given sample,

$$M \propto B / T$$

or $$\frac{M_1}{M_2} = \frac{B_1 / T_1}{B_2 / T_2}$$

Given, $B_1 = 0.84$ T, $B_2 = 0.98$ T

$T_1 = 4.2$ K and $T_2 = 2.8$ K

Thus, $$\frac{M_1}{M_2} = \frac{0.84 / 4.2}{0.98 / 2.8} = 4/7$$

or $M_2 = (7/4)\, m_1$

Initial total magnetic moment of the sample, i.e. $M_1 = 15\%$ of nm

$$M_1 = \frac{15 \times 2 \times 10^{24} \times 1.5 \times 10^{-23}}{100}$$

$$= 4.5 \text{ JT}^{-1}$$

Thus, $m_2 = (7/4)(4.5) = 7.9 \text{ JT}^{-1}$

5 (*c*) Volume of the cubic domain,

$V = (2 \times 10^{-6})\text{cm}^3 = 8 \times 10^{-18} \text{cm}^3$

Number of atoms in a domain,

$$N = \frac{\text{Total mass} \times \text{Avogadro number}}{\text{Molecular mass}}$$

$$N = \frac{\text{Volume} \times \text{Density} \times \text{Avogadro number}}{\text{Molecular mass}}$$

$$= \frac{8 \times 10^{-18} \times 7.92 \times 6.023 \times 10^{23}}{55} \times 10^6$$

$= 6.92 \times 10^{11}$ atoms

The net dipole moment of domain,

$$M_n = N \times M$$

$$= 6.92 \times 10^{11} \times 9.27 \times 10^{-27}$$

$$= 64 \times 10^{-16} \text{A-m}^2$$

So, intensity of magnetisation,

$$I = \frac{M_n}{V} = \frac{64 \times 10^{-16}}{8 \times 10^{-18}}$$

$$= 8 \times 10^2 \text{Am}^{-1}$$

6 (*c*)

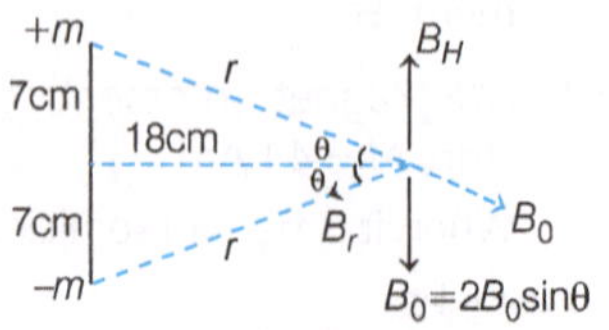

i.e. $$\frac{2\mu_0}{4\pi}\frac{m}{r^2} \times \frac{7}{r} = 0.4 \times 10^{-4}$$

$$\Rightarrow 2 \times 10^{-7} \times \frac{m \times 7}{(7^2 + 18^2)^{3/2}} \times 10^4 = 0.4 \times 10^{-4}$$

$$m = \frac{4 \times 10^{-2} \times (373)^{3/2}}{14}$$

$$M = m \times 14 \text{ cm} = m \times \frac{14}{100}$$

$$= \frac{0.04 \times (373)^{3/2}}{14} \times \frac{14}{100}$$

$$= 4 \times 10^{-4} \times 7203.82$$

$$= 2.88 \text{ J/T}$$

8 (*d*) Each magnet is identical in respect of their pole strength and magnetic moment. When north pole of one magnet is placed near the south pole of another magnet, the net pole strength will reduce to zero . Hence, the effective magnetic moment of the given combination is zero.

9 (*d*) The magnetic fields produced by these magnets at point *p* are mutually. perpendicular. Their resultant field therefore

$$B = \left[\left(\frac{\mu_0}{4\pi}\frac{m}{r^3}\right)^2 + \left(\frac{\mu_0}{4\pi}\frac{2m}{r^3}\right)^2\right]^{1/2}$$

$$= \frac{\mu_0}{4\pi}\frac{m}{r^3}(1+4)^{1/2}$$

$$B = \frac{\mu_0}{4\pi}\frac{m\sqrt{5}}{r^3}$$

10 (*b*) In first position, $T \propto \frac{1}{\sqrt{M_1 + M_2}}$

and in second position,

$$T \propto \frac{1}{\sqrt{M_1 - M_2}}$$

$$\Rightarrow \frac{3^2}{T^2} = \frac{2M - M}{2M + M}$$

$$T^2 = 9 \times 3 \text{ s}^2$$

$$\therefore \quad T = 3\sqrt{3} \text{ s}$$

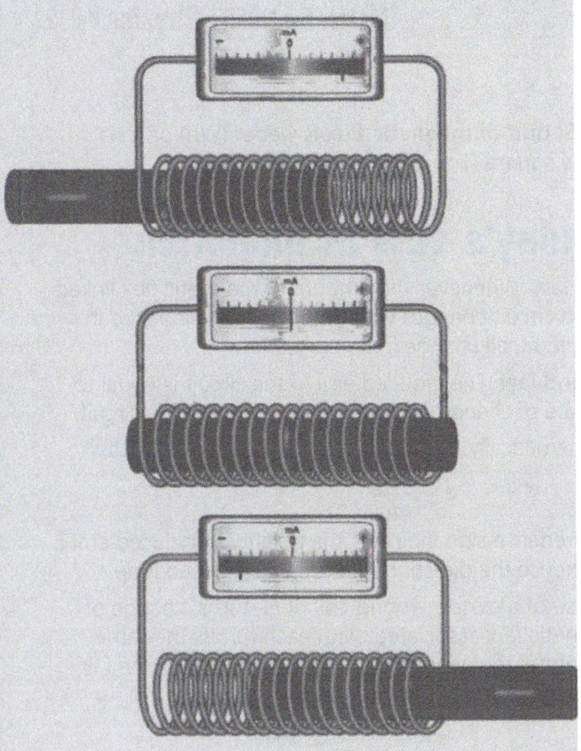

06

Scan for Physics Through Concept Master Videos

Electromagnetic Induction

Topicwise No. of Ques asked In 5 Years (NEET)

Topics	No. of Questions				
	2024	2023	2022	2021	2020
Magnetic Flux	–	–	1	–	–
Faraday's Law of Induction	1	–	1	–	1
Motional Electromotive Force	1	–	–	–	1
Inductance	–	1	–	1	1
AC Generator	–	–	–	–	–

Special Type of Ques Asked In 5 Years (NEET)

Types	Years				
	2024	2023	2022	2021	2020
A-R	–	–	–	–	–
Statement Based	–	–	–	–	–
Matching	–	–	–	–	–

Last 5 Years Weigtage (NEET)

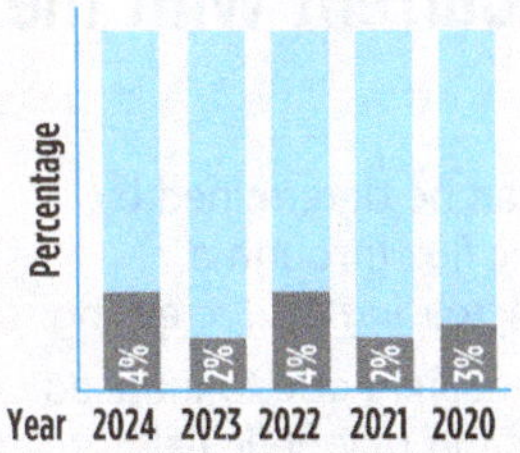

- Oersted, Ampere and few other established that **magnetic field is produced by electric current**. On the other hand, the experiments of Michael Faraday and Joseph Henry demonstrated that an **electric current can also be produced by varying magnetic field**.
- The phenomenon of generation of current or emf by changing the magnetic fields is known as **Electromagnetic Induction** (EMI).
- The emf developed in the conductor by the process of EMI is known as **induced emf** and if the conductor is in the form of a closed loop, then the current flowing in the conductor is known as **induced current**.

The Experiments of Faraday and Henry

The discovery and understanding of electromagnetic induction are based on a long series of experiments carried out by Faraday and Henry. Some of the experiments are shown below.

- **Experiment 1** When the bar magnet is pushed towards the coil, the pointer in the galvanometer G deflects as shown in figure below. This deflection indicates the presence of electric current in the coil. The deflection lasts as long as the bar magnet is in motion. The galvanometer does not show any deflection when the magnet is held stationary.

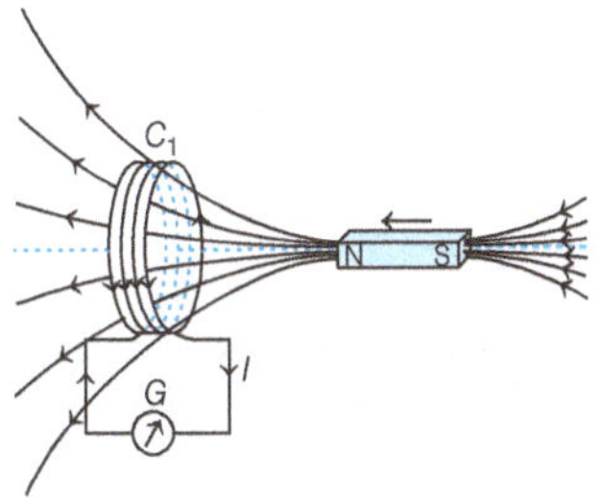

- **Experiment 2** The current is induced in coil C_1 due to motion of the current carrying coil C_2 as shown in figure below. It is the relative motion between the coils that induces the electric current.

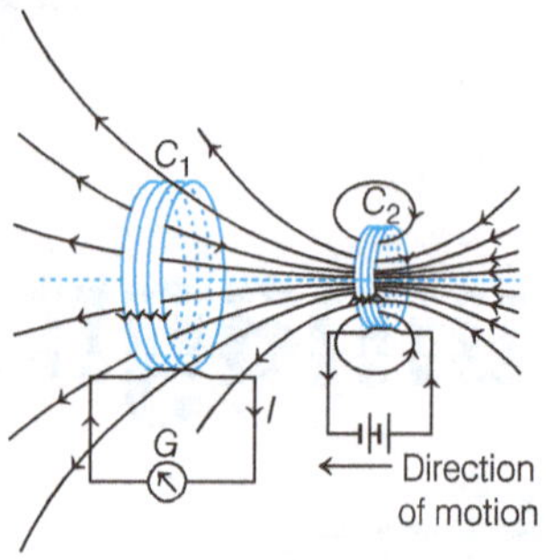

- **Experiment 3** There are two coils C_1 and C_2 held stationary. Coil C_1 is connected to galvanometer G while the second coil C_2 is connected to a battery through a tapping key K as shown in figure.

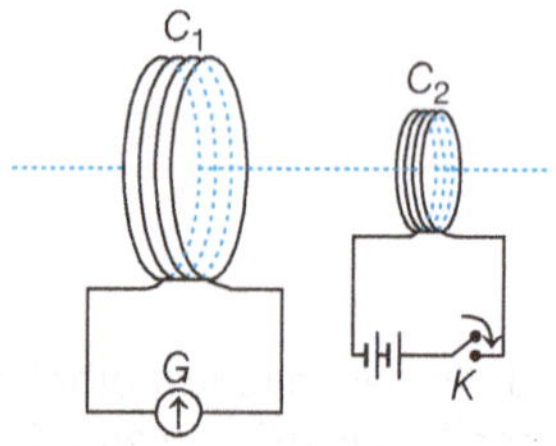

The galvanometer shows a momentary deflection when the tapping key K is pressed. The pointer in the galvanometer returns to zero immediately.

If the key is held pressed continuously, there is no deflection in the galvanometer. When the key is released, a momentary deflection is observed again, but in the opposite direction.

Magnetic Flux

- The total number of magnetic field lines crossing normally through any surface area, when it is placed in a magnetic field is known as the **magnetic flux** of that surface.
- Magnetic flux through a plane of surface area **A** placed in a uniform magnetic field **B** as shown in figure below. It is denoted as $\phi_B = \mathbf{B} \cdot \mathbf{A} = BA\cos\theta$ NEET 2022

  where, θ is angle between **B** and **A**.

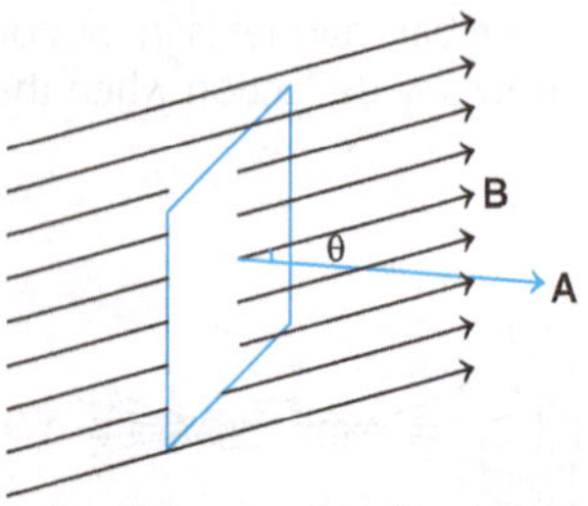

Plane of surface area **A** inclined at angle θ with uniform magnetic field **B**.

- The **SI unit of magnetic flux** is weber (Wb) or tesla metre square (Tm^2). It is a scalar quantity.

Faraday's Law of Induction

- **First law** Whenever the amount of magnetic flux linked with a circuit changes with time, an emf is induced in the circuit, till change in flux take place.
- **Second law** The induced emf in the circuit is equal to the rate of change of magnetic flux through the circuit.

  Mathematically, the induced emf is given by NEET 2020

$$\varepsilon = \frac{-d\phi_B}{dt}$$

  The negative sign indicates the polarity of induced emf ε and hence the direction of current in a closed loop.
- In case of a closely wound coil of N turns, change of magnetic flux associated with each turn is the same. Therefore, the expression for the total induced emf is given by

$$\varepsilon = \frac{-Nd\phi_B}{dt}$$ NEET 2019

- The induced emf can be increased by increasing the number of turns N in the closed coil.

Lenz's Law and Conservation of Energy

- Lenz's law states that, the direction of induced current in the circuit is such that it opposes the change in magnetic flux linked with the circuit that produced the induced current.
- The negative sign in induced emf, $e = -\frac{d\phi_B}{dt}$, shows the opposing nature of magnetic flux w.r.t. induced emf.
- In order to continue the change in magnetic flux linked with the circuit, some mechanical work has to be done against the opposition due to induced emf in the coil. This external mechanical work appears in the circuit in the form of electrical energy.
- This law is based upon law of conservation of energy.

Direction of Induced Current with the help of Lenz's Law

- Direction of induced current can be determined by checking whether the magnetic flux through a conducting loop or circuit is increasing or decreasing.
- If flux is increasing, the magnetic field due to induced current will be opposite to existing magnetic field shown in Fig.(a) in order to oppose the change in magnetic flux.

- If flux is decreasing, the magnetic field due to induced current will be along the existing magnetic field shown in Fig.(b) in order to oppose the change in magnetic flux .

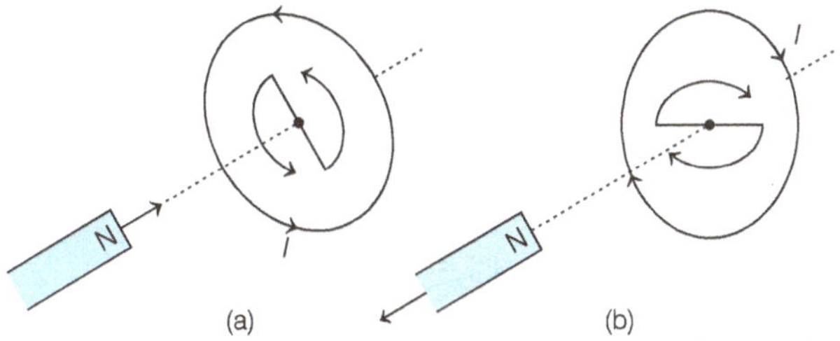

(a) The direction of induced current in the loop such that the bar magnet experiences a repulsive force

(b) The direction of induced current in the loop such that the bar magnet experiences an attractive force

Motional Electromotive Force

- The emf induced across the ends of a conductor due to its motion in magnetic field is called **motional emf**.
- When a conducting rod of length l is moving with a uniform magnetic field B (as shown below), then magnitude of induced emf will be $|\varepsilon| = Blv$.

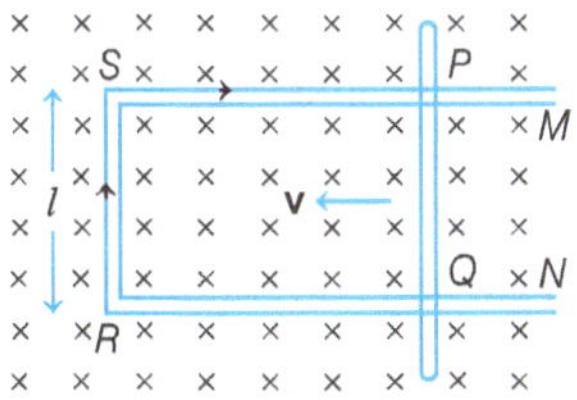

- In case of a stationary conductor, the force on its charges is given by

$$\mathbf{F} = q(\mathbf{E} + \mathbf{v} \times \mathbf{B}) = q\mathbf{E}$$

Since, $\mathbf{v} = 0$. Thus, any force on the charge must arise from the electric field term **E** alone.

Some important points related to emf are given below

- If the rod is moving, making an angle θ with the direction of magnetic field, then $|\varepsilon| = Blv \sin\theta$

  $|\varepsilon| = 0$, for motion parallel to **B**, i.e. $\mathbf{v} \parallel \mathbf{B}$.
- If a conducting rod moves on two parallel conducting rails, then again an emf is induced whose magnitude is given by

$$|\varepsilon| = Blv \qquad [\text{since, } \mathbf{v} \perp \mathbf{B}]$$

- The direction of induced current is given by **Fleming's right hand rule**.
- The induced current in the loop is given by

$$I = \frac{|\varepsilon|}{R} = \frac{Blv}{R}$$

where, R = resistance of loop.

- Due to presence of current and magnetic field , arm PQ (as shown in the above figure) experiences a magnetic force given by

$$F = BIl = \frac{B^2l^2v}{R}$$

- The force given above is directed opposite to the velocity of the rod and hence the power required to maintain constant speed v is given as

$$P = Fv = \frac{B^2l^2v^2}{R}$$

- When a metallic rod of length l is rotated at an angular speed ω normal to a uniform magnetic field B, the emf induced across the rod is given by

For Concept Master Video

$$e = \frac{1}{2}Bl^2\omega$$ NEET 2020

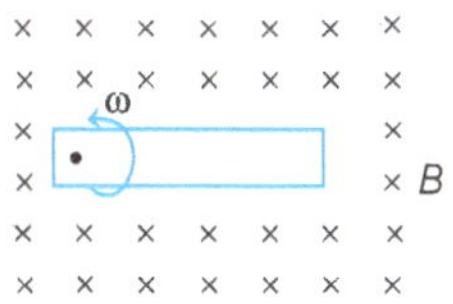

Marks Maximiser

Eddy Current

- The currents induced in bulk pieces of conductors when the magnetic flux linked with the conductor changes are known as **eddy currents**.
- The direction of the eddy currents in the conductor is determined by applying Lenz's law or Fleming's right hand rule.

Some important applications of eddy current are given below.

- Induction furnace is based on heating effect of eddy current.
- Consumption of electricity is recorded by energy meter using the concept of eddy current.
- Concept of eddy current is used in speedometer to measure instantaneous speed of a vehicle.
- Concept of eddy current is used in electromagnetic damping.

Inductance

- The tendency of electric conductor to oppose any change of current in an electrical circuit is called **inductance**.
- It plays same role in an electrical circuit as played by inertia in mechanics. It depends only on the geometry of the coil and intrinsic material properties.
- It is a scalar quantity and its SI unit is henry (H). It has dimensions of $[ML^2T^{-2}A^{-2}]$.

Self-Inductance

- The phenomenon of production of emf in a single isolated coil due to change of flux through the same coil by means of varying the current is known as **self-inductance**.
- In this case, flux linkage through the coil of N turns is proportional to the current through the coil and is expressed as

$$N\,\phi_B \propto I \text{ or } N\phi_B = LI$$

where constant of proportionality L is called the **coefficient of self-induction** of the coil. It is also called **self-inductance** of the coil.

- Induced emf due to self-induction is given by

$$\varepsilon = -\frac{d(N\phi_B)}{dt} = -L\frac{dI}{dt}$$

Thus, the self-induced emf always opposes any change (increase or decrease) of current in the coil.

- For a solenoid coil having length l, total number of turns N and cross-sectional area A, the value of self-inductance L is

$$L = \frac{\mu_0 N^2 A}{l} = \mu_0 n^2 Al = \mu_0 n^2 V$$

where, $n = N/l$ and V = volume of the solenoid $= Al$

- If we fill the inside of solenoid with a material of relative permeability μ_r, then $L = \mu_r \mu_0 n^2 Al$.
- The self-inductance of the coil depends on its geometry and on the permeability of the medium.
- The self-induced emf is also called the back emf, as it opposes any change in the current in a circuit. The self-inductance plays the role of inertia.
- Power supplied to the inductor, $P = (\varepsilon_{in})I = \left(L\frac{dI}{dt}\right)I$
- Work needs to be done against **back emf** ε in establishing the current and given by $\frac{dW}{dt} = |\varepsilon|\, I$

$$W = \int_0^I LI\,dI = \frac{1}{2}LI^2$$ NEET 2023

This work is **stored as magnetic potential energy**.

Mutual Inductance

- The phenomenon by which an opposing emf is produced in a coil as a result of change in current or magnetic flux linked with a neighbouring coupled coil is called **mutual inductance**.
- The flux linkage with coil 1 due to change in current in a neighbouring coil 2 is directly proportional to the current in coil 2.

i.e. $N_1\phi_1 \propto I_2 \Rightarrow N_1\phi_1 = M_{12}I_2$

Similarly, $N_2\phi_2 = M_{21}I_1$

The constant of proportionality M_{12} and M_{21} are called **mutual inductance** or **coefficient of mutual induction**.

- For two long co-axial solenoids S_1 and S_2 each having length l as shown in figure below. The mutual inductance or coefficient of mutual induction is

$$M_{12} = M_{21} = M = \mu_0 n_1 n_2 \pi r_1^2 l$$

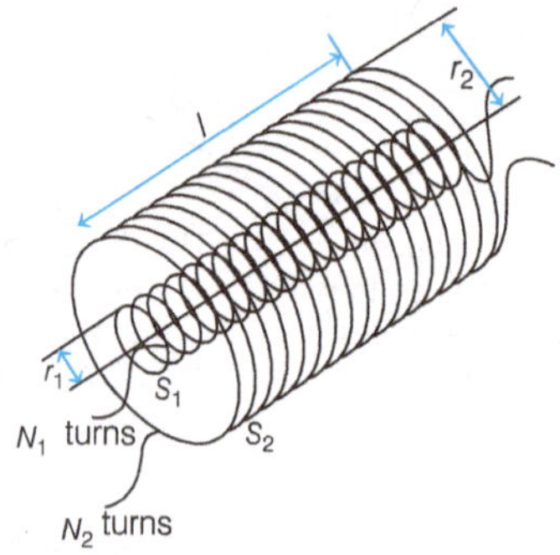

where, n_1 and n_2 are number of turns per unit length of inner and outer coils of solenoid respectively,

r_1 = radius of inner coil, r_2 = radius of outer coil

and l = length of solenoid.

- If a medium of relative permeability μ_r is present, the mutual inductance would be $M = \mu_r \mu_0 n_1 n_2 \pi r_1^2 l$.
- The induced emf in the inner coil is given by

$$\varepsilon = -M\frac{dI_2}{dt}$$

- This shows that varying current in a coil can induce emf in a neighbouring coil. The magnitude of the induced emf depends upon the rate of change of current and mutual inductance of the two coils.
- In case of current flowing simultaneously in two nearby coils, the flux linked with one coil will be the sum of two fluxes which exists independently.

$$N_1\phi_1 = M_{11}I_1 + M_{12}I_2$$

where, M_{11} represents inductance due to the same coil.

- The emf induced can be given by

$$\varepsilon_1 = -M_{11}\frac{dI_1}{dt} - M_{12}\frac{dI_2}{dt}$$

M_{11} is the self-inductance and is written as L_1.

$$\therefore \quad \varepsilon_1 = -L_1\frac{dI_1}{dt} - M_{12}\frac{dI_2}{dt}$$

- **Factors affecting mutual inductance of two solenoids**
  The mutual inductance of two solenoids depends on their geometry and the magnetic permeability of the core material explained below.

  (i) **Number of turns** Larger the number of turns in two solenoids, larger will be their mutual inductance,

  i.e. $M \propto N_1 N_2$

(ii) **Common cross-sectional area** Larger the common cross-sectional area of two solenoids, larger will be their mutual inductance.

(iii) **Relative separation** Larger the distance between two solenoids, smaller will be the magnetic flux linked with the secondary coil. Hence, smaller will be their mutual inductance.

For Concept Master Video

Marks Maximiser

- The magnetic energy stored in a solenoid in terms of magnetic field *B*, area *A* and length *l* is given by

$$U_B = \frac{1}{2\mu_0} B^2 A l$$

AC Generator

- It is an electrical machine which produces a current that alternates or changes its direction regularly after a fixed interval of time and is used to convert mechanical energy into electrical energy.
- The **essential parts of the AC generator** are coil or armature, field magnets (*N* and *S*), slip ring and brushes as shown in figure below.

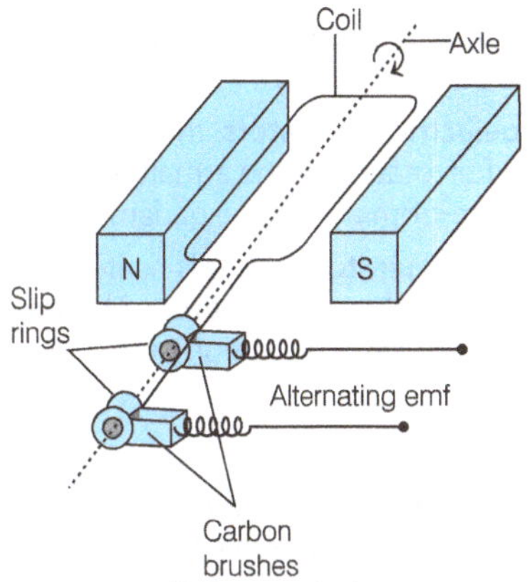

(AC generator)

- **Principle** It is based on the principle of electromagnetic induction and the magnitude of induced emf is given by

$$\varepsilon = N\frac{d\phi}{dt} = NBA\omega \sin \omega t = \varepsilon_0 \sin \omega t$$ NEET 2022

where, $\varepsilon_0 = NBA\omega$

- The **current induced in the circuit** is given by

$$i = \frac{\varepsilon}{R} = \frac{\varepsilon_0}{R} \sin \omega t = i_0 \sin \omega t$$

Working An alternating emf is generated by a loop of wire rotating in a magnetic field as shown in figure below.

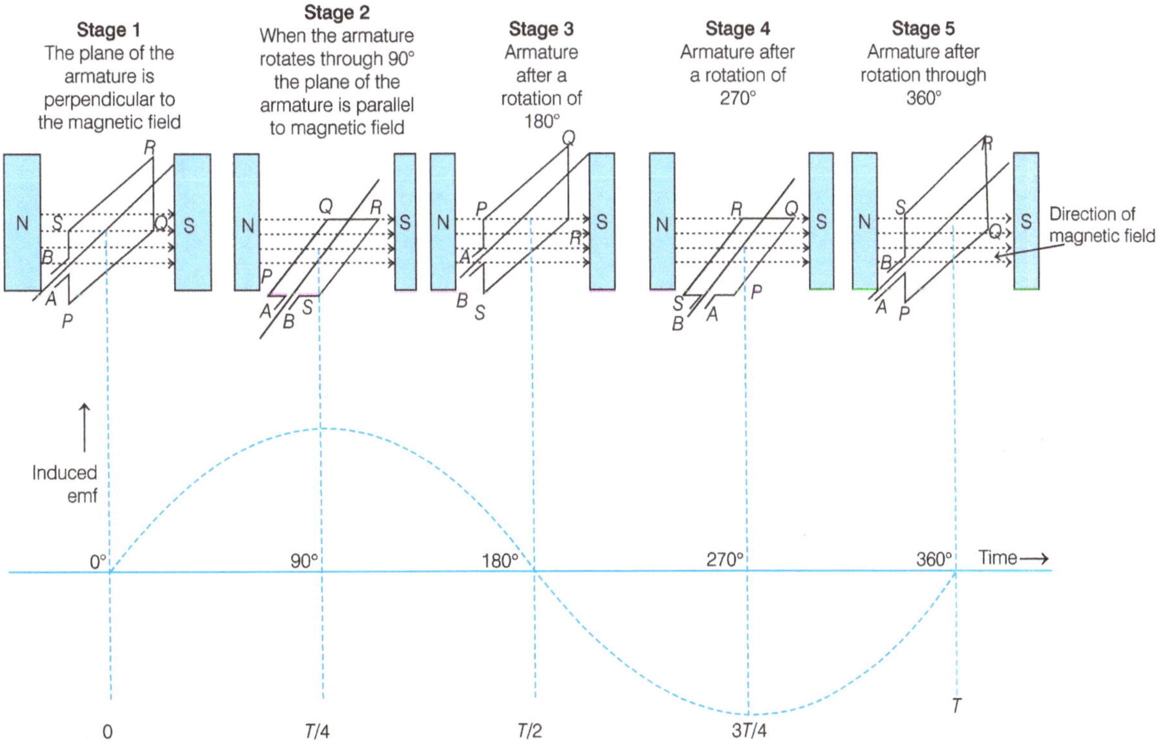

(An alternating emf is generated by a loop of wire rotating in a magnetic field)

- There are **various types of generators** depending on the source of mechanical energy
  - (i) In **hydroelectric generators**, the mechanical energy required for rotation of the armature is provided by water falling from a height, e.g. dams.
  - (ii) In **thermal generators**, water is heated to produce steam using coal or other sources. The steam at high pressure produces the rotation of the armature.
  - (iii) In **nuclear power generators**, instead of coal, nuclear fuel is used as a source.
- If instantaneous induced emf produced in a coil is $e = e_0 \sin \omega t = nBA\omega \sin \omega t$, then
  - (a) when $\omega t = 0, \pi$, i.e. coil is vertical, emf, $e = 0$
  - (b) when $\omega t = \frac{\pi}{2}$, i.e. coil is horizontal, emf, $e > 0$ (+ve) (maximum)

Caution Points

- Electricity and magnetism are related to each other. Faraday and Henry showed that a moving magnet can induce electric current.
- In a closed circuit, electric current opposes changing magnetic flux due to conservation of energy.
- Motional emf can be explained by Lorentz force on moving charges but even stationary charges in a time varying magnetic field induce emf. This suggests a symmetry between moving charges in static field and static charges in time varying field, pointing at the relevance of the principle of relativity for Faraday's law.

PYQ Notes

1. The mutual inductance of the arrangement of two concentric circular coils with radii r_1 and r_2 having number of turns n_1 and n_2, respectively are placed coaxially with centres coinciding is given by
$$M = \frac{\mu_0 n_1 n_2 \pi r_2^2}{2r_1}$$
[NEET 2021]
2. In an L-R circuit, the total charge flow through the battery after one time constant ($t = \tau$) during its current growth is given by
$$q = \int_0^\tau I dt = \int_0^\tau I_0(1 - e^{-t/\tau})\, dt$$
$$\therefore \quad q = 0.367\left(\frac{EL}{R^2}\right)$$
where, E = EMF of the battery. **[JEE Main 2020, 2019]**
3. If the magnetic flux through a coil of resistance R changes from ϕ_1 to ϕ_2, then the charge flow through the coil is given by $\Delta q = -N \cdot \frac{\Delta \phi}{R} = N \cdot \frac{(\phi_1 - \phi_2)}{R}$, where N is the number of turns in the coil. **[NEET 2019]**

Step by Step

Mastering NCERT

- Concept Builders
- Topical Questions
- Assertion and Reason Questions
- Statement Based
- Matching Type
- Numerical Type
- NCERT Exemplar
- Past Exams MCQs
- Skill Boosters

Concept Builders

1 Magnetic flux is essential to maintain an induced current in the coil. [T/F]

2 Which law tells about emf induced in a moving conductor coil in a magnetic field.

3 Faraday's law of electromagnetic induction tells about the .... (conservation of charge/conservation of energy).

4 Induced emf does not depend on material of the coil. [T/F]

5 Magnitude of induced emf is directly proportional to the relative speed of coil-magnet system. [T/F]

6 An induced current has no direction of its own. [T/F]

7 When the current in a coil changes, it induces a back emf in the same coil. [T/F]

8 A solenoid is connected to a battery, so that a steady current flows through it. If an iron core is inserted into the solenoid, the current will .... (increase/decrease/remain same).

9 When the rate of change of current is unity, the induced emf is equal to total flux linked with coil. [T/F]

10 It is .... (possible/not possible) to have mutual inductance without self-inductance.

11 Dimensional formula for the mutual inductance (M) is .... (same/different) as that of self-inductance.

12 The coefficient of mutual inductance of two coils depend on medium between the coils. [T/F]

13 The self-inductance of a long solenoid is proportional to the area of cross-section and length of the solenoid. [T/F]

14 If N is the number of turns in a coil, the value of self-inductance varies as .... (N/N^2).

15 Inductance of a solenoid at its end is .... (one fourth $\left(\frac{1}{4}\right)$, half $\left(\frac{1}{2}\right)$ of its inductance at the centre.

16 What is the coupling coefficient for perfectly coupled coils?

17 The self-inductance associated with a coil is independent of .... (induced voltage/resistance of coil)

18 What is the equivalent induction when the direction of currents in the two coils is opposite?

19 Core of a transformer is laminated to .... (increase/reduce) eddy currents.

20 The working of an AC generator is based upon magnetic effect of current. [T/F]

Topical Questions

The Experiments of Faraday and Henry

1 The demonstration of production of electric current in a closed coil when it is subjected to changing magnetic field is given by NCERT Pg. 154

(a) Newton
(b) Faraday
(c) Lenz
(d) Einstein

2 The direction of deflection of pointer of galvanometer when the bar magnet is pulled away from the coil as shown in figure, is

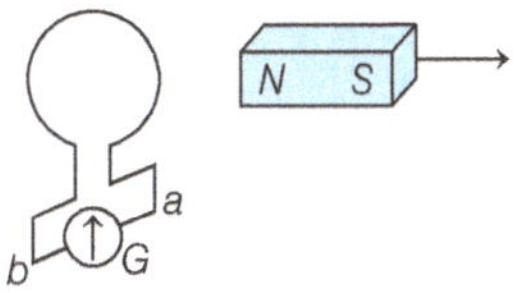

NCERT Pg. 155

(a) towards a
(b) no deflection
(c) towards b
(d) indicator oscillates between a and b

3 As shown in the figure, it is observed that the galvanometer shows a momentary deflection when the tapping key K is pressed.

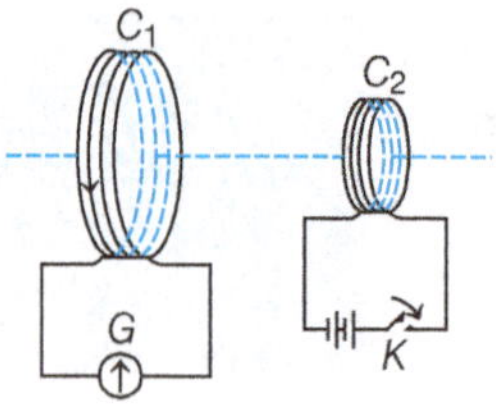

When the key is released, the current in coil C_2 and the resulting magnetic field is NCERT Pg. 156

(a) increase from zero to maximum value
(b) first increase, then decrease
(c) remains same
(d) decreases from the maximum value to zero

Magnetic Flux

4 A circular loop of radius R carrying current I lies in XY-plane with its centre at origin. The total magnetic flux through XY-plane is NCERT Pg. 156

(a) directly proportional to R
(b) directly proportional to I
(c) inversely proportional to I
(d) zero

5 Consider a circular coil of wire carrying constant current I, forming a magnetic dipole. The magnetic flux through an infinite plane that contains the circular coil and excluding the circular coil area is given by ϕ_i. The magnetic flux through the area of the circular coil area is given by ϕ_o. Which of the following option is correct? NCERT Pg. 156

(a) $\phi_i > \phi_o$ (b) $\phi_i < \phi_o$ (c) $\phi_i = \phi_o$ (d) $\phi_i = -\phi_o$

6 A circular disc of radius 0.2 m is placed in a uniform magnetic field of induction $(1/\pi)$ Wbm^{-2} in such a way that its axis makes an angle of 60° with **B**. The magnetic flux linked with the disc is NCERT Pg. 156

(a) 0.02 Wb (b) 0.06 Wb (c) 0.08 Wb (d) 0.01 Wb

7 A square of side a metre lies in the YZ-plane in a region, where the magnetic field is given by $\mathbf{B} = B_0 (3\hat{\mathbf{i}} + 3\hat{\mathbf{j}} - 4\hat{\mathbf{k}})$ T, where B_0 is constant. The magnitude of flux passing through the square (in Wb) is NCERT Pg. 156

(a) $2B_0a^2$ (b) $5B_0a^2$ (c) $3B_0a^2$ (d) $4B_0a^2$

8 Consider the following figure, a uniform magnetic field of 0.2 T is directed along the positive X-axis. The magnetic flux through top surface of the block is

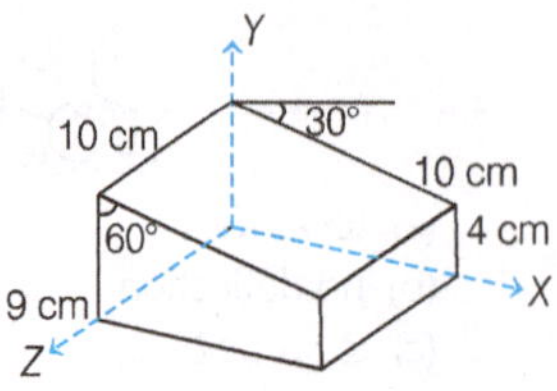

NCERT Pg. 156

(a) zero (b) 0.8 m-Wb (c) 1.0 m-Wb (d) −1.8 m-Wb

Faraday's Law of Induction

9 At time $t = 0$, magnetic field of 1000 G is passing perpendicularly through the area defined by the closed loop shown in the figure.

If the magnetic field reduces linearly to 500 G, in the next 5 s, then induced emf in the loop is NCERT Pg. 157

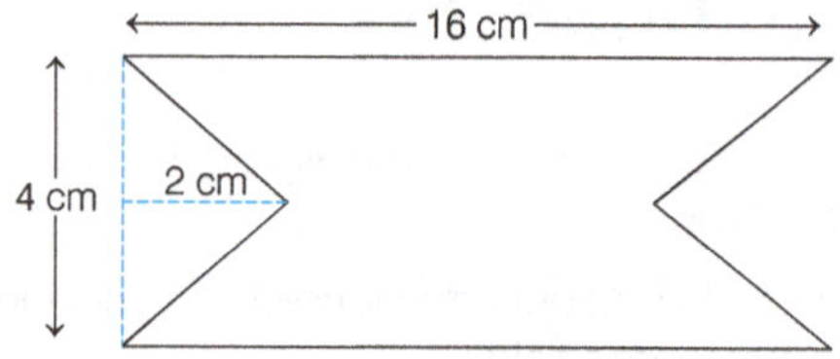

(a) 48 μV (b) 28 μV (c) 56 μV (d) 36 μV

10 The magnetic flux ϕ linked with a conducting coil depends on time t as $\phi = 3t^n - 2^n$, where n is a positive constant. If the emf induced in the coil is e, then which of the following is incorrect about e? NCERT Pg. 157

(a) If $0 < n < 1$, $e \neq 0$ and $|e|$ decrease with time
(b) If $n = 1$, e is constant
(c) If $n > 1$, $|e|$ increase with time
(d) If $n > 1$, $|e|$ decrease with time

11 The magnetic flux through a coil of resistance 20 Ω varies with time as $\phi = \left(\frac{t^3}{3} - \frac{t^2}{2} - 2t + 10\right)$ Wb.

The current in the circuit is zero at NCERT Pg. 157

(a) $t = 1$ s (b) $t = 2$ s (c) $t = 1.5$ s (d) $t = 2.5$ s

12 Whenever a magnet is moved either towards or away from a conducting coil, an emf is induced. The magnitude of which is independent of NCERT Pg. 157

(a) strength of magnetic field
(b) speed which the magnet is moving
(c) number of turns in coil
(d) resistance of coil

13 The magnetic flux through a circuit of resistance 10 Ω is changed from 20 Wb to 30 Wb in 5 ms. The charge passed through the circuit during this time is NCERT Pg. 157

(a) 4 C (b) 1 C (c) 2 C (d) 5 C

14 According to Faraday's law of electromagnetic induction, the magnitude of the induced emf in a circuit is equal to the time rate of change of NCERT Pg. 157

(a) magnetic field intensity
(b) magnetising field intensity
(c) magnetic flux
(d) electric flux

15 The magnetic flux linked with the coil varies with time as $\phi_B = 3t^2 + 4t + 9$. The magnitude of the induced emf at 2s is NCERT Pg. 157

(a) 9 V (b) 16 V (c) 3 V (d) 4 V

16 In a coil of resistance 100 Ω, a current is induced by changing the magnetic flux through it as shown in the figure. The magnitude of change in flux through the coil is NCERT Pg. 157

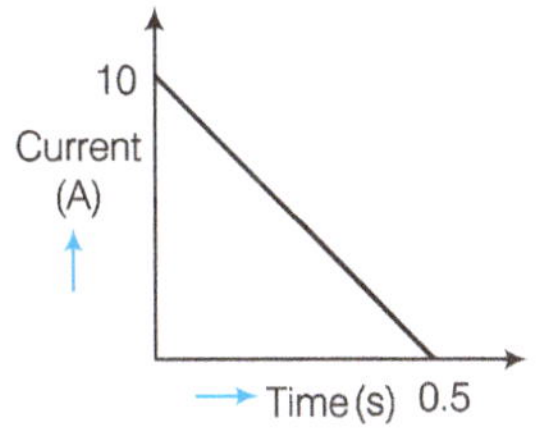

(a) 225 Wb (b) 250 Wb
(c) 275 Wb (d) 200 Wb

17 A circular coil of radius 10 cm, 500 turns and resistance 2 Ω is placed with its plane perpendicular to the horizontal component of the earth's magnetic field. It is rotated about its vertical diameter through 180° in 0.25 s. Find the magnitude of the emf induced in the coil. Horizontal component of the earth's magnetic field at the place is 3.0×10^{-5} T. NCERT Pg. 157

(a) 3×10^3 V (b) 3.8×10^{-3} mV
(c) 3.8×10^3 mV (d) 3.8×10^{-3} V

18 The flux linked with a circuit is given by $\phi_B = t^3 + 3t - 7$. The graph between time (*X*-axis) and induced emf (*Y*-axis) will be a NCERT Pg. 157

(a) straight line passing through the origin
(b) straight line with positive intercept
(c) straight line with negative intercept
(d) parabola not passing through the origin

19 A coil of resistance 400 Ω is placed in a magnetic field. If the magnetic flux ϕ_B (Wb) linked with the coil varies with time *t*(s) as $\phi_B = 50t^2 + 4$. Current at 2s is NCERT Pg. 157

(a) 0.5 A (b) 0.1 A (c) 2 A (d) 1 A

20 A square loop of wire of side length 10 cm is placed at an angle of 45° with a magnetic field that changes uniformly from 0.1 T to zero in 0.7s. The induced current in the loop (its resistance is 1Ω) is NCERT Pg. 157

(a) 1.0 mA (b) 2.5 mA (c) 3.5 mA (d) 4.0 mA

21 A square loop of side 10 cm and resistance 0.5 Ω is placed vertically in the east-west plane. A uniform magnetic field of 0.10 T is set-up across the plane in the north-east direction. The magnetic field is decreased to zero in 0.70 s at a steady rate. The magnitudes of induced emf and current during this time interval are NCERT Pg. 157

(a) 0.1 mV, 2A (b) 1 mV, 2 mA
(c) 1 V, 2 A (d) 1 mV, 0.2 A

22 If a coil of 40 turns and area 4.0 cm^2 is suddenly removed from a magnetic field, it is observed that a charge of 2.0×10^{-4} C flows into the coil. If the resistance of the coil is 80 Ω, then magnetic flux density (in Wbm^{-2}) is NCERT Pg. 157

(a) 0.5 (b) 1.0 (c) 1.5 (d) 2.0

23 A rectangular loop of sides 10 cm and 5 cm with a cut is stationary between the pole pieces of an electromagnet. The magnetic field of the magnet is normal to the loop. The current feeding the electromagnet is reduced, so that the field decreases from its initial value of 0.3 T at the rate of 0.02 Ts^{-1}. If the cut is joined and the loop has a resistance of 2.0 Ω, the power dissipated by the loop as heat is NCERT Pg. 157

(a) 5 nW (b) 4 nW (c) 3 nW (d) 2 nW

24 A rectangular wire loop of resistance 1.5 Ω placed in a region of uniform magnetic field of magnitude 0.3 T directed normal to the loop. If the area of loop decreases at a rate of 0.05 m^2/s in this magnetic field, the heat produced in it is NCERT Pg. 157

(a) 1.5×10^{-6} W (b) 15×10^{-6} W
(c) 2×10^{-6} W (d) 150×10^{-6} W

Lenz's Law and Conservation of Energy

25 Consider a metal ring kept on a horizontal plane. A bar magnet is held above the ring with its length along the axis of the ring. If the magnet is dropped freely, the acceleration of the falling magnet is (*g* is acceleration due to gravity) NCERT Pg. 160

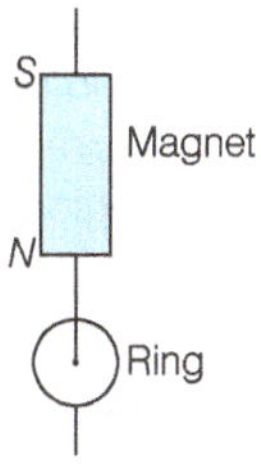

(a) More than *g*
(b) Equal to *g*
(c) Less than *g*
(d) Depend on mass of magnet

26 There is a uniform magnetic field directed perpendicular and into the plane of the paper. An irregular shaped conducting loop is slowly changing into a circular loop in the plane of the paper. Then, NCERT Pg. 160

(a) current is induced in the loop in the anti-clockwise direction
(b) current is induced in the loop in the clockwise direction
(c) AC is induced in the loop
(d) No current is induced in the loop

27 Consider a situation shown in figure. After long time, switch is opened. Then, direction of induced current in closed loop will be NCERT Pg. 160

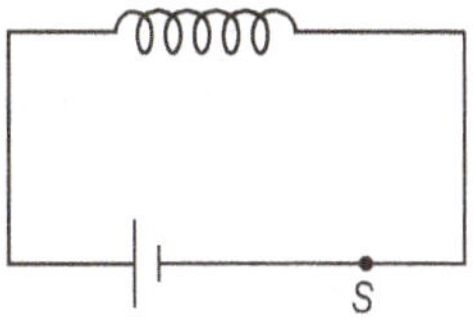

(a) clockwise (b) anti-clockwise
(c) no current will induced
(d) depends upon the resistance of the circuit

28 The polarity of induced emf is such that it tends to produce a current which opposes the change in magnetic flux that produce it, is the statement of **NCERT Pg. 160**

(a) Faraday's law (b) Lenz's law
(c) Biot-Savart's law (d) Fleming's left hand rule

29 An infinitely long cylinder is kept parallel to a uniform magnetic field B directed along positive Z-axis. This direction of induced current as seen from the Z-axis will be **NCERT Pg. 160**

(a) clockwise of the positive Z-axis
(b) anti-clockwise of the positive Z-axis
(c) zero, no current is induced
(d) along the magnetic field

30 Near a circular loop of conducting wire as shown in the figure, an electron moves along a straight line. The direction of the induced current, if any in the loop is **NCERT Pg. 160**

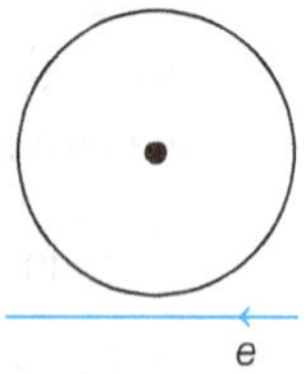

(a) variable (b) clockwise
(c) anti-clockwise (d) zero

31 A closed loop moves normal to the constant electric field between the plates of a large capacitor. Is the current induced in the loop when it is wholly inside the region between the capacitor plates? **NCERT Pg. 160**

(a) Yes (b) No
(c) May be possible (d) May not be possible

32 The north pole of a bar magnet is moved towards a coil along the axis passing through the centre of the coil and perpendicular to the plane of the coil. The direction of the induced current in the coil when viewed in the direction of the motion of the magnet is **NCERT Pg. 160**

(a) clockwise
(b) anti-clockwise
(c) no current in the coil
(d) Either clockwise or anti-clockwise

33 The north pole of a magnet is falling on a metallic ring as shown in the figure. The direction of induced current, if looked from upside, in the ring will be **NCERT Pg. 160**

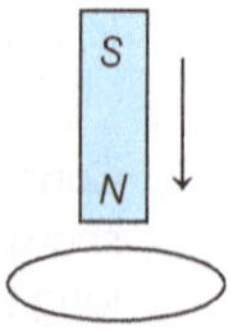

(a) clockwise or anti-clockwise depending on metal of the ring
(b) no induced current
(c) anti-clockwise
(d) clockwise

34 The magnet in figure rotates as shown on a pivot through its centre. At the instant shown, what are the directions of the induced current? **NCERT Pg. 160**

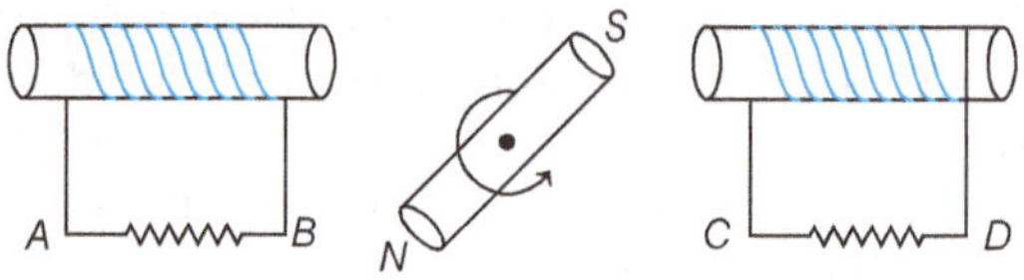

(a) A to B and C to D (b) B to A and C to D
(c) A to B and D to C (d) B to A and D to C

35 Predict the polarity of the capacitor in the situation described in the given figure. **NCERT Pg. 160**

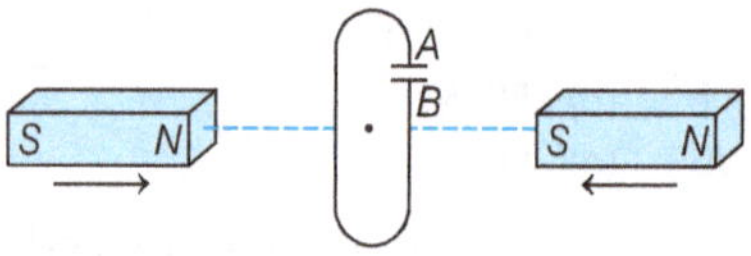

(a) Plate A will be positive
(b) Plate B will be positive
(c) Plate A will be negative
(d) No charge is developed

36 A magnet N-S is suspended from a spring and when it oscillates, the magnet moves in and out of the coil C. Then, as magnet oscillates, **NCERT Pg. 160**

(a) G shows no deflection but the amplitude steadily decreases
(b) G shows deflection to the left and right with decreasing amplitude
(c) G shows deflection to the left and right with constant amplitude
(d) G shows deflection on one side

Motional Electromotive Force

37 A conducting wire of length 1 m is placed in XY-plane. It is moved with velocity $\mathbf{v} = (\hat{\mathbf{i}} + \hat{\mathbf{j}} + 2\hat{\mathbf{k}})$ m/s through a region of magnetic induction $\mathbf{B} = (4\hat{\mathbf{j}} + 3\hat{\mathbf{k}})$ T. Then, potential difference across the ends of the wire is **NCERT Pg. 162**

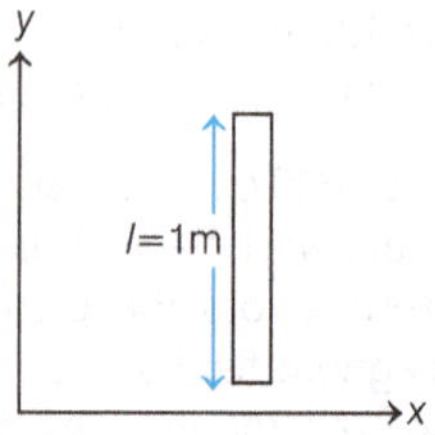

(a) 5 V (b) 2 V (c) 3 V (d) 4 V

38 A copper disc of radius 0.1 m is rotated about its centre with 10 revolutions per second in a uniform magnetic field of 0.1 T with its plane perpendicular to the field. The emf induced across the radius of disc is **NCERT Pg. 162**

(a) $\frac{\pi}{10}$ V (b) $\frac{2\pi}{10}$ V
(c) $\pi \times 10^{-2}$ V (d) $2\pi \times 10^{-2}$ V

39 A 1 m long metallic rod is rotated with angular frequency of 400 rad s^{-1} about an axis normal to the rod passing through one of its end. The other end of the rod is in contact with a circular metallic ring. A constant and uniform magnetic field of 0.5 T parallel to axis exist everywhere. The emf induced between centre and ring is NCERT Pg. 162

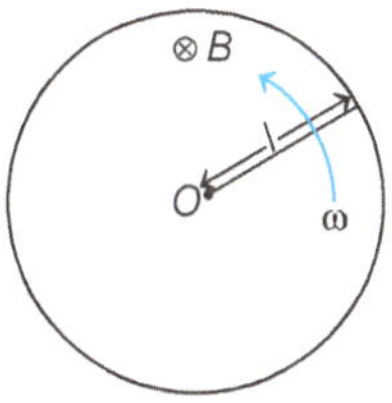

(a) 40 V (b) 100 V
(c) 160 V (d) 50 V

40 A conducting rod of length $2l$ is rotating with constant angular speed ω about its perpendicular bisector. A uniform magnetic field **B** exists parallel to the axis of rotation. The emf induced between two ends of the rod is NCERT Pg. 162

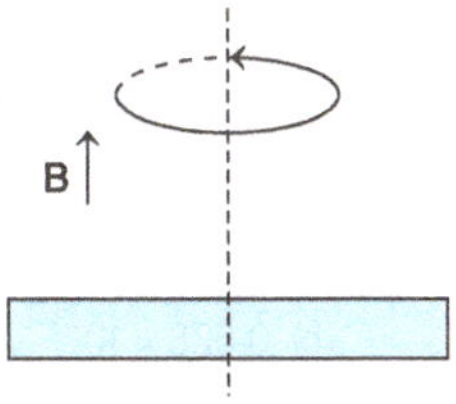

(a) $B\omega l^2$ (b) $\frac{1}{2}B\omega l^2$ (c) $\frac{1}{8}B\omega l^2$ (d) zero

41 The figure shows four wire loops, with edge lengths of either L or $2L$. All four loops will be moving into a region of uniform magnetic field **B** (directed out of the page) at the same constant velocity. Rank the four loops according to the maximum magnitude of the emf induced as they move through the field, greatest first NCERT Pg. 162

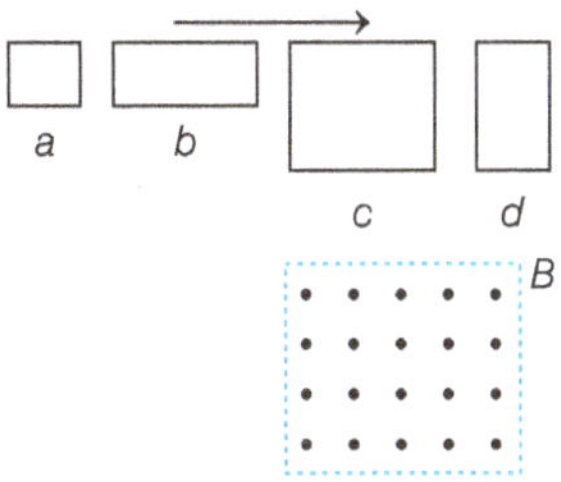

(a) $(e_c = e_d) < (e_a = e_b)$ (b) $(e_c = e_d) > (e_a = e_b)$
(c) $e_c > e_d > e_b > e_a$ (d) $e_c < e_d < e_b < e_a$

42 A conducting rod AB moves parallel to X-axis in a uniform magnetic field, pointing in the positive Z-direction. The end A of the rod gets NCERT Pg. 162

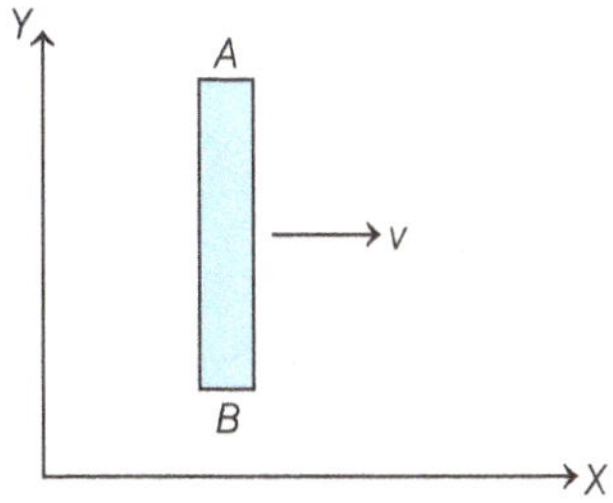

(a) positively charged
(b) negatively charged
(c) neutral
(d) first positively charged and then negatively charged

43 A conducting rod of length l is moving in a transverse magnetic field of strength B with velocity v. The induced voltage across the conducting rod is NCERT Pg. 162

(a) $\sqrt{\frac{Bvl}{2}}$ (b) $\sqrt{2Bvl}$ (c) Bvl (d) $\frac{Bvl}{2}$

44 A rectangular conductor $PQRS$ in which the arm PQ is free to move. The rod PQ is moved towards the left with a constant velocity v as shown in figure. Assume that, there is no loss of energy due to friction.

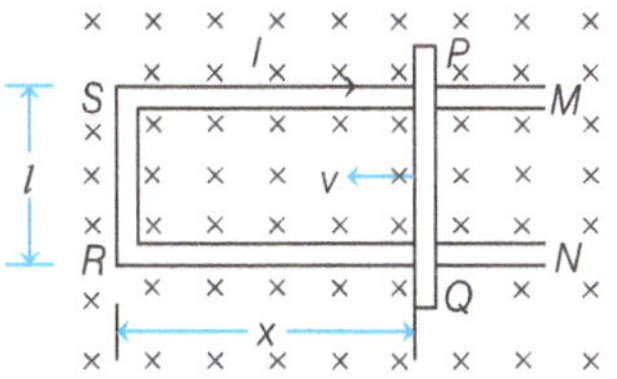

The rate of change of flux ϕ_B will induce an emf given by NCERT Pg. 162

(a) $\varepsilon = -Bx\frac{dl}{dt}$ (b) $\varepsilon = -\frac{d}{dt}(Bx)$
(c) $\varepsilon = -Bl\frac{dx}{dt}$ (d) $\varepsilon = -xl \cdot \frac{dB}{dt}$

45 A horizontal straight wire 20 m long extending from east to west is falling with a speed of 5.0 ms^{-1} at right angles to the horizontal component of the earth's magnetic field 0.30×10^{-4} Wbm^{-2}. The instantaneous value of the emf induced in the wire will be NCERT Pg. 162

(a) 6.0 mV (b) 3 mV (c) 4.5 mV (d) 1.5 mV

46 A helicopter rises vertically with a speed of 100 ms^{-1}. If helicopter has length 10 m and horizontal component of earth's magnetic field is 5×10^{-3} Wbm^{-2}, then the induced emf between the tip of nose and tail of helicopter is NCERT Pg. 162

(a) 50 V (b) 0.5 V (c) 5 V (d) 25 V

47 Two parallel rails of a railway track insulated from each other and with the ground are connected to a millivoltmeter. The distance between the rails is 1 m. A train is travelling with a velocity of 72 kmh^{-1} along the track. The reading of the millivoltmeter (in mV) is (vertical component of the earth's magnetic induction is 2×10^{-5} T) NCERT Pg. 162

(a) 1.44 (b) 0.72 (c) 0.4 (d) 0.2

48 A horizontal straight wire 10 m long extending from east to west is falling with a speed of 4.0 ms^{-1}, at right angles to the horizontal component of the earth's magnetic field of strength 0.30×10^{-2} Wbm^{-2}. The instantaneous value of the induced potential gradient in the wire from west to east is **NCERT Pg. 162**

(a) $+1.5 \times 10^{-3}$ Vm^{-1} (b) -1.5×10^{-3} Vm^{-1}
(c) $+1.2 \times 10^{-2}$ Vm^{-1} (d) -1.5×10^{-4} Vm^{-1}

49 A rectangular conductor *SPQR* is placed in a uniform magnetic field perpendicular to the plane and extending from $x = 0$ to $x = b$ as shown below. The arm *PQ* of length l is moving from $x = 0$ to $x = 2b$ with constant speed v. Find the flux and emf induced in the conductor. **NCERT Pg. 162**

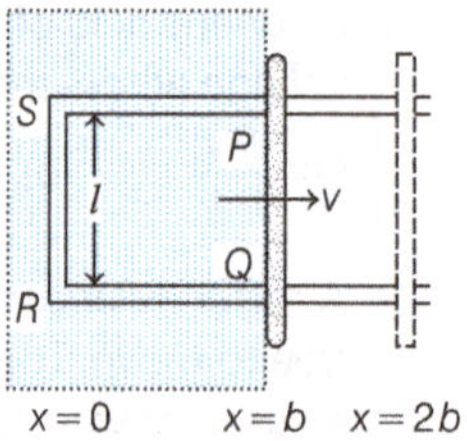

(a) $Blx, -Blv$; when $0 \le x < b$ (b) $2\,Bl, -2Bl$
(c) $Blb, 0, b \le x < 2b$ (d) $Bl, -Bl$

50 A circular coil expands radially in a region of magnetic field and no electromotive force is produced in the coil. This can be because **NCERT Pg. 162**

(a) the magnetic field is constant
(b) the magnetic field is not in the same plane as the circular coil and it may or may not vary
(c) the magnetic field has a perpendicular (to the plane of the coil) component whose magnitude is decreasing suitably
(d) there is a constant magnetic field in the perpendicular (to the plane of the coil) direction

51 An $\angle AOB$ made of a conducting wire moves along its bisector through a magnetic field B as suggested by figure. Find the emf induced between A and B, if the magnetic field is perpendicular to the plane of the paper. (where, $AO = BO = l$) **NCERT Pg. 162**

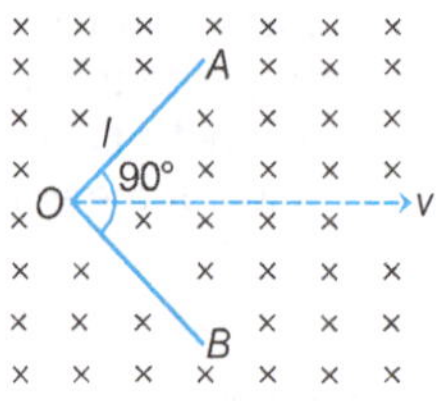

(a) $\dfrac{Bvl}{\sqrt{2}}$ (b) Bv
(c) $\sqrt{2}\,Blv$ (d) Blv

52 A simple pendulum with bob of mass m and conducting wire of length L swings under gravity through an angle θ. The earth's magnetic field component in the direction perpendicular to swing is B. Maximum emf induced across the pendulum is **NCERT Pg. 162**

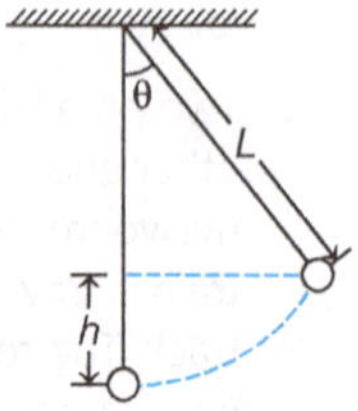

(a) $2BL \sin\left(\dfrac{\theta}{2}\right)(gL)^{1/2}$ (b) $BL \sin\left(\dfrac{\theta}{2}\right)(gL)$
(c) $BL \sin\left(\dfrac{\theta}{2}\right)(gL)^{3/2}$ (d) $BL \sin\left(\dfrac{\theta}{2}\right)(gL)^2$

53 A metallic rod of 1 m length is rotated with a frequency of 50 rev s^{-1}, with one end hinged at the centre and other end at the circumference of a circular metallic ring of radius 1 m. It is rotating about an axis passing through the centre and perpendicular to the plane of the ring as shown in figure. A constant and uniform magnetic field of 1 T parallel to the axis is present everywhere. What is the emf between the centre and the metallic ring? **NCERT Pg. 162**

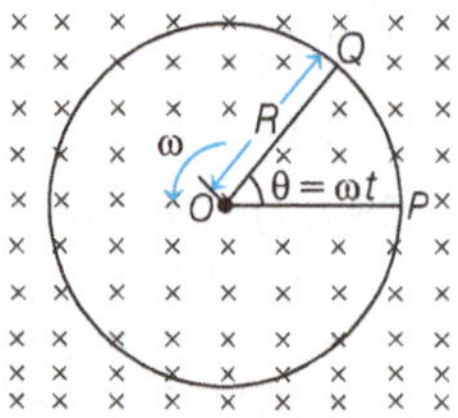

(a) 147 V (b) 157 V (c) 140 V (d) 164 V

54 A wheel with 10 metallic spokes each 0.5 m long is rotated with a speed of 120 rev/min in a plane normal to the horizontal component of earth's magnetic field H_E at a place. If $H_E = 0.4$ G at the place, what is the induced emf between the axle and the rim of the wheel? (Take, 1 G $= 10^{-4}$ T) **NCERT Pg. 162**

(a) 6.28×10^{-5} V (b) 62.8×10^{-5} V
(c) 0.628×10^{-5} V (d) 62.8×10^{-5} mV

55 A rectangular loop with a sliding connector *PQ* of length $l = 1.0$ m is situated in a uniform magnetic field $B = 2$T perpendicular to the plane of loop. Resistance of connector is $r = 2\Omega$. Two resistance of 6Ω and 3Ω are connected as shown in figure. The external force required to keep the connector moving with a constant velocity, $v = 2$ m/s is **NCERT Pg. 162**

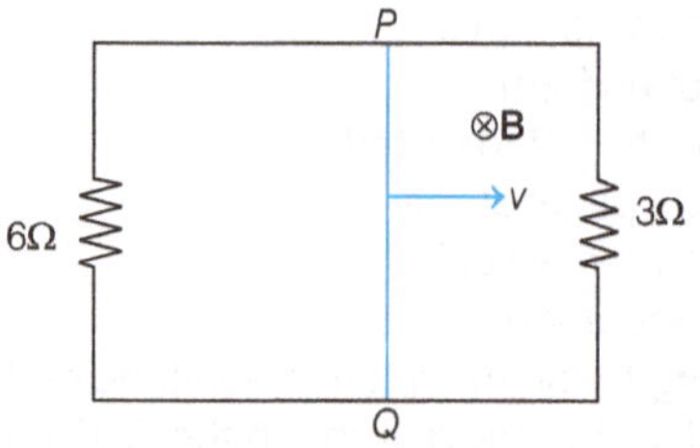

(a) 6 N (b) 4 N (c) 2 N (d) 1 N

56 A uniform conducting rod of length L is moving with velocity v_0 in a uniform transverse magnetic field B_0 as shown in figure. The emf developed across the ends of the rod is **NCERT Pg. 162**

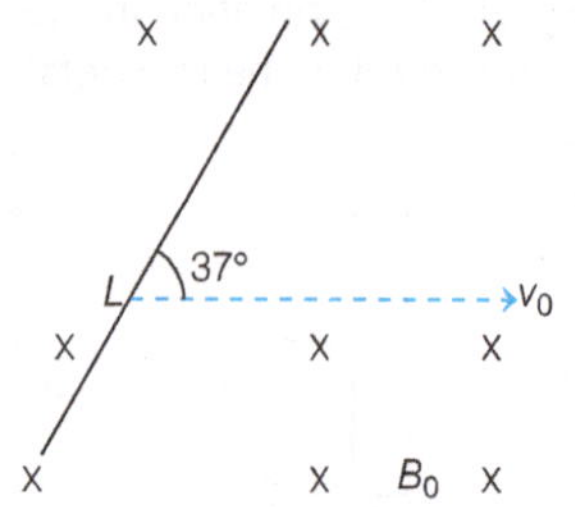

(a) $\dfrac{B_0Lv_0}{2}$ (b) $\dfrac{3}{4}\left(\dfrac{B_0Lv_0}{2}\right)$ (c) $\dfrac{3}{5}B_0Lv_0$ (d) $\dfrac{4}{5}B_0Lv_0$

57 A conducting rod of length L is moving in a transverse magnetic field of strength B with velocity v. The resistance of the rod is R. The current in the rod is NCERT Pg. 162

(a) $\frac{BLv}{R}$ (b) BLv (c) zero (d) $\frac{B^2v^2L^2}{R}$

58 Figure shows a conducting rod PQ in contact with metal rails RP and SQ, which are 25 cm apart in a uniform field of flux density 0.4 T acting perpendicular to the plane of the paper. Ends R and S are connected through a 5 Ω resistance. What is the magnitude and the direction of the current through the 5 Ω resistor when the rod moves to the right with a velocity of 5 ms^{-1}? NCERT Pg. 162

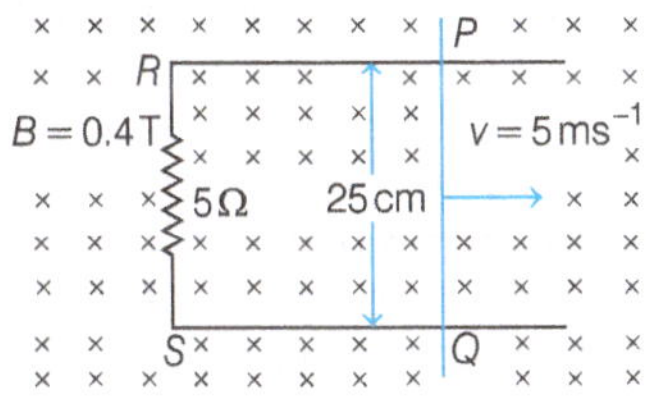

(a) 0. 1 A from R to S (b) 0.1 A from S to R
(c) 0.5 A from R to S (d) 0.5 A from S to R

Eddy Current

59 Eddy currents are produced when Old NCERT Pg. 218

(a) a metal is kept in varying magnetic field
(b) a metal is kept in a steady magnetic field
(c) a circular coil is placed in magnetic field
(d) through a circular coil current is flowing

60 A copper plate is allowed to swing like a simple pendulum between the pole pieces of a strong magnet (as shown in figure). Old NCERT Pg. 218

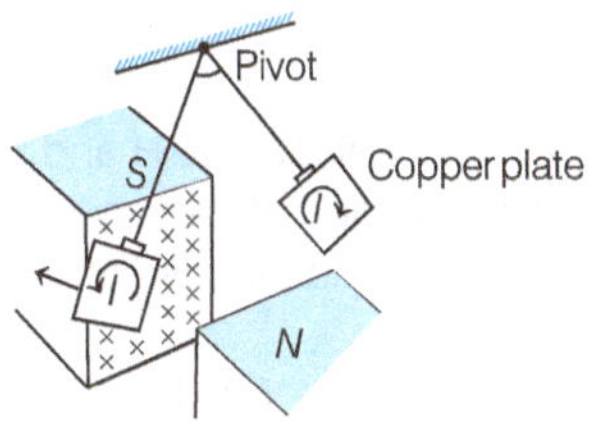

The motion of the plate and the phenomenon behind this are

(a) damped, electromagnetic induction
(b) accelerated, induced current
(c) accelerated, electromagnetic induction
(d) damped, Gauss' law

61 The shiny metal disc in the electric power meter rotates due to Old NCERT Pg. 218

(a) continuously decreasing current
(b) motor fitted inside
(c) continuously increasing current
(d) eddy current

Inductance

62 In the given L-R circuit, the magnetic energy stored in the inductor in steady state is NCERT Pg. 165

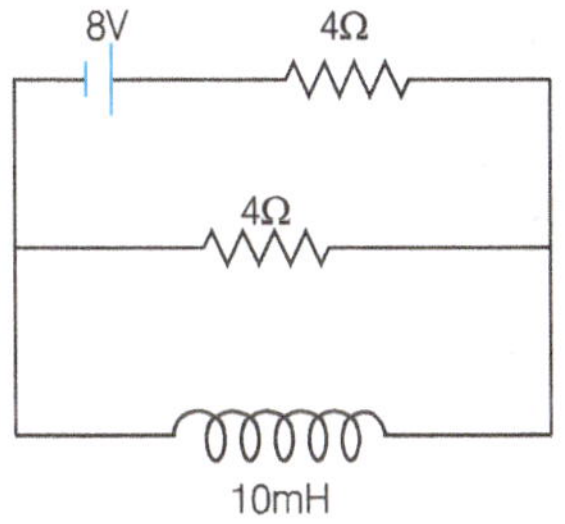

(a) 10 mJ (b)20 mJ (c) 40 mJ (d) 5 mJ

63 An inductor coil stores 32 J of magnetic field energy and dissipates energy as heat at the rate of 320 W when a current of 4 A is passed through it. The time constant of circuit when this coil is joined across ideal battery NCERT Pg. 165

(a) 0.1 s (b) 0.2 s (c) 0.3 s (d) 0.4 s

64 In a coil, when current changes from 10 A to 2 A in time 0.1 s, induced emf is 3.20 V.
What is the self-inductance of coil ? NCERT Pg. 165

(a) 4 H (b) 0.4 H (c) 0.04 H (d) 5 H

65 In the given branch PQ, a part of circuit, a current $I = (2t + 3)$ A is flowing, where t is time in second, what is the value of potential difference $(V_P - V_Q)$ at $t = 2$ s? NCERT Pg. 165

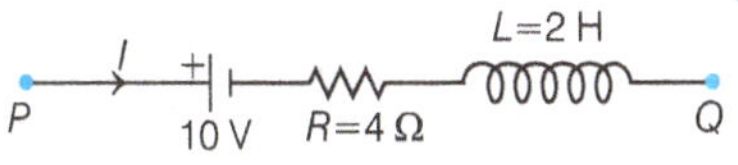

(a) 24 V (b) 36 V (c) 48 V (d) 42 V

66 The mutual inductance of a pair of coils, each of N turns is M Henry. If a current of I ampere in one of the coil is brought to zero in t second, the emf induced per turn in the other coil, (in volt), will be NCERT Pg. 165

(a) $\frac{MI}{Nt}$ (b) $\frac{MN}{It}$ (c) $\frac{NMI}{t}$ (d) $\frac{MIN^2}{t}$

67 A solenoid has 2000 turns wound over a length of 0.3 m. The area of its cross-section is 1.2×10^{-3} m^2. Around its central portion, a coil of 300 turns is wound. If an initial current of 2 A in the solenoid is reversed in 0.25 s, the emf induced in the coil is equal to NCERT Pg. 165

(a) 6×10^{-4} V (b) 48 mV (c) 6×10^{-2} V (d) 48 kV

68 In the circuit as shown in diagram $R = 10\,\Omega$, $E = 10$ V, $I = 2$ A and $L = 5$H. The current in part of the circuit is decreasing at rate of 2 A/s. What is potential difference V_{AB} at this instant? **NCERT Pg. 165**

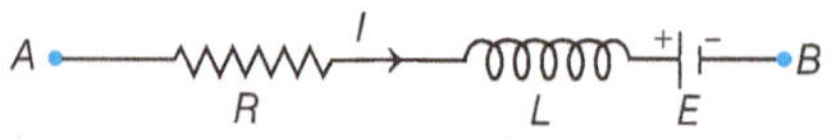

(a) 25 V (b) 35 V (c) 40 V (d) 20 V

69 A coil of Cu wire (radius r, self-inductance L) is bent in two concentric turns each having radius $\frac{r}{2}$. The self-inductance now **NCERT Pg. 165**

(a) 2 L(b) L (c) 4 L (d) $L/2$

70 Which of the following is equivalent to self-induction? **NCERT Pg. 165**

(a) Inertia of mass (b) Inertia of energy
(c) Inertia of moment (d) Inertia of current

71 An electric current can be induced in a coil by flux change produced by another coil in its vicinity or flux change produced by the same coil. In both cases, the flux through a coil is **NCERT Pg. 165**

(a) proportional to the square of current
(b) inversely proportional to the square of current
(c) proportional to the current
(d) inversely proportional to the current

72 The mutual inductance M_{12} of coil 1 with respect to coil 2 **NCERT Pg. 165**

(a) increases when they are brought nearer
(b) depends on the current passing through the coils
(c) increases when one of them is rotated about an axis
(d) is different from M_{21} of coil 2 with respect to coil 1

73 There are two identical coils A and B placed parallel along common axis, separated by some distance. A current of 2A flows through coil A and a magnetic flux of 10^{-2} Wb passes through B (no current through B). If no current passes through A and a current of 1 A passes through B, what is the flux through A? **NCERT Pg. 165**

(a) 5×10^{-3} Wb (b) 0.5×10^{-3} Wb
(c) 50×10^{-3} Wb (d) 00.5×10^{-3} Wb

74 O is the centre of two coplanar concentric circular conductors A and B, of radii r and R respectively as shown in the figure (here $r <<< R$). The mutual inductance of the system of the conductor can be given by **NCERT Pg. 165**

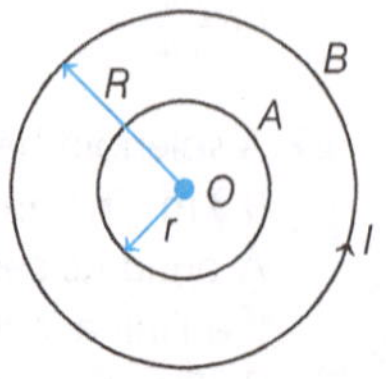

(a) $\frac{\mu_0 \pi r^2}{2R}$ (b) $\frac{\mu_0 \pi R^2}{2r}$ (c) $\frac{\pi R^2}{\mu_0 r}$ (d) $\frac{\mu_0 \pi r}{2R}$

75 Two coils P and Q are separated by some distance. When a current of 3 A flows through coil P, a magnetic flux of 10^{-3} Wb passes through Q. No current is passed through Q. When no current passes through P and a current of 2A passes through Q, the flux through P is **NCERT Pg. 165**

(a) 6.67×10^{-3} Wb (b) 6.67×10^{-4} Wb
(c) 3.67×10^{-3} Wb (d) 3.67×10^{-4} Wb

76 According to the phenomenon of mutual induction, **NCERT Pg. 165**

(a) the mutual inductance does not dependent on geometry of the two coils involved
(b) the mutual inductance depends on the intrinsic magnetic property, like relative permeability of the material
(c) the mutual inductance is independent of the magnetic property of the material
(d) ratio of magnetic flux produced by the coil 1 at the place of the coil 2 and the current in the coil 2 will be different from that of the ratio defined by interchanging the coils

77 There are two long coaxial solenoids of same length l. The inner and outer coils have radii r_1 and r_2 and number of turns per unit length n_1 and n_2, respectively. The ratio of mutual inductance to the self-inductance of the inner coil is **NCERT Pg. 165**

(a) $\frac{n_2}{n_1} \cdot \frac{r_1}{r_2}$ (b) $\frac{n_2}{n_1} \cdot \frac{r_2^2}{r_1^2}$ (c) $\frac{n_2}{n_1}$ (d) $\frac{n_1}{n_2}$

78 If induction coil is open, then L and R, respectively become **NCERT Pg. 165**

(a) $\infty, 0$ (b) $0, \infty$ (c) ∞, ∞ (d) $0, 0$

79 A current passing through a coil of self-inductance of 2 mH changes at the rate of 20 mAs^{-1}. The emf induced in the coil is **NCERT Pg. 165**

(a) 10 μV (b) 40 μV (c) 10 mV (d) 40 mV

80 The inductance of a coil is $L = 10$ H and resistance $R = 5\,\Omega$. If applied voltage of battery is 10 V and if circuit switches OFF in 1 ms, find induced emf in inductor. **NCERT Pg. 165**

(a) 2×10^4 V (b) 1.2×10^4 V
(c) 2×10^{-4} V (d) 3×10^{-4} V

81 In 0.2 s, the current in a coil increases from 1.5 A to 2.5 A. If inductance of this coil is 60 mH, then induced current in an external resistance of 3 Ω will be **NCERT Pg. 165**

(a) 1 A (b) 0.5 A
(c) 0.2 A (d) 0.1 A

82 A copper wire is wound on a wooden frame, whose shape is that of an equilateral triangle. If the linear dimension of each side of the frame is increased by a factor of 3, keeping the number of turns of the coil per unit length of the frame the same, then the self-inductance of the coil NCERT Pg. 165

(a) increases by a factor of 3
(b) decreases by a factor of $9\sqrt{3}$
(c) increases by a factor of 27
(d) decreases by a factor of 9

83 A solenoid 60 cm long has 50 turns on it and is wound on an iron rod of 7.5 mm radius. Find the flux through the solenoid when the current in it is 3A and the relative permeability of iron is 600. NCERT Pg. 165

(a) 1.66 Wb (b) 2.66 Wb
(c) 1.66 mWb (d) 1.66 μ Wb

84 Two identical induction coils each of inductance L joined in series are placed very close to each other such that the winding direction of one is exactly opposite to that of other, what is the net inductance? NCERT Pg. 165

(a) L^2 (b) $2L$ (c) $L/2$ (d) Zero

85 Three solenoid coils of same dimension, same numbers of turns and same numbers of layers of winding are taken. Coil 1 of inductance L_1 was wound using a wire of resistance $11\,\Omega m^{-1}$, coil 2 of inductance L_2 was wound using the similar wire but the direction of winding was reversed in each layer and coil 3 of inductance L_3 was wound using a superconducting wire. The self-inductance of the coils L_1, L_2 and L_3 are such that NCERT Pg. 165

(a) $L_1 = L_2 = L_3$ (b) $L_1 = L_2, L_3 = 0$
(c) $L_1 = L_3, L_2 = 0$ (d) $L_1 > L_2 > L_3$

86 The self-induced emf of a coil is 25 V. When the current in it is changed at uniform rate from 10 A to 25 A in 1s, the change in the energy of the inductance is NCERT Pg. 165

(a) 437.5 J (b) 740 J (c) 637.5 J (d) 540 J

87 The expression for the magnetic energy stored in a solenoid in terms of magnetic field B, area A and length l of the solenoid, is NCERT Pg. 165

(a) $\frac{1}{2\mu_0} BAl$ (b) $\frac{1}{2\mu_0} B^2Al$
(c) $\frac{1}{\mu_0} B^2Al$ (d) $\frac{1}{\mu_0} BA^2l$

AC Generator

88 When the coil is rotated with a constant angular speed ω, the angle θ between the magnetic field vector **B** and the area vector **A** of the coil at any instant t, is NCERT Pg. 170

(a) $\theta = \mathbf{AB}$ (b) $\theta = \mathbf{A}t$ (c) $\theta = \omega t$ (d) $\theta = \mathbf{B}t$

89 Wire loop is rotated in a magnetic field. The frequency of change of direction of the induced emf is NCERT Pg. 170

(a) once per revolution
(b) twice per revolution
(c) four times per revolution
(d) six times per revolution

90 A square coil of side 25 cm having 1000 turns is rotated with a uniform speed in a magnetic field about an axis perpendicular to the direction of the field. At an instant t, the emf induced in the coil is $\varepsilon = 200 \sin 100\,\pi t$. The magnetic induction is NCERT Pg. 170

(a) 0.50 T (b) 0.2 T (c) 10^{-3} T (d) 0.01 T

91 Kamla paddles a stationary bicycle, the paddles of the bicycle are attached to a 100 turns coil of area 0.10 m^2. The coil rotates at half a revolution per second and it is placed in a uniform magnetic field of 0.01 T perpendicular to the axis of rotation of the coil. What is the maximum voltage generated in the coil? NCERT Pg. 170

(a) 3.14 V (b) 31.4 V (c) 0.314 V (d) 314 V

92 When a circular coil of radius 1 m and 100 turns is rotated in a horizontal uniform magnetic field, the peak value of emf induced is 100 V. The coil is unwound and then rewound into a circular coil of radius 2 m. If it is rotated now with the same speed, under similar conditions, the new peak value of emf developed is NCERT Pg. 170

(a) 50 V (b) 25 V
(c) 100 V (d) 200 V

93 In a region of uniform magnetic induction $B = 10^{-2}$ T, a circular coil of radius 30 cm and resistance $\pi^2\Omega$ is rotated about an axis which is perpendicular to the direction of B and which forms a diameter of the coil. If the coil rotates at 200 rpm, the amplitude of the alternating current induced in the coil is NCERT Pg. 170

(a) $4\pi^2$ mA (b) 30 mA
(c) 6 mA (d) 200 mA

94 A rectangular coil $ABCD$ which is rotated at constant angular velocity about the horizontal axis as shown in the figure. The axis of rotation of the coil as well as the magnetic field B are horizontal.

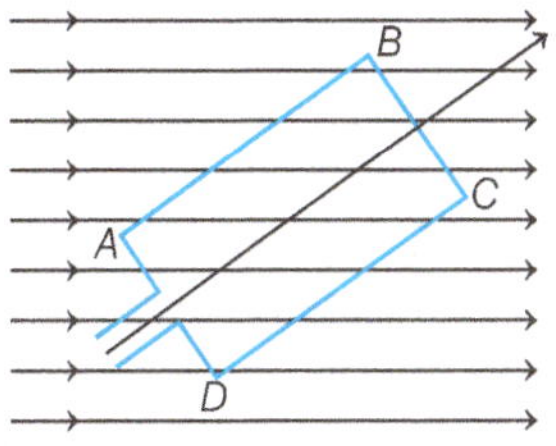

Maximum current will flow in the circuit when the plane of the coil is NCERT Pg. 170

(a) inclined at 30° to the magnetic field
(b) perpendicular to the magnetic field
(c) inclined at 45° to the magnetic field
(d) parallel to the magnetic field

95 In an AC generator, a coil with N turns, all of the same area A and total resistance R, rotates with frequency ω in a magnetic field B. The maximum value of emf generated in the coil is NCERT Pg. 170

(a) $NAB\omega$ (b) $NABR\omega$ (c) NAB (d) $NABR$

96 The working of a generator is based upon NCERT Pg. 170

(a) magnetic effect of current
(b) heating effect of current
(c) chemical effect of current
(d) electromagnetic induction

Assertion and Reason Questions

Direction (Q. Nos. 1-10) *In the following questions, a statement of Assertion is followed by a corresponding statement of Reason. Of the following statements, choose the correct one.*

(a) Both Assertion and Reason are correct and Reason is the correct explanation of Assertion.
(b) Both Assertion and Reason are correct but Reason is not the correct explanation of Assertion.
(c) Assertion is correct but Reason is incorrect.
(d) Assertion is incorrect but Reason is correct.

1 Assertion If a circular conducting coil is placed inside and parallel to a uniform magnetic field, then the magnetic flux linked with the coil is zero.

Reason The magnetic flux can be changed by changing the area of a coil. NCERT Pg. 157

2 Assertion Induced emf will always occur whenever, there is change in magnetic flux.

Reason Current always induces whenever, there is change in magnetic flux. NCERT Pg. 158

3 Assertion Only a change in magnetic flux will maintain an induced current in the coil.

Reason The presence of large magnetic flux through a coil maintains a current in the coil, if the current is continuous. NCERT Pg. 158

4 Assertion Lenz's law violates the principle of conservation of energy.

Reason Induced emf always opposes the change in magnetic flux responsible for its production. NCERT Pg. 160

5 Assertion Figure shows a metallic conductor moving in magnetic field. The induced emf across its ends is zero.

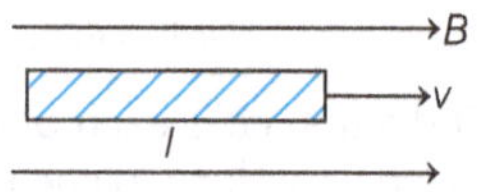

Reason The induced emf across the ends of a conductor is given by $e = Bvl \sin\theta$. NCERT Pg. 162

6 Assertion Eddy current is produced in any metallic conductor when magnetic flux is changed through it.

Reason Electric potential determines flow of charge. Old NCERT Pg. 218

7 Assertion The self-inductance of a solenoid increases with the increase in length of the solenoid for its constant number of turns.

Reason The slope of self-inductance *versus* rate of change of current gives the induced emf in the solenoid. NCERT Pg. 168

8 Assertion If the inner solenoid is much shorter than (and placed well inside) the outer solenoid, then the flux linkage $N_1\phi_1$ can still be calculated.

Reason The inner solenoid is effectively immersed in a uniform magnetic field due to the outer solenoid. NCERT Pg. 165

9 Assertion In a system of co-axial solenoids, it is extremely difficult to calculate the flux linkage with the outer solenoid when current flows in inner solenoid.

Reason The magnetic field due to the inner solenoid would vary across the length as well as cross-section of the outer solenoid (when inner solenoid is smaller in length and radius). NCERT Pg. 165

10 Assertion The self-induced emf is also called the back emf.

Reason The self-induced emf opposes any change in the current in a circuit. NCERT Pg. 165

Statement Based Questions

Direction (Q. Nos. 1-8) *In the following questions, two statements (I & II) are given. In the light of the given statements, choose the correct option given below.*

(a) Both Statement I and Statement II are false.
(b) Statement I is true but Statement II is false.
(c) Statement I is false but Statement II is true.
(d) Both Statement I and Statement II are true.

1 **Statement I** The galvanometer of a coil does not show any deflection when a magnet near the coil is stationary.

Statement II The relative motion between the magnet and the coil is responsible for generation of electric current in the coil. NCERT Pg. 155

2 **Statement I** If the plane of a coil is parallel to a uniform magnetic field, then net flux through the coil is maximum.

Statement II The magnetic flux through a coil can be changed by changing the strength of magnetic field. NCERT Pg. 156

3 **Statement I** If the same amount of magnetic flux changes through a copper coil and an aluminium coil, then the induced emf in both the coil is same.

Statement II Lenz's law is in accordance with law of conservation of momentum. NCERT Pg. 160

4 **Statement I** Inductance of an electrical circuit opposes any change of current through the circuit.

Statement II When current through a coil is constant, then no electromagnetic induction takes place. NCERT Pg. 165

5 **Statement I** Faraday's laws are consequence of conservation of energy.

Statement II Two co-axial conducting rings of different radii are placed in space. The mutual inductance of both the rings is maximum, if the rings are also co-planar. NCERT Pg. 166

6 **Statement I** Acceleration of a magnet falling through a long solenoid decreases.

Statement II The induced current produced in a circuit always flow in such direction that it opposes the change to the cause that produced it. NCERT Pg. 166

7 **Statement I** The principle of an AC generator is based on magnetic effect of current.

Statement II The current produced by an AC generator has constant magnitude, but changes its direction periodically. NCERT Pg. 170

8 **Statement I** Mutual inductance of a pair of coils does not depend upon relative orientation.

Statement II In AC generator, magnetic flux is changed by changing the effective area of loop. NCERT Pg. 171

Matching Type Questions

1 A square loop *ABCD* whose area 20 cm^2 and resistance 5 Ω is rotated in a uniform field of 2T through 180° about an axis in plane of loop and passing through its centre.

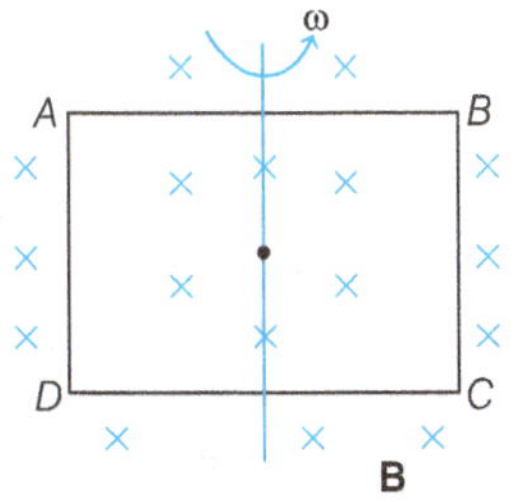

Now, match the following columns.

	Column I		Column II
A.	Current (in A) in loop at $t = 0.01$ s	1.	2.4
B.	Current (in A) in loop at $t = 0.02$s	2.	1.6
C.	Magnitude of free charge (in mC) at $t = 0.01$s	3.	0.08
D.	Magnitude of free charge (in mC) at 0.03 s	4.	0.16

NCERT Pg. 157

Choose the correct answer from the codes given below.

Codes

	A	B	C	D		A	B	C	D
(a)	1	2	3	4	(b)	4	3	2	1
(c)	3	4	1	2	(d)	3	1	2	4

2 A conductor of length l and resistance R moves through a magnetic field B with velocity v as shown below

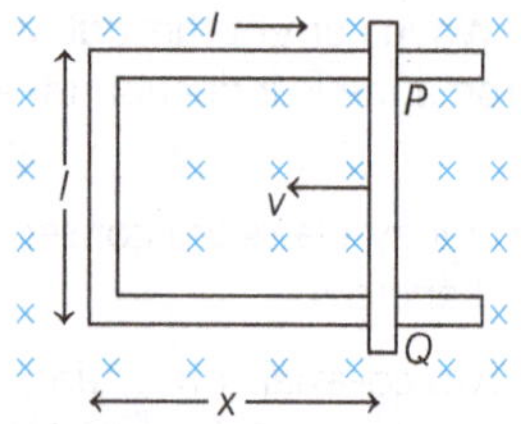

Now match the Column I with Column II.

Column I		Column II	
A.	Current induced in the loop.	1.	Bvl
B.	Force on conductor PQ	2.	Bvl/R
C.	Induced emf across PQ	3.	$\frac{B^2l^2v^2}{R}$
D.	Power delivered by external force	4.	$\frac{B^2l^2v}{R}$

NCERT Pg. 162

Choose the correct answer from the codes given below.

Codes

	A	B	C	D		A	B	C	D
(a)	2	1	4	3	(b)	2	4	1	3
(c)	4	2	3	1	(d)	4	3	2	1

3 In Column I, electromagnetic quantities are given and in Column II, mechanical quantities are given. Match the Column I and Column II.

Column I		Column II	
A.	Current	1.	Momentum
B.	Magnetic flux	2.	Potential energy
C.	Inductance	3.	Kinetic energy
D.	Magnetic energy	4.	Mass

NCERT Pg. 165

Choose the correct answer from the codes given below.

Codes

	A	B	C	D		A	B	C	D
(a)	1	2	4	3	(b)	2	4	3	1
(c)	2	1	3	4	(d)	2	1	4	3

Numerical Type Questions

1 The magnetic field B crossing normally a square metallic plate of area $2\ m^2$ is changing with time as shown in figure. The magnitude of induced emf in the plate during $t = 3$ s to $t = 5$ s, is ......mV. **NCERT Pg. 157**

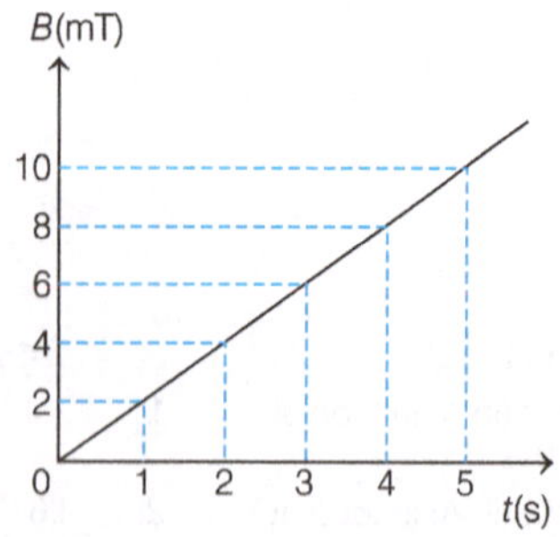

2 An insulated copper wire of 200 turns is wrapped around a wooden cylindrical core of the cross-sectional area $24\ cm^2$. The two ends of the wire are connected to a resistor. The total resistance in the circuit is $24\ \Omega$. If an externally applied uniform magnetic field in the core along its axis changes from 1.5 T in one direction to 1.5 T in the opposite direction, the charge flowing through a point in the circuit during the change of magnetic field will be ....mC. **NCERT Pg. 157**

3 In a coil of resistance $8\ \Omega$, the magnetic flux due to an external magnetic field varies with time as $\phi = \frac{2}{3}(4 - t^2)$. The value of total heat produced in the coil, till the flux becomes zero, will be $\frac{x}{27}$ J. The value of x is .... **NCERT Pg. 157**

4 In the given figure, the magnetic flux through the loop increase according to the relation $\phi_B(t) = 10t^2 + 20t$, where ϕ_B is in milliwebers and t is in seconds. The magnitude of current through $R = 10\Omega$ resistor at $t = 5$ s is ....mA. **NCERT Pg. 157**

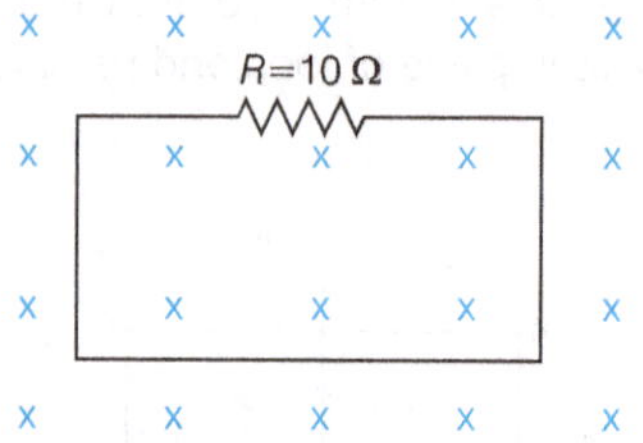

5 A conducting circular loop is placed in a uniform magnetic field to 0.2 T with its plane perpendicular to the field. Somehow, the radius of the loop starts expanding at a constant rate of 2 mm/s. The magnitude of induced emf in the loop at an instant when the radius of the loop is 2 cm will be .... μV. **NCERT Pg. 157**

6 A 15 Ω, 30 mH coil carrying constant current is connected to a battery of 20 V through a switch. Now, after switch is opened current becomes zero in 100 μs. The average emf, induced in the coil is ....V. **NCERT Pg. 157**

7 A 1 m long metal rod *XY* completes the circuit as shown in figure. The plane of the circuit is perpendicular to the magnetic field of flux density 0.15 T. If the resistance of the circuit is 10Ω, the force needed to move the rod in direction, as indicated, with a constant speed of 8 m/s will be .... $\times 10^{-3}$ N. **NCERT Pg. 162**

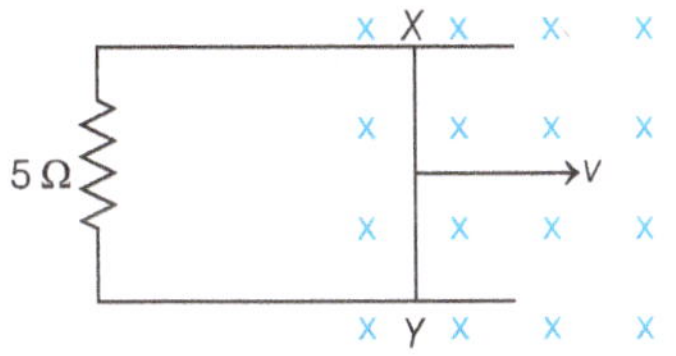

8 A 20 cm long metallic rod is rotated with 180 rpm about an axis normal to the rod passing through its one end. The other end of the rod is in contact with a circular metallic ring. A constant and uniform magnetic field 0.2 T parallel to the axis exists everywhere. The emf developed between the centre and the ring is ....mV. (Take, $\pi = \frac{22}{7}$) **NCERT Pg. 162**

9 Two concentric circular coils with radii 1 cm and 1000 cm, and number of turns 20 and 100 respectively are placed coaxially with centres coinciding. The mutual inductance of this arrangement will be ....$\times 10^{-10}$ H. (Take, $\pi^2 = 10$) **NCERT Pg. 165**

10

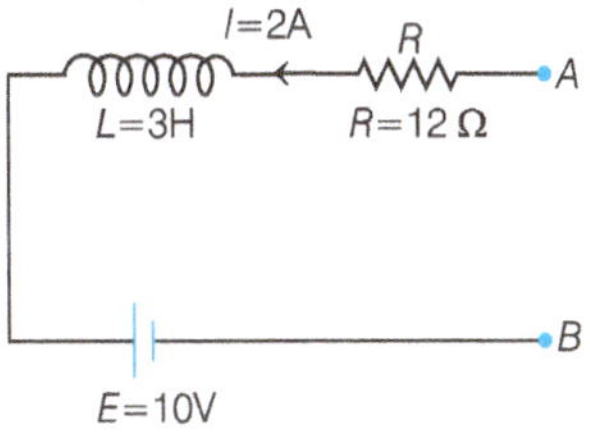

As per the given figure, if $dI/dt = -2$ A/s, then the value of V_{AB} at this instant will be ....V. **NCERT Pg. 165**

NCERT Exemplar Questions

1 A square of side *L* metres lies in the *XY*-plane in a region, where the magnetic field is given by $\mathbf{B} = B_0(2\hat{\mathbf{i}} + 3\hat{\mathbf{j}} + 4\hat{\mathbf{k}})$ T, where B_0 is constant. The magnitude of flux passing through the square is

(a) $2B_0L^2$ Wb (b) $3B_0L^2$ Wb (c) $4B_0L^2$ Wb (d) $\sqrt{29}\,B_0L^2$ Wb

2 A loop, made of straight edges has six corners at *A* (0, 0, 0), *B* (*L*, 0, 0), *C* (*L*, *L*, 0), *D* (0, *L*, 0), *E* (0, *L*, *L*) and *F* (0, 0, *L*). A magnetic field $\mathbf{B} = B_0(\hat{\mathbf{i}} + \hat{\mathbf{k}})$ T is present in the region. The flux passing through the loop *ABCDEFA* (in that order) is

(a) B_0L^2 Wb (b) $2B_0L^2$ Wb
(c) $\sqrt{2}B_0L^2$ Wb (d) $4B_0L^2$ Wb

3 A cylindrical bar magnet is rotated about its axis. A wire is connected from the axis and is made to touch the cylindrical surface through a contact. Then,

(a) a direct current flows in the ammeter *A*
(b) no current flows through the ammeter *A*
(c) an alternating sinusoidal current flows through the ammeter *A* with a time period, $T = 2\pi/\omega$
(d) a time varying non-sinusoidal current flows through the ammeter *A*

4 There are two coils *A* and *B* as shown in figure. *A* current starts flowing in *B* as shown, when *A* is moved towards *B* and stops. When *A* stops moving, the current in *B* is counter-clockwise. *B* is kept stationary when *A* moves. We can infer that

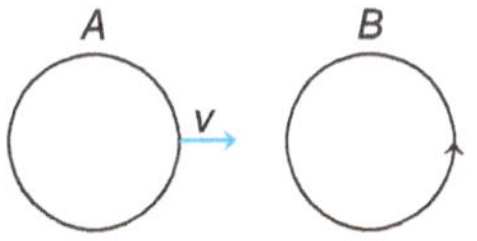

(a) there is a constant current in the clockwise direction in *A*
(b) there is a varying current in *A*
(c) there is no current in *A*
(d) there is a constant current in the counter-clockwise direction in *A*

5 Coil *A* is made to rotate about a vertical axis (shown in figure). No current flows in *B*, if *A* is at rest. The current in coil *A*,when the current in *B* (at $t = 0$) is counter-clockwise and the coil *A* is as shown at this instant, $t = 0$, is

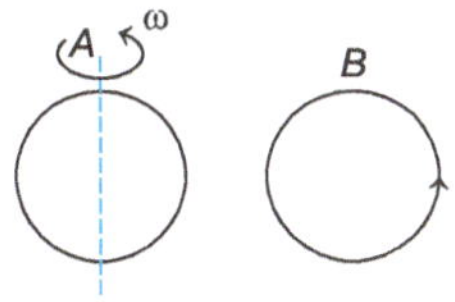

(a) constant current clockwise
(b) varying current clockwise
(c) varying current counter-clockwise
(d) constant current counter-clockwise

6 The self-inductance *L* of a solenoid of length *l* and area of cross-section *A*, with a fixed number of turns *N*, increases as

(a) *l* and *A* increase
(b) *l* decreases and *A* increases
(c) *l* increases and *A* decreases
(d) Both *l* and *A* decrease

Past Exams Questions

NEET

1 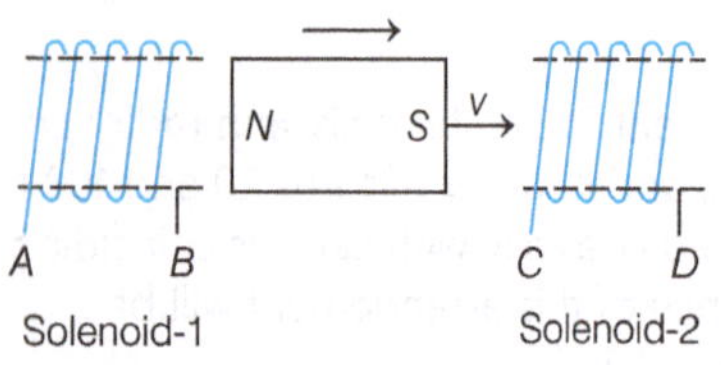

In the above diagram, a strong bar magnet is moving towards solenoid-2 from solenoid-1. The direction of induced current in solenoid-1 and that in solenoid-2, respectively, are through the directions

NCERT Pg. 163, NEET 2024

(a) AB and DC (b) BA and CD
(c) AB and CD (d) BA and DC

2 A sheet is placed on a horizontal surface in front of a strong magnetic pole. A force is needed to

NCERT Pg. 165, NEET 2024

A. hold the sheet there if it is magnetic.

B. hold the sheet there if it is non-magnetic.

C. move the sheet away from the pole with uniform velocity if it is conducting.

D. move the sheet away from the pole with uniform velocity if it is both, non-conducting and non-polar.

Choose the correct statement(s) from the options given below

(a) B and D only (b) A and C only
(c) A, C and D only (d) C only

3 The magnetic energy stored in an inductor of inductance
$4\,\mu$H carrying of 2 A is NCERT Pg. 165, NEET 2023

(a) 4 mJ (b) 8 mJ
(c) 8 μJ (d) 4 μJ

4 A square loop of side 1 m and resistance $1\,\Omega$ placed in a magnetic field of 0.5 T. If the plane of loop is perpendicular to the direction of magnetic field, the magnetic flux through the loop is NCERT Pg. 156, NEET 2022

(a) 0.5 Wb (b) 1 Wb
(c) zero (d) 2 Wb

5 Two conducting circular loops of radii R_1 and R_2 are placed in the same plane with their centres coinciding. If $R_1 >> R_2$, the mutual inductance M between them will be directly proportional to NCERT Pg. 165, NEET 2021

(a) $\frac{R_1}{R_2}$ (b) $\frac{R_2}{R_1}$ (c) $\frac{R_1^2}{R_2}$ (d) $\frac{R_2^2}{R_1}$

6 The magnetic flux linked with a coil (in Wb) is given by the equation $\phi = 5t^2 + 3t + 16$. The magnitude of induced emf in the coil at the fourth second will be

NCERT Pg. 157, NEET 2020

(a) 33 V (b) 43 V
(c) 108 V (d) 10 V

7 A cycle wheel of radius 0.5 m is rotated with constant angular velocity of 10 rad/s in a region of magnetic field of 0.1 T which is perpendicular to the plane of the wheel. The emf generated between its centre and the rim is NCERT Pg. 162, NEET 2019

(a) 0.25 V (b) 0.125 V
(c) 0.5 V (d) zero

8 The magnetic potential energy stored in a certain inductor is 25mJ when the current in the inductor is 60 mA. This inductor is of inductance.

NCERT Pg. 165, NEET 2018

(a) 1.389 H (b) 138.88 H
(c) 0.138 H (d) 13.89 H

9 A long solenoid of diameter 0.1 m has 2×10^4 turns per metre. At the centre of the solenoid, a coil of 100 turns and radius 0.01 m is placed with its axis coinciding with the solenoid axis. The current in the solenoid reduces at a constant rate to 0 A from 4 A in 0.05 s. If the resistance of the coil is $10\pi^2\Omega$, the total charge flowing through the coil during this time is

NCERT Pg. 157, NEET 2017

(a) $32\,\pi\,\mu$C (b) $16\,\mu$C
(c) $32\,\mu$C (d) $16\pi\,\mu$C

10 A uniform magnetic field is restricted within a region of radius r. The magnetic field changes with time at a rate $\frac{d\mathbf{B}}{dt}$. Loop 1 of radius $R > r$ encloses the region r and loop 2 of radius R is outside the region of magnetic field as shown in the figure. Then, the emf generated is

NCERT Pg. 157, NEET 2016

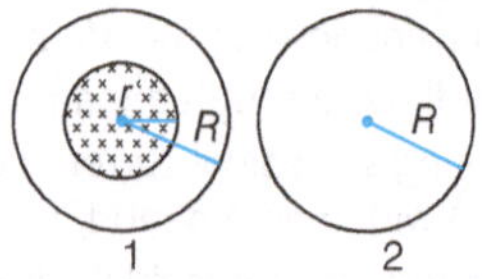

(a) zero in loop 1 and zero in loop 2

(b) $-\frac{d\mathbf{B}}{dt}\pi r^2$ in loop 1 and $-\frac{d\mathbf{B}}{dt}\pi r^2$ in loop 2

(c) $-\frac{d\mathbf{B}}{dt}\pi R^2$ in loop 1 and zero in loop 2

(d) $-\frac{d\mathbf{B}}{dt}\pi r^2$ in loop 1 and zero in loop 2

11 An electron moves on a straight path XY as shown. The $abcd$ is a coil adjacent in the path of electron. What will be the direction of current, if any induced in the coil?

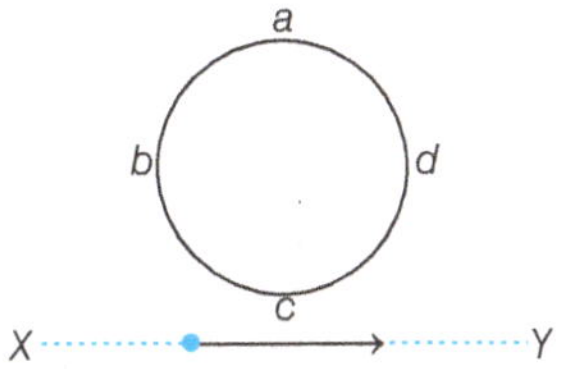

NCERT Pg. 160, AIPMT 2015

(a) $abcd$
(b) $adcb$
(c) The current will reverse its direction as the electron goes past the coil
(d) No current induced

JEE Main

12 In a coil, the current changes from –2A to +2A in 0.2 s and induces an emf of 0.1 V. The self-inductance of the cell is NCERT Pg. 165, JEE Main 2024

(a) 4 mH (b) 5 mH (c) 1 mH (d) 2.5 mH

13 A rectangular loop of length 2.5 m and width 2 m is placed at 60° to a magnetic field of 4 T. The loop is removed from the field in 10 s. The average emf induced in the loop during this time is NCERT Pg. 162, JEE Main 2024

(a) – 2 V (b) – 1 V (c) + 2 V (d) + 1 V

14 A conducting circular loop of radius $10/\sqrt{\pi}$ cm is placed perpendicular to a uniform magnetic field of 0.5 T. The magnetic field is decreased to zero in 0.5 s at a steady rate. The induced emf in the circular loop at 0.25 s is NCERT Pg. 157, JEE Main 2023

(a) emf = 5 mV (b) emf = 100 mv
(c) emf = 1 mV (d) emf = 10 mV

15 The magnetic flux through a coil perpendicular to its plane is varying according to the relation $\phi = (5t^3 + 4t^2 + 2t - 5)$ Wb. If the resistance of coil is

5Ω, then the induced current through the coil at $t = 2$ s will be NCERT Pg. 157, JEE Main 2022

(a) 15.6 A (b) 16.6 A (c) 17.6 A (d) 18.6 A

16 A conducting bar of length L is free to slide on two parallel conducting rails as shown in the figure. NCERT Pg. 162, JEE Main 2021

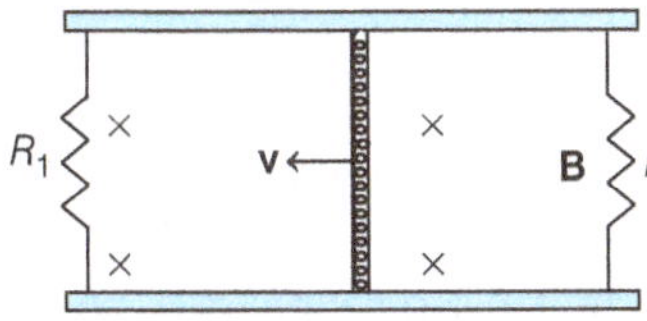

Two resistors R_1 and R_2 are connected across the ends of the rails. There is uniform magnetic field **B** pointing into the page. An external agent pulls the bar to the left at a constant speed **v**.

The correct statement about the directions of induced currents I_1 and I_2 flowing through R_1 and R_2 respectively is

(a) both I_1 and I_2 are in anti-clockwise direction.
(b) both I_1 and I_2 are in clockwise direction.
(c) I_1 is in clockwise direction and I_2 is in anti-clockwise direction.
(d) I_1 is in clockwise direction and I_2 is in clockwise direction.

17 The arm PQ of a rectangle conductor is moving from $x = 0$ to $x = 2b$ outwards and then inwards from $x = 2b$ to $x = 0$ as shown in the figure. A uniform magnetic field perpendicular to the plane is acting from $x = 0$ to $x = b$. Identify the graph showing the variation of different quantities with distance. NCERT Pg. 162, JEE Main 2021

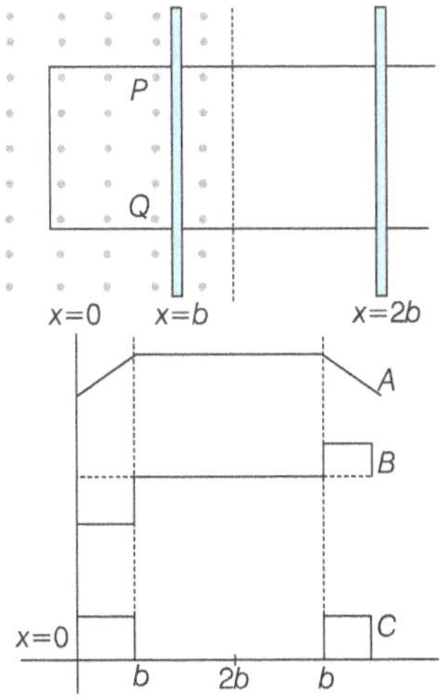

(a) A-flux, B-power dissipated, C-emf
(b) A-power dissipated, B-flux, C-emf
(c) A-flux, B-emf, C-power dissipated
(d) A-emf, B-power dissipated, C-flux

18 A coil is placed in a magnetic field B as shown below. NCERT Pg. 160, JEE Main 2021

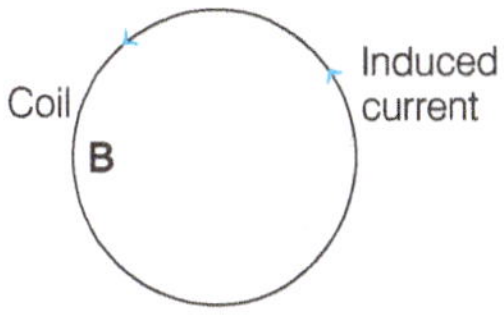

A current is induced in the coil because B is

(a) outward and decreasing with time
(b) parallel to the plane of coil and decreasing with time
(c) outward and increasing with time
(d) parallel to the plane of coil and increasing with time

Skill Boosters

1 A semicircular piece of wire is rotated about a point P (as shown) with angular velocity ω about an axis passing through P and perpendicular to plane of wire. A magnetic field of constant magnitude B exists in the region parallel to axis of rotation.

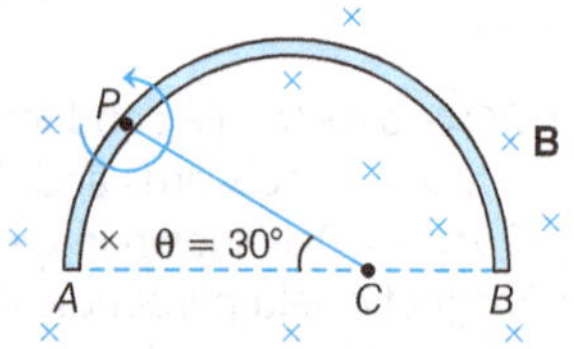

Potential difference between ends of wires (A and B) is

(a) $\frac{B\omega R^2}{2}$ (b) $\frac{B\omega R^2}{4}$

(c) $2B\omega R^2$ (d) $B\omega R^2$

2 PQ is an infinite current carrying conductor. AB and CD are smooth conducting rods on which a conductor EF moves with constant velocity v as shown in the figure. The force needed to maintain constant speed of EF is

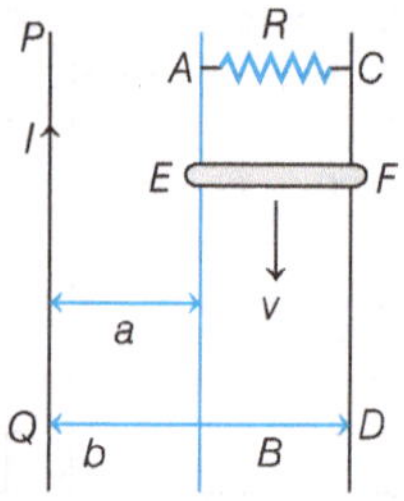

(a) $\frac{1}{vR}\left[\frac{\mu_0 Iv}{2\pi}\ln\left(\frac{b}{a}\right)\right]^2$

(b) $\left[\frac{\mu_0 Iv}{2\pi}\ln\left(\frac{b}{a}\right)\right]^2 \frac{1}{R}$

(c) $\left[\frac{\mu_0 Iv}{2\pi}\ln\left(\frac{b}{a}\right)\right]^2 \frac{v}{R}$

(d) $\frac{v}{R}\left[\frac{\mu_0 Iv}{2\pi}\ln\left(\frac{b}{a}\right)\right]^2$

3 A research associate requires an air-core solenoid with self-inductance of 1 H on the outside of a hollow plastic tube 12 cm in diameter. Such a solenoid is not available in the market. So, the associate decided to make the solenoid using a copper wire of diameter 0.81 mm. Now, help the associate in shopping different items.

Plastic tubes are available in following sizes. Pick size most suitable for the requirement, so that wastage is minimum.

(a) 100 m (b) 75 m (c) 50 m (d) 25 m

4 In figure shown, the rod has a resistance R, the horizontal rails have negligible friction. A battery of emf E and negligible internal resistance is connected between points a and b. The rod is initially at rest.

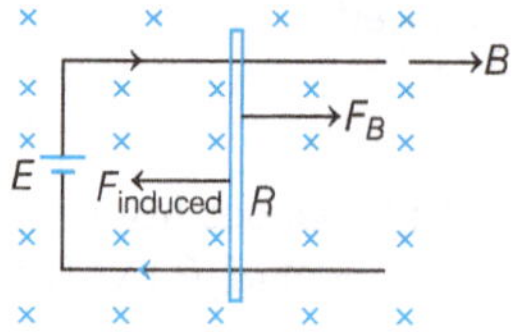

The velocity of the rod as a function of the time t (where, $\tau = mR/B^2l^2$) is

(a) $\frac{E}{Bl}(1-e^{-t/\tau})$ (b) $\frac{E}{Bl}(1+e^{-t/\tau})$

(c) $\frac{3E}{2Bl}(1-e^{-t/\tau})$ (d) $\frac{E}{2Bl}(1-e^{-t/\tau})$

5 The magnetic field in a region is given by $\mathbf{B} = B_0\left(1+\frac{x}{a}\right)\hat{\mathbf{k}}$. A square loop of edge length d is placed with its edge along the X- axis and Y-axis. The loop is moved with a constant velocity $\mathbf{v} = v_0\hat{\mathbf{i}}$. The emf induced in the loop at $t = 0$ is

(a) $\frac{v_0 B_0 d^2}{a}$ (b) $\frac{v_0 B_0 d^3}{a^2}$

(c) $v_0 B_0 d$ (d) zero

6 A square wire frame $ABCD$ of side 1 m is placed in a region of changing magnetic field whose magnitude is decreasing at a constant rate of 1 T/s.

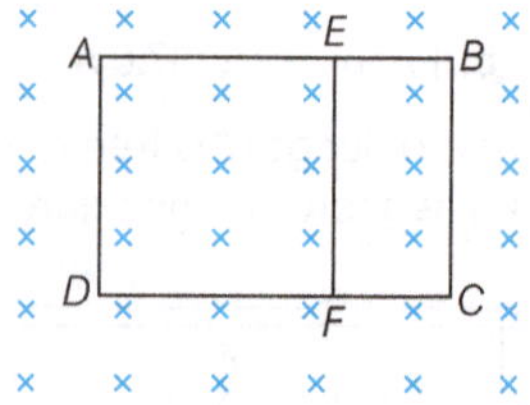

Wire segment EF is connected such that $EB = FC = 0.5$ m. Resistance per metre length of wire is $1\,\Omega$/m. Current in segment EF is $\frac{1}{11p}$ A.

Find the value of p.

(a) 5 (b) 3 (c) 2 (d) 7

7 A wire loop enclosing a semicircle of radius R is located on the boundary of a uniform magnetic field B. At the moment $t = 0$, the loop is set into rotation with constant angular acceleration α about an axis O. The clockwise emf direction is taken to be positive.

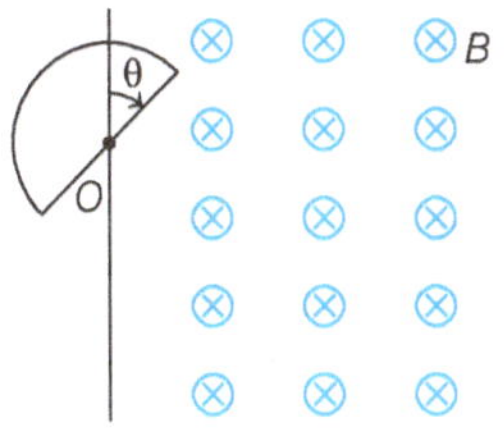

The variation of emf as a function of time is

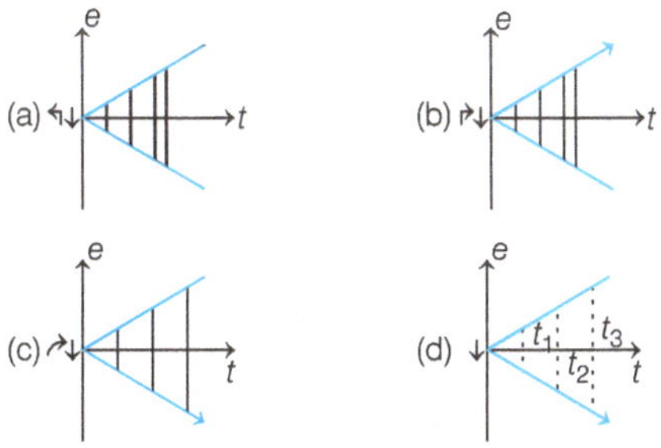

8 The figure shows certain wire segments joined together to form a coplanar loop. The loop is placed in a perpendicular magnetic field in the direction going into the plane of the figure. The magnitude of the field increases with time. I_1 and I_2 are the currents in the segments ab and cd. Then,

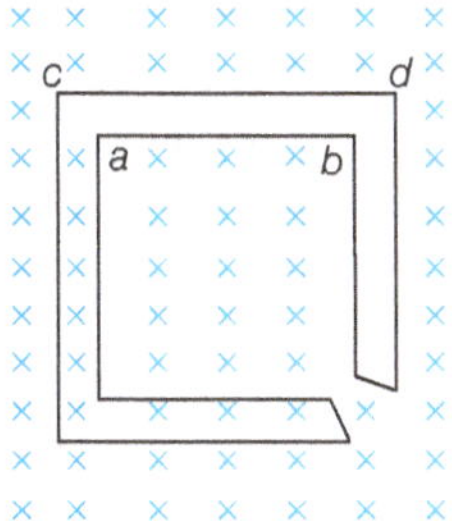

(a) $I_1 > I_2$

(b) $I_1 < I_2$

(c) I_1 is the direction ba and I_2 is in the direction cd

(d) I_1 is the direction ab and I_2 is in the direction dc

9 Two metallic rings A and B, identical in shape and size but having different resistivities ρ_A and ρ_B are kept on top of two identical solenoids as shown in the figure. When current I is switched ON in both the solenoids in identical manner, then rings A and B jump to heights h_A and h_B respectively, with $h_A > h_B$.

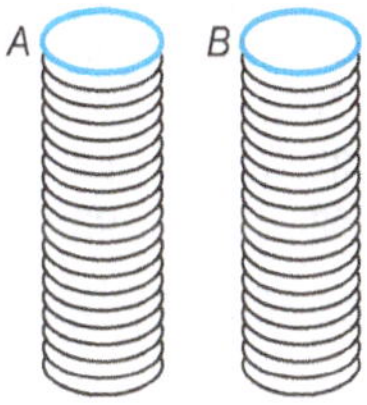

The possible relation(s) between their resistivities and their masses m_A and m_B is(are)

(a) $\rho_A > \rho_B$ and $m_A = m_B$

(b) $\rho_A < \rho_B$ and $m_A > m_B$

(c) $\rho_A > \rho_B$ and $m_A > m_B$ (d) $\rho_A < \rho_B$ and $m_A < m_B$

10 A square loop of side 2 cm is placed in region of a magnetic field, directed out of plane of paper, with magnitude $B = 4t^2 y$, where y is measured in metres with respect to the coordinate axes as shown in the figure.

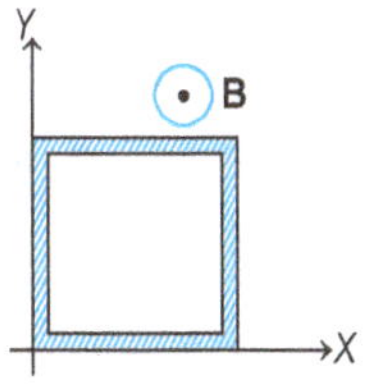

Induced emf in the loop at $t = 2.5$ s is

(a) 8×10^{-5} V anti-clockwise

(b) 8×10^{-5} V clockwise

(c) 4×10^{-3} V anti-clockwise

(d) 4×10^{-3} V clockwise

Correct Codes

Topical Questions

1 (b)	2 (c)	3 (d)	4 (d)	5 (d)	6 (a)	7 (c)	8 (c)	9 (c)	10 (d)
11 (b)	12 (d)	13 (b)	14 (c)	15 (b)	16 (b)	17 (d)	18 (d)	19 (a)	20 (a)
21 (b)	22 (b)	23 (a)	24 (d)	25 (c)	26 (a)	27 (b)	28 (b)	29 (c)	30 (a)
31 (b)	32 (b)	33 (c)	34 (a)	35 (a)	36 (b)	37 (c)	38 (c)	39 (b)	40 (d)
41 (b)	42 (b)	43 (c)	44 (c)	45 (b)	46 (c)	47 (c)	48 (c)	49 (a)	50 (c)
51 (c)	52 (a)	53 (b)	54 (a)	55 (c)	56 (c)	57 (c)	58 (a)	59 (a)	60 (a)
61 (d)	62 (b)	63 (b)	64 (c)	65 (d)	66 (a)	67 (b)	68 (d)	69 (a)	70 (a)
71 (c)	72 (a)	73 (a)	74 (a)	75 (b)	76 (b)	77 (c)	78 (b)	79 (b)	80 (a)
81 (d)	82 (c)	83 (c)	84 (d)	85 (b)	86 (a)	87 (b)	88 (c)	89 (b)	90 (d)
91 (c)	92 (d)	93 (c)	94 (d)	95 (a)	96 (d)				

Assertion and Reason Questions

1 (b)	2 (c)	3 (c)	4 (d)	5 (a)	6 (b)	7 (c)	8 (a)	9 (a)	10 (a)

Statement Based Questions

1 (d)	2 (c)	3 (b)	4 (d)	5 (d)	6 (d)	7 (a)	8 (c)

Matching Type Questions

1 (b)	2 (b)	3 (d)

Numerical Type Questions

1 (4)	2 (60)	3 (16)	4 (12)	5 (50)	6 (400)	7 (18)	8 (75)	9 (400)	10 (28)

NCERT Exemplar Questions

1 (c)	2 (b)	3 (b)	4 (d)	5 (a)	6 (b)

Past Exams Questions

1 (a)	2 (b)	3 (c)	4 (a)	5 (d)	6 (d)	7 (b)	8 (d)	9 (c)	10 (c)
11 (c)	12 (b)	13 (d)	14 (d)	15 (a)	16 (c)	17 (c)	18 (a)		

Skill Boosters

1 (d)	2 (a)	3 (c)	4 (a)	5 (a)	6 (c)	7 (d)	8 (d)	9 (d)	10 (b)

Step by Step

Decoding the Questions

Concept Builders

1 False (F)

2 Faraday's law

3 conservation of energy

4 True (T) 5 True (T)

6 True (T) 7 True (T)

8 Remain same 9 False (F)

10 not possible

11 same 12 True (T)

13 True (T) 14 N^2

15 half $\left(\frac{1}{2}\right)$ 16 1

17 resistance of coil

18 $L = L_1 + L_2 - 2M$

19 reduce 20 False (F)

Topical Questions

4 (*d*) The total magnetic flux through *XY*-plane is

$$\phi = BA\cos\theta$$
$$= BA\cos 90° \quad [\because B \perp A]$$
$$= 0$$

5 (*d*) We are given with following situation,

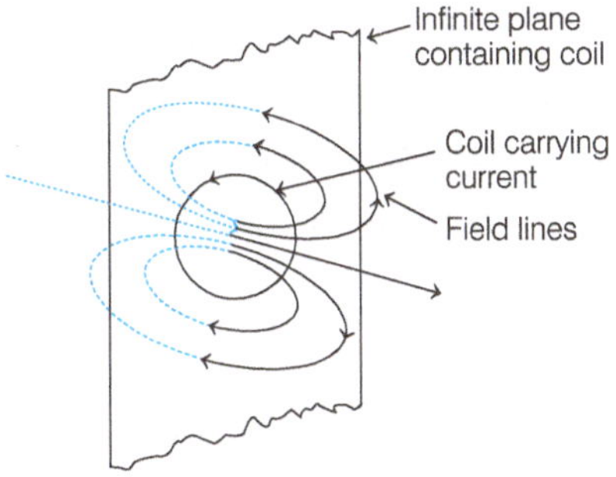

From the diagram of field lines, magnetic flux emerging from coil is equal and opposite to the flux linked with infinite plane.

So, $\phi_i = -\phi_o$

6 (*a*)

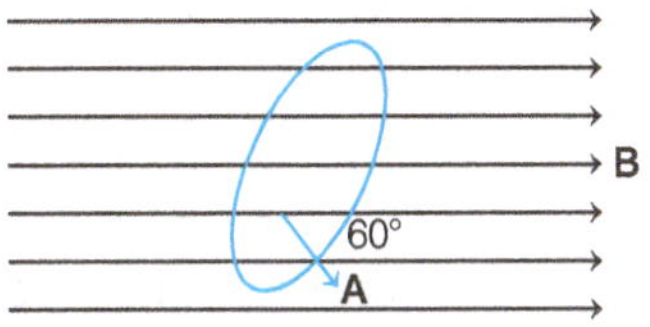

$$\therefore \quad \phi_B = BA\cos\theta$$
$$\Rightarrow \quad \phi_B = \frac{1}{\pi} \times \pi(0.2)^2 \times \cos 60°$$
$$= (0.2)^2 \times \frac{1}{2} = 0.02 \text{ Wb}$$

7 (*c*) Given, $\mathbf{B} = B_0\,(3\hat{\mathbf{i}} + 3\hat{\mathbf{j}} - 4\hat{\mathbf{k}})$ T

$$\mathbf{B}_x = (3B_0\,\hat{\mathbf{i}})\text{ T}$$

or $B_x = (3B_0)$ T = component of **B** along area **A**

Area of the square, $A = a^2 (\text{m}^2)$

Magnetic flux, $\phi_B = BA\cos\theta$

$$\Rightarrow \quad \phi_B = (B\cos\theta)A$$

= (component of **B** along **A**) A

ϕ_B (magnitude of magnetic flux)

$= B_x\, A = 3B_0 a^2\ (\text{Tm}^2) = 3\,B_0 a^2$ Wb

8 (*c*) Magnetic flux, $\phi = BA\cos\theta$

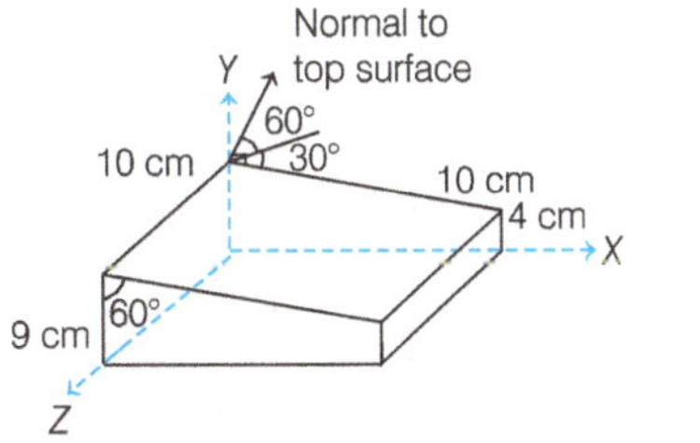

$$\therefore \phi = 0.2 \times (10 \times 10 \times 10^{-4}) \times \cos 60°$$
$$= 10^{-3} \text{ Wb} = 1.0 \text{ m-Wb}$$

9 (*c*) Induced emf in the loop,

$$E = -\left(\frac{B_2 - B_1}{\Delta t}\right)A \quad \text{...(i)}$$

$\therefore \quad A$ = Area of loop

= Area of rectangle − Area of two triangles

$$= \left(16 \times 4 - 2 \times \frac{1}{2} \times 4 \times 2\right)\text{cm}^2$$
$$= 56 \times 10^{-4} \text{ m}^2$$

Using Eq. (i), we get

$$E = \frac{(1000 - 500) \times 10^{-4} \times 56 \times 10^{-4}}{5}$$
$$= 56 \times 10^{-6} \text{ V} = 56\,\mu\text{V}$$

10 (*d*) Given, $\phi = 3t^n - 2^n$,

n = +ve constant

$\therefore$ The induced emf in the coil is

$$|e| = \frac{d\phi}{dt} = \frac{d}{dt}(3t^n - 2^n) = 3nt^{n-1}$$

If $0 < n < 1$, then $e \neq 0$ and $|e| \propto \frac{1}{t}$

If $n = 1$, then $e = 3 \times 1 \times t^0$

$= 3 =$ constant

If $n > 1$, then $|e| \propto t$, i.e. $|e|$ increase with time.

11 (*b*) The emf induced in the coil is

$$e = -\frac{d\phi}{dt} = -\frac{d}{dt}\left(\frac{t^3}{3} - \frac{t^2}{2} - 2t + 10\right)$$
$$= -(t^2 - t - 2)$$

$\therefore$ The induced current in the coil is

$$i = \frac{e}{R} = \frac{-(t^2 - t - 2)}{20} = 0$$
$$\Rightarrow \quad t^2 - t - 2 = 0$$
$$\therefore \quad t = 2\text{s}$$

12 (*d*) The magnitude of induced emf is independent of the resistance of the coil.

$$\therefore e = -d\phi/dt = -\frac{Nd}{dt}(BA)$$

Thus, e depends upon N, B and A. But induced current depends upon R.

13 (*b*) Given, $R = 10\Omega$, $\phi_1 = 20$ Wb,

$\phi_2 = 30$ Wb

$\Delta t = 5 \text{ ms} = 5 \times 10^{-3}$ s

The charge flowing through the circuit is

$$\Delta Q = \frac{\Delta\phi}{R} = \frac{\phi_2 - \phi_1}{R}$$
$$= \frac{30 - 20}{10} = 1\text{C}$$

15 (*b*) Magnitude of induced emf,

$$|\varepsilon| = \frac{d\phi_B}{dt} = \frac{d}{dt}(3t^2 + 4t + 9)$$
$$= 6t + 4$$

At $t = 2\text{s}$, $|\varepsilon|$
$$= 6 \times 2 + 4 = 16 \text{ V}$$

16 (*b*) Induced current, $I = \frac{e}{R}$

$$\Rightarrow \quad I = \frac{e}{R} = \left(\frac{d\phi}{dt}\right) \cdot \frac{1}{R}$$
$$\Rightarrow \quad d\phi = IRdt$$
$$\Rightarrow \quad \phi = \int IRdt$$

Here, R is constant.

$$\therefore \quad \phi = R\int Idt$$

$\int I \cdot dt$ = Area under I-t graph
$$= \frac{1}{2} \times 10 \times 0.5$$
$$\therefore \quad \phi = 100 \times 2.5$$
$$= 250 \text{ Wb}$$

17 (*d*) Initial flux through the coil,

$$\phi_{B(\text{initial})} = BA\cos\theta_1$$
$$= 3.0 \times 10^{-5} \times (\pi \times 10^{-2}) \times \cos 0°$$
$$= 3\pi \times 10^{-7} \text{ Wb}$$

Final flux after the rotation, about its vertical diameter through 180° is given as

$$\phi_{B(\text{final})} = BA\cos\theta_2$$
$$= 3.0 \times 10^{-5} \times (\pi \times 10^{-2}) \times \cos 180°$$
$$= -3\pi \times 10^{-7} \text{ Wb}$$
$$\Rightarrow \quad \Delta\phi_B = \phi_{B(\text{final})} - \phi_{B(\text{initial})}$$
$$= (-3\pi - 3\pi) \times 10^{-7} \text{ Wb}$$
$$= -6\pi \times 10^{-7} \text{ Wb}$$

Therefore, estimated value of the induced emf is

$$\varepsilon = -N\frac{\Delta\phi_B}{\Delta t} = -500 \times (-6\pi \times 10^{-7})/0.25$$
$$= 3.8 \times 10^{-3} \text{ V}$$

18 (*d*) ∴ Induced emf,

$$\varepsilon = -\frac{d\phi_B}{dt} = -(3t^2 + 3) = -3t^2 - 3$$

At $t = 0$, $\varepsilon = -3$ V

The above equation is in the form of $y = ax^2 + b$, which represents the equation of parabola not passing through origin.

19 (*a*) Magnitude of induced emf of coil, $|\varepsilon| = \left|-\frac{d\phi_B}{dt}\right|_t$

$$= \left|-\frac{d}{dt}(50t^2 + 4)\right|_{t=2}$$
$$= 100t|_{t=2} = 200 \text{ V}$$

Current in the coil,

$$I = \frac{|\varepsilon|}{R} = \frac{200}{400} = \frac{1}{2} = 0.5 \text{ A}$$

20 (*a*) From Faraday's law, induced emf,

$$\varepsilon = -N\frac{d\phi_B}{dt}$$
$$\Rightarrow \quad \varepsilon = -1 \cdot \frac{d}{dt}(BA\cos 45°)$$
$$= -\frac{A}{\sqrt{2}}\frac{dB}{dt}$$
$$= \frac{10^{-2}}{-\sqrt{2}} \times \frac{0.1}{0.7} = -1 \text{ mV}$$

Magnitude of current

$$= \frac{|\varepsilon|}{R} = \frac{1\text{mV}}{1\Omega} = 1.0 \text{ mA}$$

21 (*b*) The initial magnetic flux is

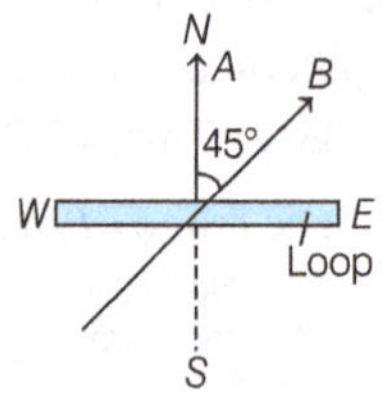

$$\phi_B = BA\cos\theta$$
$$\phi_B = 0.10 \times 10^{-2} \times \cos 45°$$
$$= \frac{0.10 \times 10^{-2}}{\sqrt{2}} \text{ Wb}$$
$$= \frac{10^{-3}}{\sqrt{2}} \text{ Wb}$$

Final flux, $\phi_{\min} = 0$

Induced emf,

$$\varepsilon = \frac{|\Delta\phi_B|}{\Delta t} = \frac{|(\phi_B - 0)|}{\Delta t}$$
$$= \frac{10^{-3}}{\sqrt{2} \times 0.70} = 1.0 \text{ mV}$$

and the magnitude of the current is

$$I = \frac{\varepsilon}{R} = \frac{1.0\text{mV}}{0.5\,\Omega} = 2 \text{ mA}$$

22 (*b*) Induced emf, $|\varepsilon| = \frac{d\phi_B}{dt}$ ...(i)

We know that,

$$i = \frac{dq}{dt} \Rightarrow q = \int idt = \int \frac{\varepsilon}{R}dt$$
$$\Rightarrow \quad q = \frac{1}{R}\int \frac{d\phi_B}{dt} \cdot dt \quad \text{[from Eq. (i)]}$$
$$= \frac{1}{R}\int d\phi_B = \frac{\phi_B}{R}$$

For N-turns, $q = \frac{N\phi_B}{R} = \frac{N}{R}(BA)$

$(\because \phi_B = BA)$

$$\Rightarrow \quad qR = NBA$$
$$\Rightarrow \quad B = \frac{qR}{NA} = \frac{2.0 \times 10^{-4} \times 80}{40 \times 4.0 \times 10^{-4}}$$
$$= 1.0 \text{ Wb m}^{-2}$$

23 (*a*) $\frac{dB}{dt} = 0.02 \text{ Ts}^{-1}$

$$|\varepsilon| = \frac{d\phi_B}{dt} = A \cdot \frac{dB}{dt}$$

[$\because \phi_B = BA$ and A is a constant]

$$= 50 \times 10^{-4} \times 0.02 = 10^{-4} \text{ V}$$

Power dissipated in the form of heat $= \frac{\varepsilon^2}{R} = \frac{10^{-4} \times 10^{-4}}{2}$

$$= 0.5 \times 10^{-8} \text{ W}$$
$$= 5 \times 10^{-9} \text{ W}$$
$$= 5\text{nW}$$

24 (*d*) Let ε be the magnitude of emf induced in the loop, then

$$\varepsilon = \frac{d\phi_B}{dt} = \frac{d(B \cdot A)}{dt}$$
$$\Rightarrow \quad \varepsilon = B \cdot \frac{dA}{dt}$$
$$= 0.3 \times 0.05 = 0.015 \text{ V}$$

or $\varepsilon = 1.5 \times 10^{-2}$ V

∴ Heat produced in the coil

$$H = P = \frac{\varepsilon^2}{R} = \frac{(1.5 \times 10^{-2})^2}{1.5}$$
$$= 150 \times 10^{-6} \text{ W}$$

26 (*a*)

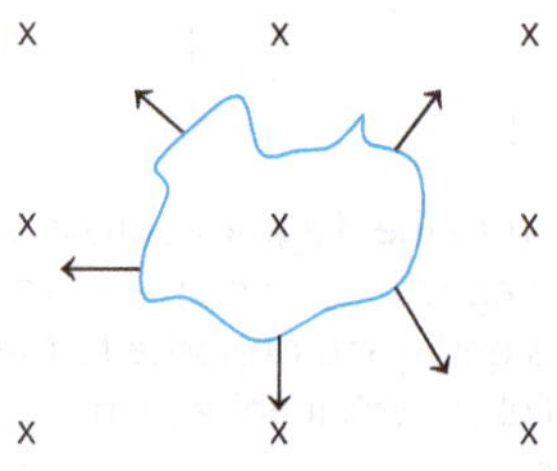

As, the irregular shaped conducting loop is slowly changing into a circular loop. So, magnetic field associated with the loop increases. By Lenz's law, an anti-clockwise current is induced in the loop to oppose the change in magnetic flux through the coil.

32 (*b*) When the north pole of the magnet is brought towards one end of the coil, then the induced current flows in the coil in such a direction, so as to oppose the motion of the north pole of the magnet towards the coil. Thus, direction of induced current is anti-clockwise as shown below.

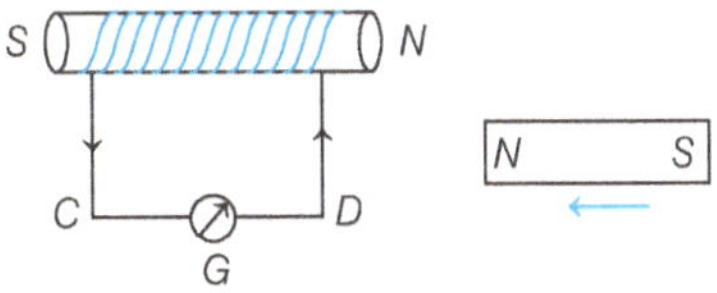

33 (*c*) By Lenz's law, the direction of induced current in the loop will be anti-clockwise, because the induced current makes the ring, a magnetic dipole with its *N*-pole upward which opposes (repel) the *N*-pole of falling magnet.

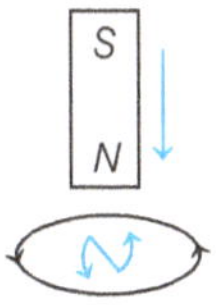

37 (*c*) The potential difference across the ends of the wire is

$$e = |(\mathbf{v} \times \mathbf{B}) \cdot \mathbf{l}|$$

$$\therefore \quad \mathbf{v} \times \mathbf{B} = \begin{vmatrix} \hat{\mathbf{i}} & \hat{\mathbf{j}} & \hat{\mathbf{k}} \\ 1 & 1 & 2 \\ 0 & 4 & 3 \end{vmatrix}$$

$$= (-5\hat{\mathbf{i}} - 3\hat{\mathbf{j}} + 4\hat{\mathbf{k}})$$

$$\therefore \; e = |(-5\hat{\mathbf{i}} - 3\hat{\mathbf{j}} + 4\hat{\mathbf{k}}) \cdot (\hat{\mathbf{j}})|$$

$$= |-3| = 3 \text{ V}$$

38 (*c*) The induced emf across the radius of the disc is given by

$$e = \frac{1}{2} B\omega R^2 = \frac{1}{2} B(2\pi f)R^2 = \pi BfR^2$$

$$= \pi \times (0.1) \times (10) \times (0.1)^2$$

$$= \pi \times 10^{-2} \text{V}$$

39 (*b*) The emf induced between the centre and the ring is

$$e = \frac{1}{2} B\omega l^2 = \frac{1}{2} \times 0.5 \times 400 \times 1^2$$

$$= 100 \text{ V}$$

40 (*d*)

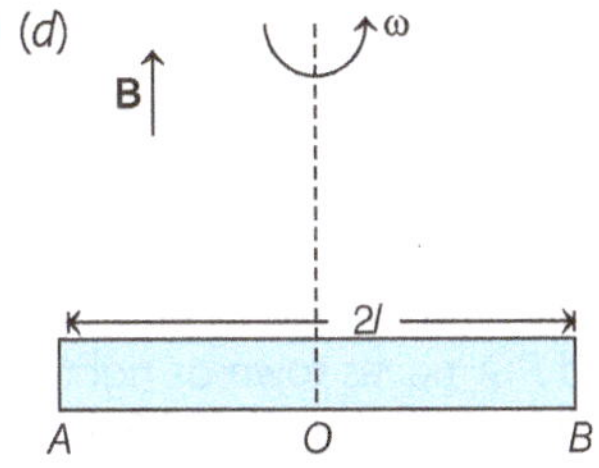

The induced emf between points *O* and *A* is

$$V_O - V_A = \frac{1}{2} B\omega l^2$$

The induced emf between points *O* and *B* is

$$V_O - V_B = \frac{1}{2} B\omega l^2$$

∴ The induced emf between two ends of the rod is

$$V_A - V_B = (V_O - V_B) - (V_O - V_A)$$

$$= \frac{1}{2} B\omega l^2 - \frac{1}{2} B\omega l^2 = 0$$

41 (*b*) The induced emf in a moving rod in a uniform magnetic field is given by

$$e = Bvl \Rightarrow e \propto l$$

As, $(l_c = l_d) > (l_a = l_b)$

$\therefore \quad (e_c = e_d) > (e_a = e_b)$

42 (*b*) The magnetic force **F** on the electron of the conductor is

$$\mathbf{F} = -e\,\mathbf{v} \times \mathbf{B}$$

∴ The direction of force **F** is given by $-\hat{\mathbf{i}} \times \hat{\mathbf{k}} = \hat{\mathbf{k}} \times \hat{\mathbf{i}} = \hat{\mathbf{j}}$

Hence, the electron will flow from *B* to *A* in the conducting rod and the end *A* of the rod becomes negatively charged.

44 (*c*) The induced emf is given by

$$\varepsilon = \frac{-d\phi_B}{dt} = -\frac{d}{dt}(Blx)$$

$$= -Bl\frac{dx}{dt} = -Blv$$

The induced emf *Blv* is called motional emf.

45 (*b*) Induced emf across the ends of wire, $\varepsilon = B_H lv$

$$= 0.30 \times 10^{-4} \times 20 \times 5.0 = 3 \text{ mV}$$

46 (*c*) The induced emf between tip of nose and tail of helicopter is given by

$$\varepsilon = B_H vl = 5 \times 10^{-3} \times 100 \times 10 = 5 \text{ V}$$

47 (*c*) ∴ Induced emf, $\varepsilon = Bvl$

$$= 2 \times 10^{-5} \times 72 \times \frac{5}{18} \times 1 = 0.4 \text{ mV}$$

48 (*c*) The induced potential gradient

$$= \frac{Bvl}{l} = Bv$$

$$= 0.30 \times 10^{-2} \times 4.0 = 0.012 \text{ Vm}^{-1}$$

$$= 1.2 \times 10^{-2} \text{ Vm}^{-1}$$

49 (*a*) Let us consider the forward motion from $x = 0$ to $x = 2b$. The flux ϕ_B linked with the circuit *SPQR* is $\quad \phi_B = Blx, \; 0 \le x < b$

The induced emf is

$$\varepsilon = -\frac{d\phi_B}{dt} = -\frac{Blx}{t}$$

$$= -Blv, \quad 0 \le x < b$$

This is because, both ϕ_B and ε are zero for $b < x \le 2b$, as *B* is zero for $x > b$.

51 (*c*) The emf induced between *A* and *B* as shown below is given by

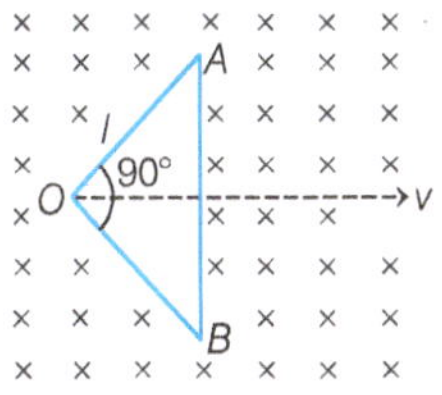

$$\varepsilon = Bv(AB)$$

In ΔAOB, $AB = \sqrt{AO^2 + BO^2}$

$$= \sqrt{l^2 + l^2} = \sqrt{2}\, l$$

$$\therefore \quad \varepsilon = Bv(\sqrt{2}\, l) = \sqrt{2}\, Bvl$$

52 (*a*) $h = L - L\cos\theta \Rightarrow h = L(1 - \cos\theta)$

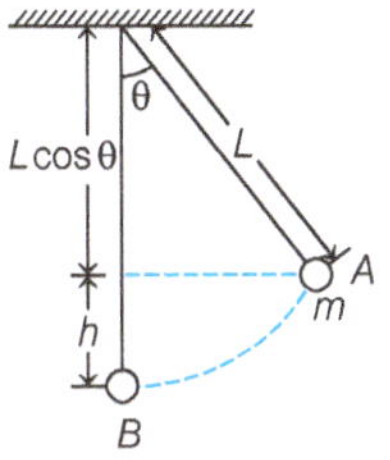

$$v^2 = u^2 + 2gh$$

$$\therefore \quad v^2 = 2gh = 2gL(1 - \cos\theta)$$

$$\Rightarrow \quad v = 2\sqrt{gL}\sin\theta/2$$

Thus, maximum emf induced,

$$\varepsilon_{max} = BvL$$
$$= B \times 2\sqrt{gL}\,(\sin\theta/2)\,L$$
$$= 2BL(\sin\theta/2)(gL)^{1/2}$$

53 (b) $d\varepsilon = Bvdr$

Hence, $\varepsilon = \int d\varepsilon = \int_0^R Bvdr$

$$= \int_0^R B\omega r dr$$
$$= B\omega\left[\frac{r^2}{2}\right]_0^R = \frac{B\omega R^2}{2}$$

$\because$ $\omega = 2\pi\nu = 2\pi \times 50 \text{ rad s}^{-1}$

$\therefore$ $\varepsilon = \frac{1}{2} \times 1 \times 2\pi \times 50 \times (1)^2$

$= 157$ V

54 (a) Induced emf, $\varepsilon = (1/2)\,\omega BR^2$

$= \frac{1}{2}\omega H_E R^2$ ($\because$ 2 rev in 1 sec)

$\omega = 2\pi\nu = 4\pi$ rad / s

$\therefore \varepsilon = (1/2) \times 4\pi \times 0.4 \times 10^{-4} \times (0.5)^2$

$= 6.28 \times 10^{-5}$ V

55 (c)

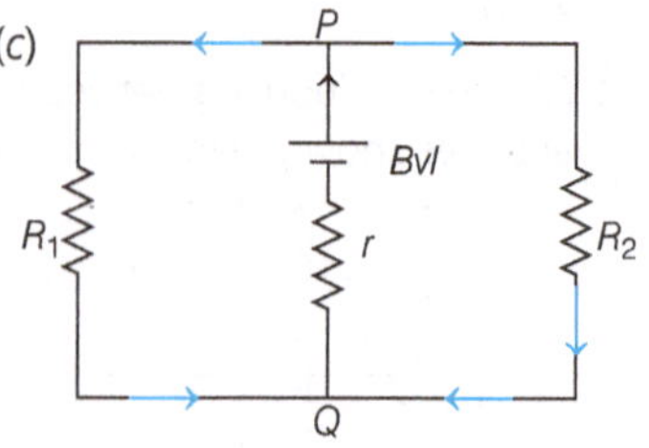

The net current through the connector is

$$i = \frac{Bvl}{\frac{R_1R_2}{R_1+R_2} + r} = \frac{2 \times 2 \times 1}{\frac{6\times3}{6+3} + 2}$$

$= 1$ A

$\therefore$ Force exerted on the connector is

$F = Bil = 2 \times 1 \times 1 = 2$ N

56 (c)

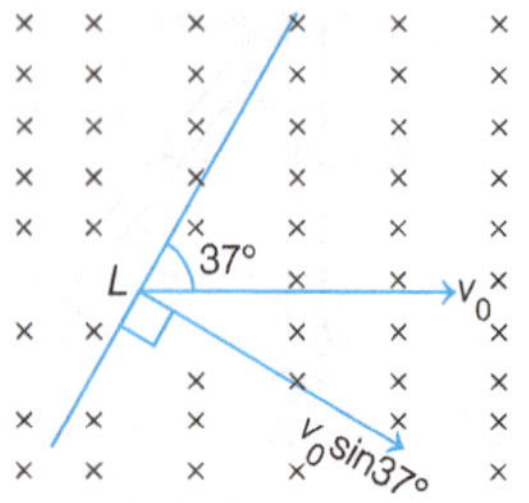

The induced emf developed across the ends of the rod is given by

$$e = B_\perp v_\perp l_\perp = B_0(v_0 \sin 37°).L$$
$$= B_0 v_0 \times \frac{3}{5}L = \frac{3}{5}B_0 v_0 L$$

58 (a) Induced emf produced is given by $\varepsilon = Blv = 0.4 \times 0.25 \times 5 = 0.5$ V

Current through the 5Ω resistance,

$$i = \frac{\varepsilon}{R} = \frac{0.5}{5} = 0.1 \text{ A}$$

According to Lenz's law, when the rod PQ moves towards right, the induced current should flow in a direction, so that the rod PQ experiences force towards left. According to Fleming's left hand rule, then the current through the rod PQ will flow from end Q to P, i.e., from end R to S through the resistance of 5Ω.

62 (b) A steady state, the inductor behaves as a closed circuit. So, the given circuit diagram can be redrawn as

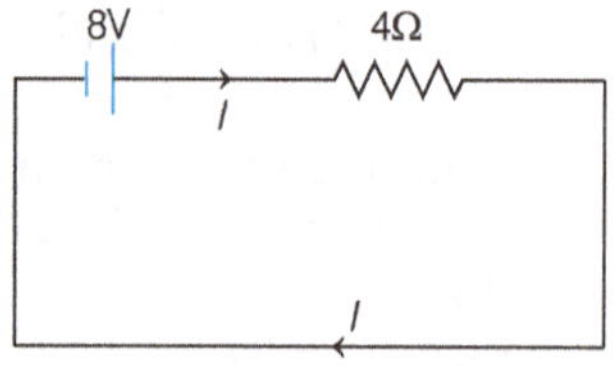

The current through the inductor is

$$I = \frac{E}{R} = \frac{8}{4} = 2\text{A}$$

$\therefore$ The magnetic energy stored in the inductor is

$$U = \frac{1}{2}LI^2 = \frac{1}{2} \times 10 \times 10^{-3} \times 2 \times 2$$

$= 20$ mJ

63 (b) The magnetic energy stored in the inductor is

$$U_L = \frac{1}{2}LI^2$$

$\Rightarrow$ $32 = \frac{1}{2} \times L \times (4)^2$

$\therefore$ $L = 4$H

The rate of heat dissipation in the resistor is

$$U_R = I^2R \Rightarrow 320 = (4)^2 \times R$$

$\Rightarrow$ $R = 20\Omega$

$\therefore$ The time constant of the circuit is

$$\tau = \frac{L}{R} = \frac{4}{20} = 0.2 \text{ s}$$

64 (c) The induced emf in the coil is

$$e = -L\left(\frac{\Delta I}{\Delta t}\right)$$
$$= -L\left(\frac{I_2 - I_1}{\Delta t}\right)$$

$\Rightarrow$ $3.20 = L \times \frac{(10-2)}{0.1}$

$\therefore$ $L = 0.04$ H

65 (d) Applying Kirchhoff's voltage law from point P to Q,

$$V_P - 10 - IR - L\frac{dI}{dt} = V_Q$$

$\therefore$ $V_P - V_Q = 10 + IR + L\frac{dI}{dt}$ ...(i)

Current at $t = 2$ s,

$$I = (2 \times 2 + 3) = 7\text{A}$$

Rate of current at $t = 2$ s, $\frac{dI}{dt} = 2$A

From Eq (i), we get

$$V_P - V_Q = 10 + 7 \times 4 + 2 \times 2$$
$$= 42 \text{ V}$$

66 (a) The current induced for N turns in the coil is

$$e = -\frac{\Delta(N\phi)}{\Delta t} = -\frac{\Delta(MI)}{\Delta t}$$
$$= M \cdot \left(\frac{I_1 - I_2}{t_2 - t_1}\right) = \frac{MI}{t}$$

$\therefore$ The emf induced per unit turn in the coil is

$$\frac{e}{N} = \frac{MI}{Nt}$$

67 (b) The mutual inductance of the coil is

$$M = \frac{\mu_0 N_1 N_2 A}{l}$$

The induced emf in the coil is

$$e_2 = M\left(\frac{\Delta I}{\Delta t}\right)$$
$$= \left(\frac{\mu_0 N_1 N_2 A}{l}\right)\left(\frac{I_1 - I'_1}{\Delta t}\right)$$
$$= \left(\frac{4\pi \times 10^{-7} \times 2000 \times 300 \times 1.2 \times 10^{-3}}{0.3}\right) \times \frac{[2-(-2)]}{0.25}$$

$\approx 48 \times 10^{-3}$ V $= 48$ mV

68 (*d*) The emf across inductor is

$$e_L = \left|L\frac{dI}{dt}\right| = |5 \times (-2)| = 10 \text{ V}$$

The equivalent circuit can be redrawn is

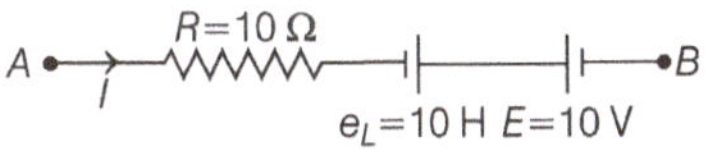

Applying Kirchhoff's law from point A to B,

$$V_A - IR + e_L - E = V_B$$

$$\Rightarrow V_A - V_B = IR - e_L + E$$

$$= 2 \times 10 - 10 + 10$$

$$= 20 \text{ V}$$

69 (*a*) The self-inductance of a coil is

$$L = \frac{N\phi}{I} = \frac{NBA}{I} = \frac{N}{I} \cdot \frac{\mu_0 IN}{2r} \cdot \pi r^2$$

$$= \frac{\mu_0 \pi N^2 r}{2}$$

$\therefore \quad L \propto N^2 r$

$$N_1 = 1, N_2 = 2, r_1 = r, r_2 = \frac{r}{2}, L_1 = L$$

$$\therefore \frac{L_2}{L_1} = \left(\frac{N_2}{N_1}\right)^2 \cdot \left(\frac{r_2}{r_1}\right) = (2)^2 \times \left(\frac{1}{2}\right)$$

$\therefore \; L_2 = 2L_1 = 2L$

73 (*a*) As, $\phi_B = M_{BA} I_A$

$$M_{BA} = \frac{\phi_B}{I_A} = \frac{10^{-2}}{2} = 5 \times 10^{-3} \text{ H}$$

When $I_B = 1$ A, $\phi_A = M_{AB} I_B$

$$= (5 \times 10^{-3} \text{ H}) (1 \text{ A})$$

$$= 5 \times 10^{-3} \text{ Wb}$$

74 (*a*) Magnetic flux linked with coil A,

$$\phi_A = BA = B \cdot \pi r^2$$

$$\Rightarrow \quad \phi_A = \frac{\mu_0 I}{2R} \cdot \pi r^2$$

$$\therefore \quad \phi_A = MI$$

$$\Rightarrow \quad M = \frac{\phi_A}{I} = \frac{\frac{\mu_0 I \cdot \pi r^2}{2R}}{I} = \frac{\mu_0 \pi r^2}{2R}$$

75 (*b*)

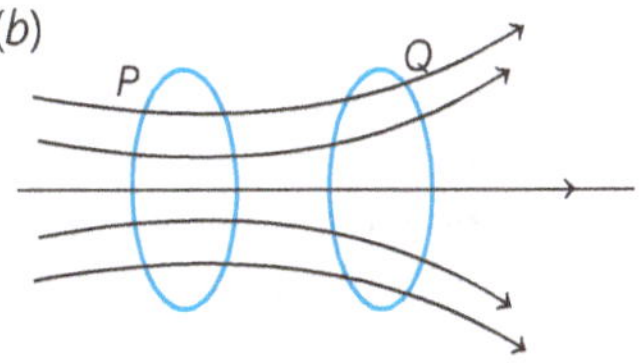

$$\therefore \quad M_{PQ} = M_{QP}$$

$$\Rightarrow \quad \frac{N_P \phi_{PQ}}{I_Q} = \frac{N_Q \phi_{QP}}{I_P}$$

$$\phi_{PQ} = \frac{I_Q \cdot \phi_{QP}}{I_P} = \frac{2}{3} \times 10^{-3}$$

$$= 0.667 \times 10^{-3}$$

$$= 6.67 \times 10^{-4} \text{ Wb}$$

77 (*c*) Mutual inductance for a coaxial solenoid of radii r_1 and r_2 and number of turns n_1 and n_2 respectively is given as,

$M = \mu_0 n_1 n_2 \, \pi r_1^2 \, l$ (for internal coil of radius r_1)

Self-inductance for the internal coil, $L = \mu_0 n_1^2 \pi r_1^2 l$

$$\therefore \quad \frac{M}{L} = \frac{n_1 n_2}{n_1^2} = \frac{n_2}{n_1}$$

78 (*b*) When coil is open, $\phi = 0$.

$$\phi \propto i \quad \Rightarrow \quad \phi = Li$$

where, L is proportionality constant known as self-inductance.

$$\therefore \quad L = \frac{\phi}{i} = 0$$

Again, since $i = 0$, hence

$$R = \frac{V}{i} = \frac{V}{0} = \infty$$

79 (*b*) The emf induced in the coil is given by

$$\varepsilon = -L\frac{dI}{dt}$$

$$\therefore \quad |\varepsilon| = 2 \times 10^{-3} \times 20 \times 10^{-3} \text{ V}$$

$$= 40 \, \mu\text{V}$$

80 (*a*) $\therefore$ Induced emf in inductor is

$$|\varepsilon| = L\frac{dI}{dt} = 10 \times \frac{2}{1 \times 10^{-3}}$$

$$= 2 \times 10^4 \text{ V}$$

81 (*d*) The emf induced in a coil is given by, $\varepsilon = -L\dfrac{\Delta i}{\Delta t}$

$$\therefore \quad \varepsilon = -\frac{60 \times 10^{-3} \times 1}{0.2} = -0.3 \text{ V}$$

Induced current,

$$i = \frac{|\varepsilon|}{R} = \frac{0.3}{3} = 0.1 \text{ A}$$

82 (*c*) Self-inductance of a coil is given by the relation

$$L = \mu_0 n^2 A \cdot l$$

$\therefore$ Area of equilateral triangle,

$$A = \frac{\sqrt{3}}{4} a^2$$

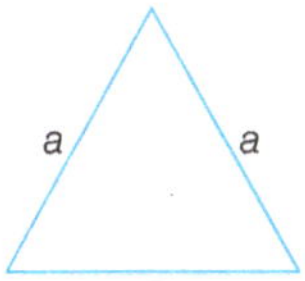

$\therefore$ Self-inductance,

$$L = \mu_0 n^2 \left[\frac{\sqrt{3}}{4} a^2\right] \cdot l$$

Here, $l = 3a \times N$

$$\therefore \quad L = \mu_0 n^2 \left[\frac{\sqrt{3}}{4} a^2\right] \times 3aN \text{ or } L \propto a^3$$

Then, $a' = 3a$

or $L' = 27L$

83 (*c*) Flux through the solenoid is

$$\phi = \mu_r \mu_0 \frac{N^2}{l} AI = \frac{\mu_r \mu_0 N^2 \pi r^2 I}{l}$$

$$\phi = 600 \times 4\pi \times 10^{-7} \times 50 \times 50 \times \pi \times \frac{(7.5 \times 10^{-3})^2 \times 3}{6 \times 10^{-1}}$$

$$= 1.66 \text{ mWb}$$

84 (*d*) Emf produced in first coil is negative and the emf produced in second coil is positive. The net inductance is

$$L = -L_1 + L_2$$

$$\therefore \quad L = -\frac{\phi}{I} + \frac{\phi}{I} \Rightarrow L = 0$$

86 (*a*) $E = \frac{1}{2} LI^2$

$$\therefore \quad \Delta E = E_2 - E_1 = \frac{1}{2} LI_2^2 - \frac{1}{2} LI_1^2 \quad \text{...(i)}$$

Now, induced emf in a coil is

$$\varepsilon = L\frac{dI}{dt}$$

Here, $\varepsilon = 25$ V,

$$dI = I_2 - I_1 = (25 - 10) = 15 \text{ A}$$

and $dt = 1$ s

$$\Rightarrow \; 25 = L \times \frac{15}{1} \text{ or } L = \frac{25}{15} = 5/3 \text{ H}$$

Putting values of L, I_1 and I_2 in Eq. (i), we get

$$\Delta E = \frac{1}{2} \times \frac{5}{3} \times [25^2 - 10^2]$$
$$= \frac{1}{2} \times \frac{5}{3} \times 525$$
$$\Rightarrow \quad \Delta E = 437.5 \text{ J}$$

87 (*b*) The magnetic energy is

$$U_B = \frac{1}{2} LI^2$$

Since, for a solenoid, $B = \mu_0 nI$ and $L = \mu_0 n^2 Al$

$$\Rightarrow \quad U_B = \frac{1}{2}(\mu_0 n^2 Al)\left(\frac{B}{\mu_0 n}\right)^2$$
$$= \frac{1}{2\mu_0} B^2 Al$$

90 (*d*) Emf induced in the coil,

$$\varepsilon = 200 \sin 100\pi t$$

Comparing with standard equation

$\varepsilon = \varepsilon_0 \sin \omega t$, we get

$$\varepsilon_0 = 200, \omega = 100\pi$$

$\because BAN\omega = \varepsilon_0$

$$\therefore \quad B = \frac{\varepsilon_0}{AN\omega}$$
$$= \frac{200}{(0.25 \times 0.25) \times 1000 \times 100\ \pi}$$
$$= 0.01 \text{ T}$$

91 (*c*) Since, coil rotates half revolution per second, hence frequency of rotation of coil,

$$\nu = \frac{1/2}{1} = \frac{1}{2} = 0.5 \text{ Hz}$$

Emf induced,

$$\varepsilon = \varepsilon_0 \sin \omega t = NBA\omega \sin \omega t$$
$$\varepsilon_{max} = \varepsilon_0 = NBA\omega \quad (\because \sin \omega t = 1)$$
$$= NBA(2\pi\nu) \quad [\because \omega = 2\pi\nu]$$
$$= 100 \times 0.01 \times 0.10 \times 2 \times 3.14 \times 0.5$$
$$= 0.314 \text{ V}$$

The maximum voltage is 0.314 V.

92 (*d*) Induced emf,

$$\varepsilon = \varepsilon_0 \sin \omega t = NBA\omega \sin \omega t$$

Initially,

Peak value, $\varepsilon_0 = N_1 BA_1 \omega = 100$ V

Here,

$$2\pi r_1 \times 100 = 2\pi r_2 \times N_2 \quad \text{(given)}$$
$$N_2 = \frac{r_1 \times 100}{r_2} = \frac{1 \times 100}{2} = 50 = \frac{N_1}{2}$$

Finally, $\varepsilon_0 = N_2 BA_2 \omega$

$$\Rightarrow \quad \varepsilon_0 = \frac{N_1}{2} \times B \times 4A_1 \times \omega$$
$$= 2 \times \text{(initial emf)}$$
$$= 2 \times 100 = 200 \text{ V}$$
$$(\because r_2 = 2r_1 \Rightarrow A_2 = 4A_1)$$

93 (*c*) Alternating emf induced is

$$\varepsilon = \varepsilon_0 \sin \omega t$$

Maximum current,

$$i_0 = \frac{\varepsilon_0}{R} = \frac{NBA\omega}{R}$$
$$A = \pi r^2 = \pi(0.3)^2 \text{ m}^2,$$
$$R = \pi^2 \ \Omega$$
$$\nu = 200 \text{ rpm} = \frac{200}{60} \text{ s}^{-1}$$

and $\omega = 2\pi\left(\frac{200}{60}\right)$

$$\therefore \quad i_0 = \frac{1 \times 10^{-2} \times \pi(0.3)^2 \times 2\pi \times 200}{60 \times \pi^2}$$
$$= 6 \times 10^{-3} \text{ A} = 6 \text{ mA}$$

94 (*d*) If ε is the emf induced in the coil, then

$$\varepsilon = -\frac{d\phi}{dt} = -\frac{d}{dt}(NAB \cos \omega t)$$
$$\Rightarrow \quad \varepsilon = -NAB\frac{d}{dt}(\cos \omega t)$$
$$= -NAB(-\sin \omega t)\,\omega$$
$$\Rightarrow \quad \varepsilon = NAB\,\omega \sin \omega t$$
$$\therefore \quad \varepsilon_{max} = \varepsilon_0 = NAB\omega \times 1$$

Therefore, ε would be maximum, hence current is maximum (as $i_0 = \varepsilon_0 / R$) when $\theta = 90°$, i.e., normal to plane of coil is perpendicular to the field or plane of coil is parallel to magnetic field.

Assertion and Reason Questions

1 (*b*) When the circular conducting coil is parallel to magnetic field, then $\theta = 90°$

$\therefore$ Magnetic flux,

$$\phi = BA \cos \theta = BA \cos 0° = 0$$

Also, $\phi \propto A$, So, magnetic flux can be changed by changing area of a coil.

Therefore, Assertion and Reason are correct but Reason is not the correct explanation of Assertion.

2 (*c*) Emf will always induces whenever, there is change in magnetic flux. The current will induced only in closed loop. Therefore, Assertion is correct but Reason is incorrect.

3 (*c*) Presence of magnetic flux cannot produce current.

Therefore, Assertion is correct but Reason is incorrect.

4 (*d*) Lenz's law is based on conservation of energy and induced emf always opposes the cause of its production, i.e. change in magnetic flux.

Therefore, Assertion is incorrect but Reason is correct.

7 (*c*) The self-inductance of a solenoid is given by

$$L = \frac{\mu_0 N^2 A}{l}$$

Number of turns, N = constant

$$L \propto \frac{1}{l}$$

Also, induced emf, $e = L \cdot \frac{dI}{dt}$

$\therefore$ The slope of induced emf e *versus* rate of change of current $\left(\frac{dI}{dt}\right)$ gives the self-inductance L.

Therefore, Assertion is correct but Reason is incorrect.

8 (*a*) If the inner solenoid is much shorter than (and placed well inside) the outer solenoid, then the flux linkage $N_1\phi_1$ can still be calculated. It is because the inner solenoid is effectively immersed in a uniform magnetic field due to the outer solenoid.

Therefore, Assertion and Reason are correct and Reason is the correct explanation of Assertion.

9 (*a*) In a system of co-axial solenoids, it is extremely difficult to calculate the flux linkage with the outer solenoid when current flows in inner solenoid.

It is because the magnetic field due to the inner solenoid would vary across the length as well as cross-section of the outer solenoid (when inner solenoid is smaller in length and radius).

Therefore, Assertion and Reason are correct and Reason is the correct explanation of Assertion.

10 (*a*) The self-induced emf is also called the back emf as it opposes any change in the current in a circuit. Physically, the self-inductance plays the role of inertia. It is an electromagnetic analogue of mass in mechanics.

Therefore, Assertion and Reason are correct and Reason is the correct explanation of Assertion.

Statement Based Questions

2 (*c*) When the plane of the coil is parallel to magnetic field, then $\theta = 90°$.

$\therefore$ Flux, $\phi = B \cdot A\cos\theta$

$= BA\cos 90° = 0$

The flux can be changed by changing the magnetic field B.

Therefore, Statement I is false but Statement II is true.

3 (*b*) Induced emf does not depend on the nature of the coil. Hence, the induced emf in both copper and aluminium coil is same.

Therefore, Statement I is true but Statement II is false.

7 (*a*) An AC generator is based on principle of electromagnetic induction. The current produces by an AC generator changes both in magnitude and direction periodically.

Therefore, Statement I and Statement II are false.

8 (*c*) Mutual inductance between a pair of coils depend on the relative orientation of coils. Therefore, Statement I is false but Statement II is true.

Matching Type Questions

1 (*b*) At $t = 0.01\,s$,

$$|e| = \frac{\Delta\phi_B}{\Delta t} = \frac{8\times10^{-3}}{0.01} = 0.8\,V$$

$$i = \frac{|e|}{R} = \frac{0.8}{5} = 0.16\,A$$

$$\Delta q = i\Delta t = 0.16 \times 0.01$$

$$= 1.6\times10^{-3}C$$

$$= 1.6\,mC$$

At $t = 0.02\,s$,

$$|e| = \frac{8\times10^{-3}}{0.02} = 0.4\,V;$$

$$i = \frac{|e|}{R} = 0.08\,A$$

$$\Delta q = i\Delta t = 0.08 \times 0.03$$

$$= 2.4\times10^{-3}\,C = 2.4\,mC$$

2 (*b*) Induced emf, $e = Bvl$

Induced current, $I = e/R = Bvl/R$

Force on conductor PQ,

$$F = IBl\sin 90° = \frac{Blv}{R}\cdot lB = \frac{B^2l^2v}{R}$$

Power delivered, $P = F\cdot v = \dfrac{B^2l^2v^2}{R}$

Numerical Type Questions

1 (4) $\therefore\ m = \tan\theta = \dfrac{10}{5} = 2$

$\because\quad B = mt \Rightarrow B = 2t$

$\therefore\quad e = \dfrac{d\phi}{dt}$

$$e = \frac{d(BA)}{dt} = \frac{A(dB)}{dt}$$

$$e = \frac{2d\,(2t)}{dt} = 2\times 2$$

$\Rightarrow\quad e = 4\,mV$

2 (60) $\Delta Q = \dfrac{\Delta\phi}{R} = \dfrac{2NBA}{R}$

$$= \frac{2\times200\times1.5\times24\times10^{-4}}{24}$$

$$= 6\times10^{-2}C = 60\,mC$$

3 (16) $\therefore$ Magnetic flux, $\phi = \dfrac{2}{3}(4 - t^2)$

$$\therefore\quad e = -\frac{d\phi}{dt} = \frac{-d}{dt}\left[\frac{2}{3}(4-t^2)\right]$$

$$= -\frac{2}{3}\times(-2t) = \frac{4}{3}t$$

Heat produced during $t = 0$ to $t = 2\,s$,

$$H = \int_0^2 \frac{e^2}{R}dt = \int_0^2 \frac{1}{8}\left(\frac{4}{3}t\right)^2 dt$$

$$= \frac{2}{9}\times\frac{8}{3} = \frac{16}{27}\,J$$

$\therefore\quad x = 16$

4 (12) As per question, flux through the loop increase according to

$$\phi_B(t) = 10t^2 + 20t \qquad \text{...(i)}$$

Induced emf, $|e| = \dfrac{d\phi}{dt}$

$$= (20t + 20)\,mV$$

Current, $i = \dfrac{|e|}{R} \Rightarrow i = \dfrac{20t+20}{10}$

$\Rightarrow i = (2t + 2)\,mA$

$\therefore$ Current, $i = (2\times5 + 2)\,mA$

$\Rightarrow\quad i = 12\,mA$

5 (50) Magnetic field, $B = 0.2\,T$

Expansion in the radius of loop

$$\left(\frac{dr}{dt}\right) = 2\,mm/s = 2\times10^{-3}\,m/s$$

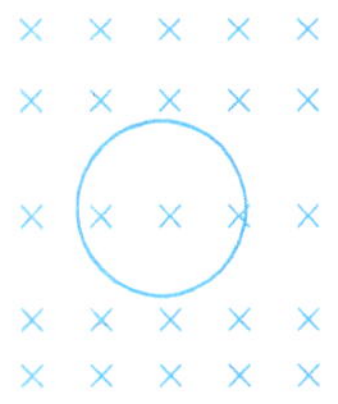

Thus, $\dfrac{dA}{dt} = 2\pi r\dfrac{dr}{dt}$

emf induced, $\varepsilon = \left(-\dfrac{d\phi}{dt}\right) = \dfrac{BdA}{dt}$

$$= B\,2\pi r\frac{dr}{dt}$$

$|\varepsilon|_r \simeq 2\times10^{-2}$

$$= 0.2\times2\times\pi\times2\times10^{-2}\times2\times10^{-3}$$

$$= 50\,\mu V$$

6 (400)

Induced emf, $e = \dfrac{\Delta\phi}{\Delta t} = L\dfrac{dI}{dt}$

$$e = I\cdot\frac{\Delta V}{R\cdot\Delta t} = \frac{30\times10^{-3}\times20\times10^{6}}{15\times100}$$

$\Rightarrow\quad e = 400\,V$

7 (18) Force on rod is given by

$$F = \frac{B^2l^2v}{R}$$

Substituting values, we get

$$F = \frac{(0.15)^2(1^2) \times 8}{10}$$

$$= 18 \times 10^{-3}\ \text{N}$$

8 (75) Given, angular speed of metallic rod,

$$\omega = 2\pi \times \frac{180}{60}\ \text{rad/s} = 6\pi\ \text{rad/s}$$

The emf induced between the centre and the ring,

$$e = \frac{1}{2}B\omega l^2 = \frac{1}{2} \times 0.2 \times 6\pi \times (0.2)^2$$

$$= 0.075\ \text{V} = 75\ \text{mV}$$

9 (400) Given, $a = 1000$ cm, $b = 1$ cm

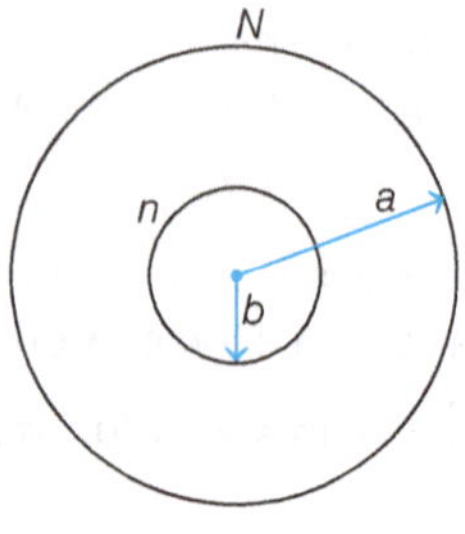

$b << a$

We will take larger coil as primary

$$B = \frac{\mu_0 i_p N}{2a}$$

Flux passing through secondary coil,

$$\phi_s = BA = \frac{\mu_0 i_p N}{2a} \times \pi b^2 \times n$$

Mutual inductance,

$$M = \frac{\phi_s}{i_p}$$

$$M = \frac{\mu_0 N n \pi b^2}{2a}$$

$$\Rightarrow M = \frac{4\pi \times 10^{-7} \times 20 \times 100 \times \pi \times 1 \times 10^{-4}}{2 \times 1000 \times 10^{-2}}$$

$$= 4\pi^2 \times 10^{-9}$$

or $M = 400 \times 10^{-10}$ H (using $\pi^2 = 10$)

10 (28) $\Rightarrow V_A - IR - \frac{Ldl}{dt} - 10 = V_B$

$$\Rightarrow \quad V_A - V_B = 2 \times 12 + 3(-2) + 10$$

$$\Rightarrow \quad V_A - V_B = 24 - 6 + 10$$

$$\Rightarrow \quad V_A - V_B = 28\ \text{V}$$

$$\Rightarrow \quad \Delta V = 28\ \text{V}$$

NCERT Exemplar Questions

1 (c) $A = L^2\hat{\mathbf{k}}$

$$\phi = \mathbf{B} \cdot \mathbf{A} = B_0(2\hat{\mathbf{i}} + 3\hat{\mathbf{j}} + 4\hat{\mathbf{k}}) \cdot L^2\hat{\mathbf{k}}$$

$$= 4B_0L^2\text{Wb}$$

2 (b)

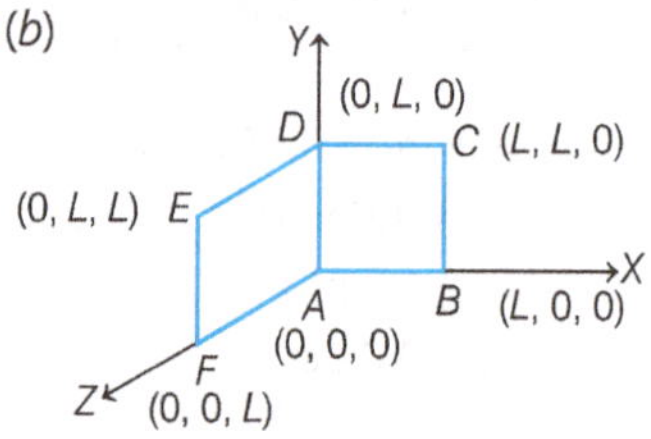

$$\phi = \mathbf{B} \cdot \mathbf{A}$$

$$\mathbf{A}_1 = L^2\hat{\mathbf{k}}$$

$$\mathbf{A}_2 = L^2\hat{\mathbf{i}}$$

$\therefore$ Total area, $\mathbf{A} = \mathbf{A}_1 + \mathbf{A}_2$

$$= L^2\hat{\mathbf{k}} + L^2\hat{\mathbf{i}}$$

and $\mathbf{B} = B_0(\hat{\mathbf{i}} + \hat{\mathbf{k}})$ T

Now, $\phi = \mathbf{B} \cdot \mathbf{A}$

$$= B_0(\hat{\mathbf{i}} + \hat{\mathbf{k}}) \cdot (L^2\hat{\mathbf{k}} + L^2\hat{\mathbf{i}})$$

$$= 2B_0L^2\ \text{Wb}$$

3 (b) When cylindrical bar magnet is rotated about its axis as shown below, no change in flux linked with the circuit takes place consequently, no emf induces and hence no current flows through the ammeter A.

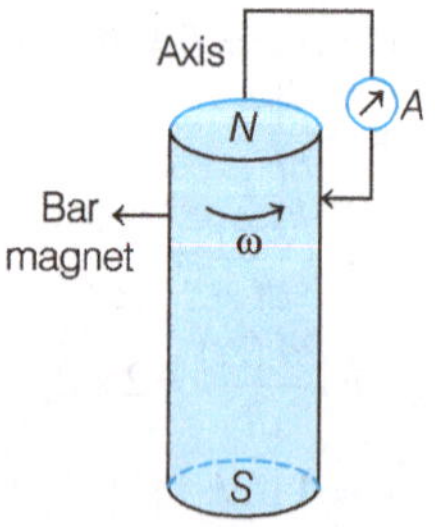

4 (d) When the A stops moving, the current in B become zero, it possible only if the current in A is constant in the counter-clockwise direction.
If the current in A would be variable, there must be an induced emf (current) in B even, if the A stops moving.

5 (a) When the current in B (at $t = 0$) is counter- clockwise, then B is equivalent to north pole of magnet and magnetic field lines are emanating towards coil A.
When coil A is rotating at $t = 0$, a constant current in clockwise direction (by Lenz's law) flow in A due to constant change in flux.

6 (b) The self-inductance of a long solenoid of cross-sectional area A and length l, having n turns per unit length, filled the inside of the solenoid with a material of relative permeability (e.g. soft iron, which has a high value of relative permeability) is given by

$$L = \mu_r \mu_0 n^2 Al$$

where, $\quad n = N / l$

$$\Rightarrow \quad L = \frac{\mu_r \mu_0 N^2 A}{l}$$

So, the self-inductance L increases as l decreases and A increases.

Past Exams' Questions

1 (a) The direction of induced current is always such that it opposes the cause which created it. For solenoid-1, the magnet is moving away. Thus, near the B-point, S-pole will be generated.

Thus, the current in solenoid-1 will be from A to B.
Similarly, the current in the solenoid-2 will be from D to C.

2 (b) If the sheet is magnetic in nature, then the flux will be linked through the sheet and a small amount of force will be needed to held the sheet. The pole will apply a force on the sheet.

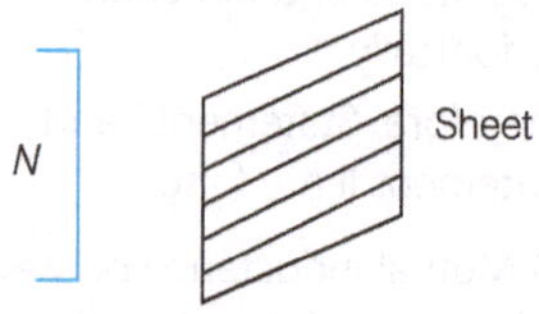

Also, to move the sheet towards or away from the magnetic pole, a force will be required.

If sheet is non-magnetic, then no force will be required either to hold it or move it when the sheet is non-conducting.

3 (c) Stored magnetic energy,

$$U = \frac{1}{2}LI^2$$

$$\therefore\ U = \frac{1}{2} \times 4 \times 10^{-6} \times 2^2 = 8 \times 10^{-6}\text{J}$$

$$= 8\,\mu\text{J}$$

4 (a) Side of square loop, $a = 1$ m

∴Area of square loop, $A = 1\ \text{m}^2$

Resistance of square loop, $R = 1\Omega$

Magnetic field, $B = 0.5$T

∴Magnetic flux passing through the loop,

$$\phi = BA\cos\theta = 0.5 \times 1 \times \cos 0°$$

$$= 0.5 \text{ Wb}$$

5 (d) Since, both conducting circular loops are in same plane and their centres are coinciding.

Hence, magnetic flux, $\phi = Mi$ ...(i)

Here, M is the mutual inductance.

Also, the magnetic flux, $\phi = BA$

Here, B is the magnetic field and ($A = \pi R_2^2$) is the area of the inner circular loop. If the current passing through the outer loop is i, then the magnetic field,

$$B = \frac{\mu_0 i}{2R_1}$$

Magnetic flux, $\phi = BA$

$$\Rightarrow \quad \phi = \frac{\mu_0 i}{2R_1}\pi R_2^2 \quad \text{...(ii)}$$

Comparing Eqs. (i) and (ii), we get

$$M = \frac{\mu_0}{2R_1}\pi R_2^2$$

Thus, the mutual inductance is directly proportional to the $\frac{R_2^2}{R_1}$.

6 (d) Magnetic flux linked with coil

$\phi = (5t^2 + 3t + 16)$ Wb

Magnitude of induced emf,

$$e = \left|-\frac{d\phi}{dt}\right| = \frac{d}{dt}(5t^2 + 3t + 16)$$

$$= 10t + 3$$

For $t = 3$ s,

$$e_3 = 10 \times 3 + 3 = 33 \text{ V}$$

For $t = 4$ s,

$$e_4 = 10 \times 4 + 3 = 43 \text{ V}$$

∴Induced emf in coil at the fourth second is given as

$$e = e_4 - e_3 = 43 - 33 = 10 \text{ V}$$

7 (b) Induced emf is given by

$$e = \frac{1}{2}B\omega r^2 \quad \text{...(i)}$$

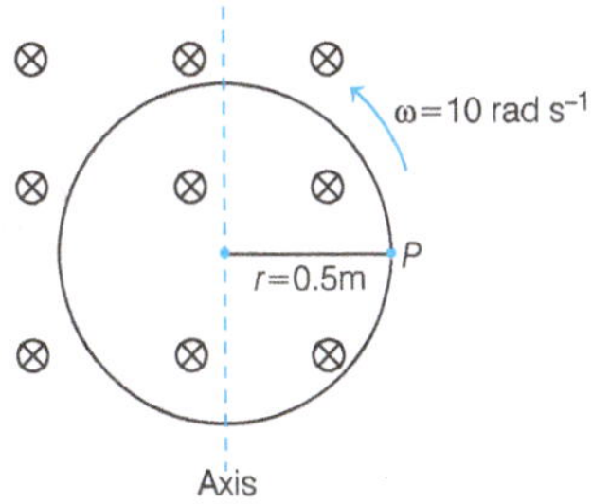

Substituting these values in Eq. (i), we get

$$e = \frac{1}{2} \times 0.1 \times 10 \times (0.5)^2$$

$$= \frac{1}{8} = 0.125 \text{ V}$$

8 (d) As, the expression for energy stored in an inductor is given as

$$U = \frac{1}{2}LI_0^2$$

Substituting the given values in above equation., we get

$$(25 \times 10^{-3}) = \frac{1}{2} \times L \times (60 \times 10^{-3})^2$$

$$\Rightarrow L = \frac{2 \times 25 \times 10^{-3}}{3600 \times 10^{-6}} = \frac{500}{36}$$

or $L = 13.89$ H

9 (c) Given, diameter of solenoid, $2r = 0.1$ m (r is radius)

Number of turns, $N = 2 \times 10^4$ turns per metre

Number of turns of coil = 100 turns

Radius = 0.01 m

Resistance of the coil = $10\,\pi^2\,\Omega$

$$\therefore \quad \varepsilon = -N\frac{d\phi}{dt}$$

$$\left|\frac{\varepsilon}{R}\right| = \frac{N}{R}\frac{d\phi}{dt}$$

$$dq = \frac{N}{R}d\phi$$

$$\Delta q = \frac{N\,(\Delta\phi)}{R}$$

$$\Delta q = \frac{(\Delta\phi_{\text{total}})}{R}$$

$$= \frac{NBA}{R} = \frac{\mu_0 ni\pi r^2}{R}$$

Putting above values, we get

$$\Delta q = \frac{4\pi \times 10^{-7} \times 100 \times \pi\,(0.001)^2}{10\pi^2}$$

$$= 32\,\mu\text{C}$$

10 (c) Induced emf in the region is given by $|e| = \frac{d\phi}{dt}$

where, $\phi = BA = \pi r^2 B$

$$\Rightarrow \quad \frac{d\phi}{dt} = -\pi r^2\frac{dB}{dt}$$

Rate of change of magnetic flux associated with loop 1

$$e_1 = -\frac{d\phi_1}{dt} = -\pi r^2\frac{dB}{dt}$$

Similarly, e_2 = emf associated with loop 2 $= -\frac{d\phi_2}{dt} = 0$ $\quad (\because \phi_2 = 0)$

11 (c) First current develops in direction of *abcd* but when electron moves away, then magnetic field inside loop decreases and current changes its direction.

12 (b) We know that, emf, $\varepsilon = -\frac{LdI}{dt}$

$$\Rightarrow \quad |\varepsilon| = \frac{LdI}{dt} \Rightarrow |\varepsilon| = L\frac{\Delta I}{\Delta t}$$

$$\Rightarrow \quad 0.1 = L\frac{[2-(-2)]}{0.2}$$

$$\Rightarrow \quad L = \frac{0.1 \times 0.2}{4}$$

$$= 5 \times 10^{-3} \text{ H} = 5 \text{ mH}$$

13 (d) $E_{\text{avg}} = \frac{\Delta\phi}{\Delta t} = \frac{BA\cos\theta}{10}$

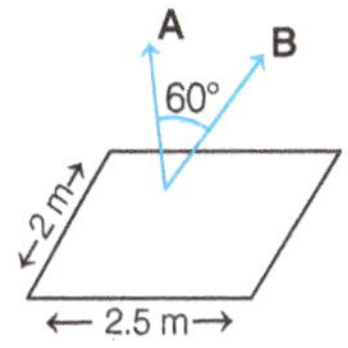

$$= 4 \times 2 \times \frac{5}{2} \times \frac{\cos 60^\circ}{10}$$

$$= 4 \times 5 \times \frac{1}{10 \times 2}$$

$$= 1\text{ V} = 1\text{ V}$$

14 (*d*) In 0.5 s, magnetic field of 0.5 T becomes zero.

So, rate of decay of magnetic field,

$$\frac{\Delta B}{\Delta t} = \frac{0 - 0.5}{0.5} = -1\text{ T/s}$$

(Negative sign shows field is reducing)

Hence, magnetic field at 0.25 s will be

$$\frac{\Delta B}{0.25} = -1\text{ T/s} \Rightarrow \frac{B_2 - B_1}{0.25} = -1$$

or $B_2 = 0.5 - 0.25 = 0.25$ T

So, magnitude of induced emf in coil at $t = 0.25$ s will be

$$\varepsilon = \frac{d}{dt}\phi = \left(\frac{dB}{dt}\right) \cdot A = \frac{\Delta B}{\Delta t} \cdot \pi r^2$$

$$= \frac{0.25}{0.25} \times \pi \times \left(\frac{10}{\sqrt{\pi}} \times 10^{-2}\right)^2$$

$$= 10^{-2}\text{ V} = 10 \times 10^{-3}\text{ V}$$

$$\Rightarrow \quad \varepsilon = 10\text{ mV}$$

15 (*a*) ∴ Induced emf,

$$e = \frac{d\phi}{dt} = 15t^2 + 8t + 2$$

At $t = 2$ s,

$$e = (15 \times 2^2) + (8 \times 2) + 2 = 78\text{ V}$$

We have, $e = IR$

∴ Induced current,

$$I = \frac{e}{R} = \frac{78}{5} = 15.6\text{ A}$$

16 (*c*) Considering this, it can be concluded that I_1 is the clockwise direction and I_2 is in the anti-clockwise direction and the effective circuit with the directions of I_1 and I_2 can be shown as follows.

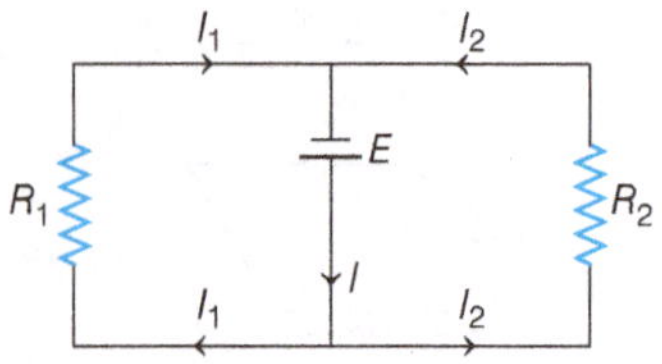

17 (*c*) As the rectangular conductor moves in field area, so flux is increasing up to $x = b$, then flux is generated on return journey from $x = b$ to $x = 0$. The flux is shown by plot *A* of the graph.

As emf, $e = -\frac{d\phi}{dt}$, which is shown by curve *B*.

and power dissipated, $P = VI$ which is shown by curve *C*.

18 (*a*) As the induced current is anti-clockwise means it forms *N*-pole on outward face.

According to the Lenz's law, the induced current always opposes the nature by which it is produced.

Hence, induced current is in the outward direction, so the strength of *N*-pole is maintained as it is decreasing.

Skill Boosters

1 (*d*)

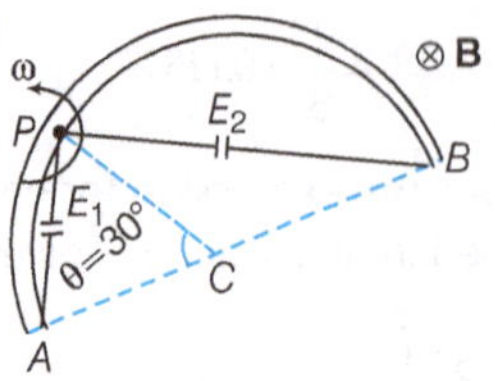

Let emf's induced in lengths *PA* and *PB* are E_1 and E_2, then potential difference between points *A* and *C* is $|E_1 - E_2|$.

Now, effective lengths of wires are

$$l_1 = AP = 2R \sin \frac{\theta}{2}$$

$$\text{and } l_2 = BP = 2R \sin\left(\frac{\pi}{2} - \frac{\theta}{2}\right)$$

$$= 2R \cos \frac{\theta}{2}$$

$$\text{So,} \quad |E_1 - E_2| = \frac{1}{2} B\omega \left(4R^2 \sin^2 \frac{\theta}{2} - 4R^2 \cos^2 \frac{\theta}{2}\right)$$

$$= 2B\omega R^2 \left(\sin^2 \frac{\theta}{2} - \cos^2 \frac{\theta}{2}\right)$$

$$= 2B\omega R^2 \cos\theta$$

$$= 2B\omega R^2 \times \frac{1}{2} = B\omega R^2$$

2 (*a*) Induced emf

$$\int_a^b BV\,dx = \int_a^b \frac{\mu_0 I}{2\pi x} \times v\,dx$$

Induced emf,

$$E = \frac{\mu_0 I v}{2\pi} \ln\left(\frac{b}{a}\right) \quad \text{... (i)}$$

Power dissipated

$$= \frac{E^2}{R}$$

Also, power $= Fv$

$$\Rightarrow \quad F = \frac{E^2}{vR}$$

Putting the value of *E* from Eq. (i), we get

$$\Rightarrow \quad F = \frac{1}{vR}\left[\frac{\mu_0 I v}{2\pi} \ln\left(\frac{b}{a}\right)\right]^2$$

3 (*c*) $L = \frac{\mu_0 N^2 A}{l} = \mu_0 n^2 A l = \frac{\mu_0 A l}{d^2}$

$$\Rightarrow l = \frac{Ld^2}{\mu_0 \pi r^2}$$

$$= \frac{1 \times (0.81 \times 10^{-3})^2}{4\pi \times 10^{-7} \times \pi \times (0.06)^2} \approx 46\text{ m}$$

So, a 50 m long tube is most suitable.

4 (*a*) The current of the battery at any instant,

$$I = \frac{E}{R}$$

The magnetic force due to this current,

$$F_B = IBl = \frac{EBl}{R}$$

This force accelerates the rod from rest. Then, motional emf developed in the rod is Blv.

So, induced current across the rod,

$$I_{\text{induced}} = \frac{Blv}{R}$$

The magnetic force due to induced current,

$$F_{\text{induced}} = I_{\text{induced}} \cdot Bl = \frac{B^2 l^2 v}{R}$$

Then, net force acting on a rod

$$\Rightarrow \quad F_B - F_{\text{induced}} = m\frac{dv}{dt}$$

$$\frac{EBl}{R} - \frac{B^2 l^2 v}{R} = m\frac{dv}{dt}$$

$$\int_0^v \frac{dv}{E - Blv} = \frac{Bl}{mR}\int_0^t dt$$

$$\frac{E - Blv}{E} = e^{-\frac{B^2l^2}{mR}t}$$

Speed of a rod, $v = \frac{E}{Bl}(1 - e^{-t/\tau})$,

where, $\tau = \frac{mR}{B^2l^2}$

5 (*a*) Magnetic field at side (1),

$$B_1 = B_0$$

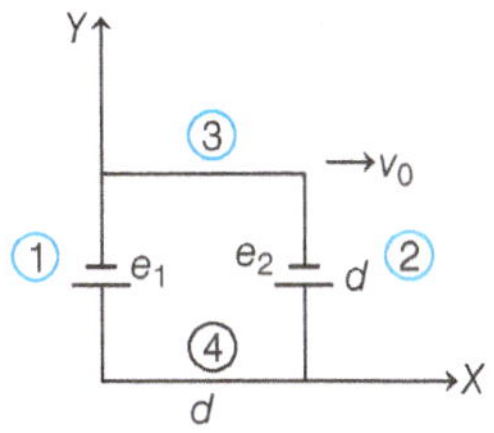

Induced emf in (1),

$$e_1 = B_0 v_0 d$$

Magnetic field at side (2),

$$B_2 = B_0\left(1 + \frac{d}{a}\right)$$

Induced emf in (2),

$$e_2 = B_0\left(1 + \frac{d}{a}\right)v_0 d$$

Induced emf in (3) and (4) will be zero.

Net emf, $e = e_2 - e_1 = \frac{B_0 v_0 d^2}{a}$

6 (*c*) Induced emf in loops *AEFD* and *EBCF* will be

$$\varepsilon_1 = \frac{d\phi_1}{dt} = A_1 \cdot \frac{dB}{dt}$$
$$= 1 \times 1 \times 1 = 1\text{ V}$$
$$\varepsilon_2 = A_2\frac{dB}{dt} = 0.5 \times 1 \times 1 = 0.5\text{ V}$$

ε_1 and ε_2 both are in anti-clockwise sense. Considering resistances of wire loops, we have

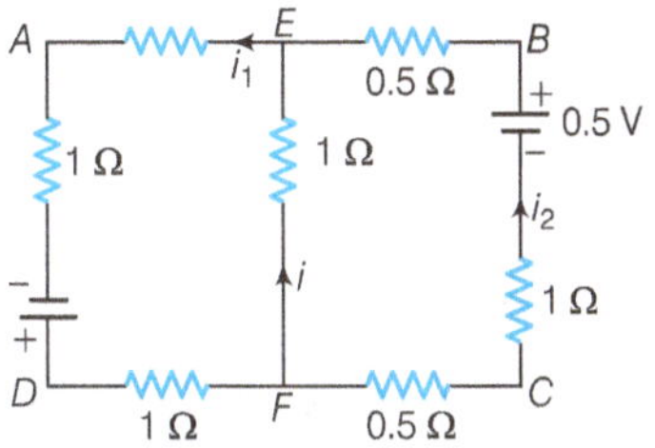

By using KVL, we have

$$i_1 = i + i_2 \quad \text{...(i)}$$
$$3i_1 + i = 1 \quad \text{...(ii)}$$
$$2i_2 - i = 0.5 \quad \text{...(iii)}$$

On solving these equations, we get

$$i = \frac{1}{22}\text{ A}$$

$\therefore \quad p = 2$

7 (*d*) Time taken to complete second half revolution

$$t_2 = \sqrt{\frac{4\pi}{\alpha}} - \sqrt{\frac{2\pi}{\alpha}}$$

We see that $t_2 < t_1$.

We can write induced emf as

$$e = (-1)^n\left[\frac{1}{2}BR^2\alpha t\right]$$

where, $n = 1, 2, 3, \ldots$ is the number of half revolutions completed by loop. Smaller time will be taken to complete the second half of revolution as compared to the previous half revolution.

8 (*d*) Magnetic field ⊗ passing from the closed loop is increasing. Therefore, from Lenz's law induced current will produce dot magnetic field. Hence, induced current is anti-clockwise.

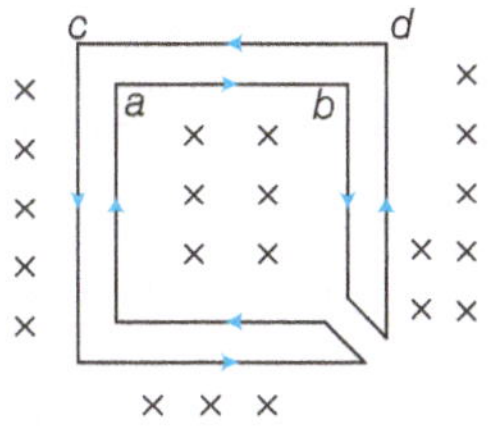

9 (*d*) Induced emf,

$$e = -\frac{d\phi}{dt}$$

For identical rings, induced emf will be same.

But current will be different.

Given, $h_A > h_B$

Hence, $v_A > v_B$ (as $v^2 = 2gh$)

When $\rho_A < \rho_B$, $l_A > l_B \Rightarrow h_A > h_B$ is fulfilled only when $m_A = m_B$.

If $\rho_A < \rho_B$, then $l_A > l_B$ this can be fulfilled if $m_A \le m_B$.

10 (*b*) As some instant *t*, flux linked with a strip with coordinate *y* is

$$d\phi = Bldy = 4lt^2y\,dy$$

where, l = length of side of square loop.

So, total flux linked with the square loop is

$$\phi = \int_0^l d\phi = \int_0^l 4lt^2ydy = 2l^3t^2$$

Hence, induced emf in the loop is

$$\varepsilon = \frac{d\phi}{dt} = \frac{d}{dt}2l^3t^2 = 4l^3t$$

$\therefore$ ε at $t = 2.5$ s

$$= 8 \times 10^{-5}\text{ V clockwise}$$

07

Scan for Physics Through Concept Master Videos

Alternating Current

Topicwise No. of Ques asked in 5 Years (NEET)

Topics	No. of Questions				
	2024	2023	2022	2021	2020
AC Voltage Applied to a Resistor	–	–	1	–	1
AC Voltage Applied to a Series L-C-R circuit	1	2	1	2	–
Power in AC circuit : The power factor	–	–	–	–	1
Transformer	1	1	–	1	–

Special Type of Ques Asked In 5 Years (NEET)

Types	Years				
	2024	2023	2022	2021	2020
A-R	–	–	–	–	–
Statement Based	–	–	–	–	–
Matching	–	–	–	–	–

Last 5 Years Weigtage (NEET)

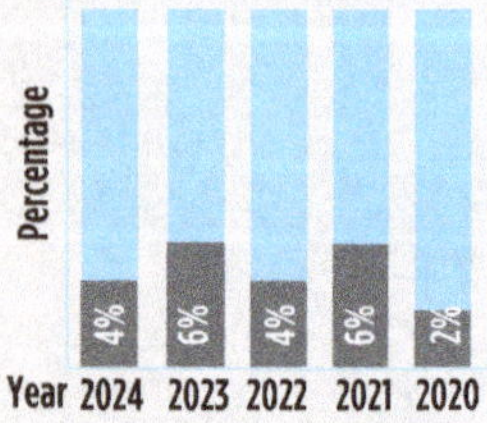

- In a circuit, when flow of electric charges changes continuously and their direction changes periodically, it is called **alternating current**.The corresponding voltage of alternating current is known as **alternating voltage** (AC voltage).
- **Direct current** is the current whose magnitude and direction do not changes with time.
- Alternating current is driven by alternating voltage. AC voltage is preferred over DC because AC voltage can be easily and efficiently converted from one voltage to the other by means of transformers.
- I-t graph of alternating current and direct current are given below.

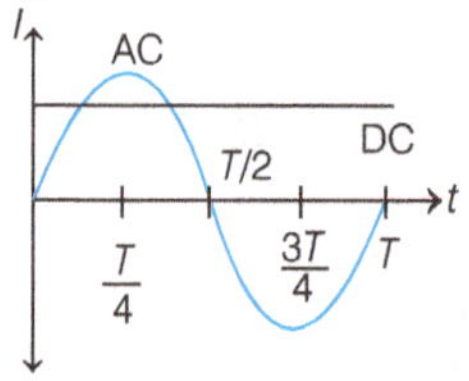

AC Voltage Applied to a Resistor

When an AC voltage source of potential difference $V = V_m \sin \omega t$, where V_m is the amplitude of the oscillating potential difference and ω is its angular frequency, is connected across a resistor R as shown in figure, then

(i) current in the circuit is $i = i_m \sin \omega t$, where $i_m = \dfrac{V_m}{R}$.

(ii) the voltage and current are in phase with each other.

- The sum of the instantaneous current values over one complete cycle is zero and the average current is also zero.
- The zero value of average current over a complete cycle does not mean that the average power consumed is zero.
- The **instantaneous power dissipated** in the resistor is

$$P_R = I^2R = I_m^2 R \sin^2 \omega t$$

- The **average power over a complete cycle** is

$$\bar{P}_R = < I_m^2 R \sin^2 \omega t > = \frac{1}{2} I_m^2 R = I_{rms}^2 R = \frac{V_{rms}^2}{R}$$

where, I_{rms} is a special value of current, which is called **root mean square current** and denoted as I_{rms}.

$$I_{rms} = I_m / \sqrt{2} = 0.707\, I_m$$

Similarly, $V_{rms} = V_m / \sqrt{2} = 0.707\, V_m$ **NEET 2022**

- The rms current (I_{rms}) is related to the peak current I_m as given in the following graph :

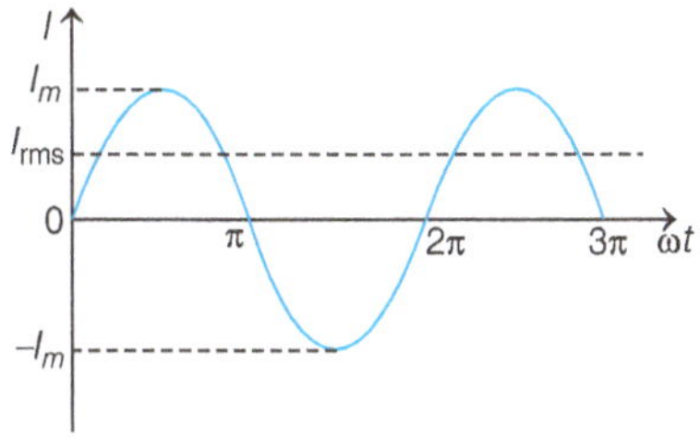

- The rms value of AC current is the equivalent to DC current that would produce the same average power loss as the alternating current.

Representation of AC Current and Voltage by Rotating Vectors Phasors

- To show phase relation between voltage and current in an AC circuit, we use the notion of **phasors**.
- A phasor is a vector which rotates about the origin with angular speed ω. The vertical components of phasors are represented as $V_m \sin \omega t_1$ and $I_m \sin \omega t_1$.
- Figure. (a) shows a **phasor diagram** for a circuit with an AC source connected to a resistor and figure (b) shows the graph of voltage V and I *versus* ωt.

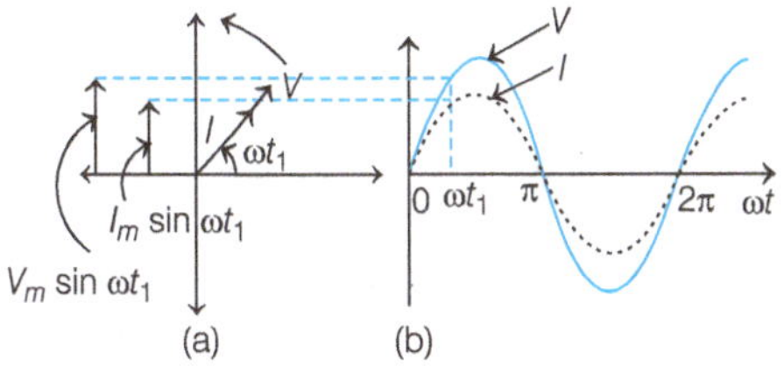

- Here, both the phasors voltage and current are in same direction, so the phase angle between the voltage and the current is zero.

AC Voltage Applied to an Inductor

- When an AC voltage source is connected to a purely inductive circuit as shown in figure, then

(i) Current in the circuit is $I = I_m \sin\left(\omega t - \frac{\pi}{2}\right)$.

(ii) The quantity ωL is analogous to the resistance and is called **inductive reactance**. It is denoted by X_L, i.e.,

$$X_L = \omega L = (2\pi\nu)L$$

Hence, the amplitude of current

$$I_m = \frac{V_m}{X_L} = \frac{V_m}{\omega L}$$

So, **the inductive reactance is directly proportional to the inductance and the frequency of alternating current.**

(iii) The dimension of inductive reactance is same as that of resistance and its SI unit is **ohm (Ω)**.

(iv) The inductive reactance limits the current in a purely inductive circuit in the same way as the resistance limits the current in a purely resistive circuit.

(v) The current in this type of circuit lags the voltage in phase by $\frac{\pi}{2}$ or one-quarter $\left(\frac{1}{4}\right)$ cycle. It means the current reaches its maximum value later than the voltage by one-fourth of a period $\left[\frac{T}{4} = \frac{\pi/2}{\omega}\right]$.

(vi) The **phasor diagram** and V and I *versus* ωt graph are as shown below.

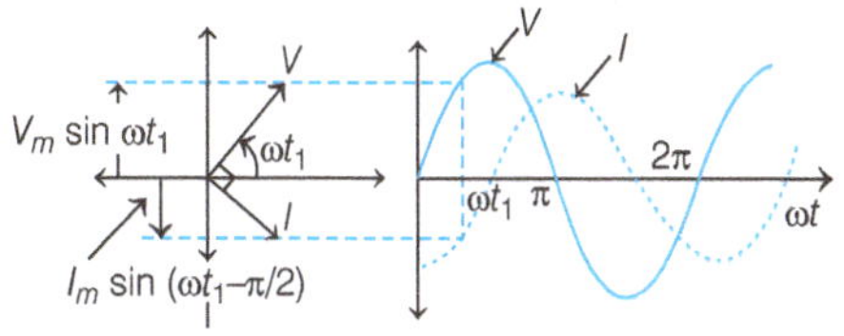

(vii) The instantaneous power supplied to the inductor is

$$P_L = I_{rms} V_{rms} = -\frac{I_m V_m}{2} \sin(2\omega t)$$

(viii) The average power of a complete cycle is

$$< P_L > = < -\frac{I_m V_m}{2} \sin(2\omega t) > = 0 \qquad [\because < \sin(2\omega t) > = 0]$$

Thus, the average power supplied to an inductor over one complete cycle is zero.

AC Voltage Applied to a Capacitor

- When a capacitor is connected to an AC voltage source in a circuit as shown in figure, then

(i) The current in the circuit is $I = I_m \sin\left(\omega t + \frac{\pi}{2}\right)$

(ii) The term $\left(\frac{1}{\omega C}\right)$ is also analogous to resistance and it is called **capacitive reactance**. It is denoted by X_C. i.e.

$$X_C = \frac{1}{\omega C} = \frac{1}{2\pi\nu C}$$ NEET 2020

So, the capacitive reactance is inversely proportional to the frequency and the capacitance.

Thus, the amplitude of the current, $I_m = \frac{V_m}{X_C} = \frac{V_m}{\left(\frac{1}{\omega C}\right)}$

(iii) The dimension of capacitive reactance is the same as that of resistance and its SI unit is ohm (Ω).

(iv) The capacitive reactance limits the amplitude of the current in a purely capacitive circuit in the same way as the resistance limits the current in a purely resistive circuit. But, it is inversely proportional to the frequency and the capacitance.

(v) The current in this circuit is ahead of voltage in phase by $\frac{\pi}{2}$ or one quarter cycle. It means the current reaches its maximum value earlier than the voltage by one-fourth of a period.

(vi) The **phasor diagram** and V and I *versus* ωt graph are as shown below

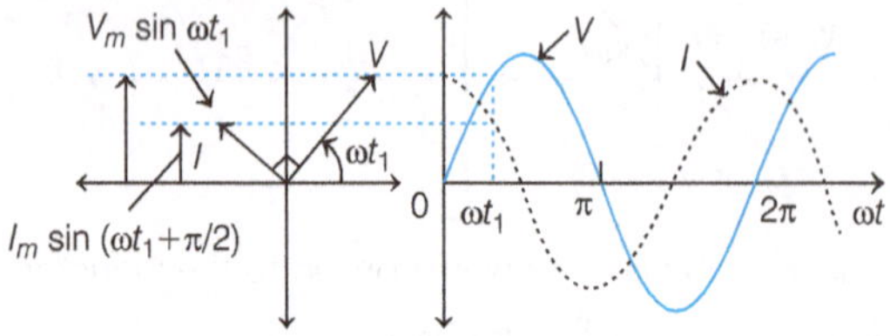

(vii) The instantaneous power supplied to capacitor is

$$P_c = I_{rms}V_{rms} = \frac{I_m V_m}{2}\sin(2\omega t)$$

(viii) The average power of a complete cycle is

$$\langle P_c \rangle = \langle \frac{I_m V_m}{2}\sin(2\omega t)\rangle = 0 \qquad [\because \langle \sin(2\omega t)\rangle = 0]$$

Thus, the average power supplied to a capacitor over one cycle is zero.

Note *When a capacitor is connected with DC source, then after being fully charged, the current in the circuit fall to zero. Whereas, when capacitor connected with AC source, it limits or regulates the current, but does not completely prevent the flow of charged (because capacitor is alternatively charged and discharged as the current reverses each half cycle).*

Marks Maximiser

Combination of *RL*, *RC* and *LC* in an AC circuit

Term	*R-L*	*R-C*	*L-C*
Circuit	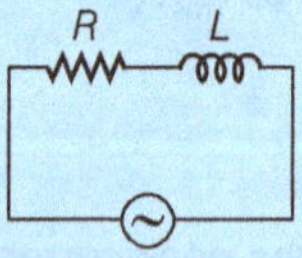 I is same in R and L	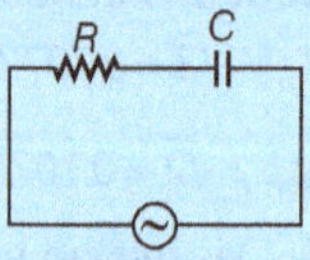 I is same in R and C	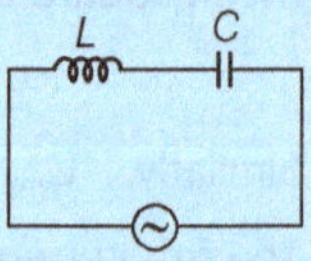 I is same in L and C
Phasor diagram	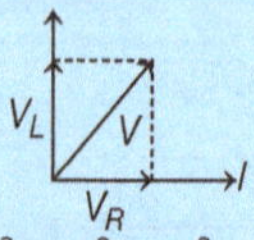 $V^2 = V_R^2 + V_L^2$	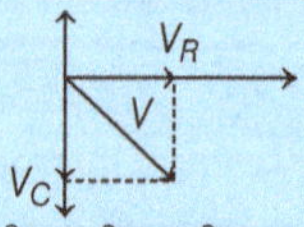 $V^2 = V_R^2 + V_C^2$	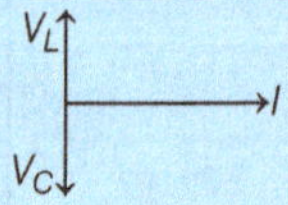 $V = V_L - V_C\ (V_L > V_C)$ $V = V_C - V_L\ (V_C > V_L)$
Phase difference between V and I	V leads I $\left(0 \text{ to } \frac{\pi}{2}\right)$	V lags $I\left(-\frac{\pi}{2} \text{ to } 0\right)$	V lags I $\left(-\frac{\pi}{2}, \text{ if } X_C > X_L\right)$ V leads I $\left(+\frac{\pi}{2}, \text{ if } X_L > X_C\right)$
Impedance	$Z = \sqrt{R^2 + X_L^2}$	$Z = \sqrt{R^2 + X_C^2}$	$Z = \lvert X_L - X_C \rvert$
At very low ν	$Z = R (X_L \to 0)$	$Z = X_C$	$Z = X_C$
At very high ν	$Z = X_L$	$Z = R (X_C \to 0)$	$Z = X_L$

AC Voltage Applied to a Series *L-C-R* Circuit

When a resistor, capacitor and an inductor are connected in series with an alternating voltage source of voltage difference, $V = V_m \sin \omega t$, then

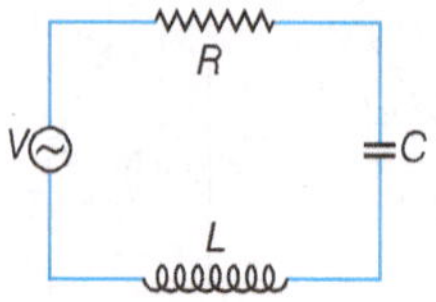

(i) voltage across the circuit is $V_m = \sqrt{V_R^2 + (V_C - V_L)^2}$

(ii) the current in the circuit is $I_m = \frac{V_m}{\sqrt{R^2 + (X_C - X_L)^2}}$

(iii) The **impedance** Z is the opposition or resistance offered by AC circuit to the flow of alternating current through it, is given as $Z = \sqrt{R^2 + (X_C - X_L)^2}$. NEET 2021

(iv) The phase angle ϕ is the angle between V_R and V can be determined from the following diagram. This diagram is called **impedance triangle**.

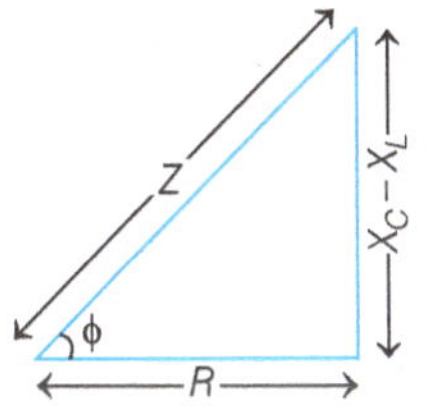

$$\tan\phi = \frac{V_C - V_L}{V_R} \quad \text{or} \quad \tan\phi = \frac{X_C - X_L}{R}$$

(v) If $X_C > X_L$, ϕ is positive and the circuit is predominantly capacitive, so the **current in the circuit leads the source voltage.**

(vi) If $X_C < X_L$, ϕ is negative and the circuit is predominantly inductive, so the **current in the circuit lags the source voltage.**

(vii) If $X_L = X_C$ then ϕ is 0. In this case, current in the circuit and source voltage are in phase.

(viii) **Phasor diagram** and V & I *versus* ωt graph are as shown below.

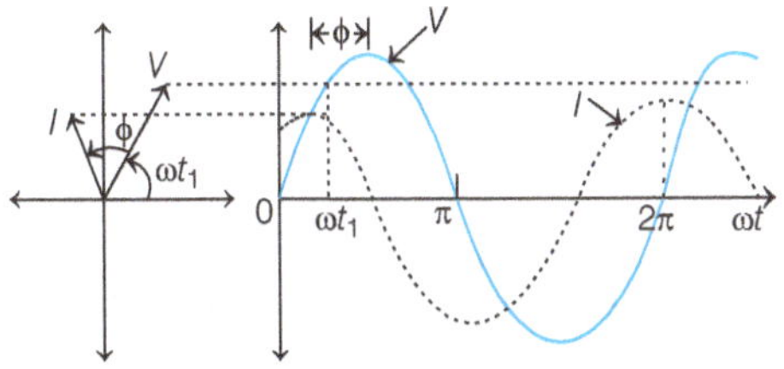

(ix) There are certain disadvantages of using the technique of phasors. These are as follows

(a) The phasor diagram say nothing about the initial condition. You can take any arbitrary value of t and draw different phasors which have relative angle difference.

(b) The solution of different phasors are different and called **steady state solutions**.

(c) The general solution consists of transit and steady solution. Over time, the transit solution vanishes and only steady solution remains, which describes the behaviour of circuit.

Resonance

It is the condition in which the impedance of series *L-C-R* circuit is minimum and the current flowing through the circuit is maximum. It is common among systems which have tendency to oscillate at a particular frequency. This frequency is called **natural frequency** of the system.

In an L-C-R circuit driven with voltage V_m and frequency ω, the current is given by

$$I_m = \frac{V_m}{Z} = \frac{V_m}{\sqrt{R^2 + (X_C - X_L)^2}}$$

At particular frequency ω_0, $X_C = X_L$, then $Z = R$.

This frequency ω_0 is called **angular resonance frequency** and given as $\omega_0 = 1/\sqrt{LC}$.

$\Rightarrow$ Resonant frequency, $\nu = \dfrac{1}{2\pi\sqrt{LC}}$ NEET 2023, 22

- At resonant frequency, the current amplitude is maximum, i.e. $I_m = \dfrac{V_m}{R}$.
- Resonance phenomenon is exhibited by a circuit if both L and C are present in it.
- Resonance does not occur in a R-L or R-C circuit.

  Figure shows the variation of I_m with ω in a L-C-R circuit with $L = 1\times 10^{-3}$H, $C = 1\times 10^{-9}$F for two values of R. i.e.

  (i) $R = 100\,\Omega$ and (ii) $R = 200\,\Omega$

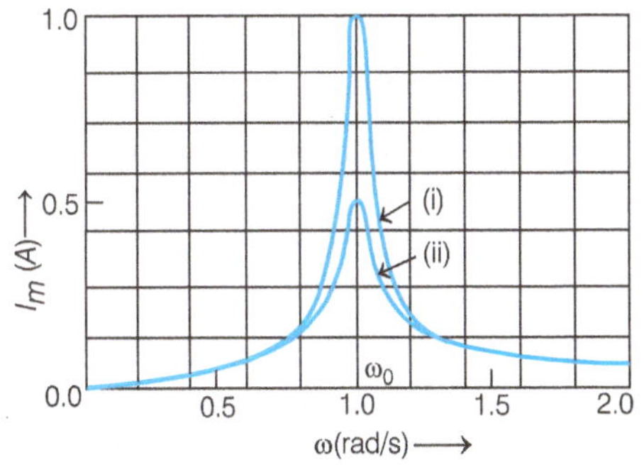

Variation of I_m with ω

For the source applied, $V_m = 100$ V

Angular resonance frequency, $\omega_0 = 1/\sqrt{LC} = 1\times 10^6$ rad/s

Here, current for $R = 100\,\Omega$ is twice to that for $R = 200\,\Omega$.

- Resonance circuits have a variety of applications. For example, in the tuning mechanism of a radio or TV set.
- In tuning, we vary the capacitance of a capacitor in the tuning circuit such that the resonant frequency of the circuit becomes nearly equal to the frequency of the radio signal received. When this happens, the amplitude of the current with the frequency of the signal of the particular radio station in the circuit is maximum.
- Resonance is exhibited by circuit only, if L and C both are present in the circuit, RL and RC circuits cannot have resonance.

For Concept Master Video

Marks Maximiser

- **Quality Factor** The ratio of the voltage developed across the inductance or capacitance at resonance to the voltage applied across resistor in a series L-C-R circuit is known as quality factor.

$$Q = \frac{\omega_0 L}{R} = \frac{1}{\omega_0 CR} = \frac{1}{R}\sqrt{\frac{L}{C}}$$

It should be maximum for better tuning of a circuit.

- **Sharpness of resonance**

$$= \frac{\omega_0}{2\Delta\omega} = \frac{\omega_0 L}{R}$$

- **Bandwidth of circuit** $2\Delta\omega = \omega_2 - \omega_1$

The smaller the $\Delta\omega$, the sharper is the resonance.

Power in AC circuit : The Power Factor

- When a voltage $V = V_m \sin \omega t$ applied to a series L-C-R circuit drives a current in the circuit is $I = I_m \sin(\omega t + \phi)$, where $I_m = \frac{V_m}{Z}$ and $\phi = \tan^{-1}\left[\frac{X_C - X_L}{R}\right]$, NEET 2019

then the **instantaneous power supplied** by source is P

$$= VI = \frac{V_m I_m}{2}[\cos\phi - \cos(2\omega t + \phi)]$$

- The average power of AC is given by

$$P_{av} = VI\cos\phi = I^2 Z\cos\phi = \frac{V_m I_m}{2}\cos\phi = V_{rms} \times I_{rms} \times \cos\phi$$

Here, the quantity $\cos\phi$ is called **power factor.** NEET 2020

- There are following cases, for power dissipation in a circuit

Case I Resistive Circuit If the circuit contains only R, then in that case, $\phi = 0 \Rightarrow \cos\phi = 1$.

Thus, there is maximum power dissipation.

Case II Purely Inductive or Capacitive Circuit If the circuit contains only an inductor or a capacitor, phase difference between voltage and current is $\frac{\pi}{2}$.

Therefore, $\cos\phi = 0$ and no power is dissipated even though a current is flowing in the circuit.

This current is sometimes referred to as **wattless current.**

Case III L-C-R Series Circuit In an L-C-R series circuit, $\phi = \tan^{-1}\left(\frac{X_C - X_L}{R}\right)$

So, ϕ may be non-zero in a R-L or R-C or R-C-L circuits. In this, power is dissipated only in the resistor.

Case IV Power Dissipated at Resonance in L-C-R Circuit

At resonance, $X_C - X_L = 0$ and $\phi = 0$, so $\cos\phi = 1$ and $P = I^2 Z = I^2 R$, i.e., maximum power is dissipated in a circuit (through R) at resonance.

For Concept Master Video

Marks Maximiser

Choke Coil

- When an inductor is connected in series with resistor, then the circuit is known as choke coil. It is used to reduce current without increasing power loss.
- Power factor of choke coil,

$$\cos\phi = \frac{R}{\sqrt{R^2 + \omega^2 L^2}} = \frac{R}{\omega L} \text{ (For } R \ll \omega L\text{)}$$

Transformer

- It is a device which converts low voltage (high current) into high voltage (low current) and *vice versa*. It is based on the principle of electromagnetic induction.

It consists of two sets of coil, insulated from each other. They are wound on a soft-iron core as given in the figure.

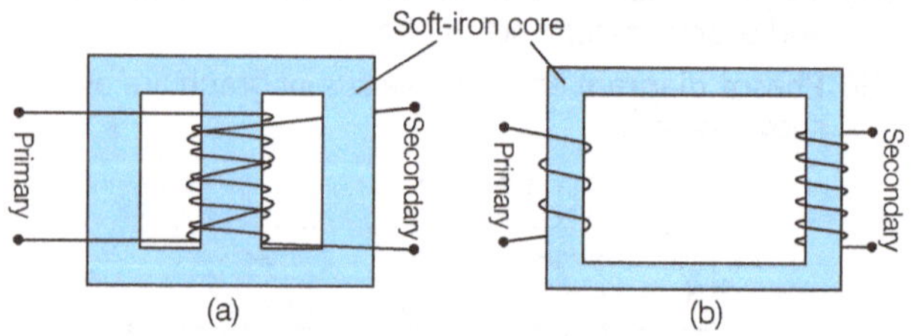

The input coil is called **primary coil** with number of turns N_p and the output coil is called **secondary coil** with number of turns N_s.

- When an alternating voltage is applied to the primary, the resulting current produces an alternating magnetic flux which links with secondary and induces an emf in it.

The value of this emf depends on the number of turns in the secondary.

For an ideal transformer,

$$\frac{\varepsilon_s}{\varepsilon_p} = \frac{V_s}{V_p} = \frac{N_s}{N_p} = \frac{I_p}{I_s}$$

(i) If $N_s > N_p$, the voltage is stepped up ($V_s > V_p$). This type of arrangement is called a **step-up transformer**.

However, there is less current in the secondary than the primary, i.e. $I_s < I_p$.

(ii) If $N_s < N_p$, we have a **step-down transformer.** In this case, $V_s < V_p$ and $I_s > I_p$, i.e., voltage is stepped down or reduced and current is increased. NEET 2021

- The **efficiency of transformer** is given by

$$\eta = \frac{V_s I_s}{V_p I_p} = \frac{\text{output power}}{\text{input power}}$$ NEET 2023

- In ideal transformer, there is no loss of energy or it is 100% efficient. Then, power input is equal to power output.
- In a transformer, some power is lost due to following reasons
  - **(i) Flux Leakage** It can be minimised by proper coupling of primary and secondary coils.
  - **(ii) Resistance of the windings** The wire used for the windings has some resistance and energy is lost due to heating effect. These are minimised by using thick wire.
  - **(iii) Eddy Currents** Iron losses due to Eddy currents produced in soft iron core. It is minimised by using laminated iron core.
  - (iv) **Hysteresis losses** Due to repeated magnetisation and demagnetisation of the core of transformer, it is minimised by using soft iron core, as area of hysteresis loop for soft iron is small and hence energy loss also becomes small.
- In large scale transmission, the power loss in the form of heat,

$$P_{\text{loss}} = I_{\text{rms}}^2 R$$

Caution Points

- The power rating of an element used in AC circuit refer to its average power rating.
- The power consumed in an AC circuit is never negative because electrical devices always use energy and do not give it back in same amount.
- Both alternating current and direct current are measured in amperes. The alternating current cannot be derived from the mutual attraction of two parallel wires carrying AC currents, as the DC derived. An AC current changes direction with source and attractive force will be zero.
- In AC circuits, voltage and current are technically not vectors but we represent them as rotating vectors on a phasor diagram. The amplitudes and phases of harmonically varying scalars combine mathematically in the same way as we added two vectors.

PYQ Notes

1. Heat generated in resistance R due to AC current $H = I_{\text{rms}}^2 Rt$ [JEE Main 2022]
2. At very high angular frequency, capacitor works as short circuit and inductor works as open circuit. [JEE Main 2021]
3. Power factor in AC circuit is also given by

$$\text{Power factor} = \cos\phi = \frac{\text{Resistance}}{\text{Total impedance}} = \frac{R}{Z}$$

[NEET 2020]

Step by Step

Mastering NCERT

- Concept Builders
- Topical Questions
- Assertion and Reason Questions
- Statement Based
- Matching Type
- Numerical Type
- NCERT Exemplar
- Past Exams MCQs
- Skill Boosters

Concept Builders

1 What is the relation between mean value of AC and rms value of AC?

2 AC is the current whose magnitude continuously changes with time. [T/F]

3 For electroplating, electrorefining, electrotyping, etc., which current is used?

4 AC voltage can be easily and efficiently converted from one voltage to other voltage by using .... (rectifier/transformer).

5 Average value of AC is always defined over half cycle. [T/F]

6 The only element that dissipates energy in an AC circuit is the .... (resistor/inductor).

7 A phasor is a .... quantity (scalar/vector).

8 Average power per cycle associated with resistor is ....

9 Inductor offers resistive path to AC and easy path to DC. [T/F]

10 What is the average power dissipation in a pure capacitive AC circuit?

11 Series resonance circuit is also known as acceptor circuit because it admits .... (minimum/maximum) current.

12 In pure capacitive circuit, the current is referred to as wattless current. [T/F]

13 What is the amplitude of the current when a capacitive reactance loaded to a circuit?

14 At resonance frequency, the impedance in series *L-C-R* circuit is .... (maximum/minimum).

15 What is the impedance in series *L-C-R* circuit?

16 What is the quality factor (*Q*-factor) in a series *L-C-R* circuit?

17 What is the dissipated power in an *L-C-R* series circuit connected to an AC source of emf ε_m?

18 At resonance, in series *L-C-R* circuit, power factor will be 0. [T/F]

19 Quantity that remains unchanged in a transformer is .... (current/frequency).

20 A laminated core is used in transformers to increase eddy currents. [T/F]

Topical Questions

AC Voltage Applied to a Resistor

1 In an AC circuit, $I = 100 \sin 200 \pi t$. The time required for the current to achieve its peak value from zero will be **NCERT Pg. 178**

(a) $\frac{1}{100}$ s (b) $\frac{1}{200}$ s (c) $\frac{1}{300}$ s (d) $\frac{1}{400}$ s

2 The electric mains in the house is marked 220 V, 50 Hz. Write down the equation for instantaneous voltage. **NCERT Pg. 178**

(a) $3.1 \sin (100\pi) t$ (b) $31.1 \cos (100\pi) t$
(c) $311.1 \sin (100\pi) t$ (d) $220 \cos (100\pi) t$

3 A resistance of 20 Ω is connected to a source of an alternating potential, $V = 220 \sin (100 \pi t)$. The time taken by current to change from its peak value to rms value is **NCERT Pg. 179**

(a) 0.2 s (b) 0.25 s
(c) 25×10^{-3} s (d) 2.5×10^{-3} s

4 An alternating current is given by the equation $i = i_1 \cos \omega t + i_2 \sin \omega t$. The rms current is given by **NCERT Pg. 179**

(a) $(1/\sqrt{2})(i_1 + i_2)$ (b) $(1/\sqrt{2})(i_1 + i_2)^2$
(c) $(1/\sqrt{2})(i_1^2 + i_2^2)^{1/2}$ (d) $(1/2)(i_1^2 + i_2^2)^{1/2}$

5 Current and voltage across a resistor in an AC circuit are
$V = 150\sin(150t)$ V, $I = 150\sin(150t)$ A
Power dissipated through the resistor is NCERT Pg. 179

(a) 150 W (b) 11250 W
(c) 5625 W (d) 0 W

6 What is the rms value of an alternating current which when passed through a resistor produces heat which is thrice of that produced by a direct current of 2 A in the same resistor? NCERT Pg. 179

(a) 6 A (b) 2 A
(c) 3.46 A (d) 0.66 A

7 The frequency of an alternating voltage is 50 cycles/s and its amplitude is 120 V, then the rms value of voltage is NCERT Pg. 180

(a) 101.3 V (b) 84.8 V
(c) 70.7 V (d) 56.5 V

8 A generator produces a voltage that is given by $V = 240\sin 120\,t$, where t is in seconds. The frequency and rms voltage are NCERT Pg. 180

(a) 60 Hz and 240 V (b) 19 Hz and 120 V
(c) 19 Hz and 170 V (d) 754 Hz and 70 V

9 The relation between an AC voltage source and time in SI unit is $V = 120\sin(100\pi t)\cos(100\pi t)$V. The value of peak voltage and frequency will be NCERT Pg. 180

(a) 130 V and 100Hz (b) $\frac{130}{\sqrt{2}}$ V and 100 Hz
(c) 60 V and 200 Hz (d) 60 V and 100 Hz

10 An alternating voltage given by $V = 140\sin 314t$ is connected across a pure resistance of 40Ω. The rms current through the resistor is NCERT Pg. 180

(a) 1.98 A (b) 8.43 A
(c) 2.39 A (d) 2.47 A

11 The rms value of potential difference V shown in the figure is NCERT Pg. 180

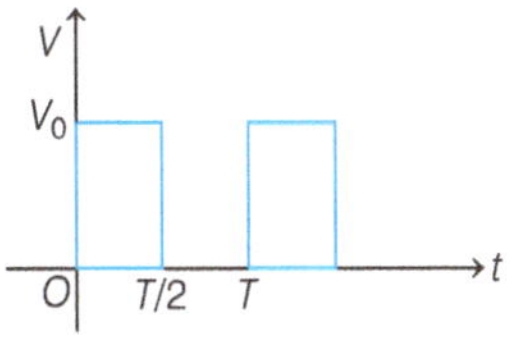

(a) V_0 (b) $\frac{V_0}{\sqrt{3}}$ (c) $\frac{V_0}{\sqrt{2}}$ (d) $\frac{V_0}{2}$

12 A 800 Ω resistor is connected to a 220 V, 50 Hz AC supply. The rms value of current in the circuit is NCERT Pg. 180

(a) 1.56 mA (b) 0.275 A
(c) 2.2mA (d) 4.0 mA

Representation of AC Current and Voltage By Rotating Vectors-Phasors

13. The phase relationship between current and voltage in a pure resistive circuit is best represented by NCERT Pg. 181

(a)
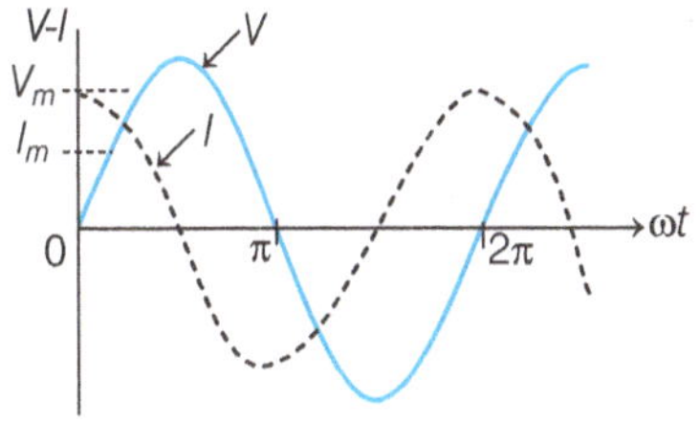

(b)
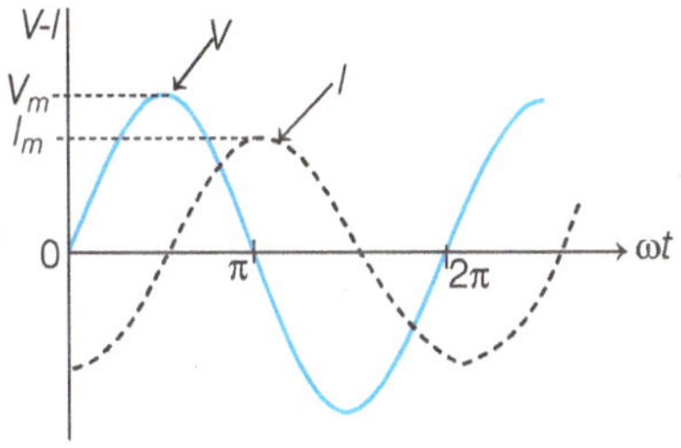

(c)
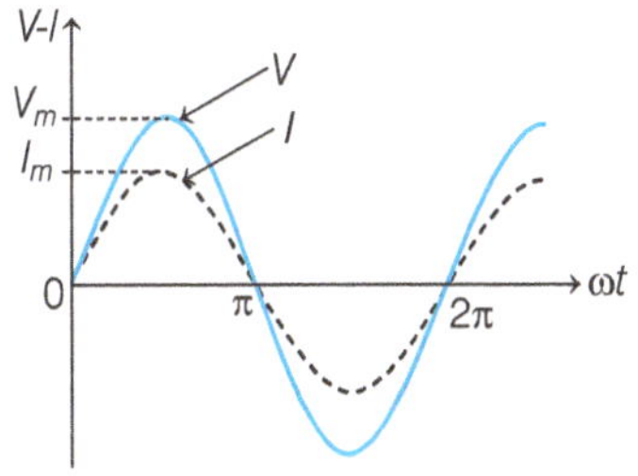

(d)
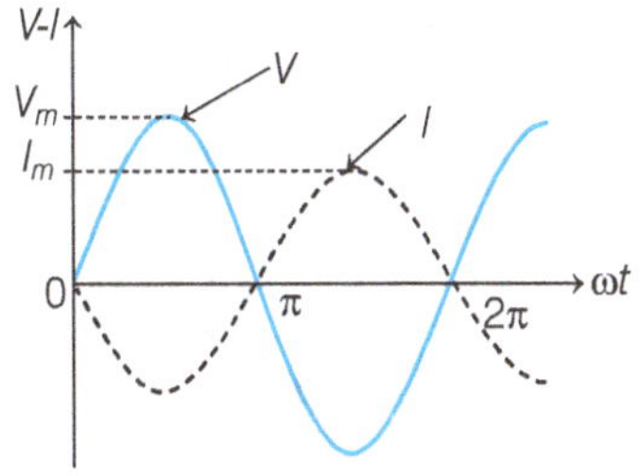

14 The phasors representing voltage and current for the case of a resistor are in the same direction. This is so for all times. This means that the phase difference between the voltage and current will be NCERT Pg. 181

(a) $\frac{\pi}{2}$ (b) $\frac{\pi}{4}$
(c) 0 (d) $\frac{3\pi}{2}$

15 The phasor is a NCERT Pg. 181
(a) vector quantity
(b) tensor quantity
(c) scalar quantity
(d) quantity having dimension in length only

AC Voltage Applied to an Inductor

16. In series AC circuit, if $V = V_0 \sin\left(\omega t + \frac{2\pi}{3}\right)$ and $I = I_0 \sin\left(\omega t + \frac{\pi}{3}\right)$, then NCERT Pg. 181

(a) voltage leads current by $\frac{2\pi}{3}$ rad

(b) voltage lags current by $\frac{2\pi}{3}$ rad

(c) voltage leads current by $\frac{\pi}{2}$ rad

(d) voltage leads current by $\frac{\pi}{3}$ rad

17 When an alternating voltage is applied to an inductor as shown in the figure, then NCERT Pg. 181

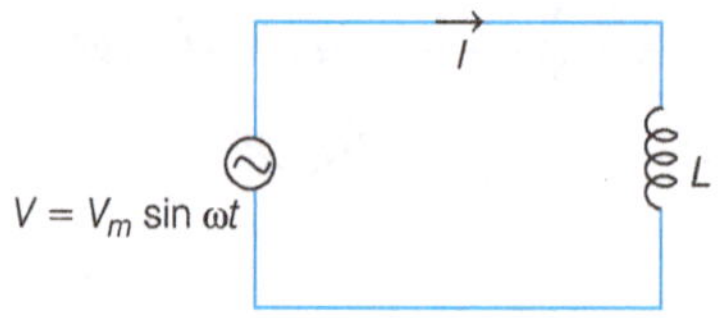

(a) $V + L\frac{dI}{dt} = 0$ (b) $V - L\frac{dI}{dt} = 0$

(c) $L + V\frac{dI}{dt} = 0$ (d) $L - V\frac{dI}{dt} = 0$

18 Which of the following graphs represents the correct variation of inductive reactance X_L with angular frequency ω? NCERT Pg. 182

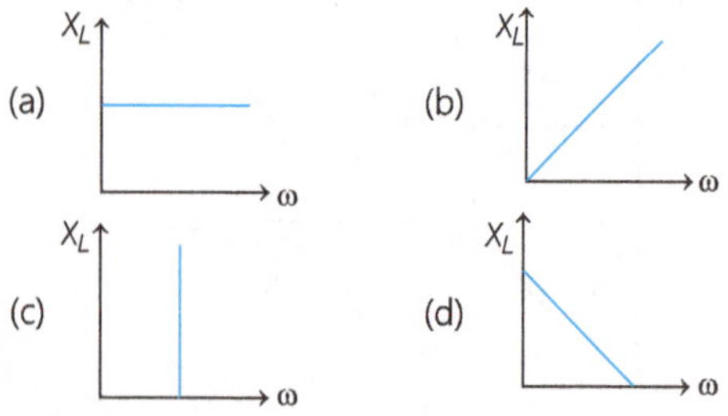

19 A pure inductor of inductance 25.0 mH is connected to a source of 220 V. Find the inductive reactance, if the frequency of the source is 50 Hz. NCERT Pg. 182

(a) 785 Ω (b) 6.50 Ω

(c) 7.85 Ω (d) 8.75 Ω

20 The rms current in the circuit containing a pure inductor of 40 mH, connected to a source 200V, 50 Hz is NCERT Pg. 182

(a) 25 A (b) 16 A (c) 11 A (d) 28 A

21 An inductance of negligible resistance, whose reactance is 120 Ω at 200 Hz is connected to a 240 V, 60 Hz, power line. The current in the inductor is NCERT Pg. 182

(a) 6.66 A (b) 6.60 A

(c) 5.45 A (d) 54.5 A

22 An arc lamp requires a direct current of 10 A at 80 V to function. If it is connected to a 220 V (rms), 50 Hz AC supply, the series inductor needed for it to work is close to NCERT Pg. 182

(a) 80 H (b) 0.08 H

(c) 0.044 H (d) 0.065 H

23 A pure resistive circuit element X when connected to an AC supply of peak voltage 200 V gives a peak current of 5 A which is in phase with the voltage. Another circuit element Y, when connected to the same AC supply also gives the same value of peak current but the current lags behind by 90°. If the series combination of X and Y is connected to the same supply, what will be the rms value of current? NCERT Pg. 182

(a) $\frac{10}{\sqrt{2}}$ A (b) $\frac{5}{\sqrt{2}}$ A

(c) $\frac{5}{2}$ A (d) 5 A

AC Voltage Applied to a Capacitor

24 In which of the following circuit, zero power dissipation is observed? NCERT Pg. 184

(a) Pure capacitive circuit

(b) Pure inductive circuit

(c) Pure resistive circuit

(d) Both (a) and (b)

25 An alternating current in a circuit is given by $I = 20\sin(100\pi t + 0.05\pi)$A. The rms value and the frequency of current, respectively are NCERT Pg. 184

(a) 10 A and 100 Hz

(b) 10 A and 50 Hz

(c) $10\sqrt{2}$ A and 50 Hz

(d) $10\sqrt{2}$ A and 100 Hz

26 A 30μF capacitor is connected to a 150 V, 60 Hz AC supply. The rms value of current in the circuit is NCERT Pg. 184

(a) 17 A (b) 1.7 A (c) 1.7 mA (d) 2.7 A

27 In a purely capacitive circuit, if the frequency of AC source is doubled, then its capacitive reactance will be NCERT Pg. 184

(a) remains same (b) doubled

(c) halved (d) zero

28 A 15.0 μF capacitor is connected to a 220 V, 50 Hz source. The capacitive reactance is **NCERT Pg. 184**

(a) 220 Ω (b) 215 Ω
(c) 212 Ω (d) 204 Ω

29 If the frequency is doubled, what happen to the capacitive reactance and the current? **NCERT Pg. 184**

(a) Capacitive reactance is halved, the current is doubled
(b) Capacitive reactance is doubled, the current is halved
(c) Capacitive reactance and the current are halved
(d) Capacitive reactance and the current are doubled

30 When a capacitor of 36 μF is connected to a 240 V, 50 Hz supply the currents (rms and peak) in the circuit are **NCERT Pg. 184**

(a) 1.47 A, 2.04 A
(b) 1.95 A, 2.73 A
(c) 2.73 A, 3.85 A
(d) 2.4 A, 1.08 A

31 An alternating voltage, $V = 200\sqrt{2}\sin(100\,t)$ is connected to a 1 μF, capacitor through an AC ammeter. The reading of the ammeter shall be **NCERT Pg. 184**

(a) 10 mA (b) 20 mA
(c) 40 mA (d) 80 mA

32 Which of the following statements is incorrect about capacitor? **NCERT Pg. 184**

(a) The current in a capacitive circuit is

$$i = i_m \sin\left(\omega t - \frac{\pi}{2}\right).$$

where, voltage is $V = V_m \sin \omega t$

(b) For a purely capacitive circuit, $\frac{1}{\omega C}$ plays the role of resistance. It is called capacitive reactance and denoted by $X_C = \frac{1}{\omega C}$

(c) The current reaches its maximum value earlier than the voltage by one-fourth of a period.

(d) In case of a capacitor, the average power,

$$P_c = \left\langle \frac{i_m V_m}{2} \sin(2\omega t) \right\rangle = 0$$

Since, $< \sin(2\omega t) > = 0$ over a complete cycle.

33 Which of the following statements is correct about the capacitive reactance? **NCERT Pg. 184**

(a) The reactance of the capacitor is directly proportional to the frequency of the current.
(b) The reactance of the capacitor is inversely proportional to the frequency of the current.
(c) Capacitive reactance is measured in farad.
(d) The reactance of a capacitor in an AC circuit is similar to the resistance of a capacitor in a DC circuit.

34 When an alternating voltage source of $V = 200\sin\left(100\pi t - \frac{\pi}{3}\right)$ is applied to a pure capacitor of capacitance 2μF, then the instantaneous value of current through the capacitor is **NCERT Pg. 184**

(a) $200\sin\left(100\pi t + \frac{\pi}{6}\right)$ (b) $0.04\pi\sin\left(100\pi t + \frac{\pi}{6}\right)$
(c) $200\sin\left(100\pi t - \frac{\pi}{6}\right)$ (d) $0.04\pi\sin\left(100\pi t - \frac{\pi}{6}\right)$

35 A 15μF capacitor is connected to a 220 V, 50 Hz source. The rms value of the current flowing through the capacitor is **NCERT Pg. 184**

(a) 2.56 A (b) 1.53 A (c) 1.04 A (d) 1.96 A

36 Same current is flowing in two alternating circuits. The first circuit contains only inductance and the second contains only a capacitance. If the frequency of the emf of AC is increased, the value of current will **NCERT Pg. 184**

(a) increase in the first circuit and decrease in the second circuit
(b) increase in both the circuits
(c) decrease in both the circuits
(d) decrease in the first circuit and increase in the second circuit

37 A capacitor of capacitance C is connected across an AC source of voltage V. The displacement current between the plates of the capacitor is given by $I_d = V_0\,\omega C\cos\omega t$, then applied voltage V is given by **NCERT Pg. 184**

(a) $V = V_0 \sin \omega t$ (b) $V = V_0 \cos \omega t$
(c) $V = V_0 \sin(2\omega t)$ (d) $V = V_0 \cos(2\omega t)$

38 Which of the following graphs represents the correct variation of capacitive reactance X_C with frequency ν? **NCERT Pg. 184**

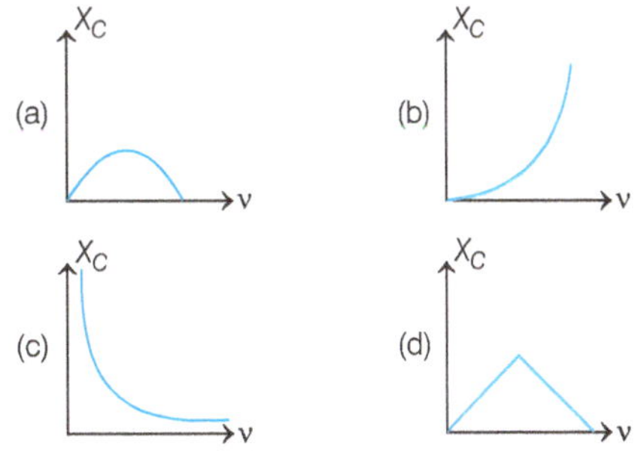

39 A 100 μF capacitor in series with a 40 Ω resistor is connected to a 100 V, 60 Hz supply. The time lag between the current maximum and the voltage maximum is **NCERT Pg. 184**

(a) 2.0×10^{-3} s (b) 3.25×10^{-3} s
(c) 1.55×10^{-3} s (d) 2.85×10^{-3} s

40 Phase difference between voltage and current in a capacitor in an AC circuit is NCERT Pg.. 185

(a) π (b) $\frac{\pi}{2}$ (c) 0 (d) $\frac{\pi}{3}$

AC Voltage Applied to a Series *L-C-R* Circuit

41 For series *L-C-R* circuit, NCERT Pg. 187

(a) applied emf and current across resistance are in same phase
(b) applied emf and current across inductor coil have phase difference of π.
(c) potential difference at capacitor and inductor have phase difference of $\pi/2$
(d) potential difference across resistance and capacitor have phase difference of π.

42 In the given circuit shown in figure. The voltmeter and ammeter readings are respectively (reactance are indicated in figure) NCERT Pg. 187

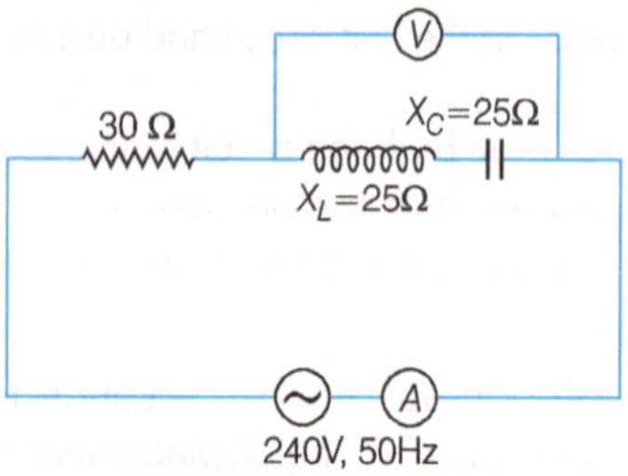

(a) 0 V, 3 A (b) 0 V, 8 A (c) 0 V, 6 A (d) 0 V, 12A

43 In a series *L-C-R* circuit, the potential difference between the terminals of the inductor is 60 V, between the terminals of the capacitor is 30 V and that across the resistor is 40 V. Then, supply voltage will be equal to NCERT Pg. 187

(a) 50 V (b) 70 V
(c) 130 V (d) 10 V

44 In a series *L-C-R* circuit, source voltage is 120 V. The voltage across inductor is 50 V and across resistor is 40 V, then determine voltage across the capacitor. NCERT Pg. 187

(a) $10(5-8\sqrt{2})$ V (b) $10(5+8\sqrt{2})$ V
(c) $20(5+8\sqrt{2})$ V (d) $10(5+7\sqrt{2})$ V

45 In a series *L-C-R* circuit, the frequency of 10 V AC voltage source is adjusted in a manner that the reactance of the inductor measures 15 Ω and that of the capacitor 11 Ω. If $R = 3\,\Omega$, the potential difference across the series combination of *L* and *C* will be NCERT Pg. 187

(a) 8 V (b) 10 V (c) 22 V (d) 52 V

46 Which of the following statement is incorrect? NCERT Pg. 187

(a) Phasor diagram say nothing about the initial condition.
(b) At any arbitrary value of *t*, if we draw different phasors which show the relative angle between different phasors. The solution, so obtained is called the steady-state solution.
(c) We do have a transient solution which exists even for $V = 0$. The general solution is the sum of transient solution and the steady-state solution.
(d) After a sufficient long time, the behaviour of the circuit is described by transient solution only.

47 Which of the following statement is correct? NCERT Pg. 187

(a) In a series *L-C-R* circuit, the AC current in each elements is different at any time, having the different amplitude and phase.
(b) By analogy to the resistance in a circuit, we introduce the impedance *Z* in an *R-L-C* series circuit given by
$$Z = \sqrt{R^2 + (X_C - X_L)^2}$$
(c) The phasor I is always parallel to phasor V_R, the phase angle ϕ is the angle between V_R and *V* and can be determined from
$$\tan\phi = \frac{V_L + V_C}{V_R}, \text{ when } V_L > V_C$$
(d) The impedance triangle is a right triangle with *Z* as its base.

48 Which of the following statement is incorrect ? NCERT Pg. 187

(a) The phenomenon of resonance is common among systems that have a tendency to oscillate at a particular frequency.
(b) If ω is varied, then at a particular frequency ω_0, $X_C > X_L$ and the impedance become maximum. This frequency is called resonant frequency.
(c) The amplitude of the current in a series *L-C-R* circuit is given by $i_m = \dfrac{V_m}{\sqrt{R^2 + \left(\omega L - \dfrac{1}{\omega C}\right)^2}}$

At $\omega = \omega_0 = \dfrac{1}{\sqrt{LC}}$, $i_m^{max} = \dfrac{V_m}{R}$
(d) In the *R-L-C* circuit, the impedance is given by
$$Z = \sqrt{R^2 + (X_C - X_L)^2}$$

49 If the reading of voltmeter V_1 is 30 V, what is the reading of voltmeter V_2? NCERT Pg. 187

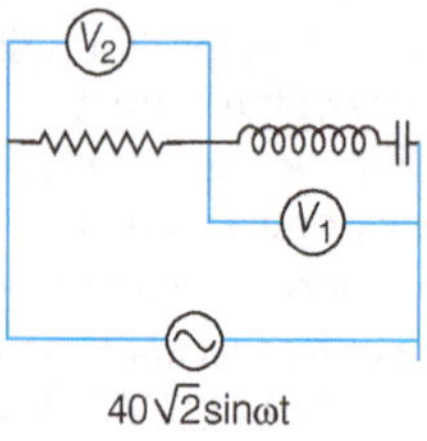

(a) 20.50 V (b) 26.45 V (c) 32.65 V (d) 15.24 V

50 In the given circuit, the readings of voltmeters V_1 and V_2 are 300 V each. The readings of the voltmeter V_3 and ammeter A are respectively **NCERT Pg. 187**

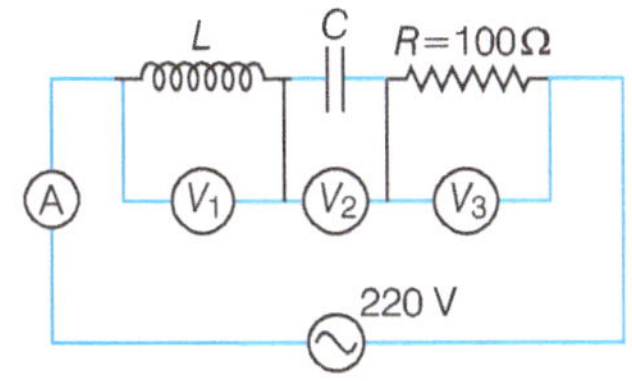

(a) 100 V, 2.0 A
(b) 150 V, 2.2 A
(c) 220 V, 2.2 A
(d) 220 V, 2.0 A

51 A resistor and a capacitor are connected in series with an AC source. If the potential drop across the capacitor is 5V and that across the resistor is 12 V, then applied voltage is **NCERT Pg. 187**

(a) 13 V (b) 17 V
(c) 5 V (d) 12 V

52 A sinusoidal voltage of peak value 300 V and an angular frequency $\omega = 400\ \text{rads}^{-1}$ is applied to a series L-C-R circuit, in which $R = 3\ \Omega$, $L = 20$ mH and $C = 625\ \mu$F. The peak current in the circuit is **NCERT Pg. 187**

(a) $30\sqrt{2}$ A (b) 60 A
(c) 100 A (d) $60\sqrt{2}$ A

53 A resistor of $200\ \Omega$ and a capacitor of $15\ \mu$F are connected in series to a 220 V, 50 Hz AC source. The current in the circuit is **NCERT Pg. 187**

(a) 755 A (b) 7.55 mA
(c) 0.755A (d) 0.755 mA

54 An inductor of inductance L, a capacitor of capacitance C and a resistor of resistance R are connected in series to an AC source of potential difference V volts as shown in figure. Potential difference across L, C and R is 90 V, 10 V and 60 V respectively. The impedance of L-C-R series circuit is $10\ \Omega$. The amplitude of current flowing through L-C-R series circuit is **NCERT Pg. 187**

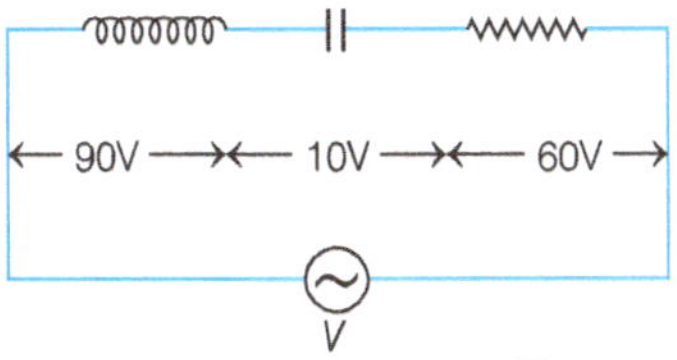

(a) $(5\sqrt{2})$ A (b) $(5/\sqrt{2})$ A
(c) $(10/\sqrt{2})$ A (d) $(10\sqrt{2})$ A

55 Which of the following graph, is correct for a series L-C-R circuit, where $X_C > X_L$? **NCERT Pg. 188**

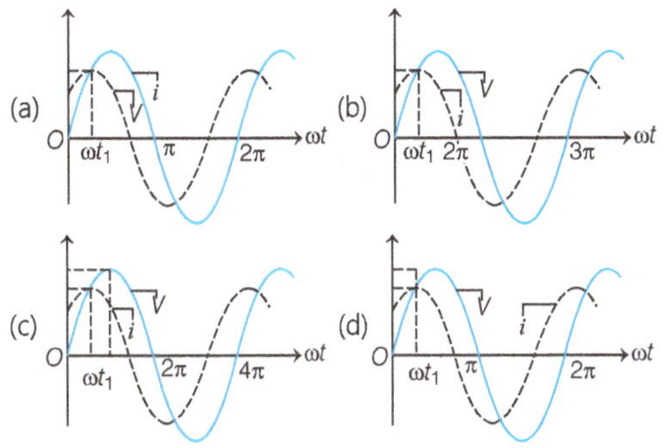

56 In a circuit L, C and R are connected in series with an alternating voltage source of frequency ν. The current leads the voltage by 45°. The value of C is **NCERT Pg. 188**

(a) $\dfrac{1}{2\pi\nu(2\pi\nu L + R)}$ (b) $\dfrac{1}{\pi\nu(2\pi\nu L + R)}$
(c) $\dfrac{1}{2\pi\nu(2\pi\nu L - R)}$ (d) $\dfrac{1}{\pi\nu(2\pi\nu L - R)}$

57 A resistance of $300\ \Omega$ and an inductance of $(1/\pi)$ H are connected in a series to an AC voltage of 20 V and 200 Hz frequency. The phase angle between the voltage and current is **NCERT Pg. 188**

(a) $\tan^{-1}(4/3)$
(b) $\tan^{-1}(3/4)$
(c) $\tan^{-1}(3/2)$
(d) $\tan^{-1}(2/5)$

58 In a series R-C circuit shown in figure, the applied voltage is 10 V and the voltage across capacitor is found to be 8V. The voltage across R and the phase difference between current and the applied voltage will respectively be **NCERT Pg. 188**

(a) 6V, $\tan^{-1}\left(\dfrac{4}{3}\right)$

(b) 3V, $\tan^{-1}\left(\dfrac{3}{4}\right)$

(c) 6V, $\tan^{-1}\left(\dfrac{5}{3}\right)$

(d) 3V, $\tan^{-1}\left(\dfrac{4}{3}\right)$

59 An AC source of angular frequency ω is fed across a circuit having resistor R and capacitor C in series. The current flowing is I. If now the frequency of source is changed to $\omega/3$ (but maintaining the same voltage), the current in the circuit is found to be halved. Calculate the ratio of reactance to resistance at the original frequency ω. **NCERT Pg. 188**

(a) $\sqrt{\dfrac{3}{5}}$ (b) $\sqrt{\dfrac{2}{5}}$ (c) $\sqrt{\dfrac{1}{5}}$ (d) $\sqrt{\dfrac{4}{5}}$

60 A series R, L and C circuit is shown here. The source frequency ν is varied, but the current is kept unchange. Which of the curves showing changes of V_C and V_L with frequency would be valid for the circuit under consideration? **NCERT Pg. 188**

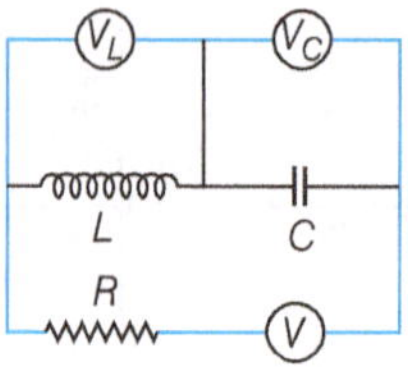

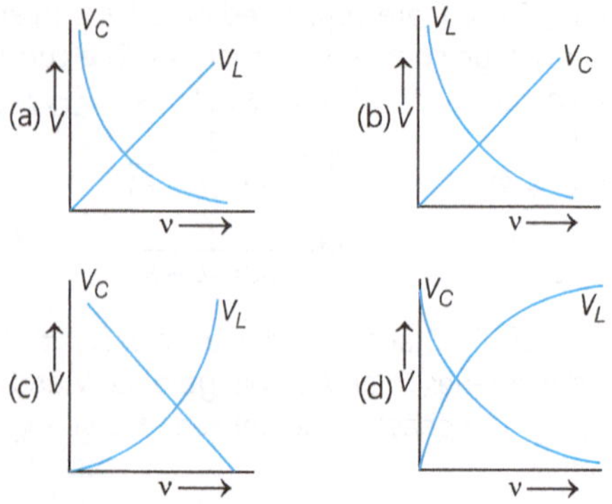

61 When an AC source of voltage $V = V_0 \sin 100t$ is connected across a circuit, the phase difference between the voltage V and current I in the circuit is observed to be $\pi / 4$, as shown in figure. If the circuit consists possibly only of R-C or R-L or L-C in series, the possible values of two elements will be **NCERT Pg. 188**

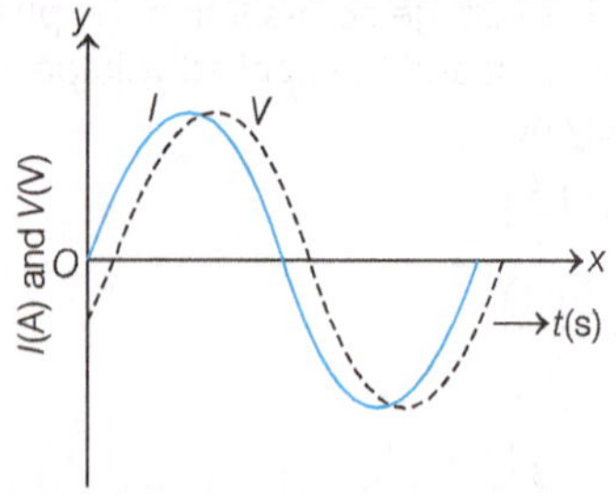

(a) $R = 1\,\text{k}\Omega, C = 10\,\mu\text{F}$ (b) $R = 1\,\text{k}\Omega, C = 1\,\mu\text{F}$
(c) $R = 1\,\text{k}\Omega, L = 10\,\text{mH}$ (d) $R = 10\,\text{k}\Omega, L = 10\,\text{mH}$

62 In series R-L-C circuit, $L = 1.00$ mH, $C = 1.00$ nF and $R = 200\,\Omega$. For the source applied with $V_m = 100$ V, the resonant frequency is **NCERT Pg. 189**
(a) 1×10^3 rad/s (b) 1×10^6 rad/s
(c) 1.56×10^6 rad/s (d) 1.75×10^3 rad/s

63 Figure shows a series L-C-R circuit, connected to a variable frequency source of 200 V with $C = 80\,\mu\text{F}$, $L = 5$ H and $R = 40\,\Omega$. The source frequency which drives the circuit at resonance is **NCERT Pg. 189**

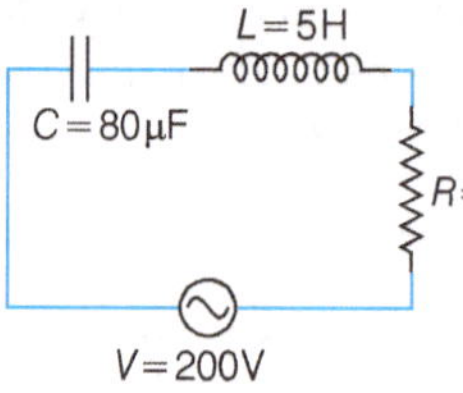

(a) 25 Hz (b) $\frac{25}{\pi}$ Hz (c) 50 Hz (d) $\frac{50}{\pi}$ Hz

64 In an L-C-R circuit, capacitance is changed from C to $2C$. For the resonant frequency to remain unchanged, the inductance should be changed from L to **NCERT Pg. 189**
(a) $4L$ (b) $2L$ (c) $L/2$ (d) $L/4$

65 For the series L-C-R circuit shown in the figure, what is the angular resonant frequency and amplitude of the current at the resonating frequency? **NCERT Pg. 189**

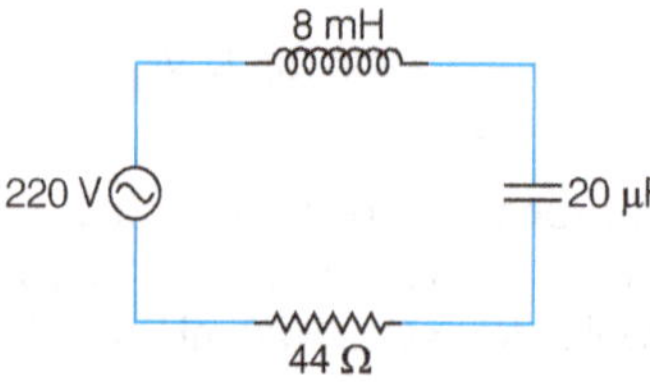

(a) 2500 rads^{-1} and $5\sqrt{2}$ A
(b) 2500 rads^{-1} and 5 A
(c) 2500 rads^{-1} and $\frac{5}{\sqrt{2}}$ A
(d) 25 rads^{-1} and $5\sqrt{2}$ A

66 In a series L-C-R circuit, the voltage across R is 100 V, $R = 1\,\text{k}\Omega$ and $C = 2\,\mu\text{F}$. The resonant frequency ω is 200 rad/s. At resonance, the voltage across L is **NCERT Pg. 189**
(a) 40 V (b) 250 V
(c) 4×10^{-3} V (d) 2.5×10^{-2} V

67 An L-C-R series circuit consists of a resistance of $10\,\Omega$, a capacitor of reactance $60\,\Omega$ and an inductor coil. The circuit is found to resonate when put across a 300 V, 100 Hz supply. The inductance of coil is (take, $\pi = 3$) **NCERT Pg. 189**
(a) 0.1 H (b) 0.01 H (c) 0.2 H (d) 0.02 H

68 An alternating emf of frequency $\nu = \left(\frac{1}{2\pi\sqrt{LC}}\right)$ is applied to a series L-C-R circuit. For this frequency of the applied emf, which statement is incorrect? **NCERT Pg. 189**
(a) The circuit is at resonance and its impedance is made up only of a resistive part.
(b) The current in the circuit is in phase with the applied emf and voltage across R equals the applied emf.

(c) The sum of the potential difference across the inductance and capacitance equals the applied emf which is 180° ahead of phase of the current in the circuit.

(d) If the phase difference between two voltage is properly taken into account the total voltage across the resistor and the capacitor equal to voltage of the source.

69 Find resonant frequency in the given circuit. **NCERT Pg. 189**

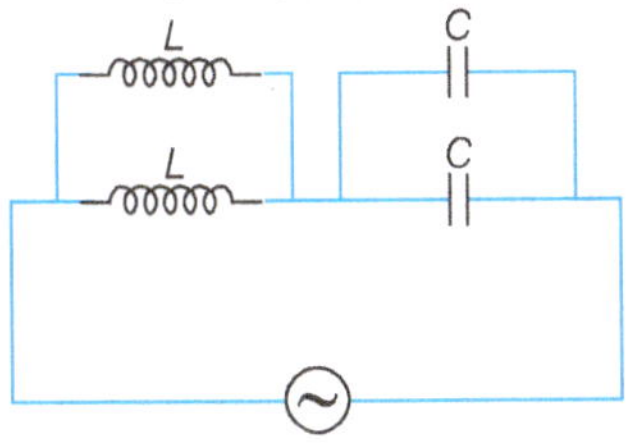

(a) $\frac{1}{\sqrt{LC}}$ (b) $\frac{2}{\sqrt{LC}}$ (c) $\frac{1}{2\sqrt{LC}}$ (d) $\frac{4}{\sqrt{LC}}$

70 In the circuit shown in figure, the AC source gives a voltage $V = 20\cos(2000t)$. Neglecting source resistance, the voltmeter and ammeter readings will be **NCERT Pg. 189**

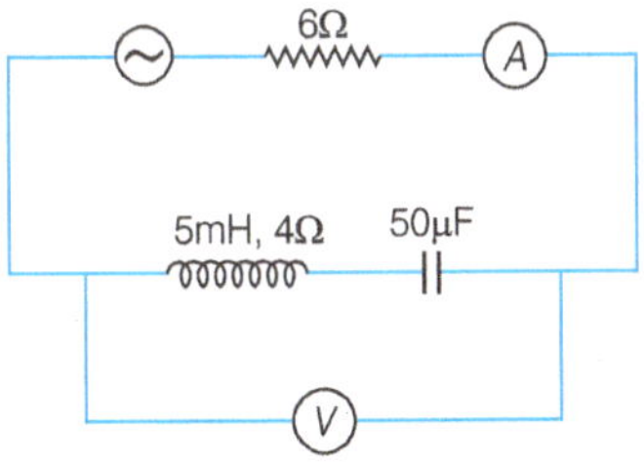

(a) 0 V, 2.0 A (b) 0 V, 1.4 A
(c) 5.6 V, 1.4 A (d) 8 V, 2.0 A

71 In the figure shown, three AC voltmeters have been connected. At resonance, the reading in voltmeter will be **NCERT Pg. 189**

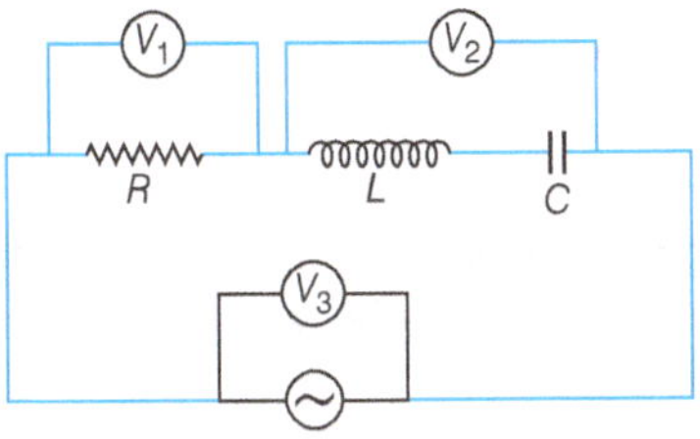

(a) V_1 is zero (b) V_2 is zero
(c) V_3 is zero (d) $V_1 = V_2 = V_3 = 0$

72 Which of the following statement is correct? **NCERT Pg. 191**

(a) In an inductive circuit, using Kirchhoff's loop rule, we get $V - L\frac{di}{dt} = 0$
where, the second term is the mutual induced emf in the inductor.

(b) The quantity ω is analogous to the conductance.

(c) The current phasor **I** is $\frac{\pi}{2}$ behind the voltage phasor.

(d) The average power supplied to an inductor over one complete cycle is zero.

Power in AC Circuit : The Power Factor

73 A group of electric lamps having total power rating of 600 W, 220V is supplied by an AC voltage $V = 169\sin(314t + 60°)$. The rms value of the current is **NCERT Pg. 191**

(a) 10 A (b) 9.04 A (c) 1.48 A (d) 8 mA

74 For a value of ω, the current amplitude becomes $1/\sqrt{2}$ times its maximum value. At this value, the power dissipated by the circuit becomes **NCERT Pg. 191**

(a) double (b) one-fourth
(c) one-third (d) half

75 A lamp consumes only 50% of peak power in an AC circuit. What is the phase difference between the applied voltage and the circuit current? **NCERT Pg. 191**

(a) $\frac{\pi}{6}$ (b) $\frac{\pi}{3}$ (c) $\frac{\pi}{4}$ (d) $\frac{\pi}{2}$

76 In an electrical circuit R, L, C and an AC voltage source are all connected in series. When L is removed from the circuit, the phase difference between the voltage and the current in the circuit is $\pi/3$. If instead, C is removed from the circuit, the phase difference is again $\pi/3$. The power factor of the circuit is **NCERT Pg. 191**

(a) 1/2 (b) $1/\sqrt{2}$ (c) 1 (d) $\sqrt{3}/2$

77 The potential difference V and the current i flowing through an instruments in an AC circuit of frequency ν are given by $V = (5\cos\omega t)$ volts and $i = (2\sin\omega t)$ amperes (where, $\omega = 2\pi\nu$).
The power dissipated in the instrument is **NCERT Pg. 191**

(a) zero (b) 10 W
(c) 5 W (d) 2.5 W

78 In an AC circuit, the instantaneous values of emf and current are $\varepsilon = (200\sin 314t)$ V and $I = \sin(314t + \pi/3)$ A. The average power consumed is **NCERT Pg. 191**

(a) 200 W (b) 100 W
(c) 50 W (d) 25 W

79 A coil of self-inductance L is connected in series with a bulb B and an AC source. Brightness of the bulb decreases when **NCERT Pg. 191**

(a) frequency of the AC source is decreased
(b) number of turns in the coil is reduced
(c) a capacitance of reactance $X_C - X_L$ is included in the same circuit
(d) an iron rod is inserted in the coil

80 A coil of inductive reactance 31 Ω has a resistance of 8 Ω. It is placed in series with a condenser of capacitive reactance 25 Ω. The combination is connected to an AC source of 110 V. The power factor of the circuit is NCERT Pg. 191

(a) 0.56 (b) 0.64 (c) 0.80 (d) 0.33

81 An inductor 20 mH, a capacitor 100 μF and a resistor 50Ω are connected in series across a source of emf, $V = 10 \sin 314\, t$. The power loss in the circuit is NCERT Pg. 191

(a) 2.74 W (b) 0.43 W
(c) 0.79 W (d) 1.13 W

82 A voltage of peak value 283 V and varying frequency is applied to a series *L-C-R* combination in which $R = 3\,\Omega$, $L = 25$ mH and $C = 400\,\mu$F. The frequency (in Hz) of the source at which maximum power is dissipated in the above circuit is NCERT Pg. 191

(a) 51.5 (b) 50.7 (c) 51.1 (d) 50.3

83 The rms current in an AC circuit is 2 A. If the wattless current be $\sqrt{3}$A, what is the power factor? NCERT Pg. 191

(a) $\frac{1}{\sqrt{3}}$ (b) $\frac{1}{\sqrt{2}}$ (c) $\frac{1}{2}$ (d) $\frac{1}{3}$

84 An inductor 200 mH, capacitor 500 μF and resistor 10Ω are connected in series with a 100 V variable frequency AC source. What is the frequency at which the power factor of the circuit is unity? NCERT Pg. 191

(a) 10.22 Hz (b) 12.4 Hz
(c) 19.2 Hz (d) 15.9 Hz

85 The power factor of the circuit as shown in figure is NCERT Pg. 191

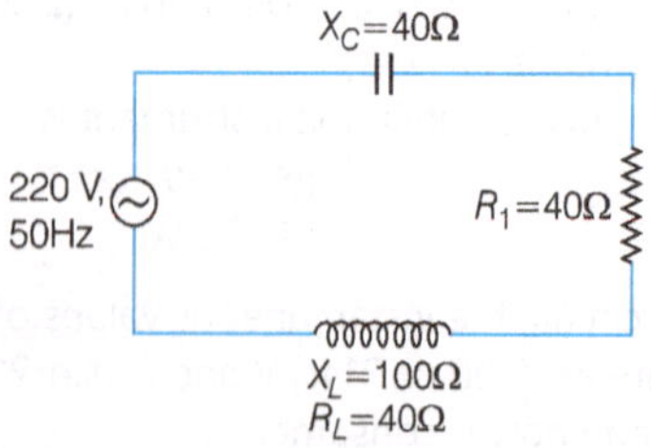

(a) 0.2 (b) 0.4
(c) 0.8 (d) 0.6

86 A series AC circuit containing an inductor (20 mH), a capacitor (120 μF) and a resistor (60 Ω) is driven by an AC source of 24 V/50 Hz. The energy dissipated in the circuit in 60 s is NCERT Pg. 192

(a) 3.39×10^3 J
(b) 5.65×10^2 J
(c) 2.26×10^3 J
(d) 5.17×10^2 J

Transformers

87 Which of the following statement(s) is correct? NCERT Pg. 194

(a) Flux leakage is reduced by winding the primary and secondary coils at different places.
(b) Resistance of windings is minimised by using thin wire.
(c) Eddy currents are reduced by using a laminated core.
(d) Hysteresis is minimised by using a non- magnetic material.

88 Electrical energy is transmitted over large distances at high alternating voltages. Which of the following statement(s) is/are incorrect? NCERT Pg. 194

(a) For a given power level, there is a lower current.
(b) Lower current implies less power loss.
(c) Transmission lines can be made thinner.
(d) It is easy to reduce the voltage at the receiving end, using step-down transformers.

89 A power transmission line feeds input power at 2300 V to a step-down transformer with its primary windings having 4000 turns. What should be the number of turns in the secondary in order to get output power at 230 V? NCERT Pg. 195

(a) 600 (b) 550
(c) 400 (d) 375

90 How much current is drawn by the primary coil of a transformer which steps down 220 V to 22 V to operate a device with an impedance of 220 Ω? NCERT Pg. 195

(a) 1 A (b) 0.25 A
(c) 0.01 A (d) 1.50 A

91 A 110 V AC is connected to a transformer of ratio 10. If resistance of secondary coil is 550 Ω, current through secondary coil will be NCERT Pg. 195

(a) 10 A (b) 2 A
(c) zero (d) 55 A

92 The ratio of secondary to primary turns is 4 : 5, for an ideal transformer, then the ratio of power output to power input is NCERT Pg. 195

(a) 4 : 9 (b) 9 : 4
(c) 5 : 4 (d) 1 : 1

93 A transformer consisting of 300 turns in the primary and 150 turns in the secondary gives output power of 2.2 kW. If the current in the secondary coil is 10 A, then the input voltage and current in the primary coil are NCERT Pg. 195

(a) 440 V and 5 A
(b) 220 V and 20 A
(c) 220 V and 10 A
(d) 440 V and 20 A

94 A transformer with turns ratio $\frac{N_1}{N_2} = \frac{50}{1}$ is connected to a 120 V AC supply. If primary and secondary circuit resistances are $1.5\,k\Omega$ and $1\,\Omega$ respectively, then find out power of output. **NCERT Pg. 195**

(a) 5.76 W (b) 11.4 W
(c) 2.89 W (d) 7.56 W

95 A transformer is used to light 140 W, 24 V lamp from 240 V AC mains. The current in the mains is 0.7 A. The efficiency of transformer is nearer to **NCERT Pg. 195**

(a) 90% (b) 80%
(c) 70% (d) 60%

96 A transformer having efficiency of 90% is working on 200 V and 3kW power supply. If the current in the secondary coil is 6 A, the voltage across the secondary coil and the current in the primary coil respectively, are **NCERT Pg. 195**

(a) 300 V, 15 A (b) 450 V, 15 A
(c) 450 V, 13.5 A (d) 600 V, 15 A

97 A step down transformer reduce the voltage of transmission line from 2200 V to 220 V. The power delivered by it is 880 W and its efficiency is 88%. The input current is **NCERt Pg. 195**

(a) 4.65 mA (b) 0.465 A
(c) 0.4545 A (d) 4.65 A

98 A village with a demand of 800 kW of electric power at 220 V is situated 15 km away from an electric plant generating power at 440 V. The resistance of the two wire line carrying power is $0.5\,\Omega$ per km. The village gets power from the line through a 4000-220 V step down transformer at a substation in the town. The line power loss in the form of heat is **NCERT Pg. 195**

(a) 400 kW (b) 600 kW
(c) 300 kW (d) 800 W

Assertion and Reason Questions

Direction (Q. Nos. 1-10) *In the following questions, a statement of Assertion is followed by a corresponding statement of Reason. Of the following statements, choose the correct one.*

(a) Both Assertion and Reason are correct and Reason is the correct explanation of Assertion.
(b) Both Assertion and Reason are correct but Reason is not the correct explanation of Assertion.
(c) Assertion is correct but Reason is incorrect.
(d) Assertion is incorrect but Reason is correct.

1 **Assertion** Today, most of the electrical devices we use, require AC voltage.
Reason Most of the electrical energy sold by power companies is transmitted and distributed as alternating current. **NCERT Pg. 177**

2 **Assertion** Phasors V and I for the case of a resistor are in the same direction.
Reason The phase angle between the voltage and the current is zero. **NCERT Pg. 178**

3 **Assertion** The alternating current lags behind the emf by a phase angle of $\pi/2$, when AC flows through an inductor.
Reason The inductive reactance increases as the frequency of AC source decreases. **NCERT Pg. 182**

4 **Assertion** When the capacitor is connected to an AC source, it limits or regulates the current, but does not completely prevent the flow of charge.
Reason The capacitor is alternately charged and discharged as the current reverses after each half-cycle. **NCERT Pg. 184**

5 **Assertion** Capacitor serves as a barrier for DC and offers an easy path to AC.
Reason Capacitive reactance is inversely proportional to frequency. **NCERT Pg. 184**

6 **Assertion** In an AC circuit, the power factor can be improved by adding a capacitor.
Reason A capacitor in parallel with the load can be provide leading reactive power, compensating for lagging reactive power in load. **NCERT Pg. 184**

7 **Assertion** If $X_C > X_L$, ϕ is positive and the circuit is predominantly capacitive. The current in the circuit leads the source voltage.

Reason If $X_C < X_L$, ϕ is negative and the circuit is predominantly inductive. The current in the circuit lags the source voltage. NCERT Pg. 186

8 **Assertion** In a series R-L-C circuit, the voltages across resistor, inductor and capacitor are 8V, 16V and 10V, respectively. The resultant emf in the circuit is 10 V.

Reason Resultant emf of the circuit is given by the relation.

$$E = \sqrt{V_R^2 + (V_L - V_C)^2}$$ NCERT Pg. 186

9 **Assertion** Resonance phenomenon is exhibited only by a circuit having both L and C.

Reason Voltage across L and C cancel each other and the current amplitude is V_m / R, the total source voltage appearing across R causes resonance. NCERT Pg. 186

10 **Assertion** A transformer can increase voltage without affecting current, violating the law of conservation of energy.

Reason A transformer operates on the principle of mutual induction, where a change in voltage is balanced by a change in current to maintain energy conservation. NCERT Pg. 195

Statement Based Questions

Direction (Q. No. 1-8) *In the following questions, two statement (I and II) are given. In the light of the given statement, choose the correct options given below.*

(a) Both Statement I and Statement II are incorrect.
(b) Statement I is correct but Statement II is incorrect.
(c) Statement I is incorrect but Statement II is correct.
(d) Both Statement I and Statement II are correct.

1 **Statement I** The alternating current lags behind the emf by a phase angle of $\frac{\pi}{2}$, when AC flows through an capacitor.

Statement II The capacitive reactance is directly proportional to frequency of AC sources. NCERT Pg. 182

2 **Statement I** Circuit containing capacitors should be handled cautiously even when there is no current.
Statement II The capacitors are very delicate and so quickly breakdown. NCERT Pg. 184

3 **Statement I** An electric lamp connected in series with a variable capacitor and AC source, its brightness increases with increase in capacitance.
Statement II Capacitive reactance decreases with increase in capacitance of capacitor. NCERT Pg. 185

4 **Statement I** At resonance, L-C-R series circuit have a minimum current.

Statement II At resonance, in L-C-R series circuit, the current and emf are in phase with each other. NCERT Pg. 189

5 **Statement I** The signal picked up in the antenna acts as a source in the tuning circuit of the radio, so the circuit can be driven at only one frequency.

Statement II The antenna of radio accepts signals from many broadcasting stations. NCERT Pg. 189

6 **Statement I** When AC circuit contains resistor only, its power is maximum.
Statement II Power of AC circuit is independent of phase angle. NCERT Pg. 191

7 **Statement I** Power will not be dissipated in purely inductive or capacitive circuit even though a current is flowing in the circuit.
Statement II When a capacitor is connected to an inductor, the charge on the capacitor and the inductor in the circuit exhibit the phenomenon of electrical oscillation. NCERT Pg. 191

8 **Statement I** A step-up transformer converts low AC voltage into high AC voltage without changing frequency of AC source.
Statement II Core of transformer is made of a magnetic material of high permeability. NCERT Pg. 195

Matching Type Questions

1 Match the Column I (AC circuit condition) with Column II (power dissipation). Choose the correct answer from the codes given below. NCERT Pg. 190

Column I	Column II
A. Resistive circuit	1. No power dissipation
B. Purely inductive or capacitive circuit	2. Maximum power dissipation because of $X_C = X_L$
C. L-C-R series circuit	3. Power dissipated only in the resistor
D. Power dissipated at resonance in L-C-R circuit	4. Maximum power dissipation

Codes

	A	B	C	D
(a)	1	2	4	3
(b)	4	1	3	2
(c)	3	1	4	2
(d)	2	1	3	4

2 Let an alternating emf $\mathbf{E} = \mathbf{E}_0 \sin \omega t$ be applied across a pure element in Column I, the instantaneous current in the circuit is given in Column II. Choose the correct answer from the codes given below. NCERT Pg. 185

Column I	Column II
A. Pure inductance	1. $i_0 = \dfrac{E_0}{2\pi f L}$
B. Pure capacitance	2. $i_0 = \dfrac{E_0}{R}$
C. Pure resistance	3. $f_0 = \dfrac{1}{2\pi}\sqrt{\dfrac{1}{LC} - \dfrac{R^2}{L^2}}$
D. In AC, parallel resonant circuit	4. $i_0 = E_0(2\pi \nu C)$

Codes

	A	B	C	D
(a)	1	4	2	3
(b)	3	2	1	4
(c)	4	3	2	1
(d)	2	1	3	4

3 For series R-L-C circuit, $R = 100\,\Omega$, $C = \dfrac{100}{\pi}\,\mu\text{F}$ and $L = \dfrac{100}{\pi}$ mH are connected to an AC source as shown in the figure. The rms value of AC voltage is 220 V and its frequency is 50 Hz. In Column I, some physical quantities are mentioned while in Column II information about quantities are provided. Match the following columns and select the correct option. (All values of Column II are in SI unit) NCERT Pg. 187

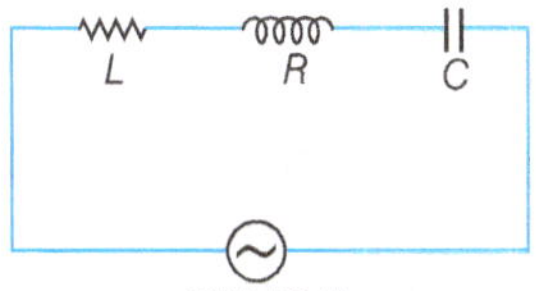

Column I	Column II
A. Impedance of the circuit	1. 265.7
B. rms value of the current through the circuit	2. 1.63
C. rms value of voltage across capacitor	3. 134.5
D. Average power dissipated across the resistor	4. 163

Codes

	A	B	C	D
(a)	3	2	4	1
(b)	1	4	3	2
(c)	3	4	2	1
(d)	4	3	1	2

Numerical Type Questions

1 An AC source is rated at 220V, 50Hz. Time taken for voltage to charge from the peak value to zero is $n \times 10^{-3}$s. The value of n is .... NCERT Pg. 179

2 A coil of inductance 300 mH and resistance 2Ω is connected to a source of voltage 2 V. The current reaches half of its steady state value in $m \times 10^{-1}$s. The value of m is .... NCERT Pg.182

3 A transmitting station releases waves of wavelength 840 m. A capacitor of 2.2 μF is used in the resonant circuit. The self-inductance of coil necessary for resonance is .... $\times 10^{-8}$H. NCERT Pg. 184

4 In an *L-C-R* series circuit, an inductor 40 mH and a resistor 1Ω are connected to an AC source of angular frequency 300 rad/s. The value of capacitance for which, the current leads the voltage by 45° is $\frac{1}{x} \times 10^{-2}$ F, then the value of x is .... NCERT Pg. 187

5 In the given circuit, the AC source had $\omega = 100$ rad/s. Considering the inductor and capacitor to be ideal, the net current through the circuit is $x \times 10^{-3}$ A. Then, the value of x is .... NCERT Pg. 187

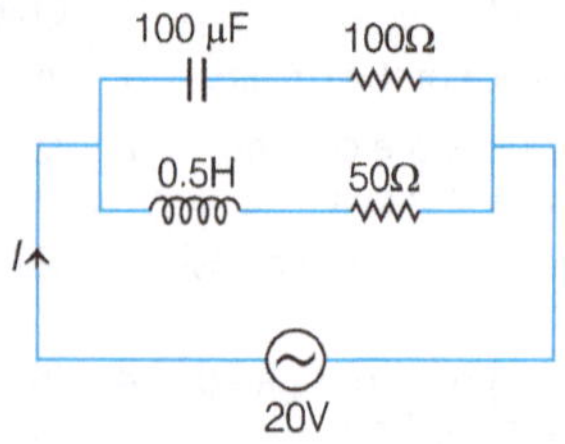

6 A sinusoidal voltage of peak value 220 V is applied to a series *L-C-R* circuit in which $R = 121\Omega$, $L = 24$ mH and $C = 60\,\mu$F. The value of power dissipated at resonant condition is x W. The value of x to the nearest integer is .... NCERT Pg. 189

7 In an *L-C-R* circuit, capacitance is changed from C to $2C$ for the resonant frequency to remain unchanged, the inductance should be charged from L to $\frac{L}{n}$. The value of n is .... NCERT Pg. 189

8 A series *L-C-R* circuit containing a resistance of $120\,\Omega$ has angular resonance frequency 4×10^5 rad s^{-1}. At resonance, the voltage across resistance and inductance are 60 V and 40 V, respectively. If the current in the circuit lags the voltage by 45°, the angular frequency of current is $x \times 10^5$ rad/s. The value of x is .... NCERT Pg. 189

9 Two circuits are shown in the figures (a) and (b). At a frequency of ....rad/s, the average power dissipated in one cycle will be same in both the circuits. NCERT Pg. 190

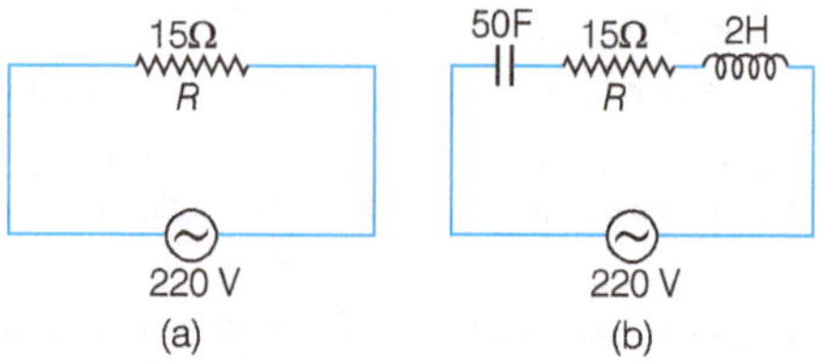

10 A circuit draws a power of 550 W from a source of 220 V, 50 Hz. The power factor of the circuit is 0.8 and the current lags in phase behind the potential difference. To make the power factor of the circuit as 1.0, value of the capacitance that will have to be connected with it is $\frac{1}{p\pi} \times 10^{-2}$ F, then the value of p is .... NCERT Pg. 191

11 Power factor of an *L-R* series is 0.6 and that of a *C-R* series circuit is 0.5. If the elements (*L*, *C*, and *R*) of the two circuits are joined in series the power factor of this circuit is found to be 1. The ratio of the resistance in the *L-R* circuit to the resistance in the *C-R* circuit is $\frac{x\sqrt{3}}{4}$ then the value of x is .... NCERT Pg. 191

12 A transformer is used to light a 140 W, 24 V lamp from 240 V AC mains. The current in the main cable is 0.7A. The efficiency of the transformation is .... (in percentage). NCERT Pg.. 194

13 An ideal transformer with purely resistive load operates at 10 kV on the primary side. It supplies electrical energy to a number of nearby houses at 220 V. The average rate of energy consumption in the houses served by the transformer is 110 kW. The value of resistive load (R_s) required in the secondary circuit will be .... mΩ. NCERT Pg. 195

14 1 MW power is to be delivered from a power station to a remote village 10 km away. If a step-up transformer is used to boost the voltage to 11000 V and transmitted through a pair of copper wires of radius 0.5 cm, then a step-down transformer is used to bring voltage to 220 V. The fraction of ohmic losses to power transmitted is ....%. ($\rho_{cu} = 1.7 \times 10^{-8}$ SI unit) NCERT Pg. 19

NCERT Exemplar Questions

1 If the rms current in a 50 Hz AC circuit is 5 A, the value of the current 1/300 s after its value becomes zero is
(a) $5\sqrt{2}$ A (b) $5\sqrt{3/2}$ A (c) (5 / 6) A (d) $(5/\sqrt{2})$ A

2 An alternating current generator has an internal resistance R_g and an internal reactance X_g. It is used to supply power to a passive load consisting of a resistance R_g and a reactance X_L. For maximum power to be delivered from the generator to the load, the value of X_L is equal to
(a) zero (b) X_g (c) $-X_g$ (d) R_g

3 When a voltage measuring device is connected to AC mains, the meter shows the steady input voltage of 220 V. This means
(a) input voltage cannot be AC voltage, but a DC voltage
(b) maximum input voltage is 220 V
(c) the meter reads not v but $<v^2>$ and is calibrated to read $\sqrt{<v^2>}$
(d) the pointer of the meter is stuck by some mechanical defect

4 To reduce the resonant frequency in an L-C-R series circuit with a generator,
(a) the generator frequency should be reduced
(b) another capacitor should be added in parallel to the first
(c) the iron core of the inductor should be removed
(d) dielectric in the capacitor should be removed

5 An inductor of reactance 1Ω and a resistor of 2Ω are connected in series to the terminals of a 6V (rms) AC source. The power dissipated in the circuit is
(a) 8 W (b) 12 W (c) 14.4 W (d) 18 W

6 The output of a step-down transformer is measured to be 24 V when connected to a 12 W light bulb. The value of the peak current is
(a) $(1/\sqrt{2})$ A (b) $\sqrt{2}$ A (c) 2 A (d) $2\sqrt{2}$ A

Past Exams Questions

NEET

1 A 10 μF capacitor is connected to a 210 V, 50 Hz source as shown in figure. The peak current in the circuit is nearly ($\pi = 3.14$). NCERT Pg. 184, NEET 2024

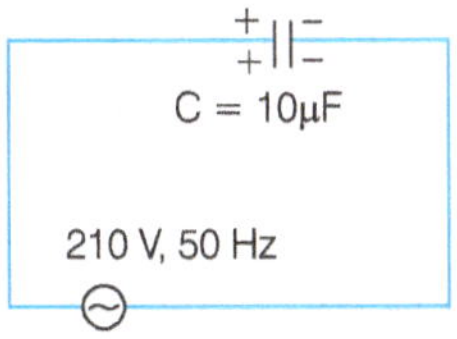

(a) 0.58 A (b) 0.93 A
(c) 1.20 A (d) 0.35 A

2 In an ideal transformer, the turns ratio is $\frac{N_p}{N_s} = \frac{1}{2}$. The ratio $V_s : V_p$ is equal to (the symbols carry their usual meaning) NCERT Pg. 195, NEET 2024
(a) 1 : 2 (b) 2 : 1 (c) 1 : 1 (d) 1 : 4

3 In a series L-C-R circuit, the inductance L is 10 mH, capacitance C is 1 μF and resistance R is 100 Ω. The frequency at which resonance occurs is NCERT Pg. 189, NEET 2023
(a) 15.9 kHz (b) 1.59 rad/s (c) 1.59 kHz (d) 15.9 rad/s

4 The net impedance of circuit (as shown in figure) will be NCERT Pg. 189, NEET 2023

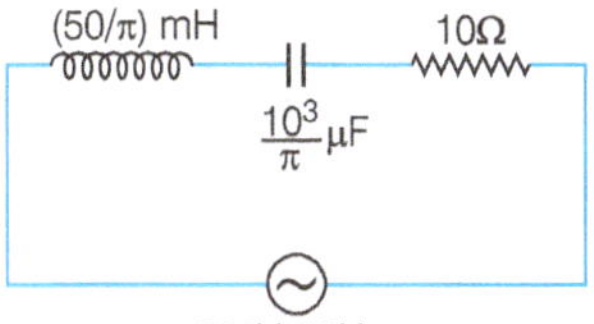

(a) 15 Ω (b) $5\sqrt{5}\ \Omega$
(c) 25 Ω (d) $10\sqrt{2}\ \Omega$

5 A 12 V, 60 W lamp is connected to the secondary of a step-down transformer, whose primary is connected to AC mains of 220 V. Assuming the transformer to be ideal, what is the current in the primary winding? NCERT Pg. 195, NEET 2023
(a) 2.7 A (b) 3.7 A (c) 0.37 A (d) 0.27 A

6 The peak voltage of the AC source is equal to NCERT Pg. 180, NEET 2022
(a) the rms value of the AC source
(b) $\sqrt{2}$ times the rms value of the AC source
(c) $1/\sqrt{2}$ times the rms value of the AC source
(d) the value of voltage supplied to the circuit

7 A series L-C-R circuit with inductance 10 H, capacitance 10 μF, resistance 50Ω is connected to an AC source of voltage, $V = 200\sin(100\,t)$ volt. If the resonant frequency

of the L-C-R circuit is ν_0 and the frequency of the AC source is ν, then NCERT Pg. 189, NEET 2022

(a) $\nu_0 = \nu = \frac{50}{\pi}$ Hz (b) $\nu_0 = \frac{50}{\pi}$ Hz, $\nu = 50$ Hz

(c) $\nu = 100$ Hz, $\nu_0 = \frac{100}{\pi}$ Hz (d) $\nu_0 = \nu = 50$ Hz

8 An inductor of inductance L, a capacitor of capacitance C and a resistor of resistance R are connected in series to an AC source of potential difference V volts as shown in figure.

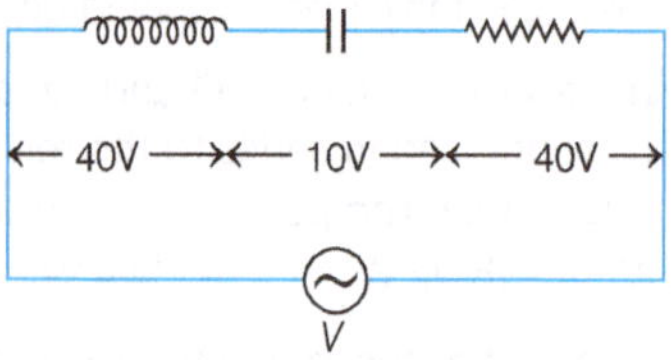

Potential difference across L, C and R is 40 V, 10 V and 40 V, respectively. The amplitude of current flowing through L-C-R series circuit is $10\sqrt{2}$ A. The impedance of the circuit is NCERT Pg. 187, NEET 2021

(a) $4\sqrt{2}\ \Omega$ (b) $5\sqrt{2}\ \Omega$ (c) $4\ \Omega$ (d) $5\ \Omega$

9 A 40 μF capacitor is connected to a 200 V, 50 Hz AC supply. The rms value of the current in the circuit is, nearly NCERT Pg. 184, NEET 2020

(a) 2.05 A (b) 2.5 A
(c) 25.1 A (d) 1.7 A

10 A circuit when connected to an AC source of 12 V gives a current of 0.2 A. The same circuit when connected to a DC source of 12 V, gives a current of 0.4 A. The circuit is NCERT Pg. 186, NEET 2019

(a) series L-R (b) series R-C
(c) series L-C (d) series L-C-R

11 An inductor 20 mH, a capacitor 100 μF and a resistor 50 Ω are connected in series across a source of emf, $V = 10\sin 314t$. The power loss in the circuit is NCERT Pg. 191, NEET 2018

(a) 0.79 W (b) 0.43 W (c) 2.74 W (d) 1.13 W

12 A 100 Ω resistance and a capacitor of 100 Ω reactance are connected in series across a 220 V source. When the capacitor is 50% charged, the peak value of the displacement current is NCERT Pg. 191, NEET 2016

(a) 2.2 A (b) 11 A (c) 4.4 A (d) $11\sqrt{2}$ A

JEE Main

13 A capacitor of capacitance 150.0 μF is connected to an alternating source of emf given by $E = 36\sin(120\pi t)$ V. The maximum value of current in the circuit is approximately equal to NCERT Pg. 184, JEE Main 2023

(a) 2 A (b) $\sqrt{2}$ A
(c) $2\sqrt{2}$ A (d) $1/\sqrt{2}$ A

14 In a series L-R circuit with $X_L = R$, power factor is P_1. If a capacitor of capacitance C with $X_C = X_L$ is added to the circuit the power factor becomes P_2. The ratio of P_1 to P_2 will be NCERT Pg. 191, JEE Main 2023

(a) 1 : 1 (b) 1 : 2 (c) 1 : 3 (d) $1 : \sqrt{2}$

15 In the given circuit, rms value of current (I_{rms}) through the resistor R is NCERT Pg. 187, JEE Main 2023

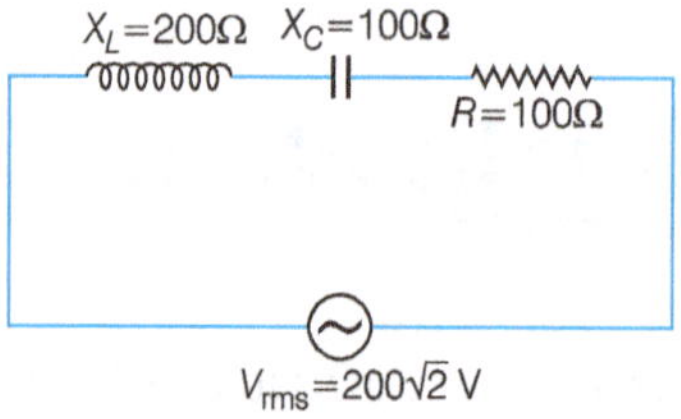

(a) 20 A (b) $2\sqrt{2}$ A (c) 2 A (d) $\frac{1}{2}$ A

16 An alternating emf $E = 440 \sin 100\pi t$ is applied to a circuit containing an inductance of $\sqrt{2}/\pi$ H. If an AC ammeter is connected in the circuit, its reading will be NCERT Pg. 182, JEE Main 2022

(a) 4.4 A (b) 1.55 A (c) 2.2 A (d) 3.11 A

17 A direct current of 4 A and an alternating current of peak value 4 A flow through resistance of 3 Ω and 2 Ω, respectively. The ratio of heat produced in the two resistances in same interval of time will be NCERT Pg. 180, JEE Main 2022

(a) 3 : 2 (b) 3 : 1 (c) 3 : 4 (d) 4 : 3

Skill Boosters

1 A transformer has an efficiency of 80%. It works at 4 kW and 100 V. If the secondary voltage is 240 V, find the primary and secondary currents.

(a) 20 A, 13.3 A (b) 40 A, 13.3 A
(c) 50 A, 40 A (d) 30 A, 20 A

2 Kanha wants to calculate the current and power dissipated in an L-C-R series circuit. He connected 100 Ω resistance to an AC source of peak value 200 V and angular frequency 300 rad/s. When he removed only the capacitance, the current was found to be lagging behind the voltage by 60°. While on removing the inductance, he found the current leading the voltage by 60°. The value of peak current and the power dissipated obtained by him will be

(a) 2 A, 200 W
(b) 4 A, 100 W
(c) 3 A, 120 W
(d) None of these

3 The line that draws power supply to your house from street has

(a) non-zero average current
(b) 220 V average voltage
(c) voltage and current out of phase by 90°
(d) voltage and current possibly differing in phase ϕ, such that $|\phi| < \pi/2$

4 Figure shows an experimental plot for discharging of a capacitor in an R-C circuit. The time constant τ of this circuit lies between

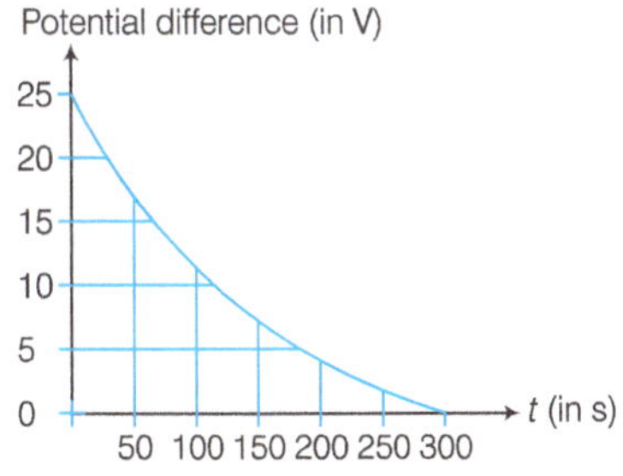

(a) 150 s and 200 s
(b) 0 s and 50 s
(c) 50 s and 100 s
(d) 100 s and 150 s

5 For an AC circuit shown in figure, the supply voltage has a constant rms value V but variable frequency f. At resonance, the circuit

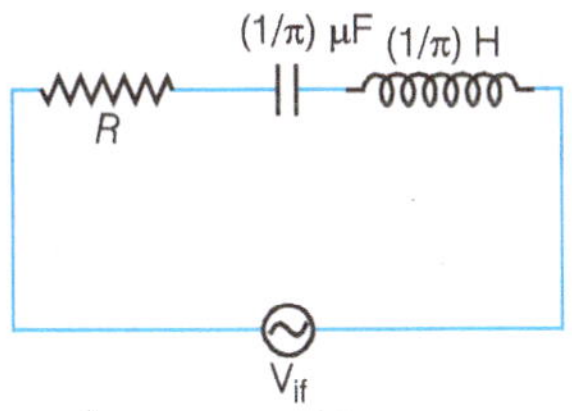

(a) has current given by $I = \frac{V}{R}$
(b) has a resonance frequency of 1000 Hz.
(c) has a voltage across the capacitor which is 90° out of phase with that across the inductor.
(d) has a current given by $I = \frac{V}{\sqrt{R^2 + \left(\frac{1}{\pi} + \frac{1}{\pi}\right)^2}}$

6 A series R-L-C circuit consisting of a resistor $R << \sqrt{\frac{44}{C}}$, is set up in the oscillations. In time $t = \log 2 \times \left(\frac{2L}{R}\right)$, instantaneous current becomes $\frac{1}{K}$ times of maximum current. Find the value of K.

(a) 1
(b) 2
(c) 3
(d) 4

7 An alternating voltage is given by $e = e_1 \sin \omega t + e_2 \cos \omega t$, then the root mean square value of voltage is given by

(a) $\sqrt{e_1^2 + e_2^2}$
(b) $\sqrt{e_1 e_2}$
(c) $\sqrt{\frac{e_1 e_2}{2}}$
(d) $\sqrt{\frac{e_1^2 + e_2^2}{2}}$

8 When 100 V DC is applied across a solenoid, a current of 1 A flows in it. When 100 V AC is applied across the same coil, the current drops to 0.5 A. If the frequency of the AC source is 50 Hz, the impedance and inductance of solenoid are

(a) 100 Ω, 0.93 H
(b) 200 Ω, 1.0 H
(c) 10 Ω, 0.86 H
(d) 200 Ω, 0.55 H

9 A series L-C-R circuit containing a resistance of 120 Ω has angular resonance frequency 4×10^3 rad/s. At resonance, the voltage across resistance and inductance are 60 V and 40 V, respectively. The values of L and C are respectively

(a) 20 mH, $\frac{25}{8}$ μF
(b) 2 mH, $\frac{1}{35}$ μF
(c) 20 mH, $\frac{1}{40}$ μF
(d) 2 mH, $\frac{25}{8}$ μF

10 For an AC voltage, $\Delta V = 100 \sin 1000t$ is applied to a series R-L-C circuit. Given, resistance is 400 Ω, capacitance is 5 μF and the inductance is 0.5 H, then

(a) current amplitude in the circuit is 2 A
(b) current amplitude in the circuit is 0.4 A
(c) average power dissipated in the circuit is 40 W
(d) average power dissipated in the circuit is 8 W

Correct Codes

Topical Questions

1 (d)	2 (c)	3 (d)	4 (c)	5 (b)	6 (c)	7 (b)	8 (c)	9 (d)	10 (d)
11 (c)	12 (b)	13 (c)	14 (c)	15 (a)	16 (d)	17 (b)	18 (b)	19 (c)	20 (b)
21 (a)	22 (d)	23 (c)	24 (d)	25 (c)	26 (b)	27 (c)	28 (c)	29 (a)	30 (c)
31 (b)	32 (a)	33 (b)	34 (b)	35 (c)	36 (d)	37 (a)	38 (c)	39 (c)	40 (b)
41 (a)	42 (b)	43 (a)	44 (a)	45 (a)	46 (d)	47 (b)	48 (b)	49 (b)	50 (c)
51 (a)	52 (b)	53 (c)	54 (d)	55 (d)	56 (c)	57 (a)	58 (a)	59 (a)	60 (a)
61 (a)	62 (b)	63 (b)	64 (c)	65 (a)	66 (b)	67 (a)	68 (c)	69 (a)	70 (c)
71 (b)	72 (a)	73 (c)	74 (d)	75 (b)	76 (c)	77 (a)	78 (c)	79 (d)	80 (c)
81 (c)	82 (d)	83 (c)	84 (d)	85 (c)	86 (d)	87 (c)	88 (c)	89 (c)	90 (c)
91 (b)	92 (d)	93 (a)	94 (a)	95 (b)	96 (b)	97 (c)	98 (b)		

Assertion and Reason Questions

1 (a)	2 (a)	3 (c)	4 (a)	5 (a)	6 (a)	7 (b)	8 (a)	9 (a)	10 (d)

Statement Based Questions

1 (a)	2 (b)	3 (d)	4 (c)	5 (d)	6 (b)	7 (d)	8 (d)

Matching Type Questions

1 (b)	2 (a)	3. (a)

Numerical Type Questions

1 (5)	2 (1)	3 (9)	4 (39)	5 (300)	6 (200)	7 (2)	8 (8)	9 (100)	10 (42)
11 (3)	12 (83.3)	13 (440)	14 (3.6)						

NCERT Exemplar Questions

1 (b)	2 (c)	3 (c)	4 (b)	5 (c)	6 (a)

Past Exams Questions

1 (b)	2 (b)	3 (c)	4 (b)	5 (d)	6 (b)	7 (a)	8 (d)	9 (b)	10 (a)
11 (a)	12 (a)	13 (a)	14 (d)	15 (c)	16 (c)	17 (b)			

Skill Boosters

1 (b)	2 (a)	3 (d)	4 (d)	5 (a)	6 (b)	7 (d)	8 (d)	9 (a)	10 (d)

Step by Step

Decoding the Questions

Concept Builders

1 $\frac{I_{av}}{0.637}=\frac{I_{rms}}{0.707}$

2 True (T)

3 DC

4 transformer

5 True (T)

6 resistor

7 vector

8 $I_{rms}\,I_{rms}$

9 True (T)

10 Zero watt

11 maximum

12 True (T)

13 $i_m=\frac{\varepsilon_m}{X_C}$

14 minimum

15 $Z=\sqrt{R^2+(X_C-X_L)^2}$

16 $Q=\frac{1}{R}\sqrt{\frac{L}{C}}$

17 $P=i_m^2R=\frac{\varepsilon_m^2R}{[R^2+(X_L-X_C)^2]}$

18 False(F)

19 frequency

20 False(F)

Topical Questions

1 (*d*) The current takes $\frac{T}{4}$ seconds to reach the peak value, where T is the time period.

From $I=I_0\sin\omega t$, we get

$$\omega=\frac{2\pi}{T}=200\,\pi$$

$$\Rightarrow\quad T=\frac{1}{100}\text{ s}$$

∴ Time required to reach the peak value $=T/4=\frac{1}{400}$ s.

2 (*c*) Given, $V_{rms}=220\text{ V}, \nu=50\text{ Hz}$

$\Rightarrow V_m=V_{rms}\sqrt{2}$

$=(220\text{ V})(1.414)=311.1\text{ V}$

Further, $\omega=2\pi\nu=2\pi\times50$

$=100\,\pi\text{ rads}^{-1}$

Thus,

$V=V_m\sin\omega t=311.1\sin(100\,\pi)\,t$

4 (*c*) Here,

$i=i_1\cos\omega t+i_2\sin\omega t$ ...(i)

Let, $i_1=A\sin\phi$ ...(ii)

and $i_2=A\cos\phi$ ...(iii)

∴ From Eq. (i), we have

$i=A\sin\phi\cos\omega t+A\cos\phi\sin\omega t$

$=A[\cos\omega t\sin\phi+\sin\omega t\cos\phi]$

$i=A\sin(\omega t+\phi)$ ...(iv)

Squaring and adding Eqs. (ii) and (iii), we get

i.e. $i_1^2+i_2^2=A^2\sin^2\phi+A^2\cos^2\phi$

$=A^2$

$\Rightarrow\quad A=(i_1^2+i_2^2)^{1/2}$

∴ From Eq. (iv), we have

$i=(i_1^2+i_2^2)^{1/2}\sin(\omega t+\phi)$ ...(v)

∴ Comparing Eq. (v) with equation, $i=i_m\sin(\omega t+\phi)$, we get

$i_m=(i_1^2+i_2^2)^{1/2}$

$\therefore\quad i_{rms}=\frac{i_m}{\sqrt{2}}=\frac{(i_1^2+i_2^2)^{1/2}}{\sqrt{2}}$

5 (*b*) Equation

$V=150\sin(150t)$ compare with

$V=V_0\sin\omega t$, we get $V_0=150$ V

and equation

$I=150\sin(150t)$ compare with

$I=I_0\sin(\omega t)$, we get

$I_0=150$ A

The power dissipated in AC circuit,

$P=\frac{1}{2}V_0I_0$

$=\frac{1}{2}\times150\times150$

$=11250$ W

6 (*c*) According to question,

Heat produced by AC = 3 × Heat produced by DC

$I_{rms}^2Rt=3I^2Rt$

$I_{rms}^2=3I^2$

$I_{rms}^2=3\times(2)^2$

$[\because I=2\text{A (given)}]$

$I_{rms}=\sqrt{3}\times2=3.46$ A

7 (*b*) Amplitude of alternating voltage = Peak voltage (V_m)

= 120 V, hence rms value of voltage, i.e.

$V_{rms}=\frac{V_m}{\sqrt{2}}=\frac{120}{1.414}=84.8$ V

8 (*c*) The voltage produced by generator, $V=240\sin120t$

$V_m=240$ V and $\omega=120$ rad/s

Frequency of a generator,

$\nu=\frac{\omega}{2\pi}=\frac{120\times7}{2\times22}$

$=19.09\simeq19$ Hz

$\Rightarrow V_{rms}=\frac{V_m}{\sqrt{2}}=\frac{240}{\sqrt{2}}$

$=120\sqrt{2}\approx170$ V

9 (*d*) $V=120\sin(100\pi t)\cos(100\pi t)$

$=60\sin(200\pi t)$

$(\because\sin2\theta=2\sin\theta\cos\theta)$

So, $V_0=60$ V

$\omega=200\pi$

$2\pi f=200\cdot\pi$

$f=100$ Hz

10 (*d*) Given, $V=140\sin314t$,

$R=40\Omega, V_0=140$ V

$\therefore\quad I_{rms}=\frac{V_{rms}}{R}=\frac{0.707V_0}{R}$

$=\frac{0.707\times140}{40}=2.47$A

11 (*c*) $V=V_0$ for $0\le t\le\frac{T}{2}$

$V=0$ for $\frac{T}{2}\le t\le T$

$$V_{rms}=\left[\frac{\int_0^T v^2dt}{\int_0^T dt}\right]^{\frac{1}{2}}$$

$$=\left[\frac{V_0^2}{T}[t]_0^{\frac{T}{2}}\right]^{\frac{1}{2}}=\frac{V_0}{\sqrt{2}}$$

12 (*b*) Given,

Resistance $= 800\Omega$

Voltage $= 220$ V

$f = 50$ Hz

$I_{rms} = \frac{V_{rms}}{R} = 0.275$ A

13 (*c*) In the pure resistive circuit current and voltage both are in phase. Hence, (c) is correct.

14 (*c*) The phase difference between the voltage and the current in resistance only circuit will be zero.

19 (*c*) $X_L = 2\pi\nu L$

$= 2 \times 3.14 \times 50 \times 25 \times 10^{-3}$

$= 7.85\ \Omega$

20 (*b*) The rms current in the circuit,

$$i_{rms} = \frac{V}{X_L} = \frac{V}{2\pi\nu L}$$

$$= \frac{200}{2 \times 3.14 \times 50 \times 40 \times 10^{-3}}$$

≈ 16 A

21 (*a*) Reactance $= 120\ \Omega$

Frequency, $\nu = 200$ Hz

$X_L = \omega L = 2\pi\nu L$

$$\Rightarrow L = \frac{X_L}{2\pi\nu} = \frac{120}{2\pi \times 200} = \frac{3}{10\pi} \text{ H}$$

If X'_L denotes the reactance of the same inductance at 60 Hz, then

$X'_L = \omega' L = 2\pi\nu' L$

$$\Rightarrow X'_L = (2\pi \times 60)\left(\frac{3}{10\pi}\right) = 36\ \Omega$$

So, $i_{rms} = \frac{V_{rms}}{X'_L} = \frac{240 \text{ V}}{36\ \Omega} = 6.66$ A

22 (*d*) $R = \frac{V}{I} = \frac{80}{10} = 8\ \Omega$

and $\omega = 50$ Hz

For AC circuit, we have

$$I = \frac{V}{\sqrt{R^2 + X_L^2}}$$

$$\Rightarrow 10 = \frac{220}{\sqrt{64 + X_L^2}}$$

$$\Rightarrow \sqrt{64 + X_L^2} = 22$$

$$\Rightarrow X_L = \sqrt{420}$$

$$\Rightarrow 2\pi\nu L = \sqrt{420}$$

Series inductor on an arc lamp,

$$L = \frac{\sqrt{420}}{2\pi \times 50} = 0.065 \text{ H}$$

23 (*c*) For circuit element *X*, current is same phase with voltage, *X* must be a resistor.

$$\therefore R = \frac{V_0}{I_0} = \frac{200}{5} = 40\Omega$$

For circuit element *Y*,

Current lags behind the voltage by 90°, thus *Y* must be a inductor.

$$X_L = \frac{V_0}{I_0} = \frac{200}{5} = 40\Omega$$

In the series combination of *R* and *L*,

$$Z = \sqrt{R^2 + X_L^2}$$

$$= \sqrt{40^2 + 40^2} = 40\sqrt{2}\ \Omega$$

$$I_{rms} = \frac{V_{rms}}{Z} = \frac{V_0}{\sqrt{2}Z}$$

$$= \frac{200}{\sqrt{2} \times \sqrt{2} \times 40} = \frac{5}{2} \text{ A}$$

25 (*c*) $I = 20\sin(100\pi t + 0.05\pi)$A

Comparing with standard equation, we get

$I_0 = 20$ A and $\omega = 100\pi$ rad/s

$$\therefore I_{rms} = \frac{I_0}{\sqrt{2}} = \frac{20}{\sqrt{2}} = 10\sqrt{2}\text{A}$$

and $\nu = \frac{\omega}{2\pi} = \frac{100\pi}{2\pi} = 50$ Hz

26 (*b*) As, $C = 30 \times 10^{-6}$F, $V_{rms} = 150$ V, $\nu = 60$ Hz

Capacitance reactance,

$$X_C = \frac{1}{\omega C} = \frac{1}{2\pi\nu C} = 88.46\ \Omega$$

$$I_{rms} = \frac{V_{rms}}{X_C} = \frac{150}{88.46} = 1.7\text{A}$$

27 (*c*) In pure capacitive circuit,

$$X_C = \frac{1}{2\pi f C}$$

$$\Rightarrow \frac{X_{C_1}}{X_{C_2}} = \frac{\nu_2}{\nu_1} = \frac{2\nu}{\nu} = 2$$

So, $X_{C_2} = \frac{X_{C_1}}{2}$

28 (*c*) Given, $C = 15\ \mu\text{F} = 15 \times 10^{-6}$F, $V = 220$ V and $\nu = 50$ Hz

Capacitive reactance,

$$X_C = \frac{1}{2\pi\nu C}$$

$$= \frac{1}{2\pi(50)(15 \times 10^{-6})}$$

$= 212\ \Omega$

29 (*a*) Capacitive reactance,

$$X_C = \frac{1}{\omega C} = \frac{1}{2\pi\nu C}$$

or $X_C \propto \frac{1}{\nu}$ ...(i)

Current,

$$I = \frac{V_{rms}}{X_C} = V_{rms} \cdot \omega C = V_{rms} \cdot 2\pi\nu C$$

$\Rightarrow I \propto \nu$ ...(ii)

From Eqs. (i) and (ii), we conclude that, if the frequency is doubled, the capacitive reactance is halved and the current is doubled.

30 (*c*) Given, $C = 36\ \mu\text{F} = 36 \times 10^{-6}$F, $V = 240$ V and $\nu = 50$ Hz

Capacitive reactance,

$$X_C = \frac{1}{2\pi\nu C}$$

$$= \frac{1}{2\pi \times 50 \times 36 \times 10^{-6}} = 88\ \Omega$$

The rms current, $i_{rms} = \frac{V_{rms}}{X_C}$

$$= \frac{240}{88} = 2.73 \text{ A}$$

The peak current, $i_m = \sqrt{2}\, i_{rms}$

= (1.41) (2.73 A) = 3.85 A

31 (*b*) Given, alternating voltage, $V = 200\sqrt{2}\sin(100t)$ and $C = 1\ \mu\text{F} = 1 \times 10^{-6}$ F

From standard equation

$V = V_m \sin \omega t$,

we get $V_m = 200\sqrt{2}$ V

and $\omega = 100$ rad/s

Reading of ammeter,

$$i_{rms} = \frac{V_{rms}}{X_C} = \frac{V_m \omega C}{\sqrt{2}} \quad \left(\because X_C = \frac{1}{\omega C}\right)$$

$$= \frac{200\sqrt{2} \times 100 \times (1 \times 10^{-6})}{\sqrt{2}}$$

$= 2 \times 10^{-2}$A = 20 mA

32 (*a*) Statement given in option (a) is incorrect and it can be corrected as

The current in a capacitive circuit is $i = i_m \sin\left(\omega t + \frac{\pi}{2}\right)$ because currents leads voltage in capacitive circuit.

33 (*b*) The capacitive reactance in an AC circuit is given by

$$X_C = \frac{1}{\omega C} = \frac{1}{2\pi\nu C}$$

In a DC circuit, frequency of current is zero, i.e.,

$$\nu = 0$$

$$\Rightarrow \quad X_C = \frac{1}{2\pi\nu C} = 0$$

So, its values are different for AC and DC circuits. Hence, statement given in option (b) is correct and rest are incorrect.

34 (*b*) Current leads the voltage by $\frac{\pi}{2}$ in case of pure capacitor, hence

$$I = I_0 \sin\left(100\pi t - \frac{\pi}{3} + \frac{\pi}{2}\right)$$

$$= \frac{V_0}{X_c} \sin\left(100\pi t + \frac{\pi}{6}\right)$$

$$= V_0 \omega C \sin\left(100\pi t + \frac{\pi}{6}\right)$$

$$= (200)(100\pi)(2 \times 10^{-6}) \sin\left(100\pi t + \frac{\pi}{6}\right)$$

$$= 0.04\pi \sin\left(100\pi t + \frac{\pi}{6}\right)$$

35 (*c*) Given, $C = 15\,\mu F = 1.5 \times 10^{-5}$ F,

$$\nu = 50 \text{ Hz}$$

$$V_{rms} = 220 \text{ V}$$

$\therefore$ Capacitive reactance,

$$X_C = \frac{1}{\omega C} = \frac{1}{2\pi f C}$$

$$= \frac{1}{2 \times 3.14 \times 50 \times 1.5 \times 10^{-5}}$$

$$= 212.2\ \Omega$$

$$\therefore I_{rms} = \frac{V_{rms}}{X_C}$$

$$= \frac{220}{212.2} = 1.04 \text{ A}$$

36 (*d*) For the first circuit, $i = \frac{V}{X_L} = \frac{V}{\omega L}$

$$\Rightarrow \quad i \propto \frac{1}{\omega}$$

For the second circuit,

$$i = \frac{V}{X_C} = \frac{V}{1/\omega C} = \omega C V$$

$$\Rightarrow i \propto \omega$$

Hence, if the frequency ω of the emf of AC is increased, the value of current will decrease in the first circuit and increase in the second circuit.

38 (*c*) As we know that,

$$X_C = \frac{1}{\omega C}$$

but $\quad \omega = 2\pi f$

$$\therefore \quad X_C = \frac{1}{2\pi f C}$$

$$X_C \propto \frac{1}{f}$$

Hence, X_C is inversely proportional to ν., so correct graph is (c).

39 (*c*) Given, $C = 100\,\mu F = 10^{-4}$ F

$$R = 40\Omega$$

Frequency, $\nu = 60$ Hz

By using,

$$\tan\phi = \frac{X_C}{R} = \frac{1}{\omega CR}$$

$$= \frac{1}{2\pi\nu CR} = \frac{1}{2\pi \times 60 \times 10^{-4} \times 40}$$

$$= 0.6634$$

$$\phi = \tan^{-1}(0.6634)$$

$$= \frac{33.56 \times \pi}{180} \text{ rad}$$

Now, time lag,

$$\Delta t = \frac{\phi}{\omega} = \frac{\frac{33.56 \times \pi}{180}}{120\,\pi}$$

$$= 1.55 \times 10^{-3} \text{ s}$$

41 (*a*) For series *L*-*C*-*R* circuit, applied emf and current across resistance are in same phase and across inductor coil have phase difference of $\frac{\pi}{2}$.

The potential difference at capacitor and inductor has phase difference of π and across resistance and capacitor is of $\pi/2$.

42 (*b*) Given, $R = 30\Omega$

$$X_C = 25\Omega$$

$$X_L = 25\Omega$$

$$V_{rms} = 240 \text{ V}$$

Here, $\quad X_L = X_C$

So, $\quad Z = R$

Therefore, potential drop across *C* and *L* is zero.

Now, current in this circuit,

$$I_{rms} = \frac{V_{rms}}{Z} = \frac{240}{30} = 8\text{A}$$

43 (*a*) In series *L*-*C*-*R* circuit, supply voltage will be

$$V_{rms} = \sqrt{V_R^2 + (V_L - V_C)^2}$$

$$= \sqrt{(40)^2 + (60-30)^2}$$

$$= \sqrt{1600 + 900}$$

$$= \sqrt{2500} = 50 \text{ V}$$

44 (*a*) Given, source voltage (resultant voltage) $V = 120$ V

Voltage across inductor,

$$V_L = 50 \text{ V}$$

Voltage across resistor,

$$V_R = 40 \text{ V}$$

In series *L*-*C*-*R* circuit,

$$V = \sqrt{V_R^2 + (V_L - V_C)^2}$$

or $\quad 120 = \sqrt{40^2 + (50 - V_C)^2}$

$$120^2 = 40^2 + (50 - V_C)^2$$

$$\Rightarrow \quad (50 - V_C)^2 = 12800$$

$$\Rightarrow \quad 50 - V_C = 80\sqrt{2}$$

$$\Rightarrow \quad V_C = 10(5 - 8\sqrt{2})$$

45 (*a*) Given, $R = 3\Omega$, $X_L = 15\Omega$, $X_C = 11\Omega$, and $V_{rms} = 10$ V

∴Current through the circuit,

$$i_{rms} = \frac{V_{rms}}{\sqrt{R^2 + (X_L - X_C)^2}} = \frac{10}{\sqrt{(3)^2 + (15-11)^2}} = \frac{10}{\sqrt{9+16}} = \frac{10}{5} = 2 \text{ A}$$

In series combination, potential difference across R is,

$$V_R = i_{rms} R = 2 \times 3 = 6 \text{ V}$$

Across L, $V_L = i_{rms} X_L = 2 \times 15 = 30$ V

Across C, $V_C = i_{rms} X_C = 2 \times 11 = 22$ V

So, potential difference,

$$V_{LC} = V_L - V_C = 30 - 22 = 8 \text{ V}$$

47 (b) In a series L-C-R circuit, the AC current in each element is the same at any time, having the same amplitude and phase.

The phasor I is always parallel to phasor V_R, the phase angle ϕ is the angle between V_R and V and can be determined from

$$\tan\phi = \frac{V_L - V_C}{V_R}$$

when $V_L > V_C$

The impedance diagram is shown below

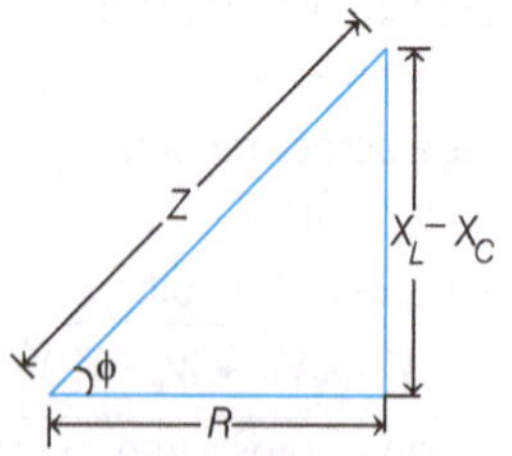

From figure, impedance,

$$Z = \sqrt{R^2 + (X_L - X_C)^2}$$

which is equivalent to the resistance in a circuit.

Hence, statement given in option (b) is correct and rest are incorrect.

48 (b) The statement given in option (b) is incorrect and it can be corrected as,

If ω is varied, then at a particular frequency ω_0, $X_C = X_L$ and the impedance is minimum ($Z = R$). This frequency is called the resonant frequency and given as

$$\omega_0 = \frac{1}{\sqrt{LC}}$$

Rest statements are correct.

49 (b) Equation of alternating voltage applied to the circuit,

$$V = 40\sqrt{2} \sin \omega t$$

AC voltmeter reads only rms value of voltage

$$\therefore V_{rms} = \frac{V_m}{\sqrt{2}} = 40 \text{ V} \quad [\because V_m = 40\sqrt{2}]$$

Again, according to the question,

$$\sqrt{V_1^2 + V_2^2} = V_{rms}$$

or $30^2 + V_2^2 = 40^2$

$$\therefore \text{Reading of } V_2 = \sqrt{40^2 - 30^2} = 26.45 \text{ V}$$

50 (c) Given, $V_L = V_C = 300$ V, $R = 100\,\Omega$ and $V_{rms} = 220$ V

Resultant voltage in L-C-R circuit,

$$V_{rms} = \sqrt{(V_L - V_C)^2 + V_R^2}$$

$$220 = \sqrt{(300-300)^2 + V_R^2}$$

or $V_R = 220$ V

Since, $V_L = V_C = 300$ V

$\Rightarrow IX_L = IX_C$

$\Rightarrow X_L = X_C$, hence given circuit is L-C-R series resonance circuit.

$$\therefore I_{rms} = \frac{V_R}{R} = \frac{220 \text{ V}}{100\,\Omega} = 2.2 \text{ A}$$

51 (a) Given, $V_R = 12$ V, $V_C = 5$ V

Let the applied voltage be V volt in given R-C circuit, then

$$V_{rms} = \sqrt{V_R^2 + V_C^2} = \sqrt{(12)^2 + (5)^2} = \sqrt{144 + 25} = \sqrt{169} = 13 \text{ V}$$

52 (b) Given, $V_m = 300$ V,

$\omega = 400 \text{ rads}^{-1}$

$R = 3\,\Omega$, $L = 20 \text{ mH} = 20 \times 10^{-3}$ H

and $C = 625\,\mu\text{F} = 625 \times 10^{-6}$ F.

The impedance of the circuit,

$$Z = \sqrt{R^2 + (X_L - X_C)^2}$$

Here,

$X_L = \omega L = 400 \times 20 \times 10^{-3} = 8\,\Omega$

and $X_C = \frac{1}{\omega C} = \frac{1}{400 \times 625 \times 10^{-6}} = 4\,\Omega$

$$\Rightarrow Z = \sqrt{(3)^2 + (8-4)^2} = 5\,\Omega$$

$$\therefore \text{Peak current, } i_m = \frac{V_m}{Z} = \frac{300}{5} = 60 \text{ A}$$

53 (c) Given, $R = 200\,\Omega$,

$C = 15\,\mu\text{F} = 15 \times 10^{-6}$ F

$V_{rms} = 220$ V and $\nu = 50$ Hz

Impedance of the circuit,

$$Z = \sqrt{R^2 + X_C^2} = \sqrt{R^2 + (2\pi\nu C)^{-2}} \quad \left[\because X_C = \frac{1}{2\pi\nu C}\right]$$

$$= \sqrt{(200)^2 + (2 \times 3.14 \times 50 \times 15 \times 10^{-6})^{-2}}$$

$$= \sqrt{(200)^2 + (212)^2} = 291.5\,\Omega$$

Therefore, the current in the circuit is

$$i_{rms} = V_{rms}/Z = \frac{220 \text{ V}}{291.5\,\Omega} = 0.755 \text{ A}$$

54 (d) Here, $Z = 10\,\Omega$

$$V_{rms} = \sqrt{V_R^2 + (V_L - V_C)^2} = \sqrt{(60)^2 + (90-10)^2} = 100 \text{ V}$$

$$I_{rms} = \frac{V_{rms}}{Z} = \frac{100}{10} = 10 \text{ A}$$

$$I_0 = 10\sqrt{2} \text{ A}$$

55 (d) For L-C-R circuit, if $X_C > X_L$, then current leads voltage by $\frac{\pi}{2}$.

56 (c) Given, $\phi = 45°$

$$\therefore \tan 45° = \frac{\omega L - \frac{1}{\omega C}}{R}$$

$$\Rightarrow 1 = \frac{\omega L - \frac{1}{\omega C}}{R}$$

$$R = \omega L - \frac{1}{\omega C}$$

$$\Rightarrow \omega C = \frac{1}{\omega L - R}$$

$$\Rightarrow C = \frac{1}{\omega(\omega L - R)} = \frac{1}{2\pi\nu(2\pi\nu L - R)}$$

57 (*a*) Given, $R = 300\,\Omega$, $L = \left(\frac{1}{\pi}\right)$ H,

$V = 20$ V and $\nu = 200$ Hz

If ϕ is the phase difference between V and I for R-L circuit, then

$$\tan\phi = \frac{\omega L}{R} = \frac{2\pi\nu L}{R} = \frac{2\pi \times 200}{300} \times \frac{1}{\pi} = \frac{4}{3}$$

$$\Rightarrow \quad \phi = \tan^{-1}(4/3)$$

58 (*a*) We know that, for series R-C circuit,

$$V^2 = V_C^2 + V_R^2$$

Given, $V = 10$ V and $V_C = 8$ V

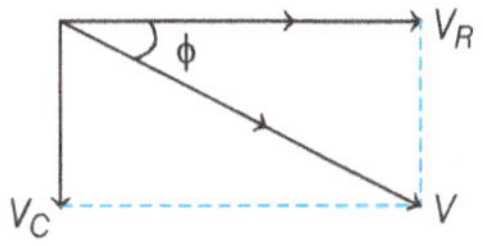

$$100 = 64 + V_R^2$$

$$\Rightarrow \quad V_R^2 = 36, \; V_R = \sqrt{36} = 6 \text{ V}$$

Also, $\tan\phi = \frac{V_C}{V_R}$

$$\Rightarrow \quad \tan\phi = \frac{8}{6} \quad \tan\phi = \frac{4}{3}$$

$$\therefore \quad \phi = \tan^{-1}\left(\frac{4}{3}\right)$$

59 (*a*) At angular frequency ω, the current in R-C circuit is given by

$$I_{rms} = \frac{V_{rms}}{\sqrt{R^2 + \left(\frac{1}{\omega C}\right)^2}} \quad \text{...(i)}$$

When frequency of source is changed to $\frac{\omega}{3}$, then

$$\frac{I_{rms}}{2} = \frac{V_{rms}}{\sqrt{R^2 + \left[\frac{1}{\omega C/3}\right]^2}} = \frac{V_{rms}}{\sqrt{R^2 + \frac{9}{\omega^2 C^2}}} \quad \text{...(ii)}$$

Dividing Eq. (i) by Eq. (ii), we get

$$\frac{I_{rms}}{\frac{I_{rms}}{2}} = \frac{V_{rms}}{\sqrt{R^2 + \frac{1}{\omega^2 C^2}}} \times \frac{\sqrt{R^2 + 9/\omega^2 C^2}}{V_{rms}}$$

$$\Rightarrow 4\left(R^2 + \frac{1}{\omega^2 C^2}\right) = R^2 + \frac{9}{\omega^2 C^2}$$

$$3R^2 = \frac{5}{\omega^2 C^2}$$

$$\Rightarrow \quad \frac{1}{\omega CR} = \sqrt{\frac{3}{5}}$$

$$\Rightarrow \quad \frac{X_C}{R} = \sqrt{\frac{3}{5}} \left[\because X_C = \frac{1}{\omega C}\right]$$

60 (*a*) Current is kept unchange.

$$V_L = i \times (2\pi\nu L)$$

$$\Rightarrow \quad V_L \propto \nu \qquad \text{(straight line)}$$

$$V_C = i \times \left(\frac{1}{2\pi\nu C}\right)$$

$$\Rightarrow \quad V_C \propto \frac{1}{\nu} \text{ (rectangular hyperbola)}$$

61 (*a*) Given, $V = V_0 \sin 100t$

$\omega = 100$ rad/s

Here phase difference is $\frac{\pi}{4}$, thus circuit can be R-C.

$$\therefore \tan\phi = \frac{X_C}{R} = \frac{1}{\omega CR}$$

$$\tan\frac{\pi}{4} = \frac{1}{\omega CR}$$

$$CR = \frac{1}{\omega} = \frac{1}{100} \Rightarrow C = \frac{1}{100\,R}$$

If $R = 1\text{k}\Omega = 1 \times 10^3\,\Omega$, then

$$C = \frac{1}{100 \times 10^3} = 10^{-5}\text{ F}$$

$$= 10 \times 10^{-6}\text{ F} = 10\,\mu\text{F}$$

62 (*b*) Given, $L = 1$ mH $= 1 \times 10^{-3}$ H and $C = 1$ nF $= 1 \times 10^{-9}$ F

Resonant frequency of R-L-C series circuit,

$$\omega_0 = \frac{1}{\sqrt{LC}} = \frac{1}{\sqrt{1 \times 10^{-3} \times 1 \times 10^{-9}}}$$

$$= 1 \times 10^6 \text{ rad / s}$$

63 (*b*) Given, $C = 80\,\mu\text{F} = 80 \times 10^{-6}$ F, $L = 5$ H and $R = 40\,\Omega$

At resonance, source frequency,

$$\nu = \frac{1}{2\pi\sqrt{LC}}$$

$$\therefore \quad \nu = \frac{1}{2\times\pi\times\sqrt{5\times 80\times 10^{-6}}} = \frac{1}{2\times\pi\sqrt{(400\times 10^{-6})}} = \frac{1}{2\times\pi\times 2\times 10^{-2}} = \frac{100}{\pi\times 4} = \frac{25}{\pi}\text{Hz}$$

64 (*c*) At resonance $X_L = X_C$

$$\Rightarrow \omega L = \frac{1}{\omega C} \Rightarrow \omega = \frac{1}{\sqrt{LC}}$$

Since, resonant frequency remains unchanged.

$$\sqrt{LC} = \text{constant}$$

$$\Rightarrow \quad L_1C_1 = L_2C_2$$

$$\Rightarrow \quad LC = L_2(2C) \qquad \text{(given)}$$

$$\Rightarrow \quad L_2 = L/2$$

65 (*a*) Given, $L = 8$ mH $= 8 \times 10^{-3}$ H, $C = 20\,\mu\text{F} = 20 \times 10^{-6}$ F, $R = 44\,\Omega$ and $V_{rms} = 220$ V

Angular resonant frequency of series L-C-R circuit,

$$\omega_0 = \frac{1}{\sqrt{LC}} = \frac{1}{\sqrt{8 \times 10^{-3} \times 20 \times 10^{-6}}}$$

$$= 2500 \text{ rads}^{-1}$$

$$\text{Resonant current} = V_m/R = \frac{V_{rms}\sqrt{2}}{R} = \frac{220\sqrt{2}}{44} = 5\sqrt{2}\text{ A}$$

66 (*b*) Given, $V_R = 100$ V, $R = 1\,\text{k}\Omega = 1000\,\Omega$, $C = 2\mu\text{F} = 2 \times 10^{-6}$ F and $\omega = 200$ rad/s

At resonance, $X_L = X_C$

$$\text{or} \quad \omega L = \frac{1}{\omega C}$$

$$\text{or } L = \frac{1}{\omega^2 C} = \frac{1}{(200)^2 \times 2\times 10^{-6}}$$

$$= 12.5 \text{ H}$$

$$\text{As, } I_0 = \frac{V_R}{R} = \frac{100}{1000} = 0.1 \text{ A}$$

$$\therefore \quad V_L = I_0 X_L = I_0\,\omega L = (0.1)(200)(12.5) = 250 \text{ V}$$

67 (*a*) Given, $R = 10\,\Omega$, $X_C = 60\,\Omega$
$V = 300$ V and $\nu = 100$ Hz

Angular velocity,

$$\omega_0 = 2\pi\nu = 2\pi \times 100$$
$$\omega_0 = 2 \times 3 \times 100 = 600 \text{ rads}^{-1} \quad (\because \pi = 3)$$

Further, $\omega_0 = \dfrac{1}{\sqrt{LC}}$ ...(i)

Also, $X_C = \dfrac{1}{C\omega_0} = 60\,\Omega$

$$\Rightarrow \quad C = \frac{1}{\omega_0 \times 60} = \frac{1}{600 \times 60}$$
$$\Rightarrow \quad C = \frac{1}{36 \times 10^3} \text{ F}$$

On putting values in Eq. (i), we get

$$600 = \frac{1}{\sqrt{L\left(\dfrac{1}{36 \times 10^3}\right)}}$$
$$\Rightarrow 36 \times 10^4 = \frac{36 \times 10^3}{L}$$
$$\Rightarrow L = \frac{36 \times 10^3}{36 \times 10^4} = \frac{1}{10} = 0.1 \text{ H}$$

69 (*a*) In the given circuit diagram, both inductors of inductance L are parallel to each other, hence

$$L_{eq} = \frac{L_1 L_2}{L_1 + L_2} = \frac{L \cdot L}{L + L} = \frac{L}{2}$$

Similarly, $C_{eq} = C_1 + C_2$
$= C + C = 2C$

$\therefore$ Resonant frequency,

$$\omega_r = \frac{1}{\sqrt{L_{eq} \cdot C_{eq}}} = \sqrt{\frac{1}{\frac{L}{2} . 2C}} = \sqrt{\frac{1}{LC}}$$

70 (*c*) $X_L = \omega L = 2000 \times 5 \times 10^{-3}$
$= 10\Omega$

$$X_C = \frac{1}{\omega C} = \frac{1}{2000 \times 50 \times 10^{-6}} = 10\Omega$$

At resonance,

$$X_L = X_C$$
$$i = \frac{V}{R} = \frac{20/\sqrt{2}}{10} = \sqrt{2}\text{A}$$
$$i = 1.4\text{A}$$
$$V = iR = 1.4 \times 4 = 5.6 \text{ V}$$

71 (*b*) Let current in the circuit is I.

Now, reading of voltmeter 1,

$$V_1 = \frac{I}{R}, \text{ which is not zero}$$

At resonance condition,

$$X_L - X_C = 0$$

So, reading of voltmeter 2,

$$V_2 = \frac{I}{Z} = \frac{I}{0} = 0$$

Reading to voltmeter 3 is equal to voltage difference of source AC current. So it is also not zero.

Hence, option (b) is correct answer.

73 (*c*) Given, $P = 600$ W, $V = 220$ V

Also, AC voltage,

$$V = 169 \sin(314t + 60°)$$

The general equation for the AC voltage is $V = V_m \sin(\omega t + \theta)$.

Comparing it with the given equation, we find that

$V_m = 169$ V, $\omega = 314$ rad s^{-1}, $\theta = 60°$

$$V_{rms} = \frac{V_m}{\sqrt{2}} = \frac{169}{\sqrt{2}} \text{V} = 119.5 \text{ V}$$

Power of electric lamp, $P = \dfrac{V^2}{R}$

$$\Rightarrow \quad R = \frac{V^2}{P} = \frac{(220)^2}{600}$$
$$i_{rms} = \frac{V_{rms}}{R} = \frac{119.5 \times 600}{(220)^2} \quad (\because V_{rms} = i_{rms} R)$$
$$= 1.48 \text{ A}$$

74 (*d*) The amplitude of the current in the series *L-C-R* circuit is given by

$$i_m = \frac{V_m}{Z} = \frac{V_m}{\sqrt{R^2 + \left(\omega L - \dfrac{1}{\omega C}\right)^2}} \quad \text{...(i)}$$

Since, $i_m = \dfrac{I_{max}}{\sqrt{2}}$

$$\Rightarrow \quad I_{max} = i_m\sqrt{2}$$
$$\Rightarrow \quad \frac{V_m}{R} = i_m\sqrt{2}$$
$$\Rightarrow \quad i_m = \frac{V_m}{\sqrt{2}R} \quad \text{...(ii)}$$

From Eqs, (i) and (ii), we have

$$\Rightarrow \quad \frac{1}{2}\frac{V_m^2}{R^2} = \frac{V_m^2}{R^2 + (\omega L - 1/\omega C)^2}$$
$$\Rightarrow \quad 2R^2 = R^2 + \left(\omega L - \frac{1}{\omega C}\right)^2$$
$$\Rightarrow \quad R^2 = (\omega L - 1/\omega C)^2$$
$$\Rightarrow \quad R = (\omega L - 1/\omega C) \quad \text{...(iii)}$$

If ϕ is the phase difference between V and I, then

$$\Rightarrow \tan\phi = \frac{\omega L - \dfrac{1}{\omega C}}{R} = \frac{\left(\omega L - \dfrac{1}{\omega C}\right)}{\left(\omega L - \dfrac{1}{\omega C}\right)} = 1$$

[from Eq. (iii)]

$$\Rightarrow \quad \tan\phi = 1 = \tan 45°$$
$$\phi = 45°$$

Power dissipated, $P = i_m^2 Z \cos\phi$

$$= \frac{I_{max}^2 \times \sqrt{R^2 + \left(\omega L - \dfrac{1}{\omega C}\right)^2}}{2} \times \cos 45°$$
$$= \frac{I_{max}^2 \times \sqrt{R^2 + R^2}}{2} \times \frac{1}{\sqrt{2}}$$
$$= \frac{I_{max}^2 \times \sqrt{2}R}{2} \times \frac{1}{\sqrt{2}} = \frac{I_{max}^2 R}{2} = \frac{P_{max}}{2}$$

Thus, power dissipated by the circuit becomes half.

75 (*b*) Power consumed by lamp,

$$P = (1/2) V_m i_m \cos\phi$$
$$\Rightarrow P = P_{peak} \cdot \cos\phi$$

Given, $P = 50\%$ of $P_{peak} = \dfrac{1}{2} P_{peak}$

$$\Rightarrow \quad \frac{1}{2}(P_{peak}) = P_{peak} \cos\phi$$
$$\Rightarrow \quad \cos\phi = \frac{1}{2} \Rightarrow \phi = \frac{\pi}{3}$$

$\therefore$ Phase different between the applied voltage and the circuit current is $\pi/3$.

76 (*c*) Given, $\phi = \dfrac{\pi}{3}$

Here, phase difference,

$$\tan\phi = \frac{X_L - X_C}{R}$$

When L is removed,

$$\tan \pi/3 = \sqrt{3} = X_C/R$$
$$\Rightarrow \quad X_C = \sqrt{3}R$$

When C is removed,

$$\tan\frac{\pi}{3} = \sqrt{3} = \frac{X_L}{R}$$
$$\Rightarrow \quad X_L = \sqrt{3}R$$

Hence, in resonant circuit,

$$\tan\phi = \frac{\sqrt{3}R - \sqrt{3}R}{R} = 0$$

$\Rightarrow \quad \phi = 0$

$\therefore$ Power factor $= \cos\phi = \cos 0 = 1$

77 (*a*) Given,

$V = 5\cos\omega t = 5\sin\left(\omega t + \frac{\pi}{2}\right)$ and

$i = 2\sin\omega t$

Power dissipated in the instrument,

$P = V_{rms} \times i_{rms} \times \cos\phi = 0$

(since, $\phi = \frac{\pi}{2}$, therefore

$\cos\phi = \cos\frac{\pi}{2} = 0$)

78 (*c*) Given, $\varepsilon = (200\sin 314t)$ V

and $\quad I = \sin(314t + \pi/3)$ A

$\therefore \quad \phi = \frac{\pi}{3}, V_m = 200$ V, $I_m = 1$ A

$$V_{rms} = \frac{V_m}{\sqrt{2}} = \frac{200}{\sqrt{2}}$$

$$i_{rms} = \frac{I_m}{\sqrt{2}} = \frac{1}{\sqrt{2}}$$

$\therefore$ Average power consumed is,

$$P = V_{rms}\, i_{rms}\cos\phi = \frac{200}{\sqrt{2}}\frac{1}{\sqrt{2}}\cos\pi/3$$

$$= \frac{200}{2} \times \frac{1}{2} = 50 \text{ W}$$

79 (*d*) As, $Z = \sqrt{R^2 + X_L^2}$

$$= \sqrt{R^2 + (2\pi f L)^2}$$

Also, $\quad i = \frac{V}{Z}$ and $P = i^2 R$

When iron rod is inserted, then inductance L of the coil increases which increases impedance Z and consequently, current i and power P of the circuit decreases. So, brightness of bulb decreases.

80 (*c*) Power factor of AC circuit is given by

$$\cos\phi = \frac{R}{Z} \qquad \text{...(i)}$$

where, R is resistance employed and Z is the impedance of the circuit.

$$Z = \sqrt{R^2 + (X_L - X_C)^2} \qquad \text{...(ii)}$$

From Eqs. (i) and (ii), we get

$$\cos\phi = \frac{R}{\sqrt{R^2 + (X_L - X_C)^2}}$$

Given,

$R = 8\,\Omega, X_L = 31\,\Omega, X_C = 25\,\Omega$

$$\therefore \quad \cos\phi = \frac{8}{\sqrt{(8)^2 + (31-25)^2}}$$

$$= \frac{8}{\sqrt{64 + 36}} = \frac{8}{10}$$

Hence, $\cos\phi = 0.80$

81 (*c*) Given, inductance,

$L = 20$ mH $= 20 \times 10^{-3}$ H

Capacitance, $C = 100\,\mu$F

$= 100 \times 10^{-6}$ F $= 10^{-4}$ F

Resistance, $R = 50\,\Omega$

emf, $V = 10\sin 314t \qquad$ ...(i)

The general equation of emf is given as

$V = V_m \sin\omega t \qquad$ ...(ii)

Comparing Eqs. (i) and (ii), we get

$V_m = 10$ V, $\omega = 314$ rad s^{-1}

The power loss associated,

$$P = V_{rms} I_{rms}\cos\phi$$

$$= V_{rms}\left(\frac{V_{rms}}{Z}\right)\left(\frac{R}{Z}\right)$$

$$= \left(\frac{V_{rms}}{Z}\right)^2 R = \left(\frac{V_m}{\sqrt{2}\cdot Z}\right)^2 R \qquad \text{...(iii)}$$

Impedance, $Z = \sqrt{R^2 + (X_L - X_C)^2}$

$$= \sqrt{R^2 + \left(\omega L - \frac{1}{\omega C}\right)^2} \qquad \text{...(iv)}$$

Substituting the given values in the above Eq. (iv), we get

$$Z = \sqrt{(50)^2 + \left[(314 \times 20 \times 10^{-3}) - \frac{1}{314 \times 10^{-4}}\right]^2}$$

$$= \sqrt{2500 + [6280 \times 10^{-3} - 0.00318 \times 10^4]^2}$$

$$= \sqrt{2500 + (25.56)^2}$$

$= 56.15\,\Omega \simeq 56\,\Omega$

Now, substituting this values in Eq. (iii), we get

$$P = \left(\frac{10}{\sqrt{2} \times 56}\right)^2 \times 50$$

$$= \frac{100}{2 \times 3136} \times 50 = 0.79 \text{ W}$$

Thus, power loss in the circuit is 0.79 W.

82 (*d*) Given, $R = 3\,\Omega, L = 25$ mH

$= 25 \times 10^{-3}$ H,

$C = 400\,\mu$F $= 400 \times 10^{-6}$ F

and $V = 283$ V

Frequency at which maximum power dissipated,

$$\nu = \frac{1}{2\pi\sqrt{LC}}$$

$$= \frac{1}{2 \times 3.14\sqrt{25 \times 10^{-3} \times 400 \times 10^{-6}}}$$

$$= \frac{1}{2 \times 3.14\sqrt{10^{-5}}} = 50.3 \text{ Hz}$$

83 (*c*) Given, $I_{rms} = 2$A

Wattless current, $I_w = \sqrt{3}$ A

As we know that,

Wattless current, $I_w = I_{rms}\sin\phi$

$$\sin\phi = \frac{I_w}{I_{rms}} = \frac{\sqrt{3}}{2}$$

$\sin\phi = \sin 60°$

$\therefore \quad \phi = 60°$

Now, power factor $= \cos\phi$

$= \cos 60° = \frac{1}{2}$

84 (*d*) Given,

$L = 200$ mH $= 0.2$ H

$C = 500\,\mu$F $= 5 \times 10^{-4}$ F

$R = 10\,\Omega$

Power factor, $\cos\phi = 1$

$\because \quad \cos\phi = R/Z$

$1 = R/Z \Rightarrow R = Z$

$R = \sqrt{R^2 + (X_L - X_C)^2}$

$R^2 = R^2 + (X_L - X_C)^2$

$X_L - X_C = 0$

$$2\pi\nu L - \frac{1}{2\pi\nu C} = 0$$

$$\nu = \frac{1}{2\pi\sqrt{LC}} = \frac{1}{2 \times 3.14\sqrt{0.2 \times 5 \times 10^{-4}}}$$

$= 15.9$ Hz

85 (*c*) Given, $R_1 = 40\,\Omega$

$R_2 = 40\,\Omega$

$X_C = 40\,\Omega$

$X_L = 100\Omega$

Now, total resistance,

$R = R_1 + R_2$

$= 40 + 40 = 80\Omega$

Impedance of the circuit,

$Z = \sqrt{R^2 + (X_L - X_C)^2}$

$= \sqrt{80^2 + (100-40)^2}$

$= \sqrt{6400 + 3600}$

$= 100\Omega$

The power factor,

$\cos\phi = \frac{R}{Z} = \frac{80}{100} = 0.8$

86 (*d*) Given that,

$L = 20\text{ mH}, C = 120\,\mu\text{F}$

$R = 60\Omega$

Impedance of this series circuit,

$Z = \sqrt{R^2 + (X_L - X_C)^2}$ ...(i)

$\because \quad X_L = \omega L = (2\pi\nu)(L)$

$= 2\pi \times 50 \times 20 \times 10^{-3}\,\Omega$

$X_L = 6.28\Omega$ ...(ii)

and $X_C = \frac{1}{\omega C} = \frac{1}{2\pi\nu C}$

$= \frac{1}{2\pi \times 50 \times 120 \times 10^{-6}}$

$= \frac{250}{3\pi}\Omega$ ...(iii)

and $X_L - X_C = \left(6.28 - \frac{250}{3\pi}\right)$

$= -20.23\,\Omega$ ...(iv)

RMS value of current in circuit,

$I_{rms} = \frac{V_{rms}}{Z} = \frac{24}{\sqrt{R^2 + (X_L - X_C)^2}}$

$I_{rms} = \frac{24}{\sqrt{60^2 + (-20.23)^2}} = \frac{24}{63.18}$

$I_{rms} = 0.379\text{ A}$

Therefore, energy dissipated is

$= I_{rms}^2 \times R \times t$

$E = (0.379)^2 \times 60 \times 60$

$= 517.10 = 5.17 \times 10^2\text{ J}$

87 (*c*) The statement given in option (c) is correct and rest are incorrect and these can be corrected as,

Flux leakage is reduced by winding the primary and secondary coils one over the other.

Resistance of windings is minimised by using thick wire.

Hysteresis is minimised by using a magnetic material because magnetic flux is passed easily through magnetic material.

88 (*c*) We have to transmit energy (power) over large distances at high alternating voltages, so current flowing through the wires will be low, for a given constant power (*P*).

For this, the transmission lines are made thicker.

i.e., $P = E_{rms}\, i_{rms}$,

i_{rms} is low, when E_{rms} is high.

i.e., Power loss $= i^2_{rms} R =$ low

($\because i_{rms}$ is low)

Now, at the receiving end high voltage is reduced by using step-down transformers.

Hence, statement given in option (c) is incorrect and rest are correct.

89 (*c*) Given, $\varepsilon_p = 2300\text{ V}, N_p = 4000$ and $\varepsilon_s = 230\text{ V}$

Let N_s be the required number of turns in the secondary

As, $\frac{\varepsilon_s}{\varepsilon_p} = \frac{N_s}{N_p} \Rightarrow N_s = N_p\left(\frac{\varepsilon_s}{\varepsilon_p}\right)$

$= 4000\left(\frac{230}{2300}\right) = 400$

90 (*c*) Given, $\varepsilon_p = 220\text{ V}, \varepsilon_s = 22\text{ V}$ and $Z = 220\,\Omega$

If i_s is the current through the secondary, then

$i_s = \frac{\varepsilon_s}{Z} = \frac{22\text{ V}}{220\,\Omega} = 0.1\text{ A}$

We know that, $\varepsilon_p i_p = \varepsilon_s i_s$

where, i_p is the current drawn by the primary coil.

Thus, $220 \times i_p = 22 \times 0.1\text{ A}$

$\Rightarrow \quad i_p = 0.01\text{ A}$

91 (*b*) Given, $V_p = 110\text{ V}, k = \frac{N_s}{N_p} = 10$

and $R_s = 550\,\Omega$

$V_s = V_p \times \frac{N_s}{N_p}$

$= 110 \times 10 = 1100\text{ V}$

Current through secondary coil,

$i_s = \frac{V_s}{R_s} = \frac{1100}{550} = 2\text{A}$

92 (*d*) In an ideal transformer, there is no energy loss and flux is completely confined within the magnetic core, i.e. perfectly coupled. So, all the input power appears across the output.

i.e. $\frac{P_{out}}{P_{in}} = 1$ or $P_{out} : P_{in} = 1:1$

93 (*a*) Given, number of turns in primary, $N_1 = 300$

Number of turns in secondary, $N_2 = 150$

Output power,

$P_2 = 2.2\text{ kW} = 2.2 \times 10^3\text{ W}$

Current in secondary coil, $I_2 = 10\text{ A}$

Output power, $P_2 = I_2 V_2$

$\Rightarrow V_2 = \frac{P_2}{I_2} = \frac{2.2 \times 10^3}{10} = 220\text{V}$ ... (i)

We know that,

$\frac{N_1}{N_2} = \frac{\text{Input voltage}}{\text{Output voltage}} = \frac{V_1}{V_2}$

$\Rightarrow V_1 = \left(\frac{N_1}{N_2}\right)V_2$

$\Rightarrow V_1 = \left(\frac{300}{150}\right) \times (220)$ [using Eq. (i)]

$V_1 = 440\text{ V}$ ... (ii)

Again, $\frac{V_1}{V_2} = \frac{I_2}{I_1}$

$\Rightarrow \quad I_1 = \left(\frac{V_2}{V_1}\right) I_2 = \frac{220}{440} \times 10$

[using Eqs. (i) and (ii)]

$\Rightarrow \quad I_1 = 5\text{A}$

94 (*a*) Given, turn ratio of a transformer,

$\frac{N_1}{N_2} = \frac{50}{1} \Rightarrow N_1 = 50N_2$

Since, $\frac{N_1}{N_2} = \frac{V_1}{V_2}$

$\Rightarrow 50 = \frac{120}{V_2}$ [$V_1 = 120$ V (given)]

$\Rightarrow V_2 = \frac{12}{5}$ V

Output power at secondary coil,

$$P_s = \frac{V_2^2}{R_2} = \frac{\left(\frac{12}{5}\right)^2}{1} = \frac{144}{25} = 5.76 \text{ W}$$

[$R_2 = 1\Omega$ (given)]

95 (*b*) Given, $P_o = 140$ W, $V_0 = 24$ V, $V_i = 240$ V and $i_L = 0.7$ A

Input power of transformer,

$P_i = V_i \times i_L = 240 \times 0.7 = 168$ W

Efficiency of transformer,

$$\eta = \frac{P_o}{P_i} \times 100 = \frac{140}{168} \times 100 \approx 80\%$$

96 (*b*) Given, initial power,

$P_1 = 3$ kW $= 3000$ W,

$V_1 = 200$ V and $i_2 = 6$ A

As efficiency is 90%, then final power,

$$P_2 = P_1 \times \frac{\eta}{100} = 3000 \times \frac{90}{100} = 2700 \text{ W}$$

As, $P_1 = V_1 i_1 = 3000$ W

$\Rightarrow i_1 = \frac{P_1}{V_1} = \frac{3000}{200} = 15$ A

Also, $P_2 = V_2 i_2 = 2700$ W

$\Rightarrow V_2 = \frac{P_2}{i_2} = \frac{2700}{6} = 450$V

97 (*c*) $\eta = \frac{\text{output power}}{\text{input power}}$

$P_{in} = \frac{880}{88} \times 100 = 1000$ W

$I_{input} = \frac{1000}{2200} = 0.4545$ A

98 (*b*) Given, power $P = 800 \times 10^3$ W

Resistance per km of wire $= 0.5\,\Omega$/km

Total resistance of wires,

$R = 0.5 \times 15 \times 2 = 15\Omega$

Here, input voltage $V_{rms} = 4000$ V

$\therefore I_{rms} = \frac{P}{V_{rms}} = \frac{800 \times 10^3}{4000} = 200$ A

Line power loss

$= I_{rms}^2 R = 200^2 \times 15$

$= 600$ kW

Assertion and Reason Questions

3 (*c*) The inductive reactance is directly proportional to the inductance and the frequency of the current as $X_L = \omega L = 2\pi\nu L$. So, it increases as the frequency of AC source increases.

5 (*a*) Capacitive reactance is inversely proportional to frequency as $X_C = \frac{1}{\omega C} = \frac{1}{2\pi\nu C}$

As DC does not have any frequency, i.e. $f = 0$

Hence, $X_C = \infty$.

So, no DC current flows through capacitor. But AC varies like a sine function with some frequency.

So, it passes easily through capacitor.

Hence, capacitor serves as a barrier for DC and offers an easy path to AC.

6 (*a*) When a load has lagging (inductive) reactive power, it can lower the power factor by adding a capacitor in parallel, it provides leading (capacitive) reactive power that counter acts the lagging reactive power thus improve the power factor.

7 (*b*) The phase difference between current and voltage in a series *R-L-C* circuit is

$$\phi = \tan^{-1}\left(\frac{X_C - X_L}{R}\right)$$

So, if $X_C > X_L$, ϕ is positive and the circuit is predominantly capacitive. The current in the circuit leads the source voltage.

If $X_C < X_L$, ϕ is negative and the circuit is predominantly inductive. The current in the circuit lags the source voltage.

8 (*a*) The resultant emf in the *L- C-R* circuit is given by

$$E = \sqrt{V_R^2 + (V_L - V_C)^2}$$

Given, $V_R = 8$ V, $V_L = 6$ V

and $V_C = 10$ V

$\Rightarrow E = \sqrt{(8)^2 + (16 - 10)^2}$

$\Rightarrow E = \sqrt{64 + 36}$

$\Rightarrow E = 10$ V

9 (*a*) It is important to note that resonance phenomenon is exhibited only by a circuit having both *L* and *C* are present in the circuit.

Only then do the voltage across *L* and *C* cancel each other (both being out of phase) and the current amplitude is V_m/R. This means that we cannot have resonance in a *R-L* or *R-C* circuit,

$$V = \sqrt{V_R^2 + (V_L - V_C)^2} = V_R \quad (\because V_L = V_C)$$

Hence, the total source voltage appears across *R* at resonance.

10 (*d*) A transformer can increase voltage (in step-up) or decrease voltage (in step-down) without violating the law of conservation of energy. Transformers work on the principle of mutual induction, where the changing magnetic field in the primary coil induces a voltage in secondary coil. The change in voltage in the secondary coil is balanced by a change in current to ensure that energy is conserved.

Statement Based Questions

1 (*a*) When pure capacitor is connected to source of an alternating emf, then instantaneous value of alternating emf is given as $E = E_0 \sin \omega t$ and corresponding alternating current is given by $I = I_0 \sin\left(\omega t + \frac{\pi}{2}\right)$ from these two equation, it follows that alternating current leads emf by phase angle of $\frac{\pi}{2}$.

Capacitive reactance $X_C = \frac{1}{\omega C}$

2 (b) Statement I is correct and Statement II is incorrect.
A charged capacitor, after removing the battery, does not discharge itself. If touched, one may feel shock due to significant amount of charge still present on the capacitor.

3 (d) Capacitive reactance $X_C = \frac{1}{\omega C}$.

When capacitance increases, the capacitive reactance decreases. Due to decrease in its values, the current in the circuit will increase $\left(I = \frac{E}{\sqrt{R^2 + X_C^2}}\right)$ and hence brightness of source will also increases.

4 (c) At resonance $X_L = X_C$ or $\omega L = \frac{1}{\omega C}$. Because of this impedance of L-C-R series circuit becomes equal to resistance of circuit and current is maximum. Whereas, corresponding phase difference is also equal to zero.

6 (b) Power, $P = E_{rms} i_{rms} \cos\phi$
where ϕ is the angle which is known as phase angle.
For pure resistive AC circuit,
$$\phi = 0 \text{ and } \cos\phi = 1$$
$$\therefore \quad P = P_{max} = E_{rms} I_{rms}$$

Matching Type Questions

3 (a) As, $X_L = \omega L = 2\pi \times 50$
$$= \frac{100}{\pi} \times 10^{-3} = 10\Omega$$
and $X_C = \frac{1}{\omega C}$
$$= \frac{1}{2\pi \times 50 \times \frac{100}{\pi} \times 10^{-6}} = 100\Omega$$

Impedance of the circuit
i.e., $Z = \sqrt{R^2 + (X_L - X_C)^2}$
$$= \sqrt{(100)^2 + (10 - 100)^2} = 134.5\Omega$$

rms value of the current through the circuit is
$$I_{rms} = \frac{220}{Z} = \frac{220}{134.5} = 1.63 \text{ A}$$

rms value of voltage drop across the capcitor is
$$V_{CV} = I_{rms} X_C = 1.63 \times 100 = 163 \text{ V}$$
Average power dissipated across the resistor is
$$P_{av} = I_{rms}^2 \times R = (1.63)^2 \times 100$$
$$= 265.7 \text{W}$$
Hence, A → 3, B → 2, C → 4, D → 1

Numerical Type Questions

1 (5) $t = \frac{T}{4}$ or $t = \frac{1}{4f} = \frac{1}{4 \times 50}$
$$t = 5 \times 10^{-3} \text{s}$$
$$\therefore \quad n = 5$$

2 (1) Here, $I = I_0\left[1 - e^{-\left(\frac{R}{L}\right)t}\right]$
$$\frac{I_0}{2} = I_0\left[1 - e^{-\left(\frac{2}{300} \times 10^3\right)t}\right]$$
$$e^{\frac{-20}{3}t} = 1 - \frac{1}{2} = \frac{1}{2}$$
$$\frac{20}{3}t = \ln 2 = 2.3026 \times \log 2$$
$$= 2.3026 \times 0.301$$
$$= 0.6931$$
or $t = \frac{0.6931}{20} \times 3 = 0.1 \text{ s}$
or 1×10^{-1}s
$\Rightarrow \quad m = 1$

3 (9) Given, wavelength of transmission signal,
$$\lambda = 840 \text{ m},$$
$$C = 2.2 \,\mu\text{F}$$
$$= 2.2 \times 10^{-6} \mu\text{F}$$

As we know, resonance frequency,
$$\nu = \frac{1}{2\pi\sqrt{LC}}$$
Also, frequency (ν)
$$\therefore \quad \frac{v}{\lambda} = \frac{1}{2\pi\sqrt{LC}}$$
$$\Rightarrow \sqrt{LC} = \frac{\lambda}{v \times 2\pi}$$
On squaring both sides, we get
$$\Rightarrow \quad LC = \frac{\lambda^2}{v^2 \times 4\pi^2}$$
$$\Rightarrow \quad L = \frac{\lambda^2}{v^2 \times 4\pi^2 \times C}$$
$$\Rightarrow \quad L = \frac{(840)^2}{(3 \times 10^8)^2 4\pi^2 \times 2.2 \times 10^{-6}}$$
$$\therefore \quad L = 9 \times 10^{-8} \text{ H}$$

4 (39) Given, Inductance, $L = 40$ mH
Resistance, $R = 1\Omega$
Angular frequency, $\omega = 300$ rad/s
We know that in L-C-R circuit,
$$\tan\phi = \frac{X_C - X_L}{R}$$
where, ϕ = phase angle = 45°
X_C = capacitive reactance = $\frac{1}{\omega C}$
X_L = inductive reactance = ωL.
$$\Rightarrow \tan 45° = \frac{X_C - X_L}{R}$$
$$\Rightarrow \quad X_C - X_L = R \qquad [\because \tan 45° = 1]$$
$$\Rightarrow \frac{1}{\omega C} - \omega L = R$$
$$\Rightarrow \frac{1}{\omega C} - 300 \times 40 \times 10^{-3} = 1$$
$$\Rightarrow \frac{1}{\omega C} = 13 \Rightarrow \omega C = \frac{1}{13}$$
$$\Rightarrow \quad C = \frac{1}{13\,\omega} \Rightarrow C = \frac{1}{13 \times 300}$$
$$\Rightarrow \quad C = \frac{1}{39} \times 10^{-2} \text{F} = \frac{1}{x} \times 10^{-2}$$
Hence, $x = 39$

5 (300) Given, $\omega = 100$ rad/s
$$L = 0.5 \text{ H}$$
$$C = 100 \,\mu\text{F} = 10^{-4} \text{F}$$
$$V = 20 \text{ V}$$
$$R_1 = 100\Omega, R_2 = 50\Omega$$
$$\therefore \quad X_L = \omega L = 100 \times 0.5 = 50\Omega$$

and $X_C = \frac{1}{\omega C} = \frac{1}{100 \times 10^{-4}}$

$= 100\,\Omega$

The impedance across capacitor,

$Z_1 = \sqrt{R_1^2 + X_C^2} = \sqrt{100^2 + 100^2}$

$= 100\sqrt{2}\,\Omega$

$\therefore$ Current, $I_1 = \frac{V}{Z_1} = \frac{20}{100\sqrt{2}}$

$= \frac{1}{5\sqrt{2}}$ A

The impedance across inductor,

$Z_2 = \sqrt{R_2^2 + X_L^2}$

$= \sqrt{(50)^2 + (50)^2}$

$= 50\sqrt{2}\,\Omega$

$\therefore$ Current, $I_2 = \frac{V}{Z_2} = \frac{20}{50\sqrt{2}} = \frac{\sqrt{2}}{5}$ A

So, the net current through the circuit,

$I = \sqrt{I_1^2 + I_2^2}$

$= \sqrt{\left(\frac{1}{5\sqrt{2}}\right)^2 + \left(\frac{\sqrt{2}}{5}\right)^2}$

$= \sqrt{\frac{1}{50} + \frac{2}{25}}$

$= \sqrt{\frac{5}{50}}$

$= 0.3 = 300 \times 10^{-3}$

$= x \times 10^{-3}$ (given)

$\therefore \quad x = 300$

6 (200) Given, $V_0 = 220$ V

$R = 121\,\Omega$, $L = 24$ mH and $C = 60\,\mu$F

We know that, at resonance power,

$P = \frac{V_{rms}^2}{R}$

$\Rightarrow \quad P = \frac{(220/\sqrt{2})^2}{121}$

$\left[\because V_{rms} = \frac{V_0}{\sqrt{2}} = \frac{220}{\sqrt{2}} \text{ V}\right]$

$= (220)^2/242 = \frac{48400}{242}$

≈ 200 W

$\Rightarrow \quad x = 200$

7 (2) At resonance,

$\omega L = \frac{1}{\omega C}$ or $\omega = \frac{1}{\sqrt{LC}}$

To keep resonant frequency unchanged, LC = constant.

or $\quad L_1C_1 = L_2C_2$

$L_2 = \frac{L_1C_2}{C_2} = \frac{LC}{2C} = \frac{L}{2}$

So, $\quad n = 2$

8 (8) Given, $R = 120\,\Omega$

$\omega_0 = 4 \times 10^5$ rad/s

$V_R = 60$ V, $V_L = 40$ V

$\phi = 45°$

Current across resistance R,

$I = \frac{V_R}{R} = \frac{60}{120} = 0.5$ A

Current across inductor,

$I = \frac{V_L}{Z} = \frac{V_L}{\omega_0 L}$

$L = \frac{V_L}{\omega_0 I} = \frac{40}{4 \times 10^5 \times 0.5}$

$= 0.2$ mH

At resonance condition,

$\omega_0 = \frac{1}{\sqrt{LC}}$

$C = \frac{1}{\omega_0^2 L} = \frac{1}{(4 \times 10^5)^2 \times 0.2 \times 10^{-3}}$

$= \frac{1}{32}\,\mu$F

As we know, $\tan\phi = \frac{X_L - X_C}{R}$

$\tan 45° = \frac{\omega L - \frac{1}{\omega C}}{R}$

$1 = \frac{\omega L - \frac{1}{\omega C}}{R}$

$R = \omega L - \frac{1}{\omega C}$

$120 = 2 \times 10^{-4}\omega - \frac{1}{\omega\left(\frac{1}{32} \times 10^{-6}\right)}$

$\omega^2 - 6 \times 10^5\omega - 16 \times 10^{10} = 0$

On solving it,

$\omega = 8 \times 10^5 = x \times 10^5$ (given)

So, $x = 8$

9 (100) For circuit (a), $P_a = \frac{V_{rms}^2}{R}$

For circuit (b), $P_b = \frac{V_{rms}^2}{Z^2} \times R$

Given that $P_a = P_b$

$\Rightarrow \frac{V_{rms}^2}{R} = \frac{V_{rms}^2}{Z^2} \times R \Rightarrow R^2 = Z^2$

$\Rightarrow 225 = (\sqrt{(X_C - X_L)^2 + (15)^2})^2$

$\Rightarrow 225 = (X_C - X_L)^2 + 225$

$\Rightarrow X_C = X_L \Rightarrow \frac{1}{\omega C} = \omega L$

$\Rightarrow \omega^2 = \frac{1}{LC} = \frac{10^6}{50 \times 2}$

$\Rightarrow \quad \omega = 100$ rad/s

10 (42) Given, power, $P = 550$ W

$V_{rms} = 220$ V, $\nu = 50$ Hz

As we know that,

power, $P = V_{rms} \times I_{rms} \times \cos\phi$

but $I_{rms} = \frac{V_{rms}}{Z}$

$\Rightarrow \quad Z = \frac{V_{rms}^2}{P}\cos\phi$

$Z = \frac{(220)^2 \times 0.8}{550} = 70.4\,\Omega$

Here, $\cos\phi = R/Z$

$R = Z\cos\phi = 70.4 \times 0.8$

$= 56.32\,\Omega$

and $\quad Z^2 = R^2 + X_L^2$

$X_L = \sqrt{Z^2 - R^2}$

$\omega L = \sqrt{(70.4)^2 - (56.32)^2}$

$= 42.2\,\Omega$

Now, according to question,

$\cos\phi = 1$

$\therefore \quad R = Z$

So, $\quad Z = \sqrt{Z^2 + \left(\omega L - \frac{1}{\omega C}\right)^2}$

$\therefore \quad \omega L = \frac{1}{\omega C}$

$C = \frac{1}{(\omega L)\omega} = \frac{1}{42.2 \times 2\pi\nu}$

$= \frac{1}{42.2 \times 2\pi \times 50}$

$C = \frac{1}{2\pi \times 50 \times 42.2}$

$\approx \frac{1}{42\pi} \times 10^{-2}$F

$= \frac{1}{p\pi} \times 10^{-2}$F

$\therefore \quad p = 42$

11 (3) For L-R circuit,

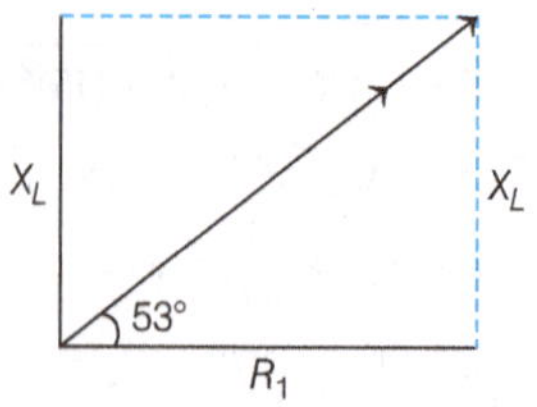

Given, $\cos\phi = 0.6$

$$\cos\phi = 3/5$$
$$\phi = 53°$$

Now, $\tan 53° = \frac{X_L}{R_1}$

$$\frac{4}{3} = \frac{X_L}{R_1} \Rightarrow X_L = \frac{4R_1}{3}$$

For C-R circuit,

$$\cos\phi = 0.5$$
$$\Rightarrow \quad \phi = 60°$$

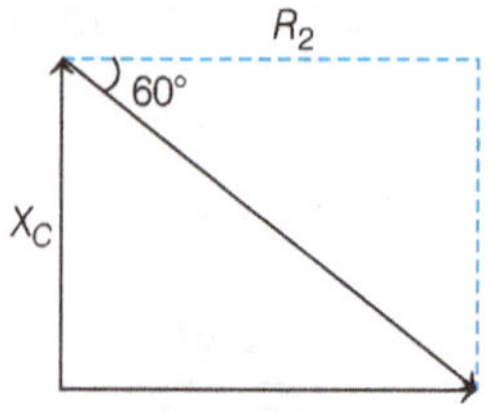

$$\tan 60° = \frac{X_C}{R_2}$$
$$\sqrt{3} = X_C / R_2$$
$$X_C = \sqrt{3}R_2$$

For L-C-R circuit,

$$\cos\phi = 1$$
$$\phi = 0°$$

So, $X_C = X_L$

$$\sqrt{3}R_2 = \frac{4R_1}{3}$$
$$\frac{R_1}{R_2} = \frac{3\sqrt{3}}{4} = \frac{x\sqrt{3}}{4} \text{ (given)}$$

so, $x = 3$

12 (83.3) Efficiency $= \frac{V_s \times I_s}{V_p \times I_p} \times 100\%$

$$= \frac{140}{240 \times 0.7} \times 100\%$$
$$= 83.3\%$$

13 (440) Given, $\frac{V_s}{V_p} = \frac{N_s}{N_p}$

$$\frac{220}{10000} = \frac{N_s}{N_p}$$
$$\frac{N_s}{N_p} = \frac{22}{1000} \quad ...(i)$$

For an ideal transformer, input power = output power and power is given by

$$P = VI$$
$$I_pV_p = I_sV_s = 110000$$
$$10000 \times I_p = 110000$$
$$I_p = 11\text{ A}$$

Now, $R_p = \frac{V_p}{I_p} = \frac{10000}{11}\,\Omega$

For secondary coil,

$$P_s = V_s \cdot I_s$$
$$I_s = \frac{P_s}{V_s} = \frac{110000}{220} = 500\text{ A}$$
$$\Rightarrow \quad R_s = \frac{V_s}{I_s} = \frac{200\text{V}}{500\text{A}}$$
$$R_s = 440 \times 10^{-3}\,\Omega$$
$$= 440\text{ m}\Omega$$

14 (3.6) Given, length $l = 10$ km

$= 10 \times 10^3$m

Radius, $r = 0.5$ cm $= 5 \times 10^{-3}$ m

$\rho = 1.7 \times 10^{-8}\,\Omega$-m

Now, resistance of both wires,

$$R = \frac{n\rho l}{A} = \frac{2 \times 1.7 \times 10^{-8} \times 10 \times 10^3}{3.14 \times (5 \times 10^{-3})^2}$$
$$= 4.3\,\Omega$$

Here, $P = 10^6$ W, $V = 11000$ V

$$\text{Current} = \frac{P}{V} = \frac{10^6}{11000} = \frac{10^3}{11}\text{ A}$$

Now, power loss,

$$I^2R = \left(\frac{10^3}{11}\right)^2 \times 4.3$$
$$P_{lost} = 3.6 \times 10^4 \text{ W}$$

$\therefore$ Ohmic loss $= \frac{P_{lost}}{P} \times 100\%$

$$= \frac{3.6 \times 10^4}{10^6} \times 100 = 3.6\%$$

NCERT Exemplar Questions

1 (b) Given, $i_{rms} = 5$A, $\nu = 50$ Hz

and $t = \frac{1}{300}$ s

$$i_0 = i_{rms}\sqrt{2}$$
$$i_0 = \sqrt{2} \times 5 = 5\sqrt{2}\text{ A}$$
$$\Rightarrow \quad i = i_0 \sin\omega t = 5\sqrt{2}\sin 2\pi f t$$
$$= 5\sqrt{2}\sin 2\pi \times 50 \times \frac{1}{300}$$
$$= 5\sqrt{2}\sin\frac{\pi}{3} = 5\sqrt{2} \times \frac{\sqrt{3}}{2}$$
$$= 5\sqrt{3/2}\text{ A}$$

2 (c) For delivering maximum power from the generator to the load, total internal reactance must be equal to the conjugate of total external reactance.

Hence, $X_{int} = X_{ext}$

$\Rightarrow \quad X_g = (X_L) = -X_L$

or $\quad X_L = -X_g$

3 (c) The voltmeter connected to AC mains reads mean value ($<v^2>$) and is calibrated in such a way that it gives value of $<v^2>$, which is multiplied by form factor to give rms value, i.e. $\sqrt{<v^2>}$.

4 (b) We know that, resonant frequency in an L-C-R circuit is given by $\nu_0 = \frac{1}{2\pi\sqrt{LC}}$

Now to reduce ν_0 either we can increase L or we can increase C.

To increase capacitance, we must connect another capacitor parallel to the first.

5 (c) Given, $X_L = 1\,\Omega$, $R = 2\,\Omega$, $V_{rms} = 6$ V

Average power dissipated in the circuit,

$$P_{av} = V_{rms}\, i_{rms} \cos\phi \quad ...(i)$$

As, $i_{rms} = \frac{i_0}{\sqrt{2}} = \frac{V_{rms}}{Z}$

where, $Z = \sqrt{R^2 + X_L^2}$

$$= \sqrt{4+1} = \sqrt{5}$$
$$\Rightarrow \quad i_{rms} = \frac{6}{\sqrt{5}}\text{ A}$$
$$\cos\phi = \frac{R}{Z} = \frac{2}{\sqrt{5}}$$
$$P_{av} = 6 \times \frac{6}{\sqrt{5}} \times \frac{2}{\sqrt{5}} \quad \text{[From Eq. (i)]}$$

$$= \frac{72}{\sqrt{5}\sqrt{5}} = \frac{72}{5} = 14.4 \text{ W}$$

6 (*a*) Secondary voltage, $V_s = 24\text{V}$

Power associated with secondary,

$$P_s = 12 \text{ W}$$

$$\Rightarrow \quad i_s = \frac{P_s}{V_s} = \frac{12}{24} = \frac{1}{2} \text{ A} = 0.5 \text{ A}$$

Peak value of the current in the secondary,

$i_0 = i_s\sqrt{2} = (0.5)\ (1.414) = 0.707$

or $\quad i_0 = 1/\sqrt{2}$ A

Past Exams Questions

1 (*b*) Given, $C = 10\,\mu\text{F} = 10 \times 10^{-6}$ F

Potential, $V = 210$ V

Frequency, $f = 50$ Hz

Reactance of circuit, $X_C = \dfrac{1}{\omega C}$

$$= \frac{1}{2\pi f C}$$

$$= \frac{1}{2 \times 3.14 \times 50 \times 10 \times 10^{-6}} = \frac{10^3}{3.14}$$

Peak current, $I_m = \dfrac{V\sqrt{2}}{X_C} = \dfrac{210 \times \sqrt{2}}{\dfrac{10^3}{3.14}}$

$$= \frac{3.14 \times 210 \times \sqrt{2}}{1000} \simeq 0.93 \text{ A}$$

2 (*b*) We know that, transformation ratio,

$$r = \frac{N_s}{N_p} = \frac{V_s}{V_p}$$

$$\because \quad \frac{N_p}{N_s} = \frac{1}{2} = \frac{V_p}{V_s}$$

$\Rightarrow V_s : V_p = 2 : 1$

3 (*c*) In series *L-C-R* circuit,

$L = 10 \text{ mH} = 10^{-2}$ H

$C = 1\,\mu\text{F} = 10^{-6}$ F, $R = 100\,\Omega$

$\therefore$ Resonant frequency,

$$f = \frac{1}{2\pi\sqrt{LC}} = \frac{1}{2\pi\sqrt{10^{-2} \times 10^{-6}}}$$

$$= \frac{1}{2\pi \times 10^{-4}} = \frac{10^4}{2\pi}$$

$= 1.59 \times 10^3$ Hz $= 1.59$ kHz

4 (*b*) Given, $L = \dfrac{50}{\pi} \text{ mH} = \dfrac{5}{\pi} \times 10^{-2}$ H

$$C = \frac{10^3}{\pi}\,\mu\text{F} = \frac{1}{\pi} \times 10^{-3} \text{ F}$$

$R = 10\,\Omega,\ \nu = 50 \text{ Hz}, V = 220$ V

$\therefore X_L = 2\pi\nu L$

$$= 2\pi \times 50 \times \frac{5}{\pi} \times 10^{-2} = 5\,\Omega$$

$$X_C = \frac{1}{\omega C} = \frac{1}{2\pi\nu C}$$

$$= \frac{1}{2\pi \times 50 \times \frac{1}{\pi} \times 10^{-3}} = \frac{1}{10^{-1}}$$

$= 10\,\Omega$

$\therefore$ Net impedance the circuit,

$$Z = \sqrt{R^2 + (X_C - X_L)^2}$$

$$= \sqrt{10^2 + (10 - 5)^2}$$

$$= \sqrt{125} = 5\sqrt{5}\,\Omega$$

5 (*d*) According to given situation,

$$V_s = 12 \text{ V}$$

$$\therefore \quad I_s = \frac{P}{V_s} = \frac{60}{12} = 5 \text{ A}$$

$\therefore$ Given, $V_p = 220$ V

For ideal transformer.

$$I_pV_p = I_sV_s$$

$$\Rightarrow \quad I_p = \frac{I_sV_s}{V_p} = \frac{5 \times 12}{220} = 0.27 \text{ A}$$

6 (*b*) We know that, peak voltage (V_0) and rms voltage (V_{rms}) are related as

$$\therefore \quad V_0 = \sqrt{2}\,V_{rms}$$

7 (*a*) Given, In series *L-C-R* circuit,

$L = 10$ H, $C = 10\,\mu\text{F} = 10^{-5}$ F

$R = 50\,\Omega$

Source voltage,

$$V = 200 \sin(100\,t) \text{ volt}$$

$$\omega = 100 \text{ rad/s}$$

$\therefore \quad 2\pi\nu = 100$

$$\Rightarrow \quad \nu = \frac{100}{2\pi} = \frac{50}{\pi} \text{ Hz}$$

Resonant frequency,

$$\nu_0 = \frac{1}{2\pi\sqrt{LC}}$$

$$= \frac{1}{2\pi\sqrt{10 \times 10^{-5}}}$$

$$= \frac{1}{2\,\pi \times 10^{-2}} = \frac{50}{\pi} \text{ Hz}$$

Hence, $\nu = \nu_0 = \dfrac{50}{\pi}$ Hz

8 (*d*) The given circuit diagram as shown below.

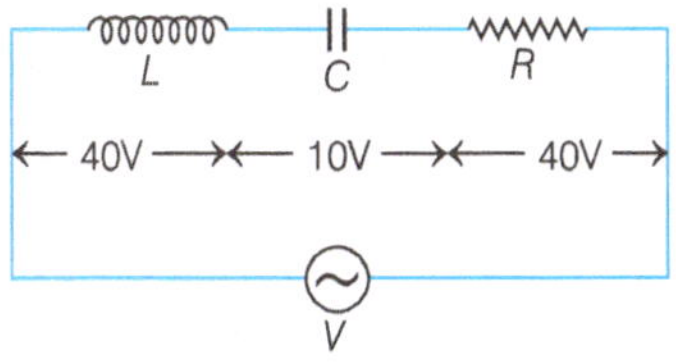

Given, $\quad V_L = 40 \text{ V}, V_C = 10$ V

and $\quad V_R = 40$ V

$$I_0 = 10\sqrt{2} \text{ A} \qquad \text{...(i)}$$

$$\therefore \quad I_{rms} = \frac{I_0}{\sqrt{2}}$$

$$\Rightarrow \quad I_{rms} = \frac{10\sqrt{2}}{\sqrt{2}} \qquad \text{[from Eq. (i)]}$$

$$\Rightarrow \quad I_{rms} = 10 \text{ A}$$

$$\therefore \quad V_{rms} = \sqrt{V_R^2 + (V_L - V_C)^2}$$

$$\Rightarrow \quad V_{rms} = \sqrt{(40)^2 + (40 - 10)^2}$$

$$\Rightarrow \quad V_{rms} = 50 \text{ V}$$

The impedance of the *L-C-R* series circuit $Z = \dfrac{V_{rms}}{I_{rms}} \Rightarrow Z = \dfrac{50}{10}$

or $\quad Z = 5\Omega$

9 (*b*) Given, $C = 40\,\mu\text{F} = 40 \times 10^{-6}$ F

$V_{rms} = 200 \text{ V}, \nu = 50$ Hz

As, $X_C = \dfrac{1}{2\pi\nu C}$

$$= \frac{1}{2\pi \times 50 \times 40 \times 10^{-6}} = \frac{250}{\pi}\,\Omega$$

$$\therefore \quad I_{rms} = \frac{V_{rms}}{X_C} = \frac{200}{\left(\dfrac{250}{\pi}\right)} = 2.5 \text{ A}$$

10 (*a*) When the circuit is connected to AC source,

Voltage, $\quad V = 12$ V

Current, $\quad I = 0.2$ A

$\Rightarrow$ Impedance $Z = \dfrac{V}{I} = \dfrac{12}{0.2} = 60\ \Omega$

When it is connected to DC source,

Voltage, $V = 12$ V, Current, $I = 0.4$ A

$\Rightarrow$ Resistance, $R = \dfrac{V}{I} = \dfrac{12}{0.4} = 30\Omega$

As in case of DC supply, the capacitor act as an open circuit and no current flows through the circuit.

So, the given circuit will not have capacitor in series combination. Therefore, the circuit should be a series *L-R* circuit.

11 (*a*) Impedance of an AC circuit,

$Z = \sqrt{R^2 + (X_C - X_L)^2}$

where X_C = capacitive reactance and X_L = inductive reactance.

Also $X_C = \frac{1}{\omega C}$ and $X_L = \omega L$

$$\therefore Z = \sqrt{(50)^2 + \left(\frac{1}{314 \times 100 \times 10^{-6}} - 314 \times 20 \times 10^{-3}\right)^2}$$

or $Z = 56\,\Omega$

The power loss in the circuit,

$$P_{av} = \left(\frac{V_{rms}}{Z}\right)^2 R$$

$$\therefore \quad P_{av} = \left(\frac{10}{(\sqrt{2})56}\right)^2 \times 50 = 0.79 \text{ W}$$

12 (*a*) Impedance of the *R-C* circuit,

$Z = \sqrt{R^2 + X_C^2}$

where, $R = 100\,\Omega$ and $X_C = 100\,\Omega$

$\Rightarrow Z = \sqrt{(100)^2 + (100)^2} = 100\sqrt{2}\,\Omega$

Peak value of the current,

$$I_{max} = \frac{V_{max}}{Z} = \frac{220\sqrt{2}}{100\sqrt{2}} = 2.2 \text{ A}$$

13 (*a*) Given, alternating AC source

$E = 36\sin(120\pi t)$ V

$C = 150\mu$F

Using $\quad Q = CV$

$Q = CE_0 \sin \omega t$

Current, $i = \frac{dQ}{dt} = CE_0 \omega \cos \omega t$

Maximum value of current

$i_0 = CE_0 \omega$

or $i_0 = 150 \times 10^{-6} \times 36 \times 120\pi$

$= 2.03 \text{ A} \approx 2\text{A}$

14 (*d*) Power factor, $\cos\phi = \frac{R}{Z}$

So, power factor, $P_1 = \frac{R}{\sqrt{X_L^2 + R^2}}$

$$= \frac{R}{\sqrt{R^2 + R^2}} \qquad (\because X_L = R)$$

So, $P_1 = \frac{1}{\sqrt{2}}$

Now, when a capacitor is added in circuit such that,

$X_L = X_C$

Then, power factor will be

$$\Rightarrow \quad P_2 = \frac{R}{\sqrt{R^2 + (X_L - X_C)^2}}$$

$$= \frac{R}{\sqrt{R^2}} = \frac{R}{R} = 1$$

Hence, ratio, $\frac{P_1}{P_2} = \frac{1}{\sqrt{2}}$

15 (*c*) Given, $X_L = 200\,\Omega$,

$X_C = 100\,\Omega$, $R = 100\,\Omega$

$V_{rms} = 200\sqrt{2}$ V

Impedance,

$$Z = \sqrt{R^2 + (X_L - X_C)^2}$$

$$= \sqrt{(100)^2 + (200 - 100)^2}$$

$$= \sqrt{100^2 + 100^2} = 100\sqrt{2}\,\Omega$$

$$\therefore I_{rms} = \frac{V_{rms}}{Z} = \frac{200\sqrt{2}}{100\sqrt{2}} = 2 \text{ A}$$

16 (*c*) Given, $E = 440 \sin 100\pi t$

$(E_0 = 440$ V and $\omega = 100\pi)$

$$L = \frac{\sqrt{2}}{\pi} \text{ H}$$

We know that, the reading of an AC ammeter gives I_{rms}.

So, let's calculate I_{rms}.

$$X_L = \omega L = 100\pi \frac{\sqrt{2}}{\pi}$$

$$= 100\sqrt{2}\,\Omega$$

$\therefore$ Peak value of current,

$$= I_0 = \frac{E_0}{X_L} = \frac{440}{100\sqrt{2}}$$

$$\Rightarrow \quad I_0 = \frac{4.4}{\sqrt{2}} = \frac{4.4\sqrt{2}}{2} = 2.2\sqrt{2}\text{A}$$

$$I_{rms} = \frac{I_0}{\sqrt{2}} = \frac{2.2\sqrt{2}}{\sqrt{2}} = 2.2 \text{ A}$$

17 (*b*) Given, for direct current,

$I_1 = 4$ A, $R_1 = 3\Omega$

For alternating peak current,

$I_0 = 4$ A

$$I_{rms} = \frac{I_0}{\sqrt{2}} = \frac{4}{\sqrt{2}} = 2\sqrt{2} \text{ A}$$

$$\frac{\text{Heat produced across } R_1(H_1)}{\text{Heat produced across } R_2(H_2)} = \frac{I_1^2 R_1 t}{I_2^2 R_2 t}$$

$$\Rightarrow \quad \frac{H_1}{H_2} = \frac{I_1^2 R_1}{(I_{rms})^2 R_2}$$

$$= \frac{4^2 \times 3}{(2\sqrt{2})^2 \times 2}$$

$$= \frac{4 \times 4 \times 3}{8 \times 2} = \frac{3}{1}$$

$\therefore H_1 : H_2 = 3 : 1$

Skill Boosters

1 (*b*) Here, $\eta = 80\%$, P_i

$= 4$ kW $= 4000$ W

$E_p = 100$ V, $E_s = 240$ V, $I_p = ?$, $I_s = ?$

As, input power $(P_i) = E_p I_p$

$$\therefore \quad I_p = \frac{P_i}{E_p} = \frac{4000}{100} = 40 \text{ A}$$

$$\text{As, } \eta = \frac{E_s I_s}{E_p I_p} \Rightarrow \frac{80}{100} = \frac{240\, I_s}{4000}$$

$$\Rightarrow \quad I_s = \frac{80 \times 4000}{100 \times 240} = 13.3 \text{ A}$$

2 (*a*) $\tan 60° = \frac{\omega L}{R}$, $\tan 60° = \frac{1/\omega C}{R}$

$$\therefore \quad \omega L = \frac{1}{\omega C}$$

$\therefore$ Impedance of the circuit,

$$Z = \left[R^2 + \left(\omega L - \frac{1}{\omega C}\right)^2\right]^{\frac{1}{2}} = R$$

Current in the circuit,

$$i_0 = \frac{V_0}{Z} = \frac{V_0}{R} = \frac{200}{100} = 2 \text{ A}$$

Average power, $\bar{P} = \frac{1}{2} V_0 i_0 \cos\phi$

But, $\tan\phi = \frac{\omega L - \frac{1}{\omega C}}{R} = 0$

$\therefore \quad \cos\phi = 1$

$\therefore \quad \bar{P} = \frac{1}{2} \times 200 \times 2 \times 1 = 200 \text{ W}$

3 (d) The line that draws power supply to our home from street supplies alternating current, whose average value/mean value is zero over a cycle. As the line has some resistance ($R \neq 0$), therefore voltage and current differ in phase ϕ such that $|\phi| < \frac{\pi}{2}$.

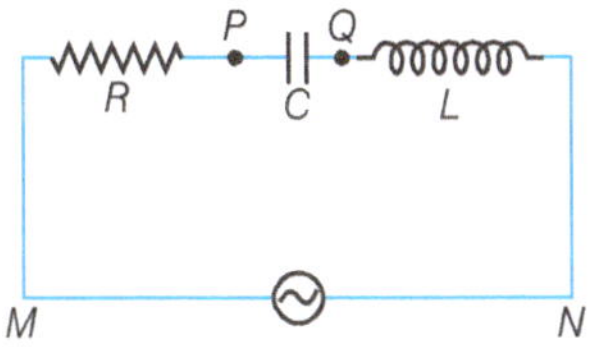

4 (d) As, potential across capacitor in discharging R-C circuit, $V = V_0 e^{-t/\tau}$, when time constant τ of this circuit, $t = \tau$.

$$V = V_0 e^{-1} = \frac{V_0}{e} = \frac{25}{2.718} = 9.2 \text{ V}$$

Corresponding to $V = 9.2$ V, t lies between 100 s and 150 s.

5 (a) In an L-C-R circuit, we have Resonant frequency,

$$f_{res} = \frac{1}{2\pi\sqrt{LC}} = \frac{1}{2\pi\sqrt{\frac{1}{\pi} \times \frac{1}{\pi} \times 10^{-6}}} = 500 \text{ Hz}$$

But at resonance, $Z = R$, we get

So, current, $I = \frac{V}{Z} = \frac{V}{R}$

When L and C are in series, then voltage across capacitor and inductor is 180° out of phase.

6 (b) $Q = Q_{max} e^{-Rt/2L} \cos(\omega dt)$

$$I_{max} \propto e^{-Rt/2L}$$

$$\frac{1}{K} = e^{-Rt/2L}$$

$$\Rightarrow -\log K = -\frac{Rt}{2L}$$

$$\Rightarrow -\log K = \frac{-R}{2L} \times \log 2 \times \frac{2L}{R}$$

$$\Rightarrow K = 2$$

7 (d) Given, $e = e_1 \sin \omega t + e_2 \cos \omega t$ rms value of alternating voltage,

$$e_{1\,rms} = \frac{e_1}{\sqrt{2}} \text{ and}$$

Similarly, $e_{2\,rms} = \frac{e_2}{\sqrt{2}}$

Using phasor diagram, we get

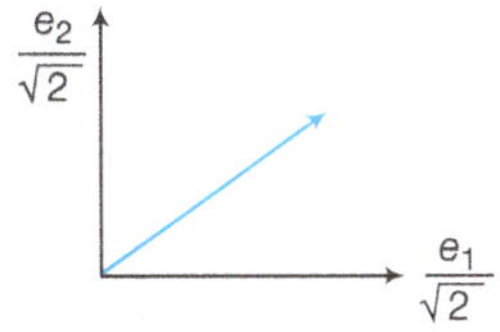

Net resultant root mean square of voltage is given by

$$e_{rms} = \sqrt{\frac{e_1^2 + e_2^2}{2}}$$

8 (d) When DC is applied across a solenoid, then resistance, $R = \frac{V}{I}$

$$R = \frac{100}{1} = 100\,\Omega$$

When AC is applied, then

$$Z = \frac{100}{0.5} = 200\,\Omega$$

Net impedance,

$$Z = \sqrt{R^2 + X_L^2}$$

$$200 = \sqrt{(100)^2 + X_L^2}$$

$$\Rightarrow (200)^2 = (100)^2 + X_L^2$$

$$\Rightarrow 30000 = X_L^2$$

$$\Rightarrow X_L = 173.205\,\Omega$$

Now, $X_L = \omega L \Rightarrow 173.205 = 2\pi\nu L$

$$\Rightarrow \frac{173.205}{2\pi \times \nu} = L$$

$$\Rightarrow \frac{173.205}{2 \times 3.14 \times 50} = L$$

$$\Rightarrow 0.55\,\Omega = L$$

$$L = 0.55\,\Omega$$

9 (a) In L-C-R series circuit, we have

$$V_R = 60 \text{ V}, V_R = IR$$

$$I = \frac{60}{120} = \frac{1}{2} \text{ A}$$

Voltage drop across inductor,

$$V_L = IX_L$$

$$40 = \frac{1}{2} X_L$$

Net reactive inductance,

$$X_L = 80\,\Omega, \text{ i.e. } \omega L = 80\,\Omega$$

$$L = \frac{80}{4 \times 10^3} = 20 \text{ mH}$$

As we know that, angular frequency, $\omega = \frac{1}{\sqrt{LC}}$

Squaring both sides, we get

$$\omega^2 = \frac{1}{LC}$$

$$(4 \times 10^3)^2 = \frac{1}{20 \times 10^{-3} \times C}$$

$$\Rightarrow C = \frac{1}{16 \times 10^6 \times 20 \times 10^{-3}}$$

$$C = \frac{25}{8} \mu\text{F}$$

10 (d) $\omega = 1000 \text{ rad s}^{-1}$, $R = 400\,\Omega$

$$C = 5 \times 10^{-6} \text{ F}, L = 0.5 \text{ H}$$

$$V_{max} = 100 \text{ V}$$

$$\omega L = 500\,\Omega, \frac{1}{\omega C} = 200\,\Omega$$

Circuit impedance,

$$Z = \sqrt{R^2 + \left(\omega L - \frac{1}{\omega C}\right)^2} = \sqrt{(400)^2 + (300)^2} = 500\,\Omega$$

$$I_{max} = \frac{\Delta V_{max}}{Z} = \frac{100}{500} = 0.2 \text{ A}$$

Average power dissipated in the circuit,

$$P = I_{rms}^2 R = \left(\frac{I_{max}^2}{2}\right) R = \frac{(0.2)}{2} \times 400 = 8 \text{ W}$$

08

Scan for Physics Through Concept Master Videos

Electromagnetic Waves

Topicwise No. of Ques asked in 5 Years

Topics	No. of Questions				
	2024	2023	2022	2021	2020
Displacement Current	1	–	–	1	–
Electromagnetic Waves	1	1	1	1	3
Electromagnetic Spectrum	–	–	–	–	1

Special Type of Ques asked in 5 Years

Types	Years				
	2024	2023	2022	2021	2020
A-R	–	–	–	–	–
Statement Based	–	–	–	–	–
Matching	–	–	1	–	–

Last 5 Years Weigtage (NEET)

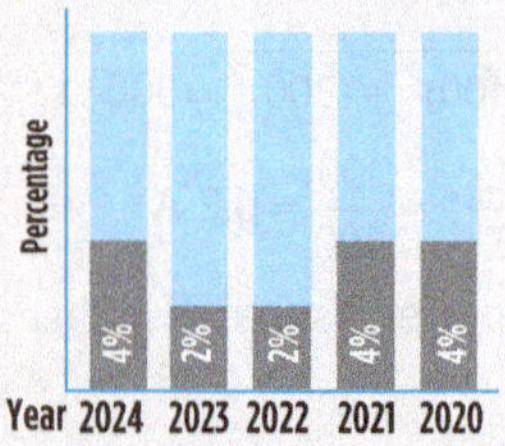

- Maxwell formulated a set of equations involving electric and magnetic fields, and their sources, the charge and current densities. These equations are known as **Maxwell's equations**.
- These equations predicted the existence of electromagnetic waves, which are time-varying electric and magnetic fields (coupled) that propagate in space.
- The speed of the waves, according to these equations, turned out to be very close to the speed of light (3×10^8 m/s), obtained from optical measurements.
- This led to the remarkable conclusion that light is an electromagnetic wave. Maxwell's work thus unified the domain of electricity, magnetism and light.

Displacement Current

- From the figure, Ampere's circuital for loop c_1 is

$$\oint_{c_1} \mathbf{B} \cdot d\mathbf{l} = \mu_0 I$$

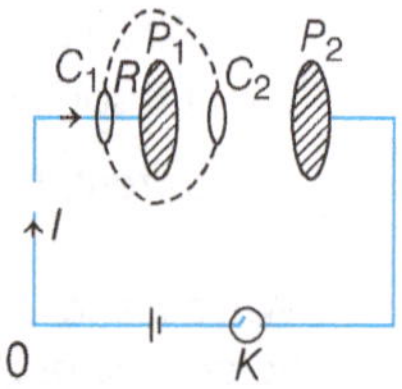

Here, $I \neq 0, \quad B \neq 0$

- Now, Ampere's circuital law for loop c_2 is $\oint_{c_2} \mathbf{B} \cdot d\mathbf{l} = 0$

because, conduction current I is zero inside the capacitor.

$\oint_{c_1} \mathbf{B} \cdot d\mathbf{l} \neq \oint_{c_2} \mathbf{B} \cdot d\mathbf{l}$ while practically, these two quantities must be equal.

- To remove this inconsistency in Ampere's circuital law, Maxwell added addition term called displacement current.
- **Displacement current** is a current which is produced due to the rate of change of electric flux with respect to time. This is also called **Maxwell's displacement current**. It is given by

$$i_d = \varepsilon_0 \frac{d\phi_E}{dt}$$ **NEET 2021,19**

For Concept Master Video

The total current i is the sum of the conduction current denoted by i_c and the displacement current denoted by i_d.

So, we have $\quad i = i_c + i_d = i_c + \varepsilon_0 \dfrac{d\phi_E}{dt}.$

- For a capacitor system outside the capacitor plates $i_c = i$ and $i_d = 0$.

  On the other hand, inside the capacitor, $i_c = 0$ and $i_d = i$.
- **Maxwell modified the Ampere's circuital law** with one difference. The new law states that, **the line integral of the magnetic field along a closed path is equal to μ_0 times the total current (i.e., sum of conduction current and displacement current) threading the surface bounded by that closed path**. It is given by

  $$\oint \mathbf{B} \cdot d\mathbf{l} = \mu_0 \left(I_c + \varepsilon_0 \frac{d\phi_E}{dt} \right)$$

  This is also known as **Ampere-Maxwell law.**

Note *The displacement current has the same physical effects as the conduction current.*

The following inference can be drawn from the above discussion.

- Time-dependent electric and magnetic fields give rise to each other. It is a consequence of the displacement current being a source of a magnetic field.
- Faraday's law of electromagnetic induction and Ampere-Maxwell law give a quantitative expression of this statement with the current being the total current.
- One very important consequence of this symmetry is the existence of electromagnetic waves.

Marks Maximiser

$$i_d = \varepsilon_0 \frac{d\phi_\varepsilon}{dt} = \varepsilon_0 A \frac{dE}{dt} = \frac{\varepsilon_0 A}{d} \frac{dV}{dt}$$

Here, $A =$ Area of plate of capacitor, $E =$ electric field, $V =$ potential difference and $d =$ distance between plates.

Maxwell's Equations

- Maxwell's equations are the basic laws of electricity and magnetism. These equations give complete description of all electromagnetic interactions. Maxwell on the basis of his equations, predicted the existence of electromagnetic waves.
- There are four Maxwell's equations which are explained as given below.

  (i) **Gauss's Law of Electrostatics** This law states that the total electric flux through any closed surface is always equal to $\dfrac{1}{\varepsilon_0}$ times the net charge enclosed by that surface. It is given by $\oint \mathbf{E} \cdot d\mathbf{S} = \dfrac{q}{\varepsilon_0}$

  This equation is called **Maxwell's first equation.**

  Conclusion can be drawn that the electric field lines are not closed continuous curves.

  (ii) **Gauss's Law in Magnetostatics** This law states that, the net magnetic flux through any closed surface is always zero. It is given by $\oint \mathbf{B} \cdot d\mathbf{S} = 0$

  This equation is called Maxwell's second equation.

  It concludes that magnetic force lines are closed and continuous curves.

  (iii) **Faraday's Law of Electromagnetic Induction** This law states that the induced emf produced in a circuit is numerically equal to rate of change of magnetic flux through it. It is given by $\oint \mathbf{E} \cdot d\mathbf{l} = -\dfrac{d\phi_B}{dt}$

  This equation is called **Maxwell's third equation.**

  It concludes that a changing magnetic field with time produces electric field.

  (iv) **Ampere-Maxwell's Circuital Law** This law states that the line integral of the magnetic field along a closed path is equal to μ_0 times the total current (i.e., sum of conduction current and displacement current) threading the surface bounded by that closed path. It is given by $\oint \mathbf{B} \cdot d\mathbf{l} = \mu_0 \left(I_c + \varepsilon_0 \dfrac{d\phi_E}{dt} \right)$

  This equation is called **Maxwell's fourth equation.**

  It shows that a changing electric field with time produces magnetic field.

Electromagnetic Waves

- These waves are produced due to the change in electric field E and magnetic field B sinusoidally at right angles to each other and propagating through space.
- **Sources of EM Waves** Maxwell found that the accelerated or oscillated charges radiate electromagnetic waves. These charges produce an oscillating electric field in space, which produce an oscillating magnetic field, which in turn, is a source of oscillating electric field and so on. The oscillating electric and magnetic fields thus regenerate each other.
- The frequency of the electromagnetic wave naturally equals the frequency of oscillation of the charge and the energy associated with the propagating wave comes at the expense of the energy of the source (the accelerated charge).

- Electromagnetic waves are also produced when fast moving electrons are suddenly stopped by metal target of high atomic number. These electromagnetic waves are called X-rays.
- **Nature of EM Waves** Electromagnetic waves are transverse in nature. In an electromagnetic wave, electric and magnetic fields are perpendicular to each other and to the direction of propagation.
- A plane electromagnetic wave propagating along the z-direction is shown below.

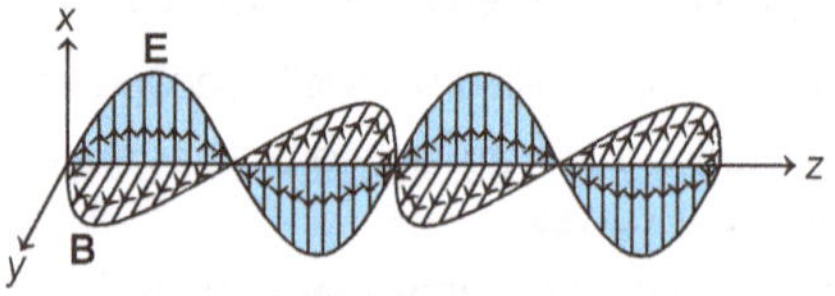

Direction of propagation

- The electric field E_x is along X-axis and the magnetic field B_y is along the Y-axis are given as $E_x = E_0 \sin(kz - \omega t)$

$$= E_0 \sin\left[2\pi\left(\frac{z}{\lambda} - \nu t\right)\right] = E_0 \sin\left[2\pi\left(\frac{z}{\lambda} - \frac{t}{T}\right)\right]$$

and $B_y = B_0 \sin(kz - \omega t) = B_0 \sin\left[2\pi\left(\frac{z}{\lambda} - \nu t\right)\right]$

$$= B_0 \sin\left[2\pi\left(\frac{z}{\lambda} - \frac{t}{T}\right)\right]$$ **NEET 2020**

where, k is propagation vector or wave vector $= \frac{2\pi}{\lambda}$

and ω is the angular frequency.

The direction of k describes the direction of propagation of the wave.

Important characteristics of EM waves are listed below

(i) The electromagnetic waves are produced by accelerated charge.

(ii) These waves do not require any material medium for propagation.

(iii) These waves travel in free space with the speed of light ($3 \times 10^8 \text{ ms}^{-1}$), given by the relation $c = 1/\sqrt{\mu_0 \varepsilon_0}$. (Also, $c = \nu\lambda$) It means that **light waves are electromagnetic in nature.**

(iv) Speed of electromagnetic wave in a medium is given by $v = 1/\sqrt{\mu\varepsilon}$, where ε and μ are the permittivity and magnetic permeability of a material medium, respectively. This means, the speed of EM wave in a medium depends on electric and magnetic properties of a medium. **NEET 2019**

(v) The direction of variations of electric and magnetic fields are perpendicular to each other and also perpendicular to the direction of wave propagation. Thus, electromagnetic waves are transverse in nature.

Marks Maximiser

- In free space, the magnitudes of electric and magnetic fields in electromagnetic waves are related by $E_0/B_0 = c$. **NEET 2023, 20**
- The energy in electromagnetic waves is divided equally between electric and magnetic fields,

$$U_e = U_m$$

where, U_e = energy of electric field

and U_m = energy of magnetic field.

- The **energy density** (energy per unit volume) in an electric field **E** in vacuum is $\frac{1}{2}\varepsilon_0 E^2$ and that in magnetic field **B** is $\frac{B^2}{2\mu_0}$.

$\therefore$ Energy associated with an electromagnetic wave is given by

$$U = \frac{1}{2}\varepsilon_0 E^2 + \frac{1B^2}{2\mu_0}$$

Also, average energy density,

$$u_{av} = \frac{1}{4}\varepsilon_0 E_0^2 + \frac{1}{4}\frac{B_0^2}{\mu_0}$$

Also, $$u_{av} = \frac{1}{2}\varepsilon_0 E_0^2 = \frac{B_0^2}{2\mu_0}$$

- Electromagnetic waves being uncharged are not deflected by electric and magnetic fields.
- The electromagnetic wave carries momentum. Since, it has momentum, these waves also exerts pressure called **radiation pressure.**

If wave is incident on a completely absorbing surface, then momentum delivered is given by $p = \frac{U}{c}$ and force exerted on the surface is $F = \frac{p}{\Delta t}$

- If the surface is a perfect reflector, then momentum transferred to the surface is given by

$$p = \frac{2U}{c}$$

- Pressure due to radiation falling normally on a surface of area A is given by

$$P = \frac{F}{A} = \frac{1}{A}\frac{d}{dt}\left(\frac{U}{c}\right) = \frac{1}{c}\frac{\left(\frac{dU}{dt}\right)}{A}$$

Here, $\frac{dU}{dt}$ is the rate at which energy is coming.

Note *Light carries energy from the sun to the earth, thus making life possible on the earth.*

Electromagnetic Spectrum

- The arrangement of electromagnetic waves in increasing and decreasing order of wavelength λ and frequency ν is called electromagnetic spectrum. These waves includes visible light waves, X-rays, gamma rays, radio waves, microwaves, ultraviolet and infrared waves.

The wavelength ranges, frequency ranges and use of various regions of electromagnetic spectrum are summarised below.

	Name of Wave	Frequency Range	Wavelength Range	Production	Detection	Uses
(*i*)	**Radio waves**	500 kHz to 1000 MHz	> 0.1 m	Rapid acceleration and decelerations of electrons in aerials.	Receiver's aerials.	• These are used in AM (Amplitude Modulation) from 530 kHz to 1710 kHz and ground wave propagation. • These are used in TV waves ranging from 54 MHz to 890 MHz. • These are used in FM (Frequency Modulation) ranging from 88 MHz to 108 MHz.
(*ii*)	**Microwaves**	1 GHz to 300 GHz	0.1m to 1mm	Klystron valve or magnetron valve.	Point contact diodes.	• These are used in RADAR systems for aircraft navigation. NEET 2022,20 • These are used in microwave oven for cooking purpose. • These are used in study of atomic and molecular structures.
(*iii*)	**Infrared waves** (heat waves)	3×10^{11}Hz to 4×10^{14}Hz	1 mm to 700 nm	Vibration of atoms and molecules.	Thermopiles bolometer and infrared photographic film.	• These are used in physical therapy. • These are used in satellites for army purpose. • These are used in weather forecasting.
(*iv*)	**Light rays** (visible rays)	4×10^{14}Hz to 7×10^{14}Hz	700 nm to 400 nm	Electrons in atoms emit light when they move from a higher energy level to a lower energy level.	Eye, photocells and photographic film.	• These are used by the optical organs of humans and animals for three primary purposes given below (i) To see things, avoid bumping into them and escape danger. (ii) To look for food. (iii) To find other living things.
(*v*)	**Ultraviolet rays**	10^{14} Hz to 10^{16} Hz	400 nm to 1 nm	Inner shell electrons in atoms moving from higher energy level to a lower energy level.	Photocells and photographic film.	• These are used in burglar alarm. • These are used in checking mineral sample. • These are used to study molecular structure. • To kill germs in water purifiers. • Used in LASIK eye surgery.
(*vi*)	**X-rays**	3×10^{16} Hz to 3×10^{21} Hz	1 nm to 10^{-3} nm	X-ray tubes or inner shell electrons, bombarding metals by high energy electrons.	Photographic film, geiger tubes and ionisation chamber.	• These are used in medicine to detect the fracture, diseased organs, stones in the body, etc. • These are used in engineering to detect fault, cracks in bridges and testing of welds. • These are used to detect metals or explosive material.

	Name of Wave	Frequency Range	Wavelength Range	Production	Detection	Uses
(vii)	**Gamma (γ) rays**	3×10^{18} Hz to 5×10^{22} Hz	$< 10^{-3}$ nm	Radioactive decay of the nucleus.	Photographic film and ionisation chamber.	• These are used to produce nuclear reactions. • These are used in radio therapy for the treatment of tumour and cancer. • These are used in food industry to kill pathogenic microorganism.

Caution Points

- All the electromagnetic waves travels at the same speed in vacuum, therefore they are differentiated on the basis of their wavelengths and frequencies. Interaction with matter of these waves is also different.
- Infrared waves can vibrate the electrons as well as the atoms or molecules of a substance. This vibration increases the internal energy which further increases the temperature of the substance. That is why they are often called heat waves.
- Human eyes are most sensitive to the colours of light because humans have vision most sensitive to the strongest wavelength coming from the sun.

PYQ Notes

1. **Intensity produced by electric field component** [JEE Main 2023]

   If the intensity produced by a point source is given by

   $$I = \frac{P}{4\pi r^2}$$

   then, intensity produced by electric field component is given by $I_E = \frac{I}{2}$.

2. **Energy on non-reflecting surface** [NEET 2020]

   For a non-reflecting surface, the energy received is given by

   energy received = average flux × surface area × time.

Step by Step

Mastering NCERT

- Concept Builders
- Topical Questions
- Assertion and Reason Questions
- Statement Based
- Matching Type
- Numerical Type
- NCERT Exemplar
- Past Exams MCQs
- Skill Boosters

Concept Builders

1 Displacement current exists due to changing electric flux. [T/F]

2 Write down the missing term in Ampere's circuital law.

3 On which factors of medium does the velocity of electromagnetic waves depends ?

4 What does an electromagnetic wave consists of?

5 In electromagnetic waves, electric and magnetic fields oscillates in .... (parallel/perpendicular) to each other.

6 Electromagnetic wave has .... (linear/angular) momentum.

7 All the electromagnetic waves of different radiations move with .... (same/different) speed in vacuum but they move with .... (same/different) speed in a medium.

8 Write down the formula for the velocity of light travelling in a medium.

9 What is the ratio of velocities of light rays of wavelength 4000 Å and 8000Å in vacuum ?

10 Which is the basic oscillatory circuit used to produce electromagnetic waves ?

11 Write the expression for the frequency of EM waves produced by *LC* oscillatory circuit.

12 Out of mircrowaves, UV-rays and infrared rays, which radiation is most effective for emission of electrons from a metallic surface ?

13 If the wavelength of an electromagnetic radiation is doubled, then the energy of the photons is halved. [T/F]

14 What is the maximum frequency range of radio waves?

15 Which electromagnetic wave is used to treat cancer?

16 Microwaves are produce due to oscillating currents in special vacuum tubes. [T/F]

17 The vibrations due to .... (ultraviolet/infrared) waves increases the internal energy and consequently the temperature of the substance.

18 .... (Infrared/Microwaves) are used for observing the movement of trains.

19 Gamma rays are produce by bombarding a metal target by high speed electrons. [T/ F]

20 Visible light has shorter wavelength than infrared radiation. [T/F]

Topical Questions

Displacement Current

1 Inconsistency in the Ampere's circuital law can be removed by the addition of NCERT Pg. 201

(a) AC current (b) DC current

(c) displacement current (d) reactance

2 The most important prediction emerge from Maxwell's equation is the existence of NCERT Pg. 201

(a) electromagnetic waves

(b) electric field

(c) magnetic field

(d) current

3 In the given figure, for which configuration, the magnetic field (say at point *P*) outside the plates of the capacitor is to be same everywhere? NCERT Pg. 202

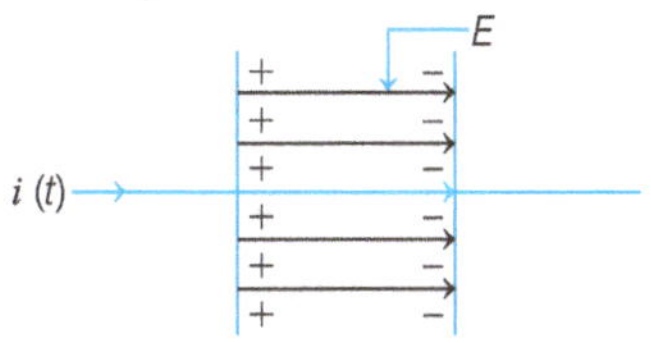

(a) Plane circular loop perpendicular to wire

(b) Plane circular loop parallel to wire

(c) Pot like surface with bottom between the plates

(d) Tiffin box like shape (without the lid)

4 The charge on a parallel plate capacitor varies as $q = q_0 \cos 2\pi\nu t$. The plates are very large and close together (area $= A$, separation $= d$). Neglecting the edge effects, find the displacement current through the capacitor. NCERT Pg. 203

(a) $-\sin 2\pi\nu t\,(2\pi\nu)$ (b) $q_0 \cos 2\pi\nu t$
(c) $2\pi\, q_0\, \nu \sin(2\pi\nu t)$ (d) $-2\pi\, q_0 \nu \sin(2\pi\nu t)$

5 What is an instantaneous rate of change of voltage for displacement current of 10A, in the space between the parallel plate capacitor of 1 μF? NCERT Pg. 203

(a) 10^5Vs^{-1} (b) 10^6Vs^{-1} (c) 10^{-6}Vs^{-1} (d) 10^7Vs^{-1}

6 A parallel plate capacitor consists of two circular plates with radius $R = 10$ cm separated by distance $d = 0.5$ mm. The capacitor is being charged at a uniform rate by applying a changing potential difference between the two plates. Calculate the displacement current for the capacitor. Assume that, the electric field is due to the displacement current only and rate at which the electric field between the plates changes is 5×10^{13} Vms^{-1}. NCERT Pg. 203

(a) 12.8 A (b) 12.6 A (c) 13.9 A (d) 10.5 A

7 A sinusoidal voltage is applied directly across an 8 μF capacitor. The frequency of the source is 3.00 kHz and the voltage amplitude is 30.0 V. Find the maximum value of displacement current between the plates of the capacitor. NCERT Pg. 203

(a) 42.5 A (b) 4.25 μA (c) 4.52 A (d) 4.52 μA

8 A parallel plate capacitor is charged to 100×10^{-6} C. Due to radiations, falling from a radiating source, the plate loses charge at the rate of 2×10^{-7} Cs^{-1}. The magnitude of displacement current is NCERT Pg. 203

(a) 10^{-6} A (b) 10^{-4} A
(c) 2×10^{-7} A (d) 2×10^{-7} mCs^{-1}

9 To establish an instantaneous displacement current of magnitude I ampere in between the plates of a parallel plate capacitor of capacitance $\frac{1}{2}$F, the value of $\frac{dV}{dt}$ is NCERT Pg. 204

(a) $2I$ (b) $\frac{I}{2}$ (c) $\frac{1}{2I}$ (d) I

10 Which statement is correct about the symmetrical counterpart and a consequence of the displacement current being a source of a magnetic field? NCERT Pg. 204

(a) An electric field changing with time gives rise to a magnetic field.
(b) A magnetic field changing with time gives rise to an electric field.
(c) An emf changing with time gives rise to an electric field.
(d) An displacement current changing with time gives rise to an electric field.

11 In order to establish an instantaneous displacement current of 1 mA in the space between the plates of 2 μF parallel plate capacitor, the rate of change of potential difference is NCERT Pg. 204

(a) 100 Vs^{-1} (b) 200 Vs^{-1}
(c) 300 Vs^{-1} (d) 500 Vs^{-1}

12 A parallel plate capacitor with plate area A and separation between the plates d, is charged by a constant current I. Consider a plane surface of area $\frac{2A}{3}$ parallel to the plates and drawn between the plates. The displacement current through the area is NCERT Pg. 203

(a) $\frac{2I}{3}$ (b) $\frac{I}{2}$ (c) $\frac{I}{4}$ (d) $\frac{I}{8}$

13 Which of the following statement is correct in regards to the Maxwell's equations? NCERT Pg. 205

(a) The most important prediction to emerge from Maxwell's equations is the existence of magnetic waves.
(b) Maxwell's equations involves only electric and magnetic fields.
(c) The total current has the same value of current i for all surfaces.
(d) We can rephrase Faraday's law of electromagnetic induction that there is an induced emf equal to the rate of change of magnetic flux.

14 Total average energy density of electromagnetic waves in vacuum is given by the relation Old NCERT Pg. 277

(a) $\frac{E^2}{2\varepsilon_0} + \frac{B^2}{2\mu_0}$ (b) $\frac{1}{2}\varepsilon_0 E^2 + \frac{1}{2}\mu_0 B^2$
(c) $\frac{E^2 + B^2}{c}$ (d) $\frac{1}{2}\varepsilon_0 E^2 + \frac{B^2}{2\mu_0}$

Electromagnetic Waves

15 An electromagnetic wave travels in vacuum along z-direction $\mathbf{E} = (E_1\hat{\mathbf{i}} - E_2\hat{\mathbf{j}})\cos(kz - \omega t)$. Find the correct statement from the following options. NCERT Pg. 206

(a) The associated magnetic field is given as
$$\mathbf{B} = \frac{1}{c}(E_1\hat{\mathbf{i}} - E_2\hat{\mathbf{j}})\sin(kz - \omega t)$$
(b) The associated magnetic field is given as
$$\mathbf{B} = \frac{1}{c}(E_1\hat{\mathbf{i}} + E_2\hat{\mathbf{j}})\cos(kz - \omega t)$$
(c) The given electromagnetic field is circularly polarised.
(d) The given electromagnetic wave is plane polarised.

16 An electromagnetic wave travelling along Z-axis is given as $\mathbf{E} = E_0 \cos(kz - \omega t)$. Choose the correct statement from the following. NCERT Pg. 206

(a) The associated magnetic field is given as $\mathbf{B} = \frac{1}{c}(\hat{\mathbf{j}} \times \mathbf{E})$.

(b) The electromagnetic field can be written in terms of the associated magnetic field as $\mathbf{E} = c(\mathbf{B} \times \hat{\mathbf{j}})$.

(c) $\hat{\mathbf{k}} \cdot \mathbf{E} = 0, \hat{\mathbf{k}} \cdot \mathbf{B} = 0$.

(d) $\hat{\mathbf{k}} \times \mathbf{E} = 0, \hat{\mathbf{k}} \times \mathbf{B} = 0$.

17 Intensity of sunlight is observed 0.099 Wm^{-2} at a point in free space. What will be the peak value of magnetic field at that point? ($\varepsilon_0 = 8.85 \times 10^{-12} C^2/N\text{-}m^2$) NCERT Pg. 206

(a) 2.88×10^{-8} T (b) 1.96×10^{-8} T

(c) 8.31 T (d) 5.88 T

18 A beam of light travelling along X-axis is described by the electric field $E_y = 300 \sin \omega(t - x/c)$. The ratio of electric force to magnetic force on a charge q moving along Y-axis with a speed of 3×10^7 ms^{-1}
(Given, speed of light $= 3 \times 10^8$ ms^{-1}) NCERT Pg. 206

(a) 1 : 1 (b) 1 : 10 (c) 10 : 1 (d) 1 : 2

19 An EM wave is propagating in a medium with a velocity $\mathbf{v} = v\hat{\mathbf{i}}$. The instantaneous oscillating electric field of this EM wave is along + Y-axis. Then, the direction of oscillating magnetic field of EM wave will be along NCERT Pg. 206

(a) − y-direction (b) + z-direction

(c) − z-direction (d) −x-direction

20 A uniform heavy string of mass M hangs vertically from a rigid ceiling. A transverse wave is sent from its free end towards fixed end. As the wave moves upward, NCERT Pg. 206

(a) its speed and frequency increases

(b) its speed and wavelength increases

(c) its speed decreases but wavelength increases

(d) its speed and wavelength decreases

21 Equation of transverse wave is given by $y = 5\sin(\pi t - 0.1\pi x)$, where x and y are in cm. The wavelength λ and velocity v of the wave respectively is NCERT Pg. 206

(a) 20 cm, 10 cm/s (b) 10 cm, 100 cm/s

(c) 10 cm, 50 cm/s (d) 20 cm, 50 cm/s

22 A wave travels on a string. The equation of the wave is $y = A\sin(\omega t - kx)$. It is reflected from a heavier string tied to an end of the lighter string at $x = 0$. If 36% of the incident energy is reflected back, then the equation of the reflected wave is NCERT Pg. 206

(a) $y = \frac{8}{10} A\sin(\omega t + kx)$ (b) $y = -\frac{6}{10} A\sin(\omega t + kx)$

(c) $y = \frac{6}{10} A\sin(kx + \omega t)$ (d) $y = -\frac{8}{10} A\sin(kx + \omega t)$

23 For a plane electromagnetic wave, direction of electric field E and magnetic field B is along $-\hat{\mathbf{i}} + \hat{\mathbf{j}}$ and $-\hat{\mathbf{i}} - \hat{\mathbf{j}}$, respectively. The direction of propagation of plane electromagnetic wave is NCERT Pg. 206

(a) +x-direction

(b) +z-direction

(c) +y-direction

(d) −x-direction

24 The electric field part of an electromagnetic wave in a medium is represented by $E_x = 0$;

$$E_y = 2.5\frac{N}{C}\cos\left[\left(2\pi \times 10^6 \frac{rad}{m}\right)t - \left(\pi \times 10^{-2}\frac{rad}{s}\right)x\right]; E_z = 0.$$

The wave is NCERT Pg. 206

(a) moving along y-direction with frequency $2\pi \times 10^6$ Hz and wavelength 200 m

(b) moving along x-direction with frequency 10^6 Hz and wavelength 100 m

(c) moving along x-direction with frequency 10^6Hz and wavelength 200 m

(d) moving along y-direction with frequency 10^6 Hz and wavelength 200 m

25 The electric field associated with an electromagnetic wave in vacuum is given by $\mathbf{E} = \hat{\mathbf{i}}\, 40\cos(kz - 6 \times 10^8 t)$, where E, z and t are in volt/m, metre and second, respectively. The value of wave vector k is NCERT Pg. 206

(a) 2 m^{-1} (b) 0.5 m^{-1}

(c) 6 m^{-1} (d) 3 m^{-1}

26 The electric field in a plane electromagnetic wave is given by $E_z = 60\sin(4\pi \times 10^9 t - \pi \times 10^3 x)$ Vm^{-1}, where x is in metre and t is in second. What is the amplitude of magnetic field and wavelength? NCERT Pg. 206

(a) 2×10^{-7} T and 2×10^{-3}m

(b) 2×10^{-7} T and 10^{-3} m

(c) 4×10^{-7} T and 10^{-3} m

(d) 4×10^{-7} T and 2×10^{-3} m

27 A wave is described by the equation $y = (0.25\text{ m})\sin(5\pi x - \pi t)$. Here, x is in metre and t is in second. The speed of the wave is NCERT Pg. 206

(a) 5 m/s (b) 0.2 m/s

(c) 0.1 m/s (d) 0.5 m/s

28 The equation of progressive wave is given as $y = 4\sin\left(4\pi t - 0.04x + \frac{\pi}{3}\right)$, where x is in metre and t in second. The speed of wave is NCERT Pg. 206

(a) 20 π m/s (b) 100 π m/s

(c) 200 π m/s (d) $\frac{100}{\pi}$ m/s

29 If the equation of the stationary wave is given by $y = 2A\sin\left(\frac{2\pi ct}{\lambda}\right)\cos\left(\frac{2\pi x}{\lambda}\right)$, then which of the following is correct? NCERT Pg. 206

(a) The unit of $\frac{c}{\lambda}$ is same as that of $\frac{x}{\lambda}$

(b) The unit of xt is same as that of λ

(c) The unit of $\frac{2\pi c}{\lambda}$ is same as that of $\frac{2\pi x}{\lambda t}$

(d) The unit of ct is same as that of $\frac{\lambda}{x}$

30 The phase difference between the two given waves is

$$y_1 = a_1\sin\left(\omega t - \frac{2\pi}{\lambda}x\right)$$

$$y_2 = a_2\cos\left(\omega t - \frac{2\pi}{\lambda}x + \phi\right)$$

NCERT Pg. 206

(a) $\frac{2\pi}{\lambda}(\phi)$ (b) ϕ (c) $\frac{\pi}{2}+\phi$ (d) $\phi - \frac{\pi}{2}$

31 An electromagnetic wave is represented by the electric field $\mathbf{E} = E_0\,\hat{\mathbf{n}}\sin[\omega t + (6y - 8z)]$. Taking unit vectors in x, y and z- directions to be $\hat{\mathbf{i}}$, $\hat{\mathbf{j}}$, $\hat{\mathbf{k}}$, the direction of propagation $\hat{\mathbf{s}}$, is NCERT Pg. 206

(a) $\hat{\mathbf{s}} = \frac{3\hat{\mathbf{i}} - 4\hat{\mathbf{j}}}{5}$ (b) $\hat{\mathbf{s}} = \frac{-4\hat{\mathbf{k}} + 3\hat{\mathbf{j}}}{5}$

(c) $\hat{\mathbf{s}} = \left(\frac{-3\hat{\mathbf{j}} + 4\hat{\mathbf{k}}}{5}\right)$ (d) $\hat{\mathbf{s}} = \frac{4\hat{\mathbf{j}} - 3\hat{\mathbf{k}}}{5}$

32 A plane electromagnetic wave of frequency 25 GHz is propagating in vacuum along the z-direction. At a particular point in space and time, the magnetic field is given by $\mathbf{B} = 5\times 10^{-8}\,\hat{\mathbf{j}}$ T. The corresponding electric field $\mathbf{E}$ is (speed of light, $c = 3\times 10^8\,\text{ms}^{-1}$) NCERT Pg. 206

(a) $-1.66\times 10^{-16}\,\hat{\mathbf{i}}$ V/m (b) $1.66\times 10^{-16}\,\hat{\mathbf{i}}$ V/m

(c) $-15\,\hat{\mathbf{i}}$ V/m (d) $15\,\hat{\mathbf{i}}$ V/m

33 A charged particle oscillates about its mean position with a frequency of 10^9 Hz. The electromagnetic waves produced NCERT Pg. 207

(a) will have frequency of 10^9 Hz

(b) will have frequency of 2×10^9 Hz

(c) will have wavelength of 0.2 m

(d) will have wavelength of 0.5 m

34 The magnetic field of an electromagnetic wave is given by $B_y = 3\times 10^{-7}\sin(10^3x + 6.28\times 10^{12}t)$, where t and x are in seconds and metres, respectively.

The wavelength of the electromagnetic wave is NCERT Pg. 207

(a) 6.28 cm (b) 3.14 cm

(c) 0.63 cm (d) 0.32 cm

35 The electric field of an electromagnetic wave in free space is given by $\mathbf{E} = 10\cos(10^7t + kx)\,\hat{\mathbf{j}}\,\text{Vm}^{-1}$, where t and x are in seconds and metres, respectively. It can be inferred that NCERT Pg. 207

(a) the wavelength λ is 188.4 m

(b) the wave number k is 0.33 radm^{-1}

(c) the wave amplitude is 20Vm^{-1}

(d) None of the above

36 Suppose that the amplitude of electric field of an electromagnetic wave is $E_0 = 120\,\text{NC}^{-1}$ and its frequency is $\nu = 50.0$ MHz. The expressions for E will be (if wave travels along X-axis) NCERT Pg. 207

(a) $[(120\,\text{NC}^{-1})\sin\{(1.05\,\text{rad m}^{-1})x - (3.14\times 10^8\,\text{rads}^{-1})t\}]\,\hat{\mathbf{i}}$

(b) $[(120\,\text{NC}^{-1})\sin\{(1.05\,\text{rad m}^{-1})x - (3.14\times 10^8\,\text{rads}^{-1})t\}]\,\hat{\mathbf{k}}$

(c) $[(120\,\text{NC}^{-1})\sin\{(1.05\,\text{rad m}^{-1})x - (3.14\times 10^8\,\text{rads}^{-1})t\}]\,\hat{\mathbf{j}}$

(d) $[(120\,\text{NC}^{-1})\cos\{(1.05\,\text{rad m}^{-1})x - (3.14\times 10^8\,\text{rads}^{-1})t\}]\,\hat{\mathbf{j}}$

37 In a plane electromagnetic wave, the electric field oscillates sinusoidally at a frequency of 2.0×10^{10} Hz and amplitude 48 Vm^{-1}. What is the amplitude of the oscillating magnetic field? NCERT Pg. 207

(a) 0.8×10^{-7} T (b) 1.6×10^{-7} T

(c) 3.2×10^{-8} T (d) 6.4×10^{-8} T

38 If the magnetic field in a plane electromagnetic wave is given by

$$\mathbf{B} = 3\times 10^{-8}\sin(1.6\times 10^3x + 48\times 10^{10}t)\hat{\mathbf{j}}\text{T},$$

then what will be expression for electric field? NCERT Pg. 207

(a) $\mathbf{E} = 60\sin(1.6\times 10^3x + 48\times 10^{10}t)\hat{\mathbf{k}}$ V/m

(b) $\mathbf{E} = 3\times 10^{-8}\sin(1.6\times 10^3x + 48\times 10^{10}t)\,\hat{\mathbf{i}}$ V/m

(c) $\mathbf{E} = 3\times 10^{-8}\sin(1.6\times 10^3x + 48\times 10^{10}t)\,\hat{\mathbf{j}}$ V/m

(d) $\mathbf{E} = 9\sin(1.6\times 10^3x + 48\times 10^{10}t)\hat{\mathbf{k}}$ V/m

39 An EM wave from air enters a medium. The electric fields are $\mathbf{E}_1 = E_{01}\hat{\mathbf{x}}\cos\left[2\pi\nu\left(\frac{z}{c} - t\right)\right]$ in air and $\mathbf{E}_2 = E_{02}\hat{\mathbf{x}}\cos[k(2z - ct)]$ in medium, where the wave number k and frequency ν refer to their values in air. The medium is non-magnetic. If ε_{r_1} and ε_{r_2} refer to relative permittivities of air and medium respectively, which of the following options is correct? NCERT Pg. 207

(a) $\frac{\varepsilon_{r_1}}{\varepsilon_{r_2}} = 4$ (b) $\frac{\varepsilon_{r_1}}{\varepsilon_{r_2}} = 2$

(c) $\frac{\varepsilon_{r_1}}{\varepsilon_{r_2}} = \frac{1}{4}$ (d) $\frac{\varepsilon_{r_1}}{\varepsilon_{r_2}} = \frac{1}{2}$

40 The refractive index and permeability of a medium are 1.7 and $7\times 10^{-7}\,\text{Hm}^{-1}$, respectively. The relative permittivity of the medium is nearly NCERT Pg. 207

(a) 25 (b) 15

(c) 10 (d) 5

41 Light with an energy flux of 20 Wcm^{-2}falls on a non-reflecting surface at normal incidence. If the surface has an area of 25 cm^2, the average force exerted on the surface during 20 min time span is Old NCERT Pg. 277

(a) 2.1×10^{-6} N (b) 1.2×10^{-6} N
(c) 1.66×10^{-6} N (d) 2.1×10^{6} N

42 A plane electromagnetic wave with electric field of amplitude 4 Vm^{-1} varies with time propagating along Z-axis. The average energy density of the magnetic field (in $J\ m^{-3}$) is Old NCERT Pg. 207

(a) 33.29×10^{-12} (b) 35.4×10^{-12}
(c) 37.72×10^{-12} (d) 30.1×10^{-12}

43 A plane electromagnetic wave of frequency 50 MHz travels in free space along the positive x-direction. At a particular point in space and time, the electric field is $\mathbf{E} = 6.3\hat{\mathbf{j}}$ V/m. The corresponding magnetic field $\mathbf{B}$ at the point will be NCERT Pg. 207

(a) $18.9 \times 10^{-8}\ \hat{\mathbf{k}}$ T (b) $6.3 \times 10^{-8}\ \hat{\mathbf{k}}$ T
(c) $2.1 \times 10^{-8}\ \hat{\mathbf{k}}$ T (d) 8

44 A plane electromagnetic wave of frequency 25 MHz travels in free space along the positive x-direction. At a particular point in space and time, $\mathbf{E} = 6.3\hat{\mathbf{j}}$ in V/cm. Then, $\mathbf{B}$ at this point will be (in T) NCERT Pg. 207

(a) $2.1 \times 10^{-6}(-\hat{\mathbf{k}})$ (b) $2.1 \times 10^{-6}(\hat{\mathbf{k}})$
(c) $2.1 \times 10^{-6}(\hat{\mathbf{j}})$ (d) $2.1 \times 10^{-6}(\hat{\mathbf{i}})$

45 In an electromagnetic wave propagating through space, peak value of electric field is 0.12 V/cm. The peak value of magnetic field induction is NCERT Pg. 207

(a) 40 pT (b) 20 nT
(c) 30 nT (d) 40 nT

46 An electromagnetic wave of frequency $\nu = 3.0$ MHz passes from vacuum into a dielectric medium with relative permittivity $\varepsilon = 4.0$. Then, NCERT Pg. 207

(a) wavelength is doubled and frequency becomes half
(b) wavelength is halved and frequency remains unchanged
(c) wavelength and frequency both remains unchanged
(d) wavelength is doubled and frequency unchanged

47 Which of the following statement is incorrect? NCERT Pg. 207

(a) Electromagnetic waves cannot be deflected by any field.
(b) The velocity of light in a medium is $v = 1/\sqrt{\mu\varepsilon}$, thus it depends on both the electric and magnetic properties of the medium.
(c) The constancy of the velocity of electromagnetic waves in vacuum is used to define a standard of time.
(d) The direction of propagation vector k describes the direction of propagation of the wave.

48 Which of the following statement is correct for a plane electromagnetic wave? NCERT Pg. 207

(a) Average value of electric field is zero only.
(b) Average value of magnetic field is zero only.
(c) Average value of both electric and magnetic fields is zero.
(d) Average value of magnetic energy is zero.

49 A radiation of energy E falls normally on a perfectly reflecting surface. The momentum transferred to the surface is Old NCERT Pg. 277

(a) $\frac{E}{c}$ (b) $\frac{2E}{c}$
(c) Ec (d) $\frac{E}{c^2}$

50 The average value of electric energy density in an electromagnetic wave is (E_0 is peak value of electric field in electromagnetic wave) Old NCERT Pg. 277

(a) $\frac{1}{2}\varepsilon_0 E_0^2$ (b) $\frac{E_0^2}{2\varepsilon_0}$
(c) $\varepsilon_0 E_0^2$ (d) $\frac{1}{4}\varepsilon_0 E_0^2$

51 Assume a bulb of efficiency 2.5% as a point source. The peak values of electric and magnetic fields produced by the radiation coming from a 100W bulb at a distance of 3m is respectively Old NCERT Pg. 277

(a) 2.5 V m^{-1}, 3.6×10^{-8} T
(b) 4.2 V m^{-1}, 2.8×10^{-8} T
(c) 4.08 V m^{-1}, 1.36×10^{-8} T
(d) 3.6 V m^{-1}, 4.2×10^{-10} T

52 The wave which had wavelength ten million times that of the light waves, could be diffracted, refracted and polarised. This established that the radiation possesses Old NCERT Pg. 277

(a) particle nature
(b) wave nature
(c) Both particle and wave nature
(d) electromagnetic nature

53 Light having an energy flux of 40 Wcm^{-2} falls on non-reflecting surface at normal incidence. If the surface has an area of 20 cm^2, the total momentum delivered (for complete absorption) during 10 min is Old NCERT Pg. 277

(a) 16×10^{-5} kg-m s^{-1} (b) 16×10^{-4} kg-ms^{-1}
(c) 102×10^{4} kg-ms^{-1} (d) 1.03×10^{7} kg-ms^{-1}

54 A 27 mW laser beam has a cross-sectional area of 10 mm^2. The magnitude of the maximum electric field in this electromagnetic wave is given by Old NCERT Pg. 277
[Take, permittivity of free space, $\varepsilon_0 = 9 \times 10^{-12}$ SI units and speed of light, $c = 3 \times 10^{8}$ m/s]

(a) 1 kV/m (b) 0.7 kV/m
(c) 2 kV/m (d) 1.4 kV/m

55 In free space, the energy of electromagnetic wave in electric field is U_E and in magnetic field is U_B. Then, Old NCERT Pg. 277

(a) $U_E = U_B$ (b) $U_E > U_B$

(c) $U_E < U_B$ (d) $U_E = \frac{U_B}{2}$

Electromagnetic Spectrum

56 Frequency of radiations arising from two close energy levels in hydrogen, known as lamb shift is 1057 MHz. This frequency falls in which range of electromagnetic wave? NCERT Pg. 209

(a) Infrared rays (b) X-rays

(c) γ-rays (d) Radio waves

57 Radio waves diffract around buildings, although light waves do not. The reason is that radio waves NCERT Pg. 209

(a) travel with speed larger than c

(b) have much larger wavelength than light

(c) are not electromagnetic waves

(d) have much longer frequency

58 The condition under which a microwave oven heats up a food item, containing water molecules, most efficiently is NCERT Pg. 209

(a) the frequency of the microwave must match the resonant frequency of the water molecules

(b) the frequency of the microwave has no relation with natural frequency of water molecules

(c) microwave are heat waves, so always produce heating

(d) infrared waves produce heating in a microwave oven

59 Which of the following statement is incorrect? NCERT Pg. 209

(a) The classification of electromagnetic waves according to frequency is called electromagnetic spectrum.

(b) The AM band is from 530 kHz to 1710 kHz.

(c) The FM radio band extends from 88 MHz to 108 MHz.

(d) Infrared waves are produced by cold bodies and molecules.

60 Which of the following statement is incorrect about UV-rays? NCERT Pg. 210

(a) Ultraviolet rays cover wavelengths ranging from 4×10^{-7} m (400 nm) to 6×10^{-10} m (0.6 nm).

(b) UV radiation is produced by special lamps and very hot bodies.

(c) The sun is an important source of ultraviolet light.

(d) The ozone layer in the atmosphere cannot absorb UV-rays.

61 Which of the following statement is incorrect? NCERT Pg. 210

(a) The wavelength of microwave is greater than that of UV-rays.

(b) The wavelength of infrared rays is lesser than that of UV-rays.

(c) The wavelength of microwave is greater than that of infrared rays.

(d) Gamma rays have shortest wavelengths in the electromagnetic spectrum.

62 Infrared radiation keep the earth's surface warm using NCERT Pg. 210

(a) greenhouse effect

(b) resonance effect

(c) radioactivity

(d) None of the above

63 Visible rays in the spectrum ranges from about NCERT Pg. 210

(a) 4×10^{14}Hz to 4×10^{11} Hz

(b) 4×10^{14} Hz to 7×10^{14} Hz

(c) 4×10^{12} Hz to 7×10^{14} Hz

(d) 4×10^{11} Hz to 7×10^{14} Hz

64 UV-radiation is absorbed by NCERT Pg. 210

(a) ordinary glass (b) prism

(c) black glass (d) Both (b) and (c)

65 X-rays, gamma rays and microwaves travelling in vacuum have NCERT Pg. 211

(a) same wavelength but different velocities

(b) same frequency but different velocities

(c) same velocity but different wavelengths

(d) same velocity and same frequency

66 In the electromagnetic spectrum, X-ray region lies NCERT Pg. 211

(a) beyond the microwave region

(b) beyond the gamma rays

(c) beyond the UV region

(d) above the infrared ray region

67 One common way to generate X-rays is that NCERT Pg. 211

(a) bombard a metal target by high energy electrons

(b) bombard a metal target by low energy neutrons

(c) bombard a metal target by low energy protons

(d) bombard a metal target by high energy neutrons

68 Wavelength of gamma rays are NCERT Pg. 211

(a) 10^{-10} m to less than 10^{-14} m

(b) 10^{-14} m to less than 10^{-10} m

(c) 10^{-11} m to less than 10^{-14} m

(d) 10^{-14} nm to less than 10^{-10} nm

69 Gamma rays can be detected by NCERT Pg. 211

(a) photocells

(b) geiger tubes

(c) thermopiles

(d) diodes

70 The frequencies of X-rays, γ-rays and UV-rays are respectively n_1, n_2, n_3, then NCERT Pg. 211

(a) $n_1 > n_2, n_2 < n_3$ (b) $n_1 < n_2, n_2 < n_3$
(c) $n_1 < n_2, n_2 > n_3$ (d) $n_1 > n_2, n_2 > n_3$

71 Arrange the following electromagnetic radiations in the order of increasing wavelength. NCERT Pg. 211

I. Blue light II. Yellow light
III. X-ray IV. Radio wave

(a) IV, II, I, III (b) I, II, IV, III
(c) III, I, II, IV (d) II, I, IV, III

72 Which of the following statement about EM waves is correct? NCERT Pg. 211

(a) Gamma rays are produced in nuclear reactions.
(b) Ultraviolet waves are used in treatment of swollen joints.
(c) Snakes cannot detect infrared rays.
(d) Electromagnetic waves do not exhibit polarisation while sound waves.

Assertion and Reason Questions

Direction (Q. Nos. 1-10) *In the following questions, a statement of Assertion is followed by a corresponding statement of Reason. Of the following statements, choose the correct one.*

(a) Both Assertion and Reason are correct and Reason is the correct explanation of Assertion.
(b) Both Assertion and Reason are correct but Reason is not the correct explanation of Assertion.
(c) Assertion is correct but Reason is incorrect.
(d) Assertion is incorrect but Reason is correct.

1 Assertion The current through surface P is zero in the cases shown in figure below.

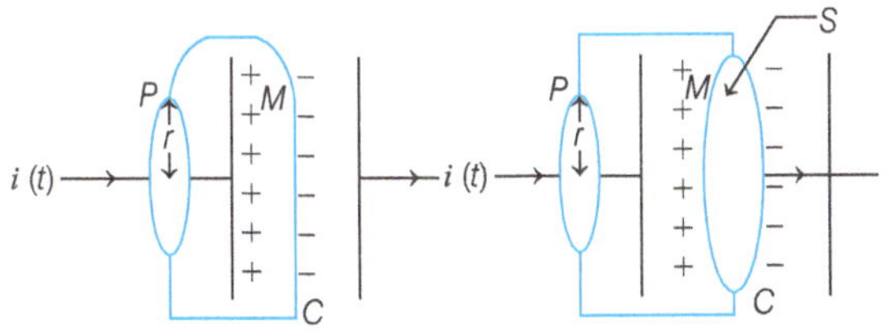

Reason While applying Ampere's circuital law to given surfaces with same perimeter, the left hand side of equation $\oint B \cdot dl = \mu_0 i(t)$ has not changed but the right hand side is zero. NCERT Pg. 203

2 Assertion An electromagnetic wave is a self-sustaining oscillating wave.

Reason An oscillating charge produces an electric field in space, which produces an oscillating magnetic field, which in turn, is a source of electric field and so on. NCERT Pg. 205

3 Assertion The electromagnetic wave is transverse in nature.

Reason Electromagnetic wave propagates parallel to the direction of electric and magnetic fields. NCERT Pg. 207

4 Assertion The velocity of electromagnetic waves depends on electric and magnetic properties of the medium.

Reason Velocity of electromagnetic waves in free space is constant. NCERT Pg. 207

5 Assertion Electromagnetic waves carry energy and momentum.

Reason Electromagnetic waves can be polarised. NCERT Pg. 207

6 Assertion When the sun shine on our hand, we feel the energy being absorbed from the electromagnetic waves (our hands get warm).

Reason Electromagnetic waves transfer momentum to our hand but because c is very large, the amount of momentum transferred is extremely small and we do not feel the pressure. NCERT Pg. 210

7 Assertion Infrared waves are sometimes referred to as heat waves.

Reason Water molecules present in most materials readily absorb infrared waves. After absorption, their thermal motion increases, i.e. they heat up and heat their surroundings. NCERT Pg. 210

8 Assertion UV-radiations are used in LASIK eye surgery.

Reason Due to shorter wavelengths, UV-radiations can be focused into very narrow beams. NCERT Pg. 210

9 Assertion The eye is most sensitive for the light of frequency 5.36×10^{14} Hz.

Reason The frequency of light is directly proportional to wavelength of light. NCERT Pg. 210

10 Assertion X-ray astronomy is possible only from satellites orbiting the earth.

Reason Efficiency of X-rays telescope is large as compared to any other telescope. NCERT Pg. 211

Statement Based Questions

Direction (Q. Nos. 1-8) *In the following questions, two statements (I & II) are given. In the light of the given statements, choose the correct option given below.*

(a) Both Statement I and Statement II are false.
(b) Statement I is true, but Statement II is false.
(c) Statement I is false, but Statement II is true.
(d) Both Statement I and Statement II are true.

1 For a parallel plate capacitor, two statements are given below.

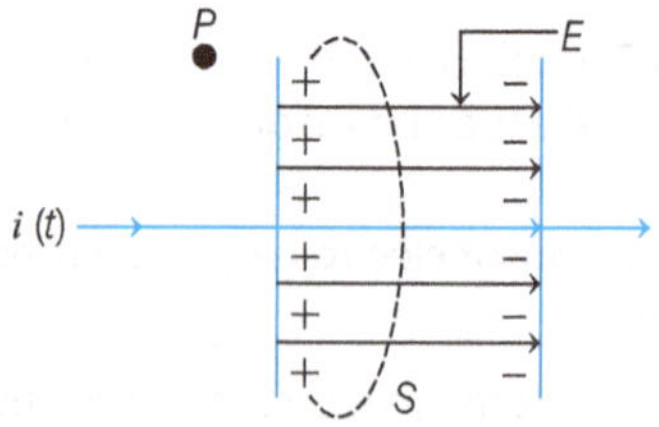

Statement I The magnitude of E is same over the area A of the capacitor plates and vanishes outside it.

Statement II The electric flux ϕ_E through the surfaces S by using the Gauss' law, is

$$\phi_E = |\mathbf{E}|A = \frac{1}{\varepsilon_0}\frac{Q}{A} \cdot A = \frac{Q}{\varepsilon_0}$$ NCERT Pg. 203

2 **Statement I** The total current i is the sum of the conduction current denoted by i_c and the displacement current denoted by

$$i_d = \varepsilon_0\left(\frac{d\phi_E}{dt}\right)$$

Statement II Outside the capacitor plates, we have both conduction current and displacement current. NCERT Pg. 203

3 **Statement I** In all respects, the displacement current has the same physical effects as the conduction current.

Statement II Due to electric fields in a conducting wire, the displacement current may be zero, since the electric field **E** does not change with time. NCERT Pg. 204

4 **Statement I** An oscillating charge is an example of accelerating charge.

Statement II The current $i = \varepsilon_0 \frac{d\phi_E}{dt}$ is due to change in electric field, therefore called conduction current. NCERT Pg. 205

5 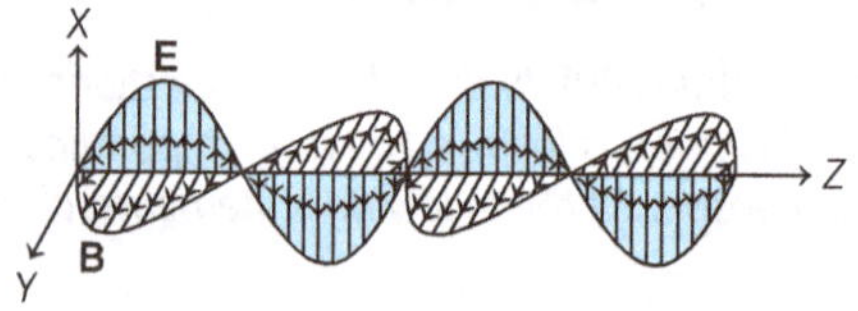

Statement I A plane electromagnetic wave propagating along the z-direction (the fields are shown as a function of the z-coordinate, at a given time t).

Statement II The electric field E is along the Y-axis and varies sinusoidally with Z, at a given time. NCERT Pg. 206

6 **Statement I** Material medium is involved in the vibrations of the electric and magnetic fields.

Statement II Sound waves in air are longitudinal waves of compression and rarefaction. NCERT Pg. 207

7 **Statement I** The great technological importance of electromagnetic waves is their capability to carry energy from one place to another.

Statement II The radio and TV signals from broadcasting stations carry energy. NCERT Pg. 209

8 **Statement I** Radio waves are produced by the accelerated motion of charges in conducting wires.

Statement II Radio waves are used in radio and television communication systems. NCERT Pg. 209

Matching Type Questions

1 Match the Column I (equation) with Column II (law) and select the correct answer from the options given below. NCERT Pg. 205

Column I	Column II
A. $\oint \mathbf{E} \cdot d\mathbf{A} = Q/\varepsilon_0$	1. Faraday's law
B. $\oint \mathbf{B} \cdot d\mathbf{A} = 0$	2. Ampere-Maxwell law
C. $\oint \mathbf{E} \cdot d\mathbf{l} = -\frac{d\phi_B}{dt}$	3. Gauss's law for electricity
D. $\oint \mathbf{B} \cdot d\mathbf{l} = \mu_0 i_c + \mu_0 \varepsilon_0 \frac{d\phi_E}{dt}$	4. Gauss's law for magnetism

Codes

	A	B	C	D		A	B	C	D
(a)	4	3	2	1	(b)	3	2	1	4
(c)	3	4	1	2	(d)	1	2	3	4

2 Match the Column I (EM wave) with Column II (frequency band) and select the correct answer from the options given below. NCERT Pg. 209

Column I	Column II
A. Radio waves	1. 54 MHz
B. Amplitude modulated	2. 54 MHz to 890 MHz
C. Short wave bands	3. 530 kHz to 1710 kHz
D. TV wave	4. 500 kHz to 1000 MHz

Codes

	A	B	C	D
(a)	3	1	4	2
(b)	1	4	2	3
(c)	4	1	3	2
(d)	4	3	1	2

3 Match the Column I (EM wave) with Column II (application association) and select the correct answer from the options given below. NCERT Pg. 210

Column I	Column II
A. Infrared waves	1. To treat muscular strain
B. Radio waves	2. For broadcasting
C. X-rays	3. To detect fracture of bones
D. Ultraviolet	4. Absorbed by the ozone layer of the atmosphere

Codes

	A	B	C	D
(a)	4	3	2	1
(b)	1	2	4	3
(c)	3	2	1	4
(d)	1	2	3	4

Numerical Type Questions

1 The magnetic field of a plane electromagnetic wave is given by $\mathbf{B} = B_0 \hat{\mathbf{i}}[\cos(kz - \omega t)] + B_1 \hat{\mathbf{j}}[\cos(kz + \omega t)]$, where $B_0 = 3 \times 10^{-5}$ T and $B_1 = 2 \times 10^{-6}$ T. The rms value of the force experienced by a stationary charge $Q = 10^{-4}$ C at $z = 0$ is .... $\times 10^{-1}$N. NCERT Pg. 207

2 A RADAR sends an electromagnetic signal of electric field $E_0 = 2.25$ V/m and magnetic field $B_0 = 1.5 \times 10^{-8}$ T which strikes a target on line of sight at a distance of 3 km in a medium. After that a pair of signal (echo) reflects back towards the RADAR with same velocity and by same path. If the signal was transmitted at time $t = 0$s from RADAR, then after $x \times 10^{-5}$ s time, echo reaches the RADAR. The value of x is .... NCERT Pg. 207

3 A red LED emits light at 0.15 W uniformly around it. The amplitude of the electric field (in Vm^{-1}) of the light at a distance of 1 m from the diode is .... Old NCERT Pg. 277

4 Electric field of plane electromagnetic wave propagating through a non-magnetic medium is given by $E = 20\cos(2 \times 10^{10} t - 200x)$ V/m. The dielectric constant of the medium is equal to .... (Take, $\mu_r = 1$) NCERT Pg. 207

5 A plane electromagnetic wave $E_y = 100\cos(6 \times 10^8 t + 4x)$ V/m is propagating in a medium. The refractive index of that medium is......... . NCERT Pg. 207

6 If a source is transmitting electromagnetic waves of frequency 8.196×10^6 Hz, then the wavelength of the electromagnetic waves transmitted from the source will be ...... cm. NCERT Pg. 207

7 The magnetic field of a beam emerging from a filter facing a flood light as given by

$B = 12 \times 10^{-8} \sin(1.20 \times 10^7 z - 36 \times 10^{15} t)$ T

The average intensity of the beam is ...... $\times 10^{-2}$ Wm^{-2}. NCERT Pg.277

8 The electric field for an electromagnetic wave in free space is $\mathbf{E} = \hat{\mathbf{i}} 30\cos(kz - 6 \times 10^8 t)$. where magnitude of $\mathbf{E}$ is in V/m. The magnitude of wave vector k is ...... rad /m. (velocity of EM wave in free space is 3×10^8 m/s) NCERT Pg. 207

9 Nearly 10% of the power of a 110W light bulb is converted to visible radiation. The change in average intensities of visible radiation, at a distance of 1 m from the bulb to a distance of 5m is $a \times 10^{-2}$ W/m^2. The value of a will be

Old NCERT Pg. 277

10 The electric field intensity produced by the radiation coming from a 100 W bulb at a distance of 3 m is E. The electric field intensity produced by the radiation coming from 55 W at the same distance is $\sqrt{\frac{x}{20}}E$, where the value of x is ....

Old NCERT Pg. 277

NCERT Exemplar Questions

1 A linearly polarised electromagnetic wave given as $\mathbf{E} = E_0 \hat{\mathbf{i}} \cos(kz - \omega t)$ is incident normally on a perfectly reflecting infinite wall at $z = a$. Assuming that the material of the wall is optically inactive, the reflected wave will be given as

(a) $\mathbf{E}_r = E_0 \hat{\mathbf{i}}(kz - \omega t)$
(b) $\mathbf{E}_r = E_0 \hat{\mathbf{i}} \cos(kz + \omega t)$
(c) $\mathbf{E}_r = -E_0 \hat{\mathbf{i}} \cos(kz + \omega t)$
(d) $\mathbf{E}_r = E_0 \hat{\mathbf{i}} \sin(kz - \omega t)$

2 The electric field intensity produced by the radiations coming from 100 W bulb at a 3 m distance is E. The electric field intensity produced by the radiations coming from 50 W bulb at the same distance is

(a) $\frac{E}{2}$
(b) $2E$
(c) $\frac{E}{\sqrt{2}}$
(d) $\sqrt{2}E$

3 The ratio of contributions made by the electric and magnetic field components to the intensity of an EM wave is

(a) $c : 1$
(b) $c^2 : 1$
(c) $1 : 1$
(d) $\sqrt{c} : 1$

Past Exams Questions

NEET

1 A parallel plate capacitor is charged by connecting it to a battery through a resistor. If I is the current in the circuit, then in the gap between the plates.

NCERT Pg. 202, NEET 2024

(a) There is no current.
(b) Displacement current of magnitude equal to I flows in the same direction as I.
(c) Displacement current of magnitude equal to I flows in a direction opposite to that of I.
(d) Displacement current of magnitude greater than I flows but can be in any direction.

2 The property which is not of an electromagnetic wave travelling in free space is that

NCERT Pg. 206, NEET 2024

(a) they are transverse in nature
(b) the energy density in electric field is equal to energy density in magnetic field
(c) they travel with a speed equal to $\frac{1}{\sqrt{\mu_0 \varepsilon_0}}$
(d) they originate from charges moving with uniform speed

3 A capacitor of capacitance C, is connected across an AC source of voltage V, given by $V = V_0 \sin \omega t$. The displacement current between the plates of the capacitor, would then be given by

NCERT Pg. 204, NEET 2021

(a) $I_d = V_0 \omega C \cos \omega t$
(b) $I_d = \frac{V_0}{\omega C} \cos \omega t$
(c) $I_d = \frac{V_0}{\omega C} \sin \omega t$
(d) $I_d = V_0 \omega C \sin \omega t$

4 For a plane electromagnetic wave propagating in x-direction, which one of the following combination gives the correct possible directions for electric field (E) and magnetic field (B) respectively?

NCERT Pg. 206, NEET 2021

(a) $\hat{\mathbf{j}} + \hat{\mathbf{k}}, \hat{\mathbf{j}} + \hat{\mathbf{k}}$
(b) $-\hat{\mathbf{j}} + \hat{\mathbf{k}}, -\hat{\mathbf{j}} - \hat{\mathbf{k}}$
(c) $\hat{\mathbf{j}} + \hat{\mathbf{k}}, -\hat{\mathbf{j}} + \hat{\mathbf{k}}$
(d) $-\hat{\mathbf{j}} + \hat{\mathbf{k}}, -\hat{\mathbf{j}} + \hat{\mathbf{k}}$

5 The magnetic field in a plane electromagnetic wave is given by $B_y = 2 \times 10^{-7} \sin(\pi \times 10^3 x + 3\pi \times 10^{11} t)$ T Calculate the wavelength.

NCERT Pg. 206, NEET 2020

(a) $\pi \times 10^3$ m
(b) 2×10^{-3} m
(c) 2×10^3 m
(d) $\pi \times 10^{-3}$ m

6 The electromagnetic wave with shortest wavelength among the following is

NCERT Pg. 211, NEET 2020

(a) UV-rays
(b) X-rays
(c) γ-rays
(d) microwaves

7 A parallel plate capacitor of capacitance 20 μF is being charged by a voltage source whose potential is changing at the rate of 3 V/s. The conduction current through the connecting wires and the displacement current through the plates of the capacitor, would be respectively

NCERT Pg. 203, NEET 2019

(a) 60 μA, 60 μA (b) 60 μA, zero
(c) zero, zero (d) zero, 60 μA

8 For a transparent medium, relative permeability and permittivity μ_r and ε_r are 1.0 and 1.44, respectively. The velocity of light in this medium would be
NCERT Pg. 207, NEET 2019

(a) 2.5×10^8 m/s (b) 3×10^8 m/s
(c) 2.08×10^8 m/s (d) 4.32×10^8 m/s

9 In an electromagnetic wave in free space the root mean square value of the electric field is $E_{rms} = 6\ \text{Vm}^{-1}$. The peak value of the magnetic field is
NCERT Pg. 207, NEET 2017

(a) 2.83×10^{-8} T (b) 0.70×10^{-8} T
(c) 4.23×10^{-8} T (d) 1.41×10^{-8} T

10 The energy of EM waves is of the order of 15 keV. To which part of the spectrum does it belong?
NCERT Pg. 211, AIPMT 2015

(a) X-rays (b) Infrared rays
(c) Ultraviolet rays (d) γ-rays

JEE Main

11 The magnetic field in a plane electromagnetic wave is $B_y = (3.5 \times 10^{-7} \sin(1.5 \times 10^3 x + 0.5 \times 10^{11} t)$ T. The corresponding electric field will be
NCERT Pg. 205, JEE Main 2024

(a) $E_z = 1.17 \sin(1.5 \times 10^3 x + 0.5 \times 10^{11} t)\ \text{Vm}^{-1}$
(b) $E_y = 1.17 \sin(1.5 \times 10^3 x + 0.5 \times 10^{11} t)\ \text{Vm}^{-1}$
(c) $E_z = 105 \sin(1.5 \times 10^3 x + 0.5 \times 10^{11} t)\ \text{Vm}^{-1}$
(d) $E_y = 10.5 \sin(1.5 \times 10^3 x + 0.5 \times 10^{11} t)\ \text{Vm}^{-1}$

12 Given below are two statements

Statement I Electromagnetic waves carry energy as they travel through space and this energy is equally shared by the electric and magnetic fields.

Statement II When electromagnetic waves strike a surface, a pressure is exerted on the surface.
NCERT Pg. 205, JEE Main 2024

In the light of the above statements, choose the most appropriate answer from the options given below.
(a) Both Statement I and Statement II are correct.
(b) Both Statement I and Statement II are incorrect.
(c) Statement I is correct but Statement II is incorrect.
(d) Statement I is incorrect but Statement II is correct.

13 In a plane EM wave, the electric field oscillates sinusoidally at a frequency of 5×10^{10} Hz and an amplitude of $50\ \text{Vm}^{-1}$. The total average energy density of the electromagnetic field of the wave is
[Use, $\varepsilon_0 = 8.85 \times 10^{-12}\ \text{C}^2/\text{N-m}^2$]
NCERT Pg. 205, JEE Main 2024

(a) $2.212 \times 10^{-10}\ \text{Jm}^{-3}$ (b) $1.106 \times 10^{-8}\ \text{Jm}^{-3}$
(c) $4.425 \times 10^{-8}\ \text{Jm}^{-3}$ (d) $2.212 \times 10^{-8}\ \text{Jm}^{-3}$

14 Which of the following Maxwell's equation is valid for time varying conditions but not valid for static conditions
NCERT Pg. 205, JEE Main 2023

(a) $\oint \mathbf{E} \cdot d\mathbf{l} = 0$ (b) $\oint \mathbf{D} \cdot d\mathbf{A} = Q$
(c) $\oint \mathbf{B} \cdot d\mathbf{l} = \mu_0 I$ (d) $\oint \mathbf{E} \cdot d\mathbf{l} = -\frac{d\phi_B}{dt}$

15 If **E** and **K** represent electric field and propagation vectors of the EM waves in vacuum, then magnetic field vector is given by (ω = angular frequency)
NCERT Pg. 206, JEE Main 2023

(a) $\omega(\mathbf{k} \times \mathbf{E})$ (b) $\mathbf{k} \times \mathbf{E}$ (c) $\frac{1}{\omega}(\mathbf{k} \times \mathbf{E})$ (d) $\omega(\mathbf{E} \times \mathbf{k})$

16 The amplitude of magnetic field in an electromagnetic wave propagating along Y-axis is 6.0×10^{-7}T. The maximum value of electric field in the electromagnetic wave is
NCERT Pg. 207, JEE Main 2023

(a) $2 \times 10^{15}\ \text{Vm}^{-1}$ (b) $180\ \text{Vm}^{-1}$
(c) $5 \times 10^{14}\ \text{Vm}^{-1}$ (d) $6.0 \times 10^{-7}\ \text{Vm}^{-1}$

17 The magnetic field of a plane electromagnetic wave is given by

$\mathbf{B} = 2 \times 10^{-8} \sin(0.5 \times 10^3 x + 1.5 \times 10^{11} t)\hat{\mathbf{j}}$ T.

The amplitude of the electric field would be
NCERT Pg. 207, JEE Main 2022

(a) $6\ \text{Vm}^{-1}$ along X-axis (b) $3\ \text{Vm}^{-1}$ along Z-axis
(c) $6\ \text{Vm}^{-1}$ along Z-axis (d) $2 \times 10^{-8}\ \text{Vm}^{-1}$ along Z-axis

18 An EM wave propagating in x-direction has a wavelength of 8 mm. The electric field vibrating in y-direction has maximum magnitude of 60Vm^{-1}. Choose the correct equations for electric and magnetic fields, if the EM wave is propagating in vacuum.
NCERT Pg. 207, JEE Main 2022

(a) $E_y = 60 \sin\left[\frac{\pi}{4} \times 10^3 (x - 3 \times 10^8 t)\right]\hat{\mathbf{j}}\ \text{Vm}^{-1}$
$E_z = 2 \sin\left[\frac{\pi}{4} \times 10^3 (x - 3 \times 10^8 t)\right]\hat{\mathbf{k}}\text{T}$

(b) $E_y = 60 \sin\left[\frac{\pi}{4} \times 10^3 (x - 3 \times 10^8 t)\right]\hat{\mathbf{j}}\ \text{Vm}^{-1}$
$B_z = 2 \times 10^{-7} \sin\left[\frac{\pi}{4} \times 10^3 (x - 3 \times 10^8 t)\right]\hat{\mathbf{k}}\ \text{T}$

(c) $E_y = 2 \times 10^{-7} \sin\left[\frac{\pi}{4} \times 10^3 (x - 3 \times 10^8 t)\right]\hat{\mathbf{j}}\ \text{Vm}^{-1}$
$B_z = 60 \sin\left[\frac{\pi}{4} \times 10^3 (x - 3 \times 10^8 t)\right]\hat{\mathbf{k}}\ \text{T}$

(d) $E_y = 2 \times 10^{-7} \sin\left[\frac{\pi}{4} \times 10^4 (x - 4 \times 10^8 t)\right]\hat{\mathbf{j}}\ \text{Vm}^{-1}$
$B_z = 60 \sin\left[\frac{\pi}{4} \times 10^4 (x - 4 \times 10^8 t)\right]\hat{\mathbf{k}}\ \text{T}$

Skill Boosters

1 Green light is travelling in vacuum with electric field **E** and magnetic field **B**. The direction of polarisation of the light is **X** and direction of propagation is **k**.
Then,
(a) $\mathbf{X} \parallel \mathbf{E}$ and $\mathbf{k} \parallel \mathbf{E} \times \mathbf{B}$
(b) $\mathbf{X} \parallel \mathbf{E}$ and $\mathbf{k} \parallel \mathbf{B} \times \mathbf{E}$
(c) $\mathbf{X} \parallel \mathbf{B}$ and $\mathbf{k} \parallel \mathbf{B} \times \mathbf{E}$
(d) $\mathbf{X} \parallel \mathbf{B}$ and $\mathbf{k} \parallel \mathbf{E} \times \mathbf{B}$

2 A plane electromagnetic wave is propagating along the direction $\frac{\hat{\mathbf{i}}+\hat{\mathbf{j}}}{\sqrt{2}}$, with its polarisation along the direction $-\hat{\mathbf{k}}$. The correct form of the magnetic field of the wave would be (Here, B_0 is a constant)
(a) $B_0\,\hat{\mathbf{k}}\cos\left(\omega t - k\frac{\hat{\mathbf{i}}+\hat{\mathbf{j}}}{\sqrt{2}}\right)$
(b) $B_0\,\frac{\hat{\mathbf{i}}-\hat{\mathbf{j}}}{\sqrt{2}}\cos\left(\omega t + k\frac{\hat{\mathbf{i}}+\hat{\mathbf{j}}}{\sqrt{2}}\right)$
(c) $B_0\,\frac{\hat{\mathbf{i}}+\hat{\mathbf{j}}}{\sqrt{2}}\cos\left(\omega t - k\frac{\hat{\mathbf{i}}+\hat{\mathbf{j}}}{\sqrt{2}}\right)$
(d) $B_0\,\frac{-\hat{\mathbf{i}}+\hat{\mathbf{j}}}{\sqrt{2}}\cos\left(\omega t - k\frac{\hat{\mathbf{i}}+\hat{\mathbf{j}}}{\sqrt{2}}\right)$

3 The electric field of a plane electromagnetic wave propagating along the x-direction in vacuum is $\mathbf{E} = E_0\hat{\mathbf{k}}\cos(\omega t - kx)$. The magnetic field at the moment $t = 2\text{s}$ is
(a) $\mathbf{B} = E_0\sqrt{\mu_0\varepsilon_0}\cos(kx)\,\hat{\mathbf{j}}$
(b) $\mathbf{B} = \frac{E_0}{\sqrt{\mu_0\varepsilon_0}}\cos(kx)\,\hat{\mathbf{k}}$
(c) $\mathbf{B} = E_0\sqrt{\mu_0\varepsilon_0}\cos(2\omega - kx)\,\hat{\mathbf{k}}$
(d) $\mathbf{B} = E_0\sqrt{\mu_0\varepsilon_0}\cos(2\omega - kx)\,\hat{\mathbf{j}}$

4 A parallel plate capacitor is charged by a constant current i. Consider a plane surface area $A/2$ parallel to the plates is drawn symmetrically between the plates, then the displacement current through this area will be (A = area of plates and d = separation between plates)
(a) $\frac{i}{4}$
(b) $\frac{i}{2}$
(c) i
(d) $\frac{i}{8}$

5 A new scientist uses X-rays for radar purpose but the radar is not able to detect target because
(a) it is not reflected by the target
(b) it is partly absorbed by the target
(c) it is not an electromagnetic wave
(d) it is completely absorbed by target

6 A square loop of side a is placed in a homogeneous magnetic field perpendicular to the plane of the loop. The field B change with time according to the equation $B = Kt$, where K is a constant and t is the time. The electric field in the loop is
(a) $\frac{Ka}{4}$
(b) $\frac{Ka^2}{4}$
(c) $\frac{K}{4a}$
(d) $\frac{K}{2a}$

7 The pressure exerted by an electromagnetic wave intensity I (W/m^2) on a perfectly black body is (c is the velocity of light)
(a) Ic
(b) Ic^2
(c) $\frac{I}{c}$
(d) $\frac{I}{c^2}$

8 A capacitor and a resistor are connected in series across a 220V source. When the capacitor is 50% charged, the peak value of the displacement current is ($R = 100\Omega$, $X_C = 100\Omega$)
(a) 2.2 A
(b) 1.56 A
(c) 4.4 A
(d) 1.1 A

Correct Codes

Topical Questions

1 (c)	2 (a)	3 (a)	4 (d)	5 (d)	6 (c)	7 (c)	8 (c)	9 (a)	10 (a)
11 (d)	12 (a)	13 (c)	14 (d)	15 (d)	16 (c)	17 (a)	18 (c)	19 (b)	20 (b)
21 (a)	22 (c)	23 (b)	24 (c)	25 (a)	26 (a)	27 (b)	28 (b)	29 (c)	30 (c)
31 (c)	32 (d)	33 (a)	34 (c)	35 (a)	36 (c)	37 (b)	38 (d)	39 (c)	40 (d)
41 (c)	42 (b)	43 (c)	44 (b)	45 (d)	46 (b)	47 (c)	48 (c)	49 (b)	50 (d)
51 (c)	52 (b)	53 (b)	54 (d)	55 (a)	56 (d)	57 (b)	58 (a)	59 (d)	60 (d)
61 (b)	62 (a)	63 (b)	64 (a)	65 (c)	66 (c)	67 (a)	68 (a)	69 (b)	70 (c)
71 (c)	72 (a)								

Assertion and Reason Questions

1 (a)	2 (a)	3 (c)	4 (b)	5 (b)	6 (b)	7 (a)	8 (a)	9 (c)	10 (c)

Statement Based Questions

1 (d)	2 (b)	3 (d)	4 (b)	5 (b)	6 (c)	7 (d)	8 (d)

Matching Type Questions

1 (c)	2 (d)	3 (d)

Numerical Type Questions

1 (6)	2 (4)	3 (3)	4 (9)	5 (2)	6 (3660)	7 (171)	8 (2)	9 (84)	10 (11)

NCERT Exemplar Questions

1 (b)	2 (a)	3 (c)

Past Exams Questions

1 (b)	2 (d)	3 (a)	4 (b)	5 (b)	6 (c)	7 (a)	8 (a)	9 (a)	10 (a)
11 (c)	12 (a)	13 (b)	14 (d)	15 (c)	16 (b)	17 (c)	18 (b)		

Skill Boosters

1 (a)	2 (d)	3 (d)	4 (b)	5 (a)	6 (a)	7 (c)	8 (a)

Step by Step

Decoding the Questions

Concept Builders

1 True (T)

2 $\varepsilon_0\left(\frac{d\phi_E}{dt}\right)$

3 Permeability (μ_0) and permittivity (ε_0)

4 Electric and magnetic fields

5 perpendicular

6 linear

7 same, different

8 $v = \frac{1}{\sqrt{\mu\varepsilon}}$

9 1

10 LC oscillatory circuit

11 $v = \frac{1}{2\pi\sqrt{LC}}$

12 UV-ray

13 True (T)

14 1000 MHz

15 γ-rays

16 True (T)

17 infrared

18 Microwaves

19 False (F)

20 True (T)

Topical Questions

4 (*d*) $i_d = \frac{dq}{dt}$

$$= \frac{d}{dt}(q) = \frac{d}{dt}(q_0 \cos 2\pi vt)$$

$$= -2\pi q_0\, v \sin(2\pi vt)$$

5 (*d*) As, displacement current,

$$i_d = \varepsilon_0 \frac{d\phi_E}{dt}$$

$$= \varepsilon_0 A \frac{d}{dt}\left(\frac{V}{d}\right) \quad \left(\because \phi_E = EA = \frac{AV}{d}\right)$$

$$\Rightarrow \quad i_d = \frac{\varepsilon_0 A}{d} \times \frac{dV}{dt} = C\frac{dV}{dt} \quad \left(\because C = \frac{\varepsilon_0 A}{d}\right)$$

Given, $i_d = 10$ A and $C = 10^{-6}$ F

$$\Rightarrow \quad \frac{dV}{dt} = \frac{i_d}{C} = \frac{10}{10^{-6}} = 10^7 \text{ Vs}^{-1}$$

Thus, an instantaneous rate of voltage is 10^7 Vs^{-1}.

6 (*c*) Given, radius of plate, $R = 10$ cm $= 0.1$ m, cross-section area of a capacitor,

$$A = \pi R^2 = \pi(0.1)^2$$

$$= 3.14 \times 10^{-2} \text{ m}^2$$

Rate of change of electric field,

$$\frac{dE}{dt} = 5 \times 10^{13} \text{ Vms}^{-1}$$

Thus, displacement current,

$$i_d = \varepsilon_0 \frac{d\phi_E}{dt} = \varepsilon_0 A \frac{dE}{dt} \quad [\because \phi_E = EA]$$

$$= (8.85 \times 10^{-12})(3.14 \times 10^{-2})(5 \times 10^{13})$$

$$\therefore \quad i_d = 13.9 \text{ A}$$

7 (*c*) $\omega = 2\pi v = 2\pi \times (3.00 \times 10^3 \text{ s}^{-1})$

$$= 6\pi \times 10^3 \text{ s}^{-1}$$

Voltage across the capacitor,

$$V = V_0 \sin \omega t$$

$$= (30.0) \sin(6\pi \times 10^3 t)$$

Displacement current,

$$i_d = i_c = \frac{dq}{dt} = \frac{d}{dt}(q)$$

$$= \frac{d}{dt}(CV) = C\frac{dV}{dt}$$

$$= (8 \times 10^{-6}) \frac{d}{dt}[30.0 \sin(6\pi \times 10^3 t)]$$

$$= (8 \times 10^{-6})(30.0)(6\pi \times 10^3) \cos(6\pi \times 10^3 t)$$

$$= 4.52 \cos(6\pi \times 10^3 t) \text{ A}$$

Hence, the displacement current varies sinusoidally with time and has a maximum value of 4.52 A.

8 (*c*) Magnitude of displacement current is given by

$$i_d = i_c = \left|\frac{dq}{dt}\right| = 2 \times 10^{-7} \text{ Cs}^{-1}$$

$$= 2 \times 10^{-7} \text{ A}$$

$\therefore$ Displacement current is 2×10^{-7} A.

9 (*a*) Let the area of capacitor is A and distance between plates is d.

The displacement current following through the capacitor is given by

$$I_d = \varepsilon_0 \frac{d\phi_E}{dt} = \varepsilon_0 \frac{d(EA)}{dt}$$

$$\Rightarrow \quad = \varepsilon_0 \frac{A}{d} \times d \times \frac{dE}{dt}$$

$$\Rightarrow \quad I_d = Cd \times \frac{dE}{dt} \quad \left(\because C = \frac{\varepsilon_0 A}{d}\right)$$

If V is the potential difference between the plates, then

$$I_d = Cd\frac{d}{dt}\left(\frac{V}{d}\right) \quad \left(\because E = \frac{V}{d}\right)$$

$$= Cd \times \frac{1}{d}\frac{dV}{dt}$$

$$\frac{dV}{dt} = \frac{I_d}{C}$$

$$\therefore \quad \frac{dV}{dt} = 2I$$

11 (*d*) Given $I_d = 1 \text{ mA} = 1 \times 10^{-3}$ A, $C = 2\mu\text{F} = 2 \times 10^{-6}$ F

As, $I_d = I_C = \frac{d}{dt}(VC) = C\frac{dV}{dt}$

$$\Rightarrow \quad \frac{dV}{dt} = \frac{I_d}{C}$$

$$= \frac{1 \times 10^{-3}}{2 \times 10^{-6}}$$

$$= 0.5 \times 10^3$$

$$= 500 \text{ Vs}^{-1}$$

12 (*a*) The charge on capacitor plates at time t is given by

$$q = It$$

Now, electric field between the plates at this instant

$$E = \frac{\sigma}{\varepsilon_0} = \frac{q}{A\varepsilon_0} = \frac{It}{A\,\varepsilon_0}$$

Flux through the area $\frac{2A}{3}$ is

$$\phi_E = \left(\frac{2A}{3}\right)E = \frac{2It}{3\varepsilon_0}$$

Therefore, displacement current is

$$I_d = \varepsilon_0 \frac{d\phi_E}{dt}$$

$$= \varepsilon_0 \frac{d}{dt}\left(\frac{2It}{3\varepsilon_0}\right)$$

$$I_d = \varepsilon_0 \times \frac{2I}{3\varepsilon_0} = \frac{2I}{3}$$

14 (*d*) Electric energy density of an electromagnetic wave is given by

$$\mu_e = \frac{1}{2}\varepsilon_0 E^2$$

Magnetic energy density of an electromagnetic wave is given by

$$\mu_m = \frac{B^2}{2\mu_0}$$

So, the total energy density is

$$\mu = \frac{1}{2}\varepsilon_0 E^2 + \frac{B^2}{2\mu_0}$$

15 (*d*) Here, in electromagnetic wave, the electric field vector is given as

$$\mathbf{E} = (E_1\hat{\mathbf{i}} - E_2\hat{\mathbf{j}})\cos(kz - \omega t)$$

The associated magnetic field vector,

$$\mathbf{B} = \frac{\mathbf{E}}{c} = \frac{E_1\hat{\mathbf{i}} - E_2\hat{\mathbf{j}}}{c}\cos(kz - \omega t)$$

Also, **E** and **B** are perpendicular to each other and the propagation of electromagnetic wave is perpendicular to **E** as well as **B**, so the given electromagnetic wave is plane polarised.

16 (*c*) An electromagnetic wave is travelling along negative *z*-direction. Its electric field is given by

$$\mathbf{E} = E_0\cos(kz - \omega t)$$

which is perpendicular to Z-axis. It acts along negative y-direction.

The associated magnetic field B in electromagnetic wave is along X-axis, i.e. along $\hat{\mathbf{k}} \times \mathbf{E}$.

As, $B_0 = \dfrac{E_0}{c}$

$$\Rightarrow \quad \mathbf{B} = \frac{1}{c}(\hat{\mathbf{k}} \times \mathbf{E})$$

The associated electric field can be written in terms of magnetic field as $\mathbf{E} = c\,(\mathbf{B} \times \hat{\mathbf{k}})$.

Angle between $\hat{\mathbf{k}}$ and **E** is 90° and between $\hat{\mathbf{k}}$ and **B** is 90°. Therefore,

$$\hat{\mathbf{k}} \cdot \mathbf{E} = E\cos 90° = 0$$

and $\hat{\mathbf{k}} \cdot \mathbf{B} = B\cos 90° = 0 \quad (\because |\hat{\mathbf{k}}| = 1)$

Also, $|\hat{\mathbf{k}} \times \mathbf{E}| = E\sin 90° = E$

and $|\hat{\mathbf{k}} \times \mathbf{B}| = B\sin 90° = B$.

17 (*a*) Given, intensity of sunlight,

$$I = 0.099\ \text{Wm}^{-2}$$

As we know that,

$$I = \frac{\varepsilon_0 c}{2}E_0^2$$

$$\Rightarrow \quad E_0 = \sqrt{2\frac{I}{\varepsilon_0 c}}$$

Since, $B_0 = \dfrac{E_0}{c} = \dfrac{1}{c}\sqrt{\dfrac{2I}{\varepsilon_0 c}}$

$$= \frac{1}{3 \times 10^8}\sqrt{\frac{2 \times 0.099}{8.85 \times 10^{-12} \times 3 \times 10^8}}$$

$$= 2.88 \times 10^{-8}\ \text{T}$$

18 (*c*) Electric field component,

$$E_y = 300\sin\omega\left(t - \frac{x}{c}\right)$$

Speed of charge moving along Y-axis,

$$v = 3 \times 10^7\ \text{m/s}$$

$$\therefore \quad \frac{\text{Electric force } (F_e)}{\text{Magnetic force } (F_m)} = \frac{qE}{Bqv}$$

$$\Rightarrow \quad \frac{F_e}{F_m} = \frac{E}{Bv} = \frac{E/B}{v} = \frac{c}{v} \quad \left(\because \frac{E}{B} = c\right)$$

$$= \frac{3 \times 10^8}{3 \times 10^7} = \frac{10}{1}$$

$$\Rightarrow F_e : F_m = 10 : 1$$

21 (*a*) $y = 5\sin(\pi t - 0.1\pi x)$

$$= A\sin(\omega t - kx)$$

$$\frac{2\pi}{\lambda} = \frac{1}{10} \times \pi$$

$$\therefore \quad \lambda = \frac{20\pi}{\pi} = 20\ \text{cm}$$

$$\therefore \quad v = \frac{\omega}{k} = \frac{\pi}{0.1\pi} = \frac{1}{0.1} = 10\ \text{cm/s}$$

22 (*c*) We have, $y = A\sin(\omega t - kx)$

Now, as we know that,

$$E \propto A^2$$

$$\therefore \quad A' = \sqrt{0.36A^2}$$

$$= 0.6\,A$$

So, the equation of reflected wave is

$$y = \frac{6}{10}A\sin(kx + \omega t)$$

23 (*b*) $\hat{\mathbf{E}} = \dfrac{-\hat{\mathbf{i}} + \hat{\mathbf{j}}}{\sqrt{2}}$ and $\hat{\mathbf{B}} = \dfrac{-\hat{\mathbf{i}} - \hat{\mathbf{j}}}{\sqrt{2}}$

$$\hat{\mathbf{E}} \times \hat{\mathbf{B}} = \frac{-\hat{\mathbf{i}} + \hat{\mathbf{j}}}{\sqrt{2}} \times \frac{-\hat{\mathbf{i}} - \hat{\mathbf{j}}}{\sqrt{2}}$$

$$= \frac{2\hat{\mathbf{k}}}{2} = \hat{\mathbf{k}}$$

24 (*c*) Comparing the given equation,

$$E_y = 2.5\frac{\text{N}}{\text{C}}\cos\left[\left(2\pi \times 10^6\ \frac{\text{rad}}{\text{m}}\right)t - \left(\pi \times 10^{-2}\ \frac{\text{rad}}{\text{s}}\right)x\right]$$

Comparing with the standard equation

$E_y = E_0\cos(\omega t - kx)$, we get

$$\omega = 2\pi f = 2\pi \times 10^6$$

$$\therefore \quad f = 10^6\ \text{Hz}$$

Moreover, we know that,

$$\frac{2\pi}{\lambda} = k = \pi \times 10^{-2}\ \text{m}^{-1}$$

$$\Rightarrow \quad \lambda = 200\ \text{m}$$

From equation of E_y direction of wave is in $+x$-direction.

25 (*a*) Speed of the electromagnetic wave, $v = \dfrac{\omega}{k}$ ...(i)

The electromagnetic wave equation given by

$$\mathbf{E} = \hat{\mathbf{i}}\,40\cos(kz - 6 \times 10^8 t) \quad \text{...(ii)}$$

On comparing Eq. (ii) with standard equation, we get

$$\omega = 6 \times 10^8$$

and $E_0 = 40$

Here, wave factor is

$$k = \frac{\omega}{c} = \frac{6 \times 10^8}{3 \times 10^8}$$

$$(\because v = c \text{ for vacuum})$$

$$\Rightarrow \quad k = 2\ \text{m}^{-1}$$

26 (*a*) We know that,

$$E = cB$$

From the EM wave equation,

$$E_0 = 60$$

$$\therefore \quad B_0 = \frac{E_0}{c} = \frac{60}{3 \times 10^8}$$

$$\Rightarrow \quad B_0 = 2 \times 10^{-7}\ \text{T}$$

So, the amplitude of magnetic field is 2×10^{-7} T.

Now, the wavelength can be given by

$$k=\frac{2\pi}{\lambda}$$

From the EM wave equation,

$$10^3\pi=\frac{2\pi}{\lambda}$$

$$\Rightarrow \quad \lambda=2\times10^{-3}\text{m}$$

27 (*b*) Given, $y=(0.25\text{ m})\sin(5\pi x-\pi t)$

Here $kx=5\pi x$

$$\frac{2\pi}{\lambda}=5\pi$$

$$\Rightarrow \quad \lambda=0.4\text{ m}$$

and $\omega t=\pi t$

$$\frac{2\pi}{T}=\pi\Rightarrow T=2\text{ s}$$

$$\therefore \quad v=\frac{\lambda}{T}=\frac{0.4}{2}$$

$$\Rightarrow \quad v=0.2\text{ m/s}$$

28 (*b*) Given,

$$y=4\sin\left(4\pi t-0.04x+\frac{\pi}{3}\right)$$

From the electromagnetic wave equation, we have

$$k=0.04$$

$$\frac{2\pi}{\lambda}=0.04$$

$$\Rightarrow \quad \lambda=50\pi$$

$$\omega=4\pi$$

$$\frac{2\pi}{T}=4\pi$$

$$\Rightarrow \quad T=\frac{1}{2}$$

The speed of wave is given by

$$v=\frac{\lambda}{T}=\frac{50\pi}{\frac{1}{2}}$$

$$\Rightarrow \quad v=100\pi\text{ m/s}$$

31 (*c*) Given expression of electromagnetic wave,

$$\mathbf{E}=E_0\hat{\mathbf{n}}\sin[\omega t+(6y-8z)]$$

$$\Rightarrow \mathbf{E}=E_0\hat{\mathbf{n}}\sin[\omega t-(8z-6y)] \quad \text{...(i)}$$

Comparing Eq. (i) with standard equation, we get

$$\mathbf{k}\cdot\hat{\mathbf{r}}=8z-6y \quad \text{...(ii)}$$

Here, $\hat{\mathbf{r}}=x\hat{\mathbf{i}}+y\hat{\mathbf{j}}+z\hat{\mathbf{k}}$ and $\mathbf{k}=k_x\hat{\mathbf{i}}+k_y\hat{\mathbf{j}}+k_z\hat{\mathbf{k}}$

$$\therefore \quad \mathbf{k}\cdot\hat{\mathbf{r}}=xk_x+yk_y+zk_z \quad \text{...(iii)}$$

From Eqs. (ii) and (iii), we get

$$xk_x=\text{zero}\Rightarrow k_x=0$$

$$yk_y=-6y\Rightarrow k_y=-6$$

$$zk_z=8z\Rightarrow k_z=8$$

Hence, $\mathbf{k}=-6\hat{\mathbf{j}}+8\hat{\mathbf{k}}$

So, direction of propagation,

$$\hat{\mathbf{s}}=\hat{\mathbf{k}}=\frac{\mathbf{k}}{|\mathbf{k}|}=\frac{-6\hat{\mathbf{j}}+8\hat{\mathbf{k}}}{\sqrt{6^2+8^2}}$$

$$=\frac{-6\hat{\mathbf{j}}+8\hat{\mathbf{k}}}{10}=\frac{-3\hat{\mathbf{j}}+4\hat{\mathbf{k}}}{5}$$

32 (*d*) Given, $\mathbf{B}=5\times10^{-8}\hat{\mathbf{j}}$ and $\mathbf{v}=3\times10^8\hat{\mathbf{k}}$

Using $\mathbf{E}=\mathbf{B}\times\mathbf{v}$, we have

$$\mathbf{E}=(5\times10^{-8}\hat{\mathbf{j}})\times(3\times10^8\hat{\mathbf{k}})$$

$$=15\hat{\mathbf{i}}\text{ Vm}^{-1}$$

34 (*c*) Given, $B_y=3\times10^{-7}\sin(10^3x+6.28\times10^{12}t)$

Comparing with the general equation, we get

$$k=10^3$$

$$\Rightarrow \quad \frac{2\pi}{\lambda}=10^3 \quad \left(\because k=\frac{2\pi}{\lambda}\right)$$

$$\Rightarrow \quad \lambda=\frac{2\pi}{10^3}$$

$$=\frac{2\times3.14}{10^3}=6.28\times10^{-3}\text{ m}$$

$$=0.63\text{ cm}$$

35 (*a*) Given,

$\mathbf{E}=10\cos(10^7t+kx)\hat{\mathbf{j}}\text{ Vm}^{-1}$

Comparing with the general equation, $E=E_0\cos(\omega t+kx)$, we get

Amplitude of wave

$$=10\text{ Vm}^{-1}$$

and angular frequency, $\omega=10^7$

$$\therefore \quad c=\frac{\omega}{k}$$

$$\Rightarrow 3\times10^8=\frac{10^7}{k}$$

$$\Rightarrow \quad k=\frac{1}{30}=0.033\text{ rad m}^{-1}$$

$$\Rightarrow \quad \frac{2\pi}{\lambda}=\frac{1}{30} \quad \left[\because k=\frac{2\pi}{\lambda}\right]$$

$$\Rightarrow \quad \lambda=2\pi\times30$$

$$=188.4\text{ m}$$

37 (*b*) Given, $\nu=2\times10^{10}$ Hz

and $E_0=48\text{ Vm}^{-1}$

Using the formula, $c=\frac{E_0}{B_0}$

The amplitude of the oscillating magnetic field,

$$B_0=\frac{E_0}{c}=\frac{48}{3\times10^8}$$

$$=1.6\times10^{-7}\text{ T}$$

39 (*c*) Speed of progressive wave is given by $v=\frac{\omega}{k}$

As electric field in air,

$$\mathbf{E}_1=E_{01}\hat{\mathbf{x}}\cos\left(\frac{2\pi\nu z}{c}-2\pi\nu t\right)$$

$$\therefore \text{ Speed in air}=\frac{2\pi\nu}{\left(\frac{2\pi\nu}{c}\right)}=c$$

$$\text{Also,} \quad c=\frac{1}{\sqrt{\mu_0\varepsilon_{r_1}\varepsilon_0}} \quad \text{...(i)}$$

In medium,

$$\mathbf{E}_2=E_{02}\hat{\mathbf{x}}\cos(2kz-kct)$$

$\therefore$ Speed in medium

$$=\frac{kc}{2k}=\frac{c}{2}$$

$$\text{Also,} \quad \frac{c}{2}=\frac{1}{\sqrt{\mu_0\varepsilon_{r_2}\varepsilon_0}} \quad \text{...(ii)}$$

As medium is non-magnetic medium,

$$\mu_{\text{medium}}=\mu_{\text{air}}$$

On dividing Eq. (i) by Eq. (ii), we have

$$2=\sqrt{\frac{\varepsilon_{r_2}}{\varepsilon_{r_1}}}\Rightarrow\frac{\varepsilon_{r_1}}{\varepsilon_{r_2}}=\frac{1}{4}$$

40 (*d*) Given, $n=1.7$,

$$\mu=7\times10^{-7}\text{ Hm}^{-1}$$

Refractive index is given by

$$n=\frac{c}{v}$$

$$\Rightarrow \quad v=\frac{c}{n}=\frac{3\times10^8}{1.7}$$

$$=1.76\times10^8\text{ m/s}$$

$$\text{Also} \quad v=\frac{1}{\sqrt{\mu\varepsilon}}=\frac{1}{\sqrt{\mu\varepsilon_0\varepsilon_r}}$$

$$\Rightarrow \quad \varepsilon_r = \frac{1}{v^2 \mu \varepsilon_0}$$

$$= \frac{1}{(1.76 \times 10^8)^2 \times 7 \times 10^{-7} \times 8.85 \times 10^{-12}}$$

$$= 5.21 \approx 5$$

41 (c) Given, energy $= 20\ \text{Wcm}^{-2}$

Area, $A = 25\ \text{cm}^2$

Time, $t = 20$ min

$= 20 \times 60$

$= 1200$ s

The total energy falling on the surface,

$$u = 20 \times 25 \times 1200 = 6 \times 10^5\ \text{J}$$

Now, the total momentum delivered for complete absorption,

$$p = \frac{u}{c} = \frac{6 \times 10^5}{3 \times 10^8} = 2 \times 10^{-3}\ \text{kg-m/s}$$

The average force exerted on the surface is

$$F = \frac{p}{t} = \frac{2 \times 10^{-3}}{0.12 \times 10^4} = 1.66 \times 10^{-6}\ \text{N}$$

42 (b) As we know that,

$$c = \frac{E_0}{B_0} \qquad \text{...(i)}$$

Average energy density of the magnetic field is given by

$$u_B = \frac{1}{4} \frac{B_0^2}{\mu_0}$$

From Eq. (i),

$$u_B = \frac{1}{4} \frac{E_0^2}{\mu_0 c^2}$$

$$= \frac{1}{4} \varepsilon_0 E_0^2 \quad \left(\because c = \frac{1}{\sqrt{\mu_0 \varepsilon_0}}\right)$$

$$= \frac{1}{4} \times 8.85 \times 10^{-12} \times 4^2$$

$$= 35.4 \times 10^{-12}\ \text{J m}^{-3}$$

43 (c) The electric field intensity due to electromagnetic wave is,

$$E_0 = 6.3\ \text{V/m}$$

As we know that, $\frac{E_0}{B_0} = c$

$$\Rightarrow \quad B_0 = \frac{E_0}{c} = \frac{6.3}{3 \times 10^8} = 2.1 \times 10^{-8}\ \text{T}$$

Since, the propagation of the wave is along X-axis and electric field vector is along Y-axis, the magnetic field of the wave should lie perpendicular to both the direction of propagation and direction of electric field.

So, **B** should be along $\hat{\mathbf{k}}$ such that $\mathbf{E} \times \mathbf{B}$ should be in x-direction.

$$\therefore \quad \mathbf{B} = 2.1 \times 10^{-8}\ \hat{\mathbf{k}}\ \text{T}$$

44 (b) We know that,

$$\frac{E_0}{B_0} = c$$

$$\therefore \quad B_0 = \frac{E_0}{c}$$

Substituting the values, we get

$$= \frac{6.3 \times 10^{+2}}{3 \times 10^8} = 2.1 \times 10^{-6}\ \text{T}$$

$\therefore$ **E** is along y-direction and wave is along x-direction, hence, **B** has to be perpendicular to both X and Y axes.

$\mathbf{E} \times \mathbf{B}$ should be along x-direction,

B should be along z-direction.

$$\therefore \quad \mathbf{B} = B_0 \hat{\mathbf{k}}$$

So, $\quad \mathbf{B} = 2.1 \times 10^{-6}\ \hat{\mathbf{k}}\ \text{T}$

45 (d) Given, $E_0 = 0.12$ V/cm

$= 0.12 \times 10^2$ V/m

Since, we know that

$$\frac{E_0}{B_0} = c$$

$$\Rightarrow \quad B_0 = \frac{E_0}{c} = \frac{0.12 \times 10^2}{3 \times 10^8}$$

$$= 40 \times 10^{-9}\ \text{T}$$

$$\Rightarrow \quad B_0 = 40\ \text{nT}$$

So, the peak value of magnetic field is 40 nT.

46 (b) Frequency of electromagnetic wave remains unchanged in medium but wavelength and velocity of wave changes with change in medium.

We know that,

$$c = \frac{1}{\sqrt{\mu_0 \varepsilon_0}} = \nu \lambda_{\text{vacuum}} \qquad \text{...(i)}$$

Velocity of electromagnetic wave in the medium,

$$v_{\text{medium}} = \frac{1}{\sqrt{\mu_0 \mu_r \varepsilon_0 \varepsilon_r}} = \frac{c}{\sqrt{\mu_r \varepsilon_r}}$$

For dielectric medium, $\mu_r = 1$

$$\therefore \quad v_{\text{medium}} = \frac{c}{\sqrt{\varepsilon_r}} \qquad \text{... (ii)}$$

Here, $\quad \varepsilon_r = 4.0$

Wavelength of the wave in medium,

$$\lambda_{\text{medium}} = \frac{v_{\text{medium}}}{\nu} = \frac{c}{2\nu} = \frac{\lambda_{\text{vacuum}}}{2}$$

[Using Eqs. (i) and (ii)]

47 (c) The statement in option (c) is incorrect and it can be corrected as,

The constancy of the velocity of electromagnetic waves in vacuum is used to define a standard of length. The meter is defined as the distance travelled by light in vacuum in a time $(1/c)$ second.

48 (c) The average value of both the electric and magnetic fields is zero as they are sinusoidal waves, whose average comes out to be zero for a complete cycle.

The average value of magnetic energy cannot be zero, since

$$U_{\text{avg}} = \frac{B_0^2}{2\mu_0}$$

where, B_0 = peak value.

49 (b) Initial momentum of surface,

$$p_i = E / c$$

Since, the surface is perfectly reflecting, so the same momentum will be reflected completely.

Final momentum, $p_f = -\frac{E}{c}$

$\therefore$ Change in momentum,

$$\Delta p = p_f - p_i = -\frac{E}{c} - \frac{E}{c} = -\frac{2E}{c}$$

Thus, momentum transferred to the surface is

$$\Delta p' = \Delta p = \frac{2E}{c}$$

50 (*d*) Electric energy density is given by

$$u_e = \frac{1}{2}\varepsilon_0 E_{rms}^2$$

$$E_{rms} = \frac{E_0}{\sqrt{2}}$$

$$\therefore \quad \mu_e = \frac{1}{4}\varepsilon_0 E_0^2$$

51 (*c*) Intensity is given by

$$I = \frac{P}{A} = \frac{100 \times 2.5}{4\pi(3)^2 \times 100}$$

$$= \frac{2.5}{36\pi}\ \text{Wm}^{-2}$$

The half of the intensity belongs to electric field and half of that to magnetic field.

$$\therefore \quad \frac{I}{2} = \frac{1}{4}\varepsilon_0 E_0^2 c$$

$$\Rightarrow \quad E_0 = \sqrt{\frac{2I}{\varepsilon_0 c}}$$

$$= \sqrt{\frac{2 \times \frac{2.5}{36\pi}}{8.85 \times 10^{-12} \times 3 \times 10^8}}$$

$$= 4.08\ \text{Vm}^{-1}$$

$$\therefore \quad B_0 = \frac{E_0}{c}$$

$$= \frac{4.08}{3 \times 10^8} = 1.36 \times 10^{-8}\ \text{T}$$

53 (*b*) Given,

time, t = 10 min = 10×60 s

Total energy falling on the surface in time t is

$$U = \phi A t = 40 \times 20 \times (10 \times 60)$$
$$= 4.8 \times 10^5\ \text{J}$$

Momentum of the incident light,

$$p = \frac{U}{c} = \frac{4.8 \times 10^5}{3 \times 10^8}$$

$$= 16 \times 10^{-4}\ \text{kg-ms}^{-1}$$

Momentum of the reflected light = 0 (complete absorption)

∴ Momentum delivered to the surface

$$= 16 \times 10^{-4} - 0$$
$$= 16 \times 10^{-4}\ \text{kg-ms}^{-1}$$

54 (*d*) Given, power of laser beam

$(P) = 27\ \text{mW} = 27 \times 10^{-3}\ \text{W}$

Area of cross-section (A)

$$= 10\ \text{mm}^2 = 10 \times 10^{-6}\ \text{m}^2$$

Intensity of electromagnetic wave is given by the relation

$$I = \frac{1}{2} n\varepsilon_0 E^2$$

where, n is refractive index, for air $n = 1$.

$$\therefore \quad I = \frac{1}{2} c \cdot \varepsilon_0 E^2 \quad \text{...(i)}$$

$$\text{Also,} \quad I = \frac{P}{A} \quad \text{...(ii)}$$

From Eqs. (i) and (ii), we get

$$\frac{1}{2} c\, \varepsilon_0 E^2 = \frac{P}{A} \text{ or } E^2 = \frac{2P}{Ac\,\varepsilon_0}$$

or

$$E = \sqrt{\frac{2 \times 27 \times 10^{-3}}{10 \times 10^{-6} \times 3 \times 10^8 \times 9 \times 10^{-12}}}$$

$$\simeq 1.4 \times 10^3\ \text{V/m} = 1.4\ \text{kV/m}$$

55 (*a*) Energy density of an electromagnetic wave in electric field, $U_E = \frac{1}{2}\varepsilon_0 \cdot E^2$ ...(i)

Energy density of an electromagnetic waves in magnetic field,

$$U_B = \frac{B^2}{2\mu_0} \quad \text{...(ii)}$$

Velocity of EM waves in given by

$$c = \frac{1}{\sqrt{\mu_0 \varepsilon_0}} \quad \text{...(iii)}$$

$$\text{and} \quad \frac{E}{B} = c \quad \text{...(iv)}$$

Dividing Eq. (i) by Eq. (ii), we get

$$\frac{U_E}{U_B} = \frac{\frac{1}{2}\varepsilon_0 E^2}{\frac{1}{2}B^2 \times \frac{1}{\mu_0}} = \frac{\mu_0 \varepsilon_0 E^2}{B^2} \quad \text{...(v)}$$

Using Eqs. (iii), (iv) and (v), we get

$$\frac{U_E}{U_B} = \frac{c^2}{c^2} = 1$$

Therefore, $U_E = U_B$

61 (*b*) The order of wavelength in electromagnetic spectrum is as shown.

$\lambda_{\gamma\text{-rays}} < \lambda_{\text{X-rays}} < \lambda_{\text{UV- rays}} < \lambda_{\text{visible ray}} < \lambda_{\text{infrared rays}} < \lambda_{\text{microwaves}} < \lambda_{\text{radio waves}}$

From this, we can conclude that wavelength of infrared rays is greater than that of UV-rays.

72 (*a*) The statement given in option (a) is correct, rest are incorrect and these can be corrected as,

UV-rays are used in the LASIK eye surgery and in water purifiers.

Snakes can detect infrared waves.

Electromagnetic waves exhibit polarisation while sound waves don't.

Assertion and Reason Questions

1 (*a*) On applying Ampere's circuital law to such surfaces with the same perimeter, we find that the left hand side of equation $\oint B \cdot dl = \mu_0 i(t)$ has not changed but the right hand side is zero.

Since, no current passes through the surface, i.e. $i = 0$, $\oint B \cdot dl = 0$.

2 (*a*) An oscillating charge produces an electric field in space, which produces an oscillating magnetic field, which in turn, is a source of electric field. Thus, EM wave is a self sustaining oscillating wave.

3 (*c*) Electric and magnetic field oscillates perpendicular to the direction of propagation of wave. Hence, these are transverse in nature. Therefore, Assertion is correct but Reason is incorrect.

7 (*a*) Infrared waves are sometimes referred to as heat waves. Because water molecules present in most materials readily absorb infrared waves (many other molecules, e.g. CO_2, NH_3 also absorb infrared waves). After absorption, their thermal motion increases, i.e. they heat up and heat their surroundings.

8 (*a*) Due to its shorter wavelengths, UV-radiations can be focused into very narrow beams for high precision applications such as LASIK eye surgery.

9 (c) The human eye is most sensitive to light having a frequency of about 5.36×10^{14} Hz, which is in the yellow-green region of the electromagnetic spectrum.

10 (c) The earth's atmosphere is transparent to visible light and radio waves but absorbs X-rays. Therefore, X-rays telescope cannot be used on earth surface.

Statement Based Questions

2 (b) Statement I is correct but Statement II is incorrect and it can be corrected as,

The total current i is the sum of the conduction current denoted by i_c and the displacement current denoted by $i_d = \varepsilon_0 \, (d\phi_E/dt)$. So, we have

$$i = i_c + i_d = i_c + \varepsilon_0 \frac{d\phi_E}{dt}$$

In explicit terms, this means that outside the capacitor plates, we have only conduction current, i.e. $i_c = i$ and no displacement current, i.e. $i_d = 0$.

4 (b) Statement I is correct but Statement II is incorrect and it can be corrected as,

The current $i = \varepsilon_0 \frac{d\phi_E}{dt}$ is due to change in electric field, therefore called displacement current.

5 (b) Statement I is correct but Statement II is incorrect and it can be corrected as,

The electric field E is along the X-axis and varies sinusoidally with Z, at a given time.

Numerical Type Questions

1 (6) As we know that, $c = \frac{E_0}{B_0}$

Given, $\mathbf{B} = B_0 \hat{\mathbf{i}}[\cos(kz - \omega t)] + B_1 \hat{\mathbf{j}} [\cos(kz + \omega t)]$

$$\therefore \quad \mathbf{E}_0 = B_0 c(-\hat{\mathbf{j}})$$
$$= (3 \times 10^{-5})\, c\, (-\hat{\mathbf{j}})$$
$$\mathbf{E}_1 = (2 \times 10^{-6})\, c(-\hat{\mathbf{i}})$$

Force on stationary charge,

$$F = QE$$
$$= Qc(\mathbf{E}_0 + \mathbf{E}_1)$$
$$= Qc[(-3 \times 10^{-5}\,\hat{\mathbf{j}}) + (-2 \times 10^{-6}\,\hat{\mathbf{i}})]$$
$$\therefore F = 10^{-4} \times 3 \times 10^8 \sqrt{(-3 \times 10^{-5})^2 + (-2 \times 10^{-6})^2}$$
$$= 3 \times 10^4 \times 3 \times 10^{-5}$$
$$F = 0.9 \text{ N}$$

So, $F_{rms} = \frac{F}{\sqrt{2}} = \frac{0.9}{\sqrt{2}} = 0.6$ N

$$= 6 \times 10^{-1} \text{N}$$

2 (4) Speed of electromagnetic signal in medium is

$$c = \frac{E_0}{B_0} = \frac{2.25}{1.5 \times 10^{-8}}$$
$$= 1.5 \times 10^8 \text{ m/s}$$

Now, the time taken to send and receive signal is

$$t = \frac{2d}{v} = \frac{2 \times 3 \times 10^3}{1.5 \times 10^8} \quad [\because v = c]$$
$$t = 4 \times 10^{-5} \text{ s}$$

So, the value of x is 4.

3 (3) Intensity of light,

$$I = u_{av} c$$

Also, $I = \frac{P}{4\pi r^2}$ and $u_{av} = \frac{1}{2} \varepsilon_0 E_0^2$

Therefore,

$$\frac{P}{4\pi r^2} = \frac{1}{2} \varepsilon_0 E_0^2 c$$

or $\quad E_0 = \sqrt{\frac{2P}{4\pi\varepsilon_0 r^2 c}}$

Here, $P = 0.15$ W, $r = 1$ m,

$$c = 3 \times 10^8 \text{ ms}^{-1}$$
$$\therefore \quad E_0 = \sqrt{\frac{2 \times 0.15 \times 9 \times 10^9}{1^2 \times 3 \times 10^8}}$$
$$= \sqrt{9} = 3 \text{ Vm}^{-1}$$

4 (9) Standard equation for electric field is

$$E = E_0 \cos(\omega t - kz) \text{ V/m}$$

After comparing it with the given equation, we get

$$k = 200,$$
$$\omega = 2 \times 10^{10} \text{rad/s}$$

$\therefore$ Speed of the wave,

$$v = \frac{\omega}{k} = \frac{2 \times 10^{10}}{200} = 10^8 \text{m/s}$$

Refractive index,

$$\mu = \frac{c}{v} = \frac{3 \times 10^8}{10^8} = 3$$

As we know, $\mu = \sqrt{\varepsilon_r \mu_r}$

$$3 = \sqrt{\varepsilon_r (1)}$$
$$\Rightarrow \quad \varepsilon_r = 9$$

5 (2) Given,

$$E_y = 100 \cos(6 \times 10^8 t + 4x)$$

On comparing the above equation with the standard equation, we get

$$\omega = 6 \times 10^8 \text{ rad/s}$$
$$k = 4$$

The velocity of wave,

$$v = \frac{\omega}{k} = \frac{6 \times 10^8}{4} = 1.5 \times 10^8$$

Now, refractive index of the medium,

$$n = \frac{c}{v} = \frac{3 \times 10^8}{1.5 \times 10^8} = 2$$

6 (3660) Given, frequency of EM waves,

$$\nu = 8.196 \times 10^6 \text{Hz}$$

Velocity of EM waves,

$$v = 3 \times 10^8 \text{m/s}$$

$\therefore$ Wavelength of EM waves is

$$\lambda = \frac{v}{\nu}$$
$$= \frac{3 \times 10^8}{8.196 \times 10^6}$$
$$= 36.60 \text{ m}$$
$$= 3660 \text{ cm}$$

7 (171) Given, $B = 12 \times 10^{-8} \sin(1.20 \times 10^7 z - 36 \times 10^{15} t)$ T

On comparing it with

$$B = B_0 \sin(kz - \omega t)$$

We get, $B_0 = 12 \times 10^{-8}$ T

$$\therefore \quad I_{av} = \frac{1}{2} \frac{B_0^2 c}{\mu_0}$$
$$= \frac{1}{2} \frac{(12 \times 10^{-8})^2 \times 3 \times 10^8}{4\pi \times 10^{-7}}$$
$$I_{av} = 171 \times 10^{-2} \text{Wm}^{-2}$$

So, the average intensity is $171 \times 10^{-2}\,Wm^{-2}$.

8 (2) Given, $\mathbf{E} = \hat{i}30\cos(kz - 6\times10^8 t)\hat{i}$

On comparing the above equation with standard equation, we get

$\omega = 6\times10^8$ rad/s

Since, $v = \frac{\omega}{k}$

$\Rightarrow k = \frac{\omega}{v} = \frac{6\times10^8}{3\times10^8} = 2$ rad/m

9 (84) Effective power of light bulb converted into visible radiation,

$$P' = 10\% \text{ of } 110\text{ W} = \frac{10}{100}\times110\text{ W} = 11\text{ W}$$

Change in average intensities of visible radiation,

$$I_1 - I_2 = \frac{P'}{4\pi r_1^2} - \frac{P'}{4\pi r_2^2}$$

Here, $r_1 = 1$ m and $r_2 = 5$ m

$$= \frac{P'}{4\pi}\left(\frac{1}{r_1^2} - \frac{1}{r_2^2}\right) = \frac{11}{4\pi}\left(\frac{1}{1^2} - \frac{1}{5^2}\right)$$

$$= \frac{11}{4\times\frac{22}{7}}\left(\frac{24}{25}\right) = \frac{7}{8}\times\frac{24}{25} = \frac{21}{25}$$

$$= 0.84 = 84\times10^{-2}\text{ W/m}^2$$

$$= a\times10^{-2}\text{ W/m}^2 \quad \text{[Given]}$$

$\therefore a = 84$

10 (11) Intensity,

$$I = \frac{\text{Energy}}{\text{Area}\times\text{Time}} = \frac{\text{Power}}{\text{Area}} = U_{av}c = \frac{1}{2}c\,\varepsilon_0 E_0^2$$

$$\Rightarrow P \propto E_0^2 \Rightarrow \frac{P_1}{P_2} = \frac{E_1^2}{E_2^2}$$

$$\Rightarrow \frac{E_1}{E_2} = \sqrt{\frac{P_1}{P_2}}$$

$$\Rightarrow \frac{E_1}{E_2} = \sqrt{\frac{100}{55}}$$

$$\Rightarrow E_2 = \sqrt{\frac{11}{20}}E_1 = \sqrt{\frac{11}{20}}E \quad (\because E_1 = E)$$

On comparing with $\sqrt{\frac{11}{20}}E$, we get

$x = 11$

NCERT Exemplar Questions

1 (b) Given that, incident electromagnetic wave is

$$\mathbf{E} = E_0\hat{i}\cos(kz - \omega t)$$

Thus, the reflected electromagnetic wave is given by

$$\mathbf{E}_r = E_0(-\hat{i})\cos[k(-z) - \omega t + \pi]$$
$$= -E_0\hat{i}\cos[-(kz + \omega t) + \pi]$$
$$= E_0\hat{i}\cos[-(kz + \omega t)]$$
$$= E_0\hat{i}\cos(kz + \omega t)]$$

$[\because \cos(\pi - \theta) = -\cos\theta$ and $\cos(-\theta) = \cos\theta]$

2 (a) Electric field intensity on a surface due to incident radiation is,

$$E = \frac{U}{At} \text{ where, } \frac{U}{t} = P \text{ (power)}$$

$\therefore E \propto P$

(for the given area of the surface)

Hence, $\frac{E'}{E} = \frac{P'}{P} = \frac{50}{100} = \frac{1}{2}$

or $E' = E/2$

3 (c) Intensity of EM wave in terms of electric field, $U_{av} = \frac{1}{2}\varepsilon_0 E_0^2$

Intensity of EM wave in terms of magnetic field, $U_{av} = \frac{1}{2}\frac{B_0^2}{\mu_0}$

As, $(U_{av})_{\text{electric field}} = \frac{1}{2}\varepsilon_0 E_0^2$

$$= \frac{1}{2}\varepsilon_0(cB_0)^2 \ (\because E_0 = cB_0)$$

$$= \frac{1}{2}\varepsilon_0 \times c^2 B_0^{\ 2}$$

But, $c = \frac{1}{\sqrt{\mu_0\varepsilon_0}}$

$\therefore (U_{av})_{\text{electric field}}$

$$= \frac{1}{2}\varepsilon_0\times\frac{1}{\mu_0\varepsilon_0}B_0^2 = \frac{1}{2}\frac{B_0^2}{\mu_0}$$

$$= (U_{av})_{\text{magnetic field}}$$

Thus, the energy in electromagnetic wave is divided equally between electric and magnetic vectors.

Therefore, the ratio of contributions by the electric field and magnetic field components to the intensity of an electromagnetic wave is 1 : 1.

Past Exams Questions

1 (b) When a capacitor is charged through a battery, its opposite plates are charged to a maximum value. There is displacement current as the capacitor is being charged,

$$I_d = \varepsilon\cdot\frac{d\phi_E}{dt}$$

Due to charging, ϕ_E changes and hence displacement current equal to conduction current arises while charging. When capacitor gets fully charged, the displacement current became zero.

2 (d) Electromagnetic waves are generated by accelerated charged particles.

Hence, option (d) is incorrect.

3 (a) Given, AC source voltage,

$$V = V_0\sin\omega t \quad \text{...(i)}$$

We know that, $Q = CV$ ...(ii)

On differentiate Eq. (ii) w.r.t. time, we get

$$\frac{dQ}{dt} = \frac{d(CV)}{dt}$$

$$\Rightarrow \frac{dQ}{dt} = \frac{Cd(V_0\sin\omega t)}{dt}$$

[From Eq. (i)]

$$\Rightarrow \frac{dQ}{dt} = C\omega V_0\cos\omega t$$

As we know, the displacement current, $I_d = \frac{dQ}{dt} = V_0\,\omega C\cos\omega t$

4 (b) We know that, in electromagnetic wave, the electric field (E) and magnetic field (B) are perpendicular to each other,

$\mathbf{E}\cdot\mathbf{B} = 0$

Consider the option (a);

$(\hat{j}+\hat{k})\cdot(\hat{j}+\hat{k}) = 1+1 = 2 \neq 0$

So, it is incorrect option.

Consider the option (b);

$(-\hat{j}+\hat{k})\cdot(-\hat{j}-\hat{k}) = 1-1 = 0$

Hence, it satisfies the condition $\mathbf{E}\cdot\mathbf{B} = 0$

Similarly, options (c) and (d) are incorrect.

6 (c) γ-rays has the shortest wavelength because it has higher frequency than UV-rays, microwaves and X-rays.

8 (a) Given, $\varepsilon_r = 1.44, \mu_r = 1$

We know that, $\varepsilon_r = \dfrac{\varepsilon}{\varepsilon_0}$

$\Rightarrow \varepsilon = \varepsilon_r \varepsilon_0$ and $\mu_r = \dfrac{\mu}{\mu_0} \Rightarrow \mu = \mu_r \mu_0$

$\therefore$Velocity of light in the medium will be

$$v = \frac{1}{\sqrt{\mu\varepsilon}} = \frac{1}{\sqrt{\mu_r \mu_0 \varepsilon_r \varepsilon_0}}$$
$$= \frac{c}{\sqrt{\mu_r \varepsilon_r}} = \frac{3 \times 10^8}{\sqrt{1 \times 1.44}}$$
$$= 2.5 \times 10^8 \text{ m/s}$$

9 (a) We know that,

$$\frac{E_{\text{rms}}}{B_{\text{rms}}} = c \text{ or } B_{\text{rms}} = \frac{E_{\text{rms}}}{c}$$

$$\Rightarrow \quad B_{\text{rms}} = \frac{6}{3 \times 10^8} = 2 \times 10^{-8} \text{ T}$$

Since, $B_{\text{rms}} = \dfrac{B_0}{\sqrt{2}}$

$$\therefore \quad B_0 = B_{\text{rms}}\sqrt{2}$$
$$= 2 \times 10^{-8} \times \sqrt{2}$$
$$B_0 \approx 2.83 \times 10^{-8} \text{ T}$$

10 (a) Given, energy of EM waves is of the order of 15 keV,

i.e. $\quad E = h\nu = h \times \dfrac{c}{\lambda}$

$$\Rightarrow \quad \lambda = \frac{h \times c}{E}$$
$$= \frac{6.624 \times 10^{-34} \times 3 \times 10^8}{15 \times 10^3 \times 1.6 \times 10^{-19}}$$
$$= 0.828 \times 10^{-10} \text{m}$$
$$= 0.828 \text{ Å}$$
$$[\because 1\text{Å} = 10^{-10} \text{m}]$$

Thus, this spectrum is a part of X-rays.

11 (c) Given,

$$B_y = (3.5 \times 10^{-7}) \sin(1.5 \times 10^3 x + 0.5 \times 10^{11} t) \text{ T}$$

We know that, $\mathbf{E} \times \mathbf{B}$ = direction of propagation of wave i.e., x-direction. Hence, E must be in z-direction.

Now, we know that, $\left|\dfrac{E_0}{B_0}\right| = c$

$$E_0 = B_0 c = 3.5 \times 10^{-7} \times 3 \times 10^8$$
$$= 105 \text{ Vm}^{-1}$$
$$\therefore E_z = E_0 \sin(1.5 \times 10^3 x + 0.5 \times 10^{11} t)$$
$$= 105 \sin(1.5 \times 10^3 x + 0.5 \times 10^{11} t) \text{ V/m}$$

14 (d) $\oint \mathbf{E} \cdot d\mathbf{l} = -\dfrac{d\phi_B}{dt}$

15 (c) Magnetic field vector is perpendicular to both direction of propagation of electromagnetic wave and direction of electric field vector.

Also, $\quad \dfrac{E}{B} = c$ and $\dfrac{\omega}{k} = c$

So, magnetic field vector can be given by

$$B = \frac{1}{\omega}(\mathbf{k} \times \mathbf{E})$$
$$\left(\because B = \frac{E}{c} = \frac{E}{\omega / k} = \frac{kE}{\omega}\right)$$

16 (b) Given, magnitude of magnetic field

$$|B| = 6 \times 10^{-7} \text{ T}$$

We know that $\left|\dfrac{E}{B}\right| = c$

$$\Rightarrow \quad E = Bc$$
$$= 6 \times 10^{-7} \times 3 \times 10^8$$
$$= 180 \text{ Vm}^{-1}$$

18 (b) We know that, $c = \dfrac{E_0}{B_0}$

$$\Rightarrow \quad B_0 = \frac{E_0}{c} = \frac{60}{3 \times 10^8}$$
$$= 2 \times 10^{-7} \text{ T}$$

$\mathbf{E} \times \mathbf{B}$ must be in direction of propagation.

Hence, direction of $\mathbf{B}$ is along $\hat{\mathbf{k}}$,

$$k = \frac{2\pi}{\lambda} = \frac{2\pi}{8} \times 10^3 = \frac{\pi}{4} \times 10^3 \text{m}^{-1}$$

So,

$$E_y = 60 \sin\left[\frac{\pi}{4} \times 10^3 (x - ct)\right] \hat{\mathbf{j}} \text{ V/m}$$

$$B_z = 2 \times 10^{-7} \sin\left[\frac{\pi}{4} \times 10^3 (x - ct)\right] \hat{\mathbf{k}} \text{ T}$$

Skill Boosters

1 (a) Polarisation occurs parallel to **E** and propagation is in direction perpendicular to **E** and **B**.

2 (d) Direction of propagation of wave is $\mathbf{E} \times \mathbf{B} \cdot \mathbf{E}$ is along $-\mathbf{k}$ and the wave propagates in $\dfrac{\hat{\mathbf{i}} + \hat{\mathbf{j}}}{\sqrt{2}}$.

If we choose $\mathbf{B} = \dfrac{-\hat{\mathbf{i}} + \hat{\mathbf{j}}}{\sqrt{2}}$, then

$$\mathbf{E} \times \mathbf{B} = -\hat{\mathbf{k}} \times \left(\frac{-\hat{\mathbf{i}} + \hat{\mathbf{j}}}{\sqrt{2}}\right) = \frac{\hat{\mathbf{i}} + \hat{\mathbf{j}}}{\sqrt{2}}$$

3 (d) Since, wave is propagating in x-direction and **E** is in z-direction, hence **B**, must be in y-direction. Also, direction of wave is given by $\mathbf{E} \times \mathbf{B}$ hence, **B** is –ve x-direction,

$$B_0 = \frac{E_0}{c} = E_0\sqrt{\mu_0 \varepsilon_0}$$
$$\Rightarrow \mathbf{B} = E_0\sqrt{\mu_0 \varepsilon_0} \cos(2\omega - kx)\hat{\mathbf{j}}$$

4 (b) Consider at time t, charge on capacitor is Q, the electric field between plates will be $E = Q/\varepsilon_0 A$.

Hence, flux will be

$$\phi = \frac{Q}{\varepsilon_0 A} \cdot \frac{A}{2} = \frac{Q}{2\varepsilon_0}$$
$$\therefore \quad i_d = \varepsilon_0 \frac{d\phi_E}{dt} = \varepsilon_0 \frac{1}{2\varepsilon_0} \frac{dQ}{dt} = \frac{i}{2}$$

5 (a) X-rays are not reflected from target , so it cannot be used for radar.

6 (a) $\oint \mathbf{E} \cdot d\mathbf{l} = \dfrac{d\phi_B}{dt}$

$$E(4a) = \frac{d}{dt}(Kt \times a^2)$$
$$E = \frac{Ka}{4}$$

7 (c) Since, the black body is a non-reflecting surface.

Hence $p = I/c$

8 (a) $(i_d)_{\max} = (i_c)_{\max} = i_0 = \dfrac{\varepsilon_0}{Z}$

$$= \frac{220\sqrt{2}}{\sqrt{100^2 + 100^2}}$$
$$\Rightarrow (i_d)_{\max} = \frac{220\sqrt{2}}{100\sqrt{2}} = 2.2 \text{ A}$$

09

Scan for **Physics Through Concept Master** *Videos*

Ray Optics and Optical Instruments

Topicwise No. of Ques asked in 5 Years (NEET)

Topics	No. of Questions				
	2024	2023	2022	2021	2020
Reflection of Light by Spherical Mirrors	-	-	-	-	1
Refraction	-	1	1	-	-
Total Internal Reflection	-	-	-	-	1
Refraction at Spherical Surfaces and by Lenses	-	2	1	2	1
Refraction Through a Prism	1	-	-	1	1
Optical Instruments	1	-	-	1	-

Special Type of Ques asked in 5 Years (NEET)

Types	Years				
	2024	2023	2022	2021	2020
A-R	-	-	-	-	-
Statement Based	-	-	-	-	-
Matching	-	-	-	-	-

Last 5 Years Weigtage (NEET)

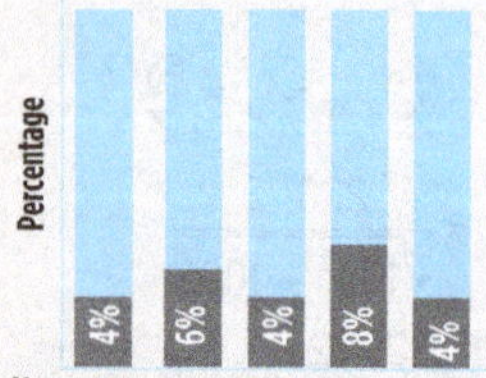

- Human eye can only see electromagnetic waves within a small range of the electromagnetic spectrum. Electromagnetic radiation belonging to this region of the spectrum (wavelength of about 400 nm to 750 nm) is called **visible light**.
- Speed of light in vacuum is $c = 2.99992458 \times 10^8$ m/s or 3×10^8 m/s. This speed in vacuum is the highest speed attainable in nature.
- Wavelength of light is very small compared to the size of ordinary objects and prefers to travel shortest distance between two points, therefore it is considered that light travels along a straight line.
- The straight line path of a light wave is called **ray of light** and a bundle of such rays constitutes a **beam of light**.

Reflection of Light by Spherical Mirrors

The phenomenon of bouncing back of light rays in the same medium on striking a surface is called **reflection of light**.

- **Laws of Reflection** There are two laws for reflection of light from a smooth reflecting surface as shown in figure below.
  - (i) The incident ray, reflected ray and the normal to the reflecting surface at the point of incidence lie in the same plane.
  - (ii) The angle of incidence, $\angle i$ = angle of reflection, $\angle r$.

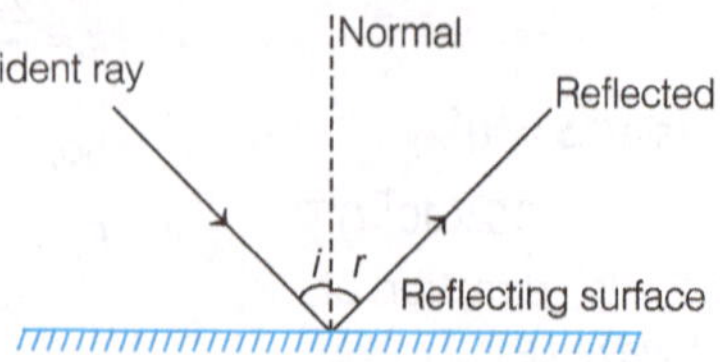

Note *These laws are valid at each point on any reflecting surface whether plane or curved.*

Marks Maximiser

- **Number of images formed by two inclined plane mirrors.**
  If two plane mirrors are inclined at an angle θ, then the number of images formed by them is given by

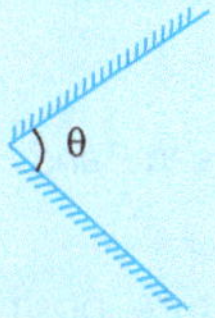

If $\frac{360^\circ}{\theta}$ is even, then $N = \frac{360^\circ}{\theta} - 1$

If $\frac{360^\circ}{\theta}$ is odd, then $N = \frac{360^\circ}{\theta}$

- **Spherical mirror** is a mirror whose reflecting surface is a part of a hollow sphere.

  Spherical mirrors are of two types : **concave** and **convex mirror.**

  (i) **Concave mirror** It is a curved mirror whose reflecting surface is on the inner side of the curved surface.

  (ii) **Convex mirror** It is a curved mirror whose reflecting surface is on outer side of curved surface.

- Some of the terms related to spherical mirrors are as follows :

  (i) The geometric centre of a spherical mirror is called its **pole**.

  (ii) The line joining the pole and centre of curvature of the spherical mirror is known as the **principal axis** (*P*).

  (iii) **Paraxial rays** are those rays that incident at points close to the pole *P* of the mirror and make small angles with the principal axis.

  (iv) **Principal focus** of the mirror is a point *F* on the principal axis at which the reflected rays converge for a concave mirror or appears to diverge for a convex mirror.

  (v) **Focal plane** of the mirror is the plane through which the reflected rays converge (or appears to diverge) when parallel paraxial beam of light were incident making some angle with the principal axis.

  (vi) The **focal length** is the distance between focus *F* and pole *P* of a spherical mirror.

  If *f* is the focal length and *R* is the radius of curvature of a spherical mirror then, $f = \frac{R}{2}$.

- These terms are depicted in the spherical (concave and convex) mirrors as shown below.

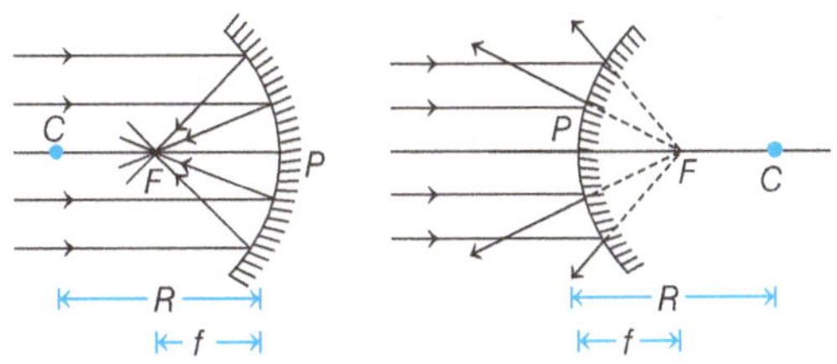

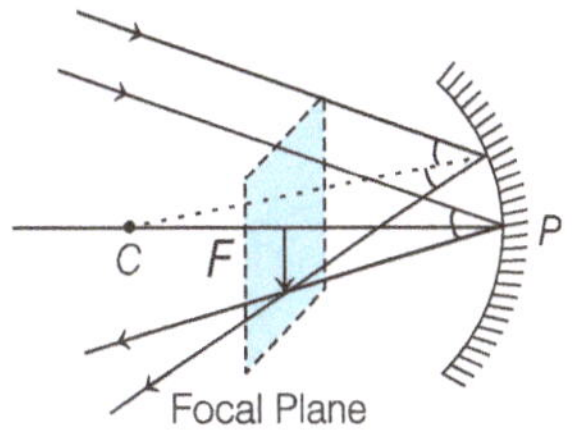

Sign Convention

- According to **cartesian sign convention,**

  (i) all the distances are measured from the pole of the mirror.

  (ii) the distances measured in the same direction as the incident light are taken as positive and those measured in the direction opposite to the direction of incident light are taken as negative.

  (iii) the height measured upwards with respect to *X*-axis and normal to the principal axis (*X*-axis) of the mirror/lens are taken as positive. The heights, measured downwards are taken as negative.

The cartesian sign convention for a mirror is shown in the figure.

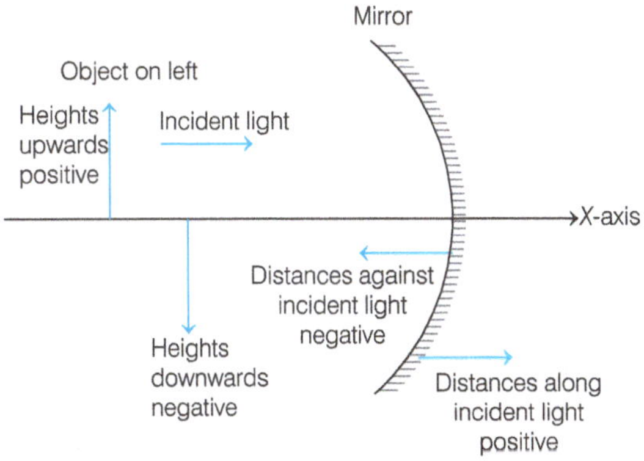

- **Image** If rays emanating from a point meet at another point after reflection and/or refraction, that point is called **image of the first point.**

  (i) The image is **real**, if the rays actually meet to converge at the point.

  (ii) The image is **virtual**, if the rays do not actually meet but appear to diverge from that point when produced backwards.

Mirror Equation and Magnification

- **Mirror Equation** As shown in the figure if an object *AB* is placed at a distance *u* from the pole of a mirror *MPN* and its image *A′B′* is formed at a distance *v* from the pole *P*. Then, according to the mirror equation

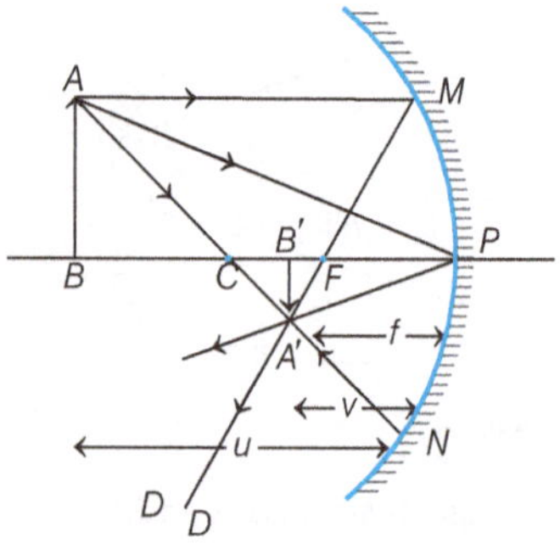

$$\frac{1}{v}+\frac{1}{u}=\frac{1}{f}$$ NEET 2020

where, f is the focal length of the mirror.

- **Linear magnification** is the ratio of the height of the image h' to the height of the object h and is given by

$$m=\frac{h'}{h}=-\frac{v}{u}=\frac{f}{f-u}=\frac{f-v}{f}$$

Marks Maximiser

Longitudinal Magnification

- For large object ($O_1 O_2$)

$$m_l=\frac{|v_1|-|v_2|}{|u_2|-|u_1|}$$

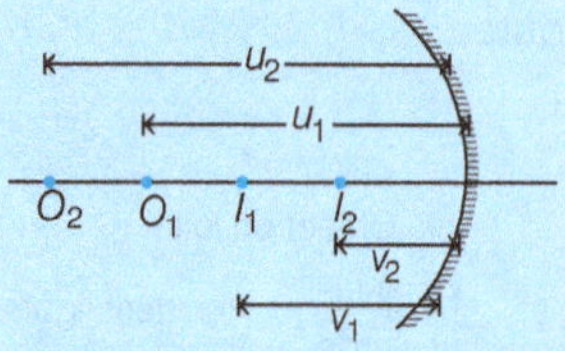

- For very small object

$$m_l=\frac{dv}{du}=\frac{-v^2}{u^2}=-(m)^2$$

- **Velocity of image by spherical mirror**

When an object is moving along principle axis with velocity v_{OM}, then the velocity of image with respect to mirror is given by

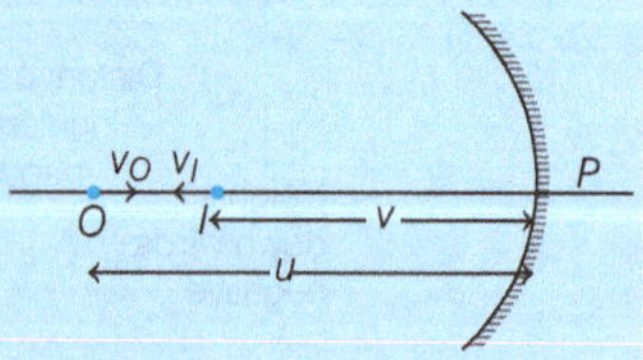

$$\mathbf{v}_{IM}=-\frac{\mathbf{v}^2}{u^2}\mathbf{v}_{OM}$$

- Image formation by a concave mirror for different positions of the object.

Position of the object	Position of the image	Size of the image	Nature of the image
At infinity	At the focus F	Highly diminished, point-sized	Real and inverted
Beyond C	Between F and C	Diminished	Real and inverted
At C	At C	Same size	Real and inverted
Between C and F	Beyond C	Enlarged	Real and inverted
At F	At infinity	Highly enlarged	Real and inverted
Between P and F	Behind the mirror	Enlarged	Virtual and erect

- Nature, position and relative size of the image formed by a convex mirror.

Position of the object	Position of the image	Size of the image	Nature of the image
At infinity	At the focus F, behind the mirror	Highly diminished, point-sized	Virtual and erect
Between infinity and the pole P of the mirror	Between P and F, behind the mirror	Diminished	Virtual and erect

Refraction

- It is the phenomena of bending of ray of light when light rays passes from one transparent medium to another depending on their optical densities.
- When a beam of light enters from one transparent medium to another, a part of light gets reflected back into the first medium while the rest part goes to other as shown in figure below.

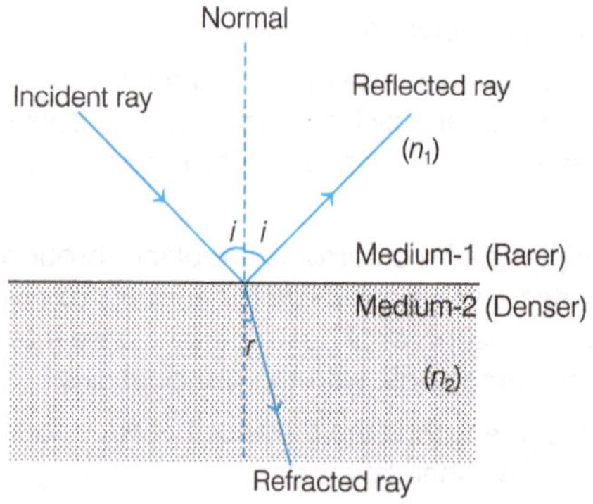

- **Laws of Refraction** There are two laws of refraction as follows:
  (i) The incident ray, the refracted ray and the normal to the interface at the point of incidence, all lie in the same plane.
  (ii) The ratio of the sine of angle of incidence i to the sine of angle of refraction r is constant, i.e. $\frac{\sin i}{\sin r}=n_{21}$

or $$n_{21}={}^1n_2=\frac{n_2}{n_1}$$ NEET 2023, 22

where, n_{21} is a constant, called the **refractive index** of the second medium with respect to the first medium.

This is known as **Snell's law of refraction**.

Refractive Index It is the ratio of velocity of light in vacuum to the velocity of light in a medium i.e., $n = \frac{c}{v}$

Note *n_{21} is a characteristic of the pair of media (and also depend on the wavelength of light) but is independent of the angle of incidence.*

- Following are few important points related to refraction of light
  (i) If $n_{21} > 1$, $r < i$, then the refracted ray bend towards the normal. In such a case, medium 2 is said to be optically denser than medium 1.
  (ii) If $n_{21} < 1$, $r > i$, the refracted ray bend away from the normal.

Note $n_{12} = \frac{1}{n_{21}}$ and $n_{32} = n_{31} \times n_{12}$

- **Lateral Shift** As shown in the figure, if a light ray passes through a rectangular glass slab, the emergent ray is parallel to the incident ray, then there is no deviation, but it does suffer **lateral displacement/shift** with respect to the incident ray.

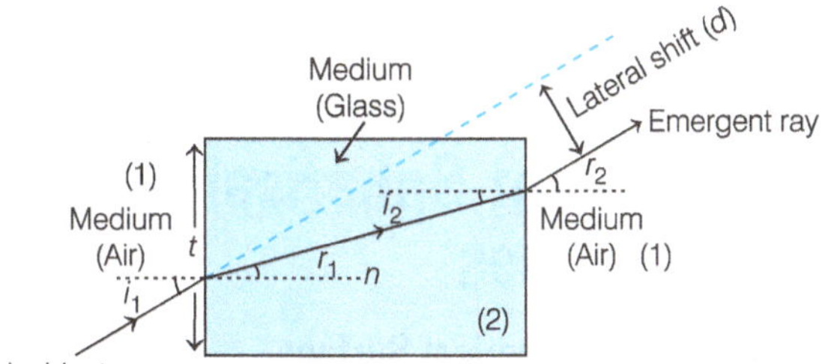

- The lateral shift in a rectangular glass slab is given by
$$d = t\frac{\sin(i_1 - r_1)}{\cos r_1}$$

- **Real and Apparent Depth** When an object is in denser medium (water) and observer is in rarer medium (air), then object appears at lesser depth (apparent depth) than its actual depth. Apparent depth for (a) normal and (b) oblique viewing is shown in the figure.

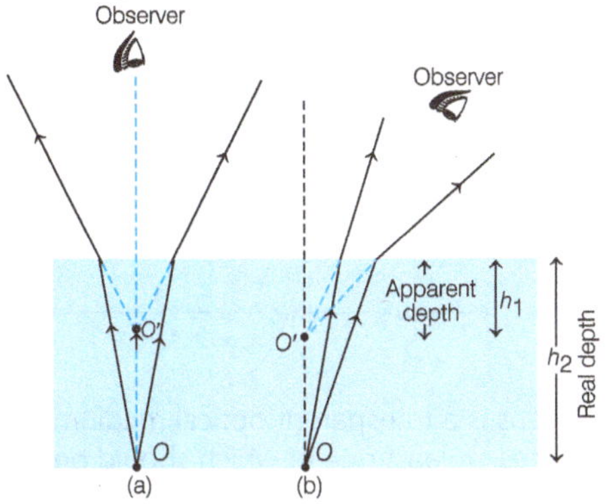

Real and apparent depth are related as follows.

$$\frac{\text{real depth } (h_2)}{\text{apparent depth } (h_1)} = n_{\text{water}}$$

i.e. Real depth > Apparent depth

Marks Maximiser

- If there is a coin at the bottom of the glass slab of thickness t, it appears to be raised by a distance d = (thickness – apparent depth).
$$= t - \frac{t}{\mu} = t\left(1 - \frac{1}{\mu}\right)$$

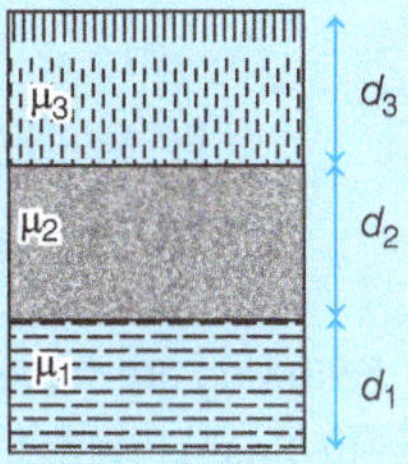

- Apparent depth of the container shown in the figure is
$$= \frac{d_1}{\mu_1} + \frac{d_2}{\mu_2} + \frac{d_3}{\mu_3}.$$

Total Internal Reflection

- When light travels from an optically denser medium to a rarer medium at the interface, it is partly reflected back into the same medium and partly refracted to the second medium. This reflection is called the **internal reflection**.
- A ray of light travelling from denser medium to a rarer medium is incident at the interface of two media at an angle greater than the critical angle for the two media, then the ray is totally reflected back to denser medium and this phenomenon is called **Total Internal Reflection** (TIR).
- The angle of incidence in denser medium corresponding to an angle of refraction 90° in rarer medium is called the **critical angle** i_c for the given pair of media, i.e. for $i = i_c$, $r = 90°$ NEET 2019

$$\sin i_c = n_{21}$$

or
$$n_{12} = \frac{1}{\sin i_c}$$

NEET 2020

For values of i larger than i_c, Snell's law of refraction cannot be satisfied, and hence, no refraction is possible. The next figure shows the refraction and internal reflection of rays from a point A in the denser medium (water) incident at different angles of incidence at the interface with a rarer medium (air). When angle of incidence is increased and becomes AO_4, refraction is not possible, and the incident ray is totally reflected.

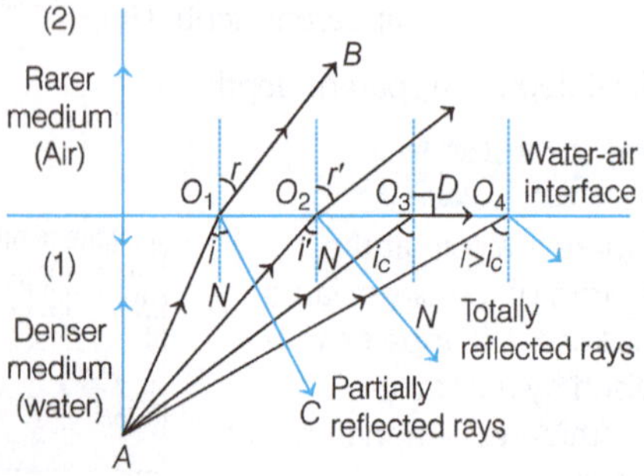

- Following are some applications of total internal reflection :
  - (i) **Prism** Prisms are designed to bend light by 90° or by 180°, making use of total internal reflection (as shown in Figs. a, b). Such prisms are also used to invert images, without changing their size as shown in Fig. (c).

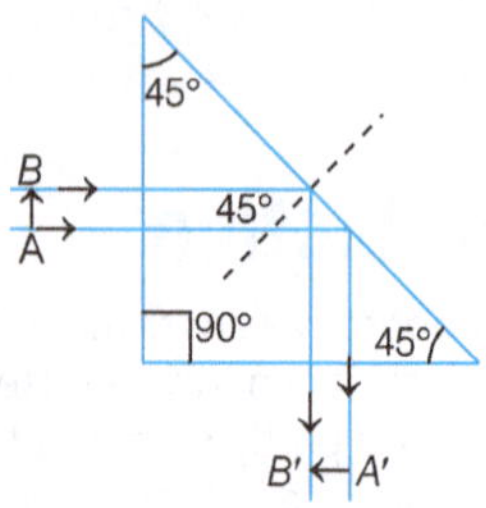

(a)

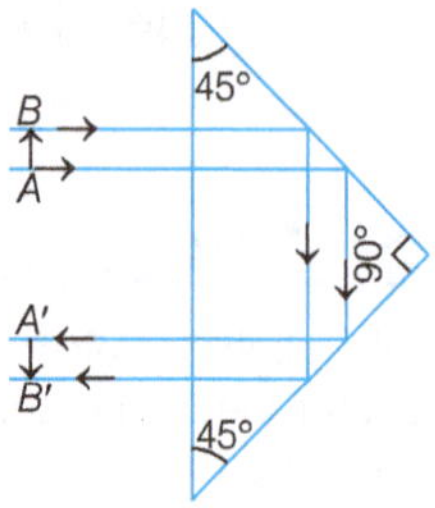

(b)

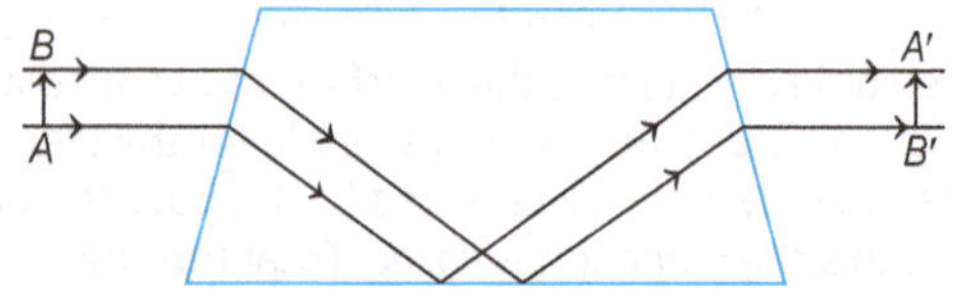

(c)

  - (ii) **Optical Fibres** Optical fibres are fabricated with high quality composite glass/quartz. Each fibre consists of a core and cladding such that refractive index of the material of the core is higher than that of the cladding.

    When a signal in the form of light is directed at one end of the fibre at a suitable angle, it undergoes repeated internal reflections along the length of the fibre and finally comes out of the other end as shown in the figure.

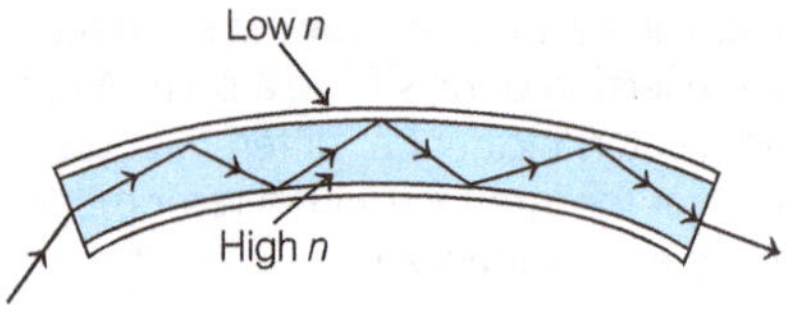

Since, light undergoes total internal reflection at each stage, there is no appreciable loss in intensity of the light signal. This can be achieved by purification and special preparation of materials such as quartz. In silica glass fibres, it is possible to transmit more than 95% of the light over a fibre length of 1 km.

Thus, these are extensively used for transmitting audio and video signals through long distances.

Optical fibres are fabricated such that light reflected at one side of inner surface strikes the other at an angle larger than the critical angle.

Even if the fibre is bent, light can easily travel along its length. Thus, an optical fibre can be used to act as an optical pipe.

Uses of optical fibre

A bundle of optical fibres can be used in several ways.

(i) These are extensively used for transmitting and receiving electrical signals, which are converted to light by suitable transducers.

(ii) These can also be used for transmission of optical signals.

Refraction at Spherical Surfaces and by Lenses

Refraction at a Spherical Surface

If an object O is placed in a medium of refractive index n_1, at a distance u from the pole of a spherical surface of radius of curvature R and after refraction, its image I is formed in a medium of refractive index n_2 at a distance v, as shown in figure below. Then, $\frac{n_2}{v} - \frac{n_1}{u} = \frac{n_2 - n_1}{R}$

Note *This equation holds for any curved spherical surface.*

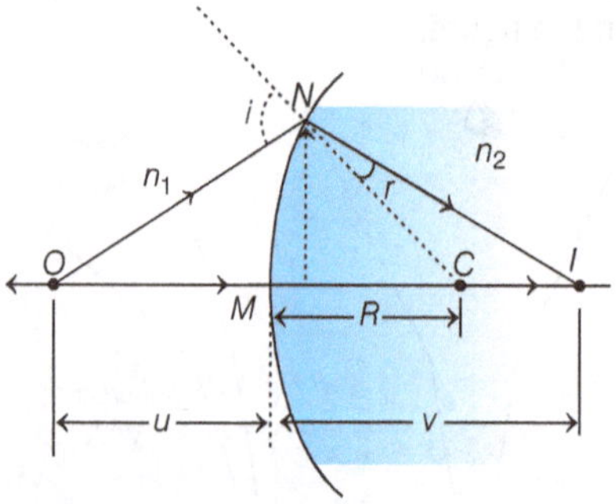

- **Lens** A lens is a transparent optical medium bounded by two surfaces, at least one of which should be spherical.

  Lens are of two types : **convex lens** and **concave lens**.

- **Convex lens** is a lens that **converges** rays of light coming parallel to its principal axis.

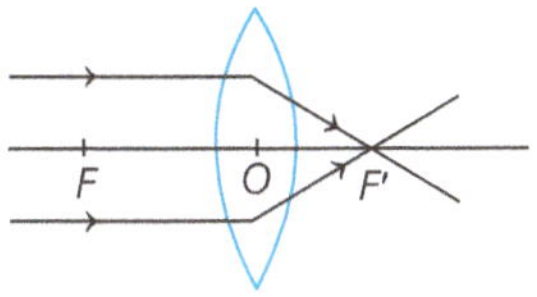

- **Concave lens** is a lens that diverges rays of light coming parallel to its principal axis.

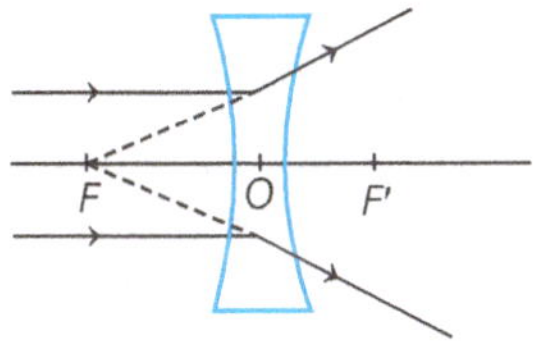

Refraction by a Lens

The Lens Maker's Formula for a double convex lens in which object O is placed at a distance u in a medium of refractive index n_1. The refractive index of material of the lens is n_2. The final image I is formed at a distance v in the same medium of refractive index n_1 as shown in figure below.

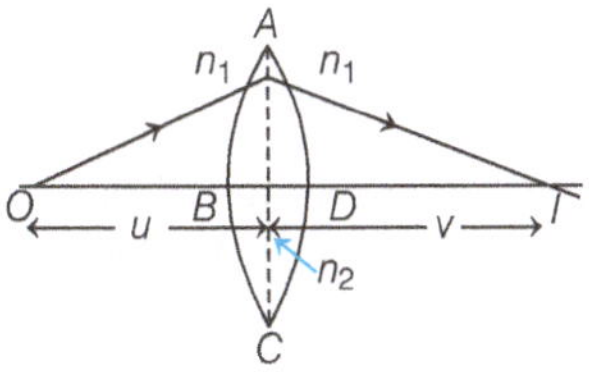

$$\frac{1}{f}=(n_{21}-1)\left(\frac{1}{R_1}-\frac{1}{R_2}\right), \text{ where } n_{21}=\frac{n_2}{n_1}$$ **NEET 2023, 21**

This formula is useful to design lenses of desired focal length using surfaces of suitable radius of curvature. It is also valid for concave lens. In that case R_1 will be negative, R_2 will be positive and therefore, f will be negative.

- If the lens is thin, then lens Maker's formula is given as

$$\frac{1}{v}-\frac{1}{u}=\frac{1}{f}$$

This is known as **thin lens formula**.

- For lens, the focus on the side of the (original) source of light is called the **first focal point**, whereas the other is called the **second focal point**.
- To find the image of an object by a lens, we can take any two rays emanating from a point of an object, trace their paths using the laws of refraction and find the point where the refracted rays meet (or appear to meet). In practice, however, it is convenient to choose any two of the following rays :

(i) A ray emanating from the object parallel to the principal axis of the lens after refraction passes through the second principal focus F' (in a convex lens) or appears to diverge (in a concave lens) from the first principal focus F.

(ii) A ray of light, passing through the optical centre of the lens, emerges without any deviation after refraction.

(iii) (a) A ray of light passing through the first principal focus of a convex lens [Fig. (a)] emerges parallel to the principal axis after refraction.

(b) A ray of light incident on a concave lens appearing to meet the principal axis at second focus point emerges parallel to the principal axis after refraction [Fig. (b)].

Figures (a) and (b) illustrate these rules.

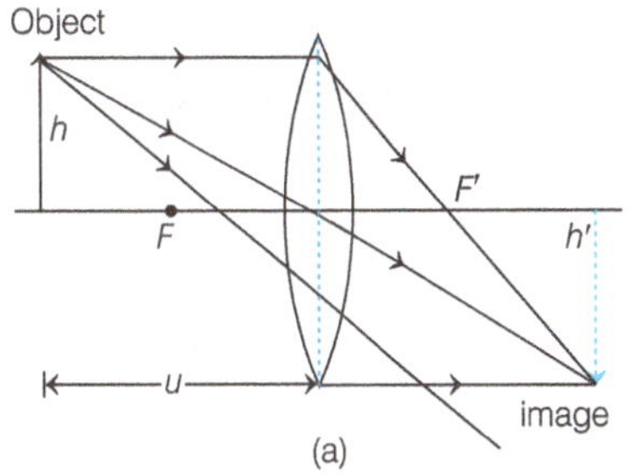

(a)

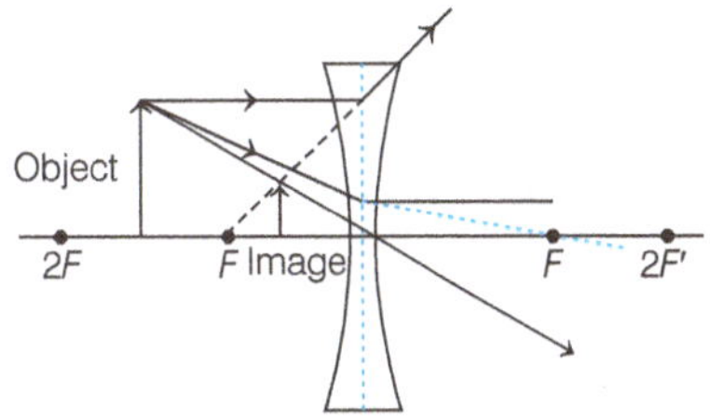

(b)

- **Magnification** m produced by lens is defined as the ratio of the size of the image to that of the object.

Mathematically, $m=\frac{h'}{h}=\frac{v}{u}$

For erect (and virtual) image, m is **positive** and for an inverted (and real) image, m is **negative.**

For Concept Master Video

Power of lens

- It is a measure of the convergence or divergence, which a lens introduces in the light falling on it.

It can be expressed mathematically as **NEET 2022**

$$P=\frac{1}{f(\text{m})}=\frac{100}{f(\text{cm})} \text{ dioptre}$$

It is also defined as the tangent of the angle by which it converges or diverges a beam of light parallel to principal axis falling at unit distance from the optical centre, i.e.

Power of lens, $\tan\delta = h/f$

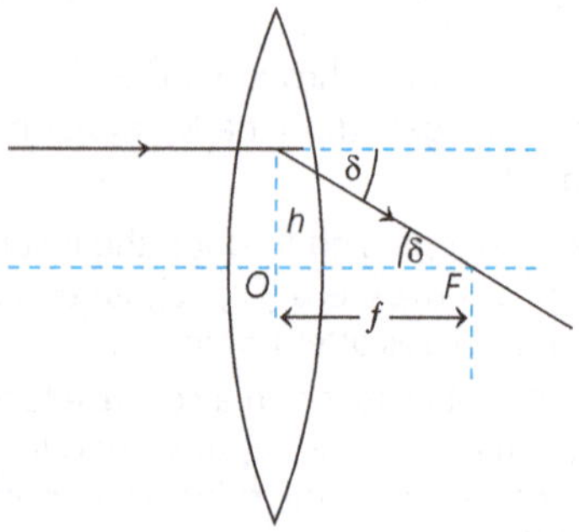

It is positive for a converging lens and negative for a diverging lens.

Combination of Thin Lenses

- If several thin lenses of focal length $f_1, f_2, f_3, \ldots$ are in contact, then the effective focal length and power of their combination is given by NEET 2023

$$\frac{1}{f} = \frac{1}{f_1} + \frac{1}{f_2} + \frac{1}{f_3}, \ldots \text{ and } P = P_1 + P_2 + P_3, \ldots$$

When two thin lenses of equal and opposite focal length (i.e., one convex and other concave) are placed in contact, then the equivalent focal length is given by

$$\frac{1}{F} = \frac{1}{f} + \frac{1}{-f} = 0 \text{ or } F = \infty$$

and power, $$P = \frac{1}{F} = 0$$

Such combination of lenses will behave as a plane glass plate.

- Combination of lenses helps to obtain diverging or converging lenses of desired magnifications. It also enhances sharpness of the image. Thus, the total magnification of such a combination is given as

$$m = m_1 m_2 m_3 \ldots$$

The system of combination of lenses is commonly used in designing lenses for cameras, microscopes, telescopes and other optical instruments.

For Concept Master Video

Marks Maximiser

Plano Convex Lens with Silvered Plane Surface

- Effective focal length ($|f|$) is given by

$$\therefore |f| = \frac{|f_L|}{2} = \frac{R}{2(\mu - 1)}, \text{ where } f_L = \text{focal length of lens}$$

- Effective power of a lens, $P = \dfrac{2(\mu - 1)}{R}$

Plano Convex Lens with Silvered Curved Surface

- Effective focal length is given by

$$\frac{1}{|f|} = \frac{2}{|f_L|} + \frac{1}{R/2} = \frac{2(\mu - 1)}{R} + \frac{2}{R} = \frac{2\mu}{R}$$

$$\therefore |f| = \frac{R}{2\mu}$$

- Effective power of a lens, $P = \dfrac{2\mu}{R}$

Refraction through a Prism

- A **prism** is a portion of a homogeneous, transparent medium bounded by two plane faces (refracting surfaces) inclined to each other at a suitable angle is known as angle of prism A.
- Refraction of light through a prism is shown in the figure given below.

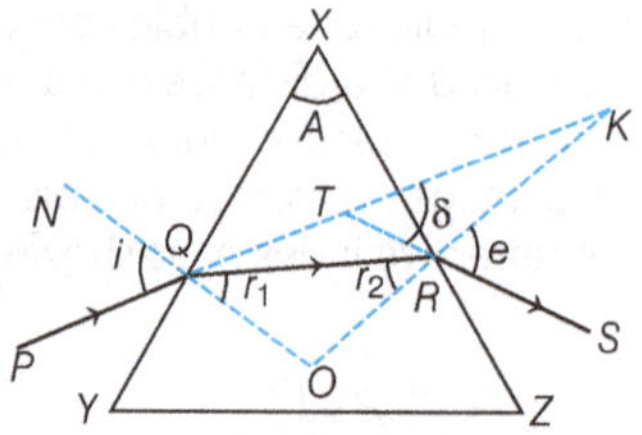

- The angle between emergent ray RS and incident ray PQ through a prism is called **angle of deviation**, i.e.,

$$\delta = i + e - A \text{ and } A = r_1 + r_2$$

where, i is the angle of incidence, e is the angle of emergence and A is the angle of prism.

- The angle of deviation depends on the angle of incidence. At the minimum deviation D_m, the refracted ray inside the prism becomes parallel to its base.
- Plot of angle of deviation (δ) *versus* angle of incidence (i) for a triangular prism is shown in the figure.

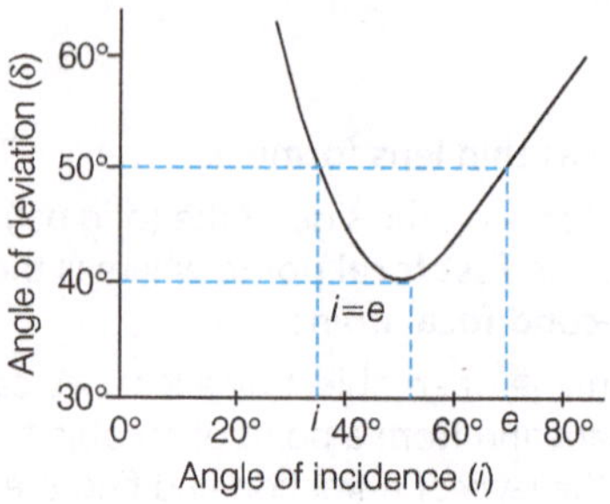

From the graph, it can be concluded that the angle of deviation δ first decreases with increase in angle of incidence i and then becomes minimum D_m at $i = e$ and then increases with increase in angle of incidence i.

In position of minimum deviation, $\delta = D_m, i = e$ and $r_1 = r_2 = \frac{A}{2}$

- Refractive index of prism material is given as

$$n_{21} = \frac{\sin\left(\frac{A + D_m}{2}\right)}{\sin(A/2)}$$

For small angle prism, $D_m = (n_{21} - 1)A$

This implies that, thin prisms do not deviate light much.

Optical Instruments

A number of optical devices and instruments have been designed utilising reflecting and refracting properties of mirrors, lenses and prisms. Some of them are as follows.

Microscope

- **A simple magnifier** or **microscope** is a converging lens of small focal length. It consists of a convex lens with object placed between its focus and optical centre and eye close to it. The image formed by simple microscope will be erect, virtual, enlarged and on the same side of the lens between object and infinity as shown in figure below.

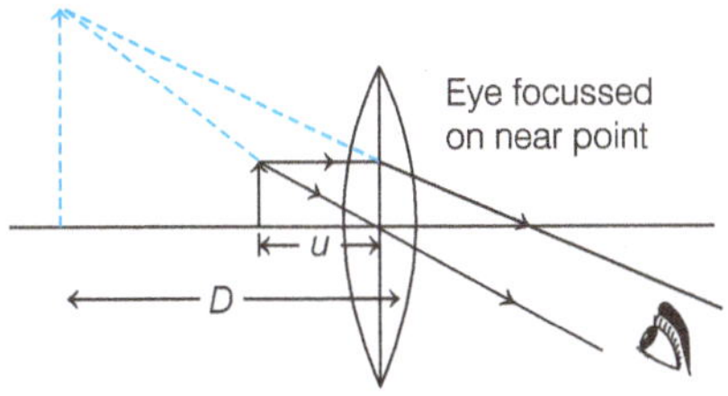

- The linear magnification m for the image formed at near point D by a simple microscope can be obtained by using the relation $m = \left(1 - \frac{v}{f}\right) = \left(1 + \frac{D}{f}\right)$
- When the image is at infinity, the angular magnification is $m = \frac{D}{f}$.
- A simple microscope has a limited maximum magnification (≤ 9) for realistic focal lengths.
- **Compound microscope** is used for much larger magnifications, one uses two lenses, one compounding the effect of the other.
- Ray diagram for the formation of image by a compound microscope is shown in the figure.

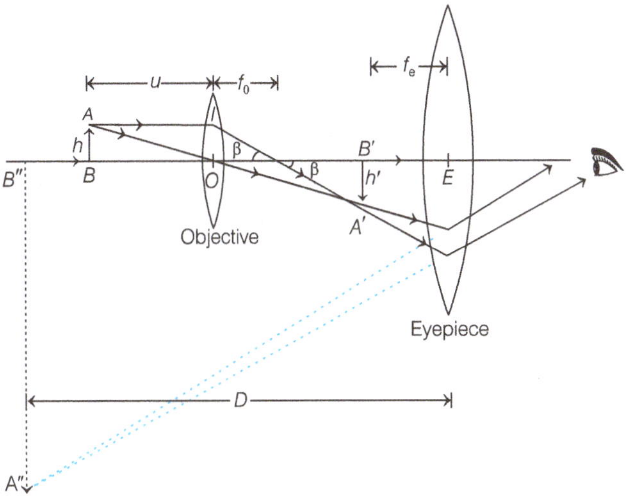

where, f_o = focal length of objective lens

and f_e = focal length of eyepiece lens.

- The lens nearest to the object, called the **objective**, forms a real, inverted, magnified image of the object. This serves as the object for the second lens, the **eyepiece**, which functions essentially like a simple microscope or magnifier, produces the final image, which is enlarged and virtual.
- The magnification due to a compound microscope is

$$m = m_o m_e$$

- The magnification m and the length of tube L of a compound microscope, when the final image is formed at least distance of distinct vision D are given by

$$m = m_o\, m_e = \left(\frac{v_o}{u_o}\right)\left(1 + \frac{D}{f_e}\right) = \left(\frac{L}{f_o}\right)\left(1 + \frac{D}{f_e}\right)$$

and $L = v_o + \left(\frac{f_e D}{f_e + D}\right)$

- The magnification m and the length of the tube L of a compound microscope, when the final image is formed at infinity (normal adjustment) are given by

$$m = m_o\, m_e = \left(\frac{v_o}{u_o}\right)\left(\frac{D}{f_e}\right) = \left(\frac{L}{f_o}\right)\left(\frac{D}{f_e}\right)$$

and $L = f_o + f_e$

Telescope

- The telescope is used to provide angular magnification of distant objects. It has objective lens of large focal length and a much larger aperture than the eyepiece.
- Ray diagram for the image formation by a refracting or astronomical telescope is shown in the figure.

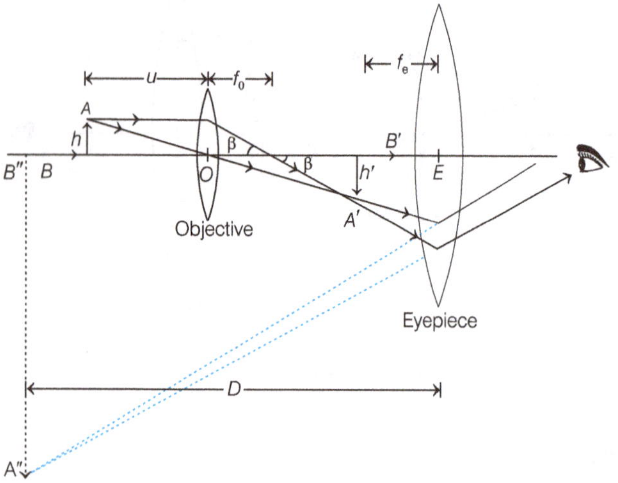

- The refracting type telescope consists of two converging lenses. The one facing the object is known as objective or field lens and has large focal length and aperture, while, the other facing the eye is known as eyepiece and has small focal length and aperture.
- The magnifying power m is the ratio of the angle β subtended at the eye by the final image to the angle α which the object subtends at the lens or the eye.

Hence, $$m = \frac{\beta}{\alpha}$$

The magnifying power m and the length of the tube L of a refracting tube L of a refracting type telescope, when the final image is formed at infinity (normal adjustment) are given by

$$m = \frac{\beta}{\alpha} = \frac{f_o}{f_e} \text{ and } L = f_o + f_e$$

The magnifying power m and the length of the tube L of a refracting type telescope, when the final image is formed at least distance of distinct vision D are given by .

$$m = \frac{\beta}{\alpha} = \frac{f_o}{f_e}\left(1 + \frac{f_e}{D}\right)$$

and $$L = f_o + \left(\frac{f_e D}{f_e + D}\right)$$

- **Terrestrial telescopes** have, in addition, a pair of inverting lenses to make the final image erect.
- **Refracting telescopes** can be used both for terrestrial and astronomical observations. The main consideration with an astronomical telescope are its light gathering power and its resolution or resolving power.
- Telescopes with mirror objective are called **reflecting telescopes**. There is no chromatic aberration in a mirror.
- A **cassegrain telescope** has the advantage of a large focal length in a short telescope.

Caution Points

- To form an image, there must be regular reflection or refraction. All the rays should continuously reach the image point.
- Dispersion is the reason for the formation of coloured images formed by thick lenses. The colour of the object is decided by the colour of light incident on it. But in case of monochromatic light, result may be entirely different.
- Without microscope, there is very small angle subtended by image when the object is kept at 25 cm. In simple microscope, magnified image is formed, when the object is much closer to eye.

PYQ Notes

1. **Two lenses placed at some distance** When two lenses of focal lengths f_1 and f_2 are placed coaxially at a distance from each other, then the equivalent focal length of the system is given by

$$\frac{1}{F} = \frac{1}{f_1} + \frac{1}{f_2} - \frac{d}{f_1 f_2}$$

and the equivalent power of the system is given by

$$P = P_1 + P_2 - d\,P_1 P_2$$

2. **Deviation of a ray from two inclined plane mirrors** When a ray falls on a system of two inclined plane mirrors as shown in the figure, it gets deviated and this deviation is given by

Total deviation $(\delta) = 360° - 2\alpha$

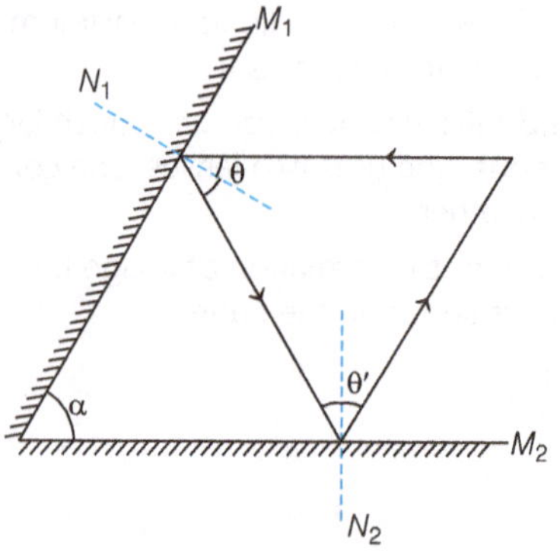

Step by Step

Mastering NCERT

- Concept Builders
- Topical Questions
- Assertion and Reason Questions
- Statement Based
- Matching Type
- Numerical Type
- NCERT Exemplar
- Past Exams MCQs
- Skill Boosters

Concept Builders

1 If a mirror is turned through an angle θ, then the reflected ray will turn through an angle .... $(\theta / 2\theta)$.

2 If an object is placed between two plane mirrors inclined at an angle θ (submultiple of 180°), with each other. What is the total number of images formed?

3 If a concave mirror is held in water, then what should be the change in the focal length of the mirror?

4 Parabolic mirrors do not show spherical aberration. [T/F]

5 What will be the minimum distance between an object and real image for a convex lens?

6 When a lens is immersed in a liquid or a medium, then its focal length always .... (increases/decreases).

7 If a source of light is situated at depth h in a liquid of refractive index μ, it will spread light in a circle of radius R such that $\mu = \sqrt{1 + h^2 / R^2}$. [T/F]

8 On what factors, does the normal shift through a refracting medium depends?

9 The lateral shift produced by a parallel side glass slab is zero when angle of incidence (i) is ...... (0°/90°) and maximum when .... (0°/90°).

10 A spherical bubble is embedded in a piece of glass. For a light ray passing through it, it behaves as a .... (convex/concave) lens.

11 The radius of curvature of each face of biconcave lens, made of glass of refractive index 1.5, is 30 cm. The focal length of the lens in air is .... (30/−30) cm.

12 One dioptre is the power of lens of focal length 100 m. [T/F]

13 The refractive index of the material of a prism depends on the angle of the prism and the angle of minimum deviation. [T/F]

14 A beam of light passing through a hollow prism gives no spectrum. [T/F]

15 The magnifying power of a microscope depends on the colour of light used. [T/F]

16 The focal length of an objective lens in compound microscope is ..... (greater/shorter) than the focal length of the eyepiece.

17 If the objective and the eyepiece of a microscope are interchanged, then it can work as a telescope. [T/F]

18 For a telescope, magnification .... (increases/decreases) with increase in length of the tube.

19 In a telescope, the objective has .... (small/large) focal length and .... (small/large) aperture.

20 An astronomical telescope forms an inverted image. As the celestial object are oval in shape, so it does not matter whether the final image is inverted or erect. [T/F]

Topical Questions

Reflection of Light by Spherical Mirrors

1 A ray of light gets reflected from the plane mirror. The incident ray and the reflected ray are perpendicular to each other. The angle of incidence is NCERT Pg. 222

(a) 60° (b) 30°
(c) 45° (d) 0°

2 A ray of light travelling in the direction $\frac{1}{2}(\hat{i} + \sqrt{3}\,\hat{j})$ is incident on a plane mirror. After reflection, it travels along the direction $\frac{1}{2}(\hat{i} - \sqrt{3}\,\hat{j})$. The angle of incidence is NCERT Pg. 222

(a) 30° (b) 45° (c) 60° (d) 75°

3 A convex mirror is formed from a sphere of radius 16 cm, then the focal length of mirror is

(a) 4 cm (b) 8 cm (c) 12 cm (d) 16 cm

4 If lower half of a concave mirror is blackened, then **NCERT Pg. 222**

(a) image distance increases
(b) image distance decreases
(c) image intensity increases
(d) image intensity decreases

5 A rod of length 30 cm lies along the principal axis of a concave mirror of focal length 10 cm in such a way that its end closer to the pole is 20 cm away from the mirror. The length of the image is **NCERT Pg. 222**

(a) 10 cm (b) 15 cm (c) 2.5 cm (d) 7.5 cm

6 A short linear object of length b lies along the axis of a concave mirror of focal length f at a distance u from the pole of the mirror. The size of the image is approximately equal to **NCERT Pg. 222**

(a) $b\left(\frac{u-f}{f}\right)^{1/2}$ (b) $b\left(\frac{f}{u-f}\right)^{1/2}$

(c) $b\left(\frac{u-f}{f}\right)$ (d) $b\left(\frac{f}{u-f}\right)^{2}$

7 The focal length of a concave mirror is 30 cm. Find the position of the object in front of the mirror (on axis), so that the image is three times the size of the object. **NCERT Pg. 222**

(a) 40 cm (b) 20 cm
(c) 50 cm
(d) Both 20 cm and 40 cm are possible

8 When an object is kept at a distance of 30 cm from a concave mirror, the image is formed at a distance of 10 m. If the object is moved with a speed of 9 m/s, the speed with which image moves is **NCERT Pg. 222**

(a) 10 cm/s (b) 1 m/s
(c) 9 m/s (d) 0.9 m/s

9 An object is placed 30 cm from concave mirror. If the image is real and 2 times magnified, then find the another location of object that image is 2 times magnified **NCERT Pg. 222**

(a) +30 cm (b) −30 cm
(c) −10 cm (d) +10 cm

10 How far should an object be from a concave spherical mirror of radius of curvature 36 cm to form a real image one-ninth in size? **NCERT Pg. 222**

(a) 120 cm (b) 140 cm
(c) 160 cm (d) 180 cm

11 An object 2 cm high is placed at a distance of 16 cm from a concave mirror, which produces a real image 3 cm high. What is the focal length of the mirror? **NCERT Pg. 222**

(a) – 9.6 cm (b) – 3.6 cm
(c) – 6.3 cm (d) – 8.3 cm

12 An object is gradually moving away from the focal point of a concave mirror along the axis of the mirror. The graphical representation of the magnitude of linear magnification (m) *versus* distance of the object from the mirror (x) is correctly given by (graphs are drawn schematically and are not to scale) **NCERT Pg. 222**

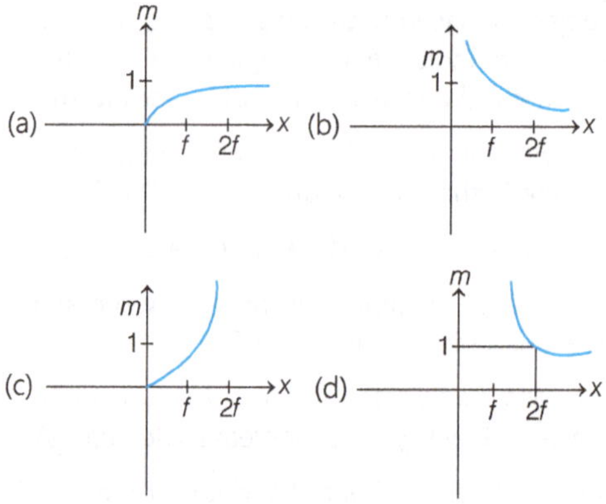

13 A concave mirror for face viewing has focal length of 0.4 m. The distance at which you hold the mirror from your face in order to see your image upright with a magnification of 5 is **NCERT Pg. 222**

(a) 0.16 m (b) 1.60 m
(c) 0.32 m (d) 0.24 m

14 Rear view mirror of a car is of radius of curvature $R = 2$ m. A jogger approaches car (from behind) at a speed of 5 ms^{-1}. The average speed of image, when jogger is 39 m from the mirror, is **NCERT Pg. 222**

(a) 0.3×10^{-2} ms^{-1}
(b) 0.1×10^{-2} ms^{-1}
(c) 0.5×10^{-2} ms^{-1}
(d) 0.5 cms^{-1}

15 Two mirrors, mounted vertically, are made to move towards each other with a speed v m/s each. A particle that can bounce back between the two mirrors starts from one mirror when the mirrors are d metres apart. On reaching the second mirror, it bounces back and so on. If the particle keeps on travelling at a constant speed of $4v$ m/s, how many trips can it make before the mirrors met with each other and what total distance does it cover ? **NCERT Pg. 222**

(a) ∞, 5.1 d (b) ∞, 2.0 d
(c) 0, 6.1 d (d) 0,1.6 d

Refraction

16 A ray of light strikes on an air-glass interface at an angle of incidence ($i = 60°$) and gets refracted at an angle of refraction r. On increasing the angle of incidence ($i > 60°$), the angle of refraction r NCERT Pg. 228

(a) decreases (b) remains same
(c) is equal to 60° (d) increases

17 As you can seen from Fig. (i) and (ii) shows refraction of light from air to glass and from air to water. Find out the value of the angle θ in the case of refraction as shown in Fig. (iii). NCERT Pg. 228

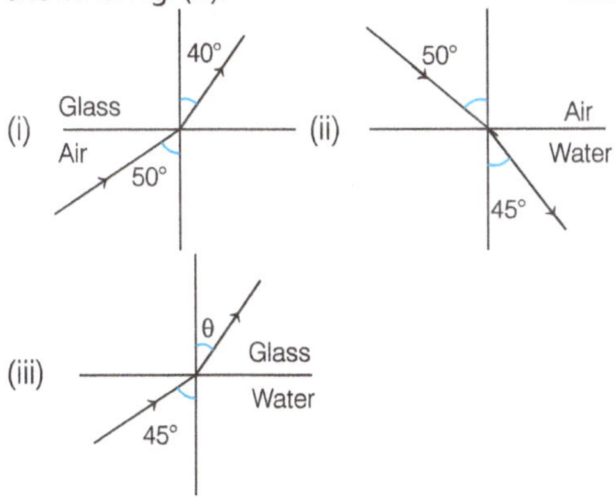

(a) 30° (b) 50° (c) 40° (d) 45°

18 A ray of light AO in vacuum is incident on a glass slab at angle 60° and refracted at angle 30° along OB as shown in the figure. The optical path length of light ray from A to B is NCERT Pg. 228

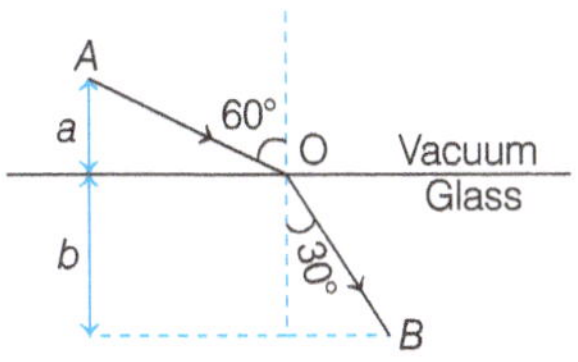

(a) $\frac{2\sqrt{3}}{a} + 2b$ (b) $2a + \frac{2b}{3}$
(c) $2a + 2b$ (d) $2a + \frac{2b}{\sqrt{3}}$

19 A ray of light strikes a material's slab at an angle of incidence 60°. If the reflected and refracted rays are perpendicular to each other, then which of the given option(s) is/are correct? NCERT Pg. 228

(a) The angle of refraction is 45°.
(b) The angle of refraction is 30°.
(c) The refractive index of the material is $\sqrt{3}$.
(d) Both (b) and (c)

20 A divergent beam of light from a point source S having divergence angle α falls symmetrically on a glass slab as shown in the figure. The angles of incidence of the two extreme rays are equal. If the thickness of the glass slab is t and its refractive index is n, then the divergence angle of the emergent beam is NCERT Pg. 228

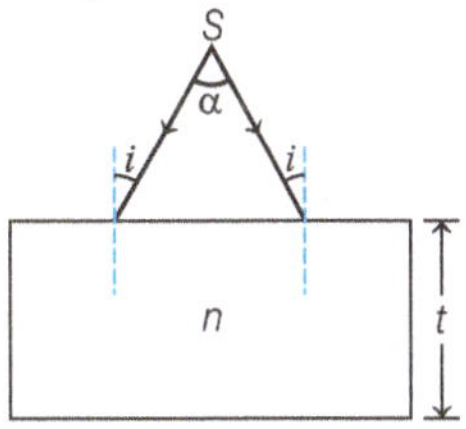

(a) zero (b) α
(c) $\sin^{-1}(1/n)$ (d) $2\sin^{-1}(1/n)$

21 A beaker contains water upto height h_1 and kerosene of height h_2 above water so that the total height (water + kerosene) is $(h_1 + h_2)$. Refractive index of water is n_1 and that of kerosene is n_2. The apparent shift in position of the bottom of the beaker when it is viewed from above is NCERT Pg. 228

(a) $\left(1 - \frac{1}{n_1}\right) h_2 + \left(1 - \frac{1}{n_2}\right) h_1$

(b) $\left(1 + \frac{1}{n_1}\right) h_1 + \left(1 + \frac{1}{n_2}\right) h_2$

(c) $\left(1 - \frac{1}{n_1}\right) h_1 + \left(1 - \frac{1}{n_2}\right) h_2$

(d) $\left(1 + \frac{1}{n_1}\right) h_2 - \left(1 + \frac{1}{n_2}\right) h_1$

22 A container is filled with water ($n = 1.33$) upto a height of 33.25 cm. A concave mirror is placed 15 cm above the water level and the image of an object placed at the bottom is formed 25 cm below the water level. The focal length of the mirror is NCERT Pg. 228

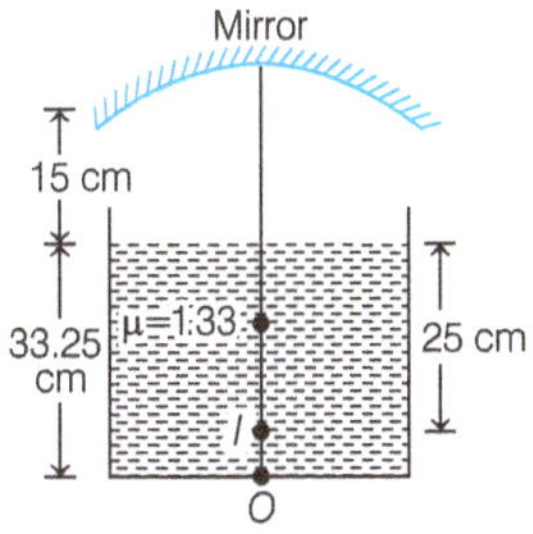

(a) 10 cm
(b) 15 cm
(c) –18.3 cm
(d) 25 cm

23 A vessel is filled with water to a height of 13 cm. The apparent depth of a screw lying at the bottom of the vessel is measured by a microscope to be 8.5 cm. If water is replaced by a liquid of refractive index 1.70 upto the same height. Find the distance at which microscope have to be moved to focus on the screw again? NCERT Pg. 228

(a) 0.85 cm (b) 0.52 cm (c) 0.65 cm (d) 1.02 cm

24 A concave mirror of radius R is kept on a horizontal table. Water (refractive index $= \mu$) is poured into it up to a height h. Where should an object be placed so that its image is formed in itself? NCERT Pg. 228

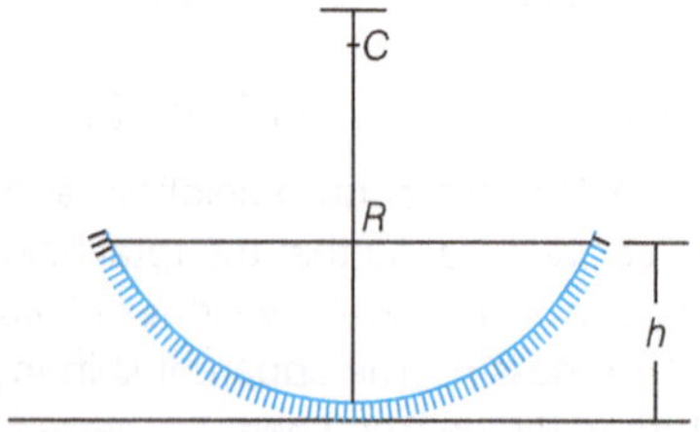

(a) $\frac{R+h}{\mu}$ (b) $\frac{R-h}{\mu}$ (c) $\frac{R-2h}{\mu}$ (d) $\frac{R+2h}{\mu}$

25 Speed of light in air is 3.0×10^8 m/s. Speed of light in the glass of refractive index 1.5 will be NCERT Pg. 228

(a) 1.5×10^8 m/s (b) 2.0×10^8 m/s
(c) 1.8×10^8 m/s (d) 2.5×10^8 m/s

26 When a light ray enters from oil to glass, then on oil-glass interface, the velocity of light changes by a factor of [given, $n_{oil} = 2$, $n_{glass} = 3/2$] NCERT Pg. 228

(a) $\frac{4}{3}$ (b) $\frac{3}{4}$ (c) 3 (d) 1

27 A point luminous object (O) is at a distance h from front face of a glass slab of width d and of refractive index μ. On the back face of slab is a reflecting plane mirror. An observer sees the image of object in mirror as shown in figure. Distance of image from front face as seen by observer will be NCERT Pg. 228

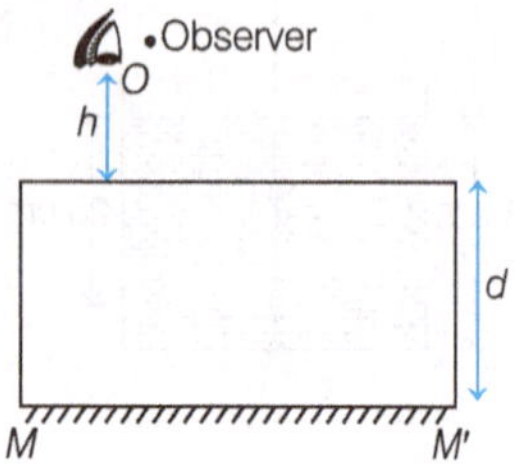

(a) $h + \frac{2d}{\mu}$ (b) $2h + 2d$
(c) $h + d$ (d) $h + \frac{f}{\mu}$

28 A vessel of depth x is half filled with oil of refractive index μ_1 and the other half is filled with water of refractive index μ_2. The apparent depth of the vessel when viewed from above is. NCERT Pg. 228

(a) $\frac{x(\mu_1 + \mu_2)}{2\mu_1\mu_2}$ (b) $\frac{x\mu_1\mu_2}{2(\mu_1 + \mu_2)}$
(c) $\frac{x\mu_1\mu_2}{(\mu_1 + \mu_2)}$ (d) $\frac{2x(\mu_1 + \mu_2)}{\mu_1\mu_2}$

29 Three immiscible liquids of densities $d_1 > d_2 > d_3$ and refractive indices $\mu_1 > \mu_2 > \mu_3$ are put in a beaker. The height of each liquid column is $h/3$. A dot is made at the bottom of the beaker. For near normal vision, the apparent depth of the dot is NCERT Pg. 228

(a) $\frac{h}{6}\left(\frac{1}{\mu_1} + \frac{1}{\mu_2} + \frac{1}{\mu_3}\right)$ (b) $\frac{h}{6}\left(\frac{1}{\mu_1} - \frac{1}{\mu_2} - \frac{1}{\mu_3}\right)$
(c) $\frac{h}{3}\left(\frac{1}{\mu_1} - \frac{1}{\mu_2} - \frac{1}{\mu_3}\right)$ (d) $\frac{h}{3}\left(\frac{1}{\mu_1} + \frac{1}{\mu_2} + \frac{1}{\mu_3}\right)$

Total Internal Reflection

30 Find the value of θ in the given figure NCERT Pg. 229

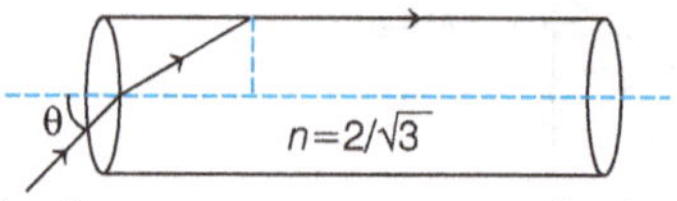

(a) $\sin^{-1}\left(\frac{2}{\sqrt{3}}\right)$ (b) $\sin^{-1}\left(\frac{1}{\sqrt{3}}\right)$
(c) $\sin^{-1}\left(\frac{1}{2}\right)$ (d) $\sin^{-1}\left(\frac{1}{\sqrt{2}}\right)$

31 If the critical angle for light travelling from medium A to B is θ. Then, find the speed of light in medium B, if speed of light is v in medium A. NCERT Pg. 229

(a) $v(1 - \cos\theta)$ (b) $\frac{v}{\cos\theta}$
(c) $\frac{v}{\sin\theta}$ (d) $v(1 - \sin\theta)$

32 Two transparent media A and B are separated by a plane boundary. The speed of light in medium A is 2×10^8 ms^{-1} and in medium B is 2.5×10^8 ms^{-1}. The critical angle for which a ray of light going from A to B is totally internally reflected is NCERT Pg. 229

(a) $\sin^{-1}\left(\frac{1}{2}\right)$ (b) $\sin^{-1}\left(\frac{2}{5}\right)$
(c) $\sin^{-1}\left(\frac{4}{5}\right)$ (d) $\sin^{-1}\left(\frac{3}{4}\right)$

33 A ray of light is incident at the glass-water interface at an angle (as shown below) and it emerges finally parallel to the surface of water, then the value of n_g would be NCERT Pg. 229

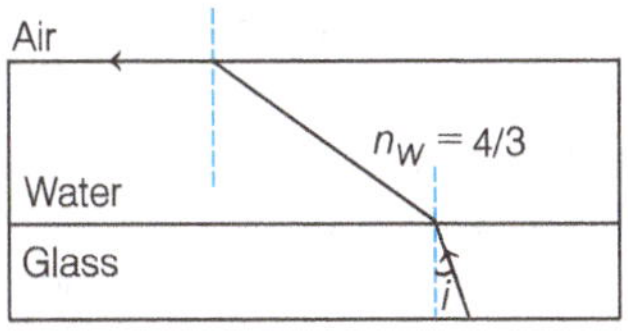

(a) $(4/3) \sin i$ (b) $1/\sin i$ (c) $4/3$ (d) 1

34 A ray of light from a denser medium strikes a rarer medium at an angle of incidence i (see figure).

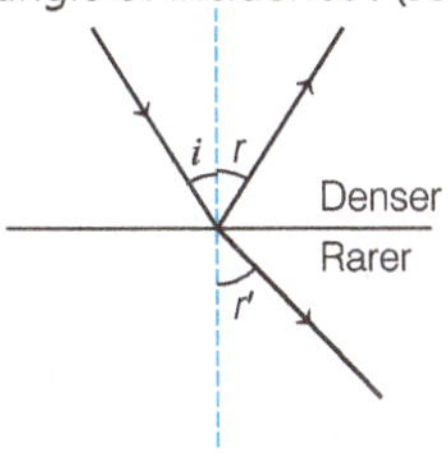

The reflected and refracted rays make an angle of 90° with each other. The angle of reflection and refraction are r and r'. The critical angle is NCERT Pg. 229

(a) $\sin^{-1}(\tan r)$ (b) $\sin^{-1}(\cot i)$
(c) $\sin^{-1}(\tan r')$ (d) $\tan^{-1}(\sin i)$

35 A parallel sides slab $ABCD$ of refractive index 2 is sandwiched between two slabs of refractive indices $\sqrt{2}$ and $\sqrt{3}$ as shown in the figure. The minimum value of angle θ such that the ray PQ suffers total internal reflection at both the surfaces AB and CD is NCERT Pg. 229

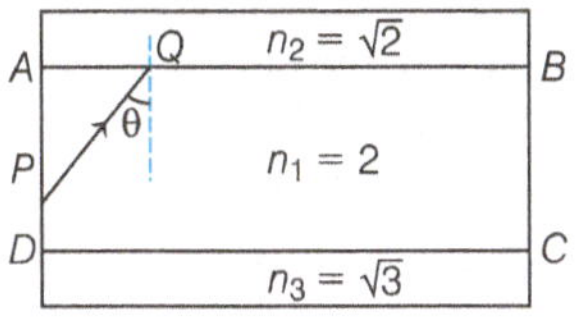

(a) 30° (b) 45° (c) 60° (d) 75°

36 A light beam is travelling from region I to region IV (refer figure). The refractive index in regions I, II, III and IV are $n_0, \frac{n_0}{2}, \frac{n_0}{6}$ and $\frac{n_0}{8}$, respectively. The angle of incidence θ for which the beam just misses entering region IV is NCERT Pg. 229

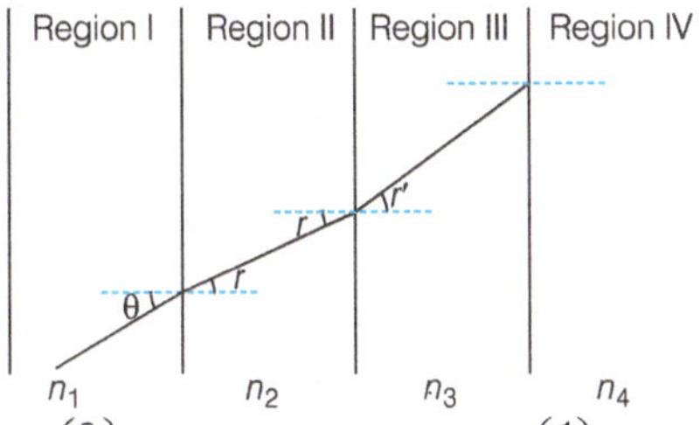

(a) $\sin^{-1}\left(\frac{3}{4}\right)$ (b) $\sin^{-1}\left(\frac{1}{8}\right)$
(c) $\sin^{-1}\left(\frac{1}{4}\right)$ (d) $\sin^{-1}\left(\frac{1}{3}\right)$

Refraction at Spherical Surfaces and by Lenses

37 From a point source a light falls on a spherical glass surface ($\mu = 1.5$ and radius of curvature $= 10$ cm). The distance between point source and glass surface is 50 cm. The position of image is NCERT Pg. 232

(a) 25 cm (b) 50 cm (c) 100 cm (d) 150 cm

38 Which of the following statement in correct? NCERT Pg. 232

(a) Power of a lens is a measure of the convergence or divergence, which a lens introduces in the light falling on it.
(b) Power is the cosine of angle of convergence of beam of light falling at unit distance from optical centre.
(c) Cutting of lenses helps to obtain diverging or converging of desired magnification.
(d) The total magnification of a combination of lenses is sum of their individual magnification.

39 Light from a point source in air falls on a spherical glass surface (whose refractive index $n = 1.5$ and radius of curvature $= 20$ cm). The distance of the light source from the glass surface is 100 cm. Image distance from the glass surface is NCERT Pg. 232

(a) 20 cm (b) 50 cm (c) 100 cm (d) 75 cm

40 An object is placed infront of a sphere of radius R and refractive index n at a distance x from the first surface. The value of x for which the light after refraction from the first surface becomes parallel to the axis is NCERT Pg. 232

(a) $\frac{R}{(n-1)}$ (b) $\frac{R}{n+1}$ (c) $\frac{2R}{(1+n)}$ (d) $\frac{Rn}{(n+1)}$

41 A mark placed on the surface of a sphere is viewed through glass from a position directly opposite as shown in the figure. The diameter of the sphere is 30 cm and refractive index of glass is 1.5. The position of the image is NCERT Pg. 232

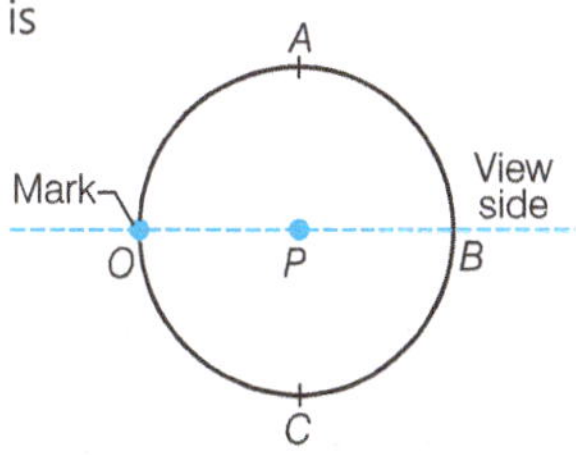

(a) at a distance of 60 cm from surface ABC in the direction of incident light
(b) at a distance of 60 cm from the surface ABC opposite to the direction of incident light
(c) at a distance of 30 cm from the surface AOC opposite to the direction of incident light on ABC
(d) Both (b) and (c)

42 A spherical surface of radius of curvature R separates air (refractive index 1.0) from glass (refractive index 1.5). The centre of curvature is in the glass. A point object P is placed in air is found to have a real image Q in the glass. The line PQ cuts the surface at a point O and $PO = OQ$. The distance PO is equal to **NCERT Pg. 232**

(a) $5R$ (b) $3R$
(c) $2R$ (d) $1.5R$

43 The image for the converging beam after refraction through the curved surface is formed at **NCERT Pg. 232**

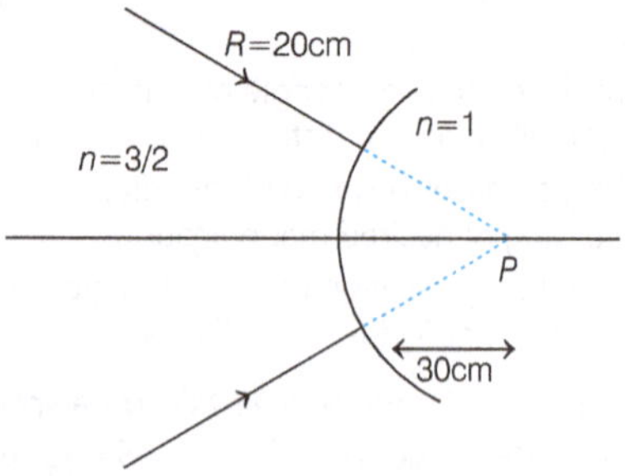

(a) 40 cm (b) $\frac{40}{3}$ cm
(c) $-\frac{40}{3}$ cm (d) 20 cm

44 When a light ray is going from vacuum to a medium, the relation between angle of incident (i) and angle of reflection r is as shown. If speed of light in the medium is nC, then value of n is (c is velocity of light in vacuum) **NCERT Pg. 232**

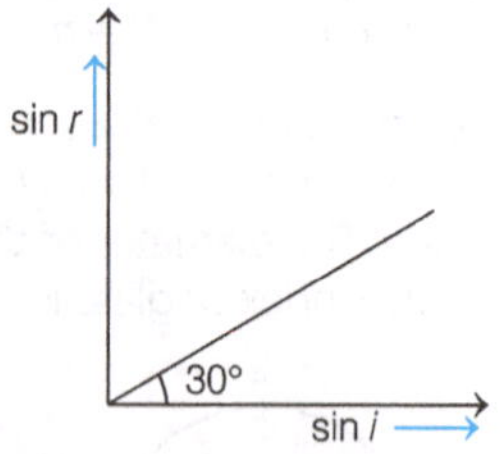

(a) 1.5 (b) 2
(c) $(2)^{-1}$ (d) $(3)^{-1/2}$

45 A thin lens made of glass (refractive index = 1.5) of focal length $f = 16$ cm in immersed in a liquid of refractive index 1.42. If its focal length in liquid is f_1, then the ratio f_1 / f is closest to the integer **NCERT Pg. 232**

(a) 1 (b) 5 (c) 9 (d) 17

46 A lens is made of flint glass (refractive index = 1.5). When the lens is immersed in a liquid of refractive index 1.25, the focal length **NCERT Pg. 232**

(a) increases by a factor of 1.25
(b) increases by a factor of 2.5
(c) increases by a factor of 1.2
(d) decreases by a factor of 1.2

47 A concave lens of glass of refractive index 1.5 has both surfaces of same radius of curvature R. On immersing it in a medium of refractive index 1.75, it will behave as a **NCERT Pg. 232**

(a) convergent lens of focal length $3.5R$
(b) convergent lens of focal length $3.0R$
(c) divergent lens of focal length $3.5R$
(d) divergent lens of focal length $3.0R$

48 A hollow double concave lens is made of very thin transparent material. It can be filled with air or either of two liquids L_1 or L_2 having refractive indices n_{L_1} and n_{L_2}, respectively (such that $n_{L_1} > n_{L_2} > 1$). The lens will diverge a parallel beam of light, if it is filled with **NCERT Pg. 232**

(a) air and placed in air
(b) air and immersed in L_1
(c) L_1 and immersed in L_2
(d) L_2 and immersed in L_1

49 A double convex lens whose refractive index is 1.33 has both radii of curvature of magnitude 10 cm. If an object is placed at a distance of 5 cm from this lens, the position of the image formed (in cm) is **NCERT Pg. 232**

(a) 7.46 same side of the object
(b) 7.46 opposite side of the object
(c) 14.45 same side of the object
(d) 14.45 opposite side of the object

50 A screen is placed 90 cm from an object. The image of an object on the screen is formed by a convex lens at two different location separated by 20 cm. The focal length of the lens is **NCERT Pg. 232**

(a) 18 cm (b) 21.4 cm
(c) 60 cm (d) 85.6 cm

51 An object is placed at a distance x_1 from the principal focus of a lens and its real image is formed at a distance x_2 from the another principal focus. The focal length of the lens is **NCERT Pg. 232**

(a) x_1x_2 (b) $\frac{x_1x_2}{2}$
(c) $\frac{x_1+x_2}{2}$ (d) $\sqrt{x_1x_2}$

52 A convex lens of radii of curvature 20 cm and 30 cm, respectively, is silvered at the surface which has smaller radius of curvature. Then, it will behave as ($\mu_g = 1.5$) **NCERT Pg. 232**

(a) concave mirror with equivalent focal length $\frac{30}{11}$ cm.
(b) concave mirror with equivalent focal length $\frac{60}{11}$ cm.
(c) convex mirror with equivalent focal length $\frac{30}{11}$ cm.
(d) convex mirror with equivalent focal length $\frac{60}{11}$ cm.

53 The graph shows how the magnification m produced by a thin lens varies with image distance v. What is the focal length of the lens used? **NCERT Pg. 232**

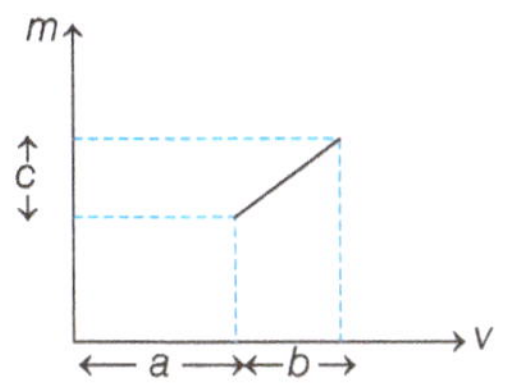

(a) $\frac{b^2c}{a}$ (b) $\frac{b^2}{ac}$ (c) $\frac{a}{c}$ (d) $\frac{b}{c}$

54 The power of a biconvex lens is 20 dioptre and the radius of curvature of each surface is 5 cm. Find the refractive index of the material of lens. **NCERT Pg. 232**
(a) $\frac{4}{3}$ (b) $\frac{3}{2}$ (c) $\frac{9}{8}$ (d) $\frac{3}{5}$

55 A convex lens of focal length 40 cm, a concave lens of focal length 40 cm and a concave lens of focal length 15 cm are placed in contact. The power of the combination in dioptre is **NCERT Pg. 232**
(a) +1.5 (b) −1.5 (c) +6.67 (d) − 6.67

56 Find the position of final image of the given object which is placed at 40 cm from first lens. Given focal length of each lens is 10 cm. **NCERT Pg. 232**

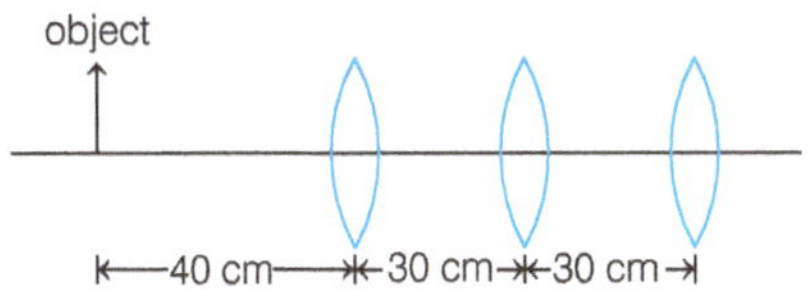

(a) 40 cm (b) 50 cm (c) 45 cm (d) 55 cm

57 A diverging lens with magnitude of focal length 25 cm is placed at a distance of 15 cm from a converging lens of magnitude of focal length 20 cm. A beam of parallel light falls on the diverging lens. The final image formed is **NCERT Pg. 232**
(a) virtual and at a distance of 40 cm from convergent lens
(b) real and at a distance of 40 cm from the divergent lens
(c) real and at a distance of 6 cm from the convergent lens
(d) real and at a distance of 40 cm from convergent lens

58 For a given lens, the magnification was found to be twice as large as when the object was 0.15 m distant from it as when the distance was 0.2 m. The focal length of the lens is **NCERT Pg. 232**
(a) 1.5 m (b) 0.20 m
(c) 0.10 m (d) 0.05 m

59 An object is placed 21 cm infront of a concave lens of radius of curvature 10 cm. A glass slab of thickness 3 cm and refractive index $\frac{3}{2}$ is then placed close to the lens in the space between the object and the lens. Distance of the near surface of the slab from the lens is 1 cm. Find the position of the final image formed **NCERT Pg. 232**
(a) 5.67 cm (b) $\frac{20}{3}$ cm
(c) 21 cm (d) 2.3 cm

60 A plano-convex lens fits exactly into a plano-concave lens. Their plane surfaces are parallel to each other. If lenses are made of different materials of refractive indices n_1 and n_2 and R is the radius of curvature of the curved surface of the lenses, then the focal length of the combination is **NCERT Pg. 232**
(a) $\frac{R}{2(n_1+n_2)}$ (b) $\frac{R}{2(n_1-n_2)}$
(c) $\frac{R}{n_1-n_2}$ (d) $\frac{2R}{n_2-n_1}$

61 Two identical thin plano-convex glass lenses (refractive index = 1.5) each having radius of curvature of 20 cm are placed with their convex surfaces in contact at the centre. The intervening space is filled with oil of refractive index 1.7. The focal length of the combination is **NCERT Pg. 232**
(a) – 20 cm (b) – 25 cm
(c) – 50 cm (d) 50 cm

Refraction Through a Prism

62 The refraction through the prisms are as shown. Pick out the wrong statements from the following path of the light ray in **NCERT Pg. 232**

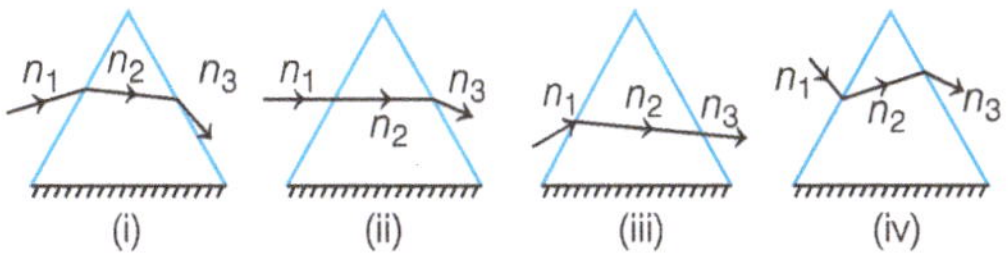

(a) (i) is correct if $n_2 > n_1$ and $n_2 > n_3$
(b) (ii) is correct if $n_1 = n_2$ and $n_2 > n_3$
(c) (ii) is correct if $n_2 > n_1$ and $n_2 = n_3$
(d) (iv) is correct if $n_1 > n_2$ and $n_2 < n_3$

63 A ray is incident at an angle of incidence i on one surface of a prism of small angle A and emerges normally from opposite surface. If the refractive index of the material of prism is μ, the angle of incidence is nearly equal to NCERT Pg. 232

(a) $\frac{A}{\mu}$ (b) $\frac{A}{2\mu}$ (c) μA (d) $\frac{\mu A}{2}$

64 Monochromatic light is incident on a glass prism of angle A. If refractive index of the material of the prism is μ,. A ray incident at an angle θ on the face AB would get transmitted through the face AC of the prism provided

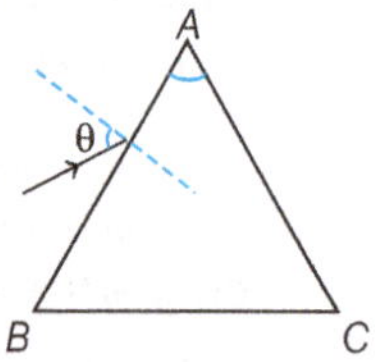

NCERT Pg. 239

(a) $\theta > \cos^{-1}\left[\mu \sin\left(A + \sin^{-1}\left(\frac{1}{\mu}\right)\right)\right]$

(b) $\theta < \cos^{-1}\left[\mu \sin\left(A + \sin^{-1}\left(\frac{1}{\mu}\right)\right)\right]$

(c) $\theta > \sin^{-1}\left[\mu \sin\left(A - \sin^{-1}\left(\frac{1}{\mu}\right)\right)\right]$

(d) $\theta < \sin^{-1}\left[\mu \sin\left(A - \sin^{-1}\left(\frac{1}{\mu}\right)\right)\right]$

65 A light ray incident normally on one of the face of a triangular prism follow the path as shown below, then the angle of refraction r_2 at the second face is NCERT Pg. 239

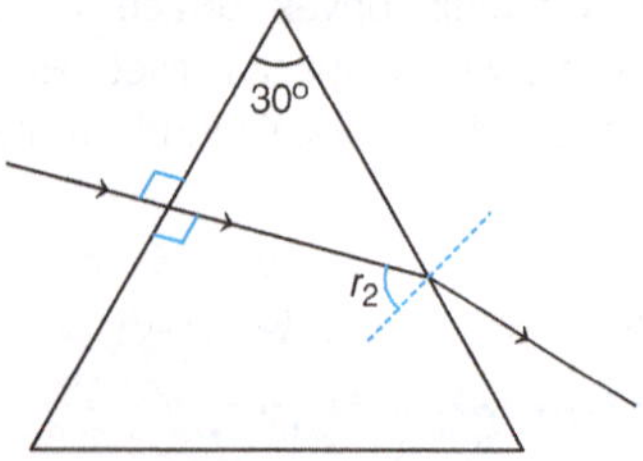

(a) 60° (b) 90° (c) 30° (d) 45°

66 The maximum value of index of refraction of a material of a prism which allows the passage of light through it when the refracting angle of prism is A is NCERT Pg. 239

(a) $\sqrt{1+\sin\left(\frac{A}{2}\right)}$ (b) $\sqrt{1+\cos\left(\frac{A}{2}\right)}$

(c) $\sqrt{1+\tan^2\left(\frac{A}{2}\right)}$ (d) $\sqrt{1+\cot^2\left(\frac{A}{2}\right)}$

67 For a prism of refractive index, 1.732, the angle of minimum deviation is equal to the angle of prism. Then, the angle of the prism is NCERT Pg. 239

(a) 60° (b) 70°

(c) 50° (d) 55°

68 If one face of prism is silvered having prism angle 30° and $n = \sqrt{2}$. What will be the angle of incidence so that the incidence ray retrace its path. NCERT Pg. 239

(a) 30° (b) 60°

(c) 90° (d) 45°

69 A light ray is incident on a glass sphere of refractive index $\mu = \sqrt{3}$ at an angle of incidence 60° as shown in the figure. The total deviation after two refractions will be NCERT Pg. 239

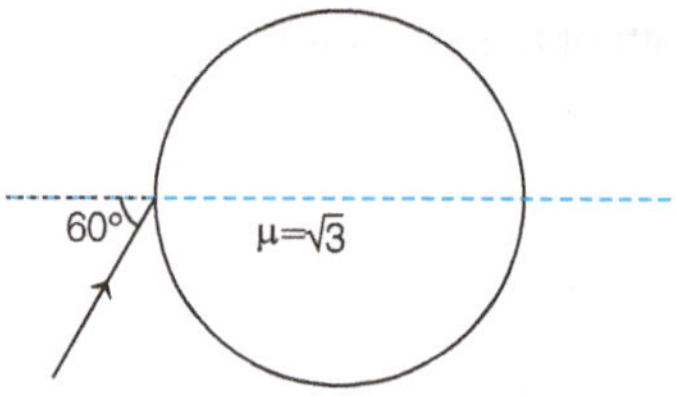

(a) 30° (b) 45°

(c) 60° (d) 120°

70 A plot of angle of deviation D *versus* angle of incidence for a triangular prism is shown below.

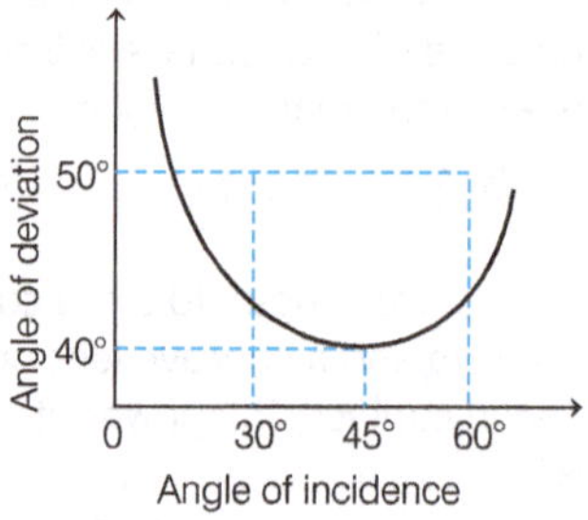

The angle of incidence for which the light ray travels parallel to the base is NCERT Pg. 239

(a) 30° (b) 60°

(c) 45° (d) Data insufficient

71 Which graph correctly represents the relation between angle of incidence and angle of deviation for a prism? NCERT Pg. 239

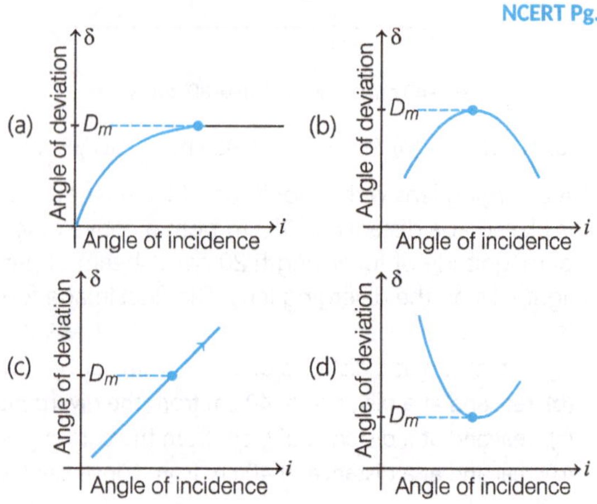

72 A ray of light passes through an equilateral prism such that, the angle of incidence is equal to the angle of emergence and the latter is equal to 3/4 the angle of prism. The angle of deviation is NCERT Pg. 239

(a) 25° (b) 30°
(c) 45° (d) 35°

73 A monochromatic light is incident at a certain angle on an equilateral triangular prism and suffers minimum deviation. If the refractive index of the material of the prism is $\sqrt{3}$, then the angle of incidence is NCERT Pg. 239

(a) 45° (b) 90° (c) 60° (d) 30°

74 The refracting angle of a prism is A, and refractive index of the material of the prism is cot $(A/2)$. The angle of minimum deviation is NCERT Pg. 239

(a) $180° - 3A$ (b) $180° - 2A$
(c) $90° - A$ (d) $180° + 2A$

75 If a light ray incident on an equilateral prism suffers minimum deviation at an angle 30°, then speed of light in the prism will be NCERT Pg. 239

(a) $\frac{3}{\sqrt{2}} \times 10^8$ m/s (b) $\frac{1}{\sqrt{2}} \times 10^8$ m/s
(c) $\frac{2}{\sqrt{3}} \times 10^8$ m/s (d) $\frac{2}{3} \times 10^8$ m/s

76 For the angle of minimum deviation of a prism to be equal to its prism angle, the prism must be made of material whose refractive index NCERT Pg. 239

(a) lies between $\sqrt{2}$ and 1
(b) lies between 2 and $\sqrt{2}$
(c) is less than 1
(d) is greater than 2

77 In an experiment for determination of refractive index of glass of a prism by i-D plot, it was found that a ray incident at an angle 35° suffers a deviation of 40° and that it emerges at an angle 79°. In that case, which of the following is closest to the maximum possible value of the refractive index? NCERT Pg. 239

(a) 1.4 (b) 1.6 (c) 1.7 (d) 1.8

78 The angle of incidence for a ray of light at a refracting surface of a prism is 45°. The angle of prism is 60°. If the ray suffers minimum deviation through the prism, the angle of minimum deviation and refractive index of the material of the prism respectively, are NCERT Pg. 239

(a) 30°; $\sqrt{2}$ (b) 45°; $\sqrt{2}$
(c) 30°; $\frac{1}{\sqrt{2}}$ (d) 45°; $\frac{1}{\sqrt{2}}$

79 A prism with refractive index $n = 1.57$ gives a deviation of 5.5°. The prism angle is NCERT Pg. 239

(a) 9.65° (b) 7.74°
(c) 5.5° (d) 8.50°

80 A prism of crown glass with refracting angle of 5° and mean refractive index = 1.51 is combined with a flint glass prism of refractive index = 1.65 to produce no deviation. Find the angle of flint glass. NCERT Pg. 239

(a) 3.92° (b) 4.68°
(c) 5.32° (d) 7.28°

81 White light is incident on one of the refracting surfaces of a prism of angle 5°. If the refractive indices for red and blue colours are 1.641 and 1.659, respectively, the angular separation between these two colours when they emerge out of the prism is NCERT Pg. 239

(a) 0.9° (b) 0.09°
(c) 1.8° (d) 1.2°

Optical Instruments

82 In a compound microscope, the focal lengths of two lenses are 1.5 cm and 6.25 cm. If an object is placed at 2 cm from objective and the final image is formed at 25 cm from eye lens. The distance between the two lenses is NCERT Pg. 240

(a) 6.00 cm (b) 7.75 cm
(c) 9.25 cm (d) 11.0 cm

83 A person with normal near point 25 cm using a compound microscope with objective of focal length 8.0 mm and an eyepiece of focal length 2.5 cm can bring an object placed at 9.0 mm from the objective in sharp focus. The separation between two lenses NCERT Pg. 240

(a) 9.47 cm (b) 3.36 cm
(c) 6.00 cm (d) 7.49 cm

84 Focal length of the lenses of an astronomical telescope are 50 cm and 5 cm. Length of the telescope when the image is formed at the least distance of distinct vision is NCERT Pg. 240

(a) 45 cm (b) 55 cm
(c) $\frac{275}{6}$ cm (d) $\frac{325}{6}$ cm

85 The final image in an astronomical telescope with respect to object is NCERT Pg. 240

(a) virtual and erect
(b) real and erect
(c) real and inverted
(d) virtual and inverted

86 A card sheet divided into square each of size 1 mm^2 is being seen through a magnifying glass lens of focal length 10 cm. The card is placed at a distance of 9 cm from the lens. The apparent area of the card through the lens is NCERT Pg. 240

(a) 1 cm^2 (b) 0.81 cm^2
(c) 0.27 cm^2 (d) 0.60 cm^2

87 In a microscope, the focal lengths of two lenses are 1.2 cm and 6.25 cm. If an object is placed at 2 cm and the final image is formed at 25 cm from eye lens. The distance between the two lenses is NCERT Pg. 240

(a) 6.00 cm (b) 8.00 cm
(c) 7.75 cm (d) 9.25 cm

88 A compound microscope has an objective with focal length $f_o = 1.0$ cm, an eyepiece with focal length, $f_e = 2.0$ cm and a tube length of 20 cm, then the magnification is NCERT Pg. 240

(a) 200 (b) 250
(c) 100 (d) 150

89 A compound microscope has an objective of focal length 2.0 cm and an eyepiece of focal length 6.25 cm and distance between the objective and eyepiece is 15 cm. If the final image is formed at the least distance of distinct vision (25 cm), the distance of the object form the objective is NCERT Pg. 240

(a) 1.5 cm (b) 2.5 cm
(c) 3.0 cm (d) 4.0 cm

90 The diameter of the moon is 3.5×10^3 km and its distance from the earth is 3.8×10^5 km. It is seen by a telescope having the focal length of the objective and the eye-piece as 4 m and 10 cm, respectively. The diameter of the image of the moon will be approximately. NCERT Pg. 240

(a) 2° (b) 20°
(c) 40° (d) 50°

91 If focal length of objective and eye lenses are 10 cm and 10 mm respectively, then angular magnification of telescope in normal adjustment is NCERT Pg. 240

(a) 10 (b) 5
(c) 100 (d) 50

92 An astronomical telescope has an angular magnification of magnitude 5 for distant objects. The separation between the objective and the eyepiece is 36 cm and the final image is formed at infinity.

The focal length f_o of the objective and the focal length f_e of the eyepiece, respectively are NCERT Pg. 240

(a) 45 cm and −9 cm
(b) − 7.2 cm and 5 cm
(c) 50 cm and 10 cm
(d) 30 cm and 6 cm

93 A reflecting telescope has an objective lens of focal length 150 cm and an eyepiece of focal length 5.0 cm. What is the separation between the objective and the eyepiece? NCERT Pg. 240

(a) 1.25 m (b) 1.55 m
(c) 1.3 m (d) 1.8 m

94 In an astronomical telescope in normal adjustment a straight black line of length L is drawn on inside part of objective lens. The eyepiece forms a real image of this line. The length of this image is l. The magnification of the telescope is NCERT Pg. 240

(a) $\frac{L}{l} + 1$ (b) $\frac{L}{l} - 1$
(c) $\frac{L+1}{L-1}$ (d) $\frac{L}{l}$

95 An observer looks at a distant tree of height 10 m with a telescope of magnifying power 20. To observer, the tree appears NCERT Pg. 240

(a) 10 times taller (b) 10 times nearer
(c) 20 times taller (d) 20 times nearer

96 F_1 and F_2 are focal lengths of objective and eyepiece. respectively, of the telescope. The angular magnification of the given telescope is equal to NCERT Pg. 240

(a) $\frac{F_1}{F_2}$ (b) $\frac{F_2}{F_1}$ (c) $\frac{F_1F_2}{F_1 + F_2}$ (d) $\frac{F_1 + F_2}{F_1F_2}$

97 A telescope consists of two thin lenses of focal lengths 0.3 m and 3 cm, respectively. It is focused on moon which subtends an angle of 0.5° at the objective. Then, the angle subtended at the eye by the final image will be NCERT Pg. 240

(a) 5° (b) 0.25°
(c) 0.5° (d) 0.35°

98 If the focal length of objective lens is increased, then magnifying power of NCERT Pg. 240

(a) microscope will increase but that of telescope will decrease
(b) microscope and telescope both will increase
(c) microscope and telescope both will decrese
(d) microscope will decrease but that of telescope will increase

99 Which of the following statement is incorrect. NCERT Pg. 240

(a) A simple microscope is a converging lens of small focal length.
(b) For microscope, the magnification in case of image formed at infinity is one more than the magnification, when image is at near point.
(c) For larger magnification, one uses two lenses, one compounding, the effect of the other know as compound microscope.
(d) The lens nearest the object is called objective and near the eye is known as eyepiece.

Assertion and Reason Questions

Direction (Q. Nos.1-10) *In the following questions, a statement of Assertion is followed by a corresponding statement of Reason. Of the following statements, choose the correct one.*

(a) Both Assertion and Reason are correct and Reason is the correct explanation of Assertion.
(b) Both Assertion and Reason are correct but Reason is not the correct explanation of Assertion.
(c) Assertion is correct but Reason is incorrect.
(d) Assertion is incorrect but Reason is correct.

1 **Assertion** A ray of light incident along the normal to the plane mirror retraces its path after reflection from the mirror.
Reason A ray of light along the normal has angle of incidence as $\pi/2$. NCERT Pg. 222

2 **Assertion** The image of an extended object placed perpendicular to the principal axis of a mirror, will be erect, if the object is real but the image is virtual.
Reason The image of an extended object, placed perpendicular to the principal axis of a mirror, will be erect, if the object is virtual but the image is real. NCERT Pg. 225

3 **Assertion** The refractive index of diamond is $\sqrt{6}$ and that of liquid is $\sqrt{3}$. If the light travels from diamond to the liquid, it will totally reflected when the angle of incidence is 30°.
Reason $n = \frac{1}{\sin i_c}$, where n is the refractive index of diamond with respect to liquid and i_c is the critical angle. NCERT Pg. 229

4 **Assertion** Propagation of light through an optical fibre is due to total internal reflection taking place at the core-clade interface.
Reason Refractive index of the material of the core of the optical fibre is greater than that of cladding. NCERT Pg. 229

5 **Assertion** The property of convergent lens of converging rays remain same in all media.
Reason Property of lens, whether the rays are diverging or converging depends on the surrounding medium. NCERT Pg. 232

6 **Assertion** If the focal length of the mirror is f and distance of the object from the focus is u, then magnification of the mirror is f/u.
Reason Magnification $= \frac{\text{Size of image}}{\text{Size of object}}$ NCERT Pg. 222

7 **Assertion** Thin prisms do not deviate light much.
Reason Thin prism have small angle A and hence, D_m (minimum deviation) is also very small as $D_m = [({}^1n_2 - 1)\,A]$, where ${}^1n_2$ is the refractive index of prism w.r.t. medium 1. NCERT Pg. 239

8 **Assertion** Refractive index of glass with respect to air is different for red light and violet light.
Reason Refractive index of a pair of media depends on the wavelength of light used. NCERT Pg. 232

9 **Assertion** When white light passes through a prism, bending of red component is most but for the violet it is least.
Reason Red colour travels faster than violet in glass. NCERT Pg. 239

10 **Assertion** The resolving power of a telescope is more, if the diameter of the objective lens is more.
Reason Objective lens of large diameter collects more light. NCERT Pg. 245

Statement Based Questions

Direction (Q. No. 1-8) *In the following questions Statement I and Statement II are given. Read then statements and choose most appropriate answer from the options given below :*

(a) Both Statement I and Statement II are incorrect
(b) Statement I is correct but Statement II is incorrect.
(c) Statement I is incorrect but Statement II is correct
(d) Both Statement I and Statement II are correct.

1 **Statement I** The incident ray, reflected ray and the normal to the reflecting surface at the point of incidence lie in two planes.
Statement II The line joining the pole and the centre of curvature of the spherical mirror is known as the principal axis. NCERT Pg. 222

2 **Statement I** For concave mirror, the reflected rays appears to diverge from a point F and for convex mirror converge at the point F (F is called principal focus of the mirror).
Statement II If parallel beam of light were incident, making some angle with the principal axis, the reflected rays would converge (or appear to diverge) from a

point in the focal plane through F normal to the principal axis. NCERT Pg. 222

3 **Statement I** The reflected ray goes through the focus of the mirror, when it is incident parallel to the principal axis.

Statement II For the ray incident at any angle at the pole, the reflected ray follows laws of reflection. NCERT Pg. 222

4 **Statement I** The velocity of light inside the glass slab is same for different colours.
Statement II A ray of white light shows no dispersion on emerging from a rectangular glass slab. NCERT Pg. 228

5 **Statement I** Optical fibre are extensively used for transmitting audio and video signals through long distances.

Statement II There is appreciable loss in the intensity of light signal. NCERT Pg. 229

6 **Statement I** Total internal reflection happens when light passes from a denser to rarer medium at an angle greater than the critical angle.
Statement II If light travelling from transparent glass to air undergoes total internal reflection at an angle of incidence of 30°, then refractive index of the glass is 1.5. NCERT Pg. 230

7 **Statement I** If angle of incidence in case of a prism is gradually increased, then deviation produced by prism will first decrease, then increase.
Statement II At minimum deviation, $r_1 = A/2$. NCERT Pg. 231

8 **Statement I** If objective and eyepiece of a microscope are interchanged, then it work as a telescope.
Statement II The objective lens of telescope has small focal length. NCERT Pg. 245

Matching Type Questions

1 A layer of ice $(n = 4/3)$ lies on a glass plate $(n = 3/2)$. A ray of light makes an angle of incidence 60° on the surface of ice as shown in the figure below. NCERT Pg. 228

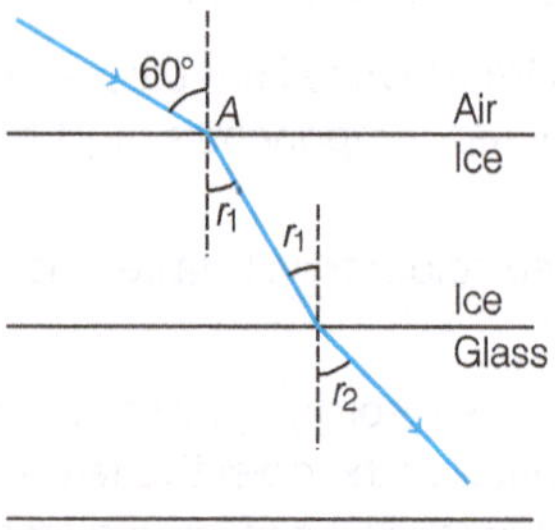

With reference to the above figure, match the Column I (parameter) with Column II (value).

Column I	Column II
A. $\sin r_1$	1. $1/\sqrt{3}$
B. $\sin r_2$	2. $3\sqrt{3}/8$
C. Refractive Index of ice w.r.t. glass	3. $8/9$
D. $\sin 60° + \frac{4}{3}\sin r_1$	4. $2 \sin 60°$

Choose the correct answer from the codes given below.

Codes

	A	B	C	D		A	B	C	D
(a)	1	4	3	2	(b)	2	1	3	4
(c)	2	3	1	4	(d)	1	3	4	2

2 A light ray passes through triangular prism with prism angle $A = 60°$ and $\mu = n = 1.5$. With reference to the above situation, match the Column I (angle) with Column II (value). NCERT Pg. 239

[Some useful data, $2\sin^{-1}(0.75) = 97°$,

$\sin^{-1}(2/3) = 42°$ and $\sin^{-1}(0.463) = 28°$]

Column I	Column II
A. Minimum deviation (D_{min})	1. 58°
B. Maximum deviation (D_{max})	2. 37°
C. The angle of refraction r_1 when maximum deviation occurs	3. 42°
D. Angle of emergence	4. 28°

Choose the correct answer from the codes given below.

Codes

	A	B	C	D		A	B	C	D
(a)	1	4	3	2	(b)	4	2	1	3
(c)	2	1	3	4	(d)	3	4	2	1

3 Radius of curvature and refractive index of all lenses are same for the following question. Regarding the focal lengths, match the Column I with Column II. NCERT Pg. 239

	Column I		Column II
A.		1.	$2f$
B.		2.	$-f$
C.		3.	f
D.		4.	$\frac{f}{2}$

Choose the correct answer from the codes given below.

Codes

	A	B	C	D		A	B	C	D
(a)	1	3	4	2	(b)	1	4	3	2
(c)	2	1	3	4	(d)	4	3	2	1

Numerical Type Questions

1 A thin cylindrical rod of length 10 cm is placed horizontally on the principal axis of a concave mirror of focal length 20 cm. The rod is placed in such a way that mid-point of the rod is at 40 cm from the pole of mirror. The length of the image formed by the mirror will be $\frac{x}{3}$ cm. The value of x is .... NCERT Pg. 222

2 Cross-section view of a prism is the equilateral triangle ABC in the figure. The minimum deviation is observed using this prism when the angle of incidence is equal to the prism angle. The time taken by light to travel from P (mid-point of BC) to A is .... $\times 10^{-10}$ s. NCERT Pg. 239

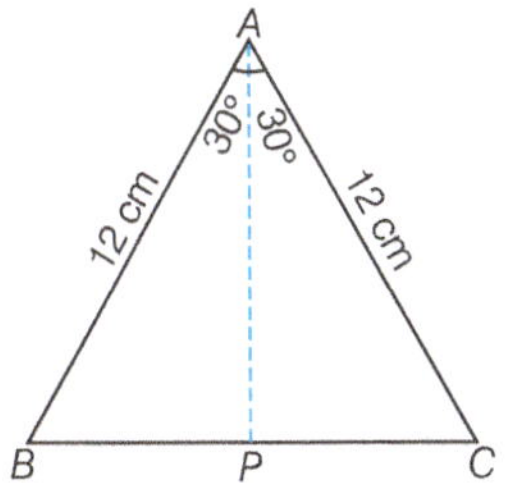

3 As shown in the figure, a combination of a thin plano concave lens and a thin plano convex lens is used to get image of an object placed at infinity. The radius of curvature of both the lenses is 30 cm and refractive index of the material for both the lenses is 1.75. Both the lenses are placed at distance of 40 cm from each other. Due to the combination, the image of the object is formed at distance $x = \ldots$ cm, from concave lens. NCERT Pg. 232

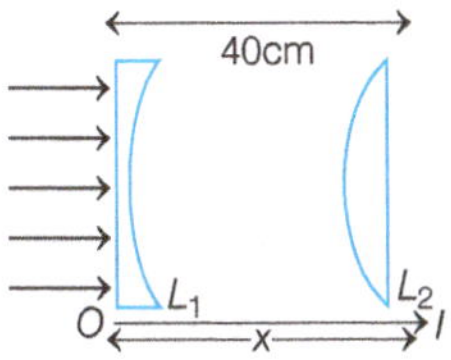

4 An object viewed from a near point distance of 30 cm, using a microscopic lens with magnification 7, gives an unresolved image. A resolved image is observed at infinite distance with a total magnification double the earlier using an eyepiece along with the given lens and a tube of length 0.7 m, if the focal length of the eyepiece is equal to .... cm. NCERT Pg. 240

5 Light enters at an angle of incidence in a transparent rod of refractive index μ. For the value $\sqrt{x}$ of the refractive index of the material of the rod such that, the light once entered into it and will not leave it through its lateral face whatsoever be the value of angle of incidence. The value of x is .... NCERT Pg. 229

6 A point source of light is placed 4 m below the surface of water of refractive index $\frac{5}{3}$. The minimum diameter of a disc which should be placed over the source on the surface of water to cut-off all light coming out of water is ...... m. NCERT Pg. 229

7 A thin glass lens of refractive index (1.5) has optical power −5D in air. Its optical power in a liquid medium with refractive index (1.6) is ...... D. NCERT Pg. 232

8 A luminous object is placed at a distance of 30 cm from the convex lens of focal length 15 cm. On the other side of the lens, at what distance (in cm) from the lens a convex mirror of radius of curvature 10 cm, be placed in order to have an upright image of the object coincident with it? NCERT Pg. 232

9 The focal length of a convex lens of refractive index 1.5 is 2 cm. Focal length of lens when immersed in a liquid of refractive index 1.25 is ...... cm. NCERT Pg. 232

10 An astronomical telescope of ten-fold angular magnification has a length of 55 cm. The focal length of the objective is ...... cm. NCERT Pg. 240

NCERT Exemplar Questions

1 An object approaches a convergent lens from the left of the lens with a uniform speed 5 ms^{-1} and stops at the focus. The image
(a) moves away from the lens with an uniform speed 5 ms^{-1}
(b) moves away from the lens with an uniform acceleration
(c) moves away from the lens with a non- uniform acceleration
(d) moves towards the lens with a non-uniform acceleration

2 The radius of curvature of the curved surface of a plano-convex lens is 20 cm. If the refractive index of the material of the lens be 1.5, it will
(a) act as a convex lens only for the objects that lie on its curved side
(b) act as a concave lens for the objects that lie on its curved side
(c) act as a convex lens irrespective of the side on which the object lies
(d) act as a concave lens irrespective of side on which the object lies

3 The direction of ray of light incident on a concave mirror is shown by PQ while directions in which the ray would travel after reflection is shown by four rays marked 1,2,3 and 4 as shown in figure. Which of the four rays correctly shows the direction of reflected ray?

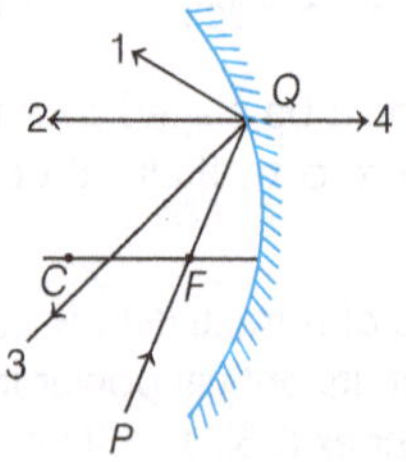

(a) 1 (b) 2 (c) 3 (d) 4

4 The optical density of turpentine is higher than that of water while its mass density is lower. Figure shows a layer of turpentine floating over water in a container. For which one of the four rays incident on turpentine in figure, the path shown is correct?

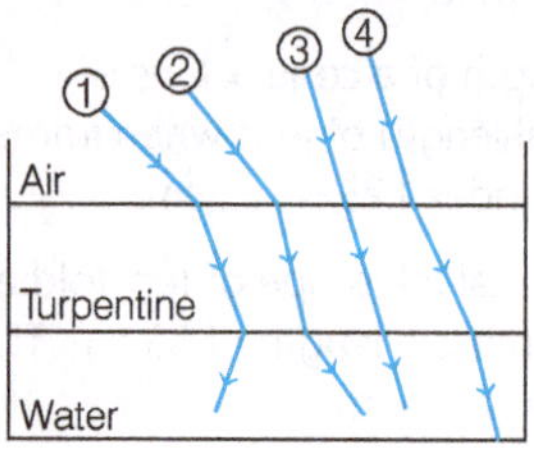

(a) 1 (b) 2 (c) 3 (d) 4

5 There are certain materials developed in laboratories which have a negative refractive index (figure shown below). A ray incident from air (medium 1) into such a medium (medium 2) shall follow a path given by

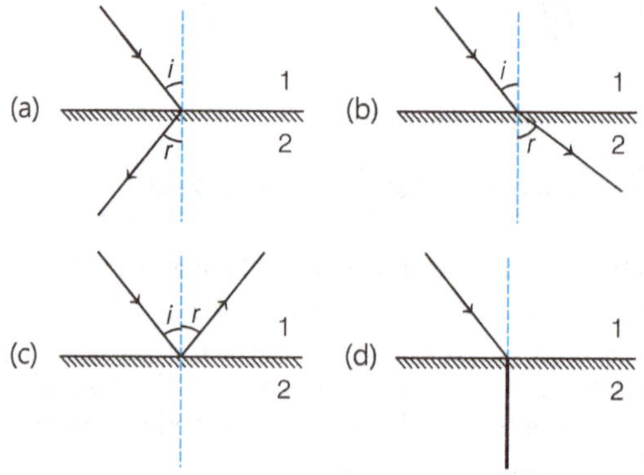

6 A rectangular block of glass $ABCD$ has a refractive index 1.6. A pin is placed midway on the face AB figure. When observed from the face AD, the pin shall

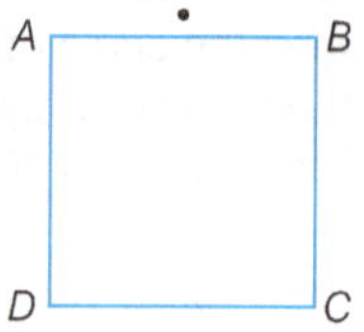

(a) appear to be near B
(b) appear to be near D
(c) appear to be at the centre of AD
(d) not be seen at all

7 The near vision of an average person is 25 cm. To view an object with an angular magnification of 10, what should be the power of the microscope?
(a) 10 D (b) 20 D (c) 40 D (d) 30 D

8 Three immiscible liquids of densities $d_1 > d_2 > d_3$ and refractive indices $n_1 > n_2 > n_3$ are put in a beaker. The height of each liquid column is $\frac{h}{3}$. A dot is made at the bottom of the beaker. For near normal vision, find the apparent depth of the dot?
(a) $\frac{h}{3}\left(\frac{1}{n_1}+\frac{1}{n_2}+\frac{1}{n_3}\right)$ (b) $3h\left(\frac{1}{n_1}+\frac{1}{n_2}-\frac{1}{n_3}\right)$
(c) $\frac{h}{3}\left(\frac{1}{n_1}-\frac{1}{n_2}+\frac{1}{n_3}\right)$ (d) $3h\left(\frac{1}{n_1}-\frac{1}{n_2}-\frac{1}{n_3}\right)$

9 For a glass prism $(n=\sqrt{3})$, the angle of minimum deviation is equal to the angle of the prism. Find the angle of the prism.
(a) 40° (b) 45° (c) 60° (d) 75°

Past Exams Questions

NEET

1 A light ray enters through a right angled prism at point P with the angle of incidence 30° as shown in figure. It travels through the prism parallel to its base BC and emerges along the face AC. The refractive index of the prism is NCERT Pg. 239, NEET 2024

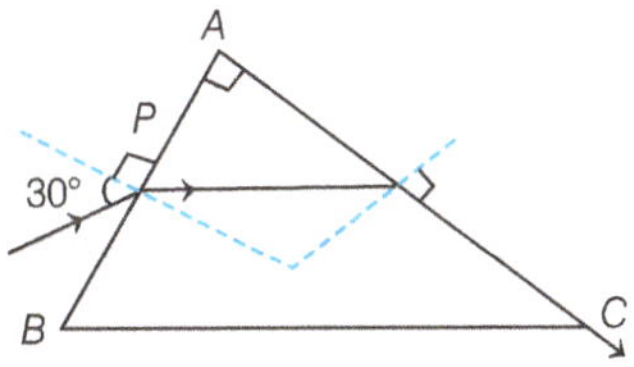

(a) $\sqrt{5}/4$ (b) $\sqrt{5}/2$ (c) $\sqrt{3}/4$ (d) $\sqrt{3}/2$

2 A small telescope has an objective of focal length 140 cm and an eyepiece of focal length 5.0 cm. The magnifying power of telescope for viewing a distant object is NCERT Pg. 240, NEET 2024

(a) 34 (b) 28 (c) 17 (d) 32

3 Light travels a distance x in time t_1 in air and $10x$ in time t_2 in another denser medium. What is the critical angle for this medium? NCERT Pg. 229, NEET 2023

(a) $\sin^{-1}\left(\frac{10t_2}{t_1}\right)$ (b) $\sin^{-1}\left(\frac{t_1}{10t_2}\right)$

(c) $\sin^{-1}\left(\frac{10t_1}{t_2}\right)$ (d) $\sin^{-1}\left(\frac{t_2}{t_1}\right)$

4 In the figure shown here, what is the equivalent focal length of the combination of lenses (Assume that all layers are thin)? NCERT Pg. 232, NEET 2023

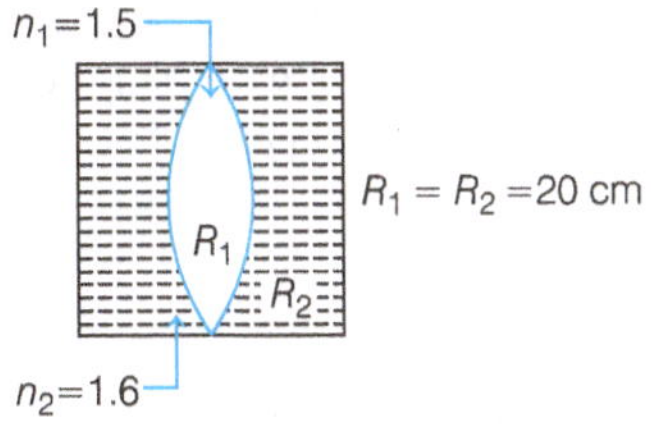

(a) – 40 cm (b) – 100 cm (c) – 50 cm (d) 40 cm

5 A biconvex lens has radii of curvature, 20cm each. If the refractive index of the material of the lens is 1.5, the power of the lens is NCERT Pg. 232, NEET 2022

(a) + 20 D (b) + 5 D (c) infinity (d) + 2 D

6 Find the value of the angle of emergence from the prism. Refractive index of the glass is $\sqrt{3}$. NCERT Pg. 239, NEET 2021

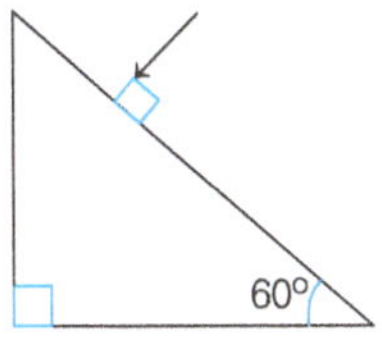

(a) 60° (b) 30°
(c) 45° (d) 90°

7 A point object is placed at a distance of 60 cm from a convex lens of focal length 30 cm. If a plane mirror were put perpendicular to the principal axis of the lens and at a distance of 40 cm from it, the final image would be formed from the plane mirror at a distance of NCERT Pg. 232, NEET 2021

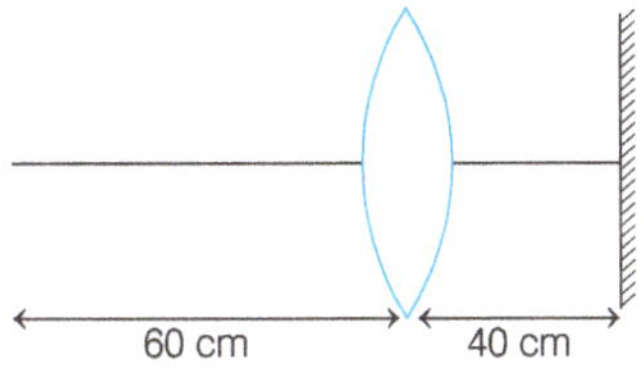

(a) 20 cm from the lens, it would be a real image
(b) 30 cm from the lens, it would be a real image
(c) 30 cm from the plane mirror, it would be a virtual image
(d) 20 cm from the plane mirror, it would be a virtual image

8 If the critical angle for total internal reflection from a medium to vacuum is 45°, then velocity of light in the medium is NCERT Pg. 239, NEET 2020

(a) 1.5×10^8 m/s (b) $\frac{3}{\sqrt{2}} \times 10^8$ m/s

(c) $\sqrt{2} \times 10^8$ m/s (d) 3×10^8 m/s

9 A ray is incident at an angle of incidence i on one surface of a small angle prism (with angle of prism A) and emerges normally from the opposite surface. If the refractive index of the material of the prism is μ, then the angle of incidence is nearly equal to NCERT Pg. 239, NEET 2020

(a) $\frac{2A}{\mu}$ (b) μA (c) $\frac{\mu A}{2}$ (d) $\frac{A}{2\mu}$

10 An equi-convex lens has power P it is cut into two symmetrical halves by a plane containing the principal axis. The power of one part will be NCERT Pg. 232, NEET 2019

(a) 0 (b) $\frac{P}{2}$ (c) $\frac{P}{4}$ (d) P

11 Two similar thin equi-convex lenses, of focal length f each, are kept co-axially in contact with each other such that the focal length of the combination is F_1. When the space between the two lenses is filled with glycerine (which has the same refractive index ($\mu = 1.5$) as that of glass) then the equivalent focal length is F_2. The ratio $F_1 : F_2$ will be NCERT Pg. 232, NEET 2019

(a) 1 : 2 (b) 2 : 3 (c) 3 : 4 (d) 2 : 1

12 The refractive index of the material of a prism is $\sqrt{2}$ and the angle of the prism is 30°. One of the two refracting surfaces of the prism is made a mirror inwards, by silver coating. A beam of monochromatic light entering the prism from the other face will retrace its path (after reflection from the silvered surface) if its angle of incidence on the prism is NCERT Pg. 232, NEET 2018

(a) 30° (b) 45°
(c) 60° (d) zero

JEE Main

13 The position of the image formed by the combination of lenses is NCERT Pg. 232, JEE Main 2024

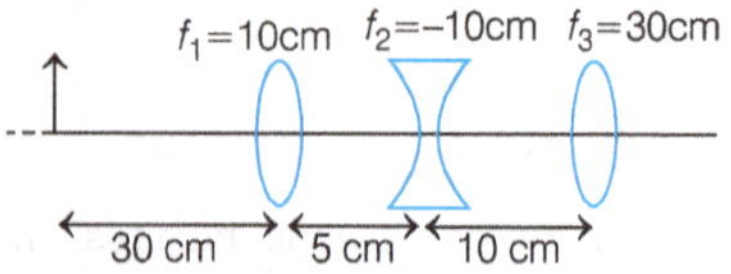

(a) 30 cm (left of third lens)
(b) 30 cm (right of third lens)
(c) 15 cm (right of second lens)
(d) 15 cm (left of second lens)

14 The following figure represents two biconvex lenses L_1 and L_2 having focal length 10 cm and 15 cm respectively. The distance between L_1 and L_2 is NCERT Pg. 232, JEE Main 2024

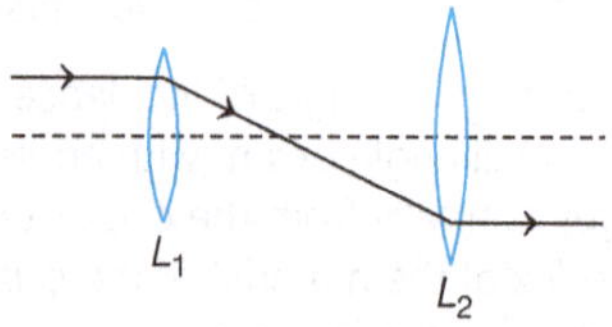

(a) 15 cm (b) 10 cm
(c) 35 cm (d) 25 cm

15 Two objects A and B are placed at 15 cm and 25 cm from the pole in front of a concave mirror having radius of curvature 40 cm. The distance between the images formed by the mirror is .... NCERT Pg. 222, JEE Main 2023

(a) 60 cm (b) 40 cm (c) 160 cm (d) 100 cm

16 The difference of speed of light in the two media A and B, $(v_A - v_B)$ is 2.6×10^7 m/s. If the refractive index of medium B is 1.47, then the ratio of refractive index of medium B to medium A is (Given : speed of light in vacuum $c = 3 \times 10^8$ ms^{-1}) NCERT Pg. 228, JEE Main 2023

(a) 1.303 (b) 1.318 (c) 1.13 (d) 0.12

17 A ray of light entering from air into a denser medium of refractive index 4 / 3, as shown in figure. The light ray suffers total internal reflection at the adjacent surface as shown. The maximum value of angle θ should be equal to NCERT Pg. 229, JEE Main 2021

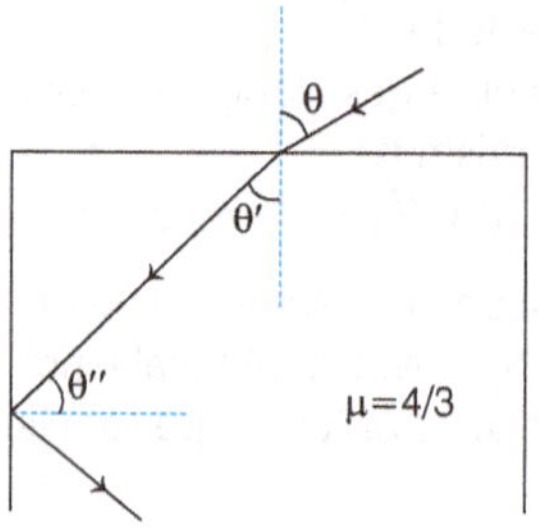

(a) $\sin^{-1}\frac{\sqrt{7}}{3}$ (b) $\sin^{-1}\frac{\sqrt{5}}{4}$
(c) $\sin^{-1}\frac{\sqrt{7}}{4}$ (d) $\sin^{-1}\frac{\sqrt{5}}{3}$

18 The magnifying power of a telescope with tube length 60 cm is 5. What is the focal length of its eyepiece? NCERT Pg. 240, JEE Main 2020

(a) 10 cm (b) 20 cm
(c) 30 cm (d) 40 cm

19 In figure, the optical fibre is $l = 2$ m long and has a diameter of $d = 20\ \mu$m. If a ray of light is incident on one end of the fibre at angle $\theta_1 = 40°$, the number of reflections it makes before emerging from the other end is close to (refractive index of fibre is 1.31 and $\sin 40° = 0.64$) NCERT Pg. 229, JEE Main 2019

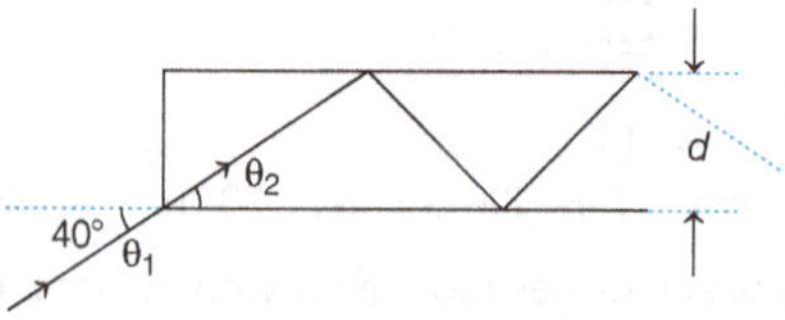

(a) 55000 (b) 66000
(c) 45000 (d) 57000

Skill Boosters

1 Three right angled prisms of refractive indices are fitted together, so that the faces of the middle prisms are in contact with one of the outside prisms. If the ray passes through the composite block and emerges without any deviation, then

(a) $\mu_1^2 + \mu_3^2 + \mu_2^2 = 1$
(b) $\mu_1^2 + \mu_3^2 - \mu_2^2 = 1$
(c) $\mu_1^2 - \mu_3^2 + \mu_2^2 = 1$
(d) $\mu_1 + \mu_2 - \mu_3 = 1$

2 A small object is placed at the bottom of a beaker containing a liquid of refractive index $\frac{10}{3}$ to a depth of 20 cm. A pin is placed horizontally over the beaker and adjusted until there is no parallax between the image of the pin formed by reflection at the liquid surface and the image of the object. The height of the pin above the liquid surface is found to be x cm, then the value of x is
(a) 6 (b) 9
(c) 4 (d) 3

3 If the optical path between two points A and B in first medium is same as the optical path between two points D and E in the second medium. Then, the ratio of time taken by light to travel from points A to B to time taken to travel from points C to D is
(a) 5 (b) 2 (c) 1 (d) 4

4 A ray of light is incident on a slab of refractive index $\mu = 2$ at an angle of incidence 60° as shown in the figure. The thickness of slab is 1 m. The lateral shifting in the ray is

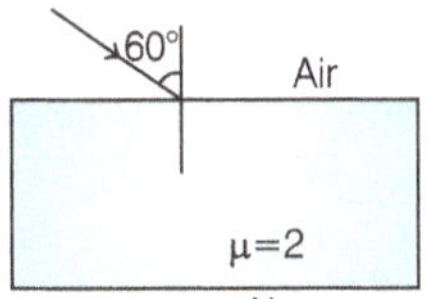

(a) 1 m (b) 0.5 m
(c) $\frac{\sqrt{3}}{2\sqrt{13}}(\sqrt{13}-1)$ m (d) 2 m

5 A rod of length L lies along the axis of a concave mirror of focal length f. The near end of the rod is at a distance $L > f$ from the mirror. Its image will have a length
(a) $\frac{Lf^2}{(L-f)(2L-f)}$ (b) $\frac{L^2f}{(L-f)(2L-f)}$
(c) $\frac{2Lf^2}{(L-f)(2L-f)}$ (d) $\frac{2L^2f}{(L-f)(2L-f)}$

6 A cube of side length 1 mm is placed at distance 30 cm from the pole of a concave mirror of focal length 20 cm. Its one side is parallel optical axis as shown in the figure. Find the magnification in the volume of cube.

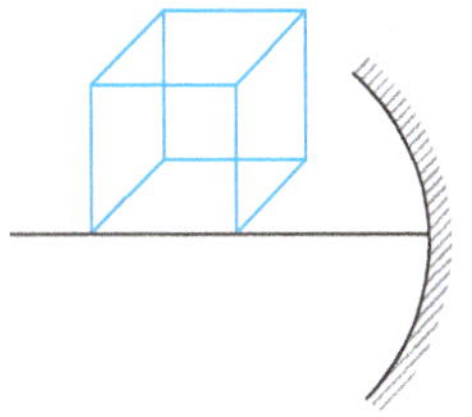

(a) 4 (b) 2 (c) 16 (d) 24

7 Two optical media have a plane boundary between them. Suppose C is the critical angle of incidence of a beam and i is the angle of incidence at which the refracted beam is perpendicular to the reflected one (the beam is assumed to come from an optically denser medium). Find the relative refracted index of these media, if $\sin C / \sin i = \eta = 1.28$.
(a) 2.25 (b) 1.25 (c) 1.50 (d) 1.75

8 A point source of light is kept on the principal axis of convex lens at a distance of 30 cm. On the side of convex lens, a convex mirror of radius of curvature 10 cm is placed in order to have an upright image of the object coincide with centre of curvature of convex mirror. The distance between lens and mirror is
(a) 25 cm (b) 50 cm
(c) 40 cm (d) 60 cm

9 A bird is flying up on an angle 37° with the vertical with a speed of 10 cms^{-1}. A fish in a pond looks at the bird. When it is vertically above the fish? $\left(\text{Take, } \mu_{water} = \frac{4}{3}\right)$
(a) The speed of image of bird is 10.24 cms^{-1}.
(b) The speed of image of bird is 10.67 cms^{-1}
(c) The angle at which bird appears to fly to the fish is $\tan^{-1}\left(\frac{9}{16}\right)$ with vertical.
(d) The angle at which bird appears to fly to the fish is $\tan^{-1}\left(\frac{16}{9}\right)$ with vertical.

Correct Codes

Topical Questions

1 (c)	2 (a)	3 (b)	4 (d)	5 (d)	6 (d)	7 (d)	8 (b)	9 (c)	10 (d)
11 (a)	12 (d)	13 (c)	14 (a)	15 (b)	16 (d)	17 (c)	18 (c)	19 (d)	20 (b)
21 (c)	22 (c)	23 (a)	24 (b)	25 (b)	26 (a)	27 (a)	28 (a)	29 (d)	30 (b)
31 (c)	32 (c)	33 (b)	34 (a)	35 (c)	36 (b)	37 (b)	38 (a)	39 (c)	40 (a)
41 (b)	42 (a)	43 (a)	44 (d)	45 (c)	46 (b)	47 (a)	48 (d)	49 (a)	50 (b)
51 (d)	52 (b)	53 (d)	54 (b)	55 (d)	56 (b)	57 (d)	58 (c)	59 (a)	60 (c)
61 (c)	62 (d)	63 (c)	64 (c)	65 (c)	66 (d)	67 (a)	68 (d)	69 (c)	70 (c)
71 (d)	72 (b)	73 (c)	74 (b)	75 (a)	76 (b)	77 (a)	78 (a)	79 (a)	80 (a)
81 (b)	82 (d)	83 (a)	84 (d)	85 (d)	86 (a)	87 (b)	88 (b)	89 (b)	90 (b)
91 (a)	92 (d)	93 (b)	94 (d)	95 (d)	96 (a)	97 (a)	98 (d)	99 (b)	

Assertion and Reason Questions

1 (c)	2 (b)	3 (d)	4 (b)	5 (d)	6 (d)	7 (a)	8 (a)	9 (d)	10 (b)

Statement Based Questions

1 (c)	2 (c)	3 (d)	4 (c)	5 (b)	6 (b)	7 (d)	8 (a)

Matching Type Questions

1 (b)	2 (c)	3 (c)

Numerical Type Questions

1 (32)	2 (6)	3 (120)	4 (30)	5 (2)	6 (6)	7 (1)	8 (20)	9 (5)	10 (50)

NCERT Exemplar Questions

1 (c)	2 (c)	3 (b)	4 (b)	5 (a)	6 (d)	7 (c)	8 (a)	9 (c)

Past Exams Questions

1 (b)	2 (b)	3 (c)	4 (b)	5 (b)	6 (a)	7 (d)	8 (b)	9 (b)	10 (d)
11 (a)	12 (b)	13 (b)	14 (d)	15 (c)	16 (c)	17 (a)	18 (a)	19 (d)	

Skill Boosters

1 (b)	2 (a)	3 (c)	4 (c)	5 (a)	6 (c)	7 (b)	8 (b)	9 (c)

Step by Step

Decoding the Questions

Concept Builders

1 2θ

2 $n = \frac{360°}{\theta} - 1$

3 No change

4 True (T)

5 $4f$

6 increases

7 True (T)

8 Thickness and refractive index

9 0°, 90°

10 concave

11 – 30

12 False (F)

13 False (F)

14 True (T)

15 True (T)

16 shorter

17 False (F)

18 decreases

19 large, large

20 True (T)

Topical Questions

1 (c)

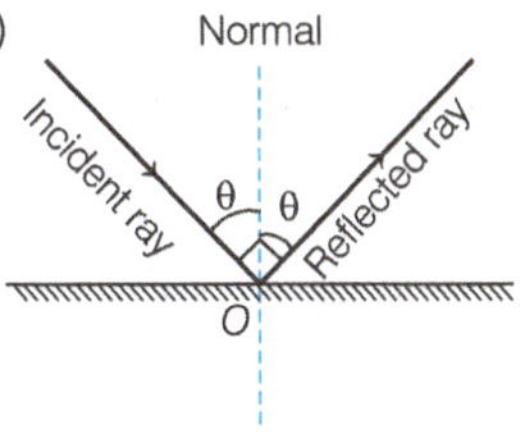

$\Rightarrow \quad \theta + \theta = 2\theta = 90°$ (from figure)

$\Rightarrow \quad \theta = 45°$

2 (a)

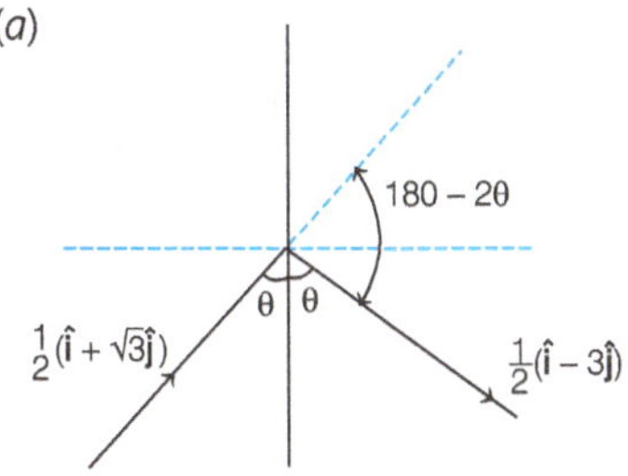

$$\cos(180° - 2\theta) = \frac{\mathbf{a} \cdot \mathbf{b}}{|\mathbf{a}||\mathbf{b}|}$$

$$= -\frac{1}{2} = \cos 120°$$

or $\quad \theta = 30°$

3 (b) The focal length of a mirror is $f = \frac{R}{2}$

where, R is the radius of curvature of mirror.

Here, $\quad R = 16$ cm

$\therefore \quad f = \frac{16}{2} = 8$ cm

5 (d)

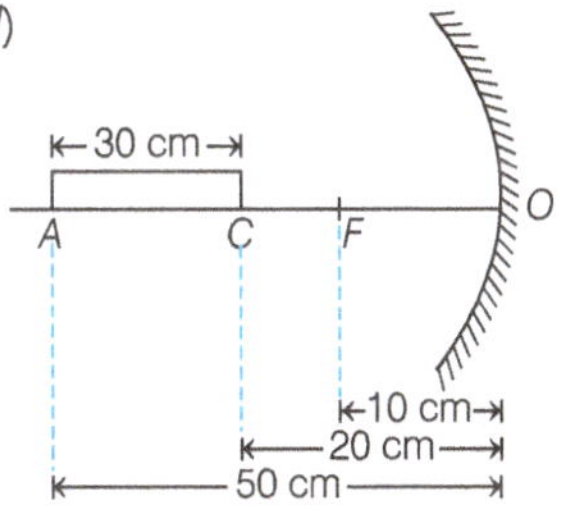

By mirror formula, image distance of point A,

$$\frac{1}{v_A} + \frac{1}{u_A} = \frac{1}{f}$$

$$\Rightarrow \quad \frac{1}{v_A} = \frac{1}{-10} - \frac{1}{(-50)}$$

$$\Rightarrow \quad v_A = -12.5 \text{ cm}$$

Similarly, image distance of C

$$\frac{1}{v_C} + \frac{1}{u_C} = \frac{1}{f}$$

$$\Rightarrow \frac{1}{v_C} - \frac{1}{20} = \frac{-1}{10} \Rightarrow v_C = -20 \text{ cm}$$

$\therefore$ The length of image $= |v_A - v_C|$

$= |-12.5 - (-20)| = 7.5$ cm

6 (d) We know that,

$$v = \left(\frac{uf}{u - f}\right) \quad \text{...(i)}$$

On differentiating Eq. (i) w.r.t. u, we get

$$\Rightarrow \quad dv = -\left(\frac{f}{u - f}\right)^2 du$$

$$|dv| = \left(\frac{f}{u - f}\right)^2 |du| \quad \text{...(ii)}$$

Here, $\quad$ image size $= |dv|$, object size $= |du| = b$

$$\text{Image size} = b\left(\frac{f}{u - f}\right)^2$$

7 (d) As a concave mirror can form a real or a virtual image, magnfication

$$m = \pm 3$$

From mirror formula,

$$\frac{1}{v} + \frac{1}{u} = \frac{1}{f}$$

Case I $\quad m = \frac{-v}{u} \Rightarrow 3 = \frac{-v}{-x}$

$$v = 3x$$

$$\therefore \quad \frac{1}{3x} - \frac{1}{x} = -\frac{1}{30}$$

$$\Rightarrow \quad x = 20 \text{ cm}$$

$$\therefore \quad u = -20 \text{ cm}$$

Case II $\quad m = -3$

$$\Rightarrow \quad \frac{f}{f - u} = -3$$

$$\Rightarrow \quad u = -40 \text{ cm}$$

8 (b) From mirror formula,

$$\frac{1}{u} + \frac{1}{v} = \frac{1}{f}, -\frac{1}{u^2}\frac{du}{dt} - \frac{1}{v^2}\frac{dv}{dt} = 0$$

$$\therefore \quad \frac{dv}{dt} = \frac{-v^2}{u^2}\left(\frac{du}{dt}\right)$$

$$= -\left(\frac{10}{30}\right)^2 \times 9 = -1 \text{ m/s}$$

$$\Rightarrow \quad \left|\frac{dv}{dt}\right| = 1 \text{ m/s}$$

9 (c) Magnification, $m = -2$ (real image)

$$\Rightarrow \quad m = -\frac{v}{u} = -2, u = -30 \text{ cm}$$

$$\Rightarrow \quad v = -60 \text{ cm}$$

Focal length is

$$\frac{i}{f} = \frac{1}{v} + \frac{1}{u} = \frac{1}{-60} + \frac{1}{-30}$$

$$\Rightarrow \quad f = -20 \text{ cm}$$

For same magnification $|m| = 2$ or $m = +2$

$\Rightarrow -\frac{v}{2} = +2$ or $v = -2u$

Let $u = -x$ then, $\frac{1}{f} = \frac{1}{v} + \frac{1}{u}$

$$\Rightarrow \frac{1}{-20} = \frac{1}{2x} + \frac{1}{-x}$$

$$\Rightarrow -\frac{1}{20} = -\frac{1}{2x} \text{ or } x = 10 \text{ cm.}$$

So, object distance is 10 cm from mirror.

10 (*d*) From mirror formula,

$$\frac{1}{v} + \frac{1}{u} = \frac{1}{f} = \frac{2}{R}$$

$$\frac{1}{v} + \frac{1}{u} = \frac{2}{-36} = \frac{1}{-18} \quad \text{...(i)}$$

Given that

$$\frac{-v}{u} = -\frac{1}{9}$$

$$\therefore \quad v = \frac{u}{9} \quad \text{...(ii)}$$

From Eqs. (i) and (ii)

$$\frac{9}{u} + \frac{1}{u} = \frac{1}{-18}$$

$$u = -180 \text{ cm}$$

11 (*a*) As, linear magnification,

$$m = \frac{h_2}{h_1} = \frac{-v}{u}$$

where, *v* is image distance.

$$\Rightarrow \quad v = \frac{-h_2}{h_1} \times u$$

$$= -\frac{(-3)}{2} \times (-16) = -24 \text{ cm}$$

Now, using mirror formula,

$$\frac{1}{f} = \frac{1}{v} + \frac{1}{u} = -\frac{1}{24} - \frac{1}{16}$$

$$= \frac{-2-3}{48} = \frac{-5}{48}$$

$$\Rightarrow \quad f = \frac{-48}{5} = -9.6 \text{ cm}$$

13 (*c*) $-\frac{v}{u} = 5$ or $v = -5u$

Using mirror formula,

$$\frac{1}{v} + \frac{1}{u} = \frac{1}{f}$$

$$\frac{1}{-5u} + \frac{1}{u} = -\frac{1}{0.4}$$

$$\Rightarrow \quad u = -\frac{1.6}{5} = -0.32 \text{ m}$$

14 (*a*) Focal length of the mirror,

$$f = \frac{R}{2} = \frac{2}{2} = 1 \text{ m}$$

Also, image distance, $u = -39$ m

From the mirror Eq. we get

$$v = \frac{fu}{u-f} \quad \text{...(i)}$$

$$v = \frac{(-39)\times 1}{-39-1} = \frac{39}{40} \text{ m}$$

$$u = -39 + (5 \times 1)$$

$$= -39 + 5 = -34 \text{ m}$$

$$\therefore \quad v = \frac{(-34)\times 1}{-34-1} = \frac{34}{35} \text{ m}$$

The shift in the position of image in 1s is

$$\frac{39}{40} - \frac{34}{35} = \frac{1365 - 1360}{1400}$$

$$= \frac{5}{1400} = \frac{1}{280} \text{ m}$$

$$= 0.3 \times 10^{-2} \text{ m/s}$$

15 (*b*) Given, speed of the mirror $= v$

∴ Relative velocity of both mirrors

$$= v - (-v)$$

$$= 2v$$

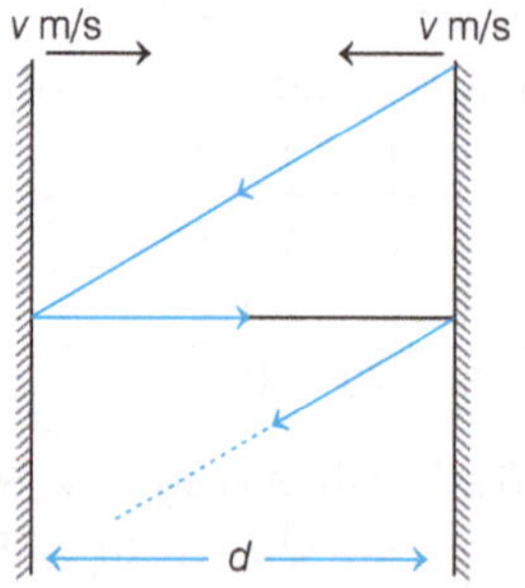

$$t = \frac{d}{2v}$$

Let in time *t* particle moves a distance of *s* m.

$$\therefore \quad s = 4v \times \frac{d}{2v}$$

$$s = 2d$$

17 (*c*) $^{a}n_g = \frac{\sin i}{\sin r} = \frac{\sin 50^\circ}{\sin 40^\circ} \quad \text{...(i)}$

Similarly,

$$^{a}n_w = \frac{\sin 50^\circ}{\sin 45^\circ} \quad \text{...(ii)}$$

$$^{w}n_g = \frac{\sin 45^\circ}{\sin \theta} \quad \text{...(iii)}$$

As, $^{a}n_w \times {}^{w}n_g = {}^{a}n_g$

$$\Rightarrow \frac{\sin 50^\circ}{\sin 45^\circ} \times \frac{\sin 45^\circ}{\sin \theta} = \frac{\sin 50^\circ}{\sin 40^\circ}$$

[using Eqs. (i), (ii) and (iii)]

$\sin\theta = \sin 40^\circ$ or $\theta = 40^\circ$

18 (*c*) From the figure,

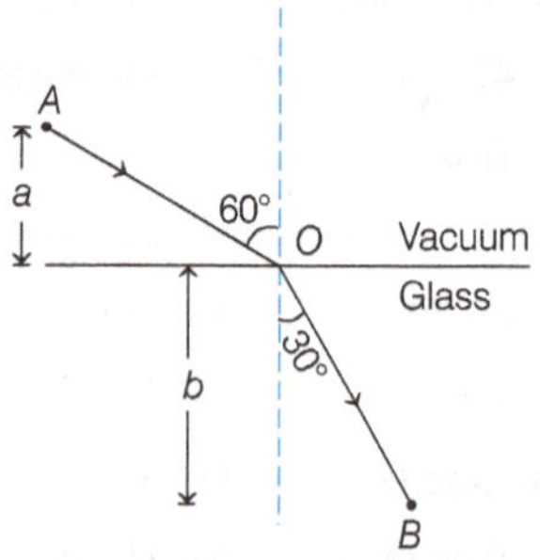

$$\Rightarrow \quad AO = \frac{a}{\cos 60^\circ} = 2a$$

$$\text{or,} \quad BO = \frac{b}{\cos 30^\circ} = \frac{2}{\sqrt{3}} b$$

Optical path length of light ray

$$= AO + \mu\,(BO)$$

Here, μ can be determined using Snell's law, i.e.

$$\mu = \frac{\sin 60^\circ}{\sin 30^\circ} = \frac{\sqrt{3}/2}{1/2} = \sqrt{3}$$

$$\therefore \text{ Optical path} = 2a + (\sqrt{3} \times \frac{2}{\sqrt{3}} b)$$

$$= 2a + 2b$$

19 (*d*)

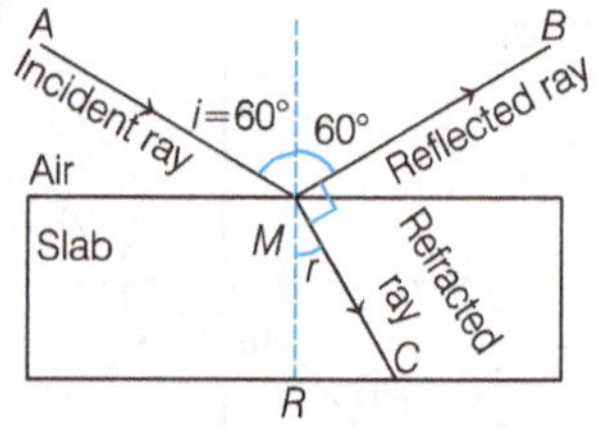

$$\angle r = 180^\circ - 90^\circ - 60^\circ = 30^\circ$$

From Snell's law,

$$\frac{\sin i}{\sin r} = \frac{n_{slab}}{n_{air}}$$

$$\Rightarrow \quad \frac{\sin 60^\circ}{\sin 30^\circ} = \frac{n_{slab}}{1.0}$$

$$\therefore \; n_{slab} = \left(\frac{\sqrt{3}}{2}\right) \times 2 = \sqrt{3}$$

20 (*b*)

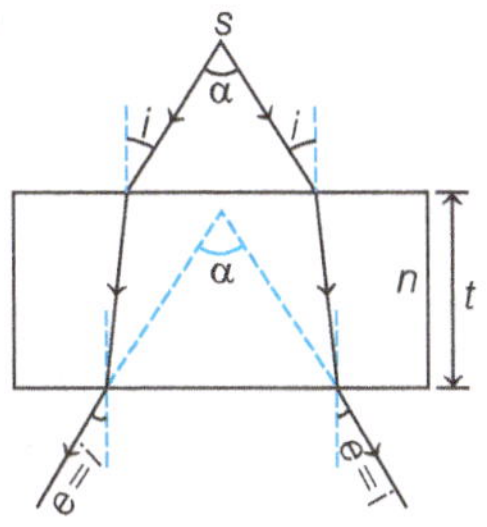

Also, $i = e$.

So, divergent angle of the emergent beam is also same, i.e. α.

21 (*c*) The given beaker is as shown below.

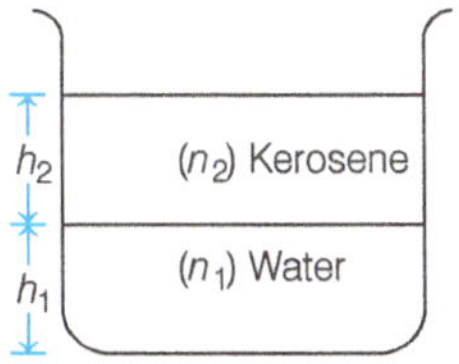

Apparent depth of the bottom of the beaker

$$= \frac{h_1}{n_1} + \frac{h_2}{n_2}$$

Thus, apparent shift = real depth − apparent depth

$$= (h_1 + h_2) - \left(\frac{h_1}{n_1} + \frac{h_2}{n_2}\right)$$

$$= h_1\left(1 - \frac{1}{n_1}\right) + h_2\left(1 - \frac{1}{n_2}\right)$$

22 (*c*) Apparent depth of the object

$$= \frac{\text{Real depth}}{\text{Refractive index}}$$

$$= \frac{33.25}{1.33} \text{ cm}$$

Distance of object from the mirror

$$= 15 + \frac{33.25}{1.33} = 40 \text{ cm}$$

Similarly, distance of image from the mirror $= 15 + \dfrac{25}{1.33}$

$$= 33.8 \text{ cm}$$

For concave mirror,

$$f = \frac{uv}{u + v}$$

$$= \frac{(-40)\,(-33.8)}{(-40 - 33.8)}$$

$$= -18.3 \text{ cm}$$

23 (*a*) $n_{water} = \dfrac{h_1}{h_2} = \dfrac{13}{8.5} = 1.53$

Let h_3 be the new apparent depth of the screw

$$\therefore \quad n' = \frac{h_1}{h_3}$$

or, $$h_3 = \frac{h_1}{n'} = \frac{13}{1.70} = 7.65 \text{ cm}$$

∴ Distance by which microscope should be moved up

$$= 8.5 - 7.65 = 0.85 \text{ cm}$$

24 (*b*)

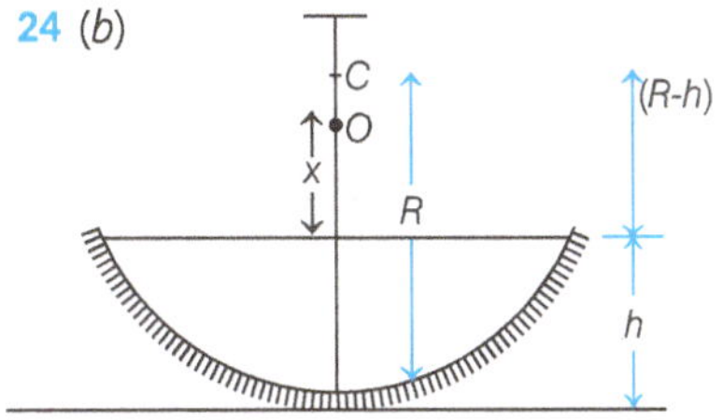

Since, $$\frac{\text{Real depth}}{\text{Apparent depth}} = \frac{1}{\mu}$$

$$\frac{x}{R - h} = \frac{1}{\mu}$$

$$\therefore \quad x = \frac{R - h}{\mu}$$

26 (*a*) Given, $n_{oil} = 2$, $n_{glass} = 3/2$

Velocity of light in oil is given by

$$v_{oil} = \frac{\text{Velocity of light } (c)}{n_{oil}} = \frac{c}{n_{oil}}$$

Similarly, $$v_{glass} = \frac{c}{n_{glass}}$$

$$\therefore \quad \frac{v_{glass}}{v_{oil}} = \frac{c/n_{glass}}{c/n_{oil}}$$

$$= \frac{n_{oil}}{n_{glass}} = \frac{2}{3/2} = \frac{4}{3}$$

27 (*a*)

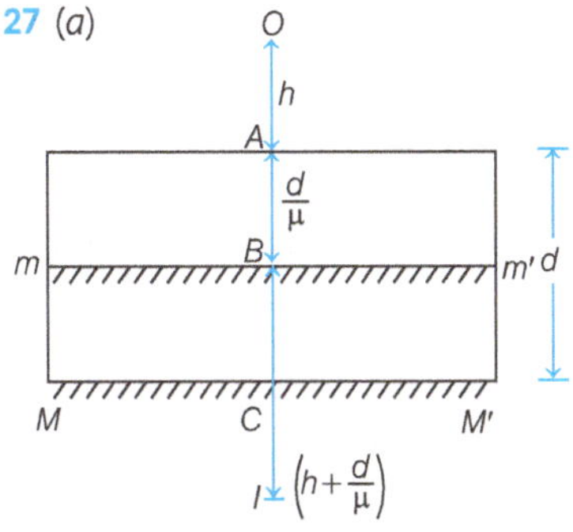

The distance of apparent mirror mm' from front face of observer is

$$AB = \frac{d}{\mu}$$

∴ Distance of image I of object O from mirror mm' is

$$BI = \left(h + \frac{d}{\mu}\right)$$

∴ Distance of image I from front face is

$$AI = \frac{d}{\mu} + \left(h + \frac{d}{\mu}\right) = \left(h + \frac{2d}{\mu}\right)$$

28 (*a*)

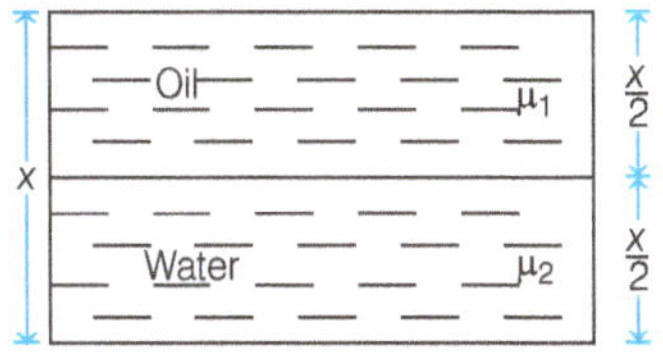

The apparent depth of vessel when it is viewed from above is

$$\text{Apparent depth} = \frac{x/2}{\mu_1} + \frac{x/2}{\mu_2}$$

$$= \frac{x(\mu_1 + \mu_2)}{2\mu_1\mu_2}$$

30 (*b*) The given figure can be drawn as follows

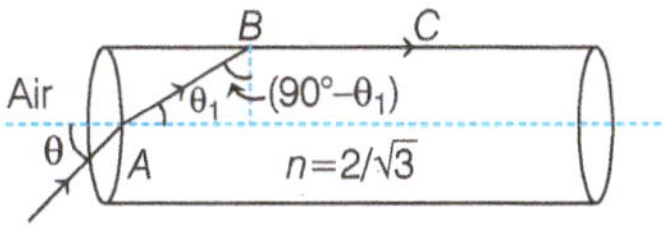

$$i_C = \sin^{-1}\frac{1}{n} \qquad \text{...(i)}$$

⇒ $(90° - \theta_1)$ = critical angle (i_C)

$$\sin(90° - \theta_1) = \frac{\sqrt{3}}{2} \text{ (using Eq. (i))}$$

$$\Rightarrow \quad \theta_1 = 30°$$

Now, using Snell's law on 1st interface,

$$n_1 \sin\theta = n_2 \sin\theta_1$$

$$\Rightarrow \quad 1 \sin\theta = \frac{2}{\sqrt{3}} \sin 30°$$

$$\Rightarrow \quad \theta = \sin^{-1}\left(\frac{1}{\sqrt{3}}\right)$$

31 (*c*) We know that, $\sin\theta = \dfrac{n_2}{n_1}$

$$\Rightarrow \quad \sin\theta = \frac{v}{v'}$$

$$\Rightarrow \quad v' = \frac{v}{\sin\theta}$$

32 (c)

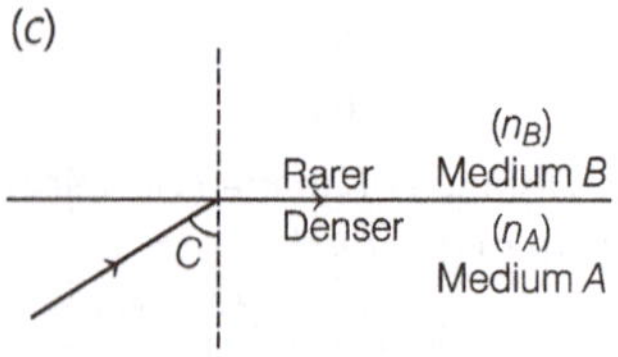

Since, critical angle for a pair of media

$$i_C = \sin^{-1}\left(\frac{n_r}{n_d}\right)$$

As, $\frac{v_A}{v_B} = \frac{n_B}{n_A} = \frac{n_r}{n_d}$

$$\frac{n_r}{n_d} = \frac{2 \times 10^8}{2.5 \times 10^8} = \frac{4}{5}$$

$\therefore \quad i_C = \sin^{-1}\left(\frac{4}{5}\right)$

33 (b)

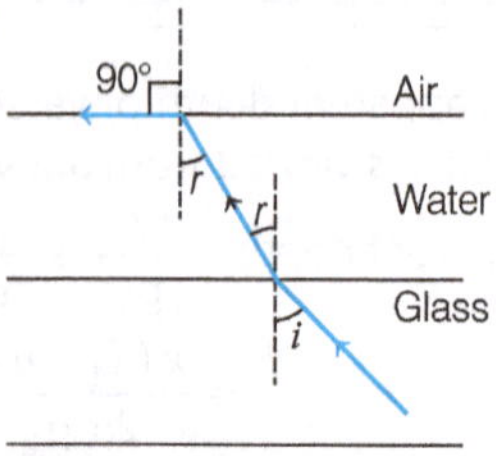

For glass-water interface, applying Snell's law

$\Rightarrow \quad n_g = \frac{n_w \sin r}{\sin i} \quad$ ...(i)

Again, $\frac{\sin r}{\sin 90°} = \frac{n_a}{n_w} = \frac{1}{n_w}$

$\Rightarrow \quad \sin r = \frac{1}{n_w} \quad$ ...(ii)

From Eqs. (i) and (ii), we get

$$n_g = \frac{(n_w) \times \left(\frac{1}{n_w}\right)}{\sin i} \Rightarrow n_g = \frac{1}{\sin i}$$

34 (a)

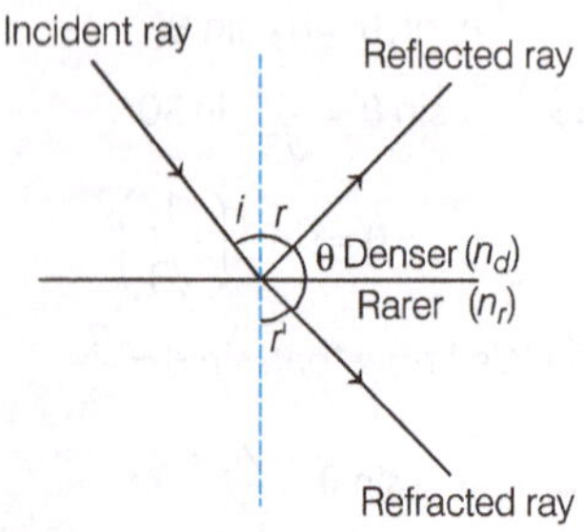

From figure, $r + \theta + r' = 180°$

or, $\quad i + r' = 90° \quad (\because i = r) \quad$ ...(i)

Applying Snell's law,

$$\frac{\sin i}{\sin r'} = \frac{n_r}{n_d} \quad \text{...(ii)}$$

Also, critical angle $= i_C = \sin^{-1}\left(\frac{n_r}{n_d}\right)$

$\Rightarrow \quad i_C = \sin^{-1}\left(\frac{\sin i}{\sin r'}\right)$ [using Eq. (ii)]

So, $i_C = \sin^{-1}\left(\frac{\sin i}{\cos i}\right) = \sin^{-1}(\tan i)$

or $\quad i_C = \sin^{-1}(\tan r) \quad (\because i = r)$

35 (c) As, critical angle, $i_C = \sin^{-1}\left(\frac{n_r}{n_d}\right)$

For total internal reflection at surface AB, $\theta > i_C$

$\Rightarrow \quad \theta > \sin^{-1}\left(\frac{\sqrt{2}}{2}\right) \quad$ ...(i)

Also, for total internal reflection at surface CD,

$$\theta > \sin^{-1}\left(\frac{\sqrt{3}}{2}\right) \quad \text{...(ii)}$$

For both Eqs. (i) and (ii) to be correct, $\theta > \sin^{-1}\left(\frac{\sqrt{3}}{2}\right)$

$\because \quad \sin^{-1}\left(\frac{\sqrt{3}}{2}\right) > \sin^{-1}\left(\frac{\sqrt{2}}{2}\right)$

Hence, for total internal reflection at both surfaces AB and CD is possible, when

$\Rightarrow \quad \theta > 60°$

$\therefore \quad \theta_{min} = 60°$

36 (b) Critical angle, $i_C = \sin^{-1}\left(\frac{n_r}{n_d}\right)$

$$= \sin^{-1}\left(\frac{n_0/8}{n_0/6}\right) = \sin^{-1}\left(\frac{3}{4}\right)$$

$\Rightarrow \sin i_C = \frac{3}{4} \quad$ ...(i)

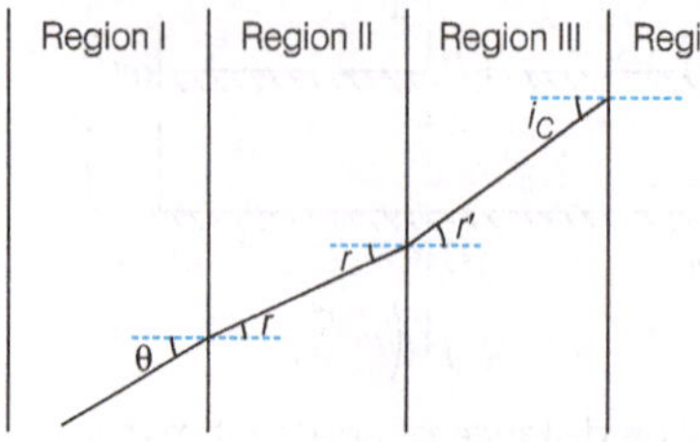

Applying Snell's law at interface,

$n_1 \sin\theta = n_2 \sin r = n_3 \sin r' =$ constant

$\Rightarrow \quad n_1 \sin\theta = n_3 \sin r'$

$\Rightarrow \quad \sin\theta = \frac{1}{6} \times \frac{3}{4} = \frac{1}{8} \quad$ [from Eq. (i)]

$\Rightarrow \quad \theta = \sin^{-1}\left(\frac{1}{8}\right)$

37 (b) $u = -50$ cm, $\mu_1 = 1$, $\mu_2 = 1.5$, $R = 10$ cm

$\therefore \quad \frac{\mu_2}{v} - \frac{\mu_1}{u} = \frac{\mu_2 - \mu_1}{R}$

$\Rightarrow \quad \frac{1.5}{v} - \frac{1}{-50} = \frac{1.5 - 1}{10}$

$\therefore \quad v = 50$ cm

39 (c) From lens Maker's formula

$$\frac{n_2}{v} - \frac{n_1}{u} = \frac{n_2 - n_1}{R}$$

$$\frac{1.5}{v} + \frac{1}{100} = \frac{0.5}{20}$$

$\Rightarrow \quad v = +100$ cm

40 (a)

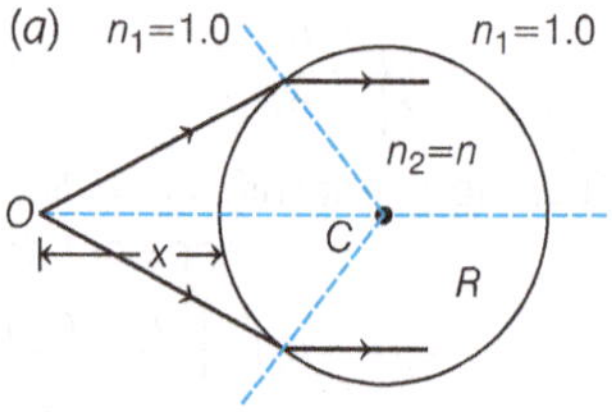

$$\frac{n_2}{v} - \frac{n_1}{u} = \frac{n_2 - n_1}{R}$$

$\Rightarrow \quad \frac{n}{\infty} - \frac{1}{(-x)} = \frac{n-1}{+R}$

$(\therefore n_1 = 1$ and $n_2 = n)$

or, $\quad x = \frac{R}{(n-1)}$

41 (b)

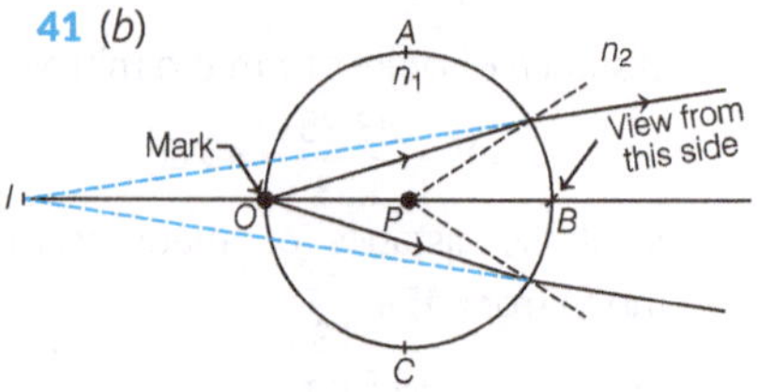

$$\frac{n_2}{v} - \frac{n_1}{u} = \frac{n_2 - n_1}{R}$$

$$\frac{1}{v} - \frac{1.5}{(-30)} = \frac{(1-1.5)}{(-15)}$$

$\Rightarrow \quad v = -60$ cm

42 (*a*) Let $PO = OQ = x$

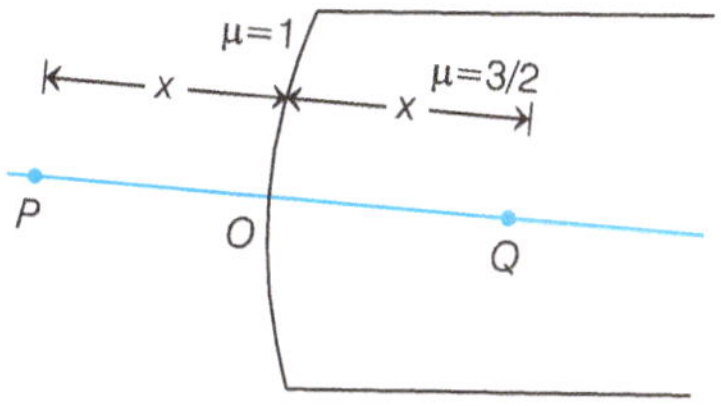

$$\frac{\mu_2}{v} - \frac{\mu_1}{u} = \frac{\mu_2 - \mu_1}{R}$$

$$\frac{\frac{3}{2}}{x} - \frac{1}{-x} = \frac{\frac{3}{2} - 1}{R}$$

$$x = 5R$$

43 (*a*) $\frac{n_2}{v} - \frac{n_1}{u} = \frac{n_2 - n_1}{R}$

$$\frac{1}{v} - \frac{\frac{3}{2}}{30} = \frac{1 - \frac{3}{2}}{20}$$

$$v = +40 \text{ cm}$$

44 (*d*) From Snell's law, $\mu = \frac{\sin i}{\sin r}$

$$\tan 30° = \frac{\sin r}{\sin i} \Rightarrow \frac{1}{\sqrt{3}} = \frac{\sin r}{\sin i} = \frac{1}{\mu}$$

$\Rightarrow$ $$\mu = \sqrt{3}$$

$\therefore$ $$n = \frac{1}{\mu} = \frac{1}{\sqrt{3}} = (3)^{-1/2}$$

45 (*c*) $\frac{1}{f} = \left(\frac{n_2}{n_1} - 1\right)\left(\frac{1}{R_1} - \frac{1}{R_2}\right)$

For a glass-lens in air, focal length,

$$\frac{1}{f_{air}} = \frac{1}{f} = \left(\frac{n_g}{n_a} - 1\right)\left(\frac{1}{R_1} - \frac{1}{R_2}\right) \quad \text{... (i)}$$

When lens is dipped in a liquid, its focal length,

$$\frac{1}{f_{liquid}} = \frac{1}{f_1} = \left(\frac{n_g}{n_l} - 1\right)\left(\frac{1}{R_1} - \frac{1}{R_2}\right) \quad \text{... (ii)}$$

From Eqs. (i) and (ii), we have

$$\frac{f_1}{f} = \frac{\left(\frac{n_g}{n_a} - 1\right)}{\left(\frac{n_g}{n_l} - 1\right)}$$

$$\frac{f_1}{f} = \frac{\left(\frac{1.5}{1} - 1\right)}{\left(\frac{1.5}{1.42} - 1\right)} = \frac{71}{8} \approx 9$$

46 (*b*) $\frac{1}{f_1} = ({}^a n_g - 1)\left(\frac{1}{R_1} - \frac{1}{R_2}\right)$ ...(i)

When lens is immersed in liquid,

$$\frac{1}{f_2} = ({}^l n_g - 1)\left(\frac{1}{R_1} - \frac{1}{R_2}\right) \quad \text{...(ii)}$$

On dividing Eq. (i) by Eq. (ii), we get,

$$\frac{f_2}{f_1} = \frac{({}^a n_g - 1)}{({}^l n_g - 1)}$$

$$\Rightarrow \quad \frac{f_2}{f_1} = \frac{(1.5 - 1)}{\left(\frac{1.5}{1.25} - 1\right)}$$

or $\quad f_2 = 2.5 f_1$

47 (*a*) Applying lens Maker's formula,

$$\frac{1}{f} = ({}^m n_g - 1)\left(\frac{1}{R_1} - \frac{1}{R_2}\right)$$

$$= \left(\frac{1.5}{1.75} - 1\right)\left(\frac{1}{-R} - \frac{1}{+R}\right)$$

$$\Rightarrow \quad f = \frac{1.75}{0.25 \times 2} R$$

$$= \frac{7}{2} R = +3.5 R$$

48 (*d*) $\frac{1}{f} = ({}^1 n_2 - 1)\left(\frac{1}{R_1} - \frac{1}{R_2}\right)$

expression $\left(\frac{1}{R_1} - \frac{1}{R_2}\right)$ is negative.

So, $({}^1 n_2 - 1) > 0 \Rightarrow \frac{n_2}{n_1} > 1$

or, $\quad n_2 > n_1$

Thus, if the lens is filled with L_2 having refractive index n_{L_2} and placed in L_1 having refractive index n_{L_1}, the above condition will be satisfied and it will diverge a parallel beam of light.

49 (*a*) Using lens Maker's formula,

$$\frac{1}{f} = (n - 1)\left(\frac{1}{R_1} - \frac{1}{R_2}\right) \quad \text{...(i)}$$

$$\frac{1}{f} = (1.33 - 1)\left(\frac{1}{10} + \frac{1}{10}\right)$$

$$\Rightarrow \quad f = 15.15 \text{ cm}$$

image distance,

$$v = \frac{uf}{u + f} = \frac{-5 \times 15.15}{-5 + 15.15}$$

$$= -7.46 \text{ cm}$$

50 (*b*)

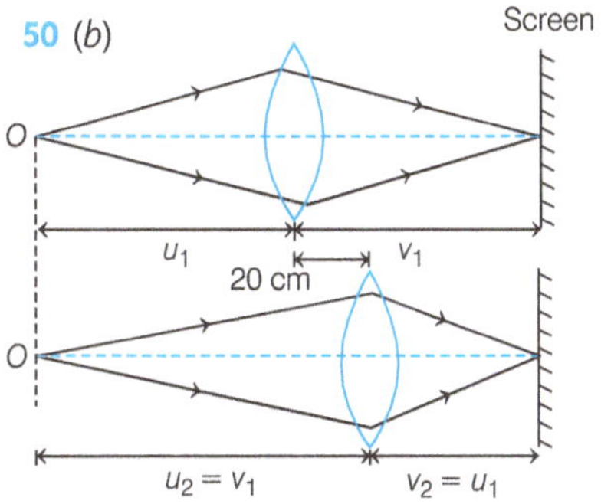

Given, $u_1 + v_1 = 90$ cm

$v_1 - u_1 = 20$ cm

Solving, $v_1 = 55$ cm, $u_1 = 35$ cm

From the lens formula,

$$\frac{1}{v_1} - \frac{1}{u_1} = \frac{1}{f}$$

$$\frac{1}{55} - \frac{1}{-35} = \frac{1}{f}$$

$$f = 21.4 \text{ cm}$$

51 (*d*)

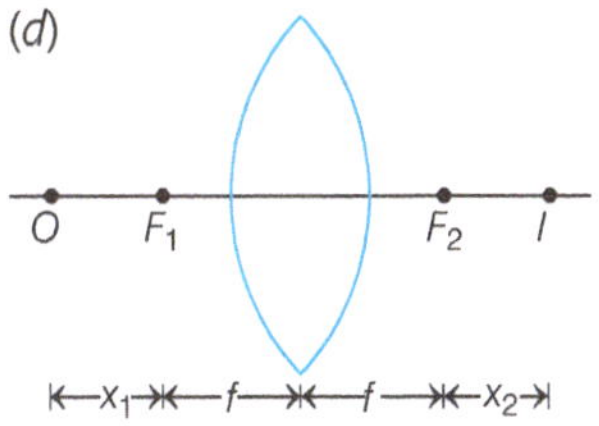

$$u = -(f + x_1), v = (f + x_2)$$

$$\frac{1}{f} = \frac{1}{v} - \frac{1}{u} = \frac{1}{f + x_2} - \frac{1}{-(f + x_1)}$$

$$f^2 = x_1 x_2 \text{ i.e. } f = \sqrt{x_1 x_2}$$

52 (*b*) From lens makers formula,

$$\frac{1}{f_2} = (\mu_g - 1)\left[\frac{1}{R_1} - \frac{1}{R_2}\right]$$

$$\therefore \quad = (1.5 - 1)\left[\frac{1}{20} - \frac{1}{-30}\right]$$

or, $f_L = \frac{120}{5} = 24$ cm

Now, focal length of mirror is,

$$f_m = \frac{R}{2} = \frac{-20}{2} = -10 \text{ cm}$$

$\therefore$ The equivalent focal length is

$$\frac{1}{f_{eq}} = \frac{-2}{f_L} + \frac{1}{f_M} = \frac{-2}{24} + \frac{1}{-10} = \frac{-11}{60}$$

$$f_{eq} = \frac{-60}{11} \text{ cm}$$

53 (*d*) $m = 1 - \frac{v}{f}$ ...(i)

Now, from given graph and from Eq. (i),

At $v = a$, magnification is

$$m_1 = 1 - \frac{a}{f} \quad \text{...(ii)}$$

At $v = a + b$, magnification is

$$m_2 = 1 - \frac{a+b}{f} \quad \text{...(iii)}$$

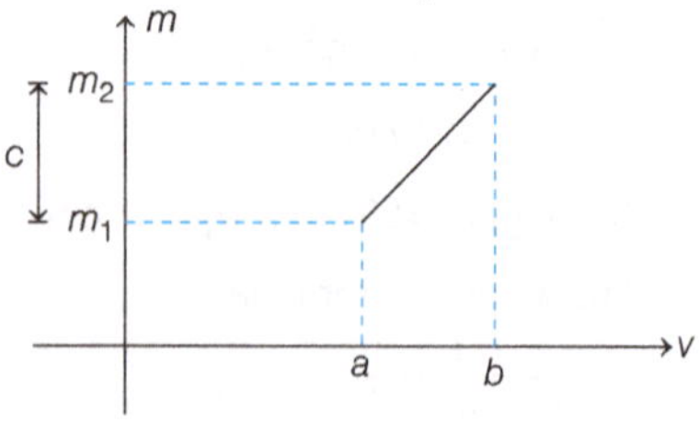

From graph, we can also say that

$$m_2 - m_1 = c \quad \text{...(iv)}$$

So, from Eqs. (ii), (iii) and (iv), we have

$$\left(1 - \frac{(a+b)}{f}\right) - \left(1 - \frac{a}{f}\right) = c$$

$$\Rightarrow \quad f = -\frac{b}{c}$$

or $|f| = \frac{b}{c}$

54 (*b*) $f = \frac{100}{20} = 5$ cm

From lens Maker's formula,

$$\frac{1}{f} = (n-1)\left(\frac{1}{R_1} - \frac{1}{R_2}\right)$$

$$\Rightarrow \quad \frac{1}{f} = (n-1)\left(\frac{1}{R} + \frac{1}{R}\right)$$

$$\frac{1}{5} = (n-1)\left(\frac{2}{5}\right)$$

$$\Rightarrow \quad n = 3/2$$

55 (*d*) For equivalent focal length,

$$\frac{1}{f} = \frac{1}{f_1} + \frac{1}{f_2} + \frac{1}{f_3}$$

$$\Rightarrow \frac{1}{f} = \frac{1}{(+40)} + \frac{1}{(-40)} + \frac{1}{(-15)}$$

$$\Rightarrow f = -15 \text{ cm}$$

Since, power, P (in D)

$$= \frac{1}{f \text{ (in m)}} = -\frac{100}{15} = -\frac{20}{3}$$

$$= -6.67 \text{ D}$$

56 (*b*)

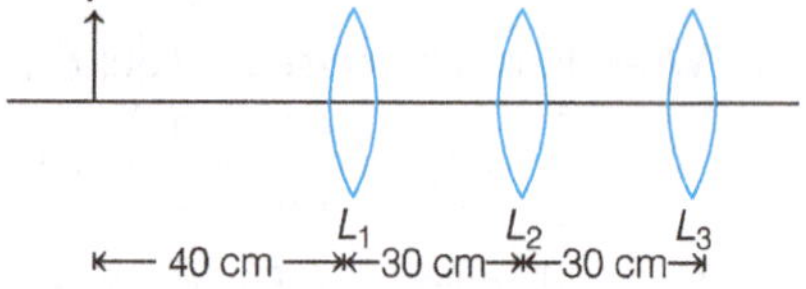

For refraction from 1st lens, L_1

$$\frac{1}{v} = \frac{1}{10} - \frac{1}{40} = \frac{3}{40} \text{ cm}$$

$$\Rightarrow \quad v = \frac{40}{3} \text{ cm}$$

This image acts as an object for 2nd lens L_2.

$\therefore$ Object distance for 2nd lens L_2

$$|u| = 30 - \frac{40}{3} = \frac{50}{3} \text{ cm}$$

Now, for refraction from L_2,

$$\Rightarrow \quad \frac{1}{v} = \frac{1}{u} + \frac{1}{f}$$

$$= \frac{1}{10} - \frac{3}{50} = \frac{2}{50}$$

$$\Rightarrow \quad v = 25 \text{ cm}$$

This image acts as an object for 3rd lens L_3

$\therefore$ Object distance for 3rd lens L_3

$$= |u| = 30 - 25 = 5 \text{ cm}$$

Similarly, for refraction from lens L_3,

$$\frac{1}{v} = \frac{1}{f} + \frac{1}{u} = \frac{1}{10} - \frac{1}{5}$$

or, $\quad v = -10$ cm

$\therefore$ Distance from L_1, i.e. the final image position

$$= 30 + (30 - 10) = 50 \text{ cm}$$

57 (*d*)

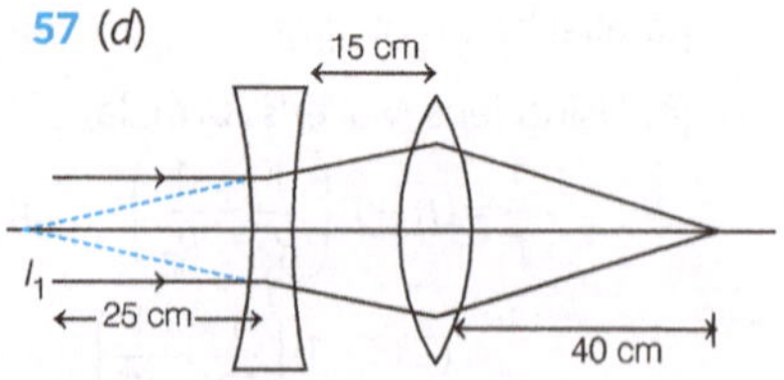

For concave lens,

$$\frac{1}{f_1} = \frac{1}{v_1} - \frac{1}{u_1}$$

$$\Rightarrow \frac{-1}{25} = \frac{1}{v_1} - \frac{1}{\infty}$$

$$\Rightarrow v_1 = -25 \text{ cm}$$

For convex lens,

$$\frac{1}{f_2} = \frac{1}{v_2} - \frac{1}{u_2}$$

$$\frac{1}{20} = \frac{1}{v_2} - \frac{1}{(-25-15)}$$

$$\frac{1}{20} = \frac{1}{v_2} - \frac{1}{-40}$$

$$\frac{1}{v_2} = \frac{1}{90} \Rightarrow v_2 = 40 \text{ cm}$$

58 (*c*) Magnification of a lens,

$$|m| = \frac{|v|}{|u|}$$

Case I $u_1 = -0.15$ m $= -15$ cm,

$v_1 = ?$ and $m_1 = ?$

Case II $u_2 = -0.2$ m $= -20$ cm,

$v_2 = ?$ and $m_2 = ?$

Given, $\quad |m_1| = 2|m_2|$

$$\Rightarrow \quad \frac{|v_1|}{|u_1|} = 2\frac{|v_2|}{|u_2|}$$

$$\Rightarrow \quad \frac{|v_1|}{|v_2|} = \frac{2 \times 15}{20} = \frac{3}{2}$$

$$\Rightarrow |v_1| = \frac{3}{2}|v_2| \text{ or } v_1 = \frac{3}{2}v_2$$

Applying thin lens formula,

$$\frac{1}{v} - \frac{1}{u} = \frac{1}{f}$$

or $\quad \frac{1}{f} = \frac{1}{v_1} - \frac{1}{u_1}$ ...(i)

and $\quad \frac{1}{f} = \frac{1}{v_2} - \frac{1}{u_2}$ ...(ii)

From Eqs. (i) and (ii),

$$\frac{1}{v_1} - \frac{1}{u_1} = \frac{1}{v_2} - \frac{1}{u_2}$$

or $\quad v_2 = +20$ cm

$$\Rightarrow \quad v_1 = \frac{3}{2} \times v_2 = \frac{3}{2} \times 20 = +30 \text{ cm}$$

From Eq. (i),

$$\frac{1}{f} = \frac{1}{+30} - \frac{1}{(-15)} = \frac{3}{30}$$

$\therefore \quad f = 10$ cm $= 0.10$ m

59 (*a*) $R = 10$ cm

Object distance $= 21$ cm

Shift due to slab

$$= t\left(1 - \frac{1}{\mu}\right) = 3\left(1 - \frac{2}{3}\right) = 1 \text{ cm}$$

along the direction of ray (incident)

So, $u = -21 + 1 = -20$ cm

$$f = \frac{R}{2} = 5 \text{ cm}$$

Now, $\frac{1}{v} - \frac{1}{u} = -\frac{1}{f}$

$$\Rightarrow \frac{1}{v} - \frac{1}{-20} = -\frac{1}{5}$$

$$v = -\frac{20}{3} \text{ cm}$$

Final position of image $= v - 1$

$$= \frac{20}{3} - 1 = \frac{17}{3} = 5.67 \text{ cm}$$

60 (c) Focal length of the combination of two given lenses,

$$\frac{1}{f} = \frac{1}{f_1} + \frac{1}{f_2} \quad \text{...(i)}$$

For plano-convex lens,

$$\frac{1}{f_1} = (n_1 - 1)\left(\frac{1}{R} - \frac{1}{\infty}\right) = \frac{n_1 - 1}{R}$$

Similarly, for plano-concave lens,

$R_1 = -R$ and $R_2 = \infty$

So, $\frac{1}{f_2} = (n_2 - 1)\left(\frac{1}{-R} - \frac{1}{\infty}\right)$

$$= \frac{-(n_2 - 1)}{R}$$

Putting these values of $\frac{1}{f_1}$ and $\frac{1}{f_2}$ in Eq. (i), we get

$$\frac{1}{f} = \frac{(n_1 - 1)}{R} - \frac{(n_2 - 1)}{R}$$

$$f = \frac{R}{n_1 - n_2}$$

61 (c) Given, situation can be depicted as follows

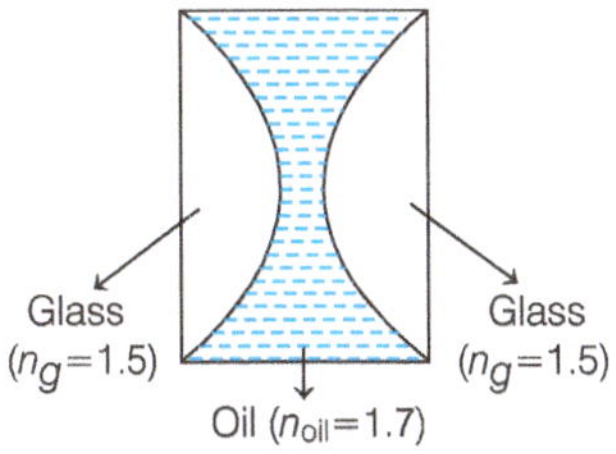

From lens Maker's formula,

$$\frac{1}{f} = (n - 1)\left[\frac{1}{R_1} - \frac{1}{R_2}\right]$$

For the plano-convex lens, $R_1 = R$ and for plane surface, $R_2 = \infty$

$$\therefore \frac{1}{f_{\text{plano-convex lens}}} = (1.5 - 1)\left(\frac{1}{R} - 0\right)$$

$$\Rightarrow \frac{1}{f_{\text{plano-convex lens}}} = \frac{0.5}{R}$$

$$\frac{1}{f_{\text{concave}}} = (1.7 - 1)\left(-\frac{1}{R} - \frac{1}{R}\right)$$

$$= \frac{-1.4}{R}$$

So, $\frac{1}{f_{eq}} = 2 \times \frac{1}{f_{\text{plano-convex lens}}} + \frac{1}{f_{\text{concave}}}$

$$= 2 \times \frac{0.5}{R} + \left(\frac{-1.4}{R}\right)$$

$$\therefore f_{eq} = -\frac{R}{0.4} = -\frac{20}{0.4} = -50 \text{ cm}$$

63 (c) As refracted ray emerges normally from opposite surface,

$\therefore \quad r_2 = 0$

$\therefore \quad r_1 + r_2 = A \Rightarrow r_1 = A$

By Snell's law

$$1 \sin i = \mu \sin r_1 = \mu \sin A$$

For small angles, $\sin i \approx i$ and $\sin A \approx A$

$\therefore \quad i = \mu A$

64 (c) Snell's law at surface AB

$$1 \sin \theta = \mu \sin r_1$$

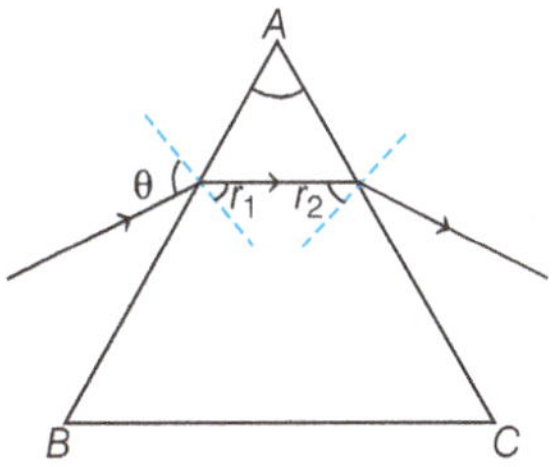

$$r_1 = \sin^{-1}\left(\frac{\sin \theta}{\mu}\right)$$

$$\therefore r_2 = A - r_1 = A - \sin^{-1}\left(\frac{\sin \theta}{\mu}\right)$$

For the ray should be transmitted through AC

$r_2 < i_C$

$$\Rightarrow A - \sin^{-1}\left(\frac{\sin \theta}{\mu}\right) < \sin^{-1}\left(\frac{1}{\mu}\right)$$

$$\therefore \theta > \sin^{-1}\left[\mu \sin\left(A - \sin^{-1}\left(\frac{1}{\mu}\right)\right)\right]$$

65 (c) The given prism can be shown as below.

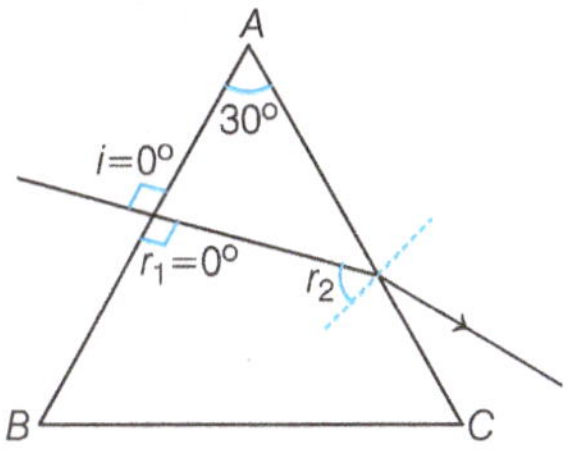

Given, $A = 30°$, $i = 0°$

$\Rightarrow \quad r_1 = 0°$

As, the angle of prism, $A = r_1 + r_2$

$\Rightarrow \quad 30° = 0 + r_2 \Rightarrow r_2 = 30°$

66 (d)

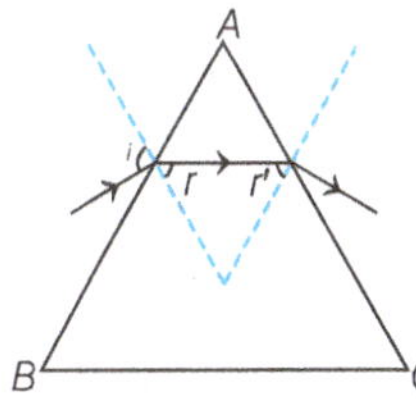

$$r' \leq C$$

$$(r + r' = A)$$

$$(A - r) \leq C$$

$$A \leq (r + C)$$

$r_{max} = C$ if $\quad i = 90°$

$$A \leq 2C$$

$$\frac{A}{2} \leq \sin^{-1}\left(\frac{1}{\mu}\right)$$

$$\mu \leq \sqrt{1 + \cot^2\left(\frac{A}{2}\right)}$$

$$\mu_{max} = \sqrt{1 + \cot^2\left(\frac{A}{2}\right)}$$

67 (a) $\quad \mu = \frac{\sin \frac{A + D_m}{2}}{\sin \frac{A}{2}}$

$$A = D_m$$

$$\therefore \quad \mu = \frac{\sin \frac{A + A}{2}}{\sin \frac{A}{2}}$$

$$1.732 = \frac{\sin A}{\sin \frac{A}{2}}$$

$$A = 60°$$

68 (*d*)

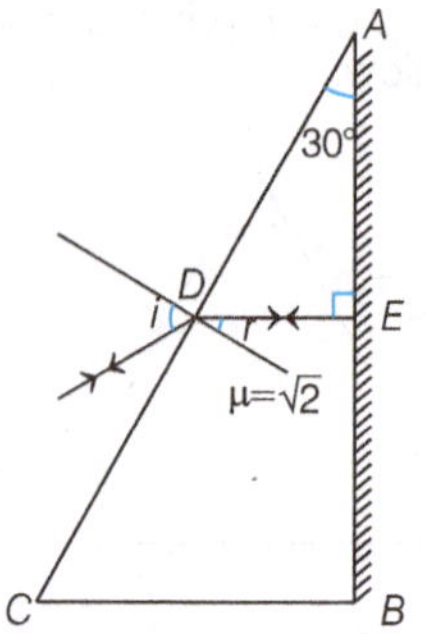

Then, the angle of refraction,

$$r = 90° - 60° = 30°$$

From Snell's law, $n_1 \sin i = n_2 \sin r$

$$1 \times \sin i = \sqrt{2} \sin 30°$$

$$i = 45°$$

69 (*c*) From Snell's law, $\dfrac{\sin i}{\sin r} = \mu$

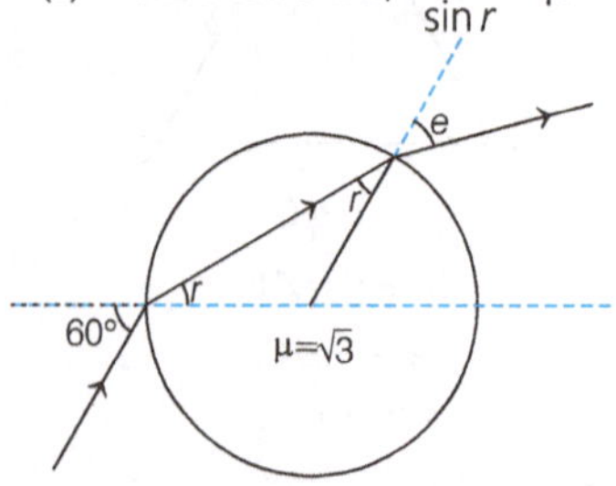

$$\frac{\sin 60}{\sin r} = \sqrt{3} \Rightarrow \frac{\sqrt{3}}{2} = \sqrt{3} \sin r$$

$$r = \sin^{-1} \frac{1}{2} = 30°$$

Again applying Snell's law at surface 2

$$\frac{\sin e}{\sin r} = \sqrt{3}$$

$$\sin e = \sqrt{3} \sin r = \sqrt{3} \times 1/2$$

$$e = 60°$$

Deviation at the first surface is

$$\delta_1 = i - r = 60 - 30 = 30°$$

Deviation at second surface

$$\delta_2 = 60° - 30° = 30°$$

Total deviation,

$$\delta_{total} = 30° + 30° = 60°$$

70 (*c*) When light ray travels parallel to the base, the light suffers minimum deviations.

So, for minimum deviation,

$D_{min} = 40°$

$i = e = 45°$ (from graph)

71 (*d*)

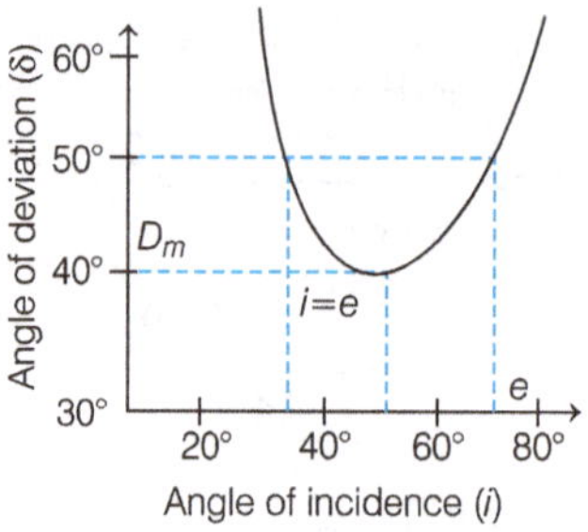

72 (*b*) For the given equilateral prism, $A = 60°$

$$i = e = \frac{3}{4} A = \frac{3}{4} \times 60° = 45°$$

From relation,

$$A + D = i + e$$

We have, $60° + D = 45° + 45°$

$$\Rightarrow \quad D = 90° - 60° = 30°$$

73 (*c*) Using prism formula,

$$n = \sqrt{3} = \frac{\sin\left(\frac{A+\delta}{2}\right)}{\sin\left(\frac{A}{2}\right)}$$

or $\dfrac{60 + \delta}{2} = 60°$

or angle of minimum deviation $\delta = 60°$

Incident angle, $i = \dfrac{60 + \delta}{2} = 60°$

74 (*b*) As, we know that refractive index of a prism $n = \dfrac{\sin\left(\frac{A+D_m}{2}\right)}{\sin\frac{A}{2}}$

$$\Rightarrow \quad \cot\frac{A}{2} = \frac{\sin\left(\frac{A+D_m}{2}\right)}{\sin\frac{A}{2}}$$

$$\Rightarrow \quad D_m = 180° - 2A$$

75 (*a*) According to prism formula,

$$n = \frac{\sin\left(\frac{A+D_m}{2}\right)}{\sin\left(\frac{A}{2}\right)}$$

$$n = \frac{\sin\left(\frac{60°+30°}{2}\right)}{\sin\left(\frac{60°}{2}\right)} = \frac{\sin 45°}{\sin 30°}$$

or $n = \sqrt{2}$

$$\Rightarrow \quad v = \frac{c}{n} = \frac{3 \times 10^8}{\sqrt{2}}$$

$$= \frac{3}{\sqrt{2}} \times 10^8 \text{ m/s}$$

76 (*b*) As, from prism formula,

$$n = \frac{\sin\left(\frac{A+D_m}{2}\right)}{\sin\left(\frac{A}{2}\right)}$$

$$\Rightarrow n = \frac{\sin\left(\frac{A+A}{2}\right)}{\sin\left(\frac{A}{2}\right)}$$

$$n = 2\left\{\cos\left(\frac{A}{2}\right)\right\}$$

In the given situation value of A varies from 0 to 90°.

$$\Rightarrow n = 2\cos\left(\frac{90°}{2}\right)$$

$$n' = 2\cos 0° = 2$$

77 (*a*) As we know, $D_m = (i_1 + i_2) - A$

$$\Rightarrow 40° = (35° + 79°) - A$$

$$\Rightarrow \quad A = 74°$$

Now, from prism formula,

$$n = \frac{\sin\left(\frac{A+D_m}{2}\right)}{\sin\left(\frac{A}{2}\right)}$$

$$n = \frac{\sin\left(\frac{74° + 40°}{2}\right)}{\sin\left(\frac{74°}{2}\right)} \approx 1.4$$

78 (*a*)

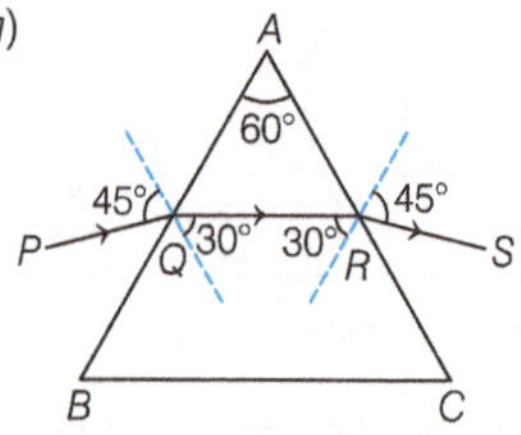

Therefore, minimum deviation suffered by the ray is

$$D_{min} = i + e - (r + r')$$

$$= 90° - 60° = 30°$$

Also we know that,

$$n=\frac{\sin\left(\frac{A+D_m}{2}\right)}{\sin\frac{A}{2}}$$

$$\therefore n=\frac{\sin\left(\frac{60^\circ+30^\circ}{2}\right)}{\sin\left(\frac{60^\circ}{2}\right)}=\frac{\sin 45^\circ}{\sin 30^\circ}$$

$$=\frac{1/\sqrt{2}}{1/2}=\frac{2}{\sqrt{2}}=\sqrt{2}$$

79 (a) $D=(n-1)A$

$$\Rightarrow A=\frac{D}{n-1}=\frac{5.5}{1.57-1}=9.65^\circ$$

80 (a) Deviation produced by crown glass,

$D=(n-1)A=(1.51-1)\times 5=2.55^\circ$

and deviation produced by flint glass,

$D'=(1.65-1)A'=0.65\,A'$

For no deviation, $D'=D$

or $0.65\,A'=2.55$

$$A'=\frac{2.55}{0.65}=3.92^\circ$$

81 (b) For blue colour light,

$D_b=(n_b-1)A$

Similarly, for red colour light,

$D_r=(n_r-1)A$

$\therefore$ Angle between the emergent blue and red rays

$=D_b-D_r=(n_b-n_r)A$

$=(1.659-1.641)\times 5$

$=0.018\times 5^\circ=0.09^\circ$

82 (d) For compound microscope,

$f_o=1.5$ cm, $f_e=6.25$ cm

$u_o=-2$ cm

$v_e=-25$ cm

For objective,

$$\frac{1}{f_o}=\frac{1}{v_o}-\frac{1}{u_o}$$

$$\Rightarrow \frac{1}{1.5}=\frac{1}{v_o}-\frac{1}{-2}$$

$\therefore v_o=6$ cm

For eyepiece,

$$\frac{1}{f_e}=\frac{1}{v_e}-\frac{1}{u_e}$$

$$\Rightarrow \frac{1}{6.25}=\frac{1}{-25}-\frac{1}{u_e}$$

$\therefore \quad u_e=-5$ cm

$\therefore$ The distance between two lenses is

$|v_o|+|u_e|=6+|-5|=11$ cm

83 (a) For compound microscope,

$D=25$ cm, $f_o=8$ mm $=0.8$ cm

$f_e=2.5$ cm, $u_o=-9$ mm

$=-0.9$ cm,

$v_e=-D=-25$ cm

For objective, $\frac{1}{f_o}=\frac{1}{v_o}-\frac{1}{u_o}$

$$\Rightarrow \frac{1}{0.8}=\frac{1}{v_o}-\frac{1}{-0.9}$$

$\therefore \quad v_o=7.2$ cm

For eyepiece, $\frac{1}{f_e}=\frac{1}{v_e}-\frac{1}{u_e}$

$$\Rightarrow \frac{1}{2.5}=\frac{1}{-25}-\frac{1}{u_e}$$

$\therefore \quad u_e=-2.27$ cm

$\therefore$ The distance between two lenses is

$|v_0|+|u_e|=7.2+|-2.27|=9.47$ cm

84 (d) For astronomical telescope,

$f_o=50$ cm, $f_e=5$ cm, $D=25$ cm

The length of the telescope when final image is formed at the least distance of distinct vision is given by

$$L=f_o+\frac{f_eD}{f_e+D}=50+\frac{5\times 25}{5+25}$$

$$=\frac{325}{6}\text{ cm}$$

86 (a) From lens formula,

$$v=\frac{uf}{u+f}=\frac{-9\times 10}{-9+10}=-90\text{ cm}$$

Magnification, $m=\frac{v}{u}=\frac{-90}{-9}=10$

$\therefore$ Apparent area of the card through the magnifying lens

$=(1\text{ mm}\times 10)\times(1\text{ mm}\times 10)$

$=100\text{ mm}^2=1\text{ cm}^2$

87 (b) For objective, $\frac{1}{v_o}-\frac{1}{u_o}=\frac{1}{f_o}$

$$\Rightarrow \frac{1}{v_o}=\frac{1}{1.2}-\frac{1}{2}$$

$\Rightarrow \quad v_o=3$ cm

For eyepiece,

$$\frac{1}{v_e}-\frac{1}{u_e}=\frac{1}{f_e}$$

$$\Rightarrow \frac{1}{-25}-\frac{1}{u_e}=\frac{1}{6.25}$$

$$\Rightarrow -\frac{1}{u_e}=\frac{1}{6.25}+\frac{1}{25}$$

$u_e=-5$ cm

Distance between two lenses

$=|v_o|+|u_e|=3+5=8$ cm

88 (b) The magnification due to objective is

$$m_0=\frac{L}{f_o}=\frac{20}{1}=20$$

and due to eyepiece is $m_e=\frac{D}{f_e}$

$$\Rightarrow \quad m_e=\frac{25}{2}=12.5$$

The magnification of compound microscope is

$$|m|=m_0m_e=\left(\frac{L}{f_o}\right)\left(\frac{D}{f_e}\right)$$

$=20\times 12.5=250$

89 (b) Image by eyepiece

$$\frac{1}{v_e}-\frac{1}{u_e}=\frac{1}{f_e}$$

$$\Rightarrow \frac{1}{-25}-\frac{1}{-u_e}=\frac{1}{\frac{25}{4}}$$

$$\frac{1}{u_e}=\frac{4}{25}+\frac{1}{25}$$

$\Rightarrow \quad u_e=5$ cm

$L=v+|u_e|$

$15=v_o+5$

$\Rightarrow \quad v_o=15-5=10$ cm

Image by objective

$$\frac{1}{v_0}-\frac{1}{u_0}=\frac{1}{f_0}$$

$$\Rightarrow \frac{1}{10}-\frac{1}{-u_o}=\frac{1}{2}$$

$$\frac{1}{u_o} = \frac{1}{2} - \frac{1}{10} = \frac{4}{10}$$

$$u_o = \frac{5}{2}\text{ cm} = 2.5\text{ cm}$$

90 (*b*) Angle subtended by moon on objective

$$\theta_0 = \frac{3.5 \times 10^3}{3.8 \times 10^5} = 9.2 \times 10^{-3}\text{ rad}$$

$$= \left(9.2 \times 10^{-3} \times \frac{180}{\pi}\right)^\circ = 0.5^\circ$$

$$|m| = \frac{f_o}{f_e} = \frac{400}{10} = 40$$

$$m = \frac{\theta}{\theta_0} \Rightarrow 40 = \frac{\theta}{(0.5)^\circ}$$

$$\theta = 20^\circ$$

92 (*d*) $\therefore$ For telescope $|m| = \frac{|f_o|}{|f_e|} = 5$

$\Rightarrow \quad |f_o| = 5|f_e| \quad$ ...(i)

and length of the telescope

$L = |f_o| + |f_e| = 36 \quad$ ...(ii)

From Eqs. (i) and (ii), we get

$$5f_e + f_e = 36$$

$$\Rightarrow f_e = 6\text{ cm and } f_o = 30\text{ cm}$$

93 (*b*) Length of tube of telescope,

$$L = f_o + f_e$$

$$\Rightarrow \quad L = 1.5 + 0.05 = 1.55\text{ m}$$

94 (*d*)

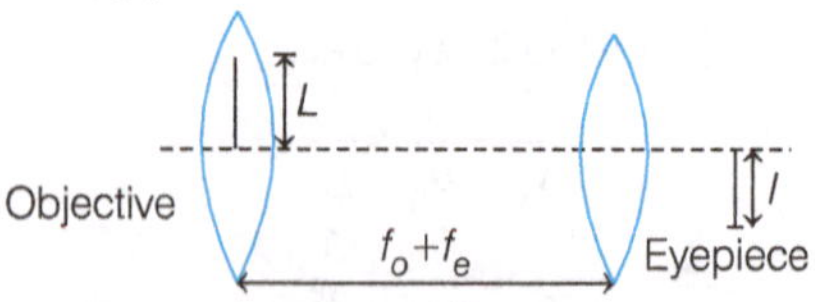

$\therefore \quad u = (f_o + f_e)$ and $f = f_e$

Using lens formula, $\frac{1}{v} - \frac{1}{u} = \frac{1}{f}$

$$\Rightarrow \frac{1}{v} - \frac{1}{(f_o + f_e)} = \frac{1}{f_e}$$

$$v = \frac{(f_o + f_e)f_e}{f_o}$$

Magnification of lens

$= \frac{v}{u} = \frac{(f_o + f_e)f_e}{f_o(f_o + f_e)} = \frac{f_e}{f_o} = \frac{I}{L} \quad$ ...(i)

$$|m| = \left|\frac{f_o}{f_e}\right|$$

$\Rightarrow \quad m = \frac{L}{I} \quad$ [using Eq. (i)]

95 (*d*) Telescope resolves and bring objects closer. Hence, the given telescope with magnifying power 20, will make the tree to appear 20 times nearer to the observer.

96 (*a*) Angular magnification for telescope,

$$|m| = \left|\frac{f_o}{f_e}\right| = \left|\frac{F_1}{F_2}\right| = \frac{F_1}{F_2}$$

97 (*a*) For a telescope,

Angular magnification, $m = \frac{\beta}{\alpha} = \frac{f_o}{f_e}$

$$\therefore \quad \frac{\beta}{0.5^\circ} = \frac{0.3}{0.03} \Rightarrow \beta = 5^\circ$$

98 (*d*) For microscope,

$$m = \frac{L}{f_o}\frac{D}{f_e} \Rightarrow m \propto \frac{1}{f_o}$$

For telescope, $|m| = \frac{f_o}{f_e} \Rightarrow m \propto f_o$

Assertion and Reason Questions

1 (*c*)

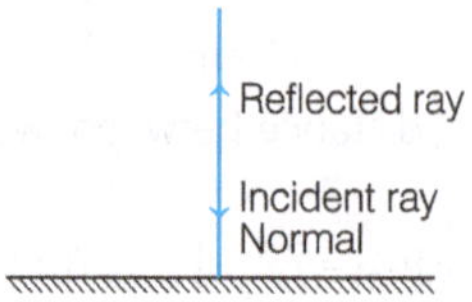

$\Rightarrow$ Angle of reflection $= 0^\circ$

(from laws of reflection)

Therefore, Assertion is correct but Reason is incorrect.

3 (*d*) Refractive index of diamond w.r.t. liquid, ${}^l n_d = \frac{1}{\sin i_c} = \frac{n_d}{n_l}$

$$\Rightarrow \frac{\sqrt{6}}{\sqrt{3}} = \frac{1}{\sin i_c}$$

$$\Rightarrow \sin i_c = \frac{1}{\sqrt{2}} = \sin 45^\circ$$

$$\therefore \quad i_c = 45^\circ$$

This means, that when the ray of light while travelling from diamond to liquid is incident at angle of 45°, then it will be totally reflected due TIR.

Therefore, Assertion is incorrect but Reason is correct.

4 (*b*) In optical fibre communication propagation of signal through optical fibre takes place, which is based on the phenomenon of total internal reflection at core-clad interface.

The refractive index of the material of the cladding is less than that of core, hence, light striking at core- cladding interface gets totally internally reflected. Therefore, Assertion and Reason are correct but Reason is not the correct expalnation of Assertion.

5 (*d*) When a convergent lens is placed inside a transparent medium having refractive index greater than that of material of lens, it behaves as a divergent lens.

Hence, property of a lens, whether the rays are converging or diverging depends on the surrounding medium. Therefore, Assertion is incorrect but Reason is correct.

6 (*d*) Magnification produced by mirror,

$$m = \frac{\text{size of image}}{\text{size of object}} = \frac{I}{O}$$

$$= \frac{f}{f - u} = \frac{f}{x}$$

where, x (say) is distance of the object from focus.

Therefore, Assertion is incorrect but Reason is correct.

7 (*a*) For thin prisms, angle of prisms A is small.

So, for minimum deviation,

$${}^1n_2 = \frac{\sin\left(\frac{A + D_{min}}{2}\right)}{\sin(A/2)} \quad \text{...(i)}$$

$$\sin\left(\frac{A + D_{min}}{2}\right) \approx \frac{A + D_{min}}{2}$$

($\because \sin\theta \approx \theta$ for small θ)

and $\quad \sin\frac{A}{2} \approx \frac{A}{2}$

Using above approximations,

$${}^1n_2 = \frac{A + D_{min}}{A}$$

$$\Rightarrow \quad D_{min} = ({}^1n_2 - 1)A$$

Hence, it can be seen that if A is small, D_{min} is also small. Thus, thin prism do not deviate light much.

Therefore, Assertion and Reason are correct and Reason is the correct explanation of Assertion.

8 (*a*) Refractive index of any pair of media is inversely proportional to wavelength of light.

As, $\lambda_v < \lambda_r \Rightarrow n_v > n_r$

Hence, refractive index of glass with respect to air is different for red light and violet light.

Therefore, Assertion and Reason are correct and Reason is the correct explanation of Assertion.

9 (*d*) When white light pass through a prism, bending of red component of white light is least while it is most for the violet.

Equivalently, red light travels faster than violet light in a glass prism.

Therefore, Assertion is incorrect but Reason is correct.

Statement Based Questions

1 (*c*) Statement II is correct but Statement I is incorrect and it can be corrected as,

According to the laws of reflection, the angle of reflection (i.e., the angle between reflected ray and the normal to the reflecting surface or the mirror) equals the angle of incidence (angle between incident ray and the normal).

The incident ray, reflected ray and the normal to the reflecting surface at the point of incidence lie in the same plane.

These laws are valid at each point on any reflecting surface whether plane or curved.

2 (*c*) The Statement I is incorrect and it can be corrected as,

The reflected ray converge at a point F on the principal axis of a concave mirror. For a convex mirror, the reflected rays appear to diverge from a point F on its principal axis. This point F is called the principal focus of the mirror.

Rest statements are correct.

4 (*c*) Velocity of light in a glass slab is different for different colours. There is no dispersion when a white ray of light emerges from a rectangular glass slab.

5 (*b*) Statement II is incorrect and can be corrected as, optical fibres are fabricated such that light reflected at one side of inner surface strikes the other at an angle larger than the critical angle.

Due to this total internal reflection takes place. Since, light undergoes total internal reflection at each stage in an optical fibre, so there is no appreciable loss in the intensity of the light signal. Even if the fibre is bent, light can easily travel along its length.

6 (*b*) Statement II is incorrect and it can be corrected as, refractive index of the glass

$$(n) = \frac{1}{\sin i_c} = \frac{1}{\sin 30°} = 2$$

8 (*a*) A microscope cannot work as a telescope by interchanging the two lenses. In a telescope, the object has much larger focal length than the eyepiece.

Matching Type Questions

1 (*b*) At A, air-ice interface

Applying Snell's law,

$$\frac{\sin i_1}{\sin r_1} = {}^{air}n_{ice} = \frac{n_{ice}}{n_{air}}$$

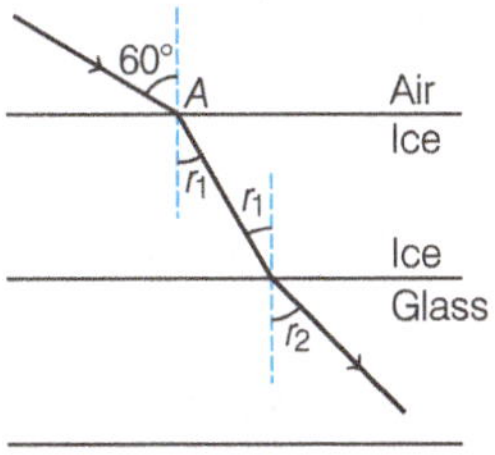

$$\Rightarrow \frac{\sin 60°}{\sin r_1} = \frac{n_{ice}}{1} \quad ...(i)$$

$$\Rightarrow \sin r_1 = \frac{\sin 60°}{n_{ice}} = \frac{\sqrt{3}/2}{4/3} = \frac{3\sqrt{3}}{8}$$

Similarly, at B, ice-glass interface

Applying Snell's law,

$$\frac{\sin r_1}{\sin r_2} = {}^{ice}n_{glass} = \frac{n_{glass}}{n_{ice}} \quad ...(ii)$$

On multiplying Eqs. (i) and (ii), we get

$$\frac{\sin 60°}{\sin r_1} \times \frac{\sin r_1}{\sin r_2} = \frac{n_{ice}}{1} \times \frac{n_{glass}}{n_{ice}}$$

$$\Rightarrow \frac{\sin 60°}{\sin r_2} = n_{glass}$$

$$\Rightarrow \sin r_2 = \frac{\sin 60°}{n_{glass}} = \frac{\sqrt{3}/2}{3/2} = \frac{1}{\sqrt{3}}$$

Also, refractive index of ice w.r.t. glass

$$\Rightarrow {}^{glass}n_{ice} = \frac{{}^{air}n_{ice}}{{}^{air}n_{glass}} = \frac{4/3}{3/2} = \frac{8}{9}$$

For air-ice interface, $n_1 \sin i = n_2 \sin r_1$

$$\Rightarrow \sin 60° = \frac{4}{3} \sin r_1$$

$$\Rightarrow \sin 60° + \frac{4}{3} \sin r_1 = 2 \sin 60°$$

Hence, A $\rightarrow$ 2, B $\rightarrow$ 1, C $\rightarrow$ 3 and D $\rightarrow$ 4.

2 (*c*) **Minimum Deviation**

$$n = \frac{\sin \frac{(A + D_{min})}{2}}{\sin \frac{A}{2}}$$

Subtituting values, we have

$$\frac{3}{2} = \frac{\sin\left(\frac{60 + D_{min}}{2}\right)}{\sin\left(\frac{60}{2}\right)}$$

$$\Rightarrow \frac{3}{4} = \sin\left(\frac{60 + D_{min}}{2}\right)$$

$$\Rightarrow 2\sin^{-1}(0.75) = 60 + D_{min}$$

$$\Rightarrow 97° = 60° + D_{min}$$

$$\Rightarrow D_{min} = 37°$$

Maximum Deviation

The deviation is maximum, when $i = 90°$ or $e = 90°$, i.e. at grazing incidence or grazing emergence.

Let we take, $i = 90°$

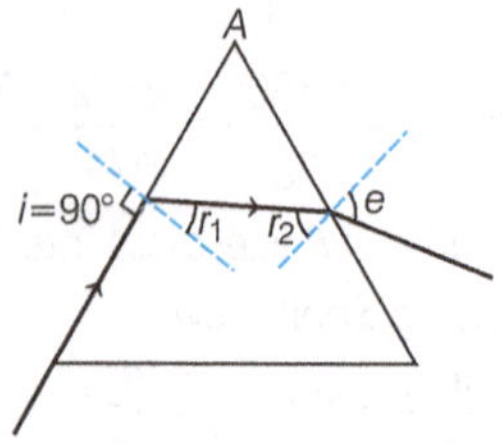

$\Rightarrow \quad r_1 = i_C = \sin^{-1}\left(\frac{n_r}{n_d}\right)$

$\Rightarrow \quad r_1 = \sin^{-1}\left(\frac{2}{3}\right) = 42°$

Also, $r_1 + r_2 = A \Rightarrow r_2 = A - r_1$
$= 60° - 42° = 18°$

Using $\frac{\sin r_2}{\sin e} = \frac{1}{n}$

$\Rightarrow \sin e = n \sin r_2 = 1.5 \sin 18°$

$\Rightarrow \sin e = 0.463 \Rightarrow e = 28°$

Deviation $= D_{max}$

$= i + e - A$

$= 90° + 28° - 60° = 58°$

Hence, A $\rightarrow$ 2, B $\rightarrow$ 1, C $\rightarrow$ 3 and D$\rightarrow$4.

Numerical Type Questions

1 (32) According to question,

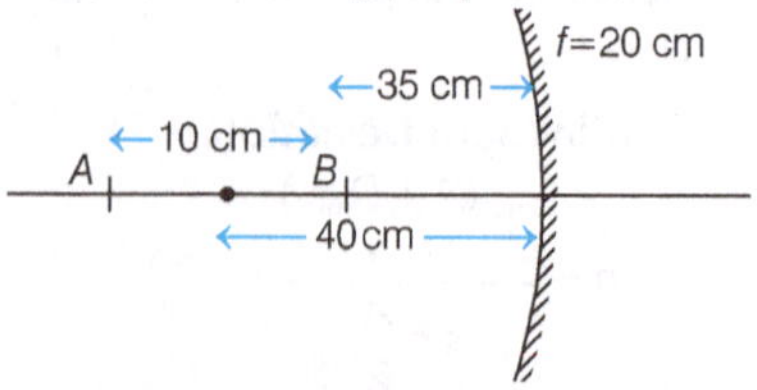

Let, the image of AB rod be $A'B'$ and distance of point A' and B' from mirror be v_A' and v_B', respectively.

From mirror formula,

For point A,

$$\frac{1}{v_A'} + \frac{1}{(-45)} = \frac{1}{-20}$$

$$\frac{1}{v_A'} - \frac{1}{45} = \frac{1}{-20}$$

$$\Rightarrow \quad v_A' = -36 \text{ cm}$$

For point B,

$$\frac{1}{v_B'} + \frac{1}{(-35)} = \frac{1}{-20}$$

$$\Rightarrow \quad \frac{1}{v_B'} - \frac{1}{35} = \frac{1}{-20}$$

$$\Rightarrow \quad v_B' = -\frac{140}{3} \text{ cm}$$

Length of rod's image

$$= |v_A' - v_B'|$$

$$\left|-36 - \left(-\frac{140}{3}\right)\right| = \left|+\frac{32}{3}\right|$$

So, $x = 32$

2 (6)

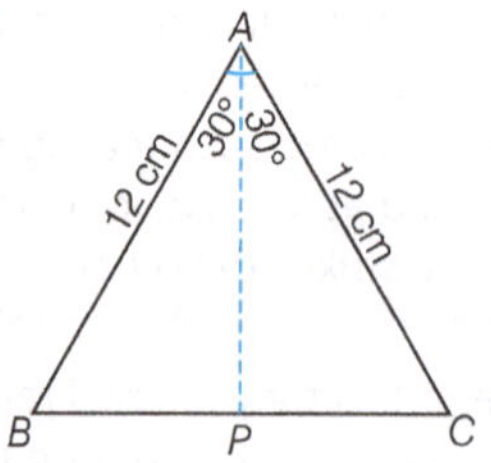

Angle of refraction,

$$r = \frac{A}{2} = \frac{60°}{2} = 30°$$

Then, by Snell's law of refraction,

$$\mu = \frac{\sin i}{\sin r} = \frac{\sin 60°}{\sin 30°} = \frac{\frac{\sqrt{3}}{2}}{\frac{1}{2}} = \sqrt{3}$$

$$d = \mu \times AP$$

$$= \sqrt{3} \times 6\sqrt{3} \times 10^{-2}$$

$$= 18 \times 10^{-2} \text{ m}$$

$$t = \frac{d}{c} = \frac{18 \times 10^{-2}}{3 \times 10^8} \text{ s} = 6 \times 10^{-10} \text{ s}$$

3 (120) Using lens Maker's formula,

$$\frac{1}{f} = (\mu - 1)\left(\frac{1}{R_1} - \frac{1}{R_2}\right)$$

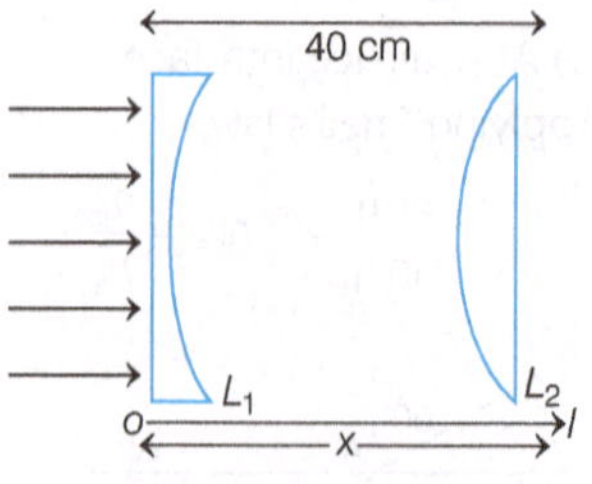

For lens, L_1

So, $\quad \frac{1}{f_1} = 0.75\left(-\frac{1}{30}\right) = -\frac{1}{40}$

or $\quad f_1 = -40$ cm

For lens L_2,

So, $\quad \frac{1}{f_2} = 0.75\left(\frac{1}{30}\right) = 40$ cm

Now, in given situation, for lens L_1,

Using, $\frac{1}{v} - \frac{1}{u} = \frac{1}{f}$

we have $\frac{1}{v} = \frac{1}{-40}$

or $\quad v = -40$ cm

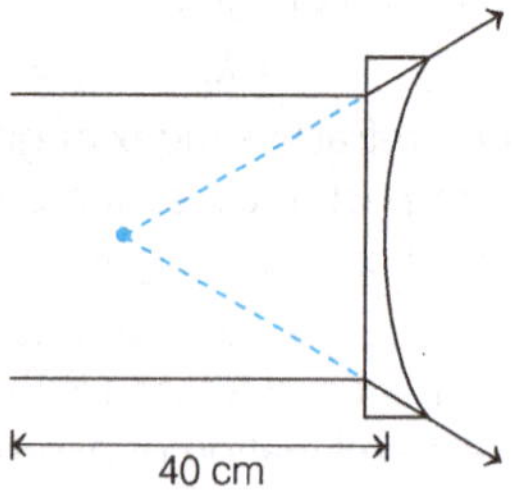

Now for lens L_2,

So, $\frac{1}{v} - \frac{1}{-80} = \frac{1}{40}$

or $\quad \frac{1}{v} = \frac{1}{40} - \frac{1}{80} = \frac{1}{80}$

or $\quad v = 80$ cm

So, distance of image from plano concave (L_1) lens is

$80 + 40 = 120$ cm.

4 (30) Given, magnification, $m = 7$

Since, we know that

$$m = 1 + \frac{D}{f_o}$$

$$\Rightarrow \quad 7 = 1 + \frac{D}{f_o}$$

$$\Rightarrow \quad f_o = 5 \text{ cm}$$

For compound microscope, magnifying power is given by

$$m = \frac{l \cdot D}{f_o f_e} = 2m_{\text{simple microscope}}$$

$$\Rightarrow 14 = \frac{70 \times 30}{5 \cdot f_e} \Rightarrow f_e = 30 \text{ cm}$$

5 (2) For no refraction at this face, $\theta > C$

$$\sin\theta > \sin C$$

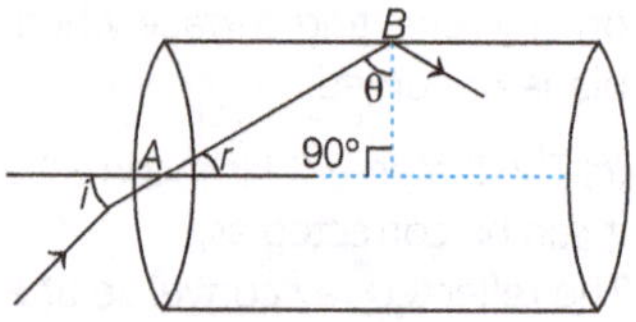

but $\quad \theta + r = 90°$

(According to geometry of figure)

$\Rightarrow \quad \theta = (90° - r)$

$\therefore \quad \sin(90° - r) > \sin C$

or $\quad \cos r > \sin C \quad$ ...(i)

Now, from Snell's law, $\mu = \dfrac{\sin i}{\sin r}$

$\Rightarrow \quad \sin r = \dfrac{\sin i}{\mu}$

$\therefore \quad \cos r = \sqrt{\left(1 - \dfrac{\sin^2 i}{\mu^2}\right)}$

$\therefore$ Eq. (i) gives,

$$\sqrt{1 - \frac{\sin^2 i}{\mu^2}} > \sin C$$

Also, $\quad \sin C = \dfrac{1}{\mu}$

$\therefore \quad \mu^2 > \sin^2 i + 1$

The maximum value of $\sin i$ is 1.

So, $\quad \mu^2 > 2$ or $\mu > \sqrt{2}$

So, the value of x is 2.

6. (6)

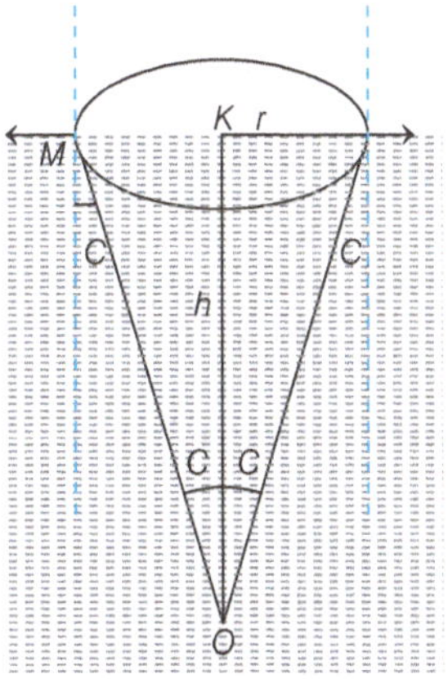

For total internal reflection of light,

$$\sin C = \frac{1}{\mu} = \frac{r}{\sqrt{r^2 + h^2}}$$

or $\quad r^2 = \dfrac{h^2}{\mu^2 - 1} = \dfrac{(4)^2}{\left(\dfrac{5}{3}\right)^2 - 1}$

So, $\quad r^2 = 9$

$\therefore \quad r = 3$ m

$\therefore$ Diameter of disc $= 2r = 6$ m

7 (1) $\dfrac{1}{f_a} = (\mu - 1)\left(\dfrac{1}{R_1} - \dfrac{1}{R_2}\right) \quad$ ...(i)

$$\frac{1}{f_a} = (1.5 - 1)\left(\frac{1}{R_1} - \frac{1}{R_2}\right)$$

and $\dfrac{1}{f_m} = \left(\dfrac{\mu_g - \mu_m}{\mu_m}\right)\left(\dfrac{1}{R_1} - \dfrac{1}{R_2}\right) \quad$ ...(ii)

$$\frac{1}{f_m} = \left(\frac{1.5}{1.6} - 1\right)\left(\frac{1}{R_1} - \frac{1}{R_2}\right)$$

Thus, $\dfrac{f_m}{f_a} = \dfrac{(1.5 - 1)}{\left(\dfrac{1.5}{1.6} - 1\right)} = -8$

or $f_m = -8 \times f_a = -8 \times \dfrac{-1}{5} = 1.6$ m

$\therefore \quad P_m = \dfrac{\mu}{f_m} = \dfrac{1.6}{1.6} = 1$ D

8 (20)

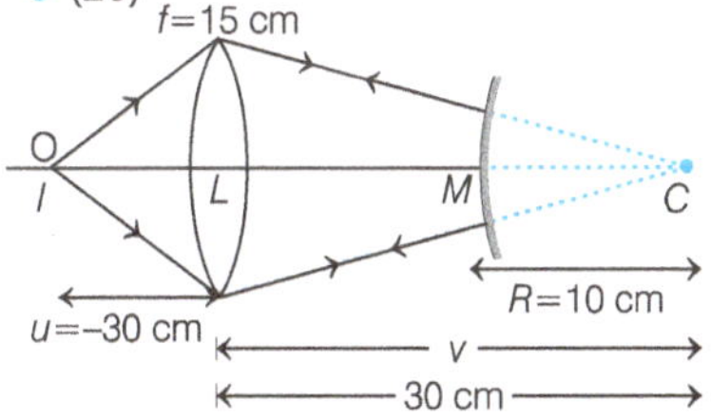

According to lens formula,

$$\frac{1}{f} = \frac{1}{v} - \frac{1}{u}$$

$\therefore \quad \dfrac{1}{15} = \dfrac{1}{v} - \dfrac{1}{-30}$

or $\quad \dfrac{1}{v} = \dfrac{1}{15} - \dfrac{1}{30} = \dfrac{2 - 1}{30} = \dfrac{1}{30}$

$\therefore \quad v = 30$ cm

$\therefore LC = v = 30$ cm

Thus, distance between lens and mirror

$$LM = 30 - 10 = 20 \text{ cm}$$

9 (5) $\dfrac{1}{f_a} = ({}_a\mu_g - 1)\left(\dfrac{1}{R_1} - \dfrac{1}{R_2}\right) \quad$ ...(i)

$$\frac{1}{f_l} = ({}_l\mu_g - 1)\left(\frac{1}{R_1} - \frac{1}{R_2}\right)$$

or, $\dfrac{1}{f_l} = \left(\dfrac{\mu_g}{\mu_l} - 1\right)\left(\dfrac{1}{R_1} - \dfrac{1}{R_2}\right) \quad$ ...(ii)

From Eqs. (i) and (ii),

$$\frac{\dfrac{1}{f_a}}{\dfrac{1}{f_l}} = \frac{(\mu_g - 1)}{\left(\dfrac{\mu_g}{\mu_l} - 1\right)}$$

or $\quad \dfrac{f_l}{f_a} = \dfrac{(\mu_g - 1)}{\left(\dfrac{\mu_g}{\mu_l} - 1\right)}$

or, $\dfrac{f_l}{f_a} = \dfrac{(1.5 - 1)}{\left(\dfrac{1.5}{1.25} - 1\right)}$

$$= \frac{\dfrac{1}{2}}{\dfrac{1}{5}} = \frac{5}{2}$$

$\therefore \quad f_l = \dfrac{5}{2} f_a = \dfrac{5}{2} \times 2 = 5$ cm

10 (50) For an astronomical telescope, where magnification, $m = \dfrac{f_o}{f_e}$

Length of telescope tube

$$L = f_o + f_e$$

$\therefore \quad \dfrac{f_o}{f_e} = 10 \quad$ ...(i)

and $\quad f_o + f_e = 55 \quad$ ...(ii)

From solving Eqs. (i) and (ii), we get

or $\quad f_o = 50$ cm

NCERT Exemplar Questions

2 (c)

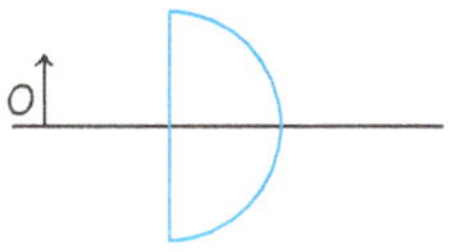

(a)

$R_1 = \infty, R_2 = -20$ cm

$\Rightarrow \dfrac{1}{f} = (n - 1)\left(\dfrac{1}{R_1} - \dfrac{1}{R_2}\right)$

$$= (1.5 - 1)\left(\frac{1}{\infty} + \frac{1}{20}\right) = \frac{1}{40}$$

$\Rightarrow \quad f = +40$ cm

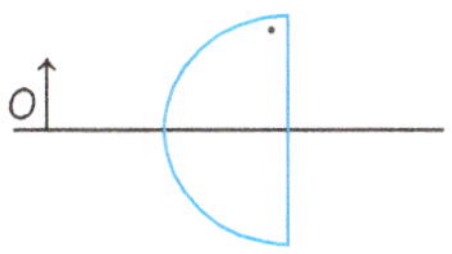

(b)

$R_1 = 20$ cm, $R_2 = \infty$.

$\Rightarrow \quad \dfrac{1}{f'} = (n - 1)\left(\dfrac{1}{R_1} - \dfrac{1}{R_2}\right)$

$= (1.5 - 1)\left(\dfrac{1}{20} - \dfrac{1}{\infty}\right) = \dfrac{1}{40}$

$\Rightarrow \quad f' = 40$ cm

Then, also the lens behaves as convex.

3 (*b*) In the given figure, PQ is a ray of light passing through focus and falling on the surface of a concave mirror.

On reflection from the mirror, the ray becomes parallel to principal axis of the mirror. Hence, the ray would travel along 2.

4 (*b*) Ray number 2 follows the correct path according to the laws of refraction.

Since, $\mu_{\text{turpentine}} > \mu_{\text{water}} > \mu_{\text{air}}$

So, as light travels from air to turpentine (i.e., from rarer to denser medium), it bends towards the normal after refraction.

Again when it strikes the turpentine-water interface, it must bend away from the normal as it travels from denser to rarer medium.

5 (*a*) For negative refractive index, i.e., n_2 is negative.

Applying Snell's law,

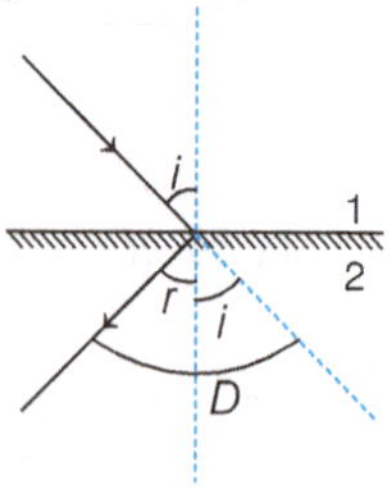

$\frac{\sin i}{\sin r} = {}^1n_2$ (refractive index of medium 2 w.r.t. medium $1 = {}^1n_2$) = negative

$\Rightarrow \sin r = \frac{\sin i}{{}^1n_2} = \frac{\text{positive}}{\text{negative}} = \text{negative}$

6 (*d*)

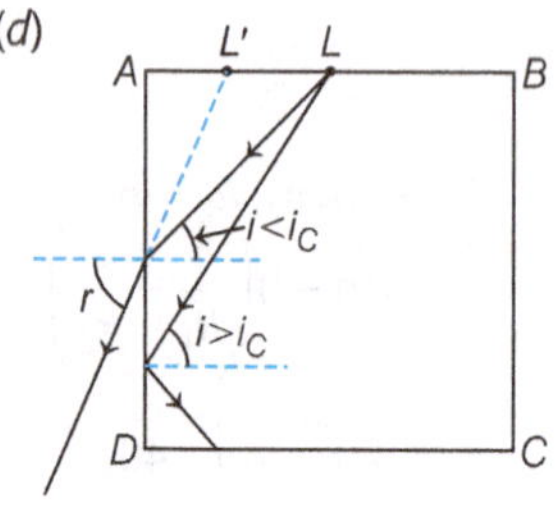

For $\mu = 1.6$, $\sin i_C = \frac{1}{n} = \frac{1}{1.6} = 0.625$

$\Rightarrow i_C = \sin^{-1}(0.625) = 38.7°$

7 (*c*) Magnification, $m = v/u = D/f$

$\Rightarrow f = \frac{D}{m} = \frac{25}{10} = 2.5 \text{ cm} = 0.025 \text{ m}$

As, $P = \frac{1}{f} = \frac{1}{0.025} = 40 \text{ D}$

This is the required power of microscope.

8 (*a*) Let the apparent depth be O_1 for the object seen from medium 2, then $O_1 = \frac{n_2}{n_1}\frac{h}{3}$ ...(i)

So, real depth = height of liquid column + O_1.

$$\Rightarrow O_2 = \frac{n_3}{n_2}\left(\frac{h}{3} + O_1\right)$$

$$= \frac{n_3}{n_2}\left(\frac{h}{3} + \frac{n_2 h}{n_1 3}\right) \text{[using Eq. (i)]}$$

$$= \frac{h}{3}\left(\frac{n_3}{n_2} + \frac{n_3}{n_1}\right)$$

$$O_3 = \frac{1}{n_3}\left(\frac{h}{3} + O_2\right)$$

$$= \frac{h}{3}\left(\frac{1}{n_1} + \frac{1}{n_2} + \frac{1}{n_3}\right)$$

This is the required expression for apparent depth.

9 (*c*) $$n = \frac{\sin\left[\frac{(A + D_m)}{2}\right]}{\sin\left(\frac{A}{2}\right)}$$

Here, $D_m = A$

$\therefore \quad n = \frac{\sin A}{\sin A/2}$

$$\Rightarrow \quad = \frac{2\sin\frac{A}{2}\cos\frac{A}{2}}{\sin\frac{A}{2}}$$

For the given value of refractive index, $n = \sqrt{3}$

we have, $\cos\frac{A}{2} = \frac{\sqrt{3}}{2}$ or $\frac{A}{2} = 30°$

$\therefore \quad A = 60°$

Past Exams Questions

1 (*b*) Given, the rays in the prism is parallel to base.

$A = r_1 + r_2$

i.e., $r_2 = 90 - r_1$ ...(i)

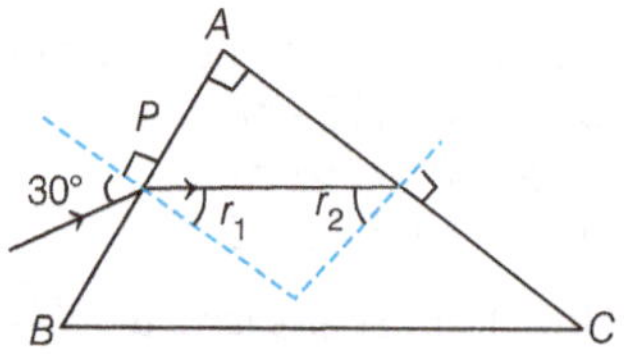

For AB interface, $\sin 30° = \mu \sin r_1$

$\Rightarrow \quad \sin r_1 = \frac{1}{2\mu}$ ...(ii)

For AC interface,

$\mu \sin r_2 = 1 \sin 90°$

$\Rightarrow \quad \sin r_2 = \frac{1}{\mu}$

$\Rightarrow \quad \sin(90 - r_1) = \frac{1}{\mu}$

$\cos r_1 = \frac{1}{\mu}$ ...(iii)

We know that, $\sin^2\theta + \cos^2\theta = 1$

From Eqs. (ii) and (iii), we get

$\sin^2 r_1 + \cos^2 r_1 = 1$

$\Rightarrow \quad \left(\frac{1}{2\mu}\right)^2 + \left(\frac{1}{\mu}\right)^2 = 1$

$\Rightarrow \quad \frac{1}{4\mu^2} + \frac{1}{\mu^2} = 1$

$\Rightarrow \quad \frac{1}{\mu^2}\left(\frac{1}{4} + \frac{1}{1}\right) = 1$

$\Rightarrow \quad \mu^2 = \frac{5}{4} \Rightarrow \mu = \frac{\sqrt{5}}{2}$

2 (*b*) Given,

Focal length of objective,

$f_o = 140 \text{ cm}$

Focal length of eyepiece, $f_e = 5 \text{ cm}$

Magnifying power, $M = \left[\frac{f_o}{f_e}\right]$

$= \left[\frac{140}{5}\right] = 28$

3 (*c*) According to given situation,

$c = \frac{x}{t_1}$ and $v = \frac{10x}{t_2}$

Since, $\sin i_c = \frac{1}{\mu}$

$$= \frac{1}{(c/v)} = \frac{v}{c} = \frac{\frac{10x}{t_2}}{\frac{x}{t_1}} = \frac{10t_1}{t_2}$$

$\Rightarrow \quad i_c = \sin^{-1}\left(\frac{10t_1}{t_2}\right)$

4 (*b*) The given situation is shown below.

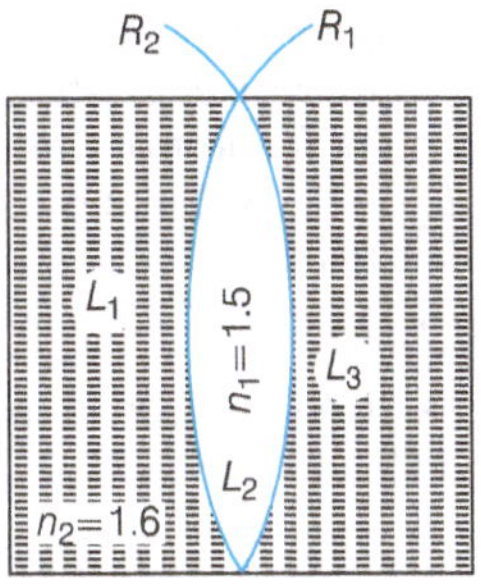

Focal length of lens L_1 is given as

$$\frac{1}{f_1} = (n_2 - 1)\left(\frac{1}{\infty} - \frac{1}{R_1}\right)$$

$$= (1.6 - 1)\left(-\frac{1}{20}\right) = -\frac{3}{100}$$

$$\Rightarrow \quad \frac{1}{f_1} = \frac{-3}{100} \text{ cm}$$

Similarly, focal length of lens L_3,

$$f_3 = \frac{-100}{3} \text{ cm}$$

Now, focal length of convex lens L_2 is given as

$$\frac{1}{f_2} = (n_1 - 1)\left(\frac{1}{R_1} - \frac{1}{R_2}\right)$$

$$= (1.5 - 1)\left(\frac{1}{20} - \frac{1}{-20}\right) = \frac{1}{20}$$

$$\Rightarrow \quad f_2 = 20 \text{ cm}$$

If F be the focal length of combination, then

$$\frac{1}{F} = \frac{1}{f_1} + \frac{1}{f_2} + \frac{1}{f_3}$$

$$= \frac{-3}{100} + \frac{1}{20} - \frac{3}{100}$$

$$\therefore \quad F = -100 \text{ cm}$$

5 (*b*) By using lens Maker's formula, we have,

$$\frac{1}{f} = (\mu - 1)\left(\frac{1}{R_1} - \frac{1}{R_2}\right)$$

$$= (1.5 - 1)\left(\frac{1}{20} - \frac{1}{-20}\right)$$

$$= 0.5\left(\frac{2}{20}\right)$$

$$\Rightarrow \quad \frac{1}{f} = 0.5 \times \frac{1}{10} \Rightarrow f = \frac{10}{0.5}$$

$$\Rightarrow \quad f = 20 \text{ cm} = 0.2 \text{ m}$$

$\therefore$ Power of the lens,

$$P = \frac{1}{f} \text{ (in metre)}$$

$$= \frac{1}{02} = +5 \text{ D}$$

6 (*a*)

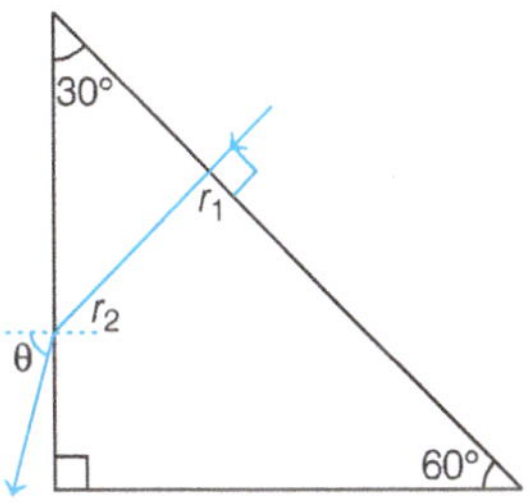

From the given figure, $r_1 = 0°$

As, $\quad A = r_1 + r_2$

where, A is the angle of prism .

$$30° = 0° + r_2 \Rightarrow r_2 = 30°$$

Using the Snell's law, in glass and air interference,

$$n_2 \sin \theta_2 = n_1 \sin \theta_1$$

$$\Rightarrow \quad n_2 \sin r_2 = n_1 \sin e$$

Given,

$$\frac{n_2}{n_1} = \frac{\sqrt{3}}{1}$$

$$\sqrt{3} \sin 30° = 1 \cdot \sin e$$

$$\frac{\sqrt{3}}{2} = \sin e$$

$$\Rightarrow \quad \sin e = \sin 60°$$

$$\Rightarrow \quad e = 60°$$

7 (*d*)

$$\frac{1}{f} = \frac{1}{v} - \frac{1}{u}$$

$$\frac{1}{+30} = \frac{1}{v} - \frac{1}{(-60)}$$

$$\Rightarrow \quad v = 60 \text{ cm}$$

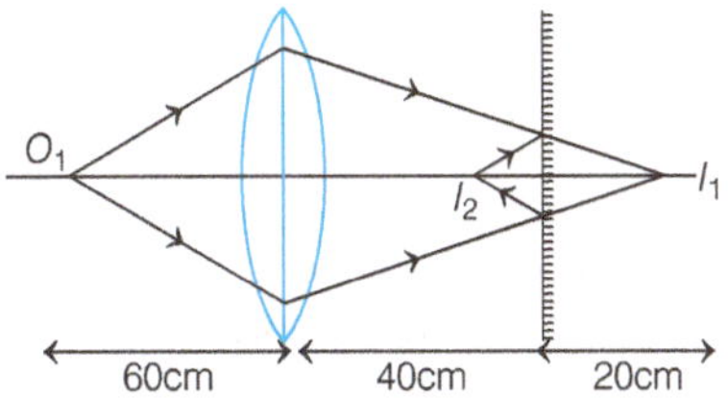

Again by using lens formula,

$$\frac{1}{v} + \frac{1}{20} = \frac{1}{30}$$

or $\quad v = -60$ cm from the lens

i.e., 20 cm from the plane mirror and virtual in nature.

8 (*b*) Critical angle, $i_c = 45°$

We know that,

$$\mu = \frac{1}{\sin i_c} = \frac{1}{\sin 45°} = \frac{1}{1/\sqrt{2}} = \sqrt{2}$$

$$\Rightarrow \mu = \sqrt{2}$$

$$\Rightarrow \frac{\text{Velocity of light in air}}{\text{Velocity of light in medium}} = \sqrt{2}$$

$$\Rightarrow \quad \frac{3 \times 10^8}{v_m} = \sqrt{2}$$

$$\Rightarrow \quad v_m = \frac{3}{\sqrt{2}} \times 10^8 \text{ m/s}$$

9 (*b*)

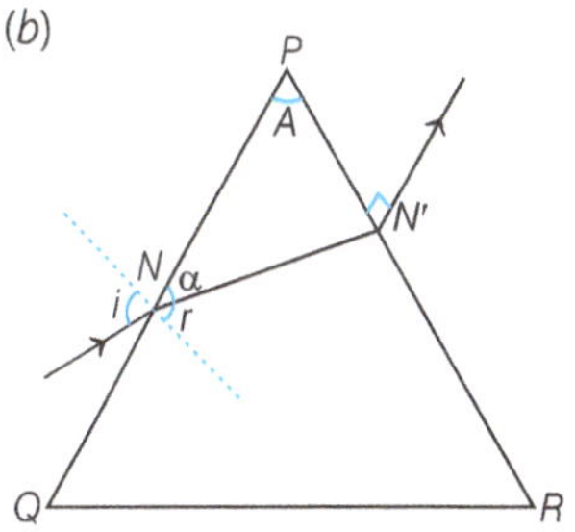

From figure in $\Delta PNN'$,

$$A + \alpha + 90° = 180°$$

$$\Rightarrow \quad \alpha = 90° - A \quad \text{...(i)}$$

Also, $\quad r + \alpha = 90°$

$$\Rightarrow \quad r = 90° - \alpha$$

$$= 90° - (90° - A) = A$$

[$\because$ from Eq. (i)]

$$\Rightarrow \quad r = A$$

From Snell's law, $\mu_1 \sin i = \mu_2 \sin r$

$$\Rightarrow \quad \sin i = \mu \sin A$$

(here, $\mu_1 = 1$ and $\mu_2 = \mu$)

For small angle, $\sin \theta \simeq \theta \Rightarrow i = \mu A$

10 (*d*) When the lens is cut along its principal axis, the focal length of the two halves will remain same because the radius of curvature of both the surfaces are still same. So, the power also remains same as $P = \dfrac{1}{f}$

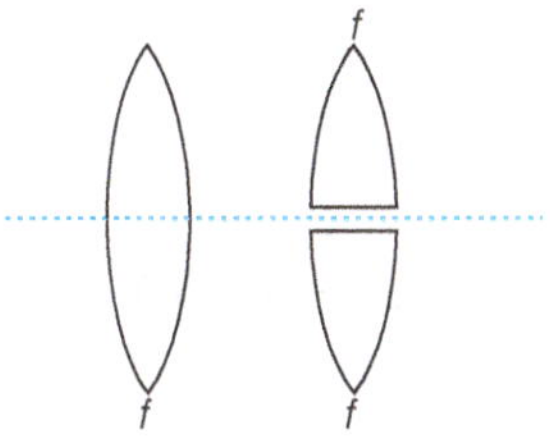

11 (*a*) **Case I**

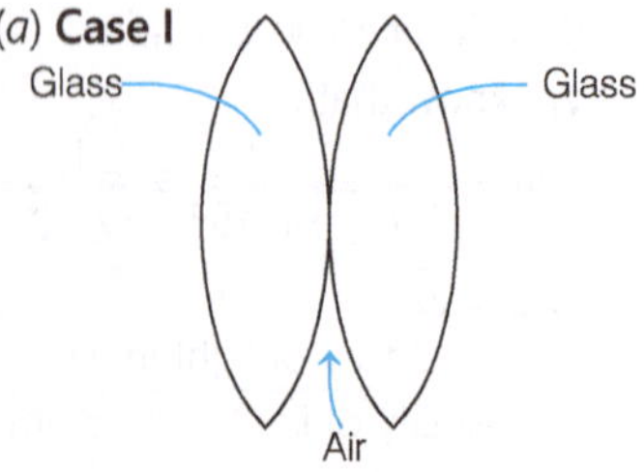

$$\frac{1}{F_1}=\frac{1}{f_1}+\frac{1}{f_2}=\frac{1}{f}+\frac{1}{f}$$

[$\because$ Here, $f_1=f_2$]

$$=\frac{2}{f} \Rightarrow F_1=\frac{f}{2} \quad \text{...(i)}$$

Case II

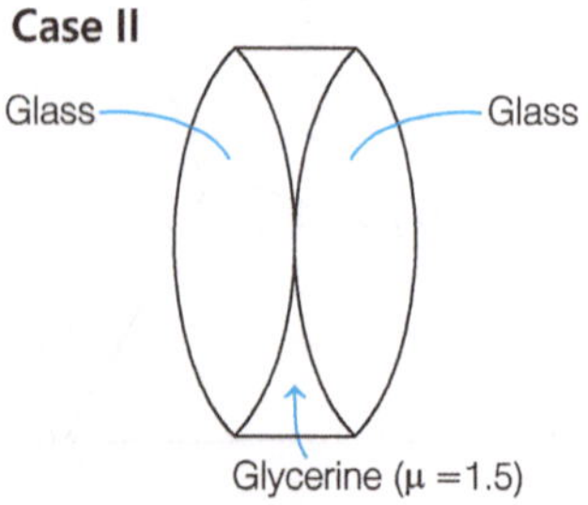

$$\frac{1}{F_2}=\frac{1}{f}+\frac{1}{(-f)}+\frac{1}{f}=\frac{1}{f}$$

$$\Rightarrow \quad F_2=f \quad \text{... (ii)}$$

From Eqs. (i) and (ii), we get

$$F_1:F_2=1:2$$

12 (*b*)

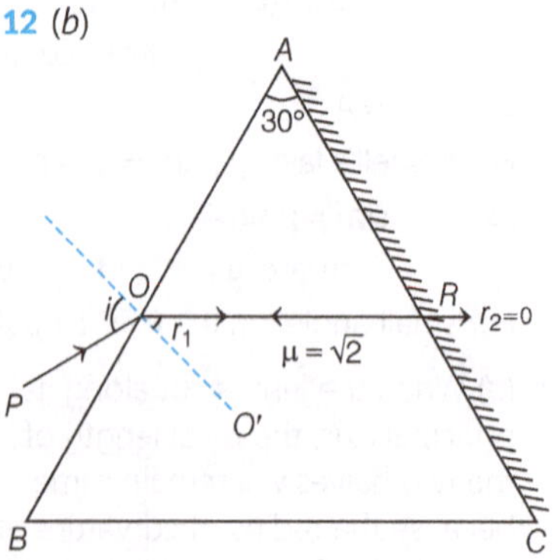

In ΔAOR,

$$\angle AOR+\angle ARO+\angle OAR=180^\circ$$

$$\Rightarrow \angle AOR+90^\circ+30^\circ=180^\circ$$

$$\Rightarrow \angle AOR=180^\circ-120^\circ=60^\circ \quad \text{...(i)}$$

As we know,

$$\angle AOR+\angle r_1=90^\circ$$

$$\Rightarrow \quad \angle r_1=90^\circ-60^\circ=30^\circ$$

[From Eq. (i)]

Applying Snell's law at the face *AB*, we get

$$\mu=\frac{\sin i}{\sin r_1}$$

Substituting the given values, we get

$$\sqrt{2}=\frac{\sin i}{\sin 30^\circ}$$

$$\Rightarrow \sin i=\sin 30^\circ\times\sqrt{2}$$

$$=\frac{1}{2}\times\sqrt{2}\left(\because \sin 30^\circ=\frac{1}{2}\right)$$

$$=\frac{1}{\sqrt{2}} \text{ or } i=\sin^{-1}\left(\frac{1}{\sqrt{2}}\right)$$

$$\Rightarrow \quad i=45^\circ \quad \left(\because \sin 45^\circ=\frac{1}{\sqrt{2}}\right)$$

13 (*b*)

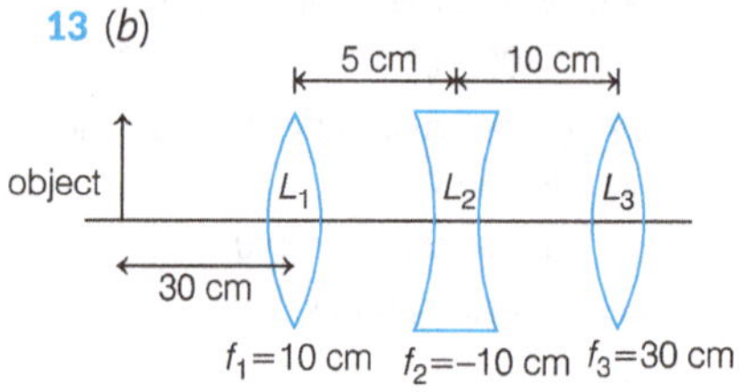

For lens L_1,

$$u=-30 \text{ cm}, f=10 \text{ cm}$$

Using, $\frac{1}{v}-\frac{1}{u}=\frac{1}{f}$, we have,

$$\frac{1}{v}-\frac{1}{(-30)}=\frac{1}{10}$$

$$\Rightarrow \frac{1}{v}=\frac{1}{10}-\frac{1}{30}=\frac{2}{30}=\frac{1}{15}$$

$$\Rightarrow \quad v=15 \text{ cm}$$

This image acts like object for L_2.

$\Rightarrow$ For L_2, $u=+10$ cm,

$$f=-10 \text{ cm}$$

$$\frac{1}{v}-\frac{1}{u}=\frac{1}{f} \Leftrightarrow \frac{1}{v}-\frac{1}{10}=\frac{1}{-10}$$

$$\Rightarrow \quad \frac{1}{v}=0 \text{ or } v=\infty$$

For L_2, rays from L_1, are directed at its second focal point

$\therefore$ rays becomes parallel after refraction.

Hence, for L_3,

$$u=\infty$$

(parallel rays falls on L_3)

$\Rightarrow$ Images is formed at focus of L_3, at 30 cm on right of L_3.

14 (*d*) iven, $f_1=10$ cm

$$f_2=15 \text{ cm}$$

From the diagram it is clear that rays from lens L_1 converges at a fixed point f_1 and from where the lens L_2 diverges the rays parallel to principal axis.

i.e. $f_1+f_2=10+15=25$ cm

15 (*c*) The given situation in question is as follows

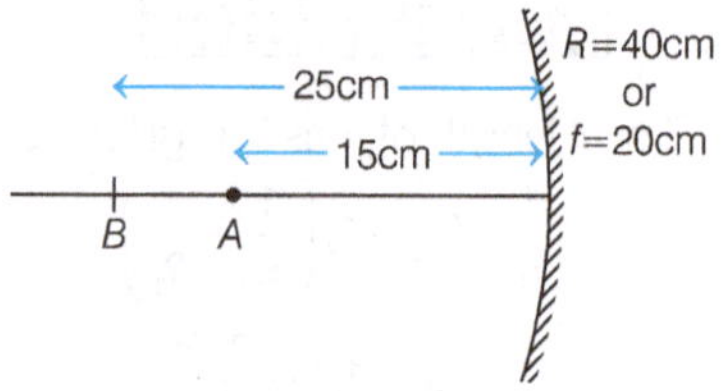

Using mirror formula, $\frac{1}{v}+\frac{1}{u}=\frac{1}{f}$

For point *A*,

$$u=-15 \text{ cm}, f=-20 \text{ cm}$$

$$\frac{1}{v_A}+\frac{1}{-15}=\frac{1}{-20}$$

$$\frac{1}{v_A}=\frac{1}{15}-\frac{1}{20}=\frac{4-3}{60}=\frac{1}{60}$$

$$v_A=+60 \text{ cm}$$

For point *B*,

$$u=-25 \text{ cm}, f=-20 \text{ cm}$$

$$\frac{1}{v_B}+\frac{1}{-25}=\frac{1}{-20}$$

$$\Rightarrow \quad \frac{1}{v_B}=\frac{1}{25}-\frac{1}{20}$$

$$=\frac{4-5}{100}=-\frac{1}{100}$$

$$\Rightarrow \quad v_B=-100 \text{ cm}$$

Hence, the distance between images formed by the mirror is

$$d=|v_A-v_B|=|60-(-100)|$$

$$\Rightarrow \quad d=160 \text{ cm}$$

16 (*c*) $v_A=\frac{c}{\mu_A}$

$$v_B=\frac{c}{\mu_B}$$

$$\because \; v_A-v_B=c\left(\frac{1}{\mu_A}-\frac{1}{\mu_B}\right)$$

$$\Rightarrow 2.6\times10^7=3\times10^8\left(\frac{1}{\mu_A}-\frac{1}{\mu_B}\right)$$

$\Rightarrow \quad \mu_A = 1.30$

So, $\quad \dfrac{\mu_B}{\mu_A} = \dfrac{1.47}{1.30} = 1.13$

17 (*a*) By using Snell's law,

$$\mu = \frac{\sin i}{\sin r} \Rightarrow \frac{4}{3} = \frac{\sin\theta}{\sin\theta'} \qquad \text{...(i)}$$

From diagram, $\theta'' = 90 - \theta'$

For total internal reflection,

$$\frac{1}{\mu} = \sin\theta''$$

$$\Rightarrow \quad \sin\theta' = \sqrt{1 - \left(\frac{3}{4}\right)^2}$$

$$= \sqrt{\frac{7}{16}} = \frac{\sqrt{7}}{4}$$

Putting value of $\sin\theta'$ in Eq. (i), we get

$$\frac{4}{3} = \frac{\sin\theta \times 4}{\sqrt{7}}$$

$$\Rightarrow \quad \sin\theta = \frac{\sqrt{7}}{3} \Rightarrow \theta = \sin^{-1}\left(\frac{\sqrt{7}}{3}\right)$$

18 (*a*) For a telescope in normal setting,

$$f_o + f_e = L$$

(length of the tube of telescope)

and $\quad \dfrac{f_o}{f_e} = m$ (magnification)

According to the given values in the question, we have

$$f_o + f_e = 60 \text{ cm and } \frac{f_o}{f_e} = 5$$

$$\Rightarrow \quad f_o = 5 f_e$$

On solving the above equations, we have

$$f_e = 10 \text{ cm}$$

19 (*d*)

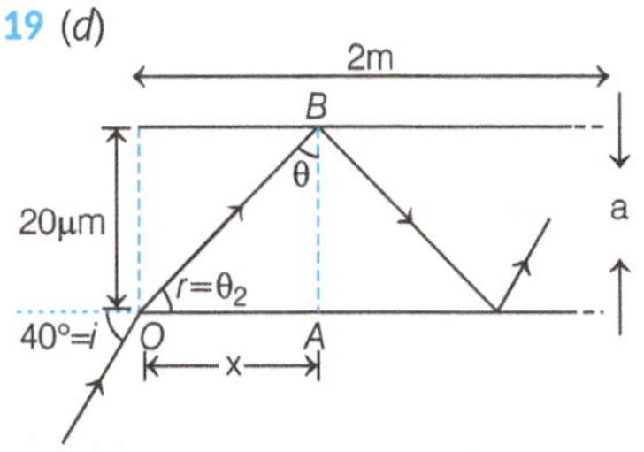

From Snell's law, $n_1 \sin i = n_2 \sin r$

where, $n_1 = 1$, $n_2 = 1.31$ and $i = 40°$

So, we get $1 \sin 40° = 1.31 \sin r$

$$\Rightarrow \quad \sin r = \frac{0.64}{1.31} = 0.49 \approx 0.5$$

So, $\quad r = 30°$

From ΔOAB, $\theta = 90 - r = 60°$

Now, $\tan\theta = \dfrac{x}{20\,\mu\text{m}}$

$\Rightarrow x = 20\sqrt{3}\,\mu\text{m}$ [$\because \tan 60° = \sqrt{3}$]

One reflection occurs in $20\sqrt{3}\,\mu$m.

$\therefore$ Total number of reflections occurring in 2 m

$$= n = \frac{2\text{ m}}{20\sqrt{3}\,\mu\text{m}}$$

$$\approx 57000 \text{ reflections}$$

Skill Boosters

1 (*b*) According to figure, relation between r_1 and r_2, r_3 and r_4 and r_5 and r_6 are given as,

$$r_1 + r_2 = 90° \qquad \text{... (i)}$$
$$r_3 + r_4 = 90° \qquad \text{... (ii)}$$
$$r_5 + r_6 = 90° \qquad \text{... (iii)}$$

Since, the emergent ray is parallel to incident ray,

$$r_7 = 90° - i \qquad \text{... (iv)}$$

$\sin i = \mu_1 \sin r_1$

$$\mu_1 \sin r_2 = \mu_2 \sin r_3$$
$$\mu_2 \sin r_4 = \mu_3 \sin r_5$$
$$\mu_3 \sin r_6 = \sin r_7$$

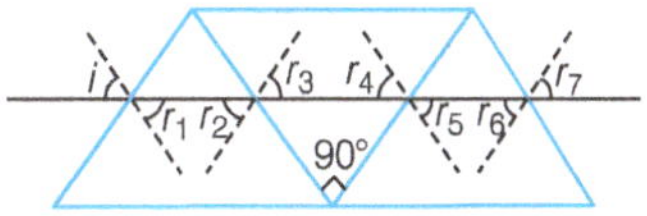

Using Eqs. (i) to (iv) in the above equations

$$\sin i = \mu_1 \sin r_1 \qquad \text{... (v)}$$
$$\mu_1 \cos r_1 = \mu_2 \sin r_3 \qquad \text{... (vi)}$$
$$\mu_2 \cos r_3 = \mu_3 \sin r_5 \qquad \text{... (vii)}$$
$$\mu_3 \cos r_5 = \cos i \qquad \text{... (viii)}$$

Carrying out the manipulation

$$(\text{Eq. v})^2 + (\text{Eq. vi})^2 + (\text{Eq. vii})^2 + (\text{Eq. viii})^2$$

We get $\quad 1 + \mu_2^2 = \mu_1^2 + \mu_3^2$

$$\mu_1^2 + \mu_3^2 - \mu_2^2 = 1$$

2 (*a*) I_1 is image of pin which is formed at x below surface, also apparent depth of object $= \dfrac{20}{\mu}$

Thus, $\quad x = \dfrac{20}{(10/3)} = 6$ cm

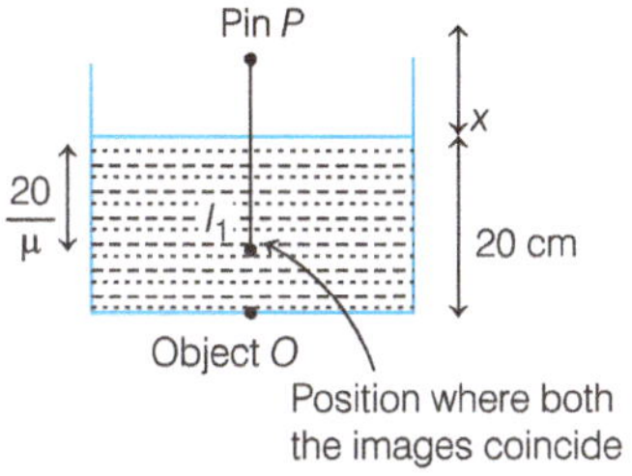

3 (*c*) According to question,

$$\mu AB = \mu' CD \Rightarrow \frac{AB}{CD} = \frac{\mu'}{\mu} \qquad \text{... (i)}$$

where, μ = refractive index of first medium

μ' = Refractive index of second medium.

If t_1 and t_2 be the time taken to travel from A to B in first medium and from C to D in second medium, then

$$t_1 v_1 = AB$$
$$t_2 v_2 = CD$$

$$\Rightarrow \quad \frac{t_1 v_1}{t_2 v_2} = \frac{AB}{CD}$$

$$\Rightarrow \quad \frac{t_1}{t_2} = \frac{AB}{CD} \cdot \frac{v_2}{v_1} \qquad \text{... (ii)}$$

Since, $\quad \mu \propto \dfrac{1}{v} \Rightarrow \dfrac{\mu}{\mu'} = \dfrac{v_2}{v_1} \quad \text{... (iii)}$

From Eqs. (i), (ii) and (iii), we have

$$\frac{t_1}{t_2} = \frac{\mu'}{\mu} \times \frac{\mu}{\mu'} = 1$$

4 (*c*) The ray diagram for given situation is shown in the following figure.

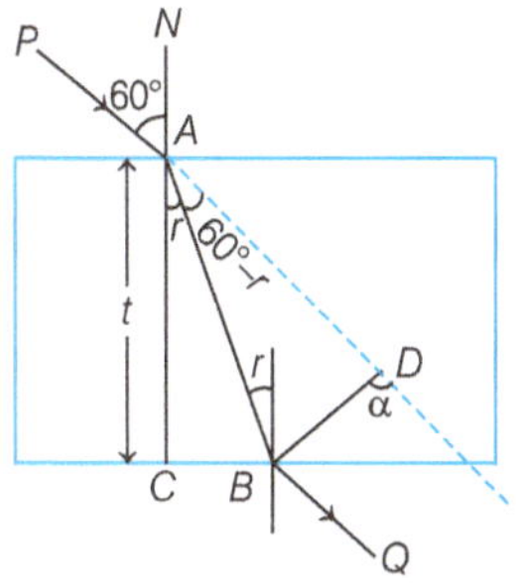

When the ray of light incident along PA and refracted along AB, then by Snell's law

$$\mu = \frac{\sin 60°}{\sin r}$$

$$\Rightarrow \quad 2 = \frac{\sqrt{3}/2}{\sin r} \Rightarrow \sin r = \frac{\sqrt{3}}{4}$$

$$\therefore \cos r = \sqrt{1-\sin^2 r}$$

$$= \sqrt{1-\left(\frac{\sqrt{3}}{4}\right)^2} = \sqrt{1-\frac{3}{16}}$$

$$= \frac{\sqrt{13}}{4} \Rightarrow \cos r = \frac{\sqrt{13}}{4}$$

In ΔABC,

$$\sec r = \frac{AB}{AC} = \frac{AB}{t} \Rightarrow AB = t\sec r$$

$\therefore$ Lateral shifting,

$$BD = AB\sin\angle BAD = AB\sin(60° - r)$$

$$\Rightarrow BD = t\sec r\,(\sin 60° \cos r - \cos 60° \sin r)$$

$$= \frac{t}{\cos r}\left[\frac{\sqrt{3}}{2}\cos r - \frac{1}{2}\sin r\right]$$

$$= \frac{1}{\sqrt{13}/4}\left[\frac{\sqrt{3}}{2}\cdot\frac{\sqrt{13}}{4} - \frac{1}{2}\cdot\frac{\sqrt{3}}{4}\right]$$

$$\Rightarrow BD = \frac{\sqrt{3}}{2\sqrt{13}}(\sqrt{13}-1)$$

5 (*a*) The given situation is shown in the figure. For the near end A of the rod, $\frac{1}{f} = \frac{1}{u} + \frac{1}{v}$

$$\Rightarrow \quad v = \frac{uf}{u-f} = \frac{Lf}{L-f}$$

For far end B of the rod,

$$\frac{1}{f} = \frac{1}{u+L} + \frac{1}{v_1}$$

$$\Rightarrow \quad \frac{1}{v_1} = \frac{1}{f} - \frac{1}{2L} = \frac{2L-f}{(f)(2L)}$$

$$\therefore \quad v_1 = \frac{(f)(2L)}{2L-f}$$

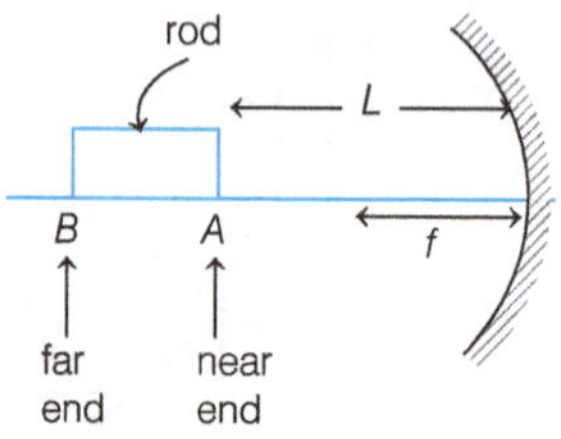

Length of image

$$= v - v_1 = \frac{Lf}{L-f} - \frac{(2L)(f)}{(2L-f)}$$

$$= \frac{Lf(2L-f) - 2Lf(L-f)}{(L-f)(2L-f)}$$

$$= \frac{Lf^2}{(L-f)(2L-f)}$$

7 (*b*) Let μ_1 and μ_2 be refractive indices of two optical media, respectively. Here, $\mu_1 > \mu_2$. PQ is the boundary separating the two media.

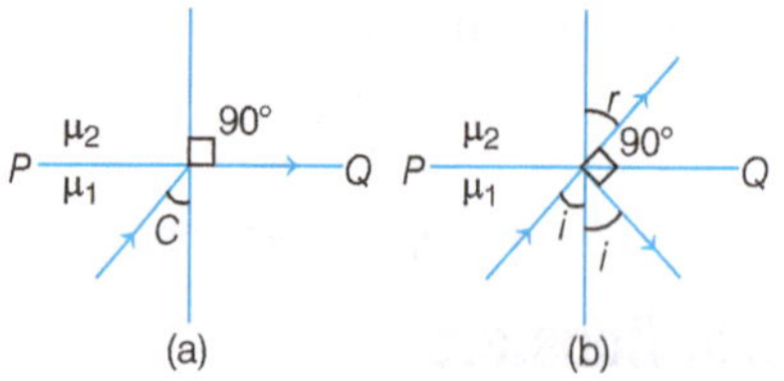

From Fig. (a) $\quad \sin C = \frac{\mu_2}{\mu_1} \quad$ ... (i)

From fig. (b), $r = (90 - i)$

We know that,

$$\frac{\mu_2}{\mu_1} = \frac{\sin i}{\sin r} = \frac{\sin i}{\sin(90-i)} = \frac{\sin i}{\cos i} = \tan i$$

Thus, $\quad \tan i = \frac{\mu_2}{\mu_1} \quad$ ... (ii)

From Eqs. (i) and (ii), we get

$$\sin C = \tan i \quad \text{... (iii)}$$

Given that $\quad \frac{\sin C}{\sin i} = \eta \quad$ ... (iv)

From Eqs. (iii) and (iv), we have

$$\frac{\tan i}{\sin i} = \eta \text{ or } \frac{1}{\cos i} = \eta$$

or $\quad \cos i = (1/\eta) \quad$ ... (v)

From Eq. (ii)

$$\frac{\mu_2}{\mu_1} = \frac{\sin i}{\cos i} = \frac{\sqrt{1-\cos^2 i}}{\cos i}$$

or $\quad \frac{\mu_2}{\mu_1} = \sqrt{(\eta^2 - 1)}$

or $\quad \frac{\mu_1}{\mu_2} = \frac{1}{\sqrt{(\eta^2-1)}}$

$$\therefore \quad \mu_{relative} = \frac{\mu_1}{\mu_2}$$

$$= \frac{1}{\sqrt{(1.28)^2 - 1}} = 1.25$$

8 (*b*) The formation of image with convex lens and convex mirror is shown below.

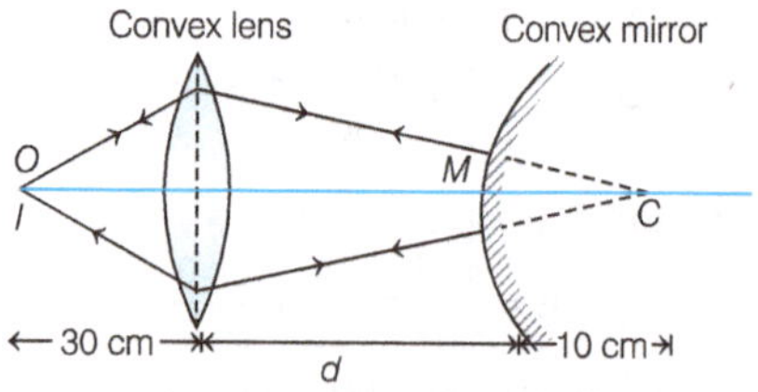

According to given condition, image of object 'O' coincide with object, as shown in the above figure.

In this situation, the rays after refraction from the lens must fall on the convex mirror normally or the rays refracted from the lens must meet at centre of curvature (C) of mirror.

For lens, $u = -30$ cm, $f = 20$ cm

$$\Rightarrow \quad \frac{1}{v} = \frac{1}{u} + \frac{1}{f} = \frac{1}{-30} + \frac{1}{20} = \frac{1}{60}$$

$$\Rightarrow \quad v = 60 \text{ cm}$$

Hence, from figure, the distance between lens and mirror, $d = v - 10$

$$= 60 - 10 = 50 \text{ cm}$$

9 (*c*) Here, $u = -y, v = -y'$

$$\mu_1 = 1, \mu_2 = \frac{4}{3}$$

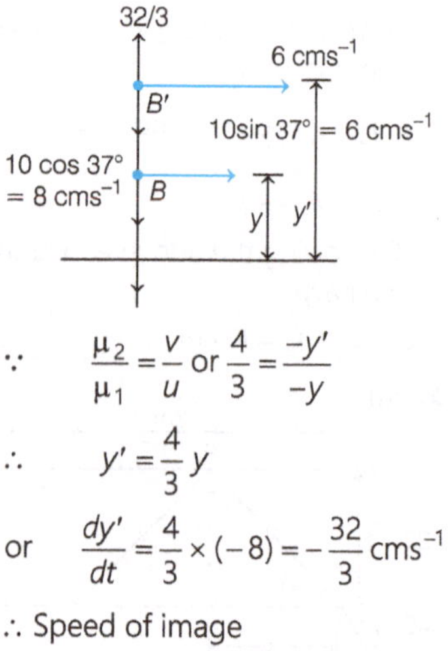

$$\because \quad \frac{\mu_2}{\mu_1} = \frac{v}{u} \text{ or } \frac{4}{3} = \frac{-y'}{-y}$$

$$\therefore \quad y' = \frac{4}{3}y$$

or $\quad \frac{dy'}{dt} = \frac{4}{3} \times (-8) = -\frac{32}{3} \text{ cms}^{-1}$

$\therefore$ Speed of image

$$= \sqrt{\left(\frac{32}{3}\right)^2 + 6^2} = 12.24 \text{ cms}^{-1}$$

$$\therefore \quad \theta = \tan^{-1}\left(\frac{9}{16}\right)$$

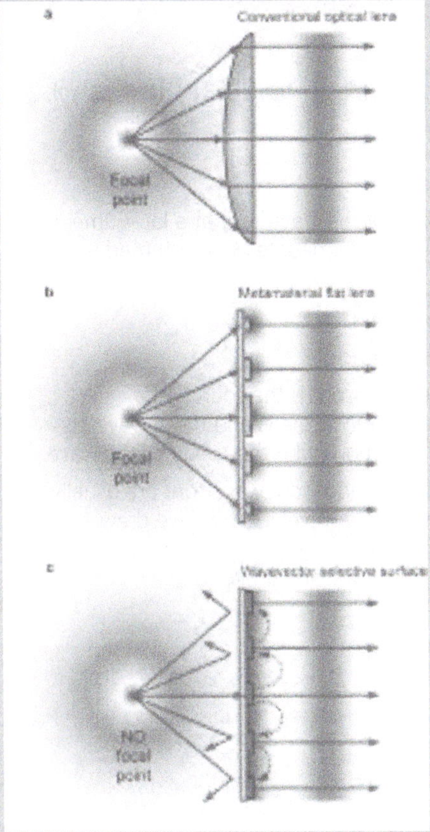

Topicwise No. of Ques asked in 5 Years (NEET)

Topics	No. of Questions				
	2024	2023	2022	2021	2020
Coherent and Incoherent Additions of Waves	–	–	–	–	1
Interference of Light Waves and Young's Experiment	1	1	1	–	2
Diffraction	–	–	–	–	1
Polarisation	1	–	1	–	1

Special Type of Ques Asked In 5 Years (NEET)

Types	Years				
	2024	2023	2022	2021	2020
A-R	–	–	–	–	–
Statement Based	–	–	–	–	–
Matching	–	–	–	–	–

Last 5 Years Weigtage (NEET)

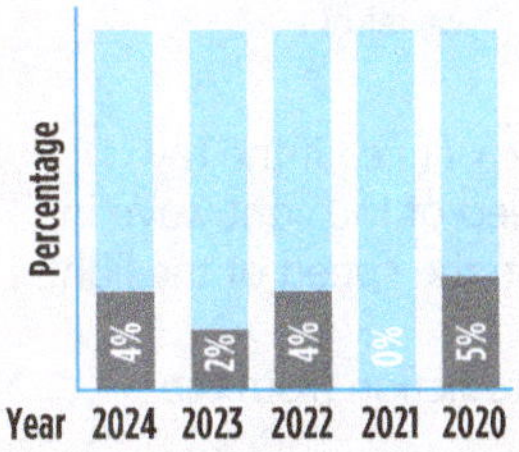

10

Scan for Physics Through Concept Master Videos

Wave Optics

- The **corpuscular model of light** predicted that , if the ray of light (on refraction) bends towards the normal, then the speed of light would be greater in the second medium.
- In 1678, the **wave model of light** was proposed by Dutch physicist Christian Huygens. It predicted that on refraction if the wave bends towards the normal, then the speed of light would be less in the second medium. This is in contradiction to the prediction made by using the corpuscular model of light.
- Later, it was confirmed by experiments that the speed of light in water is less than the speed in air. It confirmed the prediction of the wave model.
- Thomas Young performed his famous interference experiment in 1801, it was firmly established that light is indeed a wave phenomenon.
- The wavelength of visible light was measured and found to be extremely small, e.g. the wavelength of yellow light is about 0.6 μm. Light can be assumed to approximately travel in straight line, this is because of the smallness of wavelength of visible light.
- The branch of optics in which one completely neglects the finiteness of the wavelength is called **geometrical optics** and a ray is defined as the path of energy propagation in the limit of wavelength tending to zero.
- Maxwell propounded that light must be an electromagnetic wave. According to Maxwell, electromagnetic waves are coupled time-varying electric and magnetic fields that propagates in space.
- Ray optics is based on rectilinear propagation of light and deals with mirrors, lenses, reflection, refraction, etc., while wave optics consider that light travels as a wave, can bend around objects, can diffract and interfere, etc.
- The phenomena of polarisation which is based on the fact that the light waves are transverse electromagnetic waves.

Huygens' Principle

Wavefront

- The locus of all those particles which are vibrating in the same phase at any instant is called wavefront, thus a wavefront is a surface of constant phase.
- The shape of wavefront depends on the shape of source of light. Wavefront can be of three types.
    - (i) **Spherical wavefront** When the source of light is a point source, the wavefront is sphere with centre as source.

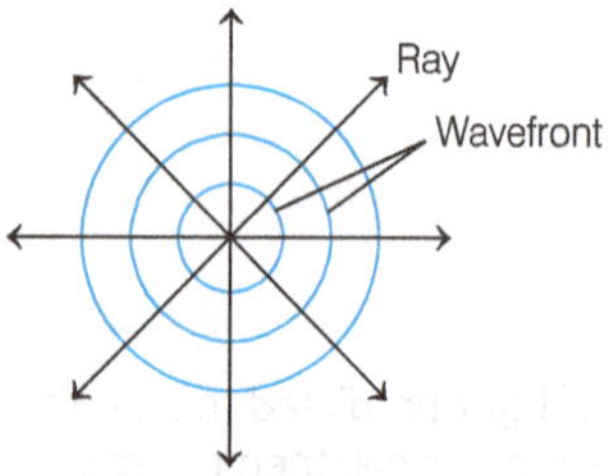

    - (ii) **Cylindrical wavefront** When the source of light is linear, then all the points equidistant from the source lie on a cylinder. Therefore, the wavefront is cylindrical in shape.

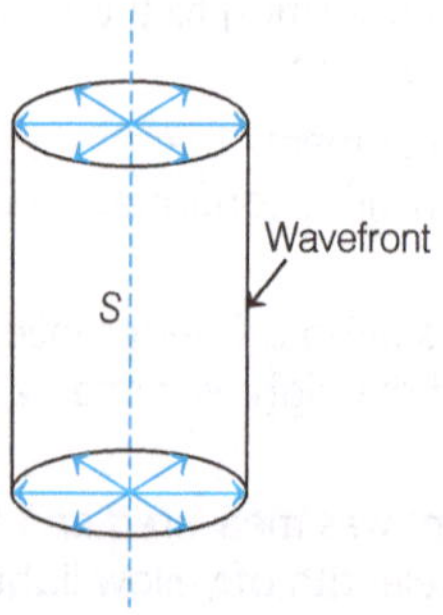

    - (iii) **Plane wavefront** When a point source or linear source of light is at very large distance, a small portion of spherical or cylindrical wavefront appears to be plane. Such wavefront is called plane wavefront.

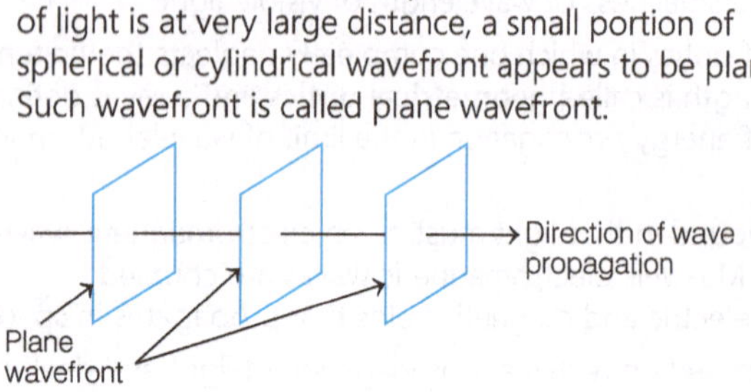

- The speed with which the wavefront moves outwards from the source is called the **speed of wave**. The energy of the wave travels in a direction perpendicular to the wavefront.
- Huygens' principle is a geometrical construction, which gives the shape of the wavefront at any time and allows us to determine the shape of the wavefront at a later time. It also tells how a wavefront propagates through medium.

Huygens' Construction

- According to Huygens' principle,
    - (i) Each point of the wavefront is the source of a secondary disturbance (wavelets) and these wavelets spread out in all directions with the speed of the wave.
    - (ii) These wavelets originating from wavefront are usually referred to as secondary wavelets and if we draw a common tangent to all these spheres, we obtain the new position of the wavefront at later time.

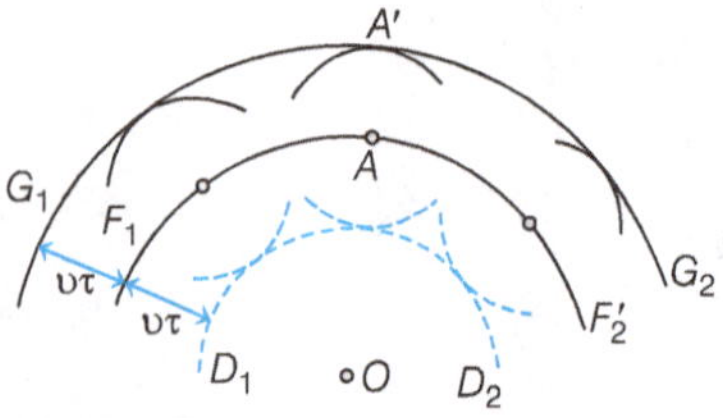

    - (iii) The secondary waves have same frequency but reduced intensity.
    Huygens' argued that the amplitude of the secondary wavelets is maximum in forward direction and zero in the backward direction. Thus, Huygens' could explain the absence of backwaves.

Refraction and Reflection of Plane Waves using Huygens' Principle

- **Refraction of a plane waves** is derived using Huygens' principle as shown in the following figure,

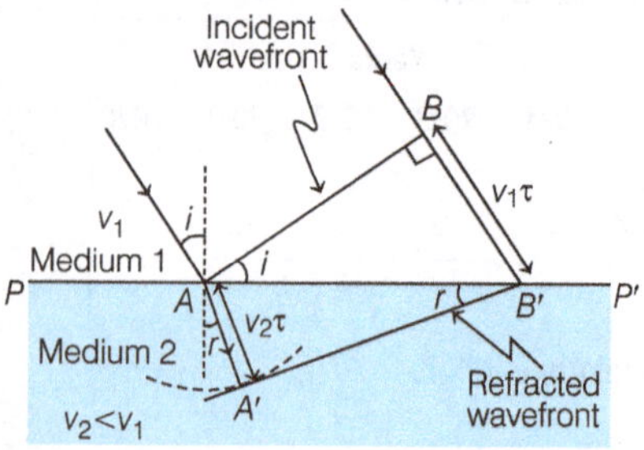

We get the important result that if $r < i$ (i.e. if the ray bends towards the normal), the speed of the light wave in second medium (v_2) will be less than the speed of the light wave in the first medium (v_1).
This prediction is opposite to the prediction from the corpuscular model of light.

This implies that **refraction of plane wave follows Snell's law**. i.e. $n_1 \sin i = n_2 \sin r$

where, i = angle of incidence of plane wave
and r = angle of refraction of plane wave.

- Speed and wavelength of plane wave in first medium are v_1 and λ_1 respectively and in second medium are v_2 and λ_2 respectively, then $\frac{\lambda_1}{\lambda_2} = \frac{v_1}{v_2}$.

  The above equation implies that, when a wave gets refracted into a denser medium ($v_1 > v_2$), the wavelength and the speed of propagation decrease but the frequency $\nu\left(=\frac{v}{\lambda}\right)$ remains the same.
- Also, the incident ray, the normal to the surface at the point of incidence and the reflected ray, all lie in same plane, which proves the second law of refraction.
- **Reflection of plane waves** is derived using Huygens principle. This implies that plane wave follows the law of reflection.
  Reflection and refraction of light on the basis of Huygens principle is shown below.

1. **Thin Prism** We consider a plane wave passing through a thin prism. Clearly, since the speed of light waves is less in glass, the lower portion of the incoming wavefront (which travels through the greatest thickness of glass) will get delayed resulting in a tilt in the emerging wavefront.

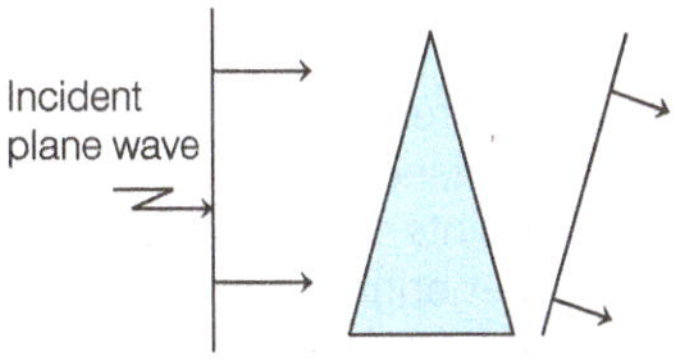

2. **Convex Lens** We consider a plane wave incident on a thin convex lens; the central part of the incident plane wave traverses thickest portion of the lens and is delayed the most. The emerging wavefront has a depression at the centre and wavefront becomes spherical and converges at point F which is called the focus.

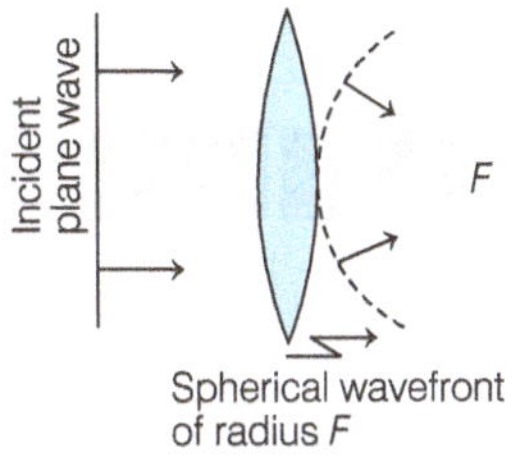

3. **Reflection of Plane wave by a Concave Mirror** A plane wave is incident on a concave mirror and on reflection, we have a spherical wave converging to the focal point F. In a similar manner, we can understand refraction and reflection by concave lenses and convex mirrors.

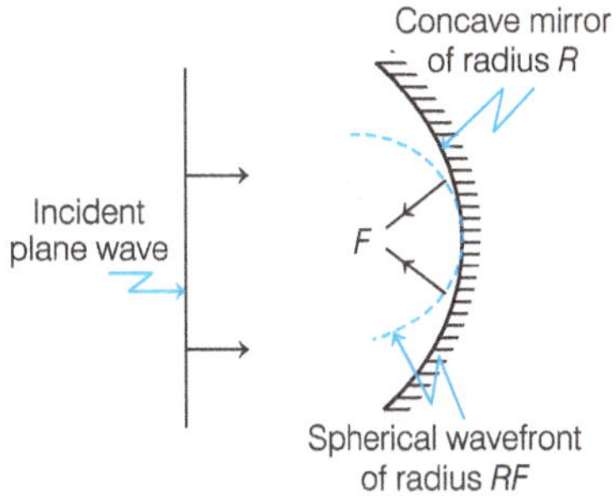

For Concept Master Video

Marks Maximiser

- Relationship among relative index, velocity and wavelength $\frac{v_1}{v_2} = \frac{\lambda_1}{\lambda_2} = \frac{\mu_2}{\mu_1}$
- $\mu = \frac{c}{v} = \frac{\text{Speed of light in vacuum}}{\text{Speed of light in medium}}$

Coherent and Incoherent Addition of Waves

- **Coherent sources** of light are the sources which emit light waves of same frequency, same wavelength and have a constant initial phase difference.
- Two sources of light, which do not emit light waves with a constant phase difference are called **incoherent sources**.
- **Superposition Principle** According to superposition principle, at a particular point in a medium, the resultant displacement produced by a number of waves is the vector sum of the displacements produced by each of the waves.
  $y = y_1 + y_2 + y_3 + y_4 + \ldots\ldots$
- The phenomenon of redistribution of energy in the region of superposition of waves is called **interference**.

  The points of maximum intensity in the regions of superposition of waves are said to be in **constructive interference** whereas the points of minimum intensity are said to be in **destructive interference**.
- Two waves of amplitudes a_1 and a_2 interfere at a point, where phase difference is ϕ, then resultant amplitude is given by

$$A^2 = a_1^2 + a_2^2 + 2a_1a_2 \cos\phi$$

  For constructive interference, $A_{max} = (a_1 + a_2)$
  For destructive interference, $A_{min} = (a_1 - a_2)$
- Resultant intensity, $I = I_1 + I_2 + 2\sqrt{I_1 I_2}\cos\phi$
  When $I_1 = I_2 = I_0$, then resultant intensity,

$$I = I_0 + I_0 + 2I_0\cos\phi = 2I_0(1 + \cos\phi)$$

or, $I = 4I_0 \cos^2\left(\frac{\phi}{2}\right)$

For constructive interference, $\phi = 0, \pm 2\pi, \pm 4\pi \dots$.

For destructive interference, $\phi = \pm \pi, \pm 3\pi, \pm 5\pi \dots$.

Marks Maximiser

- Ratio of maximum and minimum intensity is given by

$$\frac{I_{max}}{I_{min}} = \left(\frac{a_1 + a_2}{a_1 - a_2}\right)^2 = \left(\frac{\sqrt{I_1} + \sqrt{I_2}}{\sqrt{I_1} - \sqrt{I_2}}\right)^2$$

- **Addition of incoherent waves** The phase difference between the two vibrating sources changes rapidly with time such waves are incoherent.

  For these type of waves, resultant intensity,

$$I = I_1 + I_2 + \dots\dots$$

- Locus of points for which $S_1P - S_2P$ is equal to zero, $\pm\lambda, \pm 2\lambda, \pm 3\lambda$ is shown in the following graph.

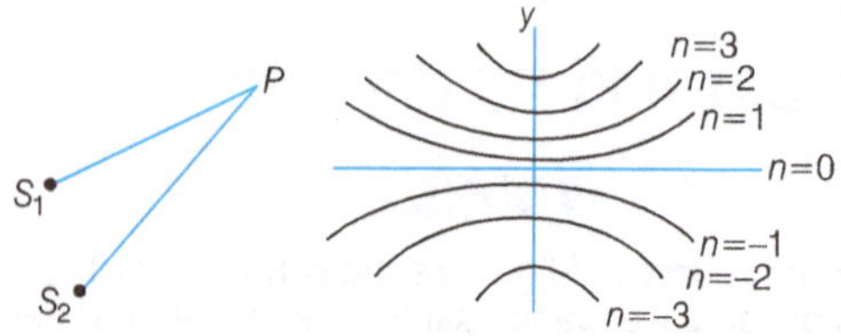

- If the two sources are coherent, then the phase difference, ϕ at any point will not change with time and we will have a stable interference pattern. The position of maxima and minima will not change with time.
- If the two needles do not maintain a constant phase difference, then the interference pattern will also change with time.
- If phase difference changes very rapidly with time, the positions of maxima and minima will also vary rapidly with time. The average intensity given by $I = 2I_0$.

Interference of Light Waves and Young's Experiment

- It two sodium lam ps illuminate two pinholes S_1 and S_2, the intensities will add up and no interference fringes will be observed on the screen. Thus, the source undergoes abrupt change in times of the order of 10^{-10} second.

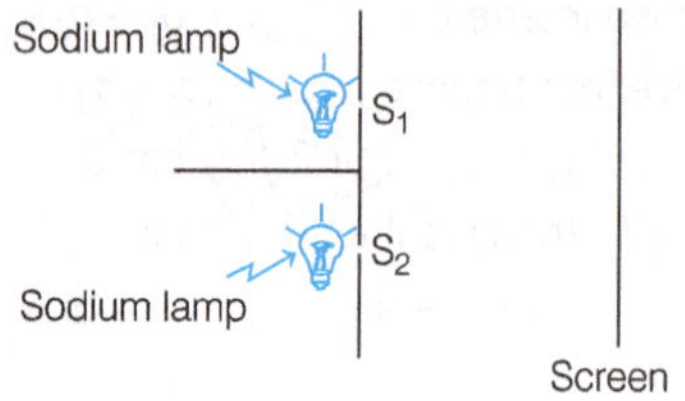

- Young used an ingenious technique to lock the phases of waves emanating from S_1 and S_2 as shown in figure (a) and (b). Spherical waves emanating from S_1 and S_2 will produce interference fringes on screen GG' as shown in figure (b).

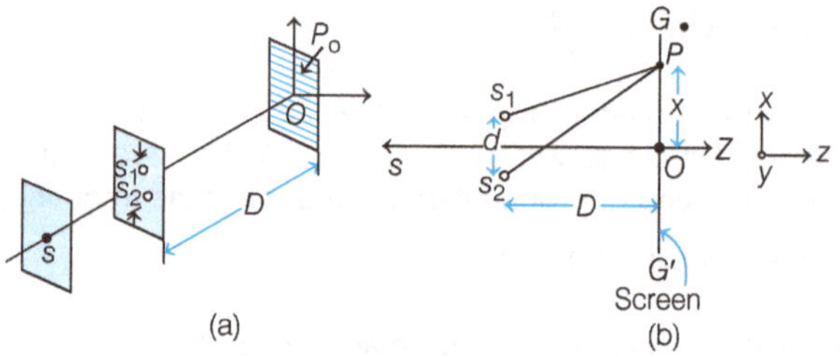

(a) (b)

- Constructive interference resulting in a bright region when $\frac{xd}{D} = n\lambda$,

  i.e. $x = x_n = \frac{n\lambda D}{d}; n = 0, \pm 1, \pm 2, \dots\dots$

- Destructive interference resulting in a dark region when $\frac{xd}{D} = \left(n + \frac{1}{2}\right)\lambda$,

  i.e. $x = x_n = \left(n + \frac{1}{2}\right)\frac{\lambda D}{d}; n = 0, \pm 1, \pm 2$

  Thus, dark and bright bands appear on the screen, such bands are called fringes. Dark and bright fringes are equally spaced.

- In YDSE, the central point O will be bright because $S_1O = S_2O$ and it will correspond to $n = 0$. Let us consider a line perpendicular to plane of the paper and passing through O, then all points on this line will be equidistant from S_1 and S_2 and get bright central fringe which is a straight line. If we had slits instead of point sources, each pair would have produced straight line fringes and increased intensities.

Intensity distribution in YDSE

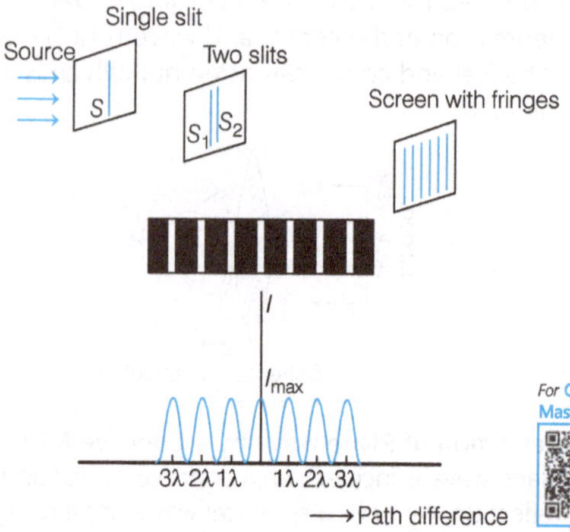

For Concept Master Video

Marks Maximiser

- The distance between two consecutive bright and dark fringe is given by $\beta = x_{n+1} - x_n = \frac{\lambda D}{d}$ [NEET 2020]
- When entire apparatus is immersed in a transparent medium of refractive index μ $\beta' = \frac{\lambda D}{\mu d} = \frac{\beta}{\mu}$.

Diffraction

- The phenomenon of bending of light around the sharp corners and the spreading of light within the geometrical shadow of the opaque obstacles is called diffraction of light.
- The amount of bending of light depends on the relative size of the aperture and wavelength of light. If the size of the aperture comparable to the wavelength, the amount of bending is considerable and easily seen with naked eye.
- When the double slit in Young's experiment is replaced by a single narrow slit (illuminated by a monochromatic source), a broad pattern with central bright region is seen. On both sides, there are alternate dark and bright regions of intensity becoming weaker away from the centre.
- **Diffraction due to a Single Slit** A parallel beam of light with a plane wavefront WW' is made to fall on a single slit AB. Width of the slit is of the order of wavelength of light, therefore diffraction occurs on passing through the slit, as shown in the diagram given below.

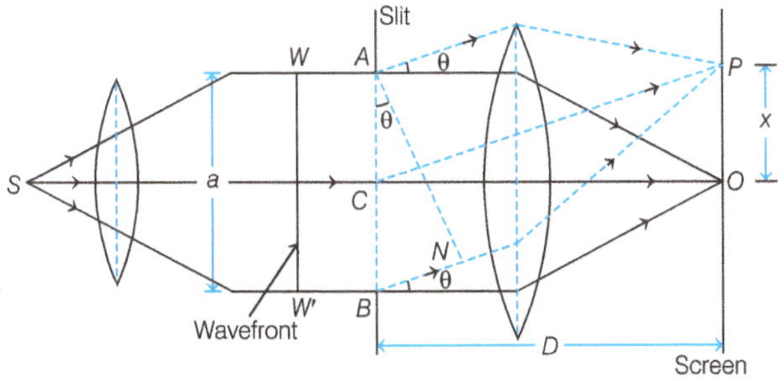

(i) ***n*th order secondary minima** is obtained when

$$a\sin\theta = n\lambda, \quad \text{where } n = 1, 2, 3, \dots$$

(ii) ***n*th order secondary maxima** is obtained when

$$a\sin\theta = \left(n + \frac{1}{2}\right)\lambda, \text{ where } n = 0, 1, 2, 3, \dots$$

(iii) **Angular separation** of *n*th minima,

$$\theta_n = \frac{n\lambda}{a}, \text{ where } n = 1, 2, 3, \dots$$

(iv) **Linear separation** of *n*th secondary minima,

$$x_n = \frac{Dn\lambda}{a}$$

(v) **Angular position** of *n*th order secondary maxima,

$$\theta_n = \left(n + \frac{1}{2}\right)\frac{\lambda}{a}$$

(vi) **Intensity of central maxima** is maximum and intensity of secondary maxima decreases with the increase of their order. The diffraction pattern is graphically shown below.

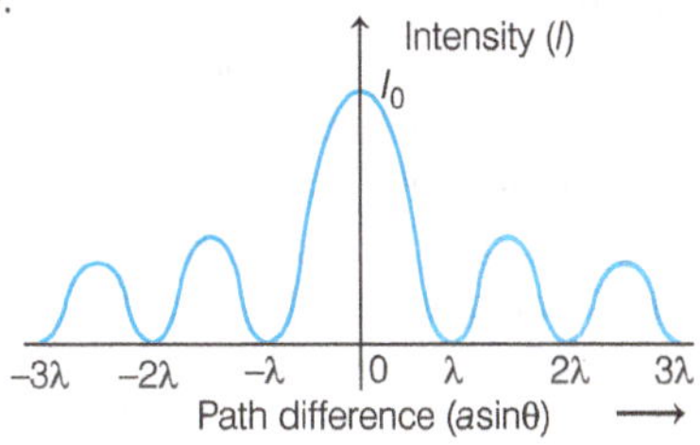

- In interference and diffraction, light energy is redistributed. If it reduces in one region (producing a dark fringe), it increases in another region (producing a bright fringe). There is no gain or loss of energy, which is consistent with the principle of conservation of energy.

Marks Maximiser

- Angular width of central maxima, $\theta = \frac{2\lambda}{a}$
- **Intensity distribution** If position of maxima on the screen is θ, then its intensity is given by $I_\theta = I_0\left(\frac{\sin\alpha}{\alpha}\right)^2$, where, $\alpha = \frac{\pi a}{\lambda}\sin\theta$ and I_0 = intensity of central maxima.

Polarisation

- The phenomenon of restricting the vibrations of light in a particular direction, perpendicular to the direction of wave motion is called polarisation of light.
- **Transverse Waves** When the displacement of the particle is perpendicular to the direction of propagation of the wave, then it is said to be transverse wave.
- **Linearly Polarised Wave** It is the wave in which the vibration of electric field vectors are confined in one plane and parallel to one unique direction. It is also referred as plane polarised wave.
- In linearly polarised wave, the vibration at all points, at all times, lie in same plane, so it is also called **plane polarised wave**.
- The linearly polarised waves are all transverse waves , i.e. the displacement of each point of the string is always at right angles to the direction of propagation of the wave. If the plane of vibration of the string is changed randomly in very short intervals of time, such waves are known as **unpolarised wave**.
- Thin film of ultramicroscopic crystals used to produce the plane polarised light is known as **polaroid**.

- If an unpolarised light wave is incident on a polaroid, then the light wave will get linearly polarised with the electric vector oscillating along a direction perpendicular to the aligned molecules, this direction is known as the pass-axis of the polaroid.
- Polaroids can be used to control the intensity, in sunglasses, windowpanes, photographic cameras and 3D movie cameras, etc.
- When a maximum and a mininum of intensity is observed through an analyser without complete darkness, then the wave is called **partially polarised**.
- **Malus' Law** According to this law, when plane polarised light is incident on an analyser, the resultant intensity of light transmitted from the analyser varies directly as the square of the cosine of the angle between the plane of transmission axis of analyser and polariser.

 i.e. $I = I_0 \cos^2 \theta$

 where, I_0 = intensity of plane polarised light,

 I = intensity of transmitted light from the analyser

 and θ = angle between axis of the polariser and the analyser.

 NEET 2017

- Fig.(a) shows the behaviour of the electric vector when light passes through two polaroids.

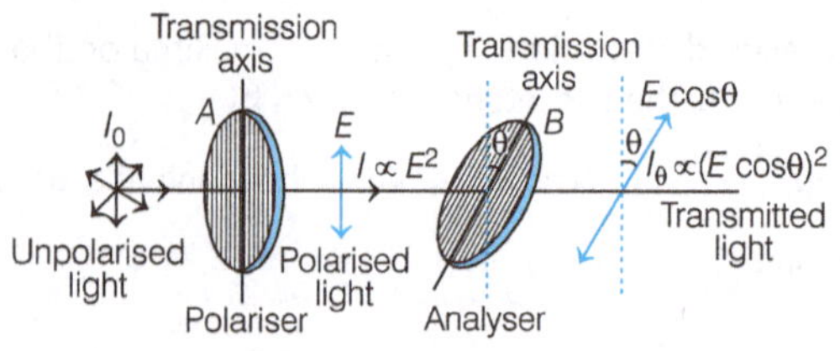

(a)

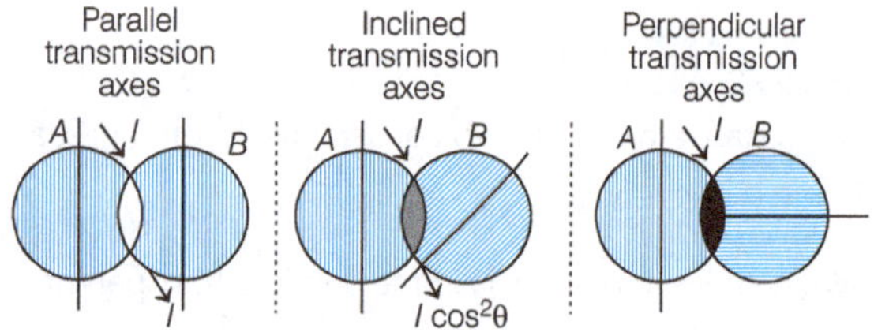

(b)

Fig.(b) shows the passage of light through two polaroids, such that the transmitted fraction falls from 1 to 0 as the angle between transmission axis varies from 0° to 90°.

Marks Maximiser

Polarisation by reflection

If $i = \theta_p$, the refracted light becomes partially polarised and reflected light becomes completely polarised.

If $i < \theta_p$ or $i > \theta_p$, both reflected and refracted rays get partially polarised.

For glass $\theta_p = \tan^{-1}(1.5) \approx 57°$, For water $\theta_p = \tan^{-1}(1.33) \approx 53°$

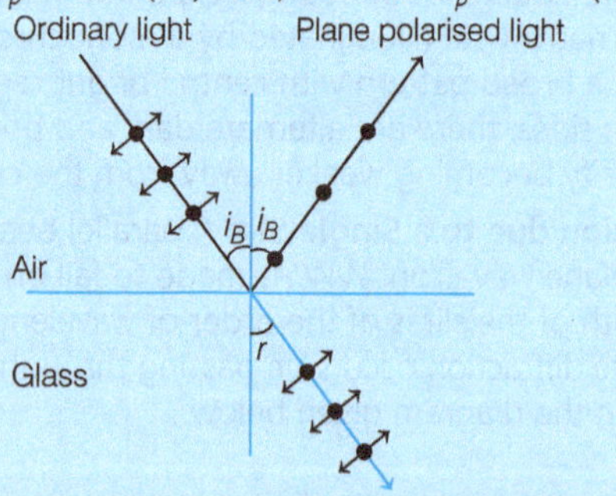

Caution Points

- Diffraction phenomenon cannot be defined by ray optics, this clearly shows the limitations of ray optics. The limit of the ability of microscopes and telescopes to distinguish very close objects is set by the wavelength of light.
- Most of the interference and diffraction phenomena exist around us even for longitudinal waves like sound in air. But polarisation can be observed only in transverse waves like light waves.

PYQ Notes

1. **Brewster's Law** According to this law, when unpolarised light is incident at polarising angle i_B on an interface separating air from a medium of refractive index μ, then the reflected light is plane polarised (perpendicular to the plane of incidence), provided $\mu = \tan i_B$.

 At polarising angle,

 $$i_B + r = \frac{\pi}{2}$$

 i.e. Reflected plane polarised light is at right angle to the refracted light. [NEET 2020]

2. **Displacement of fringes** When a glass plate of refractive index n and thickness $x\lambda$ is introduced in the path of one of the interfering beams, then the extra path difference due to glass plate is given by

 $$\Delta L = (n-1)t = (n-1)x\lambda \quad (\because t = x\lambda)$$

 and the fringe shift is given by

 $$\frac{\beta}{\lambda}(n-1)x\lambda$$

 Shift in number of N fringes,

 $$N = \frac{(n-1)t}{\lambda} \text{ or } t = \frac{N\lambda}{(n-1)}$$

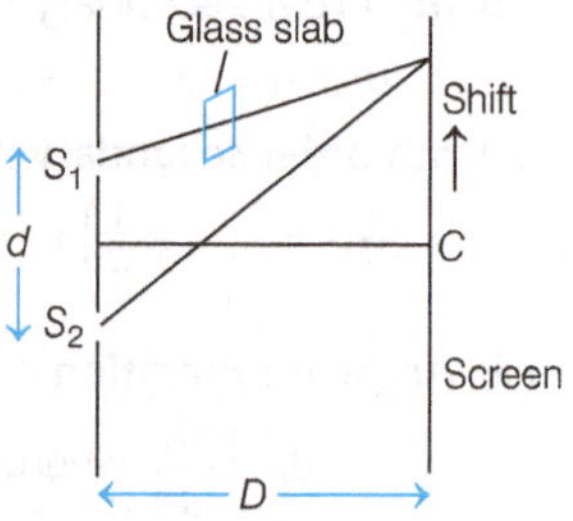

[JEE Main 2019]

Step by Step

Mastering NCERT

- Concept Builders
- Topical Questions
- Assertion and Reason Questions
- Statement Based
- Matching Type
- Numerical Type
- NCERT Exemplar
- Past Exams MCQs
- Skill Boosters

Concept Builders

1 When light goes from rarer to denser medium, frequency of light wave remains constant but wavelength and velocity both decreases. [T/F]

2 Central maxima is the maxima formed with zero optical path difference. It can be formed ...... (anywhere/at the centre) on the screen.

3 Fringe width is thicker for which light, red or blue?

4 In YDSE, the nth maxima always comes before the nth minima. [T/F]

5 For interference, fringes have equal intensity. But, in diffraction, intensity falls as the fringe order .... (increases/decreases).

6 When Young's double slit experiment is performed in water instead of air, then fringes become narrower. [T/F]

7 We can apply Malus law to .... (polarised/ polarised and ordinary both) light.

8 Which phenomena sets the limit of resolution?

9 Interference and diffraction effects are shown by both longitudinal and transverse waves. (T/F)

10 .... (Polarisation/Interference) is used to check symmetry in crystals and molecules using the phenomenon of optical activity.

11 Ray optics is a limiting case of wave optics. [T/F]

12 Polaroids are used in three dimensional motion pictures and in optical stress analyses. [T/F]

13 Interference of light does not obey the law of conservation of energy. [T/F]

14 Young's double slit experiment is performed using a source of white light. The interference fringes will be .... (coloured / black and white).

15 Diffraction from each slit affects the interference pattern in a double slit experiment. [T/F]

16 The resolving power of an astronomical telescope .... (increases/decreases) when the focal length of the objective lens is increased.

17 Diffraction is interference between different parts of the same wavefront. [T/F]

18 What would be the maximum intensity, if identical waves from n incoherent sources, each of intensity I_0, overlap at a point?

19 The value of Brewster's angle for air-glass interface is $\frac{\pi}{3}$, hence the refractive index of glass is ...... $\left(\sqrt{3}/\frac{1}{\sqrt{3}}\right)$.

20 The value of Brewster angle depends on the nature of the refracting medium and the .... (wavelength/intensity) of light.

Topical Questions

Huygens' Principle

1 Light propagates rectilinearly, due to **NCERT Pg. 257**

(a) wave nature (b) large wavelength
(c) high velocity (d) high frequency

2 Which of the following is not same in secondary wave as that of primary wave? **NCERT Pg. 257**

(a) Frequency (b) Wavelength
(c) Velocity (d) Intensity

3 Position of secondary wavefront at later time t can be obtained by drawing **NCERT Pg. 257**

(a) a sphere of diameter of $2vt$ at each point of primary wavefront.
(b) a sphere of diameter $2t$ at each point of primary wavefront.
(c) a circle of diameter vt at each point of primary wavefront
(d) a plane at a distance vt from the primary wavefront.

4 According to Huygens' principle, each point of the wavefront is the source of NCERT Pg. 257
(a) secondary disturbance (b) primary disturbance
(c) third disturbance (d) fourth disturbance

5 Huygens' principle of secondary wavelets may be used to
(a) find the velocity of light in vacuum NCERT Pg. 257
(b) explain the particle's behaviour of light
(c) find the new position of a wavefront
(d) explain photoelectric effect

6 Which of the following phenomenon is not explained by Huygens' construction of wavefront? NCERT Pg. 257
(a) Refraction (b) Reflection
(c) Diffraction (d) Origin of spectra

Refraction and Reflection of Plane Waves using Huygens' Principle

7 In the given figure, light passes from denser medium 1 to rarer medium 2. NCERT Pg. 258

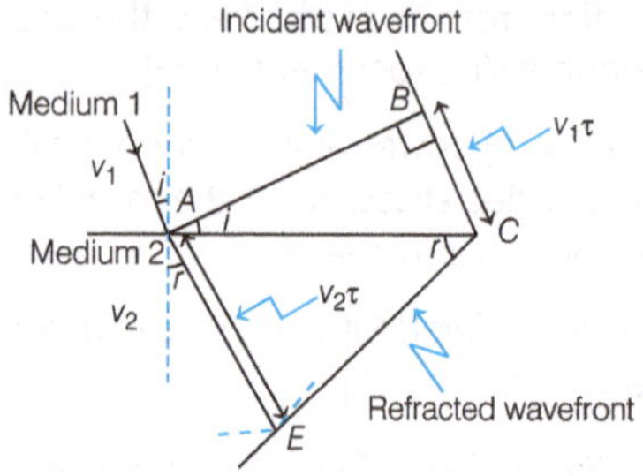

When $i > i_C$ (critical angle of incidence), then wavefront EC is
(a) formed further deep in medium 2
(b) formed closer to surface line AC
(c) formed perpendicular to AC
(d) formed in medium 1 (on the same side of AB)

8 When light is refracted into a denser medium, NCERT Pg. 259
(a) its wavelength and frequency both increases.
(b) its wavelength increases but frequency remains unchanged
(c) its wavelength decreases but frequency remains the same.
(d) its wavelength and frequency both decreases.

9 In the given figure, a plane wave AB incident at an angle i on a reflecting surface MN. NCERT Pg. 261

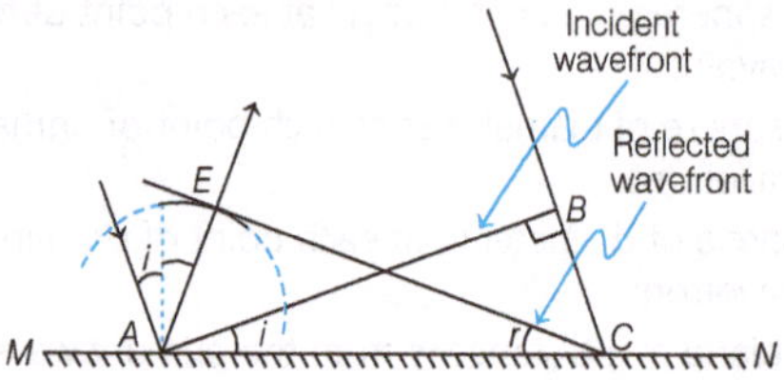

The reflected wavefront is obtained by (take, v be the speed of light and t be the time taken by it from B to C)
(a) drawing a sphere of radius vt from point A
(b) drawing a sphere of radius vt from point C
(c) drawing a perpendicular from point A
(d) drawing a perpendicular from point C

10 If ABC is incident wavefront in the figure shown below, then refracted wavefront is NCERT Pg. 261

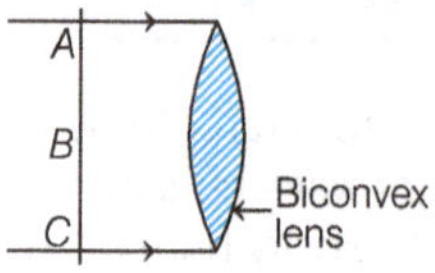

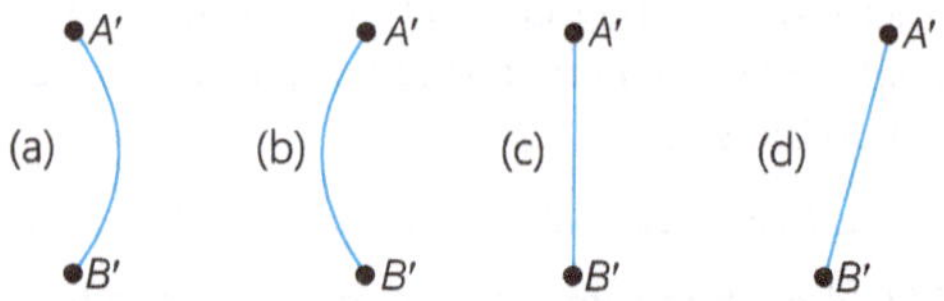

Coherent and Incoherent Addition of Waves

11 Which of the following statement is incorrect conditions for producing sustained interference? NCERT Pg. 263
(a) Phase difference between interferring waves remains constant with time.
(b) Interferring waves have nearly same amplitude levels.
(c) Interferring waves are of same frequency.
(d) Interferring waves are moving only in opposite directions.

12 Let S_1 and S_2 are two sources and if wave from S_1 reaches some common point P by covering seven time of wavelength λ and from S_2 by covering nine times of wavelength λ.

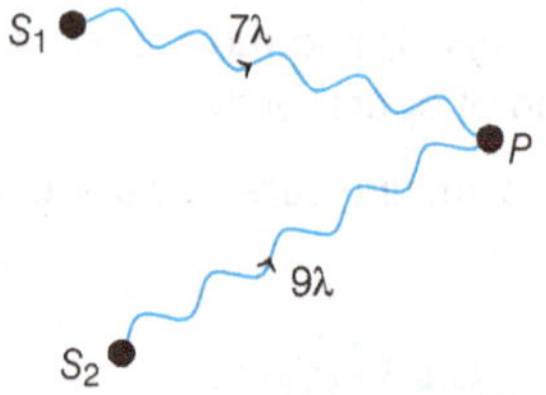

Which of the following statement is incorrect?
(a) $S_2P - S_1P = 2\lambda$ NCERT Pg. 263
(b) Waves from S_1 arrives exactly two cycles earlier than waves from S_2.
(c) At point P, waves from S_1 and S_2 are in phase.
(d) At point P, waves from S_1 and S_2 are out of phase.

13 Two waves are emanating from sources S_1 and S_2 and their displacements are given by

$y_1 = a\cos\omega t$ and $y_2 = a\cos(\omega t - 4\pi)$.

Then, on superimposing they will give rise to

(a) constructive interference NCERT Pg. 263

(b) destructive interference

(c) diffraction

(d) polarisation

14 Suppose displacement produced at some point P by a wave is $y_1 = a\cos\omega t$ and by another wave is $y_2 = a\cos\omega t$. Let I_0 represents intensity produced by each one of individual wave, then resultant intensity due to overlapping of both waves is NCERT Pg. 264

(a) I_0 (b) $2I_0$ (c) $\frac{I_0}{2}$ (d) $4I_0$

15 If the amplitude ratio of two sources producing interference is 3 : 5, then the ratio of intensities produced by each is NCERT Pg. 264

(a) 3 : 5 (b) 5 : 3 (c) 9 : 25 (d) 25 : 9

16 Two light waves superimposing at the mid-point of the screen are coming from coherent sources of light with phase difference π rad. Their amplitudes are 2 cm each. The resultant amplitude at the given point will be NCERT Pg. 264

(a) 8 cm (b) 2 cm (c) 4 cm (d) zero

17 Two identical light waves, propagating in the same direction, have a phase difference ϕ. Then, after superposing, the intensity of the resultant wave will be proportional to NCERT Pg. 264

(a) $\cos\phi$ (b) $\cos\phi/2$

(c) $\cos^2\phi/2$ (d) $\cos^2\phi$

18 Light wave from two coherent sources of intensities in ratio of 64 : 1 produces interference. The ratio of maxima and minima of the interference pattern is NCERT Pg. 264

(a) 81 : 49 (b) 64 : 25

(c) 81 : 64 (d) 49 : 81

19 Two monochromatic coherent light beams A and B have intensities I and $\frac{I}{4}$, respectively. If these waves are superposed, the maximum and minimum intensities will be NCERT Pg. 264

(a) $\frac{9I}{4}, \frac{I}{4}$ (b) $\frac{5I}{4}, 0$ (c) $\frac{5I}{4}, I$ (d) $2I, \frac{I}{2}$

Interference of Light Waves and Young's Experiment

20 In the figure shown, if a parallel beam of white light is incident on the plane of the slits then the distance of the nearest white spot on the screen from O is $\frac{d}{A}$. Find the value of A. (Assume $d << D$) NCERT Pg. 265

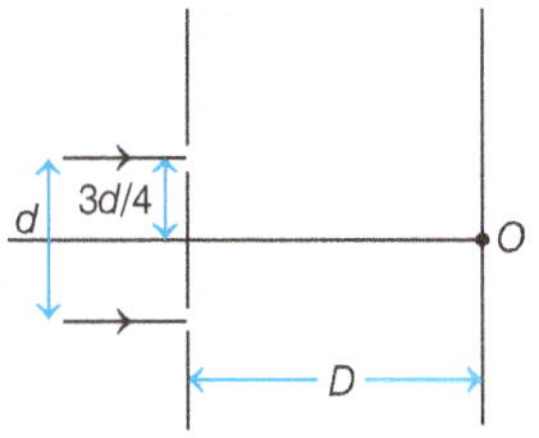

(a) 3 (b) 5

(c) 6 (d) 4

21 Two coherent sources of light emitting waves of same intensity I_0, produce fringe pattern in YDSE. At central maximum, the resultant intensity will be NCERT Pg. 265

(a) I_0 (b) $2I_0$

(c) $4I_0$ (d) $16I_0$

22 In Young's interference experiment two slits are illuminated with orange light of wavelength 6000 Å. The interference pattern is observed on screen far from slit planes. If the central bright fringe is numbered as zero, what must be path difference for light from two slits at fourth bright fringe? NCERT Pg. 265

(a) 3 μm (b) 1.6 μm

(c) 2.4 μm (d) 3.6 μm

23 A single slit is kept before two slits in YDSE. NCERT Pg. 265

(a) To reduce intensity

(b) To produce cylindrical wavefront.

(c) To produce a coherent source

(d) To produce a spherical wavefront

24 Two sources of light of wavelengths 1500Å and 2500Å are used in Young's double slit experiment simultaneously. Which orders of fringes of two wavelength patterns coincide? NCERT Pg. 266

(a) 3rd order of 1st source and 5th order of 2nd source

(b) 7th order of 1st source and 5th order of 2nd source

(c) 5th order of 1st source and 3rd order of 2nd source

(d) 5th order of 1st source and 7th order of 2nd source

25 Two slits are separated by a distance of 0.5 mm and illuminated with light of $\lambda = 6000$ Å. If the screen is placed 2.5 m from the slits, the distance of the third bright image from the centre will be NCERT Pg. 266

(a) 1.5 mm (b) 3 mm

(c) 6 mm (d) 9 mm

26 The Young's double slit experiment is performed with blue and green light of wavelengths 4360 Å and 5460 Å, respectively. If x is the distance of 4th maximum from the central one, then NCERT Pg. 266

(a) $x(\text{blue}) = x(\text{green})$ (b) $x(\text{blue}) > x(\text{green})$

(c) $x(\text{blue}) < x(\text{green})$ (d) $\frac{x(\text{blue})}{x(\text{green})} = \frac{5460}{4360}$

27 Young's double slit experiment is performed with sodium (yellow) light of wavelength 589.3 nm and the interference pattern is observed on a screen 100 cm away. The 10th bright fringe has its centre at a distance of 12 mm from the central maximum. The separation between the slits is **NCERT Pg. 266**

(a) 0.49 mm (b) 0.6 mm (c) 0.7 mm (d) 0.53 mm

28 In a Young's double slit experiment, slits are separated by 0.5 mm and the screen is placed 150 cm away. A beam of light consisting of two wavelengths 650 nm and 520 nm is used to obtain interference fringes on the screen. The least distance from the common central maximum to the point where the bright fringes due to both the wavelengths coincide, is **NCERT Pg. 266**

(a) 7.8 mm (b) 9.75 mm (c) 15.6 mm (d) 1.56 mm

29 In Young's double slit experiment, the slits are 2 mm apart and are illuminated by photons of two wavelengths $\lambda_1 = 12000$ Å and $\lambda_2 = 10000$ Å. At what minimum distance from the common central bright fringe on the screen, 2 m from the slit, will a bright fringe from one interference pattern coincide with a bright fringe from the other? **NCERT Pg. 266**

(a) 8 mm (b) 6 mm (c) 4 mm (d) 3 mm

30 The Young's double slit experiment is performed with light of wavelength 6000 Å, wherein 16 fringes occupy a certain region on the screen. If 24 fringes occupy the same region with another light of wavelength λ, then λ is **NCERT Pg. 266**

(a) 6000 Å (b) 4500 Å (c) 5000 Å (d) 4000 Å

31 In a Young's double slit experiment, the slit separation is 1mm and the screen is 1m from the slit. For a monochromatic light of wavelength 500 nm, the distance of 3rd minima from the central maxima is **NCERT Pg. 266**

(a) 0.50 mm (b) 1.25 mm (c) 1.50 mm (d) 1.75 mm

32 The intensity at the central maxima O in a Young's double slit experiment is I_0. If the distance OP equals one-third of fringe width of the pattern, then the intensity at point P would be **NCERT Pg. 266**

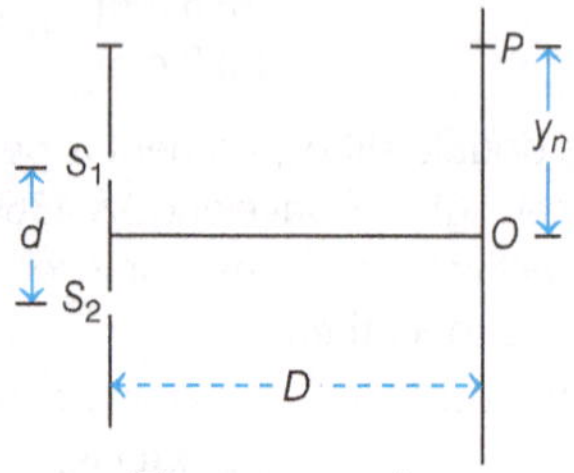

(a) $\frac{I_0}{2}$ (b) $\frac{2I_0}{3}$ (c) $\frac{I_0}{4}$ (d) $\frac{3I_0}{4}$

33 If the 5th order maxima of wavelength 400 nm in YDSE coincides with nth order maxima of the wavelength 5000 Å, then the value of n is **NCERT Pg. 266**

(a) 3 (b) 4
(c) 5 (d) 6

34 Parallel beam of monochromatic light of wavelength 450 nm passes through a long slit of width 0.2 mm. What is angular divergence in which most of the light is diffracted? **NCERT Pg. 266**

(a) 4.5×10^{-3} rad (b) 2×10^{-4} rad
(c) 4×10^{-3} rad (d) 4.5×10^{-4} rad

35 Monochromatic light is passed through double slit and interference pattern is observed on screen 2.5 m away. The separation between slits is 0.5 mm. The first bright fringe is 3.5 mm away from central fringe. The wavelength of light used is **NCERT Pg. 266**

(a) 600 nm (b) 500 nm
(c) 650 nm (d) 700 nm

36 In, YSDE, the slits are separately by 0.28 mm and the screen is placed 1.4 m away. The distance between the central bright fringe and the fourth bright fringe is measured to be1.2 cm. The wavelength of the light used in the experiment is **NCERT Pg. 266**

(a) 600 nm (b) 550 nm
(c) 400 nm (d) 750 nm

37 A narrow slit of width 1 mm is illuminated by monochromatic light of wavelength 600 nm. The distance between the first minima on either side of a screen at a distance of 2 m is **NCERT Pg. 266**

(a) 1.2 cm (b) 1.2 mm
(c) 2.4 cm (d) 2.4 mm

38 In a Young's double slit experiment, $d = 1$ mm and $D = 200$ cm. It is found that 7th bright fringe is at a distance of 6.5 mm from 1st dark fringe of fringe pattern. The wavelength of light used is **NCERT Pg. 266**

(a) 4000 Å (b) 5200 Å
(c) 5000 Å (d) 2000 Å

39 In a YSDE if $D = 1$ m, $d = 1$ mm and $\lambda = 6000$ Å, then distance of 1000th maxima from the central maxima will be **NCERT Pg. 266**

(a) $\frac{1}{2}$ m (b) $\frac{3}{5}$ m (c) $\frac{3}{4}$ m (d) $\frac{4}{5}$ m

40 In the double slit experiment, what should be the width of each slit to obtain 8 maxima of the double slit pattern within the central maxima of single slit pattern with $d = 3$ mm? **NCERT Pg. 266**

(a) 0.6 mm (b) 0.4 mm (c) 0.75 mm (d) 0.3 mm

41 In Young's double slit experiment, if source S is shifted by an angle ϕ as shown in figure. Then, central bright fringe will be shifted by angle ϕ towards NCERT Pg. 266

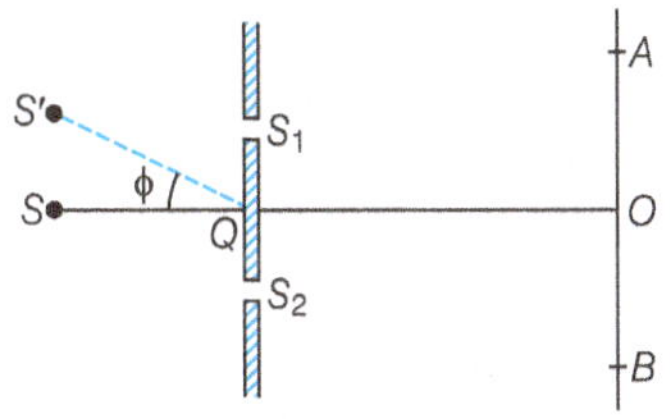

(a) end A of screen
(b) end B of screen
(c) does not shift at all
(d) Either end A and B depending on extra phase difference caused by shifting of source

42 In Young's double slit experiment two disturbance arriving at a point P have phase difference of $\pi/2$. The intensity of this point expressed as a fraction of maximum intensity I_0 is NCERT Pg. 266

(a) $\frac{3}{2}I_0$ (b) $\frac{1}{2}I_0$ (c) $\frac{4}{3}I_0$ (d) $\frac{3}{4}I_0$

43 If the intensities of the two interferring beams in Young's double slit experiment be I_1 and I_2, then the contrast between the maximum and minimum intensity is good when NCERT Pg. 266

(a) I_1 is much greater than I_2
(b) I_2 is smaller than I_2
(c) $I_1 = I_2$
(d) Either $I_1 = 0$ or $I_2 = 0$

44 In Young's double slit experiment, the slit width and the distance of slits from the screen both are doubled. The fringe width will Old NCERT pg 364

(a) increases (b) decreases
(c) remain unchanged (d) None of these

45 The fringe width in a Young's double slit interference pattern is 3.2×10^{-4} m, when red light of wavelength 5600Å is used. How much will it change, if blue light of wavelength 4200Å is used? Old NCERT pg 364

(a) 8×10^{-4} m (b) 0.8×10^{-4} m
(c) 4.2×10^{-4} m (d) 0.45×10^{-4} m

46 In Young's double slit experiment, the fringe width is 1×10^{-4} m. If the distance between the slit and screen is doubled and distance between the two slit is reduced to half and wavelength is changed from 6.4×10^{-7} m to 4.0×10^{-7} m, the value of new fringe width will be Old NCERT pg 364

(a) 0.15×10^{-4}m (b) 2.0×10^{-4} m
(c) 1.25×10^{-4} m (d) 2.5×10^{-4} m

47 Distance of 5th dark fringe from centre is 4 mm. If $D = 2$ m and $\lambda = 600$ nm, then distance between slits is Old NCERT pg 364

(a) 1.35 mm (b) 2.00 mm (c) 3.25 mm (d) 10.35 mm

48 In Young's double slit experiment, let S_1 and S_2 be the two slits and C be the centre of the screen. If the $\angle S_1CS_2 = \theta$ and λ is the wavelength, then fringe width will be Old NCERT pg 364

(a) $\frac{\lambda}{\theta}$ (b) $\lambda\theta$ (c) $\frac{2\lambda}{\theta}$ (d) $\frac{\lambda}{2\theta}$

49 In a two slit experiment with monochromatic light, fringes are obtained on a screen placed at some distance from the slits. If the screen is moved by 5×10^{-2} m towards the slits, the change in fringe width is 3×10^{-5} m. If separation between the slits is 10^{-3}m, the wavelength of light used is Old NCERT pg 364

(a) 6000 Å (b) 5000 Å (c) 3000 Å (d) 4500 Å

50 In Young's double slit experiment, if the point sources are replaced by slits as shown below, then the intensity pattern observed have Old NCERT pg 366

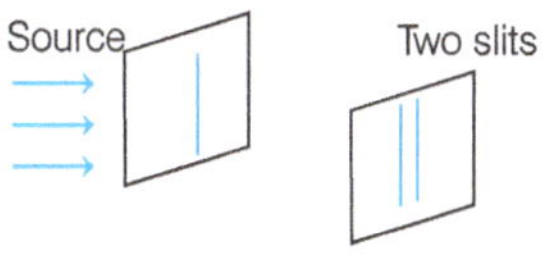

(a) point fringes with decreasing intensity
(b) point fringes with increasing intensity
(c) straight line fringes with decreasing intensities
(d) straight line fringes with increasing intensities

51 Sunlight is incident on a pinhole of width 10^3Å. Choose the correct statement among the following NCERT Pg. 267

(a) The image of the pinhole seen on a screen shall be a sharp white ring.
(b) The image of the pinhole seen on a screen shall be different from a geometrical image.
(c) The image of the pinhole seen on a screen shall be a diffused central spot with white in colour.
(d) The image of the pinhole seen on screen shall be a dark spot with white ring

Diffraction

52 In a double-slit experiment, at a certain point on the screen the path difference between the two interfering waves is $\frac{1}{8}$th of a wavelength. The ratio of the intensity of light at that point to that at the centre of a bright fringe is NCERT Pg. 267

(a) 0.568 (b) 0.853
(c) 0.760 (d) 0.672

53 A parallel beam of light of wavelength 6000 Å gets diffracted by a single slit width 0.3 mm. The angular position of the first minima of diffracted light is NCERT Pg. 267

(a) 6×10^{-3} rad (b) 1.8×10^{-3} rad
(c) 3.2×10^{-3} rad (d) 2×10^{-3} rad

54 A single slit diffraction pattern is formed with white light. For what wavelength of light, the third secondary maximum in the diffraction pattern coincides with the second secondary maximum in the pattern for red light of wavelength 6500 Å? NCERT Pg. 267

(a) 4400 Å (b) 4100Å
(c) 4642.8 Å (d) 9100 Å

55 A parallel beam of light of wavelength 600 nm is incident normally on a slit of width *d*. If the distance between the slits and the screen is 1 m and the distance of 2nd order maximum from the centre of the screen is 15 mm, the width of the slit is NCERT Pg. 267

(a) 40 μm (b) 80 μm
(c) 160 μm (d) 100 μm

56 If we observe the single-slit diffraction with wavelength λ and slit width *e*, the width of the central maximum is 2θ. On decreasing the slit width for the same λ, then NCERT Pg. 267

(a) θ increases
(b) θ remains unchanged
(c) θ decreases
(d) θ increases or decreases depending on the intensity of light

57 If a converging lens of focal length *f* is placed after the slit and the fringes are obtained on screen placed at the focus of lens in single-slit diffraction, then the size of screen is NCERT Pg. 267

(a) λ / a (b) $f \lambda / a$
(c) a / λ (d) $f a / \lambda$

Polarisation

58 An unpolarised beam of light of intensity I_0 falls on a polaroid. The intensity of the emergent beam is NCERT Pg. 270

(a) $\frac{I_0}{2}$ (b) I_0 (c) $\frac{I_0}{4}$ (d) zero

59 A beam of unpolarised light of intensity I_0 is passed through a polaroid *A* and then through another polaroid *B*, which is oriented so that its principal plane makes an angle of 45° relative to that of *A*. The intensity of the emergent light is NCERT Pg. 270

(a) I_0 (b) $I_0/2$
(c) $I_0/4$ (d) $I_0/8$

60 At which angle, the intensity of transmitted light is maximum when a polaroid sheet is rotated between two crossed polaroids? NCERT Pg. 270

(a) $\pi / 4$ (b) $\pi / 2$ (c) $\pi / 3$ (d) π

61 An unpolarised beam intensity I_0 is incident on a pair of nicol prism making an angle of 60° with each other. The intensity of light emerging from the pair is NCERT Pg. 270

(a) I_0 (b) $I_0 / 2$ (c) $I_0 / 4$ (d) $I_0 / 8$

62 Which of the following can be used to control the intensity, in sunglasses, window-panes, etc? NCERT Pg. 271

(a) Transverse wave (b) Polaroids
(c) Plane polarised wave (d) Polarised wave

63 Two polaroid sheets are arranged with their axes parallel. Second polaroid is then rotated through an angle of 60°. What is ratio of light intensity transmitted in the first instance to second instance? NCERT Pg. 270

(a) 2 : 1 (b) 4 : 1 (c) 16 : 1 (d) 1 : 1

64 Unpolarised light of intensity 32 Wm^{-2} passes through three polarisers such that transmission axis of first is crossed with third. If intensity of emerging light is 2 Wm^{-2}, what is the angle of transmission axis between the first two polarisers? NCERT Pg. 270

(a) 30° (b) 45° (c) 22.5° (d) 60°

65 Light from sodium lamp is made to pass through two polaroids placed one after the other in the path of light. Taking the intensity of the incident light as 100%, the intensity of the outcoming light that can be varied in the range NCERT Pg. 270

(a) 0% to 100% (b) 0% to 50%
(c) 0% to 25% (d) 0% to 75%

66 Unpolarised light of intensity *I* is incident on a system of two polarisers, *A* followed by *B*. The intensity of emergent light is $\frac{2I}{3}$. If a third polariser *C* is placed between *A* and *B*, the intensity of emergent light is reduced to $\frac{I}{3}$. The angle between the polarisers *A* and *C* is θ. Then, NCERT Pg. 270

(a) $\cos\theta = \left(\frac{1}{2}\right)^{\frac{1}{2}}$ (b) $\cos\theta = \left(\frac{2}{3}\right)^{\frac{1}{4}}$
(c) $\cos\theta = \left(\frac{2}{3}\right)^{\frac{1}{2}}$ (d) $\cos\theta = \left(\frac{1}{2}\right)^{\frac{1}{4}}$

67 When both the components of electric field of light waves are present such that one is stronger than the other and such light is viewed through a rotating analyser, one sees a maximum and a minimum of intensity but not complete darkness. This kind of light is called Old NCERT Pg. 377

(a) polarised (b) linearly polarised
(c) partially polarised (d) None of the above

68 When the angle of incidence is 45° on the surface of a glass slab, it is found that the reflected ray is completely polarised. The velocity of light in glass is Old NCERT Pg. 381

(a) $\sqrt{3} \times 10^8 \text{ ms}^{-1}$ (b) $3 \times 10^8 \text{ ms}^{-1}$
(c) $2 \times 10^8 \text{ ms}^{-1}$ (d) $\sqrt{2} \times 10^8 \text{ ms}^{-1}$

69 Unpolarised light is incident on a plane glass surface. What should be the angle of incidence, so that the reflected and refracted rays are perpendicular to each other? [μ for glass $=1.5$] Old NCERT Pg. 381

(a) 60° (b) 90° (c) 0° (d) 57°

70 The refractive index of a medium is 1. If the unpolarised light is incident on it at the polarising angle of the medium, the angle of refraction is Old NCERT Pg. 381

(a) 60° (b) 45°
(c) 30° (d) 0°

71 The critical angle of a certain medium is $\sin^{-1}\left(\frac{4}{5}\right)$. The polarising angle of medium is Old NCERT Pg. 381

(a) $\tan^{-1}\left(\frac{5}{4}\right)$ (b) $\sin^{-1}\left(\frac{4}{5}\right)$
(c) $\sin^{-1}\left(\frac{5}{4}\right)$ (d) $\tan^{-1}\left(\frac{4}{3}\right)$

Assertion and Reason Questions

Direction (Q. Nos. 1-10) *In the following questions, a statement of Assertion is followed by a corresponding statement of Reason. Of the following statements, choose the correct one.*

(a) Both Assertion and Reason are correct and Reason is the correct explanation of Assertion.
(b) Both Assertion and Reason are correct but Reason is not the correct explanation of Assertion.
(c) Assertion is correct but Reason is incorrect.
(d) Assertion is incorrect but Reason is correct.

1 **Assertion** In the field of geometrical optics, light can be assumed to approximately travel in straight line.

Reason The wavelength of visible light is very small in comparison to the dimensions of typical mirrors and lenses. NCERT Pg. 255

2 **Assertion** The emergent plane wavefront is tilted on refraction of a plane wave by a thin prism.

Reason The speed of light waves is more in glass and the base of the prism is thicker than the top. NCERT Pg. 257

3 **Assertion** If we have a point source emitting waves uniformly in all directions, the locus of point which have the same amplitude and vibrate in the same phase are spheres.

Reason Each point of the wavefront is the source of a secondary disturbance and the wavelets emanating from these points spread out in all directions with the speed of the wave. NCERT Pg. 257

4 **Assertion** When monochromatic light is incident on a surface separating two media, the reflected and refracted light both have the same frequency as the incident frequency.

Reason Speed of light and wavelength of light both changes in refraction and hence the ratio $\nu = c/\lambda$ is a constant. NCERT Pg. 259

5 **Assertion** The intensity at the bright band of interference pattern on the screen is maximum and equal to $4I_0$, where I_0 is the intensity of light from each sources.

Reason The intensity at the dark band is always zero irrespective of the intensity of light waves coming from the two sources. NCERT Pg. 264

6 **Assertion** Young's double slit experiment can be performed using a source of white light.

Reason The wavelength of red light is less than the wavelength of other colours in white light. NCERT Pg. 265

7 **Assertion** In interference, all the fringes are of same width.

Reason In interference, fringe width is independent of position of the fringe. NCERT Pg. 266

8 **Assertion** No interference pattern is detected when two coherent sources are infinitely close to each other.

Reason The fringe width is inversely proportional to distance between the two slits. NCERT Pg. 266

9 **Assertion** We cannot get diffraction pattern from a wide slit illuminated by monochromatic light.

Reason In diffraction pattern, all the bright bands are not of the same intensity. NCERT Pg. 267

10 **Assertion** In Young's double slit experiment, the fringe width for dark fringes is same as that for white fringes.

Reason In Young's double slit experiment, when the fringes are formed with a source of white light, then only dark and bright fringes are observed. Old NCERT Pg. 366

Statement Based Questions

Direction (Q. Nos. 1-8) *In the following questions statement I and II are given read the statements and choose the most appropriate answer from the options given below.*

(a) Both Statement I and Statement II are incorrect.
(b) Statement I is correct but Statement II is incorrect.
(c) Statement I is incorrect but Statement II is correct.
(d) Both Statement I and Statement II are correct.

1 **Statement I** A point source spherical wavefronts.

Statement II The locus of point which have the same amplitude and vibrate in same phase are spheres. NCERT Pg. 257

2 **Statement I** A ray of light is the path along which light travels. It is always normal to the wavefront.

Statement II Huygen's principle of secondary wavelets can be used to prove only law of reflection. NCERT Pg. 257

3 **Statement I** When a light wave travels from a rarer to a denser medium, it loses speed. The reduction in speed imply a reduction in energy carried by the light wave.

Statement II The energy of waves is proportional to velocity of waves. NCERT Pg. 260

4 **Statement I** All bright interference bands have the same intensity.

Statement II In interference, all bands receive same amount of light from two sources. NCERT Pg. 264

5 **Statement I** When Young's double slit experiment performed with a source of white light, only black and white fringes are observed.

Statement II White light does not disperse in different colours in case of interference. NCERT Pg. 266

6 **Statement I** In Young's double slit experiment, if wavelengths of incident monochromatic light is just doubled, number of bright fringe on the screen will decrease.

Statement II Maximum number of bright fringes on the screen is inversely proportional to the wavelength of light used. NCERT Pg. 266

7 **Statement I** In YDSE, if a thin film is introduced infront of the upper slit, then the fringe pattern shifts in the downward direction.

Statement II In YDSE, if the slit widths are unequal, the minima will be completely dark. NCERT Pg. 266

8 **Statement I** For diffraction through a single slit, the wavelength of wave must be comparable to the size of slit.

Statement II The diffraction pattern is very common to observe in sound waves but not so common in light waves. NCERT Pg. 267

Matching Type Questions

1 Match the Column I (light source) with Column II (shape of wavefront) and select the correct answer from the codes given below. NCERT Pg. 261

Column I	Column II
A. Light from a point source	1. Plane
B. Light emerging out of convex lens when point source is of its focus	2. Spherical
C. Light emerging from a thin prism	3. Plane and tilted
D. Light emerging from a line source.	4. Cylindrical

Codes

	A	B	C	D
(a)	1	2	3	4
(b)	1	4	2	3
(c)	2	1	3	4
(d)	2	3	1	4

2 Match the Column I (interference) with Column II (relation) and select the correct answer from the codes given below. NCERT Pg. 263

Column I	Column II
A. Constructive interference	1. $n\lambda$
B. Destructive interference	2. $(2n+1)\lambda/2$
C. Path difference for constructive interference	3. Waves are in phase at point of interference
D. Path difference for destructive interference	4. Waves are out of phase at point of interference

Codes

	A	B	C	D
(a)	4	1	3	2
(b)	4	3	1	2
(c)	3	4	1	2
(d)	3	4	2	1

3 Two slits are made one millimetre apart and the screen is placed 1 m away. A blue-green light of wavelength 500 nm is used. Old NCERT Pg. 364

Match the Column I (activity) with Column II (changes in fringe pattern) and select the correct answer from the codes given below.

	Column I		Column II
A.	Screen is moved away from the plane of slits	1.	Linear width of fringes β increases
B.	Source is replaced by another source of shorter wavelength	2.	Angular separation of fringe remains constant
C.	Set up of experiment is dipped completely in water	3.	Fringe separation decreases
D.	Distance between slits is reduced	4.	Fringe width become (3/4)th

Codes

	A	B	C	D		A	B	C	D
(a)	1	3	4	2	(b)	3	1	4	2
(c)	2	3	4	1	(d)	2	3	1	4

4 Match the Column I (change in YDSE) with Column II (change in fringes) and select the correct answer from the codes given below. Old NCERT Pg. 364

	Column I		Column II
A.	If sodium light is replaced by red light of same intensity	1.	All fringes are coloured except central fringe
B.	Monochromatic light is replaced by white light	2.	Fringe width will became quadrupled
C.	Distance between slits and screen is doubled and the distance betwen slits is halved	3.	The bright fringe will became less bright
D.	If one of the slits is covered by cellophone paper	4.	The fringe width will increase

Codes

	A	B	C	D
(a)	4	1	2	3
(b)	1	2	3	4
(c)	2	3	1	4
(d)	3	2	4	1

Numerical Type Questions

1 In Young's double slit experiment carried out with light of wavelength $(\lambda) = 5000$ Å, the distance between the slits is 0.4 mm and the screen is at 800 cm from the slits. Find the distance of 3rd maxima from central maxima in cm. NCERT Pg. 266

2 In a YDSE arrangement composite lights of different wavelengths $\lambda_1 = 560$ nm and $\lambda_2 = 400$ nm are used. If D=1m, d = 0.1 mm. The distance (in mm) between two completely dark regions is .... NCERT Pg. 266

3 White light is passed through a double slit and interference is observed on a screen 1.5 m away. The separation between the slits is 0.3 mm. The first violet and red fringes are formed 2.0 mm and 3.5 mm away from the central white fringes. The difference in wavelengths of red and violet light is ....nm. NCERT Pg. 266

4 In Young's double slit experiment , two coherent sources are placed 0.90 mm apart and fringes are observed one meter away. If it produces second dark fringe at a distance of 1 mm from central fringe, the wavelength of monochromatic light is used would be ...... 10^{-5} cm. NCERT Pg. 266

5 Sodium light of wavelengths 650 nm and 655 nm is used to study diffraction at a single slit of aperture 0.75 mm. The distance between the slit and the screen is 1.5 m. The separation between the positions of the first maxima of diffraction pattern obtained in the two cases is ....$\times 10^{-6}$ m. NCERT Pg. 267

6 In YDSE, the fringes are obtained on a screen placed at some distance from the slits. If the screen is moved by 5 cm towards the slit, the change in the fringe width of 3×10^{-5} m. If the distance between two slits is 10^{-3} m, the wavelength of the light used is .... Å . Old NCERT Pg. 364

NCERT Exemplar Questions

1 Consider sunlight incident on a slit of width 10^4 Å. The image seen through the slit shall
(a) be a fine sharp slit white in colour at the centre
(b) a bright slit white at the centre diffusing to zero intensities at the edges.
(c) a bright slit white at the centre diffusing to regions of different colours
(d) only be a diffused slit white in colour

2 In a Young's double slit experiment, the source is white light. One of the holes is covered by a red filter and another by a blue filter. In this case,
(a) there shall be alternate interference patterns of red and blue
(b) there shall be an interference pattern for red distinct from that for blue
(c) there shall be no distinct interference fringes
(d) there shall be an interference pattern for red mixing with one for blue

3 Figure shows a standard two slits arrangement with slits S_1, S_2. P_1 and P_2 are the two minima points on either side of P as shown in figure.

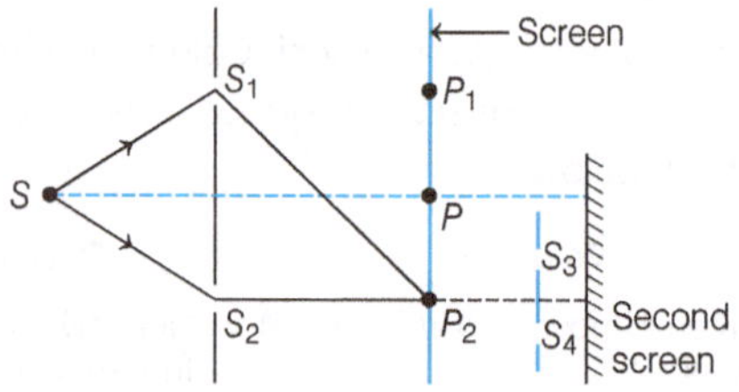

At P_2 on the screen, there is a hole and behind P_2 is a second 2-slit arrangement with slits S_3, S_4 and a second screen behind them. What pattern would you find on second screen?
(a) There would be no interference pattern on the second screen but it would be lighted
(b) The second screen would be totally dark
(c) There would be a single bright point on the second screen
(d) There would be a regular two slit pattern on the second screen

4 The human eye has an approximate angular resolution of $\phi = 5.8 \times 10^{-4}$ rad and a typical photoprinter prints a minimum of 300 dpi (dots per inch, 1 inch = 2.54 cm). At what minimum distance z should a printed page be held so that one does not see the individual dots?
(a) 14.5 cm (b) 12.5 cm (c) 19.8 cm (d) 10.25 cm

Past Exams Questions

NEET

1 An unpolarised light beam strikes a glass surface at Brewster's angle. Then **NCERT Pg. 268, NEET 2024**
(a) the reflected light will be partially polarised.
(b) the refracted light will be completely polarised.
(c) both the reflected and refracted light will be completely polarised.
(d) the reflected light will be completely polarised but the refracted light will be partially polarised.

2 If the monochromatic source in Young's double slit experiment is replaced by white light, then **NCERT Pg. 264, NEET 2024**
(a) interference pattern will disappear
(b) there will be a central dark fringe surrounded by a few coloured fringes
(c) there will be a central bright white fringe surrounded by a few coloured fringes
(d) all bright fringes will be of equal width

3 Two coherent sources of light interfere and produce fringe pattern on a screen. For central maximum, the phase difference between the two waves will be **NCERT Pg. 264, NEET 2020**
(a) zero (b) π (c) $\frac{3\pi}{2}$ (d) $\frac{\pi}{2}$

4 In a Young's double slit experiment, if there is no initial phase-difference between the light from the two slits, a point on the screen corresponding to the fifth minimum, has path difference **NCERT Pg. 266, NEET 2020**
(a) $5\frac{\lambda}{2}$ (b) $10\frac{\lambda}{2}$ (c) $9\frac{\lambda}{2}$ (d) $11\frac{\lambda}{2}$

5 Angular width of the central maxima in the Fraunhoffer diffraction for $\lambda = 6000$ Å is θ_0. When the same slit is illuminated by another monochromatic light, the angular width decreases by 30%. The wavelength of this light is **NCERT Pg. 267, NEET 2019**
(a) 1800 Å (b) 4200 Å
(c) 6000 Å (d) 420 Å

6 Two polaroids P_1 and P_2 are placed with their axis perpendicular to each other. Unpolarised light I_0 is incident on P_1. A third polaroid P_3 is kept in between P_1 and P_2 such that its axis makes an angle 45° with that of P_1. The intensity of transmitted light through P_2 is
NCERT Pg. 270, NEET 2017

(a) $\frac{I_0}{2}$ (b) $\frac{I_0}{4}$ (c) $\frac{I_0}{8}$ (d) $\frac{I_0}{16}$

7 A linear aperture whose width is 0.02 cm is placed immediately in front of a lens of focal length 60 cm. The aperture is illuminated normally by a parallel beam of wavelength
5×10^{-5} m. The distance of the first dark band of the diffraction pattern from the centre of the screen is
NCERT Pg. 261, NEET 2016

(a) 0.10 cm (b) 0.25 cm (c) 0.20 cm (d) 0.15 cm

8 In a double slit experiment, the two slits are 1 mm apart and the screen is placed 1 m away. A monochromatic light of wavelength 500 nm is used. What will be the width of each slit for obtaining ten maxima of double slit within the central maxima of single slit pattern?
NCERT Pg. 266, AIPMT 2015

(a) 0.2 mm (b) 0.1 mm (c) 0.5 mm (d) 0.02 mm

9 Two slits in Young's double slit experiment have widths in the ratio 1 : 25. The ratio of intensity at the maxima and minima in the interference pattern $\frac{I_{max}}{I_{min}}$ is
NCERT Pg. 266, AIPMT 2015

(a) $\frac{9}{4}$ (b) $\frac{121}{49}$ (c) $\frac{49}{121}$ (d) $\frac{4}{9}$

10 For a parallel beam of monochromatic light of wavelength λ, diffraction is produced by a single slit whose width a is of the order of the wavelength of the light. If D is the distance of the screen from the slit, the width of the central maxima will be
NCERT Pg. 267, AIPMT 2015

(a) $\frac{2D\lambda}{a}$ (b) $\frac{D\lambda}{a}$ (c) $\frac{Da}{\lambda}$ (d) $\frac{2Da}{\lambda}$

11 At the first minimum adjacent to the central maximum of a single slit diffraction pattern, the phase difference between the Huygens' wavelet from the edge of the slit and the wavelet from the mid-point of the slit is
NCERT Pg. 268, AIPMT 2015

(a) $\frac{\pi}{4}$ rad (b) $\frac{\pi}{2}$ rad (c) π rad (d) $\frac{\pi}{8}$ rad

JEE Main

12 When unpolarized light is incident at an angle of 60° on a transparent medium from air, the reflected ray is completely polarised. The angle of refraction in the medium is
NCERT Pg. 268, JEE Main 2024

(a) 90° (b) 45° (c) 60° (d) 30°

13 A microwave of wavelength 2.0 cm falls normally on a slit of width 4.0 cm. The angular spread of the central maxima of the diffraction pattern obtained on a screen 1.5 m away from the slit, will be
NCERT Pg. 266, JEE Main 2024

(a) 15° (b) 30° (c) 60° (d) 45°

14 When a polaroid sheet is rotated between two crossed polaroids then the transmitted light intensity will be maximum for a rotation of
NCERT Pg. 268, JEE Main 2024

(a) 45° (b) 60° (c) 90° (d) 30°

15 In a Young's double slit experiment, two slits are illuminated with a light of wavelength 800 nm. The line joining A_1P is perpendicular to A_1A_2 as shown in the figure. If the first minimum is detected at P, the value of slits separation a will be
NCERT Pg. 265, JEE Main 2023

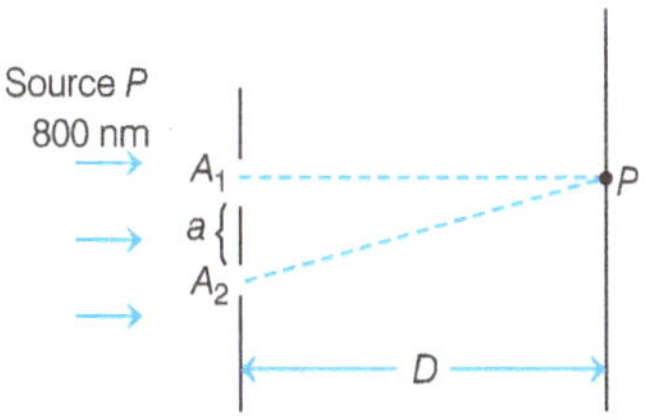

The distance of screen from slits, $D = 5$ cm

(a) 0.5 mm (b) 0.1 mm (c) 0.4 mm (d) 0.2 mm

16 n polarising sheets are arranged such that each makes an angle 45° with the preceeding sheet. An unpolarised light of intensity I is incident into this arrangement. The output intensity is found to be $I / 64$. The value of n will be
NCERT Pg. 270, JEE Main 2023

(a) 3 (b) 6 (c) 4 (d) 5

17 A polariser-analyser set is adjusted such that the intensity of light coming out of the analyser is just 10% of the original intensity. Assuming that the polariser-analyser set does not absorb any light, the angle by which the analyser need to be rotated further to reduce the output intensity to be zero, is
NCERT Pg. 270, JEE Main 2020

(a) 71.6° (b) 90° (c) 45° (d) 18.4°

18 In Young's double slit experiment with slit separation 0.1 mm, one observes a bright fringe at angle 1 / 40 rad by using light of wavelength λ_1. When the light of the wavelength λ_2 is used a bright fringe is seen at the same angle in the same set up. Given that λ_1 and λ_2 are in visible range (380 nm to 740 nm), their values are
NCERT Pg. 266 JEE Main 2019

(a) 380 nm, 525 nm (b) 400 nm, 500 nm
(c) 380 nm, 500 nm (d) 625 nm, 500 nm

Skill Boosters

1 A parallel monochromatic beam of light is incident normally on a narrow slit. A diffraction pattern is formed on a screen placed perpendicular to the direction of the incident beam. At the first minima of the diffraction pattern, the phase difference between the rays coming from the two edges of the slit is

(a) zero (b) $\pi/2$ (c) π (d) 2π

2 Upper half of the thin lens has refractive index μ and lower half has refractive index $\mu - \delta\mu$ $(\delta\mu << \mu)$, the shape the fringe on the screen is

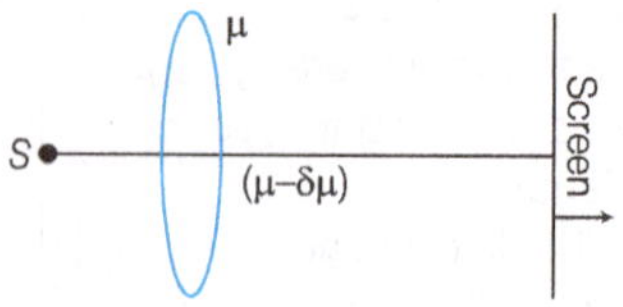

(a) hyperbolic
(b) straight line
(c) circular
(d) No sufficient information

3 Slits in Young's double slit experiment are at 1 mm separation. They are illuminated by white light (400 nm to 700 nm) on screen 1 m away interference pattern is formed. If a pinhole is made on this screen at a distance 2 mm from the central white fringe, some wavelengths will be absent in the transmitted light. The absent wavelengths are

(a) 571.4 nm and 444.4 nm
(b) 500 nm and 450 nm
(c) 402 nm, 507 nm and 609 nm
(d) 550 nm, 600 nm and 680 nm

4 A parallel beam of monochromatic light of intensity I_0 is incident on a glass plate, 25% of light is reflected by upper surface and 50% of light is reflected from lower surface. The ratio of minimum and maximum intensity in interference region of reflected light is

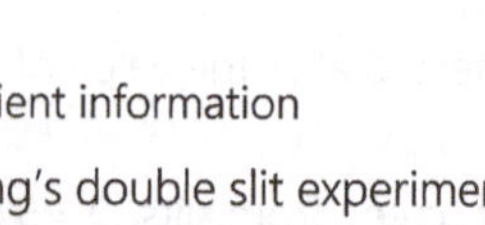

(a) $\dfrac{\left(\frac{1}{2}-\sqrt{\frac{3}{8}}\right)^2}{\left(\frac{1}{2}+\sqrt{\frac{3}{8}}\right)^2}$ (b) $\dfrac{(1-\sqrt{2})^2}{(1+\sqrt{2})^2}$

(c) $\dfrac{3}{8}$ (d) $\dfrac{4}{9}$

5 A beam of plane polarised light is incident normally on a polariser of cross-sectional area 3×10^{-4} m^2, which rotates about the axis of the ray with an angular velocity 10π rads^{-1}. The power of incident ray is 10^{-3} W.

Find the intensity of emergent beam.

(a) $\frac{1}{3}$ Wm^{-2} (b) $\frac{5}{3}$ Wm^{-2}

(c) $\frac{4}{3}$ Wm^{-2} (d) $\frac{10}{3}$ Wm^{-2}

6 The Young's double slit experiment is done in a medium of refractive index 4/3. A light of 600 nm wavelength is falling on the slits have 0.45 mm separation. The lower slit S_2 is covered by a thin glass sheet of thickness 10.4 mm and refractive index 1.5. The interference pattern is observed on a screen placed at 1.5 m. The interference pattern is observed on a screen placed 1.5 m from the slits as shown in the figure.

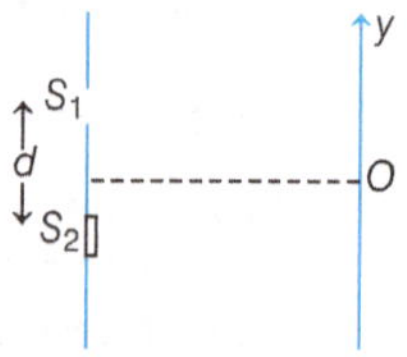

(All wavelengths in this problem are for the given medium of refractive index 4/3. Ignore dispersion.)

Find the location of central maxima (bright fringe with zero path difference) on the Y-axis.

(a) 5.22 mm (b) 4.33 mm
(c) 3.43 mm (d) 3.33 mm

7 A monochromatic light of wavelength is incident at an angle α with the normal to a plane containing two slits of separation d. Find the minimum value of α, so that a minima is formed at centre of screen.

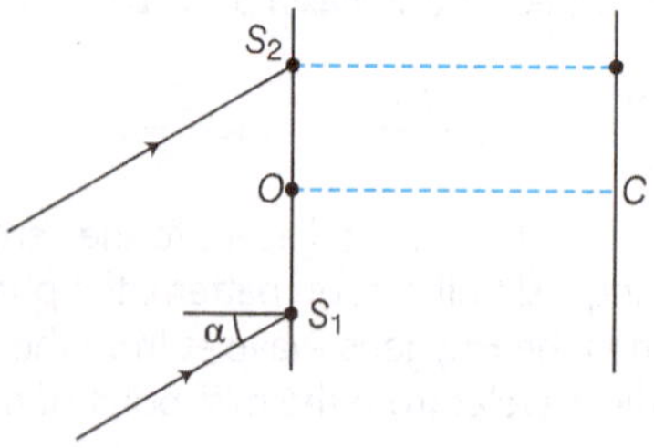

(a) $\cos^{-1}\left(\frac{\lambda}{d}\right)$ (b) $\sin^{-1}\left(\frac{\lambda}{2d}\right)$

(c) $\sin^{-1}\left(\frac{\lambda}{d}\right)$ (d) $\sin^{-1}\left(\frac{\lambda}{4d}\right)$

8 Three light waves combine at a certain point, where their electric field components are $E_1 = E_0 \cos \omega t$, $E_2 = E_0 \sin(\omega t + 53°)$ and $E_3 = E_0 \sin(\omega t - 37°)$.

Find their resultant component $E(t)$ at that point.

(a) $\frac{\sqrt{85}}{5}\sin\left(\omega t+\tan^{-1}\frac{6}{7}\right)$

(b) $E_0\sin(\omega t+60°)$

(c) $E=\frac{\sqrt{85}}{5}\sin\left(\omega t+\tan^{-1}\frac{7}{6}\right)$

(d) None of the above

9 Consider an Young's double slit experiment that has different slits width as a result, amplitudes of waves from two slits are I_0 and $4I_0$, then the intensity at a point on screen, where phase difference between waves is $\frac{2\pi}{3}$, is

(a) I_0 (b) $2I_0$ (c) $3I_0$ (d) $4I_0$

10 In Young's double slit experiment, the slits S_1 and S_2 are illuminated with coherent microwave sources, each of frequency 10^6 Hz. The initial phase difference between them is zero. The separation between slits is $d=150$ m. The intensity on screen due to each source is $1\ \text{Wm}^{-2}$. Find intensity on screen for $\theta=30°$.

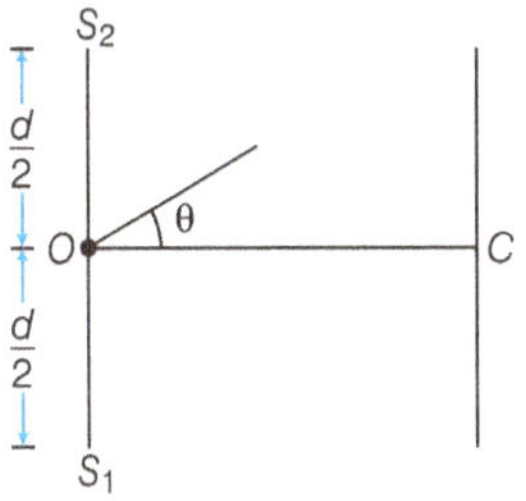

(a) $1\ \text{Wm}^{-2}$ (b) $2\ \text{Wm}^{-2}$ (c) $3\ \text{Wm}^{-2}$ (d) $4\ \text{Wm}^{-2}$

Correct Codes

Topical Questions

1 (a)	2. (d)	3 (a)	4 (a)	5 (c)	6 (d)	7 (d)	8 (c)	9 (a)	10 (b)
11 (d)	12 (d)	13 (a)	14 (d)	15 (c)	16 (d)	17 (c)	18 (a)	19 (a)	20 (d)
21 (c)	22 (c)	23 (c)	24 (c)	25 (d)	26 (c)	27 (a)	28 (a)	29 (b)	30 (d)
31 (d)	32 (c)	33 (b)	34 (a)	35 (d)	36 (a)	37 (d)	38 (c)	39 (c)	40 (c)
41 (b)	42 (b)	43 (c)	44 (c)	45 (b)	46 (d)	47 (a)	48 (a)	49 (a)	50 (d)
51 (b)	52 (b)	53 (d)	54 (c)	55 (d)	56 (a)	57 (b)	58 (a)	59 (c)	60 (a)
61 (d)	62 (b)	63 (b)	64 (c)	65 (b)	66 (d)	67 (c)	68 (b)	69 (d)	70 (b)
71 (a)									

Assertion and Reason Questions

1 (a)	2 (c)	3 (a)	4 (a)	5 (c)	6 (c)	7 (a)	8 (a)	9 (b)	10 (c)

Statement Based Questions

1 (a)	2 (b)	3 (a)	4 (b)	5 (a)	6 (c)	7 (a)	8 (d)

Matching Type Questions

1 (c)	2 (c)	3 (c)	4 (a)

Numerical Type Questions

1 (3)	2 (28)	3 (300)	4 (6)	5 (15)	6 (6000)

NCERT Exemplar Questions

1 (a)	2 (c)	3 (d)	4 (a)

Past Exams Questions

1 (d)	2 (c)	3 (a)	4 (c)	5 (b)	6 (c)	7 (d)	8 (a)	9 (a)	10 (a)
11 (c)	12 (d)	13 (c)	14 (a)	15 (d)	16 (b)	17 (d)	18 (d)		

Skill Boosters

1 (d)	2 (c)	3 (a)	4 (a)	5 (b)	6 (b)	7 (b)	8 (a)	9 (c)	10 (b)

Step by Step

Decoding the Questions

Concept Builders

1 True (T)	2 anywhere
3 Red	4 True (T)
5 increases	6 True (T)
7 polarised	8 Diffraction
9 True (T)	10 Polarisation
11 True (T)	12 True (T)
13 False (F)	14 coloured
15 True (T)	16 increases
17 True	18 $n^2 I_0$
19 $\sqrt{3}$	20 wavelength

Topical Questions

2 (*d*) Frequency, wavelength and velocity of the secondary wave remains same but intensity get reduced.

3 (*a*) By drawing sphere of radius vt at each point of primary wavefront and then drawing a common trangent at each sphere, new position of wavefront can be obtained.

5 (*c*) Every point on a given wavefront act as a secondary source of light and emits secondary wavelets which travel in all directions with the speed of light in the medium. A surface touching all these secondary wavelets tangentially in the forward direction, gives new wavefront (new position of wavefront) at that instant of time.

6 (*d*) Huygens' construction does not explain quantisation of energy, so it is not able to explain the origin of spectrum.

7 (*d*) As $i > i_C$, there cannot be any refracted wave. So, for all angles of incidence greater than the critical angle, we will not have any wavefront in medium 2. Hence, it is formed in medium 1 (on same side of *AB*).

8 (*c*) Since, $\lambda \propto \dfrac{1}{\mu}$

In denser medium, $\mu_2 > \mu_1$, so $\lambda_1 > \lambda_2$.

9 (*a*) A plane wave *AB* incident at an angle *i* on a reflecting surface *MN*, then *t* be the time taken by the wavefront to advance from point *B* to *C*. So, from the given figure the distance $BC = vt$

where, *v* is the speed of light.

For obtaining reflected wavefront, a sphere of radius vt should be drawn from the point *A* (see figure given in question). The tangent *CE* drawn on this sphere represents the reflected wavefront of *AB*.

10 (*b*) When *ABC* wavefront passes through glass lens, its velocity is reduced.

$$v_{glass} = \frac{v_{air}}{n_{glass}}$$

where, v_{glass} and v_{air} are velocities in glass and air, respectively and n_{glass} is refractive index from air to glass.

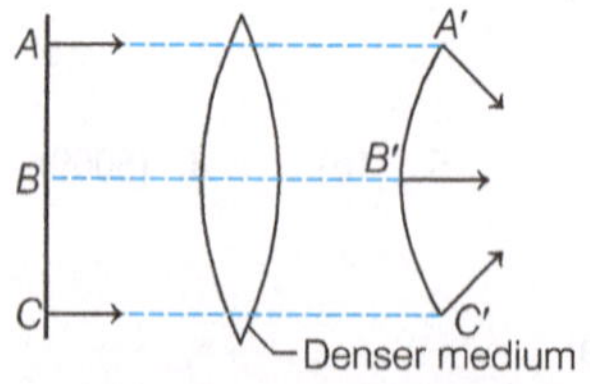

At points *A* and *C* waves remain in glass for a short duration, so they travel a larger distance while wave at *B* covers a small distance as it remains in glass for a longer duration (middle portion of glass is thick) and finally *A′ B′ C′* is the position of new wavefront. It is concave in shape as shown in the figure.

11 (*d*) The statement given in option (d) is incorrect and it can be corrected as, the motion of interferring waves can be in the same or in opposite direction. Rest statements are correct.

12 (*d*) Given, $S_1P = 7\lambda$ and $S_2P = 9\lambda$.
For constructive interference at any point, the path difference between waves should be 2λ.

Now, we have,

$$S_2P - S_1P = 9\lambda - 7\lambda$$

$$\Rightarrow \quad S_2P - S_1P = 2\lambda$$

Therefore, the sources S_1 and S_2 are said to interfere constructively.

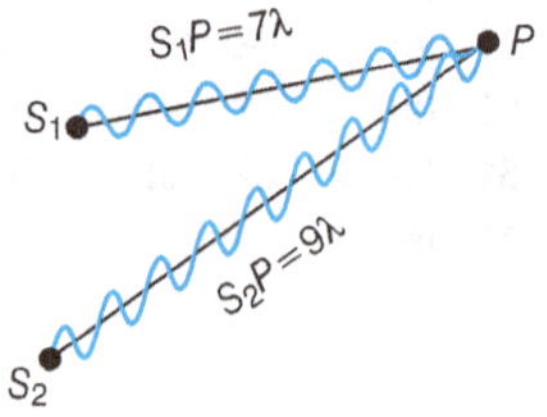

The waves emanating from S_1 will arrive exactly two cycles earlier than the waves from S_2 as $S_2P - S_1P = 2\lambda$ and will again be in phase.

13 (*a*) Given, the displacement produced by source S_1,

$$y_1 = a\cos\omega t$$

The displacement produced by source S_2,

$$y_2 = a\cos(\omega t - 4\pi)$$
$$= a\cos\omega t$$

As two displacements are in phase, so on superimposing they will give rise to constructive interference.

14 (*d*) The displacement produced by the source S_1 at the point *P* is given by $y_1 = a\cos\omega t$

The displacement produced by the sources S_2 (at the point P) is given by $y_2 = a\cos\omega t$

Thus, the resultant of displacement $y = y_1 + y_2 = 2a\cos\omega t$

Intensity, $I \propto (2a)^2$

$I = 4ka^2$

where, $I_0 = ka^2$

$I = 4I_0$

15 (c) Given, ratio of amplitudes,

$$\frac{a_1}{a_2} = \frac{3}{5}$$

Since, the intensity is proportional to the square of amplitude.

i.e. $I \propto a^2$

$$\therefore \frac{I_1}{I_2} = \left(\frac{a_1}{a_2}\right)^2 = \left(\frac{3}{5}\right)^2 = \frac{9}{25} \text{ or } 9:25$$

16 (d) Given, amplitude, $a = 2$ unit and phase difference,

$\phi = \pi$ rad

$\because$ Resultant amplitude, $A = 2a\cos\frac{\phi}{2}$

$$A = 2\times 2\times\cos\frac{\pi}{2}$$

$$A = 0$$

17 (c) The resultant amplitude of two identical superposing wave is given by

$$A = 2a\cos\frac{\phi}{2} \quad \text{... (i)}$$

The resultant intensity, $I \propto A^2$

$$\Rightarrow I \propto \cos^2\frac{\phi}{2} \quad \text{[from Eq.(i)]}$$

18 (a) Ratio of intensities of coherent sources,

i.e. $\frac{I_1}{I_2} = \frac{64}{1} = \frac{8^2}{1^2}$; $\frac{I_{max}}{I_{min}} = ?$

We have, $I_1 \propto a^2 \Rightarrow I_{max} \propto (a+b)^2$

$I_2 \propto b^2 \Rightarrow I_{min} \propto (a-b)^2$

$$\Rightarrow \frac{I_1}{I_2} = \frac{a^2}{b^2} = \frac{64}{1}$$

$$\Rightarrow \frac{a}{b} = \frac{8}{1}; a = 8b$$

So, $$\frac{I_{max}}{I_{min}} = \frac{(a+b)^2}{(a-b)^2} = \frac{(8b+b)^2}{(8b-b)^2}$$

$$= \frac{81b^2}{49b^2} = 81:49$$

19 (a) Given, $I_1 = I$

$$I_2 = \frac{I}{4}$$

Maximum intensity is given by

$$I_{max} = I_1 + I_2 + 2\sqrt{I_1, I_2}$$

$$= I + \frac{I}{4} + 2\sqrt{\frac{I\times I}{4}}$$

$$= 2I + \frac{I}{4} = \frac{9I}{4}$$

Minimum intensity is given by

$$I_{min} = I_1 + I_2 - 2\sqrt{I_1, I_2}$$

$$= I + \frac{I}{4} - 2\sqrt{\frac{I\times I}{4}} = \frac{I}{4}$$

20 (d) The nearest white spot will be at the central maxima.

$$\therefore \quad y = \frac{3d}{4} - \frac{d}{2} = \frac{d}{4}$$

So, the value of A is 4.

21 (c) The intensities due to interference of two beams of intensities I_0 with a phase difference of ϕ is

$$I_{net} = I_1 + I_2 + 2\sqrt{I_1 I_2}\cos\phi$$

Thus for central maxima, $\cos\phi = 1$

$$\Rightarrow (I_{net})_{max} = (\sqrt{I_1} + \sqrt{I_2})^2$$

$$= (2\sqrt{I_0})^2$$

$$= 4I_0$$

22 (c) Given, path difference at the centre is zero.

Path difference at 4th bright fringe

$= 4\lambda$

$= 4\times 6000\times 10^{-10}$ m $\quad (\because \lambda = 6000\text{ Å})$

$= 2.4\times 10^{-6}$ m $= 2.4\ \mu$m

23 (c) A single wide source produces many waves originating at different times. So light from a single source may be incoherent.

A single slit cuts only a part of waves from a single source.

$\therefore$ it is a coherent source.

24 (c) Let nth fringe of 1500 Å coincide with $(n-2)$ th fringe of 2500 Å.

$$\therefore \quad 1500\times n = 2500\times(n-2)$$

$$3n = 5(n-2)$$

$$3n = 5n - 10$$

$$2n = 10 \Rightarrow n = 5$$

So, $(n-2) = 3$

$\therefore$ 5th order of 1st source and 3rd order of 2nd source will coincide.

25 (d) Given, wavelength, $\lambda = 6000$ Å

Distance of screen, $D = 2.5$ m

Distance between two slits, $d = 0.5$ mm

Distance of nth bright fringe from the centre,

$$y_n = \frac{nD\lambda}{d}$$

$$\therefore \quad y_3 = \frac{3\times 2.5\times 6000\times 10^{-10}}{0.5\times 10^{-3}} \quad [\because n = 3]$$

$= 9\times 10^{-3}$ m $= 9$ mm

26 (c) Given, wavelength of blue light $= 4360$Å

and wavelength of green light $= 5460$ Å

Position of nth maximum from central maxima is

$$x_n = \frac{n\lambda D}{d} \Rightarrow x_n \propto \lambda$$

As, $\lambda_{blue} < \lambda_{green}$ (given)

So, x(blue) $< x$ (green)

27 (a) Given, wavelength, $\lambda = 589.3$ nm

$= 589.3\times 10^{-9}$ m

Distance of screen,

$D = 100$ cm $= 1$ m

Position of 10th bright fringe,

$x = 12$ mm $= 12\times 10^{-3}$ m

Position of 10th bright fringe

$$= \frac{10\lambda D}{d}$$

$$\Rightarrow \frac{10\lambda D}{d} = 12\times 10^{-3} \Rightarrow d = \frac{10\lambda D}{12\times 10^{-3}}$$

$\therefore$ The separation between the slits,

$$d = \frac{10\times 589.3\times 10^{-9}\times 1}{12\times 10^{-3}}$$

$= 4.9\times 10^{-4}$ m $= 0.49$ mm

28 (a) Let n_1th fringe formed due to first wavelength and n_2th fringe formed due to second wavelength coincide, i.e. their distance from common central maxima will be same.

i.e. $y_{n_1} = y_{n_2}$

$\Rightarrow \frac{n_1\lambda_1 D}{d} = \frac{n_2\lambda_2 D}{d}$

$\Rightarrow \frac{n_1}{n_2} = \frac{\lambda_2}{\lambda_1} = \frac{520}{650} = \frac{4}{5}$

Hence, distance of the point of coincidence from the central maxima is

$$y = \frac{n_1\lambda_1 D}{d} = \frac{n_2\lambda_2 D}{d}$$

$$= \frac{4 \times 650 \times 10^{-9} \times 1.5}{0.5 \times 10^{-3}} = 7.8 \text{ mm}$$

29 (*b*) Given, wavelengths,

$\lambda_1 = 12000$ Å and $\lambda_2 = 10000$ Å

Distance of screen, $D = 2$ m

and distance between slits,

$d = 2 \text{ mm} = 2 \times 10^{-3}$ m.

We have, $\frac{\lambda_1}{\lambda_2} = \frac{12000}{10000} = \frac{6}{5} = \frac{n_2}{n_1}$

$[\because n_1\lambda_1 = n_2\lambda_2]$

As, $x = \frac{n_1\lambda_1 D}{d}$

$$= \frac{5 \times 12000 \times 10^{-10} \times 2}{2 \times 10^{-3}}$$

$[\because n_1 = 5]$

$$= 5 \times 1.2 \times 10^4 \times 10^{-10} \times 10^3 = 6 \text{ mm}$$

30 (*d*) Given, $\lambda_1 = 6000$ Å, $n_1 = 16$ fringes and $n_2 = 24$ fringes

Position of *n*th fringe, $x_n = \frac{nD\lambda}{d}$

Now for two fringes,

$\frac{\lambda_1}{\lambda_2} = \frac{n_2}{n_1} \Rightarrow \frac{6000}{\lambda_2} = \frac{24}{16}$

$\Rightarrow \lambda_2 = \frac{6000 \times 16}{24}$

$$= \frac{96000}{24} = 4000 \text{ Å}$$

31 (*b*) Given, wavelength,

$\lambda = 500 \text{ nm} = 500 \times 10^{-9}$ m

$d = 1 \text{ mm} = 1 \times 10^{-3}$ m and $D = 1$ m

Distance of 3rd minima,

$$x_n = \left(n + \frac{1}{2}\right)\frac{\lambda D}{d}$$

$$x_3 = \left(2 + \frac{1}{2}\right)\frac{\lambda D}{d} \quad [\because n = 2]$$

$$\Rightarrow x_3 = \frac{5\lambda D}{2d}$$

$$= \frac{5 \times 500 \times 10^{-9} \times 1}{2 \times 1 \times 10^{-3}}$$

$$= 12.5 \times 10^{-4} \text{ m} = 1.25 \text{ mm}$$

32 (*c*) Given, $OP = y_n$

The distance *OP* equals one-third of fringe width of the pattern.

i.e. $y_n = \frac{\beta}{3} = \frac{1}{3}\left(\frac{D\lambda}{d}\right) = \frac{D\lambda}{3d}$

$\Rightarrow \frac{dy_n}{D} = \frac{\lambda}{3}$

Path difference $= S_2P - S_1P$

$$= \frac{dy_n}{D} = \frac{\lambda}{3}$$

$\therefore$ Phase difference,

$$\phi = \frac{2\pi}{\lambda} \times \text{Path difference}$$

$$= \frac{2\pi}{\lambda} \times \frac{\lambda}{3} = \frac{2\pi}{3}$$

If intensity at central fringe is I_0, then intensity at a point *P*, where phase difference ϕ, is given by

$I = I_0 \cos^2 \phi$

$$\Rightarrow I = I_0\left(\cos\frac{2\pi}{3}\right)^2 = I_0\left(-\cos\frac{\pi}{3}\right)^2$$

$$= I_0\left(\frac{-1}{2}\right)^2 = \frac{I_0}{4}$$

Hence, the intensity at point *P* would be $\frac{I_0}{4}$.

33 (*b*) Given,

$\lambda_1 = 400 \text{ nm} = 400 \times 10^{-9}$ m

$\lambda_2 = 5000 \text{ Å} = 5000 \times 10^{-10}$ m

$= 500 \times 10^{-9}$ m

Distance between two consecutive fringes for wavelength λ_1 is β_1 and that for wavelength λ_2 is β_2.

$\therefore \quad n_1\beta_1 = n_2\beta_2$

$\Rightarrow \quad n_1\frac{\lambda_1 D}{d} = n_2\frac{\lambda_2 D}{d}$

$\Rightarrow \quad 5 \times \frac{400 \times 10^{-9} \times D}{d}$

$$= n_2 \times \frac{500 \times 10^{-9} \times D}{d}$$

$\Rightarrow \quad n_2 = \frac{5 \times 400}{500} = 4$

34 (*a*) Most of the light is diffracted between the two first order minima. These minima occur at angles given by

$$b \sin\theta = \pm\lambda$$

$\Rightarrow \quad \sin\theta = \pm\frac{\lambda}{b}$

$$= \pm\frac{4.50 \times 10^{-9}\text{m}}{0.2 \times 10^{-3}\text{m}}$$

$$\sin\theta = \pm 2.25 \times 10^{-3}\text{rad}$$

The angular divergence

$$= 4.5 \times 10^{-3}\text{rad}$$

35 (*d*) For the first bright fringe, the distance from the centre

$$\beta = \frac{D\lambda}{d}$$

$$\Rightarrow 3.5 \times 10^{-3} = \frac{2.5 \times \lambda}{0.5 \times 10^{-3}}$$

$$\lambda = 0.7 \times 10^{-6}\text{m} = 700 \text{ nm}$$

36 (*a*) Distance between the slits,

$d = 0.28 \times 10^{-3}$m

Distance between the slits and screen, $D = 1.4$ m

Distance between the central fringe and the fourth $(n = 4)$ fringe,

$= 1.2 \times 10^{-2}$m

In case of a constructive interference, we have the relation for the distance between the two fringes as

$$y = n\lambda D/d$$

$$\Rightarrow \lambda = yd/nD = 6 \times 10^{-7} \text{ m}$$

$$= 600 \text{ nm}$$

37 (*d*) For first dark fringe on either side,

$$d \sin\theta = \lambda \text{ or } \frac{dy}{D} = \lambda$$

$\therefore \quad y = \frac{\lambda D}{d}$

Therefore, distance between two dark fringes on either side

$$= 2y = \frac{2\lambda D}{d}$$

$$= \frac{2(600 \times 10^{-6}\text{mm})(2 \times 10^3\text{mm})}{(1.0\text{mm})}$$

$$= 2.4\text{mm}$$

38 (c) Given, $D = 200\text{ cm} = 2\text{m}$

$d = 1\text{ mm} = 10^{-3}\text{m}$

Path difference

$= 6.5\text{ m} = 6.5 \times 10^{-3}\text{m}$

We know that, path difference

$$= \frac{7\lambda D}{d} - \frac{(2 \times 1 - 1)\lambda_D}{2d}$$

$$6.5 \times 10^{-3} = \frac{13\lambda D}{2d}$$

$$= \frac{13 \times \lambda \times 200 \times 10^{-2}}{2 \times 1 \times 10^{-3}}$$

$$\lambda = 0.5 \times 10^{-3} \times 10^{-3}$$

$$= 5 \times 10^{-7}\text{ m} = 5000\text{ Å}$$

39 (c) Given, $D = 1\text{ m}$

$d = 1\text{ mm} = 10^{-3}\text{ m}$

$\lambda = 6000\text{ Å}$

For 1000th maxima

$d \sin\theta = 1000\lambda$

$$\Rightarrow \quad \sin\theta = \frac{1000 \times 6000 \times 10^{-10}}{1 \times 10^{-3}}$$

$\sin\theta = 0.6, \quad \theta = 36.869$

$\therefore\ y = D\tan\theta = 1 \times \tan 36.869$

$= 0.75$

$\Rightarrow y = \frac{3}{4}\text{ m}$

40 (c) Given, $d = 3\text{ mm}$

Let width of a single slit $= a$

Path difference $= a\sin\theta \approx a\theta = \lambda$

$$\Rightarrow \quad \theta = \frac{\lambda}{a}$$

Angular width of central maxima of single slit $= 2 \times \frac{\lambda}{a}$

So, width of 8th maxima

$= 8 \times$ fringe space

$$= 8 \times \frac{\lambda}{d}$$

or $\frac{2\lambda}{a} = 8 \times \frac{\lambda}{d} \Rightarrow 4a = d$

$$a = \frac{3 \times 10^{-3}}{4}$$

$= 0.75 \times 10^{-3}\text{m}$

$\Rightarrow \quad a = 0.75\text{ mm}$

41 (b) Since, when the source S is on the perpendicular bisector, then the central bright fringe occurs at O, which is also on the perpendicular bisector.

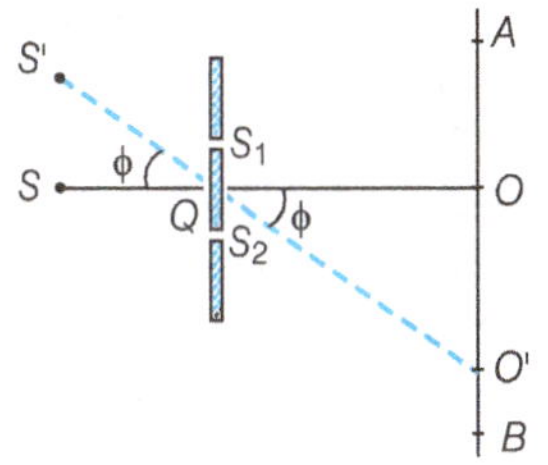

If S is shifted by an angle ϕ to point S', then the central fringe appears at a point O' at an angle ϕ (shown in figure above), which means that it is shifted by the same angle on the other side of the bisector. i.e. towards end B of screen.

42 (b) The resultant intensity,

$$I = I_0 \cos^2 \frac{\phi}{2}$$

Here, I_0 is the maximum intensity and $\phi = \frac{\pi}{2}$

$$I = I_0 \cos^2\left(\frac{\pi}{2 \times 2}\right) = I_0 \cos^2 \frac{\pi}{4}$$

$$I = \frac{I_0}{2}$$

43 (c) The contrast interference will occur when there is absolute darkness at the dark band due to destructive interference, i.e. $I_R = I_{min} = 0$ and there is complete (max) brightness at the bright band due to constructive interference, i.e. $I_R = I_{max} = 4I_0$, which is possible only when individual intensities are same.

So, $\quad I_1 = I_2 = I_0$

44 (c) As we know, fringe width,

$$\beta_1 = \frac{\lambda D}{d}$$

According to question,

$$\beta_2 = \lambda\left(\frac{2D}{2d}\right) = \frac{\lambda D}{d}$$

[$\because$ slit width and distance of screen both are doubled]

$\Rightarrow \quad \beta_1 = \beta_2$

45 (b) Given, fringe width,

$\beta_1 = 3.2 \times 10^{-4}\text{ m}$

Wavelengths, $\lambda_1 = 5600\text{ Å}$ and $\lambda_2 = 4200\text{ Å}$

Now, $\frac{\beta_2}{\beta_1} = \frac{\lambda_2}{\lambda_1} = \frac{4200}{5600} \quad [\because \beta \propto \lambda]$

or $\quad \beta_2 = \frac{6}{8} \times \beta_1 = \frac{6}{8} \times 3.2 \times 10^{-4}$

$= 2.4 \times 10^{-4}\text{ m}$

Decrease in fringe width,

$\Delta\beta = \beta_1 - \beta_2$

$= (3.2 - 2.4) \times 10^{-4}$

$= 0.8 \times 10^{-4}\text{ m}$

46 (d) Now, in YDSE fringe width,

$$\beta = \frac{\lambda D}{d}$$

$$\therefore \quad \frac{\beta_2}{\beta_1} = \frac{\lambda_2 D_2 d_1}{\lambda_1 D_1 d_2}$$

$$\Rightarrow \quad \beta_2 = \frac{\beta_1 \times \lambda_2 \times 2D_1 \times d_1}{\lambda_1 \times D_1 \times d_1/2}$$

$\left[\begin{array}{l}\therefore \text{Given } D_2 = 2D_1 \\ \text{and} \quad d_2 = d_1/2\end{array}\right]$

$$\Rightarrow \quad \beta_2 = \beta_1 \times \frac{\lambda_2}{\lambda_1} \times 4$$

$$= 1 \times 10^{-4} \times \frac{4.0 \times 10^{-7}}{6.4 \times 10^{-7}} \times 4$$

$[\because \beta_1 = 1 \times 10^{-4}\text{m}]$

$\Rightarrow \beta_2 = 2.5 \times 10^{-4}\text{ m}$

47 (a) Given, $D = 2\text{ m}$

Distance of 5th dark fringe from centre $= 4 \times 10^{-3}\text{m}$

Wavelength, $\lambda = 600\text{ nm}$

$= 6 \times 10^{-7}\text{ m}$

$\because$ Distance of 5th dark fringe from centre

$$= \beta + \beta + \beta + \beta + \frac{\beta}{2} = \frac{9\beta}{2}$$

According to question,

$$\frac{9\beta}{2} = 4 \times 10^{-3}$$

$$\frac{9}{2} \times \frac{D\lambda}{d} = 4 \times 10^{-3}$$

$$\frac{9}{2} \times \frac{2 \times 6 \times 10^{-7}}{d} = 4 \times 10^{-3}$$

$\Rightarrow \quad d = 1.35 \times 10^{-3}\text{ m}$

$= 1.35\text{ mm}$

48 (*a*) The situation is as shown below

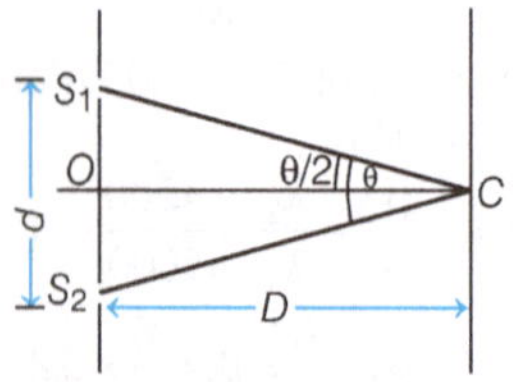

So, distance between two slits, i.e. S_1 and S_2 is

From $\Delta S_1OC, \frac{d/2}{D} = \tan\frac{\theta}{2}$

$\Rightarrow d = 2\tan(\theta/2)D$

For small angles θ, $\tan\theta \approx \theta$

$\Rightarrow \quad d = 2\times\frac{\theta}{2}\times D = D\theta$

or $\quad \frac{D}{d} = \frac{1}{\theta}$

Fringe width, $\beta = \frac{\lambda D}{d} = \frac{\lambda}{\theta}$

49 (*a*) The fringe width,

$\beta_1 = \frac{\lambda D_1}{d}$ and $\beta_2 = \frac{\lambda D_2}{d}$

So, $\beta_1 - \beta_2 = \frac{\lambda}{d}(D_1 - D_2)$

Here, $\beta_1 - \beta_2 = 3\times10^{-5}$ m,

$d = 10^{-3}$ m

and $\quad D_1 - D_2 = 5\times10^{-2}$ m

$\Rightarrow \quad 3\times10^{-5} = \frac{\lambda}{10^{-3}}(5\times10^{-2})$

$\Rightarrow \quad \lambda = \frac{3}{5}\times\frac{10^{-8}}{10^{-2}}$

$= 0.6\times10^{-6}\,\text{m} = 6000\,\text{Å}$

50 (*d*) The fringes are straight lines although S_1 and S_2 are point sources. If slits are used instead of point sources, each pair of points would have produced straight line fringes with increased intensities as shown below.

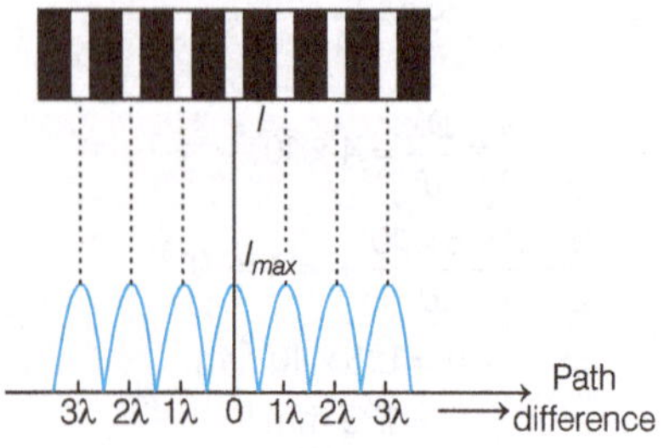

51 (*b*) Given, width of pinhole

$= 10^3\,\text{Å} = 1000\,\text{Å}$

We know that, wavelength of sunlight ranges from 4000 Å to 8000 Å.

As, the width of slit is comparable to that of wavelength, hence light is diffracted from the hole.

Due to diffraction of the sunlight, the image formed on the screen will be different from the geometrical image and overlapping of colours occur.

Thus, the statement given in option (b) is correct, rest are incorrect.

52 (*b*) In YDSE, intensity at a point is given by

$$I_{net} = 2I_0(1+\cos\phi) \quad \text{.... (i)}$$

where, ϕ = phase difference between interfering waves.

Here, $\quad \phi = \frac{1}{8}\lambda = \frac{1}{8}\times2\pi$

(a path difference of one wavelength is equivalent to a phase difference of 2π rad)

$\Rightarrow \quad \phi = \frac{\pi}{4}$

$\cos\phi = \frac{1}{\sqrt{2}} \approx 0.7$

So, I_{net} at given point *P* is

$= I_1 = 2I_0(1+0.7) = 2\times1.7I_0$

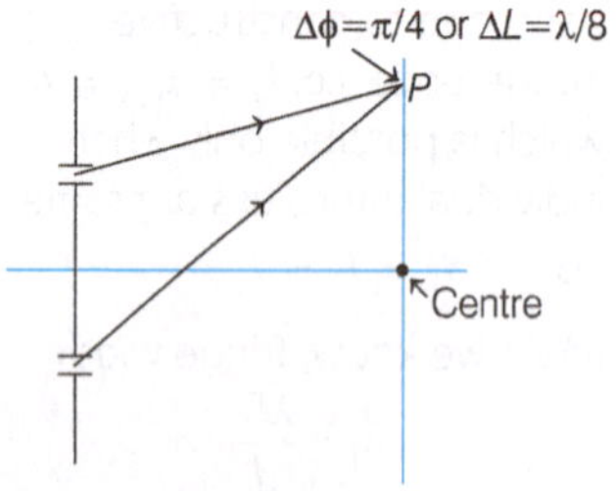

Also, intensity maxima at centre of a bright fringe is obtained by substituting

$\phi = 0, 2\pi\ldots\ n\pi$ in Eq. (i).

So, $I_{net} = I_2 = 2I_0(1+\cos0°)$

$= 4I_0$

Hence, required ratio is

$$\frac{I_1}{I_2} = \frac{2\times1.7I_0}{4I_0} = \frac{1.7}{2} = 0.853$$

53 (*d*) For minima, $d\sin\theta = m\lambda$

First minima ($m = 1$)

$\Rightarrow \quad \sin\theta = \frac{\lambda}{d}$

Angular position of 1st minima,

$\sin\theta = \theta = \frac{\lambda}{d} = \frac{6000\times10^{-10}}{0.3\times10^{-3}}$

$= 2\times10^{-3}$ rad

So, angular position of first minima is 2×10^{-3} rad.

54 (*c*) For 2nd secondary maxima using red light,

$d\sin\theta_1 = \frac{(2m+1)\lambda_1}{2}$,

where $\quad m = 2$

$d\sin\theta_1 = \frac{5\lambda_1}{2}$

$\Rightarrow \quad \sin\theta_1 = \frac{5\lambda_1}{2d} \quad$ ...(i)

When white light is used, for position of 3rd secondary maxima ($m = 3$)

$d\sin\theta_2 = \frac{7\lambda_2}{2}$

$\Rightarrow \quad \sin\theta_2 = \frac{7\lambda_2}{2d} \quad$ ...(ii)

Since, these positions coincide with each other for white and red light

$\sin\theta_1 = \sin\theta_2 \Rightarrow \frac{5\lambda_1}{2d} = \frac{7\lambda_2}{2d}$

$\Rightarrow \quad \lambda_2 = \frac{5}{7}\lambda_1 = \frac{5}{7}\times6500\,\text{Å}$

Wavelength of light,

$\lambda_2 = 4642.85\,\text{Å}$

55 (*d*) Distance of 2nd order maxima from the centre of the screen,

$x = \frac{5}{2}\frac{D\lambda}{d}$

$\Rightarrow \quad d = \frac{5}{2}\frac{D\lambda}{n}$

Given, $D = 1$ m, $x = 15$ mm

$= 15\times10^{-3}$m

$\lambda = 600$ nm $= = 600\times10^{-9}$m

$\therefore d = \frac{5}{2}\times\frac{1\times600\times10^{-9}}{15\times10^{-3}} = 100\,\mu\text{m}$

56 (*a*) Angular width of central maxima $(2\theta) = \frac{2\lambda}{d} = \frac{2\lambda}{e}$

$$\Rightarrow \quad 2\theta \propto \frac{\lambda}{e}$$

$$\Rightarrow \quad \theta \propto \frac{1}{e} \quad (\text{for } \lambda = \text{constant})$$

Thus, on decreasing slit width e, θ will increases.

57 (*b*) If a converging lens of focal length f is placed after the slit and the fringe are obtained on screen, then separation of the central maximum from the first null of the diffraction pattern is λ / a.

If f is the focal length of the lens, then the size of screen will be $f\lambda / a$.

58 (*a*) In unpolarised beam, vibrations are probable in all directions in a plane perpendicular to the direction of propagation. Therefore, θ can have any value from 0 to 2π.

$$[\cos^2\theta]_{av} = \frac{1}{2\pi}\int_0^{2\pi} \cos^2\theta \, d\theta$$

$$= \frac{1}{2\pi}\int_0^{2\pi} \left(\frac{1+\cos 2\theta}{2}\right) d\theta$$

$$= \frac{1}{4\pi}\left([\theta]_0^{2\pi} + \left[\frac{\sin 2\theta}{2}\right]_0^{2\pi}\right)$$

$$= \frac{1}{4\pi} \times 2\pi = \frac{1}{2}$$

So, using law of Malus,

$$I = I_0 \cos^2\theta$$

$$\Rightarrow \quad I = I_0 \times \frac{1}{2} = \frac{I_0}{2}$$

59 (*c*) The situation is as shown below.

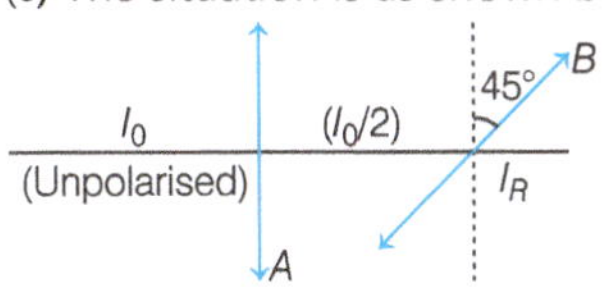

According to Malus' law,

$$I_R = \left(\frac{I_0}{2}\right)\cos^2(45°) = \frac{I_0}{2} \times \frac{1}{2} = \frac{I_0}{4}$$

60 (*a*) Suppose I_0 be the intensity of polarised light after passing through the first polariser P_1, then, the intensity of light after passing through second polariser will be

$$I = I_0 \cos^2\theta$$

where, θ is the angle between pass axes of P_1 and P_2. Since, P_1 and P_3 are crossed the angle between pass axes of P_2 and P_3 will be $\left(\frac{\pi}{2} - \theta\right)$.

Hence, the intensity of light emerging from P_3 will be

$$I = I_0 \cos^2\theta \cos^2\left(\frac{\pi}{2} - \theta\right)$$

$$= I_0 \cos^2\theta \cdot \sin^2\theta$$

$$= \left(\frac{I_0}{4}\right)\sin^2 2\theta$$

Intensity is maximum, when

$$\sin 2\theta = 1$$

$$\Rightarrow \quad 2\theta = \pi/2 \text{ or } \theta = \pi/4$$

Therefore, the transmitted intensity will be maximum when $\theta = \pi/4$.

61 (*d*) Here, angle between P_1 and $P_2 = 60°$

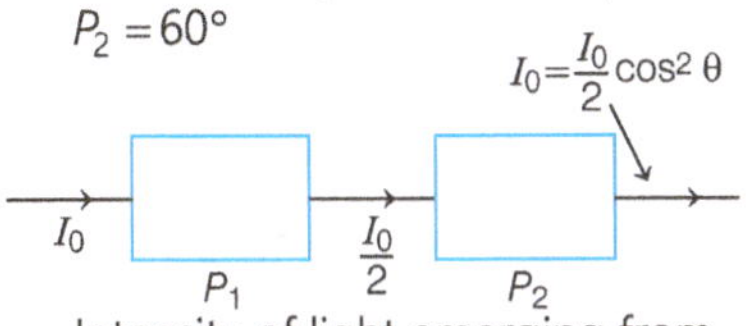

Intensity of light emerging from P_2 is $I = \frac{I_0}{2}\cos^2\theta$

where, θ = angle between P_1 and P_2.

$$\text{So,} \quad I = \frac{I_0}{2}\cos^2 60°$$

$$= \frac{I_0}{2}\left(\frac{1}{2}\right)^2 = \frac{I_0}{8}$$

62 (*b*) Polaroids can be used to control the intensity in sunglasses, window-panes, etc. The intensity can be further controlled from 50% to zero of the incident intensity by adjusting the angle between the pass-axes of two polaroids.

63 (*b*) Let I_0 be the intensity through first polaroid when axis is parallel

$\therefore$ By Malus law,

$$I_1 = I_0 \cos^2\theta$$

$$= I_0 \cos^2 0°$$

$$I_1 = I_0$$

When $\theta = 60°$

$$I_2 = I_0 \cos^2 60°$$

$$= I_0 \times \left(\frac{1}{2}\right)^2; \; I_2 = \frac{I_0}{4}$$

$$\therefore \quad \frac{I_1}{I_2} = \frac{I_0}{\left(\frac{I_0}{4}\right)} = \frac{4}{1}$$

64 (*c*) Given, $I = 2 \text{ Wm}^{-2}$

$$I_0 = 32 \text{ Wm}^{-2}$$

Let θ be the angle between the axis of first two polarisers, then $(90°-\theta)$ will be the angle between second and 3rd polariser

$$\therefore \quad I = \frac{I_0}{2}\cos^2\theta \cos^2(90 - \theta)$$

$$2 = \frac{32}{2}\cos^2\theta\cos^2(90 - \theta)$$

$$2 = 16\cos^2\theta \sin\theta^2$$

$$\frac{1}{2} = 4\cos^2\theta \sin^2\theta$$

$$\frac{1}{2} = (2\cos\theta \sin\theta)^2$$

$$\frac{1}{2} = \sin^2 2\theta$$

$$\therefore \sin 2\theta = \frac{1}{\sqrt{2}}$$

$$2\theta = \sin^{-1}\frac{1}{\sqrt{2}} = 45°$$

$$\Rightarrow \quad \theta = 22.5°$$

65 (*b*) Assume that I_0 is the intensity of incident light.

As the light coming is unpolarised, so the intensity of light emerging from the first polaroid is given by

$$I_1 = \frac{I_0}{2}$$

If θ be the angle between two polaroids, then the intensity of light emerging from the second polaroid is

$$I_2 = I_1 \cos^2\theta$$

$$= \frac{I_0}{2}\cos^2\theta$$

But, $I_0 = 100$

$\therefore \quad I_1 = \frac{100}{2} = 50$

Since, θ varies from 90° to 0°, so the intensity of the outcoming light can be varied from 0% to 50%.

66 (*d*) According to Malus law,

$$I = I_0 \cos^2 \theta$$

Let, polariser C is at angle θ with A and also with B.

$$\therefore \quad I_C = \left(\frac{2I}{3}\right)\cos^2 \theta$$

$$I_B = I_C \cos^2 \theta$$

and $\quad I_B = \frac{2I}{3}\cos^4 \theta$

Also given, $I_B = \frac{I}{3}$

$$\therefore \quad \frac{I}{3} = \frac{2I}{3}\cos^4 \theta$$

$$\Rightarrow \quad \cos^4 \theta = \frac{1}{2}; \cos \theta = \left(\frac{1}{2}\right)^{\frac{1}{4}}$$

67 (*c*) In the special situation, one of the two perpendicular components of the electric field is zero. At other angles, both components are present but one is stronger than the other.

When such light is viewed through a rotating analyser, one sees a maximum and a minimum of intensity but not complete darkness. This kind of light is called partially polarised.

68 (*b*) Given, angle of incidence = 45°

As reflected light is completely polarised, therefore

$$i_p = 45°$$

From Brewster's law, $\mu = \tan i_p$

$$= \tan 45° = 1$$

As, $\quad \mu = \frac{c}{v}$

$$\Rightarrow \quad v = \frac{c}{\mu} = \frac{3 \times 10^8}{1}$$

$$\Rightarrow \quad v = 3 \times 10^8 \text{ ms}^{-1}$$

69 (*d*) Given, $i + r = \pi / 2$

According to Brewster's law, we get

$$\tan i_B = \mu = 1.5$$

So, $\quad i_B = \tan^{-1}(1.5)$

$$\Rightarrow \quad i_B = 57°$$

i.e. This is the Brewster's angle for air to glass interface.

70 (*b*) Given, refractive index of medium, $\mu = 1$

Using Brewster's law, $\tan i_p = \mu$

$$\tan i_p = 1$$

$$i_p = \tan^{-1}(1) = 45°$$

As $\quad i_p + r = 90°$

$$r = 90° - i_p$$

$$= 90° - 45°$$

$$\Rightarrow \quad r = 45°$$

71 (*a*) Given, critical angle,

$$i_c = \sin^{-1}\left(\frac{4}{5}\right)$$

$$\therefore \quad \sin i_c = \frac{4}{5}$$

As $\quad \mu = \frac{1}{\sin i_c} = \frac{5}{4}$

According to Brewster's law, $\tan i_p = \mu$

where, i_p is the polarising angle.

$$\therefore \quad \tan i_p = \frac{5}{4}$$

$$\Rightarrow \quad i_p = \tan^{-1}\left(\frac{5}{4}\right)$$

Assertion and Reason Questions

2 (*c*) Since, the speed of light waves is less in glass, the lower portion of the incoming wavefront (which travels through the greatest thickness of glass) will get delayed resulting a tilt in the emerging wavefront as shown.

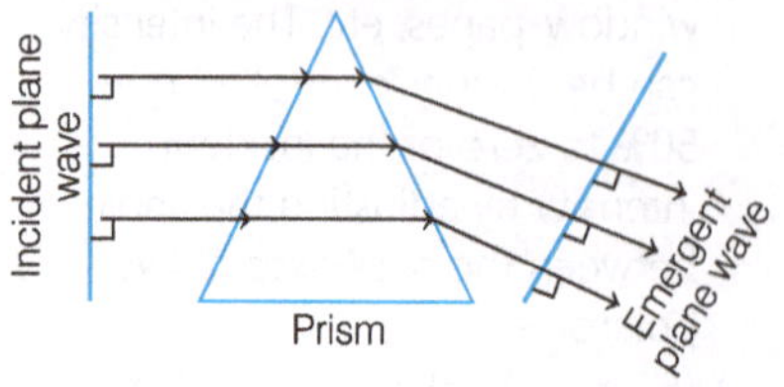

Therefore, Assertion is correct but Reason is incorrect.

5 (*c*) If I_1 and I_2 are intensity of waves coming from two sources, then the maximum intensity,

$$I_{max} = (\sqrt{I_1} + \sqrt{I_2})^2$$

$$= (2\sqrt{I_0})^2 = 4I_0$$

$$[\because I_1 = I_2 = I_0 \text{ (given)}]$$

The minimum intensity observed at dark band is given

by $\quad I_{min} = (\sqrt{I_1} - \sqrt{I_2})^2$

If $\quad I_1 = I_2 = I_0$

$$I_{min} = 0$$

If $\quad I_1 \neq I_2$

$$I_{min} \neq 0$$

Therefore, intensity of dark band is not always zero.

6 (*c*) Assertion is correct but Reason is incorrect. When source in Young's double slit experiment is white light, the central fringe is white as all colours meet there in phase.

8 (*a*) When d is negligibly small, fringe width β which is proportional to $1/d$ may become too large. Even a single fringe may occupy the whole screen. Hence, the pattern cannot be detected.

9 (*b*) When slit is wide (i.e. $a >> \lambda$), bending of light becomes so small that it cannot be detected upto a certain distance of screen from the slit. Hence, practically, no diffraction occurs.

10 (*c*) In Young's double slit experiment, fringe width for dark and white fringes are same, while in the same experiment, when a white light (as source) is used, the central fringe is white around which few coloured fringes are observed on either side.

Statement Based Questions

1 (*a*) At a large distance from the source, the small portion of the sphere can be considered as plane wave as shown in figure.

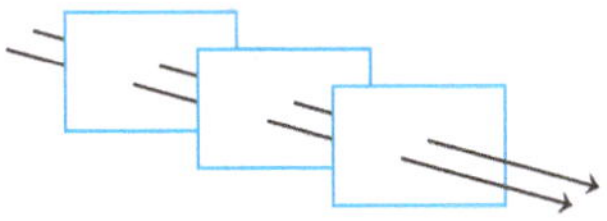

2 (*b*) Here, Huygens' principle of secondary wavelets can be used to prove law of reflection and law of refraction.

3. (*a*) When a light wave travels from a rarer to a denser medium it loses speed but energy carried by the wave does not depend on its speed. Instead, it depends on the amplitude of wave.

4 (*b*) Statement I is correct but Statement II is incorrect. Bright interference bands have the same intensity because $I_{max} \propto (a_1 + a_2)^2$, which is constant.

5 (*a*) Both Statement I and Statement II are incorrect. When Young's double slit experiment is performed by a source of white light, the central fringe will be white, there will not be a completely dark fringe and the fringe next to the central fringe will be violet.

6 (*c*) Wavelength is inversely proportional to the number of fringes, hence by doubling the wavelength the number of fringes decreases. Hence, Statement I is incorrect and Statement II is correct.

7 (*a*) If a thin film is introduced in front of the upper slit, then fringe pattern shifts in upward direction.

If slit widths are unequal, then minima will not be completely dark.

8 (*d*) Diffraction is a wave phenomenon. It is observed in electromagnetic and longitudinal waves as well.

Matching Type Questions

1 (*c*)

A. A light rays diverging from a point source.

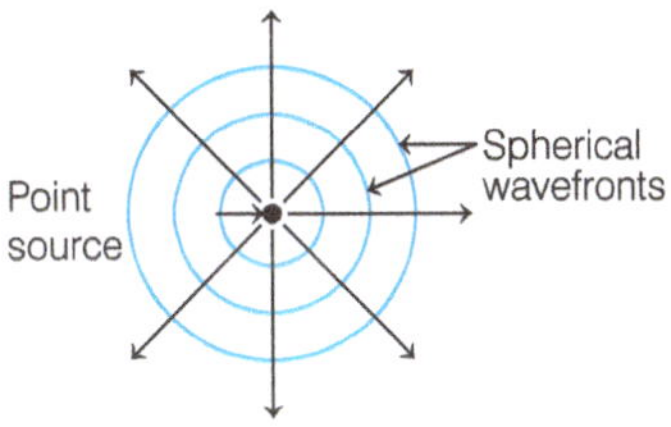

B. A light ray emerging out of convex lens when a point source is placed at its focus.

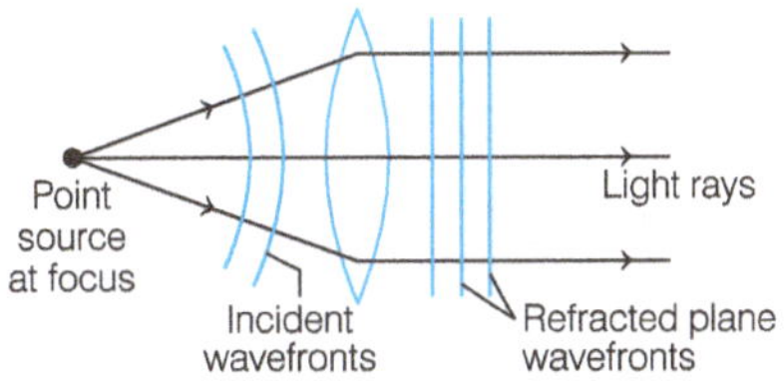

C. A plane wave incident on a thin prism.

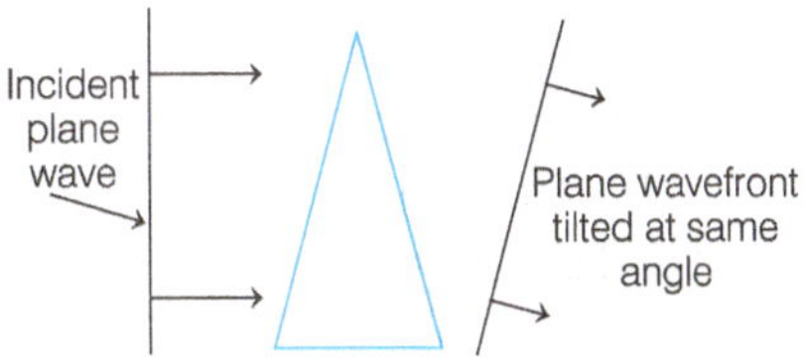

Hence, A → 2, B → 1, C → 3 and D → 4.

2 (*c*) A constructive interference is produced when waves overlaps such that a crest meets a crest and trough meet a trough, i.e. waves are in phase.

In destructive interference, waves are out of phase.

For maxima (or constructive interference), path difference

$$= n\lambda (n = 0, 1, 2, 3, \dots)$$

For minima (or destructive interference), path difference

$$= (2n + 1)\frac{\lambda}{2} \quad (n = 0, 1, 2, 3, \cdots)$$

Hence, A → 3, B → 4, C → 1 and D → 2.

3 (*c*)

A. If screen is moved away from the plane of slits, i.e. on increasing the value of *D*, the angular separation of the fringes $(= \lambda/d)$ remains constant. But the actual separation of the fringes $\left(\frac{\lambda D}{d}\right)$ increases.

B. The separation of the fringes (and also angular separation) decreases, when source is replaced by another source of shorter wavelength.

C. When medium is water, then

$$\lambda' = \frac{\lambda_{air}}{4/3} = \frac{3}{4}\lambda_{air}$$

∴ Fringe width,

$$\beta' = \frac{\lambda' D}{d} = \frac{3}{4}\left(\frac{\lambda D}{d}\right) = \frac{3}{4}\beta$$

Therefore, fringe width becomes $\left(\frac{3}{4}\right)$th.

D. Fringe width, $\beta = \frac{D\lambda}{d}$

As, $\beta \propto \frac{1}{d}$, so when distance between slits is reduced, linear width of fringes β increases.

Hence, A → 2, B → 3, C → 4 and D → 1.

4 (*a*) Fringe width, $\beta = \frac{D\lambda}{d}$

A. If sodium light ($\lambda = 589$ nm) is replaced by red light ($\lambda = 700$ nm) of same intensity,then λ is increases, so β also increases.

B. White light produces coloured fringes with centred bright fringe.

C. If D is doubled and d is halved, then $\beta\left(\frac{2\lambda D}{d/2}=\frac{4\lambda D}{d}\right)$ becomes four times.

D. If intensity of either slit is reduced by covering any slit with cellophone paper, the bright fringes became less bright.

Hence, A → 4, B → 1, C → 2 and D → 3.

Numerical Value Questions

1 (3) Here, $\lambda = 5000$ Å

$d = 0.4\text{mm} = 0.4\times10^{-3}\text{m}$

$D = 800$ cm $= 8$ m

$n = 3$

We know that, $x = (n)\lambda\frac{D}{d}$

$$= 3\times5000\times10^{-10}\times\frac{8}{0.4\times10^{-3}}$$

$$= 3\times10^{-2}\text{m} = 3\text{ cm}$$

2 (28) At total darkness both minima coincides.

The condition for the minima,

$$x_n = (2n-1)\frac{\lambda D}{2d}$$

For wavelengths λ_1 and λ_2,

$$x_n = (2n-1)\frac{\lambda_1 D}{2d}$$

$$x_m = (2m-1)\frac{\lambda_2 D}{2d}$$

For $x_n = x_m$

$$(2n-1)\frac{\lambda_1 D}{2d} = (2m-1)\frac{\lambda_2 D}{2d}$$

$$(2n-1)\frac{\lambda_1}{2} = (2m-1)\frac{\lambda_2}{2}$$

$$\frac{2n-1}{2m-1} = \frac{\lambda_2}{\lambda_1} = \frac{560\text{ nm}}{400\text{ nm}} = \frac{7}{5}$$

Possible values are ($n_1 = 4$, $m_1 = 3$) and ($n_2 = 11$, $m_2 = 8$) .... etc.

Location of there minimas is

$$y_1 = \frac{(2n_1-1)\lambda_1 D}{d}$$

and $y_2 = \frac{(2n_2-1)\lambda_1 D}{d}$

$\therefore$ Distance $= y_2 - y_1 = 42 - 14$

$= 28$ mm

3 (300) The position of bright fringe is given by

$$y_n = \frac{n\lambda D}{d}$$

Here, $D = 1.5$ m, $d = 0.3\times10^{-3}$m

and $n = 1$

$$\lambda = \frac{y_n d}{D}$$

For first violet,

$$y_n = 2\text{ mm} = 2\times10^{-3}\text{m}$$

$$\therefore\ \lambda_{violet} = 2\times10^{-3}\left(\frac{d}{D}\right)$$

For first red, $y_n = 3.5$ mm

$= 3.5\times10^{-3}$m

$$\lambda_{red} = 3.5\times10^{-3}\left(\frac{d}{D}\right)$$

$$\Delta\lambda = \lambda_{red} - \lambda_{violet}$$

$$= 3.5\times10^{-3}\left(\frac{d}{D}\right) - 2\times10^{-3}\left(\frac{d}{D}\right)$$

$$= \frac{d}{D}(1.5)\times10^{-3}$$

$$= \frac{0.3\times10^{-3}}{1.5}\times1.5\times10^{-3}$$

$$= 0.3\times10^{-6} = 0.3\times10^{-6}\times10^{3}\times10^{-3}$$

$$= 300\times10^{-9} = 300\text{ nm}$$

4 (6) Given, $d = 0.90$ mm

$= 0.9\times10^{-3}$m

$x = 1\text{ mm} = 10^{-3}$m,

$D = 1$ m, $n = 2$

For dark fringe,

$$x = (2n-1)\frac{\lambda D}{2d}$$

$$\lambda = \frac{2xd}{(2n-1)D}$$

$$= \frac{2\times10^{-3}\times0.9\times10^{-3}}{(2\times2-1)\times1}$$

$$= 0.6\times10^{-6}\text{m}$$

$$\lambda = 6\times10^{-5}\text{ cm}$$

5 (15) Given, $\lambda_1 = 650\times10^{-9}$m

$\lambda_2 = 655\times10^{-9}$m

Width of aperture,

$a = 0.75$ mm

$= 7.5\times10^{-4}$m

Distance between screen and source, $D = 1.5$ m

We know the position of first maxima,

$$a\sin\theta = 3\lambda/2$$

Since, $\sin\theta \approx \theta = \frac{y}{D}$

$$\therefore\ a.\frac{y}{D} = \frac{3\lambda}{2}$$

$$\Rightarrow\ y = \frac{3\lambda D}{2a}$$

$$\therefore\ y_1 = \frac{3\lambda_1 D}{2a}$$

and $y_2 = \frac{3\lambda_2 D}{2a}$

$$\therefore\ \Delta y = y_2 - y_1 = \frac{3\lambda_2 D}{2a} - \frac{3\lambda_1 D}{2a}$$

$$= \frac{3D}{2a}(\lambda_2 - \lambda_1)$$

$$= \frac{3\times1.5}{2\times7.5\times10^{-4}}\times(655\times10^{-9} - 650\times10^{-9})$$

$$= 15\times10^{-6}\text{m}$$

6 (6000) Given, $\Delta\beta = 3\times10^{-5}$m

$\Delta D = 5\times10^{-2}$m

$d = 10^{-3}$m

$$\Delta\beta = \frac{\lambda}{d}\Delta D$$

$$3\times10^{-5} = \frac{\lambda}{10^{-3}}\times5\times10^{-2}$$

$$\lambda = \frac{3\times10^{-5}\times10^{-3}}{5\times10^{-2}}$$

$$= 6\times10^{-7}\text{m}$$

$$= 6000\times10^{-10}\text{m}$$

$$= 6000\text{ Å}$$

NCERT Exemplar Questions

1 (*a*) Given, width of the slit

$= 10^4$ Å $= 10000$ Å

$= 10^4\times10^{-10}$ m $= 10^{-6}$m

$= 1\mu$m

Wavelength of (visible) sunlight varies from 4000 Å to 8000 Å.

As the width of slit is comparable to that of wavelength, hence, diffraction occurs with maxima at centre. So, at the centre all colours appear, i.e. mixing of colours form white patch at the centre.

Therefore, the image seen through the slit shall be a fine sharp slit white in colour at the centre.

2 (c) In a Young's double slit experiment, when one of the holes is covered by a red filter and another by a blue filter. In this case due to filteration, only red and blue lights are present, In Young's double slit experiment, monochromatic light is used for the formation of fringes on the screen. Hence, in given case, there shall be no interference fringes.

3 (d) As given, there is a hole at point P_2 (minima). The hole will act as a source of fresh light source for the slits S_3 and S_4. Therefore, there will be a regular two slit pattern on the second screen.

4 (a) Given, angular resolution of human eye, $\phi = 5.8 \times 10^{-4}$ rad and printer prints 300 dots per inch.

The linear distance between two dots,

$$l = \frac{2.54}{300} = 0.84 \times 10^{-2} \text{ cm}$$

At a distance of z cm, this subtends an angle,

$$\phi = \frac{l}{z}$$

$$\therefore \quad z = \frac{l}{\phi} = \frac{0.84 \times 10^{-2}}{5.8 \times 10^{-4}} = 14.5 \text{ cm}$$

Past Exams Questions

1 (d) At Brewster's angle, the angle between refracted and reflected rays is 90°. The reflected ray is completely linearly polarised and the refracted ray is partially polarised.

2 (c) When YDSE is performed in white light instead of monochromatic light, all wavelengths shows their maxima and minima in order of their wavelength. Thus, a central bright is observed along with few fringes that will be different colours.

3 (a) For central maximum, path difference is zero for both coherent sources in interference.

Hence, phase difference

$$= \frac{2\pi}{\lambda} \times \text{path difference}$$

$$= \frac{2\pi}{\lambda} \times 0 = 0$$

4 (c) In a YDSE, the path difference for nth minima is given by

$$\Delta y = (2n-1)\frac{\lambda}{2}$$

For 5th minima, $n = 5$

$$\therefore \quad \Delta y = [2(5)-1]\frac{\lambda}{2} = \frac{9\lambda}{2}$$

5 (b) The angular width of central maxima is given by

$$2\theta = \frac{2\lambda}{a} \quad \text{...(i)}$$

where, λ = wavelength of light used

and a = width of the slit.

For $\lambda_1 = 6000$ Å, $2\theta = \theta_0$ (given)

For another light of wavelength λ_2 (says), the angular width decreases by 30% ,

$$2\theta = \left(\frac{100-30}{100}\right)\theta_0$$

$$= \frac{70}{100}\theta_0 = 0.7\theta_0$$

As slit width is constant, so using Eq. (i) for these values, we get

$$\frac{\theta_0}{0.7\theta_0} = \frac{\lambda_1}{\lambda_2}$$

$$\Rightarrow \quad \lambda_2 = \lambda_1 \times 0.7 = 6000 \times 0.7$$

$$= 4200 \text{ Å}$$

6 (c)According to the question,

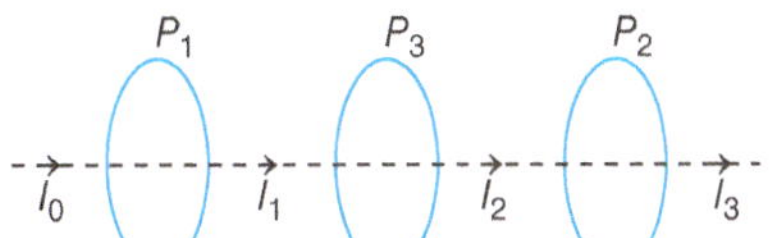

From the above diagram, intensity transmitted through P_3,

$$I_2 = \frac{I_0}{2}\cos^2 45°$$

$$\Rightarrow \quad I_2 = \frac{I_0}{2} \times \left(\frac{1}{\sqrt{2}}\right)^2$$

$$\Rightarrow \quad I_2 = \frac{I_0}{4}$$

Similarly, intensity transmitted through P_2,

$$I_3 = \frac{I_0}{4}\cos^2 45°$$

$$\Rightarrow \quad I_3 = \frac{I_0}{4} \times \left(\frac{1}{\sqrt{2}}\right)^2$$

$$\Rightarrow \quad I_3 = \frac{I_0}{4} \times \frac{1}{2}$$

$$\Rightarrow \quad I_3 = \frac{I_0}{8}$$

7 (d) For the distance of the first dark band of the diffraction pattern from the centre of the screen is given by positon of Ist minima.

i.e. $$Y = \frac{\lambda D}{a}$$

$$\Rightarrow \quad Y = \frac{(5 \times 10^{-5})(0.6)}{0.02 \times 10^{-2}} \quad \text{(given)}$$

$$\Rightarrow \quad Y = 0.15 \text{ cm}$$

8 (a) Given, $d = 1 \text{ mm} = 1 \times 10^{-3}$m

$D = 1$m

$\lambda = 500 \text{ nm} = 5 \times 10^{-7}$ m

As, width of central maxima

= width of 10 maxima

$$\therefore \quad \frac{2D\lambda}{a} = 10\left(\frac{\lambda D}{d}\right)$$

$$\Rightarrow a = \frac{d}{5} = \frac{10^{-3}}{5} = 0.2 \times 10^{-3}\text{m}$$

$a = 0.2$ mm

9 (a) Given, Young's double slit experiment, having two slits of width are in the ratio of 1 : 25.

So, ratio of intensity,

$$\frac{I_1}{I_2} = \frac{W_1}{W_2} = \frac{1}{25}$$

$$\Rightarrow \quad \frac{I_2}{I_1} = \frac{25}{1}$$

$$\therefore \quad \frac{I_{max}}{I_{min}} = \frac{(\sqrt{I_2}+\sqrt{I_1})^2}{(\sqrt{I_2}-\sqrt{I_1})^2} = \left[\frac{\sqrt{\frac{I_2}{I_1}}+1}{\sqrt{\frac{I_2}{I_1}}-1}\right]^2$$

$$\Rightarrow \left[\frac{5+1}{5-1}\right]^2 = \left(\frac{6}{4}\right)^2 = \frac{36}{16} = \frac{9}{4}$$

10 (*a*) For the condition of maxima,

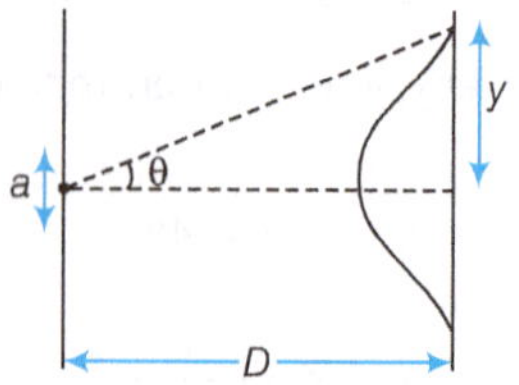

$$\sin\theta = \frac{\lambda}{a}$$

From the geometry,

$$\sin\theta \approx \theta = \frac{Y}{D} \quad \text{(for small angle)}$$

So, $\dfrac{Y}{D} = \dfrac{\lambda}{a}$

$\Rightarrow \quad Y = \dfrac{\lambda D}{a}$

Hence, width of central maxima

$$= 2Y = \frac{2\lambda D}{a}$$

11 (*c*) For first minima at *P*,

$$a\sin\theta = n\lambda$$

where, $n = 1 \Rightarrow a\sin\theta = \lambda$

So, phase difference,

$$\Delta\phi = \frac{\Delta x_1}{\lambda} \times 2\pi$$

$$= \frac{(a/2)\sin\theta}{\lambda} \times 2\pi$$

$$= -\frac{\lambda}{2\lambda} \times 2\pi = \pi \text{ rad}$$

12 (*d*) According to Brewster's rule, when polarisation of reflected ray occurs, then reflected and refracted rays are perpendicular.

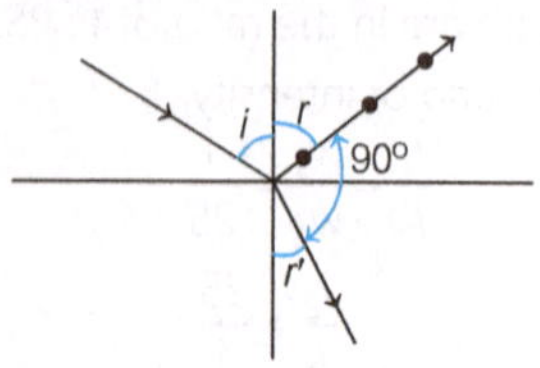

So, $\quad r + r' = 90°$

$\Rightarrow \quad r' = 90° - r = 90° - i$

$= 90° - 60° = 30°$

13 (*c*) Central maxima lies between two first minimas on either side of centre line.

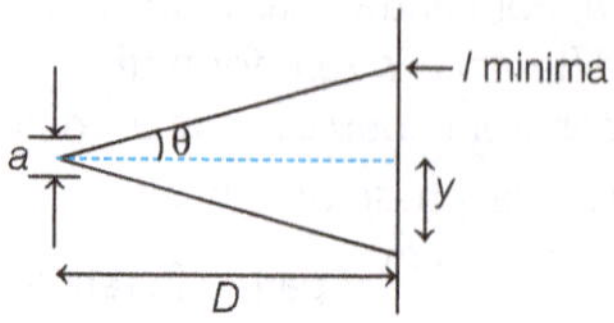

Angular width of central maxima is 2θ where,

$$\sin\theta = \frac{\lambda}{a}$$

$$\Rightarrow \quad \theta = \sin^{-1}\frac{\lambda}{a}$$

So, angular width $= 2\theta$

$$= 2\sin^{-1}\frac{\lambda}{a}$$

$$= 2\sin^{-1}\left(\frac{2}{4}\right) = 2\sin^{-1}\left(\frac{1}{2}\right)$$

$$= 2 \times 30° = 60°$$

14 (*a*) When a polaroid sheet is rotated through an angle ϕ between two crossed polaroids, then intensity of transmitted light.

$$I = I_0\cos^2\phi \cdot \sin^2\phi$$

$\therefore \quad I_{max}$ at $\phi = 45°$

$$\phi = 45°$$

15 (*d*) In given Young's double slit experiment, first minima occurs at *P*.

when $\lambda = 800$ nm.

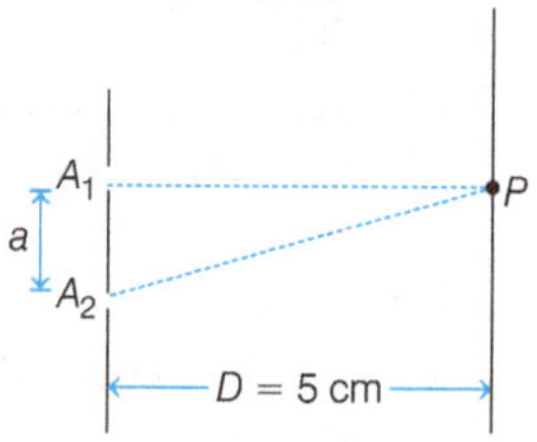

For Ist minima,

Path difference, $A_2P - A_1P$

$$= \sqrt{(5^2 + a^2)} - 5 = \frac{\lambda}{2}$$

Take length in centimeter

$$\Rightarrow \sqrt{(5^2 + a^2)} - 5 = \frac{800 \times 10^{-9} \times 100}{2}$$

$$\Rightarrow \quad \sqrt{(5^2 + a^2)} = 5 + 4 \times 10^{-5}$$

On squaring, we get

$$5^2 + a^2 = 5^2 + (4 \times 10^{-5})^2 + 40 \times 10^{-5}$$

Neglecting $(4 \times 10^{-5})^2$ being too small, we get

$$a^2 = 400 \times 10^{-6}$$

$$\Rightarrow a = 20 \times 10^{-3} \text{ cm}$$

$$= 20 \times 10^{-3} \times 10 \text{ mm} = 0.2 \text{ mm}$$

16 (*b*) If an unpolarised light is converted into plane polarised light, then its intensity becomes half i.e. $I = \dfrac{I_0}{2}$, where I_0 is intensity of unpolarised light.

According to Malus law,

$$I = I_0\cos^2\theta$$

So, $\quad I = \dfrac{I_0}{2}$

$[\cos^2 45° \times \cos^2 45° \times \ldots \times (n-1)$ times$]$

$$\Rightarrow \quad \frac{I_0}{64} = \frac{I_0}{2} \times \left(\frac{1}{2}\right)^{n-1}$$

$$\Rightarrow \quad \frac{1}{32} = \frac{1}{2^{n-1}}$$

$$\Rightarrow \quad \frac{1}{2^5} = \frac{1}{2^{n-1}}$$

$\therefore \quad n - 1 = 5$

or $\quad n = 6$

17 (*d*) By Malus' law,

Output intensity obtained from analyser,

$$I' = I_0\cos^2\theta$$

where, θ = angle between polariser and analyser.

Now, given $I' = 10\%$ of initial intensity

$$\Rightarrow \quad I' = \frac{1}{10}I_0 = I_0 \times \cos^2\theta$$

$$\Rightarrow \quad \cos^2\theta = \frac{1}{10}$$

$$\Rightarrow \quad \cos\theta = \frac{1}{\sqrt{10}}$$

$$\Rightarrow \quad \theta = \cos^{-1}\frac{1}{\sqrt{10}} \approx 71.6°$$

Now, output intensity is zero when angle between polariser and analyser is 90°.

So, analyser must be rotated by $90° - 71.6° = 18.40°$ to reduce output intensity to zero.

18 (*d*) For small value of θ,

$$\sin\theta \approx \theta$$

So, path difference $= \Delta L = d\theta$

For a bright fringe at same angular position θ, both of the rays from slits S_1 and S_2 are in phase.

Hence, path difference is an integral multiple of wavelength of light used.

i.e. $\Delta L = n\lambda$

or $d\theta = n\lambda$

$\Rightarrow \lambda = \dfrac{d\theta}{n}$

Here, $\theta = \dfrac{1}{40}$ rad, $d = 0.1$ mm

Hence, $\lambda = \dfrac{0.1}{40n}$ mm

$$= \frac{0.1 \times 10^{-3}\text{ m}}{40n}$$

$$= \frac{0.1 \times 10^{-3} \times 10^{9}}{40n}\text{ nm}$$

$\Rightarrow \quad = \dfrac{2500}{n}$ nm

So, with light of wavelength λ_1, we get

$$\lambda_1 = \frac{2500}{n_1}\text{ (nm)}$$

and with light of wavelength λ_2, we get

$$\lambda_2 = \frac{2500}{n_2}\text{ (nm)}$$

Now, choosing different integral values for n_1 and n_2, (i.e., $n_1, n_2 = 1, 2, 3$ ... etc) we find that for

$$n_1 = 4,$$
$$\lambda_1 = \frac{2500}{4} = 625\text{ nm}$$

and for $n_2 = 5$

$$\lambda_2 = \frac{2500}{5} = 500\text{ nm}$$

These values lie in given interval 500 nm to 625 nm.

Skill Boosters

1 (*d*)

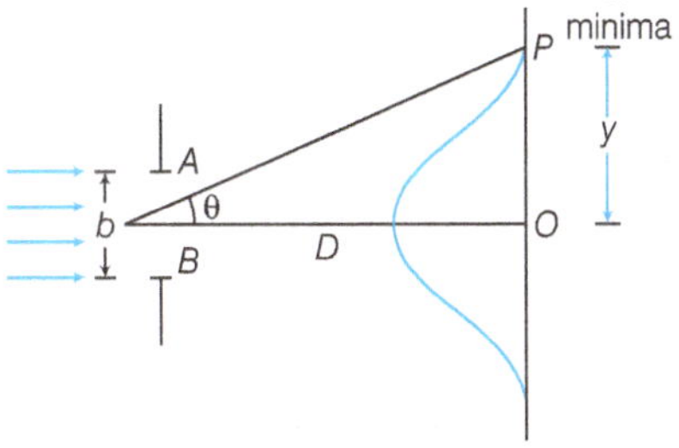

At first minima, $b\sin\theta = \lambda$

For small angle, $\sin\theta \approx \theta$

$\Rightarrow \quad b\theta = \lambda$ ...(i)

From the diagram, $\tan\theta = y/D$

For small angle, $\tan\theta \approx \theta$

$\Rightarrow \quad \theta = y/D$ ... (ii)

$$b\left(\frac{y}{D}\right) = \lambda$$

$\Rightarrow \quad y = \dfrac{\lambda D}{b}$

$\Rightarrow \quad \dfrac{yb}{D} = \lambda$ ...(iii)

Now, at P (first minima), path difference between the rays reaching from two edges (A and B) will be

$$\Delta x = \frac{yb}{D}$$

(Compare with $\Delta x = \dfrac{yd}{D}$ in YDSE)

$\Rightarrow \quad \Delta x = \lambda$ [from Eq. (i)]

Corresponding phase difference (ϕ) will be

$$\phi = \left(\frac{2\pi}{\lambda}\right)\cdot \Delta x \Rightarrow \phi = \frac{2\pi}{\lambda}\cdot\lambda = 2\pi$$

2 (*c*) Here, lens is combination of two media of refractive indices μ and $(\mu - \delta\mu)$.

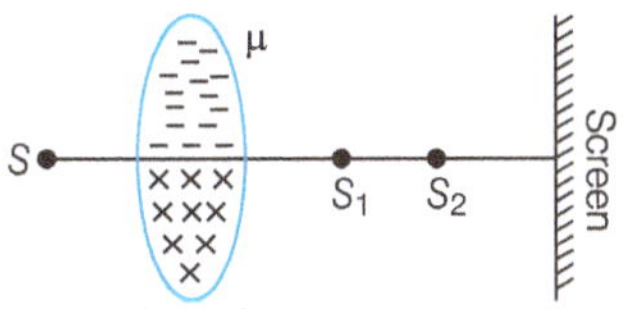

The line joining images S_1 and S_2 are perpendicular to screen. So, shape of fringe on the screen is circular.

3 (*a*) The path difference at point P is

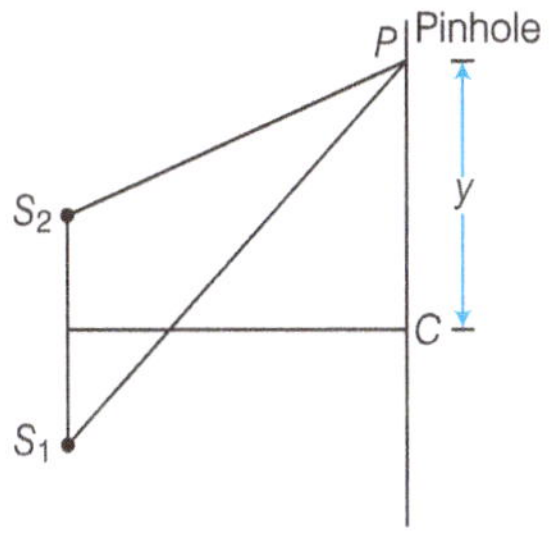

$$\Delta x = \frac{yd}{D}$$
$$= \frac{2 \times 10^{-3} \times 1 \times 10^{-3}}{1}$$
$$= 2 \times 10^{-6}$$
$$= 2000 \times 10^{-9}\text{ m} = 2000\text{ nm.}$$

For absent wavelength, minima is formed.

$\therefore \quad \Delta x = (2m - 1)\dfrac{\lambda}{2}$

or $\quad 2000 = (2m - 1)\dfrac{\lambda}{2}$

$\therefore \quad \lambda = \dfrac{4000}{2m - 1}$

Here, $m = 1, 2, 3, \cdots$

For $m = 1$, $\lambda_1 = 4000$ nm

For $m = 2$, $\lambda_2 = \dfrac{4000}{3}$ nm

For $m = 3$, $\lambda_3 = 800$ nm

For $m = 4$, $\lambda_4 = 571.4$ nm

For $m = 5$, $\lambda_5 = 444.4$ nm

For $m = 6$, $\lambda_6 = 363.6$ nm

4 (*a*) Intensity of reflected light from upper surface, $I_1 = I_0 \times \dfrac{25}{100} = \dfrac{I_0}{4}$

and intensity of transmitted light from upper surface,

$$I' = I_0 - \frac{I_0}{4} = \frac{3I_0}{4}$$

The intensity of reflected light from lower surface is

$$I_2 = \frac{3I_0}{4} \times \frac{50}{100} = \frac{3I_0}{8}$$

$$\therefore \quad \frac{I_{min}}{I_{max}} = \frac{(\sqrt{I_1} - \sqrt{I_2})^2}{(\sqrt{I_1} + \sqrt{I_2})^2}$$

$$= \frac{\left(\sqrt{\frac{I_0}{4}} - \sqrt{\frac{3I_0}{8}}\right)^2}{\left(\sqrt{\frac{I_0}{4}} + \sqrt{\frac{3I_0}{8}}\right)^2}$$

$$= \frac{\left(\frac{1}{2} - \sqrt{\frac{3}{8}}\right)^2}{\left(\frac{1}{2} + \sqrt{\frac{3}{8}}\right)^2}$$

5 (*b*) If at any instant, the axis of polariser makes an angle θ with the direction of vibration of incident light.

From law of Malus,

$I = I_0 \cos^2 \theta$

As polariser is rotating, all values of θ are possible.

$$\therefore \langle I \rangle = \langle I_0 \cos^2 \theta \rangle = \frac{I_0}{2} = \frac{\text{Power}}{2 \times \text{Area}}$$

$$= \frac{10^{-3}}{2 \times 3 \times 10^{-4}} = \frac{5}{3} \text{ Wm}^{-2}$$

6 (*b*) $\Delta x_1 = 0$

$$\Delta x_2 = \mu_w \frac{yd}{D}$$

$$\Delta x_3 = (\mu - \mu_w) t$$

$$\Delta x = \mu_w \frac{yd}{D} + (\mu - \mu_w) t$$

For bright fringes,

$$\Delta x = m\lambda$$

$$\frac{\mu_w yd}{D} + (\mu - \mu_w) t = m\lambda$$

For central bright fringe, $m = 0$

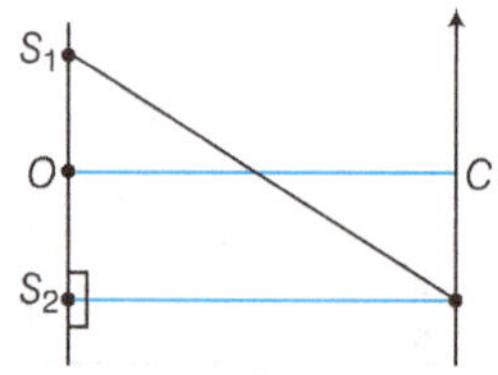

$$\frac{\mu_w yd}{D} + (\mu - \mu_w) t = 0$$

$$\frac{\mu_w yd}{D} = -(\mu - \mu_w) t$$

$$y = \frac{-(\mu - \mu_w) tD}{\mu_w d}$$

$$y = -\frac{\left[\frac{3}{2} - \frac{4}{3}\right] 10.4 \times 10^{-3} \times 3 \times 1.5}{4 \times 45 \times 10^{-5}}$$

$$y = \frac{-10.4 \times 3 \times 1.5 \times 10^{-3}}{6 \times 4 \times 45 \times 10^{-5}}$$

$\Rightarrow y = -4.33 \text{ m}$

7 (*b*) Here, $\Delta x = d \sin \alpha + d \sin \theta$

For centre of screen, $\theta = 0$

$$\therefore \Delta x = d \sin \alpha = (2m - 1) \frac{\lambda}{2}$$

$$\therefore \quad \sin \alpha = (2m - 1) \frac{\lambda}{2d}$$

$$\therefore \quad \alpha_{min} = \sin^{-1}\left(\frac{\lambda}{2d}\right)$$

8 (*a*)

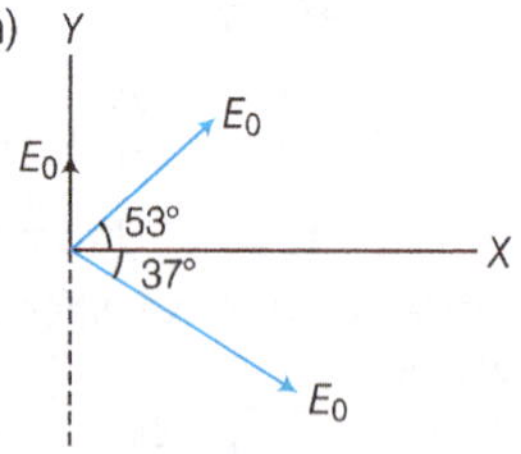

Here, $E_x = E_0 \cos 37° + E_0 \cos 53°$

$$= \frac{4}{5} E_0 + \frac{3}{5} E_0 = \frac{7}{5} E_0$$

and $E_y = E_0 + E_0 \sin 53° - E_0 \sin 37°$

$$= E_0 + \frac{4}{5} E_0 - \frac{3}{5} E_0$$

$$= E_0 + \frac{1}{5} E_0 = \frac{6E_0}{5}$$

$$\therefore E_0' = \sqrt{E_x^2 + E_y^2} = \sqrt{\frac{49}{25} + \frac{36}{25}} E_0$$

$$= \sqrt{\frac{85}{25}} E_0 = \frac{\sqrt{85}}{5} E_0$$

$$\text{Here, } \tan \phi = \frac{E_y}{E_x} = \frac{\frac{6}{5} E_0}{\frac{7}{5} E_0} = \frac{6}{7}$$

$$\therefore \quad \phi = \tan^{-1}\left(\frac{6}{7}\right)$$

Thus, $E = E_0' \sin(\omega t + \phi)$

$$= \frac{\sqrt{85}}{5} \sin\left[\omega t + \tan^{-1}\left(\frac{6}{7}\right)\right]$$

9 (*c*) Here, $I_1 = I_0$ and $I_2 = 4I_0$

$$\because \; I = I_1 + I_2 + 2\sqrt{I_1 I_2} \cos \phi$$

$$= I_0 + 4I_0 + 2 \times 2I_0\left(-\frac{1}{2}\right)$$

$$= 5I_0 - 2I_0 = 3I_0$$

10 (*b*) Here, path difference,

$$\Delta x = d \sin \theta$$

$$\therefore \text{ Phase difference, } \phi = \frac{2\pi}{\lambda} \Delta x$$

$$= \frac{2\pi}{\lambda}(d \sin \theta) = \frac{2\pi}{\frac{c}{\nu}}(d \sin \theta)$$

$$\therefore \; \phi = \frac{2\pi}{3 \times 10^8} \times 10^6 \times 150 \sin 30°$$

$$= \frac{\pi}{2}$$

$$\because \; I = 4I_0 \cos^2 \frac{\phi}{2} = 4 \times 1 \cos^2 \frac{\pi}{4}$$

$$= 4 \times \frac{1}{2} = 2 \text{ Wm}^{-2}$$

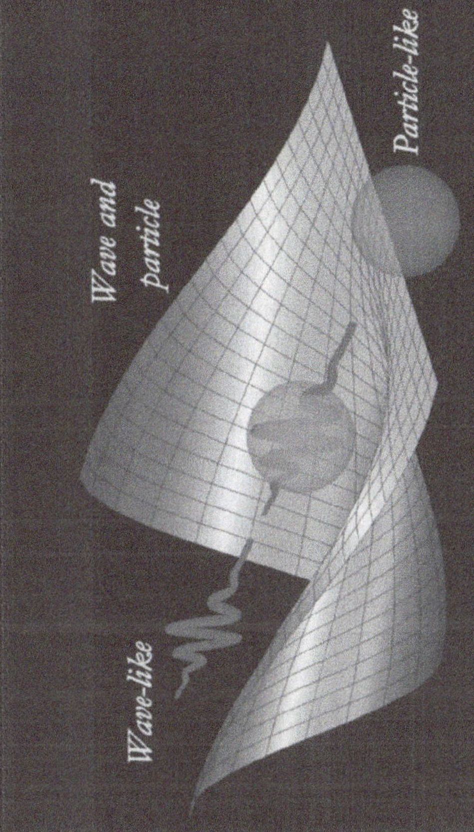

11

Scan for Physics Through Concept Master Videos

Dual Nature of Radiation and Matter

Topicwise No. of Ques asked in 5 Years (NEET)

Topics	No. of Questions				
	2024	2023	2022	2021	2020
Electron Emission	–	–	–	–	–
Experimental Study of Photoelectric Effect	–	–	–	–	–
Photoelectric Effect & Wave Theory of Light	–	–	–	–	–
Einstein's Photoelectric Equation : Energy Quantum of Radiation	–	1	1	–	1
Particle Nature of Light : the Photon	1	–	–	1	–
Wave Nature of Matter	1	–	1	1	3

Special Type of Ques Asked In 5 Years (NEET)

Types	Years				
	2024	2023	2022	2021	2020
A-R	–	–	–	–	–
Statement Based	1	–	–	–	–
Matching	–	–	–	–	–

Last 5 Years Weigtage (NEET)

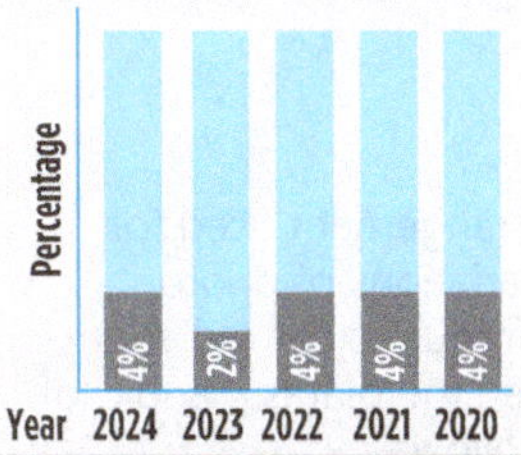

Introduction

- Maxwell's equations of electromagnetism and Hertz's experiments on generation & detection of electromagnetic waves in 1887 strongly established the wave nature of light.
- In the later years of 19th century, scientists made key discoveries: Roentgen found X-rays in 1895, and J.J. Thomson discovered electrons in 1897, advancing atomic structure knowledge.
- In 1870, William Crookes discovered **cathode rays** which was later, confirmed by Thomson in 1879 that these rays are consisted of streams of fast moving negatively charged particles.
- J.J. Thomson found the charge to mass ratio (e/m) of cathode rays. They travelled at the speed ranging from about 0.1 to 0.2 times the speed of light, with an accepted e/m value of 1.76×10^{11} C/kg.
- In 1887, metals emitted negatively charged particles under heat or light, matching $\frac{e}{m}$ ratio with cathode rays. Thomson named them electrons in 1897 and suggested as fundamental universal constituents of matter, winning a Nobel prize in 1906.
- In 1913, Millikan's oil-drop experiment found the electron's charge as 1.602×10^{-19} C, showing electric charge is quantised. It enabled the calculation of the electron's mass using charge (e) and specific charge (e/m).

Electron Emission

- Metals can conduct electricity because they have free electrons. These electrons are negatively charged particles. But normally, they can't easily escape from the metal's surface. If an electron tries to get out, the metal's surface becomes positively charged and pulls it back to the metal. So, for the electron to escape, it needs to have enough energy to overcome this attraction. This phenomenon of emission of electrons from a metal surface is called electron emission.
- The least amount of energy required for an electron to get out of the metal surface is called the **work function** of the metal.

Following are few important points related to work function

(i) It is generally denoted by ϕ_0 and measured in eV (electron-volt). One electron volt is the energy gained by an electron when it has been accelerated by a potential difference of 1 V, so that 1 eV $= 1.602 \times 10^{-19}$ J.

(ii) ϕ_0 depends on the properties of the metal and the nature of its surface.

- The minimum energy required for the electron emission from the metal surface can be supplied to the free electrons by any of the following physical processes

(i) **Thermionic Emission** By suitable heating, sufficient thermal energy can be imparted to the free electrons to enable them to come out of the metal.

(ii) **Field Emission** By applying a very strong electric field (of the order of 10^8 Vm^{-1}) to a metal, electrons can be pulled out of the metal, as in a spark plug.

(iii) **Photoelectric Emission** When light of suitable frequency illuminates a metal surface, electrons are emitted from the metal surface. This is known as **photoelectric effect**. The photo (light) generated electrons during the process are called **photoelectrons**.

Photoelectric Effect

The photoelectric effect is based upon the following observations

- **Hertz's Observations** During the production of electromagnetic waves by means of a spark discharge, Hertz observed that high voltage sparks across the detector loop were enhanced when the emitter plate was illuminated by ultraviolet light from an arc lamp.
- Hallwach and Lenard's Observations

(i) **Lenard** observed that when ultraviolet radiations were allowed to fall on emitter plate of an evacuated glass tube enclosing two electrodes (metal plates), current flows in the circuit. As soon as, the ultraviolet radiations were stopped, the current flow also stopped.

They also studied how this photocurrent varied with collector plate potential, frequency and intensity of incident light.

(ii) **Lenard** and **Hallwach** also observed that when ultraviolet light fall on the emitter plate, no electrons were emitted at all when the frequency of the incident light was smaller than a certain minimum value called **threshold frequency**. This minimum frequency depends on the nature of the material of the emitter plate.

(iii) Certain metals, like zinc, cadmium and magnesium emit electrons when exposed to ultraviolet light. Alkali metals, including lithium, sodium, potassium and rubidium can even emit electrons with visible light. These emitted electrons are termed as **photoelectrons** and the phenomenon is called the **photoelectric effect**.

Experimental Study of Photoelectric Effect

- In the experimental study of photoelectric effect an emitting electrode C with a photosensitive material is given a negative potential, while a collecting electrode A is given positive potential in a evacuated tube.
  When high frequency light from the sources S hits the emitting electrode C passing through quartz window as shown in figure below, it emits **photoelectrons** that creates a **photoelectric current**, which is directly proportional to the number of emitted photoelectrons.
- If collecting electrode A is made negative compared to emitting electrode C, it sets up an electric field in the direction of photoelectrons motion, applying a retarding force on electrons.

  This results fewer electrons reaching the collecting electrode, reducing the photoelectric current. With a strong enough negative potential V_0, no photoelectrons reach collecting electrode A, and this potential is called the **stopping potential**.

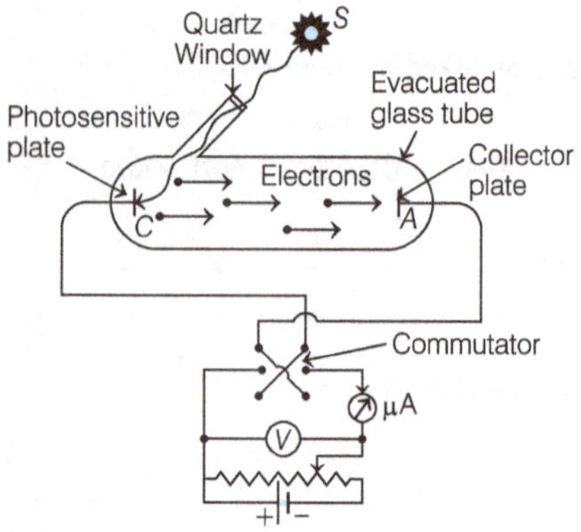

- On the basis of the experimental arrangement used for studying photoelectric effect, the variations of photo current with intensity of radiation, frequency of radiation and the potential difference between the plates A and C of photoelectric with intensity are as follows

Effect of Intensity of Light on Photocurrent

- It is found that the photocurrent increases linearly with intensity of incident light as shown in the graph below.
- Here frequency of incident radiation and the accelerating potential are fixed.

Photocurrent ∝ Intensity

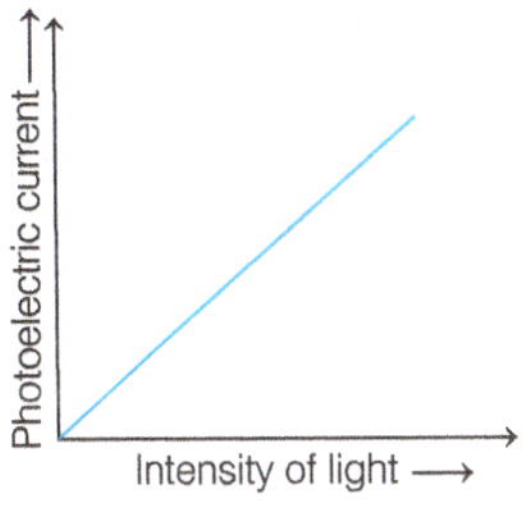

Effect of Potential on Photoelectric Current

- Effect of Potential on Photoelectric Current Variation of photocurrent with collector plate potential for different intensity of incident radiation is as shown below

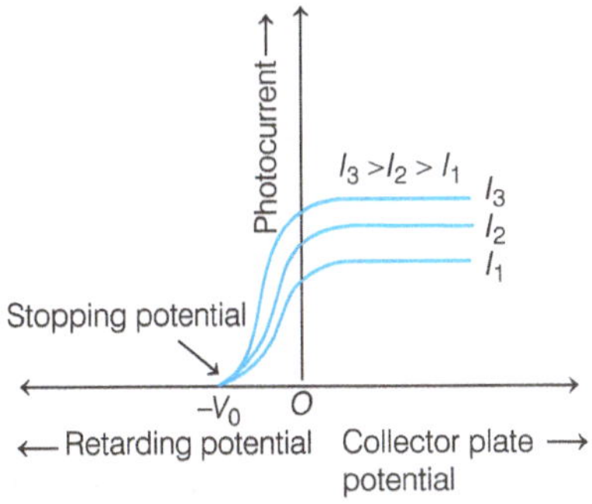

From the above graph, we can observe that,

(i) For a fixed frequency and intensity of incident radiation, the photocurrent increases with increase in the potential applied to the collector. At some stage, the photoelectric current becomes maximum or saturates.

(ii) Maximum value of photoelectric current is called **saturation current**. It corresponds to the case when all the photoelectrons emitted by the emitter plate reaches the collector plate.

(iii) For a particular frequency of incident radiation, the minimum negative (retarding) potential V_0 given to the plate A for which the photocurrent stops or becomes zero is called the **cut-off** or **stopping potential**.

(iv) Photoelectric current is zero when the stopping potential is sufficient to repel even the most energetic photoelectrons with the maximum kinetic energy K_{max}, so that $K_{max} = eV_0$.

(v) Thus, for a given frequency of the incident radiation, the stopping potential is independent of its intensity.

In other words, the maximum kinetic energy of photoelectrons depend on the light source and the emitter plate material, but it is independent of intensity of incident radiation.

Effect of Frequency of Incident Radiation on Stopping Potential

- Variation of photoelectric current with collector plate potential for different frequencies of incident radiation is as shown below

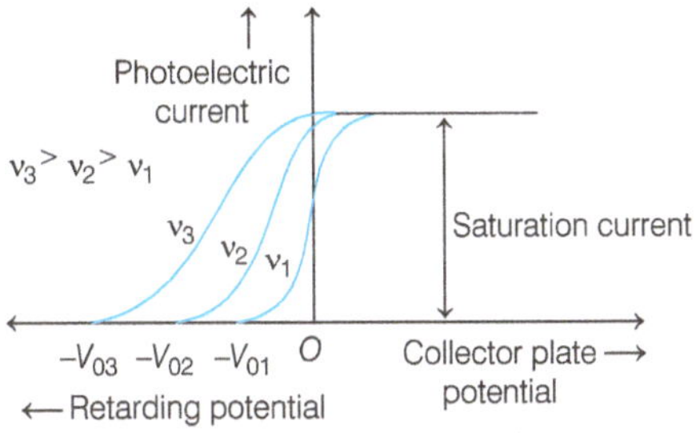

From the above graph, we observe that,

(i) Stopping potentials are in the order of $V_{03} > V_{02} > V_{01}$, if the frequencies are in the order of $\nu_3 > \nu_2 > \nu_1$.

(ii) This implies that greater the frequency of incident light, greater is the maximum kinetic energy of photoelectrons.

(iii) Consequently, greater retarding potential is required to stop them completely.

- The graph between the frequency of incident radiation and the corresponding stopping potential for different metals A and B is straight line as shown below

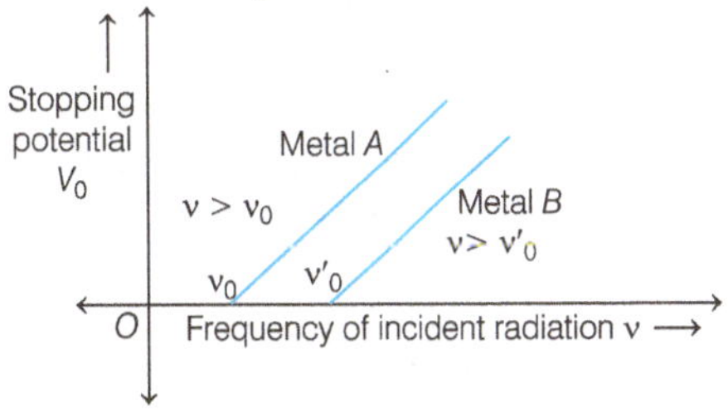

This graph shows that,

(i) the stopping potential V_0 varies linearly with the frequency of incident radiation for a given photosensitive material.

(ii) there exist a certain minimum cut-off frequency ν_0 for which the stopping potential is zero.

Note *The stopping potential is more negative for higher frequencies of incident radiations.*

- From the above observations, two implications are as follows

(i) The maximum kinetic energy of the photoelectrons varies linearly with the frequency of incident radiation, but it is independent of its intensity.

(ii) For a frequency ν of incident radiation, lower than the cut-off frequency ν_0, no photoelectric emission is possible even, if the intensity is large.
This minimum, cut-off frequency ν_0 is called the **threshold frequency**. It is different for different metals.

Note ***Threshold wavelength*** *λ_0 is the maximum wavelength of incident radiation above which no photoelectric emission takes place.*

- If frequency of incident radiation exceeds the threshold frequency, the photoelectric emission starts instantaneously without any apparent time lag (~ 10^9s or less), even if the incident radiation is very dim.

Photoelectric Effect and Wave Theory of Light

- According to wave picture, light is a type of energy that travels in waves. These waves an made up of electric and magnetic fields and they spread out as they move through space. On the basis of this theory of light, photoelectric effect can be explained as follows.

(i) Free electrons at the surface of the metal absorb the radiant energy continuously. Thus, maximum kinetic energy of the photoelectrons on the surface is then expected to increase with the increase in intensity.

(ii) No matter what the frequency of incident radiation is, a sufficiently intense beam of radiation (over sufficient time) should be able to impart enough energy to the electrons, so that they exceed the minimum energy needed to escape from the metal surface.

(iii) Since, the absorption of energy by electron takes place continuously, so it can take hours or more for a single electron to pick up sufficient energy to overcome the work function and come out of the metal.

For Concept Master Video

Thus, wave picture is unable to explain the basic features of photoelectric emission.

Einstein's Photoelectric Equation Energy Quantum of Radiation

- According to Einstein, photoelectric emission does not takes place by continuous absorption of energy from radiation.
- Radiation energy is made up of tiny units called **quanta**. Each quantum of radiant energy has energy $h\nu$, where h is Planck's constant and ν is frequency of light.
- According to Einstein's explanation, incident photons on a metal surface are completely absorbed by metal's free electrons. Each photon's energy ($h\nu$) is partly used by an electron to become free or to overcome its work function ϕ_0, and the remaining energy gives the maximum kinetic energy to the emitted photoelectrons.

$$h\nu = \frac{1}{2}mv_{max}^2 + \phi_0$$

Since, K_{max} must be non-negative. So, photoelectric emission is possible only if $h\nu > \phi_0$ or $\nu > \nu_0$

- The energy of photon $h\nu_0$ corresponding to threshold frequency ν_0 is just sufficient enough to liberate the electron i.e. it is just equal to the work function ϕ_0 of the metal i.e.

$\phi_0 = h\nu_0 = h\frac{c}{\lambda_0}$, where λ_0 = threshold wavelength

So, $h\nu = \frac{1}{2}mv_{max}^2 + h\nu_0$ or $\frac{1}{2}mv_{max}^2 = h(\nu - \nu_0)$ **NEET 2021**

This is **Einstein's photoelectric** equation.

- In terms of threshold wavelength λ_0, above equation can be written as $eV_0 = hc\left(\frac{1}{\lambda} - \frac{1}{\lambda_0}\right)$

where, λ is the wavelength of incident photon.

For Concept Master Video

Marks Maximiser

Measuring Planck's Constant and Work Function

- According to Einstein's photoelectric equation, **NEET 2021**

$$K_{max} = h\nu - \phi_0$$

$\therefore \quad eV_0 = h\nu - \phi_0 \Rightarrow V_0 = \left(\frac{h}{e}\right)\nu - \frac{h\nu_0}{e}$

From $\quad y = mx + c$

Here, $m = \tan\theta = \frac{h}{e}$ which is a slope of a straight line.

So, stopping potential V_0 *versus* frequency ν graph is straight line with slope $\left(\frac{h}{e}\right)$ as shown in figure below.

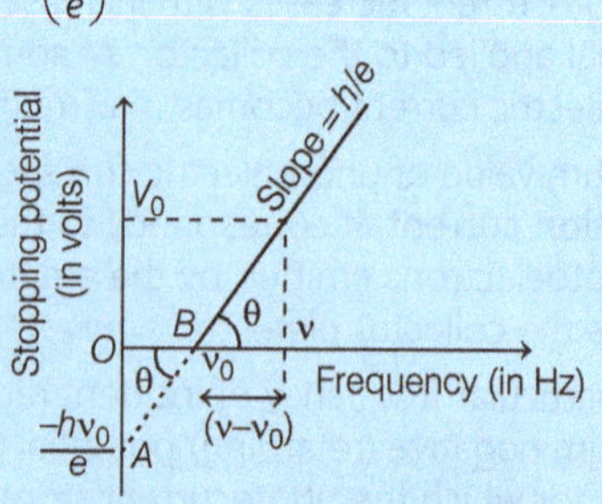

Thus, Planck's constant h can be determined by knowing the slope m.

The intercept on the potential axis is located at

$$OA = OB\tan\theta = \nu_0\frac{h}{e} \quad \text{or} \quad OA = \frac{h\nu_0}{e}$$

$\therefore \quad \phi_0 = h\nu_0 = e \times OA$

Thus, work function ϕ_0 can be determined by knowing intercept OA.

Particle Nature of Light : The Photon

- Einstein arrived at an important result, that light in interaction with matter behaves as packets of energy called quanta, each of energy $h\nu$. The light quantum can also be associated with momentum $\frac{h\nu}{c}$. A definite value of energy as well as momentum is a strong indication of the light quantum can be associated with a particle. This particle was later named **photon**.
- **Properties of photon** are as follows :
  (i) In indication of radiation with matter, radiation behaves as it is made up of particles called photons.
  (ii) Each photon has energy $E(= h\nu)$ and momentum $p\left(=\frac{h\nu}{c}\right)$ and speed of light c.
  (iii) All photons of light at a particular frequency ν or wavelength λ, have the same energy $E(= h\nu = hc/\lambda)$ and momentum $p(= h\nu/c = h/\lambda)$, whatever the intensity of radiation may be. The photon energy is independent of intensity of radiation.
  (iv) Photons are electrically neutral and are not deflected by electric and magnetic fields.
  (v) In a photon-particle collision (such as photon-electron collision), the total energy and total momentum are conserved. However, the number of photons may not be conserved in a collision. The photons may be absorbed or a new photon may be created.

Wave Nature of Matter

- With the experimental verification, it was proved that light has dual nature, in some phenomena, it behaves like wave and in some phenomena, it behaves like particle depending upon the dimensions of particle with which the light interacts.

Matter Waves : de-Broglie Waves

- In 1924, Louis Victor de-Broglie put forward a hypothesis that moving particles of matter should display wave-like properties under suitable conditions.
- According to de-Broglie, a wave is associated with moving material particle which controls the parts in every respect.

  This wave is called matter wave or de-Broglie wave whose wavelength is called de-Broglie wavelength which is given by

$$\lambda = \frac{h}{p} = \frac{h}{mv}$$ NEET 2022, 21

Marks Maximiser

de-Broglie wavelength associated with uncharged particle

(i) For neutron ($m_n = 1.67 \times 10^{-27}$ kg)

$$\lambda = \frac{h}{\sqrt{2mE}} = \frac{0.286}{\sqrt{E(\text{eV})}}\,\text{Å} = \frac{1.23}{\sqrt{V}}\,\text{nm}$$

(ii) For gas molecule, wavelength

$$\lambda = \frac{h}{m \times v_{\text{rms}}}$$

Caution Points

- Electrons in a metal don't all possess the same energy. Their energy distribution is distinct from the typical Maxwell's distribution due to the influence of electrons obey Pauli's exclusion principle.
- In the photoelectric effect, energy is absorbed in discrete units of $(h\nu)$ during the interaction between matter and light. This doesn't imply that light is made up of separate particles, each with energy $(h\nu)$.
- The matter wave's wavelength $\lambda = \frac{h}{p}$ has physical significance, but its phase velocity (v_p) has no physical significance. However, the group velocity (v_g) of the matter wave is physically meaningful and is equal to the particle's velocity.

PYQ Notes

1. If a parallel beam of light of wavelength λ and intensity I is incident on a surface of area A perpendicularly. The number of photons crossing the surface per second is given by

$$n = \frac{\text{Power}}{\text{Energy of one photon}} = \left(\frac{I.A}{hc}\right)\lambda$$

JEE Main 2023, 22

2. The de-Broglie wavelength of an ideal gas of mass m at temperature T kelvin is given by

$$\lambda = \frac{h}{\sqrt{3mk_BT}}$$

JEE Main 2022, 20

3. If a charge q is accelerated through a potential difference V, then the de-Broglie wavelength associated with the charge particle is given by

$$\lambda = \frac{h}{\sqrt{2mqV}}$$

NEET 2021, 19

Step by Step

Mastering NCERT

- Concept Builders
- Topical Questions
- Assertion and Reason Questions
- Statement Based
- Matching Type
- Numerical Type
- NCERT Exemplar
- Past Exams MCQs
- Skill Boosters

Concept Builders

1 Spectrum of atoms provide information about atomic structure. [T/F]

2 Bohr's model of atom is applicable to any atom containing only one electron. [T/F]

3 Above the threshold frequency, the number of photoelectrons emitted per second is directly proportional to the .... (frequency/intensity) of the incident radiation.

4 The .... (photon/wave) picture of electromagnetic radiation predicts nearly instantaneous photoelectric emission while the .... (photon/wave) picture requires a finite time for electrons to absorb energy before emission.

5 The de-Broglie wavelength is independent of the charge of particle. [T/F]

6 Each incident photon essentially ejects one electron from the metal surface. [T/F]

7 The dimensions of h / e (h = Planck's constant, e = electron's charge) are same as those of .... (magnetic flux/electric flux).

8 The work function of lithium and copper are 2.3 eV and 4.0 eV, respectively. Both of these metals will be useful for photoelectric cell working with visible light. [T/F]

9 The de-Broglie wavelength of an electron decreases as it moves from lowest allowed orbit to higher orbits. [T/F]

10 If an electron and a proton are accelerated through same potential, then which one will have less momentum?

11 Name the phenomenon which shows the quantum nature of electromagnetic radiation.

12 Can we use any substance as photoelectron emitter?

13 If the intensity of the incident radiation in a photocell increased, its stopping potential .... (remains same/decreases).

14 The role played by a photocell in cinematography is ....

15 The ratio of de-Broglie wavelengths associated with two electron beams accelerated through 25 V and 36 V respectively is ....

16 Kinetic energy of a particle is inversely proportional to its de-Broglie wavelength. [T/F]

17 Some .... (alkali/alkaline) metals can show photoelectric effect in visible light.

18 The ....(minimum/maximum) negative potential given to the collector plate for which photocurrent becomes zero is known as stopping potential.

19 In a photon-particle collision, the total energy and total momentum are .... (conserved/not conserved)

20 The gathering and focusing mechanism of light by the eye-lens is well described in 'the .... (wave/particle) nature. But its absorption by the rods and cones requires the .... (wave/particle) nature of light.

Topical Questions

Introduction

1 Who was the first to determine experimentally the specific charge of cathode ray particles? NCERT Pg. 274
(a) Maxwell
(b) J.J. Thomson
(c) Hertz
(d) Roentgen

2 Millikan's oil-drop experiment is used for NCERT Pg. 274
(a) measurement of charge on an electron
(b) measurement of mass of a proton
(c) measurement of specific charge on an electron
(d) measurement of specific mass of an electron

3 The specific charge on a proton is $9.6 \times 10^7 \text{ C kg}^{-1}$. The specific charge on an α-particle will be NCERT Pg. 274

(a) $9.6 \times 10^7 \text{ C kg}^{-1}$ (b) $19.2 \times 10^7 \text{C kg}^{-1}$
(c) $4.8 \times 10^7 \text{ C kg}^{-1}$ (d) $2.4 \times 10^7 \text{ C kg}^{-1}$

Electron Emission

4 Free electrons cannot normally escape out of metal surface because NCERT Pg. 275

(a) free electrons are bounded to one or other ionic core
(b) free electrons lie deep inside atom
(c) free electrons are held in metal lattice by attraction force of protons
(d) if an electron attempts to come out of metal, the metal surface acquires a positive charge and pulls the electron back to metal

5 Amongst the given metals in the following option, work function is least for which metal? NCERT Pg. 275

(a) Cesium (b) Aluminium
(c) Silver (d) Platinum

Photoelectric Effect

6 Hallwach connected an uncharged zinc plate to an electroscope as shown below.

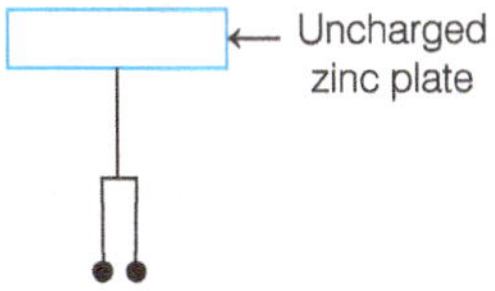

This plate is then irradiated by UV-light. The result of this is correctly shown in NCERT Pg. 276

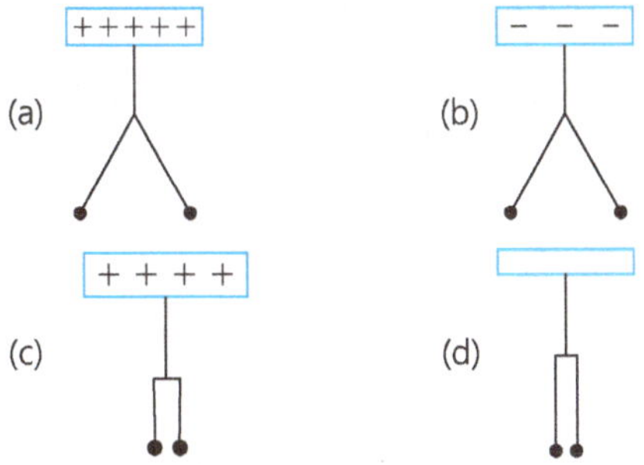

Experimental Study of Photoelectric Effect

7 When yellow light is incident over a metal surface, no electrons are emitted while green light can emit electrons. If red light is incident over the surface, then NCERT Pg. 277

(a) no electrons are emitted
(b) more electrons are emitted
(c) electrons of higher energy are emitted
(c) electrons of lower energy are emitted

8 Photoemission with visible light is possible in NCERT Pg. 277

(a) Carbon
(b) cesium
(c) zinc
(d) Magnesium

9 Variation of photoelectric current with intensity of light is correctly depicted in NCERT Pg. 277

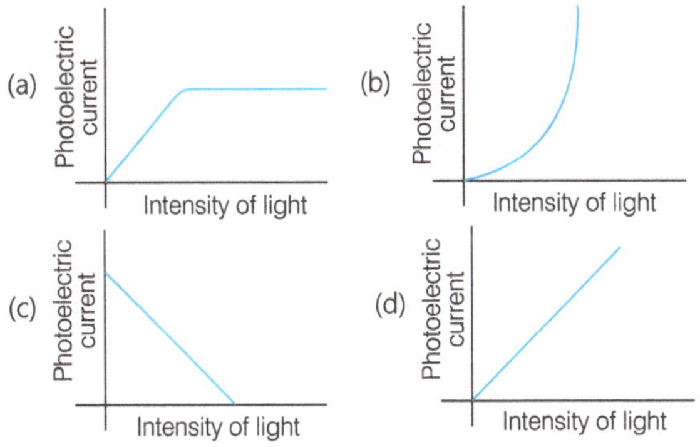

10 Number of photoelectrons emitted per second from the surface of the metal during photoemission keeping the frequency constant, increases with NCERT Pg. 277

(a) increase in intensity of incident radiation
(b) increase in angle of incidence of incident radiation
(c) decrease in potential difference between collector and emitter plates
(d) Both (a) and (b)

11 A point source of light is used in an experiment on photoelectric effect. Which of the following curves best represents the variation of photoelectric current *i* with distance *d* of the source from the emitter? NCERT Pg. 277

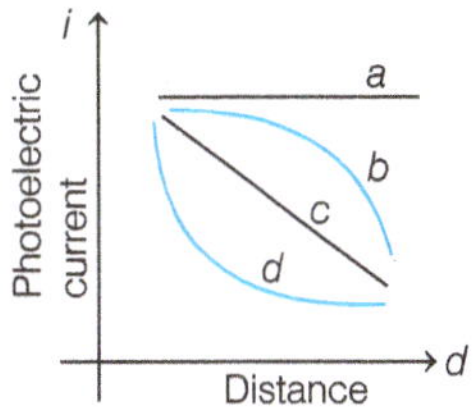

(a) *a* (b) *b*
(c) *c* (d) *d*

12 In an experiment on photoelectric effect with the increase in potential difference of emitter and collector plate, keeping the frequency and intensity fixed of the incident light, the photoelectric current NCERT Pg. 277

(a) increases
(b) decreases
(c) remains constant
(d) increases initially and then becomes constant

13 The value of stopping potential V_0 from the given graph is **NCERT Pg. 277**

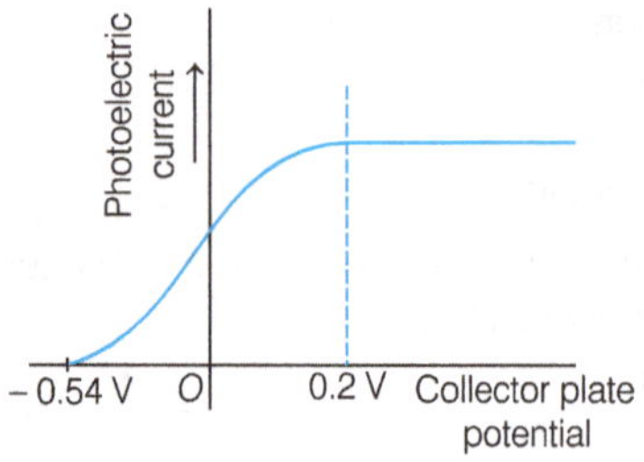

(a) −0.54 V (b) 0.54 V
(c) 0.2 V (d) −0.2 V

14 In photoelectric effect experiment, collector plate is made negative with respect to emitter plate as shown in figure below till it reach a certain potential V_0, when photocurrent is zero. **NCERT Pg. 277**

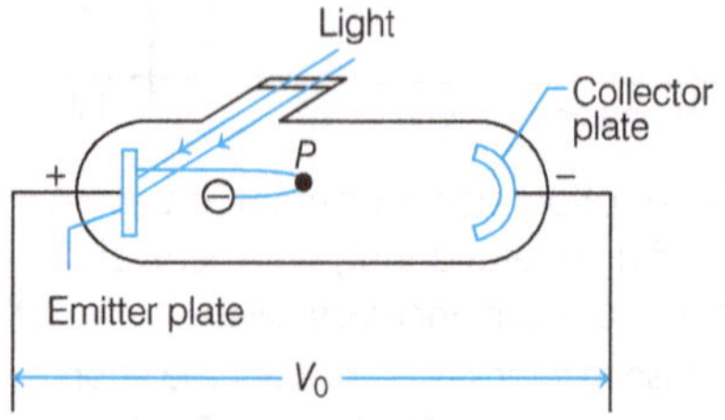

If K indicates kinetic energy of an emitted photoelectron, then
(a) $K > eV_0$
(b) $K < eV_0$
(c) $K = eV_0$
(d) $0 \leq K \leq eV_0$

15 Variation of photoelectric current with collector plate potential for different intensities $I_1$and I_2 (such that $I_1 > I_2$) at a fixed frequency is **NCERT Pg. 277**

(a)
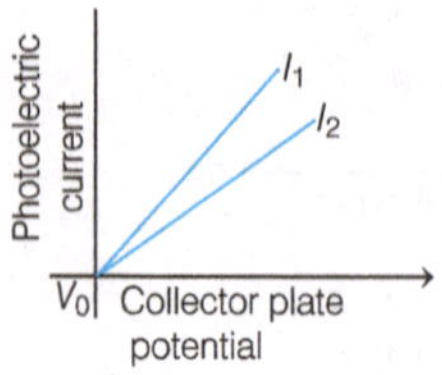

(b)
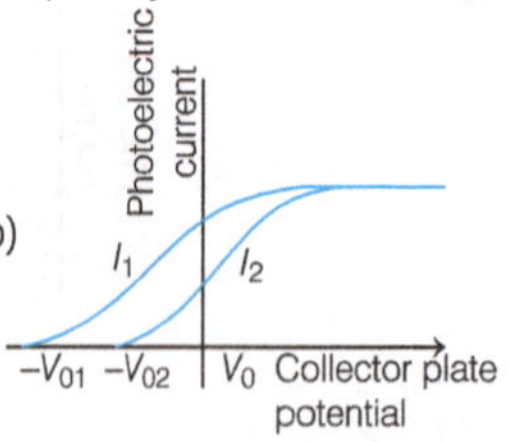

(c)
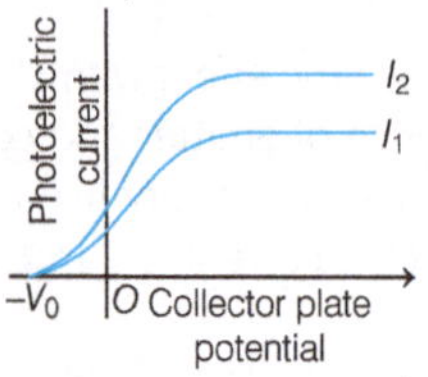

(d)
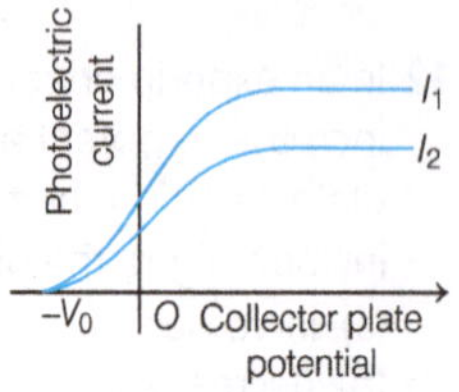

16 A student plot a graph while performing an experiment on photoelectric effect using an evacuated glass tube, for light radiation of same intensity at various frequencies as shown below **NCERT Pg. 277**

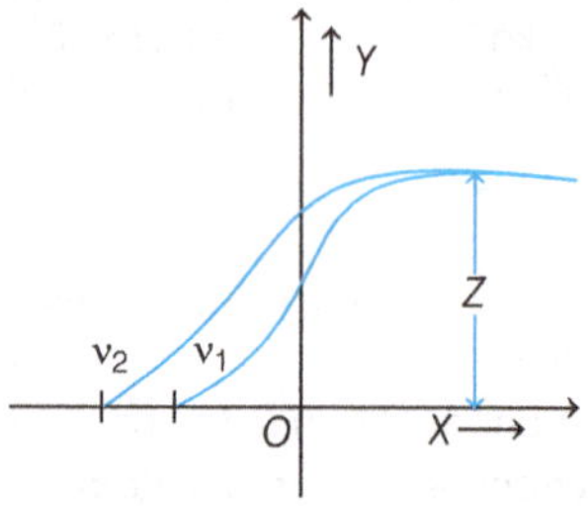

Here,
(a) $X \rightarrow$ Photoelectric current; $Y \rightarrow$ Retarding potential; $Z \rightarrow$ Stopping potential
(b) $X \rightarrow$ Retarding plate potential; $Y \rightarrow$ Photoelectric current; $Z \rightarrow$ Stopping potential
(c) $X \rightarrow$ Collector plate potential; $Y \rightarrow$ Photoelectric current $Z \rightarrow$ Saturation current
(d) $X \rightarrow$ Retarding plate potential; $Y \rightarrow$ Photoelectric current $Z \rightarrow$ Saturation current

17 Maximum kinetic energy of emitted photoelectrons depends on **NCERT Pg. 277**
(a) intensity of incident radiation only
(b) frequency of incident radiation only
(c) both on intensity and frequency of incident radiation
(d) does not depend on frequency or intensity of incident radiation

18 A beam of wavelength λ and intensity I falls over a clean surface of sodium metal. If N photoelectrons are emitted with kinetic energy E, then **NCERT Pg. 277**
(a) $N \propto I$ and $E \propto I$ (b) $N \propto I$ and $E \propto \frac{1}{\lambda}$
(c) $N \propto \lambda$ and $E \propto I$ (d) $N \propto \frac{1}{\lambda}$ and $E \propto \frac{1}{I}$

19 The cathode of a photoelectric cell is changed such that the work function changes from W_1 to W_2 $(W_2 > W_1)$. If the current before and after are i_1 and i_2, respectively and all other conditions remaining unchanged, then **NCERT Pg. 277**
(a) $i_1 = i_2$ (b) $i_1 < i_2$ (c) $i_1 > i_2$ (d) $\frac{W_1}{W_2} = \frac{i_1}{i_2}$

20 The figure shows the variation of photocurrent with anode potential for a photosensitive surface for three different radiations. Let I_a, I_b and I_c be the intensities and ν_a, ν_b and ν_c be the frequencies for the curves a, b and c, respectively.

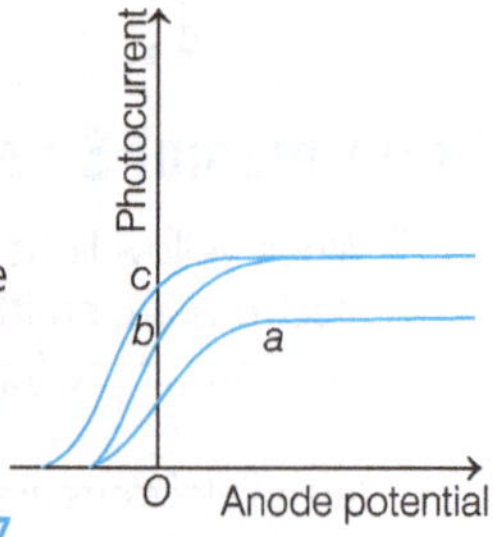

Then, **NCERT Pg. 277**
(a) $\nu_a = \nu_b$ and $I_a \neq I_b$ (b) $\nu_a = \nu_c$ and $I_a = I_c$
(c) $\nu_a = \nu_b$ and $I_a = I_b$ (d) $\nu_b = \nu_c$ and $I_b = I_c$

Photoelctric Effect and Wave Theory of Light

21 Phenomena of interference, diffraction and polarisation are explained by considering light as NCERT Pg. 280

(a) wave (b) particle
(c) corpuscles (d) quarks

22 Experimental observation of photoelectric effect, if explained in terms of wave picture of light, then NCERT Pg. 280

(a) maximum kinetic energy first increases then decreases with frequency
(b) a sufficiently intense beam of radiation is enough for photoemission
(c) time required for photoemission is around 10^{-9} s
(d) maximum kinetic energy of photoelectrons decreases with intensity

Einstein's Photoelectric Equation : Energy Quantum of Radiation

23 According to Einstein's photoelectric equation, $K_{max} \propto \nu$ because an electron is emitted NCERT Pg. 281

(a) after absorption of few photons when absorbed energies exceeds certain value
(b) after number of photons falling over surface exceeds of critical volume
(c) only, if it is present on the surface
(d) after absorption of a single photon of sufficient energy

24 The work function of platinum is 6.35 eV. The threshold frequency of platinum is NCERT Pg. 281

(a) 15.32×10^{14} Hz (b) 15.32×10^{16} Hz
(c) 15.32×10^{19} Hz (d) 15.32×10^{18} Hz

25 The work function of a photosensitive material is 4.0 eV. The longest wavelength of light that can cause photon emission from the substance is (approximately) NCERT Pg. 281

(a) 3100 nm (b) 966 nm
(c) 31 nm (d) 310 nm

26 The photoelectric threshold frequency of a metal is ν. When light of frequency 6ν is incident on the metal, the maximum kinetic energy of the emitted photoelectron is NCERT Pg. 281

(a) $4h\nu$ (b) $5h\nu$ (c) $3h\nu$ (d) $(3/2)\,h\nu$

27 Light of wavelengths λ_A and λ_B fall on two identical metal plates A and B, respectively. The maximum kinetic energy of photoelectrons is K_A and K_B respectively, then which one of the following relations is true? (Take, $\lambda_A = 2\lambda_B$) NCERT Pg. 281

(a) $K_A < \frac{K_B}{2}$ (b) $2K_A = K_B$
(c) $K_A = 2K_B$ (d) $K_A > 2K_B$

28 A metallic surface is irradiated by a monochromatic light of frequency ν_1 and stopping potential is found to be V_1. If the light of frequency ν_2 irradiates the surface, the stopping potential will be NCERT Pg. 281

(a) $V_1 + \frac{h}{e}(\nu_1 + \nu_2)$ (b) $V_1 - \frac{h}{e}(\nu_1 - \nu_2)$
(c) $V_1 + \frac{e}{h}(\nu_2 - \nu_1)$ (d) $V_1 - \frac{h}{e}(\nu_1 + \nu_2)$

29 Photoelectric emission is observed from a metallic surface for frequencies ν_1 and ν_2 of the incident light $(\nu_1 > \nu_2)$. If the maximum values of kinetic energy of the photoelectrons emitted in the two cases are in the ratio $1 : n$, then the threshold frequency of the metallic surface is NCERT Pg. 281

(a) $\frac{(\nu_1 - \nu_2)}{(n-1)}$ (b) $\frac{(n\nu_1 - \nu_2)}{(n-1)}$
(c) $\frac{(n\nu_2 - \nu_1)}{(n-1)}$ (d) $\frac{(\nu_1 - \nu_2)}{n}$

30 For a certain metal, incident frequency ν is five times the threshold frequency ν_0 and the maximum velocity of emitted photoelectrons is $8 \times 10^6\,\text{ms}^{-1}$. If $\nu = 2\nu_0$, the maximum velocity of photoelectrons will be NCERT Pg. 281

(a) 4×10^6 ms^{-1} (b) 6×10^6 ms^{-1}
(c) 8×10^6 ms^{-1} (d) 1×10^6 ms^{-1}

31 In a photoelectric experiment, the wavelength of the light incident on a metal is changed from 300 nm to 400 nm. The decrease in the stopping potential is close to $\left(\frac{hc}{e} = 1240\text{ nmV}\right)$ NCERT Pg. 281

(a) 0.5 V (b) 2.0 V
(c) 1.5 V (d) 1.0 V

32 A photoelectric surface is illuminated successively by monochromatic light of wavelengths λ and $\lambda/2$. If the maximum kinetic energy of the emitted photoelectrons in the second case is 3 times than in the first case, the work function of the surface of the material is (h = Planck's constant and c = speed of light) NCERT Pg. 281

(a) $\frac{hc}{2\lambda}$ (b) $\frac{hc}{\lambda}$
(c) $\frac{2hc}{\lambda}$ (d) $\frac{hc}{3\lambda}$

33 In a photoelectric effect experiment, the threshold wavelength of light is 380 nm. If the wavelength of incident light is 260 nm, the maximum kinetic energy of emitted electrons will be

$\left[\text{Given, } E\text{ (in eV)} = \frac{1237}{\lambda\text{(in nm)}}\right]$ NCERT Pg. 281

(a) 15.1 eV (b) 3.0 eV (c) 1.5 eV (d) 4.5 eV

34 In an experiment with rubidium photocell, the following lines from a mercury source were used $\lambda_1 = 3650$ Å, $\lambda_2 = 4047$ Å, $\lambda_3 = 4358$ Å, $\lambda_4 = 5461$ Å, $\lambda_5 = 6907$ Å and stopping potentials respectively are $V_{01} = 1.28$ V, $V_{02} = 0.95$ V, $V_{03} = 0.74$ V, $V_{04} = 0.16$ V, $V_{05} = 0$ V.

Threshold frequency and work-function of metal respectively are **NCERT Pg. 281**

(a) 4×10^{14} Hz, 1.5 eV (b) 4.3×10^{14} Hz, 1.8 eV
(c) 4×10^{14} Hz, 3 eV (d) 1.5×10^{14}Hz, 5 eV

35 Light of wavelength 600 nm from a sodium lamp falls on a photocell and causes the emission of photoelectrons for which the stopping potential is 0.5 V and with the light of wavelength 400 nm from a sodium lamp, the stopping potential is 1.5 V. With this data, the value of h/e is **NCERT Pg. 281**

(a) 4×10^{-59} V-s (b) 0.25×10^{15} V-s
(c) 4×10^{-15} V-s (d) 4×10^{-8} V-s

36 Radiation of wavelength λ is incident on a photocell. The fastest emitted electron has speed v. If the wavelength is changed to $\frac{3\lambda}{4}$, the speed of the fastest emitted electron will be **NCERT Pg. 281**

(a) $> v\left(\frac{4}{3}\right)^{1/2}$ (b) $< v\left(\frac{4}{3}\right)^{1/2}$
(c) $= v\left(\frac{4}{3}\right)^{1/2}$ (d) $= v\left(\frac{3}{4}\right)^{1/2}$

37 Monochromatic radiation of wavelength 640.2 nm ($1\text{ nm} = 10^{-9}$m) from a neon lamp irradiates photosensitive material made of caesium on tungsten. The stopping voltage is measured to be 0.54 V.

The source is replaced by an iron source and its 427.2 nm line irradiates the same photocell. Predict the new stopping voltage. **NCERT Pg. 281**

(a) 1.51 V (b) 3.5 V (c) 0.05 V (d) 2.03 V

38 In an experiment on photoelectric effect, the frequency ν of incident light is plotted against the stopping potential V_0. The work-function of the photoelectric surface is given by **NCERT Pg. 281**

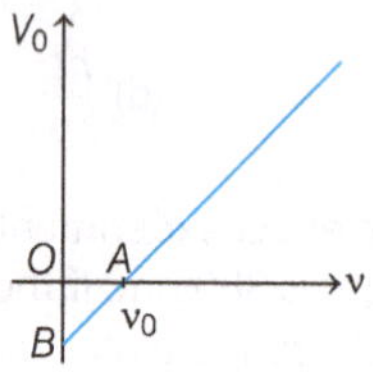

(a) $OB \times e$ (in eV)
(b) OB (in volts)
(c) OA (in eV)
(d) the slope of line AB

39 In an experiment on photoelectric effect, the slope of the cut-off voltage *versus* frequency of incident light is found to be 4.12×10^{-15} V-s. Calculate the value of Planck's constant. **NCERT Pg. 281**

(a) 6.0×10^{-34} Js
(b) 0.63×10^{-34} Js
(c) 6.59×10^{-34} Js
(d) 0

40 In a photoelectric experiment, the relation between applied potential difference V (between cathode and anode) and the photoelectric current I to be as shown in the graph below. If Planck's constant $h = 6.6 \times 10^{-34}$ J-s, the frequency of incident radiation would be nearly (in s^{-1}) (use, $\phi = 1$ eV) **NCERT Pg. 281**

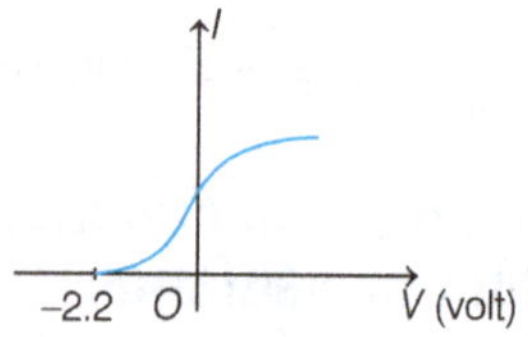

(a) 0.436×10^{18} (b) 0.436×10^{17}
(c) 0.775×10^{15} (d) 0.775×10^{16}

41 For photoelectric effect with incident photon wavelength λ, the stopping potential is V. Identify the correct variations of V_0 with $\frac{1}{\lambda}$. **NCERT Pg. 281**

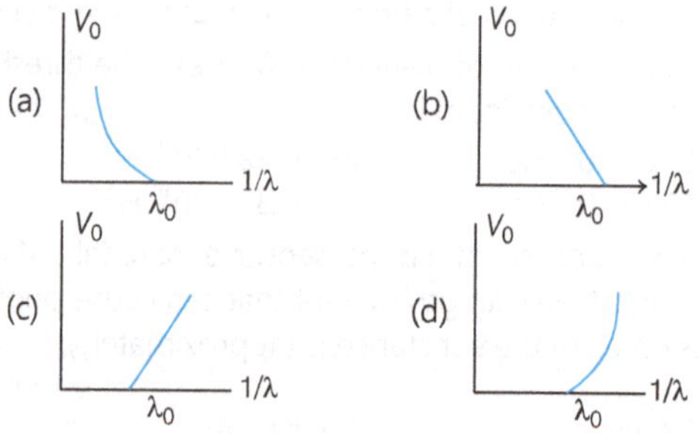

42 In photoelectric experiment, the graph of maximum kinetic energy K *versus* frequency ν of incident photon is plotted as shown. The value of θ is **NCERT Pg. 281**

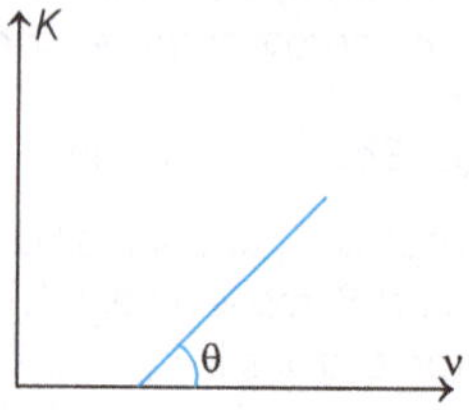

(a) $\tan^{-1}\left(\frac{h}{e}\right)$ (b) $\tan^{-1}(h)$
(c) $\tan^{-1}\left(\frac{e}{h}\right)$ (d) $\tan^{-1}\left(\frac{1}{h}\right)$

43 Light of frequency 7.21×10^{14} Hz is incident on a metal surface. Electrons with a maximum speed of $6 \times 10^5 \text{ ms}^{-1}$ are ejected from the surface. The threshold frequency for photoemission of electrons is (Given $h = 6.63 \times 10^{-34}$ Js, $m_e = 9.1 \times 10^{-31}$ kg) **NCERT Pg. 281**

(a) 2.32×10^{14} Hz (b) 2.32×10^{12} Hz
(c) 4.74×10^{14} Hz (d) 4.74×10^{12} Hz

44 A photon of energy E ejects a photoelectron from a metal surface whose work function is ϕ_0. If this electron enters into a uniform magnetic field B in a direction perpendicular to the field and describes a circular path of radius r, then the radius r is (in the usual notation) **NCERT Pg. 281**

(a) $\sqrt{\frac{2m(E-\phi_0)}{eB}}$ (b) $\sqrt{2m(E-\phi_0)eB}$
(c) $\frac{\sqrt{2e(E-\phi_0)}}{mB}$ (d) $\frac{\sqrt{2m(E-\phi_0)}}{eB}$

45 When a metallic surface is illuminated by a light of frequency f, photoelectrons of maximum kinetic energy 1 eV are emitted. When the same surface is illuminated by light of frequency $\frac{3f}{2}$, photoelectrons of maximum kinetic energy 4 eV are emitted. The work function of the metal is **NCERT Pg. 281**

(a) 5 eV (b) 4 eV
(c) 3 eV (d) 2 eV

46 All electrons ejected from a surface by incident light of wavelength 200 nm can be stopped before travelling 1 m in the direction of uniform electric field of 4 N/C. The work function of the surface is **NCERT Pg. 281**

(a) 4 eV (b) 6.2 eV (c) 2 eV (d) 2.2 eV

47 The work function of Al, K and Pt is 4.28eV, 2.30eV and 5.65 eV, respectively. The correct order of respective threshold frequency will be **NCERT Pg. 281**

(a) Pt > Al > K (b) Al > Pt > K
(c) K > Al > Pt (d) Al > K > Pt

48 When the light of frequency $2\nu_0$ (where, ν_0 is threshold frequency), is incident on a metal plate, the maximum velocity of electrons emitted is v_1. When the frequency of the incident radiation is increased to $5\nu_0$, the maximum velocity of electrons emitted from the same plate is v_2. The ratio of v_1 to v_2 is **NCERT Pg. 281**

(a) 4 : 1 (b) 1 : 4 (c) 1 : 2 (d) 2 : 1

49 The kinetic energy of an electron from a metal surface is E when the incident wavelength is λ. To increase the kinetic energy of the electron from the same surface to $2E$, the incident wavelength must be **NCERT Pg. 281**

(a) 2λ (b) $\frac{\lambda}{2}$ (c) $\frac{hc\lambda}{E\lambda + hc}$ (d) $\frac{2hc\lambda}{E\lambda + hc}$

50 The maximum velocity of an electron emitted by light of wavelength λ incident on the surface of a metal of work function ϕ is

(where h = Planck's constant, m = mass of electron and c = speed of light, when a point source is monochromatic) **NCERT Pg. 281**

(a) $\left[\frac{2(hc+\lambda\phi)}{m\lambda}\right]^{1/2}$ (b) $\frac{2(hc-\lambda\phi)}{m}$
(c) $\left[\frac{2(hc-\lambda\phi)}{m\lambda}\right]^{1/2}$ (d) $\left[\frac{2(h\lambda-\phi)}{m\lambda}\right]^{1/2}$

51 When a certain photosensitive surface is illuminated with monochromatic light of wavelength λ, the stopping potential for photoelectrons is V_0. When same surface is illuminated with wavelength 2λ, the stopping potential is $\frac{V_0}{4}$. The threshold wavelength for photoelectric emission is **NCERT Pg. 281**

(a) λ (b) 2λ (c) 3λ (d) 4λ

52 KE of photoelectron is E. When light of wavelength λ falls on them. If KE of photoelectron reduces to half i.e. $E/2$, then, wavelength of incident light will be **NCERT Pg. 281**

(a) $\frac{hc\lambda}{E\lambda - hc}$ (b) $\frac{hc(2hc - E\lambda)}{2\lambda}$
(c) 2λ (d) $\frac{\lambda}{2}$

53 When photons of energy $h\nu$ are incident on the surface of photosensitive material of work function $h\nu_0$, then **NCERT Pg. 281**

(a) the kinetic energy of all emitted electrons is $h\nu_0$
(b) the kinetic energy of the emitted electrons is $h(\nu - \nu_0)$
(c) the kinetic energy of all fastest electrons is $h(\nu - \nu_0)$
(d) the kinetic energy of all emitted electrons is $h\nu$

54 When light of maximum wavelength 300 nm falls on a photoelectric emitter, photoelectrons are liberated. For another emitter however light of maximum wavelength 600 nm causes photoelectric emission. The ratio of work functions of first emitter to second emitter will be **NCERT Pg. 281**

(a) 1 : 2 (b) 2 : 1
(c) 1 : 1 (d) 1 : 4

55 Energy levels A, B and C of a certain atom correspond to increasing values of energy, i.e., $E_A < E_B < E_C$. If λ_1, λ_2 and λ_3 are the wavelengths of radiations corresponding to transitions C to B, B to A and C to A respectively, then which of the following relations is correct ? **NCERT Pg. 281**

(a) $\lambda_3 = \lambda_1 + \lambda_2$ (b) $\lambda_3^{-1} = \lambda_1^{-1} + \lambda_2^{-1}$
(c) $\lambda_3 + \lambda_1 + \lambda_2 = 0$ (d) $\lambda_3^2 = \lambda_1^2 + \lambda_2^2$

Particle Nature of Light : The Photon

56 When intensity of a light beam is increased, NCERT Pg. 283
(a) energy of photons present increases
(b) momentum of photons present increases
(c) wavelength of photons present increases
(d) number of photons crossing a unit area per second increases

57 The linear momentum of a 6 MeV photon is NCERT Pg. 283
(a) 0.01 eV s m^{-1} (b) 0.02 eV s m^{-1}
(c) 0.03 eV s m^{-1} (d) 0.04 eV s m^{-1}

58 If h is Planck's constant, the momentum of a photon of wavelength 1 Å is NCERT Pg. 283
(a) $10^{10}\,h$ (b) h
(c) $10^{2}\,h$ (d) $10^{12}\,h$

59 An X-ray tube produces a continuous spectrum of radiation with its short wavelength end at 0.55Å. The maximum energy of a photon in the radiation is NCERT Pg. 283
(a) 32.6 eV (b) 22.6 keV
(c) 15.2 keV (d) 12.8 keV

60 In an accelerator experiment on high-energy collisions of electrons with positrons, a certain event is interpreted as annihilation of an electron-positron pair of total energy 10.2 eV into two γ-rays of equal energy. What is the wavelength associated with each γ-ray? NCERT Pg. 283
(a) 2.436×10^{-7} m (b) 1.436×10^{-7} m
(c) $2.436 \times 10^{+7}$ m (d) $1.436 \times 10^{+7}$ m

61 A laser beam of frequency 6.0×10^{14}Hz is emitted from a source of 2×10^{-3}W. Number of photons emitted per second is NCERT Pg. 283
(a) $3. \times 10^{10}$ (b) 6×10^{14}
(c) 9×10^{19} (d) 5×10^{15}

62 The energy flux of sunlight reaching the surface of the earth is 1.52×10^3 Wm^{-2}. The photons in the sunlight have an average wavelength of 520 nm. How many photons per square metre are incident on the earth per second? NCERT Pg. 283
(a) 4×10^{21} (b) 4×10^{34}
(c) 4×10^{31} (d) 4×10^{28}

63 There are two sources of light, each emitting with a power of 200 W. One emits X-rays of wavelength 2 nm and the other visible light of 400 nm. The ratio of number of photons of X-rays to the photons of visible light of the given wavelength is NCERT Pg. 283
(a) 1:100 (b) 1:200
(c) 1:500 (d) 1:300

64 A beam of 10.6 eV photons of intensity 2.0 Wm^{-2} falls on a surface of platinum of surface area $1.0 \times 10^{-4} m^2$ and the work-function of the material is 5.6 eV. Given that, 0.53% of the incident photons eject photoelectrons. The number of photoelectrons emitted per second and their maximum kinetic energy is NCERT Pg. 283
(a) 7×10^{11}, 0.0 eV
(b) 6.25×10^{11}, 5.0 eV
(c) 9×10^{10}, 6.0 eV
(d) 11×10^{11}, 2.5eV

65 If the de-Broglie wavelengths for a proton and an α-particle are equal, then ratio of their velocities will be NCERT Pg. 283
(a) 4 : 1 (b) 2 : 1
(c) 1 : 2 (d) 1 : 4

66 Which of the following statements about photon is incorrect? NCERT Pg. 283
(a) Photons exert no pressure
(b) Momentum of photon is $\frac{h\nu}{c}$.
(c) Rest mass of photon is zero.
(d) Energy of photon is $h\nu$.

67 n photons of wavelength λ are absorbed by a black body of mass m. The momentum gained by the body is NCERT Pg. 283
(a) $\frac{h}{m\lambda}$ (b) $\frac{mnh}{\lambda}$
(c) $\frac{nh}{m\lambda}$ (d) $\frac{nh}{\lambda}$

68 The wavelength of light in the visible region is about 390 nm for violet colour and about 760 nm for red colour. The energy of photon (in eV) at violet end is NCERT Pg. 283
(a) 2.32 (b) 3.19
(c) 1.42 (d) 4.13

69 A blue lamp mainly emits light of wavelength 4500Å. The lamp is rated at 150 W and 8% of the energy is emitted as visible light. The number of photons emitted by the lamp per second is NCERT Pg. 283
(a) 3×10^{19} (b) 3×10^{24}
(c) 3×10^{20} (d) 3×10^{18}

70 A 100 W sodium lamp radiates energy uniformly in all directions. The lamp is located at the centre of a large sphere that absorbs all the sodium light which is incident on it. The wavelength of the sodium light is 589 nm. The number of photons delivered per second to the sphere is NCERT Pg. 283
(a) 3×10^{15} (b) 3×10^{10}
(c) 3×10^{20} (d) 3×10^{19}

Wave Nature of Matter

71 The de-Broglie wavelength associated with an electron moving with a speed of $5.4 \times 10^6 \text{m s}^{-1}$ is NCERT Pg. 284

(a) 0.135 nm (b) 0.125 nm
(c) 0.150 nm (d) 0.145 nm

72 Which of the following figures represent the variation of particle's momentum p and the associated de-Broglie wavelength λ? NCERT Pg. 284

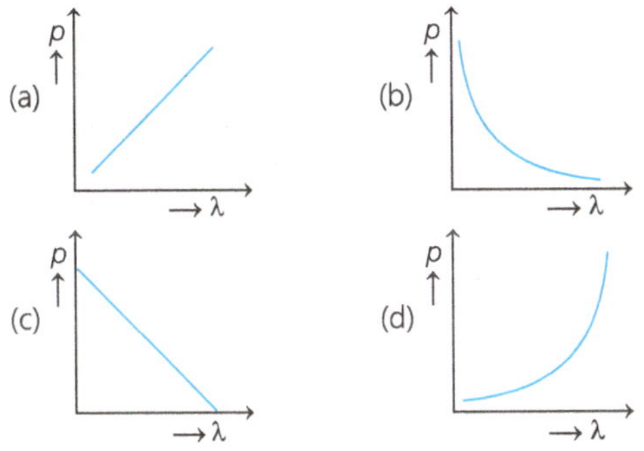

73 Wavelength of an electromagnetic wave is NCERT Pg. 284

(a) more than de-Broglie wavelength of its photon
(b) less than de-Broglie wavelength of its photon
(c) there is no relation between wavelength of a radiation and de-Broglie wavelength of its photon
(d) is equal to de-Broglie wavelength of its photon

74 If α-particle, proton and electron move with the same momentum, then their respective de-Broglie wavelengths $\lambda_\alpha, \lambda_p, \lambda_e$ are related as NCERT Pg. 284

(a) $\lambda_\alpha = \lambda_p = \lambda_e$ (b) $\lambda_\alpha < \lambda_p < \lambda_e$
(c) $\lambda_\alpha > \lambda_p > \lambda_e$ (d) $\lambda_p > \lambda_e > \lambda_\alpha$

75 A particle is moving three times as fast that of an electron. The ratio of de-Broglie wavelength of particle to that of the electron is 1.83×10^{-4}, then the particle is

(a) a meuon (b) a proton NCERT Pg. 284
(c) a neutron (d) Either a neutron or proton

76 If de-Broglie wavelength of NCERT Pg. 284

I. a bullet of mass 0.40 kg travelling with speed of 1.0 kms^{-1} is λ_1.
II. a ball of mass 0.60 kg moving at a speed of 1.0 ms^{-1} is λ_2.
III. a dust particle of mass 1.0×10^{-9} kg drifting with a speed of 2.2 ms^{-1} is λ_3.

Then,

(a) $\lambda_1 > \lambda_2 > \lambda_3$
(b) $\lambda_2 > \lambda_1 > \lambda_3$
(c) $\lambda_1 < \lambda_2 < \lambda_3$
(d) $\lambda_3 > \lambda_1 > \lambda_2$

77 Electrons with de-Broglie wavelength λ fall on the target in an X-ray tube. The cut-off wavelength of the emitted X-ray is NCERT Pg. 284

(a) $\lambda_0 = \dfrac{2mc\lambda^2}{h}$ (b) $\lambda_0 = \dfrac{2h}{mc}$
(c) $\lambda_0 = \dfrac{2m^2c^2\lambda^3}{h^2}$ (d) $\lambda_0 = \lambda$

78 The graph between the energy ($\log E$) of an electron and its de-Broglie wavelength ($\log \lambda$) will be NCERT Pg. 284

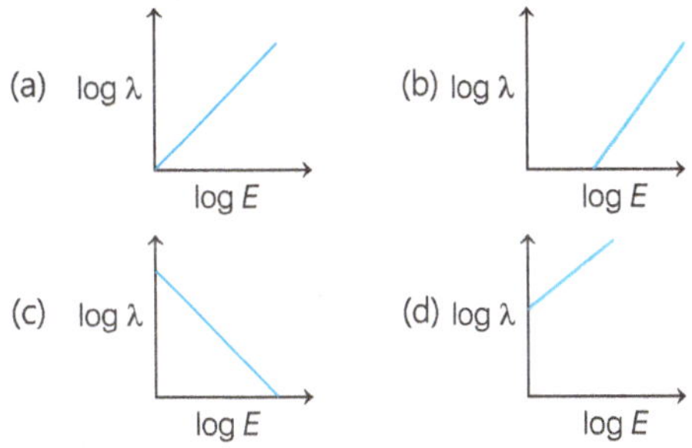

79 A particle moving with kinetic energy E has de-Broglie wavelength λ. If energy ΔE is added to its energy, the wavelength become $\lambda / 2$. Value of ΔE is NCERT Pg. 284

(a) $2E$ (b) $4E$
(c) $3E$ (d) E

80 If the kinetic energy of the particle is increased to 16 times its previous value, the percentage change in the de-Broglie wavelength of the particle is NCERT Pg. 284

(a) 25 (b) 75
(c) 60 (d) 50

81 A proton and an α-particle are accelerated from rest to the same energy. The de-Broglie wavelengths λ_p and λ_α are in the ratio NCERT Pg. 284

(a) 2 : 1 (b) 1 : 1
(c) $\sqrt{2} : 1$ (d) 4 : 1

82 Two particles A_1 and A_2 of masses m_1 and m_2 ($m_1 > m_2$) have the same de-Broglie wavelength, then NCERT Pg. 284

(a) their momenta are the same
(b) their energies are the same
(c) momenta of A_1 is less than the momenta of A_2
(d) energy of A_1 is more than energy of A_2

83 The de-Broglie wavelength of a photon is twice the de-Broglie wavelength of an electron. The velocity of the electron is $v_e = \dfrac{c}{100}$, then NCERT Pg. 284

(a) $\dfrac{E_e}{E_p} = 10^{-4}$ (b) $\dfrac{E_e}{E_p} = 10^{-2}$
(c) $\dfrac{p_e}{m_e c} = 10^{-3}$ (d) $\dfrac{p_e}{m_e c} = 10^{-4}$

84 The wavelength of light from the spectral emission line of sodium is 589 nm. Find the kinetic energy at which an electron and a neutron would have the same de-Broglie wavelength. NCERT Pg. 284

(a) $KE_e = 5 \times 10^{-25}$ J, $KE_n = 6.5 \times 10^{-28}$ J
(b) $KE_e = 6.96 \times 10^{-25}$ J, $KE_n = 3.82 \times 10^{-28}$ J
(c) $KE_e = 1.25 \times 10^{-25}$ J $KE_n = 6.23 \times 10^{-28}$ J
(d) $KE_e = 3.26 \times 10^{+25}$ J, $KE_n = 4.06 \times 10^{+28}$ J

85 An electron of mass m and a photon have same energy E. The ratio of de-Broglie wavelengths associated with them is (c being velocity of light) NCERT Pg. 284

(a) $\left(\frac{E}{2m}\right)^{1/2}$ (b) $c(2mE)^{1/2}$ (c) $\frac{1}{c}\left(\frac{2m}{E}\right)^{1/2}$ (d) $\frac{1}{c}\left(\frac{E}{2m}\right)^{1/2}$

86 An electron of mass m and charge e initially at rest gets accelerated by a constant electric field E. The rate of change of de-Broglie wavelength of the electron at time t (ignoring relativistic effect) is NCERT Pg. 284

(a) $\frac{-h}{eEt^2}$ (b) $\frac{-eEt}{h}$ (c) $\frac{-mh}{eEt^2}$ (d) $\frac{-h}{eE}$

87 A proton and an α-particle are accelerated through the same potential difference. The ratio of de-Broglie wavelength λ_p to that of λ_α is NCERT Pg. 284

(a) $\sqrt{2}:1$ (b) $\sqrt{4}:1$
(c) $\sqrt{6}:1$ (d) $\sqrt{8}:1$

88 Electrons used in an electron microscope are accelerated by a voltage of 25 kV. If the voltage is increased to 100 kV, then the de-Broglie wavelength associated with the electrons would NCERT Pg. 284

(a) decrease by 2 times (b) decrease by 4 times
(c) increase by 4 times (d) increase by 2 times

89 When photon of energy 4.25 eV strike the surface of a metal A, the ejected photoelectrons have maximum kinetic energy T_A eV and de-Broglie wavelength λ_A. The maximum kinetic energy of photoelectrons liberated from another metal B by photon of energy 4.70 eV is $T_B = (T_A - 1.5)$ eV. If the de-Broglie wavelength of these photoelectrons is $\lambda_B = 2\lambda_A$, then NCERT Pg. 284

(a) the work function of A is 3.25 eV
(b) the work function of B is 2.20 eV
(c) $T_A = 3.00$ eV
(d) $T_B = 0.5$ eV

90 The de-Broglie wavelength of a neutron in thermal equilibrium with heavy water at a temperature T kelvin and mass m, is NCERT Pg. 284

(a) $\frac{h}{\sqrt{mkT}}$ (b) $\frac{h}{\sqrt{3mkT}}$ (c) $\frac{2h}{\sqrt{3mkT}}$ (d) $\frac{2h}{\sqrt{mkT}}$

91 An electron is confined to a 1 nm wide region. Find the uncertainty in momentum using Heisenberg uncertainty principle. (Take, $h = 6.63 \times 10^{-34}$ J-s) NCERT Pg. 284

(a) 1.05×10^{-25} kg-ms^{-1} (b) 2.03×10^{-31} kg-ms^{-1}
(c) 3.05×10^{-34} kg-ms^{-1} (d) 2.49×10^{-32} kg-ms^{-1}

92 An α-particle moves in a circular path of radius 0.83 cm in the presence of a magnetic field of 0.25 Wb m^{-2}. The de-Broglie wavelength associated with the particle will be NCERT Pg. 284

(a) 1 Å (b) 0.1 Å
(c) 10 Å (d) 0.01 Å

93 A particle moves in a closed orbit around the origin, due to a force which is directed towards the origin. The de-Broglie wavelength of the particle varies cyclically between two values λ_1 and λ_2 with $\lambda_1 > \lambda_2$. NCERT Pg. 284
Which of the following statements is true?

(a) The particle could be moving in a circular orbit with origin as centre
(b) The particle could be moving in an elliptical orbit with origin as its focus.
(c) When the de-Broglie wavelength is λ_1, the particle is nearer the origin when its value is λ_2.
(d) Both (a) and (c)

94 An electron of mass m with a velocity $v = v_0\hat{\mathbf{i}}\,(v_n > 0)$ enters an electric field $E = -E_0\hat{\mathbf{i}}\,(E_0 = \text{constant} > 0)$ at $t = 0$. If λ_0 is its de-Broglie wavelength initially, then its de-Broglie wavelength at time t is NCERT Pg. 284

(a) $\lambda_0 t$ (b) $\lambda_0\left(1 + \frac{eE_0}{mv_0}t\right)$
(c) $\frac{\lambda_0}{\left(1 + \frac{eE_0}{mv_0}t\right)}$ (d) λ_0

95 The electrons used in an electron microscope are accelerated through a voltage difference of 25 kV. If the potential difference is increased to 100 kV, then the de-Broglie wavelength associated with the electrons would NCERT Pg. 284

(a) Increase by four times (b) Increase by two times
(c) Becomes half (d) Becomes one fourth

96 An electron of mass m has de-Broglie wavelength λ when accelerated through potential difference V. When proton of mass M is accelerated through potential difference 9 V, the de-Broglie wavelength associated with it will be (Assume that wavelength is determined at low voltage). NCERT Pg. 284

(a) $\frac{\lambda}{3}\sqrt{\frac{M}{m}}$ (b) $\frac{\lambda}{3}\cdot\frac{M}{m}$ (c) $\frac{\lambda}{3}\sqrt{\frac{m}{M}}$ (d) $\frac{\lambda}{3}\cdot\frac{m}{M}$

97 For a proton accelerated through V volts, de-Broglie wavelength is given as NCERT Pg. 284

(a) $\frac{12.27}{\sqrt{V}}$ Å (b) $\frac{0.286}{\sqrt{V}}$ Å (c) $\frac{0.101}{\sqrt{V}}$ Å (d) $\frac{0.202}{\sqrt{V}}$ Å

98 Two electrons are moving with non-relativistic speeds perpendicular to each other. If corresponding de-Broglie wavelengths are λ_1 and λ_2, their de-Broglie wavelength in the frame of reference attached to their centre of mass is NCERT Pg. 284

(a) $\lambda_{CM} = \frac{2\lambda_1\lambda_2}{\sqrt{\lambda_1^2 + \lambda_2^2}}$ (b) $\lambda_{CM} = \lambda_1 = \lambda_2$

(c) $\lambda_{CM} = \left(\frac{\lambda_1 + \lambda_2}{2}\right)$ (d) $\frac{1}{\lambda_{CM}} = \frac{1}{\lambda_1} + \frac{1}{\lambda_2}$

99 If the kinetic energy of a particle is reduced to one-fourth, then the percentage increase in the de-Broglie wavelength is NCERT Pg. 284

(a) 41% (b) 100% (c) 144% (d) 200%

100 A particle of mass $4m$ at rest decays into two particles of masses m and $3m$ having non-zero velocities. The ratio of the de-Broglie wavelengths of the particles 1 and 2 is NCERT Pg. 284

(a) $\frac{1}{2}$ (b) $\frac{1}{4}$ (c) 2 (d) 1

Assertion and Reason Questions

Direction (Q. Nos. 1-10) *In the following questions, a statement of Assertion is followed by a corresponding statement of Reason. Of the following statements, choose the correct one.*

(a) Both Assertion and Reason are correct and Reason is the correct explanation of Assertion.

(b) Both Assertion and Reason are correct but Reason is not the correct explanation of Assertion.

(c) Assertion is correct but Reason is incorrect.

(d) Assertion is incorrect but Reason is correct.

1 **Assertion** Electrons within a metal have the liberty to exit from the metal.

Reason Electrons within a conductor cannot exit the metal without extra energy. NCERT Pg. 275

2 **Assertion** The particle nature of light is supported by the threshold frequency of the photoelectric effect.

Reason When the frequency of incident light is lower than the threshold frequency, electrons are not released from the metal surface. NCERT Pg. 276

3 **Assertion** For $\nu > \nu_0$ (threshold frequency), photoelectric current is proportional to intensity.

Reason Greater the number of energy quanta available, greater is the number of electrons absorbing the energy quanta and greater is the number of electrons coming out of the metal. NCERT Pg. 277

4 **Assertion** Photosensitivity of a metal is high, if its work function is small.

Reason Work function $= h\nu_0$, where ν_0 is the threshold frequency. NCERT Pg. 277

5 **Assertion** The photocells, inserted in the door light, electric circuit are used as automatic door opener.

Reason Abrupt change in photocurrent, helps to open the door. NCERT Pg. 277

6 **Assertion** The strength of photoelectric current depends upon the intensity of incident radiation.

Reason A photon of energy E possesses a mass equals to E/c^2 and momentum equals to E/c. NCERT Pg. 278

7 **Assertion** The stopping potential in the photoelectric effect is independent of the intensity of incident light.

Reason The stopping potential depends only on the frequency of incident light, which determines the energy of photons. NCERT Pg. 278

8 **Assertion** Light quantum of energy is associated with a photon.

Reason Light quantum of energy is also associated with momentum. NCERT Pg. 280

9 **Assertion** Macroscopic objects in our daily life, show wave like properties prominent.

Reason Wavelength of macroscopic objects is very small. NCERT Pg. 280

10 **Assertion** The photoelectric effect will not occur if the energy of the incident radiation is insufficient to overcome the work function of the metal.

Reason If the energy of the incident radiation is equal to the work function of a metal, the kinetic energy of the photoelectrons will be zero. NCERT Pg. 281

Statement Based Questions

Direction (Q. Nos. 1-8) *In the following questions, Statement I and Statement II are given. Read the statements and choose most appropriate answer from the options given below.*

(a) Both Statement I and Statement II are incorrect.
(b) Statement I is correct but Statement II is incorrect.
(c) Statement I is incorrect but Statement II is correct.
(d) Both Statement I and Statement II are correct.

1 Statement I In the experimental set-up used for studying the photoelectric effect, a monochromatic light from the source of sufficiently short wavelength is used.

Statement II The intensity of the light incident on the emitter plate is independent of the distance of the light source from the emitter. NCERT Pg. 277

2 Statement I Low intensity means delay in electron emission.

Statement II Stopping potential V_0 *versus* frequency ν curve's slope is independent of the nature of the material. NCERT Pg. 277

3 Statement I This is a strong practical evidence that a less massive particle becomes a wave at high speeds.

Statement II When electrons or thermal neutrons are used instead of light in Young's double slit experiment, similar pattern of maxima and minima are observed. NCERT Pg. 278

4 Statement I Photoelectric saturation current increases with the increase in frequency of incident light.

Statement II Energy of incident photons increases with increase in frequency and as a result photoelectric current increases. NCERT Pg. 279

5 Statement I The kinetic energy of photoelectrons emitted from metal surface does not depend on the intensity of incident photon.

Statement II The ejection of electrons from metallic surface is not possible with frequency of incident photons below the threshold frequency. NCERT Pg. 279

6 Statement I Photoelectric effect demonstrates the wave nature of light.

Statement II The number of photoelectrons emitted is proportional to the frequency of light. NCERT Pg. 281

7 Statement I An electron is emitted from a metal surface when $h\nu < \phi_0$.

Statment II Since, K_{max} must be non-negative, so implies that photoelectric emission is only possible, if $h\nu = \phi_0$. NCERT Pg. 281

8 Statement I Whether a particle or wave description is best suited for understanding an experiment is independent of the nature of experiment.

Statement II In general, matter wave associated with an electron is a wave packet extended over some finite region of space. NCERT Pg. 284

Matching Type Questions

1 Match the quantities given in Column I with their definitions in Column II and select the correct answer from the codes given below. NCERT Pg. 280

Column I	Column II
A. Work function	1. The maximum number of photoelectrons emitted per second
B. Stopping potential	2. The number of photoelectrons emitted per second
C. Saturation current	3. The minimum retarding potential
D. Photocurrent	4. The minimum energy required by electron to escape from the metal surface

Codes

	A	B	C	D		A	B	C	D
(a)	2	4	3	1	(b)	3	2	4	1
(c)	4	3	1	2	(d)	1	2	3	4

2 Match the Column I (quantities) with Column II (expression of the values) and select the correct answer from the codes given below. NCERT Pg. 281

Column I	Column II
A. Maximum number of photons absorbed by an electron	1. $\frac{\phi_0}{\nu_0}$
B. Number of photons emitted by a source per second	2. $\frac{P}{E}$
C. Energy of a photon E	3. $h\nu$
D. Planck's constant h	4. 1

Codes

	A	B	C	D
(a)	2	4	1	3
(b)	4	2	3	1
(c)	2	4	3	1
(d)	3	1	2	4

3 Match the Column I (quantity) with Column II (formula) and select the correct answer from the codes given below. NCERT Pg. 285

	Column I		Column II
A.	Stopping potential	1.	$K_{max} = h\nu - \phi$
B.	Slope of stopping potential *versus* frequency	2.	$\lambda = h/mv$
C.	de-Broglie wavelength	3.	h/e
D.	Photoelectric equation	4.	K_{max}/e

Codes

	A	B	C	D		A	B	C	D
(a)	4	3	2	1	(b)	2	1	3	4
(c)	3	2	1	4	(d)	1	4	2	3

Numerical Type Questions

1 A beam of electrons of energy E scattered from a target having atomic spacing of 1 Å. The first maximum intensity occurs at $\theta = 60°$. Then, E (in eV) is .... NCERT Pg. 284

2 When light with a frequency twice, the threshold frequency strikes the metal plate, the maximum velocity of the emitted electron is v_1. If the frequency of incident radiation is increased to five times the threshold value, the maximum velocity of the emitted electron becomes v_2. If $v_2 = xv_1$, the value of x will be .... NCERT Pg. 281

3 Two streams of photons, with energies twice and ten times of the work function of the metal, successively strike the metal surface. The ratio of maximum velocities of the emitted photoelectrons in these two cases is $x : y$. The value of x is .... NCERT Pg. 281

4 Surface of certain metal is first illuminated with light of wavelength $\lambda_1 = 350$ nm and then by the light of wavelength $\lambda_2 = 540$ nm. It is found that the maximum speed of the photoelectrons in the two cases differ by a factor of 2. The work function of the metal (in eV) is close to (Energy of photon $= (1240 / \lambda)$ eV) ...... $\times 10^{-2}$ eV. NCERT Pg. 281

5 The energy of a photon, with a de-Broglie wavelength equal to the wavelength of an electron accelerated through a 225 V potential difference, is closest to ....keV. NCERT Pg. 284

6 From the data presented in the figure, the work function (in eV) of cesium, indicated by the stopping potential V_0 (in volts) as a function of frequency ν for a cesium emitter is ...... eV. NCERT Pg. 281

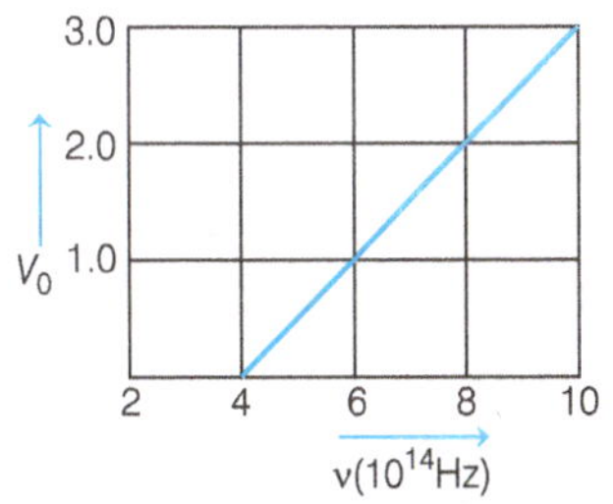

7 When light with a wavelength of 750 nm strikes on a metal, it causes photoelectrons to be emitted with a certain kinetic energy. If light with a wavelength of 450 nm is used instead, the maximum kinetic energy of the photoelectrons doubles. The work function of the metal in eV is .... (Take, $hc = 1230$ eV-nm) NCERT Pg. 281

8 The energy flux of sunlight reaching the surface of earth is 1.388×10^3 Wm^{-2}. The photons in the sunlight have an average wavelength of 600 nm. The number of photon per square metre incident on the earth's surface is $x \times 10^{21}$. Find the value of x. NCERT Pg. 283

9 Ultraviolet light of wavelength 300 nm and intensity 1.0 Wm^{-2} falls on the surface of a photosensitive material. If the incident photons produce photoelectrons, then the number of photoelectrons emitted per second from an area of 1.0 cm^2 of the surface is nearly ....$\times 10^{14}$ cm^{-2} s^{-1} NCERT Pg. 283

10 If the short wavelength limit of the continuous spectrum coming out of a coolidge tube is 10 Å, then the de Broglie wavelength of the electrons reaching the target metal in the coolidge tube is .... Å. NCERT Pg. 284

NCERT Exemplar Questions

1 A particle is dropped from a height H. The de-Broglie wavelength associated with particle is proportional to

(a) H (b) $H^{1/2}$ (c) H^0 (d) $H^{-1/2}$

2 Wavelengths of a photon needed to remove a proton from a nucleus which is bound to the nucleus with 1 MeV energy is nearly

(a) 1.2 nm (b) 1.2×10^{-3} nm
(c) 1.2×10^{-6} nm (d) 1.2×10^{1} nm

3 Consider a beam of electrons (each with energy E_0) incident on a metal surface kept in an evacuated chamber. Then,

(a) no electrons will be emitted as only photons can emit electrons
(b) electrons can be emitted but all with energy E_0
(c) electrons can be emitted with any energy, with a maximum of $E_0 - \phi$ (ϕ is the work function)
(d) electrons can be emitted with any energy, with a maximum of E_0

4 A proton, a neutron, an electron and an α-particle have same energy, then their de-Broglie wavelengths compare as

(a) $\lambda_p = \lambda_n > \lambda_e > \lambda_\alpha$ (b) $\lambda_\alpha < \lambda_p = \lambda_n < \lambda_e$
(c) $\lambda_e < \lambda_p = \lambda_n > \lambda_\alpha$ (d) $\lambda_e = \lambda_p = \lambda_n = \lambda_\alpha$

5 An electron moving with an initial velocity $\mathbf{v} = v_0\hat{\mathbf{i}}$ and is in a magnetic field $\mathbf{B} = B_0\hat{\mathbf{j}}$. Then, its de-Broglie wavelength

(a) remains constant (b) increases with time
(c) decreases with time (d) first increases decreases

6 An electron (mass m) with an initial velocity $\mathbf{v} = v_0\hat{\mathbf{i}}$ is in an electric field $\mathbf{E} = E_0\hat{\mathbf{j}}$. If $\lambda_0 = h/mv_0$, its de-Broglie wavelength at time t is given by

(a) λ_0 (b) $\lambda_0\sqrt{1 + \dfrac{e^2E_0^2t^2}{m^2v_0^2}}$

(c) $\dfrac{\lambda_0}{\sqrt{1 + \dfrac{e^2E_0^2t^2}{m^2v_0^2}}}$ (d) $\dfrac{\lambda_0}{\left(1 + \dfrac{e^2E_0^2t^2}{m^2v_0^2}\right)}$

Past Exams Questions

NEET

1 If c is the velocity of light in free space, the correct statements about photon among the following are

NCERT Pg. 283, NEET 2024

A. The energy of a photon is $E = h\nu$.
B. The velocity of a photon is c.
C. The momentum of a photon, $p = \dfrac{h\nu}{c}$
D. In a photon-electron collision, both total energy and total momentum are conserved.
E. Photon possesses positive charge.

Choose the correct answer from the options given below.

(a) A and B only
(b) A, B, C and D only
(c) A, C and D only
(d) A, B, D and E only

2 The graph which shows the variation of $\dfrac{1}{\lambda^2}$ and its kinetic energy, E is (where, λ is de-Broglie wavelength of a free particle) **NCERT Pg. 285, NEET 2024**

(a)
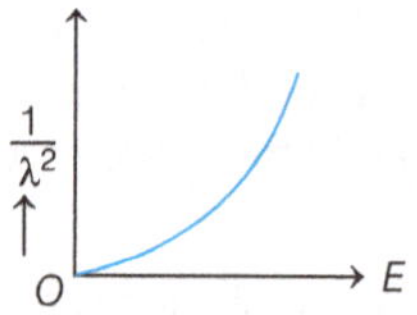

(b)
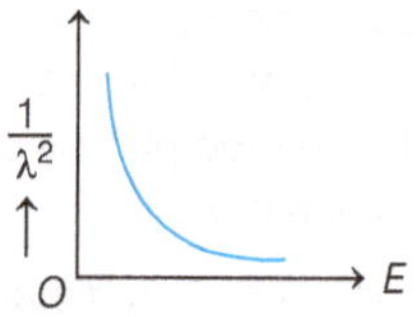

(c)
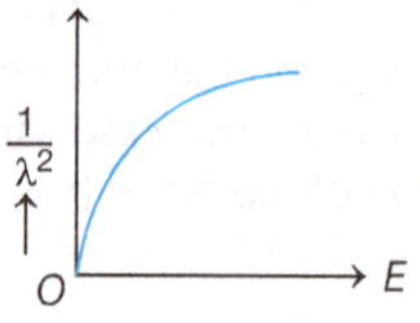

(d)
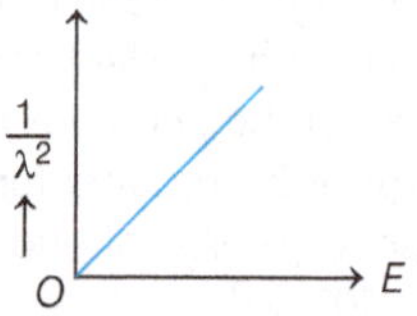

3 The work functions of caesium (Cs), potassium (K) and sodium (Na) are 2.14 eV, 2.30 eV and 2.75 eV, respectively. If incident electromagnetic radiation has an incident energy of 2.20 eV. Which of these photosensitive surfaces may emit photoelectrons?

NCERT Pg. 276, NEET 2023

(a) Both Na and K (b) K only
(c) Na only (d) Cs only

4 When two monochromatic lights of frequency, ν and $\nu/2$ are incident on a photoelectric metal, their stopping potential becomes $V_s/2$ and V_s, respectively.

The threshold frequency for this metal is
NCERT Pg. 281, NEET 2022

(a) 3ν (b) $\frac{2}{3}\nu$ (c) $\frac{3}{2}\nu$ (d) 2ν

5 An electromagnetic wave of wavelength λ is incident on a photosensitive surface of negligible work function. If m mass is of photoelectron emitted from the surface has de-Broglie wavelength λ_d, then
NCERT Pg. 284, NEET 2021

(a) $\lambda = \left(\frac{2h}{mc}\right)\lambda_d^2$ (b) $\lambda = \left(\frac{2m}{hc}\right)\lambda_d^2$

(c) $\lambda = \left(\frac{2mc}{h}\right)\lambda_d^2$ (d) $\lambda = \left(\frac{2mc}{h}\right)\lambda_d^2$

6 The number of photons per second on average emitted by the source of monochromatic light of wavelength 600 nm, when it delivers the power of 3.3×10^{-3} W will be ($h = 6.6 \times 10^{-34}$ J-s) NCERT Pg. 283, NEET 2021

(a) 10^{18} (b) 10^{17} (c) 10^{16} (d) 10^{15}

7 The de-Broglie wavelength of an electron moving with kinetic energy of 144 eV is nearly NCERT Pg. 284, NEET 2020

(a) 102×10^{-3} nm (b) 102×10^{-4} nm
(c) 102×10^{-5} nm (d) 102×10^{-2} nm

8 An electron is accelerated from rest through a potential difference of V volt. If the de-Broglie wavelength of the electron is 1.227×10^{-2} nm, the potential difference is
NCERT Pg. 284, NEET 2020

(a) 10^2 V (b) 10^3 V (c) 10^4 V (d) 10 V

9 Light of frequency 1.5 times the threshold frequency is incident on a photosensitive material. What will be the photoelectric current, if the frequency is halved and intensity is doubled? NCERT Pg 277, NEET 2020

(a) Four times (b) One-fourth
(c) Zero (d) Doubled

10 The work function of a photosensitive material is 4.0 eV. This longest wavelength of light that can cause photon emission from the substance is (approximately)
NCERT Pg. 277, NEET 2019

(a) 3100 nm (b) 966 nm (c) 31 nm (d) 310 nm

11 An electron is accelerated through a potential difference of 10000 V. Its de-Broglie wavelength is (nearly) : ($m_e = 9 \times 10^{-31}$kg) NCERT Pg. 284, NEET 2019

(a) 12.2×10^{-12}m (b) 12.2×10^{-14}m
(c) 12.2 nm (d) 12.2×10^{-13}m

12 When the light of frequency $2\nu_0$ (where, ν_0 is threshold frequency), is incident on a metal plate, the maximum velocity of electrons emitted is v_1. When the frequency of the incident radiation is increased to $5\nu_0$, the maximum velocity of electrons emitted from the same plate is v_2. The ratio of v_1 to v_2 is NCERT Pg. 281, NEET 2018

(a) 4 : 1 (b) 1 : 4 (c) 1 : 2 (d) 2 : 1

JEE Main

13 When UV light of wavelength 300 nm is incident on the metal surface having work function 2.13 eV electron emission takes place. The stopping potential is
(Given, $hc = 1240$ eV-nm) NCERT Pg. 281, JEE Main 2024

(a) 4 V (b) 4.1 V
(c) 1.5 V (d) 2 V

14 Given below are two statements

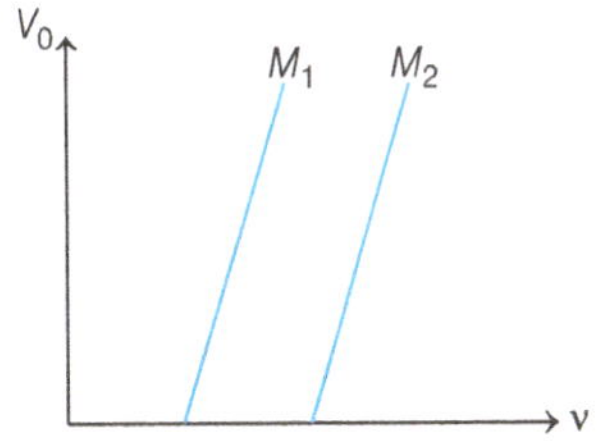

Statement I Figure shows the variation of stopping potential with frequency ν for the two photosensitive material M_1 and M_2. The slope gives value of $\frac{h}{e}$, where h is Planck's constant, e is the charge of electron.

Statement II M_2 will emit photoelectrons of greater kinetic energy for the incident radiation having same frequency. NCERT Pg. 282, JEE Main 2024

In the light of the above statements, choose the most appropriate answer from the options given below.
(a) Statement I is incorrect but Statement II is correct.
(b) Both Statement I and Statement II are incorrect.
(c) Both Statement I and Statement II are correct.
(d) Statement I is correct and Statement II is incorrect.

15 A proton and an electron have the same de-Broglie wavelength. If K_p and K_e be the kinetic energies of proton and electron respectively, then choose the correct relation. NCERT Pg. 283, JEE Main 2024

(a) $K_p = K_e$ (b) $K_p < K_e$ (c) $K_p = K_e^2$ (d) $K_p > K_e$

16 In photoelectric effect NCERT Pg. 277, JEE Main 2023

A. The photocurrent is proportional to the intensity of the incident radiation.
B. Maximum Kinetic energy with which photoelectrons are emitted depends on the intensity of incident light.
C. Maximum KE with which photoelectrons are emitted depends on the frequency of incident light.
D. The emission of photoelectrons require a minimum threshold intensity of incident radiation.

E. Maximum KE of the photoelectrons is independent of the frequency of the incident light.

Choose the correct answer from the options given below

(a) A and B only (b) B and C only
(c) A and C only (d) A and E only

17 The variation of stopping potential (V_0) as a function of the frequency (ν) of the incident light for a metal is shown in figure. The work function of the surface is

NCERT Pg. 281, JEE Main 2023

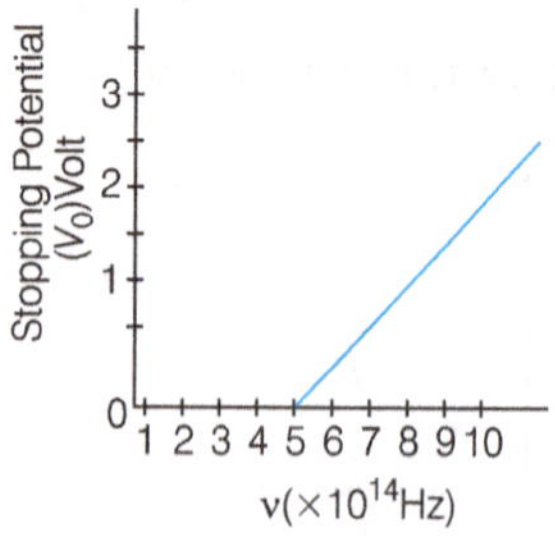

(a) 1.36 eV (b) 2.98 eV
(c) 18.6 eV (d) 2.07 eV

18 If a source of electromagnetic radiation having power 15 kW, produces 10^{16} photons per second, the radiation belongs to a part of spectrum is

(Take, Planck constant $h = 6 \times 10^{-34}$ J-s)

NCERT Pg. 283, JEE Main 2023

(a) radiowaves (b) gamma rays
(c) ultraviolet rays (d) microwaves

19 A parallel beam of light of wavelength 900 nm and intensity 100 Wm^{-2} is incident on a surface perpendicular to the beam. The number of photons crossing through area of 1 cm^2 perpendicular to the beam in one second is

NCERT Pg. 283, JEE Main 2022

(a) 3×10^{16} (b) 4.5×10^{16}
(c) 4.5×10^{17} (d) 4.5×10^{20}

20 A monochromatic neon lamp with wavelength of 670.5 nm illuminates a photo sensitive material which has a stopping voltage of 0.48 V. What will be the stopping voltage if the source light is changed with another source of wavelength of 474.6 nm?

NCERT Pg. 281, JEE Main 2021

(a) 0.96 V (b) 1.25 V (c) 0.24 V (d) 1.5 V

Skill Boosters

1 Consider the following photoelectric emission experiment.

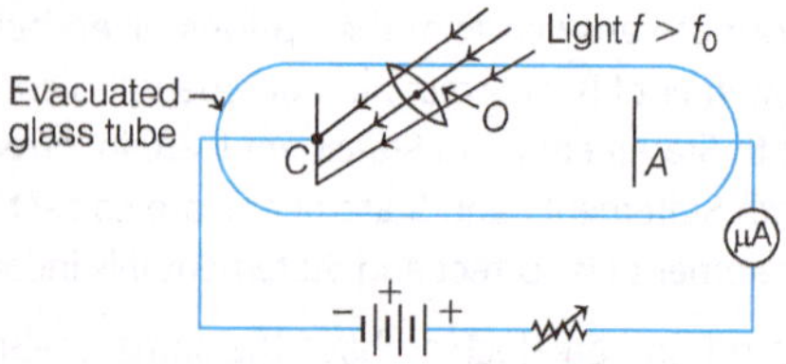

Distance of lens and centre of cathode (OC) is initially less than focal length of lens. Diameter of photosensitive cathode is more than diameter of lens. Lens is moved away from cathode slowly at a constant speed. Which of the following graphs is correct?

Assume that light falls over cathode only after passing through lens.

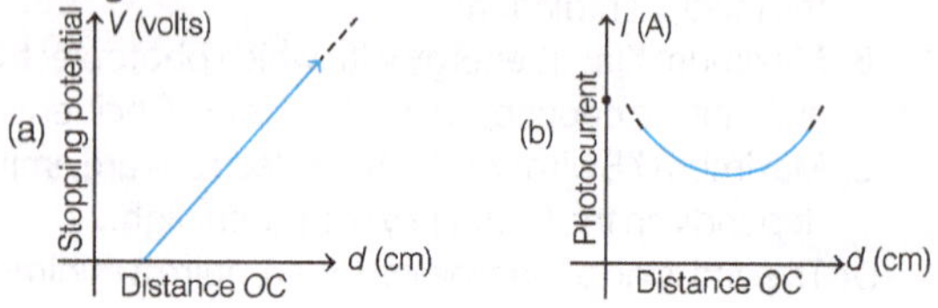

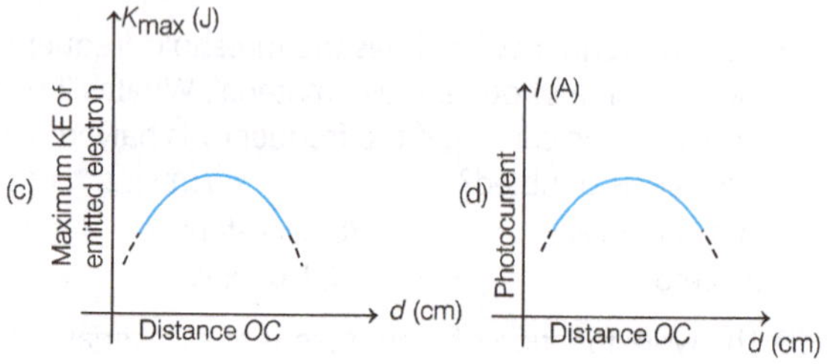

2 A point source S is placed at a distance L from a cardsheet with a hole of diameter 0.1 m. A photosensitive metal plate P is placed at a distance D from this hole at other side of cardsheet as shown in the figure.

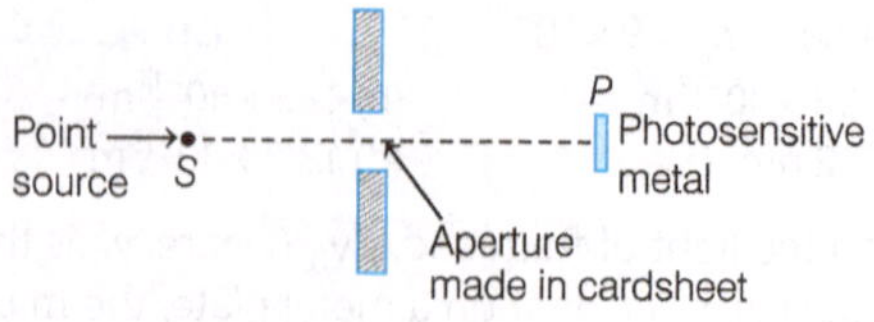

If source emits light of frequency greater than threshold frequency of the metal plate P, then mark the correct options.

(a) When a concave lens of focal length L is placed in aperture, photoemission rate of P increases.

(b) When a convex lens of focal length L is placed in aperture, photoemission rate of P decreases.

(c) When a glass slab is placed in aperture, photoemission rate of P remains the same.

(d) When a prism is placed in the aperture photoemission from P remains the same.

Assume that lens, slab or prism is of same size as that of aperture and P is much smaller than aperture.

3 Let a light beam of total intensity $1 \mu W cm^{-2}$ falls on a clean iron sample piece with work function 4.5 eV and of 1.0 cm area. Assume that iron sample reflects 96% of light and that only 3% of the absorbed energy lies in the violet region which can cause photoemission (of wavelength 250 nm). Number of electrons emitted will be

(a) 1.5×10^{10} electrons per second
(b) 3.0×10^{9} electrons per second
(c) 3.0×10^{10} electrons per second
(d) 1.5×10^{9} electrons per second

4 An electron with initial velocity $v_0 \hat{\mathbf{i}}$ is in the region of electric and magnetic fields, $-E_0 \hat{\mathbf{i}}$ and $B_0 \hat{\mathbf{j}}$, respectively. The de-Broglie wavelength of the electron at time t is given by

(a) $\lambda = \dfrac{h}{mv_0}$ (b) $\lambda = \dfrac{h}{qt(E_0)}$

(c) $\lambda = \dfrac{h}{qt(E_0^2 + B_0^2)^{1/2}}$ (d) $\lambda = \dfrac{h}{qt(E_0^2 + v_0^2 B_0^2)^{1/2}}$

5 The de-Broglie wavelength for electron in an orbit of hydrogen atom is 10^{-9} m. Principal quantum number for this electron is

(a) 1 (b) 2
(c) 3 (d) 4

6 Let I is intensity of light which falls over a metal surface with work function ϕ_0. If metal's mass density is ρ and A is its atomic mass, then photoelectric time delay assuming classical wave model is

(a) $\dfrac{\phi_0 \rho}{IA}$ (b) $\dfrac{2\phi_0}{I}\left(\dfrac{\rho}{A}\right)^{2/3}$

(c) $\dfrac{\phi_0}{I}\left(\dfrac{\rho}{A}\right)^{2/3}$ (d) $\dfrac{\phi_0}{I} \cdot \dfrac{\rho}{(A)^{1/3}}$

7 The figure shows different graphs between stopping potential (V_0) and frequency (ν) for photosensitive surface of cesium, potassium, sodium and lithium. The plots are parallel. Correct ranking of the targets according to their work function greatest first will be

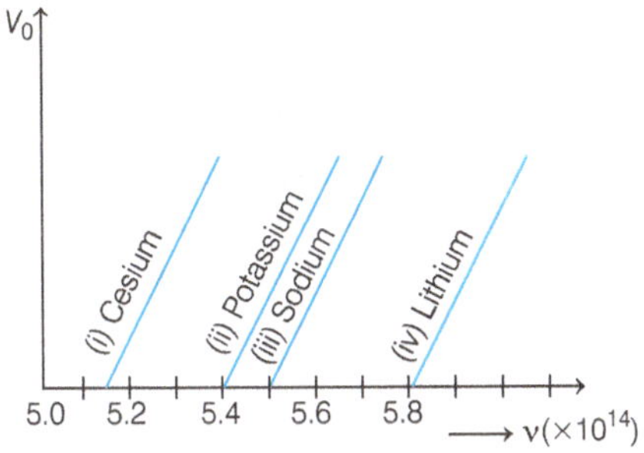

(a) (i) > (ii) > (iii) > (iv)
(b) (i) > (iii) > (ii) > (iv)
(c) (iv) > (iii) > (ii) > (i)
(d) (i) = (iii) > (ii) = (iv)

8 The graph between the stopping potential and frequency of the incident radiation is shown in figure.

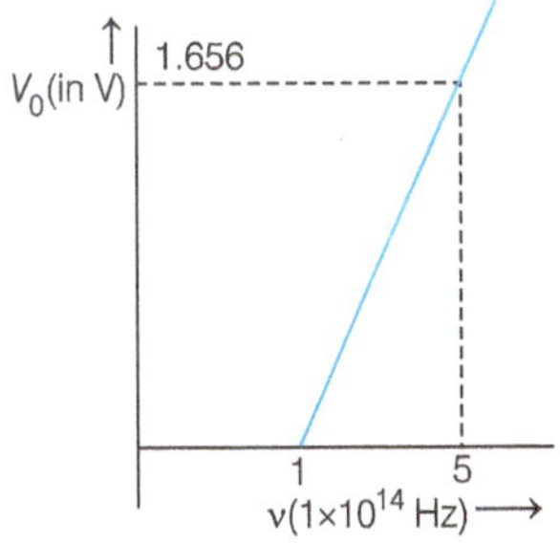

Then, ϕ_0 is

(a) 1.14 eV (b) 0.414 eV
(c) 44.14 eV (d) 441 eV

9 When photons of wavelength λ_1 are incident on an isolated sphere suspended by an insulated thread, the corresponding stopping potential is found to be V. When photons of wavelength λ_2 are used, the corresponding stopping potential was thrice the above value. If light of wavelength λ_3 is used, calculate the stopping potential for this case.

(a) $\dfrac{hc}{e}\left[\dfrac{1}{\lambda_3} + \dfrac{1}{2\lambda_2} - \dfrac{1}{\lambda_1}\right]$ (b) $\dfrac{hc}{e}\left[\dfrac{1}{\lambda_3} + \dfrac{1}{2\lambda_2} - \dfrac{3}{2\lambda_1}\right]$

(c) $\dfrac{hc}{e}\left[\dfrac{1}{\lambda_3} + \dfrac{1}{\lambda_2} - \dfrac{1}{\lambda_1}\right]$ (d) $\dfrac{hc}{e}\left[\dfrac{1}{\lambda_3} - \dfrac{1}{\lambda_2} - \dfrac{1}{\lambda_1}\right]$

10 In a photoemissive cell with executing wavelength λ the fastest electron has speed v. If the exciting wavelength is changed to $\dfrac{3\lambda}{4}$, the speed of the fastest emitted electron will be

(a) $v(3/4)^{1/2}$ (b) $v(4/3)^{1/2}$
(c) less than $v(4/3)^{1/2}$ (d) greater than $v(4/3)^{1/2}$

Correct Codes

Topical Questions

1. (b)	2. (a)	3. (c)	4. (d)	5. (a)	6. (a)	7. (a)	8. (b)	9. (d)	10. (a)
11. (d)	12. (d)	13. (a)	14. (c)	15. (d)	16. (c)	17. (b)	18. (b)	19. (a)	20. (a)
21. (a)	22. (b)	23. (d)	24. (a)	25. (d)	26. (b)	27. (a)	28. (b)	29. (b)	30. (a)
31. (d)	32. (a)	33. (c)	34. (b)	35. (c)	36. (a)	37. (a)	38. (a)	39. (c)	40. (c)
41. (c)	42. (b)	43. (c)	44. (d)	45. (a)	46. (d)	47. (a)	48. (c)	49. (c)	50. (c)
51. (c)	52. (b)	53. (b)	54. (b)	55. (b)	56. (d)	57. (b)	58. (a)	59. (b)	60. (a)
61. (d)	62. (a)	63. (b)	64. (b)	65. (a)	66. (a)	67. (d)	68. (b)	69. (a)	70. (c)
71. (a)	72. (b)	73. (d)	74. (a)	75. (d)	76. (c)	77. (a)	78. (c)	79. (c)	80. (b)
81. (a)	82. (a)	83. (b)	84. (b)	85. (d)	86. (a)	87. (d)	88. (a)	89. (d)	90. (b)
91. (a)	92. (d)	93. (b)	94 (c)	95. (c)	96. (c)	97. (b)	98. (a)	99. (b)	100. (d)

Assertion and Reason Questions

1 (d)	2 (b)	3 (a)	4 (b)	5 (a)	6 (b)	7 (a)	8 (a)	9 (d)	10 (b)

Statement Based Questions

1 (b)	2 (c)	3 (c)	4 (a)	5 (d)	6 (a)	7 (a)	8 (c)

Matching Type Questions

1 (c)	2 (b)	3 (a)

Numerical Type Questions

1 (50.47)	2 (2)	3 (1)	4 (188)	5 (15.2)	6 (1.66)	7 (0.547)	8 (4.19)	9 (1.5)	10 (0.3)

NCERT Exemplar Questions

1 (d)	2 (b)	3 (d)	4 (b)	5 (a)	6 (c)

Past Exams Questions

1 (b)	2 (d)	3 (d)	4 (c)	5 (d)	6 (c)	7 (d)	8 (c)	9 (c)	10 (d)
11 (a)	12 (c)	13 (d)	14 (d)	15 (b)	16 (c)	17 (d)	18 (b)	19 (b)	20 (b)

Skill Boosters

1 (b)	2 (a)	3 (d)	4 (d)	5 (c)	6 (c)	7 (c)	8 (b)	9 (b)	10 (d)

Step by Step

Decoding the Questions

Concept Builder

1 True (T)	2 True (T)
3 intensity	4 photon, wave
5 True (T)	6 False (F)
7 magnetic flux	8 False (F)
9 False (F)	10 Electron
11 Photoelectric effect	
12 Yes, if frequency is suitable	
13 remains same	
14 to reproduce sound	
15 6 : 5	16 True (T)
17 alkali	18 minimum
19 conserved	20 wave, particle

Topical Questions

3 (c) Specific charge on proton

$$= \frac{e}{m} = 9.6 \times 10^7 \text{ C kg}^{-1}$$

∴ Specific charge on an α-particle

$$= \frac{2e}{4m} = \frac{e}{2m} = \frac{9.6 \times 10^7}{2}$$

$$= 4.8 \times 10^7 \text{C kg}^{-1}$$

5 (a) Work function for cesium is 2.14 eV, aluminium is 4.28 eV, silver is 4.70 eV and platinum is 5.65 eV.

∴ The work function for platinum is highest while it is lowest for cesium.

11 (d) As the distance of source from the surface increases, intensity of radiation decreases.

∵ Intensity (I) $\propto \frac{1}{(\text{distance } d)^2}$ and

since, photoelectric current (i) $\propto$ intensity (I)

Thus, the variation of i *versus* d is correctly depicted by the curve d in the given figure.

13 (a) From the given graph,

The value of stopping potential, $V_0 = -0.54 \text{V}$.

14 (c) Thus, at point P (as shown in the given figure), it can be seen clearly that the electron must have been repelled, so maximum kinetic energy, $K = eV_0$.

15 (d)

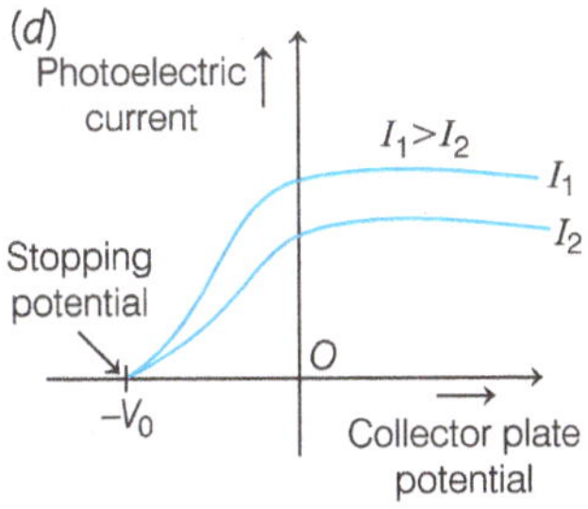

Here for greater intensity I_1, more photoelectrons are emitted and hence saturation current is more. Thus, graph corres-ponding to I_1 will be above than that of I_2. Since, the stopping potential is independent of intensity, hence the graphs converge at same value of stopping potential V_0 for both the intensities I_1 and I_2.

16 (c) For incident radiation at same intensity and at varying frequencies, the given graph represents the variation of photocurrent with collector plate potential. This can be as shown in graph below

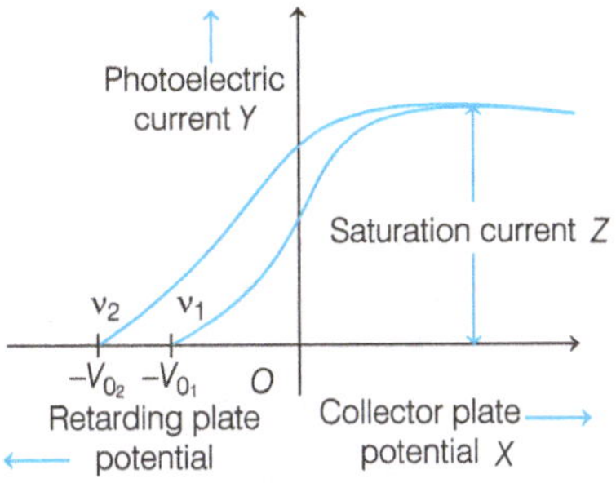

Thus, $X \to$ collector plate potential,

$Y \to$ photoelectric current

and $Z \to$ saturation current.

18 (b) Number of photoelectrons,

$$N \propto I \quad \text{...(i)}$$

As, $\nu \cdot \lambda =$ speed of light c

$$\therefore \quad \nu \propto \frac{1}{\lambda}$$

Also, $E = h\nu$

$$\Rightarrow \quad E \propto \nu$$

$$\Rightarrow \quad E \propto \frac{1}{\lambda} \quad \text{...(ii)}$$

So, from Eqs. (i) and (ii), we get

$$N \propto I \text{ and } E \propto \frac{1}{\lambda}$$

23 (d) According to Einstein's photoelectric equation, basic elementary process involved in photoelectric effect is the absorption of a single light quantum (photon) of sufficient energy by a single electron.

Thus, K_{max} depends linearly on the frequency ν of incident radiation (photon).

$$K_{max} \propto \nu$$

24 (a) $$\nu_0 = \frac{\phi_0}{h} = \frac{6.35 \times 1.6 \times 10^{-19}}{6.63 \times 10^{-34}}$$

$$= 15.32 \times 10^{14} \text{Hz}$$

25 (d) The work function of material is given by

$$\phi_0 = h\nu$$

$$\phi_0 = \frac{hc}{\lambda} \text{ or } \lambda = \frac{hc}{\phi_0} \quad \text{...(i)}$$

$$\therefore \lambda = \frac{6.63 \times 10^{-34} \times 3 \times 10^8}{4 \times 1.6 \times 10^{-19}}$$

$$= 3.108 \times 10^{-7} \text{ m} \simeq 310 \text{ nm}$$

26 (b) $K_{max} = h\nu - \phi_0 = h\nu - h\nu_0$ ...(i)

$K_{max} = h(6\nu) - h(\nu) = 5\,h\nu$

27 (*a*) According to Einstein's photoelectric equation, for metal plate *A*,

$$K_A = \frac{hc}{\lambda_A} - \phi$$

$$\Rightarrow \quad 2K_A = \frac{2hc}{\lambda_A} - 2\phi$$

or $$2K_A + \phi = \frac{2hc}{\lambda_A} - \phi \quad \text{...(i)}$$

It is given that, wavelength of metal *B* is half of metal *A*, i.e.

$$\lambda_B = \frac{\lambda_A}{2},$$

therefore

$$K_B = \frac{hc}{\lambda_B} - \phi = \frac{2hc}{\lambda_A} - \phi$$

$$\Rightarrow \quad 2K_A + \phi = K_B \quad [\because \text{Using Eq. (i)}]$$

$$\Rightarrow \quad K_A < \frac{K_B}{2}$$

28 (*b*) $K_{max} = \frac{1}{2}mv^2 = eV_1$ ...(i)

According to Einstein's photoelectric equation,

$$K_{max} = h\nu_1 - \phi_0$$

$$\Rightarrow \quad h\nu_1 = \phi_0 + eV_1 \quad \text{...(ii)}$$

[Using Eq. (i)]

Similarly,

$$h\nu_2 = \phi_0 + eV_2 \quad \text{...(iii)}$$

From Eqs. (ii) and (iii), we get

$$\therefore \quad h(\nu_1 - \nu_2) = e(V_1 - V_2)$$

$$\frac{h}{e}(\nu_1 - \nu_2) = V_1 - V_2$$

$\therefore$ Stopping potential will be

$$V_2 = V_1 - \frac{h}{e}(\nu_1 - \nu_2)$$

29 (*b*) Einstein's photoelectric equation is given as

$$h\nu - h\nu_0 = K_{max}$$

$$\therefore \quad h(\nu_1 - \nu_0) = K_1 \quad \text{...(i)}$$

Similarly, for incident light with frequency ν_2 equation will be

$$h(\nu_2 - \nu_0) = K_2 \quad \text{...(ii)}$$

Ratio of K_1 / K_2 is given in question $= 1/n$.

$\therefore$ Dividing Eq. (i) from Eq. (ii), we get

$$\frac{\nu_1 - \nu_0}{\nu_2 - \nu_0} = \frac{K_1}{K_2} = \frac{1}{n}$$

Thus, the threshold frequency of the metallic surface is

$$\nu_0 = \frac{(n\nu_1 - \nu_2)}{(n-1)}$$

30 (*a*) According to Einstein's photoelectric equation,

$$h\nu = h\nu_0 + \frac{1}{2}mv_{max}^2$$

or $$\frac{1}{2}mv_{max}^2 = h\nu - h\nu_0 \quad \text{... (i)}$$

$$v_{max} = 8 \times 10^6 \text{ ms}^{-1}$$

Incident frequency, $\nu = 5\nu_0$ (given)

$$\Rightarrow \quad \frac{1}{2}m(8 \times 10^6)^2 = h(5\nu_0 - \nu_0) \quad \text{...(ii)}$$

If $\nu = 2\nu_0$, then

$$\frac{1}{2}mv_{max}^2 = h(2\nu_0 - \nu_0) \quad \text{...(iii)}$$

On dividing Eq. (ii) by Eq. (iii), we get

$$\frac{(8 \times 10^6)^2}{v_{max}^2} = \frac{4\nu_0}{\nu_0}$$

$$v_{max} = 4 \times 10^6 \text{ms}^{-1}$$

31 (*d*) Using Einstein equation for photoelectric effect,

$$E = h\nu = \phi + eV_0 \quad \text{...(i)}$$

For λ_1,

$$E_1 = h\nu_1 = \phi + eV_{01}$$

or $$\frac{hc}{\lambda_1} = \phi + \text{e}V_{01} \quad \text{...(ii)}$$

Similarly, $$\frac{hc}{\lambda_2} = \phi + \text{e}V_{02} \quad \text{...(iii)}$$

From Eqs. (ii) and (iii), we get

or $$\frac{hc}{e}\left[\frac{1}{\lambda_1} - \frac{1}{\lambda_2}\right] = \Delta V$$

By using given values,

$$\Delta V = 1240\left[\frac{1}{300} - \frac{1}{400}\right]\frac{\text{nm-V}}{\text{nm}}$$

$$\Rightarrow \Delta V = 1.03.\ V \approx 1\text{V}$$

32 (*a*) According to Einstein's photoelectric equation,

$$E = K_{max} + \phi$$

$$\Rightarrow \quad K_{max} = E - \phi = h\nu - \phi$$

$$K_{max} = \frac{hc}{\lambda} - \phi \quad \text{...(i)}$$

Similarly, in second case

$$3K_{max} = \frac{hc}{\lambda/2} - \phi \quad \text{...(ii)}$$

Solving Eqs. (i) and (ii), we get

$$\phi = \frac{hc}{2\lambda}$$

33 (*c*) Using Einstein's relation of photoelectric effect,

$$(\text{KE})_{max} = eV_0 = h\nu - h\nu_0 \quad \text{...(i)}$$

But $$h\nu = E = \frac{1237}{\lambda(\text{nm})}\text{eV} \quad \text{(Given)}$$

$$\therefore \quad E_0 = \frac{1237}{\lambda_0(\text{nm})}\text{eV} \quad \text{...(ii)}$$

From Eqs. (i) and (ii), we get

$$(\text{KE})_{max} = E - E_0 = \left(\frac{1237}{\lambda} - \frac{1237}{\lambda_0}\right)\text{eV}$$

$$= 1237\left[\frac{1}{\lambda} - \frac{1}{\lambda_0}\right]\text{eV}$$

(λ in nm) ...(iii)

By putting values of λ and λ_0 in Eq. (iii), we get

$$(\text{KE})_{max} = 1237\left(\frac{1}{260} - \frac{1}{380}\right)\text{eV}$$

$$\Rightarrow (\text{KE})_{max} = 1.5\text{ eV}$$

34 (*b*) On calculating ν for all the wavelengths, we get following table.

$\nu \times 10^{14}$ Hz	8.219	7.412	6.884	5.493	4.343
V_0 (V)	1.28	0.95	0.74	0.16	0

As, at $V_0 = 0$, $\nu = \nu_0$ (threshold frequency)

$\therefore$ From the table, frequency, $\nu_0 = 4.343 \times 10^{14}$ Hz

Work function, $\phi_0 = h\nu_0$

$= 6.63 \times 10^{-34} \times 4.343 \times 10^{14}$

$= 2.88 \times 10^{-19}$ J

≈ 1.8 eV

Thus, the threshold frequency and work function of the metal are 4.3×10^{14} Hz and 1.8 eV, respectively.

35 (*c*) $K_{max} = eV = h\nu - \phi_0 = \frac{hc}{\lambda} - \phi_0$

Here, $\lambda = 600$ nm $= 6 \times 10^{-7}$ m and $V_0 = 0.5$ V, then

$$0.5e = \frac{hc}{6 \times 10^{-7}} - \phi_0$$

$$\Rightarrow 0.5 = \frac{h}{e}\left(\frac{c}{6\times10^{-7}}\right) - \frac{\phi_0}{e} \quad ...(i)$$

Similarly, when $\lambda = 400$ nm $= 4\times10^{-7}$ m and $V_0 = 1.5$V,

$$\text{then } 1.5 = \frac{h}{e}\left(\frac{c}{4\times10^{-7}}\right) - \frac{\phi_0}{e} \quad ...(ii)$$

Subtracting Eq. (i) from Eq. (ii), we get

$$1 = \frac{h}{e}\frac{c}{10^{-7}}\left[\frac{1}{4} - \frac{1}{6}\right]$$

$$\frac{h}{e} = 4\times10^{-15} \text{ V-s}$$

36 (*a*) $E = (\text{KE})_{max} + \phi$

or $\frac{hc}{\lambda} = (\text{KE})_{max} + \phi \quad ...(i)$

Similarly, if the wavelength of radiation is changed to $\frac{3\lambda}{4}$,

then $\frac{hc}{\left(\frac{3\lambda}{4}\right)} = (\text{KE})'_{max} + \phi$

$$\Rightarrow \frac{4}{3}\left(\frac{hc}{\lambda}\right) = (\text{KE})'_{max} + \phi \quad ...(ii)$$

Substituting the value of $\left(\frac{hc}{\lambda}\right)$

From Eq. (i) in the above Eq. (ii), we get

$$\frac{4}{3}[(\text{KE})_{max} + \phi] = (\text{KE})'_{max} + \phi$$

$$\frac{4}{3}(\text{KE})_{max} + \frac{\phi}{3} = (\text{KE})'_{max} \quad ...(iii)$$

If v and v' are the maximum speeds of emitted electron when the wavelength of light is λ and $\frac{3\lambda}{4}$ respectively, so Eq. (iii) can be written as

$$\frac{1}{2}mv'^2 = \frac{4}{3}\left(\frac{1}{2}mv^2\right) + \frac{\phi}{3}$$

i.e. $v' > v\left(\frac{4}{3}\right)^{1/2}$

37 (*a*) Work-function of photosensitive material,

$$\phi_0 = \frac{hc}{\lambda} - eV_0$$

$$= \frac{6.63\times10^{-34}\times3\times10^8}{640.2\times10^{-9}} - 1.6\times10^{-19}\times0.54$$

$$= 1.3975 \simeq 1.4 \text{ eV}$$

Now, if the material is irradiates by a iron source, then wavelength, $\lambda = 427.2$ nm

$$= 427.2\times10^{-9}\text{m}$$

Let V_0' be the new stopping potential.

$$\Rightarrow eV_0' = \frac{hc}{\lambda} - \phi_0$$

$$= \frac{6.63\times10^{-34}\times3\times10^8}{427.2\times10^{-9}\times1.6\times10^{-19}} - 1.4$$

$$= 1.51 \text{ eV}$$

38 (*a*) By Einstein's equation,

we have $eV_0 = h\nu - \phi_0$

or $V_0 = \frac{h}{e}\nu - \frac{\phi_0}{e}$

Above is an equation of straight line ($y = mx - c$) with slope $\frac{h}{e}$ and

y-intercept $= \frac{\phi_0}{e}$

$\therefore$ Work function, ϕ_0

$= e \times y$-intercept (in eV)

As in the given graph y-intercept $= OB$

$= e \times OB$ (in eV)

39 (*c*)

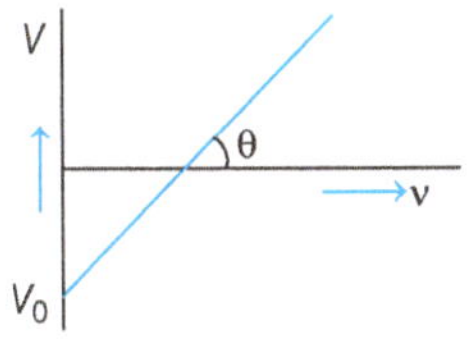

From graph, we can write

$$\tan\theta = \frac{\Delta V}{\Delta\nu}$$

As we know, for photoelectric effect, $eV = h\nu - \phi$

Differentiating both sides of the above equation, we get

$$\frac{\Delta V}{\Delta\nu} = \frac{h}{e}$$

$$\therefore \quad \frac{h}{e} = 4.12\times10^{-15}$$

$$h = 1.6\times10^{-19}\times4.12\times10^{-15}$$

$$= 6.592\times10^{-34} \text{ J-s}$$

40 (*c*) From the graph, magnitude of stopping potential,

$$V_0 = 2.2 \text{ V}$$

Since, for photoelectric effect

$$K_{max} = eV_0 = 2.2 \text{ eV}$$

From Einstein's photoelectric equation

$$\text{KE}_{max} = h\nu - \phi$$

where, work function, $\phi = 1$ eV

$$\Rightarrow h\nu = (2.2 + 1) \text{ eV} = 3.2 \text{ eV}$$

$\therefore$ The frequency of incident radiation,

$$\nu = \frac{3.2\times1.6\times10^{-19}}{h}$$

$$= 0.775\times10^{15} \text{ s}^{-1}$$

41 (*c*) $K_{max} = \frac{hc}{\lambda} - \phi_0$

$$\Rightarrow V_0 = \left(\frac{hc}{e}\right)\left(\frac{1}{\lambda}\right) - \frac{\phi_0}{e}$$

The graph between V_0 and $\frac{1}{\lambda}$ is as shown below.

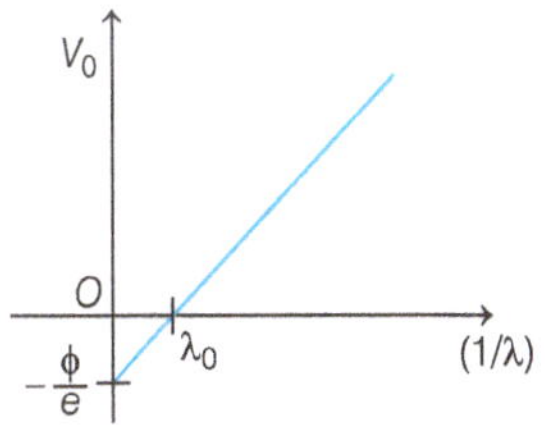

42 (*b*) $K = h\nu - h\nu_0$

$$\frac{dK}{d\nu} = h = \tan\theta$$

$$\Rightarrow \theta = \tan^{-1}(h)$$

43 (*c*) $\text{KE}_{max} = \frac{1}{2}mv^2_{max} = h(\nu - \nu_0)$

$$\frac{1}{2}mv^2_{max} = h(\nu - \nu_0)$$

$$\nu_0 = \nu - \frac{mv^2_{max}}{2h}$$

$$= 7.21\times10^{14} - \frac{9.1\times10^{-31}\times(6\times10^5)^2}{2\times(6.63\times10^{-34})}$$

$$\nu_0 = 4.74\times10^{14} \text{ Hz}$$

44 (*d*) From Einstein's equation energy of incident photon

$$E = \phi_0 + \frac{1}{2}mv^2$$

Velocity of photoelectron,

$$v = \sqrt{\frac{2(E - \phi_0)}{m}}$$

or Radius, $r = \frac{mv}{eB}$

or $r = \dfrac{m\sqrt{\dfrac{2(E-\phi_0)}{m}}}{eB}$

$\Rightarrow \quad r = \dfrac{\sqrt{2m(E-\phi_0)}}{eB}$

45 (*a*) The Einstein's equation for photoelectric effect is given by

$$E_{max} = h\nu - \phi_0$$

or $\quad h\nu = E_{max} + \phi_0$

In first case

$$f = 1 + \phi_0 \quad \text{...(i)}$$

In second case

$$\frac{3f}{2} = 4 + \phi_0 \quad \text{...(ii)}$$

dividing Eq. (ii) by Eq. (i), we get

$$\frac{\frac{3f}{2}}{\frac{f}{1}} = \frac{4+\phi_0}{1+\phi_0}$$

$\Rightarrow \quad W = 5\text{ eV}$

46 (*d*) $\frac{1}{2}mv_{max}^2 = eEd = 4\,eV$

The energy of incident photon

$$= \frac{1240}{200}$$

$$= 6.2\text{ eV}$$

From equation of photoelectric

$$\frac{1}{2}mv_{max}^2 = h\nu - \phi_0$$

$\therefore \quad \phi_0 = 6.2 - 4 = 2.2\text{ eV.}$

48 (*c*) According to the Einstein's photoelectric equation,

$$K_{max} = \frac{1}{2}mv_{max}^2$$

$$= h\nu - \phi_0 = h\nu - h\nu_0' \quad \text{...(i)}$$

When incident frequency of light, $\nu = 2\nu_0$, then

$$\frac{1}{2}mv_1^2 = h(2\nu_0) - h\nu_0 = h\nu_0 \quad \text{...(ii)}$$

If incident frequency of radiation, $\nu = 5\nu_0$, then

$$\frac{1}{2}mv_2^2 = h(5\nu_0) - h\nu_0$$

$$= 4h\nu_0 \quad \text{...(iii)}$$

$$\therefore \quad \frac{\frac{1}{2}mv_1^2}{\frac{1}{2}mv_2^2} = \frac{h\nu_0}{4h\nu_0} = \frac{1}{4}$$

$\therefore \quad v_1 : v_2 = 1:2$

49 (*c*) According to photoelectric equation,

For 1st case $E = \dfrac{hc}{\lambda} - \phi_0 \quad \text{...(i)}$

For 2nd case $2E = \dfrac{hc}{\lambda'} - \phi_0 \quad \text{...(ii)}$

From Eqs. (i) and (ii), we get

$$2E - \frac{hc}{\lambda'} = \left[-\frac{hc}{\lambda} + E\right]$$

$$\lambda' = \frac{hc\lambda}{E\lambda + hc}$$

50 (*c*) According to Einstein's photoelectric equation

$$\frac{hc}{\lambda} = \phi + \frac{1}{2}mv^2$$

$$\Rightarrow \quad v = \left[\frac{2(hc - \lambda\phi)}{m\lambda}\right]^{1/2}$$

51 (*c*) For 1st case,

$$eV_0 = \frac{hc}{\lambda} - \frac{hc}{\lambda_0} \quad \text{...(i)}$$

For 2nd case,

$$\frac{eV_0}{4} = \frac{hc}{2\lambda} - \frac{hc}{\lambda_0}$$

$$\Rightarrow \quad eV_0 = \frac{4hc}{2\lambda} - \frac{4hc}{\lambda_0} \quad \text{...(ii)}$$

From Eqs. (i) and (ii), we get

$$\Rightarrow \quad \frac{hc}{\lambda} - \frac{hc}{\lambda_0} = \frac{4hc}{2\lambda} - \frac{4hc}{\lambda_0}$$

$\Rightarrow \quad \lambda_0 = 3\lambda$

52 (*b*) $E = \dfrac{hc}{\lambda} - \phi$

$$\frac{E}{2} = \frac{hc}{\lambda'} - \phi$$

Now $\quad E - \dfrac{E}{2} = \dfrac{hc}{\lambda} - \dfrac{hc}{\lambda'}$

or $\quad \lambda' = \dfrac{hc\,(2hc - E\lambda)}{2\lambda}$

53 (*b*) $\frac{1}{2}mv_{max}^2 = h\nu - h\nu_0$

$$\frac{1}{2}mv_{max}^2 = h(\nu - \nu_0)$$

This is Einstein's equation of photoelectric effect.

54 (*b*) Work function, $\phi = \dfrac{hc}{\lambda}$

$$\frac{\phi_1}{\phi_2} = \frac{600}{300} = 2:1$$

55 (*b*) $(E_C - E_B) + (E_B - E_A)$

$$= (E_C - E_A)$$

$$\frac{hc}{\lambda_1} + \frac{hc}{\lambda_2} = \frac{hc}{\lambda_3}$$

$$\frac{1}{\lambda_3} = \frac{1}{\lambda_1} + \frac{1}{\lambda_2}$$

57 (*b*) Linear momentum of the photon, $p = \dfrac{E}{c}$

$$\Rightarrow \quad p = \frac{6\times 10^6\text{ eV}}{3\times 10^8\text{ ms}^{-1}}$$

$$= 0.02\text{ eVs m}^{-1}$$

58 (*a*) Momentum of photon,

$$p = \frac{E}{c} = \frac{h\nu}{c} = \frac{h}{\lambda}$$

$$\Rightarrow p = \frac{h}{\lambda} = \frac{h}{1\times 10^{-10}} = 10^{10}\,h$$

59 (*b*) Maximum energy of X-ray photon is

$$E_{max} = h\nu_{max} = \frac{hc}{\lambda_{min}}$$

$$= \frac{6.63\times 10^{-34}\times 3\times 10^8}{0.55\times 10^{-10}\times 1.6\times 10^{-19}}\text{ eV}$$

$$= 22.6\text{ keV}$$

60 (*a*) Energy of one γ-ray

$$= \frac{10.2}{2} = 5.1\text{ eV}$$

$$= 8.16\times 10^{-19}\text{ J}$$

Let λ be the wavelength.

Energy of each ray, $E = \dfrac{hc}{\lambda}$

or $\quad \lambda = \dfrac{hc}{E}$

$$= \frac{6.63\times 10^{-34}\times 3\times 10^8}{8.16\times 10^{-19}}$$

$$= 2.436\times 10^{-7}\text{ m}$$

61 (*d*) Energy of each photon in the laser beam

$$= h\nu$$

$$= 6.63\times 10^{-34}\times 6\times 10^{14}\text{ Unit}$$

Number of photons emitted per second

$$= \frac{2 \times 10^{-3}}{6.626 \times 10^{-34} \times 6 \times 10^{14}}$$

$$= 5 \times 10^{15} \text{ photons per second}$$

62 (*a*) No. of photons,

$$n = \frac{I}{E} = \frac{I}{hc}\lambda \qquad \left[\because E = \frac{hc}{\lambda}\right]$$

$$= \frac{1.52 \times 10^3 \times 520 \times 10^{-9}}{6.63 \times 10^{-34} \times 3 \times 10^8}$$

$$n = 4 \times 10^{21} \text{ photons per metre}^2$$

63 (*b*) Power of the source

= Number of photons emitted per second × Energy of one photon

$$\therefore \quad n_1 \frac{hc}{\lambda_1} = n_2 \frac{hc}{\lambda_2}$$

$$\Rightarrow \quad \frac{n_1}{n_2} = \frac{\lambda_1}{\lambda_2} = \frac{2}{400}$$

$$= \frac{1}{200} = 1:200$$

64 (*b*) Number of photons incident on unit area in unit time

$$= \frac{I}{E_i} = \frac{2}{16.96 \times 10^{-19}} = 1.18 \times 10^{18}$$

Therefore, number of photons incident on given area

$$= (1.18 \times 10^{18})\,(1.0 \times 10^{-4})$$

$$= 1.18 \times 10^{14}$$

∴Number of photoelectrons emitted per second (n),

$$n = \left(\frac{0.53}{100}\right)(1.18 \times 10^{14})$$

$$= 6.25 \times 10^{11}$$

$$K_{max} = E_i - \text{work function}$$

$$= (10.6 - 5.6) = 5.0 \text{ eV}$$

65 (*a*) As $\lambda = \frac{h}{mv} \Rightarrow \lambda \propto \frac{1}{mv}$

Hence, $\frac{\lambda_p}{\lambda_\alpha} = \frac{m_\alpha v_\alpha}{m_p v_p}$

$$\Rightarrow \quad \frac{1}{1} = \frac{m_\alpha v_\alpha}{m_p v_p}$$

$$\frac{v_p}{v_\alpha} = \frac{m_\alpha}{m_p} = \frac{4}{1}$$

67 (*d*) Energy of n photons,

$$E = \frac{nhc}{\lambda}$$

∴The momentum gained by the body is

$$p = \frac{E}{c} = \frac{nh}{\lambda}$$

68 (*b*) The wavelength of violet light is

$\lambda = 390 \text{ nm} = 390 \times 10^{-9} \text{ m}$

∴The energy at the violet end is

$$E = \frac{hc}{\lambda}$$

$$= \frac{6.63 \times 10^{-34} \times 3 \times 10^8}{390 \times 10^{-9} \times 1.6 \times 10^{-19}} \text{ eV}$$

$$= 3.19 \text{ eV}$$

69 (*a*) The number of photons emitted by the lamp per second is

$$n = \frac{8\% \text{ of } P}{E} = \frac{8P\lambda}{100hc}$$

$$= \frac{8 \times 150 \times 4500 \times 10^{-10}}{100 \times 6.63 \times 10^{-34} \times 3 \times 10^8}$$

$$= 3 \times 10^{19} \text{ photons per second}$$

70 (*c*) The number of photons delivered per second to the sphere is

$$n = \frac{P}{E} = \frac{P\lambda}{hc}$$

$$= \frac{100 \times 589 \times 10^{-9}}{6.63 \times 10^{-34} \times 3 \times 10^8}$$

$$= 3 \times 10^{20} \text{ photons per second}$$

71 (*a*) Momentum,

$$p = mv = 9.11 \times 10^{-31} \times 5.4 \times 10^6$$

$$= 4.92 \times 10^{-24} \text{ kg ms}^{-1}$$

de-Broglie wavelength, $\lambda = \frac{h}{p}$

$$= \frac{6.63 \times 10^{-34} \text{ J-s}}{4.92 \times 10^{-24} \text{ kg ms}^{-1}}$$

$$= 1.35 \times 10^{-10} \text{ m}$$

$$= 0.135 \text{ nm}$$

72 (*b*) The de-Broglie wavelength of a particle is given by

$$\lambda = h/p$$

$$\Rightarrow \quad p\lambda = h$$

This equation is in the form of $yx = c$, which is the equation of a rectangular hyperbola.

74 (*a*) de-Broglie wavelength,

$$\lambda = h/p \qquad \text{...(i)}$$

Given $\quad p_\alpha = p_p = p_e$

$$\therefore \quad \lambda_\alpha = \lambda_p = \lambda_e$$

[from Eq. (i)]

75 (*d*) Given, $\frac{\lambda_p}{\lambda_e} = 1.83 \times 10^{-4}$

Since, $\lambda = h/p = \frac{h}{mv}$

$$\text{or} \quad m = \frac{h}{\lambda v} \qquad \text{...(i)}$$

Using Eq. (i), we get

$$\frac{m_e}{m_p} = \frac{\lambda_p v_p}{\lambda_e v_e}$$

$$= (1.83 \times 10^{-4}) \times 3 = 5.49 \times 10^{-4}$$

$$\Rightarrow m_p = \frac{m_e}{5.49 \times 10^{-4}} = \frac{9.1 \times 10^{-31}}{5.49 \times 10^{-4}}$$

$$\approx 1.66 \times 10^{-27} \text{ kg}$$

So, the particle may be proton or a neutron.

76 (*c*) $\quad \lambda \propto \frac{1}{p} \qquad$ ...(i)

According to the question,

$$p_1 = m_1 v_1 = (0.4 \text{ kg} \times 1 \text{ kms}^{-1})$$

$$= 400 \text{ kg-ms}^{-1}$$

$$p_2 = m_2 v_2 = (0.60 \text{ kg} \times 1 \text{ ms}^{-1})$$

$$= 0.6 \text{ kg-ms}^{-1}$$

$$p_3 = m_3 v_3 = (1.0 \times 10^{-9} \times 2.2 \text{ ms}^{-1})$$

$$= 2.2 \times 10^{-9} \text{ kg-ms}^{-1}$$

$$\Rightarrow \quad p_1 > p_2 > p_3$$

$$\therefore \quad \lambda_1 < \lambda_2 < \lambda_3 \text{ [using Eq. (i)]}$$

77 (*a*) Momentum of striking electrons, $p = \frac{h}{\lambda} \qquad$ ...(i)

∴Kinetic energy of striking electrons,

$$K = \frac{p^2}{2m} = \frac{h^2}{2m\lambda^2} \qquad \text{[using Eq. (i)]}$$

This is also maximum energy of X-ray photons.

Therefore, $\frac{hc}{\lambda_0} = \frac{h^2}{2m\lambda^2}$

where, λ_0 is the cut-off wavelength $= \frac{2m\lambda^2 c}{h}$.

78 (*c*) As we know that, wavelength of an electron,

$$\lambda = \frac{h}{\sqrt{2mE}} = \frac{h}{\sqrt{2m}} \cdot \frac{1}{\sqrt{E}}$$

$$\Rightarrow \log\lambda = \log\left(\frac{h}{\sqrt{2m}}\cdot\frac{1}{\sqrt{E}}\right)$$

$$\Rightarrow \log\lambda = -\frac{1}{2}\log E + \log\frac{h}{\sqrt{2m}}$$

79 (c) de-Broglie wavelength of a moving particle is given by

$$\lambda = \frac{h}{p} = \frac{h}{\sqrt{2mK}}$$

where, K = kinetic energy of the particle.
Now, in given condition,

$$\lambda = \frac{h}{\sqrt{2mE}} \quad \text{...(i)}$$

and $$\frac{\lambda}{2} = \frac{h}{\sqrt{2m(E+\Delta E)}} \quad \text{...(ii)}$$

On dividing Eq. (i) by Eq. (ii), we get

$$2 = \frac{\sqrt{E+\Delta E}}{\sqrt{E}} \Rightarrow \Delta E = 3E$$

80 (b) So, initially de-Broglie wavelength,

$$\lambda_1 = \frac{h}{p} = \frac{h}{\sqrt{2mK}} \quad \text{...(i)}$$

$$\lambda_2 = \frac{h}{\sqrt{2m(16K)}} = \frac{h}{4\sqrt{2mK}} = \frac{\lambda_1}{4}$$

[∴ using Eq. (i)]

$\lambda_2 = 25\%$ of λ_1

Thus, there is 75% change in the de-Broglie wavelength of the particle.

81 (a) $$\lambda = \frac{h}{p}$$

$$\Rightarrow \lambda = \frac{h}{\sqrt{2m\text{KE}}}$$

$$\therefore \frac{\lambda_p}{\lambda_\alpha} = \frac{\sqrt{2m_\alpha \text{KE}_\alpha}}{\sqrt{2m_p\text{KE}_p}} \quad \text{...(i)}$$

Here, $\text{KE}_\alpha = \text{KE}_p$ and $m_\alpha = 4m_p$

$$\Rightarrow \frac{\lambda_p}{\lambda_\alpha} = \sqrt{\frac{4m_p}{m_p}} = \frac{2}{1}$$

or $\lambda_p : \lambda_\alpha = 2:1$

82 (a) $$p \propto \frac{1}{\lambda}$$

$$\therefore \frac{p_1}{p_2} = \frac{\lambda_2}{\lambda_1}$$

But $\lambda_1 = \lambda_2 = \lambda$

Then, $$\frac{p_1}{p_2} = \frac{\lambda}{\lambda} = 1$$

$$\Rightarrow p_1 = p_2 \quad \text{... (i)}$$

Thus, their momenta is same.

Also, $$E = \frac{p^2}{2m}$$

$$\Rightarrow E \propto \frac{1}{m}$$

$$\therefore \frac{E_1}{E_2} = \frac{m_2}{m_1} < 1 \quad [\because m_1 > m_2]$$

$$\Rightarrow E_1 < E_2$$

83 (b) $$\lambda_e = \frac{h}{m_e v_e}$$

$$= \frac{h}{m_e(c/100)} = \frac{100\,h}{m_e c} \quad \text{...(i)}$$

As, de-Broglie wavelength,

$$\lambda_e = \frac{h}{\sqrt{2m_eE_e}}$$

$$\Rightarrow E_e = \frac{h^2}{2\lambda_e^2 m_e} \quad \text{...(ii)}$$

$$E_p = \frac{hc}{\lambda_p} = \frac{hc}{2\lambda_e} \quad \text{...(iii)}$$

$[\because \lambda_p = 2\lambda_e$ (given)$]$

Dividing Eq. (iii) from Eq. (ii), we get

$$\therefore \frac{E_p}{E_e} = \frac{hc}{2\lambda_e} \times \frac{2\lambda_e^2 m_e}{h^2}$$

So, $$\frac{E_e}{E_p} = \frac{1}{100} = 10^{-2} \quad \text{[using Eq. (i)]}$$

84 (b) Using formula, $\lambda = \dfrac{h}{\sqrt{2\text{KE}m_e}}$

(i) Kinetic energy of electron,

$$\text{KE}_e = \frac{h^2}{2\lambda^2 m_e}$$

$$= \frac{(6.63\times 10^{-34})^2}{2\times(589\times 10^{-9})^2\times 9.1\times 10^{-31}}$$

$$= 6.96\times 10^{-25}\text{ J}$$

(ii) Kinetic energy of neutron,

$$\text{KE}_n = \frac{h^2}{2\lambda^2 m_n}$$

$$= \frac{(6.63\times 10^{-34})^2}{2\times(589\times 10^{-9})^2\times 1.67\times 10^{-27}}$$

$$\approx 3.82\times 10^{-28}\text{ J}$$

85 (d) de-Broglie wavelength for an electron will be given as

$$\lambda_e = \frac{h}{\sqrt{2mE}} \quad \text{...(i)}$$

de-Broglie's wavelength of photon.

$$\lambda_p = \frac{hc}{E} \quad \text{...(ii)}$$

Now, dividing Eq. (i) by Eq. (ii), we get

$$\Rightarrow \frac{\lambda_e}{\lambda_p} = \frac{1}{c}\cdot\sqrt{\frac{E}{2m}} = \frac{1}{c}\left(\frac{E}{2m}\right)^{\frac{1}{2}}$$

86 (a) $$a = \frac{eE}{m}$$

$$\therefore v = u + at = 0 + \frac{eE}{m}t$$

$$\Rightarrow v = \frac{eEt}{m}$$

de-Broglie wavelength, $\lambda = \dfrac{h}{mv}$

$$= \frac{h}{m(eEt/m)} = \frac{h}{eEt}$$

Rate of change of de-Broglie wavelength,

$$\frac{d\lambda}{dt} = \frac{h}{eE}\left(-\frac{1}{t^2}\right) = \frac{-h}{eEt^2}$$

87 (d) As de-Broglie wavelength,

$$\lambda = \frac{h}{\sqrt{2\,mqV}}$$

$$\therefore \lambda \propto \frac{1}{\sqrt{mq}}$$

$$\therefore \frac{\lambda_p}{\lambda_\alpha} = \frac{\sqrt{m_\alpha q_\alpha}}{\sqrt{m_p q_p}}$$

As we know, $m_\alpha = 4\,m_p$, $q_\alpha = 2q_p$

⇒ The ratio of

$$\frac{\lambda_p}{\lambda_\alpha} = \frac{\sqrt{4m_p\times 2e}}{\sqrt{m_p\times e}} = \sqrt{8}:1$$

88 (a) The de-Broglie wavelength associated with an electron accelerated through a potential of V volts is given as

$$\lambda = \frac{12.27}{\sqrt{V}}\,\text{Å}$$

$$\therefore \frac{\lambda_1}{\lambda_2} = \sqrt{\frac{V_2}{V_1}}$$

or $\lambda_2 = \lambda_1 \sqrt{\frac{V_1}{V_2}}$

$\Rightarrow \lambda_2 = \lambda_1 \sqrt{\frac{25}{100}}$

$\Rightarrow \lambda_2 = \lambda_1 \sqrt{\frac{1}{4}} = \frac{\lambda_1}{2}$

89 (*d*) As, maximum kinetic energy,

$$K_{max} = E - \phi_0 \quad \text{...(i)}$$

metal *A*,

$$T_A = 4.25 - (\phi_0)_A \quad \text{...(ii)}$$

metal *B*,

$$T_B = 4.70 - (\phi_0)_B \quad \text{...(iii)}$$

It is given that,

$$T_B = T_A - 1.5$$

$$4.25 - (\phi_0)_A - 1.5 = 4.70 - (\phi_0)_B$$

$$(\phi_0)_B - (\phi_0)_A = 1.95 \text{ eV} \quad \text{... (iv)}$$

As, de-Broglie wavelength,

or $\lambda = \frac{h}{\sqrt{2mK}}$

$\Rightarrow \lambda \propto \frac{1}{\sqrt{K}}$

or $\frac{\lambda_B}{\lambda_A} = \sqrt{\frac{K_A}{K_B}} = \sqrt{\frac{T_A}{T_B}} = \sqrt{\frac{T_A}{T_A - 1.5}}$

Given, $\lambda_B = 2\lambda_A$

$\Rightarrow 2 = \sqrt{\frac{T_A}{T_A - 1.5}} \Rightarrow T_A = 2 \text{ eV}$

and $T_B = T_A - 1.5$

$= (2 - 1.5) \text{ eV} = 0.5 \text{ eV}$

$T_B = 0.5 \text{ eV}$

Also, from Eq. (i), we get

$2 = 4.25 - (\phi_0)_A$

$\Rightarrow (\phi_0)_A = 2.25 \text{ eV}$

Now, from Eq. (iv), we get

$(\phi_0)_B - 2.25 = 1.95$

$\Rightarrow (\phi_0)_B = 4.2 \text{ eV}$

90 (*b*) de-Broglie wavelength of the neutron,

$$\lambda = \frac{h}{p} = \frac{h}{\sqrt{2m(KE)}} = \frac{h}{\sqrt{2m \times \frac{3}{2}kT}}$$

$$= \frac{h}{\sqrt{3mkT}}$$

91 (*a*) Uncertainty in momentum,

$$\Delta p = \frac{\hbar}{\Delta x} = \frac{h}{2\pi \Delta x} \quad \left(\because \hbar = \frac{h}{2\pi}\right)$$

$$= \frac{6.63 \times 10^{-34}}{2 \times 3.14 \times 10^{-9}}$$

$$\approx 1.05 \times 10^{-25} \text{ kg ms}^{-1}$$

92 (*d*) $mv = RBq$

$mv = 0.83 \times 10^{-2} \times 0.25 \times 2 \times 1.6 \times 10^{-19}$

de-Broglie wavelength,

$$\lambda = \frac{h}{mv}$$

$$= \frac{6.6 \times 10^{-34}}{0.83 \times 10^{-2} \times 0.25 \times 2 \times 1.6 \times 10^{-19}}$$

$$\lambda = 1 \times 10^{-12} = 0.01 \text{ Å}$$

94 (c) According to the question,

$$v = v_0 \hat{\mathbf{i}}, E = -E_0 \hat{\mathbf{i}}$$

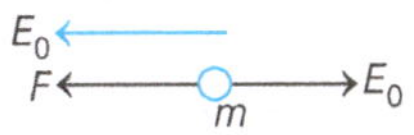

$|\mathbf{F}| = q|\mathbf{E}| \Rightarrow F = eE_0$

From Newton's second law of motion

$\therefore F = ma = eE_0$

$\Rightarrow a = \frac{eE_0}{m} \quad \text{...(i)}$

or $a = \frac{(-e)(-E_0\hat{\mathbf{i}})}{m} = \frac{eE_0\hat{\mathbf{i}}}{m}$

From first equation of motion,

$$v = u + at$$

Here, *u* (initial velocity) $= v_0$

$\Rightarrow v = v_0 + \frac{eE_0}{m}t \quad \text{...(ii)}$

[from Eq (i)]

Initial de-Broglie wavelength of the electron is given as

$$\lambda_0 = \frac{h}{mv_0}$$

$\Rightarrow h = \lambda_0 m v_0 \quad \text{...(iii)}$

After time *t*, de-Broglie wavelength is given as $\lambda = \frac{h}{mv}$

$$\lambda = \frac{h}{m\left(v_0 + \frac{eE_0}{m}t\right)}$$

$\therefore \lambda = \frac{\lambda_0}{\left[1 + \frac{eE_0}{mv_0}t\right]}$

95 (*c*) From $\lambda \propto \frac{1}{\sqrt{V}}$

$\Rightarrow \frac{\lambda_1}{\lambda_2} = \frac{\sqrt{V_2}}{\sqrt{V_1}} = \frac{\sqrt{100}}{\sqrt{25}} = 2$

$\Rightarrow \lambda_2 = \frac{\lambda_1}{2}$

96 (*c*) de-Broglie wavelength

$$\lambda = \frac{h}{\sqrt{2meV}}$$

$\Rightarrow \lambda \propto \frac{1}{\sqrt{mV}}$

$\frac{\lambda_2}{\lambda_1} = \sqrt{\frac{m_1 V_1}{m_2 V_2}}$

or $\frac{\lambda_2}{\lambda} = \sqrt{\frac{mV}{M(9V)}}$

$\Rightarrow \lambda_2 = \frac{\lambda}{3}\sqrt{\frac{m}{M}}$

97 (*b*) $\lambda = \frac{h}{\sqrt{2meV}}$

$$\lambda = \frac{6.6 \times 10^{-34}}{\sqrt{2 \times 1.67 \times 10^{-27} \times 1.6 \times 10^{-19}}}$$

$$\lambda \approx \frac{0.286}{\sqrt{V}} \text{ Å}$$

98 (*a*) The velocity of centre of mass is

$$\mathbf{v}_{CM} = \frac{mv_1\hat{\mathbf{i}} + mv_2\hat{\mathbf{j}}}{(m+m)}$$

$\Rightarrow \mathbf{v}_{CM} = \frac{1}{2}\sqrt{v_1^2 + v_2^2}$

$\Rightarrow \frac{h}{m\lambda_{CM}} = \frac{1}{2}\sqrt{\left(\frac{h}{m\lambda_1}\right)^2 + \left(\frac{h}{m\lambda_2}\right)^2}$

$\therefore \lambda_{CM} = \frac{2\lambda_1\lambda_2}{\sqrt{\lambda_1^2 + \lambda_2^2}}$

99 (*b*) Final kinetic energy of the particle is

$$K_2 = \frac{K_1}{4}$$

The de-Broglie wavelength of the particle is

$$\lambda = \frac{h}{\sqrt{2mK}}$$

$$\frac{\lambda_2}{\lambda_1} = \sqrt{\frac{K_1}{K_2}} = 2$$

$\therefore \lambda_2 = 2\lambda_1$

$\therefore$% increase in de-Broglie wavelength is

$$\left(\frac{\lambda_2-\lambda_1}{\lambda_1}\times 100\right)\%$$

$$=\left(\frac{2\lambda_1-\lambda_1}{\lambda_1}\times 100\right)\%$$

$$=100\%$$

100 (*d*) By conservation of momentum,

$$4m\times 0 = m\mathbf{v}_1 + 3m\mathbf{v}_2$$

$$\Rightarrow \quad \mathbf{v}_2 = -\frac{\mathbf{v}_1}{3}$$

$$\therefore \quad v_2 = \frac{v_1}{3}$$

$\therefore$The ratio of de-Broglie wavelength of particles 1 and 2 is

$$\frac{\lambda_1}{\lambda_2} = \frac{m_2v_2}{m_1v_1}$$

$$= 3\times\frac{1}{3} = 1$$

Assertion and Reason Quesitons

1 (*d*) Electrons in a metal can move freely within the material under a constant potential but require additional energy to exit the metal.

2 (*b*) Photoelectrons are not emitted unless the incident lights frequency is above a certain threshold, regardless of its intensity. In the photoelectric effect, it involves a collision with a single particle.

Intensity is represented as the product of the individual photons, energy ($h\nu$) and the total photon count (N). In wave theory, intensity is proportional not only to the frequency squared but also to the square of the amplitude.

In the quantum theory proposed by Einstein for the same frequency, increasing intensity only leads to a higher number of photons.

3 (*a*) According to the Einstein's principle of photoelectric effect, intensity of the radiation is proportional to the number of energy quanta per unit area per unit time. Thus, greater the number of the energy quanta available, greater is the number of electrons absorbing the energy quanta and therefore greater is the number of electrons coming out of the metal.

Hence, for $\nu > \nu_0$ photoelectric current is proportional to intensity.

4 (*b*) Work function is the minimum energy required to eject the photoelectron from photosensitive metal.

Hence for metal to have high photosensitivity, the work function should be small.

Mathematically, work function is given as $h\nu_0$, where ν_0 is the threshold frequency.

5 (*a*) A person approaching a doorway may intrupt a light beam which is incident on photocell.

This interuption will leads to abrupt change in the amount of photocurrent. Thus, this change in photocurrent helps to start a motor which is fitted in the doorway which opens the door.

6 (*b*) Photoelectric current is directly proportional to intensity of incident radiation as each photon ejects one electron constituting photocurrent.

8 (*a*) Light when interacted with matter behaves as, if it is made up of quanta or packet of energy, each packet of energy $h\nu$. Einstein later arrived at a important result that, the light quantum can also be associated with momentum $\left(\frac{h\nu}{c}\right)$.

Thus, a definite value of energy as well as momentum is a strong sign that the light quantum can be associated with a particle. This particle was later named photon.

9 (*d*) Wavelength associated with a particle is given as

$$\lambda = \frac{h}{p} = \frac{h}{mv}$$

$$\Rightarrow \quad \lambda \propto \frac{1}{m} \text{ or } \lambda \propto \frac{1}{v}$$

Thus, we can say that wavelength λ is smaller for heavier particles. As, macroscopic objects are heavier in nature so their wavelength is so small, that it is beyond any measurement.

This is the reason why macroscopic objects in our daily life do not show wave like properties.

10 (*b*) The work function of a metal, which is the minimum energy needed to release electrons from its surface, is equal to the minimum energy required to eject electrons. Consequently in accordance with Einstein's photoelectric equation, the kinetic energy of the emitted electrons can be expressed as $KE = h\nu - \phi_0$.

If $h\nu = \phi_0$, then $KE = 0$

Statement Based Questions

1 (*b*) Statement I is correct and statement II is incorrect and it can be corrected as,

In the experimental set-up used for studying the photoelectric effect, the intensity of light can be varied by changing the distance of the light source from the emitter.

As, intensity $\propto \frac{1}{(\text{distance})^2}$

2 (*c*) In Einstein's picture, the basic elementary process involved in photoelectric effect is the absorption of a light quantum of an electron. This process is instantaneous. Thus, whatever may be the intensity, i.e. the number of quanta of radiation per unit area per unit time, photoelectric emission is instantaneous.

Hence, low intensity does not mean delay in electron emission.

From photoelectric equation,

$$eV_0 = h\nu - \phi_0$$

or $V_0 = \left(\frac{h\nu}{e}\right) - \frac{\phi_0}{e}$

So, it predicts that V_0 *versus* ν curve is a straight line with slope $\left(\frac{h}{e}\right)$ and it is independent of the nature of the material.

3 (c) Statement I is incorrect but Statement II is correct. A particle behaves like a wave not become a wave.

4 (a) Both Statement I and Statement II are incorrect. Photoelectric saturation current is independent of frequency. It only depends on intensity of light.

6 (a) Photoelectric effect demonstrates the particle nature of light. The number of photoelectrons emitted is proportional to the intensity of incident light. Therefore, both Statement I and Statement II are incorrect.

7 (a) Einstein's photoelectric equation is $K_{max} = h\nu - \phi_0$

where, K_{max} = maximum KE of emitted electrons,

h = Planck's constant, ν = frequency of incident radiation and ϕ_0 = work function of metal.

Since, K_{max} must be non-negative. So, photoelectric emission is possible only, if

$$h\nu > \phi_0$$

or $\nu > \nu_0$,

where, $\nu_0 = \frac{\phi_0}{h}$

So, more tightly bound electrons will emerge with kinetic energies less than the maximum value.

∴ Kinetic energy of emitted photoelectrons lies between 0 to K.

8 (c) Whether a particle or wave description is best suited for understanding an experiment depends on the nature of the experiment.

e.g. In the familiar phenomenon of seeing an object by our eye, both the following given descriptions are important.

Firstly, the gathering and focussing mechanism of light by the eye lens is well described in the wave picture.

Secondly, its absorption by rods and cones (of the retina) requires the photon picture of light.

Matching Type Questions

2 (b) An electron absorbs a single photon of light and if the energy carried by photon is more than work function of the metal, the electron is emitted.

From source, total emitted power = P (total energy per second),

Energy carried by each photon = E

So, number of photons emitted by the source = P/E

Energy of a photon $E = h\nu$.

For the cut-off or threshold frequency, the energy $h\nu_0$ of the incident radiation must be equal to work function ϕ_0, so that $h\nu_0 = \phi_0$

$$\Rightarrow \quad h = \frac{\phi_0}{\nu_0}$$

Hence, A → 4, B → 2, C → 3 and D → 1.

Numerical Type Questions

1 (50.47)

$$\therefore \quad \lambda = \frac{h}{p} = \frac{h}{\sqrt{2mE}}$$

for maximum intensity,

$$2d\sin\theta = \lambda$$

$$2d\sin 60° = \frac{h}{\sqrt{2mE}}$$

$$2\times 10^{-10} \times \frac{\sqrt{3}}{2} = \frac{6.64\times 10^{-34}}{\sqrt{2\times 9.1\times 10^{-31}E}}$$

$= 50.47$ eV

2 (2) According to Einstein's photoelectric equation,

$$\frac{1}{2}mv^2 = h\nu - h\nu_0$$

Case I $\nu_1 = 2\nu_0$

i.e., $\frac{1}{2}mv_1^2 = h\nu_1 - h\nu_0$

$$= h\cdot 2\nu_0 - h\nu_0$$

$$= h\nu_0$$

$$\Rightarrow \frac{1}{2}mv_1^2 = h\nu_0 \quad \text{...(i)}$$

Case II $\nu_2 = 5\nu_0$

$$\frac{1}{2}mv_2^2 = h\nu_2 - h\nu_0$$

$$= 5h\nu_0 - h\nu_0$$

$$\frac{1}{2}mv_2^2 = 4h\nu_0 \quad \text{...(ii)}$$

Dividing Eq. (i) by Eq. (ii), we get

$$\frac{\frac{1}{2}mv_1^2}{\frac{1}{2}mv_2^2} = \frac{h\nu_0}{4h\nu_0}$$

$$\Rightarrow \quad v_2 = 2v_1$$

$$\therefore \quad x = 2$$

3 (1) Given, first incident energy, $E_1 = 2\phi_0$

Second incident energy, $E_2 = 10\,\phi_0$

$$\text{KE} = E_1 - \phi_0$$

$$\therefore \quad \frac{1}{2}mv_1^2 = 2\phi_0 - \phi_0 = \phi_0 \quad \text{...(i)}$$

and $\frac{1}{2}mv_2^2 = 10\,\phi_0 - \phi_0 = 9\phi_0$ ...(ii)

on dividing Eq. (i) by Eq. (ii), we get

$$\Rightarrow \quad \frac{v_1}{v_2} = \frac{1}{3} = \frac{x}{y}$$

$$x = 1$$

4 (188) Using Einstein photoelectric equation,

$$E - \phi = \frac{1}{2}mv^2$$

$$E_1 = \phi + \frac{1}{2}(2v)^2 \quad \text{...(i)}$$

$$E_2 = \phi + \frac{1}{2}(v)^2 \quad \text{...(ii)}$$

Dividing Eq. (i) by Eq. (ii), we get

$$\Rightarrow \quad \frac{E_1 - \phi}{E_2 - \phi} = 4$$

$$\frac{\frac{hc}{\lambda_1}-\phi}{\frac{hc}{\lambda_2}-\phi}=4$$

$$\phi=\left(\frac{hc}{3}\right)\left(\frac{4}{\lambda_2}-\frac{1}{\lambda_1}\right)$$

$$=\left(\frac{1240}{3}\right)\left[\frac{4\times 350-540}{350\times 540}\right]$$

$$=188\times 10^{-2}\text{ eV}$$

5 (15.2) de-Broglie wavelength associated with electron accelerated under a potential difference V is,

$$\lambda=\frac{12.27}{\sqrt{V}}\text{ Å}$$

$$=\frac{12.27}{\sqrt{225}}\text{ Å}=0.818\text{ Å}$$

Energy of photon,

$$E=\frac{hc}{\lambda}$$

$$=\frac{6.63\times 10^{-34}\times 3\times 10^{8}}{0.818\times 10^{-10}\times 1.6\times 10^{-19}}\text{ eV}$$

$$\approx 15.2\text{ keV}$$

6 (1.66) Einstein's equation for photoelectric effect

$$h\nu=\phi+eV_0$$

$$V_0=\frac{h\nu}{e}-\frac{\phi}{e}$$

From the given graph $V_0=0$ at

$$\nu=4\times 10^4\text{ Hz}$$

$$0=\frac{h\times 4\times 10^{14}}{1.6\times 10^{-19}}-\frac{\phi}{e}$$

$$\phi=4\times 10^{14}\times 6.6\times 10^{-34}\text{ J}$$

$$=1.66\text{ eV}$$

7 (0.547) Using Einstein's photoelectric equation,

$$K_m=\frac{hc}{\lambda}-\phi$$

$$K=\frac{1230}{750}-\phi \quad \text{...(i)}$$

and $$2K=\frac{1230}{450}-\phi \quad \text{...(ii)}$$

Using Eqs. (i) and (ii), we get

$$\Rightarrow \frac{2\times 1230}{750}-2\phi=\frac{1230}{450}-\phi$$

$$\Rightarrow \phi=\frac{2\times 1230}{750}-\frac{1230}{450}$$

$$=0.547\text{ eV}$$

8 (4.19) Number of photons incident on earth's surface per second per square metre is

$$n=\frac{I}{E}=\frac{I\lambda}{hc}$$

$$=\frac{1.388\times 10^{3}\times 600\times 10^{-9}}{6.63\times 10^{-34}\times 3\times 10^{8}}$$

$$=4.19\times 10^{21}$$

$$\Rightarrow x=4.19$$

9 (1.5) $n=\dfrac{\text{Power}}{hc/\lambda}$

$$=\frac{300\times 10^{-9}}{6.6\times 10^{-34}\times 3\times 10^{8}}$$

$$=1.5\times 10^{18}\text{ m}^{-2}\text{ s}^{-1}$$

$$=1.5\times 10^{14}\text{ cm}^{-2}\text{s}^{-1}$$

10 (0.3) We have KE $=\dfrac{p^2}{2m_e}=\dfrac{hc}{\lambda_{min}}$

$$p=\sqrt{\frac{2hcm_e}{\lambda_{min}}}$$

Also, $\lambda_{\text{de-Broglie}}=\dfrac{h}{p}=\sqrt{\dfrac{h\times\lambda_{min}}{2m_ec}}$

for $\lambda_{min}=10\text{ Å}$

$$\lambda_{\text{de-Broglie}}\cong 0.3\text{ Å}$$

NCERT Exemplar Questions

1 (*d*) From equation of motion,

$$v^2-u^2=2gH,$$

As, $u=0$

$\Rightarrow$ Velocity gained by particle,

$$v=\sqrt{2gH}$$

$$\therefore \lambda=\frac{h}{p}=\frac{h}{mv}=\frac{h}{m\sqrt{2gH}}$$

$$\Rightarrow \lambda\propto H^{-1/2}$$

2 (*b*) Given, $E=1$ MeV

Energy of a photon, $E=\dfrac{hc}{\lambda}$

$$\Rightarrow \lambda=\frac{6.63\times 10^{-34}\times 3\times 10^{8}\times 10^{9}\text{eV-nm}}{1.6\times 10^{-19}\times 1\text{ MeV}}$$

$$\simeq\frac{1240\text{ eV - nm}}{1\text{ MeV}}=1.2\times 10^{-3}\text{ nm}$$

4 (*b*) We know that, the relation between λ and K is given by

$$\lambda=\frac{h}{\sqrt{2mK}}$$

Thus, $\lambda\propto\dfrac{1}{\sqrt{m}}$

$$\therefore \lambda_p:\lambda_n:\lambda_e:\lambda_\alpha$$

$$\Rightarrow =\frac{1}{\sqrt{m_p}}:\frac{1}{\sqrt{m_n}}:\frac{1}{\sqrt{m_e}}:\frac{1}{\sqrt{m_\alpha}}$$

Since, $m_p=m_n$, hence $\lambda_p=\lambda_n$

As, $m_\alpha>m_p$,

therefore $\lambda_\alpha<\lambda_p$

As, $m_e<m_n$,

therefore $\lambda_e>\lambda_n$

Hence, $\lambda_\alpha<\lambda_p=\lambda_n<\lambda_e$

5 (*a*) Given, $\mathbf{v}=v_0\hat{\mathbf{i}}$ and $\mathbf{B}=B_0\hat{\mathbf{j}}$

Force on charged particle moving in external magnetic field $=q(\mathbf{v}\times\mathbf{B})$

or $\mathbf{F}=q(v_0\hat{\mathbf{i}}\times B_0\hat{\mathbf{j}})$

or $\mathbf{F}=qB_0v_0\hat{\mathbf{k}}$

$\because q$ is negative, force is in direction of $-\hat{\mathbf{k}}$ (into the plane of paper). For force perpendicular to velocity, the particle executes uniform circular motion. Since, magnitude of velocity v_0 is constant.

de-Broglie wavelength,

$$\lambda=\frac{h}{mv}=\frac{h}{mv_0}=\text{constant}$$

6 (*c*) Initial de-Broglie wavelength of electron,

$$\lambda_0=\frac{h}{mv_0}$$

Force on electron in electric field,

$$\mathbf{F}=-e\mathbf{E}=-eE_0\hat{\mathbf{j}}$$

Acceleration of electron,

$$\mathbf{a}=\frac{\mathbf{F}}{m}=-\frac{eE_0}{m}\hat{\mathbf{j}}$$

It is acting along negative Y-axis.

The initial velocity of electron along X-axis, $\mathbf{v}_{x0}=v_0\hat{\mathbf{i}}$, Initial velocity of electron along Y-axis,

$$\mathbf{v}_{y0}=0.$$

and velocity of electron after time t along X-axis,

$$\mathbf{v}_x=v_0\hat{\mathbf{i}}$$

(since, there is no acceleration of electron along X-axis)

Velocity of electron after time t along Y-axis,

$$\mathbf{v}_y = 0 + \left(-\frac{eE_0}{m}\hat{\mathbf{j}}\right)t = -\frac{eE_0}{m}t\,\hat{\mathbf{j}}$$

Magnitude of velocity of electron after time t,

$$|\mathbf{v}| = \sqrt{v_x^2 + v_y^2}$$

$$= \sqrt{v_0^2 + \left(\frac{-eE_0}{m}t\right)^2}$$

$$= v_0\sqrt{1 + \frac{e^2E_0^2t^2}{m^2v_0^2}}$$

de-Broglie wavelength,

$$\lambda = \frac{h}{mv} = \frac{h}{mv_0\sqrt{1 + \frac{e^2E_0^2t^2}{(m^2v_0{}^2)}}}$$

(here, $\lambda_0 = \frac{h}{mv_0}$)

$$= \frac{\lambda_0}{\left(1 + \frac{e^2E_0{}^2t^2}{m^2v_0^2}\right)^{1/2}}$$

Past Exams Questions

1 (*b*) Photon is quanta of energy. It is a massless and chargeless particle. The rest mass of photon is zero. In free space, it moves with velocity c and energy of photon is equal to $h\nu$. The momentum of the photon is given as $p = \frac{E}{c} = \frac{h\nu}{c}$.

2 (*d*) We know that $\lambda = \frac{h}{p} = \frac{h}{\sqrt{2mE}}$

Here, E = kinetic energy

Thus, $\lambda^2 = \frac{h^2}{2mE} \Rightarrow \frac{1}{\lambda^2} = \frac{2mE}{h^2}$

$$\frac{1}{\lambda_2} \propto E$$

Hence, option (d) is correct.

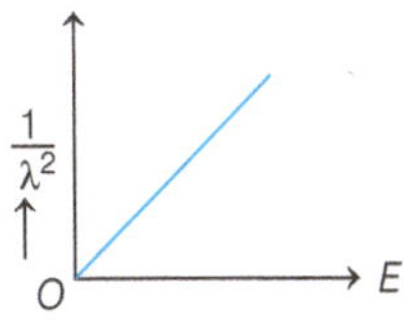

4 (*c*) Using Einstein's photoelectric equation,

$$eV' = h\nu' - h\nu_0$$

when $\nu' = \nu$

and $V' = V_s/2$, then

$$\therefore \quad \frac{eV_s}{2} = h\nu - h\nu_0 \quad \text{...(i)}$$

Again when $\nu' = \frac{\nu}{2}$ and $V' = V_s$ then

$$\therefore \quad eV_s = \frac{h\nu}{2} - h\nu_0 \quad \text{...(ii)}$$

Dividing Eq. (i) by Eq. (ii), we get

$$\frac{eV_s/2}{eV_s} = \frac{h\nu - h\nu_0}{\frac{h\nu}{2} - h\nu_0}$$

$$\Rightarrow \quad \nu_0 = \frac{3}{2}\nu$$

5 (*d*) Since, work function is negligible. Therefore, kinetic energy of emitted electron

= Energy of incident photon

i.e., $\frac{1}{2}mv^2 = h\nu$

$$\Rightarrow \quad \frac{p^2}{2m} = \frac{hc}{\lambda}$$

$$\Rightarrow \quad p = \sqrt{\frac{2mhc}{\lambda}}$$

de-Broglie wavelength of emitted electrons is

$$\lambda_d = \frac{h}{p} = \frac{h}{\sqrt{\frac{2mhc}{\lambda}}}$$

$$\Rightarrow \quad \lambda_d = \sqrt{\frac{h\lambda}{2mc}}$$

$$\Rightarrow \quad \lambda = \left(\frac{2mc}{h}\right)\lambda_d^2$$

6 (*c*) We know that, $P = \frac{nhc}{\lambda}$

$$3.3 \times 10^{-3} = \frac{n \times 6.6 \times 10^{-34} \times 3 \times 10^8}{600 \times 10^{-9}}$$

$$\Rightarrow \quad n = 10^{16}$$

7 (*d*) Kinetic energy of electron,

$$K = 144 \text{ eV}$$

$$\Rightarrow \quad eV = 144 \text{ eV}$$

$$\Rightarrow \quad V = 144 \text{ V}$$

$\therefore$ de-Broglie wavelength

$$\lambda = \frac{1.227}{\sqrt{V}}\text{Å} = \frac{1.227}{\sqrt{144}}\text{Å} = \frac{1.227}{12}\text{Å}$$

$$= 0.102\text{Å} = 1.02 \text{ nm}$$

$$= 102 \times 10^{-2} \text{ nm}$$

8 (*c*) Given, $\lambda = 1.227 \times 10^{-2}$ nm

$$= 1.227 \times 10^{-11} \text{ m}$$

Relation for de-Broglie wavelength for moving electron is

$$\lambda = \frac{12.27}{\sqrt{V}}\text{Å}$$

$$\Rightarrow \sqrt{V} = \frac{12.27}{\lambda} \times 10^{-10}\text{m}$$

$$= \frac{12.27 \times 10^{-10}}{1.227 \times 10^{-11}} = 10^2$$

$$\Rightarrow \quad V = 10^4 \text{ V}$$

9 (*c*) Initially, frequency of light,

$$\nu = 1.5\nu_0$$

But when the frequency of incident light is halved,

then $\nu' = \frac{\nu}{2} = 0.75\nu_0$

Thus, it becomes less than the threshold frequency. In that case, no photoelectric effect takes place. Hence, photoelectric current becomes zero.

Hence, correct option is (c).

10 (*d*) The work function of material is given by

$$\phi = h\nu$$

$$\phi = \frac{hc}{\lambda} \quad \text{...(i)}$$

$$\Rightarrow 4 \times 1.6 \times 10^{-19} = \frac{6.63 \times 10^{-34} \times 3 \times 10^8}{\lambda}$$

or $\lambda = \frac{6.63 \times 10^{-34} \times 3 \times 10^8}{4 \times 1.6 \times 10^{-19}}$

$$= 3.108 \times 10^{-7} \text{ m} = 310 \text{ nm}$$

11 (*a*) If electron is accelerated through a potential of V volt, then the wavelength associated with it is given by

$$\lambda = \frac{12.27}{\sqrt{V}}\text{Å} = \frac{12.27}{\sqrt{10000}} \times 10^{-10}$$

$$= 12.27 \times 10^{-12} \text{ m}$$

12 (*c*) According to the Einstein's photoelectric equation,

$$K_{max} = \frac{1}{2}mv_{max}^2 = h\nu - \phi_0$$

$$= h\nu - h\nu_0 \quad \text{...(i)}$$

When incident frequency of light, $\nu = 2\nu_0$

Substituting the value of ν in Eq. (i), we get

$$\frac{1}{2}mv_1^2 = h(2\nu_0) - h\nu_0 = h\nu_0 \quad \text{...(ii)}$$

If incident frequency of radiation, $\nu = 5\nu_0$

Substituting the value of ν in Eq. (i), we get

$$\frac{1}{2}mv_2^2 = h(5\nu_0) - h\nu_0 = 4h\nu_0 \quad \text{...(iii)}$$

On dividing Eq. (ii) by Eq (iii), we get

$$\frac{\frac{1}{2}mv_1^2}{\frac{1}{2}mv_2^2} = \frac{h\nu_0}{4h\nu_0}$$

$$\therefore \quad v_1 : v_2 = 1:2$$

13 (*d*) Given, $\lambda = 300$ nm

$\phi_0 = 2.13$ eV

According to Einstein's equation,

$$\frac{hc}{\lambda} - \phi_0 = K_{max}$$

$$\Rightarrow \frac{hc}{\lambda} - \phi_0 = eV_0$$

$$\Rightarrow \left(\frac{1240}{300} - 2.13\right)\text{eV} = eV_0$$

$$\Rightarrow V_0 = 2\text{ V}$$

14 (*d*) Statement I is correct but Statement II is incorrect. The correct form is,

We know from work function equation, $eV_0 = h\nu - \phi$

$$V_0 = \frac{h}{e}\nu - \frac{\phi}{e}$$

Now, material M_2 has higher work function, so it will have lower kinetic energy.

15 (*b*) de-Broglie wavelength is given by

$$\lambda = \frac{h}{p} = \frac{h}{\sqrt{2mK}}$$

Given, $\lambda_{proton} = \lambda_{electron}$

$$\Rightarrow \frac{h}{\sqrt{2m_pK_p}} = \frac{h}{\sqrt{2m_eK_e}}$$

$$\Rightarrow m_pK_p = m_eK_e$$

$$\Rightarrow \frac{K_p}{K_e} = \frac{m_e}{m_p} = \frac{1}{1836}$$

$$\therefore m_p \approx 1836 m_e$$

$$\Rightarrow \frac{K_p}{K_e} < 1 \text{ or } K_p < K_e$$

16 (*c*) In photoemission; Intensity $\propto$ photocurrent. Maximum KE of emitted electrons depends on frequency of incident light.

Photoemission is possible only when frequency is greater than threshold frequency.

So, statements A and C are correct.

17 (*d*) From Einstein's photoelectric equation,

we have, $eV_0 = h\nu - \phi$

$$\Rightarrow 0 = h\nu - \phi$$

$$\Rightarrow \phi = h\nu = 6.6 \times 10^{-34} \times 5 \times 10^{14}$$

$$= 2.07 \text{ eV}$$

18 (*b*) As we know that power,

$$P = \frac{E}{t} = n\frac{hc}{\lambda}$$

$$\Rightarrow \lambda = \frac{nhc}{P}$$

$$= \frac{10^{16} \times 6 \times 10^{-34} \times 3 \times 10^8}{15 \times 10^3}$$

$$= 1.2 \times 10^{-13} = 0.0012 \text{ Å}$$

This wavelength corresponds to gamma rays.

19 (*b*) The energy of each photon,

$$E_1 = \frac{hc}{\lambda} = \frac{6.63 \times 10^{-34} \times 3 \times 10^8}{9 \times 10^{-7}}$$

$$= 2.21 \times 10^{-19} \text{ J}$$

We know that, intensity of light wave,

$$I = \frac{P}{A}$$

$$\Rightarrow P = IA$$

$$= 100 \times 10^{-4} = 10^{-2} \text{ W}$$

$$= 10^{-2} \text{ J/s}$$

$\therefore$ Total energy of light beam in one second, $E = P \times t$

$$= 10^{-2} \times 1 = 10^{-2} \text{ J}$$

Number of photons

$$= \frac{\text{Total energy } (E)}{\text{Energy of one photon } (E_1)}$$

$$= \frac{10^{-2}}{2.21 \times 10^{-19}} = 4.5 \times 10^{16}$$

20 (*b*) $\lambda_1 = 670.5$ nm, $V_1 = 0.48$ V

$\lambda_2 = 474.6$ nm

By using Einstein photoelectric equation, $eV_1 = \frac{hc}{\lambda_1} - \phi_0$

$\therefore \phi_0$ is work function

$$eV_1 = \frac{hc}{\lambda_1} - eV_1 \quad \text{... (i)}$$

and similarly, $eV_2 = \frac{hc}{\lambda_2} - \phi_0$

$$\Rightarrow \phi_0 = \frac{hc}{\lambda_2} - eV_2 \quad \text{...(ii)}$$

From Eqs. (i) and (ii), we get

$$\therefore \frac{hc}{\lambda_1} - eV_1 = \frac{hc}{\lambda_2} - eV_2$$

$$\Rightarrow V_2 = V_1 + \frac{hc}{e}\left(\frac{1}{\lambda_2} - \frac{1}{\lambda_1}\right)$$

$$= 0.48 + \frac{6.63 \times 10^{-34} \times 3 \times 10^8}{1.6 \times 10^{-19}}\left(\frac{1}{474.6} - \frac{1}{670.5}\right)$$

$$= 1.25 \text{ V}$$

Skill Boosters

1 (*b*) When lens is moved away, initially it is focused over cathode forming an intense spot of less area.

So, intensity over a smaller area increases. This results in lowering of emission rate as area over which light is focused is reduced.

2 (*a*) Concave lens forms image of source S at S'.

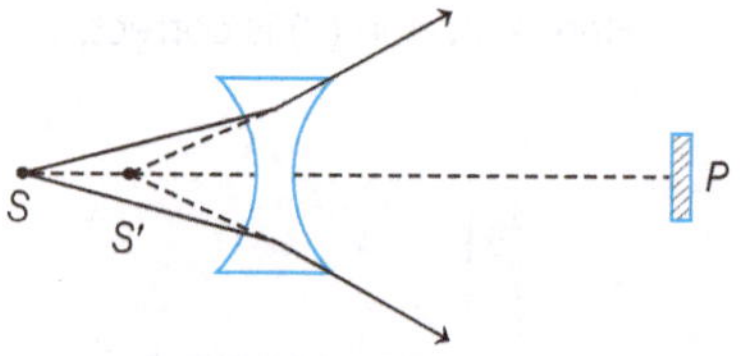

So, S' now acts like a source and as its distance is less, photoemission rate increases.

With a convex lens in place of aperture, it delivers all photons reaching upto the lens to metal surface.

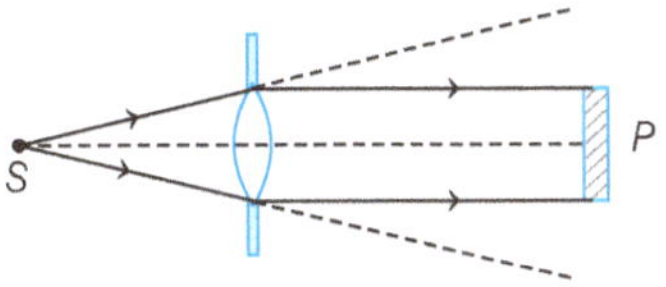

$\therefore$ Photoemission rate increases.

When a glass slab is placed in place of aperture. It absorbs a part of light and delivered remaining part reducing photoemission rate.

When a prism is placed in place of aperture, it may deviates light beam (monochromatic).

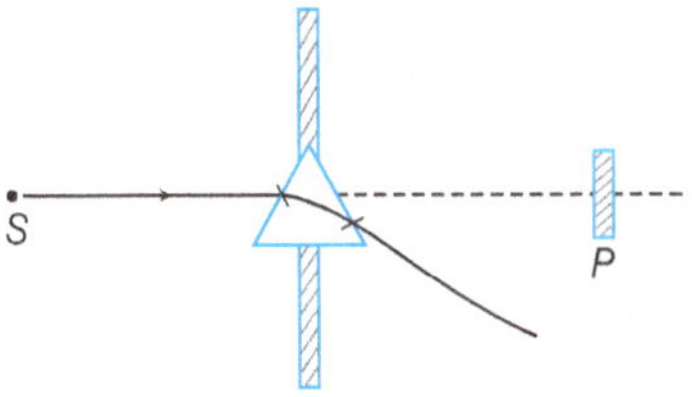

Upto such an extent that light does not reach P. So, option (a) is correct.

3 (*d*) Only 4% of energy is absorbed and only 3% of this can cause photoemission, part of intensity available for photoemission is

$I' = 0.03 \times 0.04 I_0 = 1.2\ \text{nWcm}^{-2}$

$\therefore$ Number of electrons/second

$$= \frac{1.2 \times 10^{-9}\ \text{W}}{hf} = 1.5 \times 10^{9}\ \text{electrons}$$

per second.

4 (*d*) Net force on electron at any instant,

$$= q(\mathbf{E} + \mathbf{v} \times \mathbf{B})$$
$$= q(-E_0\hat{\mathbf{i}} + v_0\hat{\mathbf{i}} \times B_0\hat{\mathbf{j}})$$
$$= q(-E_0\hat{\mathbf{i}} + v_0B_0\hat{\mathbf{k}})$$

Acceleration of electron,

$$a = \frac{F}{m} = \frac{q}{m}(-E_0\hat{\mathbf{i}} + v_0B_0\hat{\mathbf{k}})$$

Velocity after t seconds $= u + at$

$$= 0 + \frac{q}{m}(-E_0\hat{\mathbf{i}} + v_0B_0\hat{\mathbf{k}}) \cdot t$$

So, momentum of electron after t seconds is

$$\mathbf{p} = m\mathbf{v} = q(-E_0\hat{\mathbf{i}} + v_0B_0\hat{\mathbf{k}})t$$

or $|\mathbf{p}| = \sqrt{E_0^2q^2t^2 + v_0^2B_0^2q^2t^2}$

or $\mathbf{p} = qt\sqrt{E_0^2 + (v_0B_0)^2}$

Thus, λ = Wavelength associated with moving electron

$$= \frac{h}{p} = \frac{h}{qt(\sqrt{E_0^2 + (v_0B_0)^2})}$$

5 (*c*) $2\pi r_1 n = \lambda$

$$\Rightarrow \quad n = \frac{\lambda}{2\pi r_1}$$

$$\Rightarrow \quad n = \frac{10^{-9}}{2 \times 3.14 \times 5.13 \times 10^{-11}}$$

$$\Rightarrow n = 3$$

6 (*c*) Let there is one free electron per atom in metal

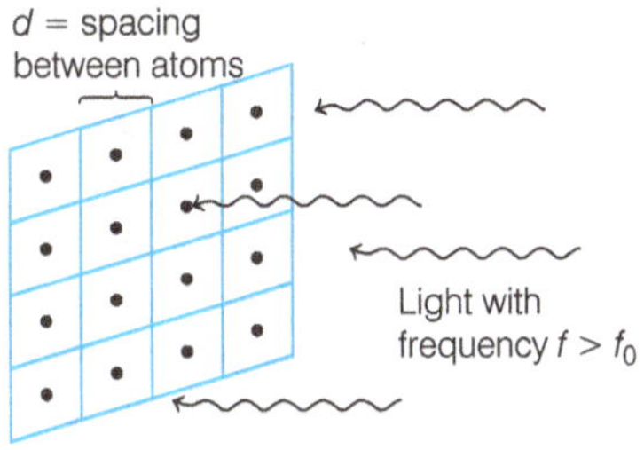

Total amount of energy falling, over each atom per unit time

$$= \frac{dE}{dt} = Id^2 \begin{pmatrix} d^2 = \text{Area} \\ I = \text{Intensity} \end{pmatrix}$$

Energy absorbed in time, $t = Id^2t$

As volume of a cube of side d is d^3 and we assume that there is one atom in d^3 volume.

So, number of atoms per unit volume is

$$N = \frac{1}{d^3}$$

But $\quad N = \frac{\rho}{A}$

So, $\quad d = \left(\frac{A}{\rho}\right)^{1/3}$

For photoemission, absorbed energy = Work function

$\therefore \quad Id^2t = \phi_0$

or $\quad t = \dfrac{\phi_0}{Id^2}$

$$\Rightarrow \quad t = \text{time lag} = \frac{\phi_0}{I}\left(\frac{\rho}{A}\right)^{2/3}$$

7 (*c*) The graph between V_0 and ν cut the Y-axis at V_0.

where, V_0 represents the stopping potential.

For the given graphs,

$$(V_0)_{(iv)} > (V_0)_{(iii)} > (V_0)_{(ii)} > (V_0)_{(i)}$$

$$\therefore (W_0)_{(iv)} > (W_0)_{(iii)} > (W_0)_{(ii)} > (W_0)_{(i)}$$

10 (*d*) From photoelectric equation,

$$h\nu - W_0 = \frac{1}{2}mv_{max}^2$$

$$\Rightarrow \quad \frac{hc}{\lambda} - \frac{hc}{\lambda_0} = \frac{1}{2}mv_{max}^2$$

$$\Rightarrow hc\left(\frac{\lambda_0 - \lambda}{\lambda\lambda_0}\right) = \frac{1}{2}mv_{max}^2$$

$$\Rightarrow \quad v_{max} = \sqrt{\frac{2hc}{m}\left(\frac{\lambda_0 - \lambda}{\lambda\lambda_0}\right)}$$

When wavelength is λ and velocity is v, then

$$v = \sqrt{\frac{2hc}{m}\left(\frac{\lambda_0 - \lambda}{\lambda\lambda_0}\right)} \quad \text{...(i)}$$

When wavelength is $\dfrac{3\lambda}{4}$ and velocity is v, then

$$v' = \sqrt{\frac{2hc}{m}\left[\frac{\lambda_0 - (3\lambda/4)}{(3\lambda/4) \times \lambda_0}\right]} \quad \text{...(ii)}$$

Dividing Eq. (ii) by Eq. (i), we get

$$\frac{v'}{v} = \sqrt{\frac{[\lambda_0 - (3\lambda/4)]}{\frac{3}{4}\lambda\lambda_0} \times \frac{\lambda\lambda_0}{\lambda_0 - \lambda}}$$

$$v' = v\left(\frac{4}{3}\right)^{1/2}\sqrt{\frac{[\lambda_0 - (3\lambda/4)}{\lambda_0 - \lambda}}$$

i.e. $v' > v\left(\dfrac{4}{3}\right)^{1/2}$

12

Scan for **Physics Through Concept Master** Videos

Atoms

Topicwise No. of Ques asked in 5 Years (NEET)

Topics	No. of Questions				
	2024	2023	2022	2021	2020
α-Particle Scattering and Rutherford's Nuclear Model of Atom	1	–	–	–	–
Bohr Model of the Hydrogen Atom	–	1	1	–	2
The Line spectra of the Hydrogen Atom	1	2	–	–	–

Special Type of Ques Asked In 5 Years (NEET)

Types	Years				
	2024	2023	2022	2021	2020
A-R	–	–	–	–	–
Statement Based	1	–	–	–	–
Matching Type	1	–	–	–	–

Last 5 Years Weigtage (NEET)

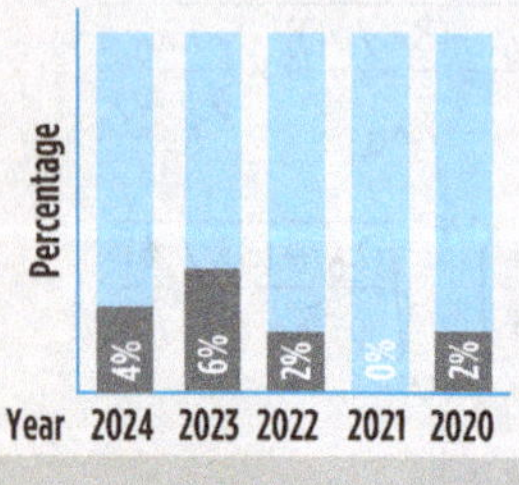

- The **first model of atom** was proposed by **JJ Thomson in 1898**. According to this model, the positive charge of the atom is uniformly distributed throughout the volume of the atom and the negatively charged electrons are embedded in it like seeds in a watermelon.
- This model was called **plum pudding model** of atom. However, further studies on atoms, shows that the distribution of electrons and protons are very different from that proposed in this model.
- Atoms of condensed matter (solids and liquids) and dense gases at all temperatures emit electromagnetic radiation in which a continuous distribution of several wavelengths is present.
- **In the early nineteenth century**, it was established that each element is associated with a characteristic spectrum of radiation.

  It suggested a relation between structure of atom and spectrum of radiation emitted it.
- To investigate the atomic structure, Rutherford proposed an experiment of α-particle scattering by atom in 1906. This experiment was performed by **Hans Geiger and Ernest Marsden** in 1911. The results of this experiment led to the birth of Rutherford's planetary model, which is also called the **nuclear model of the atom**.
- Rutherford's planetary model explains the atomic structure very well. However, it could not explain the discrete levels of hydrogen spectrum.

α-Particle Scattering and Rutherford's Nuclear Model of Atom

- In Geiger-Marsden experiment, a beam of 5.5 MeV α-particle emitted from ${}^{214}_{83}Bi$ radioactive source was directed at a gold foil of thickness 2.1×10^{-7} m as shown in figure.

  The scattered α-particles were observed through a rotatable detector with zinc sulphide screen.

- The entire apparatus is placed in a vacuum chamber.

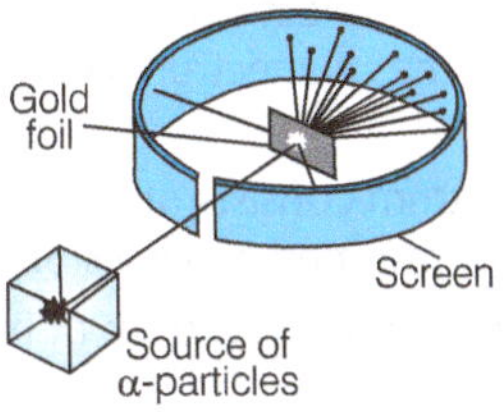

The scattered α-particles produced scintillations by striking on the screen. The distribution of these scintillations may be studied as a function of angle of scattering.

- The schematic arrangement of Rutherford's α-particle scattering experiment (also called **Geiger-Marsden experiment)** is shown below.

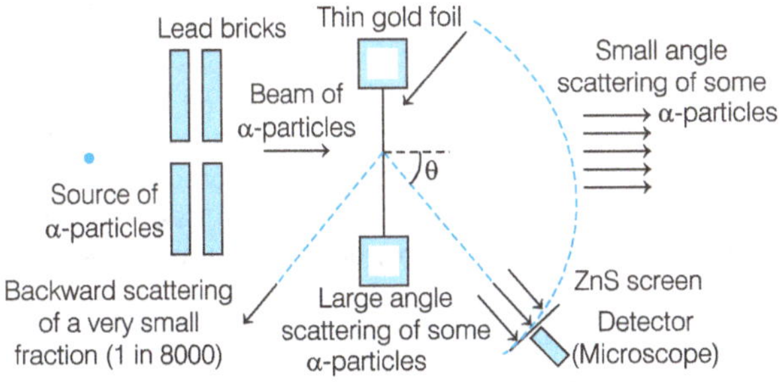

- **Observations of this experiment** are as follows
  (i) Many of the α-particles pass through the foil without deflection. It means, most of the space in an atom is empty.
  (ii) Only about 0.14% of the incident α-particles scattered by more than 1°.
  (iii) Only about one α-particle in every 8000 α-particles are deflected by more than 90°. This shows that entire positive charge and most of the mass m are concentrated at atom's core called **nucleus**.
  (iv) The number of α-particles scattered per unit area $N(\theta)$ at scattering angle θ varies inversely as $\sin^4 \frac{\theta}{2}$.

$$N(\theta) \propto \frac{1}{\sin^4\left(\frac{\theta}{2}\right)}$$

Experimental data points on scattering of α-particles by a thin foil at different angles obtained by Geiger and Marsden is shown in figure.

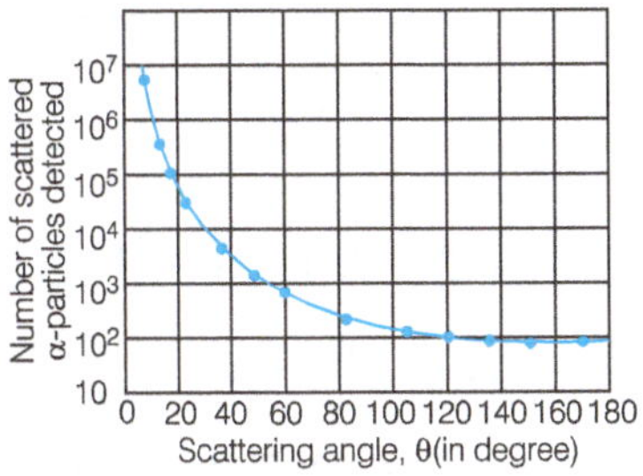

- The trajectory of the α-particle can be computed by employing Newton's second law of motion and the Coulomb's law for electrostatic force of repulsion between the α-particle and the positively charged nucleus. The magnitude of this force is

$$F = \frac{1}{4\pi\varepsilon_0} \frac{(2e)(Ze)}{r^2}$$

where, r is the distance between the α-particle and the nucleus.

- The magnitude and direction of the force on an α-particle continuously changes as it approaches nucleus and recedes away from it.
- **Trajectory of the α-particles** in the Coulomb field of a target nucleus is as shown in the figure below.

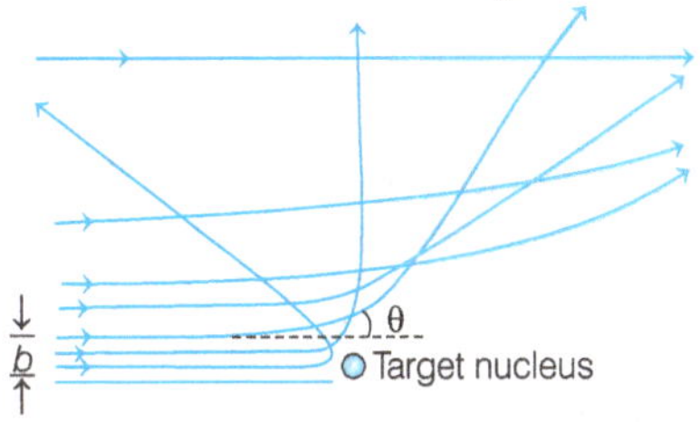

- **Impact parameter** (b) is the perpendicular distance of the initial velocity vector of the α-particle from the centre of the nucleus.

Marks Maximiser

- The trajectory of α-particle depends on the impact parameter.
  Rutherford had calculated the impact parameter
  as $b = \dfrac{Ze^2 \cot\frac{\theta}{2}}{4\pi\varepsilon_0 E_K}$
  where, E_K is kinetic energy of incident α-particle.
  (i) For head-on collision, impact parameter is zero and α-particle rebounds back i.e., if $b = 0$, then $\theta = 180°$.
  (ii) For large impact parameter, α-particle goes nearly undeviated i.e., if $b = \infty$, then $\theta = 0°$.

- The minimum distance from the nucleus upto which the α-particle approaches is called the **distance of closest approach** (r_0).
  At this distance, whole of the kinetic energy of α-particles converts into electrostatic potential energy.
  It is given as, $r_0 = \dfrac{2Ze^2}{4\pi\varepsilon_0 E_K}$

Postulates of Rutherford's Atomic Model

- Based on these observations, Rutherford proposed a nuclear model of atom, also called **planetary model**, in which entire positive charge and most of the mass of atom are concentrated in a small volume called the **nucleus.**

- Rutherford's experiment suggested that the size of nucleus to be about 10^{-15} m to 10^{-14} m. From kinetic theory, the size of an atom is known to be 10^{-10} m. Thus, most of an atom is empty space.
- Electrons are revolving in a large empty space around a nucleus. A centripetal force is provided by the electrostatic force of attraction between electron and nucleus.
- The atom is neutral overall, so the total positive charge on nucleus is equal to the total negative charge on electrons.

For Concept Master Video

Drawbacks of Rutherford's Atomic Model

(i) According to classical electromagnetic theory, the electrons must radiate energy in the form of electromagnetic wave. Due to this continuous loss of energy of the electrons, the radii of their orbits should be continuously decreasing, and ultimately, the electron should fall into the nucleus.

(iii) As the electrons follow a spiral path, their angular velocities and frequencies changes continuously, and so the frequency of emitted light will also change. They would emit a continuous spectrum instead of the actually observed line spectrum.

Electron Orbits

- For a dynamically stable orbit in a hydrogen atom, electrostatic force of attraction F_e between the revolving electrons and the nucleus provides the requisite centripetal force F_c. Thus, $F_e = F_c \Rightarrow \dfrac{e^2}{4\pi\varepsilon_0 r^2} = \dfrac{mv^2}{r}$
- The **relation between the orbit radius and the electron velocity** is $r = \dfrac{e^2}{4\pi\varepsilon_0\, mv^2}$.
- The **kinetic energy *K* and electrostatic potential energy *U* of the electron in hydrogen atom** are

$$K = \frac{e^2}{8\pi\varepsilon_0 r} \quad \text{and} \quad U = \frac{-e^2}{4\pi\varepsilon_0 r}$$ NEET 2019

- **The total energy *E* of the electron in a hydrogen atom** is

$$E = \frac{-e^2}{8\pi\varepsilon_0 r}$$

Negative sign implies the fact that electron is bound to the nucleus.

- If *E* were positive, an electron will not follow a closed orbit around the nucleus.

Atomic Spectra

- Each element has a characteristic spectrum of radiation, which it emits.
- When an atomic gas or vapour is excited at low pressure, usually by passing an electric current through it, the emitted radiation has a spectrum containing specific wavelengths only.

This type of spectrum consists of bright lines on a dark background and is termed as **emission line spectrum.**

- The emission lines in the spectrum of hydrogen are shown below.

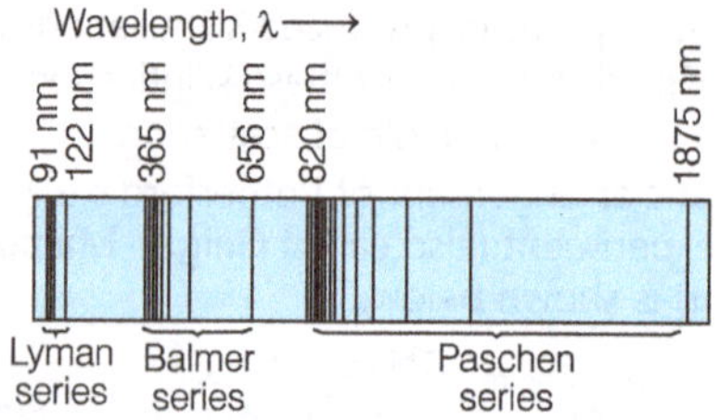

- When white light passes through a gas, we found that the transmitted light consists of some dark lines in the spectrum. These dark lines correspond precisely to those wavelengths which were found in the emission spectrum of gas. This is called the **absorption spectrum of the gas.**

Marks Maximiser

Spectral Series

- The radiation emitted by the excited hydrogen atom consists of certain specific wavelengths or frequencies, whose value depends on quantum numbers n_1 and n_2. The relation is called **Rydberg formula,** given by

$$\bar{v} = \frac{1}{\lambda} = R\left(\frac{1}{n_1^2} - \frac{1}{n_2^2}\right)$$ NEET 2023

Series Name	Spectral formula	No. of last orbit	Region
Lyman series	$\frac{1}{\lambda} = R\left(\frac{1}{(1)^2} - \frac{1}{(n)^2}\right)$	$n = 2, 3, 4 \ldots$	Ultraviolet
Balmer series	$\frac{1}{\lambda} = R\left(\frac{1}{(2)^2} - \frac{1}{(n)^2}\right)$	$n = 3, 4, 5 \ldots$	Visible
Paschen series	$\frac{1}{\lambda} = R\left(\frac{1}{(3)^2} - \frac{1}{(n)^2}\right)$	$n = 4, 5, 6 \ldots$	Near Infrared
Brackett series	$\frac{1}{\lambda} = R\left(\frac{1}{(4)^2} - \frac{1}{(n)^2}\right)$	$n = 5, 6, 7 \ldots$	Infrared
Pfund series	$\frac{1}{\lambda} = R\left(\frac{1}{(5)^2} - \frac{1}{(n)^2}\right)$	$n = 6, 7, 8 \ldots$	Far Infrared

Bohr Model of the Hydrogen Atom

- Bohr combined classical and early quantum concepts and gave his theory in form of three postulates.

These three postulates are as given below.

(i) An electron in an atom could revolve in certain stable orbits (known as stationary orbits) without the emission of radiant energy. Thus, each atom has definite states and each possible state has definite total energy.

(ii) The electron revolves around the nucleus only in those orbits for which the angular momentum is some integral multiple of $\frac{h}{2\pi}$, where h is called the Planck's constant (6.6×10^{-34} J-s).

Thus, the angular momentum L of the orbiting electron is quantised, i.e.,

$$L = \frac{nh}{2\pi}$$

(iii) An electron might make a transition from higher unstable orbit to lower stable orbit. When it does so, a photon is emitted having energy equal to the energy difference between the initial and final states. The frequency of the emitted photon is given by

$$\nu = \frac{E_i - E_f}{h}$$

where, E_i and E_f are the energies of the initial and final states and $E_i > E_f$.

- The **orbital radius** of an electron in nth orbit is

$$r_n = \left(\frac{n^2}{m}\right)\left(\frac{h}{2\pi}\right)^2 \frac{4\pi\varepsilon_0}{e^2} \Rightarrow r_n \propto n^2$$

Bohr's radius ($n = 1$) is given as

$$r_1 = a_0 = \frac{h^2\varepsilon_0}{\pi me^2} = 5.29 \times 10^{-11} \text{m}$$

- **Total energy of electron** in the stationary states of hydrogen atom is given as

$$E_n = \frac{-me^4}{8n^2\varepsilon_0^2h^2}$$

$$= \frac{-2.18 \times 10^{-18}}{n^2} \text{J}$$ NEET 2023, 19

$$= \frac{-13.6}{n^2} \text{eV}$$ NEET 2022, 20

Here, negative sign means that this much energy will be required to remove the electron from hydrogen atom.

Marks Maximiser

- The **orbital velocity** of an electron in nth orbit is

$$v_n = \frac{1}{n}\frac{e^2}{4\pi\varepsilon_0}\frac{1}{\left(\frac{h}{2\pi}\right)} \Rightarrow v_n \propto \frac{1}{n}$$

Velocity of electron in first orbit ($n = 1$) of H-atom is

$$v_1 = \frac{e^2}{2h\varepsilon_0} = \frac{c}{137}$$

Energy Levels

- The energy of an atom is the least (largest negative value) when its electron is revolving in an orbit closest to the nucleus.
- The lowest state of the atom is called **ground state**. At room temperature, most of the hydrogen atoms are in ground state.
- The minimum energy required to free the electron from the ground state of the hydrogen atom is 13.6 eV and is called the **ionisation energy of the hydrogen atom**.
- The highest energy state corresponds to $n = \infty$ and has an energy of 0 eV. This is the energy of the atom when the electron is completely removed from the nucleus and is at rest.
- The energy required to excite an electron from the lower energy state n_i to higher energy state n_f ($n_i < n_f$) is,

$$\Delta E = E_{n_f} - E_{n_i}$$

- Electron can jump back from excited states to initial state by emitting a photon.
- As the excitation of hydrogen atom increases (i.e., value of n increases) the value of minimum energy required to make electron free from the excited atom decreases.
- The energy level diagram for stationary states of hydrogen atom is given in figure below.

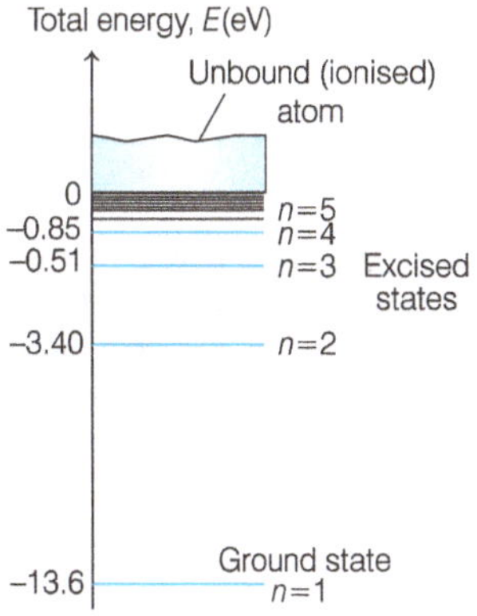

The Line Spectra of the Hydrogen Atom

- When an atom makes a transition from the higher energy state with quantum number n_i to the lower energy state with quantum n_f ($n_f < n_i$) in hydrogen like atom, the difference of energy is carried away by a photon of frequency ν_{if} such that

$$h\nu_{if} = E_{n_i} - E_{n_f}$$

- The various lines in the atomic spectra are produced when electrons jump from higher energy state to a lower energy state and photons are emitted. These spectral lines are called **emission lines**.

Number of transition possible for an electron in nth orbit is $n(n-1)/2$.

For Concept Master Video

- When an atom absorbs a photon that has same energy needed by the electron in a lower energy state to make transitions to a higher energy state, the process is called **absorption**.

de-Broglie's Explanation of Bohr's Second Postulate of Quantisation

- According to Bohr's second postulate, the angular momentum of the electron orbiting around the nucleus is quantised.
- It was explained by de-Broglie on the basis of his hypothesis that all material particles, such as electrons in its circular orbit must be seen as a particle wave. Similar to waves travelling in a string, particle waves too can lead to standing waves under resonant condition.

For an electron moving in nth orbit of radius r_n, as shown in figure.

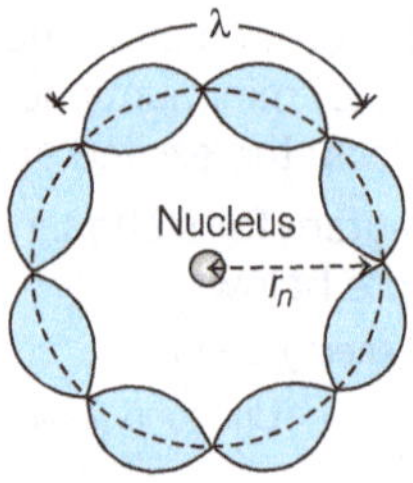

$$2\pi r_n = n\lambda, \; n = 1, 2, 3, \ldots \qquad \left[\because \lambda = \frac{h}{mv_n}\right]$$

or $$mv_n r_n = \frac{nh}{2\pi}$$

This is quantum condition proposed by Bohr.

Thus, de-Broglie hypothesis explained Bohr's second postulate for the quantisation of angular momentum of the orbiting electron.

- The quantised electron orbit and energy states are due to the wave nature of the electron and only resonant standing waves can persist.
- **Limitations of Bohr's model** are given below.
  (i) Bohr model is applicable to hydrogenic atoms only. It cannot be extended even to two electron atoms such as helium.
  (ii) Bohr's model is unable to explain the relative intensities of the frequencies in the spectrum.
  (iii) Bohr's theory does not explain the further splitting of spectral lines in a magnetic field (zeeman effect) or in electric field (stark effect).
  (iv) It does not explain the distribution of electrons in different orbits.
  (v) It is unable to explain the cause of weak and strong intensities in visible frequencies of hydrogen emission spectrum.

Caution Points

- Thomson and Rutherford models are unstable because of electrostatic instability and the electron's electromagnetic radiation, respectively.
- Bohr choose to quantise angular momentum because dimension of h is same as dimension of angular momentum, which is relevant for a circular orbit.
- Unlike in the solar system, electron-electron forces in atoms are significant, making Bohr model unsuitable for multi-electron atoms.
- In Bohr model, electron orbit frequency doesn't match with spectral line frequency. For large quantum number transitions, they coincide.

PYQ Notes

1. When a metal target is bombarded with high energy electrons, then X-rays are emitted. [JEE Main 2023]
2. Orbital angular momentum of revolving electron,
$$\mu_L = \frac{-ev_n r_n}{2} = \frac{-eL}{2m}$$ [JEE Main 2022]
3. Time period of revolution of an electron in its nth orbit of H-atom, $$T_n = \frac{2\pi r_n}{v_n} = n^3 T_1$$
where, T_1 is time period in ground state. [NEET 2017]

Step by Step

Mastering NCERT

- Concept Builders
- Topical Questions
- Assertion and Reason Questions
- Statement Based
- Matching Type
- Numerical Type
- NCERT Exemplar
- Past Exams MCQs
- Skill Boosters

Concept Builders

1 Which model of the atom assumes nearly a continuous distribution of mass in it ?

2 Rutherford model is unstable because of orbiting electrons. [T/F]

3 The size of the nucleus can be estimated by the scattering of which particles ?

4 About one α-particle in every 8000 α-particles deviate by more than 90°. [T/F]

5 For a projectile of given energy, the scattering angle .... (increases / decreases) with the increase in impact parameter.

6 The kinetic energy of an electron in Bohr's atomic model increases with the increase in orbital radius. [T/F]

7 The potential energy of an electron in a stationary Bohr orbit increases with the increase in orbital radius. [T/F]

8 Rutherford's atomic model cannot explain the stability of an atom. [T/F]

9 Bohr's model is applicable only to hydrogenic atoms (single electron). [T/F]

10 According to Bohr's atomic model, the radii of the stationary orbits are inversely proportional to the square of the quantum number n. [T/F]

11 In the first orbit of hydrogen atom, the frequency of revolution of electron is 6.57×10^5 rps. [T/F]

12 The dimensions of Planck's constant are same as that of .... (angular momentum/linear momentum).

13 The value of Rydberg constant is ....
($1.09 \times 10^7 \text{ m}^{-1}$ / $2.5 \times 10^6 \text{ m}^{-1}$).

14 The energy required to excite an electron in H-atom to its first excited state is .... (– 13.6 eV/10.2 eV).

15 What is the maximum number of spectral lines emitted by a H-atom when it is in the fourth excited states?

16 What is the potential energy of an electron when it is far away from the nucleus ?

17 The ratio of the energies of the hydrogen atom in its first to second excited state is .... (9 : 4 / 3 : 5).

18 Which spectral series of hydrogen lies in the UV-region?

19 .... (Paschen / Balmer) series of the hydrogen spectrum lies in the visible part of the electromagnetic spectrum.

20 The shortest and longest wavelengths in the Balmer series have wavelength 911 Å and 1215 Å. [T/F]

Topical Questions

α-Particle Scattering and Rutherford's Nuclear Model of Atom

1 In Geiger-Marsden experiment, detection of scattered α-particles at a particular angle is done by NCERT Pg. 292

(a) counting flashes produced by α-particles on a ZnS coated screen
(b) counting spots produced on a photographic film
(c) using a galvanometer detector
(d) using a Geiger-counter

2 Choose the incorrect statement regarding the observations of Geiger-Marsden experiment. NCERT Pg. 292

(a) Many of α-particles pass straight through the gold foil.
(b) Only about 2% of α-particles scatter by more than 1°.
(c) About 1 in 8000 of α-particles is deflected more than 90°.
(d) Very few α- particles are reflected back.

3 Graph of total number of α-particles scattered at different angles is NCERT Pg. 293

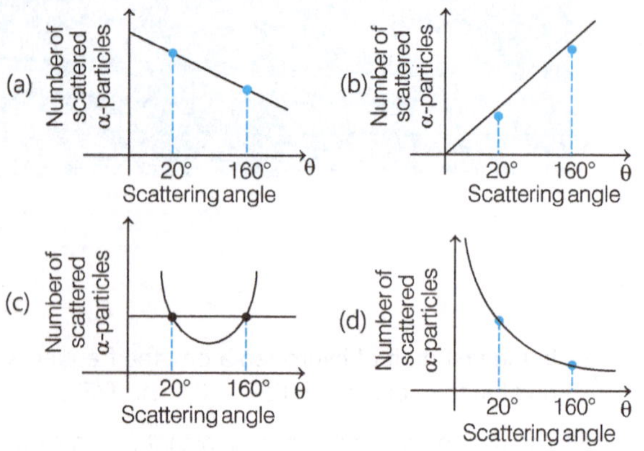

4 Trajectory of an α-particle is shown in the figure below, then impact parameter is NCERT Pg. 294

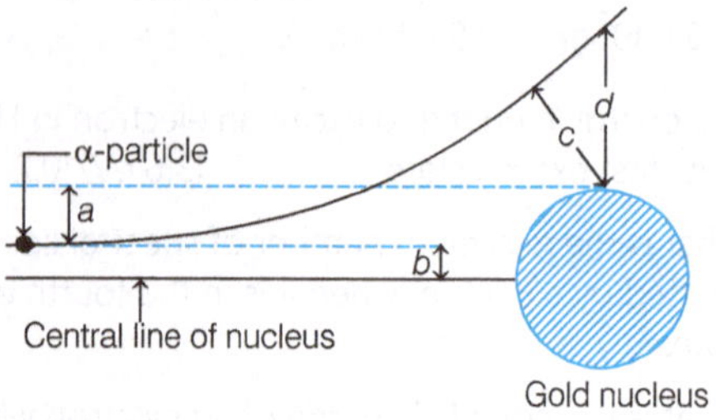

(a) a (b) b
(c) c (d) d

5 A given beam of α-particles has a distribution of impact parameter b, so that the beam is scattered in various direction as shown below. NCERT Pg. 294

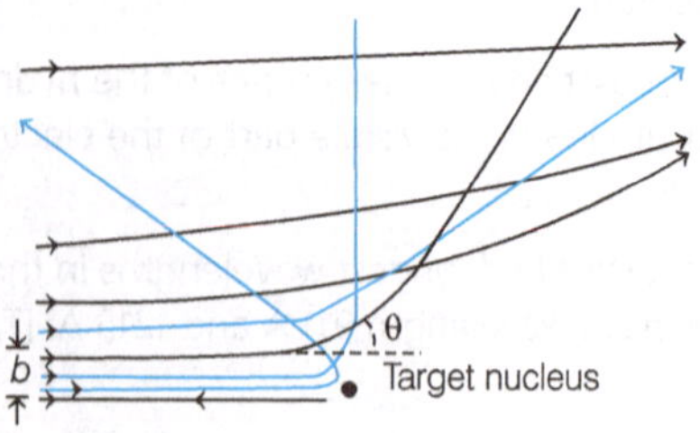

Then,
(a) b = minimum and $\theta \cong 0$
(b) b = maximum and $\theta \cong \pi$
(c) b = minimum and $\theta \cong \pi$
(d) b = maximum and θ at all values

6 In a Geiger-Marsden experiment, find the distance of closest approach to the nucleus of a 7.7 MeV α-particle before it comes momentarily to rest and reverse its direction. (Z for gold nucleus = 79) NCERT Pg. 295
(a) 10 fm (b) 20 fm
(c) 30 fm (d) 40 fm

7 In α-scattering experiment, in a head-on collision between an α-particle and a gold nucleus, the minimum distance of separation or closest approach is 4×10^{-14} m. The energy of α-particle is (Take, atomic number of gold = 79) NCERT Pg. 296
(a) 5.68 MeV (b) 8 MeV
(c) 4.47 MeV (d) 7.24 MeV

8 In a Geiger-Marsden experiment, an α-particle of 7.7 MeV energy approaches a gold nucleus head-on, it comes momentarily to rest and reverses its direction. We can conclude that (for gold, $Z = 79$) NCERT Pg. 296
(a) radius of gold nucleus is 3.0×10^{-14} m
(b) radius of gold nucleus is more than 3.0×10^{-14} m
(c) radius of gold nucleus is less than 3.0×10^{-14} m
(d) radius cannot be estimated by given data

9 If the orbital radius of the electron in a hydrogen atom is 4.7×10^{-11} m. Compute the kinetic energy of the electron in hydrogen atom. NCERT Pg. 296
(a) 15.3 eV (b) – 15.3 eV
(c) 13.6 eV (d) –13.6 eV

10 It is found experimentally that 13.6 eV energy is required to separate a hydrogen atom into a proton and an electron. Then, the velocity of the electron in a hydrogen atom is NCERT Pg. 296
(a) 10^{15} m/s (b) 2.2×10^6 m/s
(c) 4.2×10^8 m/s (d) 3×10^8 m/s

11 An elementary particle of mass m and charge $+e$ is projected with velocity v towards a much more massive particle of charge Ze, where $Z > 0$. What is the closest possible distance of approach of the incident particle? NCERT Pg. 296

(a) $\dfrac{Ze^2}{2\pi\varepsilon_0 mv^2}$ (b) $\dfrac{Ze}{4\pi\varepsilon_0 mv^2}$
(c) $\dfrac{Ze^2}{8\pi\varepsilon_0 mv^2}$ (d) $\dfrac{Ze}{8\pi\varepsilon_0 mv^2}$

Atomic Spectra

12 An emission line spectrum is observed when NCERT Pg. 296
(a) a gas is excited by heating or by passing an electric discharge through it
(b) a gas is excited by applying pressure
(c) a gas under low pressure condition is excited by heating or by passing an electric discharge through it
(d) a gas under high pressure condition is excited by heating or by passing an electric discharge through it

13 When white light is passed through an unexcited gas, then transmitted light consists of NCERT Pg. 297

(a) few bright lines in dark background
(b) few dark lines in bright background
(c) alternate dark and bright lines
(d) alternate dark and bright bands

14 The total energy of an electron in an orbit of hydrogen atom is −1.51 eV. Its kinetic and potential energies are, respectively NCERT Pg. 297

(a) 1.51 eV, 1.51 eV (b) 1.51 eV, 3.02 eV
(c) 1.51 eV, −3.02 eV (d) −1.51 eV, −1.51 eV

15 Hydrogen atom emits light when it changes from $n = 5$ energy level to $n = 2$ energy level. Which colour of light would the atom emit ? NCERT Pg. 297

(a) Red (b) Yellow (c) Green (d) Violet

16 Which of the following correctly shows the Balmer series in the emission spectrum of hydrogen? Old NCERT Pg. 421

(a)
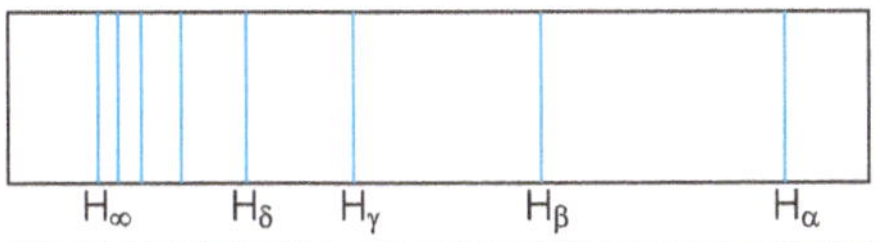

(b)
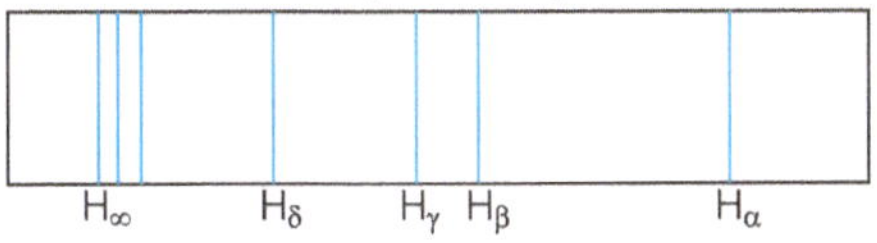

(c)
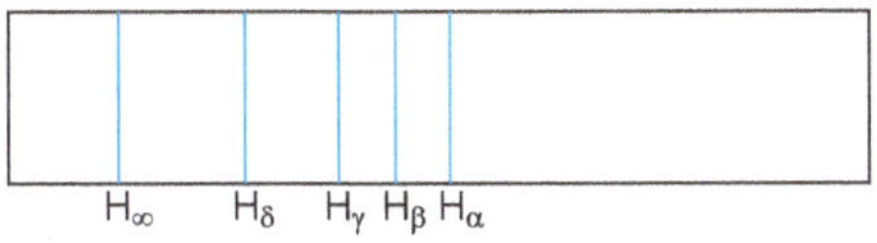

(d)
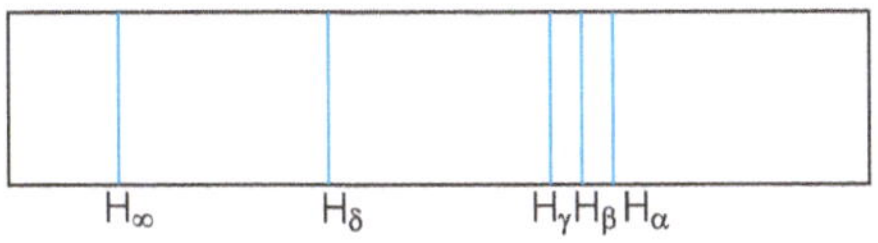

17 Shortest wavelength or series limit in Balmer series is Old NCERT Pg. 421

(a) 128 nm (b) 486 nm
(c) 656 nm (d) 364 nm

18 The wavelength of the first line of Lyman series for hydrogen atom is equal to that of the second line of Balmer series for a hydrogen like ion. The atomic number Z of hydrogen like ion is Old NCERT Pg. 421

(a) 3 (b) 4 (c) 1 (d) 2

19 The wavelength of the first line of Lyman series is 1215 Å, the wavelength of first line of Balmer series will be Old NCERT Pg. 422

(a) 4545 Å (b) 5295 Å (c) 6561 Å (d) 6750 Å

20 The first line of the Lyman series in a hydrogen spectrum has a wavelength of 1210 Å. The corresponding line of a hydrogen like atom of $Z = 11$ is equal to Old NCERT Pg. 422

(a) 4000 Å (b) 100 Å (c) 40 Å (d) 10 Å

21 If the series limit frequency of the Lyman series is ν_L, then the series limit frequency of the Pfund series is Old NCERT Pg. 422

(a) $25\,\nu_L$ (b) $16\,\nu_L$
(c) $\frac{\nu_L}{16}$ (d) $\frac{\nu_L}{25}$

22 The ratio of wavelengths of the last line of Balmer series and the last line of Lyman series is Old NCERT Pg. 422

(a) 2 (b) 1
(c) 4 (d) 0.5

23 In Pfund series, ratio of maximum to minimum wavelength of emitted spectral lines is Old NCERT Pg. 422

(a) $\frac{\lambda_{max}}{\lambda_{min}} = \frac{4}{3}$ (b) $\frac{\lambda_{max}}{\lambda_{min}} = \frac{9}{5}$
(c) $\frac{\lambda_{max}}{\lambda_{min}} = \frac{16}{7}$ (d) $\frac{\lambda_{max}}{\lambda_{min}} = \frac{36}{11}$

24 In the spectrum of hydrogen, the ratio of the largest wavelength in the Lyman series to the largest wavelength in the Balmer series is Old NCERT Pg. 422

(a) $\frac{4}{9}$ (b) $\frac{9}{4}$ (c) $\frac{27}{5}$ (d) $\frac{5}{27}$

25 A 12.75 eV electron beam is used to bombard gaseous hydrogen at room temperature, then wavelengths emitted are in Old NCERT Pg. 422

(a) either Paschen, Lyman or Balmer series
(b) either Brackett, Pfund or Lyman series
(c) either Paschen, Brackett or Balmer series
(d) either Lyman, Balmer or Brackett series

Bohr Model of the Hydrogen Atom

26 Bohr model is applied to singly ionised helium. Consider the lines that lie in the visible region of the spectrum. Which of the following transitions can give a photon of visible light ? NCERT Pg. 297

(a) $n = 5$ to $n = 4$ (b) $n = 7$ to $n = 4$
(c) $n = 2$ to $n = 1$ (d) $n = 8$ to $n = 3$

27 The electric current I created by the electron in the ground state of H-atom using Bohr model in terms of Bohr radius (a_0) and velocity of electron in first orbit v_0 is NCERT Pg. 297

(a) $\frac{ev_0}{2\pi a_0}$ (b) $\frac{2\pi a}{ev_0}$ (c) $\frac{2\pi a}{v_0}$ (d) $\frac{v_0}{2\pi a}$

28 An electron in the ground state of hydrogen atom is revolving in anti-clockwise direction in circular orbit of radius R. The orbital magnetic dipole moment of the electron will be **NCERT Pg. 297**

(a) $\frac{eh}{4\pi m}$ (b) $\frac{eh}{2\pi m}$ (c) $\frac{eh^2}{4\pi m}$ (d) $\frac{e^2h}{4\pi m}$

29 The speed of an electron in ground state energy level is $2.6 \times 10^6 \text{ ms}^{-1}$, then its speed in fourth excited state will be **NCERT Pg. 297**

(a) $5.6 \times 10^6 \text{ ms}^{-1}$ (b) $6.5 \times 10^5 \text{ ms}^{-1}$
(c) $5.5 \times 10^5 \text{ ms}^{-1}$ (d) $4.3 \times 10^6 \text{ ms}^{-1}$

30 When an electron in hydrogen atom is excited from its 4th to 5th stationary orbit, the change in angular momentum of electron is **NCERT Pg. 297**

(a) 4.6×10^{-34} J-s (b) 3.32×10^{-34} J-s
(c) 1.05×10^{-34} J-s (d) 2.08×10^{-34} J-s

31 Which amongst the following statements are incorrect regarding Bohr's atomic model? **NCERT Pg. 298**

(a) Electrons in a quantised orbit will not radiate the energy.
(b) Mass of electrons varies during revolution.
(c) Emission or absorption of energy results to transition of electron from one orbit to another.
(d) Angular momentum of orbital electron is quantised.

32 In which of the following Bohr's orbit (n), a hydrogen atom emits the photons of lowest frequency? **NCERT Pg. 299**

(a) $n = 2$ to $n = 1$ (b) $n = 4$ to $n = 2$
(c) $n = 4$ to $n = 1$ (d) $n = 4$ to $n = 3$

33 A 10 kg satellite revolves around the earth once every 2 h in an orbit having a radius of 8000 km. Assuming that Bohr's angular momentum postulate applies to a satellite just as it does to an electron in the hydrogen atom, then the quantum number of the orbit of satellite is **NCERT Pg. 299**

(a) 5.3×10^{40} (b) 5.3×10^{45} (c) 7.8×10^{48} (d) 7.8×10^{50}

34 The radius of electron orbit and the speed of electron in the ground state of hydrogen atom is 5.30×10^{-11} m and $2.2 \times 10^6 \text{ m s}^{-1}$, respectively, then the orbital period of this electron in first excited state will be **NCERT Pg. 299**

(a) 1.21×10^{-14} s (b) 1.21×10^{-12} s
(c) 1.21×10^{-10} s (d) 1.21×10^{-15} s

35 In accordance with the Bohr's model, the quantum number that characterises the earth's revolution around the sun in an orbit of radius 1.5×10^{11} m with orbital speed $3 \times 10^4 \text{ ms}^{-1}$ is (Mass of earth $= 6 \times 10^{24}$ kg) **NCERT Pg. 299**

(a) 5.98×10^{86} (b) 2.57×10^{38}
(c) 8.57×10^{64} (d) 2.57×10^{74}

36 An electron in hydrogen atom makes a transition from n_1 to n_2. If the time period of electron in initial state is 27 times that in the final state, then (Symbols have their usual meanings) **NCERT Pg. 299**

(a) $n_1 = 3n_2$ (b) $n_2 = 3n_1$
(c) $n_2 = 9n_1$ (d) $n_2 = 4n_1$

37 Positronium is like a H-atom with the proton replaced by positron (a positively charged antiparticle of the electron which is as massive as electron). The ground state energy of positronium would be **NCERT Pg. 299**

(a) -3.4 eV (b) -5.2 eV (c) -6.8 eV (d) -10.2 eV

38 Time of revolution of an electron around a nucleus of charge Ze in nth Bohr orbit is proportional to **NCERT Pg. 299**

(a) n (b) $\frac{n^3}{Z^2}$ (c) $\frac{n^2}{Z}$ (d) $\frac{Z}{n}$

39 The graph of radius r_n of electron in nth orbit *versus* atomic number Z is **NCERT Pg. 299**

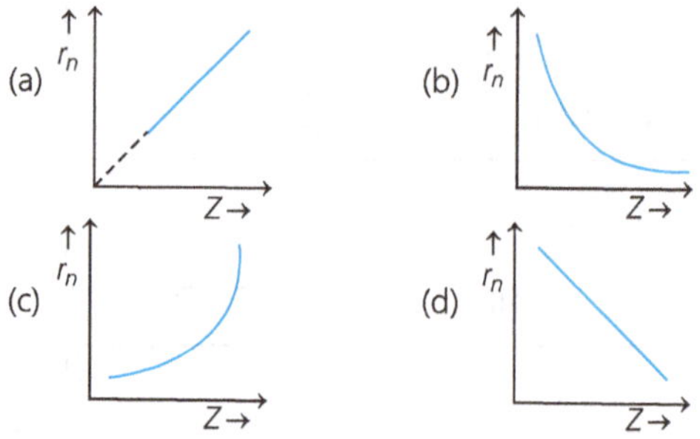

40 In Bohr's atomic model, speed and time period of revolution of an electron in $n = 3$ level are respectively **NCERT Pg. 299**

(a) $v = 1.09 \times 10^6 \text{ ms}^{-1}, T = 1.52 \times 10^{-16}$ s
(b) $v = 2.19 \times 10^6 \text{ ms}^{-1}, T = 1.52 \times 10^{-16}$ s
(c) $v = 7.31 \times 10^6 \text{ ms}^{-1}, T = 1.22 \times 10^{-16}$ s
(d) $v = 7.31 \times 10^5 \text{ ms}^{-1}, T = 4.08 \times 10^{-15}$ s

41 In the Auger process, an atom makes a transition to a lower state without emitting a photon. The excess energy is transferred to an outer electron which may be ejected by the atom. (This is called an Auger electron). Assuming the nucleus to be massive, the kinetic energy (in keV) of an $n = 4$ Auger electron emitted by chromium by absorbing the energy from a transition of $n = 2$ to $n = 1$ **NCERT Pg. 299**

(a) 4.6 (b) 7.5 (c) 5.38 (d) 2.68

42 The ratio of kinetic energy to the total energy of an electron in a Bohr orbit of the hydrogen atom is **NCERT Pg. 299**

(a) 2 : – 1 (b) 1 : – 1 (c) 1 : 1 (d) 1 : – 2

43 The total energy of an electron in a Bohr orbit of the hydrogen atom is –3.4 eV. Its kinetic and potential energies are respectively NCERT Pg. 299

(a) –3.4 eV, –6.8 eV (b) 3.4 eV, –6.8 eV
(c) 3.4 eV, 3.4 eV (d) – 3.4 eV, –3.4 eV

44 As the electron in Bohr orbit of hydrogen atom passes from state $n=2$ to $n=1$, the kinetic energy K and potential energy U changes as NCERT Pg. 299

(a) K becomes one-fourth and U becomes four times
(b) K becomes four times, U becomes twice
(c) Both K and U become four times
(d) Both K and U become twice

45 If energy of a hydrogen atom in nth orbit is E_n, then energy of a singly ionised helium (He^+) atom in nth orbit will be NCERT Pg. 299

(a) $4E_n$ (b) $E_n/4$
(c) $2E_n$ (d) $E_n/2$

46 If the binding energy of the electron in a hydrogen atom is 13.6 eV, then energy required to remove electron from first excited state of Li^{2+} is NCERT Pg. 299

(a) 122.4 eV (b) 30.6 eV
(c) 13.6 eV (d) 3.4 eV

47 Energy of an electron in an excited state of hydrogen atom is –3.4 eV. Its angular momentum will be NCERT Pg. 299

(a) 1.11×10^{34} J-s (b) 1.51×10^{-31} J-s
(c) 2.10×10^{-34} J-s (d) 3.72×10^{-34} J-s

48 A hydrogen atom and Li^+ ion are both in the second excited state. If L_H and L_{Li} are their respective electronic angular momenta and E_H and E_{Li} their respective energies, then NCERT Pg. 299

(a) $L_H > L_{Li}$ and $|E_H| > |E_{Li}|$
(b) $L_H = L_{Li}$ and $|E_H| < |E_{Li}|$
(c) $L_H = L_{Li}$ and $|E_H| > |E_{Li}|$
(d) $L_H > L_{Li}$ and $|E_H| < |E_{Li}|$

49 A He^+ ion is in its first excited state. Its ionisation energy is NCERT Pg. 299

(a) 54.40 eV (b) 13.60 eV
(c) 48.36 eV (d) 6.04 eV

50 As excitation of hydrogen atom increases (i.e. n increases), the value of minimum energy required to free the electron from the excited state NCERT Pg. 299

(a) increases
(b) decreases
(c) remains same
(d) first increases then decreases

51 An electron with kinetic energy 5eV is incident on a H-atom in its ground state. The collision NCERT Pg. 299

(a) must be elastic
(b) must be partially elastic
(c) must be completely inelastic
(d) may be completely inelastic

52 In a mixture of hydrogen gas and He^+ gas (He^+ is singly ionised He atom), H-atoms and He^+ ions are excited to their respective first excited states. Subsequently, H-atoms transfer their total excitation energy to He^+ ions (by collisions). The quantum number n of the state finally populated in He^+ ions is NCERT Pg. 299

(a) 2 (b) 3
(c) 4 (d) 5

53 An energy of 15 eV is given to an electron in 4th orbit of H-atom. Then, find its final energy when it comes out of H-atom. NCERT Pg. 299

(a) 14.15 eV (b) 13.6 eV
(c) 12.08 eV (d) 15.85 eV

54 Ionisation potential of hydrogen atom is 13.6 eV. If a hydrogen atom in ground state is excited by monochromatic radiation of photon energy 12.1 eV. The spectral lines emitted by hydrogen atom will be NCERT Pg. 299

(a) only one (b) two in number
(c) three in number (d) four in number

55 If muonic hydrogen atom is an atom in which a negatively charged muon μ of mass about 207 m_e revolves around a proton, then first Bohr radius of this atom is ($r_e = 0.53 \times 10^{-10}$ m) NCERT Pg. 299

(a) 2.56×10^{-10} m (b) 2.56×10^{-11} m
(c) 2.56×10^{-12} m (d) 2.56×10^{-13} m

56 An electron is revolving around nucleus of charge Ze. If 40.8 eV of energy is needed to excite an electron from $n=1$ to $n=2$ state. What is value of Z? NCERT Pg. 299

(a) 2 (b) 3
(c) 4 (d) 5

57 A hydrogen atom initially in the ground level absorbs a photon and is excited to $n=4$ level, then the wavelength of photon is NCERT Pg. 299

(a) 790 Å (b) 870 Å
(c) 970 Å (d) 1070 Å

58 Choose the incorrect statement from the following option regarding hydrogen atom. NCERT Pg. 299

(a) Linear momentum is directly proportional to the number of orbit n.
(b) Bohr's model assumed that electronic orbits are circular.

(c) When a hydrogen atom receives energy by processes such as electron emission, it is said to be in excited state.
(d) de-Broglie wavelength of an electron in first Bohr's orbit is equal to circumference of orbit.

59 As an electron makes a transition from an excited state to the ground state of a hydrogen like atom/ion. Then, choose the correct statement. NCERT Pg. 299
(a) Its kinetic energy increases but potential energy and total energy decrease.
(b) Kinetic energy, potential energy and total energy decrease.
(c) Kinetic energy decreases, potential energy increases but total energy remains same.
(d) Kinetic energy and total energy decrease but potential energy increases.

60 The diagram shows the energy levels for an electron in a certain atom. Which transition shown represents the emission of a photon with the most energy? NCERT Pg. 300

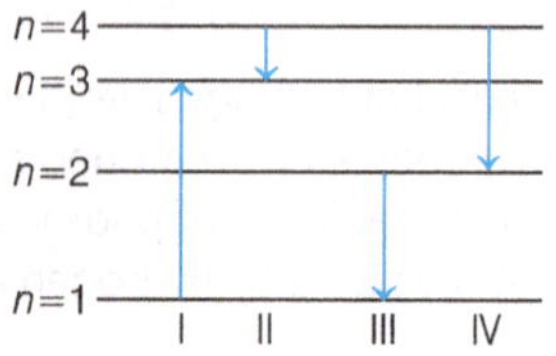

(a) I (b) II (c) III (d) IV

61 Energy is absorbed in the hydrogen atom giving absorption spectra when transition takes place from NCERT Pg. 300
(a) $n = 1 \rightarrow n'$ where $n' > 1$
(b) $n = 2 \rightarrow 1$
(c) $n' \rightarrow n$
(d) $n \rightarrow n' = \infty$

The Line Spectra of the Hydrogen Atom

62 An atom makes a transition from higher energy state n_i to the lower energy state n_f, then the difference of energy of a photon is (where, n stands for principal quantum number) NCERT Pg. 301
(a) $h = -E_{n_i} - E_{n_f}$
(b) $h\nu_{if} = E_{n_i} + E_{n_f}$
(c) $h\nu_{if} = E_{n_f} - E_{n_i}$
(d) $h\nu_{if} = E_{n_i} - E_{n_f}$

63 Frequency of radiation emitted when a hydrogen atom is de-excites from level n to level $(n-1)$ is NCERT Pg. 301
(a) $\frac{me^4 (2n-1)}{(4\pi)^3 \varepsilon_0^2 (h/2\pi)^3 n^2 (n-1)^2}$
(b) $\frac{me^4 (1-2n)}{4\pi^2 \varepsilon_0^2 (h/2\pi)^3 n^2}$
(c) $\frac{me^4 (1-2n)}{4\pi^2 \varepsilon_0 (h/2\pi)^2 (n-1)^2}$
(d) $\frac{me^4 (2n-1)}{(4\pi)^3 \varepsilon_0^2 (h/2\pi)^3 (n-1)^2}$

64 An electron jumps from the 4th orbit to 2nd orbit of the hydrogen atom. Given, Rydberg's constant $R = 10^7 \text{ cm}^{-1}$, the frequency in hertz of emitted radiation will be NCERT Pg. 301
(a) $\frac{3}{16} \times 10^5$ (b) $\frac{3}{16} \times 10^{15}$
(c) $\frac{9}{16} \times 10^{15}$ (d) $\frac{3}{4} \times 10^{15}$

65 Transition from state $n = 4$ to $n = 3$ in a hydrogen like atom results in a UV radiation. IR radiation will be obtained in the transition, when NCERT Pg. 301
(a) $2 \rightarrow 1$ (b) $3 \rightarrow 2$
(c) $1 \rightarrow 2$ (d) $5 \rightarrow 4$

66 Some energy levels of a molecule are shown in the figure. The ratio of the wavelengths $r = \lambda_1 / \lambda_2$ is given by NCERT Pg. 301

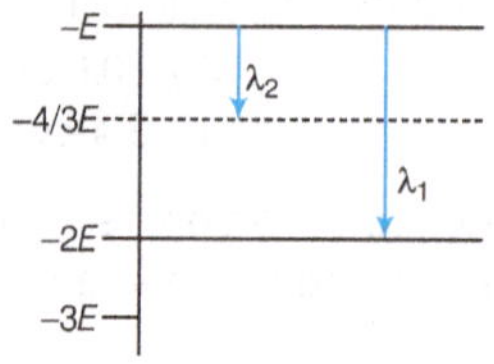

(a) $r = \frac{2}{3}$ (b) $r = \frac{3}{4}$
(c) $r = \frac{1}{3}$ (d) $r = \frac{4}{3}$

67 Radiation coming from transitions $n = 2$ to $n = 1$ of hydrogen atoms fall on He^+ ions in $n = 1$ and $n = 2$ states. The possible transition of helium ions as they absorb energy from the radiation is NCERT Pg. 301
(a) $n = 2 \rightarrow n = 3$ (b) $n = 1 \rightarrow n = 4$
(c) $n = 2 \rightarrow n = 5$ (d) $n = 2 \rightarrow n = 4$

68 Electron in hydrogen atom first jumps from third excited state to second excited state and then from second excited to the first excited state. The ratio of the wavelengths $\lambda_1 : \lambda_2$ emitted in the two cases is NCERT Pg. 301
(a) $\frac{7}{5}$ (b) $\frac{27}{20}$
(c) $\frac{27}{5}$ (d) $\frac{20}{7}$

69 Hydrogen atom from excited state comes to the ground state by emitting a photon of wavelength λ. If R is the Rydberg constant, then the principal quantum number n of the excited state is NCERT Pg. 301

(a) $\sqrt{\frac{\lambda R}{\lambda R+1}}$ (b) $\sqrt{\frac{\lambda}{\lambda R-1}}$
(c) $\sqrt{\frac{\lambda R^2}{\lambda R-1}}$ (d) $\sqrt{\frac{\lambda R}{\lambda-1}}$

70 Hydrogen $({}_1H^1)$, deuterium $({}_1H^2)$, singly ionised helium $({}_2He^4)^+$ and doubly ionised lithium $({}_3Li^8)^{2+}$ all have one electron around the nucleus. Consider an electron transition from $n=2$ to $n=1$. If the wavelengths of emitted radiation are $\lambda_1, \lambda_2, \lambda_3$ and λ_4 respectively for four elements, then approximately which one of the following is correct? NCERT Pg. 301

(a) $4\lambda_1 = 2\lambda_2 = 2\lambda_3 = \lambda_4$
(b) $\lambda_1 = 2\lambda_2 = 2\lambda_3 = \lambda_4$
(c) $\lambda_1 = \lambda_2 = 4\lambda_3 = 9\lambda_4$
(d) $\lambda_1 = 2\lambda_2 = 3\lambda_3 = 4\lambda_4$

71 The wavelength of yellow line of sodium is 5896 Å, its wave number is NCERT Pg. 301

(a) 50883 per cm (b) 16961 per cm
(c) 17581 per cm (d) 50833 per cm

72 The energy levels of the hydrogen spectrum is shown in figure.

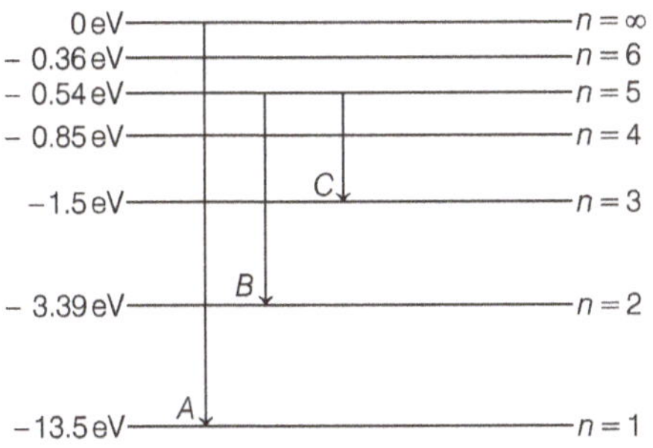

Transitions A, B and C represent NCERT Pg. 301

(a) first member of Lyman series, third spectral line of Balmer series and second line of Paschen series
(b) ionisation potential of hydrogen, second spectral line of Balmer series and third spectral line of Paschen series
(c) series limit of Lyman series, third spectral line of Balmer series and second spectral line of Paschen series
(d) series limit of Lyman series, second spectral line of Balmer series and third spectral line of Paschen series

73 If ν_1 is the frequency of the series limit of Lyman series, ν_2 is the frequency of the first line of Lyman series and ν_3 is the frequency of the series limit of the Balmer series. Then, NCERT Pg. 301

(a) $\nu_1 - \nu_2 = \nu_3$
(b) $\nu_1 = \nu_2 - \nu_3$
(c) $\frac{1}{\nu_2} = \frac{1}{\nu_1} + \frac{1}{\nu_3}$
(d) $\frac{1}{\nu_1} = \frac{1}{\nu_2} + \frac{1}{\nu_3}$

74 The Bohr model for the spectra of a H-atom NCERT Pg. 301

(a) will not be applicable to hydrogen in the molecular form
(b) is applicable for multi-electron atom
(c) explain continuous as well as discrete spectral lines
(d) Both (a) and (b)

de-Broglie Explanation of Bohr's Second Postulate of Quantisation

75 The radius of the orbit of an electron in a hydrogen like atom is 4.5 a_0, where a_0 is the Bohr radius. Its orbital angular momentum is $\frac{3h}{2\pi}$. It is given that h is Planck constant and R is Rydberg constant. Which amongst the following is not a possible wavelength(s), when the atom de-excites? NCERT Pg. 301

(a) $\frac{9}{32R}$ (b) $\frac{9}{16R}$
(c) $\frac{9}{5R}$ (d) $\frac{1}{3R}$

76 An electron of a hydrogen like atom is in excited state. If total energy of the electron is -4.6 eV, then de-Broglie wavelength of the electron is NCERT Pg. 301

(a) 6.27 nm (b) 2.48 mm
(c) 0.57 nm (d) 8 nm

77 In second orbit of hydrogen atom, wavelength of revolving electron is λ. What is its circumference? NCERT Pg. 302

(a) λ (b) 2λ
(c) 3λ (d) 4λ

Assertion and Reason Questions

Direction (Q. Nos. 1-10) *In the following questions, statement of Assertion is followed by a corresponding statement of Reason. Of the following statements, choose the correct one.*

(a) Both Assertion and Reason are correct and Reason is the correct explanation of Assertion
(b) Both Assertion and Reason are correct but Reason is not the correct explanation of Assertion
(c) Assertion is correct but Reason is incorrect
(d) Assertion is incorrect but Reason is correct

1 Assertion Most of the space of an atom is empty.

Reason From Rutherford's experiment, size of the nucleus is 10^{-10} m and from kinetic theory, size of the atom is 10^{-15} m. NCERT Pg. 293

2 Assertion Electrons in an atom are held due to Coulomb forces.

Reason The atom is stable only because the centripetal force due to Coulomb's law is balanced by the centrifugal force. NCERT Pg. 293

3 Assertion The force of repulsion between atomic nucleus and α-particle varies with distance according to inverse square law.

Reason Rutherford did α-particle scattering experiment. NCERT Pg. 294

4 Assertion If the electrons in an atom were stationary, then they would fall into the nucleus.

Reason Electrostatic force of attraction acts between negatively charged electrons and positive nucleus. NCERT Pg. 295

5 Assertion Light emitted from rarefied gases heated in a flame or excited electrically in a glow tube like mercury vapour light has only certain discrete wavelengths.

Reason Energy levels of atoms have fixed energy values. NCERT Pg. 296

6 Assertion The energy of an electron in a hydrogen atom in the first excited state is approximately -5.45×10^{-19} J.

Reason The energy of an electron in a hydrogen atom can be found by $-\dfrac{m^2 l^2}{8n^2 \varepsilon_0 h^2}$.

where, m is mass of electron, e is elementary charge, n is principal quantum number and h is Planck's constant. NCERT Pg. 299

7 Assertion Bohr postulated that electrons in stationary orbits around the nucleus do not radiate.

Reason According to classical physics, all moving electrons radiate. NCERT Pg. 299

8 Assertion Highest energy state corresponds with the electron revolving in an orbit closest to the nucleus.

Reason Energies of the excited states come closer and closer together as n increases. NCERT Pg. 300

9 Assertion The electron in the hydrogen atom passes from energy level $n = 4$ to $n = 1$ level. The maximum and minimum number of photon that can be emitted are six and one, respectively.

Reason Photons are emitted when electron make a transition from higher energy state to lower energy state. NCERT Pg. 300

10 Assertion A hydrogen atom cannot absorb a photon whose energy is greater than 13.6 eV, its binding energy.

Reason The extra energy will manifest as KE of the electron. NCERT Pg. 300

Statement Based Questions

Direction (Q. Nos. 1-8) *In the following questions, Statement I and Statement II are given. Read the statements and choose the most appropriate answer from the options given below.*

(a) Both Statement I and Statement II are incorrect
(b) Statement I is correct but Statement II is incorrect
(c) Statement I is incorrect but Statement II is correct
(d) Both Statement I and Statement II are correct

1 Statement I According to JJ Thomson's atomic model, negative charge of the atom is uniformly distributed and positive charges are embedded in it.

Statement II Condensed matter and dense gases at all temperatures emit EM radiations in which a continuous distribution of several wavelengths is present, though with different intensities. NCERT Pg. 290

2 In Geiger-Marsden experiment, two statements are given below.

Statement I α-particles emitted from a $^{214}_{83}U$ radioactive source at a thin metal foil made of gold.

Statement II α-particle were collimated into a narrow beam by their passage through lead bricks. NCERT Pg. 292

3 **Statement I** The positively charged nucleus of an atom has a radius of almost 10^{-15} m.
Statement II In α-particle scattering experiment, the distance of closest approach for α-particles is $\approx 10^{-15}$ m NCERT Pg. 294

4 **Statement I** If total energy of an electron in H-atom is positive, then the electron will be bound to the nucleus.

Statement II In Geiger-Marsden experiment, gold foil is very thin, so α-particle will not suffer more than one scattering during their passage through it. NCERT Pg. 296

5 **Statement I** Bohr model is valid for both one electron atom and multi-electron atom.

Statement II Orbital is the one electron wave function that gives the probability of finding an electron in a certain region of space around the nucleus. NCERT Pg. 297

6 **Statement I** Bohr's model is not applicable to the singly ionised helium atom.
Statement II Lyman series lies in infrared region while Brackett series lies in ultraviolet region. NCERT Pg. 297

7 **Statement I** Hydrogen atom consists of only one electron but its emission spectrum has many lines.
Statement II The spectrum of hydrogen atom is only absorption spectrum. NCERT Pg. 297

Matching Type Questions

1 For Balmer spectral series of hydrogen, match the Column I (Balmer spectral series) with Column II (wavelength) and select the correct answer from the codes given below. Old NCERT Pg. 421

Column I		Column II	
A.	H_α	1.	410.2 nm
B.	H_β	2.	434.1 nm
C.	H_γ	3.	486.1 nm
D.	H_δ	4.	656.3 nm

Codes

	A	B	C	D		A	B	C	D
(a)	4	1	2	3	(b)	4	3	2	1
(c)	2	2	4	4	(d)	2	3	4	1

2 For spectral series of hydrogen atom, match the Column I (spectral series) with Column II (region) and select the correct answer from the codes given below. NCERT Pg. 297

Column I		Column II	
A.	Lyman series	1.	Ultraviolet region
B.	Balmer series	2.	Infrared region
C.	Paschen series	3.	Visible region
D.	Brackett series	4.	Near Infrared region

Codes

	A	B	C	D		A	B	C	D
(a)	1	3	4	2	(b)	2	1	3	4
(c)	2	1	3	4	(d)	1	4	2	3

3 Match the Column I (spectral series) with Column II (maximum wavelength of the series) and select the correct answer from the codes given below.
(R = Rydberg's constant) Old NCERT Pg. 421

Column I		Column II	
A.	Lyman series	1.	$400/9R$
B.	Balmer series	2.	$144/7R$
C.	Paschen series	3.	$36/5R$
D.	Brackett series	4.	$4/3R$

Codes

	A	B	C	D		A	B	C	D
(a)	2	3	4	1	(b)	3	4	1	2
(c)	4	3	2	1	(d)	4	3	1	2

4 For atomic model of hydrogen atom given by Niels Bohr, match the Column I (quantities) with Column II (proportionalities) and select the correct answer from the codes given below. NCERT Pg. 299

Column I		Column II	
A.	Angular momentum	1.	$1/n$
B.	Velocity of electron	2.	n^2
C.	Radius of electron	3.	$1/n^2$
D.	Energy of electron	4.	n

Codes

	A	B	C	D		A	B	C	D
(a)	1	2	3	4	(b)	4	3	2	1
(c)	4	1	3	2	(d)	4	1	2	3

Numerical Type Questions

1 $\sqrt{d_1}$ and $\sqrt{d_2}$ are the impact parameters corresponding to scattering angles 60° and 90° respectively, when an α-particle is approaching a gold nucleus. If the ratio of d_1 and d_2 is x, then the value of x is .... NCERT Pg. 294

2 An alpha particle of initial energy 10 MeV is scattered by an inverse square field that produced by a nucleus of $Z = 79$. For the scattering angle 90°, the impact parameter is $p \times 10^{-15}$ m. The value of p is .... NCERT Pg. 294

3 A particle of mass 250 MeV/c^2 collides with a hydrogen atom at rest. Soon after the collision, the particle comes to rest and the atom recoils and goes to its second excited state. The initial kinetic energy of the particle (in eV) is $\frac{48.32}{N}$. The value of N is ....

(Given, the mass of the hydrogen atom to be 1 GeV/c^2) NCERT Pg. 296

4 In Bohr's atomic model, the electron is assumed to revolve in second circular orbit of radius 8.4 Å. If the speed of electron is 1.32×10^6 m/s, then the current associated with the electron will be ....$\times 10^{-2}$ mA $\left[\text{Take}, \pi = \frac{22}{7}\right]$ NCERT Pg. 296

5 A hydrogen atom make a transition from first excited state to ground state and emits a photon. This photon strikes a doubly ionised lithium atom ($Z = 3$) in excited state and completely removes the orbiting electron. The least quantum number for the excited state of the ion for this process is .... NCERT Pg. 297

6 A light of energy 10.2 eV is incident on a hydrogen atom in its ground state. The atom absorbs the radiation and reaches to one of its excited states. The angular momentum of the atom in the excited state is $x/\pi \times 10^{-17}$ eV-s. The value of x is ....

(Use $h = 4.14 \times 10^{-15}$ eV-s, $c = 3 \times 10^8$ ms^{-1}). NCERT Pg. 297

7 A photon from Balmer series in hydrogen spectrum are incident on a metal surface of work function 1.4 eV. The maximum kinetic energy of one photo-electron is ....eV. NCERT Pg. 297

8 The transition of electron from $n = 3$ to $n = 1$ have in hydrogen atom and emits a photon. This photon is incident on a photosensitive material of unknown work function. The photoelectron are emitted from the material with a maximum kinetic energy of 9 eV. The threshold wavelength of the material is $p \times 10^{-7}$ m. The value of p is .... NCERT Pg. 297

9 An electron jumps from the second excited state to the first excited state of the hydrogen atom, the wavelength of photon emitted is λ_0. If the electron jumps from the third excited state to the second excited state of the hydrogen atom, the wavelength of the photon emitted will be $\frac{x\lambda_0}{35}$. The value of x is .... NCERT Pg. 299

10 The ionisation energy of a hydrogen like atom is 9 Rydberg. The radius of first orbit of this atom as compared to the radius of first orbit of hydrogen atom is $\frac{1}{x}$ times. The value of x is .... NCERT Pg. 299

NCERT Exemplar Questions

1 Taking Bohr radius $a_0 = 53$ pm, the radius of Li^{2+} ion in its ground state on the basis of Bohr model will be

(a) 53 pm (b) 27 pm
(c) 18 pm (d) 13 pm

2 For ground state, electron in H-atom has an angular momentum $= h$, according to the simple Bohr model. As angular momentum is a vector and hence there will be infinitely many possibilities of orbits with vector pointing in all possible directions. In actuality, this is not true

(a) because Bohr model gives incorrect values of angular momentum
(b) because only one of these would have a minimum energy
(c) angular momentum must be in the direction of spin of electrons
(d) because electrons go around in horizontal orbits only

3 Two H-atoms in the ground state collide inelastically. The maximum amount by which their combined kinetic energy is reduced, is

(a) 10.20 eV (b) 20.40 eV (c) 13.6 eV (d) 27.2 eV

4 A set of atoms in an excited state decays

(a) in general to any of the states with lower energy
(b) into a lower state only when excited by an external electric field
(c) all together simultaneously into a lower state
(d) to emit photons only when they collide

Past Exams Questions

NEET

1 Given below are two statements.

Statement I Atoms are electrically neutral as they contain equal number of positive and negative charges.

Statement II Atoms of each element are stable and emit their characteristic spectrum.

NCERT Pg. 296, NEET 2024

In the light of the above statements, choose the most appropriate answer from the options given below.

(a) Both Statement I and Statement II are correct.
(b) Both Statement I and Statement II are incorrect.
(c) Statement I is correct but Statement II is incorrect.
(d) Statement I is incorrect but Statement II is correct.

2 Match List I with List II.

	List I (Spectral lines of Hydrogen for transitions from)		List II (Wavelengths (nm))
A.	$n_2 = 3$ to $n_1 = 2$	I.	410.2
B.	$n_2 = 4$ to $n_1 = 2$	II.	434.1
C.	$n_2 = 5$ to $n_1 = 2$	III.	656.3
D.	$n_2 = 6$ to $n_1 = 2$	IV.	486.1

NCERT Pg. 300, NEET 2024

Choose the correct answer from the options given below.

(a) A-II, B-I, C-IV, D-III (b) A-III, B-IV, C-II, D-I
(c) A-IV, B-III, C-I, D-II (d) A-I, B-II, C-III, D-IV

3 The radius of innermost orbit of hydrogen atom is 5.3×10^{-11} m. What is the radius of third allowed orbit of hydrogen atom? NCERT Pg. 296, NEET 2023

(a) 1.06 Å (b) 1.59 Å (c) 4.77 Å (d) 0.53 Å

4 The total energy of an electron in the nth stationary orbit of the hydrogen atom can be obtained by

NCERT Pg. 299, NEET 2020

(a) $E_n = \frac{13.6}{n^2}$ eV (b) $E_n = -\frac{13.6}{n^2}$ eV
(c) $E_n = -\frac{1.36}{n^2}$ eV (d) $E_n = -13.6 \times n^2$ eV

5 When an α-particle of mass m moving with velocity v bombards on a heavy nucleus of charge Ze, its distance of closest approach from the nucleus depends on m as

NCERT Pg. 295, NEET 2016

(a) $\frac{1}{\sqrt{m}}$ (b) $\frac{1}{m^2}$ (c) m (d) $\frac{1}{m}$

6 Consider 3rd orbit of He^+ (Helium), using non-relativistic approach, the speed of electron in this orbit will be (given $K = 9 \times 10^9$ constant, $Z = 2$ and h (Planck's constant) $= 6.6 \times 10^{-34}$ J-s)

NCERT Pg. 299, AIPMT 2015

(a) 2.92×10^6 m/s (b) 1.46×10^6 m/s
(c) 0.73×10^6 m/s (d) 3.0×10^8 m/s

JEE Main

7 The longest wavelength associated with Paschen series is (Given, $R_H = 1.097 \times 10^7$ Si unit)

NCERT 296, JEE Main 2024

(a) 1.094×10^{-6} m (b) 3.646×10^{-6} m
(c) 1.876×10^{-6} m (d) 2.973×10^{-6} m

8 The energy of He^+ ion in its first excited state is, (The ground state energy for the hydrogen atom is -13.6 eV)

NCERT 299, JEE Main 2023

(a) -27.2 eV (b) -3.4 eV
(c) -54.4 eV (d) -13.6 eV

9 A small particle of mass m moves in such a way that its potential energy $U = \frac{1}{2} m\omega^2 r^2$, where ω is constant and r is the distance of the particle from origin. Assuming Bohr's quantisation of momentum and circular orbit, the radius of nth orbit will be proportional to

NCERT Pg. 302, JEE Main 2023

(a) $\frac{1}{n}$ (b) n (c) $\sqrt{n}$ (d) n^2

10 A photon is emitted in transition from $n = 4$ to $n = 1$ level in hydrogen atom. The corresponding wavelength for this transition is (given, $h = 4 \times 10^{-15}$ eV-s)

NCERT Pg. 299, JEE main 2023

(a) 94.1 nm (b) 99.3 nm
(c) 974 nm (d) 941 nm

11 The momentum of an electron revolving in nth orbit is given by (Symbols have their usual meanings)

NCERT Pg. 302, JEE Main 2022

(a) $\frac{nh}{2\pi r}$ (b) $\frac{nh}{2r}$ (c) $\frac{nh}{2\pi}$ (d) $\frac{2\pi r}{nh}$

12 Find the ratio of energies of photons produced due to transition of an electron of hydrogen atom from its

(i) second permitted energy level to the first level, and
(ii) the highest permitted energy level to the first permitted level. NCERT Pg. 299, JEE Main 2022

(a) 3 : 4 (b) 4 : 3
(c) 1 : 4 (d) 4 : 1

13 A hydrogen atom is in ground state absorbs 10.2 eV of energy. The angular momentum of electron of the hydrogen atom will increase by the value of (Given, Planck's constant $= 6.6 \times 10^{-34}$ J-s)
NCERT Pg. 299, JEE Main 2022

(a) 2.10×10^{-34} J-s
(b) 1.05×10^{-34} J-s
(c) 3.15×10^{-34} J-s
(d) 4.2×10^{-34} J-s

Skill Boosters

1 Monochromatic wavelength λ is made incident over a hydrogen sample at room temperature. Hydrogen atom absorb energy and subsequently emits radiations of 10 different wavelengths. The value of λ is

(a) 95 nm (b) 103 nm
(c) 73 nm (d) 88 nm

2 Ionisation energy of a hydrogen like Bohr atom is 4 Rydberg. Radius of ground state orbit of electron in this atom is

(a) 0.53 Å (b) 0.265 Å
(c) 0.1325 Å (d) 1.06 Å

3 Wavelengths and frequencies of photons in transitions having serial numbers 1, 2 and 3 of a hydrogen like atom are $\lambda_1, \lambda_2, \lambda_3$ and f_1, f_2, f_3 respectively. Then, mark the correct option(s).

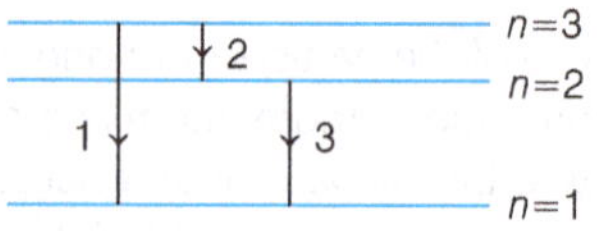

(a) $\lambda_3 = \lambda_1 + \lambda_2$ (b) $\lambda_3 = \dfrac{\lambda_1 \lambda_2}{\lambda_1 + \lambda_2}$

(c) $f_3 = \dfrac{f_1 + f_2}{f_1 f_2}$ (d) $f_3 = \dfrac{f_1 f_2}{f_1 + f_2}$

4 A neutron moving with a speed v strikes a hydrogen atom which is in ground state and moving towards neutron in same line and with same speed.
The minimum speed of the neutron for which inelastic collision (complete or partial) may takes place is nearly,

(a) 3×10^4 ms^{-1} (b) 3×10^8 ms^{-1}
(c) 3×10^8 ms^{-1} (d) 3×10^6 ms^{-1}

5 Bohr's atomic theory is first successful theory which explains line emission spectrum is put forward in 1913. Bohr's work is creditable because when in 1924 de-Broglie's hypothesis comes into light, the results are found exactly the same.
In H-atom in $n = 4$ state, the de-Broglie's wavelength λ associated with electron is

(a) λ = circumference of Bohr's orbit
(b) $\lambda = 4 \times$ circumference of Bohr's orbit
(c) $\lambda = \dfrac{1}{4} \times$ circumference of Bohr's orbit
(d) No relation exists

6 A neutron of kinetic energy K undergoes a head-on collision with a hydrogen atom at rest in ground state and is free to move.

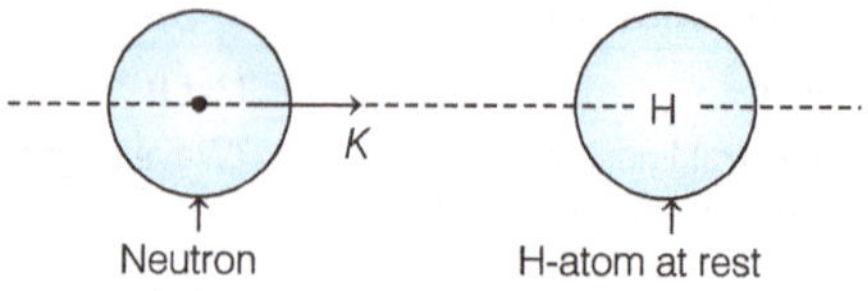

Then, mark the correct option(s).

(a) For $K < 20.4$ eV, collision is perfectly elastic
(b) For $K > 20.4$ eV, collision is perfectly inelastic
(c) For $K \geq 20.4$ eV, collision may be elastic or it may be perfectly inelastic
(d) For $K = 24.4$ eV, collision may be elastic, inelastic or perfectly inelastic

7 For the ground state, the electron in H-atom has an angular momentum of $h/2\pi$. According to simple Bohr model, angular momentum is a vector and hence there will be infinitely many orbits with the vector pointing in all possible directions.In reality, this is not correct because

(a) Bohr model gives incorrect value of angular momentum
(b) only one of these orientations corresponds to minimum energy
(c) angular momentum is in the direction of spin of electron
(d) electrons go around in horizontal orbits

8 In α-particle scattering experiment for a given angle θ, fraction of α-particles scattered by angle θ or more by a foil of thickness t and containing n atoms per unit volume will be

(a) $nt\pi b^2$ (b) $nt^2\pi b$
(c) $n^2t^3b^3$ (d) $n\pi$

9 An α-particle is scattered by a nucleus as shown in the figure.

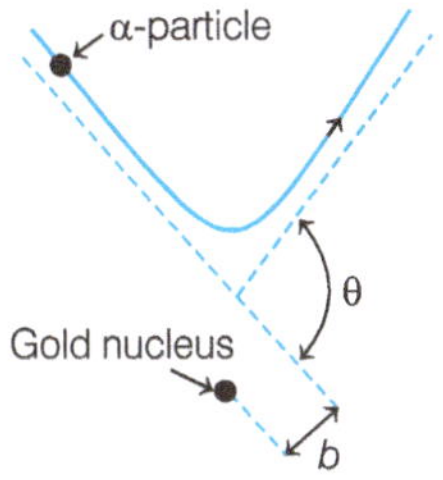

Let mass of α-particle is m and its speed is v. Assuming nucleus remains stationary, change in momentum of α-particle is

(a) $2\,mv\sin\theta$
(b) $2\,mv\cos\theta$
(c) $2\,mv\cos\frac{\theta}{2}$
(d) $2\,mv\sin\frac{\theta}{2}$

10 In some of Rutherford's experiments, a silver foil is used. Let kinetic energy of α-particles is 4.8 MeV, mass of α-particles is 6.64×10^{-27} kg, charge on silver nucleus is $47e$. For a head-on collision, impact parameter for an α-particle, which is scattered at an angle of 45°, is

(a) 2.8×10^{-14} m
(b) 3.36×10^{-14} m
(c) 1.41×10^{-14} m
(d) 5.60×10^{-14} m

Correct Codes

Topical Questions

1 (a)	2 (b)	3 (d)	4 (b)	5 (c)	6 (c)	7 (a)	8 (c)	9 (a)	10 (b)
11 (a)	12 (c)	13 (b)	14 (c)	15 (d)	16 (a)	17 (d)	18 (d)	19 (c)	20 (d)
21 (d)	22 (c)	23 (d)	24 (d)	25 (a)	26 (b)	27 (a)	28 (a)	29 (b)	30 (c)
31 (b)	32 (d)	33 (b)	34 (d)	35 (d)	36 (a)	37 (c)	38 (b)	39 (d)	40 (d)
41 (c)	42 (b)	43 (b)	44 (c)	45 (a)	46 (b)	47 (c)	48 (b)	49 (b)	50 (b)
51 (a)	52 (c)	53 (a)	54 (c)	55 (d)	56 (a)	57 (c)	58 (a)	59 (a)	60 (c)
61 (a)	62 (d)	63 (a)	64 (c)	65 (d)	66 (c)	67 (d)	68 (d)	69 (a)	70 (c)
71 (b)	72 (c)	73 (a)	74 (a)	75 (b)	76 (c)	77 (b)			

Assertion and Reason Questions

1 (c)	2 (c)	3 (b)	4 (a)	5 (a)	6 (c)	7 (b)	8 (d)	9 (b)	10 (d)

Statement Based Questions

1 (c)	2 (c)	3 (d)	4 (c)	5 (c)	6 (a)	7 (b)

Matching Type Questions

1 (b)	2 (a)	3 (c)	4 (d)

Numerical Type Questions

1 (3)	2 (11)	3 (3)	4 (4)	5 (4)	6 (414)	7 (2)	8 (4)	9 (100)

NCERT Exemplar Questions

1 (c)	2 (a)	3 (a)	4 (a)

Past Exams Questions

1 (c)	2 (b)	3 (c)	4 (b)	5 (d)	6 (b)	7 (c)	8 (d)	9 (c)	10 (a)
11 (a)	12 (a)	13 (b)							

Skill Boosters

1 (a)	2 (b)	3 (b)	4 (a)	5 (c)	6 (a)	7 (a)	8 (a)	9 (d)	10 (b)

Step by Step

Decoding the Questions

Concept Builders

1 Thomson model

2 True (T)

3 Alpha particles

4 True (T) 5 decreases

6 False (F) 7 True (T)

8 True (T) 9 True (T)

10 False (F) 11 True (T)

12 angular momentum

13 $1.09 \times 10^7 \text{ m}^{-1}$ 14 10.2 eV

15 6 16 Zero

17 9:4 18 Lyman series

19 Balmer 20 False (F)

Topical Questions

2 (*b*) According to Geiger-Marsden experiment, only about 0.14% of the incident α-particles scatter by more than 1°.

The statement given in option (b) is incorrect, rest are correct.

6 (*c*) Given, $K = 7.7$ MeV

$$= 1.2 \times 10^{-12} \text{ J}$$

$$Z = 79$$

Let r be the distance of closest approach.

From the law of conservation of energy,

initial kinetic energy of α-particle = final potential energy of system

As $K = \frac{1}{4\pi\varepsilon_0} \frac{(2e)(Ze)}{r}$

$$\Rightarrow r = \frac{1}{4\pi\varepsilon_0} \frac{2Ze^2}{K}$$

$$r = \frac{9 \times 10^9 \times 2 \times 79 \times (1.6 \times 10^{-19})^2}{1.2 \times 10^{-12}}$$

$$= 30 \times 10^{-15} \text{ m} = 30 \text{ fm}$$

8 (*c*) Let d be the centre-to-centre distance between the α-particle and the gold nucleus when the α-particle is at its stopping point. Then, we can write the conservation of energy $E_i = E_f$ as

$$K = \frac{1}{4\pi\varepsilon_0} \frac{(2e)(Ze)}{d} = \frac{2Ze^2}{4\pi\varepsilon_0 d}$$

Thus, the distance of closest approach d is given by

$$d = \frac{2Ze^2}{4\pi\varepsilon_0 K} = \frac{2kZe^2}{K}$$

$$K = 7.7 \times 1.6 \times 10^{-19} \text{ J} = 1.2 \times 10^{-12} \text{ J}$$

$$\therefore \; d = \frac{(2)(9.0 \times 10^9)(1.6 \times 10^{-19})^2 Z}{1.2 \times 10^{-12}}$$

$$= 3.84 \times 10^{-16} Z \text{ m}$$

The atomic number of foil material of gold is $Z = 79$, so that

$$d(\text{Au}) = 3.84 \times 10^{-16} \times 79$$

$$= 3.0 \times 10^{-14} \text{ m}$$

The radius of gold nucleus is therefore less than 3.0×10^{-14} m.

10 (*b*) Total energy of the electron in hydrogen atom is –13.6 eV.

$$\Rightarrow \quad E = -13.6 \times 1.6 \times 10^{-19} \text{ J}$$

$$= -2.2 \times 10^{-18} \text{ J}$$

As we know, total energy E of the electron in a hydrogen atom is

$$E = \frac{-e^2}{8\pi\varepsilon_0 r} \Rightarrow r = \frac{-e^2}{8\pi\varepsilon_0 E}$$

$$\Rightarrow \quad r = -\frac{(9 \times 10^9) \times (1.6 \times 10^{-19})^2}{2 \times (-2.2 \times 10^{-18})}$$

$$= 5.3 \times 10^{-11} \text{ m}$$

As, electron revolves around the nucleus, by centripetal force, so the electrostatic force required to separate electron from atom should be equal to this centripetal force.

i.e., $\quad F_c = F_e$

$$\Rightarrow \quad \frac{mv^2}{r} = \frac{1}{4\pi\varepsilon_0} \frac{e^2}{r^2}$$

$$\Rightarrow \quad v = \frac{e}{\sqrt{4\pi\varepsilon_0 mr}}$$

$$\Rightarrow v = \frac{1.6 \times 10^{-19}}{\sqrt{4 \times 3.14 \times 8.85 \times 10^{-12} \times 9.1 \times 10^{-31} \times 5.3 \times 10^{-11}}}$$

$$= 2.2 \times 10^6 \text{ m/s}$$

14 (*c*) Given, total energy = –1.51 eV

Total energy = – Kinetic energy

$\therefore$ Kinetic energy = –(–1.51 eV)

Kinetic energy = 1.51 eV

Now, Potential energy

= 2 × Total energy

= 2 × (–1.51) eV

= –3.02 eV

15 (*d*) $\frac{1}{\lambda} = R\left[\frac{1}{2^2} - \frac{1}{5^2}\right] = R\left[\frac{1}{4} - \frac{1}{25}\right]$

$$\frac{1}{\lambda} = \frac{21R}{100}$$

$$\therefore \quad \lambda = \frac{100}{21R} = \frac{100}{21 \times 1.1 \times 10^7}$$

$$= \frac{100}{23.1 \times 10^7}$$

$$\lambda = 4329 \text{Å}$$

This wavelength correspond to Violet.

Hence, the atom will emit violet light.

18 (*d*) The wavelength of first line of the Lyman series for hydrogen atom is given by

$$\frac{1}{\lambda} = R\left[\frac{1}{1^2} - \frac{1}{2^2}\right] \quad \text{...(i)}$$

The wavelength of second line of Balmer series for hydrogen atom is given by

$$\frac{1}{\lambda'} = Z^2R\left[\frac{1}{2^2} - \frac{1}{4^2}\right] \quad \text{...(ii)}$$

As given,

$$\lambda = \lambda'$$

From Eqs. (i) and (ii),

$$R\left[\frac{1}{1^2}-\frac{1}{2^2}\right]=Z^2R\left[\frac{1}{2^2}-\frac{1}{4^2}\right]$$

$$\Rightarrow \quad \frac{3}{4}=\frac{3Z^2}{16}$$

$$\Rightarrow \quad Z^2=4 \quad \Rightarrow \quad Z=2$$

19 (c) Given, $\lambda_L = 1215$ Å

For the first line of Lyman series,

$$\frac{1}{\lambda_L}=R\left[\frac{1}{1^2}-\frac{1}{2^2}\right]$$

$$=R\left[\frac{3}{4}\right]=\frac{3R}{4}$$

$$\therefore \quad \lambda_L=\frac{4}{3R} \quad \text{...(i)}$$

For first line of Balmer series,

$$\frac{1}{\lambda_B}=R\left[\frac{1}{2^2}-\frac{1}{3^2}\right]$$

$$=R\left[\frac{1}{4}-\frac{1}{9}\right]$$

$$\Rightarrow \quad \frac{1}{\lambda_B}=\frac{5R}{36}$$

$$\therefore \quad \lambda_B=\frac{36}{5R} \quad \text{...(ii)}$$

From Eqs. (i) and (ii), we get

$$\frac{\lambda_B}{\lambda_L}=\frac{36/5R}{4/3R}$$

$$\frac{\lambda_B}{1215}=\frac{36\times 3}{4\times 5}$$

$$\therefore \quad \lambda_B=\frac{108}{20}\times 1215$$

$$\Rightarrow \quad \lambda_B = 6561\text{Å}$$

20 (d) Given, $\lambda = 1210$ Å (for Lyman series)

For first line of Lyman series,

$$n_1=1,\ n_2=2$$

and $$\frac{1}{\lambda}=Z^2R\left[\frac{1}{1^2}-\frac{1}{2^2}\right]$$

For hydrogen atom, $Z=1$

$$\therefore \quad \frac{1}{\lambda}=R\frac{3}{4} \quad \text{...(i)}$$

For hydrogen like atom,

$$Z=11$$

$$\therefore \quad \frac{1}{\lambda'}=121\times R\frac{3}{4}$$

$$\Rightarrow \quad \frac{1}{\lambda'}=121\frac{3R}{4} \quad \text{...(ii)}$$

From Eqs. (i) and (ii), we get

$$\frac{\lambda'}{\lambda}=\frac{3R/4}{121R\times 3/4}=\frac{1}{121}$$

$$\Rightarrow \quad \lambda'=\frac{\lambda}{121}=\frac{1210}{121}$$

$$\Rightarrow \quad \lambda'=10\text{ Å}$$

21 (d) Series limit occurs in the transition $n_2=\infty$ to $n_1=1$ in Lyman series and $n_2=\infty$ to $n_1=5$ in Pfund series. For Lyman series,

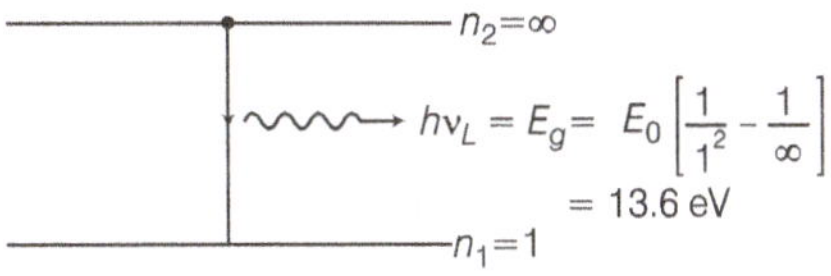

$$h\nu_L = 13.6\text{ eV} \quad \text{...(i)}$$

In Pfund series

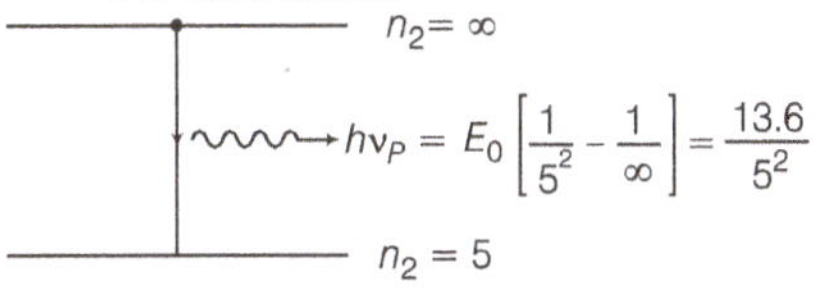

$$h\nu_P=\frac{13.6}{5^2}\text{ eV} \quad \text{...(ii)}$$

From Eqs. (i) and (ii), we get

$$25h\nu_P = h\nu_L$$

$$\therefore \quad \nu_P=\frac{\nu_L}{25}$$

22 (c) For last line of Balmer series,

$n_1=2$ and $n_2=\infty$

$$\Rightarrow \quad \frac{1}{\lambda_B}=R\left(\frac{1}{2^2}-\frac{1}{\infty^2}\right)=\frac{R}{4} \quad \text{... (i)}$$

Similarly, for last line of Lyman series,

$$n_1=1 \text{ and } n_2=\infty$$

$$\Rightarrow \quad \frac{1}{\lambda_L}=R\left(\frac{1}{1^2}-\frac{1}{\infty^2}\right)=R \quad \text{...(ii)}$$

From Eqs. (i) and (ii), we get

$$\frac{\frac{1}{\lambda_B}}{\frac{1}{\lambda_L}}=\frac{R/4}{R}$$

$$\Rightarrow \quad \frac{\lambda_L}{\lambda_B}=\frac{1}{4}\Rightarrow\frac{\lambda_B}{\lambda_L}=4$$

23 (d) In Pfund series,

$$\frac{1}{\lambda}=R\left(\frac{1}{5^2}-\frac{1}{n^2}\right),\text{ where } n=6, 7,\ldots$$

Maximum wavelength is given by

$$\frac{1}{\lambda_{max}}=R\left(\frac{1}{5^2}-\frac{1}{6^2}\right)=R\left(\frac{11}{900}\right) \quad \text{...(i)}$$

Minimum wavelength is given by

$$\frac{1}{\lambda_{min}}=R\left(\frac{1}{5^2}-\frac{1}{\infty}\right)=\frac{R}{25} \quad \text{...(ii)}$$

From Eqs. (i) and (ii), we get

$$\frac{\lambda_{max}}{\lambda_{min}}=\frac{R/25}{11R/900}=\frac{36}{11}$$

24 (d) For largest wavelength in Lyman series, $n_1=1$ and $n_2=2$

$$\frac{1}{\lambda_1}=R\left[\frac{1}{1^2}-\frac{1}{2^2}\right] \quad \text{...(i)}$$

For largest wavelength in Balmer series, $n_1=2$ and $n_2=3$

$$\frac{1}{\lambda_2}=R\left[\frac{1}{2^2}-\frac{1}{3^2}\right] \quad \text{...(ii)}$$

Dividing Eq. (ii) by Eq. (i), we get

$$\frac{\lambda_1}{\lambda_2}=\frac{R\left[\frac{1}{4}-\frac{1}{9}\right]}{R\left[1-\frac{1}{4}\right]}=\frac{\frac{5}{36}}{\frac{3}{4}}$$

$$\Rightarrow \quad \frac{\lambda_1}{\lambda_2}=\frac{5}{36}\times\frac{4}{3}=\frac{5}{27}$$

25 (a) When electron beam of 12.75 eV is incident over hydrogen gas, energy of H-atoms will be

$= -13.6 + 12.75 = -0.85$ eV

This corresponds to $n=\sqrt{\frac{13.6}{0.85}}=4$

excited state.

Various transitions, for $n=4$ are shown below

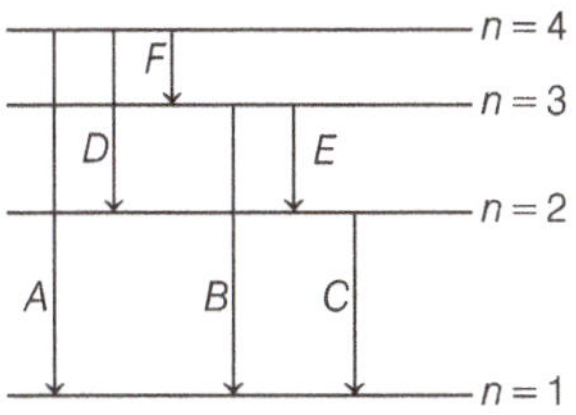

Clearly, emitted radiation lies in **Lyman series** (A, B and C).

Few emissions are in **Balmer series** (D and E).

One of them ($n=4$ to $n=3$) lies in Paschen series (F).

26 (b) $\frac{1}{\lambda}=RZ^2\left(\frac{1}{n^2}-\frac{1}{m^2}\right)$

For visible region transition is from $n = 3, 4, 5$ .... etc to $n = 2$

Here $Z = 2$

$$\frac{1}{\lambda} = R\left(\frac{Z^2}{n^2} - \frac{Z^2}{m^2}\right)$$

$$= R\left(\frac{4}{4^2} - \frac{4}{m^2}\right)$$

$m = 6$ to 4, 7 to 4, ...

28 (*a*) According to Bohr's theory of atom, $mvr = n\frac{h}{2\pi}$

For $n = 1$,

$$mvr = \frac{h}{2\pi} \Rightarrow v = \frac{h}{2\pi mr} \quad ...(i)$$

The rate of flow of current is given by

$$I = e\left(\frac{v}{2\pi r}\right)$$

From Eq. (i),

$$I = \frac{e}{2\pi r} \times \frac{h}{2\pi mr} = \frac{eh}{4\pi^2 mr^2}$$

Now, the magnetic dipole moment M is

$$M = IA = \frac{eh}{4\pi^2 mr^2} \times \pi r^2$$

$$\Rightarrow M = \frac{eh}{4\pi m}$$

30 (*c*) Change in angular momentum,

$$\Delta L = L_2 - L_1 = \frac{n_2 h}{2\pi} - \frac{n_1 h}{2\pi}$$

$$= \frac{h}{2\pi}(n_2 - n_1)$$

$$\therefore \quad \Delta L = \frac{6.6 \times 10^{-34}}{2 \times 3.14} \times (5 - 4)$$

$$= 1.05 \times 10^{-34} \text{ J-s}$$

31 (*b*) The statement given in option (b) is incorrect and it can be corrected as,

According to Bohr's atomic model, electron revolves in stationary stable orbits without emission of radiant energy. Thus, its mass remains constant.

32 (*d*) Frequency of a photon emission is given by $\nu_n = \frac{\Delta E}{h}$

Now, $E = R\left(\frac{1}{n_1^2} - \frac{1}{n_2^2}\right)$

$$E_{4 \to 3} = R\left(\frac{1}{3^2} - \frac{1}{4^2}\right)$$

$$= R\left(\frac{1}{9} - \frac{1}{16}\right) = 0.05\,R$$

$\therefore$ The lowest energy is for $n = 4$ to $n = 3$ transition, so the frequency of photons emitted in this transition will have lower frequency.

33 (*b*) Given, $M = 10$ kg,

$r_n = 8000 \text{ km} = 8 \times 10^6 \text{ m}$,

$T = 2\text{h} = 2 \times 60 \times 60$

$= 7200$ s

Velocity of nth orbit is given by

$$v_n = \frac{2\pi r_n}{T} \quad ...(i)$$

From Bohr's model,

$$Mv_n r_n = \frac{nh}{2\pi} \quad ...(ii)$$

From Eqs. (i) and (ii),

$$Mr_n\left(\frac{2\pi r_n}{T}\right) = \frac{nh}{2\pi}$$

$$\Rightarrow \quad n = \frac{2\pi}{h} \times \frac{2\pi r_n}{T} \times M \times r_n$$

$$= \frac{(2\pi r_n)^2 M}{T \times h}$$

$$= \frac{(2 \times 3.14 \times 8 \times 10^6)^2 \times 10}{7200 \times 6.64 \times 10^{-34}}$$

$$= 5.3 \times 10^{45}$$

34 (*d*) Given, $r_1 = 5.30 \times 10^{-11}$ m,

$v_1 = 2.2 \times 10^6 \text{ ms}^{-1}$

For the first excited state,

$$r_n = n^2 r_1$$

and $\quad v_n = \frac{v_1}{n}$

$$\therefore \quad r_2 = 4r_1 \quad (\because n = 2)$$

$$= 4 \times 5.30 \times 10^{-11}$$

$$r_2 = 2.12 \times 10^{-10} \text{ m}$$

and $\quad v_2 = \frac{v_1}{2} = \frac{2.2 \times 10^6}{2}$

$$= 1.1 \times 10^6 \text{ ms}^{-1}$$

Orbital period is given by

$$T = \frac{2\pi r_2}{v_2}$$

$$= \frac{2 \times 3.14 \times 2.12 \times 10^{-10}}{1.1 \times 10^6}$$

$$= 1.21 \times 10^{-15} \text{ s}$$

37 (*c*) According to Bohr's model, the ground state energy of an atom is given by

$$E = \frac{-me^4}{8\,\varepsilon_0^2 h^2} \quad ...(i)$$

where, m is the reduced mass of electron and positron in the positronium and is given by

$$m = \frac{M_e M_p}{M_e + M_p}$$

$$= \frac{M_e}{2} \quad (\because M_p = M_e)$$

From Eq. (i), the ground state energy is

$$E = -\frac{\left(\frac{M_e}{2}\right)e^4}{8 \cdot \varepsilon_0^2 h^2}$$

as $\frac{M_e e^4}{8\varepsilon_0^2 h^2} = 13.6$ eV

$$\therefore \quad E = -\frac{1}{2}\left(\frac{M_e e^4}{8\varepsilon_0^2 h^2}\right) = -\frac{13.6}{2}$$

$$\Rightarrow \quad E = -6.8 \text{ eV}$$

38 (*b*) Here, T_n = period of revolution $= \frac{2\pi r_n}{v_n}$

Here, $r_n = \frac{n^2 h^2 \varepsilon_0}{\pi m Z e^2}$

and $v_n = \frac{Ze^2}{2\varepsilon_0 nh}$

So, $\quad T_n = 2\pi \times \frac{n^2 h^2 \varepsilon_0}{\pi m Z e^2} \times \frac{2\varepsilon_0 nh}{Ze^2}$

$$= \frac{4\varepsilon_0^2 n^3 h^3}{mZ^2 e^4} \Rightarrow T_n \propto \frac{n^3}{Z^2}$$

40 (*d*) Velocity of electron,

$$v_n = \frac{2\pi kZe^2}{nh}$$

$$v_3 = \frac{2 \times \pi \times 9 \times 10^9 \times 1 \times (1.6 \times 10^{-19})^2}{3 \times 6.6 \times 10^{-34}}$$

$$= 7.31 \times 10^5 \text{ ms}^{-1}$$

Also, time period, $T_n = \frac{2\pi r_n}{v_n}$

where, $r_n = \frac{n^2 h^2 \varepsilon_0}{\pi m Z e^2}$

$$\Rightarrow r_3 = \frac{(3)^2 \times (6.6 \times 10^{-34})^2 \times 8.85 \times 10^{-12}}{\pi \times 9.1 \times 10^{-31} \times 1 \times (1.6 \times 10^{-19})^2}$$

$$= 4.75 \times 10^{-10} \text{ m}$$

$$\Rightarrow \therefore T_3 = \frac{2\pi r_3}{v_3} = \frac{2\pi \times 4.75 \times 10^{-10}}{7.31 \times 10^5}$$

$$= 4.08 \times 10^{-15} \text{s}$$

41 (c) In the transition from

$n = 2$ to $n = 1$

$$\Delta E = RhcZ^2\left[\frac{1}{1^2} - \frac{1}{2^2}\right]$$

$$= RhcZ^2\left[\frac{3}{4}\right] \quad \text{...(i)}$$

The energy required to eject an electron from $n = 4$,

$$E' = \frac{RhcZ^2}{n^2} = \frac{RhcZ^2}{16} \quad \text{...(ii)}$$

Now, kinetic energy of Auger electron,

$$KE = \Delta E - E'$$

From Eqs (i) and (ii),

$$KE = \frac{3}{4} RhcZ^2 - \frac{RhcZ^2}{16}$$

$$= RhcZ^2\left[\frac{3}{4} - \frac{1}{16}\right]$$

$$= RhcZ^2\left[\frac{11}{16}\right]$$

Here, $Rhc = 13.6$ eV, $Z = 24$, then

$$KE = \frac{13.6 \times (24)^2 \times 11}{16}$$

$$= 5.38 \times 10^3 \text{ eV} = 5.38 \text{ keV}$$

42 (b) The velocity of an electron in nth orbit of Bohr's atom is

$$v_n = \frac{e^2 \times 2\pi}{4\pi\varepsilon_0 nh} = \frac{e^2}{2\varepsilon_0 nh}$$

$\therefore$ Kinetic energy,

$$(KE)_n = \frac{1}{2} mv_n^2 = \frac{1}{2} m\left(\frac{e^2}{2\varepsilon_0 nh}\right)^2$$

$$= \frac{me^4}{8\varepsilon_0^2 n^2 h^2} \quad \text{...(i)}$$

Total energy of electron in hydrogen atom is

$$(TE)_n = -\frac{e^2}{8\pi\varepsilon_0 r_n}$$

where, $r_n = \frac{n^2h^2 4\pi\varepsilon_0}{m 4\pi^2 e^2} = \frac{n^2h^2\varepsilon_0}{\pi me^2}$

$$\Rightarrow \quad (TE)_n = -\frac{e^2}{8\pi\varepsilon_0} \times \frac{\pi me^2}{n^2h^2\varepsilon_0}$$

$$= \frac{-me^4}{8n^2\varepsilon_0^2 h^2} \quad \text{...(ii)}$$

From Eqs. (i) and (ii), we get

$$(KE)_n : (TE)_n = \frac{me^4}{8\varepsilon_0^2 n^2 h^2} : \frac{-8\varepsilon_0^2 n^2 h^2}{me^4}$$

$$= 1 : -1$$

43 (b) According to Bohr's model,

$$KE = \frac{me^4}{8\varepsilon_0^2 n^2 h^2} \quad \text{... (i)}$$

Similarly, potential energy is given by

$$PE = -\frac{me^4}{4\varepsilon_0^2 n^2 h^2} \quad \text{... (ii)}$$

$\therefore$ Total energy, $E = PE + KE$

$$= -\frac{me^4}{8\varepsilon_0^2 n^2 h^2}$$

[from Eqs. (i) and (ii)]

$\Rightarrow \quad KE = -E$ and $PE = 2E$

Given, $E = -3.4$ eV

$\therefore \quad KE = -(-3.4) = 3.4$ eV

and $\quad PE = 2(-3.4) = -6.8$ eV

46 (b) Energy of electron in first excited state of hydrogen,

$$E_n = -\frac{13.6}{n^2} = -\frac{13.6}{2^2}$$

$$= -3.40 \text{ eV}$$

($n = 2$ in first excitation)

So, for doubly ionised lithium ($Z = 3$), energy will be

$$E_n = (E_H) Z^2 = -3.40 \times 9$$

$$= -30.6 \text{ eV}$$

$\therefore$ Energy required to remove electron, $-E_n = 30.6$ eV

48 (b) Angular momentum of an electron, $L = \frac{nh}{2\pi}$

As in 2nd excited state, $n = 3$, for both H and Li^+.

$\Rightarrow \quad L_H = L_{Li}$

Energy, $E_n = \frac{-Z^2(13.6)}{n^2}$

$\Rightarrow \quad E_n \propto Z^2$

As, $Z_H = 1$ and $Z_{Li^+} = 3$

$\therefore \quad |E_{Li}| > |E_H|$

49 (b) Energy of a hydrogen atom like ion by Bohr's model is

$$E_n = -13.6 \frac{Z^2}{n^2}$$

For a He^+ ion in first excited state,

$n = 2, Z = 2$

$$\therefore \quad E_2 = -13.6 \times \frac{4}{4} = -13.6 \text{ eV}$$

So, it's ionisation energy

$$= -(E_2) = 13.6 \text{ eV}.$$

52 (c) Energy of electron,

$$E_n = \frac{-13.6}{n^2} Z^2$$

In first excited state,

$$E_{H_2} = \frac{-13.6(1)^2}{(2)^2} = -3.4 \text{ eV}$$

$$\text{and } E_{He} = \frac{-13.6(2)^2}{(2)^2} = -13.6 \text{ eV}$$

H-atom gives excitation energy ($13.6 - 3.4 = 10.2$ eV) to helium atom.

Now, energy of He ion

$$= -13.6 + 10.2$$

$$= -3.4 \text{ eV}$$

Again, $E = \frac{-13.6}{n^2} \times Z^2$

$$\Rightarrow \quad n = \sqrt{\frac{13.6 \times 4}{3.4}} = 4$$

54 (c) When electron absorbs photon of energy 12.1 eV, energy of electron will be = initial energy + absorbed energy

$$E = -13.6 \text{ eV} + 12.1 \text{ eV}$$

$$\Rightarrow \quad E = -1.5 \text{ eV}$$

which corresponds to $n = \sqrt{\frac{13.6}{1.5}} = 3$

excited state.

So, number of possible transitions are

$$N = \frac{n(n-1)}{2} = 3$$

i.e. $\quad n = 3 \to n = 2$

$\Rightarrow n = 2 \to n = 1$

$\Rightarrow \quad n = 3 \to n = 1$

$\therefore$ The spectral lines emitted by hydrogen atom are three in number.

56 (*a*) Energy of an electron in nth state for hydrogen like atom is

$$E_n = \frac{Z^2}{n^2}(E_1)_H = -13.6\frac{Z^2}{n^2} \text{ eV}$$

$\therefore$ The energy required to excite the electron from $n = 1$ to $n = 2$ is

$$E = E_2 - E_1$$

$$40.8 = -13.6\, Z^2\left(\frac{1}{2^2} - \frac{1}{1^2}\right)$$

$$40.8 = \frac{13.6\, Z^2 \cdot 3}{4}$$

$$Z^2 = \frac{40.8 \times 4}{13.6 \times 3} \Rightarrow Z = 2$$

57 (*c*) Absorption of energy is given by

$$E = E_2 - E_1$$

As, $\quad E_n = -\frac{13.6}{n^2}$ eV

Then, $\quad E_2 - E_1 = -\frac{13.6}{4^2}$ eV $-\left(-\frac{13.6}{1^2}\right)$ eV

$$= 2.04 \times 10^{-16} \text{ J}$$

As $E = \frac{hc}{\lambda} \Rightarrow \lambda = \frac{hc}{E}$

$$= \frac{6.6 \times 10^{-34} \times 3 \times 10^8}{2.04 \times 10^{-16}}$$

$$= 970 \times 10^{-10} = 970 \text{ Å}$$

58 (*a*) As, linear momentum, $p = mv$

$\Rightarrow p \propto v$

As $\quad v \propto \frac{1}{n} \Rightarrow p \propto \frac{1}{n}$

i.e. linear momentum is inversely proportional to the number of orbit n.

Thus, the statement given in option (a) is incorrect, rest are correct.

59 (*a*) As we know that, kinetic energy of an electron is KE $\propto \left(\frac{Z}{n}\right)^2$

When the electron makes transition from an excited state to the ground state, then n decreases and kinetic energy increases.

We know that, potential energy is lowest for ground state. Also, total energy = – kinetic energy, so total energy also decreases as n increases.

Thus, the statement given in option (a) is correct, rest are incorrect.

63 (*a*) Emitted frequency ν is given by $h\nu = \Delta E$

$$\Rightarrow \quad \nu = \frac{\Delta E}{h} = \frac{E_n - E_{n-1}}{h}$$

As, $\quad E_n = \frac{-me^4}{(4\pi)^3 \varepsilon_0^2 \frac{h^2}{(2\pi)^3}}\left(\frac{1}{n^2}\right)$

$$\Rightarrow \nu = -\frac{me^4}{(4\pi)^3\, \varepsilon_0^2 \left(\frac{h}{2\pi}\right)^3}\left\{\frac{1}{n^2} - \frac{1}{(n-1)^2}\right\}$$

$$= \frac{me^4\,(2n-1)}{(4\pi)^3\, \varepsilon_0^2 \left(\frac{h}{2\pi}\right)^3 n^2\,(n-1)^2}$$

64 (*c*) We know that, frequency,

$$\nu = \frac{c}{\lambda} = c \cdot R\left(\frac{1}{n_1^2} - \frac{1}{n_2^2}\right)$$

$$= 3 \times 10^8 \times 10^7\left(\frac{1}{2^2} - \frac{1}{4^2}\right)$$

$$= \frac{9}{16} \times 10^{15} \text{ Hz}$$

66 (*c*) We have, $\lambda = \frac{hc}{\Delta E}$

$\therefore$ So, ratio of wavelengths

$$\frac{\lambda_1}{\lambda_2} = \frac{hc/\Delta E_1}{hc/\Delta E_2} = \frac{\Delta E_2}{\Delta E_1}$$

$$= \frac{\left(\frac{4}{3}E - E\right)}{2E - E} = \frac{1}{3}$$

67 (*d*) De-excitation energy of hydrogen electron in transition $n = 2$ to $n = 1$ is

$$E = 13.6 \times \left(\frac{1}{n_f^2} - \frac{1}{n_i^2}\right) \text{eV}$$

$$= 13.6\left(\frac{1}{1^2} - \frac{1}{2^2}\right) = 10.2 \text{ eV}$$

Now, energy levels of helium ion's (He^+) electron are

(For helium, $Z = 2$)

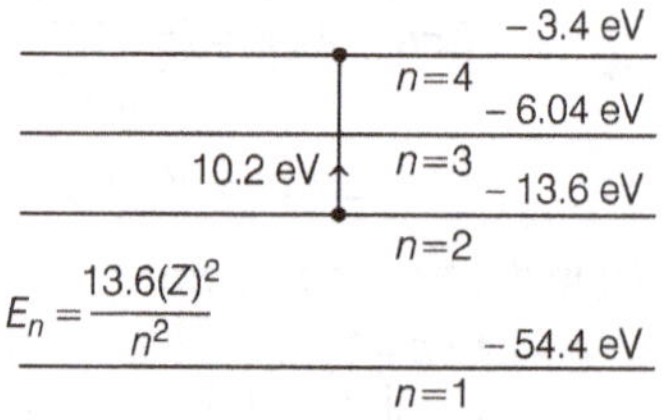

So, a photon of energy 10.2 eV can cause a transition $n = 2$ to $n = 4$ in a He^+ ion.

68 (*d*) Here, for wavelength λ_1, $n_1 = 4$ and $n_2 = 3$

and for λ_2, $n_1 = 3$ and $n_2 = 2$

We have, $\frac{1}{\lambda} = -R\left[\frac{1}{n_2^2} - \frac{1}{n_1^2}\right]$

So, for λ_1, $n_2 = 4$ and $n_1 = 3$

$$\Rightarrow \frac{1}{\lambda_1} = -R\left[\frac{1}{(4)^2} - \frac{1}{(3)^2}\right]$$

$$\frac{1}{\lambda_1} = R\left[\frac{7}{144}\right] \quad \text{...(i)}$$

Similarly, for λ_2, $n_2 = 3$ and $n_1 = 2$

$$\Rightarrow \frac{1}{\lambda_2} = -R\left[\frac{1}{(3)^2} - \frac{1}{(2)^2}\right]$$

$$\frac{1}{\lambda_2} = R\left[\frac{5}{36}\right] \quad \text{...(ii)}$$

From Eqs. (i) and (ii), we get

$$\frac{\lambda_1}{\lambda_2} = \frac{5R}{36} \times \frac{144}{7R} = \frac{20}{7}$$

69 (*a*) Wavelength emitted by photon during its transition is given by

$$\frac{1}{\lambda} = RZ^2\left(\frac{1}{n_1^2} - \frac{1}{n_2^2}\right)$$

$Z = 1$ (for H), $n_1 = n$, $n_2 = 1$ (ground state)

$$\frac{1}{\lambda} = R(1)^2\left(\frac{1}{n^2} - \frac{1}{1}\right)$$

$$\frac{1}{n^2} = \frac{1}{\lambda R} + 1$$

$$n = \sqrt{\frac{\lambda R}{\lambda R + 1}}$$

73 (a) We know that, frequency,

$$\nu = Rc\left(\frac{1}{n_1^2} - \frac{1}{n_2^2}\right)$$

For series limit of Lyman series,

$n_1 = 1, n_2 = \infty.$

$$\nu_1 = Rc\left(\frac{1}{1^2} - \frac{1}{\infty}\right) = Rc$$

For first line, $n_1 = 1, n_2 = 2.$

$$\nu_2 = Rc\left(\frac{1}{1^2} - \frac{1}{4}\right) = \frac{3}{4}Rc$$

For series limit of Balmer series, $n_1 = 2, n_2 = \infty.$

$$\nu_3 = Rc\left(\frac{1}{4} - \frac{1}{\infty}\right) = \frac{Rc}{4}$$

$$\Rightarrow \nu_1 - \nu_2 = Rc - \frac{3}{4}Rc = \frac{Rc}{4} = \nu_3$$

75 (b) As angular momentum, L

$$\frac{nh}{2\pi} = \frac{3h}{2\pi} \Rightarrow n = 3$$

Also, $a_0 \times \frac{n^2}{Z} = 4.5a_0$

$$\Rightarrow \frac{n^2}{Z} = 4.5$$

$$\Rightarrow Z = 2$$

According to Rydberg's formula,

$$\frac{1}{\lambda} = RZ^2\left(\frac{1}{n_1^2} - \frac{1}{n_2^2}\right)$$

$$\Rightarrow \frac{1}{\lambda_1} = R \times 2^2\left[\frac{1}{1^2} - \frac{1}{3^2}\right]$$

$$\Rightarrow \frac{1}{\lambda_1} = 4R \times \frac{8}{9}$$

$$\frac{1}{\lambda_2} = 4R\left[\frac{1}{2^2} - \frac{1}{3^2}\right]$$

$$\Rightarrow \frac{1}{\lambda_2} = 4R \times \frac{5}{36}$$

$$\frac{1}{\lambda_3} = 4R\left[\frac{1}{1^2} - \frac{1}{2^2}\right]$$

$$\Rightarrow \frac{1}{\lambda_3} = 4R \times \frac{3}{4}$$

$$\Rightarrow \lambda_1 = \frac{9}{32R}, \lambda_2 = \frac{9}{5R}, \lambda_3 = \frac{1}{3R}$$

Hence, $\lambda = \frac{9}{16R}$ is not possible.

76 (c) Given, $E = -4.6$ eV

$$K = -E = -(-4.6) = 4.6 \text{ eV}$$

de-Broglie wavelength, $\lambda = \frac{h}{\sqrt{2mK}}$

$$= \frac{6.6 \times 10^{-34}}{\sqrt{2 \times 9.1 \times 10^{-31} \times 4.6 \times 1.6 \times 10^{-19}}}$$

$= 0.57 \times 10^{-9}$ m $= 0.57$ nm

77 (b) From de-Broglie, the circumference of the orbit is equal to $n\lambda$.

$$\therefore \quad 2\pi r = n\lambda$$

As the electron is revolving in second orbit.

$$\therefore \quad 2\pi r = 2\lambda \quad (\because n = 2)$$

So, the circumference of the orbits is 2λ.

Assertion and Reason Questions

2 (c) According to postulates of Bohr's atom model, the electron revolves around the nucleus in fixed orbit of definite radii. As long as the electron is in a certain orbit, it does not radiate any energy. Therefore, Assertion is correct but Reason is incorrect.

3 (b) Rutherford confirmed that the repulsive force on α-particle due to nucleus varies with distance according to inverse square law and that the positive charges are concentrated at the centre and not distributed throughout the atom.

Therefore, Assertion and Reason are correct but Reason is not the correct explanation of Assertion.

5 (a) In such gases, the average spacing between atoms is large. Hence, the radiation emitted can be considered due to individual atoms because of interaction between atoms or molecules.

Therefore, Assertion and Reason are correct and Reason is the correct explanation of Assertion.

6 (c) The energy of electron in nth orbit of hydrogen atom is,

$$E_n = -\frac{me^4}{8n^2\varepsilon_0^2h^2} = \frac{-2.18 \times 10^{-18}}{n^2}$$

For first excited state ($n = 2$)

$$E_2 = -\frac{2.18 \times 10^{-18}}{4}$$

$$= -5.45 \times 10^{-19} \text{ J}$$

Therefore, Assertionis correct but Reason is incorrect.

7 (b) Bohr postulated that electrons in stationary orbits around the nucleus do not radiate. This is the one of Bohr's postulate. According to this, the moving electrons radiates only when they go from one orbit to the lower orbit.

Therefore, Assertion and Reason are correct but Reason is not the correct explanation of Assertion.

8 (d) The energy of an atom is the least when its electron is revolving in an orbit closest to the nucleus, i.e., the one for which $n = 1$.
However, the highest energy state corresponds to $n = \infty$ and has an energy of 0 eV.

Since, $E_n \propto \frac{1}{n^2}$

So, as the value of n increases, energies of excited states comes closer and closer.
Therefore, Assertion is incorrect but Reason is correct.

9 (b) Maximum number of photons is given by all the transitions possible $= {}^4C_2 = 6$
Minimum number of transition $= 1$
i.e., directly jump from 4 to 1.

Therefore, Assertion and Reason are correct but Reason is not the correct explanation of Assertion.

10 (d) It can absorb a photon with energy greater than 13.6 eV, the balance showing up as KE.
Therefore, Assertion is incorrect but Reason is correct.

Statement Based Questions

6 (a) Both Statement I and Statement II are incorrect. Bohr's model is applicable to singly ionised helium (He^+) as it describes the behaviour of electrons in hydrogen like ions. Lyman series lies in ultraviolet region while Brackett series lies in infrared region.

7 (b) Statement I is correct but Statement II is incorrect. Hydrogen atom have both emission and absorption spectrum.

Matching Type Questions

1 (b) For Balmer series,

$$\frac{1}{\lambda}=R\left(\frac{1}{2^2}-\frac{1}{n^2}\right)$$

A. For $n=3$,

$$(H_{\alpha\text{-series}})\frac{1}{\lambda_\alpha}=1.097\times10^7\left(\frac{1}{2^2}-\frac{1}{3^2}\right)$$
$$=1.097\times10^7\times\frac{5}{36}\,\text{m}^{-1}$$
$$\lambda_\alpha=\frac{36}{5\times1.097\times10^7}$$
$$=656.3\times10^{-9}\,\text{m}=656.3\,\text{nm}$$

B. For $n=4$,

$$(H_{\beta\text{-series}})\frac{1}{\lambda_\beta}=1.097\times10^7\left(\frac{1}{2^2}-\frac{1}{4^2}\right)$$
$$=1.097\times10^7\times\frac{3}{16}\,\text{m}^{-1}$$
$$\Rightarrow\lambda_\beta=\frac{16}{3\times1.097\times10^7}$$
$$=486.1\times10^{-9}\,\text{m}=486.1\text{ nm}$$

C. For $n=5$,

$$(H_{\gamma\text{-series}})\frac{1}{\lambda_\gamma}=1.097\times10^7\left(\frac{1}{2^2}-\frac{1}{5^2}\right)$$
$$=1.097\times10^7\times\frac{21}{100}\,\text{m}^{-1}$$
$$\Rightarrow\lambda_\gamma=\frac{100}{21\times1.097\times10^7}=434.1\,\text{nm}$$

D. For $n=6$,

$$(H_{\delta\text{-series}})\frac{1}{\lambda_\delta}=1.097\times10^7\left(\frac{1}{2^2}-\frac{1}{6^2}\right)$$
$$=1.097\times10^7\times\frac{8}{36}\,\text{m}^{-1}$$
$$\Rightarrow\quad\lambda_\delta=\frac{36}{8\times1.097\times10^7}$$
$$=410.2\,\text{nm}$$

Hence, A $\rightarrow$ 4, B $\rightarrow$ 3, C $\rightarrow$ 2 and D $\rightarrow$ 1.

3 (c) Lyman series

$$\frac{1}{\lambda}=R\left(\frac{1}{1^2}-\frac{1}{n^2}\right)\quad n=2,3,4,\ldots$$

Balmer series

$$\frac{1}{\lambda}=R\left(\frac{1}{2^2}-\frac{1}{n^2}\right),\ n=3,4,5,\ldots$$

Paschen series

$$\frac{1}{\lambda}=R\left(\frac{1}{3^2}-\frac{1}{n^2}\right),\quad n=4,5,6,\ldots$$

Brackett series $\quad\frac{1}{\lambda}=R\left(\frac{1}{4^2}-\frac{1}{n^2}\right),$

$n=5,6,7,\ldots$

To obtain maximum wavelengths we substitute

$\therefore$ For Lyman;

$$\lambda_{max}=\frac{1}{R\left(1-\frac{1}{4}\right)}=\frac{4}{3R}$$

For Balmer;

$$\lambda_{max}=\frac{1}{R\left(\frac{1}{4}-\frac{1}{9}\right)}=\frac{36}{5R}$$

For Paschen;

$$\lambda_{max}=\frac{1}{R\left(\frac{1}{9}-\frac{1}{16}\right)}=\frac{144}{7R}$$

For Brackett;

$$\lambda_{max}=\frac{1}{R\left(\frac{1}{16}-\frac{1}{25}\right)}=\frac{400}{9R}$$

Hence, A $\rightarrow$ 4, B $\rightarrow$ 3, C $\rightarrow$ 2 and D $\rightarrow$ 1.

4 (d) As we know,

A. Angular momentum,

$$L=\frac{nh}{2\pi}\Rightarrow L\propto n$$

B. Velocity of electrons,

$$v_n=\frac{1}{n}\frac{e^2}{4\pi\varepsilon_0}\cdot\frac{1}{(h/2\pi)}$$
$$\Rightarrow\quad v_n\propto1/n$$

C. Radius of an electron,

$$r_n=\frac{n^2}{m}\left(\frac{h}{2\pi}\right)^2\frac{4\pi\varepsilon_0}{e^2}$$
$$\Rightarrow\quad r_n\propto n^2$$

D. Potential energy,

$$U_n=-\frac{me^4}{4n^2\varepsilon_0^2h^2}$$
$$\therefore\quad U_n\propto1/n^2$$

Hence, A $\rightarrow$ 4, B $\rightarrow$ 1, C $\rightarrow$ 2 and D $\rightarrow$ 3.

Numerical Type Questions

1 (3)

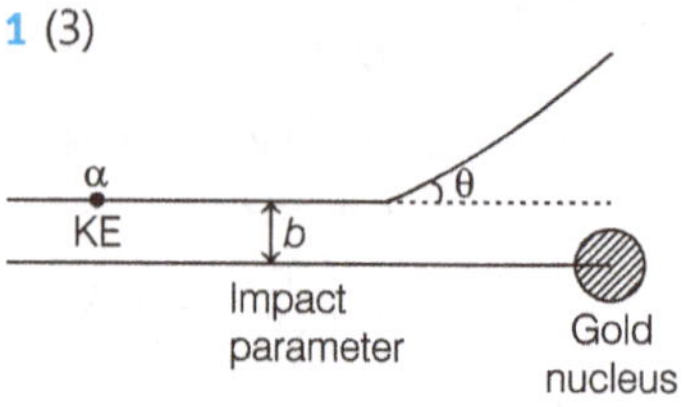

Impact parameter b is given by

$$b=\frac{Ze^2\cdot\cot(\theta/2)}{4\pi\varepsilon_0(\text{KE})}\text{ or }b\propto\cot\frac{\theta}{2}$$

With given values, we get

$$\therefore\frac{\sqrt{d_1}}{\sqrt{d_2}}=\frac{\cot(60^\circ/2)}{\cot(90^\circ/2)}=\frac{\cot30^\circ}{\cot45^\circ}$$

or $$\frac{\sqrt{d_1}}{\sqrt{d_2}}=\frac{\sqrt{3}}{1}$$

On squaring both sides,

$$\frac{d_1}{d_2}=3\text{ and }\frac{d_1}{d_2}=x\text{ (given)}$$

So, $x=3$

2 (11) Given, $\theta=90^\circ$, $Z=79$

$$E_K=10\text{ MeV}=1.6\times10^{-12}\text{ J}$$

Now, impact parameter,

$$b=\frac{Ze^2\cot(\theta/2)}{4\pi\varepsilon_0E_K}$$
$$=\frac{79\times9\times10^9\times(1.6\times10^{-19})^2\times\cot45^\circ}{1.6\times10^{-12}}$$
$$=79\times9\times1.6\times10^{-17}\text{ m}$$
$$=11\times10^{-15}\text{ m}$$
$$\therefore p=11$$

3 (3) Mass of the particle,

$$m_p=250\text{ MeV}/c^2$$

Mass of the hydrogen atom,

$$m_H=\frac{1\text{GeV}}{c^2}=1000\text{ MeV}/c^2$$
$$\therefore m_H=4m_p$$

Using law of conservation of linear momentum,

$$m_pv_p+0=0+m_Hv_H$$
$$m_pv_p=4m_pv_H$$
$$v_H=v_p/4$$

When atom goes to its second excited state,

$$\Delta E = \left[\frac{-13.6}{(3)^2}\right] \text{eV} - \left(\frac{-13.6}{(1)^2}\right) \text{eV}$$

$$= -1.51 + 13.6 = 12.08 \text{ eV} \quad \text{...(i)}$$

Loss of kinetic energy,

$$\Delta E = \frac{1}{2} m_p v_p^2 - \frac{1}{2}(4m_p) v_H^2$$

$$= \frac{1}{2} m_p v_p^2 - \frac{1}{2}(4 m_p)\left(\frac{v_p}{4}\right)^2$$

$$= \frac{1}{2} m_p v_p^2 \left(1 - \frac{1}{4}\right)$$

$$\Delta E = \frac{3}{4} K \left[\because K = \frac{m_p v_p^2}{2}\right] \quad \text{...(ii)}$$

From Eqs. (i) and (ii), we get

$$\frac{3}{4} K = 12.08$$

$$\Rightarrow \quad K = \frac{12.08 \times 4}{3} = \frac{48.32}{3} \text{ eV}$$

$$= \frac{48.32}{N}$$

$$\therefore \quad N = 3$$

4 (4) Radius,

$$r = 8.4 \text{ Å} = 8.4 \times 10^{-10} \text{m}$$

Speed, $v = 1.32 \times 10^6$ m/s

Current associated due to moving electron,

$$I = \frac{e}{T} = \frac{e\omega}{2\pi} \Rightarrow I = \frac{e}{2\pi} \cdot \frac{v}{r}$$

$$= \frac{1.6 \times 10^{-19} \times 1.32 \times 10^6 \times 7}{2 \times 22 \times 8.4 \times 10^{-10}}$$

$$\therefore \quad I = 4 \times 10^{-2} \text{mA}$$

5 (4) Here, $n_2 = 1$, $n_1 = 2$

The energy of emitted photon,

$$\Delta E = \left(\frac{1}{n_2^2} - \frac{1}{n_1^2}\right) \times 13.6 \text{ eV}$$

$$= \left(\frac{1}{1} - \frac{1}{2^2}\right) 13.6 = 10.2 \text{ eV}$$

Suppose, energy required to remove the electron from nth excited state of doubly ionised lithium is E'.

$$\therefore \quad E' = \frac{13.6 Z^2}{n^2}$$

As $\Delta E \geq E'$

$$10.2 \geq \frac{13.6 Z^2}{n^2}$$

$$\Rightarrow \quad n^2 \geq \frac{13.6 \times 9}{10.2}$$

$$\Rightarrow \quad n^2 \geq 12$$

$$\Rightarrow \quad n \geq 3.46$$

Therefore, least quantum number of the excited state should be 4.

6 (414) Energy of photon, $E = 10.2$ eV

Let the electron makes transition from ground states ($n = 1$) to ($n - 1$)th excited state (or nth shell), then we can write

$$E = 13.6\left(\frac{1}{1^2} - \frac{1}{n^2}\right) \times Z^2 \text{ (in eV)}$$

For hydrogen atom, $Z = 1$,

$$E = 13.6\left(\frac{1}{1} - \frac{1}{n^2}\right)$$

$$10.2 = 13.6\left(1 - \frac{1}{n^2}\right) \Rightarrow n = 2$$

Angular momentum, $L = \dfrac{nh}{2\pi}$

$$= 2 \times \frac{4.14 \times 10^{-15}}{2\pi} \text{ eV-s}$$

$$\Rightarrow \quad L = \frac{414}{\pi} \times 10^{-17} \text{ eV-s.}$$

$$\Rightarrow \quad x = 414$$

7 (2) Balmer series have transition from $n = 3, 4, 5 \ldots\ldots \infty$ to $n = 2$

$$\therefore \Delta E_{max} = E_\infty - E_2$$

$$= 0 - \left(\frac{-13.6}{(2)^2}\right) = \frac{13.6}{4} \text{ eV}$$

$$= 3.4 \text{ eV}$$

So, maximum kinetic energy,

$$K_{max} = \Delta E_{max} - \text{work function}$$

$$= 3.4 - 1.4 = 2 \text{ eV}$$

8 (4) Given, $n_1 = 3$, $n_2 = 1$

$$(\text{KE})_{max} = 9 \text{ eV}$$

The energy of emitted photon,

$$E = E_1 - E_3 = 13.6\left[\frac{1}{1^2} - \frac{1}{3^2}\right]$$

$$h\nu = 12.1 \text{ eV}$$

As we know that,

$$h\nu = (\text{KE})_{max} + W_0$$

$$W_0 = h\nu - (\text{KE})_{max}$$

$$= (12.1 - 9) \text{ eV}$$

$$= 3.1 \text{ eV} = 3.1 \times 1.6 \times 10^{-19} \text{J}$$

$$= 4.96 \times 10^{-19} \text{J}$$

Now, $W_0 = \dfrac{hc}{\lambda_0} \Rightarrow \lambda_0 = \dfrac{hc}{W_0}$

$$= \frac{6.62 \times 10^{-34} \times 3 \times 10^8}{4.96 \times 10^{-19}}$$

$$= 4 \times 10^{-7} \text{ m}$$

$$= p \times 10^{-7} \text{m (given)}$$

$$\therefore \quad p = 4$$

9 (100) According to first condition,

$$\frac{hc}{\lambda_0} = \frac{-13.6}{3^2} - \left(\frac{-13.6}{2^2}\right)$$

$$\Rightarrow \quad \frac{hc}{\lambda_0} = \frac{13.6 \times 5}{36}$$

According to second condition,

$$\frac{hc}{\lambda'} = \frac{-13.6}{4^2} - \left(\frac{-13.6}{3^2}\right)$$

$$\frac{hc}{\lambda'} = \frac{13.6 \times 7}{16 \times 9} \quad \text{...(ii)}$$

On dividing Eq. (i) by Eq. (ii), we get

$$\frac{\frac{hc}{\lambda_0}}{hc/\lambda'} = \frac{13.6 \times 5}{36} \times \frac{16 \times 9}{13.6 \times 7}$$

$$\Rightarrow \quad \frac{\lambda'}{\lambda_0} = \frac{20}{7}$$

$$\Rightarrow \quad \lambda' = \frac{100}{35} \lambda_0 = \frac{x}{35} \lambda_0$$

$$\therefore \quad x = 100$$

NCERT Exemplar Questions

2 (*a*) In the simple Bohr model, only the magnitude of angular momentum is kept equal to some integral multiple of $\dfrac{h}{2\pi}$, where h is Planck's constant and thus the Bohr model gives incorrect values of angular momentum.

3 (*a*) The total energy associated with the two H-atoms in the ground state collide in elastically,

$$E = 2 \times 13.6 \text{ eV}$$

$$= 27.2 \text{ eV}$$

The total energy associated with the two H-atoms after the collision,

$$E' = E_2 + E_1 = \left(\frac{13.6}{2^2}\right) + 13.6$$

$$= 17.0 \text{ eV}$$

Therefore, maximum loss of their combined kinetic energy,

$$\Delta E = E - E' = 27.2 - 17.0 = 10.2 \text{ eV}$$

Past Exams Questions

1 (c) Atoms are electrically neutral as they contain equal number of protons and electrons.
Statement II is incorrect because atom of radioactive elements are not stable.
So, option (c) is correct.

3 (c) Radius of third allowed orbit of H-atom.

$$r_3 = r_0 n^2 = r_0 (3)^2$$
$$= 9 \times 5.3 \times 10^{-11}$$
$$= 4.77 \times 10^{-10} \text{m} = 4.77 \text{ Å}$$

4 (b) Total energy of an electron in the nth stationary orbit of the hydrogen atom is given by

$$E_n = \frac{-Rhc}{n^2} = \frac{-13.6}{n^2} \text{ eV}$$
$$[\because Rhc = 13.6 \text{ eV}]$$

6 (b) Energy of electron in the 3rd orbit of He^+ is

$$E_3 = -13.6 \times \frac{Z^2}{n^2} \text{ eV}$$
$$= -13.6 \times \frac{4}{9} \times 1.6 \times 10^{-19} \text{ J}$$

From Bohr's model,

$$E_3 = -K$$
$$E_3 = -\frac{1}{2} m_e v^2$$
$$\Rightarrow -\left(\frac{1}{2} \times 9.1 \times 10^{-31} \times v^2\right)$$
$$= -13.6 \times \frac{4}{9} \times 1.6 \times 10^{-19}$$
$$\Rightarrow v^2 = \frac{136 \times 16 \times 4 \times 2 \times 10^{+11}}{9 \times 91}$$

or, $v = 1.46 \times 10^6 \text{m/s}$

8 (d) For He^+,

$$E = -13.6 \frac{Z^2}{n^2} = -13.6 \times \frac{4}{4}$$
$$= -13.6 \text{ eV}$$

9 (c) Angular momentum,

$$L = mvr = \frac{nh}{2\pi}$$

or $mr^2\omega = \dfrac{nh}{2\pi}$

$$r^2 \propto n \Rightarrow r \propto \sqrt{n}$$

10 (a) Energy released during transition from $n = 4$ to $n = 1$,

$$\Delta E = \frac{-13.6}{4^2} - \left(-\frac{13.6}{1^2}\right)$$
$$= 13.6 - \frac{13.6}{4^2} = 13.6\left(1 - \frac{1}{16}\right)$$
$$= 12.75 \text{ eV}$$

Since, $\Delta E = \dfrac{hc}{\lambda} \Rightarrow \lambda = \dfrac{hc}{\Delta E}$

$$= \frac{4 \times 10^{-15} \times 3 \times 10^8}{12.75} \text{m}$$
$$= 0.941 \times 10^{-7}$$
$$= 94.1 \times 10^{-9} = 94.1 \text{ nm}$$

11 (a) We know that, angular momentum,

$$L = \frac{nh}{2\pi}$$

As, $L = mvr$

$$\Rightarrow \quad mvr = \frac{nh}{2\pi}$$
$$\Rightarrow \quad mv = \frac{nh}{2\pi r}$$

or $\quad p = mv = \dfrac{nh}{2\pi r}$

Skill Boosters

1 (a) As sample is at room temperature, initially all of atoms are in ground state. In de-excitation (after being excited by wavelength λ), 10 wavelengths are emitted, this indicates 10 different transitions .

Now, using $\frac{n}{2}(n-1) = 10$, we have

$$n = 5$$

So, incident wavelength is able to excite atom to $n = 5$ state.

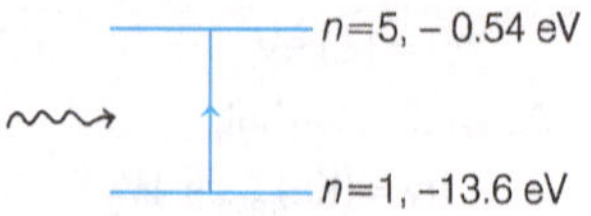

So, energy of incident photon

$$= [-0.54 - (-13.6)] \text{ eV}$$
$$= 13.06 \text{ eV}$$

As, energy of photon, $E = \dfrac{hc}{\lambda}$

$$= \frac{1240 \text{eV-nm}}{\lambda \text{nm}}$$

We have, $\lambda = \dfrac{1240}{13.06}$ nm

$$= 94.9 = 95 \text{ nm}$$

2 (b) 1 Rydberg $= 2.2 \times 10^{-18}$ J $= Rhc$
Ionisation energy of H-like atom

$$= 4 \text{ Rydberg}$$
$$= 4 \times 2.2 \times 10^{-18} \text{ J}$$
$$= \frac{4 \times 2.2 \times 10^{-18}}{1.6 \times 10^{-19}} \text{ eV} = 55 \text{ eV}$$

So, energy in first orbit $= -55$ eV

$$= -13.6 \times Z^2$$
$$\Rightarrow \quad Z^2 = \frac{-55\text{eV}}{-13.6\text{eV}} = 4$$
$$\Rightarrow \quad Z = 2$$

Now, radius of ground state

$$= \frac{0.53}{Z} \text{ Å} = 0.265 \text{Å}$$

3 (b) For transitions 1, 2 and 3,

$$E_{31} = E_{32} + E_{21}$$
$$\Rightarrow h \times f_{31} = h \times f_{32} + h \times f_{21}$$
$$\Rightarrow \quad f_3 = f_2 + f_1$$
$$\Rightarrow \quad \frac{c}{\lambda_3} = \frac{c}{\lambda_2} + \frac{c}{\lambda_1}$$
$$\Rightarrow \quad \frac{1}{\lambda_3} = \frac{\lambda_1 + \lambda_2}{\lambda_2 . \lambda_1}$$
$$\Rightarrow \quad \lambda_3 = \frac{\lambda_1 \lambda_2}{\lambda_1 + \lambda_2}$$

4 (a) Let's consider a perfectly inelastic collision. For this, neutron and hydrogen atom will be moving together after collision (speed let v').

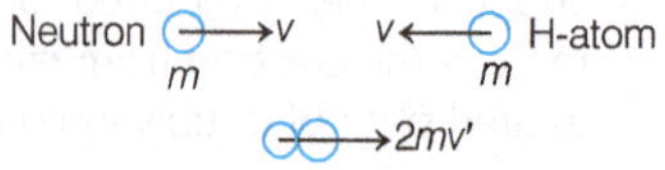

Conservation of momentum gives
$v' = 0$

So, complete energy is converted into excitation energy. This must be at least 10.2eV.

$$\Rightarrow \quad 2 \times \frac{1}{2} mv^2 = 10.2 \times 1.6 \times 10^{-19}$$

$$\Rightarrow \quad v^2 = \frac{10.2 \times 1.6 \times 10^{-19}}{1.6 \times 10^{-27}}$$

$$= 10.2 \times 10^8 \approx 4.0 \times 10^4 \text{ ms}^{-1}$$

5 (c) In $n = 4$ state, an electron behaves like a wave of such wavelength, which covers complete circumference in 4 wavelengths.

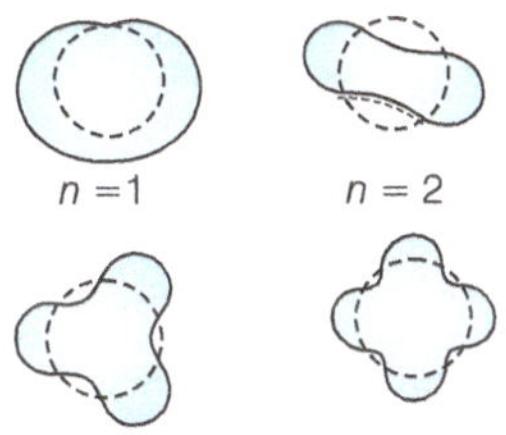

$$\therefore \quad 2\pi r = 4\lambda \Rightarrow \lambda = \frac{1}{4} \times 2\pi r$$

6 (a) Loss of KE of collision will be used to excite the atom from one level to another.

So, $\Delta E = 0, 10.2\text{ eV}, 12.09\text{ eV}, 12.75\text{ eV}, 13.06\text{ eV}, \ldots\ldots, 13.6\text{ eV}$

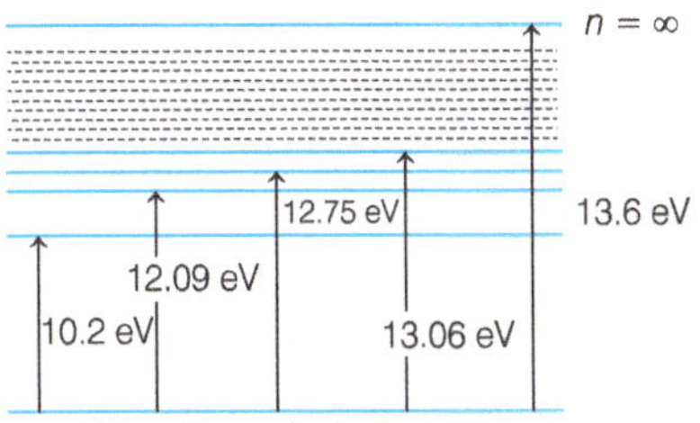

Transitions of a hydrogen atom

Let v_0 = initial speed of neutron and let a perfectly inelastic collision results. If v_f = final common speed, then by momentum conservation,

$$mv_0 = mv_f + mv_f$$

$$\Rightarrow \quad v_f = \frac{v_0}{2}$$

So, final KE $= \frac{1}{2} \times 2m \times \frac{v_0^2}{4} = \frac{K_i}{2}$

So, maximum loss of KE,

$$\Delta K = K_i - K_f = K - \frac{K}{2} = \frac{K}{2}$$

So, possible values of ΔK are 0 and $\frac{K}{2}$.

$$\Rightarrow \quad \Delta K = \left[0, \frac{K}{2}\right]$$

So, for $K < 20.4, \Delta K < 10.2\text{eV}$, which is possible when collision is elastic.

Hence, collision is always elastic for $K = 20.4$, $\Delta K = 0$ or 10.2 eV.

$\Rightarrow$ Collision may perfectly inelastic or perfectly elastic.

For $\quad K = 24.18$ eV,

$\Delta K = 12.09$, collision is perfectly inelastic.

When $\Delta K = 0$, collision is elastic.

When $\Delta K = 10.20$, collision is inelastic.

7 (a) In Bohr's atomic model, only orbital angular momentum is considered. No account is taken for spin or orientation of electron and so Bohr's model gives inaccurate value of angular momentum.

8 (a)

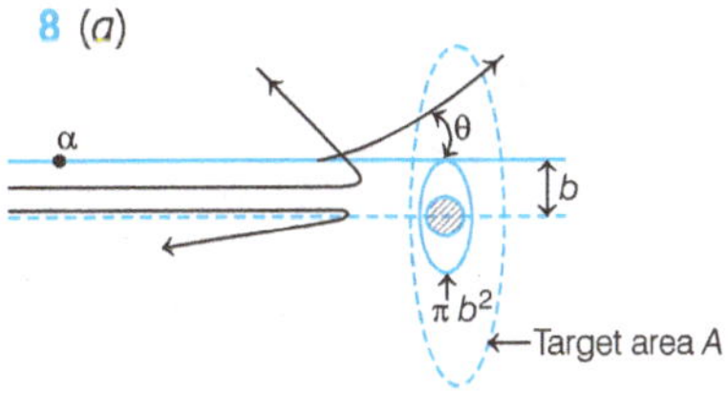

α-particle is scattered before it reaches near to nucleus and hence it does not pass with in a distance b of it.

Now, fraction of α-particles, which are scattered by angle θ or more,

$$f = \frac{\alpha\text{-particles scattered by angle } \theta \text{ or more}}{\text{Total member of incident } \alpha\text{-particles}}$$

$$= \frac{\text{Aggregate cross-section}}{\text{Target area}}$$

Now, when α-particle beam is targetted over area A, it encounters ntA nuclei. But an α particle which is initially directed anywhere in area πb^2 is scattered, through θ or more.

where, $\cot \frac{\theta}{2} = \frac{2\pi\varepsilon_0 mv^2}{Ze^2} \cdot b$

So, $f = \frac{\text{aggregate cross-section}}{\text{area}}$

$$= \frac{ntA \times \pi b^2}{A} = nt\pi b^2$$

9 (d) By law of sines,

$$\frac{\Delta p}{\sin\theta} = \frac{mv}{\sin\left(\frac{\pi - \theta}{2}\right)}$$

As, $\sin\left(\frac{\pi - \theta}{2}\right) = \cos\frac{\theta}{2}$

and $\quad \sin\theta = 2\sin\frac{\theta}{2}\cos\frac{\theta}{2}$

We have, $\frac{\Delta p}{2\sin\frac{\theta}{2}\cos\frac{\theta}{2}} = \frac{mv}{\cos\frac{\theta}{2}}$

$$\Rightarrow \quad \Delta p = 2mv \cdot \sin\frac{\theta}{2}$$

13

Scan for **Physics Through Concept Master** Videos

Nuclei

Topicwise No. of Ques asked in 5 Years (NEET)

Topics	No. of Questions				
	2024	2023	2022	2021	2020
Atomic Masses and Composition of Nucleus	1	–	1	–	–
Size of Nucleus	–	–	1	–	–
Radioactivity	–	1	–	2	2
Nuclear Energy	–	–	–	1	2

Special Type of Ques Asked In 5 Years (NEET)

Types	Years				
	2024	2023	2022	2021	2020
A-R	–	–	–	–	–
Statement Based	–	–	–	–	–
Matching	–	–	–	–	–

Last 5 Years Weigtage (NEET)

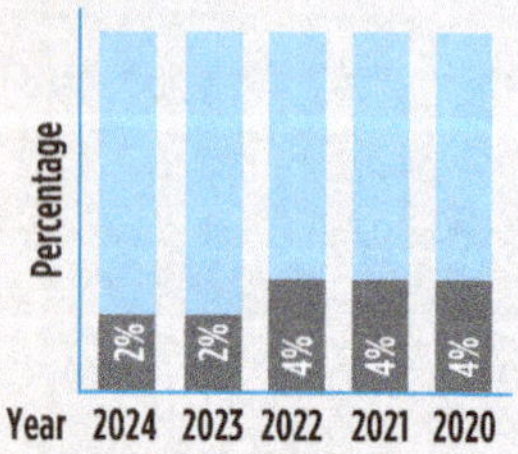

Atomic Masses and Composition of Nucleus

- In every atom, the positive charge and mass are densely concentrated at the centre of the atom forming its nucleus.
- The overall dimension of a nucleus are much smaller than those of an atom.
- Mass of an atom is very small compared to a kilogram, so atomic masses are expressed using a different unit. This unit is **atomic mass unit** (u), defined as $\frac{1}{12}$th of the mass of the carbon (^{12}C) atom, i.e. according to this definition,

$$1\,u = \frac{\text{mass of one } ^{12}C \text{ atom}}{12}$$

$$\therefore \quad 1\ u = 1.660539 \times 10^{-27}\ kg$$

- Also, the atomic masses of various elements expressed in atomic mass unit (u) are close to integral multiple of the mass of hydrogen atom, but there are notable exception, such as the atomic mass of chlorine is 35.46 u.
- **Composition of Nucleus** The composition of the nucleus can be described using the following terms and symbols.
  $Z \rightarrow$ atomic number = number of protons = number of electrons
  $N \rightarrow$ number of neutrons
  $A \rightarrow$ mass number $= Z + N =$ total number of protons and neutrons.
- **Nuclear species** or **nuclides** are shown by the notation,
  $^{A}_{Z}X$; X = chemical symbol of an element

Properties of Nucleons

Name	Symbol	Charge	Mass	Rest energy
Proton	p	$+e$	1.007276 u	938.28 MeV
Neutron	n	0	1.008665 u	939.57 MeV

Note *(i) All the electrons of an atom are outside the nucleus.*

(ii) The term nucleons refers to a proton and a neutron.

- **Isotopes** The atoms of an element having same atomic number but different mass number are called isotopes.

  e.g. Hydrogen (^1_1H), deuterium (^2_1H) and tritium (^3_1H). The masses of the nuclei of hydrogen, deuterium and tritium are in the ratio of 1 : 2 : 3. They are placed at the same place in the periodic table of elements.

Note *Tritium nuclei, being unstable do not occur naturally.*

- Fig. (a) shows the isotopes of hydrogen and Fig. (b) shows the isotopes of lithium.

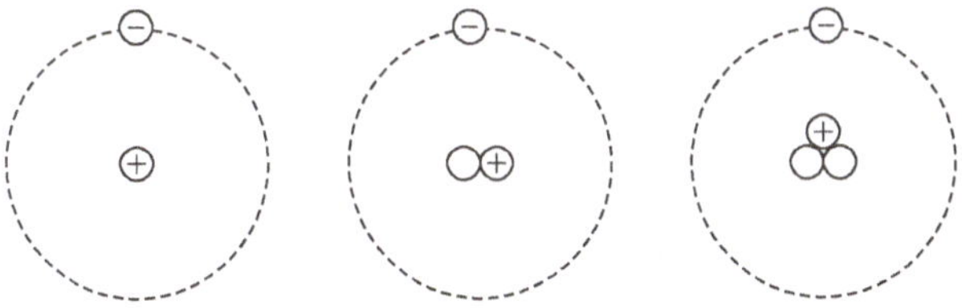

(a)

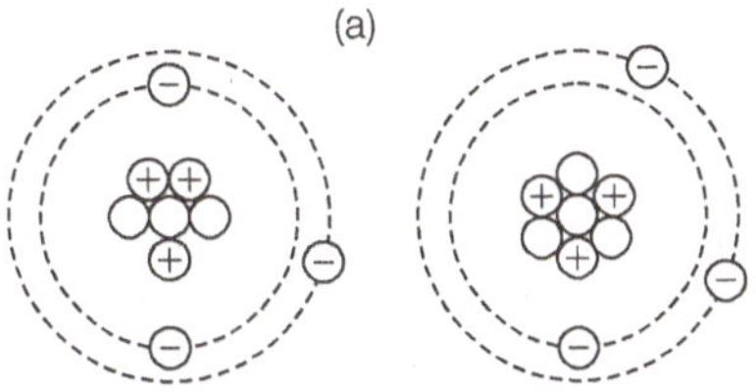

(b)

- **Isobars** The atoms of different elements having same atomic mass but different atomic number are called isobars. e.g. ^3_1H and ^3_2He, $^{37}_{17}Cl$ and $^{37}_{16}S$.
- **Isotones** Nuclides with same neutron number N but different atomic number Z are called **isotones**. e.g. $^{198}_{80}Hg$ and $^{197}_{79}Au$.
- **Isomers** Nuclei with same atomic number and mass number but existing in different energy state.

Size of Nucleus

- Radius of nucleus is smaller than the radius of an atom by a factor of about 10^4. Thus, its volume is 10^{-12} times the volume of the atom. It also contains most of the mass of an atom (more than 99.9%). In other words, **an atom is almost empty**.
- The **radius of a nucleus** depends only on its mass number A, according to the relation $R = R_0\, A^{1/3}$ NEET 2022

  where, R_0 is a constant having value 1.2×10^{-15} m or 1.2 fm.

  This means that the volume of the nucleus is directly proportional to the atomic mass (A) of the nucleus.

$$V \propto R^3 \Rightarrow V \propto (R_0 A^{1/3})^3$$

  So, $V \propto A$

  where, A = atomic mass of an element.

- **Density of nucleus** is a constant, independent of A, for all nuclei, according to the relation, $\rho = \dfrac{3m}{4\pi R_0^3}$.

  m = average mass of a nucleon

  Its value is approximately 2.3×10^{17} kg-m^{-3}.

  – Density of the nuclei of all the atoms is same as it is independent of mass number.

  – Matter is not distributed uniformly inside the nucleus. Density is maximum at centre of nucleus and reduces towards its edges. So, nucleus does not have sharp boundaries.

  – The high density of the nucleus ($\approx 10^{17}$ kg m^{-3}) suggest that nucleus is highly compact.

Mass-Energy and Nuclear Binding Energy

- Einstein showed that mass is another form of energy. The **mass-energy equivalence** relation is NEET 2020

$$E = mc^2$$

  This relation has been achieved in the study of nuclear reactions amongst nucleons.

- The **conservation law of energy** states that the initial and the final energies are equal, provided the energy associated with mass is also included.
- While the nucleus is composed of neutrons and protons, one might anticipate that its mass would be equals to the combined mass of these individual particles. Surprisingly, the nuclear mass (M) is consistently found to be less than this sum.
- Difference between the sum of the masses of the nucleons constituting a nucleus and the rest mass of nucleus is called **mass defect** (ΔM). It is expressed as

$$\Delta M = Zm_{\text{protons}} + (A - Z)m_{\text{neutrons}} - m_{\text{nucleus}}$$

- The energy required for binding the nucleons together in a nucleus is called the **binding energy**.

  If ΔM is the mass defect, then according to Einstein's mass-energy relation, $E_b = \Delta Mc^2$

  $\therefore E_b = [(Zm_p + (A - Z)m_n) - M] \times c^2$

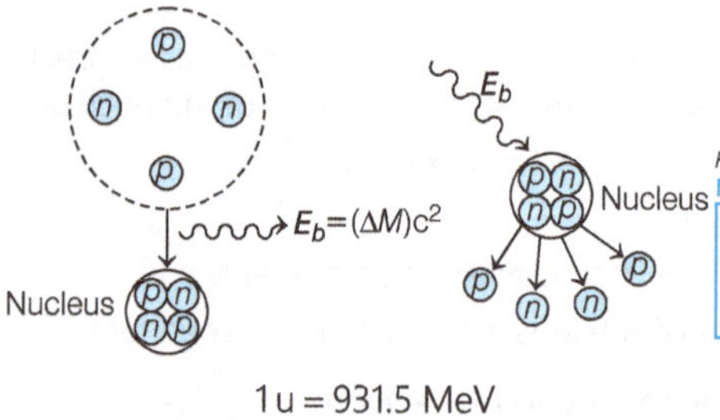

For Concept Master Video

$1\,u = 931.5$ MeV

- **Binding energy per nucleon** E_{bn} is the ratio of the binding energy E_b of a nucleus to the number of the nucleons A in that nucleus.

$$E_{bn} = \frac{E_b}{A}$$

E_{bn} can also be defined as the average energy per nucleon needed to separate a nucleus into its individual nucleons.

Marks Maximiser

- Gain in BE = BE of product − BE of reactant
  (BE = Binding Energy) NEET 2021

Binding Energy Curve

- A graph of the binding energy per nucleon E_{bn} *versus* the mass number A for a large number of nuclei is as shown below.

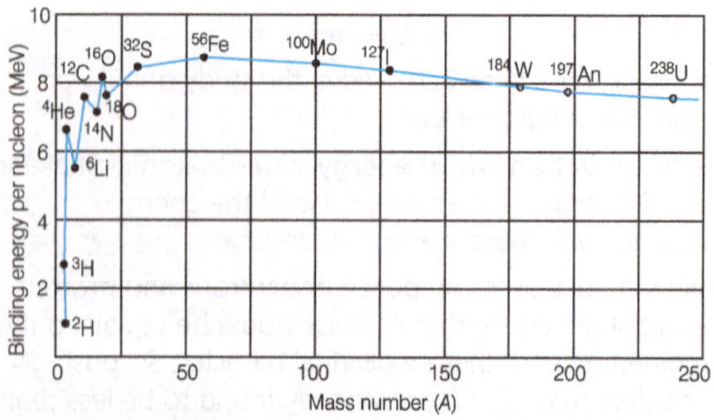

Main features of the graph are as follows

(i) **The binding energy per nucleon E_{bn} is practically constant**, i.e. independent of A for nuclei of middle mass number ($30 < A < 170$).

(ii) The curve has maximum 8.75 MeV for A = 56 and has a value of 7.6 MeV for $A = 238$.

(iii) **E_{bn} is lower for both very light nuclei (A < 30) and very heavy nuclei (A > 170)** i.e. **most stable nuclei have the highest binding energy per nucleon whereas lower binding energy per nucleon makes it easier to break the nucleus into its constituent nucleons.**

- Conclusions from the observations of E_{bn} *versus A* graph are as follows

  (i) Nuclear force is attractive and sufficiently strong to produce E_{bn} of a few MeV per nucleon.

  (ii) The constancy of E_{bn} in the range $30 < A < 170$ is the consequence of the fact that the nuclear force is short-ranged.

  (iii) **Nuclear Fission** A very heavy nucleus (say $A = 240$) can be splitted into two lighter nuclei (say $A = 120$) near the flat maximum of the curve, such that E_{bn} of product nuclei will increase. Hence, energy will be released in this process of fission.

  The binding energy per nucleon is higher in two smaller fragments nuclei than the original nucleus.

  (iv) **Nuclear Fusion** Two very light nuclei ($A \le 10$) joined together to form a heavier nucleus. E_{bn} of the fused nuclei becomes more than that of lighter nuclei. Again, energy would be released in such as process of fusion. This is the energy source of sun.

Nuclear Force

- The repelling electrostatic force inside the nucleus is very strong as compared to the attractive gravitational force because the ratio of electrostatic force and gravitational force between two protons is

$$\frac{F_e}{F_g} = 10^{36} \text{ is huge}$$

- It is the nuclear force, which is one of the strongest force in nature, only works over extremely short distances, about 4.2 fm.
- It effectively balances out the electrostatic repulsion between protons in the nucleus, keeping the nucleons closely bound together in the nucleus.
- **Following are few important properties of the nuclear forces**

  (i) It is much stronger than the Coulomb force acting between the charges or the gravitational force between masses.

  (ii) A nucleon only interact with its nearest neighbouring nucleon, it does not interact with nucleons which are not interacting directly with it. This is called **saturation property**.

Nuclear force between two nucleons falls rapidly to zero as their distance is increases more than few femtometres (fm).

This leads to saturation of forces or a large sized nucleus, which is the reason for **constancy of binding energy per nucleon** E_{bn}.

The graph illustrates the potential energy between two nucleons as a function of their separation.

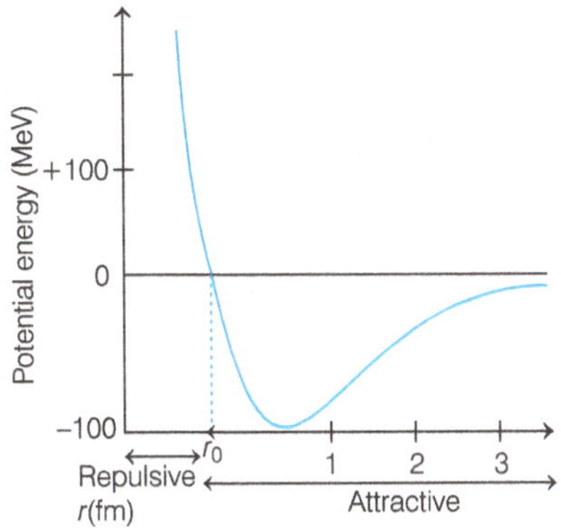

It highlights, the fact that the **nuclear force has a short-range nature**. Beyond a separation of $r_0 (< 1\,\text{fm})$, the force is attractive, but within the distance less than r_0, the force becomes highly repulsive.

(iii) Nuclear force between neutron-neutron, proton-neutron and proton-proton is approximately the same. The attractive nuclear force is due to exchange of π mesons. It does not depend on the electric charge.

Radioactivity

- Antoine Henri Becquerel discovered radioactivity in 1896.
- It is a nuclear phenomenon in which an unstable nucleus undergoes a decay with the emission of some particles (α, β) and electromagnetic radiation (γ-rays). This is also referred as **radioactive decay**.
- Three types of radioactive decay occur in nature which are as follows
  - (i) **α-Decay** It is the phenomenon of emission of nucleus of helium ($_2He^4$) from a radioactive nucleus. NEET 2019
  - (ii) **β-Decay** It is a spontaneous emission of an electron (β^--decay) or positron (β^+-decay). Positrons are the particles with same mass as electrons, but with a charge exactly opposite to that of electron.
  - (iii) **γ-Decay** When a nucleus in excited state spontaneously decays to its ground state, a photon is emitted with energy equal to the difference in the two energy levels of the nucleus. This is called γ-decay.

Marks Maximiser

- Atomic number Z decreases by 2 after one α-decay.
- Atomic number Z decreases by 1 after one β^+-decay.
- Atomic number Z increases by 1 after one β^--decay. NEET 2021

Nuclear Energy

- It is the energy released during the transformation of nuclei.

  A nuclear reaction can be written as

  $$A + a \rightarrow B + b + Q$$

  where A and a are **parent nuclei**, B and b are **product nuclei** and Q is the **energy released**.
- **Q-value** The equivalent energy of the difference between the rest masses of parent nuclei $[A + a]$ and of product nuclei $[B + b]$ is called **nuclear reaction energy** or **Q-value** of nuclear reaction.

  Q-value is positive for exothermic reactions and negative for endothermic reactions.
- In nuclear reactions,
  - the number of nucleons are conserved (i.e., atomic mass).
  - atomic number or charge is also conserved.
  - the linear momenta of product nuclei $(B + b)$ is always equal to the sum of parent linear momenta $(A + a)$.
- Two distinct ways of obtaining energy from nucleus are as follows

  (i) Nuclear fission (ii) Nuclear fusion

Nuclear Fission

- It is the process of splitting of a heavy nucleus ($_{92}U^{235}$ or $_{92}U^{239}$) into two lighter nuclei of comparable masses along with the release of a large amount of energy after bombarded by slow neutrons.
- When a uranium isotope $^{235}_{92}U$ bombarded with a neutron breaks into two intermediate mass nuclear fragments.

  $$^1_0n + ^{235}_{92}U \longrightarrow ^{236}_{92}U \longrightarrow ^{144}_{51}Ba + ^{89}_{36}Kr + 3^1_0n + Q \text{ (energy released)}$$ NEET 2020
- Here, the energy released is represented as Q-value. It can be calculated using the following formula-

  Q = final KE of product − Initial KE of reactants
- Also, due to the conservation of mass-energy.

  Q = (Sum of initial masses of reactants − Sum of final masses of product) × c^2
- The fragment products are radioactive nuclei they emit β-particles in succession to achieve stable product.

  In the above fission reaction of U-235, the energy released per fission is about 200 MeV.

- The disintegration energy in fission reaction first appears as the kinetic energy of the fragments and neutrons, then it is transferred to the surrounding in the form of heat.
- Nuclear fission is the source of energy in nuclear reactor, which produces electricity.
- The enormous energy released in an atom bomb comes from uncontrolled nuclear fission.

Marks Maximiser

Output Power of a Nuclear Reactor

- If n number of fissions are taking place per second and each fission produces E energy, then
$$P = nE$$
- If mass of nuclear fuel is X gram and mass number is A undergoes fission in time t second, then
$$P = \frac{N_A E X}{At}$$
(E = Energy relased per fission and N_A = Avogadro number)

Nuclear Fusion : Energy Generation in Stars

- It is a phenomenon in which two light nuclei fuse to form a larger nucleus and energy is released. e.g.
$$^1_1\text{H} + {}^1_1\text{H} \longrightarrow {}^2_1\text{H} + e^+ + \nu + 0.42 \text{ MeV}$$
$$^2_1\text{H} + {}^2_1\text{H} \longrightarrow {}^3_2\text{He} + n + 3.27 \text{ MeV}$$
$$^2_1\text{H} + {}^2_1\text{H} \longrightarrow {}^3_1\text{H} + {}^1_1\text{H} + 4.03 \text{ MeV}$$
- In order to fuse two nuclei, they must come close enough, so that attractive short range nuclear force is able to affect them. For this, they must overcome coulomb repulsion of positive charges which could only be achieved at high temperature.
- **Thermonuclear fusion** When fusion is achieved by raising the temperature of the system, so that particles have enough kinetic energy to overcome the coulomb repulsive behaviour due to which it is also called **thermonuclear fusion.**
- It is the source of energy output in the interior of stars. The interior of the Sun has a temperature of 1.5×10^7 K, which is considerably less than the estimated temperature required for fusion of particles of average energy.
- The fusion process in the Sun involves several reactions, ultimately converting hydrogen into helium and releasing energy.
- This process is known as **proton-proton cycle**, which is represented as follows

1. $^1_1\text{H} + {}^1_1\text{H} \longrightarrow {}^2_1\text{H} + e^+ + \nu + 0.42 \text{ MeV}$
2. $e^+ + e^- \longrightarrow \gamma + \gamma + 1.02 \text{ MeV}$
3. $^2_1\text{H} + {}^1_1\text{H} \longrightarrow {}^3_2\text{He} + \gamma + 5.49 \text{ MeV}$
4. $^3_2\text{He} + {}^3_2\text{He} \longrightarrow {}^4_2\text{He} + {}^1_1\text{H} + {}^1_1\text{H} + 12.86 \text{ MeV}$

For the fourth reaction to occur the first three reactions must happen twice, leading to the combination of $4{}^1_1\text{H}$ atoms into a ^4_2He atom, releasing 26.7 MeV of energy.
$$4{}^1_1\text{H} + 2e^- \longrightarrow {}^4_2\text{He} + 2\nu + 6\gamma + 26.7 \text{ MeV}$$

- In stars, helium fuses to form heavier elements, but it can't create elements beyond thė binding energy peak. The Sun aged 5 billion years, has enough hydrogen for 5 billion more. Eventually, it will cool, collapse and become a red giant.
- In **controlled fusion reactors**, steady power is generated by heating the nuclei fuel to a temperature in the range of 10^8 K. At these temperature, the fuel is a mixture of positive ions and electrons (plasma).
- Global efforts are focused on confining high temperature plasma in fusion reactors to provide virtually limitless power for humanity. India is among the countries working on this promising technology.
- Uncontrolled release of large nuclear energy is called an atomic explosion. High temperature conditions for fusion reactions can be created by exploding a fission bomb.

Caution Points

- Electron scattering yields a nucleus radius slightly different from α-particle scattering because it detects charge distribution, while α-particles sense nuclear matter.
- Einstein's $E = mc^2$ showed that mass and energy are equivalent, leading to a unified law of conservation of mass and energy. This principle is most evident in nuclear physics and essential for understanding of nuclear energy and harnessing it as a source of power. Also, this principle allows expressing Q value of nuclear processes in terms of initial and final masses.
- Exothermic nuclear reactions occur through nuclear fusion of light nuclei or fission of a heavy nucleus, as seen in the binding energy (per nucleon) curve.
- Fusion demands high temperature because light nuclei need the sufficient initial energy to overcome the Coulomb potential barrier for interaction.
- The binding energy curve is generally smooth still exhibit peaks at nuclides like ^{4}He and ^{16}O, signifying an atom- like shell structure of nucleus.
- Electrons and positrons are particle- anti particle pair with identical mass and opposite charges. (Electron and positron collision results in mutual annihilation, releasing energy as γ-ray photons).
- Radioactivity signifies nuclear instability. Stability demands a balanced neutron to proton ratio; approximately 1:1 for light nuclei and about 3:2 for heavy ones, as more neutrons counteract proton repulsion. Nuclei deviating from this ratio are unstable.

Step by Step

Mastering NCERT

- Concept Builders
- Topical Questions
- Assertion and Reason Questions
- Statement Based
- Matching Type
- Numerical Type
- NCERT Exemplar
- Past Exams MCQs
- Skill Boosters

Concept Builders

1 The radius of a nucleus is smaller than the radius of an atom by a factor of .... $(10^4/10^6)$.

2 The density of nuclear matter is independent of the size of the nucleus. [T/F]

3 The density of nucleus is maximum at its centre and .... (increases/decreases) as we move outward from the nucleus.

4 What is the ratio of radii of the nuclei with mass numbers 8 and 27?

5 If two small nuclei are combined to form a relatively heavy nucleus, then how the binding energy per nucleon will change?

6 When a boron nucleus ($^{10}_{5}B$) is bombarded by neutrons, α-particles are emitted. The resulting nucleus is of the element .... (Li/Be).

7 What does the difference between the mass of nucleus and the total mass of its constituents called?

8 What is the binding energy per nucleon of $^{235}_{92}U$?

9 Among all the elements, which element has the maximum binding energy per nucleon and what is the value?

10 Nuclear forces are non-central forces. This shows that distribution of nucleons in a nucleus is spherically symmetric. [T/F]

11 Nuclear forces are charge dependent in nature. (T/F)

12 γ-rays .... (can/cannot) be deflected by both electric and magnetic fields.

13 In α-decay, an α-particle is emitted from the parent nucleus and mass number of the atom decreases by .... (2/4) and atomic number decreases by .... (2/4).

14 In γ-decay, ... (lower/higher) energy photons are emitted.

15 Among α, β and γ-rays, α-particles have maximum penetrating power. [T/F]

16 Mass is not conserved but mass and energy are conserved as a single entity called mass-energy. [T/F]

17 What is the average number of neutrons released in the fission of $^{235}_{92}U$ nucleus?

18 What is the source of stellar energy?

19 A fusion reaction is initiated at .... (low/high) temperature.

20 .... (Fission/Fusion) reactors can supply almost unlimited power to humanity if successful.

Topical Questions

Atomic Masses and Composition of Nucleus

1 What is approximate ratio of volume of a nucleus to the volume of an atom? NCERT Pg. 306

(a) 10^{-34} (b) 10^{-20} (c) 10^{-15} (d) 10^{-10}

2 Two stable isotopes $^{6}_{3}Li$ and $^{7}_{3}Li$ have respective abundances of 7.5% and 92.5%. These isotopes have masses 6.01512 u and 7.01600 u respectively. The atomic weight of lithium is NCERT Pg. 307

(a) 6.941 u (b) 3.321 u (c) 5.561 u (d) 7.621 u

3 Chlorine has two isotopes having masses 34.98 u and 36.98 u with relative abundance of 75.4% and 24.6 %, respectively. The average atomic mass of chlorine is NCERT Pg. 307

(a) 34.98 u (b) 36.98 u
(c) 35.47 u (d) 35 u

4 The natural boron of atomic weight 10.81 is found to have two isotopes ^{10}B and ^{11}B. The ratio of abundance of isotopes of natural boron should be NCERT Pg. 307

(a) 11 : 10 (b) 81 : 19
(c) 10 : 11 (d) 19 : 81

5 If m, m_n and m_p are the masses of $_Z X^A$ nucleus, neutron and proton respectively, then NCERT Pg. 308
(a) $m < (A - Z) m_n + Zm_p$
(b) $m = (A - Z) m_n + Zm_p$
(c) $m = (A - Z) m_p + Zm_n$
(d) $m > (A - Z) m_n + Zm_p$

6 If the nucleus of $^{27}_{13}$Al has a nuclear radius of about 3.6 fm, then $^{125}_{52}$Te would have its radius approximately as NCERT Pg. 309
(a) 9.6 fm (b) 12 fm (c) 4.8 fm (d) 6 fm

7 The set which represents the isotope, isobar and isotone respectively is NCERT Pg. 309
(a) ($^2_1$H, $^3_1$H), ($^{197}_{79}$Au, $^{198}_{80}$Hg) and ($^3_2$He, $^2_1$H)
(b) ($^3_2$He, $^1_1$H), ($^{197}_{79}$Au, $^{198}_{80}$Hg) and ($^1_1$H, $^3_1$H)
(c) ($^3_2$He, $^3_1$H), ($^2_1$H, $^3_1$H) and ($^{197}_{79}$Au, $^{198}_{80}$Hg)
(d) ($^2_1$H, $^3_1$H), ($^3_2$He, $^3_1$H) and ($^{197}_{79}$Au, $^{198}_{80}$Hg)

8 The ratio of mass densities of nuclei of ^{40}Ca and ^{16}O is close to NCERT Pg. 309
(a) 5 (b) 2 (c) 0.1 (d) 1

9 Two nuclei have their mass numbers in the ratio of 1:27. The ratio of their volume is NCERT Pg. 309
(a) 3:1 (b) 1:27 (c) 9:1 (d) 27:1

Size of Nucleus

10 Surface area of a nucleus (assuming it to be a perfect sphere), is (where, A = mass number) NCERT Pg. 309
(a) $(1.8 \times 10^{-29}) A^{1/3}$ (b) $(1.8 \times 10^{-29}) A^2$
(c) $(1.8 \times 10^{-29}) A^{2/3}$ (d) $(1.8 \times 10^{-29}) A^3$

11 The ratio of the nuclear radii of the gold isotope $^{197}_{79}$Au and silver isotope $^{107}_{47}$Ag, is NCERT Pg. 309
(a) 1.23 (b) 0.216 (c) 2.13 (d) 3.46

12 If the nuclear radius of ^{27}Al is 3.6 fm, the approximate nuclear radius of ^{64}Cu in fm is NCERT Pg. 309
(a) 2.4 (b) 1.2 (c) 4.8 (d) 3.6

13 Mass number of two nuclei are in the ratio of 4 : 3. Their nuclear densities will be in the ratio of NCERT Pg. 309
(a) 4 : 3 (b) $\left(\frac{3}{4}\right)^{1/3}$ (c) 1 : 1 (d) $\left(\frac{4}{3}\right)^{1/3}$

14 The nucleus which has radius one third of the radius of Cs^{189} is NCERT Pg. 309
(a) Be^9 (b) Li^7 (c) F^{19} (d) Cl^2

15 Mass of iron nucleus is 55.85 u and $A = 56$. Its nuclear density will be (take, $R_0 = 1.2 \times 10^{-15}$ m) NCERT Pg. 310
(a) 4.28×10^{17} kg m^{-3} (b) 2×10^{10} kg m^{-3}
(c) 2.29×10^{17} kg m^{-3} (d) 9×10^{10} kg m^{-3}

Mass-Energy and Nuclear Binding Energy

16 Energy equivalent of 2 g of a substance is NCERT Pg. 310
(a) 18×10^{13} mJ (b) 18×10^{13} J
(c) 9×10^{13} mJ (d) 9×10^{13} J

17 How much mass has to be converted into energy to produce electric power of 200 MW for one hour? NCERT Pg. 310
(a) 2×10^{-6} kg (b) 8×10^{-6} kg
(c) 1×10^{-6} kg (d) 3×10^{-6} kg

18 Mass defect of helium ($_2He^4$) is [use, mass of proton, m_p = 1.0072676 u, mass of neutrons, m_n = 1.008665 u and mass of $_2He^4$ = 4.001506 u] NCERT Pg. 311
(a) 0.016767 u (b) 1.00726 u
(c) 2.00686 u (d) 0.0303592 u

19 Given, mass of a neutron = 1.00866 u, mass of a proton = 1.00727 u and mass of $^{16}_8$O = 15.99053 u. Then, the energy required to separate $^{16}_8$O into its constituents is NCERT Pg. 311
(a) 12.7 MeV (b) 931.5 MeV
(c) 1.49×10^{-10} J (d) 127.5 MeV

20 Given, m ($^{56}_{26}$Fe) = 55.934939 u, m_{proton} = 1.007825 u and $m_{neutron}$ = 1.008665 u. Then, BE per nucleon of Fe is, NCERT Pg. 312
(a) 8.790 MeV (b) 7.75 MeV
(c) 7.5 MeV (d) 9.28 MeV

21 If the binding energy per nucleon of deuteron is 2.115 MeV, then its mass defect in atomic mass unit is NCERT Pg. 312
(a) 0.0024 u (b) 25.62 u
(c) 96.264 u (d) 0.0045 u

22 The curve of binding energy per nucleon as function of atomic mass number has a sharp peak for lithium nucleus. This implies that lithium NCERT Pg. 312
(a) can be used as fissionable material
(b) is highly radioactive
(c) can be easily broken up
(d) is very stable

23 Consider the binding energy of $_{17}Cl^{35}$ and $_{15}P^{31}$ are 287.67 MeV and 262.48 MeV, respectively. Then, NCERT Pg. 312
(a) $_{17}Cl^{35}$ is more stable than $_{15}P^{31}$
(b) $_{15}P^{31}$ is more stable than $_{17}Cl^{35}$
(c) stability of both the elements is equivalent
(d) cannot be estimated from the given data

24 A nucleus with mass number 240 breaks into two fragments of mass number 110 and 130 having binding energy per nucleon 7.8 MeV and 8.0 MeV respectively. If binding energy per nucleon of unfragmented nuclei is 7.5 MeV. The energy released in the process is NCERT Pg. 312

(a) 216 MeV (b) 153 MeV
(c) 124 MeV (d) 98 MeV

25 Mass numbers of the elements A, B, C and D are 30, 60, 90 and 120, respectively. The binding energy per nucleon of them are 5 MeV, 8.5 MeV, 8 MeV and 7 MeV respectively. Then, in which of the following reaction/s energy is released? NCERT Pg. 312

(i) $D \to 2B$ (ii) $C \to B + A$
(iii) $B \to 2A$

(a) Only in (i) (b) in (ii), (iii)
(c) in (i), (iii) (d) in (i), (ii) and (iii)

26 Binding energy per nucleon *versus* mass number curve for nuclei is shown in the figure, W, X, Y and Z are four nuclei indicated on the curve. The process that would release energy is NCERT Pg. 312

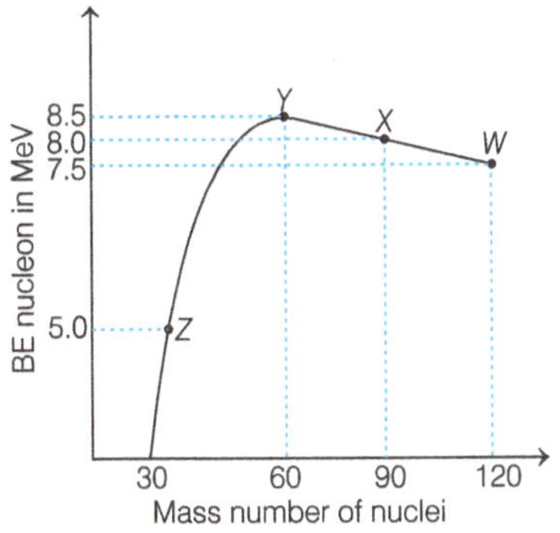

(a) $Y \to 2Z$ (b) $W \to X + Z$
(c) $W \to 2Y$ (d) $X \to Y + Z$

Nuclear Force

27 If a nucleon can have a maximum of p-neighbours within the range of nuclear force, then on increasing A by adding nucleons, the binding energy per nucleon NCERT Pg. 312

(a) increases abruptly
(b) decreases gradually
(c) remains constant
(d) first increases sharply and then decreases gradually

28 Which amongst the following is a correct graph of potential energy U of a pair of nucleons as a function of their separation r? NCERT Pg. 313

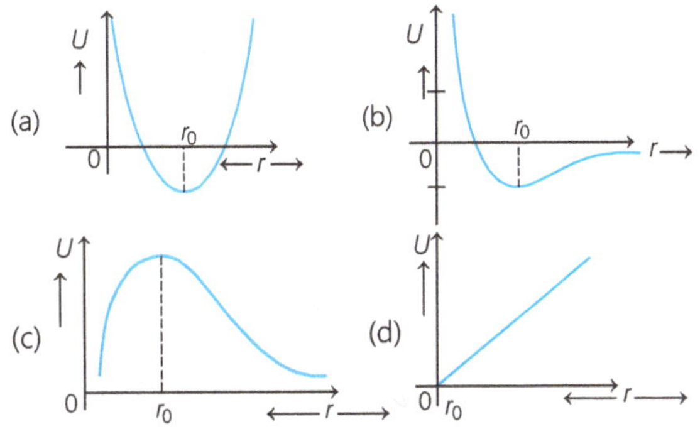

29 Two nucleons are at a separation of 1 fermi. The net force between them is F_1 if both are neutrons, F_2 if both are protons and F_3 if one is proton and the other is a neutron, then NCERT Pg. 313

(a) $F_1 > F_2 > F_3$ (b) $F_1 = F_3 > F_2$
(c) $F_2 > F_1 > F_3$ (d) $F_1 = F_2 > F_3$

30 Two protons are kept at a separation of 40 Å. If F_n is the nuclear force and F_e is the electrostatic force between them, then NCERT Pg. 313

(a) $F_n << F_e$ (b) $F_n \approx F_e$ (c) $F_n >> F_e$ (d) $F_n = F_e$

31 Nuclear forces are NCERT Pg. 313

(a) Short ranged attractive and charge independent
(b) Short ranged attractive and charge dependent
(c) Long ranged repulsive and charge independent
(d) Long ranged repulsive and charge dependent

Radioactivity

32 α-particle consists of NCERT Pg. 314

(a) 2 electrons, 2 protons and 2 neutrons
(b) 2 electrons and 4 protons
(c) 2 protons only
(d) 2 protons and 2 neutrons

33 In the nuclear reaction ${}^{238}_{92}U \longrightarrow X + {}^{4}_{2}He$. The nucleus X is NCERT Pg. 314

(a) ${}^{234}_{90}Th$ (b) ${}^{235}_{90}U$
(c) ${}^{237}_{91}Pa$ (d) ${}^{140}_{54}Xe$

34 During negative β-decay, an antineutrino is also emitted along with the emitted electron. Then, NCERT Pg. 314

(a) only linear momentum will be conserved
(b) total linear momentum and total angular momentum but not total energy will be conserved
(c) total linear momentum and total energy but not total angular momentum will be conserved
(d) total linear momentum, total angular momentum and total energy will be conserved

35 An electron emitted in beta radiation originates from NCERT Pg. 314

(a) inner orbits of atom
(b) free electrons existing in the nuclei
(c) decay of neutron in a nuclei
(d) photon escaping from the nucleus

Nuclear Energy

36 The binding energy per nucleon is 8.5 MeV for $A = 121$ and is 7.6 MeV for mass number $A = 242$. If a nucleus with $A = 242$ breaks into two nuclei of nearly equal mass numbers, the energy released in the process is NCERT Pg. 314

(a) 192 MeV (b) 217.8 MeV
(c) 220 MeV (d) 208.2 MeV

37 Ratio of charge on positron to mass of positron is approximately NCERT Pg. 314

(a) $+2 \times 10^{11}$ C/kg (b) $+5 \times 10^{12}$ C/kg
(c) -2×10^{11} C/kg (d) -5×10^{11} C/kg

38 The binding energy per nucleon of ${}^7_3\text{Li}$ and ${}^4_2\text{He}$ nuclei are 5.60 MeV and 7.06 MeV, respectively. In the nuclear reaction ${}^7_3\text{Li} + {}^1_1\text{H} \rightarrow {}^4_2\text{He} + {}^4_2\text{He} + Q$, the value of energy Q released is NCERT Pg. 315

(a) 19.6 MeV (b) −2.4 MeV
(c) 8.4 MeV (d) 17.3 MeV

39 Given, atomic masses are ${}^{238}_{92}\text{U} = 238.05079\text{u}$, ${}^4_2\text{He} = 4.00260\text{u}$ and ${}^{234}_{90}\text{Th} = 234.04363\text{u}$. The nuclear energy released during the α-decay of ${}^{238}_{92}\text{U}$ is NCERT Pg. 315

(a) 4.25 MeV (b) 4.5 MeV
(c) 6 MeV (d) 5 MeV

40 If a nucleus with mass number $A = 240$ with $E_{bn} = 7.6$ MeV breaks into two fragments of $A = 120$ and $E_{bn} = 8.5$ MeV, then released energy is around NCERT Pg. 315

(a) 216 MeV (b) 200 MeV
(c) 100 MeV (d) 156 MeV

41 On bombarding U^{235} by slow neutron, 200 MeV energy is released. If the output power is 1.6 MW, then the rate of fission will be NCERT Pg. 315

(a) $5 \times 10^{22}\ \text{s}^{-1}$ (b) $5 \times 10^{16}\ \text{s}^{-1}$
(c) $8 \times 10^{16}\ \text{s}^{-1}$ (d) $20 \times 10^{16}\ \text{s}^{-1}$

42 Which of the following is/are fission reaction(s)?

I. ${}^1_0n + {}^{235}_{92}\text{U} \rightarrow {}^{236}_{92}\text{U} \rightarrow {}^{144}_{56}\text{Ba} + {}^{89}_{36}\text{Kr} + 3{}^1_0n$
II. ${}^1_0n + {}^{235}_{92}\text{U} \rightarrow {}^{236}_{92}\text{U} \rightarrow {}^{133}_{51}\text{Sb} + {}^{99}_{41}\text{Nb} + 4{}^1_0n$
III. ${}^1_0n + {}^{235}_{92}\text{U} \rightarrow {}^{140}_{54}\text{Xe} + {}^{94}_{38}\text{Sr} + 2{}^1_0n$
IV. ${}^2_1\text{H} + {}^2_1\text{H} \rightarrow {}^3_2\text{He} + {}^1_0n$ NCERT Pg. 315

(a) I, II and IV (b) Both III and IV
(c) II, III and IV (d) I, II and III

43 A nucleus of uranium decays at rest into nuclei of thorium and helium, then NCERT Pg. 315

(a) the helium nucleus has more kinetic energy than the thorium nucleus
(b) the helium nucleus has less momentum than the thorium nucleus
(c) the helium nucleus has more momentum than the thorium nucleus
(d) the helium nucleus has less kinetic energy than the thorium nucleus

44 Fusion reaction in the sun involves the following reactions. NCERT Pg. 315

${}^1_1\text{H} + {}^1_1\text{H} \longrightarrow {}^2_1\text{H} + e^+ + \nu + 0.42$ MeV (A)
$e^+ + e^- \longrightarrow \gamma + \gamma + 1.02$ MeV (B)
${}^2_1\text{H} + {}^1_1\text{H} \longrightarrow {}^3_2\text{He} + \gamma + 5.49$ MeV (C)
${}^3_2\text{He} + {}^3_2\text{He} \longrightarrow {}^4_2\text{He} + {}^1_1\text{H} + {}^1_1\text{H} + 12.86$ MeV (D)

For the fourth reaction (D) to occur, the combination of the above three reactions will be NCERT Pg. 316

(a) A + B + C (b) 2A + 2B + C
(c) A + 2B + C (d) 2A + 2B + 2C

45 In the fusion reaction,

$${}^2_1\text{H} + {}^2_1\text{H} \longrightarrow {}^3_2\text{He} + {}^1_0n$$

the masses of deuteron, helium and neutron expressed in amu are 2.015, 3.017 and 1.009, respectively. If 1 kg of deuterium undergoes complete fusion, find the amount of total energy released. (1 amu = 931.5 MeV.) NCERT Pg. 315

(a) 9.0×10^{13} J (b) 20×10^5 J
(c) 5×10^{16} J (d) 8×10^5 J

46 If in a nuclear fusion reaction, mass defect is 0.3%, then energy released in fusion of 1 kg mass is NCERT Pg. 315

(a) 27×10^{10} J (b) 27×10^{11} J
(c) 27×10^{12} J (d) 27×10^{13} J

47 A nuclear fusion reaction is given by $4({}^4_2\text{He}) \rightarrow {}^{16}_8\text{O}$. If atomic mass of He is 4.0026 amu and that of O is 15.9994 amu, then the Q-value of the reaction will be approximately NCERT Pg. 315

(a) 5.4 MeV (b) 10.2 MeV
(c) 18.6 MeV (d) 20.4 MeV

48 The binding energy of deuteron ${}^2_1\text{H}$ is 1.112 MeV per nucleon and an α-particle ${}^4_2\text{He}$ has a binding energy of 7.047 MeV per nucleon. Then in the fusion reaction ${}^2_1\text{H} + {}^2_1\text{H} \rightarrow {}^4_2\text{He} + Q$, the energy Q released is NCERT Pg. 315

(a) 1 MeV (b) 11.9 MeV
(c) 23.8 MeV (d) 931 MeV

49 Fusion reaction takes place at high temperature as NCERT Pg. 316

(a) molecules break at higher temperature
(b) nuclei break at high temperature
(c) atoms get ionised at high temperature
(d) kinetic energy is enough to overcome the coulomb repulsive force between nuclei at high temperature.

50 In a nuclear fusion reaction, two nuclei A and B, fuse to produce a nucleus C, releasing an amount of energy ΔE in the process. If the mass defects of the three nuclei are ΔM_A, ΔM_B and ΔM_C respectively, then which of the following relations holds? Here, c is the speed of light. NCERT Pg. 316

(a) $\Delta M_A + \Delta M_B = \Delta M_C - \Delta E / c^2$
(b) $\Delta M_A + \Delta M_B = \Delta M_C + \Delta E / c^2$
(c) $\Delta M_A - \Delta M_B = \Delta M_C - \Delta E / c^2$
(d) $\Delta M_A - \Delta M_B = \Delta M_C + \Delta E / c^2$

Assertion and Reason Questions

Direction (Q. Nos. 1-10) *In the following questions, a statement of Assertion is followed by a corresponding statement of Reason. Of the following statements, choose the correct one.*

(a) Both Assertion and Reason are correct and Reason is the correct explanation of Assertion.
(b) Both Assertion and Reason are correct but Reason is not the correct explanation of Assertion.
(c) Assertion is correct but Reason is incorrect.
(d) Assertion is incorrect but Reason is correct.

1 **Assertion** For an element generally $N \geq Z$ (N = number of neutrons, Z = atomic number).

Reason Neutrons do not always experience attractive nuclear force. NCERT Pg. 308

2 **Assertion** Initially, it was believed that mass and energy are conserved separately in a nuclear reaction.

Reason According to Einstein, one can convert mass-energy into other forms of energy. NCERT Pg. 310

3 **Assertion** Binding energy per nucleon is practically constant for middle mass numbers ($30 < A < 170$).

Reason Nuclear force is short ranged in nature. NCERT Pg. 312

4 **Assertion** Nuclide $^{30}_{13}Al$ is less stable than $^{40}_{20}Ca$.

Reason Nuclides having odd number of protons and neutrons are generally unstable. NCERT Pg. 312

5 **Assertion** Unlike electric forces and gravitational forces, nuclear force has limited range.

Reason Nuclear forces do not follow the inverse square law. NCERT Pg. 313

6 **Assertion** Nuclear force between neutron-neutron, proton-neutron and proton-proton is approximately the same.

Reason The nuclear force does not depend on the electric charge. NCERT Pg. 314

7 **Assertion** Binding energy is liberated during the fission of heavy nuclei or fusion of light nuclei.

Reason The binding energy per nucleon rises as Z increases for heavy nuclei, whereas for light nuclei, it decreases as Z increases. NCERT Pg. 315

8 **Assertion** Mass spectrometer can be used to separate isotopes of an element.

Reason The separation of isotopes is possible due to variations in the number of electrons among different isotopes. NCERT Pg. 315

9 **Assertion** Thermonuclear fusion reaction is not possible on earth naturally.

Reason For thermonuclear fusion reaction to take place, extreme condition of temperature and pressure are required. NCERT Pg. 317

10 **Assertion** Thermonuclear fusion reactions have the potential to provide mankind with an unlimited amount of energy.

Reason A single fusion event with hydrogen isotopes yields more energy than nuclear fission of $^{235}_{93}U$. NCERT Pg. 317

Statement Based Questions

Direction (Q. Nos 1-8) *In the following questions, Statement I and Statement II are given. Read the statements and choose most appropriate answer from the options given below*

(a) Both Statement I and Statement II are incorrect.
(b) Statement I is correct but Statement II is incorrect.
(c) Statement I is incorrect but Statement II is correct.
(d) Both Statement I and Statement II are correct.

1 **Statement I** Atomic masses of various elements expressed in atomic mass unit are close to being integral multiple of the mass of H-atom.

Statement II Mass spectrometer is used to measure accurate atomic masses. NCERT Pg. 307

2 **Statement I** Positive charge in the nucleus is due to the protons.
Statement II Charge of electrons may be greater than $-Ze$ in an atom. NCERT Pg. 308

3 **Statement I** Positive value of packing fraction implies a large value of binding energy.
Statement II The ratio of the difference between the atomic mass of nucleus and the mass number of the nucleus to that of atomic mass is called packing fraction. NCERT Pg. 309

4 **Statement I** When a very heavy nucleus, $A = 240$ is broken into two $A = 120$ nuclei, BE of formed nucleus is more than that of initial nucleus.

Statement II When two very light nuclei ($A \leq 10$) joined to form a heavier nucleus, BE of formed nucleus is more than that of initial nucleus. NCERT Pg. 312

5 **Statement I** Nuclear force is both attractive and repulsive and it is sufficient to produce E_{bn} of few eV per nucleon.

Statement II Saturation property of the forces is the reason for constancy of E_{bn}. NCERT Pg. 313

6 **Statement I** Neutron-induced nuclear reaction is fusion.
Statement II The disintegration energy in fission first appears as kinetic energy of fragments and neutrons. NCERT Pg. 315

7 **Statement I** Hydrogen bomb involves fusion of isotopes of hydrogen, deuterium and tritium.
Statement II After the estimated life of sun, its outer envelope will convert into red giant. NCERT Pg. 317

8 In the interior of star, as the hydrogen in the core gets depleted and becomes helium, the core starts to cool. Then, star begins to collapse under its gravity, which leads to

Statement I Decrease in temperature of the core and star.

Statement II Increase in temperature of the core and if $T > 10^8$ K, then fusion takes place of helium into carbon. NCERT Pg. 317

Matching Type Questions

1 Match correctly Column I and Column II for the gold nucleus $^{197}_{79}$Au. NCERT Pg. 308

	Column I		Column II
A.	Number of protons	1.	118
B.	Number of neutrons	2.	197
C.	Number of nucleons	3.	1.264×10^{-17}
D.	Total positive charge in coulomb	4.	79

Choose the correct answer from the codes given below.

Codes

	A	B	C	D		A	B	C	D
(a)	1	2	3	4	(b)	4	1	2	3
(c)	2	1	3	4	(d)	4	1	3	2

2 Assuming that protons and neutrons have equal masses. Given that nuclear radius is given by $R = 1.2 \times 10^{-15} A^{1/3}$ metre and mass of nucleon $= 1.677 \times 10^{-27}$ kg.

On the basis of above condition, match Column I (terms) with Column II (values). NCERT Pg. 309

	Column I		Column II
A.	Nuclear mass (in kg)	1.	2.307×10^{14}
B.	Nuclear volume (in m^3)	2.	$1.67 \times 10^{-27} A$
C.	Nuclear density (in kg m^{-3})	3.	$7.24 \times 10^{-45} A$
D.	Ratio of nuclear density to density of water	4.	2.307×10^{17}

Choose the correct answer from the codes given below.

Codes

	A	B	C	D
(a)	2	3	4	1
(b)	3	2	1	4
(c)	3	4	2	1
(d)	4	3	2	1

3 Match the nuclear reactions given in Column I with the energy involved in these reactions in Column II. NCERT Pg. 310

Column I	Column II
A. ${}_1^2H + {}_1^2H \longrightarrow {}_1^3H + {}_1^1H + E_1$	1. 17.6 MeV
B. ${}_1^3H + {}_1^2H \longrightarrow {}_2^4He + {}_0^1n + E_2$	2. 18.3 MeV
C. ${}_1^2H + {}_1^2H \longrightarrow {}_2^3He + {}_0^1n + E_3$	3. 4 MeV
D. ${}_2^3H + {}_1^2H \longrightarrow {}_2^4He + E_4$	4. 13.3 MeV

Choose the correct answer from the codes given below.

Codes

	A	B	C	D		A	B	C	D
(a)	1	4	3	2	(b)	3	1	4	2
(c)	1	2	3	4	(d)	3	4	2	1

Numerical Type Questions

1 Assuming equal masses for protons and neutrons, with a nucleon mass of 1.6×10^{-27} kg and a nuclear radius of $1.5 \times 10^{-15} A^{1/3}$m. The approximate ratio of the nuclear density and water density is $n \times 10^{13}$. The value of n is .... NCERT Pg. 309

2 The sun radiates energy in all directions. The average radiations received on the earth surface from the sun is 1.4 kW/m^2. The average earth-sun distance is 1.5×10^{11} m. The mass lost by the sun per day is ....$\times 10^{14}$ kg (1 day = 86400 s) NCERT Pg. 311

3 A nucleus with a mass number of 240 and a binding energy per nucleon of 7.6 MeV splits into two fragments, each with mass number of 120 and binding energy per nucleon of 8 MeV. The total increase in binding energy is ...... MeV. NCERT Pg. 311

4 The binding energy per nucleon for ${}_6^{12}C$ nucleus is .... MeV. (Nuclear mass of ${}_6^{12}C = 12.0000$ u, Mass of hydrogen nucleus $= 1.007825$ u, Mass of neutron $= 1.008665$ u) NCERT Pg. 312

5 A nucleus splits into two nuclear parts in such a way that ratio of their velocities is 2 : 1. Their respective nuclear size have a ratio of $1 : (n)^{1/3}$. The value of n is NCERT Pg. 315

6 The energy liberated during the fission of a nucleus of ${}^{240}X$ is 200 MeV. The energy released, if all the atoms in 60 g of pure ${}^{240}X$ undergo fission is ....$\times 10^{25}$ MeV.

(Given, $N_A = 6 \times 10^{23}$) NCERT Pg. 315

7 In a single fission of ${}_{95}^{235}U$, 220 MeV energy is released, the fissions which are required to produce a power of 1.5 kW is ....$\times 10^{13}$. NCERT Pg. 315

8 An electric lamp of 100 W can be kept glowing for .... $\times 10^4$ years by the fusion of 2 kg of deuterium. (Round off to nearest whole number)

The fusion reaction can be taken as

${}_1^2H + {}_1^2H \longrightarrow {}_2^3He + n + 3.2$ MeV NCERT Pg. 315

9 When a slow moving neutron collides with Uranium 235 atom (${}_{92}^{235}U$), following reaction occurs.

$${}_0^1n + {}_{92}^{235}U \longrightarrow {}_{92}^{236}U \longrightarrow {}_{40}^{99}Zr + {}_{52}^{134}Te + 3{}_0^1n$$

If kinetic energy of neutrons is neglected (as it is very small), then the Q of reaction is $37 \times K$ MeV. The value of K is .... Use following data

$m(U^{235}) = 235.0439$ u, $m(n) = 1.0087$ u,

$m(Zr^{99}) = 98.9165$ u, $m(Te^{134}) = 133.9115$ u. NCERT Pg. 315

10 A star initially has 10^{40} deuterons. It produces energy *via* the processes, ${}_1H^2 + {}_1H^2 \rightarrow {}_1H^3 + p$

${}_1H^2 + {}_1H^3 \rightarrow {}_2He^4 + n$

The masses of the nuclei are as follows

$m(H^2) = 2.014$ amu, $M(p) = 1.007$ amu,

$m(n) = 1.008$ amu, $M(He^4) = 4.001$ amu

If the average power radiated by the star is 10^{16} W, the deuteron supply of the star is exhausted in a time .... $\times 10^9$ s. NCERT Pg. 317

NCERT Exemplar Questions

1 Heavy stable nuclei have more neutrons than protons. This is because of the fact that

(a) neutrons are heavier than protons
(b) electrostatic force between protons is repulsive
(c) neutrons decay into protons by beta decay
(d) nuclear force between neutrons is weaker than protons

2 The gravitational force between a H-atom and another particle of mass m will be given by Newton's law

$$F = G\,\frac{M \cdot m}{r^2}, \text{ where } r \text{ is in km and}$$

(a) $M = m_{\text{proton}} + m_{\text{electron}}$
(b) $M = m_{\text{proton}} + m_{\text{electron}} - \frac{B}{c^2}\,(B = 13.6 \text{ eV})$.
(c) M is not related to the mass of the hydrogen atom.
(d) $M = m_{\text{proton}} + m_{\text{electron}} - \frac{|V|}{c^2}$ ($|V|$) = magnitude of the potential energy of electron in the H-atom.

Past Exams Questions

NEET

1 $^{290}_{82}X \xrightarrow{\alpha} {}^{286}_{80}Y \xrightarrow{e^+} Z \xrightarrow{\beta^-} P \xrightarrow{e^-} Q$

In the nuclear emission stated above, the mass number and atomic number of the product Q respectively are **NCERT Pg. 309, NEET 2024**

(a) 280, 81 (b) 286, 80 (c) 288, 82 (d) 286, 81

2 In the given nuclear reaction, the element X is **NCERT Pg. 315, NEET 2022**

$$^{22}_{11}\text{Na} \longrightarrow X + e^+ + \nu$$

(a) $^{23}_{10}\text{Ne}$ (b) $^{22}_{10}\text{Ne}$ (c) $^{22}_{12}\text{Mg}$ (d) $^{23}_{11}\text{Na}$

3 A nucleus of mass number 189 splits into two nuclei having mass number 125 and 64. The ratio of radius of two daughter nuclei, respectively is **NCERT Pg. 309, NEET 2022**

(a) 4 : 5 (b) 5 : 4
(c) 25 : 16 (d) 1 : 1

4 A nucleus with mass number 240 breaks into two fragments each of mass number 120, the binding energy per nucleon of unfragmented nuclei is 7.6 MeV, while that of fragments is 8.5 MeV. The total gain in the binding energy in the process is **NCERT Pg. 315, NEET 2021**

(a) 0.9 MeV (b) 9.4 MeV (c) 804 MeV (d) 216 MeV

5 The energy equivalent of 0.5 g of a substance is **NCERT Pg. 310, NEET 2020**

(a) 4.5×10^{13} J (b) 1.5×10^{13} J
(c) 0.5×10^{13} J (d) 4.5×10^{16} J

6 When a uranium isotope $^{235}_{92}\text{U}$ is bombarded with a neutron, it generates $^{89}_{36}\text{Kr}$, three neutrons and **NCERT Pg. 315, NEET 2020**

(a) $^{91}_{40}\text{Zr}$ (b) $^{101}_{36}\text{Kr}$
(c) $^{103}_{36}\text{Kr}$ (d) $^{144}_{56}\text{Ba}$

7 A nucleus of uranium decays at rest into nuclei of thorium and helium. Then, **NCERT Pg. 315, AIPMT 2015**

(a) the helium nucleus has more kinetic energy than the thorium nucleus
(b) the helium nucleus has less momentum than the thorium nucleus
(c) the helium nucleus has more momentum than the thorium nucleus
(d) the helium nucleus has less kinetic energy than the thorium nucleus

8 The binding energy per nucleon of ^7_3Li and ^4_2He nuclei are 5.60 MeV and 7.06 MeV, respectively. In the nuclear reaction $^7_3\text{Li} + {}^1_1\text{H} \rightarrow {}^4_2\text{He} + {}^4_2\text{He} + Q$, the value of energy Q released is **NCERT Pg. 312, AIPMT 2015**

(a) 19.6 MeV (b) – 2.4 MeV
(c) 8.4 MeV (d) 17.3 MeV

9 If radius of the $^{27}_{13}\text{Al}$ nucleus is taken to be R_{Al}, then the radius of $^{125}_{53}\text{Te}$ nucleus is nearly **NCERT Pg. 309, AIPMT 2015**

(a) $\left(\frac{53}{13}\right)^{\frac{1}{3}} R_{\text{Al}}$ (b) $\frac{5}{3} R_{\text{Al}}$ (c) $\frac{3}{5} R_{\text{Al}}$ (d) $\left(\frac{13}{53}\right)^{\frac{1}{3}} R_{\text{Al}}$

JEE Main

10 The atomic mass of $_6\text{C}^{12}$ is 12.000000 u and that of $_6\text{C}^{13}$ is 13.003354 u. The required energy to remove a neutron from $_6\text{C}^{13}$, if mass of neutron is 1.008665 u, will be **NCERT Pg. 311, JEE Main 2024**

(a) 4.95 MeV (b) 62.5 MeV
(c) 49.5 MeV (d) 6.25 MeV

11 The mass number of nucleus having radius equal to half of the radius of nucleus with mass number 192 is **NCERT Pg. 309, JEE Main 2024**

(a) 20 (b) 32 (c) 24 (d) 40

12 Binding energy of a certain nucleus is 18×10^8 J. How much is the difference between total mass of all the nucleons and nuclear mass of the given nucleus ?
NCERT Pg. 315, JEE Main 2024

(a) 20 μg (b) 2 μg (c) 0.2 μg (d) 10 μg

13 The mass of proton, neutron and helium nucleus are respectively 1.0073 u, 1.0087 u and 4.0015 u. The binding energy of helium nucleus is
NCERT Pg. 311, JEE Main 2023

(a) 14.2 MeV (b) 28.4 MeV (c) 7.1 MeV (d) 56.8 MeV

14 The Q-value of a nuclear reaction and kinetic energy of the projectile particle, K_p are related as
NCERT Pg. 315, JEE Main 2022

(a) $Q = K_p$ (b) $(K_p + Q) < 0$ (c) $Q < K_p$ (d) $(K_p + Q) > 0$

15 Which of the following figures represents the variation of $\left(\frac{R}{R_0}\right)$ with ln A (If R = radius of a nucleus and A = its mass number)?
NCERT Pg. 309, JEE Main 2022

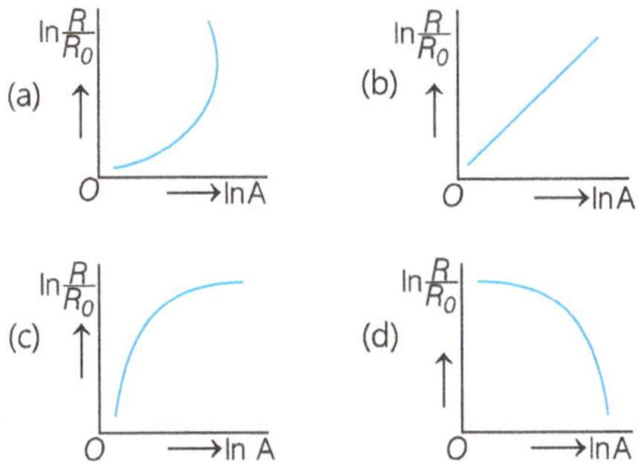

16 Nucleus A is having mass number 220 and its binding energy per nucleon is 5.6 MeV. It splits in two fragments B and C of mass numbers 105 and 115. The binding energy of nucleons in B and C is 6.4 MeV per nucleon. The energy Q released per fission will be
NCERT Pg. 315, JEE Main 2022

(a) 0.8 MeV (b) 275 MeV
(c) 220 MeV (d) 176 MeV

17 A nucleus with mass number 184 initially at rest emits an α-particle. If the Q-value of the reaction is 5.5 MeV, calculate the kinetic energy of the α-particle.
NCERT Pg. 315, JEE Main 2021

(a) 5.0 MeV (b) 5.5 MeV
(c) 0.12 MeV (d) 5.38 MeV

18 Find the binding energy per nucleon for $^{120}_{50}$Sn. Mass of proton $m_p = 1.00783$ u, mass of neutron $m_n = 1.00867$ u and mass of tin nucleus $m_{Sn} = 119.902199$ u.
(Take, 1 u = 931 MeV) NCERT Pg. 312, JEE Main 2020

(a) 9.0 MeV
(b) 7.5 MeV
(c) 8.0 MeV
(d) 8.5 MeV

19 You are given that mass of $^7_3$Li = 7.0160 u, mass of $^4_2$He = 4.0026 u and mass of $^1_1$H = 1.0079 u.
When 20g of $^7_3$Li is converted into $^4_2$He by proton capture, the energy liberated (in kWh), is [Mass of nucleon = 1 GeV/c^2] NCERT Pg. 311, JEE Main 2020

(a) 4.5×10^5 (b) 8×10^6
(c) 6.82×10^5 (d) 1.33×10^6

Skill Boosters

1 Consider the reaction,

$$^{14}\text{N}(\alpha, p)^{17}\text{O}$$

The masses involved are

^{14}N = 14.00307 u, ^{4}He = 4.00260 u

^{1}H = 1.00783 u, ^{17}O = 16.99913 u

Then,

(a) reaction is spontaneous
(b) reaction is possible when α-particle has a KE of 1.54 MeV
(c) reaction is possible when α-particle has a KE of 0.54 MeV
(d) Q-value of reaction is 1.54 MeV

2 One of the process of separating the isotopes ^{235}U and ^{238}U is based on the difference of radii of their paths in a magnetic field. Assume that, singly ionised atoms of uranium starts from a common source and move perpendicular to a uniform magnetic field. Maximum spatial separation of beams, when the two isotopes have same energies is

(a) $\frac{2\sqrt{2K}}{BZ}(\sqrt{m_2} - \sqrt{m_1})$ (b) $\frac{2\sqrt{2K}}{BZ}(\sqrt{m_2} - \sqrt{m_1})$
(c) $\frac{2\sqrt{2K}(m_2 - m_1)}{BZ}$ (d) zero

3 In order to fuse two nuclei, they must be brought at a separation of about 2 fm or less. Let two deuterium nuclei may be brought to fuse together by colliding them with equal and opposite velocities.
Minimum speed required for above process must be around

(a) 5.8×10^{12} ms^{-1} (b) 5.8×10^{10} ms^{-1}
(c) 5.8×10^{6} ms^{-1} (d) 5.8×10^{4} ms^{-1}

4 When a slow moving neutron collides with a uranium 235 atom ($^{235}_{92}U$), following reaction occurs.

$$^{1}_{0}n + ^{235}_{92}U \longrightarrow ^{236}_{92}U \longrightarrow ^{99}_{40}Zr + ^{134}_{52}Te + 3^{1}_{0}n$$

If kinetic energy of neutrons is neglected (as it is very small), then the Q-value of reaction is $37 \times K$ MeV. Find the value of K. Use following data,

$m(U^{235}) = 235.0439$ u, $m(n) = 1.0087$ u,
$m(Zr^{99}) = 98.9165$ u, $m(Te^{134}) = 133.9115$ u.

(a) 7 (b) 5 (c) 2 (d) 3

5 A proton is bombarded over a lithium nucleus. Due to collision, two α-particles are produced.

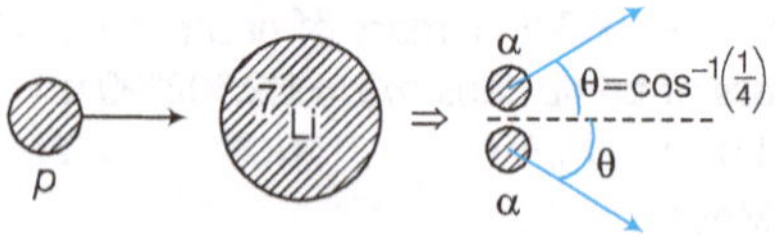

If direction of motion of the α-particles with the direction of bombarding proton is at an angle of $\cos^{-1}(1/4)$, then the correct relation between KE of proton (K_p) and KE of α-particle (K_α) is

(a) $K_p = 2K_\alpha$ (b) $K_p = \frac{1}{2}K_\alpha$
(c) $2K_p = 3K_\alpha$ (d) $K_p = K_\alpha$

6 Consider the plot of N (neutron number) *versus* Z (photon number) for the different nuclei. Let three nuclides A, B and C are at the positions as shown in the figure.

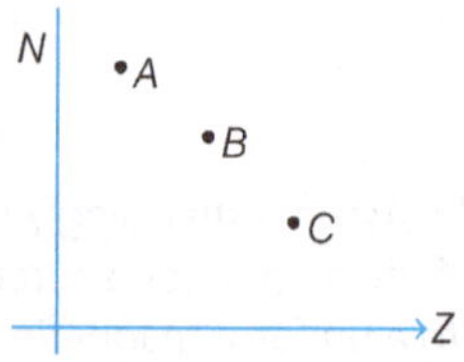

The order of their stability may be

(a) $A > B > C$ (b) $A < B < C$
(c) $B > A > C$ (d) $C < A < B$

7 Which of the following is not a requirement for a fusion reaction?

(a) High temperature
(b) High density
(c) High time
(d) High mass number

8 A nuclear reactor of efficiency 40% produces 250 MeV energy per fission. If 10^{14} fissions are taking place per second, then the power output of the reactor is

(a) 2000 W (b) 4000 W
(c) 1600 W (d) 3200 W

9 Consider the following reaction

$$^{2}_{1}H + ^{2}_{1}H \longrightarrow ^{3}_{2}He + ^{1}_{0}n$$

$m(^{2}_{1}H) = 2.014082$ u, $m(^{3}_{2}He) = 3.016029$ u
$m(^{1}_{0}n) = 1.008665$ u

Mark the correct option.

(a) The reaction will start if more than 3.23 MeV energy is supplied.
(b) Reaction occurs when total KE of reactants exceeds 3.23 MeV.
(c) Reaction occurs such that final total KE is 3.23 MeV lesser than total initial KE.
(d) No threshold energy is required for the reaction.

10 In the following reaction, about 20 MeV energy is released.

$$^{2}_{1}H + ^{2}_{1}H \longrightarrow ^{1}_{0}n + ^{4}_{2}He$$

If a nuclear reactor of power 1 MW, then mass of $^{2}_{1}H$ consumed per day is

(a) 0.001 g (b) 0.1 g
(c) 10.0 g (d) 1000 g

Correct Codes

Topical Questions

1 (c)	**2** (a)	**3** (c)	**4** (d)	**5** (a)	**6** (d)	**7** (d)	**8** (d)	**9** (b)	**10** (c)
11 (a)	**12** (c)	**13** (c)	**14** (b)	**15** (c)	**16** (b)	**17** (b)	**18** (d)	**19** (d)	**20** (a)
21 (d)	**22** (d)	**23** (b)	**24** (d)	**25** (a)	**26** (c)	**27** (c)	**28** (b)	**29** (b)	**30** (a)
31 (a)	**32** (d)	**33** (a)	**34** (d)	**35** (c)	**36** (b)	**37** (a)	**38** (d)	**39** (a)	**40** (a)
41 (b)	**42** (d)	**43** (a)	**44** (d)	**45** (a)	**46** (d)	**47** (b)	**48** (c)	**49** (d)	**50** (a)

Assertion and Reason Questions

1 (d)	**2** (b)	**3** (a)	**4** (b)	**5** (b)	**6** (a)	**7** (c)	**8** (c)	**9** (a)	**10** (c)

Statement Based Questions

1 (d)	**2** (b)	**3** (b)	**4** (d)	**5** (c)	**6** (c)	**7** (d)	**8** (d)

Matching Type Questions

1 (b)	**2** (a)	**3** (b)

Numerical Type Questions

1 (11)	**2** (3.8)	**3** (96)	**4** (7.6)	**5** (2)	**6** (3)	**7** (4.26)	**8** (5)	**9** (5)	**10** (1290)

NCERT Exemplar Questions

1 (b)	**2** (b)

Past Exams Questions

1 (d)	**2** (b)	**3** (b)	**4** (d)	**5** (a)	**6** (d)	**7** (a)	**8** (d)	**9** (b)	**10** (a)
11 (c)	**12** (a)	**13** (b)	**14** (d)	**15** (b)	**16** (d)	**17** (d)	**18** (d)	**19** (d)	

Skill Boosters

1 (b)	**2** (b)	**3** (c)	**4** (b)	**5** (d)	**6** (c)	**7** (d)	**8** (c)	**9** (d)	**10** (b)

Step by Step

Decoding the Questions

Concept Builders

1 10^4
2 True (T)
3 decreases
4 $\frac{2}{3}$
5 Increases
6 Li
7 Mass defect
8 7.6 MeV/nucleon
9 Fe, 8.8 MeV/nucleon.
10 False (F)
11 False (F)
12 cannot
13 4, 2
14 higher
15 False (F)
16 True (T)
17 2.5
18 Nuclear fusion
19 high
20 Fusion

Topical Questions

1 (c) R radius of Nucleus $\approx 10^{-15}$ m

r radius of atom $\approx 10^{-10}$ m

$$\frac{\text{Volume of Nucleus}}{\text{Volume of atom}} = \left(\frac{R}{r}\right)^3 = \left(\frac{10^{-15}}{10^{-10}}\right)^3$$

$$\frac{V\,(\text{Nucleus})}{V\,(\text{atom})} = (10^{-5})^3 \approx 10^{-15}$$

2 (a) Atomic weight = Average weight of isotopes

$$= \frac{6.01512 \times 7.5 + 7.01600 \times 92.5}{7.5 + 92.5}$$

$= 0.45113 + 6.4898 = 6.941$ u

3 (c) The average atomic mass of a chlorine atom is obtained by the weighted average of the masses of the two isotopes, which is

Average atomic mass

$$= \frac{75.4 \times 34.98 + 24.6 \times 36.98}{100}$$

$= 35.47$u

4 (d) Let ^{10}B be present as $x\%$ and percentage of $^{11}B = (100 - x)$

Average atomic mass

$$= \frac{10x + (100 - x)11}{100}$$

$$10.81 = \frac{10x + 1100 - 11x}{100}$$

$$x = 1100 - 1081 = 19$$

% of ^{11}B is $(100 - 19) = 81$

and % of $^{10}B = 19$

So, ratio is 19 : 81.

6 (d) Given, $A_{Al} = 27$, $r_{Al} = 3.6$ fm

$$A_{Te} = 125$$

$$R = R_0 A^{1/3}$$

$$\therefore \frac{R_{Te}}{R_{Al}} = \left(\frac{A_{Te}}{A_{Al}}\right)^{1/3} = \left(\frac{125}{27}\right)^{1/3} = \frac{5}{3}$$

$$\Rightarrow \quad R_2 = \frac{5}{3} R_1$$

$$\therefore \quad R = \frac{5}{3} \times 3.6 = 6 \text{ fm}$$

9 (b) The volume of the nucleus $\propto$ Atomic mass

So, $V_1 \propto A_1$ ...(i)

and $V_2 \propto A_2$ ...(ii)

Given, $\frac{A_1}{A_2} = \frac{1}{27}$

[From Eqs. (i) and (ii)]

So, $\frac{V_1}{V_2} = \frac{1}{27}$

10 (c) Surface area of nucleus,

$$S_A = 4\pi R^2 = 4\pi (R_0 A^{1/3})^2 = 4\pi R_0^2 \cdot A^{2/3}$$

Substituting constant (R_0) value $= 1.2 \times 10^{-15}$ m, we get

$$S_A = 4\,(3.14)(1.2 \times 10^{-15})^2 A^{2/3} = (1.8 \times 10^{-29})\, A^{2/3}$$

11 (a) Given, atomic mass of gold isotopes, $A_1 = 197$

and atomic mass of silver isotope, $A_2 = 107$

As, radius of nucleus, $R = R_0 A^{1/3}$

$$\therefore \quad \frac{R_1}{R_2} = \left(\frac{A_1}{A_2}\right)^{1/3} = \left(\frac{197}{107}\right)^{1/3} = 1.225 \simeq 1.23$$

The ratio of nuclear radii of the gold isotope $^{197}_{97}Au$ and silver isotope $^{107}_{47}Ag$ is 1.23.

12 (c) Nuclear radius, $R \propto A^{1/3}$, where A is mass number.

For ^{27}Al,

$$R = R_0 A^{1/3} = R_0 (27)^{1/3} = 3R_0$$

$$R_0 = \frac{3.6}{3} = 1.2 \text{ fm}$$

[$\because R = 3.6$ fm, for Al]

For ^{64}Cu,

$$R = R_0\, A^{1/3} = 1.2\,(64)^{1/3} = 4.8 \text{ fm}$$

14 (b) Let nucleus be X^A

$$\therefore \quad \frac{R_X}{R_{Cs}} = \left(\frac{A}{189}\right)^{1/3} \quad (\because R = R_0 A^{1/3})$$

$$\Rightarrow \quad \frac{\frac{R}{3}}{R} = \left(\frac{A}{189}\right)^{1/3}$$

$$\Rightarrow \quad A = \frac{189}{27} = 7$$

$\therefore$ Nucleus is Li^7

15 (c) Given, $m_{Fe} = 55.85$,

$$u = 55.85 \times 1.66 \times 10^{-27} \text{ kg} = 9.27 \times 10^{-26} \text{ kg},$$

$A = 56$ and $R_0 = 1.2 \times 10^{-15}$ m

Nuclear density

$$= \frac{\text{Mass}}{\text{Volume}} = \frac{m_{Fe}}{(4/3)\pi R_0^3 A}$$

$$= \frac{9.27 \times 10^{-26}}{(4\pi/3)\,(1.2 \times 10^{-15})^3} \times \frac{1}{56}$$

$$= 2.29 \times 10^{17} \text{ kg m}^{-3}$$

16 (b) According to mass-energy equivalence relation,

Energy, $E = mc^2$

We have, $E = 2 \times 10^{-3} \times (3 \times 10^8)^2$

$$\Rightarrow \quad E = 2 \times 10^{-3} \times 9 \times 10^{16} = 18 \times 10^{13} \text{ J}$$

17 (*b*) We have,

$P = 200\text{ MW} = 200 \times 10^6\text{ W}$
$= 2 \times 10^8\text{ W}$
$t = 1\text{ h} = 3600\text{ s}$

As energy,
$E = P \times t = 2 \times 10^8 \times 3600$

Also, $E = mc^2$

$\Rightarrow \quad m = \frac{E}{c^2} = \frac{2 \times 10^8 \times 3600}{(3 \times 10^8)^2}$
$= 8 \times 10^{-6}\text{ kg}$

18 (*d*) Mass defect, Δm
$= [Zm_p + (A - Z)\, m_n] - M_n$

Here, mass number, $A = 4$

Number of neutrons
$= A - Z = 4 - 2 = 2$

Mass of nucleon in $_2He^4$
= Mass of 2 protons + Mass of 2 neutrons
$= 2 \times 1.0072676 + 2 \times 1.008665$

$\therefore \Delta m = 2 \times 1.0072676 + 2 \times 1.008665 - 4.001506$
$= 0.0303592\text{ u}$

19 (*d*) Given, mass of a neutron $= 1.00866$ u,

Mass of a proton $= 1.00727$ u, mass of $^{16}_{8}O = 15.99053$ u

Number of neutrons $= (A - Z) = 8$

Therefore, mass of 8 neutrons
$= 8 \times 1.00866$ u

Mass of 8 protons $= 8 \times 1.00727$ u

So, the expected mass of $^{16}_{8}O$ nucleus,
$= 8 \times (1.00866 + 1.00727)$
$= 8 \times 2.01593\text{ u} = 16.12744\text{ u}$

Thus, mass defect,
$\Delta m = 16.12744\text{ u} - 15.99053\text{ u}$
$= 0.13691\text{ u}$

Since, $1\text{ u} = 931.5$ MeV.

For $^{16}_{8}O$, $\Delta m = 0.13691$ u

$\Rightarrow \quad E = 0.13691 \times 931.5$
$= 127.5$ MeV

20 (*a*) Given, $m(^{56}_{26}Fe) = 55.934939$ u,
$m_p = 1.007825$ u
and $\quad m_n = 1.008665$ u

Also, $A = 56$ and $Z = 26$

$^{56}_{26}Fe$ nucleus has 26 protons and $(56 - 26) = 30$ neutrons.

$\therefore$ Mass defect
$= [26(1.007825) + 30(1.008665)] - 55.934939$
$= 0.528461$ u

Total BE $= \Delta m \times 931.5$ MeV
$= 0.528461 \times 931.5$ MeV
$= 492.26$ MeV

$\therefore$ Binding energy per nucleon
$= \frac{\text{Total BE}}{A} = \frac{492.26}{56}$
$= 8.790$ MeV

21 (*d*) Binding energy per nucleon is

$$E_{bn} = \frac{E_b}{A} \quad \text{...(i)}$$

For deuteron, atomic mass,
$A = 2$ and $E_{bn} = 2.115$ MeV

Substituting these values in Eq. (i), we get

$2.115 = \frac{E_b}{2}$
$E_b = 2 \times 2.115$ MeV

As, $\quad E_b = \Delta mc^2$

$\Rightarrow \quad \Delta m = \frac{E_b}{c^2}$

$\therefore$ Mass defect,
$\Delta m = \frac{2 \times 2.115\, u}{931.5} = 0.0045$ u

23 (*b*) Given, E_b of chlorine
$= 287.67$ MeV

and E_b of phosphorus
$= 262.48$ MeV

Binding energy per nucleon of $_{17}Cl^{35}$
$= \frac{\text{Binding energy}}{\text{Mass number}}$
$= \frac{287.67}{35} = 8.22$ MeV

Similarly,
Binding energy per nucleon of
$_{15}P^{31} = \frac{262.48}{31} = 8.47$ MeV

Since, BE of $_{15}P^{31}$ is more than BE of $_{17}Cl^{35}$, hence $_{15}P^{31}$ is more stable.

24 (*d*) $X^{240} \rightarrow Y^{110} + Z^{130}$

$Q = (BE)_{product} - (BE)_{reactant}$
$= [(7.8 \times 110) + (8 \times 130)] - [240 \times 7.5]$
$= 1898 - 1800 = 98$ MeV

25 (*a*) Total BE for *A*,
$E_A = 5 \times 30 = 150$ MeV

BE for *B*,
$E_B = 8.5 \times 60 = 510$ MeV

BE for *C*,
$E_C = 8 \times 90 = 720$ MeV

BE for *D*,
$E_D = 7 \times 120 = 840$ MeV

Now differences of final and initial energies for each reaction,

Reaction (i) $D \rightarrow 2B$,
$\Delta E = 2E_B - E_D = 2(510) - 840$
$\Delta E = 180\text{ MeV} \Rightarrow \Delta E > 0$

Energy released

Reaction (ii) $C \rightarrow B + A$,
$\Delta E = E_B + E_A - E_C$
$\Delta E = -60\text{ MeV}, \Delta E < 0$

Energy absorbed

Reaction (iii) $B \rightarrow 2A$,
$\Delta E = 2E_A - E_B$
$\Delta E = -210\text{ MeV}, \Delta E < 0$

Energy absorbed

So, only in reaction (i), the energy is released.

26 (c) Total BE for *W*,
$E_W = 120 \times 7.5 = 900$ MeV

BE for *X*, $E_X = 90 \times 8.0 = 720$ MeV

BE for *Y*, $E_Y = 60 \times 8.5 = 510$ MeV

BE for *Z*, $E_Z = 30 \times 5 = 150$ MeV

Now, differences of final and initial energies for each reaction

Reaction (a) $Y \rightarrow 2Z$,
$\Delta E = 2E_Z - E_Y = -210$ MeV
$\Delta E < 0$, Energy absorbed

Reaction (b) $W \rightarrow X + Z$,
$\Delta E = E_X + E_Z - E_W = -30$ MeV
$\Delta E < 0$, Energy absorbed.

Reaction (c) $W \rightarrow 2Y$,
$\Delta E = 2E_Y - E_W = 120$ MeV
$\Delta E > 0$, Energy released

Reaction (d) $X \rightarrow Y + Z$,

$\Delta E = E_Y + E_Z - E_X$

$= -60$ MeV

$\Delta E < 0$, Energy absorbed

So, only in reaction (c), the energy is released.

27 (c) If a nucleon can have a maximum of p-neighbours within the range of nuclear force, then its binding energy would be proportional to p.

If we increase, A by adding nucleons, they will not change the binding energy of a nucleon, inside.

This is because most of the nucleons in a large nucleus interacts only with their immediate neighbours.

∴The binding per nucleons remains constant in the given case.

29 (b) Attractive nuclear force is same for

neutron – neutron;

proton – proton;

ploton – neutron

But for two protons, the net force = Nuclear force – repulsion, electrostatic force

So, $F_1 = F_3 > F_2$

36 (b) The reaction is given by

$$\underset{\left(\begin{smallmatrix}A=242\\ \frac{BE}{A}=7.6\,\text{MeV}\end{smallmatrix}\right)}{P} \rightarrow \underset{\left(\begin{smallmatrix}A=121\\ \frac{BE}{A}=8.5\,\text{MeV}\end{smallmatrix}\right)}{2Q} + \underset{\left(\begin{smallmatrix}\text{Energy}\\ \text{released}\end{smallmatrix}\right)}{\Delta E}$$

Total initial BE $= 242 \times 7.6$ MeV

$= 1839.2$ MeV

Total final BE $= 121 \times 2 \times 8.5$ MeV

$= 2057$ MeV

Energy released

$= (2057 - 1839.2)$ MeV

$= 217.8$ MeV

37 (a) Ratio of, charge on positron to mass of positron is,

$$\frac{q}{m} = \frac{1.6 \times 10^{-19}}{9.1 \times 10^{-31}} = 1.75 \times 10^{11}$$

$\simeq 2 \times 10^{11}$ C/kg

38 (d) Given, nuclear reaction is

$${}^7_3\text{Li} + {}^1_1\text{H} \longrightarrow {}^4_2\text{He} + {}^4_2\text{He} + Q$$

$\Rightarrow Q = 2 \times 4\,(E_{bn}$ of He$) - 7(E_{bn}$ of Li$)$

where, E_{bn} is the binding energy per nucleon.

Substituting given values, we get

Energy released,

$Q = 2\,(4 \times 7.06) - 7 \times 5.60$

$= 17.28$ MeV $\simeq 17.3$ MeV

39 (a) The nuclear reaction of ${}^{238}_{92}$U is given by

$${}^{238}_{92}\text{U} \rightarrow {}^{234}_{90}\text{Th} + {}^4_2\text{He} + Q$$

The energy released in this process is given by

$Q = \Delta mc^2 = (M_U - M_{Th} - M_{He})\,c^2$

Substituting the given values of atomic masses, we get

$Q = (238.05079 - 234.04363 - 4.00260)\text{u} \times c^2$

$= (0.00456\ \text{u})c^2$

$= (0.00456\ \text{u})\ (931.5\ \text{MeV/u})$

$= 4.25$ MeV

40 (a) Given, E_{bn} for $A = 240$ nucleus is about 7.6 MeV.

E_{bn} for the two $A = 120$ fragment nuclei is about 8.5 MeV.

So, gain in binding energy of nucleon is about (8.5–7.6 =) 0.9 MeV.

Hence, the total gain in binding energy is $240 \times 0.9 = 216$ MeV.

41 (b) Energy released on bombarding U^{235} by neutron

$= 200$ MeV

$= 200 \times 10^6 \times 1.6 \times 10^{-19}$ J

Power output of atomic reactor

$= 1.6$ MW $= 1.6 \times 10^6$ W

∴ Rate of fission

$$= \frac{1.6 \times 10^6}{200 \times 10^6 \times 1.6 \times 10^{-19}}$$

$= 5 \times 10^{16}\ \text{s}^{-1}$

43 (a) According to question,

$${}_{92}U^{238} \longrightarrow {}_{90}Th^{234} + {}_2He^4$$

According to law of conservation of linear momentum, we have,

$|p_{Th}| = |p_{He}| = p$

As, kinetic energy of an object,

$$\text{KE} = \frac{p^2}{2M}$$

where, M is the mass of the object.

Thus, $\text{KE} \propto \frac{1}{M}$

As, $M_{He} < M_{Th}$

$\Rightarrow \text{KE}_{He} > \text{KE}_{Th}$

i.e. The helium nucleus has more kinetic energy than the thorium.

44 (d) For the fourth reaction (D) to occur, the first three reaction must occur twice in which two light helium nuclei (${}^3_2$He) unite to form ordinary helium nucleus (${}^4_2$He).

So, the correct combination will be 2A + 2B + 2C.

45 (a) Given, fusion reaction is,

$${}^2_1\text{H} + {}^2_1\text{H} \longrightarrow {}^3_2\text{He} + {}^1_0n$$

Mass defect, Δm = Mass of 2(${}^2_1$H) – Mass of (${}^3_2$He + ${}^1_0n$)

$\Delta m = 2(2.015) - (3.017 + 1.009)$

$= 0.004$ amu

∴ Energy released

$= (0.004 \times 931.5)$ MeV

$= 3.726$ MeV

Energy released per deuteron

$$= \frac{3.726}{2} = 1.863\ \text{MeV}$$

Number of deuterons in 1 kg

$= (6.023 \times 10^{23}) \times$ (Number of moles)

$$= (6.023 \times 10^{23})\frac{1000}{2} = 3.01 \times 10^{26}$$

∴Energy released per kg of deuterium fusion

$= (3.01 \times 10^{26} \times 1.863)$

$= 5.6 \times 10^{26}$ MeV

$= 5.6 \times 10^{26} \times 10^6 \times 1.6 \times 10^{-19}$ J

$\approx 9.0 \times 10^{13}$ J

46 (d) Given $\Delta M = 0.3\%$ of kg

$$= \frac{0.3}{100} \times 1\ \text{kg}$$

$= 3 \times 10^{-3}$ kg

∴ $\Delta E = (\Delta m)c^2$

$= 3 \times 10^{-3} \times (3 \times 10^8)^2$

$\Delta E = 27 \times 10^{13}$ J

47 (*b*) The reaction is given as

$$4(^4_2He) \longrightarrow ^{16}_8O + Q$$

$Q = \Delta M \times 931$ MeV [1 u = 931 MeV]

$Q = (4 \times 4.0026 - 15.994) \times 931$ MeV

$= 0.011 \times 931$ MeV

$Q = 10.2$ MeV

48 (*c*) Given reaction,

$$^2_1H + ^2_1H \longrightarrow ^4_2He + Q$$

$Q =$ BE of product − BE of reactants

$= (4 \times 7.047 - 2 \times 2 \times 1.112)$ MeV

$= (28.188 - 4.448)$ MeV

$Q = 23.8$ MeV

49 (*d*) For fusion reaction to take place, the two nuclei must come close enough, so that the attractive short range nuclear force is able to affect them. Also, they must have suitable energy, enough to overcome the coulomb repulsive force barrier.

This could only be achieved, if the reaction is taking place at high temperature.

50 (*a*) The nuclear reaction given by

$A + B \longrightarrow C + \Delta E$

BE of $A = \Delta M_A c^2$

BE of $B = \Delta M_B c^2$

BE of $C = \Delta M_C c^2$

Energy released (ΔE)

= BE of C − (BE of A + BE of B)

$\Delta E = \Delta M_C c^2 - (M_A c^2 + M_B c^2)$

$\Delta M_A + \Delta M_B = \Delta M_C - \frac{\Delta E}{c^2}$

Assertion and Reason Questions

1 (*d*) For an element, it is not always true that atomic number Z is less than or equal to number of neutrons (N). e.g. In hydrogen atom, there is no neutron but it has one proton.

Therefore, atomic number of hydrogen atom is greater than number of neutrons.

i.e. $Z > N$, for hydrogen atom.

The force between neutrons in the nucleus is attractive only upto the range of 1 fm. But this attractive force become highly repulsive when neutrons came nearer to about 0.6 to 0.7 fm. Therefore, neutrons do not always experience attractive nuclear force.

2 (*b*) Before the advent of special theory of relativity, it was presented that mass and energy were conserved separately in a reaction.

However, Einstein showed that mass is another form of energy and one can convert mass-energy into other forms of energy, say kinetic energy and *vice-versa*.

3 (*a*) The constancy of the binding energy per nucleon in the range $30 < A < 170$ is a consequence of the fact that the nuclear force is short ranged in nature.

4 (*b*) Upto atomic mass of 20, stable nuclei possess neutron to proton ratio $\left(\frac{n}{p}\right) = 1$.

$$\frac{n}{p}(^{30}_{13}Al) = \frac{30 - 13}{13} = 1.3 > 1,$$

So, Al is unstable.

$$\frac{n}{p}(^{40}_{20}Ca) = \frac{20}{20} = 1, \text{ stable}$$

Also, the oddness of both protons and neutrons tend to lower the nuclear binding energy, making odd nuclei generally less stable.

5 (*b*) As we know that, gravitational force is the weakest force in nature but has infinite range.

Also, the electric forces has infinite range but nuclear force works within the nucleus, hence it is short range force. So, assertion is true.

Reason is true as nuclear forces do not follow inverse square law but not a correct explanation of the short-range nature of nuclear forces.

7 (*c*) As we know that, energy is released when heavy nuclei undergo fission or light nuclei undergo fusion. Hence, assertion is correct.

The reason is false because for heavy nuclei BE per nucleon decreases with increasing Z and for light nuclei, BE per nucleon increases with increasing Z.

8 (*c*) This is fact that isotopes can be separated using mass spectrometer, so Assertion is correct but Reason is incorrect because in isotopes the number of neutrons differs not electrons.

9 (*a*) Thermonuclear reaction are those fusion reactions which is achieved by raising the temperature and pressure of the system so that particles have enough kinetic energy to overcome the coulomb repulsive barrier.

Since, at earth such conditions are very difficult to attain naturally, so this reaction is not possible.

10 (*c*) Assertion is correct but the Reason is incorrect because much more energy is released in a single fission than in a single fusion.

(The amount of energy released in single fusion with H-isotopes = 17.5890 MeV while the energy released in single nuclear fission of U-235 is 201.7588 MeV).

Statement Based Questions

2 (*b*) Statement II is incorrect and it can be corrected as,

We know that, the number of electrons outside the nucleus of the atom is Z, the atomic number.

The total charge of the atomic electrons is thus $(-Ze)$ and since the atom is neutral, the charge of the nucleus is $(+Ze)$.

3 (*b*) Statement I is correct and Statement II is incorrect. Mass defect per nucleon is called the packing fraction.

i.e. $p = \frac{\Delta m}{A} = \frac{m - A}{A}$

Positive value of p does not mean that Δm is large and binding energy will be calculated by

$$E = \Delta m \times c^2$$

4 (*d*) A very heavy nucleus, say $A = 240$ has lower binding energy per nucleon compared to that of nucleus with $A = 120$.

Thus, if a nucleus, $A = 240$ breaks into two $A = 120$ nuclei, nucleons get more lightly bound.

Similarly, consider two very light nuclei $[A \le 10]$ joining to form a heavier nucleus. The binding energy per nucleon of the fused heavier nuclei is more than the BE per nucleon of the lighter nuclei. Thus, in both the cases BE of formed nucleus is more than that of initial nucleus.

5 (*c*) The nuclear force between two nucleons falls rapidly to zero as their distance is more than a few femtometers. This leads to saturation of forces in a medium or a large sized nucleus, which is the reason for the constancy of the binding energy per nucleon.

However, nuclear force is attractive and sufficiently strong to produce binding energy of a few MeV per nucleon.

6 (*c*) Neutron induced nuclear reactions are fission reactions. The disintegration energy in fission first appears as kinetic energy of the fragments and neutrons. Eventually, it will be transferred to surrounding matter, which appears as heat.

8 (*d*) As hydrogen in the core gets depleted and becomes helium, the core starts to cool. The star begins to collapse under its own gravity which increases the temperature of the core.

If this temperature increases to about 10^8 K, fusion takes place again, this time fusion take place of helium nuclei into carbon. This kind of process through fusion can generate higher mass elements.

Matching Type Questions

1 (*b*) In $^{197}_{79}$Au nucleus,

No. of protons $= Z = 79$

No. of neutrons $= (A - Z)$

$= 197 - 79 = 118$

No. of nucleons $= A = 197$

Total positive charge $= Ze$

$= (79 \times 1.6 \times 10^{-19})$ C

$= 1.264 \times 10^{-17}$ C

So, option (b) is correct

$(A \to 4; B \to 1; C \to 2; D \to 3)$

2 (*a*) Here, $R = 1.2 \times 10^{-15} A^{1/3}$ m,

Mass of nucleon,

$m = 1.67 \times 10^{-27}$ kg

Nuclear mass

$= mA = 1.67 \times 10^{-27} \times A$ kg

Nuclear volume $= \frac{4}{3}\pi R^3$

$= \frac{4}{3}\pi(1.2 \times 10^{-15} A^{1/3})^3$ m^3

$= 7.24 \times 10^{-45} A$m^3

Nuclear density,

$$\rho_{nu} = \frac{1.67 \times 10^{-27} \times A}{\frac{4}{3}\pi(1.2 \times 10^{-15} A^{1/3})^3}$$

$= 2.307 \times 10^{17}$ kg m^{-3}

Now, density of water,

$\rho_{water} = 10^3$ kg m^{-3}

$\therefore \frac{\rho_{nu}}{\rho_{water}} = \frac{2.307 \times 10^{17}}{10^3}$

$= 2.307 \times 10^{14}$

3 (*b*) $E_1 = [2m({}_1H^2) - m({}_1H^3) - m({}_1H^1)] \times 931.5$ MeV $= 4$ MeV

$E_2 = [-m({}_2He^4) - m({}_0n^1) + m({}_1H^3) + m({}_1H^2)] \times 931.5$ MeV

$= 17.6$ MeV

$E_3 = [-m({}_2He^3) - m({}_0n^1) + 2m({}_1H^2)] \times 931.5$ MeV $= 13.3$ MeV

$E_4 = [m({}_2He^3) - m({}_1n^2) + m({}_2He^4) + m({}_1H^1)] \times 931.5$ MeV $= 18.3$ MeV

Hence, $A \to 3$, $B \to 1$, $C \to 4$, $D \to 2$.

Numerical Type Questions

1 (11) Mass of one nucleon

$= 1.6 \times 10^{-27}$ kg

Volume of nucleus

$= \frac{4}{3}\pi R^3$

$= \frac{4}{3}\pi(1.5 \times 10^{-15} A^{1/3})^3$

$= \frac{4}{3}\pi(1.5 \times 10^{-15})^3 A$

A = no. of nucleons in nucleus

So, nuclear density

$= \frac{\text{mass}}{\text{volume}}$

$= \frac{A \times 1.6 \times 10^{-27}}{\frac{4}{3}\pi(1.5 \times 10^{-15})^3 A}$ kg/m^3

$= \frac{1.6 \times 10^{-27}}{\frac{4}{3}\pi \times (1.5)^3 \times 10^{-45}}$ kg/m^3

$= 1.1 \times 10^{17}$ kg/m^3

and density of water $= 1000$ kg/m^3

Hence, the ratio,

$\frac{\rho_{nucleus}}{\rho_{water}} = \frac{1.1 \times 10^{17}}{10^3} = 1.1 \times 10^{14}$

$\frac{\rho_{nucleus}}{\rho_{water}} = 11 \times 10^{13}$

$\therefore \quad n = 11$

2 (3.8) Average radiations received by Earth $= 1.4$ kW/m^2 $= 1.4$ kJ/s-m^2

$= \frac{1.4 \text{ kJ}}{\frac{1}{86400} \text{ day m}^2}$

$= \frac{1.4 \times 86400}{\text{day m}^2}$ kJ

Total radiation received by Earth/day

$$= \frac{4\pi r^2 \times 1.4 \times 86400}{1} \frac{\text{kJ}}{\text{day}} = E$$

r = average earth-sun distance

$= 1.5 \times 10^{11}$ m

$$E = 4\pi(1.5 \times 10^{11})^2 \times 1.4 \times 86400 \times 10^3$$

Now, $E = mc^2$

$$m = \frac{E}{c^2}$$

$$m = \frac{4\pi \times (1.5 \times 10^{11})^2 \times 1.4 \times 86400 \times 10^3}{(3 \times 10^8)^2} \text{ kg}$$

$m = 3.79 \times 10^{11} \times 10^3$ kg

The mass lost by the sun per day is

$m = 3.8 \times 10^{14}$ kg.

3 (96) The above reaction given as

$$\underset{\left(\substack{A=240 \\ \frac{BE}{A}=7.6\,\text{MeV}}\right)}{X} \longrightarrow \underset{\left(\substack{A=120 \\ \frac{BE'}{A}=8\,\text{MeV}}\right)}{2Y}$$

Total initial BE = 240×7.6 MeV

= 1824 MeV

Total Final BE = $120 \times 2 \times 8$ MeV

= 1920 MeV

Gain in BE = (1920 − 1824) MeV

Gain in BE = 96 MeV

4 (7.6) Mass defect in carbon nucleus,

$$\Delta m = [Zm_p + (A - Z)m_n - m_C]$$

$$= [6 \times 1.007825 + 6(1.008665) - 12.00000] \text{ u}$$

$$\Delta m = (12.09894 - 12.00000) \text{ u}$$

$$= 0.09894 \text{ u}$$

Binding Energy = $\Delta m \times 931.5$ MeV

[1 u = 931.5 MeV]

= 0.09894×931.5 MeV

= 92.16 MeV

Binding energy per nucleon,

$$\frac{BE}{A} = \frac{92.16}{12} = 7.68 \text{ MeV}$$

5 (2) Since, the linear momentum of the system must be conserved.

So, $m_1 v_1 - m_2 v_2 = 0$

$$\Rightarrow \frac{m_1}{m_2} = \frac{v_1}{v_2} = \frac{1}{2}$$

Since, the density of both particles is same.

$$\therefore \quad \frac{\rho \frac{4}{3}\pi r_1^3}{\rho \frac{4}{3}\pi r_2^3} = \frac{1}{2}$$

$$\frac{r_1^3}{r_2^3} = \frac{1}{2} \Rightarrow \frac{r_1}{r_2} = \frac{1}{(2)^{1/3}}$$

$\therefore \quad n = 2$

6 (3) Molar mass of given isotope $(^{240}X) = 240$ g

So, in 240 g number of nucleus present = $N_A = 6 \times 10^{23}$

∴ In 60 g, number of nucleus present

$$\frac{N_A}{4} = \frac{6 \times 10^{23}}{4} = 1.5 \times 10^{23}$$

1 nucleus gives 200 MeV of energy in fission.

So, total energy obtained by fission of 60 g of ^{240}X will be

$= 1.5 \times 10^{23} \times 200$

$= 3 \times 10^{25}$ MeV

7 (4.26) Energy released per fission

= 220 MeV

$= 220 \times 10^6 \times 1.6 \times 10^{-19}$

$= 352 \times 10^{-13}$ J

Total energy released per second

= 1.5 kW = 1500 J/s

Therefore, the no. of fissions occuring per second to produce a power of 1500 J/s is

$$n = \frac{1500}{352 \times 10^{-13}}$$

$$n = 4.26 \times 10^{13}$$

8 (5) Number of atoms present in 2g of deuterium = 6×10^{23}

Number of atoms present in 2 kg of deuterium

$$= \frac{6 \times 10^{23} \times 2000}{2}$$

$= 6 \times 10^{26}$

Given that, energy released by fusion of 2 deuterium atoms

= 3.2 MeV

Total energy released by fusion of 2 kg of deuterium = $\frac{3.2}{2} \times 6 \times 10^{26}$

$= 9.6 \times 10^{26}$ MeV

$= 9.6 \times 10^{26} \times 10^6 \times 1.6 \times 10^{-19}$ J

$= 15.34 \times 10^{13}$ J

Energy consumed by electric lamp per second = 100×1 J = 100 J

Time for which bulb will glow

$$= \frac{15.34 \times 10^{13}}{100} \text{ s}$$

$$= \frac{15.34 \times 10^{11}}{3.15 \times 10^7} \text{ years}$$

(1 year = 3.15×10^7 s)

$= 4.869 \times 10^4$ years

$\approx 5 \times 10^4$ years

9 (5) Mass defect

$$\Delta m = [m(\text{U}^{235}) + m(n')] - [m(\text{Zr}^{99}) + m(\text{Te}^{134}) + 3m(n')]$$

$$\Delta m = [235.0439 + 1.0087] - [98.9165 + 133.9115 + 3(1.0087)]$$

$$\Delta m = \{236.0526 - 235.8541\} \text{ u}$$

$$\Delta m = 0.1985 \text{ u}$$

As we know 1 u = 931.5 MeV

So, Q-value of reaction is

$Q = \Delta m \times 931.5$

$= 0.1985 \times 931.5$ MeV

$Q \approx 185$ MeV

$Q = 37 \times 5$ MeV

$\therefore \quad K = 5$

10 (1290) The given reactions are

$${}_1^2\text{H} + {}_1^2\text{H} \rightarrow {}_1^3\text{H} + p \quad \text{...(i)}$$

$${}_1^2\text{H} + {}_1^3\text{H} \rightarrow {}_2^4\text{He} + n \quad \text{...(ii)}$$

Adding Eqs. (i) and (ii), we get

$$3({}_1^2\text{H}) + {}_1^3\text{H} \rightarrow {}_1^3\text{H} + {}_2^4\text{He} + n + p$$

$$3({}_1^2\text{H}) \rightarrow {}_2^4\text{He} + n + p \quad \text{...(iii)}$$

Mass defect, Δm =

$$[3 \times m({}_1^2\text{H}) - m({}^4\text{He}) - m(n) - m(p)] \text{ u}$$

$$= [3 \times 2.014 - 4.001 - 1.008 - 1.007] \text{ u}$$

$\Delta m = 0.026$ u

Energy released = $\Delta m \times 931.5$ MeV

$= 0.026 \times 931.5$

= 24.219 MeV

Energy released = 24.219 MeV

$= 24.219 \times 10^6 \times 1.6 \times 10^{-19}$ J

$= 38.75 \times 10^{-13}$ J

$= 3.875 \times 10^{-12}$ J

This is the energy produced by consumption of 3 deuteron atoms.

Energy released by 10^{40} deuterons

$= 10^{40} \times 3.875 \times 10^{-12}$

$= 1.29 \times 10^{28}$ J

Power radiated by star

$= 10^{16}$ W or 10^{16} J/s

Total time to exhaust all deuterons of the star, $t = \dfrac{1.29 \times 10^{28}}{10^{16}}$

$= 1.29 \times 10^{12}$ s

$= 1290 \times 10^{9}$ s

NCERT Exemplar Questions

1 (*b*) Force between neutrons is only attractive and is short range force. However, force between protons is repulsive.

$\therefore$ For stable nuclides, either

$$\frac{N}{Z} = 1 \text{ or } \frac{N}{Z} > 1$$

So, heavy stable nuclei have more neutrons than protons.

Past Exams Questions

1 (*d*) Given,

$${}^{290}_{82}X \xrightarrow{\alpha} Y \xrightarrow{e^+} Z \xrightarrow{\beta^-} P \xrightarrow{e^-} Q$$

From $X \to Y$, α-particle is emitted thus ${}^{286}_{80}Y$.

Now, $Y \to Z, e^+$ is emitted, thus ${}^{286}_{79}Z$.

Again $Z \to P, \beta^-$ is emitted thus ${}^{286}_{80}P$.

Again $P \to Q, e^-$ is emitted thus ${}^{286}_{81}Q$.

2 (*b*) The given nuclear reaction is represented as

$${}^{22}_{11}\text{Na} \longrightarrow {}^{M}_{Z}X + e^+ + \nu$$

Since, atomic number and mass number are same for both side of reaction.

Hence, for atomic number,

$11 = Z + 1 \Rightarrow Z = 10$

For mass number, $22 = M$

$\therefore \quad {}^{M}_{Z}X = {}^{22}_{10}\text{Ne}$

3 (*b*) Given, mass number of parent nucleus, $A = 189$

Mass number of daughters nuclei,

$A_1 = 125$

and $\quad A_2 = 64$

We know that, $R = R_0(A^{1/3})$

$$\therefore \quad \frac{R_1}{R_2} = \left(\frac{A_1}{A_2}\right)^{1/3} = \left(\frac{125}{64}\right)^{1/3}$$

$$= \left[\left(\frac{5}{4}\right)^3\right]^{1/3} = \frac{5}{4}$$

$\therefore R_1 : R_2 = 5 : 4$

4 (*d*) A nucleus with mass number 240 breaks into two fragment each of mass number 120.

$$X^{240} \longrightarrow Y^{120} + Z^{120}$$

Given, the binding energy per nucleon of unfragmented nuclei, X = 7.6 MeV

The binding energy per nucleon of fragmented nuclei,

$Y = Z = 8.5$ MeV

Now, we shall determine the total gain in binding energy.

Gain in binding energy = Binding energy of products − Binding energy of reactants

Gain in binding energy

$= 2 \times 120 \times 8.5 - 240 \times 7.6$

$= 216$ MeV

5 (*a*) Given,

$m = 0.5 \text{ g} = 0.5 \times 10^{-3}$ kg

Relation for energy equivalent of mass is $\quad E = mc^2$

where, c is speed of light.

$= 0.5 \times 10^{-3} \times (3 \times 10^8)^2 \quad (\because c = 3 \times 10^8)$

$= 4.5 \times 10^{13}$ J

6 (*d*) Here,

$${}^{235}_{92}\text{U} + {}^{1}_{0}n \longrightarrow {}^{89}_{36}\text{Kr} + {}^{A}_{Z}X + 3({}^{1}_{0}n)$$

According to the law of conservation,

$(\text{Atomic number})_{\text{Reactant}} = (\text{Atomic number})_{\text{Product}}$

$92 + 0 = 36 + Z$

$\Rightarrow \quad Z = 92 - 36 = 56$

Similarly,

$(\text{Atomic masses})_{\text{Reactant}} = (\text{Atomic masses})_{\text{Product}}$

$235 + 1 = 89 + A + 3 \times 1$

$\Rightarrow \quad A = 144$

$\therefore$ Other element is ${}^{144}_{56}\text{Ba}$.

7 (*a*) ${}_{92}\text{U}^{238} \longrightarrow {}_{90}\text{Th}^{234} + {}_{2}\text{He}^{4}$

According to law of conservation of linear momentum, we have

$|p_{\text{Th}}| = |p_{\text{He}}| = p$

$\Rightarrow$ As, kinetic energy of an element,

$$\text{KE} = \frac{p^2}{2m}$$

where, m is mass of an element.

Thus, $\text{KE} \propto \dfrac{1}{m}$

So, $m_{\text{He}} < m_{\text{Th}} \Rightarrow K_{\text{He}} > K_{\text{Th}}$

8 (*d*) The binding energy for ${}_1\text{H}^1$ is around zero and also not given in the question so we can ignore it

$Q = 2(\text{E}_{\text{bn}} \text{ of He}) - (\text{E}_{\text{bn}} \text{ of Li})$

$Q = [2\,(4 \times 7.06) - (7 \times 5.60)]$ MeV

$\therefore Q = 17.28$ MeV

$\simeq 17.3$ MeV

9 (*b*) Radius of the nucleus is given by

$R = R_0 A^{1/3} \Rightarrow R \propto A^{1/3}$

$$\frac{R_{\text{Al}}}{R_{\text{Te}}} = \left(\frac{A_{\text{Al}}}{A_{\text{Te}}}\right)^{1/3} = \left(\frac{27}{125}\right)^{1/3} = \frac{3}{5}$$

$$R_{\text{Te}} = \frac{5}{3} R_{\text{Al}}$$

10 (*a*) Given, ${}_6\text{C}^{12} = 12.000000$ u

${}_6\text{C}^{13} = 13.003354$ u

${}_0n^1 = 1.008665$ u

Mass defect,

$\Delta M = [12.000000 + 1.008665] - 13.003354$

$= 0.005311$ u

The required energy,

$\Delta E = 0.005311 \times 931.5$

$= 4.9471 \approx 4.95$ MeV

11 (*c*) Radius of nucleus is, $R = R_0 A^{1/3}$

For nucleus of mass number 192, radius is

$R = R_0\,(192)^{\frac{1}{3}} \quad$ ...(i)

For nucleus of radius $\frac{R}{2}$ let mass number is A', then

$$\frac{R}{2} = R_0 A'^{1/3} \quad ...(ii)$$

Dividing Eq. (i) by Eq. (ii), we get

$$2A'^{1/3} = 192^{1/3} \Rightarrow 8A' = 192$$

$$\Rightarrow \quad A' = \frac{192}{8} = 24$$

12 (*a*) Binding energy,

$$E = \Delta M \cdot c^2 \quad ...(i)$$

ΔM = mass defect,

$c = 3 \times 10^8$ m/s

$E = 18 \times 10^8$ J

Substituting values in Eq. (i), we get

$$\Delta M = \frac{E}{c^2} = \frac{18 \times 10^8}{(3 \times 10^8)^2}$$

$$= 2 \times 10^{-8} \text{ kg} = 2 \times 10^{-8} \times 10^3 \text{ g}$$

$$= 2 \times 10^{-5} \text{ g} = 20 \times 10^{-6} \text{ g}$$

$$= 20 \, \mu\text{g}$$

13 (*b*) Binding energy $= \Delta mc^2$

$$= [Zm_p + (A - Z)m_n - m_{He}]c^2$$

$$= [Zm_p + (A - Z)m_n - m_{He}] \times 931.5 \text{ MeV}$$

$$= (2 \times 1.0073 + (4 - 2) \times 1.0087 - 4.00154) \times 931.5$$

Binding energy = 28.4 MeV

14 (*d*) For an exothermic reaction

$Q > 0$, also $K_p > 0$

Hence, $Q + K_p > 0$

If reaction is endothermic then,

$$K_p > 0 \text{ and } Q < 0$$

Hence, $K_p + Q > 0$

So, $K_p + Q > 0$, for any type of nuclear reaction.

15 (*b*) Radius of nucleus is given by

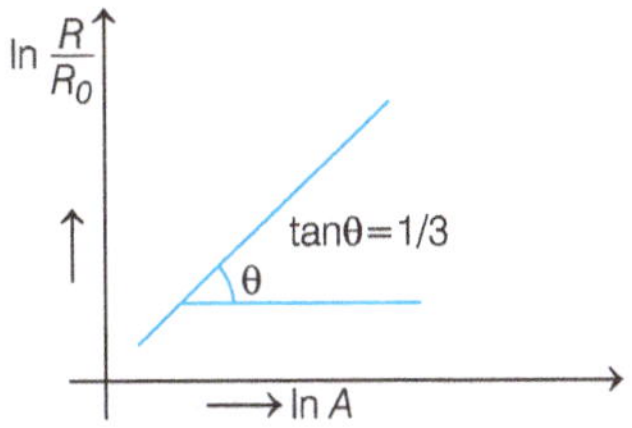

$$R = R_0 A^{1/3} \Rightarrow \frac{R}{R_0} = A^{1/3}$$

$$\Rightarrow \ln \frac{R}{R_0} = \frac{1}{3} \ln A$$

On comparing it with the equation of straight line $y = mx + c$, we get $m = \frac{1}{3}$ and $c = 0$.

16 (*d*) Binding energy per nucleon of nucleus A,

$$E_A = 5.6 \text{ MeV}$$

$$M_A = 220$$

Binding energy per nucleon of nucleus B and C,

$$E_B = E_C = E = 6.4 \text{ MeV}$$

$$M_B = 105, M_C = 115$$

∴ Released energy per fission

Q = Total binding energy of products nuclei – Total binding energy of reactants nuclei

$$= (M_B + M_C)E - M_A \times E_A$$

$$= (105 + 115)(6.4) - 220 \times 5.6$$

$$= 176 \text{ MeV}$$

17 (*d*) Given, initial mass number be A is 184

and Q value is 5.5 MeV.

Equation of α-emission is

$$X_Z^A \longrightarrow Y_{Z-2}^{A-4} + \alpha + Q$$

$$X_Z^{184} \longrightarrow Y_{Z-2}^{180} + \alpha + Q$$

$p_Y, p_\alpha, m_Y, m_\alpha$, KE_Y and KE_α be the momentum, mass, kinetic energy of Y and α, respectively.

By using conservation of momentum, momentum of α = momentum of Y

$$\Rightarrow \quad p_\alpha = p_Y$$

$$\therefore \quad \sqrt{2m_\alpha E_\alpha} = \sqrt{2m_Y E_Y}$$

$$[\because \text{Momentum, } p = \sqrt{2mE}]$$

$$\Rightarrow \quad E_\alpha = \frac{180}{4} E_Y = 45E_Y$$

$$\Rightarrow \quad E_Y = \frac{E_\alpha}{45}$$

By using conservation of energy,

$$Q = KE_Y + KE_\alpha = \frac{KE_\alpha}{45} + KE_\alpha$$

$$\Rightarrow \quad 5.5 = KE_\alpha \left(\frac{46}{45}\right)$$

$$\Rightarrow \quad KE_\alpha = \frac{5.5 \times 45}{46}$$

$$= 5.38 \text{ MeV}$$

18 (*d*) $m_{theoretical} = Zm_p + (A - Z)m_n$

$$= 50(1.00783 \text{ u}) + (120 - 50) + (1.00867 \text{ u})$$

$$= 50.391500 \text{ u} + 70.606900 \text{ u}$$

$$= 120.998400 \text{ u}$$

$m_{experimental} = 119.902199$ u

So, mass defect,

$$\Delta m = m_{theoretical} - m_{experimental}$$

$$= 120.998400 \text{ u} - 119.902199 \text{ u}$$

$$= 1.096201 \text{ u}$$

Now, total binding energy,

$$\text{BE} = \Delta m \times 931 \text{ MeV}$$

$$= 1.096201 \times 931 \text{ MeV}$$

$$= 1020.563131 \text{ MeV}$$

Therefore, binding energy per nucleon,

$$(\text{BE})_{\text{per nucleon}} = \frac{\text{BE}}{\text{Total number of nucleons}}$$

$$= \frac{1020.563131}{120}$$

$$= 8.50469275833 \text{ MeV}$$

$$\simeq 8.5 \text{ MeV}$$

19 (*d*) Given that $m({}_3^7\text{Li}) = 7.0160$ u

$m({}_2^4\text{He}) = 4.0026$ u

$m({}_1^1\text{H}) = 1.0079$ u

Nuclear reaction ;

$${}_3^7\text{Li} + {}_1^1\text{H} \longrightarrow {}_2^4\text{He} + {}_2^4\text{He}$$

Energy released in one nuclear reaction,

$$Q = \Delta mc^2 = \Delta m \times 931 \text{ MeV}$$

$$= (7.0160 + 1.0079 - 2 \times 4.0026) \times 931 \text{ MeV}$$

$$= 17.41 \text{ MeV}$$

Number of atoms in 20 g of Li

$$= \frac{20}{7} \times 6.023 \times 10^{23} = 1.72 \times 10^{24}$$

∴ Total energy liberated

$$= Q \times \text{Total number of Li atoms}$$

$$= (17.41 \text{ MeV}) \times (1.72 \times 10^{24}) \times 1.6 \times 10^{-19}$$

$$= 4.79 \times 10^{12} \text{ J}$$

$$\text{Energy (in kWh)} = \frac{4.79 \times 10^{12}}{3.6 \times 10^6}$$

$$(\because 1 \text{ kWh} = 3.6 \times 10^6 \text{ J})$$

$$= 1.33 \times 10^6 \text{ kWh}$$

Skill Boosters

1 (*b*) Reaction is

$${}_2^4He + {}_7^{14}N \longrightarrow {}_8^{17}O + {}_1^1H$$

Q-value of reaction is

$$Q = 931.5 \times [m({}_7^{14}N) + m({}_2^4He)] - \{m({}_8^{17}O) + m({}_1^1H)\}$$

$$= 931.5\,(14.00307 + 4.00260 - 1.00783 - 16.99913)$$

$$= -1.20 \text{ MeV}$$

As *Q*-value is negative, hence reaction is endothermic and cannot proceed without external energy.

Minimum KE of α-particle to initiate this reaction would be

$$K_{min} = |Q| \times \left(\frac{m_\alpha}{m_N} + 1\right)$$

$$= 1.20 \times \left(\frac{4.00260}{14.00307} + 1\right)$$

$$= 1.54 \text{ MeV}$$

2 (*b*) For a charged particle, radius of path, $r = \frac{mv}{qB}$

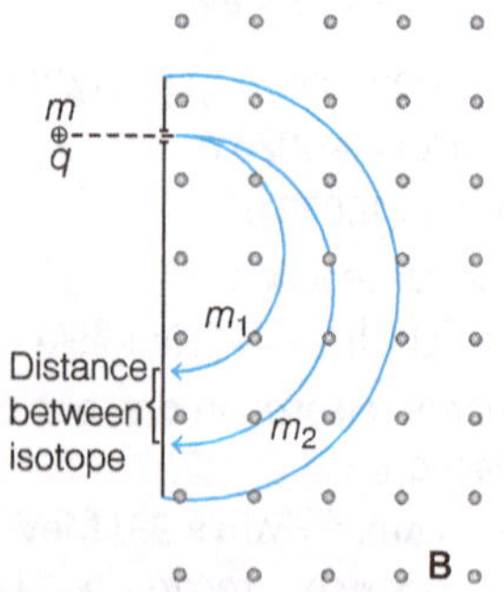

$$\Rightarrow \quad r = \frac{mv}{qB} = \frac{\sqrt{2mK}}{Bq}$$

When particles (nuclei of 2-different isotopes) have same energies, then

$$r_1 = \frac{\sqrt{2m_1K}}{BZ}$$

and $$r_2 = \frac{\sqrt{2m_2K}}{BZ}$$

Separation between two traces,

$$d = 2r_2 - 2r_1 \qquad \text{(see figure)}$$

$$= \frac{2\sqrt{2m_2K}}{BZ} - \frac{2\sqrt{2m_1K}}{BZ}$$

$$= \frac{2\sqrt{2K}}{BZ}(\sqrt{m_2} - \sqrt{m_1})$$

3 (*c*) The complete process is a shown in the figure.

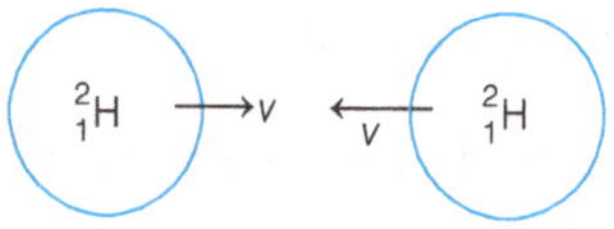

Potential energy barrier for 2 fm separation, $U = \frac{kq_1q_2}{r}$

$$= \frac{9 \times 10^9 \times (1.6 \times 10^{-19})^2}{2 \times 10^{-15}}$$

$$= 1.15 \times 10^{-13} \text{ J}$$

On equating this with available KE, we get

$$2 \times \frac{1}{2}mv^2 = 1.15 \times 10^{-13}$$

$$\Rightarrow \quad v^2 = \frac{1.15 \times 10^{-13}}{2 \times 1.67 \times 10^{-27}}$$

$$\Rightarrow \quad v \approx 5.8 \times 10^6 \text{ ms}^{-1}$$

4 (*b*) $\Delta M = \{m(U^{235}) + m(n)\} - \{m(Zr^{99}) + m(Te)^{134} + 3\,m(n)\}$

$$= 0.1985 \text{ u}$$

So, *Q* value of reaction is

$$Q = \Delta M \times 931.5$$

$$= 185 \text{ MeV}$$

$$= 5 \times 37 \text{ MeV}$$

Given, $K \times 37$

$$K = 5$$

5 (*d*) By momentum conservation, $\Sigma p_x = \text{constant}$

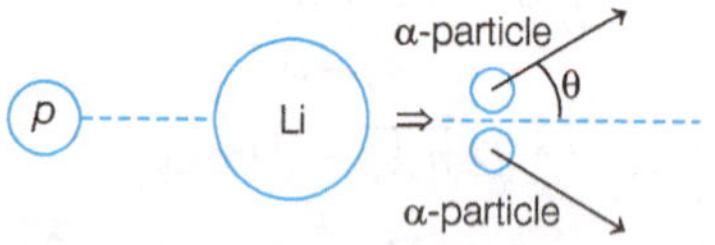

$$p_p + p_{Li} = 2p_\alpha \cos\theta$$

$$\sqrt{2m_pK_p} + 0 = 2(\sqrt{2m_\alpha K_\alpha})\cos\theta$$

$$\Rightarrow \quad 2m_pK_p = 2^2 \times 2m_\alpha K_\alpha \cos^2\theta$$

$$\Rightarrow m_pK_p = 4 \times 4\,m_p \times K_\alpha \times \frac{1}{16}$$

$$\Rightarrow \quad K_p = K_\alpha$$

6 (*c*) Most stable, $N = Z(B)$. Nucleus with more neutron number (*N*) is slightly more stable than nucleus which have more atomic number (*Z*).

So, order of stability is $B > A > C$.

7 (*d*) Option (d) is not correct because fusion involves 2 lighter nuclei and nuclei with high mass number undergoes fission. All other options are correct.

8 (*c*) Total energy released per second

$$= 250 \times 1.6 \times 10^{-13} \times 10^{14} = 4000 \text{ J}$$

$$\text{Power output} = 4000 \times \frac{40}{100}$$

$$= 1600 \text{ W}$$

9 (*d*) As, $m({}_1^2H) = 2.014082$ u

and $m({}_2^3He) = 3.016029$ u

and $m({}_0^1n) = 1.008665$ u

Δm = mass defect

$$= 2m({}_1^2H) - m({}_2^3He) - m({}_0^1n)$$

$$= 2 \times 2.014082 - 3.016029 - 1.008665$$

$$\Delta m = 0.003470$$

$\Rightarrow$ *Q*-value = Energy liberated in reaction

Q = [mass (reactants) – mass (products)] × 931.5

$$= \Delta m \times 931.5 \text{ MeV}$$

$$= 3.232 \text{ MeV}$$

As *Q*-value is positive, so no threshold energy is required.

10 (*b*) $P = 10^6$ W

Time = 1 day = $24 \times 36 \times 10^2$ s

Energy produced,

$$U = Pt = 10^6 \times 24 \times 36 \times 10^2$$

$$= 24 \times 36 \times 10^8 \text{ J}$$

Energy released per fusion reaction

$$= 20 \text{ MeV} = 32 \times 10^{-13} \text{ J}$$

Energy released per atom of ${}_1H^2 = 32 \times 10^{-13}$ J

Number of ${}_1H^2$ atoms used

$$= \frac{24 \times 36 \times 10^8}{32 \times 10^{-13}}$$

$$= 27 \times 10^{21}$$

Mass of 6×10^{23} atoms = 2 g

∴ Mass of 27×10^{21} atoms

$$= \frac{2}{6 \times 10^{23}} \times 27 \times 10^{21} \simeq 0.1 \text{ g}$$

14

Scan for **Physics Through Concept Master** *Videos*

Semiconductor Electronics: Materials, Devices and Simple Circuits

Topicwise No. of Ques asked in 5 Years (NEET)

Topics	No. of Questions				
	2024	2023	2022	2021	2020
Intrinsic Semiconductor	–	–	–	–	1
Extrinsic Semiconductor	–	–	–	1	1
p-n Junction	–	–	–	–	1
Semiconductor Diode	1	–	1	–	1
Application of Junction Diode as Rectifier	–	1	1	–	–
Special Purpose *p-n* Junction Diode	1	–	–	1	–
Digital Electronics and Logic Gates	2	1	1	–	2

Special Type of Ques Asked In 5 Years (NEET)

Types	Years				
	2024	2023	2022	2021	2020
A-R	–	–	–	–	–
Statement Based	1	1	–	–	–
Matching	–	0	–	0	0

Last 5 Years Weigtage (NEET)

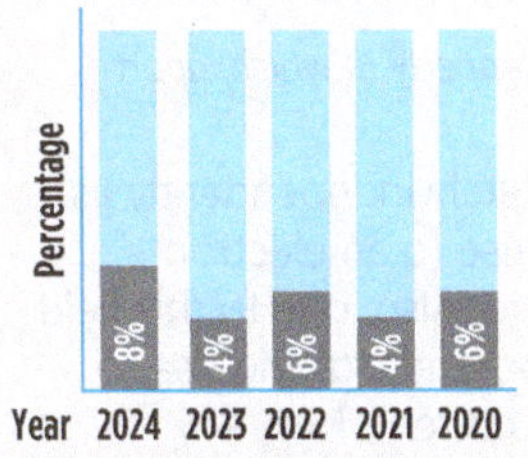

- Electronic circuits are the basic building blocks of all those devices in which a controlled flow of electrons can be obtained. Before the discovery of transistors, vacuum tubes were mostly used.
- In 1930, it was realised that some solid-state semiconductors and their junctions offers the possibility of controlling the number and the direction of flow of charge carriers through them. Simple excitations like light, heat or small applied voltage can change the number of mobile charges in a semiconductor.
- The supply and flow of charge carriers in the semiconductor devices are within the solid itself.
- No external heating or large evacuated space is needed by the semiconductor devices. They are small in size, consume low power, operate at low voltage and have long life and highly reliable.

Classification of Metals, Conductors and Semiconductors

- **On the basis of the relative values of electrical conductivity** (σ) or resistivity ($\rho = 1/\sigma$), solids are broadly classified as
  (i) **Metals** They possess very low resistivity (or high conductivity).
  $$\rho \sim 10^{-2}\text{-}10^{-8}\ \Omega\text{-m};\ \sigma \sim 10^{2}\text{-}10^{8}\ \text{Sm}^{-1}$$
  (ii) **Semiconductors** They have resistivity or conductivity intermediate to metals and insulators.
  $$\rho \sim 10^{-5}\text{-}10^{6}\ \Omega\text{-m};\ \sigma \sim 10^{5}\text{ - }10^{-6}\ \text{Sm}^{-1}$$
  (iii) **Insulators** They have high resistivity (or low conductivity).
  $$\rho \sim 10^{11}\text{-}10^{19}\Omega\text{-m};\ \sigma \sim 10^{-11}\text{ - }10^{-19}\ \text{Sm}^{-1}$$

Energy Bands in Solids

- Inside the crystal of a solid, each electron has a unique position and no two electrons see exactly the same pattern of surrounding charges. Because of this, each electron will have a different energy level. These different energy levels with continuous energy variation are called **energy bands**.

  These bands are of two types

  (i) **Valence band** The range of energies possessed by valence electrons is called valence band.

  (ii) **Conduction band** The range of energies possessed by conduction electrons is called conduction band.

Note *With no external energy, all the valence electrons will reside in the valence band.*

Forbidden Energy Gap or Energy Band Gap

- The gap between the top of the valence band and the bottom of the conduction band is called the **energy band gap**.
- If λ is the wavelength of radiation used to excite the electron so that it can jump from valence band to conduction band, then the energy band gap is

$$E_g = h\nu = \frac{hc}{\lambda}$$

  The energy gap in a semiconductor depends on the temperature.
- **Fermi energy** It is the maximum possible energy possessed by free electron of a material at absolute zero temperature. i.e., 0K.
- **On the basis of the energy band gap**, solids can be classified as

  (i) **Metals** In metals, either conduction band is partially filled and valence band is partially empty or conduction and valence bands overlap. When there is overlap electrons from the valence band can easily move into the conduction band. Therefore, resistance of such materials is low or the conductivity is high. It is as shown in the figure below.

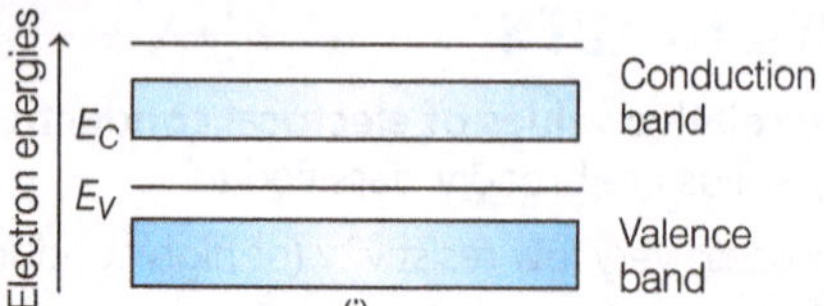

(i)

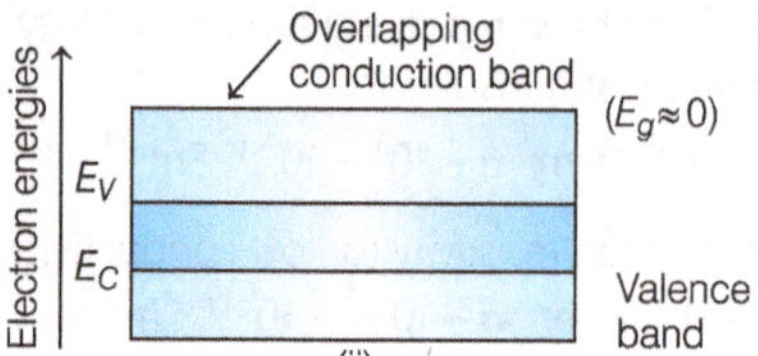

(ii)

  (ii) **Insulators** In insulators, a large band gap E_g exists ($E_g > 3$ eV). There are no electrons in the conduction band and therefore no electrical conduction is possible. It is as shown in the figure below.

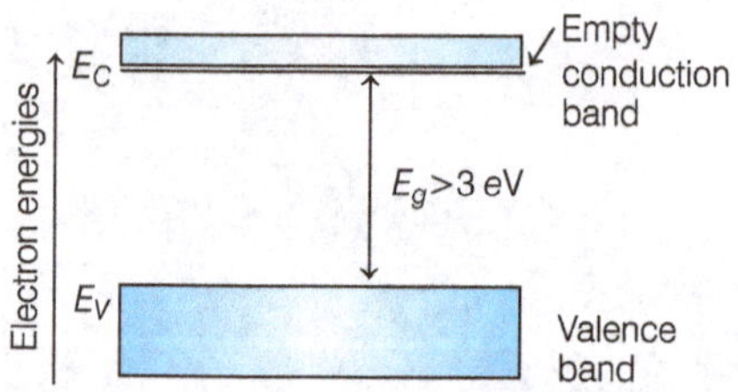

  (iii) **Semiconductors** In semiconductors finite but small energy gap exists ($E_g < 3$ eV). Due to this reason at room temperature, some electrons from the valence band can move to conduction band.

  Thus, the resistance of these materials is not as high as that of the insulators. It is as shown in the figure.

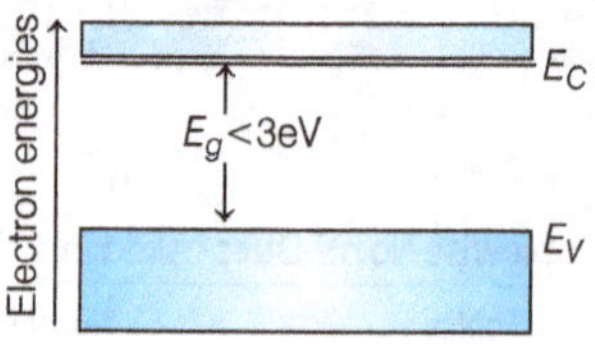

  In semiconductor, the energy band gap is of the order of 1 eV. For silicon, it is 1.1 eV and for germanium, it is 0.72 eV.

  At absolute zero, semiconductor behaves as a perfect insulator.

  (iv) **Hole** A vacancy is created in the valence band when an electron get excited and moves to conduction band. A hole is a seat of positive charge. Mobility of hole is smaller than that of electron.

For Concept Master Video

Intrinsic Semiconductor

- A pure semiconductor which does not contain any impurity is called an **intrinsic semiconductor.** e.g. Silicon, germanium, etc. Following are few important points related to this

  (i) In intrinsic semiconductors, the number of free electrons n_e is equal to the number of holes n_h.

  i.e. $n_e = n_h = n_i$

  where, n_i is called **intrinsic carriers concentration**.

Note *Semiconductor possess the unique property in which, apart from electrons, the holes also move.*

  (ii) The free electron moves completely independently as conduction electron and gives rise to an electron current I_e, under an applied field. Also, due to this field holes move towards negative potential giving rise to hole current I_h. Therefore, total current, $I = I_e + I_h$ $= n_i eA (v_e + v_h)$

Marks Maximiser

- Conductivity of intrinsic semiconductor,
$$\sigma = n_i e(\mu_e + \mu_h)$$
- Resistivity of intrinsic semiconductor
$$\rho = \frac{1}{\sigma} = \frac{1}{en_i(\mu_e + \mu_h)}$$

(iii) During the process of generation of conduction electrons and holes, a simultaneous process of recombination occurs in which electrons recombine with the holes. At equilibrium, the rate of generation is equal to the rate of recombination of charge carriers. The recombination occurs due to the electron colliding with a hole.

- **Effect of temperature on conductivity of intrinsic semiconductor** The conductivity of an intrinsic semiconductor depends on its temperature but at room temperature, its conductivity is very low.
- With rising temperature, the density of electron-hole pairs increases which increases the conductivity of an intrinsic semiconductor.
- Following figure shows the schematic two dimensional representation of Si or Ge structure showing covalent bonds at low temperature (all bonds intact) and +4 symbol shows inner cores of Si or Ge.

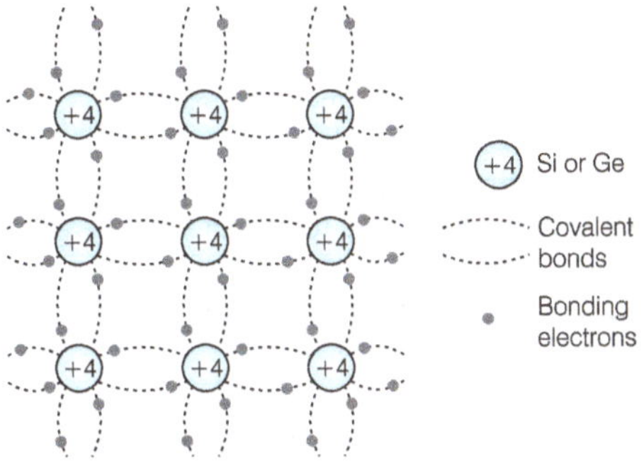

- Following figure shows the simplified representation of possible thermal motion of a hole. The electron from the lower left hand covalent bond (site 2) goes to the earlier hole (site 1), leaving a hole at its site indicating an apparent movement of the hole from site 1 and site 2.

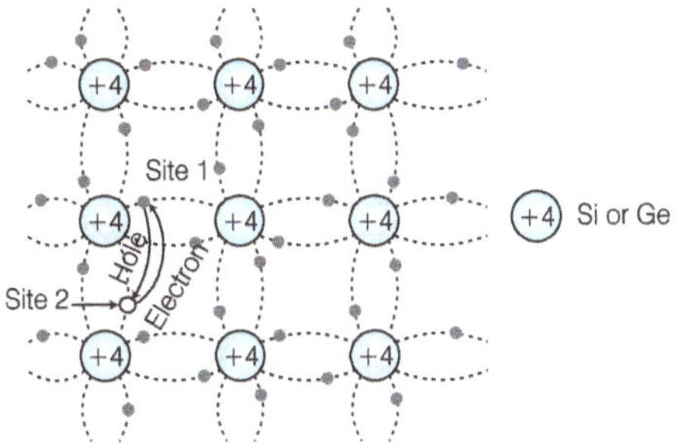

Energy Band Diagram of Intrinsic Semiconductor

- The valence band is completely filled with electrons at absolute temperature, i.e., at $T = 0$ K, while the conduction band is empty. Hence, an intrinsic semiconductor behaves like an insulator at $T = 0$ K. At high temperature ($T > 0$K), some electrons from the valence bands gets excited after gaining some energy and jump to the conduction band, creating equal number of holes in the valence band.

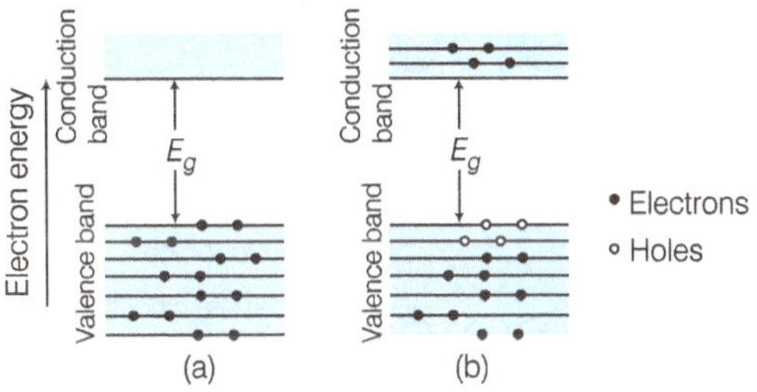

Extrinsic Semiconductor

- When a small amount of specific impurity is added to a pure semiconductor to increase its conductivity, then the semiconductor created is called **extrinsic semiconductor or impure semiconductor**.
- The deliberate addition of a desirable impurity is called **doping** and the impurity atoms are called **dopants**, so extrinsic semiconductors are also called **doped semiconductors**.
- For doping, size of the dopant and the semiconductor atoms should be nearly same.
- There are two types of dopants used in doping.
  - (i) **Pentavalent** (valency 5) ; like arsenic (As), antimony (Sb), phosphorous (P), etc.
  - (ii) **Trivalent** (valency 3); like indium (In), boron (B), aluminium (Al), etc.
- Based on impurity (or dopant) extrinsic semiconductor is of two types: *n*-type and *p*-type semiconductors.
  - (i) ***n*-type semiconductors** It is obtained when a pure semiconductor of Si or Ge (i.e. tetravalent) is doped with a group V pentavalent impurity like arsenic (As), phosphorus (P), etc.
- The pentavalent impurity atoms added in the semiconductor is called the **donor atoms**.
- In *n*-type semiconductor, the conduction of current is due to electrons, i.e. electrons are majority carriers and holes are minority carriers. Therefore, they are called *n*-type semiconductor.
- For *n*-type semiconductor, we have $n_e >> n_h$.
- The conductivity of *n*-type semiconductor is $\sigma_n = en_e\mu_e$
- Fig. (a) shows pentavalent donor atom (As, Sb, P, etc.) doped for tetravalent Si or Ge giving *n*-type semiconductor and Fig. (b) shows commonly used schematic

representation for n-type material which shows only the fixed cores of the substituent donors with one additional positive charge and its associated extra electron.

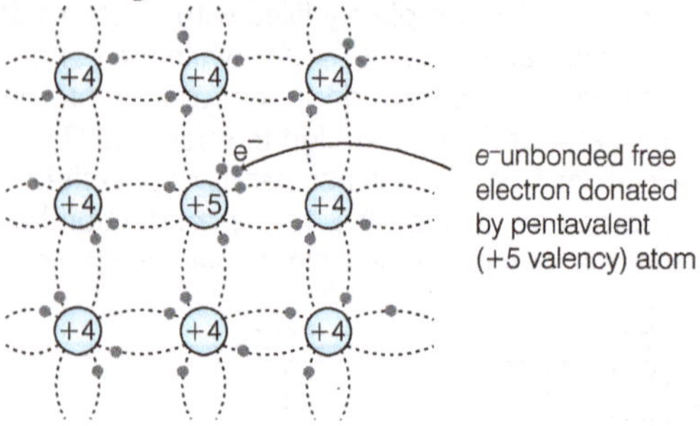

(a)

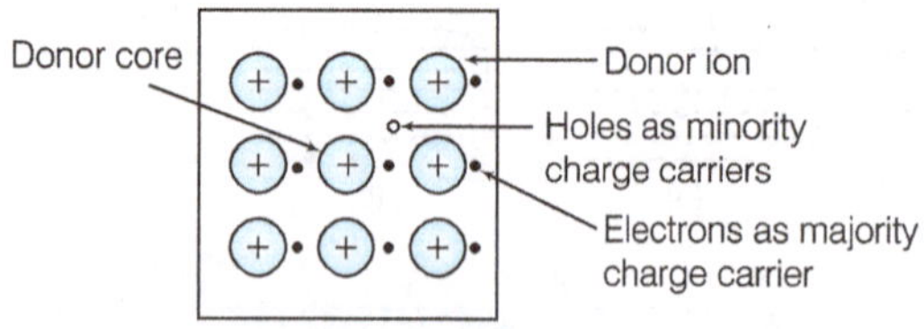

(b)

(ii) ***p*-type semiconductors** It is obtained when a pure semiconductor of Si or Ge is doped with a group III trivalent impurity like aluminium (Al), boron (B), etc.

- The trivalent impurity atom added in the semiconductor is called **acceptor atom**.
- In p-type semiconductor, the conduction of current is due to holes, i.e. holes are majority carriers and electrons are minority carriers, therefore they are called p-type semiconductor.
- For p-type semiconductor, the recombination process will reduce the number n_i of intrinsically generated electrons to n_e, we have $n_h >> n_e$ **NEET 2019**
- The conductivity of p-type semiconductor is $\sigma_p = en_h\mu_h$.
- Fig. (a) shows trivalent acceptor atom (In, Al, B, etc.) doped in tetravalent Si or Ge lattice giving p-type semiconductor. Fig. (b) shows commonly used schematic representation of p-type material which shows only the fixed core of the substituent acceptor with one effective additional negative charge and its associated hole.

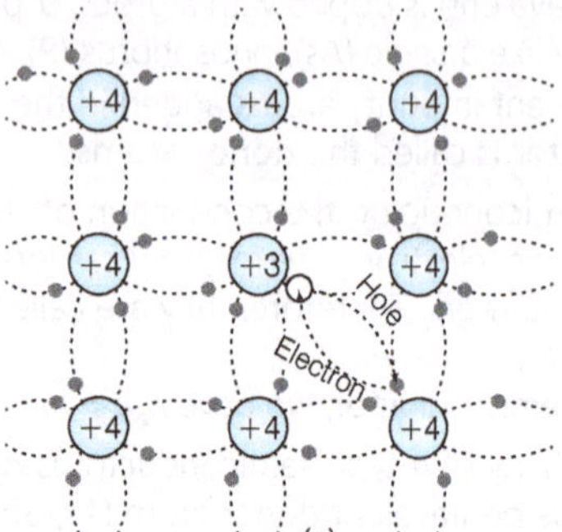

(a)

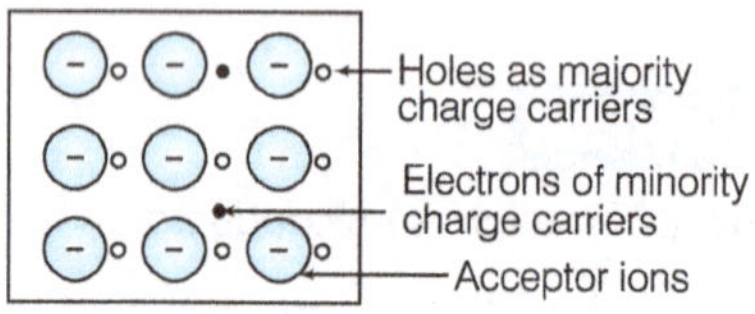

(b)

- Doped crystal maintains an overall charge neutrality as the charge of additional charge carriers is just equal and opposite to that of the ionised cores in the lattice.
- **Semiconductor's energy band** structure is also affected by doping. In the case of

  (i) ***n*-type semiconductor**, the donor energy level E_D exists slightly below the bottom E_C of conduction band and electrons from this level move into the conduction band with very small supply of energy.

- Figure shows energy band of n-type semiconductor at $T > 0$ K.

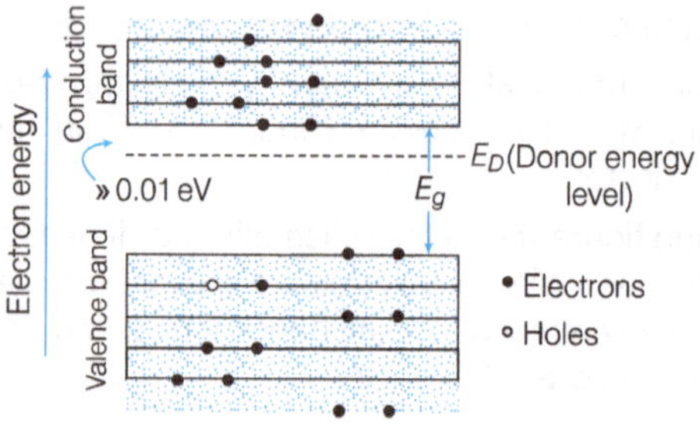

(a) $T > 0$ K
One thermally generated electron-hole pair +9 electrons from donor atoms

(ii) ***p*-type semiconductor**, an acceptor energy level E_A exists slightly above the top E_V of the valence band. With very small supply of energy an e^- from valence band can jump to level E_A and ionise the acceptor negatively.

- The electron and hole concentration in an extrinsic semiconductor in thermal equilibrium is given by

$$n_e n_h = n_i^2$$

- Figure shows energy band of p-type semiconductor at $T > 0$ K.

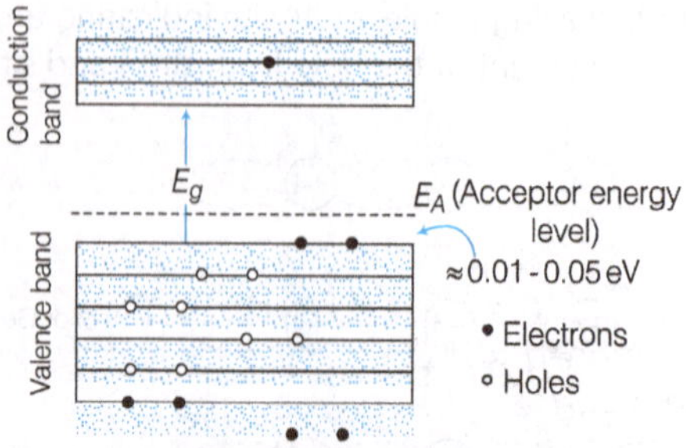

(b) p-type semiconductor at $T > 0$ K

Marks Maximiser

- Conductivity of a metal, $\sigma = \frac{nev}{E}$
  (n = number density of electrons, v = drift speed, E = electric field, e = charge of electron)
- Current flowing in a semiconductor due to electrons and holes, $I = eA(n_e v_e + n_h v_h)$
  (A = cross-section area)
- Conductivity of intrinsic semiconductor
  $\sigma_i = n_i e(\mu_e + \mu_h)$ (μ = mobility)
- Minimum energy required to create a electron-hole pair, $E_g = h\nu_{min} = \frac{hc}{\lambda_{max}}$
- Variation of conductivity with temperature,
  $$\sigma = \sigma \exp\left(\frac{-E_g}{2k_B T}\right)$$

p-n Junction

- A *p-n* junction is an interface or boundary between a *p*-type and a *n*-type semiconductor.
- It is the basic building block of many semiconductor devices like diodes, transistors, etc.
- During the formation of *p-n* junction, and due to the concentration gradient across *p*-side and *n*-side, holes diffuse from *p*-side to *n*-side (*p-n*). This motion of charge carriers gives rise to current.
- **Current** flowing across a *p-n* junction are of two types as follows
  (i) **Diffusion Current** (I_{df}) Current flowing from *p*-side to *n*-side due to diffusion of electrons and holes because of concentration difference.
  (ii) **Drift Current** (I_{dr}) Current flowing from *n*-side to *p*-side due to electrons-hole pairs (because of thermal collision) created in depletion region.
- As the holes continue to diffuse, a layer of negative charge (or negative space-charge region) on the *p*-side of the junction is developed. Similarly, as e^- diffuses from $n \rightarrow p$ it leaves behind a layer of positive charge on the *n*-side of the junction. This space-charge region on either side of the junction together is known as **depletion region** as the electrons and holes taking part in the initial movement across the junction depleted the region of its free charges as shown in the figure. The thickness of depletion region is of the order of one-tenth of a micrometre.

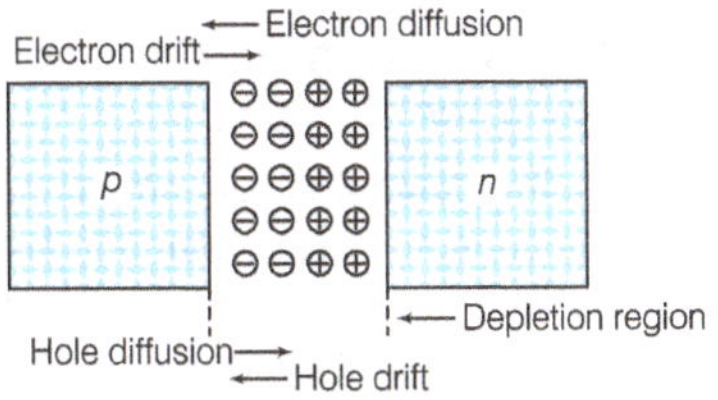

- Initially, diffusion current is large and drift current is small. As the diffusion process continues, the space-charge regions on either side of the junction extend, thus increasing the electric field strength and hence drift current. This process continuous until the diffusion current equals the drift current. Thus, a *p-n* junction is formed. In a *p-n* junction under equilibrium, there is no net current.
- The loss of e^- from the *n*-region and the gain of e^- by the *p*-region causes a difference of potential across the junction of two regions. This potential tends to prevent the movement of electrons from *n*-region to *p*-region and is often called a **barrier potential**.

Semiconductor Diode

- It is basically a *p-n* junction with metallic contacts provided at the ends for application of an external voltage (bias). It is a two terminal device. Diode and its symbol are shown below.

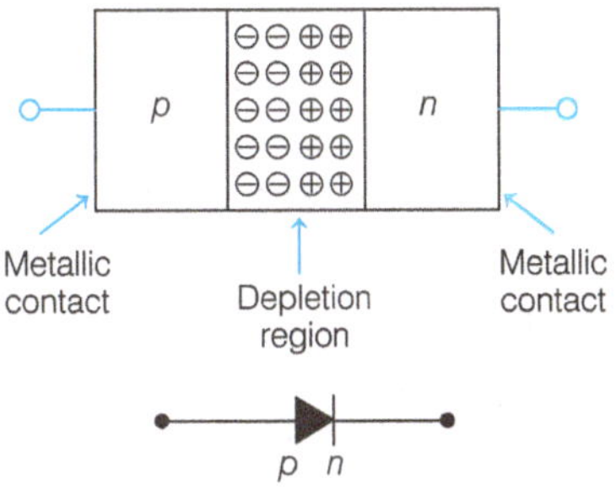

- The direction of arrow indicates the conventional direction of current (when the diode is under forward bias). The equilibrium barrier potential can be altered by applying an external voltage V across the diode.

p-n Junction Diode under Forward Bias

- When an external voltage V is applied across a semiconductor diode such that *p*-side is connected to the positive terminal of the battery and *n*-side to the negative terminal of the battery, then it is said to be **forward biased**.

  Following are few important points related to it
  (i) The effective barrier height under forward bias is $(V_0 - V)$.
  (ii) Due to applied voltage, electrons from *n*-side cross the depletion region and reach *p*-side. Similarly, holes from *p*-side cross the junction and reach the *n*-side. This process under forward bias is called **minority carrier injection**.
  (iii) The total diode forward current is the sum of hole diffusion current and conventional current of electron diffusion. The magnitude of current is in mA.

(iv) *p-n* junction diode under forward bias as shown in Fig. (a) and barrier potential for different cases (1) without battery, (2) low battery voltage and (3) high voltage battery is shown in Fig. (b).

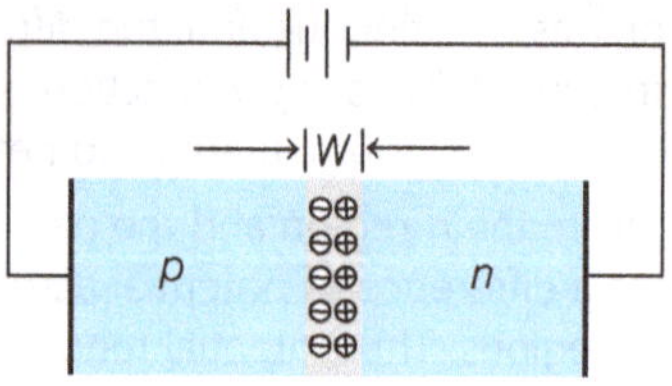

(a)

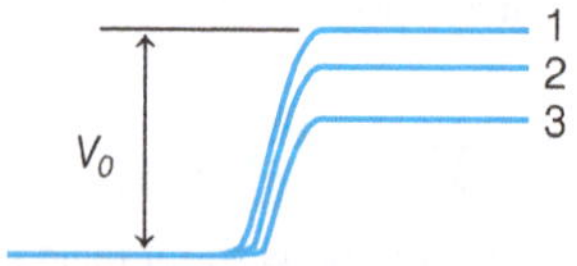

(b)

p-n Junction Diode under Reverse Bias

- When an external voltage V is supplied across the diode such that *n*-side is connected to positive terminal of the battery and *p*-side is connected to negative terminal of the battery, then it is said to be **reverse biased**.

Following are few important points related to it.

(i) The direction of applied voltage is same as the direction of barrier potential, so effective barrier height will be $(V_0 + V)$ and the depletion region widers due to change in electric field. NEET 2020

In reverse biased, the drift of carriers is responsible for the rise in current (i.e., drift current). The drift current is of the order of a few microampere.

(ii) The current under reverse bias is essentially voltage independent upto a critical reverse bias voltage, known as **breakdown voltage** (V_{br}). When $V = V_{br}$, the diode reverse current increases sharply.

(iii) *p-n* junction diode under reverse bias and barrier potential under reverse bias is shown in Figs. (a) and (b), respectively.

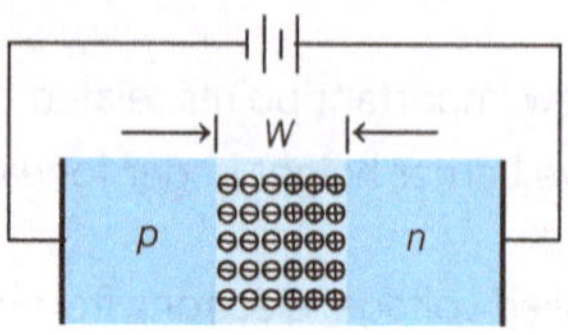

(a)

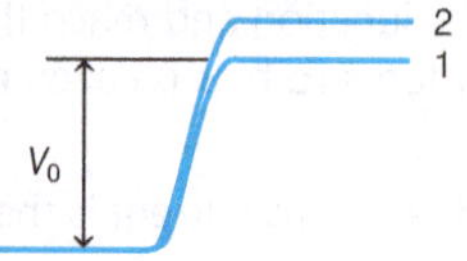

(b)

For Concept Master Video

Knee voltage or Threshold voltage

The forward voltage beyond which the current through the junction starts increasing rapidly with voltage is called knee voltage or threshold voltage.

V-I Characteristic of a Diode

The circuit arrangement for studying the *V-I* characteristics of a diode are shown in Figs. (a) and (b).

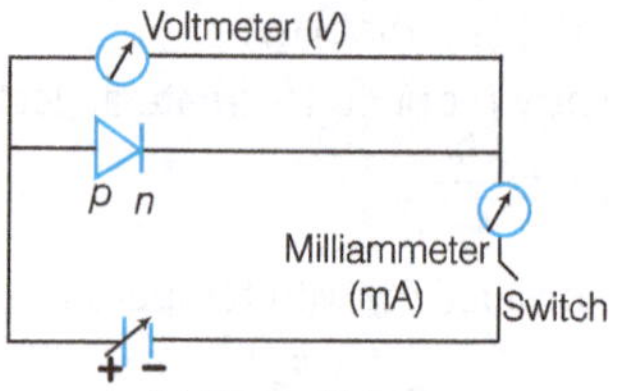

(a) Forward bias

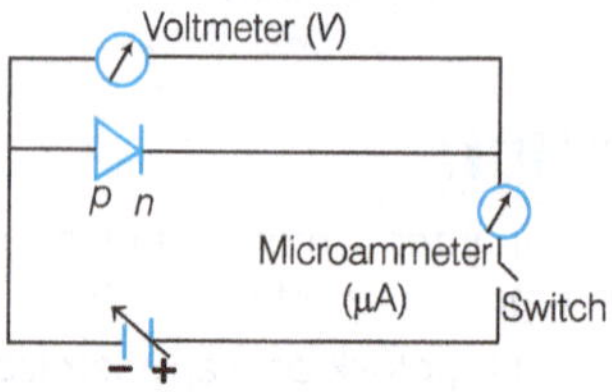

(b) Reverse bias

- The *V-I* characteristics (i.e. variation of current as a function of applied voltage) of a silicon diode is as follows.

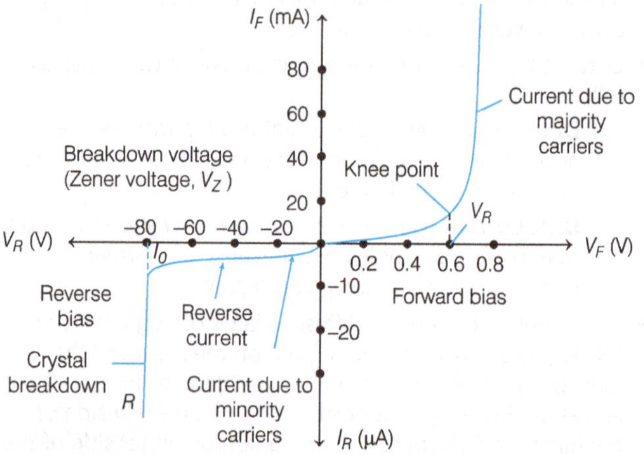

From the above graph,

(i) In forward bias, the current first increases very slowly, almost negligible till the voltage across the diode crosses a certain value. After the characteristic voltage, the diode current increases significantly. This voltage is called the **threshold voltage** or **cut-in voltage** (~ 0.2 V for Ge and ~ 0.7 V for Si).

(ii) In reverse bias, the current is very small (~ μA) and almost remains constant with change in bias. It is called **reverse saturation current**. However, at breakdown voltage, the current suddenly increases.

(iii) **Dynamic resistance** is defined as the ratio of small change in voltage ΔV to a small change in current ΔI,

i.e. $$r_d = \frac{\Delta V}{\Delta I}$$

Note *p-n junction diode primarily allows the flow of current only in one direction (forward bias).*

Marks Maximiser

- The temperature dependent current through junction diode is $I = I_0 (e^{eV/kT} - 1)$
(I_0 = reverse saturation current, V = voltage, k = Boltzmann constant and T = absolute temperature)

Application of Junction Diode as a Rectifier

- **Rectifier** It is a device which converts alternating current to direct current by using one or more *p-n* junction diodes. A diode behaves as a one-way valve that allows current to flow in a single direction.
- If an alternating voltage is applied across a diode, the current flows only in that part of the cycle when the diode is forward biased. This property is used to rectify alternating voltages and the circuit used for this purpose is called a rectifier. It is of two types **half-wave rectifier** and **full-wave rectifier**.
- **Half-wave rectifier** It is a circuit in which, an alternating voltage is applied across a diode in series with a load. The diode conducts corresponding to positive half-cycle and does not conduct during negative half-cycle. Hence, a unidirectional pulsating DC voltage across the load will appear. This process is known as half-wave rectification. It is as shown in the figure below.

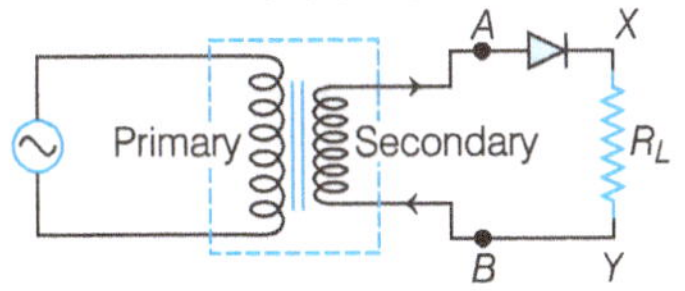

- Input AC voltage and output voltage waveforms from the half-wave rectifier are shown below.

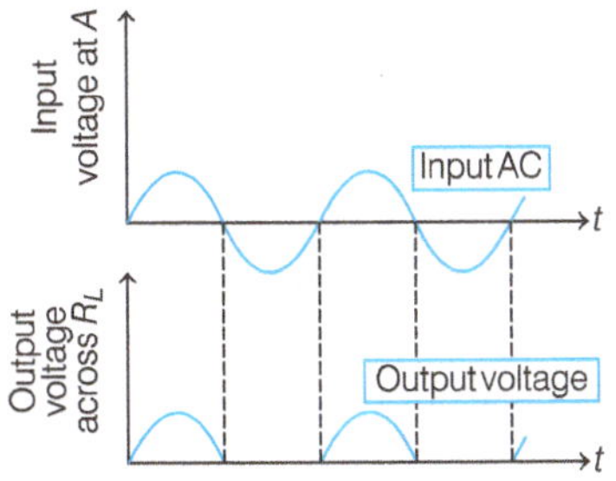

- Relation between input frequency and output frequency is $f_{out} = f_{in}$ NEET 2022
- **Full-wave rectifier** It is a circuit which gives output rectified voltage corresponding to both the positive as well as negative half of the AC cycle. It is as shown below.

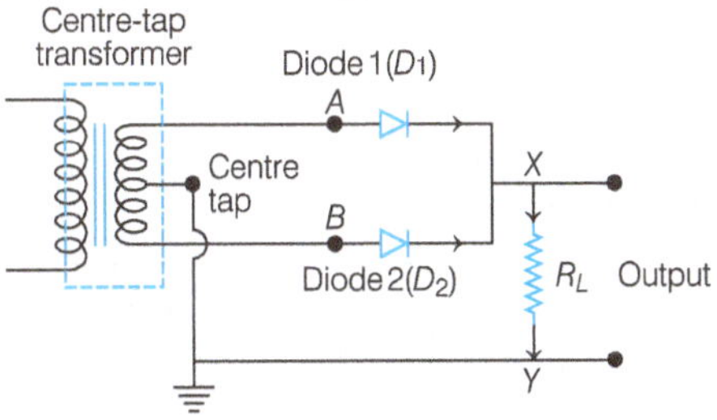

- For full wave rectifier, the secondary coil of the transformer is provided with a centre tapping and so, it is called **centre-tap transformer**.
- Input waveforms given to D_1 at A, D_2 at B and output across R_L connected in a full wave rectifier is as follows.

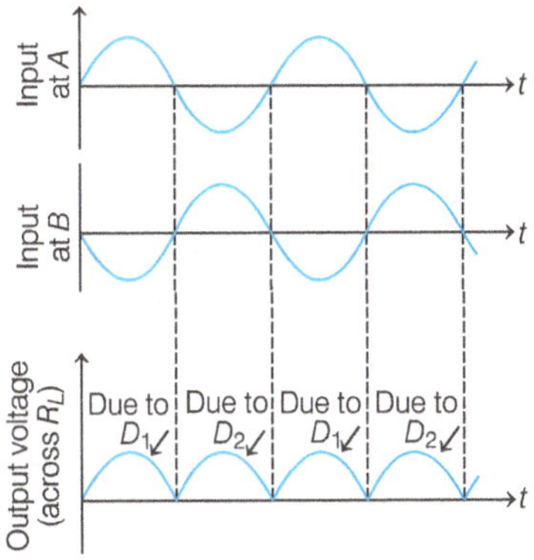

- Relation between input frequency and output frequency is
$$f_{out} = 2 \times f_{in}$$
- Rectified voltage in the rectifier are in the form of pulses. To get steady DC output from pulsating voltage, a capacitor in parallel or an inductor in series is connected with R_L.
Since, the additional circuit filter out the AC ripple and gives pure DC voltage, so they are called **filters**. NEET 2023
- The rate of fall of voltage across the capacitor in filters depends inversely upon the product of capacitance C and the effective resistance R_L used in the circuit and is called **time constant**, $\tau = R_L C$
- A full wave rectifier with capacitor filter is shown in Fig. (a). Fig. (b) shows the input and output voltage of rectifier in (a).

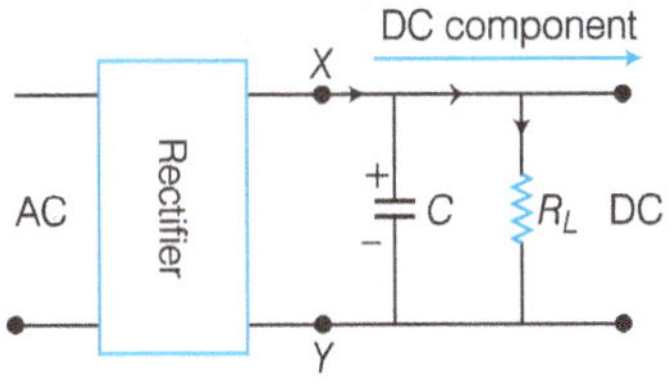

(a)

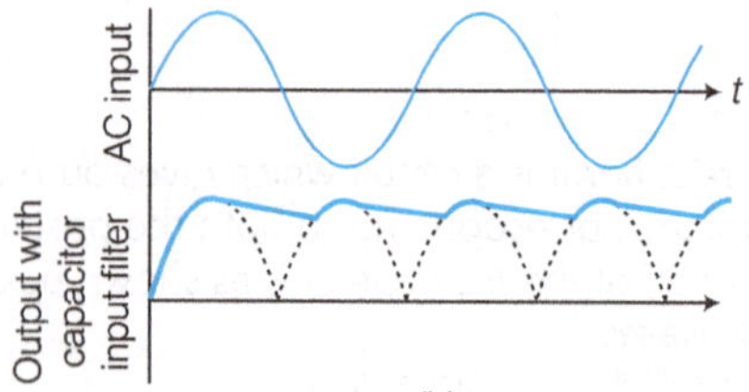

(b)

Marks Maximiser

p-n Junction diode as half-wave rectifier	p-n Junction diode as full wave rectifier
Average output in one cycle	
(i) $V_{DC} = \frac{V_0}{\pi}$; $I_{DC} = \frac{I_0}{\pi}$	$V_{DC} = \frac{2V_0}{\pi}$, $I_{DC} = \frac{2I_0}{\pi}$
(ii) rms output	
$I_{rms} = \frac{I_0}{2}$, $V_{rms} = \frac{V_0}{2}$	$V_{rms} = \frac{V_0}{\sqrt{2}}$, $I_{rms} = \frac{I_0}{\sqrt{2}}$

*Special Purpose *p-n* Junction Diodes

There are many types of *p-n* junction diodes based on their purpose are available. Some of them are discussed here.

Zener Diode

- It is a special purpose semiconductor diode designed to operate under reverse bias in the breakdown region and used as voltage regulator.
- Zener diode is fabricated by heavily doping both *p* and *n*-side of the junction. Due to this, depletion region formed is very thin ($<10^{-6}$ m) and electric field of the junction is extremely high ($\sim 5 \times 10^6$ V/m) even for a small reverse bias voltage of about 5V.
- Its symbol is as shown below.

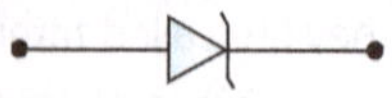

- *I-V* characteristics is as follows

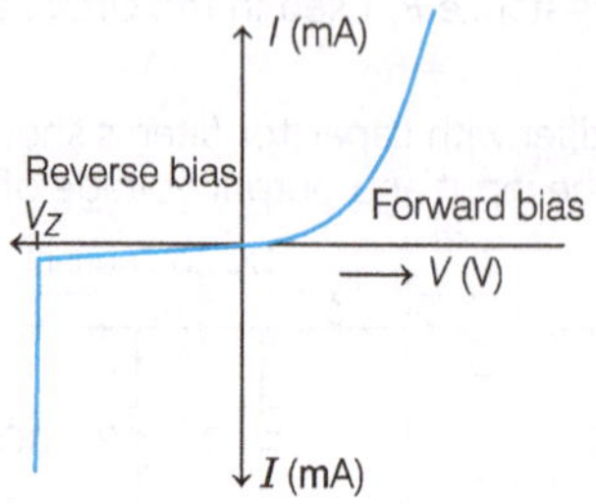

- Zener diode can be used as a **voltage regulator**, in which the constant output voltage is taken across a load resistance connected in parallel with it.

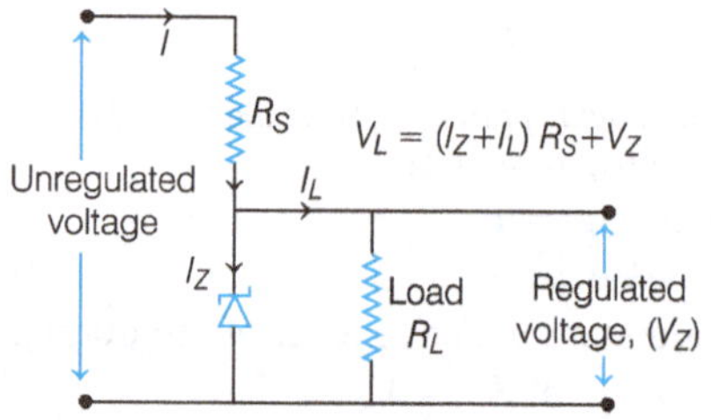

Optoelectronic Junction Devices

Semiconductor diodes in which carriers are generated by photons (photoexcitation) are called optoelectronic devices. e.g. Photodiodes, LED, photovoltaic cell (solar cell), etc.

- **Photodiode** is a junction diode fabricated with a transparent window to allow light to fall on the diode. It is operated under reverse bias. When it is illuminated with light of photon energy greater than the energy graph (E_g) of the semiconductor, electron-hole pairs are generated in near depletion region.
  - (i) An illuminated photodiode under reverse bias is as shown below.

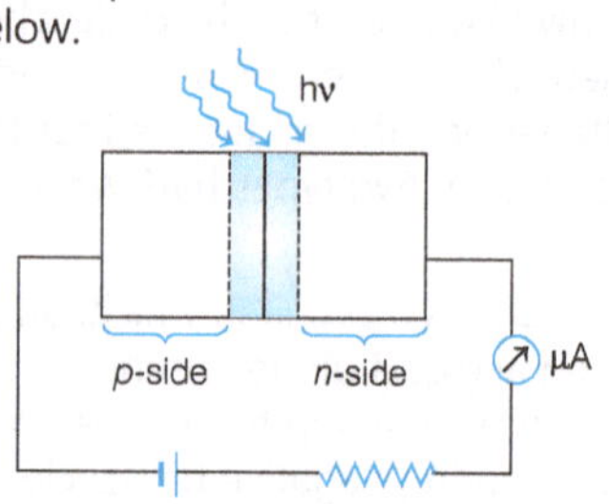

  - (ii) *I-V* characteristics of it is as follows

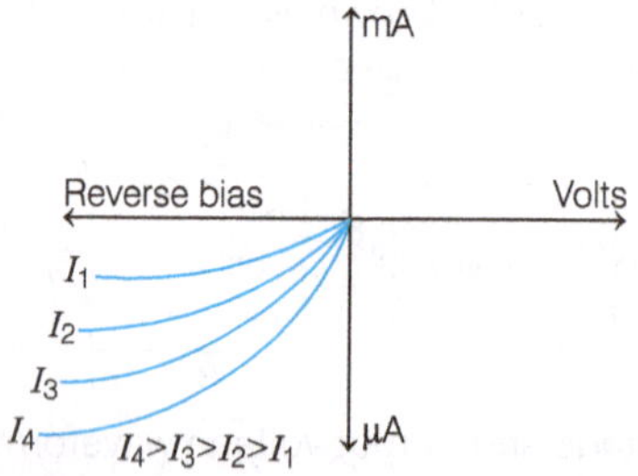

  - (iii) It can be used as photodetectors to detect optical signals.
- **Light Emitting Diode** (LED) converts electrical energy into light energy. It is a heavily doped *p-n* junction which under forward bias emits spontaneous radiation.
  - (i) Its *I-V* characteristics is similar to that of a Si junction diode but the threshold voltages are much higher and slightly different for each colour.
  - (ii) The reverse breakdown voltages of LED's very low.

* *This topic is not included in latest rationalised NCERT. But it is given in latest NEET syllabus.*

(iii) These are used in remote controls, burglar alarm systems, etc.

Symbol of LED is shown below.

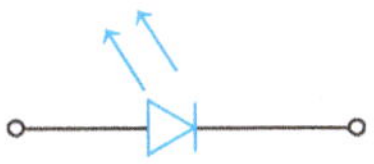

- Advantages of LEDs over incandescent low light lamps.
  (i) Low operational voltage and less power.
  (ii) Fast action and no warm-up time required.
  (iii) It is nearly monochromatic.
  (iv) Long life and ruggedness.
  (v) Fast on-off switching capability.
- **Solar cell** is basically a *p-n* junction which generates emf when solar radiation falls on it.
- **The generation of emf by a solar cell** when light falls on. It is due to the following three basic processes: generation, separation and collection.
  (i) **Generation** of *e-h* pairs due to light (with $h\nu > E_g$) close to the junction.
  (ii) **Separation** of electrons and holes due to electric field of the depletion region. Electrons are swept to *n*-side and holes to *p*-side.
  (iii) The electrons reaching the *n*-side are collected by the front contact and holes reaching *p*-side are collected by the back contact. Thus, *p*-side becomes positive and *n*-side becomes negative giving rise to photovoltage.
  (a) An illuminated *p-n* junction solar cell is shown below as

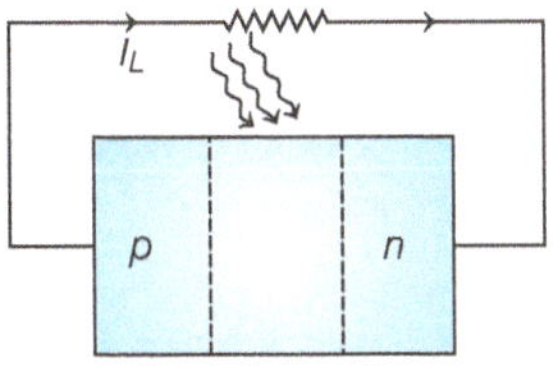

Depletion region

(b) *I-V* characteristics of it is as follows

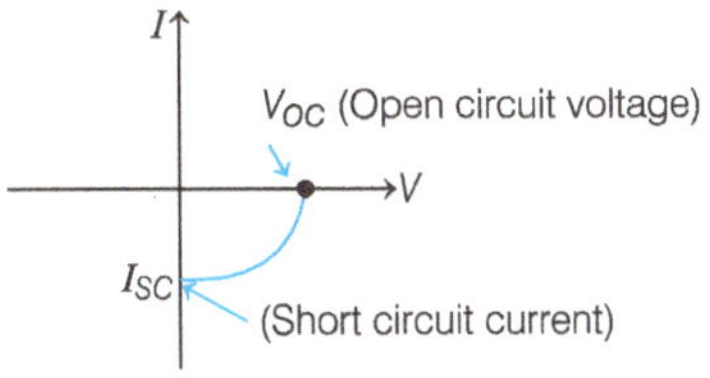

Note *Semiconductors with band-gap close to 1.5 eV are ideal materials for solar cell fabrication.*

*Digital Electronics and Logic Gates

- **Logic gates** are the basic building blocks of digital electronics, which process the digital signals in a specific manner. It follows a logical relationship between the input and output voltages.

Note *Each logic gate is indicated by a symbol and its function is defined by a truth table that rows are the possible input logic level combinations with their respective output logic levels.*

- There are three basic logic gates are as follows
  (i) **NOT gate** is a basic logic gate with one input *A* and one output *Y*. It produces an inverted version of input at its output and is known as **inverter**.

  The boolean expression for NOT gate is $Y = \overline{A}$.

  Its symbol and truth table is as shown below.

Input	Output
A	$Y = \overline{A}$
0	1
1	0

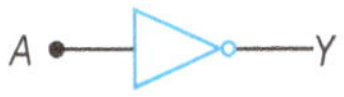

  (ii) **OR gate** has two or more inputs with one output. The output is 1 when either input *A* or *B* or both are 1, i.e. if any of the input is high output is high.

  The boolean expression for OR gate is $Y = A + B$.

  Its symbol and truth table is as shown below.

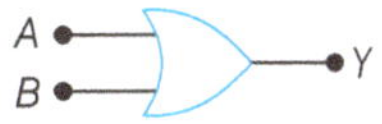

Input		Output
A	B	$Y = A + B$
0	0	0
0	1	1
1	0	1
1	1	1

  (iii) **AND gate** has two or more inputs and one output. The output *Y* of AND gate is 1 only when both inputs *A* and *B* are 1.

  The boolean expression for AND gate is $Y = A \cdot B$.

  Its symbol and truth table is as shown below.

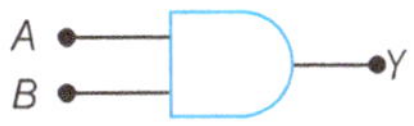

Input		Output
A	B	$Y = A \cdot B$
0	0	0
0	1	0
1	0	0
1	1	1

*Combination of logic gates

(iv) **NAND gate** is an AND gate followed by NOT gate. If both inputs *A* and *B* are 1, the output *Y* will not be 1. It is

* *This topic is not included in latest rationalised NCERT. But it is given in latest NEET syllabus.*

also called **universal gate**, since by using it, other basic gates OR, AND and NOT can be realised.

The boolean expression for NAND gate is $Y = \overline{A \cdot B}$.

Its symbol and truth table is as shown below.

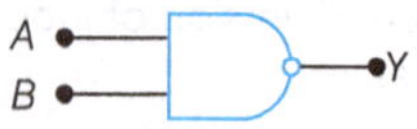

Input		Output
A	B	$Y = \overline{A \cdot B}$
0	0	1
0	1	1
1	0	1
1	1	0

(v) **NOR gate** is a gate with NOT operation applied after OR gate. Its output Y is 1 only when both inputs A and B are 0. It is also an universal gate.

The boolean expression for NOR gate is $Y = \overline{A + B}$.

Its symbol and truth table is as shown below.

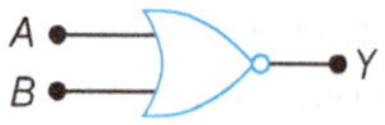

Input		Output
A	B	$Y = \overline{A + B}$
0	0	1
0	1	0
1	0	0
1	1	0

Caution Points

- The concept of energy bands (E_c or E_v) is a hypothetical concept, these bands are not actually present in the solid.
- The energies are the overall averages. E_c and E_v should be taken simple as bottom of conduction band energy levels and top of valence band energy levels, respectively.

PYQ Notes

XOR Gate

1. Its symbol and truth table are given below.

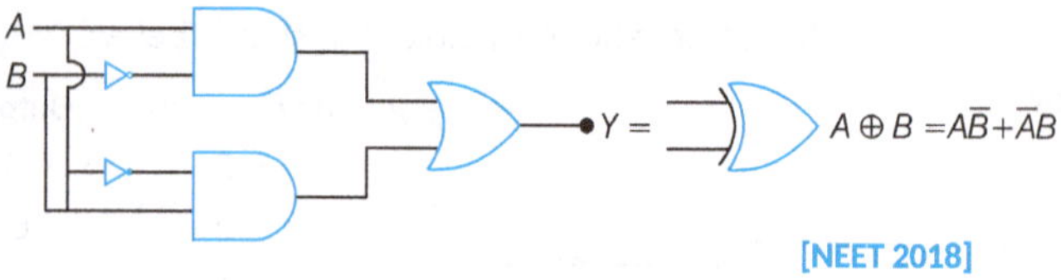

[NEET 2018]

A	B	$A \oplus B$
0	0	0
0	1	1
1	0	1
1	1	0

* *This topic is not included in latest rationalised NCERT. But it is given in latest NEET syllabus.*

Step by Step

Mastering NCERT

- Concept Builders
- Topical Questions
- Assertion and Reason Questions
- Statement Based
- Matching Type
- Numerical Type
- NCERT Exemplar
- Past Exams MCQs
- Skill Boosters

Concept Builders

1 What elements other than indium and gallium can be used to form a *p*-type semiconductor?

2 The *p-n* type junction can act as a semiconductor diode. [T/F]

3 The intensity of emitted light in a LED depends on the doping level of the semiconductor used. [T/F]

4 In *p-n* junction diode there is a .... (diffusion/drift) of majority carrier across the junction in forward bias.

5 The number of electrons in the valence shell of a pure semiconductor is .... (3/4).

6 A *p-n* junction with reverse bias can be used as a photodiode to measure intensity of light. [T/F]

7 Light emitting diodes give out light radiations when reverse biased. [T/F]

8 What is the resistivity of a pure semiconductor at absolute zero?

9 A zener diode can be used as a voltage reference. [T/F]

10 *p*-type semiconductor is better than *n*-type semiconductor as electrons have more mobility than holes. [T/F]

11 The frequency of light emitted by an LED depends on the ....

12 An ideal junction diode can act as a closed switch when forward biased and an open switch when reverse biased. [T/F]

13 The vacancy created by the removal of an electron from a covalent bond of semiconductor is called a ....

14 In an unbiased *p-n* junction diode, the *p*-side of the junction is at .... potential as compared to that on the *n*-side of the junction.

15 GaAs is a commonly used semiconductor used in the making of a solar cell. [T/F]

16 Name any one important process involved in the formation of the *p-n* junction.

17 The energy gap in the semiconductor .... (decreases/increases) due to the creation of acceptor energy level just above the top of the valence band.

18 The output of a NAND gate is .... (low/high) when both inputs are high.

19 A .... is a digital circuit that follows a logical relationship between input and output voltages.

20 Diffusion current is set up across the junction due to the concentration differences of the majority charge carriers on the two sides of the junction. [T/F]

Topical Questions

Introduction

1 For the flow of electrons in a vacuum tube like vacuum diode, vacuum is required in the interelectrode space otherwise, **NCERT Pg. 323**

(a) electrons will not be ejected from cathode
(b) extraction of electrons from remaining gas molecules or atoms will increase abruptly
(c) work function of cathode will be reduced
(d) electrons may lose their energy on collision with air molecules in their path

2 The vaccum tubes are

(a) bulky and consume high power
(b) small in size and consume high power
(c) bulky and consume less power
(d) reliable and have long life

Classification of Metals, Conductors and Semiconductors

3 Correct order of relative values of electrical conductivity σ for different types of solid is **NCERT Pg. 324**

(a) $\sigma_{semiconductor} > \sigma_{insulator} > \sigma_{metal}$
(b) $\sigma_{metal} > \sigma_{semiconductor} > \sigma_{insulator}$
(c) $\sigma_{semiconductor} > \sigma_{metal} > \sigma_{insulator}$
(d) $\sigma_{insulator} > \sigma_{semiconductor} > \sigma_{metal}$

4 Choose the incorrect statement(s) from the following. NCERT Pg. 324

(a) Vacuum tetrode has four electrodes.

(b) Liquid crystal display monitors has been replaced by cathode rays tube.

(c) Vacuum diode is usually referred as valves.

(d) Both (a) and (b)

5 Energy band gap of a certain material is neither very large nor zero. However, with the help of some external energy, conduction takes place due to (i.e., at room temperature) NCERT Pg. 325

(a) vacancies in conduction band

(b) electrons in valence band

(c) electrons in conduction band

(d) all electrons are bound to valence band

6 In the energy band diagram of material *A*, conduction band is partially filled and valence band is partially empty and for material *B*, both conduction and valence band overlaps each other. Then, materials *A* and *B* respectively are NCERT Pg. 325

(a) insulator and semiconductor

(b) semiconductor and conductor

(c) Both are semiconductors

(d) Both are conductors

7 If the energy of a photon of sodium light ($\lambda = 580\,\text{nm}$) equals the band gap of semiconductor, the minimum energy required to create hole-electron pair is NCERT Pg. 325

(a) 1.5 eV (b) 3.2 eV

(c) 2.1 eV (d) 4.1 eV

Intrinsic Semiconductor

8 The probability of electrons to be found in the conduction band of an intrinsic semiconductor at a finite temperature NCERT Pg. 327

(a) increases exponentially with increasing band gap

(b) decreases exponentially with increasing band gap

(c) decreases with increasing temperatrue

(d) is independent of the temperature and band gap

9 An intrinsic semiconductor has a resistivity of $0.50\,\Omega\text{m}$ at room temperature. Find the intrinsic carrier concentration if the mobilities of electrons and holes are $0.39\ \text{m}^2\ \text{V}^{-1}\text{s}^{-1}$ and $0.11\ \text{m}^2\ \text{V}^{-1}\text{s}^{-1}$, respectively. NCERT Pg. 327

(a) $1.2 \times 10^{18}\ \text{m}^{-3}$

(b) $2.5 \times 10^{19}\ \text{m}^{-3}$

(c) $1.9 \times 10^{20}\ \text{m}^{-3}$

(d) $3.1 \times 10^{21}\ \text{m}^{-3}$

10 At an elevated temperature ($T > 0$ K), few of covalent bonds of Si or Ge are broken and a vacancy in the bond is created. Effective charge of the vacancy or hole is NCERT Pg. 327

(a) positive

(b) negative

(c) neutral

(d) either positive or negative depending upon the material

11 At equilibrium condition, the rate of generation of electron-hole pairs in Ge crystal NCERT Pg. 328

(a) is more than rate of recombination of electron and hole pairs

(b) is less than rate of recombination of electron and hole pairs

(c) equals to rate of recombination of electron and hole pairs

(d) is always zero

12 Energy band gap E_g diagram for an intrinsic semiconductor at temperature $T > 0$ K is

(Here, E_c is energy for conduction band and E_v is energy for valence band) NCERT Pg. 329

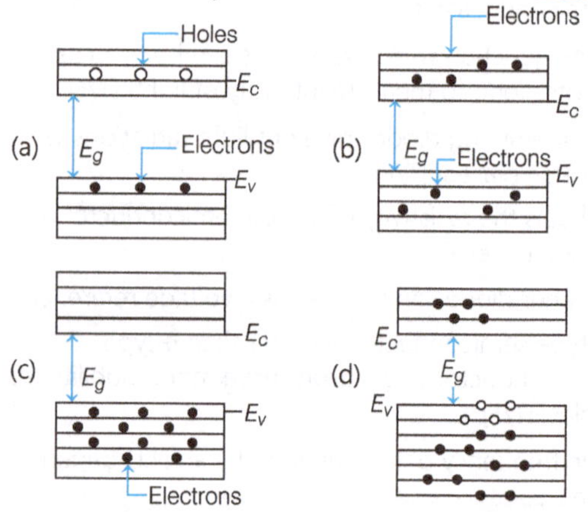

Extrinsic Semiconductor

13 Choose the incorrect statement from the following. NCERT Pg. 329

(a) In intrinsic semiconductor, number of free electrons is equal to number of holes.

(b) If the lowest level in the conduction band is lower than the highest level of valence band, then conduction takes place.

(c) In semiconductors apart from electrons, holes also move.

(d) Size of the dopant can be greater than the semiconductor atoms.

14 In extrinsic *p*-type and *n*-type semiconductor materials, the ratio of the impurity atoms to the pure semiconductor atoms is about NCERT Pg. 329

(a) 1 (b) 10^{-1} (c) 10^{-4} (d) 10^{-7}

15 For an extrinsic semiconductor, NCERT Pg. 329

(a) the conduction band and valence band overlaps
(b) the gap between conduction band and valence band is more than 16 eV
(c) the gap between conduction band and valence band is near about 1 eV
(d) the gap between conduction band and valence band will be 100 eV and more

16 In an *n*-type semiconductor, which of the following statement is true? NCERT Pg. 330

(a) Electrons are majority charge carriers and trivalent atoms are the dopants.
(b) Electrons are minority charge carriers and pentavalent atoms are the dopants.
(c) Holes are minority charge carriers and pentavalent atoms are the dopants.
(d) Holes are majority charge carriers and trivalent atoms are the dopants.

17 Number of electrons available for conduction due to doping atom in an extrinsic semiconductor NCERT Pg. 330

(a) increases with increase in temperature
(b) decreases with increase in temperature
(c) is independent of change in ambient temperature
(d) reduces to zero at temperature above room temperature

18 Schematic two-dimensional representation of Si structure is as shown below. NCERT Pg. 331

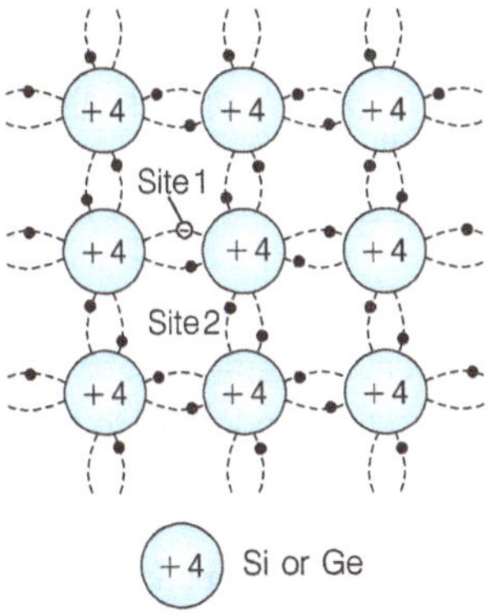

Here, o→ hole, •→ electrons. Then, at $T = 0$ K

(a) it behaves as an insulator
(b) a free electron might have been thermally excited from site 1
(c) an electron from site 2 can jump to site 1
(d) Both (b) and (c)

19 For a *p*-type semiconductor, which of the following statement is true? NCERT Pg. 331

(a) Holes are the majority carriers and trivalent atoms are the dopants.
(b) Holes are the majority carriers and pentavalent atoms are the dopants.
(c) Electrons are the majority carriers and pentavalent atoms are the dopants.
(d) Electrons are the majority carriers and trivalent atoms are the dopants.

20 A Ge specimen is doped with Al. The concentration of acceptor atom is ~ 10^{21} atoms per m^3. Given that the intrinsic concentration of electron-hole pairs is ~ 10^{19} per m^3, the concentration of electrons in the specimen is NCERT Pg. 332

(a) 10^{17} per m^3 (b) 10^{15} per m^3
(c) 10^4 per m^3 (d) 10^2 per m^3

21 Let a pure Si crystal has 5×10^{28} atoms m^{-3}. It is doped by one parts per million concentration of pentavalent arsenic. If number of intrinsic pairs is $1.5 \times 10^{16} m^{-3}$, then number of holes in doped crystal is NCERT Page 332

(a) $4.5 \times 10^9 \ m^{-3}$ (b) ~ $10^{16} \ m^{-3}$
(c) $2.25 \times 10^{32} \ m^{-3}$ (d) $5 \times 10^{22} \ m^{-3}$

22 The number of silicon atoms per m^3 is 5×10^{28}. This is doped simultaneously with 5×10^{22} atoms per m^3 of arsenic and 5×10^{20} per m^3 atoms of indium. Given that, $n_i = 1.5 \times 10^{16} m^{-3}$. Number of electrons and holes (in per metre cube of sample) are respectively, NCERT Pg. 332

(a) 4.95×10^{22}, 4.54×10^9 (b) 4.54×10^9, 4.54×10^9
(c) 4.54×10^9, 4.95×10^{22} (d) 4.95×10^{22}, 4.95×10^{22}

p-n Junction

23 Which of these graphs shows potential difference between *p*-side and *n*-side of a *p-n* junction in equilibrium? NCERT Pg. 333

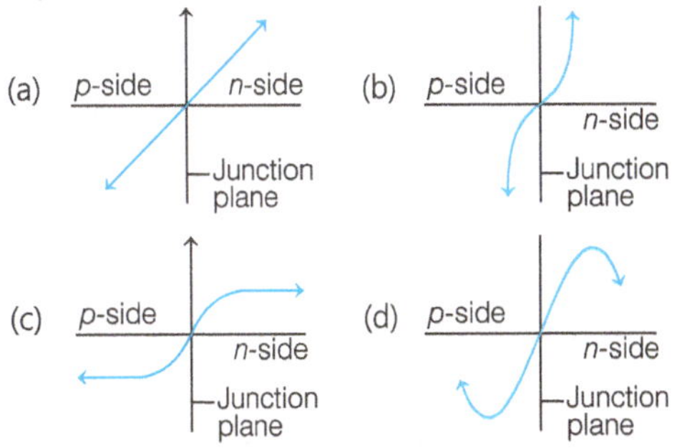

24 If no external voltage is applied across *p-n* junction, there would be NCERT Pg. 333

(a) no electric field across the junction
(b) an electric field pointing from *n*-type to *p*-type side across the junction
(c) an electric field pointing from *p*-type to *n*-type side across the junction
(d) a temporary electric field during formation of *p-n* junction that would subsequently disappear

25 The dominant mechanism for motion of charge carriers in forward and reverse biased silicon *p-n* junction are NCERT Pg. 333

(a) drift in forward bias, diffusion in reverse bias
(b) diffusion in forward bias, drift in reverse bias
(c) diffusion in both forward and reverse bias
(d) drift in both forward and reverse bias.

26 Potential barrier developed in a junction diode opposes the flow of NCERT Pg. 334

(a) minority carrier in both regions only
(b) majority carriers only
(c) electrons in *p* region
(d) holes in *p* region

27 In an unbiased *p-n* junction, holes diffuse from the *p*-region to *n*-region because NCERT Pg. 333

(a) free electrons in the *n*-region attract them
(b) they move across the junction by the potential difference
(c) hole concentration in *p*-region is more as compared to *n*-region
(d) All of the above

Semiconductor Diode

28 The arrow in the symbol of a *p-n* junction diode as shown below indicates the direction of NCERT Pg. 334

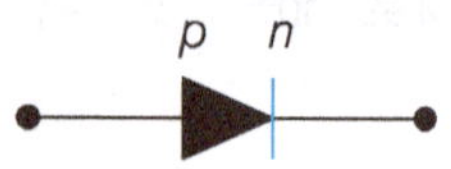

(a) drift current
(b) flow of holes
(c) conventional current (when it is forward biased)
(d) electric field

29 The forward biased diode connection among the following is NCERT Pg. 334

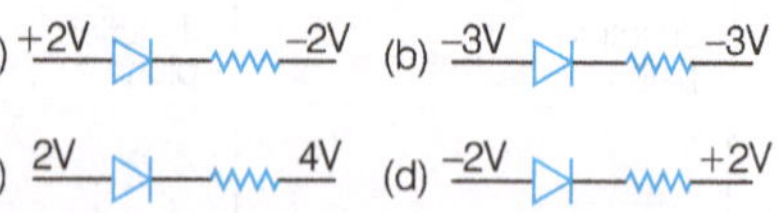

30 In the following circuit of *p-n* junction diodes D_1, D_2 and D_3 are ideal, then *i* is NCERT Pg. 334

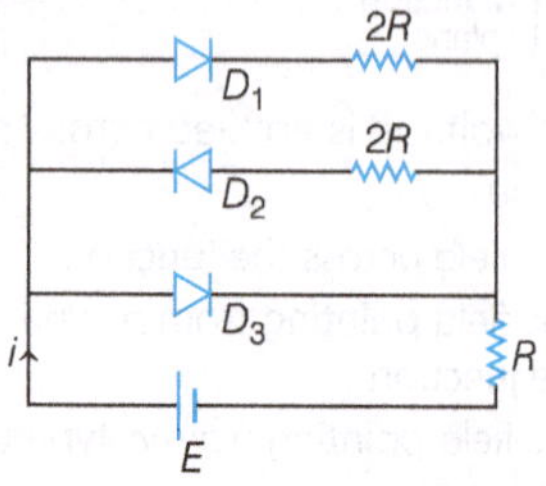

(a) E/R (b) $E/2R$ (c) $2E/3R$ (d) zero

31 Four silicon diodes are connected as shown in the figure. Assume the diodes to be ideal. The current through the resistance *R* is NCERT Pg. 334

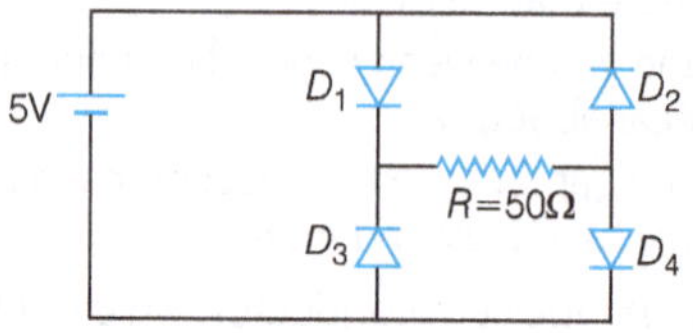

(a) 0.2 A (b) 0.1 A
(c) 0.3 A (d) 0.5 A

32 If *V* is applied potential difference in forward bias and V_0 is barrier potential of a *p-n* junction, then effective barrier height under forward bias is NCERT Pg. 335

(a) V (b) $V_0 - V$
(c) $V_0 + V$ (d) V_0

33 In the case of forward biasing of *p-n* junction, which one of the following figures correctly depicts the process of minority charge injection. NCERT Pg. 335
Here, e^- refers to electron and *o* refers to hole

(a)
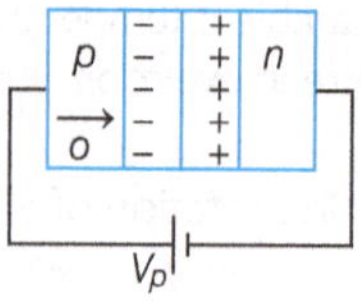

(b)
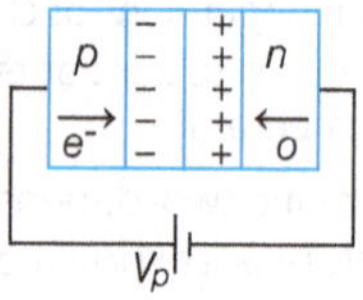

(c)
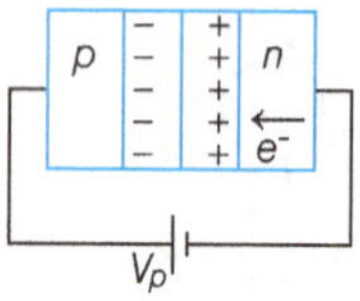

(d) Both (a) and (c)

34 In a reverse biased *p-n* junction diode, NCERT Pg. 335

(a) current is not much dependent on applied voltage
(b) current is directly proportional to applied voltage
(c) current initially depends on applied voltage, then it becomes independent
(d) no current flows in reversed bias

35 The breakdown in a reverse biased *p-n* junction diode is more likely to occurs due to NCERT Pg. 335

(a) small velocity of minority charge carriers, if the doping is small
(b) large velocity of minority charge carriers, if the doping is large
(c) strong electric field in depletion region, if the doping concentration is small
(d) strong electric field in depletion region, if the doping concentration is large

36 If V_0 is the barrier potential of an unbiased *p-n* junction diode, then on reverse bias the barrier potential is correctly depicted in NCERT Pg. 336

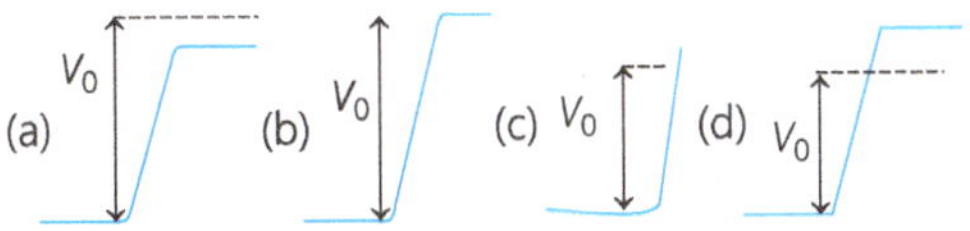

37 If reverse biasing potential is increased beyond a certain critical (breakdown) value, then NCERT Pg. 336

(a) diode gets destroyed due to overheating
(b) no current flows through the diode
(c) a heavy current flows from *p* to *n*-side
(d) potential barrier becomes zero

38 The *V-I* characteristic curve of a silicon diode is NCERT Pg. 336

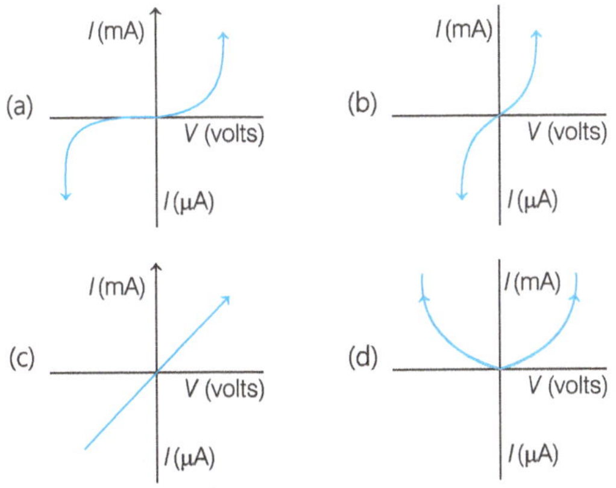

39 The *V-I* characteristics of a non-linear device is shown in the figure. The region showing negative resistance is NCERT Pg. 336

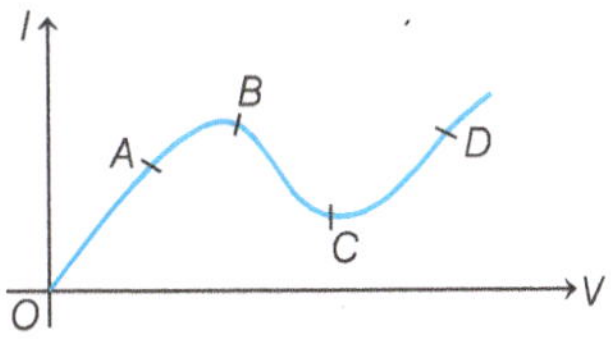

(a) *OA* (b) *AB*
(c) *CD* (d) *BC*

40 When the voltage drop across a *p-n* junction diode is increased from 0.65 V to 0.70 V, the change in the diode current is 5 mA. The dynamic resistance of diode is NCERT Pg. 337

(a) 5 Ω (b) 10 Ω
(c) 20 Ω (d) 25 Ω

41 *V-I* characteristics of a silicon diode is shown. NCERT Pg. 337

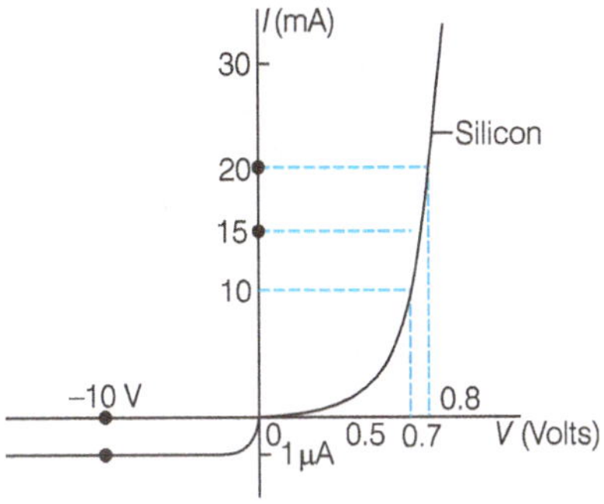

The ratio of resistance of diode at $I_D = 15$ mA and $V_D = -10$ V, is

(a) 10^{-3} (b) 10^{-4}
(c) 10^{-5} (d) 10^{-6}

42 The current *I* in the network is NCERT Pg. 337

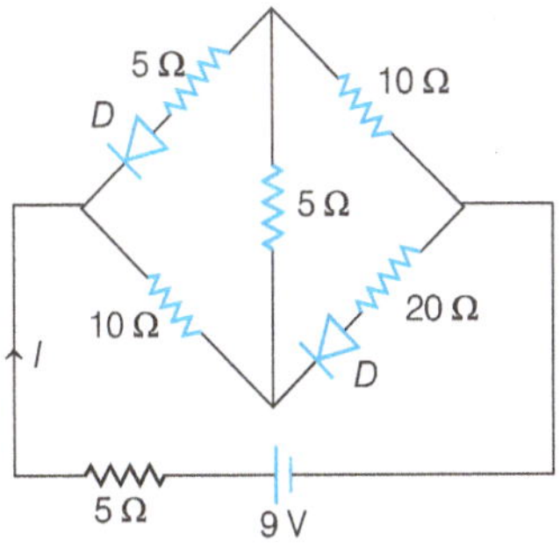

(a) 0.2 A (b) 0 A (c) 0.6 A (d) 0.3 A

43 The diode used in the circuit shown in the figure has a constant voltage drop of 0.5 V at all currents and a maximum power rating of 100 mW. Value of maximum current *I* and potential drop V_R across distance *R* is NCERT Pg. 337

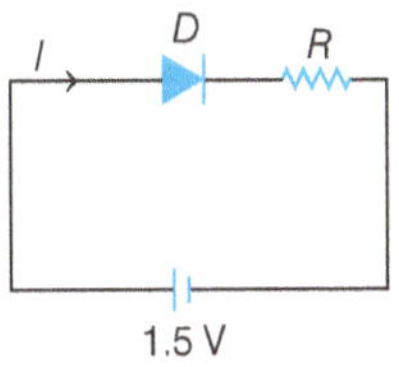

(a) $I = 200$ mA, $V_R = 1$ V (b) $I = 200$ mA, $V_R = 10$ V
(c) $I = 100$ mA, $V_R = 2$ V (d) $I = 100$ mA, $V_R = 10$ V

44 When a forward bias voltage of a diode is changed from 0.6 V to 0.7 V, the current changes from 5 mA to 15 mA. Then, its forward biased resistance is NCERT Pg. 337

(a) 6 Ω (b) 5 Ω (c) 10 Ω (d) 3 Ω

Application of Junction Diode as a Rectifier

45 Diodes are most commonly used for rectification of alternating voltages. Then, which amongst the following property of diode is responsible for this? NCERT Pg. 338

(a) Current flow in one direction
(b) Forward bias resistance is low compared to reverse bias
(c) Reverse current is independent of voltage applied
(d) Both (a) and (b)

46 For any practical half-wave rectifier circuit, the reverse breakdown voltage of diode NCERT Pg. 338

(a) greater than the peak AC voltage
(b) greater than the rms AC voltage
(c) greater than the mean AC voltage
(d) smaller than the rms AC voltage

47 Input to an half-wave rectifier is given as follows NCERT Pg. 338

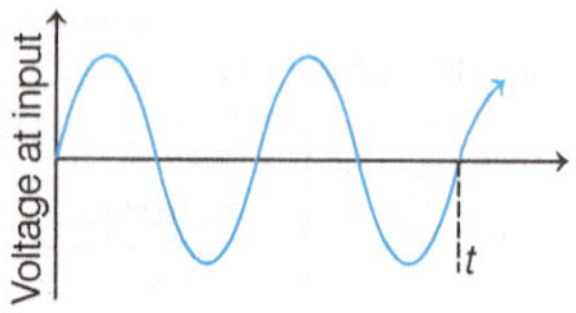

Its output (voltage across load resistance, R_L) will be

(a)
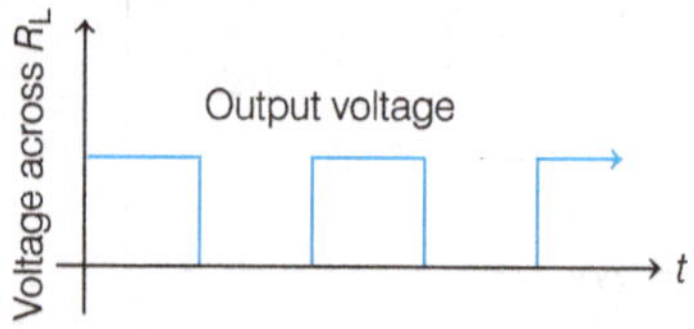

(b)
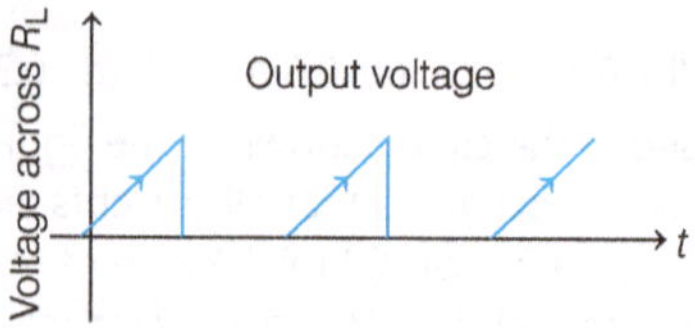

(c)
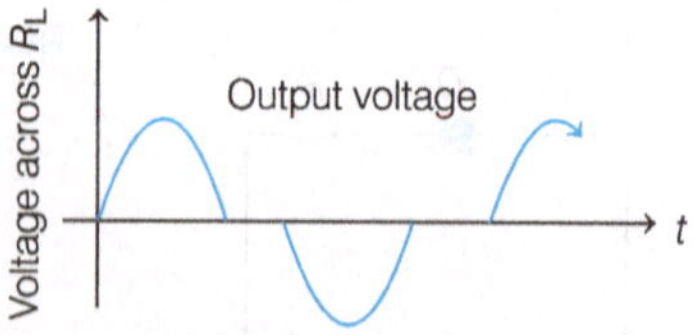

(d)
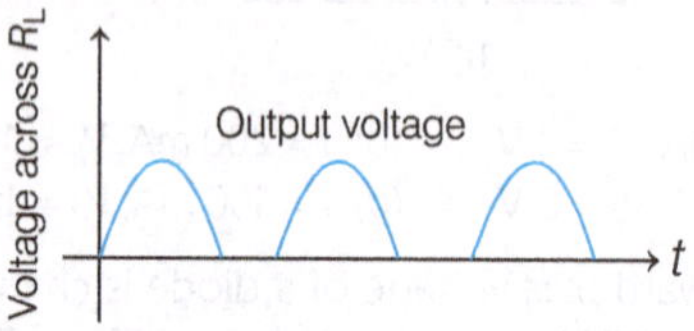

48 If in a *p*-*n* junction, a square input signal of 10 V is applied as shown NCERT Pg. 338

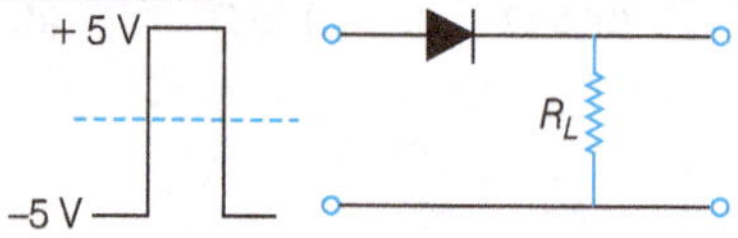

Then, the output across R_L will be

(a)

(b)

(c)

(d)

49 The ratio of output frequencies of full wave rectifier and a half-wave rectifier, when an input of frequency 50 Hz is fed at input is NCERT Pg. 338

(a) 1 : 2 (b) 2 : 1 (c) 4 : 1 (d) 1 : 4

50 If a centre tap transformer is used with 2 diodes for full wave rectification, then output voltage of rectifier w.r.t. each diode is NCERT Pg. 339

(a) $2 \times$ secondary voltage of transformer
(b) $(2/3) \times$ secondary voltage of transformer
(c) $(1/2) \times$ secondary voltage of transformer
(d) $(3/2) \times$ secondary voltage of transformer

51 In the given circuit,

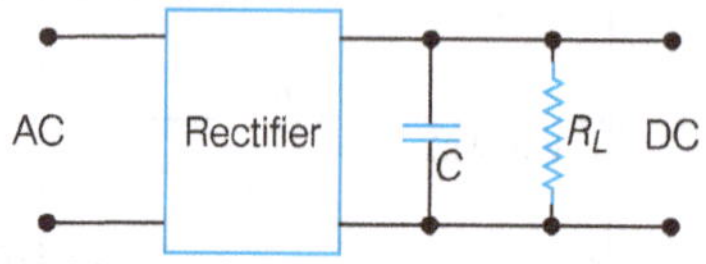

Capacitor *C* is used NCERT Pg. 339

(a) for storing potential energy
(b) as a bypass to DC component to get AC in R_L
(c) to remove sparking
(d) as a bypass to AC component to get DC in R_L

52 If in a full wave rectifier circuit, a capacitor *C* is connected in parallel to the load R_L (across output terminal), then rate of fall of voltage across *C* is proportional to NCERT Pg. 339

(a) $R_L C$ (b) $\frac{C}{R_L}$ (c) $\frac{1}{R_L C}$ (d) $\frac{R_L}{C}$

Special Purpose *p*-*n* Junction Diode

53 During the internal field emission or field ionisation in zener diode, Old NCERT Pg. 485

(a) valence electrons accelerated from $n \to p$
(b) holes are accelerated from $p \to n$
(c) resistance of the diodes becomes infinite
(d) valence electrons accelerates from $p \to n$

54 *I*-*V* characteristics curve of a zener diode is as shown below. Old NCERT Pg. 485

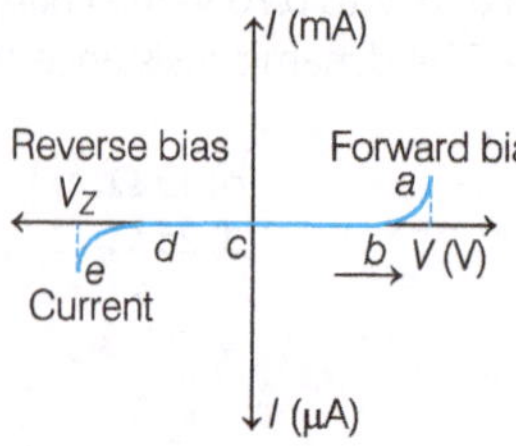

Which amongst the parts labelled above is suitable for the operation of voltage regulation?

(a) *ab* (b) *bc* (c) *cd* (d) *de*

55 A photodiode in reverse bias is irradiated with light of suitable frequencies and current in circuit is measured. Characteristics of diode for different illumination intensities I_1, I_2, I_3 and I_4 are drawn as follows. Old NCERT Pg. 487

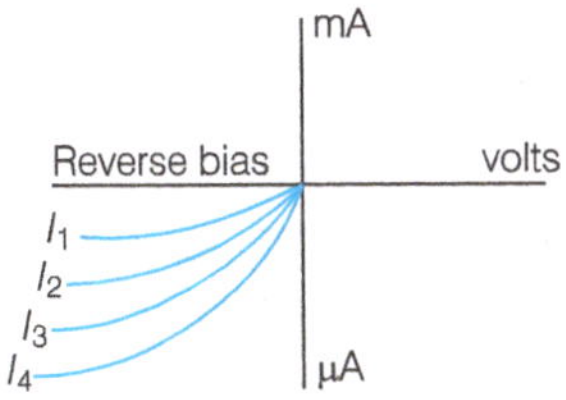

Then, the maximum intensity amongst these is

(a) I_1 (b) I_2 (c) I_3 (d) I_4

56 A *p-n* photodiode is made of a material with a band gap of 2 eV. The minimum frequency of the radiation that can be absorbed by the material is nearly (take, $hc = 1240$ eV-nm) Old NCERT Pg. 487

(a) 1×10^{14} Hz (b) 20×10^{14} Hz
(c) 10×10^{14} Hz (d) 5×10^{14} Hz

57 A *p-n* photodiode is made of a material with a band gap of 1.0 eV. The maximum wavelength of radiation that can be absorbed by the material is nearly Old NCERT Pg. 487

(a) 10^{-2}m (b) 1.2×10^{-7}m
(c) 1.2×10^{-10}m (d) 1.6×10^{-6}m

58 Semiconductors used to fabricate LED to produce visible light must have energy gap E_g such that Old NCERT Pg. 488

(a) $1.1 \text{ eV} < E_g$ (b) $E_g > 3$ eV
(c) $1.8 \text{ eV} < E_g < 3$ eV (d) $1.1 \text{ eV} < E_g < 2.8$ eV

59 The given graph represents *V-I* characteristic for a semiconductor device. Old NCERT Pg. 489

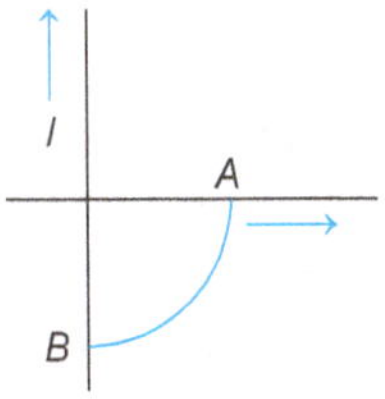

Which of the following statements is correct?

(a) It is *V-I* characteristic for solar cell, where point *A* represents open circuit voltage and point *B* represents short circuit current.
(b) It is for a *p-n* junction and points *A* & *B* represent open circuit voltage & current, respectively.
(c) It is for a photodiode and points *A* & *B* represent open circuit voltage and current, respectively.
(d) It is for a LED and points *A* & *B* represents open circuit voltage & short circuit current, respectively.

Digital Electronics and Logic Gates

60 In the given circuit, value of *Y* is Old NCERT Pg. 502

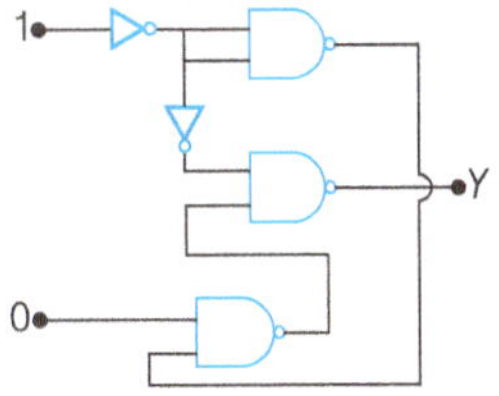

(a) toggles between 0 and 1 (b) 1
(c) 0 (d) will not execute

61 The output (*Y*) of the logic circuit shown in the figure is Old NCERT Pg. 502

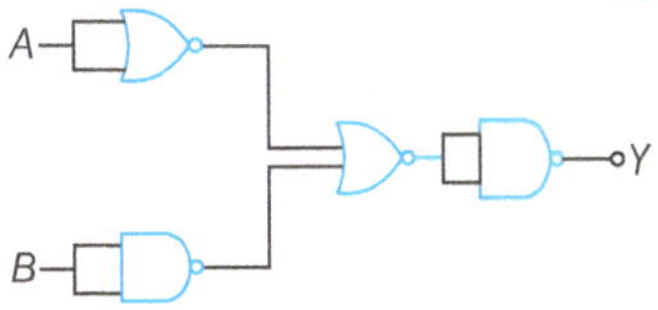

(a) $\overline{A+B}$ (b) AB (c) $A \oplus B$ (d) $\overline{A \cdot B}$

62 The output of the given logic circuit is Old NCERT Pg. 502

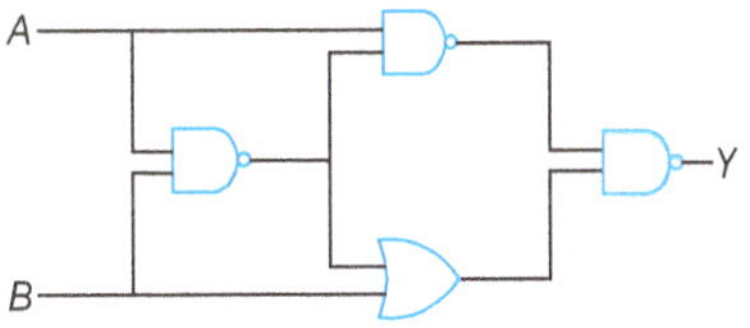

(a) $\bar{A}B$ (b) $A\bar{B}$ (c) $AB + \overline{AB}$ (d) $A\bar{B} + \bar{A}B$

63 Following circuit will act as Old NCERT Pg. 504

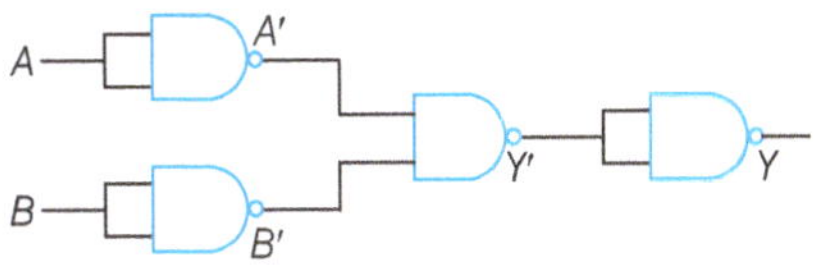

(a) NOR gate (b) NAND gate
(c) AND gate (d) OR gate

64 The correct Boolean operation represented by the circuit diagram drawn is Old NCERT Pg. 505

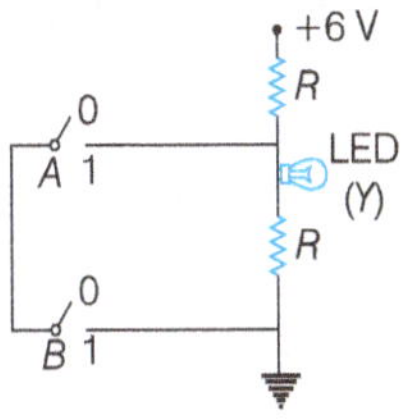

(a) OR (b) NAND (c) NOR (d) AND

Assertion and Reason Questions

Direction (Q. Nos. 1-10) *In the following questions, a statement of Assertion is followed by a corresponding statement of Reason. Of the following statements, choose the correct one.*

(a) Both Assertion and Reason are correct and Reason is the correct explanation of Assertion.
(b) Both Assertion and Reason are correct but Reason is not the correct explanation of Assertion.
(c) Assertion is correct but Reason is incorrect.
(d) Assertion is incorrect but Reason is correct.

1 **Assertion** The total current I in a semiconductor is the sum of electron current and hole current.

Reason In a semiconductor, I_h arises due to the motion of holes towards positive potential and free electrons under an applied electric field. NCERT Pg. 328

2 **Assertion** The resistance of an intrinsic semiconductor decreases with increase in its temperature.

Reason As the temperature of an intrinsic semiconductor increases, the number of conduction electrons as well as holes also increases. NCERT Pg. 329

3 **Assertion** The probability of electrons to be found in the conduction band of an intrinsic semiconductor at a finite temperature decreases exponentially with increase in band gap.

Reason It will be more difficult for the electron to cross over the large band gap while going from valence band to conduction band. NCERT Pg. 329

4 **Assertion** In a n-type semiconductor, number of holes is less than number of conduction electrons.

Reason Rate of recombination of holes is increased. NCERT Pg. 330

5 **Assertion** An electron on p-side of a p - n junction moves to n-side just an instant after drifting of charge carriers occurs across junction plane.

Reason Drifting of charge carriers reduces the concentration gradient across junction plane. NCERT Pg. 333

6 **Assertion** In a p-n junction, under equilibrium, no net current flows across the junction.

Reason A stable p-n junction is only formed when drift and diffusion currents are equal. NCERT Pg. 333

7 **Assertion** The applied voltage (in forward bias of a p-n junction) mostly drops across the depletion region and the voltage drop across the p-side and n-side of the junction is negligible.

Reason Resistance of depletion region is large compared to resistance of n or p-side. NCERT Pg. 333

8 **Assertion** The value of current through p-n junction in the given figure will be 20 mA.

Reason In the figure, p-side is at higher potential than n-side.

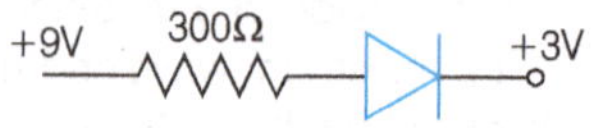

NCERT Pg. 333

9 **Assertion** Photodiodes are operated under reverse bias.

Reason Current in forward bias is known to more (~ mA) than the current in reverse bias (~ μA). NCERT Pg. 487

10 **Assertion** NAND and NOR gates are called digital building blocks.

Reason The repeated use of NAND or NOR gates can produce all basic or complicated gates. NCERT Pg. 505

Statement Based Questions

Direction (Q. No. 1-8) *In the following questions statement I and Statement II are given. Read then statements and choose most appropriate answer from the options given below.*

(a) Both Statement I and Statement II are incorrect
(b) Statement I is correct but Statement II is incorrect.
(c) Statement I is incorrect but Statement II is correct
(d) Both Statement I and Statement II are correct.

1 **Statement I** In metals when conduction band is partially empty electrons from its lower level can move to higher level making conduction possible.

Statement II In insulators, energy gap is so large that electrons cannot be excited from the valence band to the conduction band by thermal excitation. NCERT Pg. 327

2 **Statement I** Number of electrons made available for conduction by dopant atoms is independent of any increase in dopant level.

Statement II When the electrical conductivity of semiconductor is due to breaking of its covalent bond, then the semiconductor is extrinsic in nature. NCERT Pg. 329

3 Commonly used schematic representation of p-type material is as shown below.

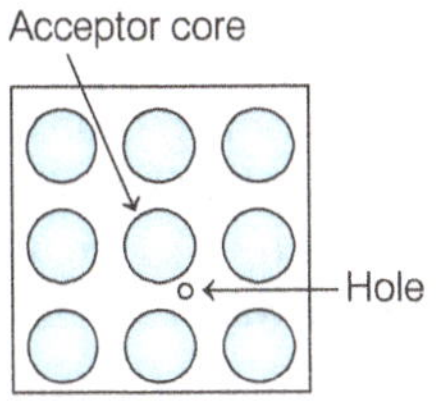

Statement I The dopant can be treated as core of one positive charge.
Statement II With very small supply of energy an electron can jump from valence band to the acceptor energy level.

4 **Statement I** A p-type semiconductor is a positive type crystal.
Statement II A p-type semiconductor is an uncharged crystal. NCERT Pg. 331

5 **Statement I** Silicon is preferred over germanium for making semiconductor devices.
Statement II The energy gap in germanium is more than the energy gap in silicon. NCERT Pg. 332

6 Due to diffusion of electron from n to p-side.
Statement I a layer of negative charge is developed on n-side.
Statement II an ionised donor is left in the n-region. NCERT Pg. 333

7 **Statement I** When zener diode is used as DC voltage regulator, then with the increase in input voltage V_i, zener voltage V_z remains unchanged. But when V_i decreases, then V_z also decreases.
Statement II LED's requires low operational voltage and less power as comare to incandescent lamp. Old NCERT Pg. 485

8 **Statement I** A p-n junction with reverse bias can be used as a photodiode to measure light intensity.
Statement II In a reverse bias condition the current is small but it is more sensitive to changes in incident light intensity. Old NCERT Pg. 487

Matching Type Questions

1 Match column I (type of semiconductors) with column II (properties) given below and select the correct answer from the codes given below. NCERT Pg. 332

Column I		Column II	
A.	p-type semiconductor	1.	Doped with impurity
B.	n-type semiconductor	2.	Pure semiconductor
C.	Extrinsic semiconductor	3.	Majority carriers are holes
D.	Intrinsic semiconductor	4.	Majority carriers are electrons

Codes

	A	B	C	D		A	B	C	D
(a)	3	4	1	2	(b)	1	3	2	1
(c)	2	1	3	4	(d)	4	2	1	3

2 Match the column I (types of semiconductor of physical quantity) with column II (their properties) and select the correct answer from the codes given below. NCERT Pg. 327

Column I		Column II	
A.	p-type semiconductor	1.	No-impurity
B.	n-type semiconductor	2.	Mobility × Electric field
C.	Intrinsic semiconductor	3.	Impurity of IIIrd group
D.	Drift velocity	4.	Impurity of fifth group

Codes

	A	B	C	D
(a)	1	2	4	3
(b)	4	3	2	1
(c)	2	1	3	4
(d)	3	4	1	2

3 Match the Column I (symbol) with Column II (their respective logic gate) and select the correct answer from the codes given below. Old NCERT Pg. 501

Column I		Column II	
A.		1.	OR
B.		2.	AND
C.		3.	NAND
D.	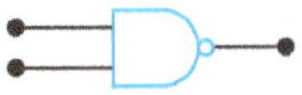	4.	NOT

Codes

	A	B	C	D
(a)	1	2	3	4
(b)	3	1	2	4
(c)	3	1	4	2
(d)	4	1	2	3

Numerical Type Questions

1 In a semiconductor, if the ratio of the concentration of electrons to that of holes is $\frac{K}{4}$, the ratio of currents is $\frac{9}{4}$ and the ratio of their drift velocities is $\frac{9}{7}$, then the value of K is .... NCERT Pg. 333

2 Pure silicon at 300 K has equal electron and hole concentrations of $1.5 \times 10^{16}/\text{m}^3$. Doping by indium increases the hole concentration to $4.5 \times 10^{22}/\text{m}^3$. The new electron concentration in the doped silicon is ....$\times 10^9$ m^{-3}. NCERT Pg. 333

3 The circuit has two oppositely connected ideal diodes in parallel. The current flowing in the circuit is ....A. NCERT Pg. 334

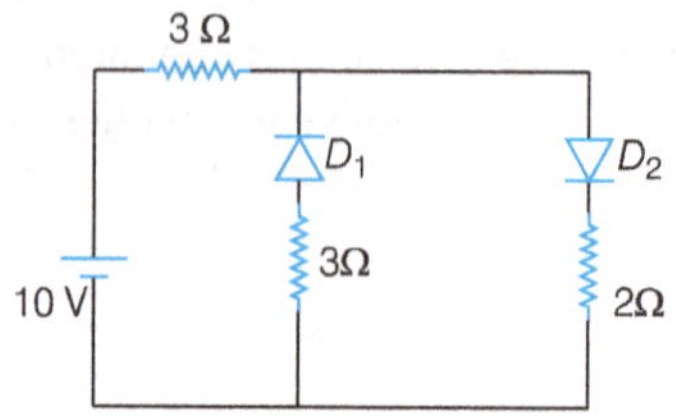

4 The junction diode in the following circuit requires a minimum current of 1 mA to be above the knee point (0.5 V) of its I-V characteristic curve. The voltage across the junction diode is independent of current above the knee point. If $V_B = 4.5$ V, then the maximum value of R, so that voltage is above knee point will be ....$\times 10^3 \Omega$. NCERT Pg. 336

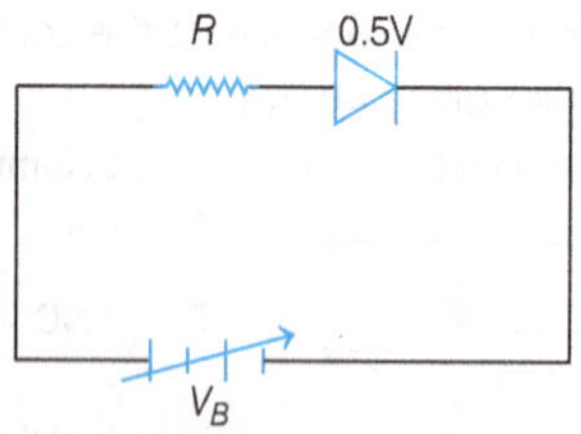

5 A semiconductor diode is used as a half-wave rectifier having internal resistance 150Ω. The voltage applied is given by $V = (50 \sin \omega t)$ V and load resistance is 850Ω. Then the maximum output current is ....$\times 10^{-3}$ A. NCERT Pg. 338

6 A full wave diode rectifier is applied with a voltage from a 60 V–0 – 60 V transformer. Load and diode forward resistance are 100Ω and 10Ω, respectively. The average output voltage of the rectifier circuit is ....V. (Round off to nearest integer value)

7 A 5V zener diode along with a series resistance R is connected across a 10 V supply. If the maximum zener current is 20 mA, then the minimum value of R will be ....Ω.

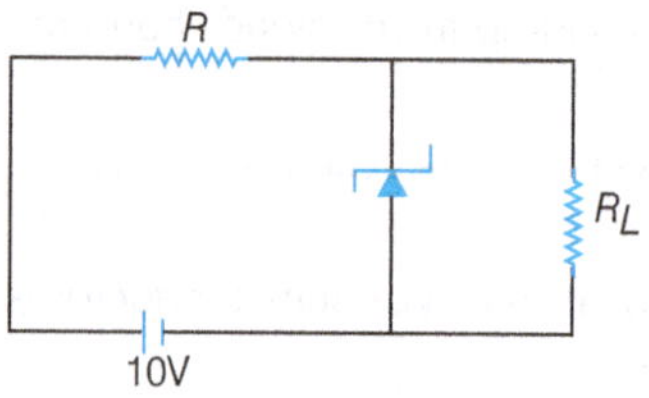

8 An LED is constructed from a p-n junction diode using GaAsP. The energy gap is 1.9 eV. The wavelength of the light emitted will be equal to ....$\times 10^{-9}$ m. (Round off to nearest integer value) Old NCERT Pg. 488

[$h = 6.626 \times 10^{-34}$ Js and 23×10^8 ms^{-1}]

9 In the logic circuit shown in the figure, if inputs of A and B are 0 and C is 1, the output at Q would be x. Then the value of $\bar{x}$ is .... Old NCERT Pg. 502

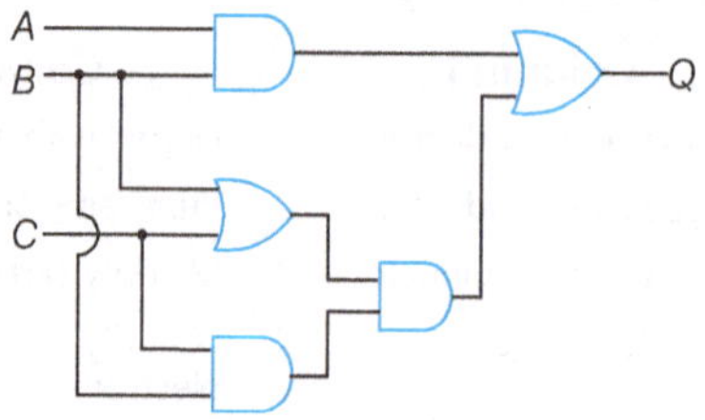

10 For the given combination of logic gates, if the logic states of A and B are 1 and 0, respectively, then the logic state of output R is ....

Old NCERT Pg. 502

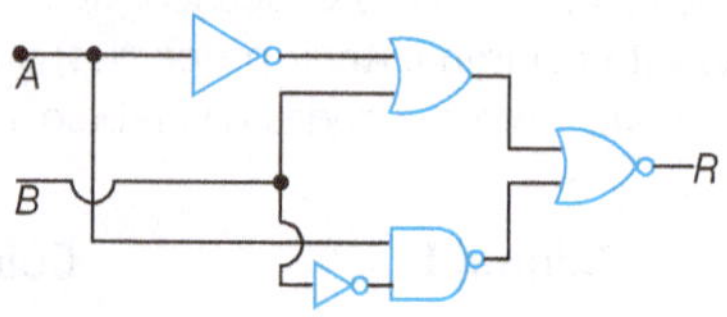

NCERT Exemplar Questions

1 A hole is
(a) an anti-particle of electron
(b) a vacancy created when an electron leaves a covalent bond
(c) absence of free electrons
(d) an artificially created (particle)

2 Conductivity of a semiconductor increases with increase in temperature, because
(a) number density of free charge carriers increases
(b) relaxation time increases
(c) both number density of free charge carriers and relaxation time increases
(d) number density of free charge carriers increases and relaxation time decreases but effect of decrease in relaxation time is much less than increase in number density

3 Assuming diodes to be ideal,

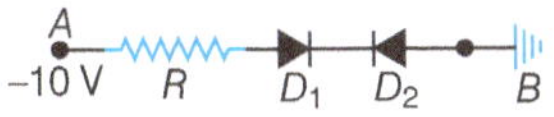

(a) D_1 is forward biased and D_2 is reverse biased, so current flows from A to B
(b) D_2 is in forward bias and D_1 is in reverse bias and hence no current flows from B to A and *vice-versa*
(c) D_1 and D_2 both are in forward bias, so current flows from A to B
(d) D_1 and D_2 both are in reverse bias, so no current flows from A to B

4 A 220 V AC supply is connected between points A and B.

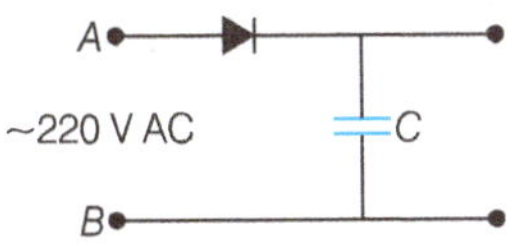

What will be potential difference across capacitor C ?
(a) 220 V (b) 110 V
(c) 0 V (d) $220\sqrt{2}$ V

5 Output of the circuit shown below will be

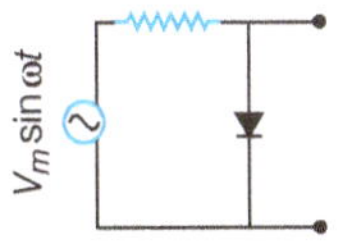

(a) zero all the times
(b) like half wave rectifier with positive cycles in output
(c) like half wave rectifier with negative cycles in output
(d) like that of a full wave rectifier

6 In the circuit shown, the voltage difference between A and B, if the diode forward voltage drop is 0.3 V, is

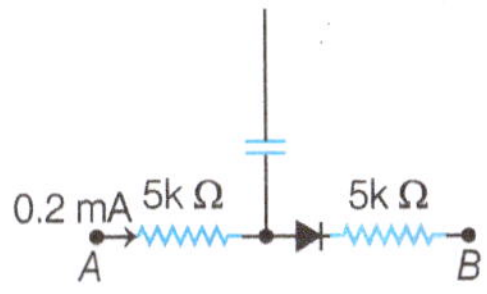

(a) 1.3 V (b) 2.3 V (c) 0 (d) 0.5 V

7 In figure given below V_o is the potential barrier across a p-n junction. When no battery is connected across the junction, then

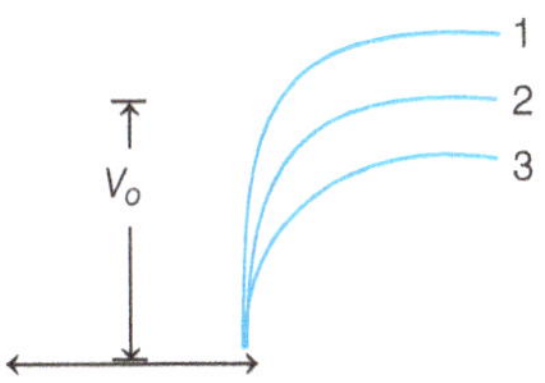

(a) 1 and 3 both correspond to forward bias of junction
(b) 3 corresponds to forward bias of junction and 1 corresponds to reverse bias of junction
(c) 1 corresponds to forward bias and 3 corresponds to reverse bias of junction
(d) 3 and 1 both correspond to reverse bias of junction

Past Exams Questions

NEET

1 A logic circuit provides the output Y as per the following truth table. **Old NCERT Pg. 502, NEET 2024**

A	B	Y
0	0	1
0	1	0
1	0	1
1	1	0

The expression for the output Y is
(a) $A.B+\overline{A}$ (b) $A.\overline{B}+\overline{A}$ (c) $\overline{B}$ (d) B

2 The output Y of the given logic gate is similar to the output of an/a **Old NCERT Pg. 502, NEET 2024**

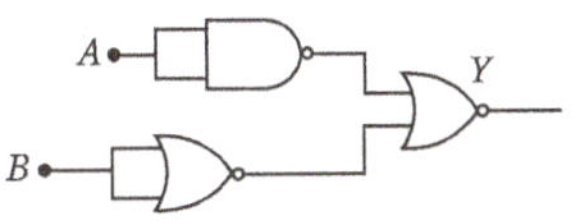

(a) NAND gate (b) NOR gate
(c) OR gate (d) AND gate

3 A full wave rectifier circuit consists two *p-n* junction diodes, a centre-tapped transformer, capacitor and a load resistance. Which of these components remove the AC ripple from the rectified output?
NCERT Pg. 339, NEET 2023

(a) *p-n* junction diodes (b) Capacitor
(c) Load resistance (d) A centre-tapped transformer

4

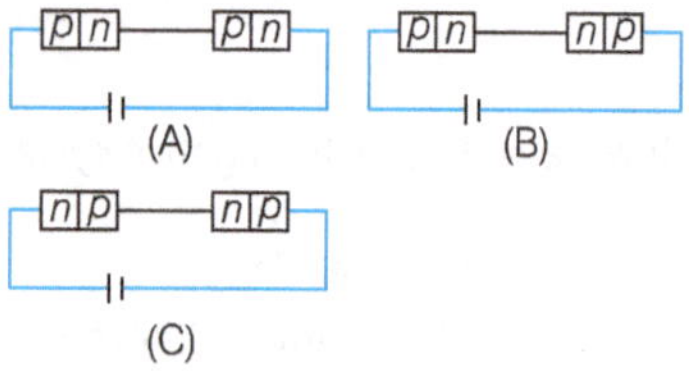

In the given circuits (*A*), (*B*) and (*C*) the potential drop across the two *p-n* junctions are equal in
NCERT Pg. 333, NEET 2022

(a) Circuit (*B*) only (b) Circuit (*C*) only
(c) Both circuits (*A*) and (*C*) (d) Circuit (*A*) only

5 The electron concentration in an *n*-type semiconductor is the same as hole concentration in a *p*-type semiconductor. An external field (electric) is applied across each of them. Compare the currents in them.
NCERT Pg. 331, NEET 2021

(a) Current in *n*-type = Current in *p*-type
(b) Current in *p*-type > Current in *n*-type
(c) Current in *n*-type> Current in *p*-type
(d) No current will flow in *p*-type, current will only flow in *n*-type

6 In a *p-n* junction diode, change in temperature due to heating
NCERT Pg. 333, NEET 2018

(a) does not affect resistance of *p-n* junction
(b) affects only forward resistance
(c) affects only reverse resistance
(d) affects the overall *V-I* characteristics of *p-n* junction

7 Which one of the following represents forward bias diode?
NCERT Pg. 335, NEET 2017

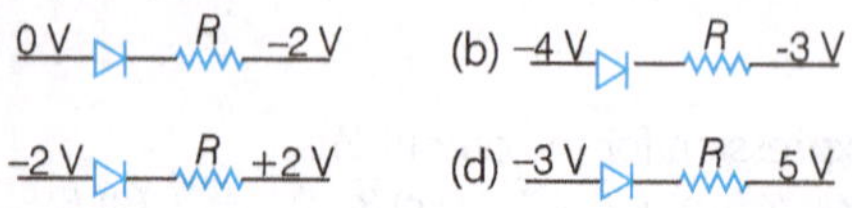

8 Consider the junction diode as ideal. The value of current flowing through *AB* is
NCERT Pg. 334 NEET 2016

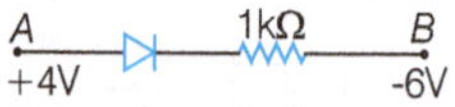

(a) 10^{-2} A (b) 10^{-1} A
(c) 10^{-3} A (d) 0 A

9 The barrier potential of a *p-n* junction depends on
(i) type of semiconductor material
(ii) amount of doping
(iii) temperature
NCERT Pg. 334, AIPMT 2014

Which one of the following is correct?
(a) (i) and (ii) only (b) (ii) only
(c) (ii) and (iii) only (d) (i), (ii) and (iii)

JEE Main

10 The output *Y* of following circuit for given inputs is

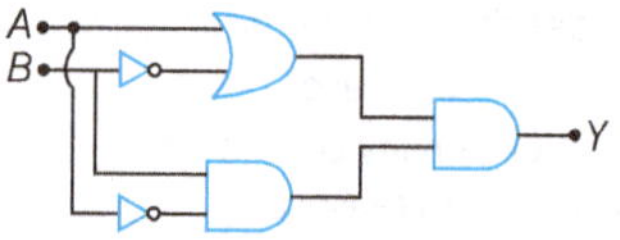

Old NCERT Pg. 502, JEE Main 2024

(a) 0 (b) $A \cdot B(A+B)$ (c) $\bar{A} \cdot B$ (d) $A \cdot B$

11 The *I-V* characteristics of an electronic device shown in the figure. The device is
NCERT Pg. 333, JEE Main 2024

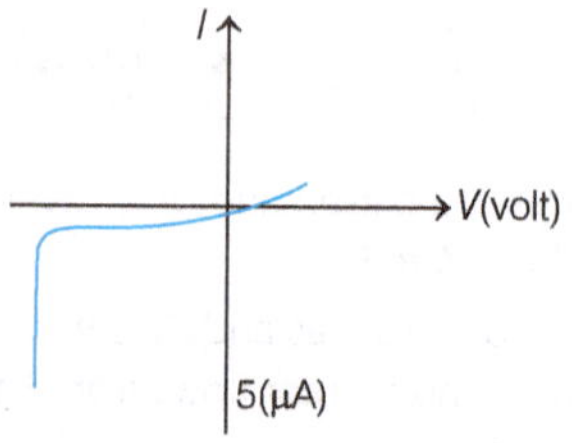

(a) a diode which can be used as a rectifier
(b) a transistor which can be used as an amplifier
(c) a zener diode which can be used as a voltage regulator
(d) a solar cell

12 Identify the logic operation performed by the given circuit.

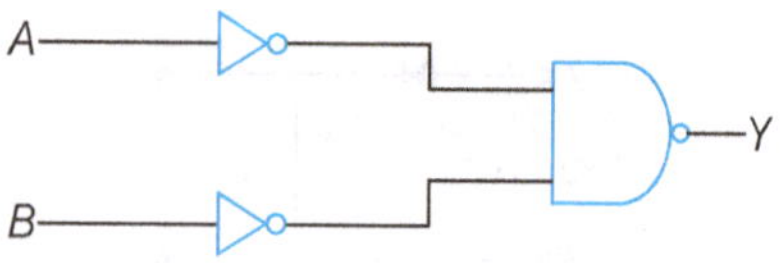

Old NCERT Pg. 502, JEE Main 2024

(a) NAND (b) AND (c) NOR (d) OR

13 In the figure, potential difference between *A* and *B* is
NCERT Pg. 324, JEE Main 2020

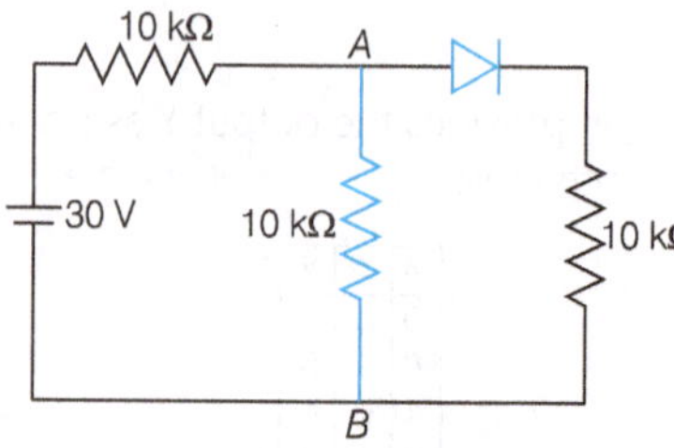

(a) zero (b) 10 V (c) 5 V (d) 15 V

Skill Boosters

1 Two time varying functions are as follows

$$A=\begin{cases}0, & 0\le t<1,\\ 1, & 1\le t\le 2,\\ 0, & 2<t\le 3,\end{cases}\quad B=\begin{cases}0, & 0\le t<\frac{1}{2}\\ 1, & \frac{1}{2}\le t\le\frac{5}{2}\\ 0, & \frac{5}{2}<t\le 3\end{cases}$$

Output of a NAND gate will be

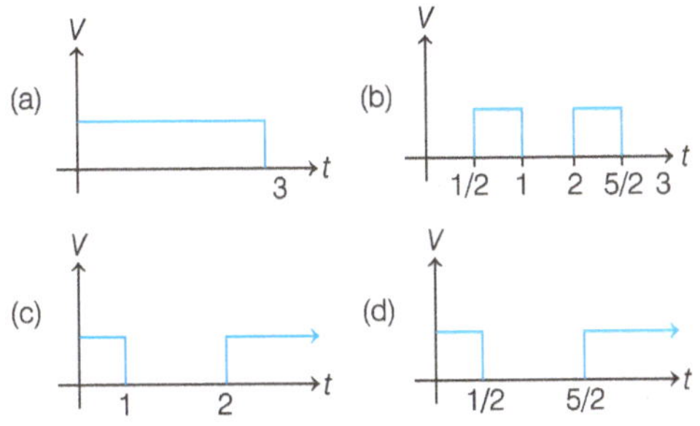

2 Logic gates X and Y have the truth tables shown below.

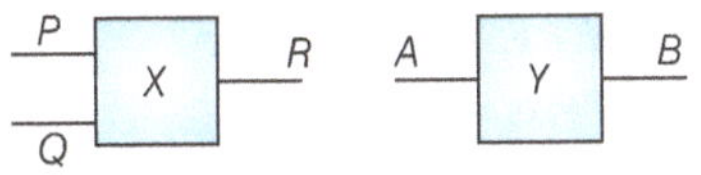

P	Q	R	A	B
0	0	0	0	1
1	0	0	1	0
0	1	0		
1	1	1		

When the output of X of connected to the input of Y, the resulting combination is equivalent to a single

(a) NOT gate (b) OR gate
(c) NAND gate (d) AND gate

3 Consider given input waveforms A and B

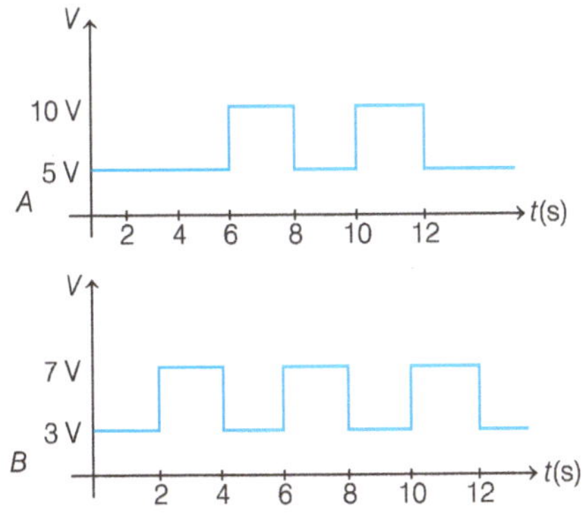

When the inputs are fed to a NAND gate with a negative logic, output is

(a) 000101 (b) 010101
(c) 101000 (d) 100100

4 Let we have a half-wave rectifier using one p-n junction and a full wave rectifier using two p-n junctions and a centre tap transformer. All of p-n junctions used are identical and ideal. Ratio of rectifier efficiencies in half-wave and full wave rectification is

(a) $1:\sqrt{2}$ (b) $\sqrt{2}:1$ (c) $1:2$ (d) $2:1$

5 Minimum potential energy of each ion due to its intraction with other ions in the crystal is where, (r_0 = equilibrium separation of positive and negative ions)

(a) $U_0=\dfrac{-\alpha e^2}{4\pi\varepsilon_0 r_0}$ (b) $U_0=\dfrac{-\alpha e^2}{4\pi\varepsilon_0 r_0 m}$

(c) $U_0=\dfrac{-\alpha e^2}{4\pi\varepsilon_0 r_0 m^2}$ (d) $U_0=\dfrac{-\alpha e^2}{4\pi\varepsilon_0 r_0}\left(1-\dfrac{1}{m}\right)$

6 A typical diode characteristics curve A is drawn at temperature $T_2(K)$.

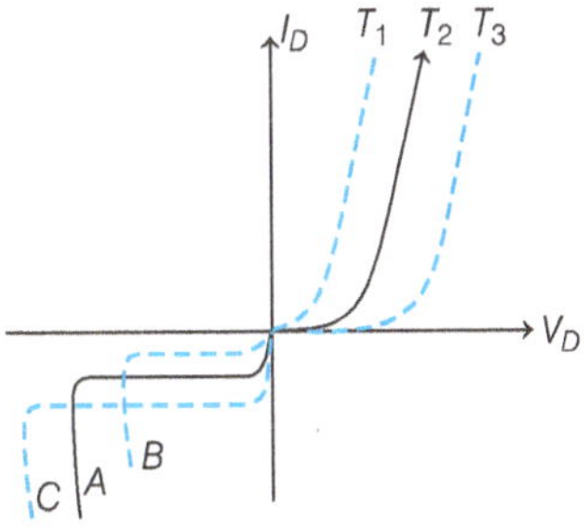

Let curves B and C are drawn at temperatures T_3 and T_1, respectively (under same set up and for same diode). What will be the possible relation between temperatures T_1, T_2 and T_3?

(a) $T_1>T_2>T_3$ (b) $T_1<T_2<T_3$

(c) $T_2=\dfrac{T_1+T_3}{2}$ (d) $T_1=T_2=T_3$

7 2 In figure given below V_0 is the potential barrier across a p-n junction, when no battery is connected across the junction

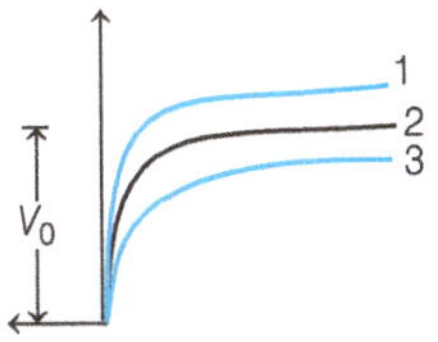

(a) 1 and 3 both correspond to forward bias of junction
(b) 3 corresponds to forward bias of junction and 1 corresponds to reverse bias of junction
(c) 1 corresponds to forward bias and 3 corresponds to reverse bias of junction
(d) 3 and 1 both correspond to reverse bias of junction

8 In the following circuits, *p-n* junction diodes D_1, D_2 and D_3 are ideal for the following potential of A and B, the correct increasing order of resistance between A and B will be

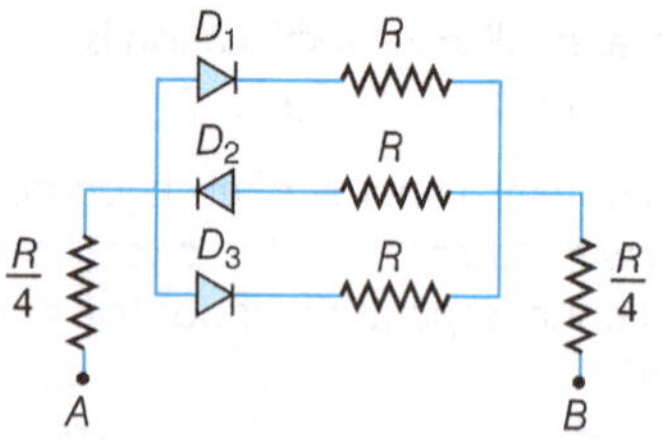

(i) $-10\,V, -5\,V$
(ii) $-5\,V, -10\,V$
(iii) $-4\,V, -12\,V$

(a) (i) < (ii) < (iii)
(b) (iii) < (ii) < (i)
(c) (iii) = (ii) < (i)
(d) (i) = (iii) < (ii)

9 Two logical circuits are equivalent when they produce same outputs for same inputs. Now, you have given following circuit.

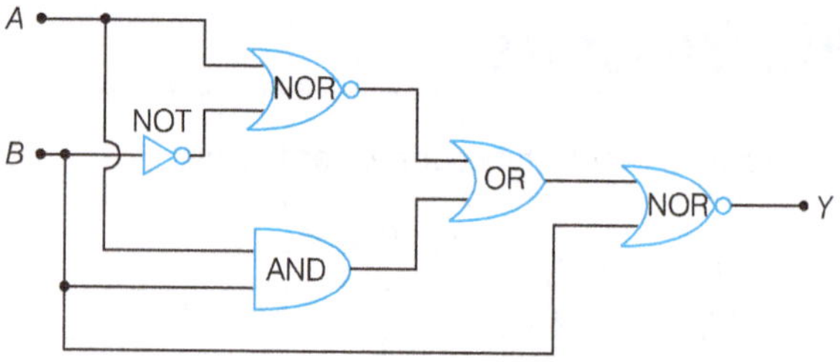

(a) 

(b) 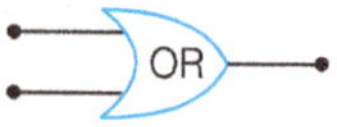

(c) 

(d) 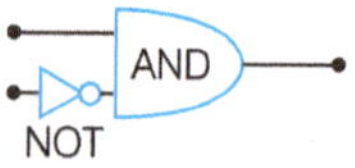

10 For the given logic circuit,

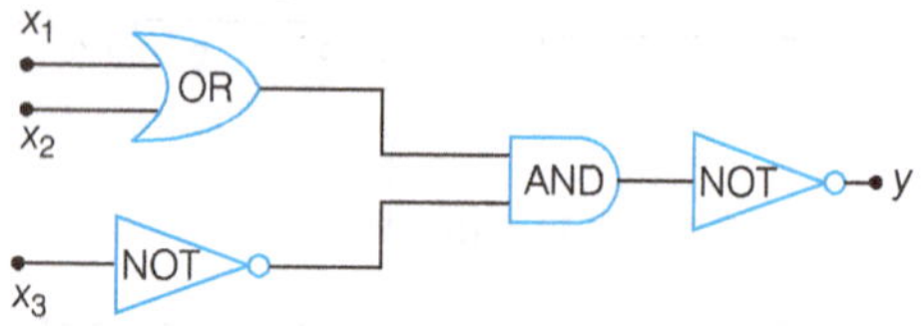

Which of these is correct?
(a) $y = 0$ for $x_1 = x_3 = 0$ and $x_2 = 1$
(b) $y = 0$ for $x_1 = x_2 = x_3 = 0$
(c) $y = 1$ for $x_1 = x_2 = x_3 = 1$
(d) $y = 1$ for $x_1 = x_2 = 1$ and $x_3 = 0$

Correct Codes

Topical Questions

1 (d)	2 (a)	3 (b)	4 (b)	5 (c)	6 (b)	7 (c)	8 (b)	9 (b)	10 (a)
11 (c)	12 (d)	13 (d)	14 (d)	15 (c)	16 (c)	17 (c)	18 (a)	19 (a)	20 (a)
21 (a)	22 (a)	23 (c)	24 (b)	25 (b)	26 (b)	27 (c)	28 (c)	29 (a)	30 (a)
31 (b)	32 (b)	33 (d)	34 (a)	35 (d)	36 (d)	37 (a)	38 (a)	39 (d)	40 (b)
41 (d)	42 (d)	43 (a)	44 (c)	45 (d)	46 (a)	47 (d)	48 (d)	49 (b)	50 (c)
51 (d)	52 (c)	53 (d)	54 (d)	55 (d)	56 (d)	57 (d)	58 (c)	59 (a)	60 (c)
61 (d)	62 (b)	63 (a)	64 (b)						

Assertion and Reason Questions

1 (c)	2 (a)	3 (a)	4 (a)	5 (b)	6 (b)	7 (a)	8 (b)	9 (b)	10 (a)

Statement Based Questions

1 (c)	2 (a)	3 (c)	4 (c)	5 (b)	6 (c)	7 (c)	8 (d)

Matching Type Questions

1 (a)	2 (d)	3 (d)

Numerical Type Questions

1 (7)	2 (5)	3 (2)	4 (4)	5 (50)	6 (49)	7 (250)	8 (654)	9 (1)	10 (1)

NCERT Exemplar Questions

1 (c)	2 (c)	3 (b)	4 (d)	5 (b)	6 (b)	7 (b)

Past Exams Questions

1 (c)	2 (d)	3 (b)	4 (c)	5 (c)	6 (d)	7 (a)	8 (a)	9 (d)	10 (a)
11 (c)	12 (d)	13 (b)							

Skill Boosters

1 (c)	2 (c)	3 (a)	4 (c)	5 (d)	6 (a)	7 (b)	8 (c)	9 (a)	10 (a)

Step by Step

Decoding the Questions

Concept Builder

1 Aluminium	2 True (T)
3 True (T)	4 diffusion
5 4	6 True (T)
7 False (F)	8 infinity
9 True (T)	10 False (F)
11 band gap	12 True (T)
13 hole	14 lower
15 True (T)	16 Drift
17 decreases	18 low
19 logic gate	20 True (T)

Topical Questions

1 (*d*) In a vacuum tube like vacuum diode, the electrons are supplied by a heated cathode and the controlled flow of these electrons in vacuum is obtained by varying the voltage between its different electrodes. Vacuum is required in the interelectrode space; otherwise the moving electrons may lose their energy on collision with the air molecules in their path.

4 (*b*) The statement given in option (b) is incorrect and it can be corrected as, Cathode ray tubes used in television and computer monitors work on the principle of vacuum tubes are being replaced by liquid crystal display (LCD) monitors with supporting solid state electronics.
Rest statements are correct.

5 (*c*) Electrons in the valence band may gain external energy to cross the gap between the conduction band and the valence band. Thus, these electrons will move into the conduction band. At the same time, they will create vacant energy levels in the valence band where other valence electrons can move.

Thus, the process creates the possibility of conduction due to electrons in conduction band as well as due to vacancies in the valence band.

7 (*c*) If the energy of a photon of sodium light equals the band gap of semiconductor, so $E = E_g = \frac{hc}{\lambda}$

Wavelength of sodium light,

$$\lambda = 580 \text{ nm} = 580 \times 10^{-9} \text{ m}$$

$$\Rightarrow E_g = \frac{6.6 \times 10^{-34} \times 3 \times 10^8}{580 \times 10^{-9}} \text{ J}$$

$$= \frac{6.6 \times 10^{-34} \times 3 \times 10^8}{580 \times 10^{-9} \times 1.6 \times 10^{-19}} \text{ eV}$$

$$= 2.1 \text{ eV}$$

13 (*d*) The statement given in option (d) is incorrect and it can be corrected as,
For doping a semiconductor, dopant has to be such that it does not distort the original pure semiconductor lattice. It occupies only a very few of the original semiconductor atoms sites in the crystal. A necessary condition to attain is that the sizes of the dopant and the semiconductor atoms should be nearly the same.
Rest statements are correct.

14 (*d*) Dopant concentration in extrinsic semiconductor is usually 1 to 10 ppm (parts per million).
So, the ratio of impurity atoms to the pure semiconductor atom is

$$\frac{1}{10^7} \approx 10^{-7}$$

15 (*c*) In an extrinsic semiconductor, due to doping, energy states due to donor impurity E_d and acceptor impurity E_a also exist which facilitates the conduction at room temperature. However, the energy gap between the conduction and valence bands remain the same (about 0.72 eV for Ge and 1.1 eV for Si).

17 (*c*) The number of electrons made available for conduction by dopant atoms depends strongly upon the doping level and is independent of any increase in ambient temperature. However, number of free electrons generated in semiconductor atom increases weakly with temperature.

20 (*a*) For extrinsic semiconductor,

$$n_i^2 = n_e n_h$$

Here, number of intrinsic electron hole pairs,

$$n_i = 10^{19} \text{ per m}^3$$

Number acceptor atom of Al

$\approx$ Number of holes,

$$n_h = 10^{21} \text{ per m}^3$$

$$\Rightarrow (10^{19})^2 = n_e (10)^{21}$$

$$\Rightarrow n_e = \frac{10^{38}}{10^{21}} = 10^{17} \text{ per m}^3$$

21 (*a*) Thermally generated electrons ($n_i \sim 10^{16}$ m^{-3}) are negligibly small as compared to those produced by doping.
Therefore, $n_e \approx N_D$
Given, total number of atoms

$$= 5 \times 10^{28} \text{m}^{-3}$$

$$n_i = 1.5 \times 10^{16} \text{ m}^{-3}$$

For every 10^6 atoms, only one atom is doped and 1 As contribute only $1e^-$

$$n_e = 5 \times 10^{28}/10^6$$

$$= 5 \times 10^{22}$$

Since, $n_e n_h = n_i^2$
The number of holes

$$n_h = \frac{n_i^2}{n_e} = \frac{(1.5 \times 10^{16})^2}{5 \times 10^{22}}$$

$$= \frac{2.25 \times 10^{32}}{5 \times 10^{22}}$$
$$= 4.5 \times 10^{9}\ m^{-3}$$

22 (a) Given, $N = 5 \times 10^{28}$ atoms/m^3,

Number of acceptor atom of indium,

$$N_A = 5 \times 10^{20} \text{ per } m^3$$
$$= 0.05 \times 10^{22} \text{ atoms}/m^3$$

Number of donor atoms of arsenic,

$$N_D = 5 \times 10^{22} \text{ atoms}/m^3$$
$$n_i = 1.5 \times 10^{16}\ m^{-3}$$

$$\Rightarrow N_D - N_A = n_e - n_h$$

and $n_e n_h = n_i^2$

$$\therefore\ N_D - N_A = n_e - \frac{n_i^2}{n_e}$$

$$\Rightarrow n_e^2 - (N_D - N_A)\, n_e - n_i^2 = 0$$

$$\Rightarrow n_e = \frac{(N_D - N_A) \pm \sqrt{(N_D - N_A)^2 + 4n_i^2}}{2}$$

On substituting values, the given values in the above equation, we get, $n_e = 4.95 \times 10^{22}/m^3$

$$\therefore\ n_h = \frac{n_i^2}{n_e} = \frac{(1.5 \times 10^{16})^2}{4.95 \times 10^{22}}$$
$$= 4.54 \times 10^{9} m^{-3}$$

$\therefore$ Number of electrons n_e and holes n_h are $4.95 \times 10^{22}/m^3$ and $4.54 \times 10^{9}\ m^{-3}$, respectively.

Note Observe that doping level $\frac{10^{22}}{10^{28}} = 10^{-6}$ ppm nearly.

23 (c) In a p-n junction, the loss of electrons from the n-region and the gain of electrons by the p-region causes a difference of potential across the junction of the two regions.

The polarity of this potential is such as to oppose further flow of carriers, so that a condition of equilibrium exists. Since, the n-side has lost electrons and p-side has acquired electrons. So, the potential of n-side is thus positive to that p-side.

24 (b) In a p-n junction, when no external voltage is applied, there is an inherent electric field that forms across the junction. This electric field points from the n-type region to the p-type region creating a barrier for the flow of charge carriers and resulting in the depletion region.

27 (c) In an unbiased p-n junction, the diffusion of charge carriers across the junction takes place from higher concentration to lower concentration.

30 (a) Diodes D_1 and D_3 are forward biased and D_2 is reverse biased, so the circuit can be redrawn as follows.

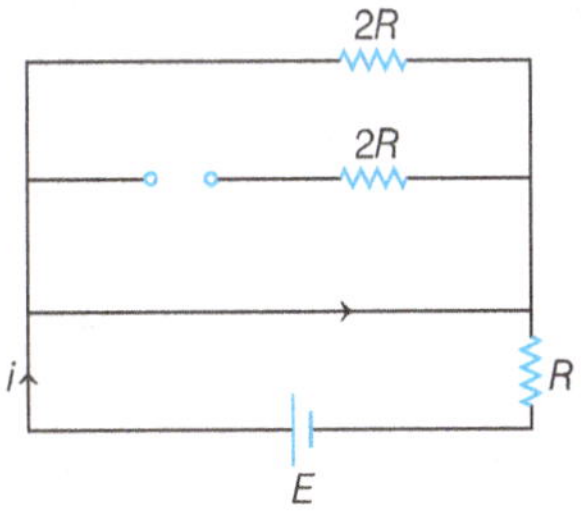

As i follows the minimum resistive path

$$\Rightarrow \quad i = \frac{E}{R}$$

31 (b) Only D_1 and D_4 are forward biased, D_2 and D_3 are reverse biased. In the conductive path of D_1 and D_4

$$i = \frac{E}{R_{D_1} + R_{50} + R_{D_4}}$$
$$= \frac{5}{0 + 50 + 0} = 0.1 \text{ A}$$

32 (b) When p-n junction is forward biased, the direction of the applied voltage is opposite to the built in potential V_0 (i.e., barrier potential). As a result, the depletion layer width decreases and the barrier height is reduced.

$\therefore$ The effective barrier height under forward bias is $V_0 - V$.

33 (d) In the minority injection process, in the case of forward biasing, due to the applied voltage, electrons from n-side cross the depletion region and reach p-side (where they are minority). Similarly, holes from p-side cross the junction and reach the n-side (where they are minority carriers).

34 (a) In a reverse biased p-n junction diode, current is not very much dependent on the applied voltage, even a small voltage is sufficient to sweep the minority charge carriers from one side of the junction to the other side of the junction.

$\therefore$ The current is not limited by the magnitude of the applied voltage but is limited due to the concentration of the minority charge carrier on either side of the junction.

35 (d) In reverse biased p-n junction diode, the minority charge carriers will be accelerated due to reverse biasing which on colliding with atoms cause ionisation that results in secondary electrons. This increases the number of charge carriers.

Thus, when doping concentration is large, there will be large number of ions in the depletion region, which will give rise to a strong electric field.

37 (a) The current under reverse bias is essentially voltage independent upto a critical reverse bias voltage known as breakdown voltage (V_{br}). When $V = V_{br}$, the diode reverse current increases sharply from n to p-side.

Even a slight increase in the bias voltage causes large change in the current. If the reverse current is not limited by an external circuit, the p-n junction will get destroyed due to overheating.

40 (*b*) Dynamic resistance,

$$r_d = \frac{\Delta V}{\Delta I}$$

Here, $\Delta V = 0.70\text{ V} - 0.65\text{ V} = 0.05\text{ V}$

$$\Delta I = 5\text{ mA} = 5 \times 10^{-3}\text{ A}$$

$$\therefore \quad r_d = \frac{0.05}{5 \times 10^{-3}} = 10\,\Omega$$

41 (*d*) From the graph $I = 20$ mA, V is 0.8 V and at $I = 10$ mA, $V = 0.7$ V

$$r_{FB} = \frac{\Delta V}{\Delta I} = \frac{0.8 - 0.7}{20 - 10}$$

$$= \frac{0.1\text{ V}}{10\text{ mA}} = \frac{0.1\text{ V}}{10 \times 10^{-3}\text{ A}}$$

$$= 10\,\Omega$$

Also, at $V = -10$ V, $I = -1\,\mu$A

$$r_{RB} = \frac{10\text{ V}}{1\,\mu\text{A}} = \frac{10\text{ V}}{1 \times 10^{-6}\text{ A}}$$

$$= 1 \times 10^{7}\,\Omega$$

$$\therefore \quad \text{Ratio} = \frac{r_{FB}}{r_{RB}} = \frac{10}{10^7} = 10^{-6}$$

42 (*d*) As both diodes are in reverse bias, so given circuit is equivalent to the circuit as shown in the figure.

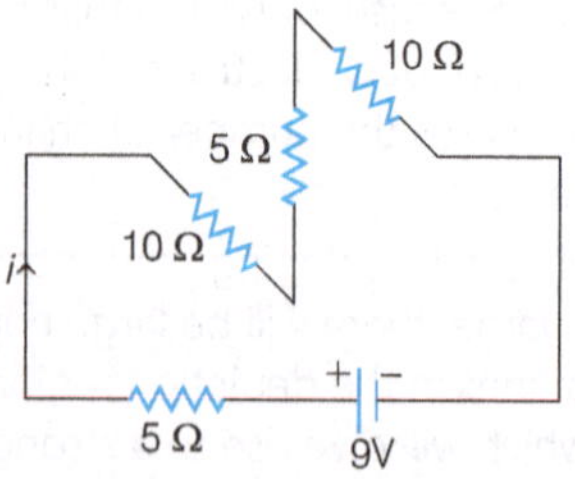

Equivalent resistance of circuit,

$$R = 5 + 10 + 5 + 10 = 30\Omega$$

$$\therefore \text{ Circuit current, } I = \frac{V}{R} = \frac{9}{30} = 0.3\text{ A}$$

43 (*a*) Current in circuit,

$$I = \frac{P}{V_d} = \frac{100 \times 10^{-3}}{0.5}$$

$$= 200 \times 10^{-3}\text{ A} = 200\text{ mA}$$

Voltage across resistance R,

$$V_R = 1.5 - 0.5 = 1.0\text{ V}$$

Thus, resistance, $R = \frac{V_R}{I}$

$$= \frac{1.0}{200 \times 10^{-3}} = 5\,\Omega$$

44 (*c*) $r = \frac{\Delta V}{\Delta I}$

$$= \frac{(0.7 - 0.6)\text{V}}{(15 - 5)\text{ mA}} = \frac{0.1}{10^{-2}} = 10\Omega$$

45 (*d*) *p-n* junction diode primarily allows the flow of current only in one direction, i.e. only in forward bias condition.

Also, the forward bias resistance is low as compared to reverse bias resistance.

So, if an alternating voltage is applied across a diode, the current flows only in that part of the cycle when diode is forward biased. This property is thus used to rectify alternating voltages.

46 (*a*) As we know, the reverse saturation current of a diode is negligible and can be considered equal to zero for practical purposes. Thus, the reverse breakdown voltage of the diode in a rectifier circuit must be sufficiently greater than the peak AC voltage at the secondary of the transformer to protect the diode from reverse breakdown.

49 (*b*) For full wave rectifier, output frequency = 2 × input frequency

and for half-wave rectifier,

output frequency = input frequency.

Given, input frequency = 50 Hz

∴ Ratio of output frequency of full wave rectifier to half-wave rectifier

$$= \frac{2 \times 50}{50} = \frac{2}{1}$$

50 (*c*) If a centre tap transformer is used with 2 diodes for full wave rectification, then output voltage of rectifier w.r.t. each diode is (1/2) × secondary voltage of transfomer.

51 (*d*) Capacitor helps to filter out the AC ripple and give a pure DC voltage or bypass AC component to get DC.

This could be as shown in the waveform below.

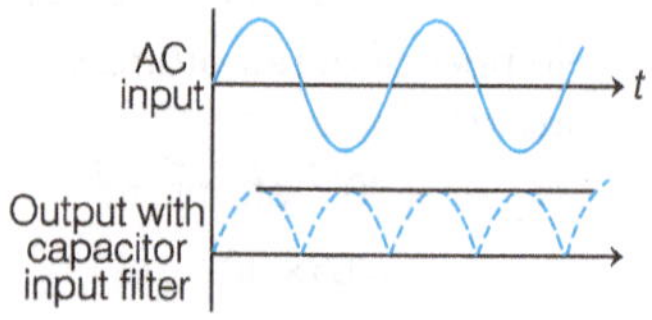

52 (*c*) For a full wave rectifier circuit with a capacitor C as filter, the rate of fall of the voltage across the capacitor depends inversely upon the product of capacitance C and the effective resistance R_L used in the circuit.

53 (*d*) When the reverse bias voltage $V = V_Z$, then the electric field strength is high enough to pull valence electrons from the host atoms on the *p*-side which are accelerated to *n*-side. These electrons account for high current observed at the breakdown. Thus, the emission of electrons from the host atoms due to the high electric field is known as internal field emission or field ionisation.

54 (*d*) For voltage regulation operation, increase/decrease in applied voltage should not affect the voltage drop across zener diode.

For this feature to be satisfied, from the graph given for zener diode the part *de* is best suitable for its operation.

55 (*d*) The magnitude of the photocurrent depends on the intensity of the incident light as the photocurrent is proportional to incident light intensity. So, when intensity is increased, reverse saturation current also increases.

For the given, I-V characteristics of a photodiode for different illumination intensity, the order will be

$$I_4 > I_3 > I_2 > I_1$$

Thus, maximum illumination of intensity is I_4.

56 (*d*) Given, $E_g = 2\text{ eV}$

Wavelength of radiation corresponding to this energy,

$$\lambda = \frac{hc}{E_g} = \frac{1240\text{ eV-nm}}{2\text{eV}} = 620\text{ nm}$$

$$\text{Frequency, } \nu = \frac{c}{\lambda} = \frac{3\times10^8\text{ms}^{-1}}{620\times10^{-9}\text{m}}$$

$$= 5\times10^{14}\text{Hz}$$

57 (*d*) For absorbing minimum frequency of radiation the condition is given below.

Energy of radiation = band gap energy

i.e., $h\nu = 1.0\text{ eV}$

$$\nu = \frac{1.0\times1.6\times10^{-19}}{6.6\times10^{-34}} \approx 2.42\times10^{14}\text{ s}^{-1}$$

Now we need wavelength

$$\lambda = \frac{c}{\nu} = \frac{3.8\times10^8}{2.42\times10^{14}} = 1.6\times10^{-6}\text{m}$$

58 (*c*) As, emitted energy of radiation = Band gap value when an electron moves from conduction band to valance band.

If λ is wavelength of emitted radiation, then

$$E_g = \frac{hc}{\lambda}$$

$$\Rightarrow \quad \lambda = \frac{hc}{E_g} \quad \text{...(i)}$$

Taking $hc = 1240$ eV-nm and $450\text{ nm} \le \lambda \le 750\text{ nm}$ for visible region, we get

$$450 \le \lambda \le 750$$

$$\Rightarrow \quad 450 \le \frac{hc}{E_g} \le 750 \quad \text{[using Eq. (i)]}$$

$$\Rightarrow \quad E_g \le \frac{hc}{450} = \frac{1240\text{ eV-nm}}{450\text{ nm}} \approx 2.8\text{ eV}$$

$$\text{and} \quad E_g \ge \frac{hc}{750} = \frac{1240\text{ eV nm}}{750\text{ nm}} \approx 1.7\text{ eV}$$

So, we have $1.8\text{ eV} \le E_g \le 3\text{ eV}$

59 (*a*) V-I characteristic of a solar cell is shown in the question, where A represents open circuit voltage and B shows short circuit current.

$\therefore$ Statement given in option (a) is correct but rest are incorrect.

60 (*c*) We are showing intermediate outputs on the circuit as given below.

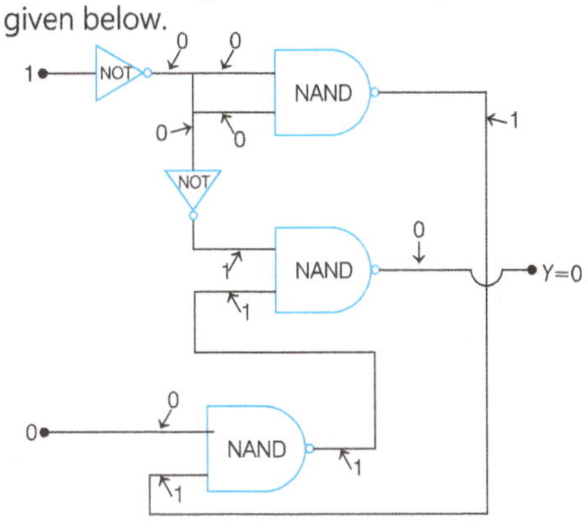

Output of above circuit at given inputs is zero.

To calculate output, we use truth tables of NAND and NOT gates.

NAND gate

A	*B*	*Y*
0	0	1
1	0	1
0	1	1
1	1	0

NOT gate

Y_{in}	Y_{out}
0	1
1	0

61 (*d*)

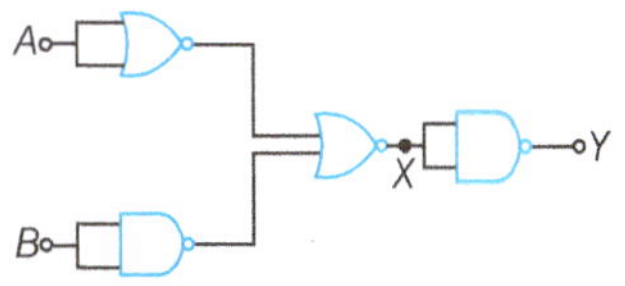

$$Y = \overline{X} = \overline{\overline{\overline{A}+\overline{B}}} = \overline{\overline{\overline{A}}\cdot\overline{\overline{B}}} = \overline{AB}$$

62 (b)

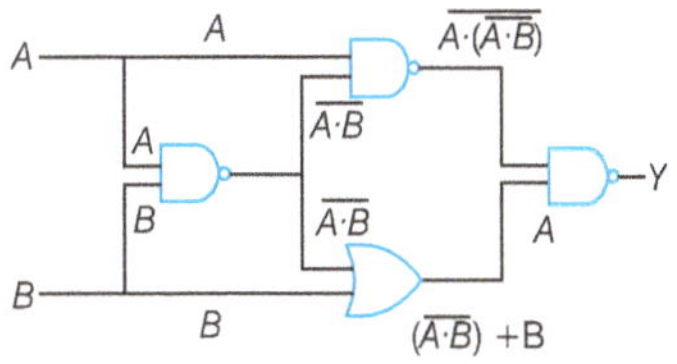

$$Y = \overline{\overline{A\cdot\overline{\overline{(A\cdot B)}}}\cdot(\overline{A\cdot B}+B)} = \overline{\overline{A\cdot\overline{AB}}} + \overline{\overline{AB}+B}$$

$$= A\cdot\overline{AB} + \overline{\overline{AB}}\cdot\overline{B} = A(\overline{A}+\overline{B}) + AB\cdot\overline{B}$$

$$= A\overline{A} + A\overline{B} + AB\cdot\overline{B} = A\overline{B}$$

63 (*a*) The given circuit can be shown as

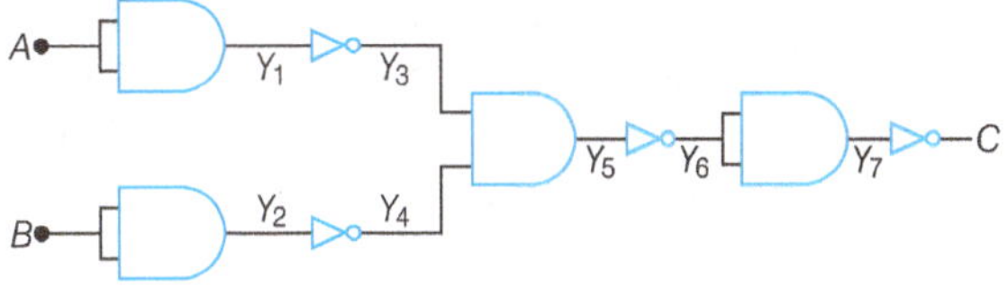

Truth table for the given circuit is

A	B	Y_1	Y_2	Y_3	Y_4	Y_5	Y_6	Y_7	C
0	0	0	0	1	1	1	0	0	1
0	1	0	1	1	0	0	1	1	0
1	0	1	0	0	1	0	1	1	0
1	1	1	0	0	0	0	1	1	0

Output of the given circuit matches with the output of NOR gate. Thus, this is NOR gate.

64 (*b*) The LED in the given circuit in the question will glow when the current flows through it, i.e. when the voltage across it is high.

∴The truth table can be formed from this circuit diagram is

A	B	Y
0	0	1
0	1	1
1	0	1
1	1	0

The output Y is same as that come for NAND gate.

Thus, the correct Boolean operation represented by the given circuit diagram is drawn by NAND gate.

Assertion and Reason Questions

1 (*c*) Free electrons move completely as conduction electron and give rise to an electron current I_e, under an applied electric field. Under the action of an electric field holes move towards negative potential giving the hole current I_h.

The total current I is thus the sum of the electron current I_e and hole current I_h,

$$I = I_e + I_h$$

2 (*a*) As temperature increases, more electron-hole pairs are generated, leading to an increase in the number of charge carriers. This causes the conductivity of semiconductor to increase.

The number of conduction electrons and holes increases as the temperature of an intrinsic semiconductor increases.

3 (*a*) In intrinsic semiconductors, electrons in the valence band needs to gain sufficient energy to surpass the band gap and move to the conduction band. This energy acquisition through thermal excitation decreases exponentially with an increasing band gap.

Thus, the probability of electrons transitioning from valence band to conduction band decreases.

4 (*a*) In n-type semiconductor, the rate of recombination of holes increases due to increase in the number of electrons, this results is the reduction of number of holes.

5 (*b*) During the drift, charge carriers move instantly, this movement is due to the applied electric field across the junction. This drifting of charge carriers reduces the concentration gradient across the junction plane.

6 (*b*) Initially, in a p-n junction diffusion current is large and drift current is small.

As the diffusion process continues through the space, charge regions on the either side of the junction extend. Thus, this increases the electric field strength and hence the drift current.

This process continues until the diffusion current equals the drift current. Thus, a p-n junction is formed.

∴ In a p-n junction under equilibrium, there is no net current as drift current is opposite to the diffusion current.

7 (*a*) As resistance of depletion region is large, potential drop occurs mainly in depletion region.

So, the applied voltage mostly drop across the depletion region and the voltage drop across the p-side and n-side of the junction is negligible.

8 (*b*) The p-side of p-n junction is at higher potential of +9 V and n-side is at lower potential of +3 V, so p-n junction is forward biased.

For ideal $p-n$ junction diode, resistance is zero in forward bias.

$$I = \frac{V}{R} = \frac{9-3}{300\,\Omega}$$

$$I = \frac{6}{3\times 10^2}\text{ A}$$

$$I = 2\times 10^{-2}\text{A}$$

$$I = 20\text{ mA}$$

9 (*b*) The drift of carrier gives rise to drift current, which is of the order of few μA. This is quite low because it is due to motion of carriers from their minority side to their majority side, across the junction. This drift current is also there under forward bias but it is negligible (~ μA) when compared with current due to injected carriers whch is usually in mA. Photodiode are prefereably used in reverse bias. Condition for measuring light intensity.

Statement Based Questions

1 (*c*) The statement II is correct but I is incorrect and it can be corrected as, In metals/conductors, although conduction band is partially filled but as valence band is partially empty, electrons from its lower level can move to higher level making conduction possible.

2 (*a*) The statements I and II are incorrect and these can be corrected as, number of electrons made available for conduction by dopant atoms depends strongly upon the doping level and is independent of any increase in ambient temperature. With proper doping level, the number of conduction electrons can be made

much larger than the number of holes.

In intrinsic semiconductor, conductivity occurs due to excitation of electrons when they absorb energy and break covalent bonds.

3 (*c*) In a *p*-type semiconductor, the dopant has one valence electron less than pure semiconductor (Si or Ge). Therefore, this atom can form covalent bonds with neighbouring three Si atoms but does not have any electron to offer fourth Si atom.

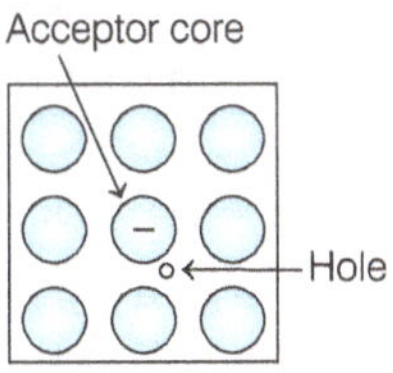

So, the bond between the fourth neighbour and trivalent atom has a vacancy or hole. So, the trivalent foreign atom (the doping impurity) becomes effectively negatively charged when it shares fourth electron with neighbouring Si atom (pure semiconductor). Therefore, the dopant atom of *p*-type material can be treated as core of one negative charge along with its associated hole, as shown.

Also, for *p*-type semiconductor, the energy band diagram E_A is slightly above the top of E_V of the valence band. So, with very small supply of energy an electron from the valence band can jump to the level E_A and ionise the acceptor negatively.

So, statement II is correct but I is incorrect.

4 (*c*) Statement I is incorrect and Statement II is correct. There is no charge on *p*-type semiconductor, because each atom of semiconductor is itself neutral.

5 (*b*) Statement I is correct but Statement II is incorrect.
Silicon is cheaper than germanium, so it is preferred over germanium. But energy gap in germanium is smaller than silicon.

6 (*c*) The statement II is correct but statement I is incorrect and can be corrected as,

When an electron diffuses from $n \to p$, it leaves behind an ionised donor (species which has become ion by donating electron) on *n*-side.

This ionised donor (positive charge) is immobile as it is bonded to the surrounding atoms. As the electrons continue to diffuse from $n \to p$, a layer of positive charge (or positive space-charge region) on *n*-side of the junction is developed. However, when hole diffuses from $p \to n$, it leaves behind an ionised acceptor.

7 (*c*) The statement I is incorrect and it can be corrected as,
When zener diode is used as DC voltage regulator, then it is connected through a series resistance R_s such that the zener diode is reverse biased. If the input voltage increases, the current through R_s and zener diode also increases. This increases the voltage drop across R_s without any change in the voltage across the zener diode. This is because in the breakdown region, zener voltage remains constant even though the current through the zener diode changes. Similarly, if the input voltage decreases, the current through R_s and zener diode also decreases. The voltage drop across R_s decreases without any change in the voltage across the zener diode.

Thus, any increase/decrease in the input voltage results in, increase/ decrease of the voltage drop across R_s without any change in voltage across the zener diode.

Rest statements are correct.

Matching Type Questions

2 (*d*) (A) *p*-type semiconductor is formed when trivalent (IIIrd-group) doping is used.

Intrinsic + Trivalent $\to$ *p*-Type semiconductor

Semiconductor doping (IIIrd group)

(B) *n*-type semiconductor is formed when pentavalent (Vth group) doping is used.

Intrinsic semiconductor + pentavalent doping (Vth group) $\to$ *n*-type semiconductor.

(C) Intrinsic semiconductor is pure semiconductor. (No doping)

(D) Drift velocity $(V_d) =$ Mobility $(\mu) \times$ Electric field **E**.

Numerical Type Questions

1 (7) We know that, $I = n_e A v_d$

$$\frac{I_e}{I_h} = \frac{n_e (v_d)_e}{n_n (v_d)_h}$$

Given, $\frac{n_e}{n_h} = \frac{K}{4}, \frac{I_e}{I_h} = \frac{9}{4}$

and $\frac{(v_d)_e}{(v_d)_h} = \frac{9}{7}$

So, $\frac{9}{4} = \frac{K}{4} \times \frac{9}{7}$

$$K = 7$$

2 (5) The initial concentration (n_i) $= 1.5 \times 10^{16}$ m^{-3} of holes or electron

After doping, hole (n_h) concentration $= 4.5 \times 10^{22}$ m^{-3}

As we know,

$$n_e n_h = (n_i)^2$$

$$n_e = \frac{(n_i)^2}{n_h}$$

$$n_e = \frac{(1.5 \times 10^{16})^2}{4.5 \times 10^{22}} \text{ m}^{-3}$$

$$n_e = 5 \times 10^9 \text{ m}^{-3}$$

The new electron concentration in doped silicon is $5 \times 10^9\ m^{-3}$

3 (2) In the given circuit, diode D_1 is reverse biased while D_2 is forward biased, so the circuit can be redrawn as

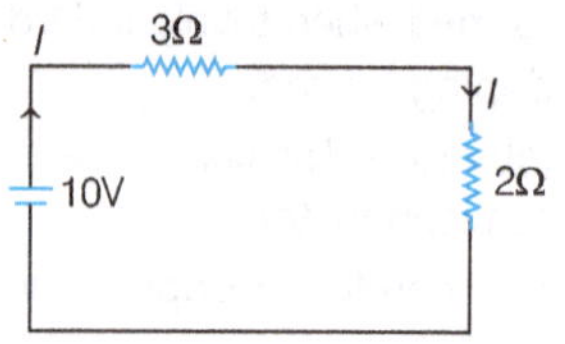

So, total current

$$I = \frac{V_{Total}}{R_{Total}}$$

$$I = \frac{10}{3+2}$$

$$\Rightarrow \quad I = 2A$$

4 (4) The voltage across V_B is given as

$$V_B = V_{Knee} + IR$$

Given $V_B = 4.5\ V, V_{knee} = 0.5\ V$

and $I = 1\ mA$

So, $4.5 = 0.5 + 1 \times 10^{-3} R$

$$\frac{4.5 - 0.5}{10^{-3}} = R$$

$$\Rightarrow \quad R = 4 \times 10^3 \Omega$$

5 (50) Here, $V = (50 \sin \omega t)\ V$

Comparing it with general equation,

$$(V = V_0 \sin \omega t)$$

we get, $V_0 = 50\ V$

Given, (Load Resistance)

$$R_L = 850 \Omega$$

(internal Resistance of rectifier)

$$r_d = 150 \Omega$$

Maximum Output Current,

$$I_0 = \frac{V_0}{r_d + R_L}$$

$$I_0 = \frac{50}{(150 + 850)}$$

$$I_0 = \frac{50}{1000} = 0.05\ A$$

$$I_0 = 50 \times 10^{-3} A$$

6 (49) The above full wave rectifier circuit is shown as

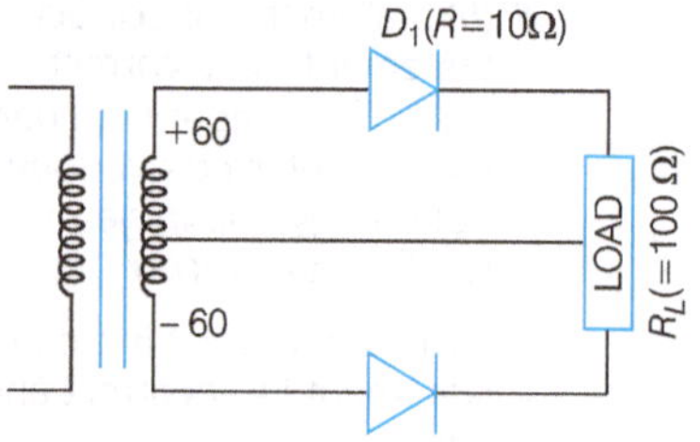

Given $V_{rms} = 60\ V$

$$V_0 = 60\sqrt{2}\ V$$

R_L is the forward diode resistance (10Ω)

R_L is the load resistance (100Ω)

During the first half cycle the circuit is shown below.

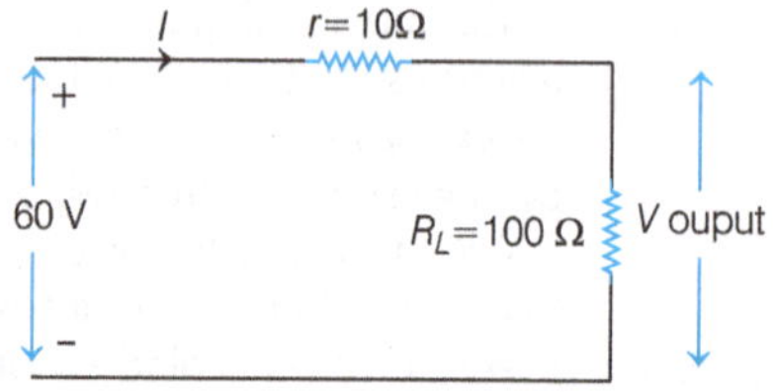

D_1 diode is forward biased and D_2 diode is reverse biased.

The output voltage = Voltage drop across Load (100Ω)

$$= IR_L = \frac{V_0}{R_L + r} \times R_L$$

$$V_{output} = \frac{60\sqrt{2}}{100 + 10} \times 100$$

$$V_{output} = 54.545\sqrt{2}\ V$$

Now, average output voltage

$$V_{avg} = \frac{2V_{output}}{\pi}$$

$$V_{avg} = \frac{2 \times 54.545\sqrt{2}}{\pi}$$

$$V_{avg} = 49.1\ V$$

$$V_{avg} \approx 49\ V$$

7 (250) The circuit diagram for the given situation is shown below

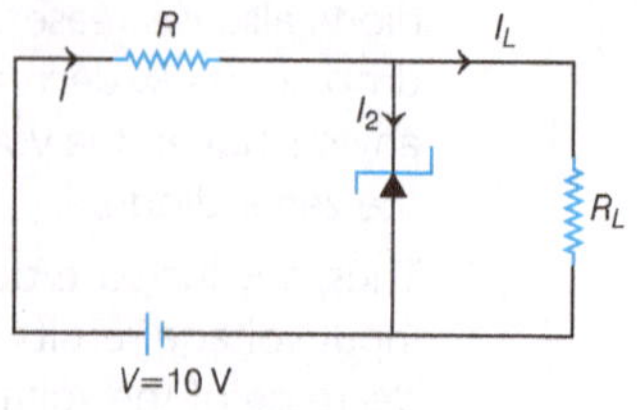

Given, $V_Z = 5\ V$

$$I = \frac{V - V_Z}{R} = \frac{10 - 5}{R}$$

$$I = \frac{5}{R} \quad ...(i)$$

Given, $(I_z)_{max} = 20\ mA$

$$= 20 \times 10^{-3}\ A \quad ...(ii)$$

$$\therefore (I_Z)_{max} = I$$

$$20 \times 10^{-3} = \frac{5}{R}$$

(from (i) and (ii))

$$R = \frac{5}{20 \times 10^{-3}} \Omega$$

$$R = 0.25 \times 10^3 \Omega$$

$$R = 250 \Omega$$

8 (654) Energy gap of LED is 1.9 eV

$$E = 1.9 \times 1.6 \times 10^{-19}\ J$$

$$E = h\nu = \frac{hc}{\lambda}$$

$$h = 6.626 \times 10^{-34}\ Js$$

$$c = 3 \times 10^8\ ms^{-1}$$

So, $\lambda = \frac{hc}{E}$

$$= \frac{6.626 \times 10^{-34} \times 3 \times 10^8}{1.9 \times 1.6 \times 10^{-19}}\ m$$

$$\lambda = 6.538 \times 10^{-7}\ m$$

$$\lambda = 653.8 \times 10^{-9}\ m$$

$$\lambda \approx 654 \times 10^{-9}\ m$$

9 (1) Consider the figure given in the question and solving it using Boolean identities.

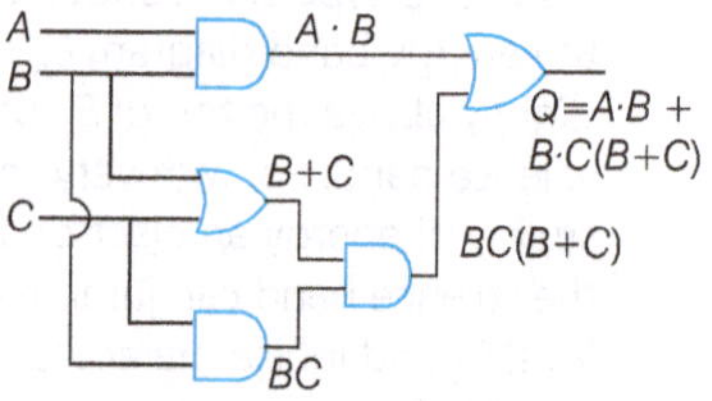

Now, $Q = AB + BC(B + C)$, put the values of A, B and C.

We get $Q = 0 \times 0 + 0 \times 1(0 + 1)$

$$= 0 + 0(1)$$

$$Q = 0$$

So, x is 0

So, the value of $\bar{x}$ is 1.

10 (1) Consider the figure given in the question & solving it using Boolean identities.

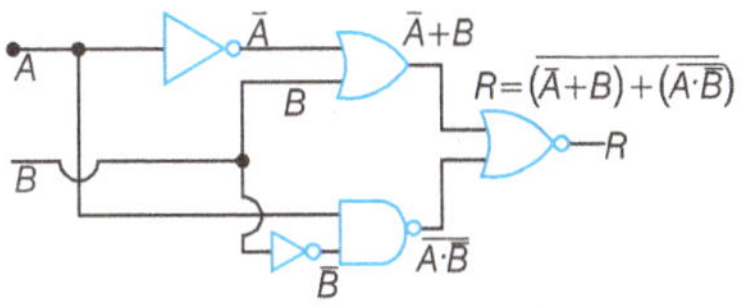

The output $R=\overline{(\bar{A}+B)+(A\cdot\bar{B})}$

$$=\overline{(\bar{A}+B)}\cdot\overline{(A\cdot\bar{B})}$$

$$=(A\cdot\bar{B})\cdot(A\cdot\bar{B})=A\cdot\bar{B}$$

So, R on simplification becomes,

$$R=A\cdot\bar{B}$$

Now put the values of A and B, we get

$$A=1, B=0$$
$$R=1\times\bar{0}$$
$$R=1\times1=1$$
$$R=1$$

NCERT Exemplar Questions

3 (*b*) In the given circuit, *p*-side of *p*-*n* junction, diode D_1 is connected to lower voltage and *n*-side of D_1 to higher voltage. Thus, D_1 is reverse biased. Similarly, the *p*-side of *p*-*n* junction diode D_2 is at higher potential and *n*-side of D_2 is at lower potential. Thus, D_2 is forward biased.

Hence, no current flows through the junction B to A.

4 (*d*) As *p*-*n* junction conducts during positive half cycle only, the diode connected here will work in positive half cycle.

Thus, the potential difference across C = peak voltage of the given AC voltage $V_0=V_{rms}\sqrt{2}=220\sqrt{2}$ V.

5 (*b*) For each positive half cycle of the input voltage, the diode will be forward biased but for each negative half cycle, it will be reverse biased. So, the output of the given circuit will only contains positive halves of voltage like a half-wave rectifier.

6 (*b*) Since, diode is forward biased, so no current goes through side branch after capacitor is charged.

$$\therefore V_{AB}-0.3=I_{AB}\times R_{AB}$$
$$=0.2\times10^{-3}\times10\times10^{3}$$
$$V_{AB}=2+0.3\text{ V}=2.3\text{ V}$$

Option (b) is most appropriate, extra 0.3 V occurs due to voltage drop of diode.

7 (*b*) When *p*-*n* junction is forward biased, it opposes the potential barrier junction resulting in decrease in barrier. When *p*-*n* junction is reverse biased, it supports the potential barrier junction, resulting increase in potential barrier across the junction.

So, the curve 3 in given graph (question) represents the forward bias of junction and curve 1 represents reverse bias of junction.

Past Exams Questions

1 (*c*) Output from the truth table

$$Y=\bar{A}\bar{B}+A\bar{B}$$
$$=\bar{B}(A+\bar{A})$$
$$Y=\bar{B}$$

So, correct option is (c).

2 (*d*) The given combination of gates can be taken as

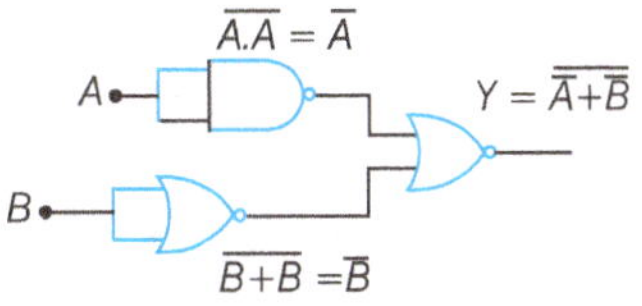

$$Y=\overline{\bar{A}+\bar{B}}=\bar{\bar{A}}\cdot\bar{\bar{B}}=A\cdot B$$

Hence, the output Y of the given logic gate is similar to AND gate.

3 (*b*) When AC is converted into DC using a rectifier circuit, then converted DC is an unstable current that includes ripples.

A capacitor is used to remove these ripples and maintain a constant voltage across load.

4 (*c*) In the circuit diagram (A) and (C), both the *p*-*n* junction diodes are in same biasing conditions.

So, both diodes offers equal resistances.

Since, both diodes are in series, therefore equal potential will drop across the junction.

5 (*c*) Given, the electron concentration in *n*- type semiconductor is equal to the hole's concentration in *p*-type semiconductor.

When electric field is applied across the semiconductor, the electrons and holes will move opposite to each other. Since, the electrons in mobility of *n*-type semiconductor is greater than mobility of holes in *p*-type semiconductor.

$\therefore$ The current in the *n*-type semiconductor is greater than current in the *p*-type semiconductor.

6 (*d*) Due to increase in temperature because of heating, thermal collision between the electron and holes increases.

Thus, net electron-hole pairs increase. This leads to increase in the current in diode and overall resistance of the diode changes.

This in turn changes both the forward biasing and the reverse biasing.

Thus, the overall *I*-*V* characteristics of *p*-*n* junction diode gets affected.

7 (*a*) In the forward biasing of *p*-*n* junction, *p* side of junction diode is connected to higher potential and *n* side of junction diode is connected to lower potential.

8 (*a*) Let us assume that current through the diode is *I*.

From the given condition,

$\because \quad I = \frac{V_A - V_B}{R} = \frac{4-(-6)}{1\,\text{k}\Omega}$

$= \frac{10}{1 \times 10^3} = 10^{-2}\,\text{A}$

9 (*d*) Barrier potential depends on all the three options given. Barrier potential depends on the material used to make *p-n* junction diode (whether it is Si or Ge).

It also depends on amount of doping due to which the number of majority carriers will change.

It also depends on temperature due to which the number of minority carriers will change.

10 (*a*)

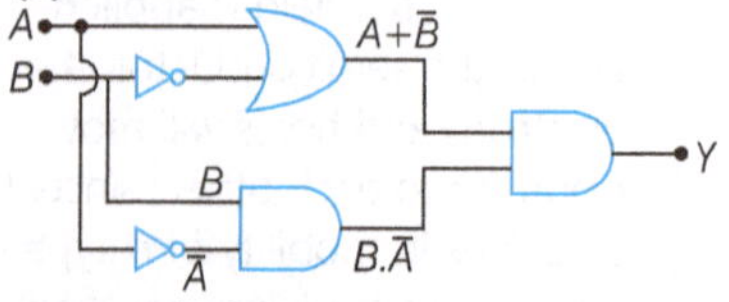

$Y = (A + \overline{B}) \cdot (B \cdot \overline{A})$

$= (AB + \overline{B}B) \cdot \overline{A} = (AB + 0) \cdot \overline{A}$

$= AB\overline{A} = (A\overline{A})B = 0B = 0$

11 (*c*) The device shows a rapid current increase in reverse biasing after a certain point. This is a zener diode operating in reverse biased connection. It can also be used as a voltage regulator as a small voltage difference creates a large change in current after breakdown voltage.

12 (*d*)

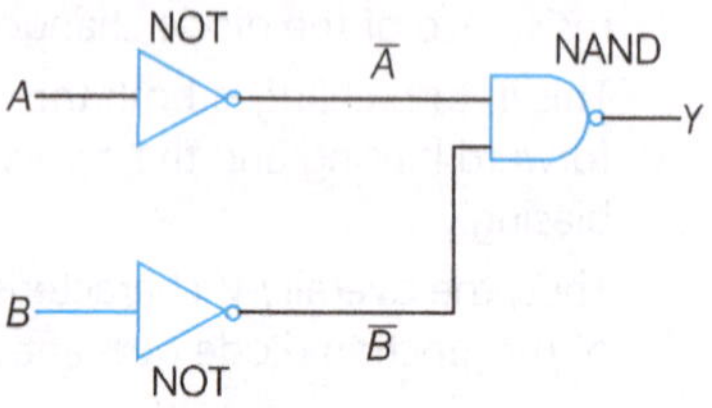

$\therefore Y = \overline{\overline{A} \cdot \overline{B}} = \overline{\overline{A}} + \overline{\overline{B}} = A + B$

= output of OR gate

13 (*b*) In ideal condition, a forward biased *p-n* junction acts like a conductive path of zero resistance.

So, given circuit is equivalent to circuit shown below

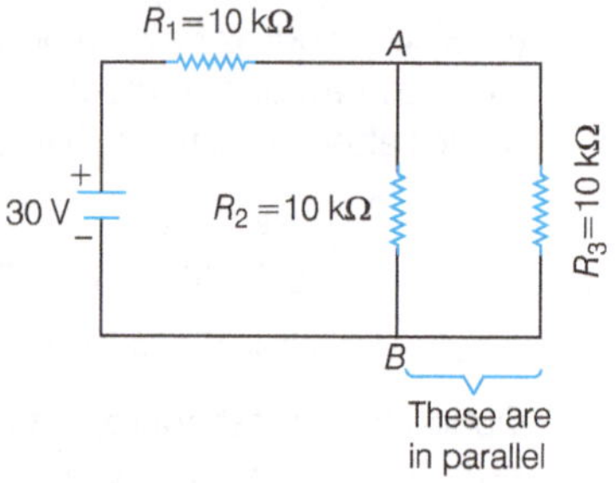

$R_{eq} = \frac{10 \times 10}{10 + 10} + 10 = 15\,\text{k}\Omega$

So, total current in the circuit,

$I = \frac{V}{R_{eq}} = \frac{30}{15\,\text{k}\Omega}$

$= 2 \times 10^{-3}\,\text{A}$

Now, potential drop across R_1, $(10\,\text{k}\Omega)$,

$V_{R_1} = IR_1$

$= 2 \times 10^{-3} \times 10 \times 10^3$

$= 20\,\text{V}$

$V_{AB} = 30 - 20$

$= 10\text{V}$

This can be seen in the figure below.

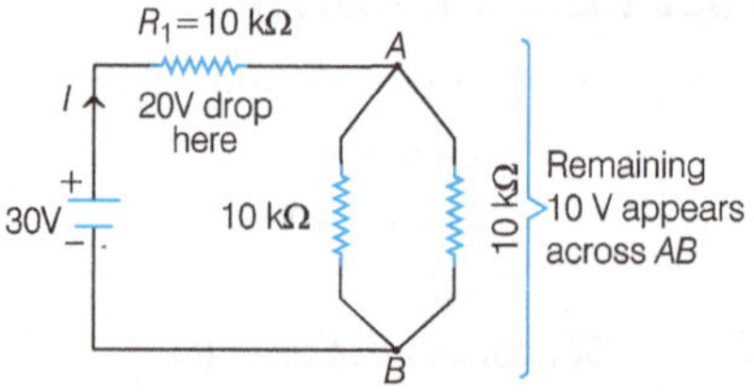

Skill Boosters

1 (*c*) Waveforms of inputs are

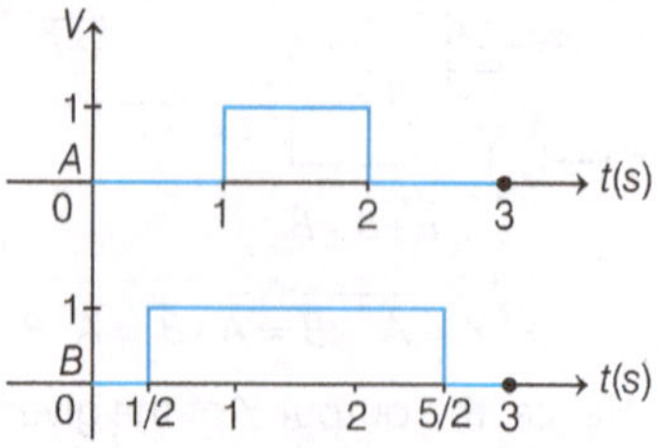

AND gate gives an output when both inputs are at higher voltage level and hence, output is

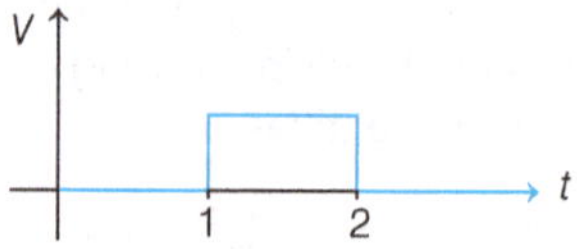

When this is fed to a NOT gate output will be

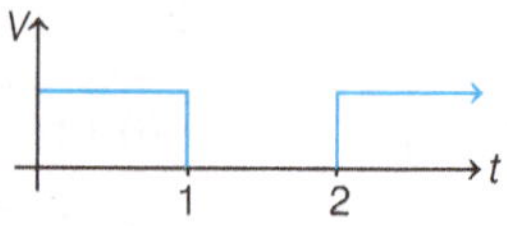

2 (*c*) The truth table of the resulting logic circuit by connecting *X* to *Y* is as follows

P	*Q*	*R*	*R′*
0	0	0	1
1	0	0	1
0	1	0	1
1	1	1	0

Hence, from the truth table, the combination is equivalent to a single NAND gate.

(*X* is an AND gate and *Y* is a NOT gate, thus the combination is NOT-AND gate, i.e., a NAND gate)

3 (*a*) Output of NAND gate is

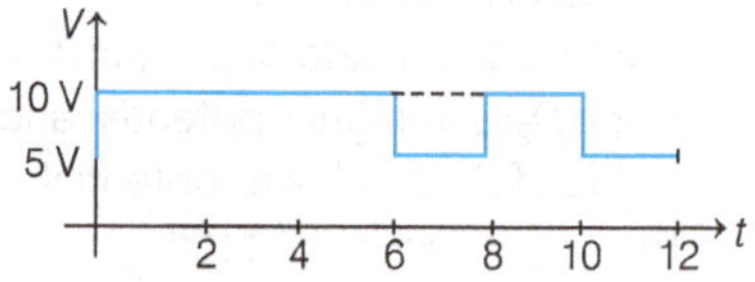

We can write this, output in positive logic as 111010.

But in negative logic it becomes to 000101.

4 (*c*) Rectifier efficiency

$\eta = \frac{P(\text{output})}{P(\text{input})} = \frac{I_{DC}^2 R_L}{I_{rms}^2 R_L}$

As diodes are ideal, we are not considering forward resistance of *p-n* junctions.

Now, for half-wave rectification,

$I_{rms} = \frac{I_0}{2}, \; I_{DC} = \frac{I_0}{\pi}$

$\eta_{\text{half-wave}} = \frac{2^2}{\pi^2} = \frac{4}{\pi^2} = 0.4$

For full wave rectification,

$$I_{rms} = \frac{I_0}{\sqrt{2}}, I_{DC} = \frac{2I_0}{\pi}$$

$$\eta_{\text{half wave}} = \frac{4}{\pi^2} \times 2 = \frac{8}{\pi^2} = 0.8$$

So, efficiency ratio $= \frac{1}{2}$

5 (*d*) As, $U = U_{\text{coloumb}} + U_{\text{repulsive}}$

$$= \frac{-\alpha e^2}{4\pi\varepsilon_0 r} + \frac{B}{r^m} \quad \text{...(i)}$$

At equilibrium separation, $r = r_0$ potetnail energy must be minimum.

So, $\frac{dU}{dr} = 0$

$$\Rightarrow \frac{\alpha e^2}{4\pi\varepsilon_0 r_0^2} - \frac{mB}{r_0^{m+1}} = 0$$

$$\Rightarrow B = \frac{\alpha e^2}{4\pi\varepsilon_0 m} r_0^{m-1}$$

Substituting the value of B and $r = r_0$ in Eq. (i), we get

$$U = U_0 = -\frac{\alpha e^2}{4\pi\varepsilon_0 r_0}\left(1 - \frac{1}{m}\right)$$

6 (*a*) With increase of temperature, more electron-hole pairs are generated and so, forward characteristics are more ideal But in reverse bias region, reverse saturation current also increases with corresponding increase in reverse breakdown voltage.

So, $T_1 > T_2 > T_3$

7 (*b*) When *p-n* junction is forward biased, it opposes the potential barrier junction. When *p-n* junction is reverse biased, it supports the potential barrier junction, resulting increase in potential barrier across the junction.

8 (*c*) For (i) We have,

$V_A = -10$ V

and $V_B = -5$ V

Diodes D_1 and D_3 are reverse biased and D_2 is forward biased.

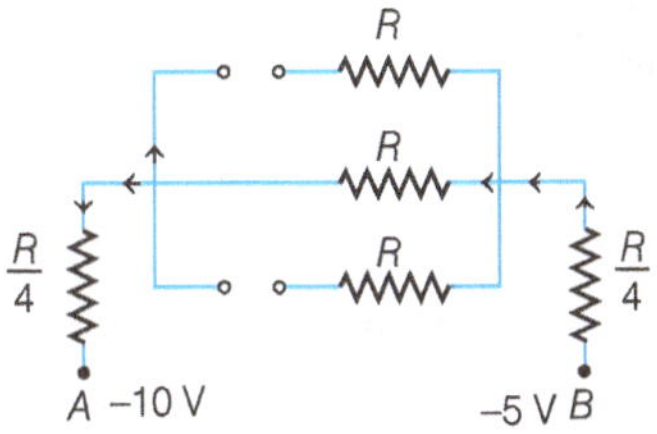

$$\Rightarrow R_{AB} = R + \frac{R}{4} + \frac{R}{4} = \frac{3}{2} R$$

For (ii) When $V_A = -5$ V and $V_B = -10$ V

Diodes D_2 is reverse biased and D_1 and D_3 are forward biased.

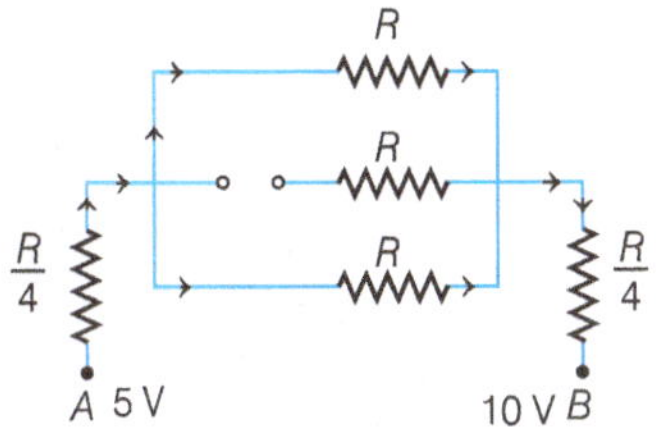

$$\Rightarrow R_{AB} = \frac{R}{4} + \frac{R}{2} + \frac{R}{4} = R$$

For (iii), In this case, equivalent resistance between A and B is also R.

Hence, correct order is (ii) = (iii) < (i)

9 (*a*) Truth table for given logic circuit is

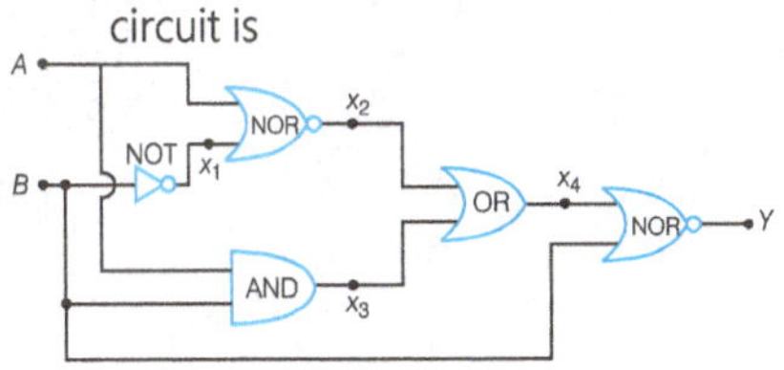

A	B	x_1	x_2	x_3	x_4	Y
0	0	1	0	0	0	0
1	0	1	1	0	1	0
0	1	0	0	0	0	0
1	1	0	0	1	1	1

Clearly above circuit is equvalent to AND gate.

10 (*a*) When $x_1 = x_3 = 0$ and $x_2 = 1$, inputs to AND gate are 1 and 1 so $y = 0$ due to inversion of NOT gate.

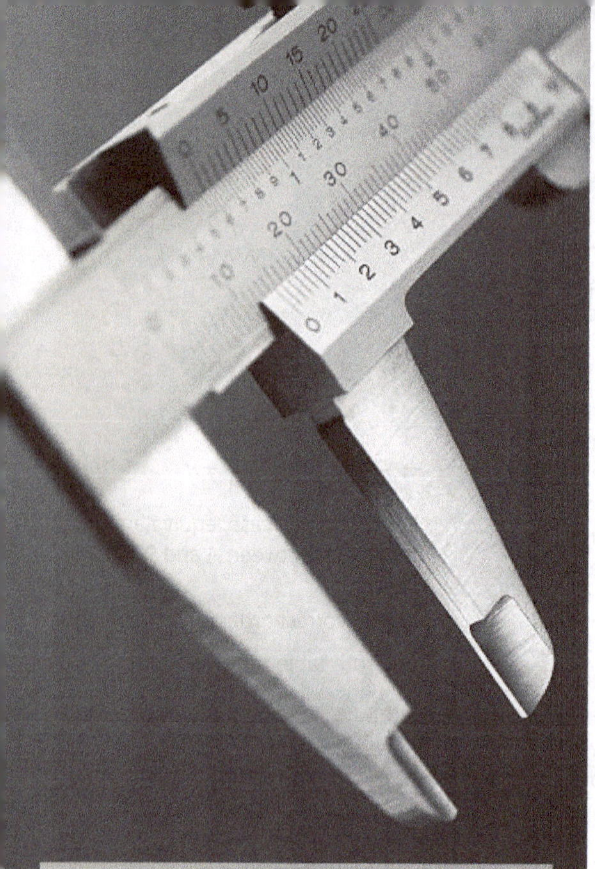

15

Experimental Physics

Topicwise No. of Ques asked in 5 Years (JEE Main)

Topics	No. of Questions				
	2024	2023	2022	2021	2020
Experiment 1	2	–	3	2	–
Experiment 2	–	1	1	–	2
Experiment 3	1	–	–	1	1
Experiment 4	1	–	2	–	–
Experiment 8	–	–	2	–	–
Experiment 10	1	2	1	–	–
Experiment 11	–	1	1	1	–
Experiment 13	–	1	–	–	–
Experiment 15	–	1	–	–	–

Special Type of Ques Asked In 5 Years (JEE Main)

Types	Years				
	2024	2023	2022	2021	2020
A-R	–	–	–	–	–
Statement Based	–	–	–	–	–
Matching	–	–	–	–	–

Last 5 Years Weigtage (JEE Main)

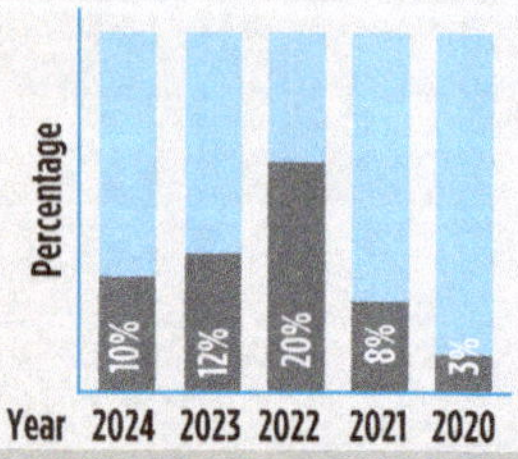

Experiment 1

Vernier callipers – to measure the internal and external diameter and depth of a vessel.

- It is designed to measure accurately upto $\left(\frac{1}{10}\right)$th of a millimeter of linear measurements.
- It comprises of two scales, namely the main scale and vernier scale. The main scale is fixed but the vernier scale (also called auxiliary scale) is movable. The vernier scale slides along the main scale is shown below.

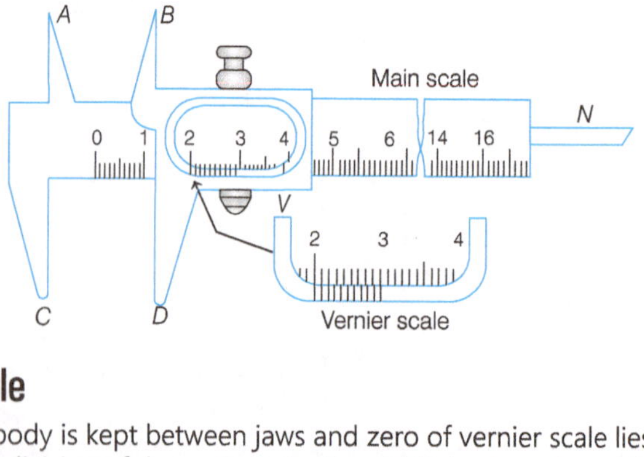

Principle

- If the body is kept between jaws and zero of vernier scale lies ahead of Nth division of the main scale, then MSR (main scale reading) = N.
- If nth division of vernier scale coincides with any division of main scale, then vernier scale reading (VSR) = $n \times$ (LC)

  where, LC = least count of vernier callipers.

  Total reading = MSR + VSR = $N + n \times$ (LC)

  The least count of a vernier calliper is given by

$$LC = \frac{\text{Size of smallest main scale division}}{\text{The total number of divisions on the vernier scale}}$$

$$LC = \left(\frac{1\,\text{mm}}{10}\right) = 0.1\,\text{mm}$$

Also, $LC = 1\,\text{MSD} - 1\,\text{VSD}$

Zero Error

Due to some mechanical errors, or wear and tear of jaws due to prolonged use, the zero mark of the vernier scale does not coincide with zero mark of the main scale. This gives rise to an error called **zero error.** This error can result in incorrect measurement.

There are two types of zero error in a vernier callipers.

(i) **Positive zero error** This occurs when the zero mark on the vernier scale is to the right of the zero mark on the main scale when the jaws of the callipers are closed. This means that the callipers reads a value that is greater than actual.

(ii) **Negative zero error** This occurs when the zero mark on the vernier scale is to the left of the zero mark on the main scale when the jaws of the calliper are closed. This means that the callipers read a value that is smaller than actual value.

It is important to identify and correct these errors when using a vernier callipers to ensure accurate measurements. Zero error can be corrected by subtracting the zero error the observed value.

True value = Observed value − Zero error

Experiment 2

Screw Gauge – to determine thickness/diameter of a thin sheet/wire.

- Screw gauge is a precision instrument used to measure small distances and thickness.
- It consists of a calibrated screw called **spindle** that moves through threaded **sleeve** called the **thimble** when the thimble is rotated.
- The spindle has a flat end (the anvil) and a pointed end (the spindle tip) that can be brought into contact with the object being measured.

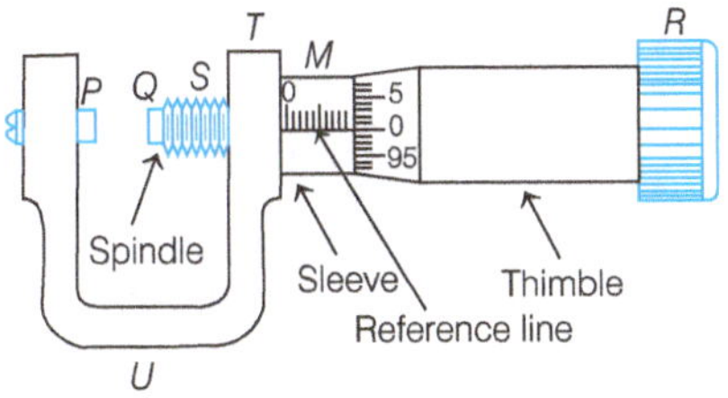

Principle

- When the wire or sheet is kept between plane faces P and Q and edge of the cup lies ahead of Nth division of linear scale.

  Then, linear scale reading (LSR) = N
- If the nth division of circular scale lies over reference line, then,

  Circular scale reading (CSR) = $n \times LC$

  where, LC = least count of screw gauge.

  Least count of screw gauge can be calculated as

$$LC = \frac{\text{Pitch}}{\text{Total number of divisions on circular scale}}$$

Types of errors in screw gauge

- **Zero error** This occurs when the zero mark on the thimbles does not align perfectly with the zero mark on the main scale when the jaws of the screw gauge are closed.

  (i) Positive zero error When the zero mark on the thimble is to the right of the zero mark on the main scale when jaws of the screw gauge are closed. In this case, the screw gauge will read a value that is larger than actual value.

  (ii) Negative zero error When zero mark on the thimble is to the left of the zero mark on the main scale after closing the jaws of the screw gauge. In this case, the screw gauge will read a value which is too small when measuring an object.
- **Parallax Error** When the observer's eye is not directly in line with the measurement being taken, causing the measurement to appear larger or smaller than it actually is.
- **Backlash Error** This occurs when there is small amount of movement in the screw gauge, causing the measurement to be slightly inaccurate. This can be minimised by ensuring that the screw gauge is properly calibrated and maintained.

Experiment 3

Simple Pendulum - Dissipation of energy by plotting a graph between square of amplitude and time.

- A simple pendulum consists of an adjustable thin long string with upper end screwed in a torsion screw fixed to a rigid support and a metal bob is suspended from its lower end.

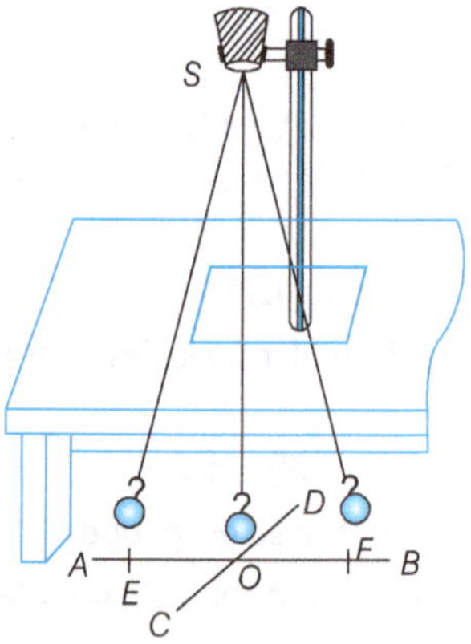

Principle

- The total force due to a simple harmonic oscillation will be the sum of restoring force and drag force, given by
$$F = -kx - bv$$
- For damp oscillator, the mechanical energy is not constant and decreases with time
i.e., $E = E_0 e^{-\lambda t}$
where, $\lambda = \dfrac{b}{m}$

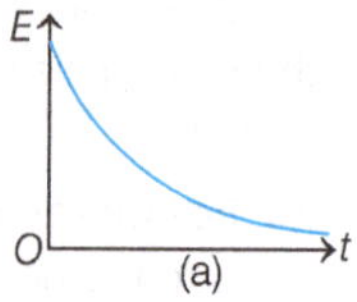

- The plot for E *versus* t is shown in Fig. (a)
- The amplitude A at any given time t is
$$A = A_0 \cdot e^{\frac{-b}{m}t} \quad \text{or} \quad A = A_0 \cdot e^{-\lambda t}$$
- The graph (b) shows the dissipation of energy with time.

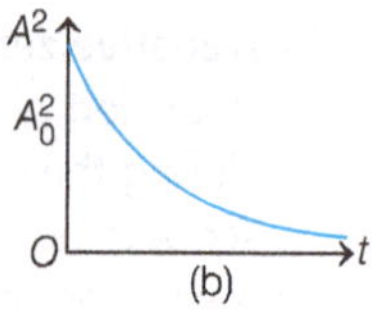

Experiment 4

To measure mass of a meter scale by the principle of moments.

If a body of mass m is suspended at one end A of a meter scale and a body of unknown mass M is suspended at the end B and then position of point O is adjusted, so that the meter scale is in equilibrium.

By the principle of moments,

$$(mg) \times OA = (Mg) \times OB, \quad OA = l_1 \text{ and } OB = l_2$$

$$mg \times l_1 = Mg \times l_2, \quad m = M\left(\frac{l_2}{l_1}\right)$$

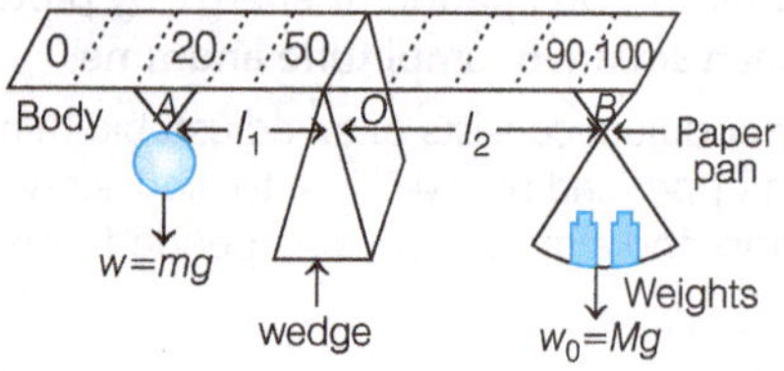

Experiment 5

- **Young's modulus using the Searle's apparatus.**
- Searle's apparatus consists of two long wires, a fixed weight, a $\left(\frac{1}{2}\text{ kg}\right)$ hanger along with $\left(\frac{1}{2}\right)$ kg slotted weights, a meter scale, a plumb line with long thread and a screw gauge.

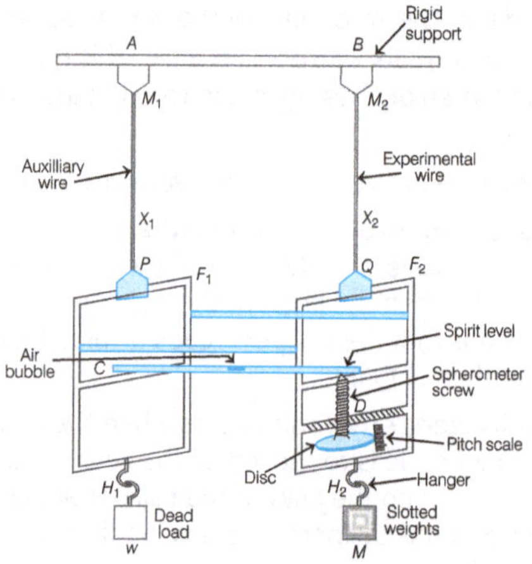

Principle

- According to Hooke's law, if stress developed in a body lies within a certain limit called elastic limit, then strain produced is directly proportional to the stress and the proportionality constant is called Young's modulus.
$$Y = \frac{\text{Stress}}{\text{Strain}} = \frac{F/A}{\frac{\Delta L}{L}} = \frac{mgL}{\pi r^2 \Delta L}$$

Experiment 6

Surface tension of water by capillary rise and effect of detergent

- The capillary rise method is a technique used to measure the surface tension of liquid by observing the height of liquid rises in a narrow tube called capillary tube.

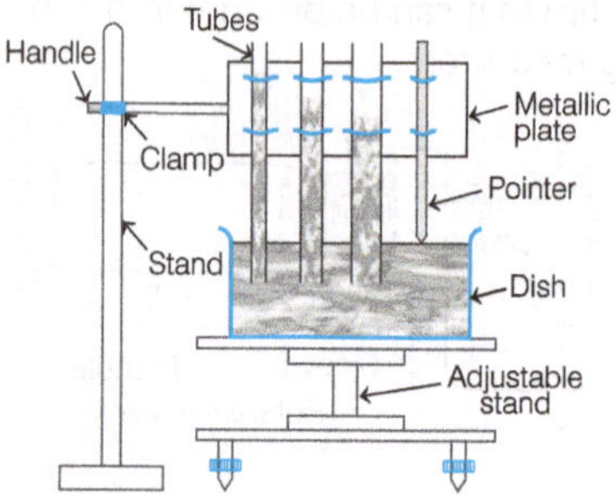

Principle

- When a liquid is placed in a capillary tube, the liquid molecules at the surface of the liquid are attracted to each other by cohesive forces, while the liquid molecules at the interface between the liquid and the tube are attracted to the tube by adhesive forces. As a result, liquid rises in the tube until the adhesive forces are balanced by the cohesive force.
- When a capillary of radius r is immersed in a liquid of density ρ, the height h to which the liquid rises is given by surface tension T.

$$T = \frac{r\left(h + \frac{r}{3}\right)\rho g}{2\cos\theta}$$

For water, $T = \frac{r\left(h + \frac{r}{3}\right)\rho g}{2}$, as θ is small.

- The rise of water in capillary tube decreases with the addition of detergent in pure water. This implies that the detergent reduces the surface tension of water.

Experiment 7

Coefficient of viscosity of a given viscous liquid by measuring terminal velocity of given spherical body.

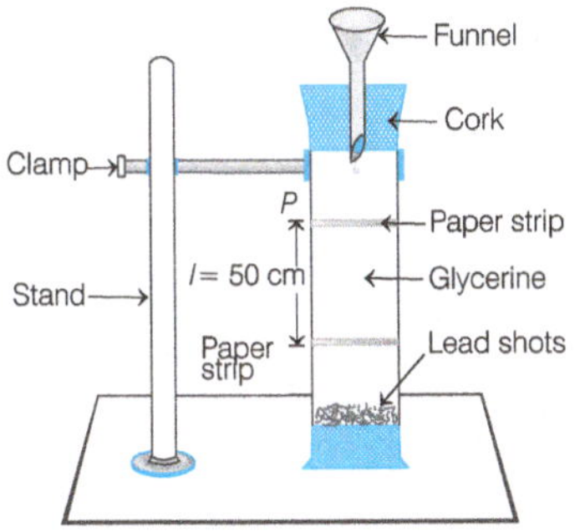

- When a solid falls in a liquid, it experiences a resistive force due to viscosity of the liquid. This is given by

$$F = 6\pi r\eta v$$

where, r = radius of spherical body,

η = coefficient of viscosity of fluid

and v = velocity.

- Due to this resistive force, acceleration of the body decreases and after sometime, it attains a constant velocity called terminal velocity which is given by

$$v_t = \frac{2r^2(\rho - \sigma)g}{9\eta}$$

Thus, $$\eta = \frac{2}{9}\frac{r^2(\rho - \sigma)g}{v_t}$$

where, ρ = density of the material of the sphere, σ = density of fluid and v_t = terminal velocity.

Experiment 8

Speed of sound in air at room temperature using a resonance tube.

- The resonance tube apparatus is an instrument used to measure the speed of sound in air.
- It consists of a glass tube with one end closed and the other end open, a water reservoir and a tuning fork.
- The closed end submerged in the water and the tuning fork is struck and held over the open end of the tube.

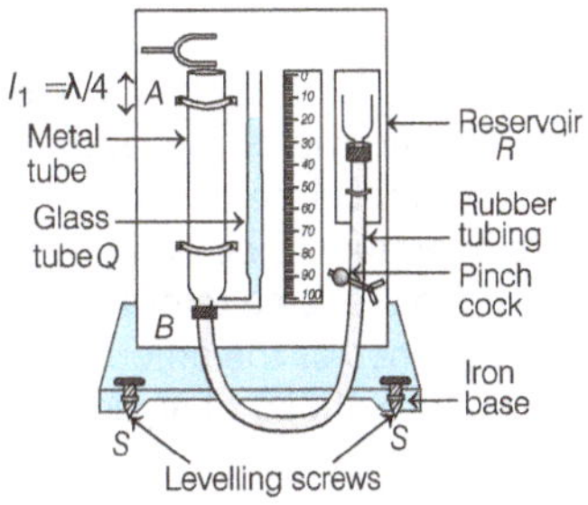

Principle

- Resonance tube apparatus is based on the principle of resonance.
- When tuning fork is struck, it produces a sound wave with a specific frequency. If the length of the air column in the tube is such that the sound wave produced by the tuning fork matches the natural frequency of the air column, resonance occurs, and the wave is amplified.
- This results in a loud sound being heard at the open end of the tube.

Speed of sound in air, $v = 2\nu(l_2 - l_1)$

where, ν = frequency of tuning fork,

l_1 = length of the air column at first resonance

and l_2 = length of the air column in second resonance with tuning fork.

Experiment 9

Specific heat capacity of a solid and liquid by method of mixtures.

- The method of mixture is a technique used to determine the specific heat of a substance which is the amount of heat required to raise the temperature of a unit mass of the substance by one degree celsius.

- This method involves mixing of a known mass of a substance with a known mass of water at a known temperature and measuring the final temperature of the mixture.

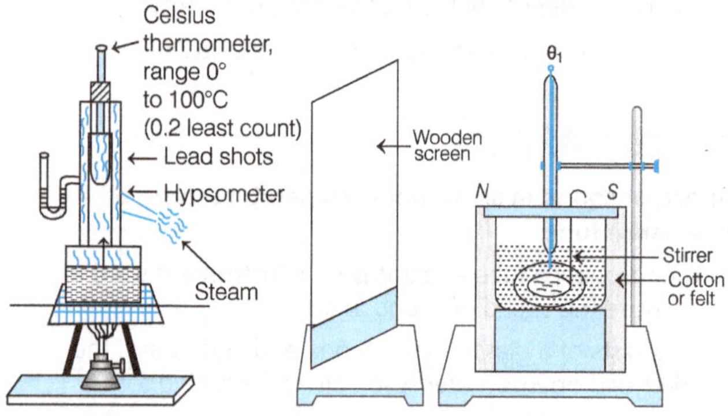

Heating of lead shot in steam using hypsometer   Calorimeter in jacket containing

Principle

- The basis of this method is principle of calorimetry, according to which when two bodies at different temperatures are brought close in contact, heat flows from body at higher temperature to body at lower temperature till both bodies acquire the same temperature, specific heat of a given liquid is defined as the amount of heat required to raise the temperature of 1 kg of liquid through 1°C.
- From the principle of calorimetry,

$$\text{Heat lost} = \text{Heat gained}$$

$$m_s s_s(\theta_s - \theta_e) = (m_w \cdot s_w + m_c \cdot s_c)(\theta_e - \theta_w)$$

where, s_s, s_w and s_c are the specific heats of the solid, water and calorimeter. From the above equation, s_s is determined.

Experiment 10

The resistivity of the material of a given wire using meter-bridge.

- Meter bridge is based on Wheatstone bridge. Diagram of meter-bridge and its comparison with Wheatstone bridge are shown below.
- The resistance R, the unknown resistance X, the wire length l and the wire of length $(100-l)$ acts as four arms of the Wheatstone bridge.

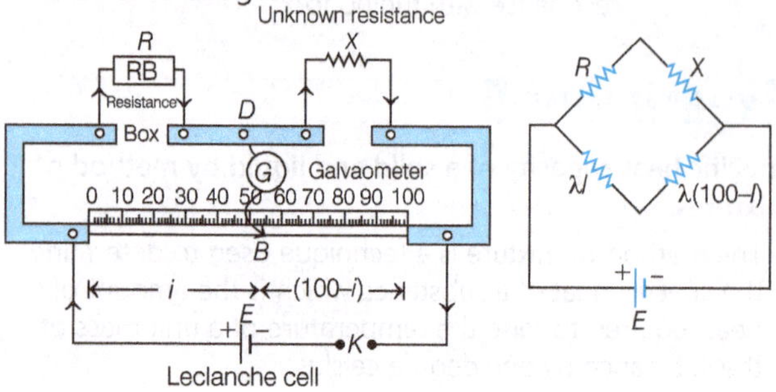

(λ = resistance per unit length)

- According to the principle of wheatstone bridge,

$$\frac{R}{X} = \frac{\lambda l}{\lambda(100-l)}$$

$$\Rightarrow \qquad X = \frac{R}{l}(100-l)$$

Experiment 11

The resistance of a given wire using Ohm's law.

- The following arrangement is used in this method.

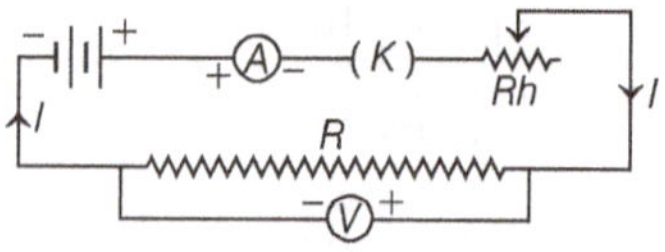

Principle

- If I be the current flowing through a conductor and V be the potential difference across its ends, then according to Ohm's law,

$$V \propto I \quad \Rightarrow \quad V = RI$$

where, R is the constant of proportionality. It is known as resistance of the conductor.

or $$\frac{V}{I} = R$$

- The graph of V *versus* I is shown below.

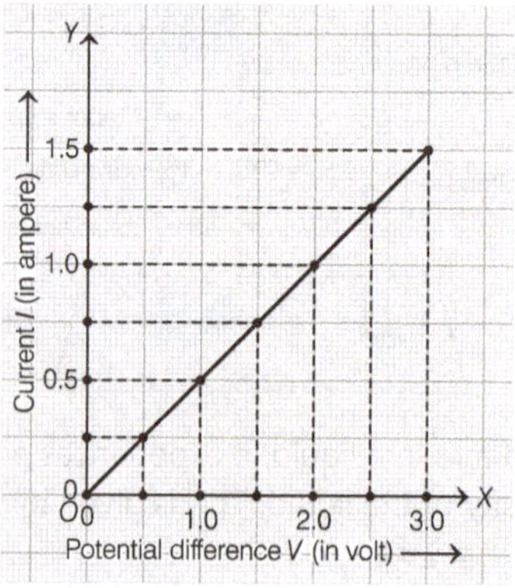

Experiment 12

Resistance and figure of merit of a galvanometer by half deflection method.

- Galvanometer is a device used for detecting feeble electric current in circuits.
- It consists of a coil of wire suspended between the poles of permanent magnet.

- The principle behind the moving coil galvanometer is based on the interaction between magnetic field and electric field, which causes the coil to rotate.
- When a current flows through the coil, it experiences a torque due to magnetic field, causing it to rotate.
- The amount of rotation is proportional to the current flowing through the coil making the galvanometer a sensitive instrument for measuring small currents.
- If A is area of galvanometer, N be number of turns and I is current, then deflecting torque is given by

$$\tau_{def} = NAIB$$

- Let τ be the restoring torque per unit twist of spring, then at equilibrium,

$$\Rightarrow \qquad I = \frac{c}{NAB}\theta = k\theta$$

where, $k = \frac{c}{NAB}$, called galvanometer constant.

Current Sensitivity

- Deflection produced due to flow of unit current in its coil is called current sensitivity of the galvanometer. It is S_I.

From relation, $I = \frac{c}{NAB}\theta \Rightarrow S_I = \frac{\theta}{I} = \frac{NAB}{c}$

Voltage Sensitivity

- Deflection produced due to current produced by unit potential difference between ends of the galvanometer coil, is called voltage sensitivity of the galvanometer. Its symbol is S_V.

For coil of resistance R, $I = \frac{V}{R}$

Hence, $\frac{V}{R} = \frac{c}{NAB}\theta \Rightarrow S_V = \frac{\theta}{V} = \frac{NAB}{cR} = \frac{S_I}{R}$

Resistance of Galvanometer

- The connections for finding the resistance of a galvanometer by half deflection method is shown in the figure. When key K_1 is closed and K_2 is open, then current flowing through the galvanometer is given by,

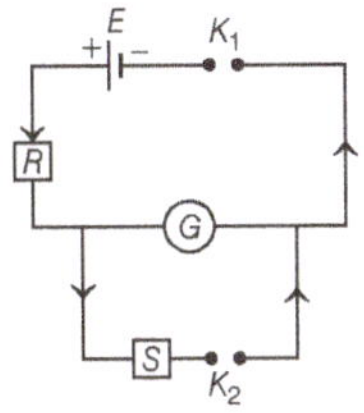

$$I = \frac{E}{R+G} = k\theta$$

where, G is resistance of galvanometer and θ is the deflection.

- The resistance of galvanometer is given by

$$G = \frac{RS}{R-S}$$

where, S is shunt resistance.

Figure of Merit of a Galvanometer

- It is a measure of sensitivity and it is defined as the current required to produce a full-scale deflection of the galvanometer. It is denoted by k.
- When current I produces a deflection of θ in the galvanometer, then

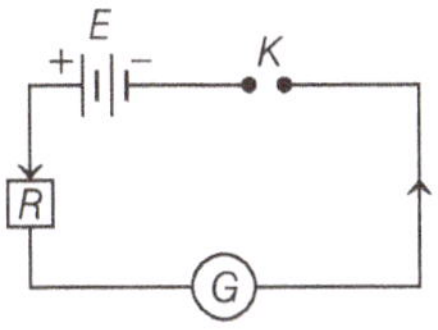

$$k = \frac{I}{\theta} = \frac{E}{(R+G)\theta}$$

- If n is the number of divisions in galvanometer scale, then current required to produce full scale deflection is given by $I_g = nk$.

Experiment 13

The focal length of (i) convex mirror, (ii) concave mirror and (iii) convex lens, using the parallax method.

(i) Convex Mirror

- The convex mirror is a curved mirror with a reflective surface that bulged outward towards the observer.
- The experiment involves placing an object in front of the convex mirror and observing the image formed by the mirror.
- Focal length of the mirror is given by

$$\frac{1}{f} = \frac{1}{v} + \frac{1}{u}$$

where, f = focal length,

u = object distance from pole

and v = image distance from pole.

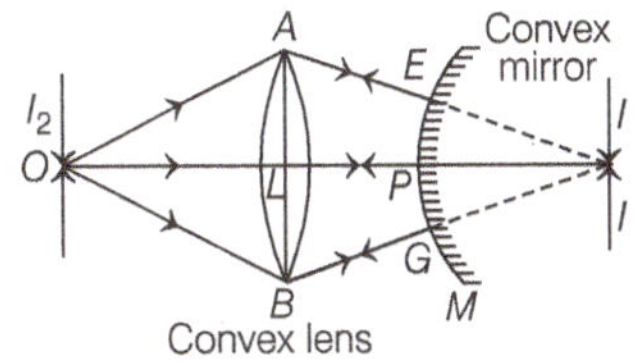

Properties of Image Formed by a Convex Mirror

(a) The image formed by a convex mirror is always virtual i.e., it appears to be located behind the mirror.

(b) The image formed is always smaller than the object.

(c) The image formed is always upright.

(ii) Concave Mirror

- The concave mirror is a curved mirror with a reflective surface that curves inward, away from the observer.

- The focal length of the concave mirror is given by mirror formula

$$\frac{1}{f}=\frac{1}{v}+\frac{1}{u}$$

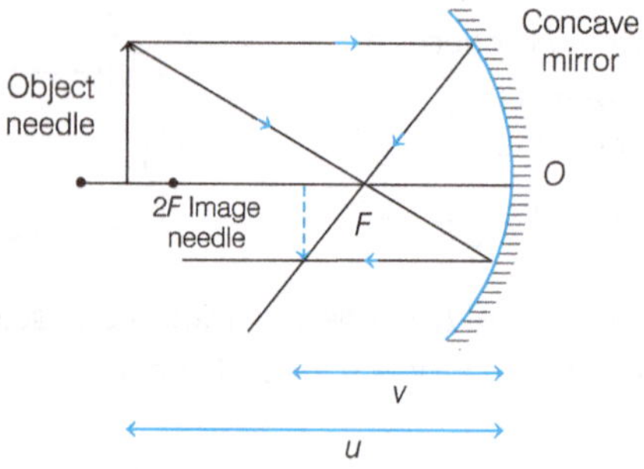

Properties of Image Formed by a Concave Mirror

(a) The image formed by a concave mirror can be either real or virtual, depending on the position of the object relative to the focal point of the mirror.

(b) If the object is located beyond the focal point, the image is real and inverted and if the object is located between the focal point and mirror, the image is virtual and upright.

(c) The image formed by concave mirror is either magnified or reduced in size. If the object is located beyond $2F$, the image is reduced in size, and if it is placed between $2F$ and mirror, then image is magnified.

(iii) Convex Lens

- The parallax method is a technique used to determine the focal length of a convex lens.
- It involves observing the apparent shift in the position of an object when viewed through lens from different distances.
- The convex lens is a curved lens with a thicker middle and thinner edges which causes light rays passing through the lens to converge at focal point.
- Focal length of the lens is given by the lens formula

$$\frac{1}{f}=\frac{1}{v}-\frac{1}{u}$$

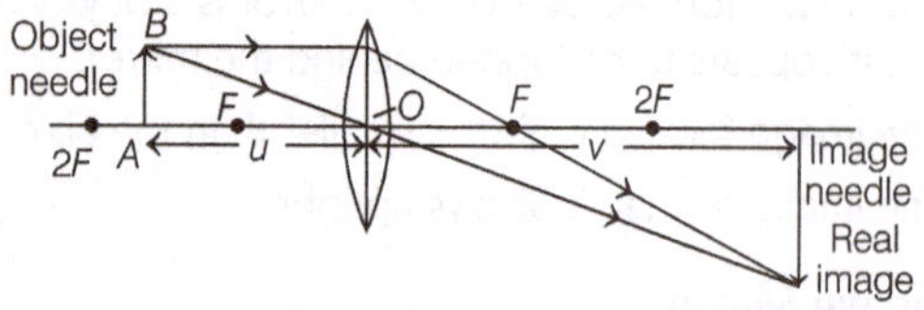

Properties of the Image Formed

(a) The image formed can be real or virtual, depending on the position of the object relative to the focal point.

(b) If the object is placed beyond the focal length, the image is real and inverted, and if the object is between focal point and lens, the image is virtual and upright.

(c) If the object is located beyond $2F$, the image is reduced and if the object is between the $2F$ and the lens, the image size will be magnified.

Experiment 14

Angle of minium deviation for a triangular prism.

- Prism is a homogeneous transparent medium enclosed by two plane surface inclined at an angle. These surfaces are called the refracting surfaces and angle between them is called refracting angle or angle of prism denoted by A.
- The angle between the incident ray and the emergent ray is known as the angle of deviation. It is denoted by δ.
- For refraction through prism, $\delta_m = i + e - A$

  where, $A = r_1 + r_2$

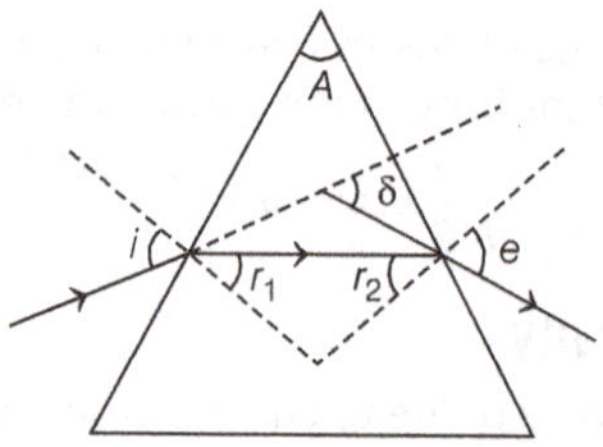

- To find the refractive index of the material of the prism, the following formula is used $\mu = \dfrac{\sin\left(\dfrac{A+\delta_m}{2}\right)}{\sin\left(\dfrac{A}{2}\right)}$
- The plot for the angle of deviation δ *versus* angle of incidence for a triangular prism is shown in the figure below.

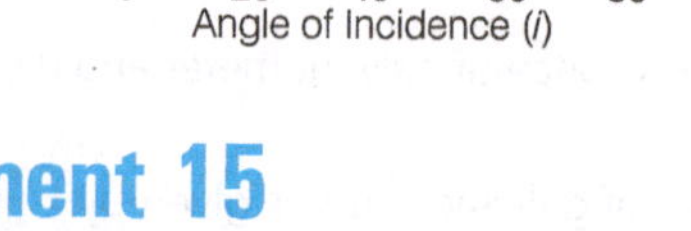

Experiment 15

Refractive index of a glass slab using a travelling microscope.

- Refraction is a phenomenon of propagation of light from one transparent medium into other, such that the light deviates from its original path.

- The ratio of the velocity of light in the first medium to that in the second medium is called refractive index of the second medium with respect to first medium.
- The bottom surface of the slab appears to be raised, such that the apparent thickness is less than the real thickness. The refractive index of the slab is defined as the ratio of real thickness to the apparent thickness.

i.e. $$\mu = \frac{\text{real thickness}}{\text{apparent thickness}}$$

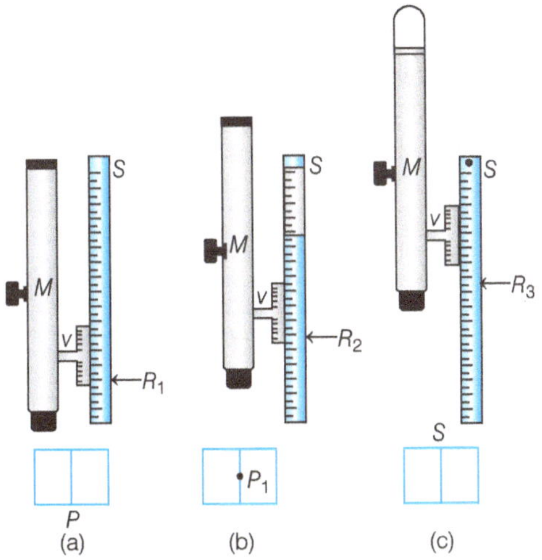

Real and apparent thickness

Travelling Microscope

- A travelling microscope is a precision instrument used to measure small distances of object with high accuracy.
- It is a compound microscope mounted on a carriage that can be moved along a graduated scale.
- It has a magnification system that allows us to view the object being measured with high precision.

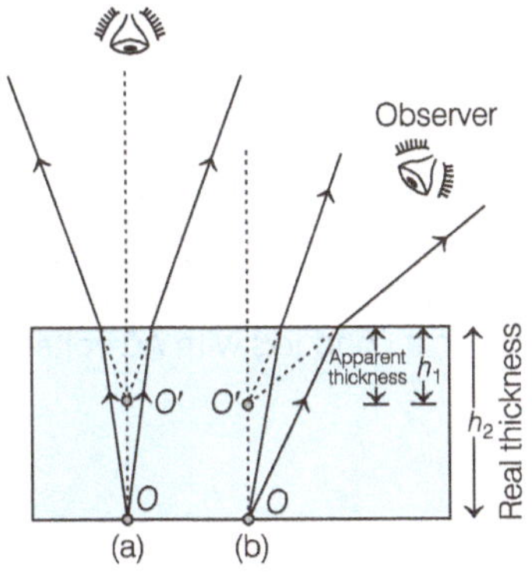

Apparent thickness for (a) Normal and (b) Oblique viewing

Experiment 16

Characteristic curves of a *p-n* junction diode in forward and reverse bias.

(i) The circuit of a *p-n* junction diode in forward bias is shown.

- In forward biased *p-n* junction diode, with increase in bias voltage, the forward current increases slowly in the beginning and then rapidly. At about 2.4 V, the current increases suddenly.

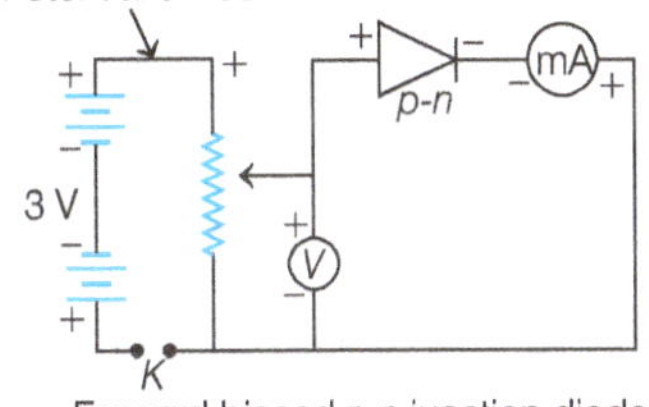

Forward biased *p-n* junction diode

- Junction resistance for forward bias is given by

$$R_f = \frac{\Delta V_F}{\Delta I_F}$$

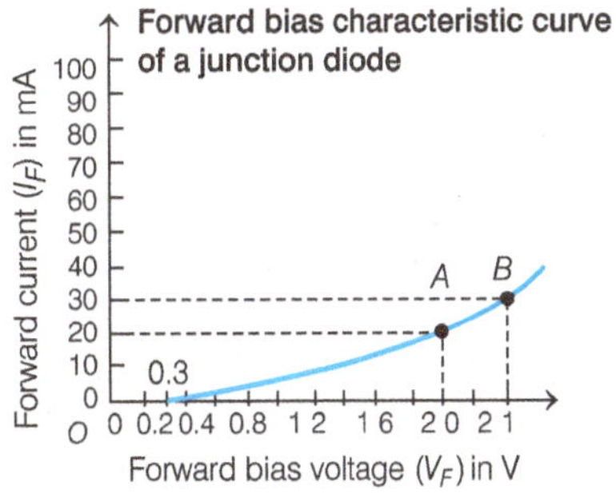

(ii) The circuit of a *p-n* junction diode in reverse bias is shown.

- In reverse biased *p-n* junction diode, in starting no appreciable reverse current flows. At about 5 V, a feeble current starts flowing. With increase in bias voltage, the current slowly increases. At about 25 V, the reverse current increases suddenly.

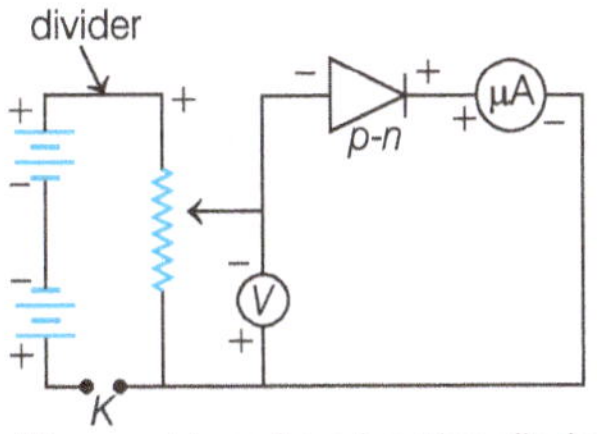

Reverse biased *p-n* junction diode

- Junction resistance for reverse bias is given by

$$R_R = \frac{\Delta V_R}{\Delta I_R}$$

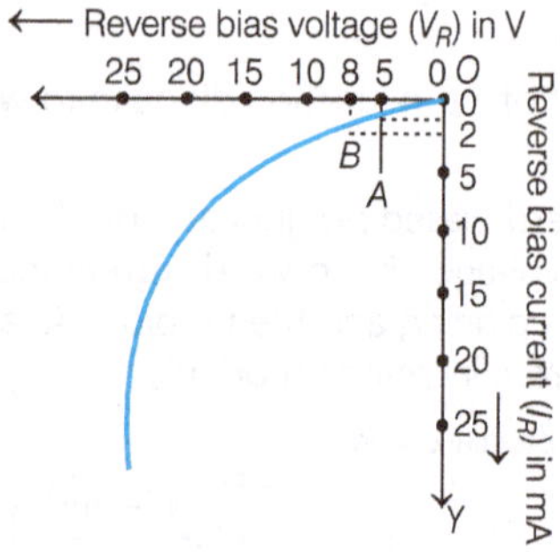

Experiment 17

Characteristic curves of a zener diode and finding reverse breakdown voltage.

- **Zener diode** is a semiconductor diode, having *n*-type and the *p*-type sections heavily doped. This heavy doping results in a low value of reverse breakdown voltage.

Avalanche Effect

- Avalanche effect in a zener diode occur when the reverse-biased voltage across the diode exceeds a certain threshold, called zener voltage. This causes the generation of electron-hole pairs through impact ionisation, resulting in a rapid increase in the reverse current flowing through the diode. This effect is used in zener diodes to regulate voltage and provide a stable output voltage.
- The reverse breakdown voltage of a zener diode is called zener voltage (V_Z). The reverse current that results after the breakdown, is called zener current (I_z).

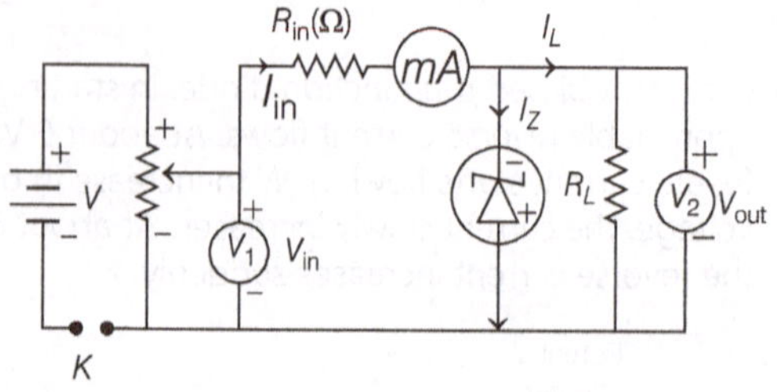

(i) **Relations**

$$I_L = I_{in} - I_Z \quad \text{...(i)}$$

$$V_{out} = V_{in} - R_{in} I_{in} \quad \text{...(ii)}$$

$$V_{out} = R_L I_L \quad \text{...(iii)}$$

Initially, as V_{in} is increased, I_{in} increases a little, then V_{out} increases.

- At breakdown, increase of V_{in}, I_{in} increases by large amount, so that $V_{out} = V_{in} - R_{in} I_{in}$ becomes constant.

  This constant value of V_{out} which is the reverse breakdown voltage, is called zener voltage, given by,

$$V_{out} = V_{in} - R_{in} I_{in}$$

  Constant value of V_{out} gives reverse breakdown voltage.

- Plot a graph between input voltage and output voltage along *X*-axis and along *Y*-axis respectively. The graph is shown below.

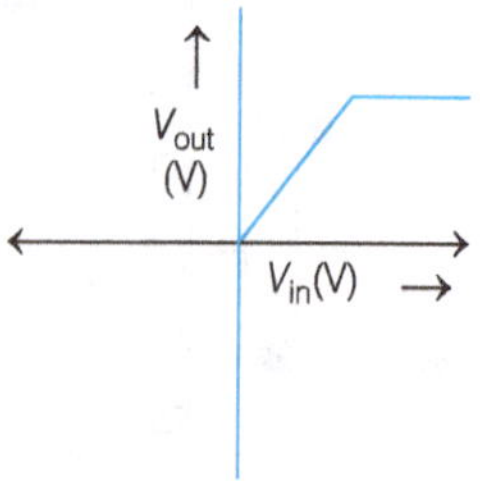

Experiment 18

Identification of Diode, LED, Resistor, Capacitor from a mixed collection of such items.

For the identification, appearance and working of each item will is considered.

(i) **Diode** is a two terminal device. It conducts in forward bias and does not conduct when connected in reverse biased.

(ii) **LED** LED stands for light emitting diode. It consists of two terminals and conducts when connected in forward bias and does not conduct in reverse biased. While conducting, LED emits light.

(iii) **Resistor** A resistor is also a two terminal device. It conducts in both forward and reverse biased. It conducts in AC and DC voltage.

(iv) **Capacitor** A capacitor consists of two terminals and it does not conduct when either in forward bias or reverse bias. However, it conducts with AC voltage.

Step by Step

Mastering NCERT

- Concept Builders
- Topical Questions
- Assertion and Reason Questions
- Statement Based
- Matching Type
- Numerical Type
- Past Exams MCQs
- Skill Boosters

Concept Builders

1 .... (Resolution/Least count) is the difference between the value of one main scale and one vernier scale division.

2 The lowest main scale division of vernier callipers is .... (0.1 mm/1mm).

3 In a screw gauge, the frame is the C-shaped body that contains the anvil and barrel. [T/F]

4 Ratchet in a screw gauge aids in marking the main scale and baseline. [T/F]

5 The energy dissipated in a damped oscillation decays .... (linearly/exponentially).

6 Total energy in a damped oscillation of pendulum is not conserved. [T/F]

7 A couple is formed if two equal and opposing forces act at a .... (perpendicular/parallel) distance.

8 What is the dimension of Young's modulus?

9 What kind of shape is observed in stress *versus* strain graph (within the elastic limit)?

10 Water has a higher surface tension than oil. [T/F]

11 Which type of fluids have surface tension equal to zero?

12 The viscosity of liquids .... (increases/decreases) with increase in temperature.

13 Resonance tube method is used to find speed of sound in air at 300 K. [T/F]

14 Velocity of sound is dependent on temperature T as .... ($\sqrt{T}$ / $T^{3/2}$).

15 Specific heat of a solid depends on volume of the solid. [T/F].

16 What is the resistance of open key?

17 Meter bridge experiment is used to calculate the value of unknown resistance using Ohm's law. [T/F].

18 What is the angle of deviation of ray when it falls normally on one of the faces of a glass prism of apex 30°?

19 Real image of a distant tree can be obtained by .... (convex/concave) lens.

20 Zener diode is used as .... (voltage regulator/ ampilfier) in .... (DC/AC) circuit.

Topical Questions

Experiment-1 Vernier Callipers

1 In an unusual vernier, 9 vernier scale divisions coincide with 6 main scale divisions, then the least count of the vernier is

(a) $\frac{1}{2}$ mm (b) 0.2 mm
(c) 0.33 mm (d) 0.8 mm

2 In a vernier callipers, each cm on the main scale is divided into 15 equal parts. If 8th vernier scale division coincides with 6th main scale division, then the value of vernier constant is

(a) 0.10 mm (b) 0.16 mm
(c) 0.19 mm (d) 0.20 mm

3 The vernier constant of vernier callipers is 0.2 mm and it has zero error of – 0.08 cm. While measuring diameter of a sphere, the main scale reading is 1.4 cm and coinciding vernier division is 6. The corrected diameter will be

(a) 1.46 cm (b) 1.5 cm (c) 1.56 cm (d) 1.6 cm

4 In an experiment, the angles are required to be measured using an instrument. 44 divisions of the main scale exactly coincide with the 45 divisions of the vernier scale. If the smallest division of the main scale is 0.5°, then the least count of the instrument is

(a) one minute (b) one and half minute
(c) one degree (d) half degree

5 The least count of vernier callipers is defined as
(a) ratio of a main scale division and a vernier scale division.
(b) difference between a main scale division and a vernier scale division.
(c) product of a main scale division and a vernier scale division.
(d) sum of a main scale division and a vernier scale division.

Experiment-2 Screw Gauge

6 The least count of the main scale of a screw gauge is 2 mm. The minimum number of divisions on its circular scale required to measure 8 μm diameter of a wire is
(a) 250 (b) 200 (c) 300 (d) 150

7 A screw gauge with a pitch of 0.4 mm and a circular scale with 20 divisions is used to measure the thickness of a thin sheet of aluminium. Before starting the measurement, it is found that when the two jaws of the screw gauge are brought in contact, the 25th division coincides with the main scale line and that the zero of the main scale is barely visible. What is the thickness of the sheet if the main scale reading is 0.6 mm and the 15th division coincides with the main scale line?
(a) 0.95 mm (b) 1.05 mm
(c) 1.00 mm (d) 0.90 mm

8 A screw gauge gives the following reading when used to measure the diameter of a wire.
Main scale reading : 1 mm
Circular scale reading : 62 divisions
Given that 2 mm on main scale corresponds to 100 divisions of the circular scale.
The diameter of wire from the above data is
(a) 0.022 cm (b) 0.422 cm
(c) 0.042 cm (d) 0.224 cm

9 In a screw gauge, 5 complete rotations of the screw cause it to move a linear distance of 0.20 cm. There are 50 circular scale divisions. The thickness of a wire measured by this screw gauge gives a reading of 6 main scale divisions and 40 circular scale divisions. Assuming negligible zero error, the thickness of the wire is
(a) 0.312 cm (b) 0.272 cm
(c) 0.252 cm (d) 0.432 cm

10 Which of the following can be measured by a screw gauge?
(a) To measure length of a wire.
(b) To measure diameter of lead shot.
(c) To measure weight of lead shot.
(d) To measure diameter of a glass plate.

Experiment-3 Dissipation of Energy of Pendulum

11 In a damped oscillation with damping constant b. The time taken for amplitude of oscillation to drop to half its value is ?
(a) $\frac{b}{m}\ln 2$ (b) $\frac{b}{2m}\ln 2$
(c) $\frac{m}{b}\ln 2$ (d) $\frac{2m}{b}\ln 2$

12 Three students S_1, S_2 and S_3 perform an experiment for determining the acceleration due to gravity (g) using a simple pendulum. They use different lengths of pendulum and record time for different number of oscillations. The observations are as shown in the table.

Student no.	Length of pendulum (cm)	No. of oscillations n	Total time for n oscillations (t)	Time period (s)
1.	60	7	84	12
2.	40	8	80	10
3.	60	8	96	12

(Least count of length = 0.1 cm, least count for time = 0.1 s)
If E_1, E_2 and E_3 are the percentage errors in g for students 1, 2 and 3 respectively, then the minimum percentage error is obtained by student number is
(a) 3 (b) 2
(c) Both 1 and 2 (d) 1

13 In an experiment to determine acceleration due to gravity, the length of the pendulum is measured as 98 cm by a meter scale of least count of 1 cm. The period of swing/oscillations is measured with the help of a stop watch having a least count of 1s. The time period of 50 oscillations is found to be 98 s. Express value of g with proper error limits.
(a) $(10.1 \pm 0.5)\ ms^{-2}$
(b) $(10.1 \pm 0.2)\ ms^{-2}$
(c) $(10.1 \pm 0.3)\ ms^{-2}$
(d) $10.1 ms^{-2}$

14 Time period of simple pendulum inside the satellite orbiting earth is
(a) zero (b) infinite
(c) T (d) None of these

15 The graph between the length and the square of the time period of a simple pendulum is a
(a) parabola (b) circle
(c) straight line (d) hyperbola

Experiment-4 Meter Scale

16 The wedge is kept below the 50 cm mark on the meter scale. Known masses of 2 kg and 3 kg are hung at the 25 cm and 35 cm mark, respectively. Where will a 5 kg mass be hung on the meter scale to balance it? (Neglect mass of meter scale)

(a) 65 cm (b) 69 cm (c) 73 cm (d) 71 cm

17 When a meter scale is balanced above a wedge, 2 kg mass is hung at 20 cm mark and a 3 kg mass is hung at 100 cm mark. To which mark on the meter scale, the fulcrum be shifted (neglect mass of meter scale) to balance the scale?

(a) 78 cm (b) 48 cm (c) 68 cm (d) 58 cm

18 In the experiment of balancing moments, suppose the fulcrum is at the 60 cm mark and a known mass of 4 kg is used on the longer arm. The greatest mass of m which can be balanced against 4 kg such that the minimum distance of either of the masses from the fulcrum is atleast 15 cm. (Neglect mass of meter scale)

(a) 16 kg (b) 18 kg (c) 20 kg (d) 12 kg

19 In the scale and wedge experiment, m is situated at x from the wedge and M is situated at y from wedge at equilibrium. Now, if $M < m$, then what is the relation between x and y?

(a) $x = y$

(b) $x < y$

(c) $x > y$

(d) Nothing can be said about x and y

20 When the moment of force is maximum, then what is the angle between force and position vector of the force?

(a) 0° (b) 45° (c) 90° (d) 180°

Experiment-5 Young's Modulus

21 A load of mass M kg is suspended from a steel of wire of length 2 m and radius 1.0 mm in Searle's apparatus experiment. The increase in length produced in the wire is 6.0 mm. Now, the load is fully immersed in a liquid of relative density 3. The relative density of the material of load is 9. The new value of increase in length of the steel wire is

(a) 4 mm (b) 3 mm
(c) 5 mm (d) 6 mm

22 A solid cylindrical steel column is 5 m long and 10 cm in diameter. ($Y_{steel} = 1.9 \times 10^{11}$ N/m^2). The decrease in length of the column, while carrying a load of 7×10^4 kg is

(a) 2.35 mm (b) 2.29 mm
(c) 3.45 mm (d) 4.35 mm

23 A thin 2m long rod has a radius of 6 mm. A force of 72 π kN is applied at one end to determine its Young's modulus. Assume that the force is exactly known. If the least count in the measurement of all lengths is 0.02 mm, which of the following statement is correct?

(a) The maximum value of Y that can be determined is 2×10^{14} N/m^2.

(b) $\frac{\Delta Y}{Y}$ gets minimum contribution from the uncertainty in the length.

(c) $\frac{\Delta Y}{Y}$ gets its maximum contribution from the uncertainty in strain.

(d) The figure of merit is the largest for the length of its rod.

24 The Young's modulus of a wire is dependent on which property?

(a) Stress (b) Strain
(c) Ultimate tensile stress (d) Material of wire

25 The breaking stress of a wire depends upon

(a) material of wire (b) length of wire
(c) radius of wire (d) shape of cross-section

Experiment-6 Surface Tension of Liquid

26 By how much depth will the surface of a liquid be depressed in a glass tube of radius 0.3 mm, if the angle of contact of the liquid is 120° and the surface tension is 0.75 N/m?

(Density of the liquid is 15.5×10^3 kg m^{-3})

(a) 2.5 cm (b) 1.6 cm (c) 1.2 cm (d) 3.2 cm

27 To what height can mercury be filled in a vessel without any leakage, if there is a pin hole of diameter 0.4 mm at the bottom of the vessel. (Density of mercury $= 13.6 \times 10^3$ kg m^{-3}, surface tension of mercury $= 650 \times 10^{-3}$ N m^{-1}, angle of contact with the vessel for mercury = 60°).

(a) 0.450 m (b) 0.042 m
(c) 0.024 m (d) 0.240 m

28 The amount of energy evolved when 27 droplets of mercury (surface tension = 0.55 N/m) of radius 0.5 mm each combine into one drop, is

(a) 31.1 μJ (b) 37.7 μJ (c) 35.3 μJ (d) 29.9 μJ

29 In the case of liquids that do not wet the walls of the vessel,

(a) adhesive forces are larger than cohesive forces.

(b) cohesive forces are larger than adhesive forces.

(c) both adhesive and cohesive forces are equal in magnitude.

(d) None of the above

30 Two capillary tubes of different diameters are dipped in water. The rise of water is
(a) the same in both tubes.
(b) greater in the tube of larger diameter.
(c) greater in the tube of smaller diameter.
(d) independent of the diameter of the tube.

Experiment-7 Coefficient of Viscosity by using v_t

31 A steel ball of diameter 4 mm falls under gravity through an oil of density 980 kg m^{-3} and viscosity 1.78 N sm^{-2}. The density of steel may be taken as 7980 kg m^{-3}. The terminal velocity of the ball is
(a) 4.4×10^{-2} m/s (b) 3.4×10^{-2} m/s
(c) 2.4×10^{-3} m/s (d) 5.4×10^{-3} m/s

32 A steel ball bearing of diameter 5 mm falls through glycerine and covers a distance of 30 cm in 15 s. The specific gravity of steel and glycerine are 9.8 and 2.2 respectively. The viscosity of glycerine is about
(a) 62 poise (b) 56 poise (c) 52 poise (d) 48 poise

33 Three spherical raindrops of equal size are falling vertically through air with a terminal velocity of 3 m/s. What would be the terminal speed, if these three drops were to coalesce to form a large spherical drop?
(a) 4.2 m/s (b) 7.2 m/s (c) 5.2 m/s (d) 6.2 m/s

34 What happens to the coefficient of viscosity of a liquid if the temperature increases?
(a) Increases
(b) Decreases
(c) Remains the same.
(d) Independent of temperature.

35 A body just floats in sea water but sinks in river water because
(a) sea water has lesser density than river water.
(b) sea water has greater density than river water.
(c) sea water exerts less upthrust on the body than river water.
(d) river water is more contaminated than sea water.

Experiment-8 Speed of Sound using Resonance Tube

36 A tuning fork having frequency of 300 Hz is vibrated just above a cylindrical tube. The height of the tube is 125 cm. Water is slowly poured in. The minimum height of water for resonance is ($v = 276$ m/s).
(a) 12 cm (b) 8 cm (c) 32 cm (d) 20 cm

37 A resonance tube is old and has jagged end. It is still used in the laboratory to determine velocity of sound in air. A tuning fork of frequency 1500 Hz produces first resonance when the tube is filled with water to a mark 15 cm below a reference mark, near the open end of the tube. The experiment is repeated with another fork of frequency 500 Hz which produces first resonance when water reaches a mark 30 cm below the reference mark. The velocity of sound in air, obtained in the experiment, is close to
(a) 450 m/s (b) 400 m/s
(c) 250 m/s (d) 500 m/s

38 The internal radius of a 1 m long resonance tube is measured as 3.0 cm. A tuning fork of frequency 2000 Hz is used. The first resonating length is measured as 4.6 cm and the second resonating length is measured as 14.0 cm. Percentage error in calculation of end correction *e* is
(a) 100% (b) 80% (c) 94% (d) 75%

39 When you increase the loudness of the ringtone of your mobile phone, the frequency of ringtone
(a) increases (b) decreases
(c) remains same (d) can't be determined

40 When the length of a closed air column is increased, then the frequency will
(a) decrease (b) increase
(c) remain same (d) can't same

Experiment-9 Specific Heat of Liquid/Solid by Mixtures

41 150 g of a solid ball at 30°C is dropped in an equal amount of water at 90°C. The resulting temperature is 45°C. This means that specific heat of solid is
(a) one-third of water
(b) same as water
(c) twice of water
(d) three times of water

42 In an experiment, a sphere of aluminium of mass 0.30 kg is heated upto 160°C. Immediately, it is put into water of volume 160 cc at 27°C kept in a calorimeter of water equivalent to 0.040 kg. Final temperature of the system is 60°C. The specific heat of aluminium is (take 4.2 J = 1 cal)
(a) 952 J/kg°C (b) 924 J/kg°C
(c) 864 J/kg°C (d) 964 J/kg°C

43 The temperature of equal masses of three different liquids *A*, *B* and *C* are 12°C, 19°C and 28°C, respectively. The temperature when *A* and *B* are mixed is 16°C and when *B* and *C* are mixed is 23°C. The temperature when *A* and *C* are mixed, is
(a) 18.2°C (b) 22°C
(c) 20.2°C (d) 25.2°C

44 Which of the following statement is incorrect for heat?
(a) The temperature of the two bodies are same, even if their heat contents are different.
(b) When two bodies are mixed, total heat is equal to the sum of the heat contents of the two bodies.
(c) It is measured by the principle of calorimetry.
(d) Heat content of body depends on its mass, temperature and nature.

45 The sprinkling of water reduces slightly the temperature of a closed room because
(a) water is a bad conductor of heat.
(b) water has large latent heat of vaporisation.
(c) temperature of water is less than that of the room.
(d) specific heat of water is high.

Experiment-10 Resistance Using Meter Bridge

46 In a meter bridge experiment, the corresponding observation table is shown in figure.

S.No.	R(Ω)	l (cm)
1.	1000	55
2.	100	11
3.	10	1.2
4.	1	1

Which of the reading is inconsistent?
(a) 109 (b) 70 (c) 99 (d) 98

47 In a simple meter bridge circuit, the gaps are bridged by coils P and Q having the smaller resistance. A balance is obtained when the jockey key makes contact at a point of the bridge wire 45 cm from the P end. On shunting the coil Q with a resistance of 50 Ω, the balance point is moved through 5 cm. The resistance P and Q are
(a) $P = \frac{100}{11}, Q = \frac{100}{9}$
(b) $P = \frac{100}{9}, Q = \frac{100}{11}$
(c) $P = \frac{100}{7}, Q = \frac{100}{9}$
(d) $P = \frac{100}{13}, Q = \frac{100}{11}$

48 In a meter bridge experiment, S is a standard resistance and R is a resistance wire. It is found that, balancing length is $l = 25$ cm. If R is replaced by a wire of half length and half diameter that of R of same material, then find the balancing distance l'.

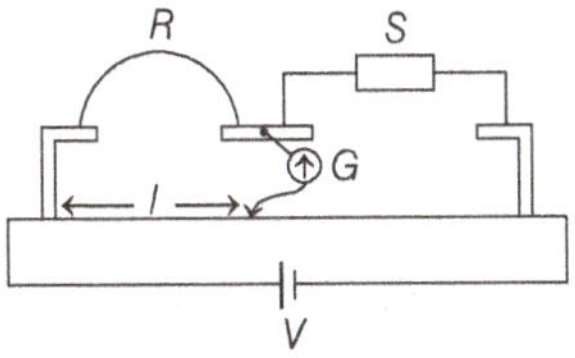

(a) 20 cm (b) 30 cm (c) 40 cm (d) 50 cm

49 The meter bridge is used to
(a) measure the electric current in a circuit.
(b) measure the potential difference across a resistance.
(c) measure the resistance of a resistor.
(d) measure the power supplied in the circuit.

50 If the radius of the wire of the meter bridge is doubled, what will happen to the balancing length?
(a) The balancing length will become zero.
(b) The balancing length will also get doubled.
(c) The balancing length will remains the same.
(d) The balancing length will get reduced.

Experiment-11 Resistance using Ohm's Law

51 The current taken from the 45 V soruce and the current through the 12 Ω resistor are respectively

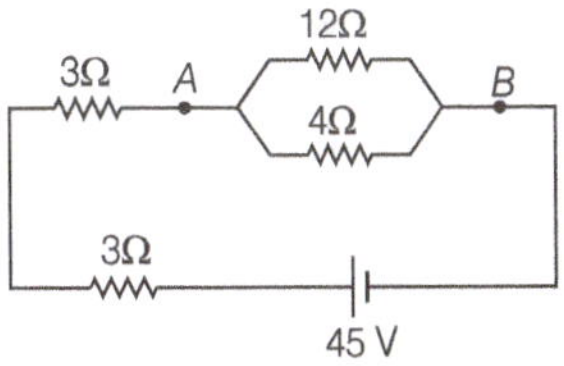

(a) 5 A, 1.25 A (b) 5A, 1.5 A
(c) 6A, 1.5 A (d) 6A, 1.25 A

52 If a copper wire is stretched to make it $n = 0.2\%$ longer, then the percentage change in its resistance is
(a) 0.2% (b) 0.6%
(c) 0.4% (d) 0.8%

53 The temperature coefficient of resistance of a wire is $0.00145°C^{-1}$. At 100 °C, its resistance is 2 Ω. At what temperature the resistance of the wire will be 3 Ω?
(a) 767.8 K (b) 567.5 K
(c) 928.3 K (d) 727.56 K

54 Resistivity of a wire depends on
(a) length of wire (b) cross-section area
(c) material (d) All of the mentioned

55 Ohm's law is obeyed by many substances, but it is not a fundamental law of nature.It fails, if
(a) V depends on I non-linearly.
(b) The relation between V and I is non-unique.
(c) The relation between V and I depends on the sign of V for the same absolute value of V.
(d) More than one V for same I.

Experiment-12 Resistance by Half-deflection Method

56 The scale of a galvanometer of resistance 150 Ω contains 50 divisions. It gives a deflection of 1 division on passing a current of 5×10^{-4} A. The resistance in ohm to be added to it, so that it may become a voltmeter of range 5 V is
(a) 50 Ω (b) 75 Ω (c) 25 Ω (d) 100 Ω

57 A moving coil galvanometer has 200 equal divisions. Its current sensitivity is 20 divisions per milliampere and voltage sensitivity is 5 divisions per millivolt. In order that each division reads 1 V, the resistance (in ohm) needed to be connected in series with the coil will be
(a) $10^5 - 4$ (b) 9996 (c) $10^3 - 4$ (d) 19996

58 A galvanometer can be converted into a voltmeter by connecting
(a) a low resistance in series
(b) a high resistance in series
(c) a low resistance in parallel
(d) a high resistance in parallel

59 Which of the following is the correct statement regarding current sensitivity of a galvanometer?
(a) Sensitivity increases with increase in magnetic field.
(b) Sensitivity decreases with increase in area of coil.
(c) Sensitivity decreases with increase in number of turns.
(d) More than one of the above

Experiment-13 Focal Length of Lenses and Mirror Using Parallax

60 At what distance from a convex lens of focal length 30 cm an object should be placed, so that the size of image be (1/4)th of the object?
(a) 30 cm (b) 60 cm
(c) 15 cm (d) 150 cm

61 A concave lens of focal length f forms an image which is n times the size of the object. The distance of the object from the lens is
(a) $(1 + n) f$ (b) $(1 - n) f$
(c) $\left(\frac{1+n}{n}\right) f$ (d) $\left(\frac{1-n}{n}\right) f$

62 A convex lens of focal length f is placed somewhere in between an object and a screen. The distance between the object and the screen is x. If the numerical value of the magnification produced by the lens is m, the focal length of the lens is
(a) $\frac{mx}{(m+1)^2}$ (b) $\frac{(m+1)^2}{m} x$ (c) $\frac{(m-1)^2}{m} x$ (d) $\frac{mx}{(m-1)^2}$

63 To find the focal length of a convex lens which produces a virtual image at a distance of 50 cm of an object placed 20 cm in front of it. The focal length is
(a) $\frac{50}{3}$ cm (b) $\frac{100}{3}$ cm (c) 100 cm (d) 20 cm

64 In finding experimentally, the u of a liquid using a convex lens and a plane mirror, parallax is removed when
(a) object needle is at $2f$.
(b) object needle lies between f and $2f$.
(c) object needle is at the focus of the lens.
(d) None of the above

Experiment-14 Angle of Deviation versus Incidence for Prism

65 A prism having refractive index $\sqrt{2}$ and refracting angle 30°, has one of the refracting surfaces polished. A beam of light incident on the other refracting surface will trace its path, if the angle of incidence is
(a) 20° (b) 30° (c) 45° (d) 60°

66 A ray falls on a prism ABC ($AB = BC$) and travels as shown in figure. The minimum refractive index of the prism material should be

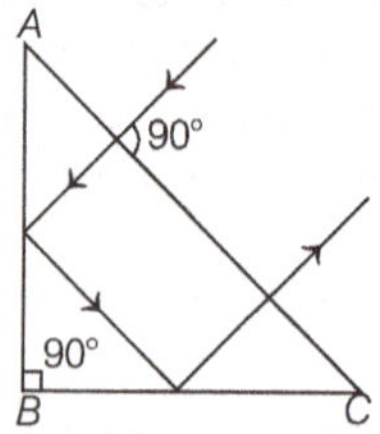

(a) $\sqrt{2}$ (b) $\sqrt{3}$ (c) 1.5 (d) $\frac{4}{3}$

67 A ray of light passes through an equilateral glass prism in such a manner that the angle of incidence is equal to the angle of emergence and each of these angles is equal to $\frac{3}{4}$ of the angle of the prism. The angle of deviation is
(a) 30° (b) 20° (c) 39° (d) 45°

68 The minimum deviation produced by a glass prism of angle 60° is 30°. If the velocity of light in vacuum is 3×10^8 m/s, then the velocity of light in glass (in m/s) is
(a) 2.9×10^8 (b) 2.72×10^8
(c) 3.1×10^8 (d) 2.121×10^8

69 A ray of light passes through an equilateral prism such that the angle of incidence is equal to emergence and later is equal to (2/3)rd the angle of prism. The angle of deviation is
(a) 45° (b) 20°
(c) 40° (d) 30°

Experiment-15 Refractive Index using Microscope

70 To determine refractive index of glass slab using travelling microscope, minimum number of readings required are
(a) one (b) two (c) three (d) four

71 The magnifying power of a microscope with an objective of 5 mm focal length is 400. The length of its tube is 20 cm. Then, the focal length of the eye-piece is
(a) 1.5 cm (b) 2.5 cm (c) 0.1 cm (d) 10 cm

72 An experiment is performed to find the refractive index of glass using a travelling microscope. In this experiment, distances are measured by
(a) a vernier scale provided on the microscope
(b) a standard laboratory scale
(c) a screw gauge provided on the microscope
(d) a meter scale provided on the microscope

73 A travelling microscope is used to determine the refractive index of a glass slab. If 40 divisions are there in 1 cm on main scale and 50 vernier scale divisions are equal to 49 main scale divisions, the least count of the travelling microscope is
(a) 5×10^{-6} m (b) 6×10^{-6} m
(c) 8×10^{-6} m (d) 2×10^{-6} m

74 For the angle of minimum deviation of a prism to be equal to its refracting angle, the prism must be made of a material whose refractive index
(a) lies between 2 and $\sqrt{2}$ (b) lies between $\sqrt{2}$ and 1
(c) is greater than 2 (d) is less than 1

Experiment-16 *p-n* Junction Diode in Forward and Reverse Bias

75 Four silicon diodes and a 10Ω resistor are connected as shown in figure below. Each diode has a resistance of 3Ω. Find the current flows through the 10 Ω resistor?

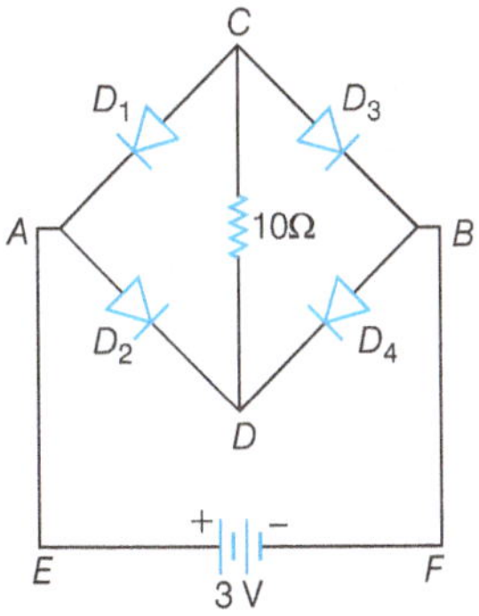

(a) 0.1 A (b) 0.2 A
(c) 0.3 A (d) 0.4 A

76 In the figure, potential difference between *A* and *B* is

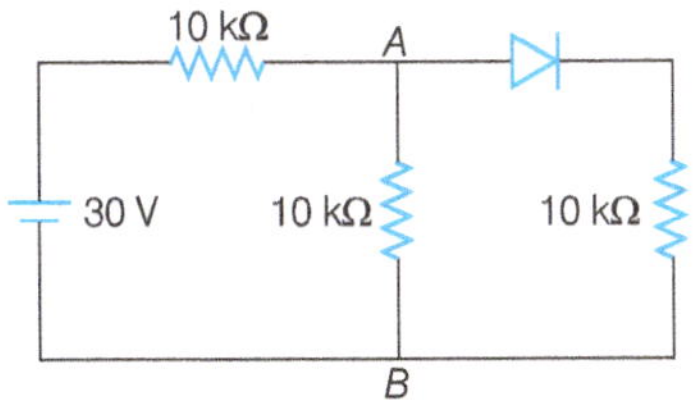

(a) zero (b) 10 V
(c) 5 V (d) 15 V

77 The current *i* in the network is

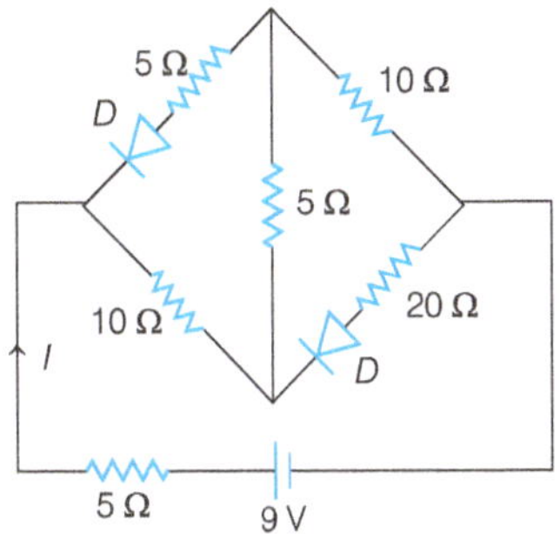

(a) 0.2 A (b) 0 A
(c) 0.6 A (d) 0.3 A

78 The reason of current flow in *p-n* junction in forward bias is
(a) drifting of minority charge carriers.
(b) drifting of majority charge carriers.
(c) diffusion of minority charge carriers.
(d) diffusion of majority charge carriers.

79 Which option is correct for making *p-n* junction as a conducting diode?
(a) Barrier potential is less than the value of reverse biased.
(b) Barrier potential should be less than the value of forward biased.
(c) Barrier potential should be greater than the value of reverse biased.
(d) Barrier potential should be greater than the value of forward biased.

Experiment-17 Zener Diode

80 An experiment is performed to determine the *I-V* characteristics of a zener diode, which has a protective resistance of 75 Ω and a maximum power of dissipation rating of 3W. The minimum voltage range of the DC source in the circuit is
(a) 0-35 V (b) 0-28 V
(c) 0-20 V (d) 0-15 V

81 Find the current through the zener diode when the load resistance is 2 kΩ. Use diode, approximation.

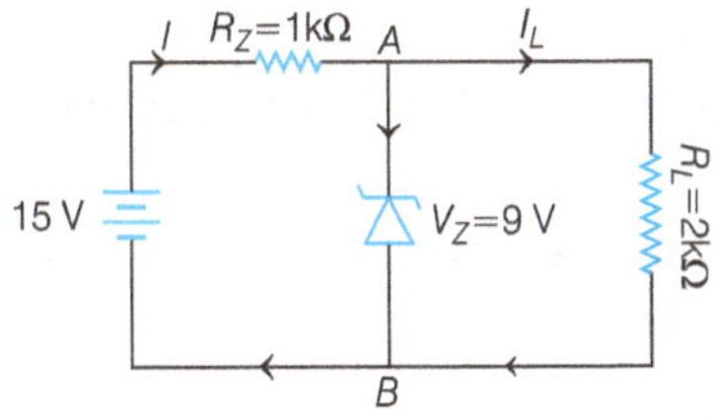

(a) 1 mA (b) 2 mA
(c) 1.5 mA (d) 2.5 mA

82 Figure shows a DC voltage regulator circuit with a zener diode of breakdown voltage = 6 V. If the unregulated input voltage varies between 10 V to 16 V, then what is the maximum zener current?

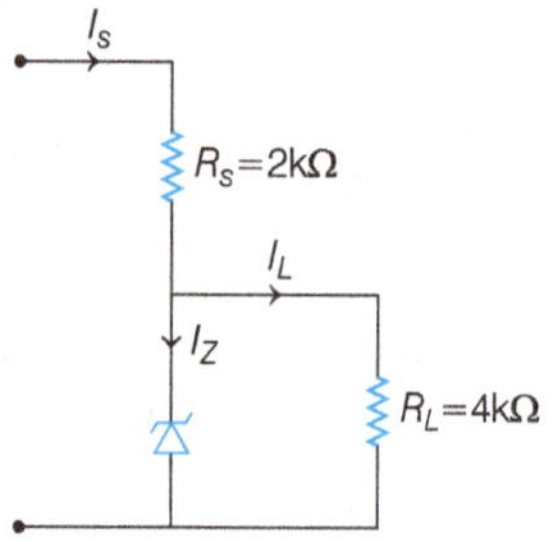

(a) 2.5 mA (b) 1.5 mA
(c) 7.5 mA (d) 3.5 mA

83 A zener diode when used as a voltage regulator is connected
(a) in forward bias in parallel with load
(b) in reverse bias in parallel with load
(c) in forward bias in series with load
(d) in reverse bias in series with load

84 By narrowing the space charge region, the amount of reverse voltage needed to cause zener breakdown
(a) reduces to zero (b) increases
(c) decreases (d) has no effect

Assertion and Reason Questions

Direction (Q. Nos. 1-10) *In the following questions, a statement of Assertion is followed by a corresponding statement of Reason. Of the following statements, choose the correct one.*
(a) Both Assertion and Reason are correct and Reason is the correct explanation of Assertion.
(b) Both Assertion and Reason are correct but Reason is not the correct explanation of Assertion.
(c) Assertion is correct but Reason is incorrect.
(d) Assertion is incorrect but Reason is correct.

1 **Assertion** The least count of vernier callipers is dependent on its design.

Reason The least count of vernier callipers is the ratio of pitch to number of vernier scale division.

2 **Assertion** The accuracy of a standard screw gauge is more than the accuracy of a standard vernier callipers.

Reason The least count of standard screw gauge is more than the least count of standard vernier callipers.

3 **Assertion** The viscosity of gases increases with increase in temperature.

Reason The viscosity of gases is directly proportional to the square of temperature.

4 **Assertion** Solids have the highest heat capacity as compared to liquids.

Reason Gases have the least value of specific heat capacity.

5 **Assertion** With the addition of detergent in pure water, the rise in capillary tube increases.

Reason The addition of detergent in water decrease its surface tension.

6 **Assertion** When a concave mirror is held under water, its focal length will increase.

Reason The focal length of a concave mirror is independent of the medium in which it is placed.

7 **Assertion** At high temperature, metal wires have a greater chance of short circuiting.

Reason Both resistance and resistivity vary with temperature.

8 **Assertion** If the angles of the base of the prism are equal, then in the position of minimum deviation, the refracted ray will pass parallel to the base of prism.

Reason In the case of minimum deviation, the angle of incidence is equal to the angle of emergence.

9 **Assertion** When two semiconductors of *p* and *n* types are brought in contact, they form *p-n* junction which act like a rectifier.

Reason A rectifier is used to convert alternating current into direct current.

10 **Assertion** In zener diode, depletion layer is thin.

Reason In reverse bias, strong electric field exists across the potential barrier.

Statement Based Questions

Direction (Q. Nos. 1-8) *In the following questions, Statement I and Statement II are given. Read the statements and choose the most appropriate answer from the options given below.*

(a) Both Statement I and Statement II are incorrect
(b) Statement I is correct but Statement II is incorrect
(c) Statement I is incorrect but Statement II is correct
(d) Both Statement I and Statement II are correct

1. **Statement I** When zero mark of the vernier scale lies towards the right side of zero of the main scale is called zero error positive.

   Statement II Zero correction is equal in magnitude but opposite in sign to zero error.

2. **Statement I** A screw gauge having a smaller value of pitch has greater accuracy.

   Statement II The least count of screw gauge is directly proportional to the number of divisions on circular scale.

3. **Statement I** The value of Young's modulus (Y) increases, if the diameter of the wire decreases.

   Statement II The value of Young's modulus (Y) decreases with the rise in temperature.

4. **Statement I** If liquid rise in the capillary tube is greater than height of a tube, then the liquid does not overflow.

   Statement II Product of radius of meniscus and height of liquid in capillary tube always remains constant.

5. **Statement I** Coefficient of viscosity decreases with increases in density of liquid.

   Statement II Viscosity of liquid does not depend on temperature.

6. **Statement I** In meter bridge, wires of nichrome, constantan are used due to their high resistivity.

   Statement II For constantan wire, the coefficient of resistance α increase with rise in temperature.

7. **Statement I** The resolving power of an electron microscope is higher than that of an optical microscope.

   Statement II The wavelength of electron is more than the wavelength of visible light.

8. **Statement I** If angle of incidence in the case of a prism is gradually increased, then deviation produced by prism will first decrease then increase.

   Statement II At minimum deviation, $r_1 = \frac{A}{2}$.

Matching Type Questions

1. Match the Column I with the Column II and choose the correct option from the codes given below.

	Column I		Column II
A.	Intrinsic semiconductor	1.	Prepared by adding antimony
B.	n-type semiconductor	2.	Immobile ion
C.	p-type semiconductor	3.	Silicon
D.	Depletion region	4.	Prepared by adding layer indium

Codes

	A	B	C	D
(a)	1	2	3	4
(b)	3	2	4	1
(c)	2	1	3	4
(d)	3	1	4	2

2. Match the Column I with the Column II and choose the correct option from the codes given below.

	Column I		Column II
A.	Resonance column method	1.	Only external measurement
B.	Searle's experiment	2.	Young's modulus of elasticity
C.	Vernier calliper	3.	Both internal and external measurements
D.	Screw gauge	4.	Speed of sound in air

Codes

	A	B	C	D
(a)	2	1	3	4
(b)	4	2	3	1
(c)	4	3	2	1
(d)	4	2	1	3

Numerical Type Questions

1. On measuring the diameter of a spherical body using vernier callipers, main scale reading = 1.3 cm, 5th vernier scale division is coinciding with any main scale division and zero error is – 0.03 cm, what will be corrected reading in cm?

2. Students I_1, J_1, J_3 and I_2 perform an experiment for measuring the acceleration due to gravity (g) using a simple pendulum. They use different lengths of the pendulum and record time for different number of oscillations. The observations are shown in the table. Least count for length = 0.1 cm and least count for time = 1 s.

Students	Length of Pendulum (cm)	No. of Oscillations (n)	Time period of Pendulum (s)
I_1	100.0	20	20
J_1	400.0	10	40
J_3	100.0	10	20
I_2	400.0	20	40

If P_1, P_2, P_3 and P_4 are the percentage error in g for students I_1, J_1, J_3 and I_2 respectively, then find ratio $\frac{P_2}{P_1}$.

3. In measurement of mass of a given object by the principle of moments, the meter scale is hung from its mid-point. A known weight of mass 2 kg is hung at one end of meter scale and unknown weight of mass m kg is hung at 20 cm from the centre on other side. The value of m is ....

4. In Searle's method to determine the Young's modulus of wire, a steel wire of length 156 cm and diameter 0.054 cm is taken as experimental wire. The average increase in length for 1.5 kg-wt is found to be 0.050 cm, then the Young's modulus of the wire is $x \times 10^{11}$ N/m,^{2} where the value of x is ....

5. In the measurement of surface tension of water, the capillary rise in the glass tube is not exceeding 0.2 mm of water. The minimum size, given that surface tension for water in contact with air is 0.0725 N/m is .... cm.

6. In the experiment of measuring speed of sound by resonance tube, it is observed that for tuning fork of frequency $\nu = 480$ Hz, length of air column $l_1 = 30$ cm, $l_2 = 70$ cm, then v_1 is equal to .... ms^{-1}.

7. In an experiment, one kilogram of ice at 0°C is mixed with one kilogram of water at 80°C. What will be the final temperature (in °C) of the mixture?

(Take, specific heat of water = 4200 J kg^{-1} K^{-1} and latent heat of ice = 336 kJ/kg)

8. In the circuit shown, a meter bridge is in its balanced state. The meter bridge wire has a resistance 0.1 Ω/cm. The value of unknown resistance X is ....

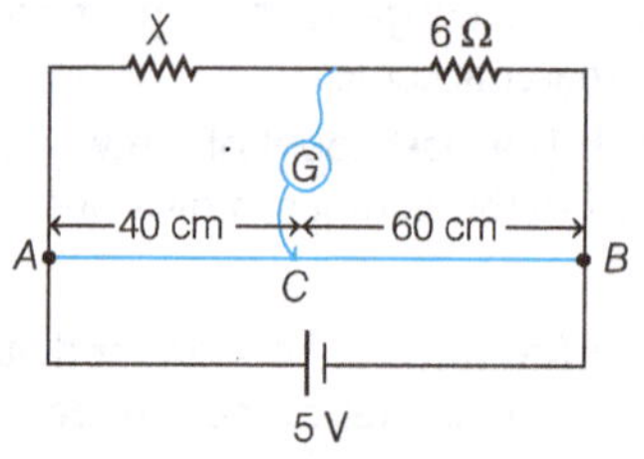

9. The light ray is incidence at angle of 60° on a prism of angle 45°. When the light ray falls on the other surface at 90°, refractive index of the material of prism μ is $\sqrt{\frac{x}{2}}$.

What is the value of x ?

10. The value of power dissipated across the zener diode ($V_Z = 15$ V) connected in the circuit as shown in the figure is $x \times 10^{-1}$ watt.

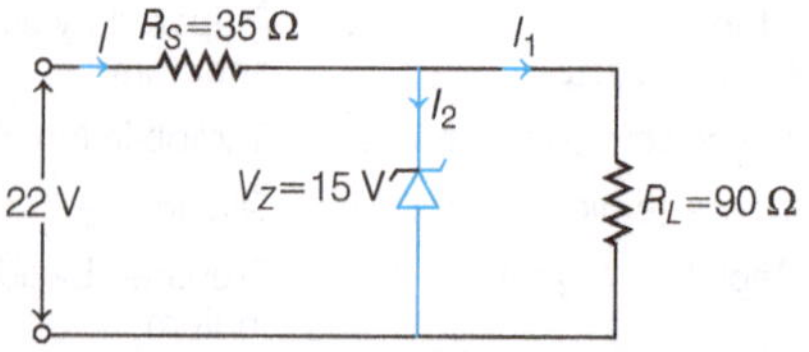

The value of x, to the nearest integer, is ....

Past Exams Questions

1. In vernier calliper, when both jaws touch each other, zero of the vernier scale shifts towards left and its 4th division coincides exactly with a certain division on main scale. If 50 vernier scale divisions equal to 49 main scale divisions and zero error in the instrument is 0.04 mm, then how many main scale divisions are there in 1 cm? **JEE Main 2024**

(a) 10 (b) 20 (c) 40 (d) 5

2. In finding out refractive index of glass slab the following observations were made through travelling microscope 50 vernier scale division = 49 MSD; 20 divisions on main scale in each cm

For mark on paper

MSR = 8.45 cm, VC = 26

For mark on paper seen through slab

MSR = 7.12 cm, VC = 41

For powder particle on the top surface of the glass slab

MSR = 4.05 cm, VC = 1

(MSR = Main Scale Reading, VC = Vernier Coincidence)

Refractive index of the glass slab is **JEE Main 2024**

(a) 1.24 (b) 1.42 (c) 1.35 (d) 1.52

3. Least count of a vernier caliper is $\frac{1}{20N}$ cm. The value of one division on the main scale is 1 mm. Then, the number of divisions of main scale that coincide with N divisions of vernier scale is **JEE Main 2024**

(a) $\left(\frac{2N-1}{20N}\right)$ (b) $(2N-1)$ (c) $\left(\frac{2N-1}{2N}\right)$ (d) $\left(\frac{2N-1}{2}\right)$

4. The time period of a simple pendulum is given by $T = 2\pi\sqrt{\frac{l}{g}}$. The measured value of the length of pendulum is 10 cm known to a 1 mm accuracy. The time for 200 oscillations of the pendulum is found to be 100 s using a clock of 1s resolution. The percentage accuracy in the determination of g using this pendulum is x. The value of x to the nearest integer is **JEE Main 2021**

(a) 2% (b) 3%
(c) 5% (d) 4%

5. The vernier scale used for measurement has a positive zero error of 0.2 mm. If while taking a measurement, it was noted that 0 on the vernier scale lies between 8.5 cm and 8.6 cm. Vernier coincidence is 6, then the correct value of measurement is ...... cm. (Least count = 0.01 cm) **JEE Main 2021**

(a) 8.36 cm (b) 8.54 cm
(c) 8.58 cm (d) 8.56 cm

6. One main scale division of a vernier callipers is a cm and nth division of the vernier scale coincide with $(n-1)$th division of the main scale. The least count of the callipers (in mm) is **JEE Main 2021**

(a) $\frac{10\,na}{(n-1)}$ (b) $\frac{10a}{(n-1)}$
(c) $\left(\frac{n-1}{10n}\right)a$ (d) $\frac{10\,a}{n}$

7. If the screw on a screw gauge is given six rotations, it moves by 3 mm on the main scale. If there are 50 divisions on the circular scale, the least count of the screw gauge is **JEE Main 2020**

(a) 0.001 cm (b) 0.01 cm
(c) 0.02 cm (d) 0.001 cm

8. A simple pendulum is being used to determine the value of gravitational acceleration g at a certain place. The length of the pendulum is 25.0 cm and a stop watch with 1s resolution measures the time taken for 40 oscillations to be 50 s. The accuracy in g is **JEE Main 2020**

(a) 2.40% (b) 5.40%
(c) 4.40% (d) 3.40%

Skill Boosters

1. A spherical ball of radius r and density ρ is falling into a tank full of water. Before entering into the tank, the covers a distance h in air. If terminal velocity of ball in the water is same as its velocity just before entering the water surface, then the value of r is proportional to

(a) $h^{\frac{1}{2}}$ (b) h^4 (c) $h^{\frac{1}{4}}$ (d) h^2

2. Mass of a 1 m long uniform beam is 2 kg. A force F at 100 cm mark is applied to lift if vertically up. The minimum value of F is

(a) 20 N
(b) 10 N
(c) 100 N
(d) 50 N

3. A 0.1 kg mass is suspended from a wire of negligible mass. The length of the wire is 1 m and its cross-sectional area is 4.9×10^{-7} m^2. If the mass is pulled a little in the vertically downward direction and released, it performs SHM with angular frequency 140 rad s^{-1}. The Young's modulus of the material of the wire is

(a) 3.5×10^7 (b) 6.2×10^7
(c) 2.0×10^8 (d) 4×10^9

4. Water in a clean aquarium forms a meniscus, as shown in the figure. Calculate the difference in height (h) between the centre and edge of the meniscus. Given, the surface tension of water, $T = 0.073$ N m^{-1} and density of water, $\rho = 1000$ kgm^{-3}.

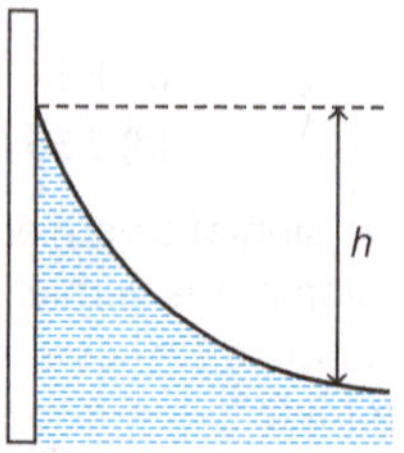

(a) $h \simeq 4$ mm (b) $h \simeq 2$ mm
(c) $h \simeq 1$ mm (d) $h \simeq 5$ mm

5. A galvanometer, having a resistance of 60 Ω, gives a full scale deflection for a current of 0.04 A. The length (in m) of a resistance wire of area of cross-section 3.50×10^{-2} cm^2 that can be used to convert the galvanometer into an ammeter which can read a maximum of 4A current is (specific resistance of wire $= 6 \times 10^{-7}$ Ω-m)

(a) 3 (b) 4.5
(c) 3.5 (d) 4

6. A student wants to choose a particular wavelength λ_0 for which the ray passes through the interface BC of combination of two prism as shown in the figure, without deviation.

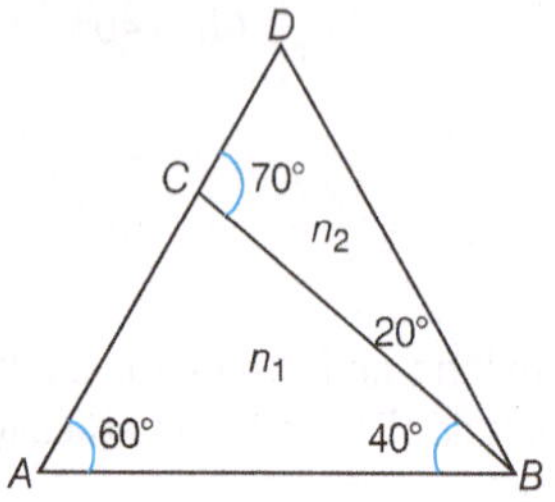

The refractive indices of prism are $n_1 = 1.2 + \dfrac{10.8 \times 10^4}{\lambda^2}$

and $n_2 = 1.45 + \dfrac{1.80 \times 10^4}{\lambda^2}$, where λ is in nm.

For a light of wavelength λ_0, find the angle of incidence i on the face AC such that the deviation produced by the combination of prisms in minimum.

(a) $\cos^{-1}\dfrac{3}{4}$ (b) $\tan^{-1}\dfrac{3}{4}$
(c) $\sin^{-1}\dfrac{3}{4}$ (d) $\sec^{-1}\dfrac{3}{4}$

7. A diode has a given characteristics.

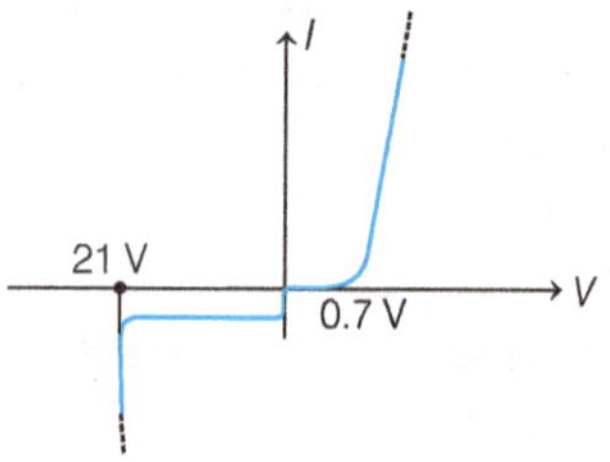

This diode is connected in a circuit as

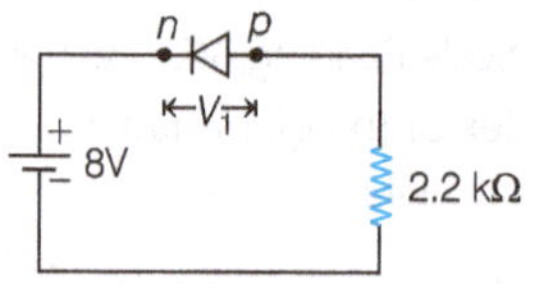

and then as

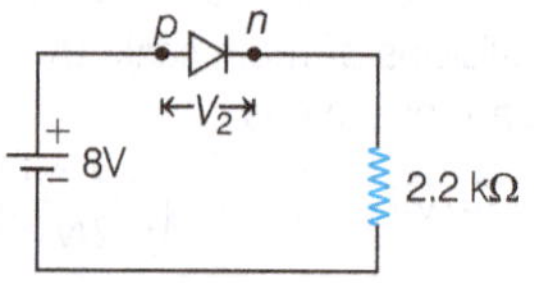

Ratio of potential drops $V_1 : V_2$ (in given circuits) will be

(a) 0 (b) $\dfrac{80}{70}$ (c) $\dfrac{80}{7}$ (d) $\dfrac{79}{1}$

8. An ice cube of mass 0.1 kg at 0°C is placed in an isolated container at 227°C. Specific heat of container is given by $S = A + BT$, where $A = 100$ cal kg^{-1}K^{-1} and $B = 2 \times 10^{-2}$ cal kg^{-2}K^{-2}. If final temperature after stabilisation is 27°C, then which of these are correct ?
(Take, $L_{water} = 80$ cal g^{-1}K^{-1} and $C_{water} = 10^3$ cal kg^{-1} K^{-1})

(a) Ice receives a total of 10800 cal of heat
(b) Container lost around 10700 cal of heat
(c) Container has a mass of around 0.5 kg
(d) Water equivalent of container is 300 g

9. A thin convex lens of focal length is able to slide along optical axis. The distance between object plane and screen is 180 cm. The magnification of image produced by initial position of lens is 2.

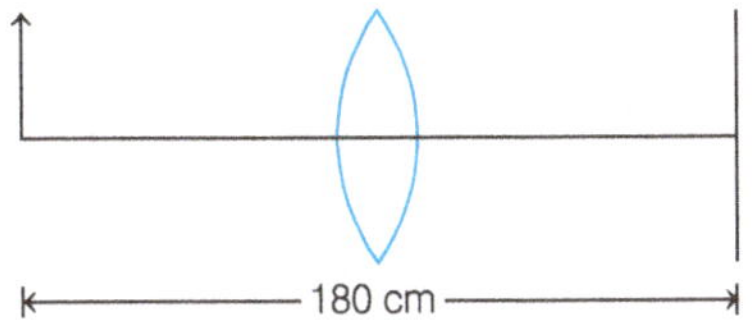

(a) The focal length of lens is 50 cm.
(b) The distance through which lens is shifted to form again real image on the screen is 60 cm.
(c) The distance through which lens is shifted to form again real image on screen is 30 cm.
(d) The focal length of lens is 60 cm.

Correct Codes

Topical Questions

1 (c)	2. (b)	3 (d)	4 (b)	5 (b)	6 (a)	7 (c)	8 (d)	9 (b)	10 (b)
11 (d)	12 (a)	13 (c)	14 (b)	15 (c)	16 (b)	17 (c)	18 (a)	19 (b)	20 (c)
21 (a)	22 (b)	23 (a)	24 (d)	25 (a)	26 (b)	27 (c)	28 (a)	29 (b)	30 (c)
31 (b)	32 (c)	33 (d)	34 (b)	35 (b)	36 (b)	37 (a)	38 (c)	39 (c)	40 (a)
41 (d)	42 (b)	43 (c)	44 (b)	45 (b)	46 (c)	47 (a)	48 (c)	49 (c)	50 (c)
51 (a)	52 (c)	53 (a)	54 (c)	55 (d)	56 (a)	57 (d)	58 (b)	59 (a)	60 (d)
61 (d)	62 (a)	63 (b)	64 (c)	65 (c)	66 (a)	67 (a)	68 (d)	69 (b)	70 (c)
71 (b)	72 (a)	73 (a)	74 (a)	75 (a)	76 (b)	77 (d)	78 (d)	79 (b)	80 (a)
81 (c)	82 (d)	83 (b)	84 (c)						

Asertion and Reason Questions

1 (a)	2 (c)	3 (c)	4 (b)	5 (d)	6 (d)	7 (b)	8 (a)	9 (b)	10 (a)

Statement Based Questions

1 (d)	2 (b)	3 (c)	4 (d)	5 (a)	6 (d)	7 (b)	8 (d)

Matching Type Questions

1 (d)	2 (b)

Numerical Type Questions

1 (1.38)	2 (0.87)	3 (5)	4 (2)	5 (14.8)	6 (384)	7 (0)	8 (4)	9 (3)	10 (5)

Past Exams Questions

1 (b)	2 (b)	3 (d)	4 (b)	5 (b)	6 (d)	7 (d)	8 (c)

Skill Boosters

1 (c)	2 (b)	3 (d)	4 (a)	5 (c)	6 (c)	7 (c)	8 (c)	9 (b)

Step by Step

Decoding the Questions

Concept Builders

1 Least count
2 1 mm
3 True (T)
4 False (F)
5 exponentially
6 False (F)
7 perpendicular
8 $[ML^{-1}T^{-2}]$
9 Straight line
10 True (T)
11 Ideal fluids
12 decreases
13 True (T)
14 $\sqrt{T}$
15 False (F)
16 Infinite
17 False (F)
18 15°
19 convex
20 voltage regulator, DC

Topical Questions

1 (*c*) Given, 6MSD = 9 VSD

We can rewrite it as,

$$9\text{MSD} - 3\text{MSD} = 9\text{VSD}$$

$$9\text{MSD} - 9\text{VSD} = 3\text{MSD}$$

$$9\ (\text{MSD} - \text{VSD}) = 3\text{MSD}$$

$$(\text{MSD} - \text{VSD}) = \frac{3}{9}\ \text{MSD}$$

$$(\text{MSD} - \text{VSD}) = 0.33\ \text{MSD}$$

So, least count of the vernier is 0.33 mm.

2 (*b*) Given,

1 cm is divided into 15 divisions

$$1\ \text{MSD} = \frac{1}{15}\ \text{cm} \quad \text{...(i)}$$

$$6\ \text{MSD} = 8\ \text{VSD}$$

$$1\ \text{VSD} = \frac{6}{8}\ \text{MSD}$$

So, $\text{LC} = 1\ \text{MSD} - 1\ \text{VSD}$

$$= 1\ \text{MSD} - \frac{6}{8}\ \text{MSD}$$

$$= \frac{2}{8}\ \text{MSD} = \frac{1}{4}\ \text{MSD}$$

$$= \frac{1}{4} \times \frac{1}{15} \quad \text{[From Eq. (i)]}$$

$$= \frac{1}{60}\ \text{cm}$$

$$\text{LC} = 0.16\ \text{mm}$$

3 (*d*) Given, LC = 0.2 mm

Zero error = – 0.08 cm

MSR = 1.4 cm

$n = 6$

So, $\text{VSR} = n \times \text{LC}$

$$= 6 \times 0.2$$

$$= 1.2\ \text{mm}$$

$$= 0.12\ \text{cm}$$

Diameter = MSR + VSR – Zero error

$$= 1.4 + 0.12 - (-0.08)$$

$$= 1.4 + 0.12 + 0.08$$

$$= 1.4 + 0.20$$

$$= 1.6\ \text{cm}$$

4 (*b*) Least count

$$= \frac{\text{Value of 1 main scale division}}{\text{No. of divisions on vernier scale}}$$

Here, n vernier scale division

= $(n-1)$ main scale division

$$1\ \text{VSD} = \frac{n-1}{n}\ \text{MSD}$$

So, LC = 1 MSD – 1 VSD

$$\text{LC} = 1\ \text{MSD} - \left(\frac{n-1}{n}\right)\text{MSD}$$

$$\text{LC} = \frac{1\text{MSD}}{n}$$

$$\text{LC} = \frac{0.5}{45}$$

$$\text{LC} = \frac{1}{90}^{\circ}$$

LC = One and half minute

Or

LC = One minute 30 sec.

5 (*b*) The least count of vernier callipers is also known as vernier constant. It is a difference between one main scale division and one vernier scale division.

6 (*a*) Given,

least count = 2 mm

$$= 2 \times 10^{-3}\ \text{m}$$

diameter of a wire = 8 μm

$$= 8 \times 10^{-6}\ \text{m}$$

N_d (No. of divisions)

$$= \frac{\text{LC}}{\text{diameter of wire}}$$

$$= \frac{2 \times 10^{-3}}{8 \times 10^{-6}} = \frac{1}{4} \times 10^{3} = 250$$

7 (*c*) Given, Pitch = 0.4 mm

$(\text{CSD})_a$, circular scale division (after) = 20

$(\text{CSD})_i$, circular scale division (initially) = 25

(MSR) main scale reading = 0.6 mm

(CSR) circular scale reading = 15

So,

$$\text{LC} = \frac{\text{Pitch}}{(\text{CSD})_a} = \frac{0.4}{20} = 0.02\ \text{mm}$$

Zero error

$$= [(\text{CSD})_{\text{after}} - (\text{CSD})_{\text{initial}}] \times \text{LC}$$

$$= (20 - 25) \times 0.02$$

$$\Rightarrow -5 \times 0.02$$

$$\Rightarrow -0.10\ \text{mm}$$

Thickness of sheet

$$= \text{MSR} + (\text{CSR} \times \text{LC}) - \text{Zero error}$$

$$= 0.6 + (15 \times 0.02) - (-0.10)$$

$$= 0.6 + .30 + 0.10$$

$$= 1\ \text{mm}$$

8 (*d*) Given,

Pitch = 2 mm

Circular scale division = 100

Main scale reading = 1 mm

Circular scale reading = 62 divisions

So, LC

$$= \frac{\text{Pitch}}{\text{No. of divisions on circular scale}}$$

$$= \frac{2}{100} = 0.02\ \text{mm}$$

Diameter of wire = Main scale reading + Circular scale reading × LC − Zero error

$= 1 + (62 \times 0.02) - 0$

$= 1 + 1.24 = 2.24$ mm

$= 0.224$ cm

9 (*b*) Given,

Number of rotations = 5

Pitch = 0.20 cm

Circular scale division = 50

(MSR) Main scale reading = 6

(CSR) Circular scale reading = 40

So, LC

$$= \frac{\text{Pitch}}{\text{Number of rotation} \times \text{Number of division on circular scale}}$$

$$= \frac{0.20}{5 \times 50}$$

$$= 8 \times 10^{-4} \text{ cm}$$

Thickness of wire

= MSR + (CSR × LC) − Zero error

$$= 6 \times \frac{0.20}{5} + 40 \times 8 \times 10^{-4} - 0$$

$= 0.240 + 0.032$

$= 0.272$ cm

11 (*d*) For damped oscillation, amplitude

$$A = A_0 e^{-\left(\frac{bt}{2m}\right)}$$

Let, time to drop to half of initial value be T'.

Then, $\frac{A_0}{2} = A_0 \cdot e^{-\left(\frac{bT'}{2m}\right)}$

$\therefore \left[\text{When } A = \frac{A_0}{2}, t = T'\right]$

So, $\frac{1}{2} = e^{-\left(\frac{bT'}{2m}\right)}$

Taking log both sides, we get

$$\ln\left(\frac{1}{2}\right) = \ln e^{-\left(\frac{bT'}{2m}\right)}$$

$$-\ln 2 = -\left(\frac{bT'}{2m}\right)$$

$$2m \cdot \ln 2 = bT'$$

$$T' = \frac{2m}{b} \ln 2$$

12 (*a*) Time period,

$$T = 2\pi\sqrt{\frac{l}{g}}$$

where, L is pendulum length and g is the acceleration due to gravity.

Also, $T^2 = 4\pi^2 \frac{L}{g}$

$$g = 4\pi^2 \frac{L}{T^2}$$

% error in g,

$$\frac{\Delta g}{g} \times 100 = \frac{\Delta L}{L} \times 100 + \frac{2\Delta t}{t} \times 100$$

$$E_1 = \left(\frac{0.1}{60} + \frac{2 \times 0.1}{84}\right) \times 100 = 0.404\%$$

$$E_2 = \left(\frac{0.1}{40} + \frac{2 \times 0.1}{80}\right) \times 100 = 0.50\%$$

$$E_3 = \left(\frac{0.1}{60} + \frac{2 \times 0.1}{96}\right) \times 100 = 0.375\%$$

So, E_3 is minimum.

So, minimum percentage error is obtained by student number 3.

13 (*c*) As, $T = 2\pi\sqrt{\frac{l}{g}}$ ... (i)

Now, time period of 50 oscillations is 98 s.

∴ Time period of one oscillation

$$= \frac{98}{50} = 1.96 \text{ s}$$

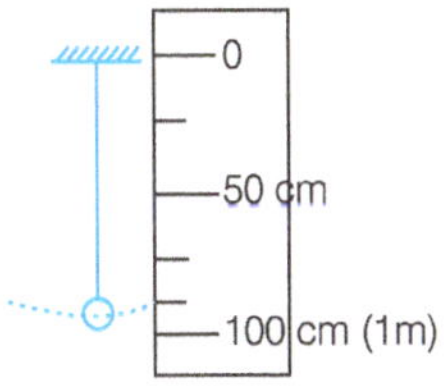

$\Rightarrow g = \frac{4\pi^2 l}{T^2}$ [from Eq. (i)]

$$= 4 \times (3.14)^2 \times \frac{0.98}{1.96 \times 1.96}$$

$$= 10.06 \text{ m/s}^2$$

Now, % error in $g = \frac{\Delta g}{g} \times 100$

$$= \left(\frac{\Delta l}{l} + \frac{2\Delta T}{T}\right) \times 100$$

$$\Rightarrow \Delta g = 10 \times \left(\frac{1}{98} + \frac{2 \times 1}{98}\right)$$

(∵ least count of meter scale is 1 cm and least count of stop watch is 1s)

$\therefore \Delta g = 0.3$ m/s^2

So, final result can be expressed as (10.1 ± 0.3) ms^{-2}

14 (*b*) As we know that

$$T \propto \frac{1}{g}$$

On an artificial satellite, orbiting the earth, net gravity is zero.

As, $g = 0$, so $T = \infty$

15 (*c*) We know that, $T = 2\pi\sqrt{\frac{l}{g}}$

Squaring both sides

$$T^2 = 4\pi^2 \frac{l}{g}$$

$$l = \frac{g}{4\pi^2} T^2 \quad \text{...(i)}$$

Take, $m = \frac{g}{4\pi^2}$ and $T^2 = x$

So, Eq. (i) becomes

$l = mx$

Comparing it with the straight line equation, $y = mx$.

So, the graph between the length and the square of the time period of a simple pendulum is a straight line.

16 (*b*)

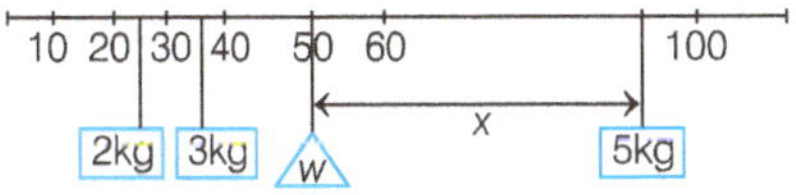

The anticlockwise moments due to 2 kg and 3 kg are

= (2 kg wt) (50 − 25) cm + (3 kg wt) (50 − 35) cm

$= 2 \times 25 + 3 \times 15 = 95$ kg wt cm

The clockwise moment due to 5 kg

= 5 kg wt × x cm

$95 = 5 \times x$

$x = 19$ cm

So, the 5 kg mass must be hung at (50 cm + x cm)

$= 50 + 19$

= 69 cm mark to balance the scale.

17 (c)

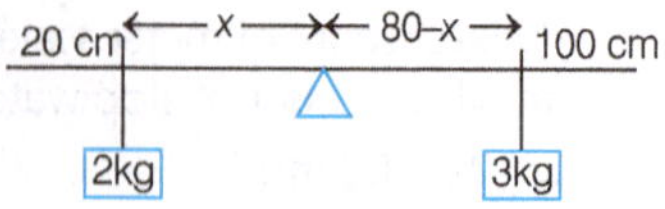

Balancing moments

$$2 \times x = 3(80 - x)$$
$$2x = 240 - 3x$$
$$5x = 240$$
$$x = 48 \text{ cm}$$

So, fulcrum is at $20 + 48 = 68$ cm mark.

18 (a) Given, $Y_{max} = 60$ cm

$$X_{min} = 15 \text{ cm}$$
$$m = 4 \text{ kg}$$

Then, from $m = M\left(\frac{Y}{X}\right)$

$$m_{max} = M\left(\frac{Y_{max}}{X_{min}}\right)$$
$$m_{max} = 4 \times \left(\frac{60}{15}\right)$$
$$m_{max} = 16 \text{ kg}$$

19 (b) m is at x from wedge and M is at distance y from wedge.

For equilibrium,

$$mg \cdot x = Mg \cdot y$$

i.e., $mx = My$

Given $m > M$, hence x has to be lowest than y

$\therefore \quad x < y$

20 (c) We know that,

$$\tau = F \cdot r \sin \theta$$

For τ_{max}, $\sin \theta$ will be 1.

$$\sin \theta = 1$$
$$\sin \theta = \sin 90°$$
$$\theta = 90°$$
$$\tau_{max} = F \cdot r$$

21 (a) Let, ρ and σ be the density of the liquid and material of the load, respectively.

In first case, the extension in the wire is

$$x = \frac{Mg}{K} = V\rho g / K \quad ...(i)$$

When the load is immersed in the liquid, Weight of the load = upthrust + internal force due to extension in wire

$$V\rho g = V\sigma g + Kx_1$$
$$x_1 = \frac{Vg(\rho - 6)}{K} \quad ...(ii)$$

Putting the value of K from Eq. (i)

$$x_1 = \frac{Vgx}{Vg\rho}(\rho - 6)$$
$$x_1 = x\left(1 - \frac{6}{\rho}\right)$$
$$x_1 = 6\left(1 - \frac{3}{9}\right)$$
$$x_1 = \frac{6 \times 6}{9}$$
$$x_1 = 4 \text{ mm}$$

22 (b) Given,

$$L = 5 \text{ m}$$
$$Y = 1.9 \times 10^{11} \text{ N/m}^2$$
$$d = 10 \text{ cm}$$

then, $r = 5 \text{ cm} = 5 \times 10^{-2}$ m

$$m = 7 \times 10^4 \text{ kg}$$
$$F = mg$$
$$= 7 \times 10^4 \times 9.8$$

So, $\quad Y = \frac{FL}{A \cdot l}$

$$l = \frac{F \cdot L}{A \cdot Y}$$
$$l = \frac{7 \times 10^4 \times 5 \times 7 \times 9.8}{22 \times 5 \times 5 \times 10^{-4} \times 1.9 \times 10^{11}}$$
$$l = \frac{49 \times 10^4 \times 10^{-7} \times 9.8}{110 \times 1.9}$$
$$l = 2.29 \times 10^{-3} \text{ m}$$
$$l = 2.29 \text{ mm}$$

23 (a) Given,

$$L = 2 \text{ m}$$
$$r = 6 \text{ mm} = 6 \times 10^{-3} \text{ m}$$
$$F = 72\pi \text{ kN} = 72\pi \times 10^3 \text{ N}$$

(l) LC of all lengths $= 0.02$ mm

$$= 2 \times 10^{-5} \text{ m}$$
$$Y = ?$$

We know that,

$$\text{Young's modulus of wire} = \frac{\text{Stress}}{\text{Strain}}$$
$$Y = \frac{F \cdot L}{\pi r^2 \cdot l}$$
$$Y = \frac{72 \times \pi \times 2 \times 10^3}{\pi \times (6 \times 10^{-3})^2 \times 2 \times 10^{-5}}$$
$$Y = \frac{72 \times 2 \times 10^3}{36 \times 10^{-6} \times 2 \times 10^{-5}}$$
$$Y = 2 \times 10^{14} \text{ N/m}^2$$

So, the maximum value of Y that can be determined is 2×10^{14} N/m^2.

24 (d) The value of Young's modulus depends upon the nature of the material of the body and the manner in which the body is deformed.

25 (a) The breaking stress of wire depends on the material of the wire. It means two wires made of different material will have different breaking stress.

26 (b) Given,

$$s = 0.75 \text{ N/m}$$
$$\theta = 120°$$
$$\rho = 15.5 \times 10^3 \text{ kg/m}^3$$
$$g = 9.8 \text{ m/s}^2$$
$$r = 0.3 \times 10^{-3} \text{ m}$$
$$h = ?$$

We know that,

$$h = \frac{2s\cos\theta}{\rho \cdot g \cdot r}$$
$$h = \frac{2 \times 0.75 \times \cos 120°}{15.5 \times 10^3 \times 9.8 \times 0.3 \times 10^{-3}}$$
$$h = \frac{-0.75}{45.57}$$
$$h = -0.0164 \text{ m}$$
$$h = -1.6 \text{ cm}$$

27 (c) Given,

$$d = 0.4 \text{ mm}$$
$$\rho = 13.6 \times 10^3 \text{ kg/m}^3$$
$$s = 650 \times 10^{-3} \text{ N/m}$$
$$\theta = 60°$$

Mercury will start leaking when,

$$\rho gh = \frac{2s\cos\theta}{r}$$
$$h_{min} = \frac{2s\cos\theta}{\rho g r} = \frac{2s \cdot 2 \cdot \cos\theta}{\rho \cdot g \cdot d}$$

$[\because r = d/2]$

$$h_{min} = \frac{4 \times 650 \times 10^{-3} \times \cos 60°}{13.6 \times 10^3 \times 9.8 \times 0.4 \times 10^{-3}}$$

$$h_{min} = \frac{2 \times 650 \times 10^{-3}}{13.6 \times 9.8 \times 0.4}$$

$$h_{min} = 24.38 \times 10^{-3} \text{ m}$$

$$h_{min} = 0.024 \text{ m}$$

28 (*a*) Given,

$r = 0.5 \text{ mm} = 5 \times 10^{-4}$ m

$s = 0.55$ N/m

So,

Area of 27 droplets $= 27(4\pi r^2)$
$= 108\pi r^2$

When drops combine, volume remains constant.

$$\frac{4}{3}\pi R^3 = 27 \times \frac{4}{3}\pi r^3$$

$$R = 3r$$

Area of big drop $= 4\pi R^2$
$= 4\pi(3r)^2$
$= 36\pi r^2$

Loss of surface area
$= 108\pi r^2 - 36\pi r^2 = 72\pi r^2$

$\therefore$ Loss of energy = Loss of surface area × Surface tension
$= 72 \times 3.14 \times (5 \times 10^{-4})^2 \times 0.55$
$= 3108.60 \times 10^{-8}$
$= 31.08 \times 10^{-6}$

So, loss of energy $= 31.1\ \mu$J

29 (*b*) When a liquid does not wet the walls of a vessel, it suggest that the adhesive forces between the liquid and the surface are weaker than the cohesive forces between the liquid molecules i.e., cohesive forces are larger than adhesive forces.

30 (*c*) The rise in water is given by,

$$h = \frac{2T \cos \theta}{rdg}$$

$$h \propto \frac{1}{r}$$

So, the smaller the radius or diameter of the tube, the greater the rise in water.

31 (*b*) Given,

$d = 4$ mm

$r = 2 \text{ mm} = 2 \times 10^{-3}$ m

$\sigma = 980 \text{ kg/m}^3$

$\eta = 1.78 \text{ Ns/m}^2$

$\rho = 7980 \text{ kg/m}^3$

$v_t = ?$

We know that,

$$v_t = \frac{2}{9} \cdot \frac{r^2(\rho - \sigma)}{\eta} \cdot g$$

$$= \frac{2}{9} \cdot \frac{4 \times 10^{-6}(7980 - 980) \cdot (9.8)}{1.78}$$

$$= \frac{2}{9} \cdot \frac{4 \times 9.8 \times 10^{-6} \times 7 \times 10^3}{1.78}$$

$$= \frac{548.8 \times 10^{-3}}{16.02}$$

$$= 34.25 \times 10^{-3}$$

$$v_t = 3.4 \times 10^{-2} \text{ m/s}$$

32 (*c*) Given,

distance $= 30 \text{ cm} = 30 \times 10^{-2}$ m,

time = 15 s

Velocity of steel ball,

$$v_t = \frac{30 \times 10^{-2}}{15} = 2 \times 10^{-2} \text{ m},$$

$\rho = 9.8 \times 10^3 \text{ kg/m}^3$,

$\sigma = 2.2 \times 10^3 \text{ kg/m}^3$,

$d = 5$ mm,

$r = 2.5 \times 10^{-3}$ m.

The viscosity of glycerine

$$\eta = \frac{2}{9} \frac{r^2(\rho - \sigma)g}{v_t}$$

$$\eta = \frac{2}{9} \times \frac{(2.5 \times 10^{-3})^2 (9.8 - 2.2) \times 10^3 \times 9.8}{2 \times 10^{-2}}$$

$$\eta = \frac{2}{9} \times \frac{(2.5)^2 \times 10^{-6} \times 7.6 \times 10^3 \times 9.8}{2 \times 10^{-2}}$$

$$\eta = \frac{186.2 \times 10^{-3} \times 2.5}{9 \times 10^{-2}}$$

$$\eta = 20.6 \times 10^{-1} \times 2.5$$

$\eta = 5.172$ SI unit

$\eta = 51.72 \approx 52$ poise

33 (*d*) As, $v_t \propto r^2$ ...(i)

$v_t = 3$ m/s

Let, r be the radius, of small raindrops and R is the radius of large drop.

Equating the volume, we have

$$\frac{4}{3}\pi R^3 = 3\left(\frac{4}{3}\pi r^3\right)$$

$$\frac{R}{r} = 3^{1/3}$$

From Eq. (i),

$$\therefore \quad \frac{v_t'}{v_t} = \left(\frac{R}{r}\right)^2$$

$$v_t' = \left(\frac{R}{r}\right)^2 \cdot v_t$$

$$v_t' = \left(3^{\frac{1}{3}}\right)^2 \cdot 3$$

$$v_t' = 3^{\frac{2}{3}} \cdot 3$$

$$v_t' = 3^{\frac{5}{3}}$$

$v_t' = 6.19$ m/s

$v_t' = 6.2$ m/s

34 (*b*) With the increase in temperature, the coefficient of viscosity of fluid decreases. This happens due to the weakening of bonds between the molecules. Because of its dash pot coefficient, the flow attains peak deformation.

35 (*b*) Sea water is denser than river due to the addition of salt. Density of a substance is defined as the mass per unit volume.

36 (*b*) Given, $v = 276$ m/s

Height of tube = 125 cm

Frequency $\nu = 300$ Hz

So, for resonance,

$$\nu = \frac{nv}{4L}, \text{ where } n = 1, 3, 5, \ldots$$

$$\text{or } L = \frac{nv}{4\nu} m = \frac{nv}{4\nu} \times 100 \text{ cm}$$

$$L = n \cdot \frac{276}{4 \times 300} \times 100 = 23 \cdot n$$

So, L = 23, 69, 115 cm, 161 cm

[For n = 1, 3, 5, 7 ..]

Height of water column $= (125 - L)$

$\Rightarrow$ 102 cm, 56 cm, 10 cm, – 36 × cm

So, the minimum height of water is 8 cm.

37 (a) Due to jagged end,

$$\frac{v}{4(15-x)\times 10^{-2}}=1500 \quad ...(i)$$

$$\frac{v}{4(30-x)\times 10^{-2}}=500 \quad ...(ii)$$

From Eq. (i) and (ii),

$$\frac{v}{4(15-x)\times 10^{-2}}=\frac{3v}{4(30-x)\times 10^{-2}}$$

$$3(15-x)=(30-x)$$

$$45-3x=30-x$$

$$2x=15$$

$$x=7.5 \text{ cm}$$

From Eq. (ii),

$$\frac{v}{4(30-7.5)\times 10^{-2}}=500$$

$$v=20\times 22.5$$

∴Velocity of sound in air,

$$v=450 \text{ m/s}$$

38 (c) Maximum percentage error in measurement of e, as given by Rayleigh's formula.

(Given, error in measurement of radius is 0.1 cm)

$\Delta e=0.6\,\Delta R=0.6\times 0.1=0.06$ cm

Percentage error is

$$\frac{\Delta e}{e}\times 100=\frac{0.06}{0.6\times 3}\times 100=3.33\%$$

End correction obtained in the experiment,

$$e=\frac{l_2-3l_1}{2}=\frac{14.0-3\times 4.6}{2}$$

$$=0.1 \text{ cm}$$

So, percentage error in the calculation of e with respect to theoretical value. Percentage error

$$=\frac{0.6\times 3-0.1}{0.6\times 3}\times 100$$

$$=94.44\%\simeq 94\%$$

39 (c) Loudness $\propto$ (amplitude)^2

the loudness of sound waves does not depend on the frequency of the sound waves.

40 (a) Frequency $(f)=\frac{(2n-1)\cdot v}{4L}$,

where, $n=0, 1, 2, 3, ...$

For the above formula of the frequency, the frequency is inversely proportional to the length of the air column.

When the length of a closed air column is increased, then the frequency will decrease.

41 (d) Let,

specific heat of solid is S_s and

specific heat of water is S_w

By principle of calorimetry,

$$Q_{given}=Q_{used}$$

$$150\times S_s\times(45°-30°)=150\times S_w \times(90°-45°)$$

$$S_s\times 15=S_w\times 45$$

$$S_s=3\times S_w$$

$S_s=$ three times of specific heat of water

42 (b) Let S be the specific heat of aluminium

Heat capacity of water $=1$ cal/g°C

By principle of calorimetry,

$$Q_{given}=Q_{used}$$

$$\underset{(gm)}{300}\times S\times(160°-60°)=160\times 1\times(60-27)+\underset{(gm)}{40}\times 1\times(60-27)$$

$$S\times 300\times 100=160\times 33+40\times 33$$

$$S=\frac{33\times 200}{300\times 100}=\frac{22}{100}$$

$$S=.220 \text{ cal/g°C}$$

$$S=.220\times 10^3\times 4.2 \text{ J/kg-°C}$$

$$S=924 \text{ J/kg°C}$$

43 (c) By applying calorimetry method, we get

Heat gain = Heat lost

$$C_A(16-12)=C_B(19-16)$$

$$\Rightarrow \frac{C_A}{C_B}=\frac{3}{4}$$

and $C_B(23-19)=C_C(28-23)$

$$\Rightarrow \frac{C_B}{C_C}=\frac{5}{4}$$

$$\Rightarrow \frac{C_A}{C_C}=\frac{C_A}{C_B}\times\frac{C_B}{C_C}$$

$$=\frac{3}{4}\times\frac{5}{4}=\frac{15}{16} \quad ...(i)$$

If θ is the temperature when A and C are mixed, then

$$C_A(\theta-12)=C_C(28-\theta)$$

$$\Rightarrow \frac{C_A}{C_C}=\frac{28-\theta}{\theta-12} \quad ...(ii)$$

On solving Eqs. (i) and (ii), we have

$$\frac{28-\theta}{\theta-12}=\frac{15}{16}$$

$$\Rightarrow 448-16\theta=15\theta-180$$

$$\therefore \quad \theta\approx 20.2° \text{ C}$$

44 (b) The sum of the heat of an individual body will always be equal to the total amount of heat, unless the heat energy is not transformed into another form of energy.

45 (b) When water is sprinkled over a large area, the evaporation of the water takes place when the water evaporates, it absorbs the heat from the surroundings because the latent heat of vaporisation is large for water.

46 (c) $\because \frac{R}{X}=\frac{l}{100-l}$

So, $X=\frac{R(100-l)}{l}$

So, $X_1=\frac{1000(100-55)}{55}$

$$=\frac{1000\times 45}{55}=818.18\,\Omega$$

$$X_2=\frac{100(100-11)}{11}$$

$$=\frac{100\times 89}{11}=809.09\,\Omega$$

$$X_3=\frac{10(100-1.2)}{1.2}$$

$$=\frac{10\times 98.8}{1.2}$$

$$=823.33\,\Omega$$

$$X_4=\frac{1(100-1)}{1}=\frac{1\times 99}{1}=99\,\Omega$$

So, 99 Ω is inconsistent.

47 (a) $\frac{P}{45}=\frac{Q}{55}$ ...(i)

On shunting Q with 50 Ω, the resistance of the arm containing Q comes down, so length also must shorten to keep the ratio same.

$$\frac{P}{45+5}=\frac{\frac{50Q}{50+Q}}{(55-5)}$$

$$\frac{P}{50}=\frac{50Q}{(50+Q)\cdot 50}$$

$$P=\frac{50Q}{(50+Q)} \quad \text{...(ii)}$$

Solving Eqs. (i) and (ii), we get

$$P=\frac{100}{11}\Omega$$

$$Q=\frac{100}{9}\Omega$$

48 (c)

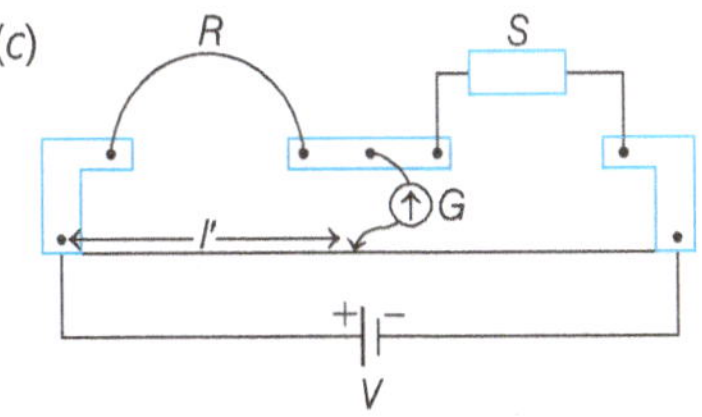

Given, balance length, $l=25$ cm

At balance point, $\frac{R}{l}=\frac{S}{100-l}$

$$\Rightarrow \quad \frac{R}{25}=\frac{S}{75}$$

$$\Rightarrow \quad R=\frac{S}{3}\Omega \quad \text{...(i)}$$

When R is replaced by some other resistance of half length and half diameter, then resistance in left gap,

$$R'=\frac{\rho\frac{l}{2}}{\frac{\pi}{4}\left(\frac{d}{2}\right)^2}=2\left\{\frac{\rho l}{(\pi d^2)}\right\}$$

$\Rightarrow R'=2R$

Now, if balance is obtained at length l', then

$$\frac{R'}{l'}=\frac{S}{(100-l')}$$

$$\Rightarrow \frac{2R}{l'}=\frac{S}{100-l'}$$

Substituting the value of S from Eq. (i), we get

$$\frac{2R}{l'}=\frac{3R}{100-l'}$$

$\Rightarrow 200-2l'=3l'$ or $l'=40$ cm

49 (c) $\frac{Q}{P}=\frac{(100-l)}{l}$

Also, $\frac{P}{Q}=\frac{R}{S}$

$$S=\frac{(100-l)}{l}\cdot R$$

Here, S is unknown resistance that can be measured with the help of the meter bridge.

50 (c) The balance point of the meter bridge is independent of the radius of the wire. Hence, the balancing length will not get affected.

51 (a) The net resistance of the circuit is

$$R=3+3+\frac{4\times 12}{12+4}=6+3$$

$$R=9\Omega$$

Given, $V=45$ V

So, $\quad i=\frac{V}{R}=\frac{45}{9}$

$$i=5\text{ A}$$

Voltage across 12Ω

$R=3\Omega$

(net resistance across AB)

$$V_{12}=i\cdot R=5\times 3$$

$$V_{12}=15\text{ V}$$

So, current on 12Ω

$$i_{12}=\frac{V}{R}$$

$$i_{12}=\frac{15}{12}$$

$$i_{12}=1.25\text{ A}$$

52 (c) We know that

$$R=\frac{\rho\cdot l}{A}$$

Taking log both sides

$$\ln R=\ln\rho+\ln l-\ln A$$

$$\frac{dR}{R}=0+\frac{dl}{l}-\frac{dA}{A} \quad \text{...(i)}$$

Now, $V=l\cdot A$ and volume is constant.

Taking log both sides

$$\ln V=\ln A+\ln l$$

$$\frac{dV}{V}=\frac{dl}{l}+\frac{dA}{A}$$

$$0=\frac{dl}{l}+\frac{dA}{A} \quad \text{...(ii)}$$

[$\because$ Volume is constant]

Adding Eqs. (i) and (ii), we get

$$\frac{dR}{R}=2\frac{dl}{l} \text{ [As } n=0.2\%, dl=0.2\%]$$

$$\frac{dR}{R}=2\times 0.2\%$$

$$\frac{dR}{R}=0.4\%$$

53 (a) Using the relation,

$$R=R_0(1+\alpha T)$$

$$R_1=R_0(1+\alpha T_1)$$

$\therefore \quad 2=R_0(1+0.00145\times 100) \quad$ ...(i)

and $R_2=R_0(1+\alpha T_2)$

$\therefore \quad 3=R_0(1+0.00145\times T_2) \quad$ ...(ii)

On dividing Eq. (ii) by Eq. (i), we get

$$\frac{3}{2}=\frac{1+0.00145T_2}{1+0.00145\times 100}$$

or $\quad T_2=494.8°\text{C}=767.8\text{ K}$

54 (c) Resistivity of a wire is a constant and it depends on the type of material used.

55 (d) If V and I is non-unique, then there are more than one value for V for same I.

56 (a) For full scale deflection,

$$I_g=nk$$

$\therefore \quad I_g=50\times 5\times 10^{-4}$

$$=25\times 10^{-3}\text{ A}$$

Now, $R=\frac{V}{I_g}-G$

$$=\frac{5}{25\times 10^{-3}}-150$$

$$=\frac{1000}{5}-150$$

$$=200-150$$

$$R=50\Omega$$

57 (d) Resistance of galvanometer

$$G=\frac{\text{Current sensitivity}}{\text{Voltage sensitivity}}=\frac{20}{5}$$

$$G=4\Omega$$

Here,

$I_g=$ Full scale deflection current

$$I_g=\frac{200}{20}=10\text{ mA}$$

Here, V = Voltage to be measured

$= 200\text{ V}$

[each division reads 1 V]

So, $R = \frac{V}{I_g} - G$

$= \frac{200}{10 \times 10^{-3}} - 4$

$= 2 \times 10^4 - 4$

$R = 19996\,\Omega$

58 (*b*) A voltmeter is a device that is used to measure the potential difference between the two points in a circuit. The resistance of an ideal voltmeter is infinite.

59 (*a*) As the sensitivity, $S_i = \frac{NBA}{k}$

when the magnetic field increases, then sensitivity also increases.

60 (*d*) Image is real, because virtual image is enlarged.

$\therefore \quad \frac{1}{v} - \frac{1}{u} = \frac{1}{f}$

$\Rightarrow \quad \frac{1}{\frac{x}{4}} + \frac{1}{x} = \frac{1}{30} \qquad (\because u = -x)$

$\Rightarrow \quad \frac{5}{x} = \frac{1}{30}$

$\Rightarrow \quad x = 150\text{ cm}$

61 (*d*) For concave lens

$\frac{1}{v} - \frac{1}{u} = \frac{1}{f}$

or $\quad \frac{u}{v} - 1 = \frac{u}{f}$

or $\quad \left(\frac{1}{n} - 1\right) = \frac{u}{f}$

$\left[\because \frac{v}{u} = n\text{ (given)}\right]$

$\therefore \quad u = \left(\frac{1-n}{n}\right) f$

62 (*a*) $x = -u + v$

$m = \frac{f}{(f+u)} = \frac{(f-v)}{f}$

For real image, m is negative

$\therefore \quad -m = \frac{f}{(f+u)}$

$\Rightarrow -mf - mu = f$

$\Rightarrow \quad u = \frac{-(m+1)}{m} f$

and $\quad -m = \frac{(f-v)}{f}$

$\Rightarrow \quad -mf = f - v$

$\Rightarrow \quad v = (m+1) f$

$\therefore \quad x = (m+1) f + \frac{(m+1)}{m} f$

$\Rightarrow \quad f = \frac{mx}{(m+1)^2}$

63 (*b*) Given, $v = 50$ cm, $u = 20$ cm

Since, the image is virtual, it will be formed on the same side of the object.

From lens formula

$\frac{1}{f} = \frac{1}{v} - \frac{1}{u}$

$\frac{1}{f} = \frac{1}{-50} - \frac{1}{-20}$

$\frac{1}{f} = \frac{3}{100}$

$f = \frac{100}{3}\text{ cm}$

64 (*c*) Parallax is removed when object needle is at focus of the lens. On refraction through convex lens, rays are rendered parallel. They fall normally on the plane mirror and retrace their path after reflection. The image of the object is formed at infinity. That is why parallax is removed.

65 (*c*) Light should fall normally on the silvered face, i.e.,

$r_2 = 0$

$\therefore \quad r_1 = A = 30°$

$\mu = \frac{\sin i_1}{\sin r_1}$

$\Rightarrow \sqrt{2} = \frac{\sin i_1}{\sin 30°}$

Angle of incidence, $i_1 = 45°$

66 (*a*) Angle i at both faces will be 45°.

For TIR to take place,

$i > \theta_C$ or $\sin i > \sin \theta_C$

$\therefore \quad \frac{1}{\sqrt{2}} > \frac{1}{\mu} \quad \Rightarrow \quad \mu > \sqrt{2}$

67 (*a*) Given,

$i = e = \frac{3}{4} A = \frac{3}{4} \times 60° = 45°$

In the position of minimum deviation,

$2i = A + \delta_m$

$\delta_m = 2i - A$

$= 2 \times 45° - 60° = 30°$

68 (*d*) $\mu = \frac{\sin \frac{(A+\delta_m)}{2}}{\sin \frac{A}{2}} = \frac{\sin \frac{(60+30)}{2}}{\sin\left(\frac{60}{2}\right)}$

$= \frac{\sin 45°}{\sin 30°} = \frac{0.7070}{0.5000} = 1.414$

Now, velocity of light in glass $= \frac{c_{air}}{\mu}$

$\Rightarrow c_g = \frac{3 \times 10^8\text{ m/s}}{1.414}$

$= 2.121 \times 10^8$ m/s

69 (*b*) Given, angle of prism, $A = 60°$

Angle of incidence, i = Angle of emergence e,

$e = \frac{2}{3} A$

As, $\delta = i + e - A$

$\delta = e + e - A$

$\delta = 2e - A$

$\delta = \frac{2 \times 2}{3} A - A$

$\delta = \left(\frac{4-3}{3}\right) A$

$\delta = \frac{A}{3} = \frac{60}{3} = 20°$

70 (*c*) We need to calculate at least three readings to calculate real thickness as well as apparent thickness.

Therefore, we need at least three readings for the experiment.

71 (*b*) We assume that, final image is formed at infinity and

$M_\infty = \frac{(L_\infty - f_o - f_e) \cdot D}{f_o f_e} = \frac{LD}{f_o f_e}$

$400 = \frac{20 \times 25}{0.5 \times f_e}$

$\therefore \quad f_e = 2.5\text{ cm}$

72 (*a*) If an experiment is performed to find the refractive index of glass using a travelling microscope, distances are measured by a vernier scale which is provided on the microscope.

73 (*a*) 50 VSD = 49 MSD

$$1\text{ VSD} = \frac{49}{50}\text{ MSD}$$

$$LC = 1\text{ MSD} - 1\text{ VSD}$$

$$= \left(1 - \frac{49}{50}\right)\text{MSD}$$

$$= \frac{1}{50}\text{ MSD}$$

$$1\text{ MSD} = \frac{1}{40}\text{ cm}$$

$$LC = \frac{1}{50} \times \frac{1}{40} = \frac{1}{2} \times 10^{-3}\text{ cm}$$

$$= 0.5 \times 10^{-3}\text{ cm}$$

$$= 5 \times 10^{-4}\text{ cm}$$

$$LC = 5 \times 10^{-6}\text{ m}$$

75 (*a*) In the given circuit, D_2 and D_3 are in forward bias, so they conduct current while D_1 and D_4 are in reverse bias, so they do not conduct current. So, the equivalent circuit will be

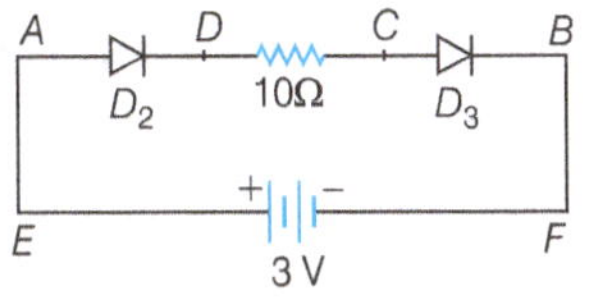

The effective resistance is

$$R_{eff} = D_2 + R + D_3$$

$$R_{eff} = 3 + 10 + 3$$

$R_{eff} = 16\,\Omega$ [$\because$ D_2 and D_3 is given]

Here, silicon diodes are used.

$\therefore$ Barrier potential for Si is 0.7 V.

Net potential $(V_{net}) = 3 - 0.7 - 0.7$

$$V_{net} = 1.6\text{ V}$$

$$\therefore \text{ Current } (I) = \frac{V_{net}}{R_{eff}}$$

$$I = \frac{1.6}{16} \Rightarrow I = 0.1\text{ A}$$

76 (*b*) In ideal condition, a forward biased *p-n* junction acts like a conductive path of zero resistance.

So, given circuit is equivalent to circuit shown below.

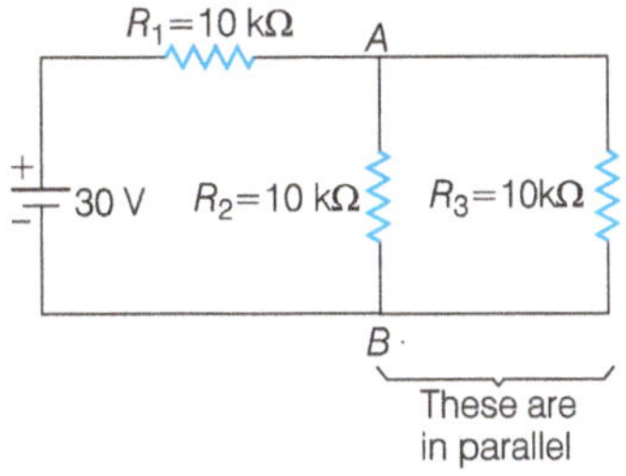

Total resistance of circuit,

$R = (R_3$ is parallel with $R_2)$

and these are in series with R_1

$$= \frac{10 \times 10}{10 + 10} + 10 = 15\text{ k}\Omega$$

So, total current in the circuit,

$$I = \frac{V}{R} = \frac{30\text{ V}}{15\text{ k}\Omega} = 2 \times 10^{-3}\text{ A}$$

So, total resistance across AB,

$$R_{AB} = 5\text{ k}\Omega$$

$$V_{AB} = I \cdot R_{AB}$$

$$V_{AB} = 2 \times 10^{-3} \times 5 \times 10^3 = 10\text{ V}$$

77 (*d*) As both diodes are in reverse bias, so given circuit is equivalent to the circuit as shown in the figure.

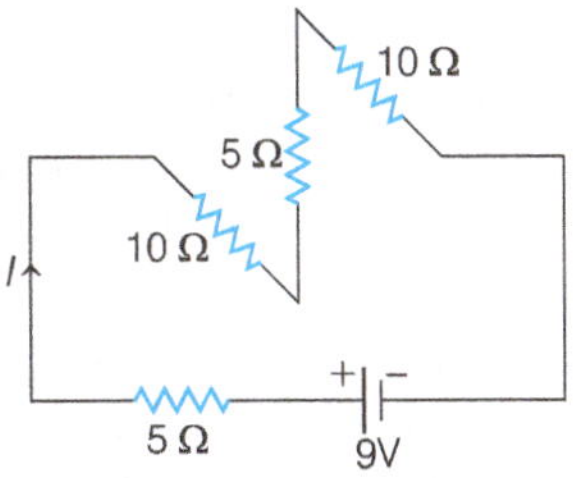

Equivalent resistance of circuit,

$$R = 5 + 10 + 5 + 10 = 30\,\Omega$$

$$\therefore \text{Circuit current, } I = \frac{V}{R} = \frac{9}{30} = 0.3\text{ A}$$

78 (*d*) In forward biasing of *p-n* junction diode, current mainly flows due to the diffusion of majority charge carriers.

79 (*b*) *p-n* junction diode conducts when the value of forward bias is more than the potential barrier.

80 (*a*)

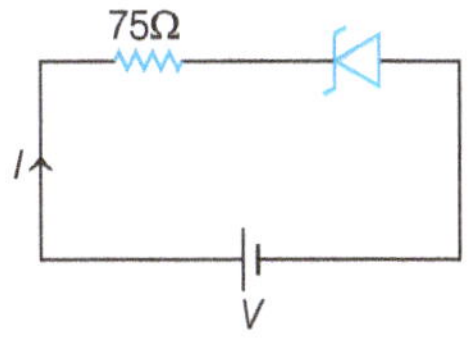

Potential drop across zener diode

$$V_Z = V - IR$$

$$V_Z = V - 75\,I$$

$\therefore$ Power $P = V_Z I_Z$

$$= (V - 75I) \cdot I$$

But, $P = 3$ W (given)

$$\therefore \quad (V - 75I) \cdot I = 3$$

$$75I^2 - VI + 3 = 0$$

For I to be real,

$$V^2 - 4 \times 75 \times 3 \geq 0$$

$$V \geq 30$$

81 (*c*) Voltage across AB is $V_Z = 9$ V

Voltage drop across R

$$= 15 - 9 = 6\text{ V}$$

Therefore, current through the resistor R_Z,

$$I = \frac{V}{R_Z} = \frac{6}{1 \times 10^3}$$

$$I = 6\text{ mA}$$

Voltage across load resistor,

$$= V_{AB} = 9\text{ V}$$

Current through load resistor,

$$I_L = \frac{V_{AB}}{R_L} = \frac{9}{2 \times 10^3} = 4.5\text{ mA}$$

So, the current through the zener diode,

$$I_Z = I - I_L$$

$$= (6 - 4.5)\text{ mA}$$

$$I_Z = 1.5\text{ mA}$$

82 (*d*) In given voltage regulator circuit, breakdown of zener occurs at 6 V.

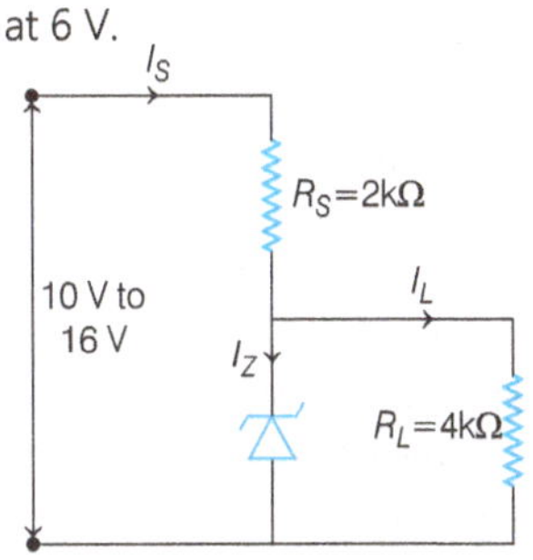

After breakdown, voltage across load resistance ($R_L = 4\ k\Omega$),

$$V = V_Z = 6\ V$$

$\therefore$ Load current after breakdown,

$$I_L = \frac{V_Z}{R_L} = \frac{6}{4000} = 1.5 \times 10^{-3}\ A$$

When unregulated supply is of 16 V, potential drop occurring across series resistance ($R_S = 2\ k\Omega$),

$$V_S = V - V_Z$$
$$= 16 - 6 = 10\ V$$

So, current across series resistance,

$$I_S = \frac{V_S}{R_S} = \frac{10}{2 \times 10^3}$$
$$= 5 \times 10^{-3}\ A$$

So, current across zener diode,

$$I_Z = I_S - I_L = 5 \times 10^{-3} - 1.5 \times 10^{-3}$$
$$= 3.5 \times 10^{-3}\ A = 3.5\ mA$$

83 (*b*) The zener diode when used as a voltage regulator is connected in reverse bias and a load is connected in parallel to zener diode for output voltage.

84 (*c*) In zener diode, depletion region between *p* and *n* becomes very narrow and the electric field is quite high.

The breakdown easily occurs in reverse biased conditions because of the narrow junctions in zener diode.

In case, we narrow the space charge region, it is obvious that with the decreased reverse voltage applied, reverse breakdown will occur.

Assertion and Reason Questions

1 (*a*) Both Assertion and Reason are correct and Reason is the correct explanation of Assertion.

The least count of vernier callipers depends on its extra-ordinary design, which helps it to make such small and precise measurements.

Also, it depends upon the pitch and the number of the vernier scale divisions present on the calliper.

$$\text{LC of VC} = \frac{\text{Pitch}}{\text{No. of VSD}}$$

2 (*c*) Assertion is correct but Reason is incorrect and it can be corrected as,

The least of standard screw gauge is less than the least count of standard vernier calliper.

3 (*c*) Assertion is correct but Reason is incorrect and it can be corrected as,

The viscosity of gases is directly proportional to the square root of temperature.

$$\eta \propto \sqrt{T}$$

4 (*b*) The intermolecular forces present in solids and liquids are stronger than that in gases. This cause the specific heat capacity of solids to be more than other forms of matter.

5 (*d*) Assertion is incorrect and it can be corrected as,

With the addition of detergent in pure water, the rise in capillary tube decreases.

This is happen because the adhesive force of water molecules towards the tube surface is increases.

6 (*d*) Focal length of mirror is a measure of the radius of curvature of the sphere from which the spherical mirror was obtained and it is totally independent of the medium in which the mirror is placed.

7 (*b*) Both Assertion and Reason are correct but correct Reason for Assertion is by increasing temperature. Flow of electrons increases which cause more heat dissipation and melts wire insulation and can produce short-circuit in the cable.

8 (*a*) In a prism with equal base angles, the deviation is minimum therefore the refracted ray becomes parallel to the base of the prism. As in the case of minimum deviation, angle of incidence is equal to the angle of emergence.

9 (*b*) Study of junction diode characteristics shows that the junction diode offers a low resistance path when forward biased and high resistance path when reverse biased. This feature of junction diode enables it to be used as a rectifier.

10 (*a*) Due to heavy doping, strong electric field exists across the barrier potential making the depletion layer thin in case of zener diode.

Statement Based Questions

1 (*d*) Zero correction = – (Zero error with its proper sign)

2 (*b*) Statement I is correct and Statement II is incorrect and it can be corrected as,

Least count of screw gauge is inversely proportional to the number of divisions on circular scale.

3 (*c*) Statement I is incorrect and it can be corrected as,

The value of *Y* does not depend upon the length or the diameter of wire. It depends on nature of the material of the wire.

4 (*d*) $h = \frac{2T}{Rdg} \Rightarrow hR = \frac{2T}{dg}$

$[\because hR = \text{constant}]$

Hence when the tube is of insufficient length, radius of curvature of the liquid meniscus increases, so as to maintain the product *hR* a finite constant.

5 (*a*) Both Statement I and Statement II are incorrect and these can be corrected as,

Viscosity of liquid decreases with rise in temperature as well as it is free from density of liquid.

6 (*d*) The nichrome or constantan wire has low temperature coefficient and high resistivity. The resistivity for constantan is 49×10^{-8} Ω-m.

7 (*b*) Statement II is incorrect and it can be corrected as,

The wavelength of wave associated with electrons is less than that of visible light.

8 (*d*) At minimum deviation,

$$r_1 = r_2 = \frac{A}{2}$$

So, $i = e$

(angle of incidence = angle of emergence)

Numerical Type Questions

1 (1.38) As, TR = MSR + $n\times$ LC

$= 1.3 + 5 \times 0.01 = 1.35$ cm

Zero error $= -0.03$ cm

Zero correction $= + 0.03$ cm

Corrected reading

$= 1.35 + 0.03 = 1.38$ cm

2 (0.87) $\therefore T = 2\pi\sqrt{\frac{l}{g}}$

So, $\frac{\Delta g}{g} = \frac{\Delta l}{l} + \frac{2\Delta T}{T}$

Therefore, $P = \left(\frac{\Delta l}{l} + \frac{2\Delta T}{T}\right) \times 100$

$$\Rightarrow P_1 = \left(\frac{0.1}{100} + \frac{2(1)}{400}\right) \times 100 = 0.6\%,$$

$$P_2 = \left(\frac{0.1}{400} + \frac{2(1)}{400}\right) \times 100 = 0.52\%$$

$$\therefore \frac{P_2}{P_1} = \frac{0.52}{0.6} = 0.87$$

3. (5) Taking moments about the point *O*,

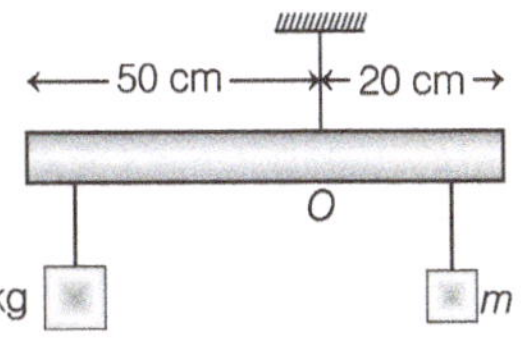

$$2g \times 0.5 = mg \times 0.2$$

$$\Rightarrow \quad m = 5 \text{ kg}$$

4. (2) Young's modulus is given by

$$Y = \frac{Fl}{A\Delta l} = \frac{mgl}{A\Delta l}$$

$$= \frac{1.5 \times 10 \times 156 \times 10^{-2}}{3.14 \times (2.7 \times 10^{-4})^2 \times 5 \times 10^{-4}}$$

$$Y = 2.002 \times 10^{-11} \text{ N/m}^2$$

So, the value of *x* is 2.

5. (14.8) Given, $h = 0.2$ mm,

$\rho = 1000$ kg/m^3

$\sigma = 0.0725$ N/m, $\theta = 0°$

The capillary rise is given by

$$h = \frac{4\sigma\cos\theta}{\rho g d}$$

$$0.2 \times 10^{-3} = \frac{4 \times 0.0725}{10^3 \times 9.81 \times d}$$

$$d = \frac{4 \times 0.0725}{0.2 \times 10^{-3} \times 10^3 \times 9.81} = 14.8 \text{ cm}$$

6. (384) $v = 2v(l_2 - l_1)$

$$= 2 \times 480 \times \frac{(70-30)}{100}$$

(convert cm in m)

$$= 2 \times 480 \times \frac{40}{100} = 384 \text{ ms}^{-1}$$

7. (0) Let θ_{mix} be the temperature of mixture and is given by

$$\theta_{mix} = \frac{m_w\theta_w - \frac{m_iL_i}{C_w}}{m_i + m_w}$$

As, $m_i = m_w$

$$\therefore \theta_{mix} = \frac{\theta_w - \frac{L_i}{C_w}}{2}$$

$$= \frac{80 + 0 - \frac{336}{4.2}}{2} = 0°\text{C}$$

8. (4) In *AC*,

$$R_{AC} = 0.1 \times 40 = 4\Omega$$

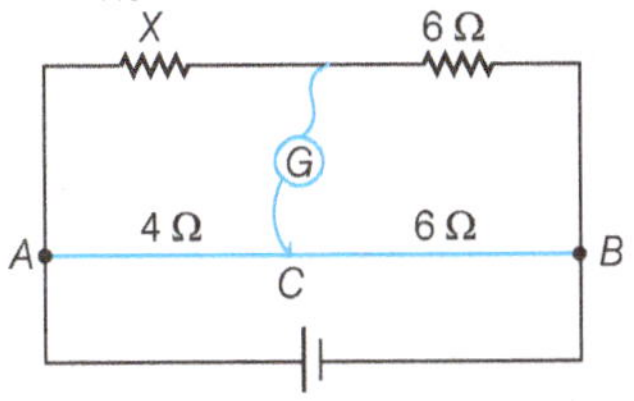

In *ABC*,

$$R_{BC} = 0.1 \times 60 = 6\Omega$$

In balanced condition,

$$\frac{X}{6} = \frac{4}{6}$$

$$\Rightarrow \quad X = 4\Omega$$

9. (3) From figure, $\angle e = \angle r_2 = 0$

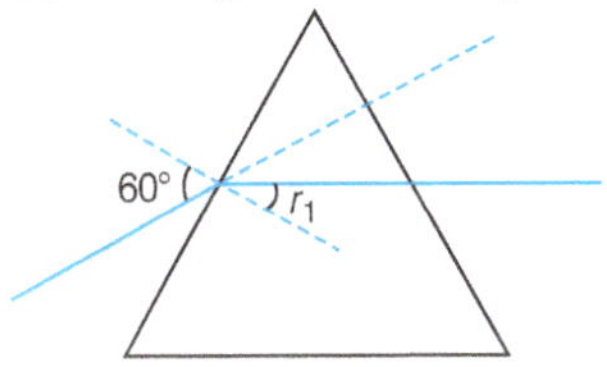

From $A = r_1 + r_2$

$$\Rightarrow \quad r_1 = A = 45°$$

$$\therefore \quad \mu = \frac{\sin i}{\sin r_1} = \frac{\sin 60°}{\sin 45°} = \sqrt{\frac{3}{2}}$$

So, according to question,

$x = 3$

10. (5) From given figure,

Voltage across $R_S = 22 - 15 = 7$ V

Current through R_S, $I = \frac{7}{35} = \frac{1}{5}$ A

Current through 90Ω,

$$I_2 = \frac{15}{90} = \frac{1}{6} \text{ A}$$

Current through zener

$$= \frac{1}{5} - \frac{1}{6} = \frac{1}{30} \text{ A}$$

Power through zener diode,

$P = VI$

$$P = 15 \times \frac{1}{30} = 0.5 \text{ W}$$

$P = 5 \times 10^{-1}$ W

$\because \quad P = x \times 10^{-1}$ W (given)

$\therefore \quad x = 5$

Past Exams Questions

1. (*b*) Let 1 MSD $= x$

According to question,

50 VSD matches with 49 MSD $= 49x$

Least count, LC $= \frac{49}{50}x$

LC = 1 MSD − 1 VSD

$$= x - \frac{49}{50}x = \frac{x}{50}$$

Zero error = MSR + VSR (LC)

$$0.04 \text{ mm} = 0 + 4\left(\frac{x}{50}\right)$$

$$\Rightarrow x = 0.5 \text{ mm}$$

Number of main scale division in 1 cm

$$= \frac{1 \text{ cm}}{0.5 \text{ mm}} = 20$$

2. (*b*) $1 \text{ MSD} = \frac{1 \text{ cm}}{20} = 0.05 \text{ cm}$

$$1 \text{ VSD} = \frac{49}{50} \text{ MSD} = \frac{49}{50} \times 0.05 \text{ cm}$$

$$= 0.049 \text{ cm}$$

$$\text{LC} = 1\text{MSD} - 1\text{VSD}$$

$$= 0.001 \text{ cm}$$

For mark on paper,

$$L_1 = 8.45 + 26 \times 0.001 \text{ cm}$$

$$= 84.76 \text{ mm}$$

For mark on paper through slab,

$$L_2 = (7.12 + 41 \times 0.001) \text{ cm}$$

$$\Rightarrow L_2 = 71.61 \text{ cm}$$

For the powder on the top of surface.

Zero error = 4.05 cm + 1 × 0.001 cm

= 40.51 mm

$\therefore$ Actual, $L_1 = 84.76 - 40.51$

= 44.25 mm

Actual, $L_2 = 71.61 - 40.51$

= 31.10 mm

$$\therefore \quad L_2 = \frac{L_1}{\mu} \Rightarrow \mu = \frac{L_1}{L_2} = \frac{44.25}{31.10} = 1.42$$

3. (*d*) Given,

$$\text{Least count} = \frac{1}{20N} \text{ cm} = \frac{10}{20N} \text{ mm}$$

1 MSD = 1 mm

Now, Least count = 1 MSD − 1 VSD

Let

x MSD = N VSD then,

$$\Rightarrow \frac{10}{20N} = 1 - \frac{x}{N} \Rightarrow \frac{1}{2N} = 1 - \frac{x}{N}$$

$$= \frac{N - x}{N}$$

$$\Rightarrow N - x = \frac{1}{2} \quad \text{or} \quad N - \frac{1}{2} = x$$

or $\quad x = \frac{2N - 1}{2}$ divisions

4. (*b*) $g = \frac{4\pi^2 l}{T^2}$

$$\frac{\Delta g}{g} = \frac{\Delta l}{l} + 2\frac{\Delta T}{T} = \frac{0.1}{10} + 2\left(\frac{\frac{1}{200}}{0.5}\right)$$

$$\frac{\Delta g}{g} = \frac{1}{100} + \frac{1}{50} \Rightarrow \frac{\Delta g}{g} \times 100 = 3\%$$

5. (*b*) Positive zero error = 0.2 mm

Main scale reading = 8.5 cm

Vernier scale reading

= 6 × 0.01 = 0.06 cm

Final reading

= 8.5 + 0.06 − 0.02 = 8.54 cm

6. (*d*) $(n-1)a = n(a')$

$$a' = \frac{(n-1)a}{n}$$

$$\therefore \quad \text{LC} = 1 \text{ MSD} - 1 \text{ VSD}$$

$$= (a - a') \text{ cm}$$

$$= a - \frac{(n-1)a}{n}$$

$$= \frac{na - na + a}{n} = \frac{a}{n} \text{ cm}$$

$$= \left(\frac{10a}{n}\right) \text{mm}$$

7. (*d*) Pitch of screw of a screw gauge

$$= \frac{\text{Distance moved by screw}}{\text{Number of rotations}}$$

$$= \frac{3 \text{ mm}}{6} = 0.5 \text{ mm}$$

and least count of screw gauge

$$= \frac{\text{Pitch}}{\text{Number of circular scale divisions}}$$

$$= \frac{0.5 \text{ mm}}{50} = 0.01 \text{ mm} = 0.001 \text{ cm}$$

8. (*c*) Given, length of pendulum, $l = 25.0$ cm, so there is an uncertainty of 0.1 cm in measurement of length.

Resolution of stop watch is 1s, so uncertainty in measurement of time is 1s.

Now using,

$$T = 2\pi\sqrt{\frac{l}{g}} \quad \text{or} \quad g = \frac{4\pi^2 l}{T^2}$$

We have, $\frac{\Delta g}{g} = \frac{\Delta l}{l} + \frac{2\Delta T}{T}$

$$\Rightarrow \frac{\Delta g}{g} \times 100\%$$

$$= \left(\frac{\Delta l}{l} + \frac{2\Delta T}{T}\right) \times 100\%$$

Accuracy in measurement of g is

$$\frac{\Delta g}{g} \times 100\% = \left(\frac{0.1}{25} + \frac{2 \times 1}{50}\right) \times 100\%$$

$$= (0.004 + 0.04) \times 100\%$$

$$= 4.40\%$$

Skill Boosters

1. (*c*) Velocity of ball after falling a distance h, $v = \sqrt{2gh}$

Terminal velocity of ball in water tank,

$$v_T = \frac{2}{9}\frac{r^2(\rho - \sigma)g}{\eta}$$

where, ρ = density of ball and σ = density of water.

Now, according to question,

$$\sqrt{2gh} = \frac{2}{9}\frac{r^2(\rho - \sigma)g}{\eta}$$

$$\Rightarrow \quad h \propto r^4 \Rightarrow r \propto h^{\frac{1}{4}}$$

2. (*b*)

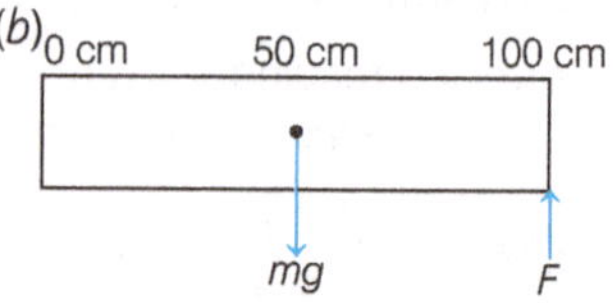

For system to be in equilibrium, $\Sigma M = 0$

On applying moment about 0 cm point, we get

$$mg \times 50 = F \times 100$$

$$F = \frac{mg}{2} \quad (\text{Take, } g = 10 \text{ m/s}^2)$$

$$= \frac{2 \times 10}{2} = 10 \text{ N}$$

3. (*d*) Force constant of the wire,

$$k = \frac{F}{\Delta L} = \frac{F}{FL/AY} = \frac{YA}{L}$$

$$\omega = \sqrt{\frac{k}{m}} = \sqrt{\frac{YA}{Lm}}$$

$$\therefore \quad \sqrt{\frac{YA}{Lm}} = 140$$

$$\Rightarrow \frac{Y \times 4.9 \times 10^{-7}}{1 \times 0.1} = 140 \times 140$$

$$Y = \frac{140 \times 140}{49 \times 10^{-7}} = 4 \times 10^{9}$$

4. (a) The pressure of the water changes linearly with the increase in height. At the bottom of the meniscus, it is equal to the external atmospheric pressure p_0 and at the top, it is equal to $p_0 - \rho gh$. The average pressure exerted on the wall is $p_{av} = p_0 - \frac{\rho gh}{2}$. The force corresponding to this value, for an aquarium with side walls of length L is $F_1 = Lh\,p_{av}$

or $F_1 = Lh\left(p_0 - \frac{\rho gh}{2}\right)$

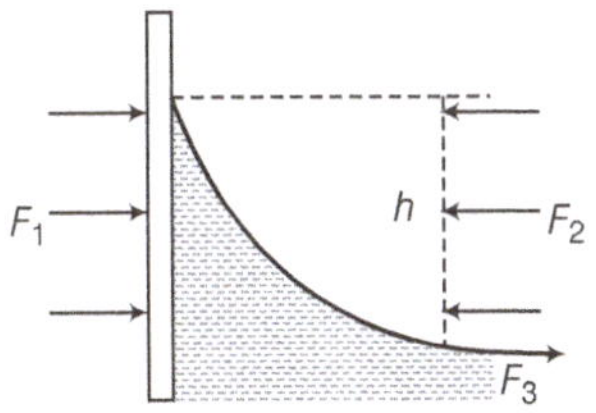

Consider the horizontal forces acting on the volume of water enclosed by the dashed lines in the figure. F_1 is towards right. (F_1 is by the wall). External air pushes it to the left with a force $F_2 = p_0 Lh$ and due to surface tension along a line of length L, a force $F_3 = LT$ acts towards right due to remaining water.

The volume itself is at rest.

$\therefore \quad F_1 + F_3 - F_2 = 0$

$$Lh\left(p_0 - \frac{\rho gh}{2}\right) + LT - p_0 Lh = 0$$

$$\frac{\rho gh^2 L}{2} = LT$$

$$\Rightarrow \quad h = \sqrt{\frac{2T}{\rho g}}$$

$$\text{or} \quad h = \sqrt{\frac{2 \times 0.073}{1000 \times 9.8}}$$

$$= 0.00386\text{m} \simeq 4\text{mm}$$

5. (c) $\therefore$ We know that,

$$(I - I_g)S = I_g \cdot G$$

$$\therefore \quad I = \left(\frac{G+S}{S}\right) \cdot I_g$$

Therefore, $4 = \left(\frac{60+R}{R}\right) 0.04$

$$100R = 60 + R$$

$$R = \frac{60}{99}\,\Omega$$

Further, $R = \frac{\rho \cdot l}{A}$

$$l = \frac{R \cdot A}{\rho} = \frac{3.5 \times 10^{-2} \times 10^{-4} \times 60}{6 \times 10^{-7} \times 99}$$

$$= l = \frac{35 \times 10^{-6} \times 10^{7}}{99}$$

$$l = 3.5\text{ m}$$

6. (c) Since, ray goes without deviation,

$\therefore \quad n_1 = n_2$

or $\quad 1.2 + \frac{10.8 \times 10^4}{\lambda^2} = 1.45 + \frac{1.80 \times 10^4}{\lambda^2}$

$\Rightarrow \lambda = 600\text{ nm}$

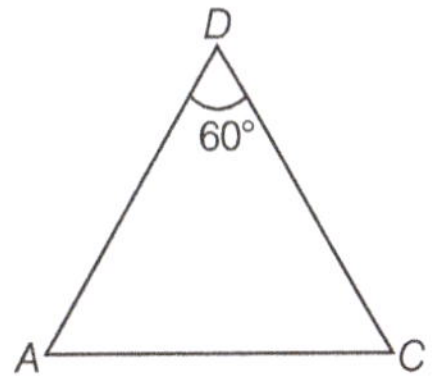

Here, $\mu = 1.2 + \frac{10.8 \times 10^4}{600 \times 600}$

$$= 1.2 + 0.3 = 1.5$$

For minimum deviation, $i = i'$, $r = r'$

But $r + r' = A = 60°$

$\therefore \quad r = 30°$

$\therefore 1 \times \sin i = \mu \sin r$

$$\sin i = 1.5 \times \frac{1}{2} = \left(\frac{3}{4}\right)$$

$$\therefore \quad i = \sin^{-1}\left(\frac{3}{4}\right)$$

7. (c) **Case I** Diode is in reversed bias,

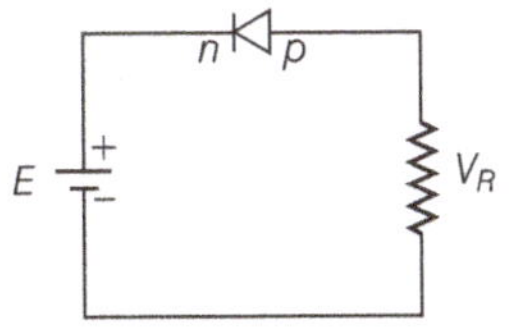

$E - V_D - V_R = 0$ (by Kirchhoff's law)

$$V_D = E - V_R$$

$$V_R = 0 \text{ or } I = 0$$

$$V_D = E = 8\text{ V}$$

Case II Diode is in forward bias, since the diode is around knee voltage = 0.7 V

So, ratio $= \frac{8}{0.7} = \frac{80}{7}$

8. (c) Heat received by ice

$= mL + mC\,\Delta T = 10700$ cal

Heat given by container, then

$$= -\int_{500}^{300} m_c(A + BT)\,dT$$

$$= -m_C\left[AT + \frac{BT^2}{2}\right]_{500}^{300}$$

$$= 21600\,m_C$$

Heat lost = Heat gained

$\therefore 10700 = 21600\,m_C$

$$\Rightarrow m_C = \frac{10700}{21600} \approx 0.495 \approx 0.5\text{kg}$$

Also, heat lost by container $\approx 0.5 \times 21600 \approx 10800$ cal

9. (b)

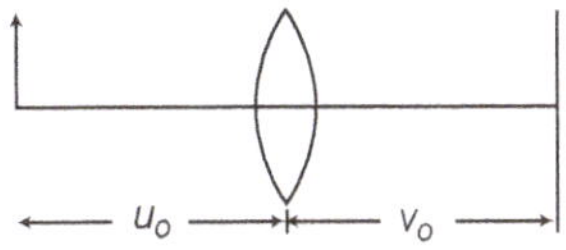

Here, $u_o + v_o = 180$ and $\frac{v_o}{u_o} = 2$

$\therefore \quad v_o = 2u_o$

$\because \; u_o + v_o = 180$

or $\quad u_o + 2u_o = 180$

$\therefore \quad u_o = 60$ cm

and $\quad v_o = +120$ cm

$\because \; \frac{1}{v} - \frac{1}{u} = \frac{1}{f}$

or $\quad \frac{1}{120} + \frac{1}{60} = \frac{1}{f}$

or $\quad \frac{1+2}{120} = \frac{1}{f}$

$\therefore \quad f = \frac{120}{3} = 40$ cm

$$f = \frac{D^2 - x^2}{4D} = \frac{180^2 - x^2}{4 \times 180}$$

or $40 = \frac{180^2 - x^2}{720}$

or $x^2 = 180^2 - 40 \times 720$

$\therefore \quad x = 60$ cm

Chapter at a Glance

Completely Coloured Glorified Infographics to map all the Key points of the chapters for quick review.

Electric Charges and Fields (Chapter at a Glance)

Basic Property of Charge

- **Additivity**
The total charge of a system is the algebraic sum of all the individual charges located at different points inside the system. If a system contain charges $q_1, q_2, ... q_n$, then its total charge is
$q = q_1 + q_2 + ... + q_n$
- **Quantization of electric charge**
The total charge (q) of a body is always an integral multiple of a basic quantum of charge (e), i.e.,
$q = \pm ne$ where, $n = 1, 2, 3 ...$
- **Conservation of Charge**
The law of conservation of charge states that
(i) The total charge of an isolated system remains constant.
(ii) The electric charge can neither be created nor destroyed, they can only be transferred from one body to another.

Conductors and Insulators

- **Conductors** The substances through which electric charges can flow easily are called conductors.
Examples Metals, human and animal bodies, graphite, acids, etc. are conductors.
- **Insulators** The substances through which electric charges cannot flow easily are called insulators.
Examples Most of the non-metals like glass, diamond, plastic, wood, nylon, etc. are insulators.

Electric Charge

Electric charge is an intrinsic property of elementary particles of matter which gives rise to electric force between various objects. It is a scalar quantity. Its SI unit is coulomb (C).

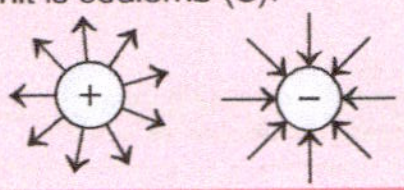

Line Charge Distribution

The line charge density at any point on this line as the charge per unit length of the line at that point, i.e.,

$$\lambda = \frac{dq}{dL}$$

The SI unit for λ is $C\text{-}m^{-1}$.

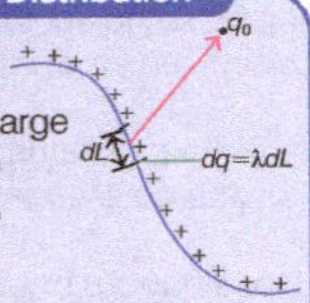

Surface Charge Density

It is a charge distribution spread over a two-dimensional surface S in space, as shown in figure. We define the surface charge density at any point on this surface as the charge per unit area at that point, i.e.,

$$\sigma = \frac{dq}{dS}$$

The SI unit for σ is $C\text{-}m^{-2}$.

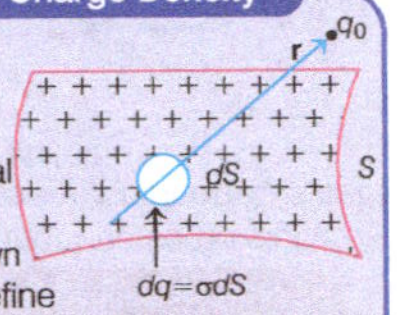

Volume Charge Distribution

It is a charge distribution spread over a three dimensional volume or region V of space as shown in figure. We define the volume charge density at any point in this volume as the charge contained per unit volume at that point, i.e., $\rho = \frac{dq}{dV}$

The SI unit for ρ is coulomb per cubic metre ($C\text{-}m^{-3}$).

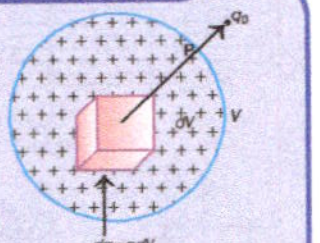

Gauss's Theorem

The total flux through a closed surface is $1/\varepsilon_0$ times the net charge enclosed by the closed surface.
Mathematically, it can be expressed as

$$\phi_E = \oint_S \mathbf{E}.d\mathbf{S} = \frac{q}{\varepsilon_0}$$

Electric Flux

The total number of electric lines of force passing normally through that area.
If an electric field **E** passes normally through an area element ΔS, then the electric flux through this area is $\Delta \phi_E = E\Delta S$

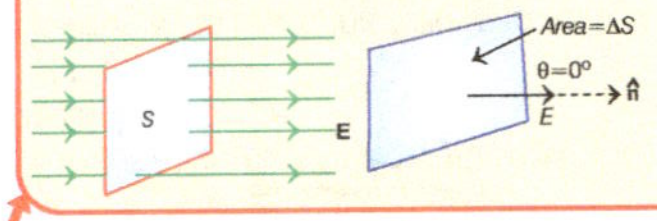

Field Due to an Infinitely Long Charged Wire

Consider a thin infinitely long straight wire having a uniform linear charge density (i.e., charge per unit length) λ. This wire is symmetrical about linear axis.

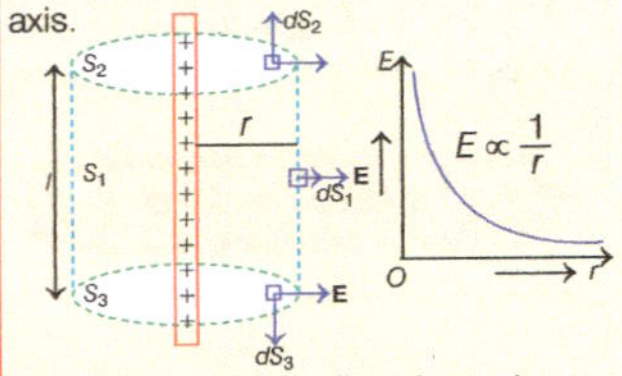

The electric field of a line charge is inversely proportional to the distance from the line charge.
Vectorially, $\mathbf{E} = \frac{\lambda}{2\pi\varepsilon_0 r}\hat{\mathbf{n}}$

Uniformly Charged Infinite Plane Sheet

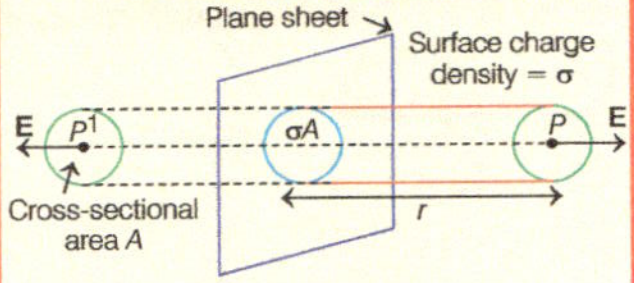

According to Gauss's theorem,

$$2EA = \frac{\sigma A}{\varepsilon_0} \text{ or } E = \frac{\sigma}{2\varepsilon_0}$$

$\therefore$ Vector form, $\mathbf{E} = \frac{\sigma}{2\varepsilon_0}\hat{\mathbf{n}}$

where, $\hat{\mathbf{n}}$ is the unit vector normal to the plane and going away from it.

Uniformly Charged Thin Spherical Shell

For spherical shell, $E = \frac{1}{4\pi\varepsilon_0}\cdot\frac{q}{r^2}$

Vectorially form, $\mathbf{E} = \frac{q}{4\pi r^2}\hat{\mathbf{r}}$

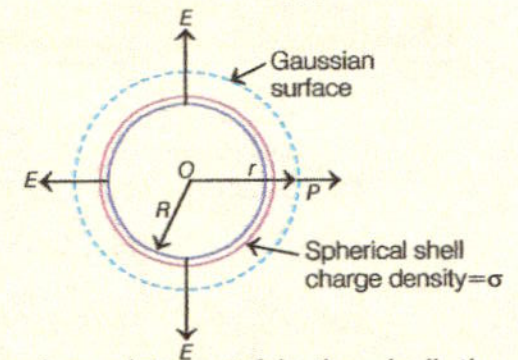

Hence, for points outside the shell, the field due to a uniformly charged shell is as if the entire charge of the shell is concentrated at its centre.

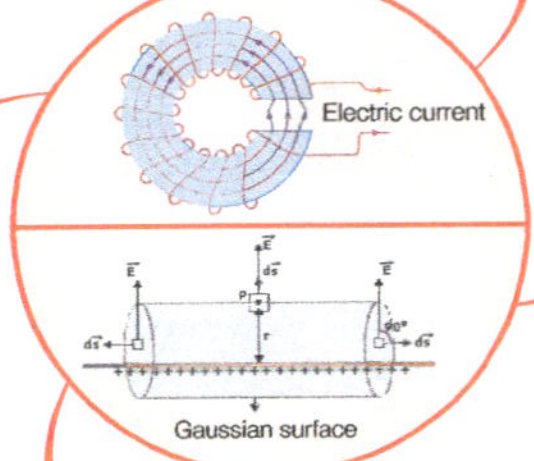

Coulomb's Law

If two statonary point charges q_1 and q_2 are kept at a distance r, then force of attraction or repulsion between them is

$$F \propto \frac{q_1q_2}{r^2} \Rightarrow F = \frac{1}{4\pi\varepsilon_0}\cdot\frac{q_1q_2}{r^2} \text{ Newton}$$

Vector form of Coulomb's law

$$\mathbf{F}_{12} = \frac{1}{4\pi\varepsilon_0}\cdot\frac{q_1q_2}{r^2}\mathbf{r}_{21} \text{ for like charges}$$

$$\mathbf{F}_{21} = \frac{q_1q_2}{4\pi\varepsilon_0 r^2}\mathbf{r}_{12} \text{ for like charges}$$

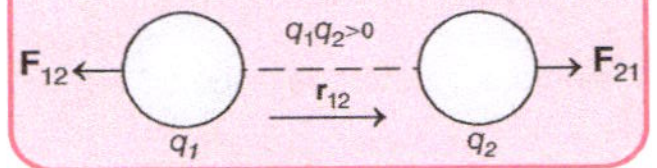

Electric Field

The electric field intensity at any point is defined as the force experienced by a unit positive charge placed at that point.

$$E = \frac{F}{q_0} = \frac{kq}{r^2}$$

$$\text{SI unit} = \frac{\text{Newton}}{\text{Coulomb}} = \frac{\text{volt}}{\text{meter}}$$

Dimension : $[E] = [MLT^{-3} A^{-1}]$

Basic Characteristics

- Fields lines start from positive charge and end at negative charges.
- Electrostatic fields lines do not form any closed loops.
- Two fields lines can never cross each other.

Electric Dipole

Every dipole is associate with a dipole moment **p** whose magnitude is equal to the product of the magnitude of either charge (q) and the distance $2a$ between the charges, i.e., $\mathbf{p} = q \times (2a)$

Torque

- **Uniform Electric Field**

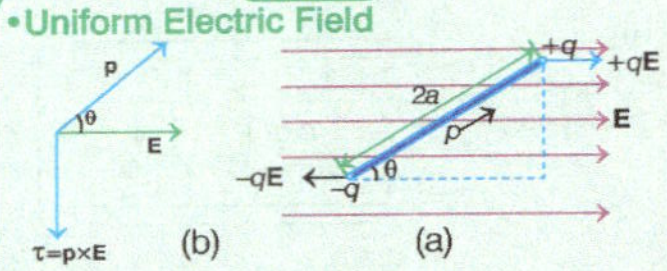

(a) Direction of torque as given by right hand screw rule.
The torque on the dipole will be maximum when the dipole is held perpendicular to **E**.
Thus,
$\tau_{max} = pE \sin 90° = pE$

- **Non-Uniform Electric Field**

In a non-uniform electric field, the $+q$ and $-q$ charges of a dipole experience different forces (not equal and opposite) at slightly different positions in the field and hence, a net force acts on the dipole in a non-uniform field. Also, a net torque acts on the dipole which depends on the location of the dipole in the non-uniform field.

$$\tau = \mathbf{p} \times \mathbf{E}(\mathbf{r})$$

The Superposition Principle

When a number of charges are interacting, the total force on a given charge is the vector sum of the force exerted on it due to all other charges. The force between two charges is not affected by the presence of other charge.
The total force on charge q_1 is given by

$$\mathbf{F}_1 = \mathbf{F}_{12} + \mathbf{F}_{13} + ... + \mathbf{F}_{1N}$$

Equatorial Point

The direction of electric field at any point on the equatorial line will be anti-parallel to the dipole moment **p**.

$$\mathbf{E}_{eq} = -\frac{1}{4\pi\varepsilon_0}\cdot\frac{p}{r^3}\cdot\hat{\mathbf{p}}$$

At general point,

$$E_{eq} = \frac{1}{4\pi\varepsilon_0}\cdot\frac{p}{r^3}\sqrt{3\cos^2\theta + 1}$$

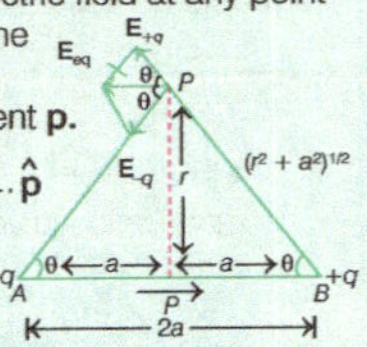

Axial Point

Electric field at any axial point of the dipole acts along the dipole axis from negative to positive charge i.e., in the direction of dipole moment **p**.

$$\mathbf{E}_{axial} = \frac{1}{4\pi\varepsilon_0}\cdot\frac{2p}{r^3}\cdot\hat{\mathbf{p}}$$

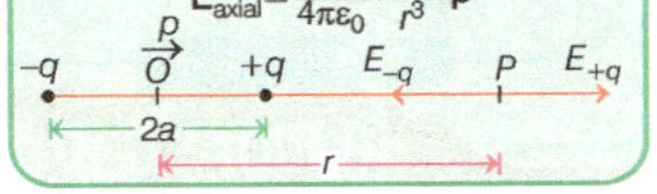

Electrostatic Potiential and Capacitance (Chapter at a Glance)

Torque acting on Dipole

The torque will be given as
$\tau = qE \times 2a \sin\theta = pE \sin\theta$
where, $q \times 2a = p$, is the dipole moment.

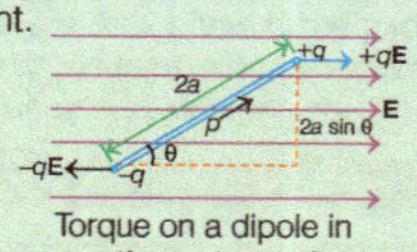

Torque on a dipole in a uniform electric field.

∴ The potential energy of the dipole will be

$$PE = -pE\cos\theta = -\mathbf{p}\cdot\mathbf{E}$$

At an Axial Point

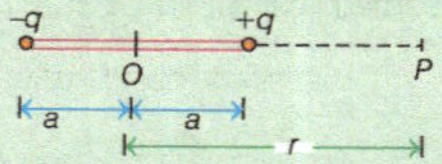

Potential at an axial point of a dipole.

$$V = \frac{1}{4\pi\varepsilon_0}\cdot\frac{p}{r^2}$$

At an Equatorial Point

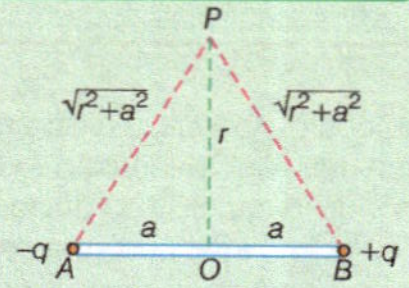

Electric potential at point P due to the dipole is

$$V = V_1 + V_2 = \frac{1}{4\pi\varepsilon_0}\cdot\frac{-q}{AP} + \frac{1}{4\pi\varepsilon_0}\cdot\frac{q}{BP}$$

$$= -\frac{1}{4\pi\varepsilon_0}\cdot\frac{q}{\sqrt{r^2+a^2}} + \frac{1}{4\pi\varepsilon_0}\cdot\frac{q}{\sqrt{r^2+a^2}} = 0$$

At any General Point

$$\therefore V = \frac{1}{4\pi\varepsilon_0}\cdot\frac{p\cos\theta}{r^2}$$

$$V = \frac{1}{4\pi\varepsilon_0}\cdot\frac{\mathbf{p}\cdot\mathbf{r}}{r^3} = \frac{1}{4\pi\varepsilon_0}\frac{\mathbf{p}\cdot\hat{\mathbf{r}}}{r^2}$$

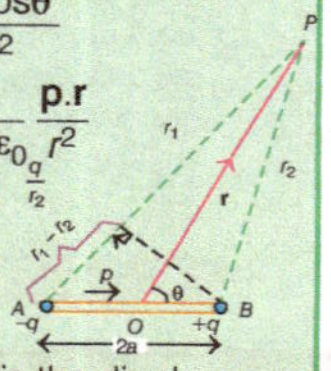

Here, $p = q \times 2a$, is the dipole moment and $\hat{\mathbf{r}} = \mathbf{r}/r$, is a unit vector along the positive vector $\mathbf{OP} = \mathbf{r}$

Uniformly Charged Thin Spherical Shell

Consider a uniformly charged spherical shell of radius R and carrying charge q.

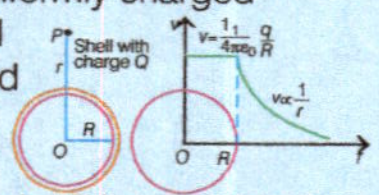

(i) When the point P lies outside the shell,

$$V = \frac{1}{4\pi\varepsilon_0}\frac{q}{r}\ [r > R]$$

(ii) When point P lies on the surface of the shell,

$$V = \frac{1}{4\pi\varepsilon_0}\frac{q}{R}\ [r = R]$$

(iii) When point P lies inside the shell,

$$V = \frac{1}{4\pi\varepsilon_0}\frac{q}{R}\ [r < R]$$

Potential Difference

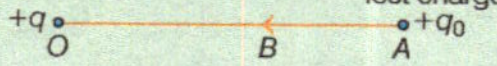

Potential difference between points A and B $\quad V = V_B - V_A = \dfrac{W_{AB}}{q_0}$

The SI unit of potential difference is volt (V).

A System of Charges

Potential at a point due to a system of N point charges.

$$V = \frac{1}{4\pi\varepsilon_0}\sum_{i=1}^{N}\frac{q_i}{r_i}$$

The electric potential at a point whose position vector is $\mathbf{r}$, would be

$$V = \frac{1}{4\pi\varepsilon_0}\sum_{i=1}^{N}\frac{q_i}{|\mathbf{r}-\mathbf{r}_i|}$$

Potential Energy of System of Charges

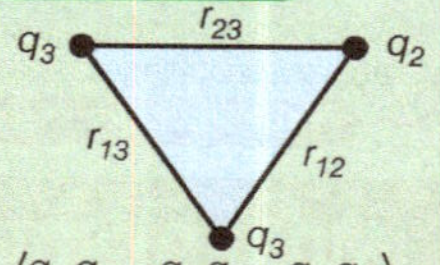

$$U = \frac{1}{4\pi\varepsilon_0}\left(\frac{q_1 q_2}{r_{12}} + \frac{q_1 q_3}{r_{13}} + \frac{q_2 q_3}{r_{23}}\right)$$

Point Charge

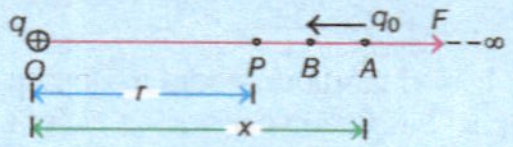

Electric potential due to a point charge at point P.

$$V = \frac{W}{q_0} \text{ or } V = \frac{1}{4\pi\varepsilon_0}\cdot\frac{q}{r}$$

Electric Potential

The electric potential at a point located far away from a charge is taken to be zero.
Electric potential $= \dfrac{\text{Work done}}{\text{Charge}}$

The SI unit of electric potential is volt (V).

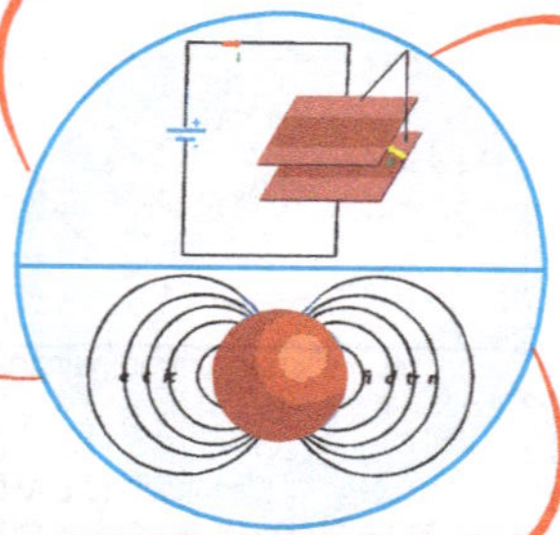

Equipotential Surface and their Properties

Any surface that has same electric potential at every point on it, is called an equipotential surface.

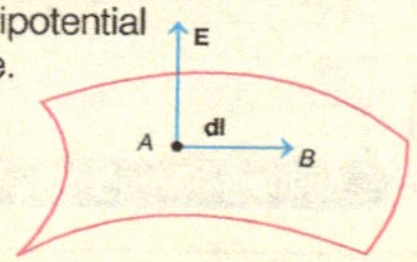

Properties

1. No work is done in moving a test charge.
2. Electric field is always normal to the equipotential surface at every point.
3. Equipotential surfaces are closer together in the regions of strong field and farther apart in the regions of weak fields.
4. No two equipotential surfaces can intersect each other.

Dielectric Slab

The capacitance of the capacitor on introduction of dielectric slab becomes,

$$C = \frac{Q}{V} = \frac{\varepsilon_0 A}{\left(d - t + \frac{t}{k}\right)}$$

t= thickness, k= dielectric constant

A Conducting Slab

Capacitance of the capacitor in the presence of conducting slab becomes,

$$C = \left(\frac{d}{d-t}\right)\cdot C_0$$

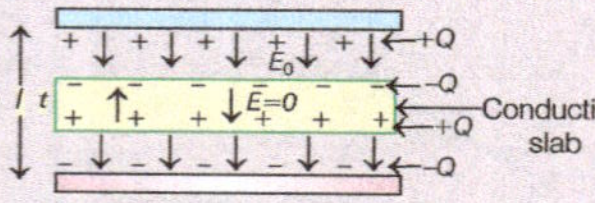

Capacitance

The measure of its ability to hold electric charge.
$Q \propto V$ or $Q = CV$
It depends upon the following factors:
1. Size and shape of the conductor.
2. Nature (permittivity) of the surrounding medium.
3. Presence of the other conductors in its neighbourhood.

Various Charge Systems

(i) Equipotential surfaces of a positive point charge.

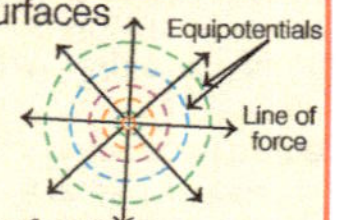

(ii) Equipotential surfaces of two equal and opposite point charges.

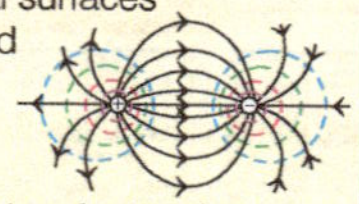

(iii) Equipotential surfaces of two equal positive charges.

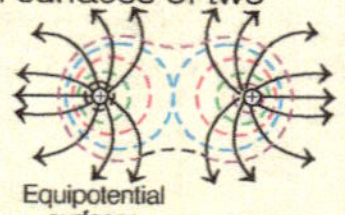

(iv) The lines of force are parallel straight lines and equipotential surfaces are equidistant parallel planes perpendicular to the lines of force.

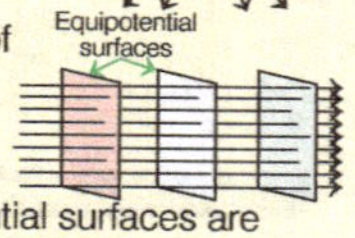

Air filled Parallel Plate Capacitor

$$C_0 = \frac{A\varepsilon_0}{d}$$

- **Energy density of capacitor**

$$u = \frac{U}{V} = \frac{1}{2}\varepsilon_0 E^2$$

- **Energy stored in a capacitor**

$$U = \frac{1}{2}CV^2 = \frac{1}{2}QV = \frac{1}{2}\frac{Q^2}{C}$$

Parallel Plate Capacitor

The simplest and the most widely used capacitor is the parallel plate capacitor. It consists of two large plane parallel conducting plates separated by a small distance.

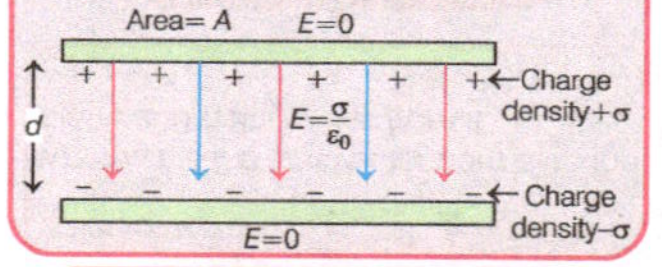

Combination of Capacitors in Series and in Parallel

Capacitors in series

$$\frac{1}{C_s} = \frac{1}{C_1} + \frac{1}{C_2} + \ldots + \frac{1}{C_n}$$

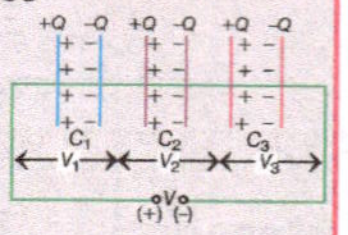

Capacitors in parallel

$$C_p = C_1 + C_2 + \ldots + C_n$$

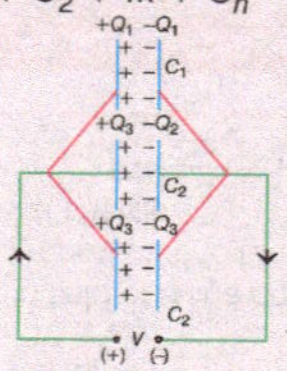

Capacitance of an Isolated Spherical Capacitor

The potential at any point on the surface of the spherical conductor will be

$$V = \frac{1}{4\pi\varepsilon_0}\cdot\frac{Q}{R}$$

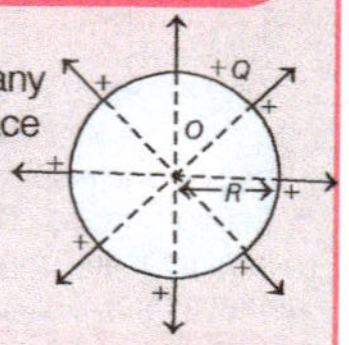

$$C = \frac{Q}{V} = \frac{Q}{\left(\frac{1}{4\pi\varepsilon_0}\cdot\frac{Q}{R}\right)} = 4\pi\varepsilon_0 R$$

Current Electricity (Chapter at a Glance)

Conductivity

The reciprocal of the resistivity of a material is called its conductivity and is denoted by σ.

$$\text{Conductivity} = \frac{1}{\text{Resistivity}}$$

$$\sigma = \frac{1}{\rho}$$

Conductance

The conductance of a conductor is the ease with which electric charges flow through it. It is equal to the reciprocal of its resistance and is denoted by G.

$$\text{Conductance} = \frac{1}{\text{Resistance}}$$

$$G = \frac{1}{R}$$

Current Density

The amount of charge flowing per second through a unit area held normal to the direction of the flow of charge at that point. $j = I/A$

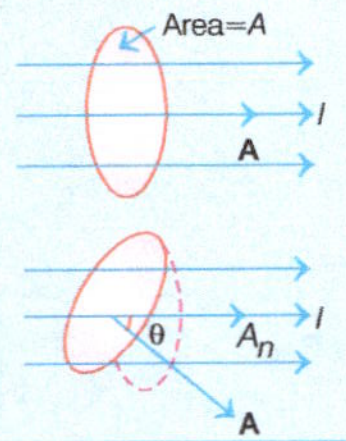

Cells in Series

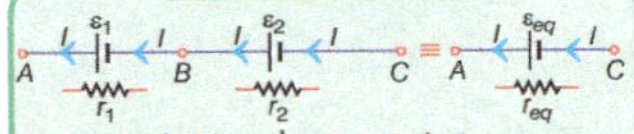

$\varepsilon_{eq} = \varepsilon_1 + \varepsilon_2$ and $r_{eq} = r_1 + r_2$

Cells in Parallel

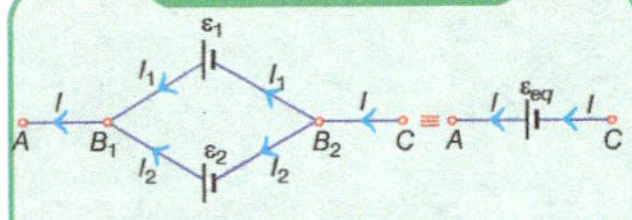

$$\varepsilon_{eq} = \frac{\varepsilon_1 r_2 + \varepsilon_2 r_1}{r_1 + r_2} \quad \text{and}$$

$$r_{eq} = \frac{r_1 r_2}{r_1 + r_2}$$

Carriers of Current

In Solids The electric current is due to the drift of electrons from low to high potential regions. In *n*-type semiconductors, electrons are the majority charge carriers while in *p*-type, holes are the majority charge carriers.

In liquids In electrolytic liquids, the charge carriers are positively and negatively charged ions.

Example $CuSO_4$ solution has Cu^{2+} and SO_4^{2-} ions, which act as the charge carriers.

In gases In ionised gases, positive and negative ions and electrons are the charge carriers.

Electric Conductance

The reciprocal of resistance is called electric conductance.

Its SI unit is mho or ohm^{-1} (Ω^{-1}).

Dimensions of electric conductance are $[M^{-1}L^{-2}T^3A^2]$.

Electric Current

The flow of electric charges through a conductor constitutes an electric current.

$$\text{Electric current} = \frac{\text{Electric charge}}{\text{Time}} \quad \text{or } I = \frac{Q}{t}$$

Electromotive Force : EMF

The work done by the source in taking a unit positive charge from lower to the higher potential. SI unit of emf is volt.

$$\text{emf} = \frac{\text{Work done}}{\text{Charge}} \text{ or } \varepsilon = \frac{W}{q}$$

Potential Difference of a Cell

The potential drop across the terminals of a cell when a current is being drawn from it is called its **terminal potential difference** (V).

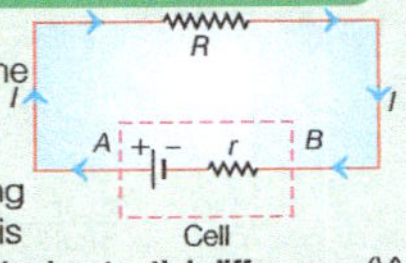

Terminal PD=emf – potential drop across the internal resistance

$$r = \frac{\varepsilon - V}{I} = \frac{\varepsilon - V}{V/R} = \left(\frac{\varepsilon - V}{V}\right)R$$

Special Cases

(i) When cell is an open circuit, i.e. I=0, we have $V_{open} = \varepsilon$

(ii) A real cell has always some internal resistance r, so when current is being drawn from cell, we have $V < \varepsilon$.

Mobility of Charge Carriers

Conductivity of any material is due to its mobile charge carriers.

These may be electrons in metals, positive and negative ions in electrolytes; and electrons and holes in semiconductors.

SI unit of mobility = $m^2 V^{-1} s^{-1}$

$$\text{Mobility, } \mu = \frac{v_d}{E} = \frac{e\tau}{m}$$

Drift Velocity

The average velocity gained by the free electrons of a conductor in the opposite direction of the externally applied electric field is called drift velocity.

$$\mathbf{v}_d = \mathbf{a}\tau = -\frac{e\mathbf{E}\tau}{m}$$

$\therefore \mathbf{v}_d$ is called drift velocity.

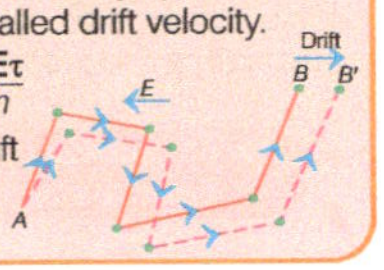

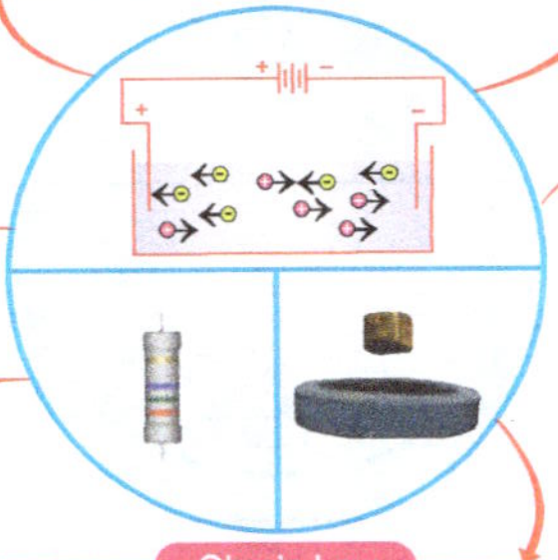

Ohm's Law

The current flowing through a conductor is directly proportional to the potential difference applied across its ends, provided the temperature and other physical conditions remain unchanged.

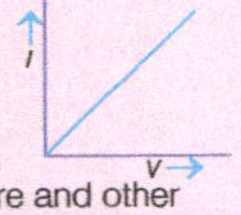

$$I \propto V \Rightarrow V = IR$$

Ohmic Conductors

The conductors which obey Ohm's law are called ohmic conductor.

Thus the V-I graph for Ohmic conductor is a straight line passing through the origin.

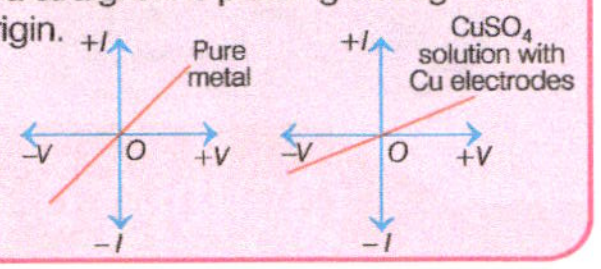

Metre Bridge

It is the simplest practical application of the wheatstone bridge that is used to measure an unknown resistance.

$$S = R\left(\frac{100 - l}{l}\right)$$

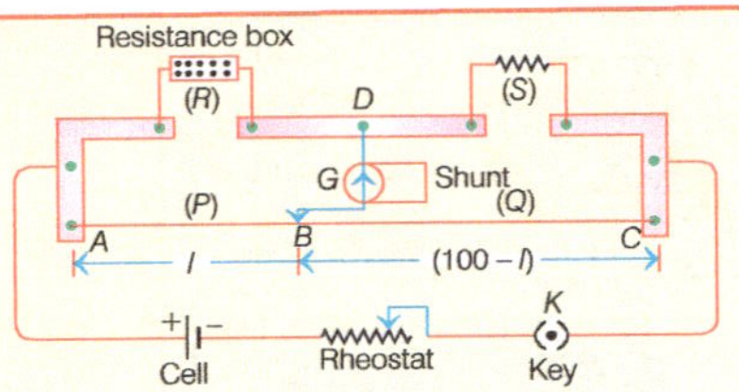

Wheatstone Bridge

It is an arrangement of four resistances used to determine one of these resistances quickly and accurately in terms of the remaining three resistances.

$$\frac{P}{Q} = \frac{R}{S}$$

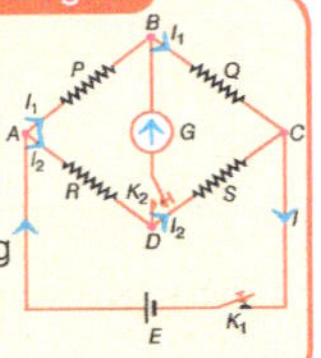

Kirchhoff's First Law or Junction Rule

In an electric circuit, the algebraic sum of currents at any junction is zero.

$\Sigma I = 0$

$I_2 = I_1 + I_3 + I_4 + I_5$

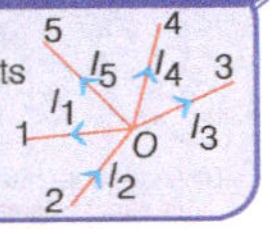

Meissener Effect

The expulsion of the magnetic flux from a superconducting material when it is cooled to a temperature below the critical temperature in a magnetic field is called Meissner effect.

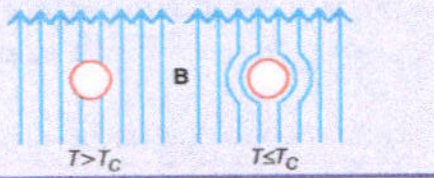

Resistance

The resistance of a conductor is the property by virtue of which it opposes the flow of charges through it. SI unit of resistance is ohm. $R = \frac{V}{I}$

Non-ohmic Conductors

The conductors which do not obey ohm's law are called non-ohmic conductors.

The V-I graph does not pass through the origin.

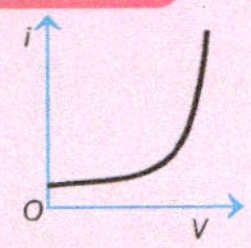

V-I relationship is non-linear.

V-I relationship is non-unique.

V-I relationship depends on the sign of V for the same absolute value of V.

Kirchhoff's Second Law or Loop Rule

The algebraic sum of the emf's in any loop of a circuit is equal to the sum of the product of currents and resistances in it.

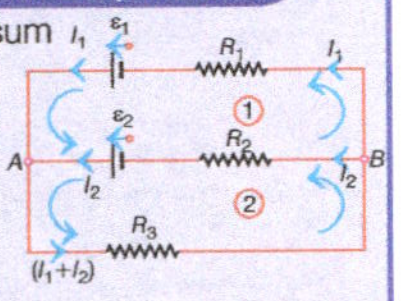

$$\Sigma \Delta V = 0 \text{ or } \Sigma\varepsilon = \Sigma IR$$

Resistivity of Specific Resistance

The resistance of a conductor of that material having unit length and unit area of cross-section or, it is the resistance offered by the unit cube of the material of a conductor.

Temperature Dependence of Resistivity

The resistivity of any material depends on the number density n of free electrons and the mean collision time τ.

$$\rho = \frac{m}{ne^2\tau}$$

The resistivity of a metal ($\rho \propto 1/\tau$) increases and the conductivity decreases with the increase in temperature.

$$\alpha = \frac{\rho - \rho_0}{\rho_0(T - T_0)} = \frac{1}{\rho_0} \cdot \frac{d\rho}{dT}$$

Factors Affecting the Resistance

- **Length** The resistance R of a conductor is directly proportional to its length. i.e. $R \propto l$
- **Area of cross-section** The resistance R of a uniform conductor is inversely proportional to its area of cross-section A. i.e. $$R \propto \frac{l}{A}$$
- **Nature of the material** The resistance of a conductor also depends on the nature of its material. $$R = \rho\frac{l}{A}$$

Moving Charges and Magnetism (Chapter at a Glance)

Magnetic Field

- **At the Centre of Circular Current Loop**

$B = \frac{\mu_0 I}{2r}$

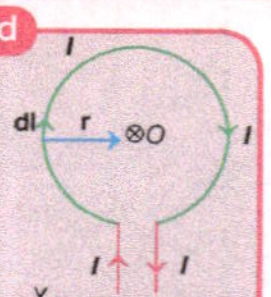

- **A Long Straight Current Carrying Conductor**

$B = \frac{\mu_0 I}{4\pi a}[\sin\phi_1 + \sin\phi_2]$

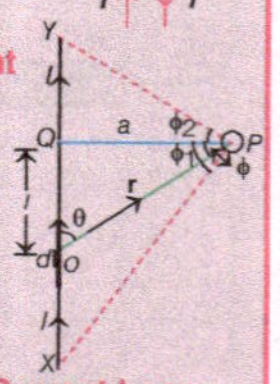

- **The Axis of a Circular Current Loop**

Field **B** at an axial point *P* at a distance from the centre *C*.

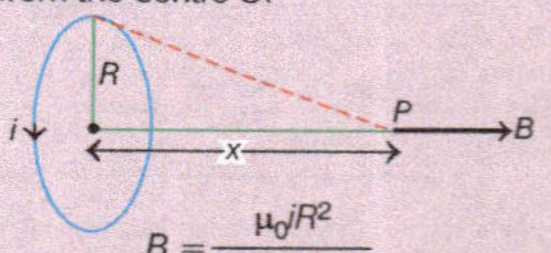

$B = \frac{\mu_0 I R^2}{2(x^2+R^2)^{3/2}}$

- **A Long Straight Wire**

$\therefore B = \frac{\mu_0 I}{2\pi r}$

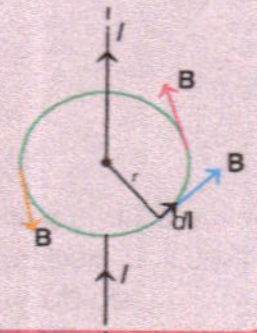

Biot-Savart Law

The magnetic field d**B** at a point *P* due to a length element d**s** that carries a steady current *I* is

$d\mathbf{B} = \frac{\mu_0}{4\pi}\cdot\frac{Idl\sin\theta}{r^2}$

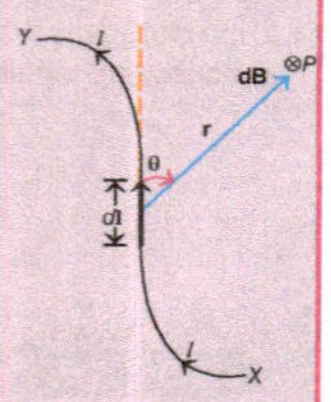

Ampere's Circuital Law

The line integral of the magnetic field **B** around any closed path is equal to μ_0 (permeability constant) times the current *I* threading or passing through this closed path.

$\oint \mathbf{B}.d\mathbf{l} = \mu_0 I$

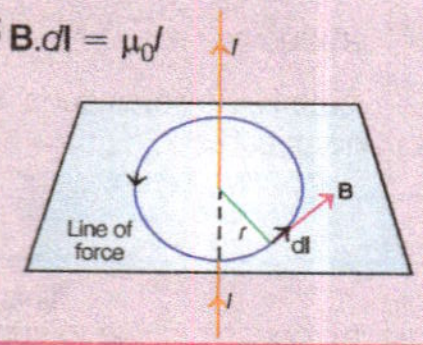

Magnetic Field of a Finite Solenoid

The polarity of any end of the solenoid can be determind by using clock rule or Ampere's right hand rule.

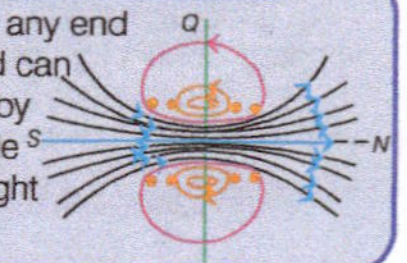

Magnetic Field Inside a Straight Solenoid

A solenoid means an insulated copper wire wound closely in the form of a helix. By a long solenoid, we mean that the length of the solenoid is very large as compared to its diameter.

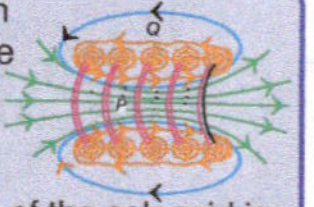

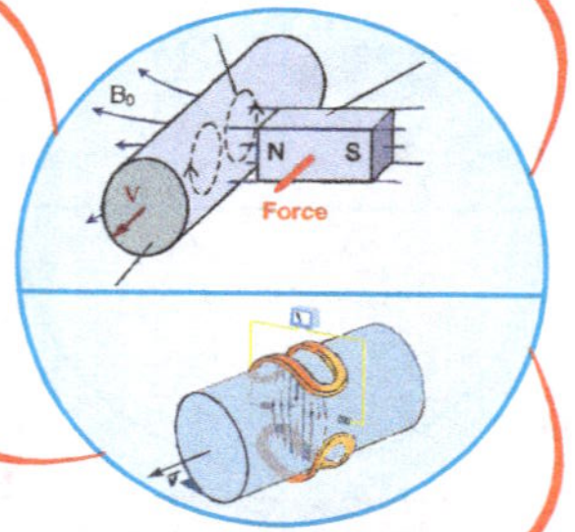

Moving Coil Galvanometer

A galvanometer is a device to detect current in a circuit. The commonly used moving coil galvanometer is named so because it uses a current-carrying coil that rotates (or moves) in a magnetic field due to the torque acting on it.

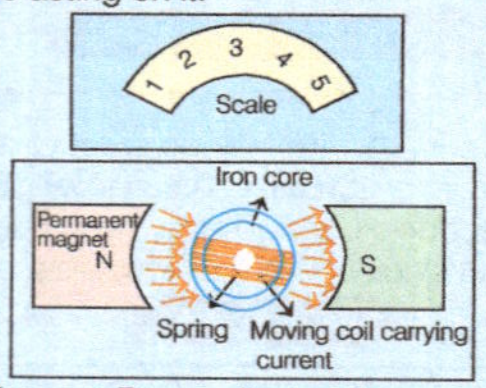

τ = Force × Perpendicular distance = *NIBA*

$\tau_{restoring} \propto \alpha$ or $\tau_{restoring} = k\,\alpha$

where *k* is the torsion constant of the springs.

Restoring torque = Deflecting torque

$k\,\alpha = NIBA$

Also, $I = \frac{k}{NBA}\cdot\alpha = G\,\alpha$

Right Hand Thumb Rule

If we hold the straight conductor in the grip of our right hand in such a way that the extended thumb points in the direction of current, then the direction of the curl of the fingers will give the direction of the magnetic field.

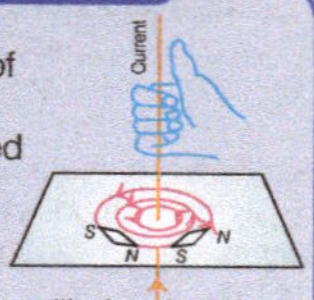

Shunt

A low resistance which is connected in parallel with a galvanometer (or ammeter) to protect, if from strong currents.

Uses of Shunt

1. To prevent a galvanometer from being damaged due to large current.
2. To convert a galvanometer into ammeter.
3. To increase the range of an ammeter.

Sensitivity of a Galvanometer

Current Sensitivity

$I_s = \frac{\alpha}{I} = \frac{NBA}{k}$

Voltage Sensitivity

$V_s = \frac{\alpha}{V} = \frac{\alpha}{IR} = \frac{NBA}{kR}$

Voltage sensitivity $= \frac{\text{Current sensitivity}}{R}$

Motion of a Charge in Perpendicular Magnetic and Electric Fields

A beam of charged particles, say electrons, possessing a range of speeds passes through a slit S_1 and then enters a region in which crossed electric and magnetic field exist. The electric field **E** acts in the downward direction and deflects the electrons in the upward direction. The magnetic field **B** acts normally into the plane of paper and deflects the electrons in the downward direction.

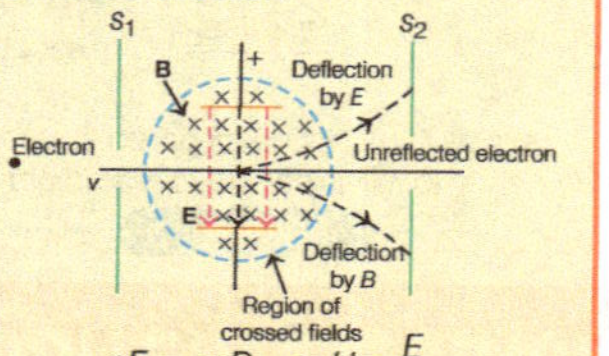

$eE = evB$ or $U = \frac{E}{B}$

Lorentz Force

The total force experienced by a charged particle moving in a region where both electric and magnetic fields are present is called Lorentz force.

$\therefore \mathbf{F} = q(\mathbf{E} + \mathbf{v}\times\mathbf{B})$

Forces between Two Parallel Current-Carrying Conductors

Consider two long parallel wires carrying currents I_1 and I_2. Let *r* be the separation between them.

The magnetic field produced by current I_1 at a distance *r* is B_1. Force per unit length is *F*.

$B_1 = \frac{\mu_0 I_1}{2\pi r}$, $f = \frac{F_2}{L} = \frac{\mu_0 I_1 I_2}{2\pi r}$

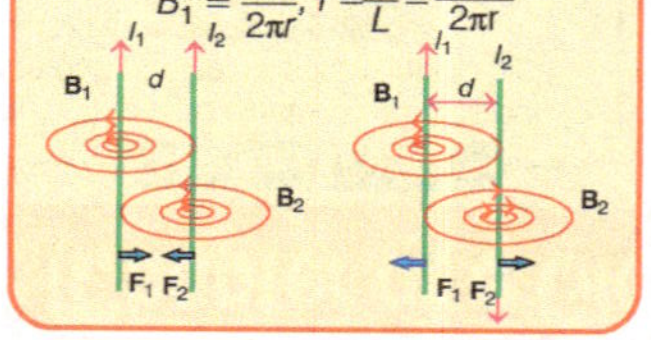

Force on a Moving Charge in a Magnetic Field

The electric charges moving in a magnetic field experience a force, while there is no such force on static charges. The charge *q* moving in the magnetic field **B** experiences a force **F** such that,

$\mathbf{F} \propto v\sin\theta$, $\mathbf{F} = q(\mathbf{v}\times\mathbf{B})$

$\therefore \mathbf{F} = qvB\sin\theta$

Fleming's Left Hand Rule

Stretch the thumb and the first two fingers of the left hand mutually perpendicular to each other. If the forefinger points in the direction of the magnetic field, central finger in the direction of current, then the thumb gives the direction of the force on the charged particle.

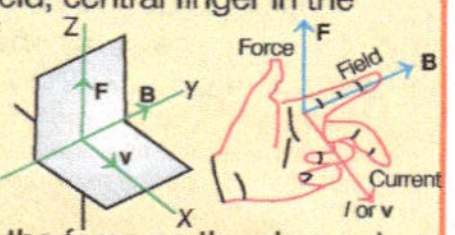

Three Cases are Possible

1. When the initial velocity is parallel to the magnetic field.

Here, $\theta = 0°$, so

$F = qvB\sin 0° = 0$.

2. When the initial velocity is perpendicular to the magnetic field.

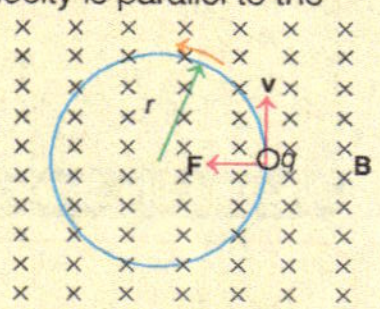

Here, $\theta = 90°$, so $F = qvB\sin 90° = qvB$ = a maximum force.

The radius of circular path

$r = \frac{mv}{qB}$

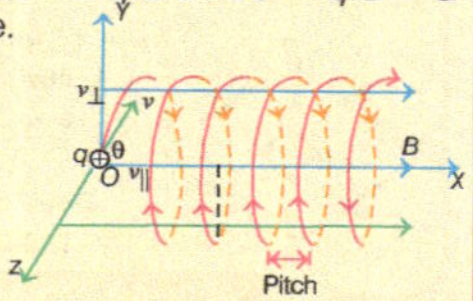

Period of revolution $= \frac{\text{Circumference}}{\text{Speed}}$

or, $T = \frac{2\pi r}{v} = \frac{2\pi}{v}\cdot\frac{mv}{qB} = \frac{2\pi m}{qB}$

The frequency of revolution is

$f_c = \frac{1}{T} = \frac{qB}{2\pi m}$

3. When the initial velocity makes an arbitrary angle with the field direction.

The radius of the circular path is

$r = \frac{mv_\perp}{qB} = \frac{mv\sin\theta}{qB}$

The period of revolution, $T = \frac{2\pi m}{qB}$

Conversion of a Galvanometer

- **Galvanometer into Ammeter**

$S = \frac{I_g}{I - I_g}\times G$

- **Galvanometer into Voltmeter**

$R = \frac{V}{I_g} - G$

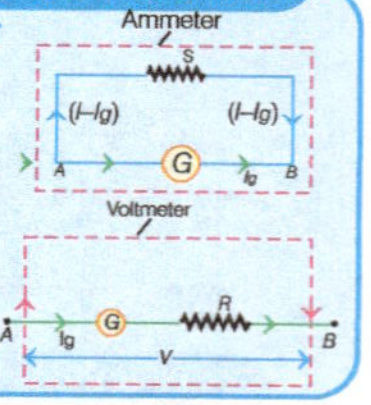

Torque Experienced by a Current Loop

Torque experienced is given by

τ = force × perpendicular distance

If the rectangular loop has *N* turns, the torque increases *N* times i.e.,

$\tau = NIBA\sin\theta$

$\tau = \mathbf{m}\times\mathbf{B}$

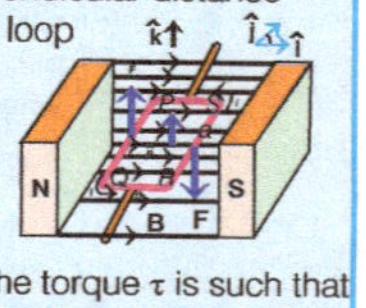

The direction of the torque τ is such that it rotates the loop anticlockwise about the axis of suspension.

Magnetism and Matter (Chapter at a Glance)

Solenoid as Equivalent Bar Magnet

- Each turns of the solenoid can be regarded as a small magnetic dipole, then the solenoid becomes a small magnetic dipole.
- The number of magnetic dipole is equal to the number of turns in the solenoid.

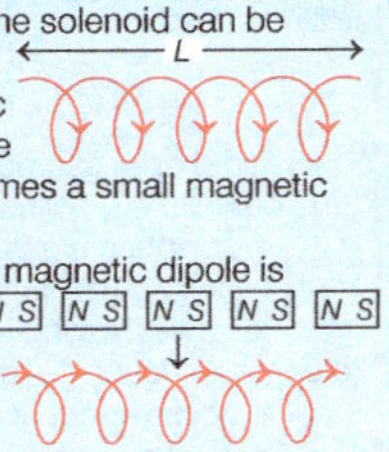

- For a solenoid of length $2l$ and radius a consisting n turns per unit length, the magnetic field is given by

$B = \frac{\mu_0 2M}{4\pi r^3}$ (where, M = magnetic moment of Solenoid = $n\,(2l)(\pi a^2)$)

Magnetic Dipole in Magnetic Field

Torque on a magnetic dipole (bar magnet),
τ = force x perpendicular distance between coupled forces
$\tau = MB\sin\theta$
$\theta = 90° \Rightarrow \tau = MB$ (Max)
$\theta = 0° \Rightarrow \tau = 0$ (Min
Potential energy of magnetic dipole,
$U = -MB\cos\theta$

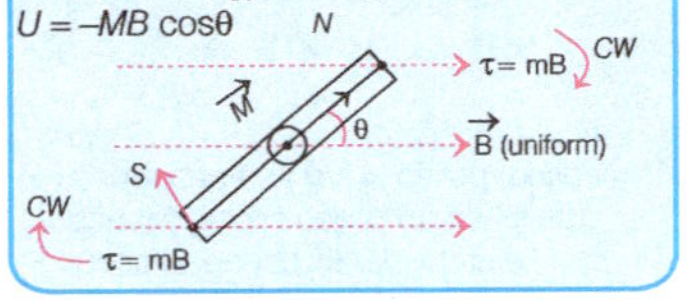

Directive Property

When a magnet is suspended, it aligns itself in the geographical north-south direction.

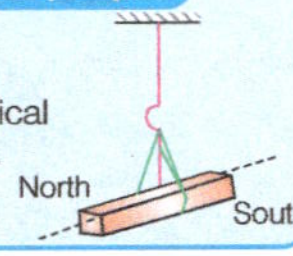

Properties of Magnetic Lines of Force

- Magnetic lines of force are closed curves which start from the N-pole and end at the S-pole, then return to the N-pole through the interior of the magnet.
- The lines of force never cross each other. If they do so, there are two directions of the magnetic field at that point which is impossible.
- The lines of force have a tendency to contract lengthwise and expand sidewise.
- The relative closeness of the lines of force gives a measure of the strength of the magnetic field which is maximum at the poles.

Bar Magnet

A bar magnet is a circular or rectangular cross-section. It is made up of iron, steel or any other ferromagnetic substance or ferromagnetic composite, having permanent magnetic properties.

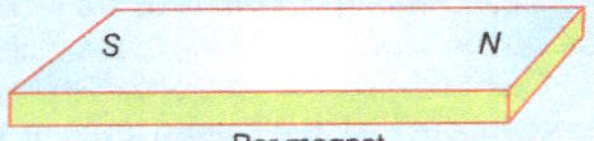

Bar magnet

Magnetism

A magnet is a material that has both attractive and directive properties. It attracts small pieces of iron, nickel, cobalt, etc. This property of attraction is called magnetism.

Magnetic Field Lines

The curve whose tangent at any point gives the direction of the magnetic field or the path along which a unit north pole would tend to move, if free to do so.

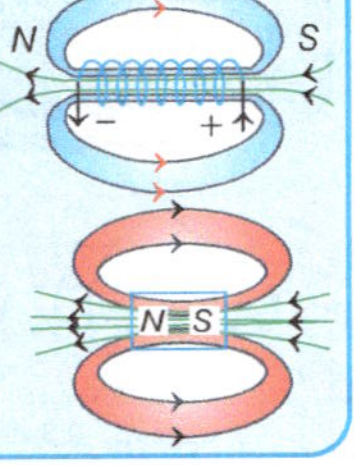

Coulomb's Law of Magnetic Force

This law states that the force of attraction or repulsion between two magnetic poles is directly proportional to the product of their pole strengths and inversely proportional to the square of the distance between them.

$$F = \frac{\mu_0}{4\pi}\cdot\frac{q_{m_1} q_{m_2}}{r^2}$$

Magnetic Dipole and Magnetic Moment

- **Magnetic dipole**

An arrangement of two equal and opposite magnetic poles separated by a small distance is called a magnetic dipole.

- **Magnetic dipole moment**

The product of its pole strength and magnetic length. It is a vector quantity, directed from S-pole to N-pole.

$$\mathbf{m} = q_m \times 2\mathbf{l}$$

SI unit is ampere metre^2(Am^2) or joule per tesla (JT^{-1}).

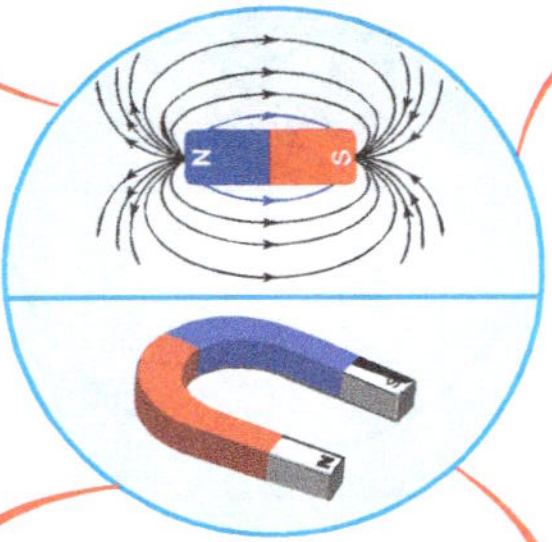

Consequences of Gauss's Law

- The magnetic poles always exist as unlike pairs of equal strengths.
- If a number of magnetic lines of force enter a closed surface, then an equal number of lines of force must leave that surface.

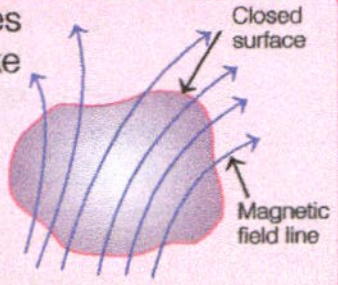

Gauss's Law in Magnetism

The surface integral of a magnetic field over a closed surface is always zero.

$$\oint_S \mathbf{B}.d\mathbf{S} = \oint_S \mathbf{B}.d\mathbf{S} = 0$$

Magnetising Field

The magnetic field that exists in vacuum and induces magnetism is called magnetising field.

$$B_0 = \mu_0 nI$$

Magnetic Induction

The total number of magnetic lines of force crossing per unit area normally through a material. The SI unit of magnetic induction is tesla (T).

Magnetising Field Intensity

The ability of magnetising field to magnetise a material medium is expressed by a vector **H**, called magnetising field intensity or magnetic intensity. $H = nI$

$\therefore \quad B_0 = \mu_0 nI = \mu_0 H$ or $H = \frac{B_0}{\mu_0}$

Properties of Diamagnetic Substances

- When a rod of diamagnetic material is suspended freely between two magnetic poles, then its axis becomes perpendicular to the magnetic field.

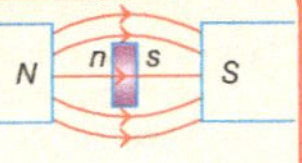

- If a diamagnetic solution is poured into a U-tube and one arm of this U-tube is placed between the poles of a strong magnet, the level of the solution in that arm is depressed.

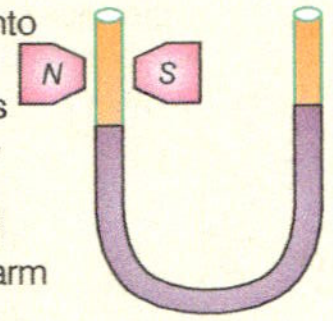

- The susceptibility of a diamagnetic substance is independent of the magnetising field and the temperature.

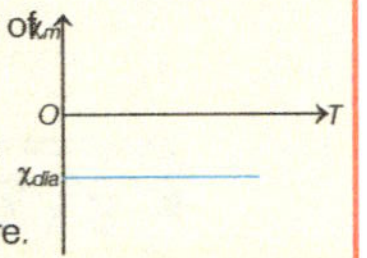

- The magnetisation of a diamagnetic substance lasts so long as the magnetising field is applied.

Magnetic Susceptibility

The ratio of the intensity of magnetisation M to the magnetising field intensity H. It is denoted by χ_m.
Thus,

$$\chi_m = \frac{M}{H}$$

Relative Permeability

The ratio of the permeability of the medium to the permeability of free space.

$$\therefore \mu_r = \frac{\mu}{\mu_0}$$

Magnetic Permeability

The magnetic permeability of a material defined as the ratio of its magnetic induction B to the magnetising field intensity H.

$$\mu = \frac{B}{H}$$

Intensity of Magnetisation

The magnetic moment developed per unit volume of a material when placed in a magnetising field is called intensity of magnetisation.

$$\mathbf{M} = \frac{\mathbf{m}}{V}$$

Properties of Paramagnetic Substances

- When a rod of paramagnetic material is suspended freely between two magnetic poles, then its axis becomes parallel to the magnetic field.

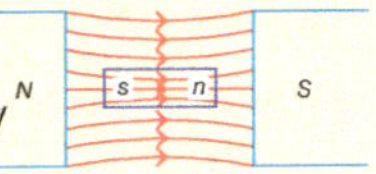

- Liquid level in that limb rises up.
- The magnetic susceptibility of a paramagnetic material varies inversely as the absolute temperature, i.e.,

$$\chi_m = \frac{C}{T}$$

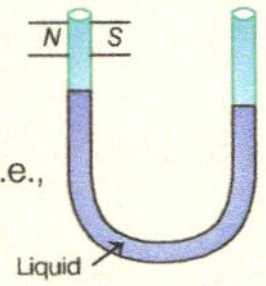

- As soon as the magnetising field is removed, a paramagnetic substance looses its magnetism.

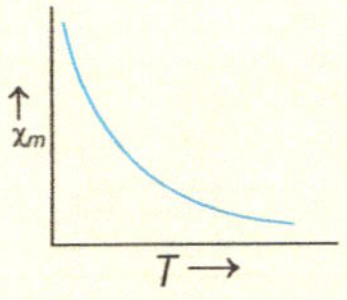

Properties of Ferromagnetic Substances

- They are strongly attracted towards the magnetic field.
- These are strongly magnetised in the direction of applied magnetic field.
- Liquid level in that limb rises up very much.

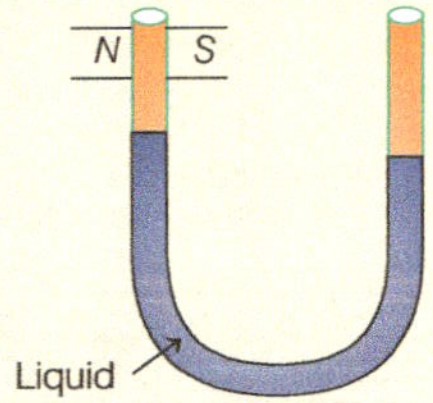

- The susceptibility of ferromagnetic material decreases with temperature in accordance with Curie-Weiss law

$$\chi_m = \frac{C'}{T - T_C}$$

- A ferromagnetic substance retains magnetism even after the magnetising field is removed.

Electromagnetic Induction (Chapter at a Glance)

Lenz's Law

The direction of the induced emf is always such as to result in opposition to the change producing it.

From Faraday's,

$$\varepsilon = -N\frac{d\phi}{dt}$$

$$I = \frac{\text{Induced emf}}{\text{Resistance}} = -\frac{1}{R}\frac{d\phi}{dt}$$

Expression for induced charge

$$dq = i_{in}\,dt = -\frac{1}{R}\left(\frac{d\phi}{dt}\right)dt = -\frac{d\phi}{R}$$

$$\Delta q = -\frac{\Delta\phi}{R}$$

It is a consequence of the law of conservation of energy.

Motional Emf

The emf induced across the ends of a conductor due to its motion in a magnetic field is called motional emf. The induced emf Blv is called motional emf.

$\varepsilon = Blv$

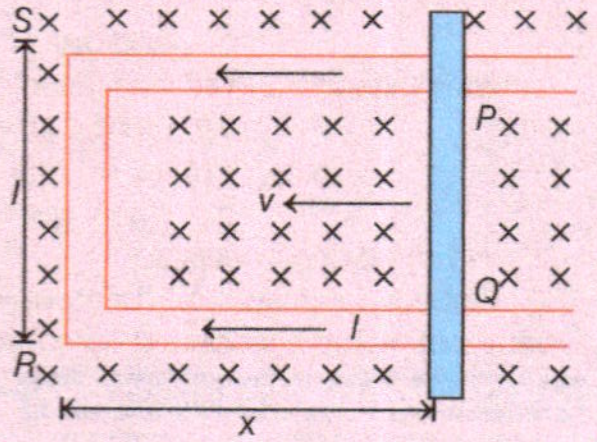

Fleming's Right Hand Rule

If we stretch the thumb and the first two fingers of our right hand in mutually perpendicular directions and if the forefinger points in the direction of the magnetic field, thumb in the direction of motion of the conductor, then the central finger points in the direction of current induced in the conductor.

This rule is also called the dynamo or generator rule and has wide practical applications.

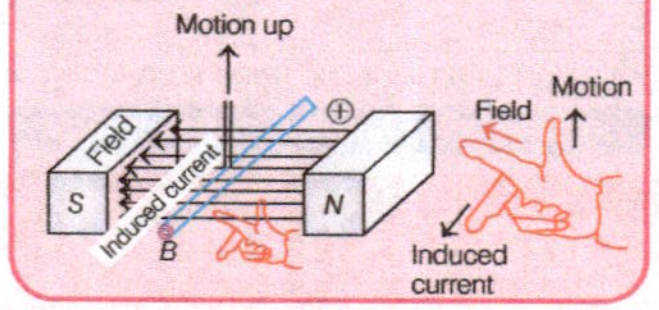

Faraday's Law

(i) Whenever the magnetic flux linked with a conducting loop or coil changes, an emf is induced in it.

(ii) The induced emf is directly proportional to the rate of change of magnetic flux through the coil.

$$\varepsilon = -N\times\frac{d\phi}{dt}$$

The negative sign indicates that the induced emf opposes the cause that produces it.

Magnetic Flux

The magnetic flux through any surface placed in a magnetic field is the total number of magnetic lines of force crossing this surface normally. SI unit of magnetic flux is weber (Wb).

$\phi = \mathbf{B}\cdot\mathbf{A}$ or $\phi = BA\cos\theta$

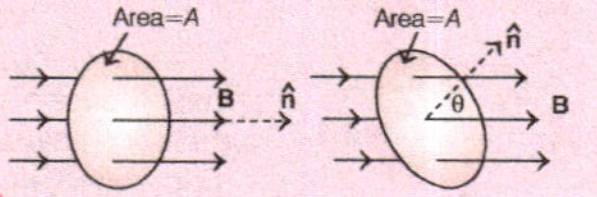

Eddy Current

Whenever the magnetic flux linked with a metal sheet changes, induced current are produced in it. The flow of these current look like swirling eddies. This is known as eddy currents.

Applications of Eddy Current

- **Induction furnace** If a metal specimen is placed in a changing magnetic field, very large eddy currents are set up. The heat produced is sufficient to even melt the metal.
- **Electric brakes** A strong magnetic field is applied to the rotating drum attached to the wheel. Eddy currents set up in the drum exert a torque on the drum, so as to stop the train.
- **Inductothermy** Eddy currents can be used to heat localised tissues of the human body. This branch is called inductothermy.
- **Energy meters** In energy meters used for measuring electric energy, the eddy currents induced in an aluminium disc are made use of.

Motional Emf from Lorentz Force and Energy Consideration

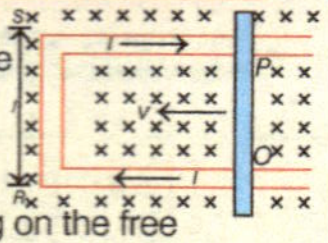

A conductor has a large number of free electrons. When it moves through a magnetic field, a Lorentz force acting on the free electrons can set up a current.

$F_m = F_e$ or, $qvB = qE$ or $vB = E$

Current induced in the loop

$$I = \frac{\varepsilon}{R} = \frac{Blv}{R}$$

Force on the movable arm

$$F = \frac{B^2l^2v}{R}$$

Power delivered by the external force

$$P = Fv = \frac{B^2l^2v^2}{R}$$

Power dissipated as joule loss

$$P_J = I^2R = \left(\frac{Blv}{R}\right)^2 R = \frac{B^2l^2v^2}{R}$$

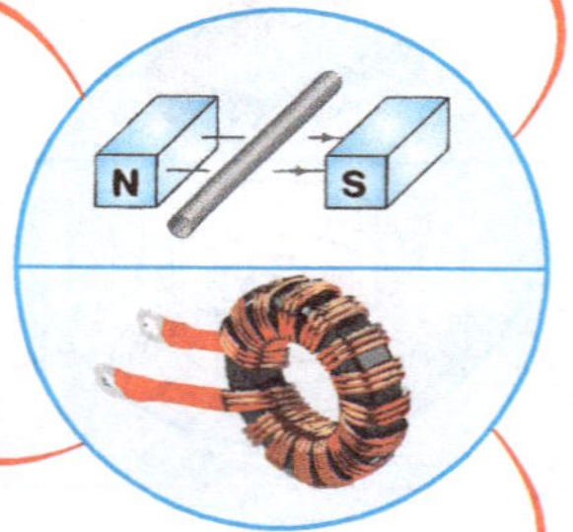

Mutual Induction

The phenomenon of production of induced emf in one coil due to a change of current in the neighbouring coil.

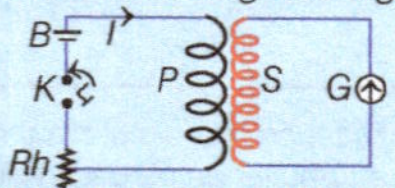

Coefficient of mutual induction

Here, $\varepsilon = -d\phi/dt = -M\,dI/dt$

Mutual Inductance of Two Long Solenoids

Mutual inductance will be

$$M = \mu_0 N_1 N_2 A/l = \mu_0 n_1 n_2 A l = \mu_0 n_1 n_2 \pi r_1^2\, l$$

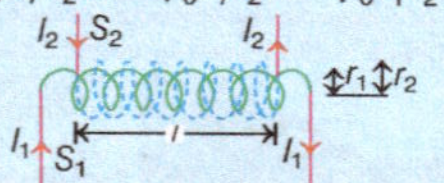

Methods of Generating Induced Emf

An induced emf can be produced by changing the magnetic flux linked with a circuit. The magnetic flux,

$$\phi = BA\cos\theta$$

Induced Emf by Changing the Magnetic Field B

(i) Moving a magnet towards a stationary coil.

(ii) Moving a coil towards a stationary magnet

(iii) Varying current in the neighbouring coil.

Self Induction

The phenomenon of electromagnetic induction in which on changing the current in a coil, an opposing induced emf is set up in that very coil is called self induction.

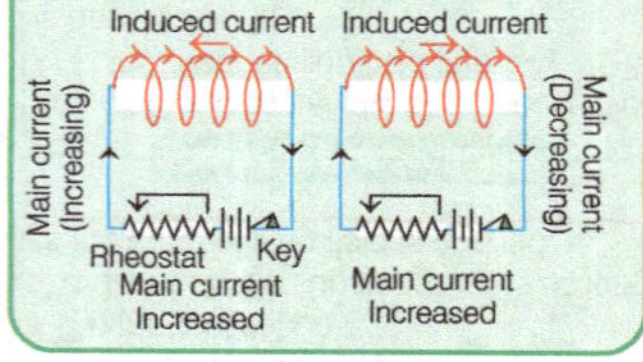

Factors Affecting Mutual Inductance

- **Number of turns** Larger the number of turns in the two solenoids, larger will be their mutual inductance.

$$M \propto N_1N_2$$

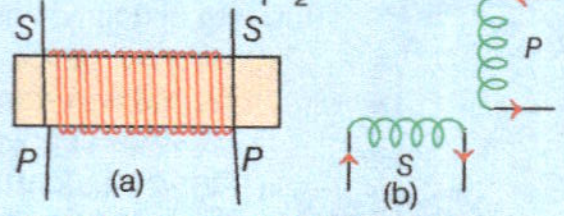

- **Relative separation** Larger the distance between two solenoids, smaller well be the magnetic flux linked with secondary coil due to current in the primary coil.
- **Common cross-sectional area** Larger the common cross-sectional area of two solenoids, larger will be their mutual inductance.
- **Relative orientation of the two coils** Mutual inductance will be maximum, when they placed coaxially to each other whereas minimum, when they are perpendicular to each other.

AC Generator

Consider a coil *PQRS* free to rotate in a uniform magnetic field **B**. The axis of rotation of the coil is perpendicular to the field **B**.

$\phi = BA\cos\theta$

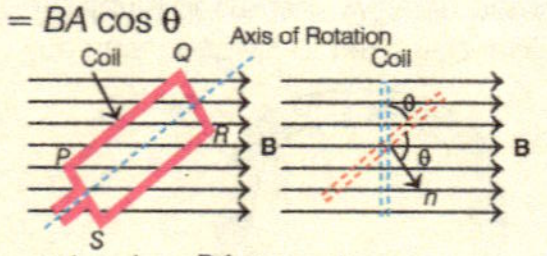

$\theta = \omega t \;\therefore\; \phi = BA\cos\omega t$

An induced emf $\varepsilon = BA\omega\sin\omega t$

For N numbers of turns

$\therefore\; \varepsilon = NBA\omega\sin\omega t$

$\varepsilon_0 = NBA\omega = 2\pi\nu NBA$

$\varepsilon = \varepsilon_0\sin\omega t = \varepsilon_0\sin 2\pi\nu t$

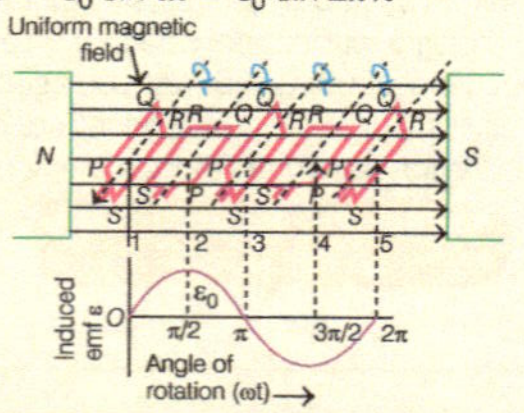

Coefficient of Self-Induction

The magnetic flux ϕ linked with a coil is proportional to the current I through it,

i.e, or, $\phi = LI \;\therefore\; \varepsilon = -\dfrac{d\phi}{dt} = -L\dfrac{dI}{dt}$

Self Inductance of a Long Solenoid

Consider a long solenoid of length l and radius r with $r << l$ and having n turns per unit length.

$B = \mu_0 nI$

$\therefore$ Self inductance of the long solenoid is

$$L = \mu_0 n^2 lA$$

$$\therefore\quad L = \frac{\mu_0 N^2 A}{l}$$

Factors Affecting Self Inductance

- **Number of turns**

Larger the number of turns in the solenoid, larger is its self-inductance.

- **Area of cross-section**

Larger the area of the cross-section of the solenoid, larger is its self-inductance.

- **Permeability of the core material**

The self-inductance of a solenoid increases μ_r times, if it is wound over an iron core of relative permeability μ_r.

Alternating Current (Chapter at a Glance)

Phasors and Phasor Diagram

- A rotating vector that represents a sinusoidally varying quantity is called a phasor.
- A diagram that represents alternating current voltage of the same frequency as rotating vectors along with proper phase angle between them is called phasor diagram or Argand diagram.

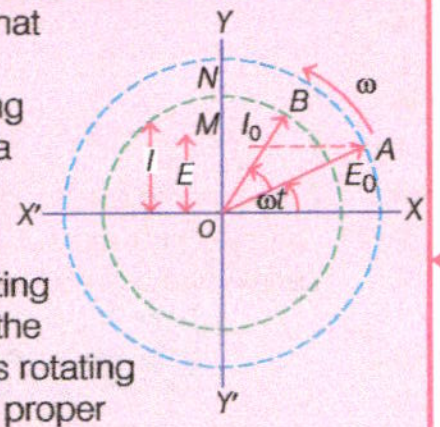

Choke Coil

- It is simply an inductor with large reactance which is used to reduce current in AC circuits without much loss of energy.

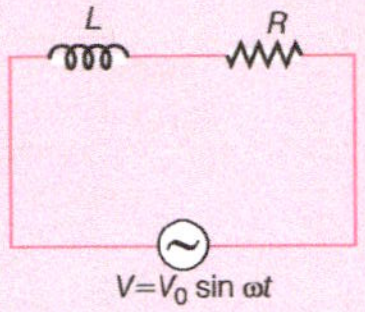

- **Uses**
  –It is used in car audio systems.
  –It also has a wide range of uses in computer cables.

Root Mean Square value of an Alternating EMF

- It is defined as that value of steady voltage that produces the same amount of heat in a given resistance as is produced by the given alternating emf when applied to the same resistance for the same time.
- It is also called virtual or effective value.
- It is denoted by ε_{rms} or ε_{eff} or ε_v.
- $\varepsilon_{rms} = \frac{\varepsilon_0}{\sqrt{2}} = 0.707\varepsilon_0$

Inductive Reactance (X_L)

- The inductive reactance is the effective opposition offered by the inductor to the flow of current in the circuit.
- Its SI unit is ohm.
- $X_L = \omega L = 2\pi f L$

Capacitance Reactance (X_C)

- The capacitive reactance is the effective opposition offered by a capacitor to the flow of current in the circuit.
- Its SI unit is ohm (Ω).
- $X_C = \frac{1}{\omega C} = \frac{1}{2\pi f C}$

Alternating Current

- **Alternating Current and Direct Current**
  An alternating current is that current whose magnitude changes continuously with time and direction reverses periodically. A direct current is that current which flows with a constant magnitude in the same direction, as shown in fig.
  $\varepsilon = \varepsilon_0 \sin \omega t$ (emf of Alternating current)
  $I = \frac{\varepsilon}{R} = \frac{\varepsilon_0}{R} \sin \omega t$

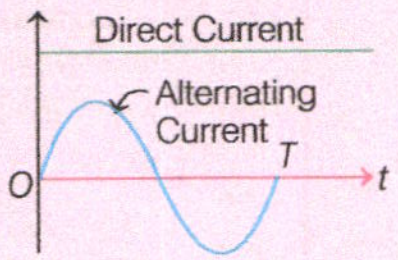

- **Amplitude** The maximum value attained by an alternating current in either direction is called its amplitude.
  It is denoted by I_0
- **Time period**
  $$\text{Time period} = \frac{\text{Angular displacement in a complete cycle}}{\text{Angular velocity}}$$
- **Frequency** It is the number of cycles completed per unit second.
- $I = I_0 \sin \omega t = I_0 \sin 2\pi ft = I_0 \sin \frac{2\pi}{T} t$
  $I_{av} = \frac{2}{\pi} I_0 = 0.637\, I_0$
  $I_{rms} = \frac{I_0}{\sqrt{\pi}} = 0.707\, I_0$

AC Circuit containing only Capacitor

- A pure capacitor C connected across a source of alternating emf ε given by
- PD across the capacitor plates applied emf
  $V = \varepsilon = \varepsilon_0 \sin \omega t$
  $Q = CV = C\varepsilon_0 \sin \omega t$
  ∴ Current at any instant is
  $I = I_0 \cos \omega t = I_0 \sin(\omega t + \pi/2)$
  where, $I_0 = \omega C\varepsilon_0 = \frac{\varepsilon_0}{1/\omega C} =$

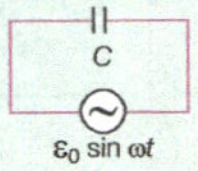

- **Phase relationship between ε and I.**
  The current leads the emf in phase by π/2 rad, So the current phasor I makes an angle π/2 rad, so the current phasor I makes an angle π/2 rad with phasor ε in anticlockwise direction.

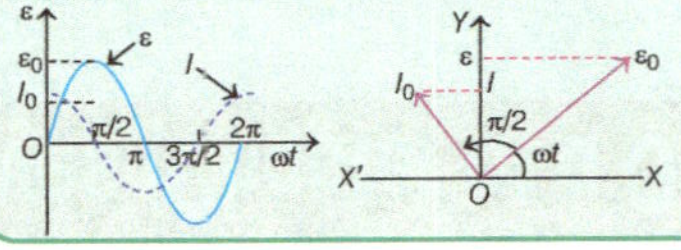

Transformer

A transformer is an electrical device for converting an alternating current at low voltage into that at high voltage or *vice-versa*.

- **Step up transformer**
  If it increases the input voltage it is called step up transformer.

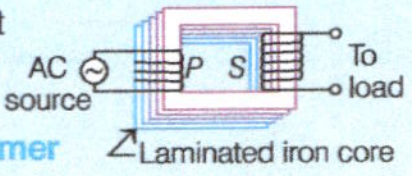

- **Step down transformer**
  If it decreases the input voltage it is called step down transformer.

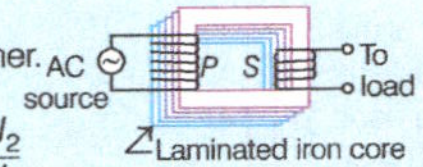

- **Induced emf,** $\frac{\varepsilon_2}{\varepsilon_1} = \frac{N_2}{N_1}$
- **Current,** $\frac{I_1}{I_2} = \frac{\varepsilon_2}{\varepsilon_1} = \frac{N_2}{N_1}$
- **Efficiency** $\eta = \frac{\text{Power output}}{\text{Power input}} \times 100\%$

The efficiency of real transformers is fairly high (90 to 99%) though not 100%.

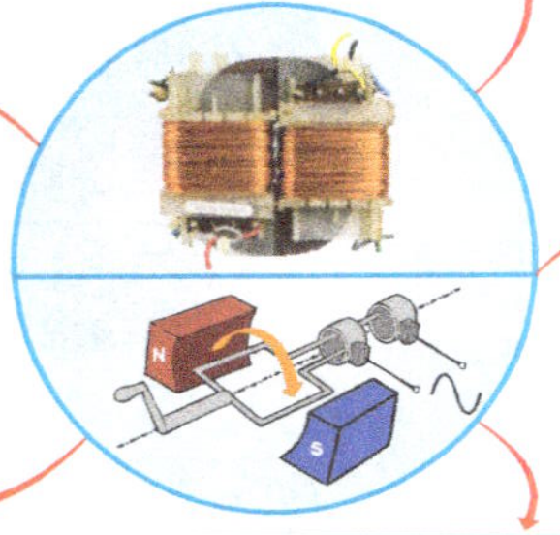

AC Circuit containing only a Resistor

- A resistor of resistance R is connected to a source of alternating emf ε given by
  $\varepsilon = \varepsilon_0 \sin \omega t$
- Current in the circuit,
  $I = I_0 \sin \omega t$

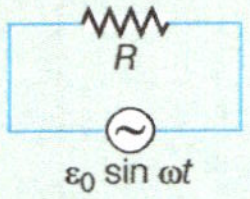

- **Phase relationship between ε and I.**
  The emf ε and current I are in same phase in a purely resistive circuit. This means that both and attain their zero, minimum and maximum values at the same respective times.

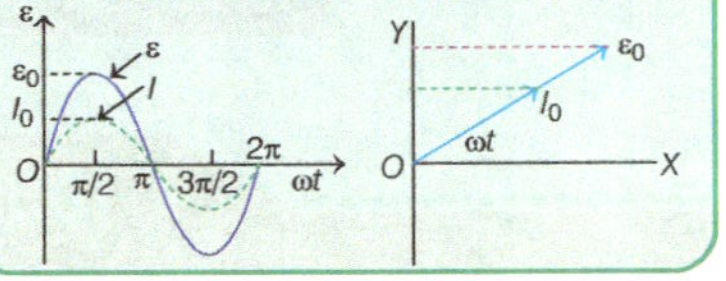

Series L-C-R Circuit

A resistance R an inductance L and capacitance C are connected in series to a source of alternating emf given by $\varepsilon = \varepsilon_0 \sin \omega t$

1. Voltage $V_R = RI$ across the resistance R will be phase with the current I. $V_0R = I_0R$
2. Voltage $V_C = X_CI$ across the capacitance C lags behind the current I in phase by π/2 rad. $V_{OC} = I_0X_C$
3. Voltage $V_L = X_LI$ across the inductance L is ahead of current I in phase by π/2 rad. So, phasor V_L lies π/2 rad anticlockwise w.r.t the phasor I. Its amplitude is $V_{OL} = I_0X_L$

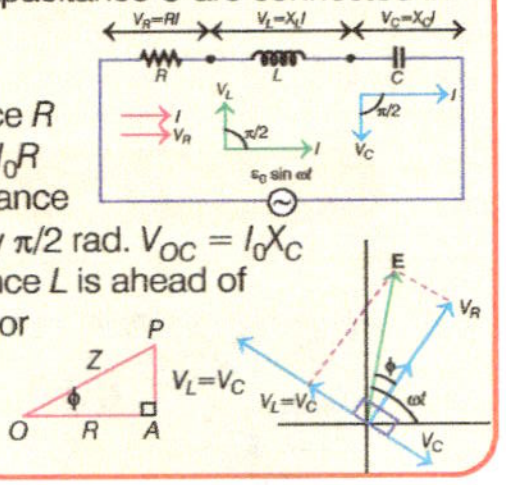

Resistor and Capacitor in Series

A resistor and capacitor connected in series to a source of alternating emf given by
$\varepsilon = \varepsilon_0 \sin \omega t$

1. Voltage $V_R = RI$ across the resistance R will be phase with the current I.
   $V_0R = I_0R$
2. Voltage $V_C = X_C I$ across the capacitance C lags behind the current I in phase by π/2 rad.Thus, $V_{0C} = I_0X_C$

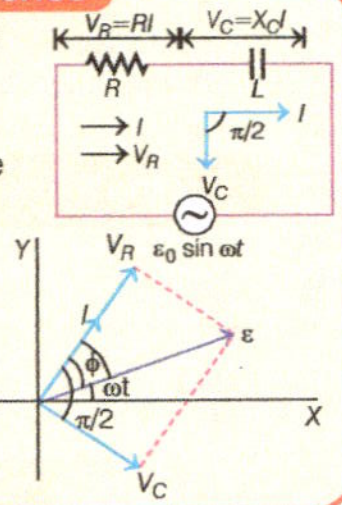

Resistor and Inductor in Series

A resistor and inductance connected in series to a source of alternating emf given by
$\varepsilon = \varepsilon_0 \sin \omega t$

1. Voltage $V_R = RI$ across the resistance R will be phase with the current I.
   $V_0R = I_0R$
2. Voltage $V_L = X_L I$ across the inductance is ahead of the current I in phase by π/2 rad.
   Thus, $V_{0L} = I_0X_L$

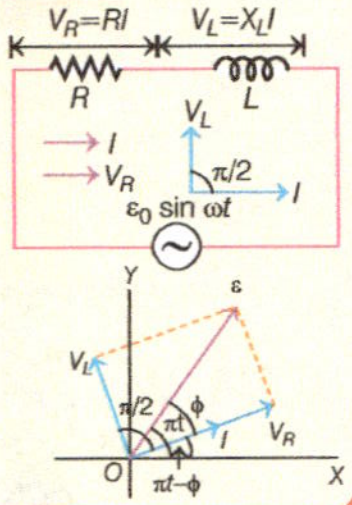

AC Circuit Containing Only an Inductor

- Suppose an inductor of inductance L is connected to a source of alternating emf given by $\varepsilon = \varepsilon_0 \sin \omega t$

  Net Instantaneous emf, $\varepsilon = L\frac{dI}{dt}$

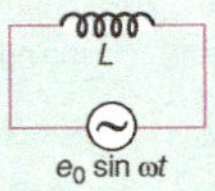

- **Phase relationship between ε and I.**
  The voltage is ahead of the current in phase by 90°.

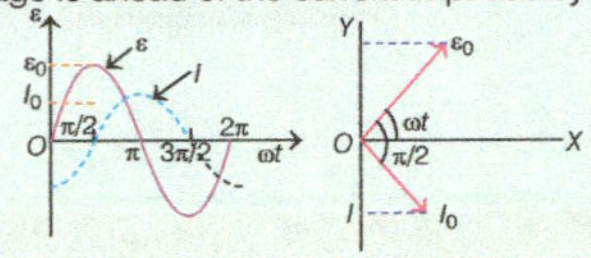

Electromagnetic Waves (Chapter at a Glance)

Production of Electromagnetic Waves

An electromagnetic wave consists of oscillating electric and magnetic fields. The various possible frequencies of electromagnetic waves form a spectrum, and a small part of which is visible light. Electromagnetic waves along

X-axis : $E_x = E_m \sin(kx - \omega t)$

Y-axis : $B_y = B_m \sin(kx - \omega t)$

Transverse Nature of Electromagnetic Waves

A changing electric field produces a changing magnetic field and vice-versa which give rise to a transverse wave known as electromagnetic wave.
The variation of electric field (E) and magnetic field (B) are mutually perpendicular to each other as well as the direction of the propagation of the wave i.e., the electromagnetic waves are transverse in nature.

Intensity of Electromagnetic Waves

Intensity of electromagnetic wave is defined as the energy crossing per unit area per unit time perpendicular to the direction of propagation of the wave.

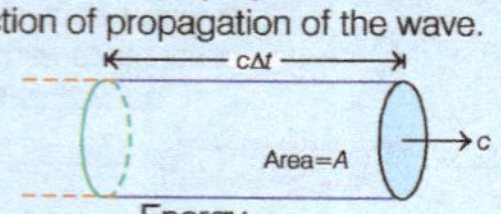

$$\text{Intensity} = \frac{\text{Energy}}{\text{Area x Time}}$$

Energy density of Electromagnetic Waves

Energy density of electromagnetic wave is defined as the energy per unit volume of the space in which it travels.

$U_E = \frac{1}{2}\varepsilon_0 E^2$

$U_B = \frac{B^2}{2\mu_0}$

$U_{av} = \frac{1}{2}\varepsilon_0 E^2_{rms} + \frac{B^2_{rms}}{2\mu_0}$

$U_{av} = \frac{\varepsilon_0 E_0^2}{4} + \frac{\varepsilon_0 E_0^2}{4} = \frac{1}{2}\varepsilon_0 E_0^2 = \varepsilon_0 E^2_{rms}$

$U_E = U_B$

Modified Ampere's Law

It implies the fact that not only a conduction current but a displacement current associated with changing electric field also produces a magnetic field.

$$\oint \mathbf{B}\cdot d\mathbf{l} = \mu_0 (I_C + I_D)$$

$$= \mu_0 I_C + \varepsilon_0 \frac{d\phi_E}{dt}$$

Displacement Current

It is a current which is produced due to the rate of change of electric flux w.r.t. time.

$$I_D = \varepsilon_0 \frac{d\phi_E}{dt}$$

Ampere's Circuital Law

The line integral of magnetic field around any closed path in vacuum is equal to the μ_0 times the total current passing through that closed path.

$$\oint \mathbf{B}\cdot d\mathbf{l} = \mu_0 \mathbf{I}$$

Characteristics / Properties of Electromagnetic Waves

1. Speed of electromagnetic waves in a medium is given by

$$v = \frac{1}{\sqrt{\mu\varepsilon}}$$

where, μ and ε are the permeability and permittivity.

2. Speed of electromagnetic wave in a free space or vacuum is given by

$$c = \frac{1}{\sqrt{\mu_0\varepsilon_0}} = 3 \times 10^8 \text{ ms}^{-1}$$

3. The amplitudes of electric field (E_0) and amplitude of magnetic field (B_0) are related to each other by relation.

$$c = \frac{E_0}{B_0}$$

4. Electromagnetic waves carry energy as they travel from one point to another point in the space without any material medium or actual transfer of material medium. The average energy densities of an electromagnetic wave is given by

$$\frac{1}{2}\varepsilon_0 E_0^2$$

5. Intensity of an EM wave depends upon the amplitude of electric field

$$I = \frac{1}{2}\varepsilon_0 E_0^2 c$$

Maxwell's Equations

1. Gauss's Law in Electrostatics

$$\oint \mathbf{E}\cdot d\mathbf{s} = \frac{q}{\varepsilon_0}$$

2. Gauss's Law in Magnetostatics

$$\oint \mathbf{B}\cdot d\mathbf{s} = 0$$

3. Faraday's Law of Electromagnetic Induction

$$\oint \mathbf{E}\cdot d\mathbf{l} = -\frac{d\phi_B}{dt}$$

4. Ampere's-Maxwell's circuital Law

$$\oint \mathbf{B}\cdot d\mathbf{l} = \mu_0\left(I_C + \varepsilon_0 \frac{d\phi_E}{dt}\right)$$

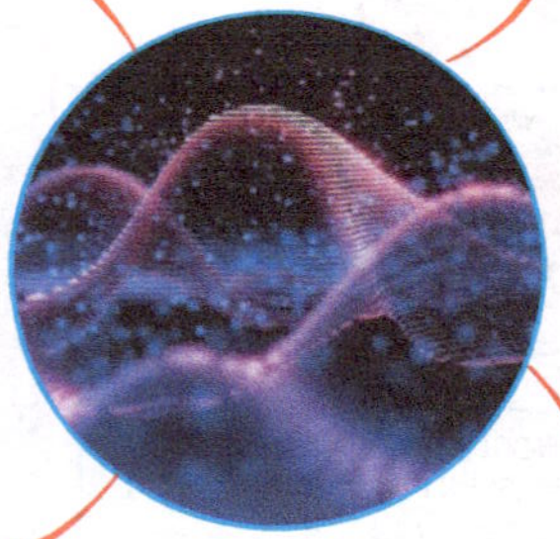

Electromagnetic Spectrum

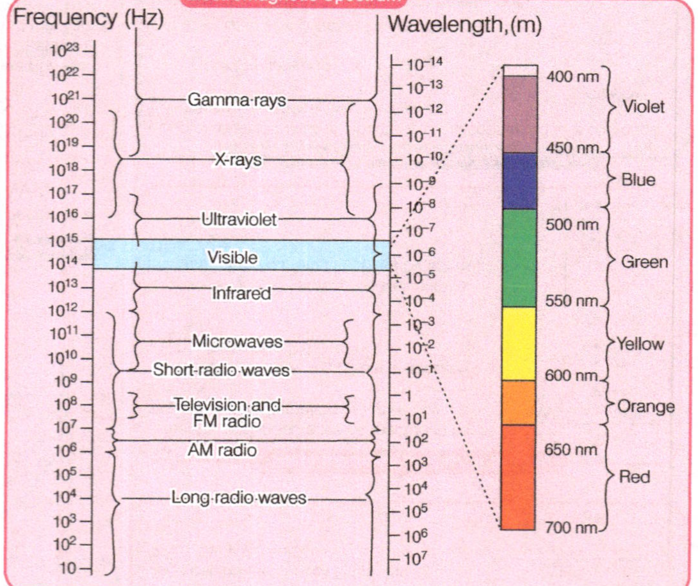

Gamma Rays

- In the treatment of cancer and tumours.
- To produce nuclear reaction.

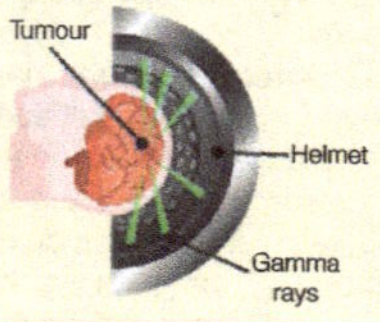

X-rays

- Penetrate matter (e.g., radiography).
- Ionise gases.
- Cause fluorescence.
- Cause photoelectric emission from metals.

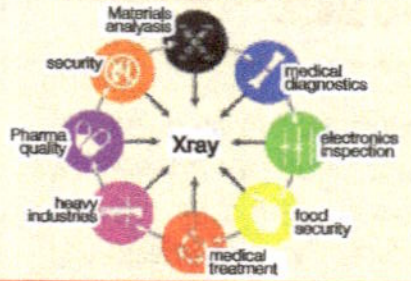

Ultraviolet Rays

- Can cause many chemical reactions, e.g., the tanning of the human skin.
- Ionise atoms in atmosphere, resulting in the ionosphere.

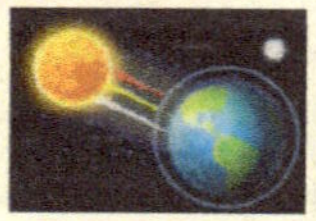

Visible Light

- Detected by stimulating nerve endings of human retina.
- Can cause chemical reaction.

Radiowaves

- Used in radio communication.

Infrared Rays

- Useful for elucidating molecular structure.
- Useful for haze photography.

Microwaves

- Radar communication.
- Analysis of fine details of molecular and atomic structure.

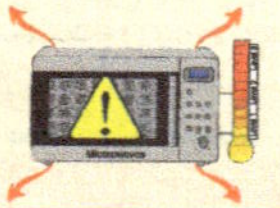

Ray Optics and Optical Instruments (Chapter at a Glance)

Sign Convention

- All the distances are measured from pole (P) of mirror
- The distances measured in the direction of incident ray are taken positive, otherwise negative .
- Heights measured upward and perpendicular to the principal axis are +ve and otherwise -ve.

Reflection By Spherical Mirrors

Mirror formula, $\frac{1}{u}+\frac{1}{v}=\frac{1}{f}=\frac{2}{R}$

Magnification, $m=-\frac{v}{u}=\frac{h_i}{h_o}$

If the image is upright or erect with respect to the object then m is positive. m is negative if the image is inverted with respect to the object.

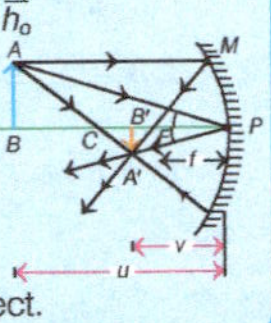

Refractive Index

The refractive index of a medium for a light of given wavelength may be defined as the ratio of the speed of light in vacuum to its speed in that medium.

$$\mu = \frac{c}{v}$$

Laws of Refraction of Light

- **First Law** The incident ray, the refracted ray and the normal to the interface at the point of incidence all lie in the same plane.
- **Second Law** The ratio of the sine of the angle of incidence and the sine of the angle of refraction is constant for a given pair of media.

Mathematically, $\frac{\sin i}{\sin r} = {}^1\mu_2$

Lens Maker Formula

This formula relates the focal length of a lens to the refractive index of the lens material and the radii of curvature of its two surfaces.

$$\Rightarrow \frac{1}{f} = (\mu - 1)\left[\frac{1}{R_1} - \frac{1}{R_2}\right]$$

Power of Lens

The tangent of the angle by which it converges or diverges a beam of light falling at unit distance from the optical centre $P = \frac{1}{f}$

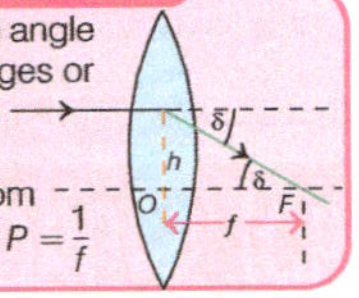

Reflection from Plane Surface

- The Image formed by a plane mirror is virtual and erect w.r.t object and of the same size as the object
- If keeping the the incident ray fixed the plane mirror is rotated through an angle θ, the reflected ray turns through double the angle i.e., 2θ in that direction.
- Deviation suffered by a light ray incident at angle i is given by

$$\delta = (180° - 2i)$$

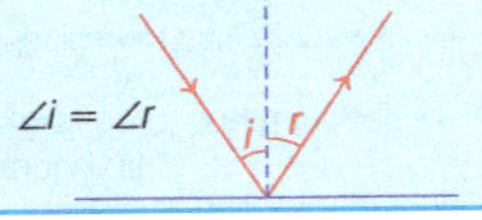

Laws of Reflection of Light

(i) The angle of incidence is equal to the angle of reflection.

i.e. $\angle i = \angle r$.

(ii) The incident ray, the reflected ray and the normal at the point of incidence all lie in the same plane.

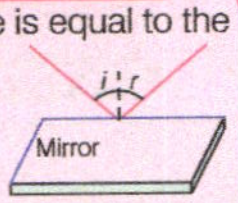

Refraction of Light

The phenomenon of the change in the path of light as it passes obliquely from one transparent medium to another is called refraction of light.

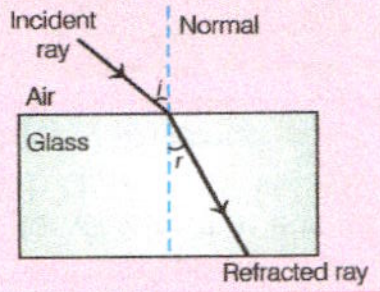

Principle of Reversibility of Light

This principle states that if the final path of a ray of light after it has suffered several reflections and refractions is reversed,
it retraces its path exactly.

$${}^1\mu_2 = \frac{1}{{}^2\mu_1}$$

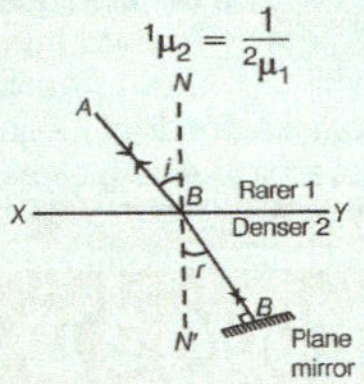

Simple Microscope

Magnifying power

- For final image is formed at D (least distance),

$$m = \frac{\text{Angle subtended by the image at } D}{\text{Angle subtended by the object at infinity}}$$

$$= 1 + \frac{D}{f}$$

- For final image formed at infinity, $m = \frac{D}{f}$

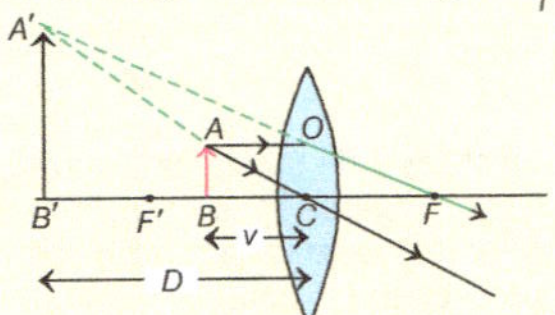

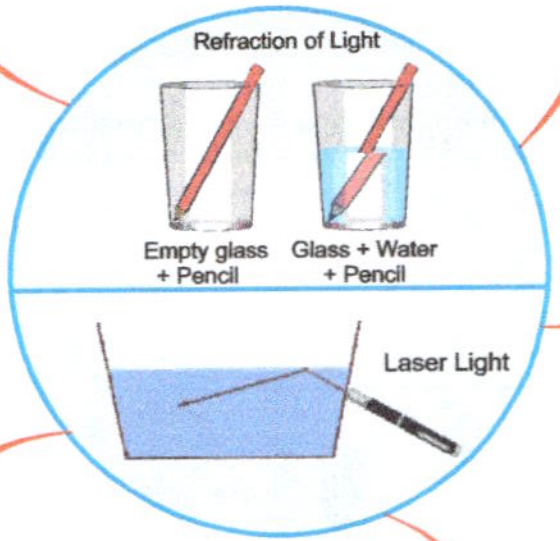

Real and Apparent Depths

It is on account of refraction of light that the apparent depth of an object placed in denser medium is less than the real depth.

$$\text{Apparent depth} = \frac{\text{Real depth}}{\text{Refractive Index}}$$

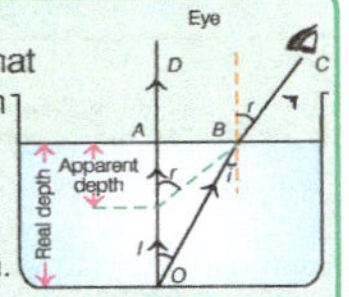

Refraction Through Lateral Shift

Lateral shift is the perpendicular distance between the incident and emergent rays, when light is incident obliquely on a refracting slab with parallel faces.

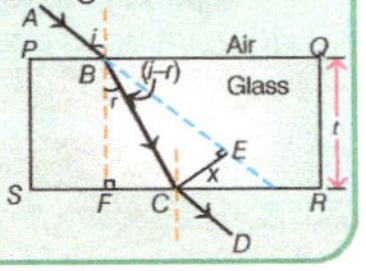

Compound Microscope

Magnifying power, $m = m_o \times m_e$

- For final image formed at D (least distance)

$$m = \frac{\beta}{\alpha} = \frac{v_o}{u_o}\left(1 + \frac{D}{f_e}\right) = -\frac{L}{f_o}\left(1 + \frac{D}{f_e}\right)$$

- For final image formed at infinity

$$m = -\frac{L}{f_o} \cdot \frac{D}{f_e}$$

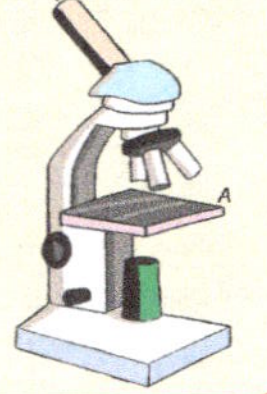

Total Internal Reflection

The phenomenon in which a ray of light travelling at an angle of incidence greater than the critical angle from denser to a rarer medium is totally reflected back into denser medium is called total internal reflection.

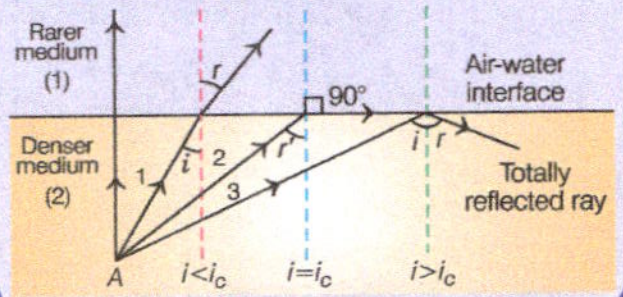

Refraction through a prism

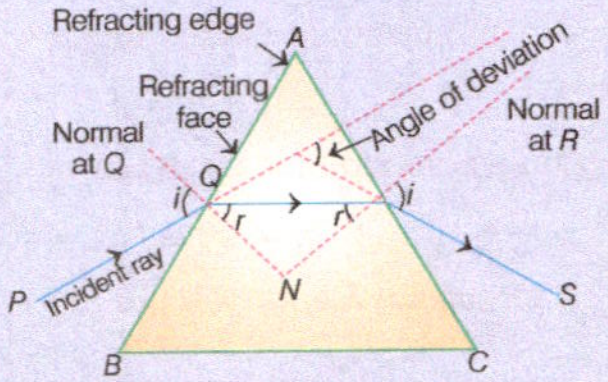

Angle of deviation,

$\delta = i + i' - A$ or $i + i' = A + \delta$

Refractive index of prism,

$$\mu = \frac{\sin\left(\frac{A + \delta_m}{2}\right)}{\sin\left(\frac{A}{2}\right)}$$

Optical Fiber

An optical fiber is a flexible glass or plastic fiber that can transmit light from one end to the other.

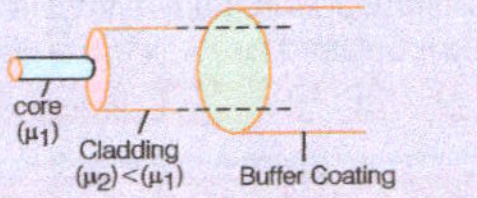

Astronomical Telescope

Magnifying power

- For final image is formed at D (least distance),

$$m = \frac{\text{Angle subtended by the image at } D}{\text{Angle subtended by the object at infinity}}$$

$$m = \frac{\beta}{\alpha} = \frac{-f_o}{f_e}\left(1 + \frac{f_e}{D}\right)$$

- In normal adjustment, image formed at infinity,

$$m = -f_o/f_e$$

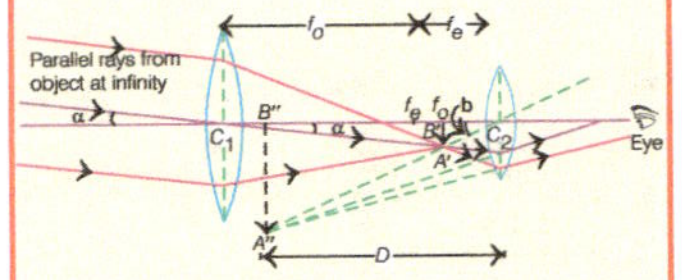

Reflecting Telescope

Magnifying power

When the final image is formed at D,

$$m = \frac{f_o}{f_e}\left(1 + \frac{f_e}{D}\right)$$

When the final image is formed at infinity

$$m = \frac{f_o}{f_e} = \frac{R/2}{f_e}$$

Newtonian reflecting telescope

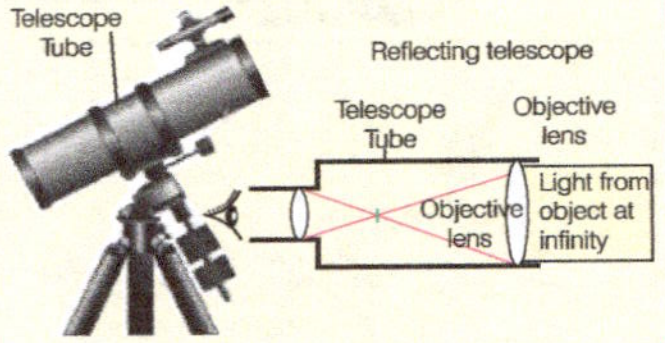

Terrestrial Telescope

For final image is formed at D,

$$m = \frac{f_o}{f_e}\left(1 + \frac{f_e}{D}\right)$$

For final image is formed at infinity,

$$m = \frac{f_o}{f_e}$$

A terrestrial telescope

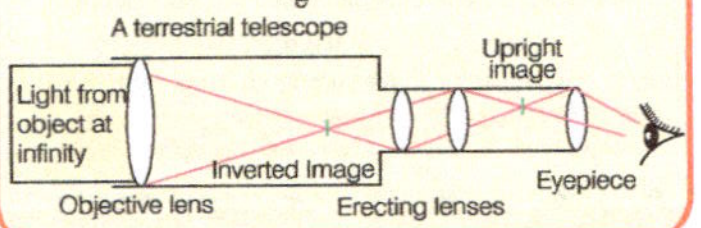

Wave Optics (Chapter at a Glance)

Wavefronts

The continuous locus of all such particles of the medium which are vibrating in the same phase at any instant.

- **Spherical Wavefront** In case of waves travelling in all directions from a point source, the wavefronts are spherical in shape.

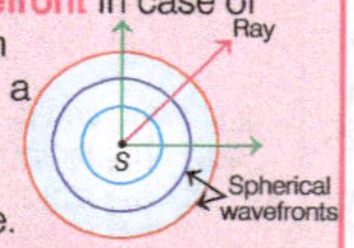

- **Cylindrical Wavefront** When the source of light is linear in shape, the wavefronts are cylindrical.

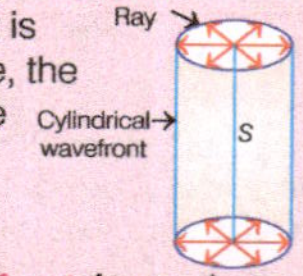

- **Plane Wavefront** At very large distances from the source, a portion of spherical or cylindrical wavefront is plane wavefront.

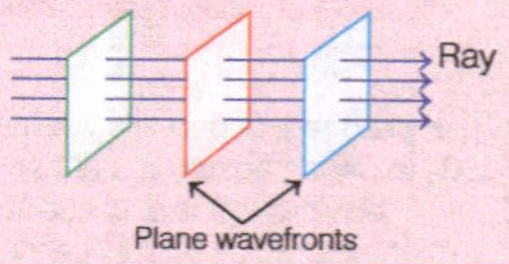

Huygens Principle

The wave theory of light tells how a wavefront propagates through a medium.

- **Assumptions**

(i) Each point on a wavefront acts as a source of new disturbance called secondary waves or wavelets.

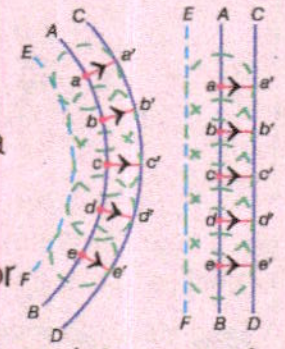

(ii) The secondary wavelets spread out in all directions with the speed of wave in the given medium.

(iii) The wavefront at any later time is given by the forward envelope of the secondary wavelets at that time.

Diffraction of Light

The phenomenon of bending of light around the corners of small obstacles or apertures and their consequent spreading into the regions of geometrical shadow is called diffraction of light.

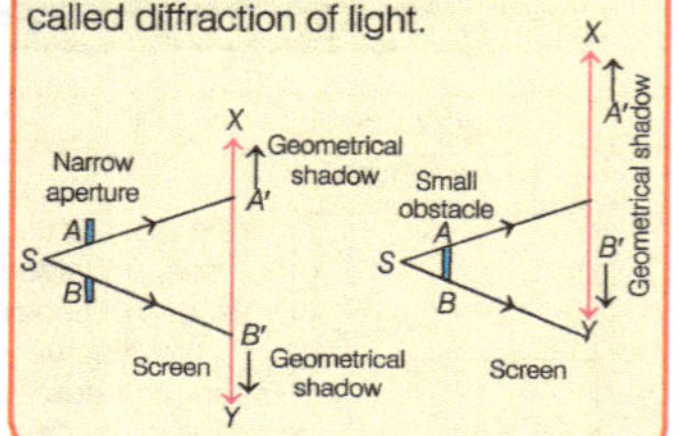

Diffraction due to a Single Slit

When a plane wave passing through a narrow slit, it suffers diffraction producing a central bright fringe and creates pattern of maxima and minima.

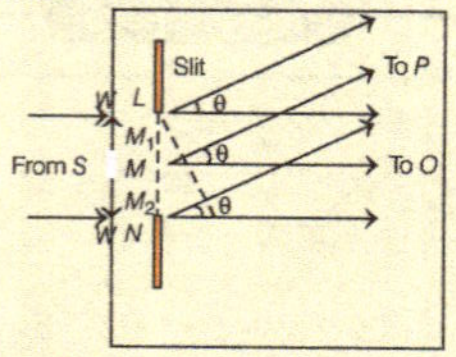

- **For nth minimum**

$a \sin \theta_n = n\lambda, n = 1, 2, 3, ...$

- **For nth secondary maximum**

$a \sin \theta_n = (2n-1)\frac{\lambda}{2}, n=1, 2, 3, ...$

- **Width of a secondary maximum**

$$\beta = \frac{D\lambda}{a}$$

- **Width of central maximum**

$$\beta_0 = 2\beta = \frac{2D\lambda}{a}$$

Diffraction at a Circular Aperture

Diffraction at a circular aperture. For diffraction of light at a circular aperture of diameter a, the angular spread of central maximum is

$$\theta = \frac{1.22\lambda}{a}$$

Brewster Law

This law states that the tangent of the polarising angle of incidence of a transparent medium is equal to its refractive index.

$\mu = \tan i_p$

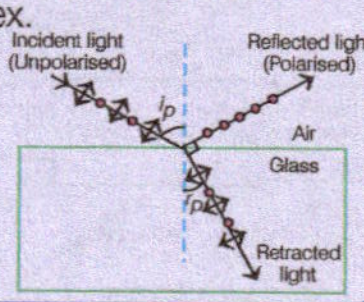

Malus Law

The intensity of transmitted light passed through an analyser is

$$I = I_0 \cos^2 \theta$$

(θ = angle between transmission directions of polariser and analyser).

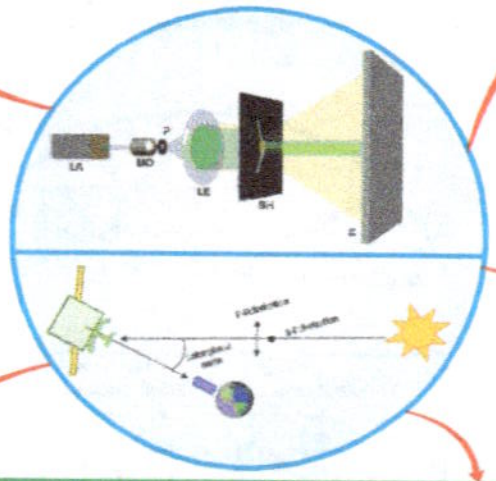

Coherent and Incoherent Sources

- Two sources of light which continuously emit light waves of same frequency (or wavelength) with a zero or constant phase difference between them are called coherent sources.
- Two sources of light which do not emit light waves with a constant phase difference are called incoherent sources.

Polarisation of Waves

The phenomenon of restricting the oscillations of a wave to just one direction in the transverse plane is called polarisation of waves.

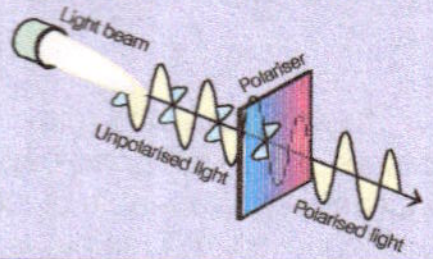

Polaroids

Polaroids are thin commercial sheets which make use of the property of selective absorption to produce an intense beam of plane polarised light.

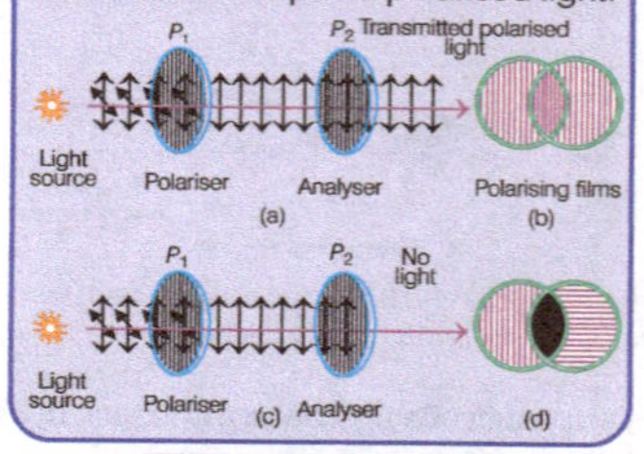

Coherent and Incoherent Addition of Waves

Resultant intensity,

$I_R = I_1 + I_2 + 2\sqrt{I_1 I_2}\cos\phi$

for bright fringes, $I_{max} = (\sqrt{I_1} + \sqrt{I_2})^2$ at $\phi = 0°, 2\pi, 4\pi, ...$

for dark fringes, $I_{min} = (\sqrt{I_1} - \sqrt{I_2})^2$ at $\phi = \pi, 3\pi, 5\pi, ..$

for $I_1 = I_2 = I_0$; $I_R = 4I_0 \cos^2 \frac{\phi}{2}$

Interference of Light

The superposition of two coherent waves resulting in a pattern of alternating dark and bright fringes of equal width.

- Position of bright fringes $x_n = \frac{n\lambda D}{d}$
- Position of dark fringes $x'_n = \frac{(2n-1)\lambda D}{2d}$
- Fringe width $\beta = \frac{\lambda D}{d}$
- Ratio of slit width and intensity $\frac{W_1}{W_2} = \frac{I_1}{I_2} = \frac{a_1^2}{a_2^2}$

Young's Double-Slit Experiment

Two identical narrow slits S_1 and S_2 are placed symmetrically with respect to narrow slit S illuminated with monochromatic light. The interference pattern is obtained on an observation screen placed at large distance D from S_1 and S_2.

The position of nth bright fringe from the centre of screen is

$$x_n = n\frac{D\lambda}{d}$$

The position of nth dark fringe from the centre of the screen is

$$x'_n = (2n-1)\frac{D\lambda}{2d}$$

Expression for Fringe Width

Fringe width is the separation between two successive bright or dark fringes and is given by

$$\beta = \frac{D\lambda}{d}$$

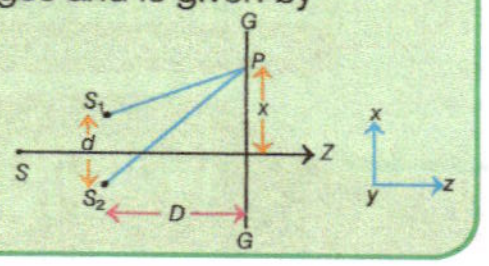

Polarised Light

If the vibrations of a wave are present in one direction, perpendicular to the direction of propagation.

In a linearly polarised wave, the vibrations at all points, at all times, lie in the same plane, so it is also called a plane polarised wave.

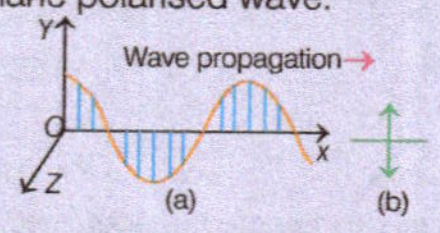

Pictorial representation of polarised light

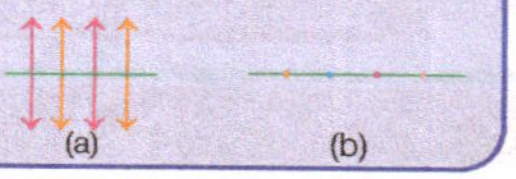

Condition for Sustained Interference

The interference pattern in which the positions of maxima and minima of intensity on the observation screen do not change with time is called a sustained or permanent interference pettern.

- Intensity ratio of maxima and minima

$$\frac{I_{max}}{I_{min}} = \frac{(a_1 + a_2)^2}{(a_1 - a_2)^2} = \left(\frac{r+1}{r-1}\right)^2$$

where, $r = \frac{a_1}{a_2}$

Fringe Shift

- Path difference produced by a slab $\Delta x = (\mu - 1)$
- Fringe shift, $\Delta x = \frac{\beta}{\lambda}(\mu-1)t = \frac{D}{d}(\mu-1)t$
- Number of fringes shifted

$$= \frac{\text{Shift}}{\text{Fringe width}} = \frac{(\mu-1)t\,D/d}{\lambda D/d} = \frac{(\mu-1)t}{\lambda}$$

Uses of Polaroids

(i) Polaroids are used in goggles and cameras to avoid glare of light.

(ii) Polaroids are useful in three dimensional motion pictures i.e., in holography.

(iii) They are used to eliminate the head light, glare in motor cars.

(iv) They are used to improve contrast in old oil paintings.

(v) They are used as window glasses to control the intensity of incoming light.

Dual Nature of Radiation and Matter (Chapter at a Glance)

Electron Volt (eV)

- It is the kinetic energy gained by an electron when it is accelerated through a potential difference of 1 volt. $1 eV = 1.6 \times 10^{-19} J$
- The work function of a metal is generally measured in electron volt (eV).

Electron Emission

The phenomenon of emission of electrons from a metal surface is called electron emission.

- **Themionic emission**
  The electrons are emitted from the metal surface with the help of thermal energy.
- **Field or cathode emission**
  Electrons are emitted from a metal surface by subjecting it to a very high electric field.
- **Photoelectric emission**
  Electrons are emitted from a metal surface with the help of suitable electromagnetic radiations.
- **Secondary emission**
  Electrons are ejected from a metal surface by striking fast moving electrons over it.

Wave Nature of Matter : de-Broglie Waves

- The waves associated with material particles in motion are called matter or de-Broglie waves and their wavelength is called de-Broglie wavelength.
- Since, radiation has dual nature. Therefore, de-Broglie predicted that matter must also possess dual nature. de-Broglie's wave equation,

$$\lambda = \frac{h}{p} = \frac{h}{mv}$$

de-Broglie Wavelength of an Electron

- Consider an electron of mass m and charge e. Let v, be the final velocity attained by the electron when it is accelerated from rest through the potential difference of V volts.

$$\lambda = \frac{h}{p} = \frac{h}{\sqrt{2mK}} = \frac{h}{\sqrt{2meV}}$$

Work Function

- The minimum amount of energy required by an electron to just escape from the metal surface is called work function of the metal. The work function depends on
  (i) the nature of the metal and
  (ii) the conditions of its surface.

Free Electrons in Metals

- In metals, the electrons in the outer shells of the atoms are loosely bound. They move about freely throughout the lattice of positive ions. Such loosely bound electrons are called free electrons.

Particle Nature of Light : The Photon

- In the interaction of radiation with matter, radiation behaves as if it is made of particles, called photons.
- Each photon has energy ($E = h\nu$) and momentum ($p = h\nu/c = h/\lambda$), and speed (c = speed of light in vacuum).
- Photons are electrically neutral and are not deflected by electric and magnetic fields.
- In a photon-particle collision, the total energy and total momentum are conserved.

Laws of Photoelectric Emission

(i) For a given metal and a radiation of fixed frequency, the rate of emission of photoelectrons is proportional to the intensity of incident radiation.
(ii) For every metal, there is a certain minimum frequency below which no photoelectrons are emitted.
(iii) The photoelectric emission is an instantaneous process.
(iv) For the radiation of frequency higher than the threshold frequency, the maximum kinetic energy of the photoelectrons is directly proportional to the frequency of incident radiation and is independent of the intensity of incident radiation.

Einstein's Theory of Photoelectric Effect

Einstein explained photoelectric effect with the help of Planck's quantum theory. Einstein's photoelectric equation is

$$K_{max} = \frac{1}{2} mv_{max}^2 = eV_0 = h\nu - W_0 = h(\nu - \nu_0)$$

where, W_0 is the work function of the metal and υ_0 is the threshold frequency. All the experimental observations can be explained on the basis of Einstein's photoelectric equation.

Failure of Wave Theory to Explain Photoelectric Effect

The classical wave theory of radiation could not explain the main features of photoelectric effect. Its picture of continuous absorption of energy from radiation could not explain
(i) the independence of K_{max} on intensity.
(ii) the existence of threshold frequency υ_0.
(iii) the instantaneous nature of the phenomenon.

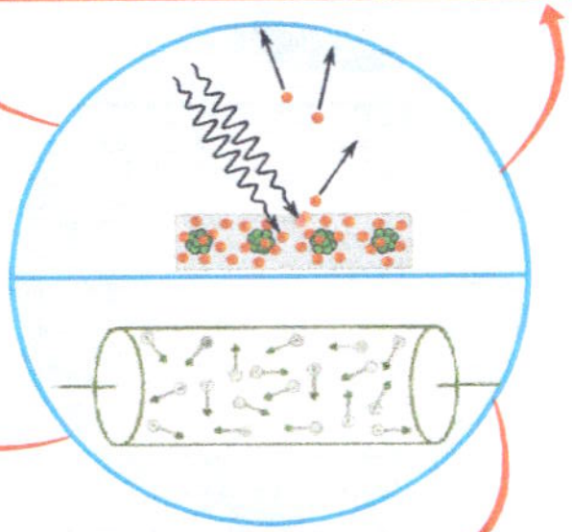

Photoelectric Effect

When light of suitable frequency illuminates a metal surface, electrons are emitted from the metal surface. The phenomenon is called photoelectric effect. The photo (light)-generated electrons are called photoelectrons.

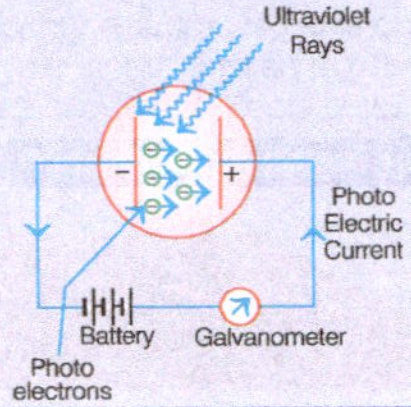

Effect of Frequency of Incident Radiation on Stopping Potential

The greater frequency of the incident radiation, greater is the maximum kinetic energy of the photoelectrons and hence, greater is the retarding potential required to stop such electrons completely.

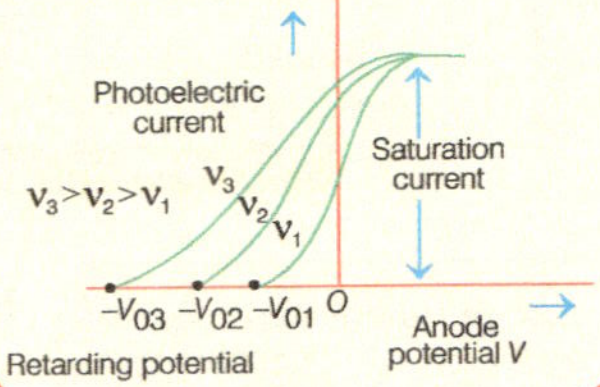

Effect of Intensity of Light

The number of photoelectrons emitted per second is proportional to the intensity of incident radiation.

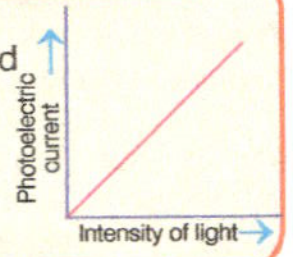

Experimental Study of Photoelectric Effect

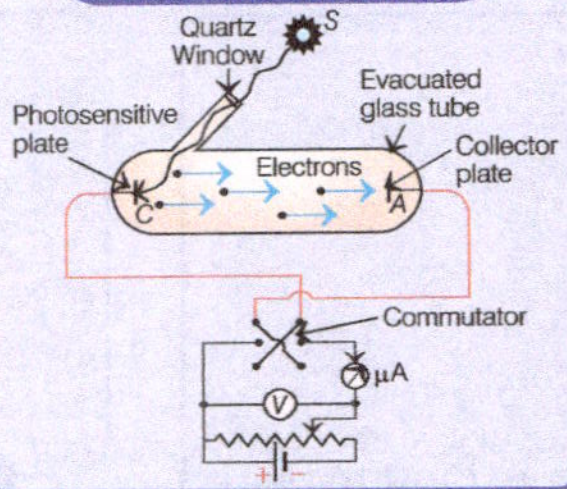

Photoelectric Current

The current constituted by photoelectrons is called photoelectric current. Its values depends on
(i) the intensity of light.
(ii) the potential difference applied between the two electrodes, and
(iii) the nature of the cathode material.

Threshold Frequency

The minimum value of the frequency of incident radiation below which the photoelectric emission stops altogether is called threshold frequency. It is denoted by ν_0 and is a characteristic of the metal.

Effect of Potential

The photoelectric current increases with the increase in accelerating potential till a stage is reached when the photoelectric current becomes maximum and does not increase further with the increase in the accelerating potential.

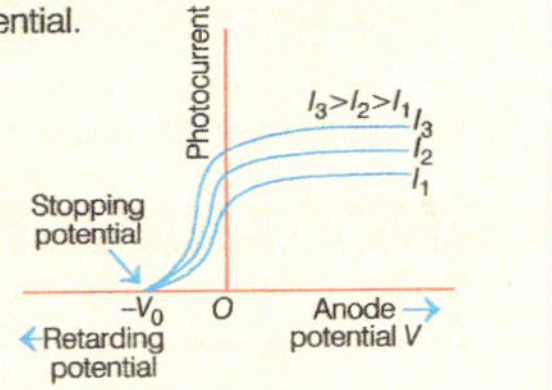

$$K_{max} = \frac{1}{2} mv_{max}^2 = eV_0$$

Hertz's Observations

Hertz found that high voltage sparks passed across the metal electrodes of the detector loop more easily when the cathode was illuminated by ultraviolet light from an arc lamp. The ultraviolet light falling on the metal surface caused the emission of negatively charged particles, which are known to be electrons.

Hallwach's and Lenard's Observations

Hallwach connected a zinc plate to an electroscope. He allowed ultraviolet light to fall on a zinc plate. He observed that the zinc plate became
(i) uncharged if initially negatively charged.
(ii) positively charged if initially uncharged.
(iii) more positively charged if initially positively charged.

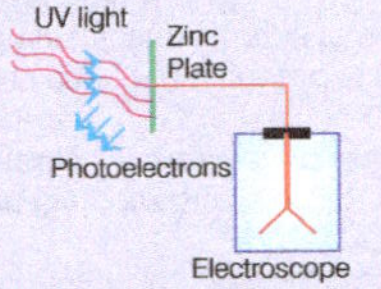

Concluded Some negatively charged particles emitted by the zinc plate.

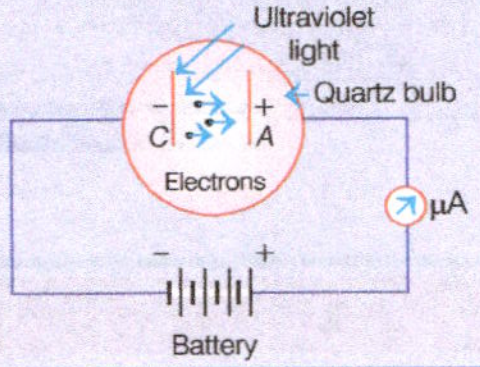

Atoms (Chapter at a Glance)

Distance of Closest Approach

When an α-particle of mass m and velocity v moves directly towards a nucleus of atomic number Z, its distance of closest approach is given by

$$r_0 = \frac{2kZe^2}{E} = \frac{4kZe^2}{mv^2}$$

where, $E = \frac{1}{2}mv^2$

and $k = \frac{1}{4\pi\varepsilon_0} = 9 \times 10^9 \text{ Nm}^2\text{C}^{-2}$

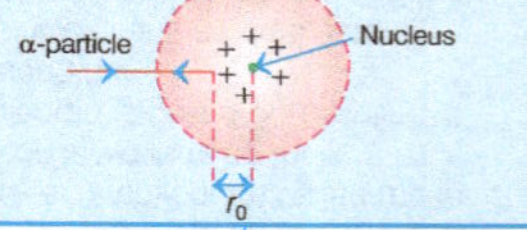

Impact Parameter

The perpendicular distance of the velocity vector of the α-particle from the centre of the nucleus, when it is far away from the atom.

$$b = \frac{1}{4\pi\varepsilon_0}\cdot\frac{Ze^2\cot\frac{\theta}{2}}{E} = \frac{1}{4\pi\varepsilon_0}\cdot\frac{Ze^2\cot\frac{\theta}{2}}{\frac{1}{2}mv^2}$$

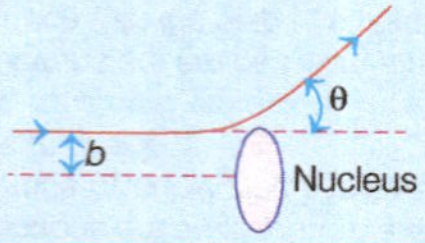

Limitations of Rutherford's Atomic Model

An electron revolving around the nucleus is under continuous acceleration towards the centre. It should continuously lose its energy and move in orbits of gradually decreasing radii. The electron should follow the spiral path and finally, it should collapse into the nucleus. Thus, the Rutherford's model cannot explain the stability of an atom. As the electrons spiral inwards, their angular velocities and frequencies would change continuously, and the frequency of emitted light will also change. They would emit a continuous spectrum instead of the actually observed line spectrum.

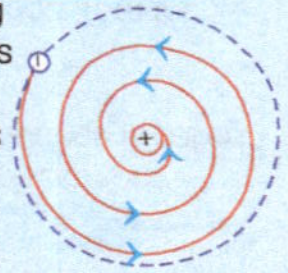

Rutherford's Model

About Experiment

(i) Most of the α-particles pass straight through the gold foil or suffer only small deflection.

(ii) A few α-particles, about 1 in 8000, get deflected through 90° or more.

(iii) Occasionally, an α-particle gets rebounded from the gold foil, suffering a deflection of nearly 180°.

Thomson's Model

An atom consists of a sphere of positively charged matter in which the negatively charged electrons are uniformly embedded like plums in a pudding. This model could not explain scattering of α-particles through thin foils and hence discarded.

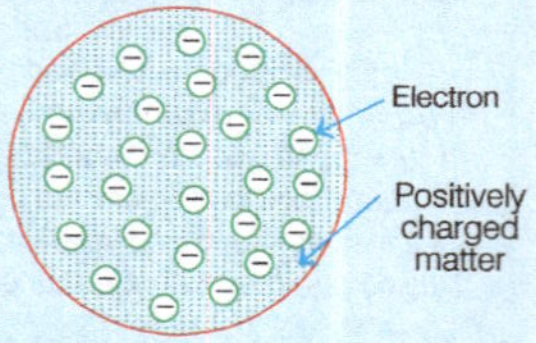

Hydrogen Line Spectrum

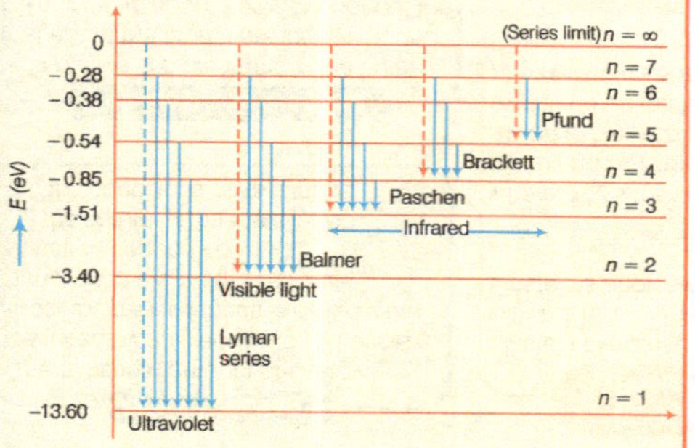

$$\therefore E_n = \frac{E_1}{n^2} = -\frac{13.6}{n^2} \text{ eV}$$

Limitations of Bohr's Theory

- This theory is applicable only for H-like single electron atoms. It failed to explain the atomic spectrum of atoms with two or more electrons.
- It does not explain why only circular orbits should be chosen when elliptical orbits are also possible.
- It failed to explain Zeeman effect and stark effect i.e., splitting of spectral lines in presence of electric field.

Bohr's Theory of Hydrogen Spectra

- Radius of permitted orbit

$$r = \frac{n^2h^2}{4\pi^2mkZe^2} = a_0\frac{n^2}{Z} \text{ Å}$$

where, a_0 is Bohr's radius

- Velocity of electron

$$v = \frac{2\pi kZe^2}{nh} = 2.2 \times 10^6 \frac{Z}{n} \text{ m/s}$$

- Energy of electron,

$$E_n = \frac{-2\pi^2mk^2Z^2e^4}{n^2h^2} = -21.8\times10^{-19} \times \frac{Z^2}{n^2} \text{ J}$$

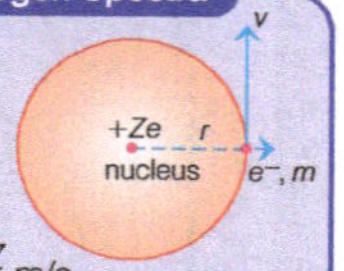

Bohr's Atomic Model : Postulates

1. Quantum Condition All the possible circular orbits allowed by the classical theory, the electrons are permitted to circulate only in such orbits in which the angular momentum of an electron is an integral multiple of $\frac{h}{2\pi}$, h being Planck's constant.

$$L = mvr = \frac{nh}{2\pi}, n = 1, 2, 3 \ldots$$

2. Stationary Orbit While revolving in the permissible orbits, an electron does not radiate energy. These non-radiating orbits are called stationary orbits.

3. Frequency Condition An atom can emit or absorb radiation in the form of discrete energy photons only when an electron jumps from a higher to a lower orbit or from a lower to a higher orbit.

$$h\nu = E_2 - E_1$$

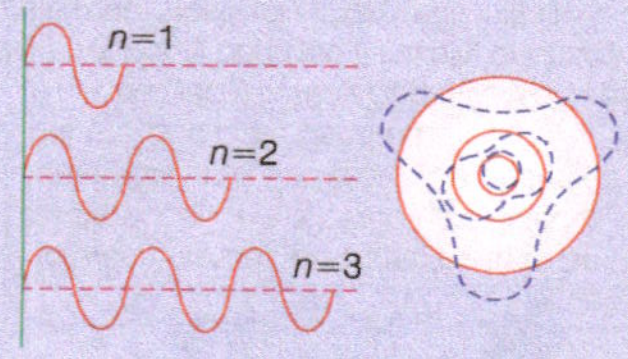

Excitation and Ionisation Potential

- **Excitation Potential**

It is that accelerating potential which gives to a bombarding electron sufficient energy to excite the target atom by raising one of its electrons from an inner to an outer orbit.

First excitation potential of hydrogen = − 3.4 − (− 13.6) = 10.2 V

Second excitation potential of hydrogen = − 1.51 − (− 13.6) = 12.09 V.

- **Ionisation Potential**

It is that accelerating potential which gives to a bombarding electron sufficient energy to ionise the target atom by knocking one of its electrons completely out of the atom.

Ionisation potential of hydrogen = 0 − (− 13.6) = 13.6 V.

Spectral Series of Hydrogen Atom

The transitions corresponding to maximum energy or smallest wavelength of a given series of hydrogen spectrum is called **series limit**.

To calculate wavelength corresponding to a series limit, we use $n_2 = \infty$.

$$\bar{\nu} = \frac{1}{\lambda} = R\left(\frac{1}{n_1^2} - \frac{1}{n_2^2}\right) \text{cm}^{-1}; R = 109677 \text{ cm}^{-1}$$

Series	n_1	n_2	**Region of Spectrum**
Lyman	1	2, 3, 4, ...	Ultraviolet
Balmer	2	3, 4, 5, ...	Visible
Paschen	3	4, 5, 6, ...	Near Infrared
Brackett	4	5, 6, 7, ...	Infrared
Pfund	5	6, 7, 8, ...	Far Infrared

Excitation and Ionisation Energy

- **Excitation Energy**

The energy required by an electron of an atom to jump from its ground state to any one of its excited states.

First excitation energy = $E_2 - E_1$ = 10.2 eV

Second excitation energy = $E_3 - E_1$ = 12.09 eV

- **Ionisation Energy**

The energy required to remove an electron from an atom, i.e, the energy required to take an electron from its ground state to the outermost orbit ($n = \infty$).

Ionisation energy of hydrogen = $E_\infty - E_1$ = 13.6 eV

Nuclei (Chapter at a Glance)

Nuclear Stability

When the atom of an element has an equal number of neutrons or protons, it does not create extra energy in the nucleus. Thus, it will behave save stable nucleus.

Nuclear Unstability

When the atom of an element have extra neutrons or protons, it create extra energy in the nucleus and causes the atom to become unbalanced or unstable.

Packing Fraction

The packing fraction of a nucleus is its mass defect per nucleon.

$$\text{PF of a nucleus} = \frac{\text{Mass defect}}{\text{Mass number}} = \frac{\Delta m}{A}$$

It is directly related to the availability of nuclear energy and the stability of the nucleus.

Binding Energy Curve

The value of binding energy per nucleon of a nucleus gives a measure of the stability of that nucleus. Greater is the binding energy per nucleon of a nucleus, more stable is the nucleus.

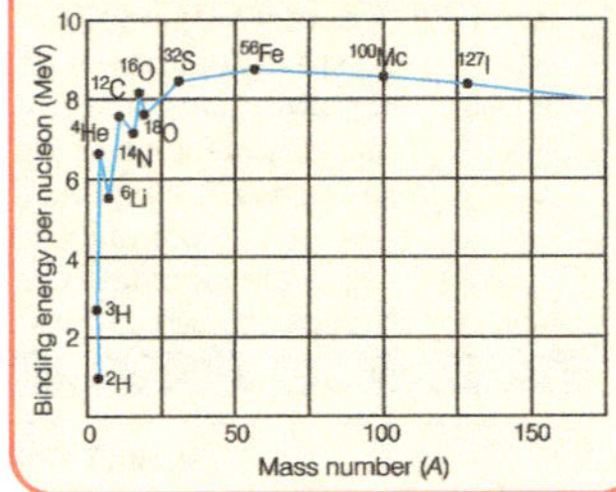

Binding Energy Per Nucleon

Average energy required to extract one nucleon from the nucleus. It is obtained by dividing the binding energy of a nucleus by its mass number.

$$\Delta E_{bn} \text{ or } \bar{B} = \frac{BE}{A}$$

$$= \frac{[Zm_H + (A-Z)M_n - m]\,c^2}{A}$$

Nuclear Size and density

- **Nuclear Size**
The volume of a nucleus is directly proportional to the number of nucleons in it.
$R = R_0 A^{1/3}$
- **Nuclear density**
The density of a nucleus is independent of the size of the nucleus and is given by

$$\rho_{nu} = \frac{\text{Nuclear mass}}{\text{Nuclear volume}} = \frac{m_{nu}}{\frac{4\pi R^3}{3}}$$

The nuclear density is of the order of 10^{17} kg m^{-3}.

Composition of A Nucleus

- **Nucleons** Protons and neutrons present in the nuclei of atoms are collectively known as nucleons.
- **Atomic number** The number of protons in the nucleus is called the atomic number of the element. It is denoted by Z.
- **Mass Number** The total numbers of protons and neutrons present in a nucleus is called the mass number of the element. It is denoted by A.
- **Nuclear Mass** The total mass of the protons and neutrons present in a nucleus is called the nuclear mass.
- **Nuclide** A nuclide is a specific nucleus of an atom characterised by its atomic number Z and mass number A, represented as, $^{A}_{Z}X$

Binding Energy

The energy required to break up a nucleus into its constituent protons and neutrons and to separate them to such a large distance that they may not interact with each other.

The binding energy of a nucleus $^{A}_{Z}X$ is given by

$\Delta E_b = [Zm_p + (A-Z)m_n - m]c^2$

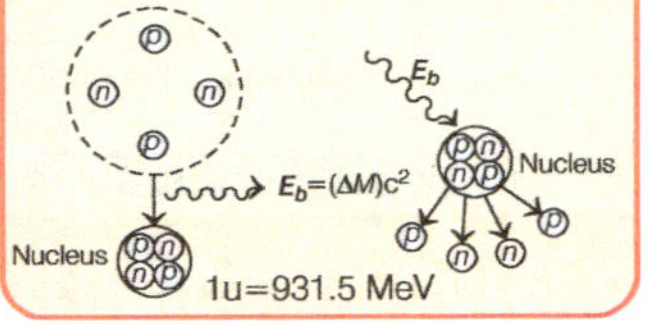

Nuclear Force

It is one of the strongest force in nature.
it acts only in the range of the order of few fermi meters ($\approx 4.2 \times 10^{-15}$m)
It balances the electrostatic force between protons in the nucleus.

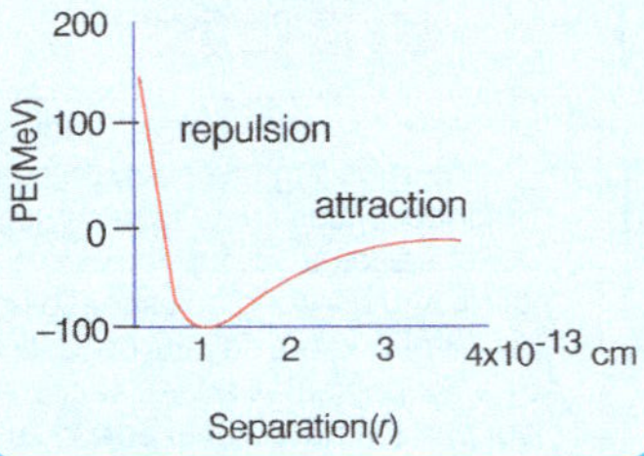

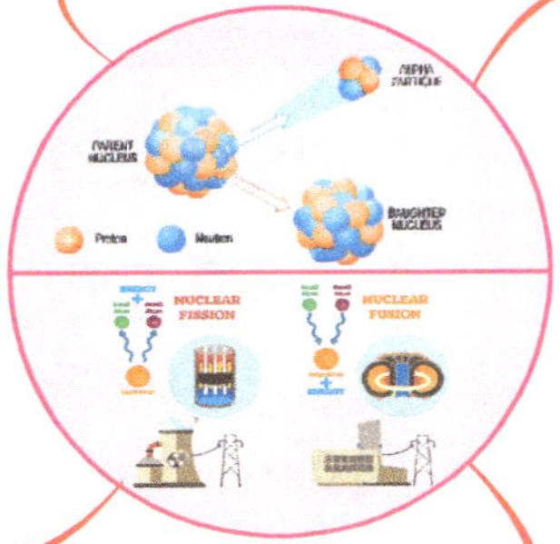

Mass Defect

The difference between the rest mass of a nucleus and the sum of the rest masses of its constituent nucleons.

$\Delta m = Zm_p + (A - Z)m_n - m$

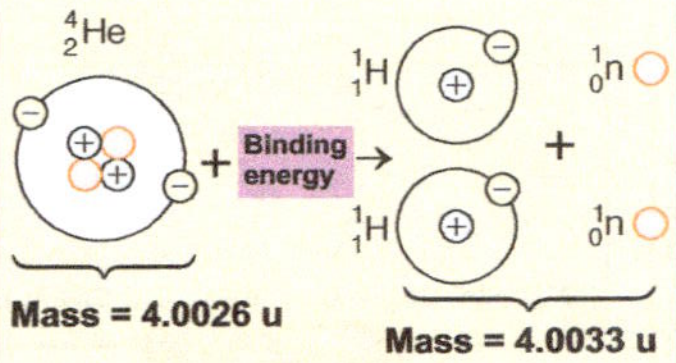

Necessary Conditions for Nuclear Fusion

The high temperature is necessary for the light nuclei to have sufficient kinetic energy, so that they can overcome their mutual coulombic repulsions and come closer than the range of nuclear force. That is why, the fusion reaction is also called thermonuclear reaction.

Nuclear Fusion

It is the process of fusion of two smaller nuclei into a heavier nucleus with the liberation of large amount of energy.

Example

$^{2}_{1}H + ^{3}_{1}H \longrightarrow ^{4}_{2}He + ^{1}_{0}n + \text{Energy}$

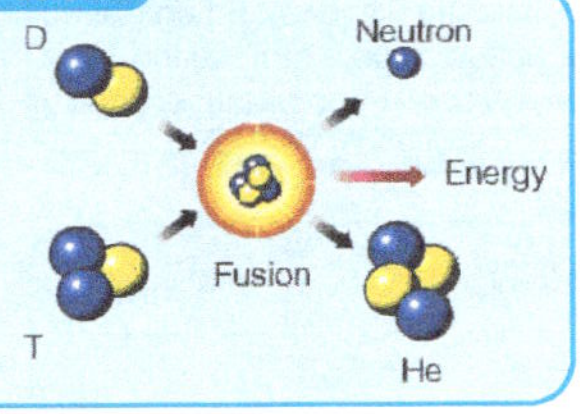

Nuclear Fission

It is the process in which a heavy nucleus ($A > 230$), when excited gets split up into two smaller nuclei of nearly comparable masses.

Example

$^{235}_{92}U + ^{1}_{0}n \longrightarrow ^{144}_{56}Ba + ^{89}_{36}Kr + 3\,^{1}_{0}n + Q.$

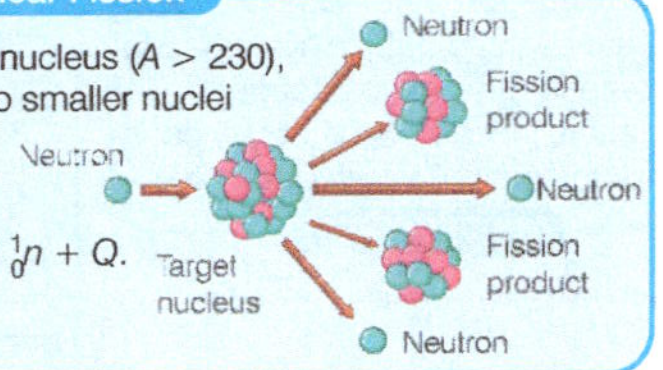

Nuclear Fission As a Source of Energy

The sum of the masses of the final products is less than the sum of the masses of the reactant components. The difference in masses is called mass defect, is converted into energy according to Einstein's mass-energy relationship ($E = mc^2$)

$$^{235}_{92}U + ^{1}_{0}n \longrightarrow ^{144}_{56}Ba + ^{89}_{36}Kr + 3\,^{1}_{0}n + Q.$$

Isotopes, Isobars, Isotones and Isomers

- **Isotopes** The atoms of an element, which have the same atomic number but different mass number are called isotopes.

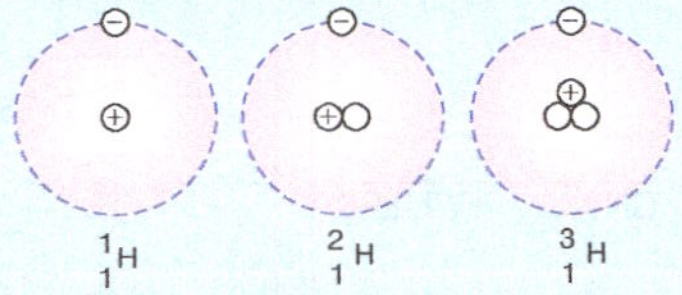

- **Isobars** The atoms of different elements (different atomic number) but having the same mass number are called isobars.
Example $^{3}_{1}$H and $^{3}_{2}$He, as both have same A=3.
- **Isotones** The nuclides having the same number of neutrons are called isotones.
Example $^{37}_{17}$Cl and $^{39}_{19}$K are isotones, as both contain the same number of neutrons.

Semiconductor Electronics (Chapter at a Glance)

Semiconductor

A solid substance that allows heat or electricity to pass through it.
They have much higher resistivity than metals. They have considerably lower number density of charge carriers than metals. Semiconductors may be elemental (Si, Ge) and compound (GaAs, CdS, etc.)

Classification of Semiconductors

- **Intrinsic Semiconductor** The pure semiconductors are called intrinsic semiconductors.
The numbers of excited electrons is equal to number of holes.
- **Extrinsic Semiconductor** When a small amount few parts per million (ppm) impurity is added to the pure semiconductor, the conductivity of semiconductor is increased.
- **Doping** When some suitable impurity is added to intrinsic semiconductors, then this process is called doping.
(i) Pentavalent dopants such as Sb and P. These are also called donors.
(ii) Trivalent dopants such as In (indium), B (boron) and Al (aluminium).

Types of Extrinsic Semiconductor

- ***n*-type semiconductors**
The pentavalent impurity is used in this type of semiconductor.
In *n*-type semiconductors, electrons are the majority charge carriers and holes are the minority charge carriers.

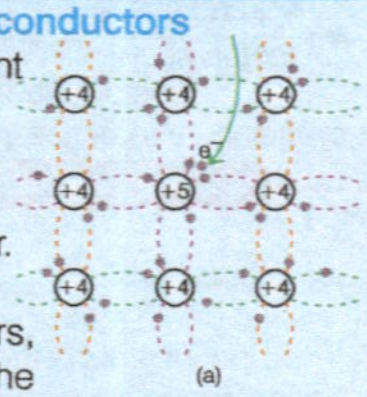

- ***p*-type semiconductors**
The trivalent impurity atoms are called acceptors because they create holes which can accept electrons from the nearby bonds. In *p*-type semiconductor, holes are the majority carriers and electrons are the minority charge carriers.

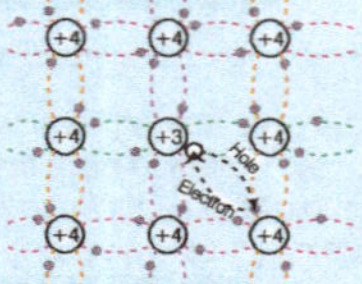

Energy Bands in Solids

- **Valence band(VB)**
– It is the range of energies of valence electron.
- **Conduction band(CB)**
– It is the range of energies of conduction electron.
(a) For insulators $E_g > 3eV$
(b) For conductors $E_g \approx 0$
(c) For semiconductor $E_g < 3eV$

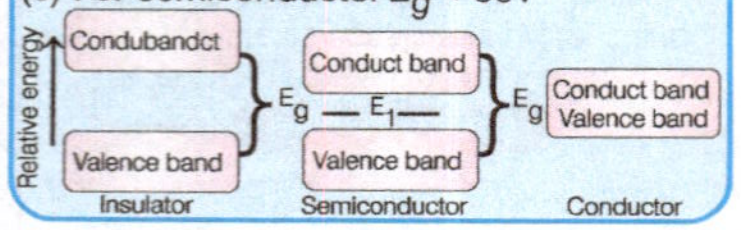

Classification of Solids on the Basis of Their Electrical Properties

(i) Metals Have very low resistivity or high conductivity.
$\rho \approx 10^{-2} - 10^{-8}\ \Omega m$
$\sigma \approx 10^{2} - 10^{8}\ Sm^{-1}$
(ii) Insulators Have high resistivity or low conductivity.
$\rho \approx 10^{11} - 10^{-18}\ \Omega m$
$\sigma \approx 10^{-11} - 10^{-19}\ Sm^{-1}$
(iii) Semiconductor Possess resistivity or conductivity intermediate to metals and insulators.
$\rho \approx 10^{-5} - 10^{+6}\ \Omega m$
$\sigma \approx 10^{5} - 10^{-6}\ Sm^{-1}$

Semiconductor Diode

A semiconductor diode is basically a *p-n* junction with metallic contacts provided at the ends for the application of an external voltage. It is a two terminals device.

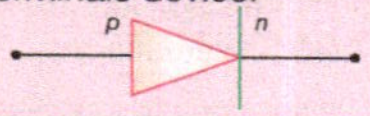

Forward Biasing

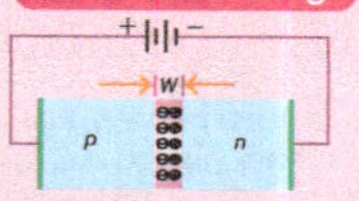

p connected to (+) terminal of battery.
n connected to (–) terminal of battery.
Width of depletion layer and potential barrier reduced

NOT Gate

It inverts the input signal. It is described by the Boolean expression,
$\overline{A} = Y$

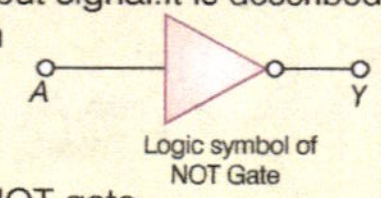

Truth table of NOT gate

A	Y
0	1
1	0

Logic Gate

A logic gate is a digital circuit that has one or more inputs but only one output. It follows a logical relationship between input and output voltages.

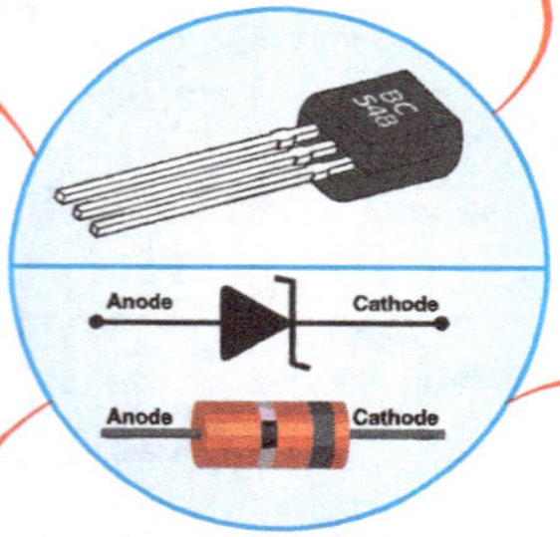

p-n Junction

It is a single crystal of Ge or Si doped in such a manner that one half-portion of it acts as *p*-type semiconductor and the other half as *n*-type semiconductor. The term junction implies the boundary or region of transition between *n*-type and *p*-type semiconductor materials. *p-n* junction used in many semiconductor devices like diodes, LED, solar cell, transistors.

Reverse Biasing

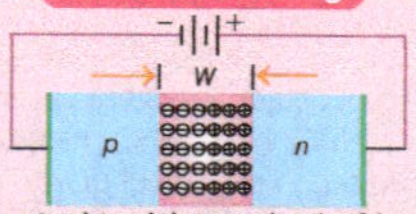

p connected to (–) terminal of battery.
n connected to (+) terminal of battery.
Width of depletion layer and potential barrier increases

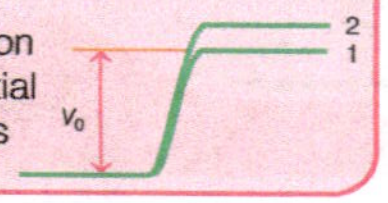

AND Gate

It gives a high output (1), if inputs *A* and *B* are both high (1). It is described by the Boolean expression,
$A.B = Y$

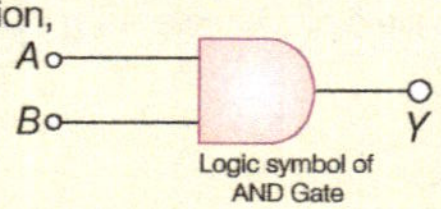

Truth table of AND gate

A	B	Y
0	0	0
0	1	0
1	0	0
1	1	1

Diode as a Rectifier

A device which rectifiers AC to DC.

- **Half wave rectifier**
– Average output per cycle
– Ripple frequency = Frequency of AC input

$I_{dc} = \frac{I_o}{\pi}; V_{dc} = \frac{V_o}{\pi}$

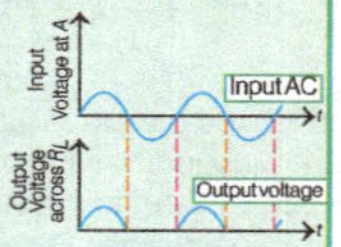

- **Full wave rectifier**
– Average output per cycle
– Ripple frequency = 2 x frequency of AC input

$I_{DC} = \frac{2I_o}{\pi}; V_{DC} = \frac{2V_o}{\pi}$

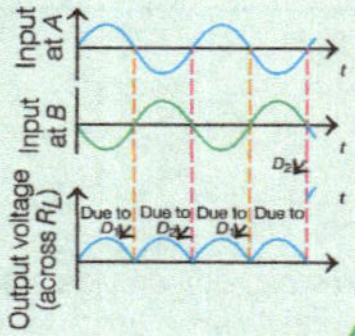

Zener Diode

A junction diode specially designed to operate only in the reverse breakdown region continuously (without getting damaged).

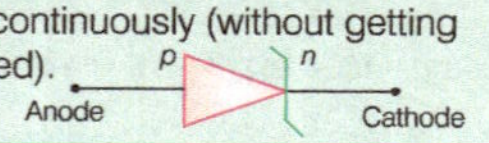

Zener Diode As A Voltage Regulator

When a zener diode is operated in the reverse breakdown region, the voltage across it remains constant for a large change in the reverse current. This will used as voltage regulator.

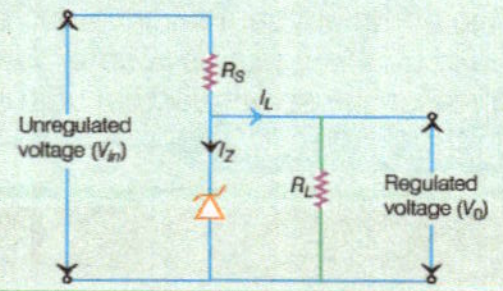

NAND Gate

Its input is high, if both inputs *A* and *B* are not high. It is described by the Boolean expression,
$\overline{A.B} = Y$

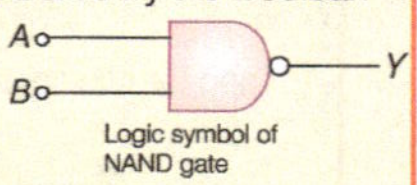

Truth table of NAND gate

A	B	Y
0	0	1
0	1	1
1	0	1
1	1	0

OR Gate

It gives a high output, if either input *A* or *B* or both are high (1)
$A + B = Y$

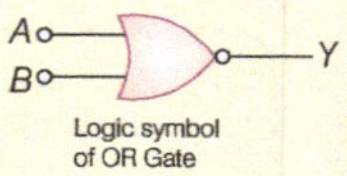

Truth table of OR gate

A	B	Y
0	0	0
0	1	1
1	0	1
1	1	1

Photodiode

– A special type of junction diode used for detecting optical signal.
– It is fabricated with a transparent cover to allow light to fall on the diode and operated under reverse bias.

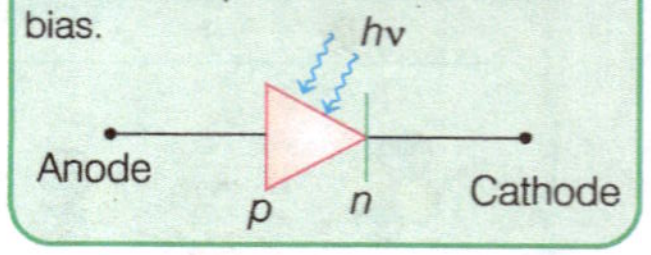

Solar Cell

It is a junction diode which converts solar energy into electricity and is based on photovoltaic effect.

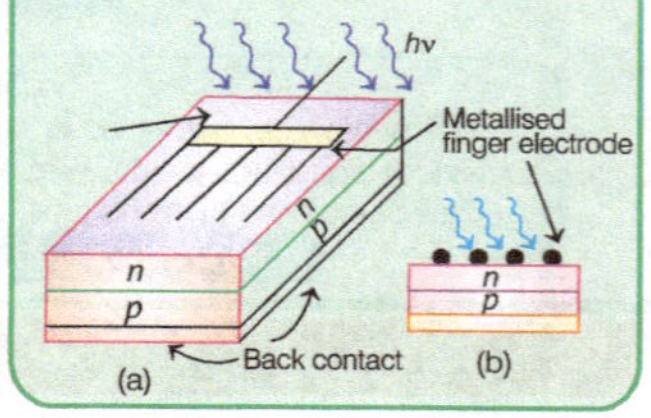